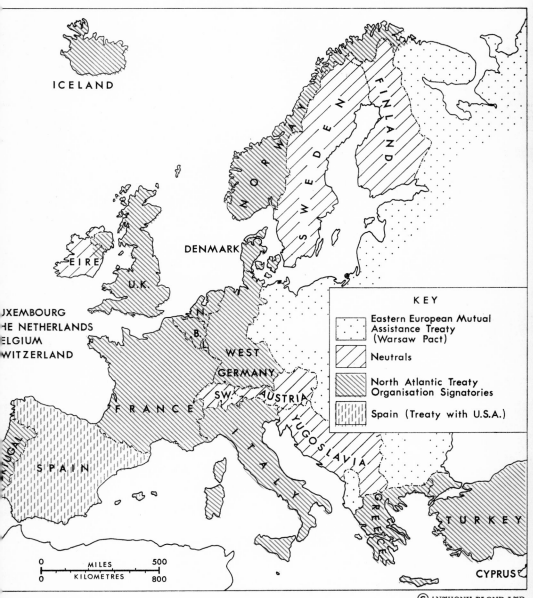

ICELAND

NORWAY

SWEDEN

FINLAND

EIRE

U.K.

DENMARK

LUXEMBOURG
THE NETHERLANDS
BELGIUM
SWITZERLAND

N.

B.

WEST
GERMANY

SW.

AUSTRIA

FRANCE

ITALY

YUGOSLAVIA

PORTUGAL

SPAIN

GREECE

TURKEY

CYPRUS

KEY

Eastern European Mutual
Assistance Treaty
(Warsaw Pact)

Neutrals

North Atlantic Treaty
Organisation Signatories

Spain (Treaty with U.S.A.)

MILES
0   500

KILOMETRES
0   800

© ANTHONY BLOND LTD

WESTERN EUROPE

WESTERN EUROPE
A Handbook

Edited by
JOHN CALMANN

FREDERICK A. PRAEGER, *Publishers*
New York · Washington

BOOKS THAT MATTER

Published in the United States of America in 1967
by Frederick A. Praeger, Inc., Publishers
111 Fourth Avenue, New York, N.Y. 10003

Library of Congress Catalog Card Number: 67–23393

Printed in Great Britain

CONTRIBUTORS

Richard Bailey
R. Colin Beever
Tony Burgess
John Calmann
Sarah Child
William Clarke
Ian Dunlop
Charles Ford
Marianne Gellner
Vic George
Harry Graham
Miron Grindea
Brian Holmes
Jacques Mallet
Richard Mayne
Richard Moore
José Antonio Novais

John Pinder
Roy Pryce
Laurance Reed
Anthony Sharp
Werner von Simson
Joseph R. Starobin
John Russell Taylor
David Tonge
Ossia Trilling
Pierre Uri
C. M. W. Vasey
Anthony Verrier
Stephen Walsh
T. K. Warley
John White
Glen Garfield Williams
Philip Windsor

Salomon Wolff

CONTENTS

PART ONE: THE COUNTRIES OF WESTERN EUROPE

Basic Information *compiled by Anthony Sharp*

PART TWO: GENERAL

PART THREE: WESTERN EUROPEAN INTEGRATION

A*

MAPS

GENERAL KEY

=====	Motorways
=======	Projected motorways
———	Other main roads
+—+—+	Railways
~~	Rivers
🝆	Lakes
•—•—•	International frontiers
•—•—•	Internal regional boundaries
◑	Large towns (sizes of spheres indicate relative sizes of towns within each map; they are not relative from map to map)

Type-faces

VAASA Internal administrative regions

OSLO Capital cities

Malmö Other large towns

Mt Etna Relief features

x

ILLUSTRATIONS

EDITOR'S PREFACE

THE PURPOSE of this book is to provide essential information on an area stretching from Iceland to Turkey and containing some of the fastest changing communities in the world. The subject matter and its presentation have been selected so as to provide a basic guide to the area for many years to come. Twenty-seven states have been included on the basis that they are European but non-Communist; this means that all countries west of the Iron Curtain are covered except Yugoslavia, which has not yet fully identified itself with the Western bloc.

The aim is not to stress the differences between the countries of Western Europe, but to point out the large areas of common interest as well as the high degree of integration that has already been achieved between them in a number of fields. Individual countries have not, however, been neglected. The reader will find basic information on each country, with maps and statistical tables, in Part One. Part Two covers a large number of subjects affecting all or much of Western Europe. (Social security is covered in Part One as the complexity of the subject made it impossible to deal with in a single chapter.) Part Three deals with Western European integration: the Common Market (EEC) and the European Free Trade Association (EFTA) are fully described, as well as the outlook for European integration in the future; there will also be found a brief guide to the principal Western European organisations. The index covers the whole of Parts Two and Three and the *Recent History* sections in Part One; the rest of Part One is self-indexing. Each chapter contains a list for further reading.

Inevitably in a work of reference of this kind, statistics will have been released by governments and international organisations after the book has gone to press. Every effort has been made, however, to provide the reader with the latest figures available and to ensure that where comparisons are made they are between figures that are comparable.

Thanks are due to Dr. Peter Odell of the Department of Geography, London School of Economics and Political Science, who planned the maps, and to Mrs. M. E. Sinclair, the cartographer, who prepared them; to Stephen Edgell who prepared the economic section of the Basic Information and the Comparative Statistics; to Miss E. M. J. Campbell and Dr. J. F. Davis of the Department of Geography, Birkbeck College, University of London who prepared the geography section of the Basic Information; to Mrs. Nona Blenkin who compiled the index; and to Miss Angela Grandage and Mrs. Marie Gordon who assisted in checking proofs.

Among the many people who have given useful advice, the editor would like to acknowledge those who have been particularly helpful: François

Duchêne, who made many useful suggestions on the conception as well as the content of the work; and Antony Wood, without whose devotion and tenacity it would not have appeared at all.

J. C.

INTRODUCTION

JOHN CALMANN

THIS book is about an area that has emerged only in the last twenty years. In 1945 most of the countries described were at war with each other, and when the war was over their future was as bleak as their devastated cities and their abandoned farms and factories. Now Western Europe—which we have taken to include all the non-Communist countries of Europe and Turkey—has become a rich, highly integrated, recognisable unit, with a variety of more or less free institutions, and a vast spread of prosperity, surpassed only in North America. Politically and economically it has become separated from the Communist countries of Europe, and while that separation may now be drawing to its close, the gap between the two areas is still a strong factor in the condition of Europe. Thus Western and Eastern Europe can still both be treated as distinct and recognisable regions with their own economic and political systems, their own cultural development, and their own diversity.

This book, unlike the others in the series, emphasises the similarities of the problems which the various countries face, rather than their national characteristics. Indeed, the oddest thing about Western Europe is that it still has such a variety of structures to deal with what is really much the same business; thus while each country is still expected to cope with its own problems it finds this less and less easy to do without the support and interest of its neighbours. Just as during the pre-war depression it was gradually realised that even the rich were to some extent dependent on the well-being of the poor, so governments in Western Europe have come to regard each other as having the same objectives rather than necessarily being in competition with each other. One of the regrettable effects of the present regime in France may be that those who still hanker after the apparent freedom of national independence will be encouraged to follow General de Gaulle's example, and attempt to dismantle the integration so far achieved. The General's policies may also give rise to the illusion that the surviving national structures are in themselves powerful enough to secure independence for one area or one ethnic group in Western Europe. Certainly it is still widely supposed that the mere fact that a national government has survived, and that the nation-states in Western Europe are still there, means that the range of actions nationally and internationally open to them is still large. The intention behind the shape of this book is to show how little this corresponds to reality; if the object of a handbook on Western Europe is to give the basic facts about the area, then it must stress the interdependence of the nations of which it is made up, and the community of needs and expectations formed by its peoples.

This is not to ignore the survival of the nation-states—they are amply covered in the section providing basic information—but rather to show how they have changed since pre-war days, in spite of the continuity of their institutions, of their political parties, even of their politicians. In fact the essays in this book bring out two opposed elements common to all the nation-states: first that they are bound to act in concert in a large number of fields because their interests are complementary, and secondly that their national structures impose limitations on their joint action which are detrimental to their prosperity and progress. What Western European countries have been seeking since the war—and this includes Britain—is to find a method or methods of resolving this contradiction. It is certainly not a proof of the eternal vigour of the nation-state that the difficulty of doing so remains. The feebleness of the states was revealed during the second world war itself, when they nearly all collapsed before Hitler's armies. (Their interdependence was also revealed in this catastrophe.) A more intelligent and more constructive change in their relationships is being wrought more slowly today by a common recognition of economic circumstances and by some common institutions.

Part Three of this book covers these institutions, and more particularly the Common Market, or European Economic Community, of the Six. The reason for this emphasis on the Treaties of Paris and Rome is that they represent a revolutionary challenge to the traditional concept of the European state. Their effects as well as their aims go far beyond the large number of other organisations such as the OECD or EFTA which group Europeans together. Their aim, unlike that of Bismarck's 'blood and iron', is to marry states to each other without individual loss of life or property. Their success is proved by the fact that they have survived some rather violent crises, more or less intact, and that now those states—mainly the EFTA countries— that felt unable to join the Community in the first place are continually knocking at its door. Indeed the presence of the European Community is felt in the formulation of nearly every major decision which the countries described in this book take. Quite apart from broad generalities of economic policy, in the discussion of specific industrial, agricultural, transport, energy or even social questions, all Western European governments, whether they are inside the Community or outside, look to see what is being done in Brussels. Naturally the influence of the Community is largest in the member countries, but in the others there is a constant preoccupation with knowing how to 'fit in' with Community policies, or how to 'be ready' when the time comes to join. There are, however, two fields largely exempt from this process, as Pierre Uri points out in his chapter on the limits of economic union—defence and diplomacy.[1] Even in the Community these aspects of policy are largely conducted with purely national aims in mind, and interdependence has only been recognised in theory, very rarely in practice.

This is of course particularly clear in the present NATO crisis, which at the time of writing remains unresolved. Quite apart from the fundamental differences of view between France and her partners in the alliance, there is the inability of the Western European countries as a whole to agree on what kind of defence they need. Indeed their present clinging to the alliance is a reflection of their lack of new ideas—not necessarily a sign of the alliance's importance or effectiveness. Sometimes it appears as if the allies, apart from France, feel that as they must have some formal institution, it is better to keep NATO than have nothing at all. The NATO question is further complicated by the presence of the Americans, who are needed for the protection

[1] See page 601.

they offer, but who cannot participate in the integration of Western Europe, and who do not want to do so. Thus NATO is no help in providing a framework in which Europeans can act by themselves, which for economic and political reasons the Americans have long wanted them to do. For Europeans to find such a framework requires a much larger recognition by all those involved that their defence interests are linked, if not identical, than they are willing to give at present. In particular there is no sign of this either in Britain or in France, and in the absence of any real wish for military integration from these two countries, neither Germany nor Italy, let alone the smaller poorer states, can be expected to do anything but seek further guarantees from the United States.

The defence question is a more complicated one than the economic one, for the simple reason that traditionally military power has been conceived as a national responsibility in a way that economic power has not. The crown, or the head of the republic, and after them the heads of government, have been linked to the military in Western European states from time immemorial; the encroachment of government on economic affairs has been a more modern development. Military power also contains in it the choice of peace or war—a choice to which the nation-states would like to cling, even though it has already been taken away from them. It is inconceivable that any Western European states should ever go to war alone in Europe again—and if they went to war they would not be alone for long, possibly no more than for a few minutes. With the disappearance of the empires the British alone remain with a large-scale international commitment, and it is not likely that that will continue into the far distant future. Thus the political circumstances in which each country needed its national defence system have come to an end—not to mention the very great changes on the military and strategic side that have been wrought by the existence of the American nuclear deterrent, and the American commitment to defend Western Europe against possible Soviet attacks. But not surprisingly, as Anthony Verrier shows,[1] the countries of Western Europe are unable to agree on a method for reorganising their defence on a joint basis, or on how it is to be linked to that of the Americans, whose association with Western Europe in one way or another is thought necessary by most countries in the area. The adaptation to the idea of a Defence Community from traditional attitudes to defence and the power to declare war, still regarded as essential to real power in some countries, is bound to take time, and while the change is taking place there are bound to be serious aberrations, as in France today.

Leaving aside the personal predilections of General de Gaulle, it is probably true to say that French policy, preoccupied as it is with the preservation of the nation and the myth of French independence, reflects the last agonies of a primarily agricultural society as it is forced to realise that territory alone is not decisive in establishing a people's influence and prosperity. Even though some Frenchmen realised the need to be integrated with their neighbours—it was a Frenchman, Jean Monnet, who inspired both the Paris and the Rome treaties—de Gaulle's government is pursuing a policy of establishing a network of bilateral defence and economic links with other countries, mainly European but also non-European, that will provide France with various mercantile advantages, but not commit her to work within any institutional framework. But this framework is necessary, at least if the authors of the European Treaties are to be believed, because without it the long-term advantages of integration—stability, a large market,

[1] See pages 265 ff.

a more rational use of resources, greater opportunities for political and economic growth—will never be realised. An economic depression in one country of Western Europe, just as much as a military attack, would affect all, since they are all dependent on each other for prosperity. It is possible that the countries of Western Europe will soon need the Eastern European countries and the Soviet Union in the same way as well.

It is sometimes suggested that NATO—and the wholly European organisations like the Common Market also—are more divisive than cohesive, since they serve to perpetuate the gap between Eastern Europe and Western Europe. This has hardly been borne out by the experience of the last few years. The existence of the European Community has served as a magnet to the great revival of interest in Western Europe on the part of the smaller Communist countries. Poland, Hungary, Czechoslovakia, even East Germany, have once again looked to their traditional markets in the West, now more prosperous than ever, and are seeking means of re-entering them. In the meanwhile Yugoslavia, as usual the first to move, has joined GATT, and declared herself ready for reforms that will bring her economic system closer to the market economy. This movement has not been hindered by the economic integration of the West—it has been encouraged by it. And it has taken place in spite of the fact that NATO still exists, that the Berlin Wall still stands, that the hostility to West Germany is fostered by continual hate campaigns and irrelevant anti-Nazi propaganda. In other words trade is more important than slogans or military alliances, for the good reason that Eastern Europe, like the West, is having to reassess the military threat. As in the West, all this is provoking a lively discussion and there are still plenty of backward-looking conservatives standing in the way—but the movement is perceptible.

The obvious lesson for Western Europe is to continue with the work of coordinating and improving its common institutions, and providing firmer foundations for its prosperity through integration. This will make the region more attractive to Eastern Europe than any disbanding of NATO or bilateral treaties of non-aggression. The way to the hearts of the Eastern Europeans is economic; trade and business will reduce the fear of war much more rapidly than vaguer if more high-flown concessions. The problem of Germany is of course a real one and not likely to be solved until much closer relations have been established with the Eastern European countries than are possible at present. This is probably the only way round the dilemma posed by the division of Germany; certainly independent démarches by the French alone are not going to help. Mr Gromyko's suggestion that the problem can be solved by Europeans without the Americans can be seen as a simple trick to divide the West.

Thus the preoccupation which Western Europe has had with its economic revival since the war is spreading to Europe as a whole. States, in the East or in the West, are today more interested in competing in trade than in arms or for territory—whatever impression a few voices calling for an Austrian South Tyrol, a Germany beyond the Oder or a separate Walloon state may give to the contrary. It is the opportunity to better himself, to live more prosperously, to enjoy the advantages of the mass society, that the ordinary European seeks, even if the methods he chooses, and the aspects of prosperity he prefers, may differ a good deal from one part of the continent to another. To facilitate this economic unity, institutions and organisations have multiplied; it already looks as if they will gradually be extended or added to so that East Europe can join.

All this is a slow process, and is of necessity carried on in the dim language of technicians, lawyers and civil servants, whose political talents are today being used to implement a new kind of revolution. The language of integration is certainly dull compared with the more heroic and much less materialistic battle cries of the old nation-states. But these slogans and banners, with their 'Fatherlands' and 'honour' and 'glory of the race', refer less and less to the ordinary experience of the people who now live in Western Europe. (On the more emotional side, the wide support given at one time to pacifist movements like the Campaign for Nuclear Disarmament in Britain is also a symptom of the erosion of the old faith in the nation and the need to defend it by all available means.) The impetus for economic integration has come from a recognition of real needs and interests; a Frenchman's interests lie more in the kind of house he can get or the car he can afford to buy than in General de Gaulle's prestige visits to South America, which have led to nothing. For the time being a European's charity begins at home. This explains the heavy emphasis on economic subjects in this book, for it is these which concern Western Europe most just now.

One effect of the new prosperity is that it is gradually destroying the traditional Europe which, while more backward economically, still had the aesthetic and cultural attractions of the past. The half-forgotten world of Spain and Italy and Greece has been invaded by tourists and their hotels and villas, and in the more industrial north, the countryside of the more heavily populated areas has been destroyed without thought or care for the pleasure or welfare of the people who will live there in the future. Cheapness, shoddiness, lack of forethought have been combined to turn some of the best sites in the world into some of the most unpleasant. And this has been done not by poor, ill-equipped societies or individuals, but by some of the richest in the world. Thus the materialism which in the countries of Western Europe has fostered a desire to live peaceably and to work together with neighbour-countries has also contributed to the partial destruction of Europe's own peculiar heritage; the cities, landscape and way of life that grew gently out of the past, and made Europe the most varied and exciting region of the world. In other words the mass society from which all wish to profit has very serious disadvantages.

So far this aspect of Europe has hardly been discussed at all. It is therefore perhaps worthwhile to mention it here for it may be of fundamental importance in the future. At the same time, one of the striking things about post-war Western Europe is the complete absence of political thinkers; there are teachers of political thought in the universities, and there are plenty of politicians and civil servants telling Western Europeans how they should or should not set about their business, but the discussion of the objectives of society, of the values which should inform its laws and policies, has come to a halt. Society is simply there and no-one bothers to be an anarchist. Protest is registered against specific acts or people and technical problems are continually posed and answered, but there is no Locke or Rousseau or even Marx preparing people for the revolution to come. Instead the revolution is being carried out in treaties by highly intelligent but culturally almost lifeless bureaucrats. This may sound ungrateful, but a reading of the speeches and other works of officials of the Common Market Commission, or their many colleagues in other European organisations, who have certainly worked tirelessly for a more stable world, reveals a marked lack of concern about what kind of European society they ultimately want. They are also extremely wary of discussing the aims and powers of the federal institutions which they advocate, which has led some of their opponents to suppose that they do not want a really integrated Europe at all. This is another good reason why their concentration on administrative and technical problems cannot make up for the lack of discussion about the ends towards which they are working—just as prosperity by itself cannot make up for the gradual disappearance of privacy and individuality in everyday life. As Richard Moore points out in his chapter on parliamentarianism in Western Europe,[1] this absence of strongly felt and valid ideals has caused considerable damage to the effectiveness of democratic institutions in the area.

This situation is not only the result of an absence of imagination in Europe, it is a reaction against the huge burden of ideals and ideologies which Europeans carried for so long, and from whose workings they have suffered immeasurable damage. The effect of Nazism and Communism has in fact been to frighten the intellectuals away from a systematic approach to revolutionary action—and in a sense the Community's implications are revolutionary—and from ideological constructions. Instead they prefer to stick rather aridly to the problems in hand. Even socialism has had to become an anodyne shadow of the fighting movement of the earlier part of this century; the reason is obvious—the circumstances which bred such a class-based view of the world have changed. Altogether, compared to the situation in the United States, political idealism in Western Europe is dead. And this is not because of an absence of problems, but because the problems are seen to be largely technical, and because the institutions and political organisations which could harness the idealism of the young and energetic are mostly bureaucratic rather than democratic.

Indeed it is the policy of some governments in the European Community to make sure that the common Parliamentary institutions (whose role is specified in the Treaties) are kept in a secondary position for as long as possible, because they fear the effect that a directly elected 'European' body could have on existing national authorities. At the same time, people who earlier in this century might have been 'activists' or 'agitators' or leaders of movements go into hiding, as it were, in international organisations, research institutes, universities and newspapers, where their function is to organise or comment on present conditions rather than to think independently or to rouse the populace. The ideas of such people on the nature of society tend (in so far as they have any) to be conservative and unimaginative, their private lives fitting comfortably into a pattern of bourgeois rectitude. This is not meant to sound disparaging; perhaps it is a good thing that so much energy is being put into organising our material existence. Perhaps a concentration on wider issues would lead to a vast quantity of fuzzy good-will (or dangerous theorising about Europe as a world power) and no effective action. Nevertheless it does seem important to think about some of the problems of the 'mass society' now, even before Europeans have fully accepted that this is the direction in which they are probably moving. This need not be done only in the pseudo-precise terms of popular sociology; for a change, it might be conceived as a philosophical task, in which the thinker might consider Europe's variety itself as a highly desirable aspect of his ideal state. This kind of political philosopher is badly lacking in Western Europe today.

A Western European mass society poses particular problems of its own, both because the sub-continent is immensely crowded, and also because its prosperity is largely related to its trade. Internally therefore it is vulnerable to the pressure of its growing population, so that without careful thought

[1] See page 297.

the region may become increasingly unattractive compared with emptier parts of the world; externally the sub-continent is deeply involved with its trading partners elsewhere. The population pressure will soon be such that it will be extremely hard to preserve the special attractions of Europe's countryside and cities, without extensive planning and control; an important part in this could be played by a federal institution which would be able to encourage local or national authorities with money and expertise to keep these attractions alive. A different question is that of justice; European countries as a whole could do much more to bring the misfits, the criminals, the poor and the lonely, into society. In this too a federal agency could play a stimulating part: a comparison of methods and experiences from one country to the next, the federal application of jointly conceived programmes, these are ways in which a highly materially developed society, such as Western Europe is rapidly becoming, might refine its sense and its administration of justice.

Another problem, possibly of even more immediate urgency, is the need for some form of technological union which, like the American government, could harness vast resources to be invested in research and development in advanced products, techniques and services, ranging from computers to medicine or even transport (not to mention weapons). The efforts in this field of individual European countries, while they may be brave and even fruitful, are inevitably so limited in scale that their future prosperity may be endangered unless they manage to pool their resources in some way. On the external side, Europe's relations with the developing countries are becoming more and more important, since looked at purely materially their backwardness and poverty hinders Europe's own economic growth. If they could gradually become equal trading partners instead of remaining second-class citizens in the world economy, this would be as much to Europe's advantage as to theirs. In the absence of a joint approach by Europeans to this problem, the resentments harboured by the developing countries against them will grow, and will provide a new cause for international instability and militant alignments against the West. (This question is discussed at length in this book by John Pinder and John White.[1])

These are some of the great questions of the future on which Western Europe has hardly begun to work. The choices offered by our Eastern neighbours have been firmly rejected since the war, and Western Communists themselves, where they remain influential, have changed their approach, as Joseph Starobin shows.[2] In the West, the American experience of a mass society is certainly instructive but its lessons are not entirely applicable to Europe, for the United States is a highly integrated society with vast resources of land at its disposal, and no comparable divergences of structure or tradition. The difficulty in Europe is to bring together a series of entrenched national administrations into one system, in which they do not compete with each other but instead work together. The difficulty is enormous because it means abandoning the possessive view of government which has been traditional in Europe since the days of the feudal kings; this requires new methods and new approaches peculiar to the problems and the people involved. In this book we have tried to contribute to this vision of Europe by presenting the countries involved in a common political, economic and cultural perspective.

Roman Europe, which comprised most of the countries described here

[1] See pages 346–7 and 433–4.
[2] See pages 299 ff.

(and a few Balkan ones which are not), seemed to the medieval world which followed it a golden age, in which there was an ease of communication and degree of stability which it seemed was never again to be possible. This unity is now within the grasp of Western Europe—without the need for the tyrannical elements which in the end weakened and divided ancient Rome. The great question is whether the peoples of Western Europe believe that unity is possible; in theory they generally favour it, but they seem to fear that in practice they will lose their peace of mind, and the familiar advantages of independence. Although the European Community has gone some way in allaying this fear, it can only be regarded as a beginning; the real business of creating a European society is still to come. It is to be hoped that the same originality that was shown in the writing of the Treaties of Paris and Rome will emerge in the discussion of this wider problem, involving as it does a much more systematic vision of democracy than most of the 'technocrats' are as yet willing to adopt. It is to be feared that without this vision Western Europe may be devastated by its own prosperity, and the 'inherent contradictions of capitalism' may emerge in new and unexpected forms.

PART ONE

THE COUNTRIES OF WESTERN EUROPE

BASIC INFORMATION

Compiled by

ANTHONY SHARP

ANDORRA

GEOGRAPHY AND POPULATION

Features: A mountainous country seldom below 2,500 ft/760 m. *Area:* 180 sq. miles/465 sq. km. *Total population:* About 15,000 of whom about 60 per cent are foreigners. *Capital:* Andorra la Vella (2,200). *Language:* Catalan. *Religion:* Roman Catholic.

CONSTITUTIONAL SYSTEM

Constitution: Andorra has existed as an independent principality since 1278. It is now ruled by two Co-Princes, the Spanish Bishop of Urgell and the President of the French Republic.

Executive and legislature: The permanent delegate of the French Co-Prince to Andorra is the Prefect of the Pyrénées Orientales resident in Perpignan. The delegate of the Bishop is his Vicar-General resident in La Seu d'Urgell. Both delegates are represented in Andorra by locally resident civil servants (*veguers*). Proposals are submitted to the delegates by the General Council of the Valleys which numbers 24 members elected by universal suffrage for four years. The President of the Council is the Chief Syndic assisted by a Second Syndic, both of whom are elected by the Council, but are not members of it. The two Syndics and the senior Councillors of each Parish—eight in all—make up the Junta General whose function is to make provisional decisions that are afterwards submitted to the Council for confirmation. *Political figures:* Francesc Escudé-Ferrero (Chief Syndic), Eduard Rossell-Pujal (Second Syndic).

Local government: Six Parishes are administered by municipal authorities (*comúns*) of about ten members. Each *comú* elects a Senior and Junior Consul as Mayor. Villages are administered by *quarts*.

Judicial system: Civil law is exercised in the first instance by two civil judges (*batlles*), one appointed by each Co-Prince. The litigant may apply to either. Appeals are heard by the Appeal Judge, who is appointed for life by the two Co-Princes alternately. Final appeal is to the Supreme Court of Andorra in Perpignan or to the Court of Urgell. Criminal law is administered by the Tribunal de les Corts consisting of two members of the Council, the two Batlles, the two Veguers and the Appeal Judge, and is based on the French and Spanish legal codes.

ECONOMY

Main agricultural products are cereals, potatoes, vegetables and tobacco. Lead, stone, alum, timber and iron are also produced. Sheep-rearing and tourism—over 1 million in 1966—are the main industries. As there are no

4

customs duties, apart from 2 per cent on the invoice price of exports, Andorra has become a great market for European goods. There is no income-tax or death-duty and only a 3 per cent levy on alcohol and motor-fuels.

SOCIAL SECURITY

Andorra's first social security scheme was introduced in 1966 to cover the 4,000 Andorran, 3,500 Spanish and 500 French employees in the country. Its annual cost of F350,000 ($71,400) will be met by a return of half the profits on the sale of French stamps in the Principality. A new modern clinic, mainly for maternity care, is expected to provide free services. A private clinic is already in existence and there are several resident doctors and dentists; also ambulance and fire services.

EDUCATION

Primary schools teach mainly in French and Spanish. The General Council has constructed a primary school in each of the six Parishes and a secondary school in Andorra la Vella, all teaching in Catalan. Previously children were compelled to go to Barcelona or Toulouse for secondary education. Whereas in the past all teachers were supplied by France and Spain, the Council now reserves the right of selecting its teachers from any nationality.

MASS MEDIA

The press: Under a Franco-Spanish agreement no newspapers as such may be published in Andorra in Catalan or any other language, but national newspapers are supplied by both countries. The only Catalan magazines are *Serra d'Or* published by the Catalan Monks of Montserrat in Catalonia, *Vida Nova* published in Montpellier, and the ski-ing quarterly *Neu* published in Barcelona.

Broadcasting: Under the same Franco-Spanish agreement, neither country may give political information on the other over the Spanish-owned Radio-Andorra or the French-owned Radio des Vallées d'Andorre.

WESTERN EUROPE

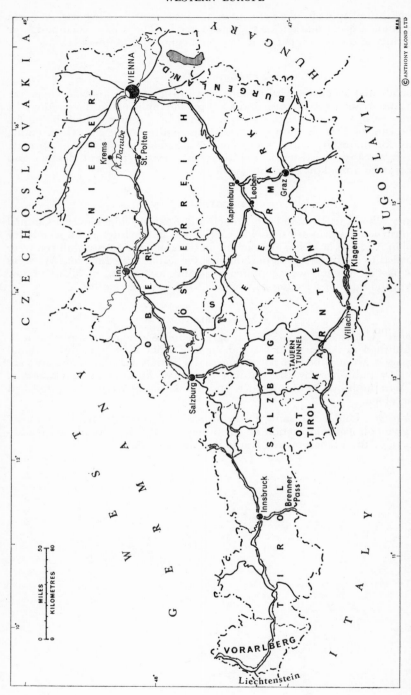

AUSTRIA

6

AUSTRIA

GEOGRAPHY

Features: Austria is essentially an Alpine country although it contains sections of other major European physical regions. North of the Danube is an area of rolling granite uplands with elevations of 1,200–2,500 ft/365–760 m. and incised valleys. South of the Danube is the Alpine foreland which is covered with glacial material and contains a number of lakes. The loess-covered Vienna basin, an eastern continuation of this region, provides a lowland break between the Alps and the Carpathians. South-east is the Styrian lowland centred on Graz. The largest geographical region is the Alpine zone with Vienna and Salzburg standing on its northern edge. Variations between limestone, sandstone and crystalline rocks give the variations in scenery for which the Alps are famous. Heights of over 10,000 ft/3,000 m. are common and the only major areas of level ground are to be found along the river valleys.

The most fertile areas are the loess regions of the Vienna and Styrian basins, and some parts of the Alpine foreland area; in the Alpine zone agriculture is concentrated on the alluvial and glacial fans and terraces of the latitudinal valleys. In the mountainous areas, however, there is much summer pasture. Principal natural resources are HEP, oil (from a field in the east), lignite and iron ore (Styria and Linz). Industry is concentrated mainly around Vienna, Salzburg, Styria and Linz.

Area: 32,355 sq. miles/83,850 sq. km. *Mean max. and min. temperatures:* Vienna (48° N, 16° 30′ E; 660 ft/200 m.) 75°F/24°C (July), 26°F/−3°C (Jan.); Innsbruck (47° 30′ N, 11° 30′ E; 1,900 ft/580 m.) 78°F/26°C, 20°F/−7° C; Graz (47° N, 15° 30′ E; 1,200 ft/370 m.) 87°F/31°C, 10°F/−12°C. *Relative humidity:* Vienna 82 per cent; Innsbruck 87 per cent; Graz 84 per cent. *Mean annual rainfall:* Vienna 59 in./1,500 mm.; Innsbruck 34 in./860 mm.; Graz 34 in./860 mm.

POPULATION

Total population: (1964 est.) 7,215,000. *Chief towns and populations:* (1961) VIENNA (1,628,000), Graz (237,000), Linz (196,000), Salzburg (108,000), Innsbruck (101,000). *Distribution:* In 1961 57 per cent of the population lived in Municipalities and Communes of up to 10,000 inhabitants and 43 per cent in towns of over 10,000 inhabitants. *Language:* 98 per cent of the population speak German, and minorities Czech, Croat and Slovene. *Religion:* 89 per cent Roman Catholic, 6 per cent Protestant.

CONSTITUTIONAL SYSTEM

Constitution: Austria is a federal republic. The 1929 constitution was reintroduced in 1945 unaltered. *Head of state:* President Franz Jonas (Austrian

7

Socialist Party). *Head of government:* Federal Chancellor Josef Klaus (Austrian People's Party).

Executive: The Federal President is elected by popular vote for six years. Although invested with special emergency powers, he normally acts on the authority of the government. The government is composed of Chancellor, Vice-Chancellor and ministers. The President selects the Chancellor from the party with the greatest representation in the National Council and appoints the other ministers on the Chancellor's advice. Ministers need not be members of the National Council and must resign after a personal vote of no-confidence.

Legislature: Legislative power rests with the National Council (Nationalrat), which is composed of 165 members elected for four years by all Austrians over 20 by proportional representation, and the Federal Council (Bundesrat). The latter is composed of 50 members representing the Länder. Legislation originates exclusively in the Nationalrat. The Bundesrat has delaying powers but no power of veto over legislation except in matters relating to its own composition. *Referendum:* The constitution provides for the use of the referendum. Further, any petition to the government having the support of 200,000 electors must be laid by the government before the National Council.

Political parties: The two main parties are the Catholic-conservative Austrian People's Party and the Austrian Socialist Party. The only other party represented in the Nationalrat is the liberal Austrian Freedom Party. In 1966 the Democratic Progressive Party was formed, led by Franz Olah, an ex-Socialist Minister of the Interior. The Austrian Communist Party instructed its followers to support the Socialists in 1966 where there was no Communist candidate. There are three other small parties—the European Federalist Party which instructed its supporters to abstain in 1966, the newly-formed Liberal Party, and the Marxist-Leninist Party that supports the Chinese Communist line. The present government was formed in April 1966 from the Austrian People's Party which gained an absolute majority over all other parties in the March 1966 elections. The Socialist Party then went into opposition after having governed in coalition with the People's Party for twenty years.

Election results:

Party	1962 Percentage of poll	Seats	1966 Percentage of poll	Seats
People's Party . .	45.43	81	48.35	85
Socialist Party . .	44.00	76	42.56	74
Freedom Party . .	7.05	8	5.35	6
Progressive Democrats			3.28	—
Communists . .	3.04	—	0.41	—
Others	0.08	—	0.05	—

Leading political figures: Austrian People's Party—Josef Klaus (Federal Chancellor), Fritz Bock (Vice-Chancellor), Lujo Toncic-Sorinj (Foreign Minister), Georg Prader (Defence Minister). Socialist Party—Bruno Kreisky (Party Chairman and former Foreign Minister), Bruno Pittermann (former Party Chairman).

Local government: Each *Land* has its own parliament (*Landtag*) elected in the same way as the Nationalrat. The Landtag elects its own government

8

(*Landesregierung*) consisting of the Governor (*Landeshauptmann*) and his Councillors (*Landesräte*), which is responsible to the Landtag. The Landeshauptmann acts in a dual capacity as chief provincial officer for the central administration, and as Land premier. The administration of the Land is the responsibility of Prefectures (*Bezirkshauptmannschaften*) composed of civil servants and of the Mayors and executive committees responsible to elected Communal Councils.

Judicial system: The constitution provides for the separation of the judiciary from the legislative and administrative authorities. Professional judges are appointed by the President on the recommendation of the Minister of Justice and may be neither dismissed nor transferred. Some cases are heard by non-professional Magistrates (*Schöffen*). The lowest courts are the Local Courts (*Bezirksgerichte*) which are competent in minor civil cases and cases involving minor misdemeanours. All other civil cases and criminal cases involving sentences up to 10 years are heard by the Provincial and District Courts (*Landes-* and *Kreisgerichte*). These also act as appeal courts for the Bezirksgerichte. The more serious criminal cases are heard by the Jury Courts (*Geschworenengerichte*) composed of three judges and eight jurors; the jury determines the sentence together with the judges. The four Higher Provincial Courts (*Oberlandsgerichte*) sit with three judges and hear appeals from the lower courts in civil and criminal cases. The final court of appeal for civil and criminal cases, as well as from the Commercial Courts (*Handelsgerichte*) and the Juvenile Courts (*Jugendgerichte*), is the Supreme Court (Oberster Gerichtshof) sitting with five judges. The Constitutional Court (Verfassungsgerichtshof) deals with all matters concerning the interpretation of the constitution and with disputes between the Länder and the central government, and examines the legality of administration and legislation. There is no death penalty.

RECENT HISTORY

After the second world war Austria was occupied by the United States, France, the Soviet Union and Britain. An abortive Communist putsch took place in 1950. In May 1955 Austria regained its independence under the Austrian State Treaty and in October 1955 opted for permanent neutrality. Austria was a founder-member of EFTA but in 1965 opened negotiations to become an associate member of the EEC.

Defence: The Federal President is commander-in-chief of the armed forces. The State Treaty forbids Austria the possession of atomic, biological and chemical weapons, missiles and heavy bombers. Compulsory national service for all men between 18 and 50 lasts for nine months. Austria has a small defence force (Bundesheer) of 54,000 which includes a regular force (Kaderbestand) of about 21,000. A small air force of about 7,000 men is an integral part of the Bundesheer. In addition there is a frontier defence force (Grenzschutztruppen) of about 12,000 which is to be increased. The 1965 defence budget was Sch2,750 million ($106 million) which represented about 1·4 per cent of GNP.

ECONOMY

Background: In the 1950s the base of the Austrian economy shifted from agriculture to industry, and in the process a consistently high rate of economic

9

growth was achieved. The movement of the working population from agriculture to industry (especially manufacturing) and services was accompanied by greater diversification of industry. After a boom in 1960 price-rises accelerated and in 1964–5 short- and long-term counter-measures were introduced. Budgetary policy was tightened and a more liberal import policy adopted.

From 1953 to 1964 the average annual growth rate of GNP at constant prices was 5.7 per cent—the highest among EFTA countries for this period. In 1964 GNP rose by 6 per cent compared to an increase of 4.4 per cent in 1963 and an estimated increase of 3 per cent in 1965. The main growth industries in recent years have been iron and steel, hydroelectric power, electrical engineering, paper and wood processing and building. The origin of GDP at factor cost in 1964 was:

Sector	Percentage
Agriculture . . .	10
Industry	52
Services	38
GDP	100

Industrial production in 1964 increased by over 8 per cent in volume compared with an increase of 3·8 per cent in 1963 and 2·3 per cent in 1962. Agricultural production rose by 5 per cent in 1964 compared to increases of 3·2 per cent in 1963 and 5·8 per cent in 1962. The main agricultural products are cereals, potatoes, sugar beet, wine, cattle and pigs.

Foreign trade: There was a balance of payments surplus from 1962 to 1964 (in 1964 it amounted to Sch1,490 million or $57 million). Exports of manufactured products accounted in 1964 for 74 per cent of total exports, the remainder consisting of raw materials and energy 17 per cent, chemicals 5 per cent and food, tobacco and beverages 4 per cent. Imports in 1964 were: manufactured products 59 per cent of total imports, raw materials and energy 20 per cent, food, tobacco and beverages 12 per cent and chemicals 9 per cent. Exports amounted to 17 per cent of GNP and imports to 22 per cent. The EEC received 48 per cent of all Austrian exports in 1964; EFTA received 18 per cent. Imports were similarly distributed; the EEC supplied 59 per cent of total imports and EFTA 14 per cent. Austria also has significant trade links with Eastern European countries—about 13 per cent of total trade.

Employment: The total labour force in 1963 was 3.3 million, of whom 21 per cent were employed in agriculture, 40 per cent in industry and 38 per cent in services; unemployment was 1 per cent. In 1965 the labour market became tighter, and in 1965 the government increased the quota for foreign workers.

Price and wage trends: From 1960 to 1962 consumer prices rose by about 9 per cent, in 1963 by 2·7 per cent and in 1964 by 3·8 per cent. From 1960 to 1962 hourly wages of industrial and building workers in the Vienna region rose by about 22 per cent; in 1963 they increased by 6·9 per cent, and in 1964 by 8·9 per cent. This proportionate rise in earnings was largely due to negotiated adjustments and shortage of labour.

Consumption: Private consumption rose less steeply in 1964 (3·6 per cent) compared with the two previous years—5 per cent in 1963 and 5.3 per cent in 1962. Private consumption accounted for 61 per cent of GNP in 1964 and public consumption for 14 per cent. Public consumption rose by 6 per cent in 1964 compared with increases of 5·6 per cent in 1963 and 1·9 per cent in 1962.

SOCIAL SECURITY

The Ministry of Social Administration supervises health, pensions and accident insurance and directly administers unemployment insurance through provincial and local unemployment offices. Contributions and benefits described below refer to 1964 except where otherwise stated.

Health insurance: Insurance with funds is compulsory for employees and pensioners (medical benefits only). There are special funds for railwaymen, public employees, miners and self-employed. All funds are self-governing bodies managed by elected representatives of insured persons and employers. Finance is provided by employees (wage-earners 3·6 per cent and self-employed 2·4 per cent of annual earnings up to Sch39,000 or $1,500) and employers at the same rate. The government provides 50 per cent of cash maternity benefits. Pension insurance institutes pay 8·7 per cent towards pensioners' medical insurance. Pensioners themselves pay between 1 and 2·5 per cent of their pension. Medical benefits are provided without limit usually by services under contract to the funds. Patients pay Sch3 ($0·10) per doctor's visit, Sch2 ($0·08) per prescription and up to 20 per cent of dental costs. Sickness benefits are paid for 26 weeks (some funds 52 weeks) and are 50 per cent of earnings, rising to 60 per cent after six weeks illness, with dependant's supplement of up to 10 per cent for a wife and 5 per cent for each child. Maternity benefits are 100 per cent of earnings paid for six weeks both before and after confinement, daily nursing benefits of between Sch2 and 5 for eight to 26 weeks after confinement, and a lump sum maternity grant of Sch40–100 ($1·5–4). Dependants receive the same medical benefits as the insured except that they pay 10 to 20 per cent of costs for hospitalisation and medicines and receive a larger maternity grant of Sch600–1,000 ($23–38·5).

Accident insurance: Benefits are paid by the General Accident Insurance Institution. There are separate institutions for agricultural and railway employees. Contributions are collected by sick funds which pass them on to accident insurance institutes. Accident insurance covers all employed and self-employed persons. Employers pay 2 per cent for wage-earners and 0·5 per cent for salaried employees of annual earnings up to Sch62,400 ($2,400). The self-employed pay Sch30 ($1·15) per year. Full medical benefits including appliances and rehabilitation are supplied for 45 days by sickness insurance, and thereafter by accident insurance bodies, until earning capacity is restored. Temporary disability benefit is provided by sickness funds in the form of ordinary sickness benefits for the first 26 weeks. Thereafter, for permanent disability greater than 20 per cent, the insured receives a pension from the accident institution amounting for employed persons to two-thirds of earnings up to Sch62,400 (far less for self-employed persons) for total disability, with supplements of 10 per cent for each child under 18 (25 if studying, no limit if invalid) up to a maximum of one-third of earnings, and an allowance of 50 per cent of pension if the insured is in need of constant attendance. For partial disability a proportion of the full pension is paid according to the degree of disability above 20 per cent. This is converted into a lump sum if it is less than 25 per cent of the full pension. Widow's pensions, also payable to dependant widowers, amount to 40 per cent of the insured's earnings if she is aged 60 or invalid, otherwise

11

20 per cent. Orphan's pensions are 20–30 per cent of earnings. Other eligible survivors may receive 20 per cent of earnings.

Pensions insurance: This covers compulsorily all wage-earners and salaried employees, for whom there are separate but similar systems. Contributions are collected by sick funds which transmit them to separate pension insurance institutes that administer benefits for wage-earners, salaried employees, agricultural workers, railwaymen, miners and the self-employed. These autonomous institutes are managed by elected representatives of the insured and employers. Wage-earners and salaried employees respectively pay 7·5 per cent and 7 per cent of earnings up to Sch62,400; this is matched by the employer, except that he pays higher contributions for wage-earners in agriculture and mining—8·5 and 13 per cent respectively. The state contributes annual grants to the wage-earner and agricultural systems.

Old-age pensions are paid at 65 (60 for women) or 60 (55 for women) after a year of sickness or unemployment, and amount to 30 per cent of average earnings—up to an annual maximum of Sch62,400—over the last five years plus increments related to the number of years of insurance. Pensions are reduced by any earnings greater than Sch710 ($27·30) per month. Bonuses of one month's pension are paid twice per year. Other supplements are for constant attendance (50 per cent of pension with a monthly minimum of Sch300 or $11·50) and for each child (5 per cent of earnings). Where the pension is small, means-tested supplemental equalisation payments are made, raising the insured's monthly pension to Sch870 ($33·50), plus Sch345 ($13·30) for his wife and Sch100 ($4) for each child. Invalidity pensions, supplements and equalisation payments paid upon loss of 50 per cent of normal earning capacity are the same as for old-age pensions, except that an additional supplement of 10 per cent of earnings (subject to the maximum) is paid, so long as this does not cause the pension and supplements to exceed 50 per cent of maximum earnings.

Widow's pensions are 50 per cent of the insured's invalidity pension; if the widow is over 40 or is caring for a child the minimum pension must be at least 25 per cent of the insured's earnings. Orphan's pensions are 40–60 per cent of the widow's pension, payable to each orphan under 18, under 25 if studying and without limit if invalid. Supplement equalisation payments in case of hardship raise the widow's monthly pension to Sch870 plus Sch315 ($12) for each child, and the monthly orphan's pension to Sch475 ($18·30).

Unemployment insurance: This covers all employed persons save casual labour and public employees. Both insured and employer pay 1 per cent of annual earnings up to Sch28,800 ($1,108). Benefits—reduced by the amount of earned income above Sch1,200 ($46) per month—are 30 to 60 per cent of earnings up to the above annual maximum varying inversely to wage-levels, with a weekly maximum of Sch156 ($6), plus weekly supplements of Sch30 ($1·15) for the first, and Sch22 ($0·80) for each other dependant, up to a maximum of 80 per cent of the insured's earnings. Benefits are payable for 12 to 36 weeks depending upon the number of contributions paid. Unemployment assistance is available for the needy in addition to insurance benefits.

Other benefits: The Ministry of Finance administers the family allowance scheme through its Family Allowance Equalisation Fund. The scheme covers all employed and self-employed persons and social insurance and assistance beneficiaries with one or more children and is financed by the insured (3 per cent of payable income tax), the employers (6 per cent of earnings) and grants from the Länder. Family allowances are paid at the monthly rate of Sch155 ($6) for the first, Sch175 ($6·70) for the second, Sch 205 ($8) for the third and Sch265 ($10) for each subsequent child. One month's allowances are paid as a bonus twice a year. Each family receives an additional monthly supplement of Sch175 if there are three or more children in the family. A lump-sum grant of Sch500 ($19·20) is paid for each birth, plus infant's grants of Sch600 ($23), paid after the first and sixth months of each child's life.

EDUCATION

The Federal Minister of Education has control over all schools. Education is free and compulsory from the age of six to 14. Religious education is compulsory in all schools.

Primary education: This is given in the *Volksschule.* In the first four years of 'basic school' (*Grundschule*) all children receive the same education. Those not admitted to secondary education go on to the *Hauptschule* for four more years, where they receive a general and practical education in preparation for vocational training. Admission to the Hauptschule is dependent upon the satisfactory completion of the fourth year of Grundschule and a certificate stating that the pupil is capable of attending the Hauptschule. There is provision for a ninth year of compulsory schooling: a one-year polytechnic course to consolidate basic general education with a special emphasis on the future occupation of those who neither remain at primary school nor take intermediate or secondary education. This course is organised either as an adjunct to primary or vocational schools, or as a separate school.

Secondary education: Admission to secondary schools is dependent upon the successful completion of the Grundschule and passing an entrance examination. Secondary education generally lasts for nine years—four years in the lower and five in the upper divisions. Secondary schools are of four main categories: the Arts Grammar School (*Gymnasium*), the Science Grammar School (*Realgymnasium*), the Domestic Science College (*Wirtschaftskundliches Realgymnasium*) for girls, and special categories of general secondary schools. The latter include the *musisch-pädagogisches Realgymnasium* which admits pupils who have successfully completed primary education for five-year courses, preparing them for entry into teacher-training colleges and social service occupations; the Intermediate Grammar School (*Aufbaugymnasium* and *Aufbaurealgymnasium*) which provides a one-year transition grade and a five-year upper division for pupils who have successfully completed Volksschule and wish to attain secondary education standards; the Grammar School for Employed Persons (*Gymnasium* and *Realgymnasium für Berufstätige*) which provides ten half-yearly courses for persons over 18 who have completed vocational education or are employed. Other special secondary schools provide courses for non-commissioned officers and physically handicapped children. All secondary education terminates with a leaving examination (*Reifeprüfung*) which is the qualification for entry into the universities and the institutes of higher education.

Special education: There are special schools, organised either as separate institutions or attached to primary schools, for mentally or physically handicapped children as well as some sanatorium schools.

Technical and vocational education: There are four types of vocational school: part-time, intermediate, secondary and those for social work. For those

13

serving apprenticeships in commerce and trade attendance is compulsory at a part-time vocational school (*berufsbildende Pflichtschule*). Intermediate schools (*berufsbildende mittlere Schulen*) generally admit as students those who have completed primary school and passed the entrance examination. Courses last from one to four years. Trade, technical and arts and crafts schools have four-year courses ending either with a final proficiency examination (*Abschlussprüfung*) or—after a special course—the Master Craftsman's Examination (*Meisterprüfung*). Other schools exist for domestic science, business and commerce and for social workers. In the last case courses last from one to two years, and students must be at least 18. Secondary schools (*berufsbildende höhere Schulen*) have the same entrance qualifications as the *berufsbildende mittlere Schulen*; courses last for five years and end, like those at the secondary schools, with the Reifeprüfung which qualifies the pupil to study a related discipline in a higher educational institute. The School for Social Work (*Lehranstalt für gehobene Sozialberufe*) offers courses lasting four semesters to students who have passed the Reifeprüfung.

University and higher education: Austria has ten institutions of university standard empowered to grant degrees of equivalent standing. All are self-governing public institutions. The four universities proper—Vienna, Graz, Salzburg and Innsbruck—are run on the principle of freedom of studies, but attendance at a certain number of lectures is obligatory. There are two technological universities, in Vienna and in Graz. There are four other specialised institutes each with university status: schools of agriculture, veterinary medicine and commerce, all in Vienna, and a school of mining in Loeben. In addition there are three academies of music—in Vienna, Salzburg and Graz—and one each of fine arts and applied art, both in Vienna. Students must meet the costs of university fees. Scholarships are available.

Educational Institutions 1964–5:

	Institutions	Staff	Students
Primary	4,523	25,153	581,713
Secondary	1,074	17,186	280,446
Special (1957–8)	120[1]	1,276	19,301
Technical and vocational (1963–4)	489	9,211	188,586
Universities, etc.	15	4,672	51,402

[1] Refers to schools only. In the same year there were 303 special classes attached to regular primary schools.

Adult education: This is provided mainly by adult education regional and local centres. In addition there are a few public boarding schools maintained by the church and the trade unions. In 1963 there were over 2,600 public libraries.

MASS MEDIA

The press:

Dailies: Kurier, Vienna, independent, 334,000; *Express*, Vienna, ind., 312,000; *Illustrierte Kronen-Zeitung*, Vienna, ind., 179,000; *Arbeiter-Zeitung*, Vienna, organ of Socialist Party, 109,000; *Kleine Zeitung*, Graz, ind., 95,000; *Volksblatt*, Vienna, People's Party, 94,000; *Neues Österreich*, Vienna, ind., 62,000; *Oberösterreichische Nachrichten*, Linz, ind., 54,000; *Die Neue Zeit*, Graz,

Socialist, 53,000; *Wiener Zeitung*, Vienna, official government paper, 50,000; *Die Presse*, Vienna, ind. liberal, 47,000; *Südost Tagespost*, Graz, organ of People's Party, 47,000; *Tiroler Tageszeitung*, Innsbruck, ind., 44,000; *Salzburger Nachrichten*, Salzburg, ind., 42,000; *Volkstimme*, Vienna, organ of Communist Party, 40,000.

Periodicals: Neue Illustrierte Wochenschau (w), Vienna, illustrated, 388,000; *AT Auto-Touring* (f), Vienna, motoring, 290,000; *Der Sozialist* (m), Vienna, Soc., 283,000; *Wiener Wochenausgabe* (w), Vienna, general review, 196,000; *Wiener Wochenblatt* (w), Vienna, ind., 186,000; *Die Frau*, Vienna, woman's, 177,000; *Echo* (w), Vienna, ind. international review, 146,000; *Welt am Montag* (w), Vienna, Soc., 129,000; *Der Erzähler* (w), Vienna, literary/film, 69,000; *Austria-SKI-Sport* (2m), Innsbruck, journal of Austrian Skiing Association, 50,000; *Agrar-Post* (w), Vienna, agriculture, 34,000; *Internationale Wirtschaft* (w), Vienna, economics.

Broadcasting: Popular demand for reform of the Austrian Broadcasting Corporation (Österreichische Rundfunk GmbH), a state-supported private company, in particular to free it from the political appointments of the coalition period, led to a new law governing the Corporation from 1 January 1967. The supreme authority of the Corporation is a convention on which both Federal and Länder governments are represented. This body appoints a board of directors representing the nine Länder, religion, science, art, education and sport, and the main parties (proportionately) in the National-rat. The board chooses the director-general and departmental directors of the Corporation. None of these may concurrently hold any political office, and the director-general must not have held any such office in the five years prior to his appointment. Proportional broadcasting time is given to the parties represented in the Nationalrat. Daily commercial broadcasting is limited to 20 minutes on TV and two hours on radio.

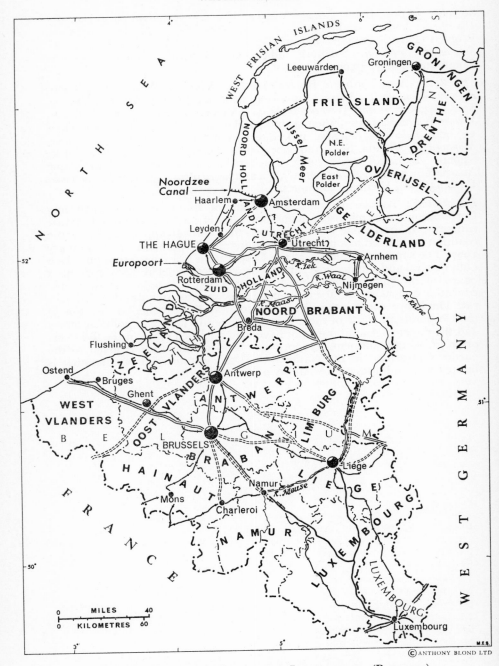

BELGIUM, THE NETHERLANDS AND LUXEMBOURG (BENELUX)

BELGIUM

Geography

Features: Belgium may be divided into a series of NE–SW bands. South-east is a continuation of the low plateau and scarplands of the Province of Luxembourg. To the north lie the Ardennes, a dissected plateau which is a western continuation of the German Rhine uplands; at its greatest elevation it reaches nearly 2,000 ft/610 m., but much is no more than 1,000 ft (Low Ardenne). The narrow but deep Sambre-Meuse Valley, following the line of the coalfield outcrop, is marked by a series of important industrial towns and marks a divide between the Ardennes and the lower plateau areas to the north—Hainaut, Brabant and Hesbaye, largely loess-covered chalk areas of about 250 ft/75 m. which slope gradually to the lower lands of Flanders to the north. Flanders consists of an inner, undulating, partly sandy plain, and an outer flat maritime plain immediately behind the coastal dunes. Finally, in the north lies the area of coarse gravels and sands known as the Campine (Kempenland), drained by the Scheldt river. This was largely a waste area till reclamation was undertaken in the 19th century.

Agriculture is mainly concentrated in the low loess-covered plateau and in Flanders. The chief mineral is coal, worked in the Sambre-Meuse Valley and the Campine coalfield. Industry is concentrated around both these coalfields and Brussels and Antwerp.

Area: 11,780 sq. miles/30,500 sq. km. *Mean max. and min. temperatures:* Brussels (51° N, 4° 30' E; 330 ft/100 m.) 73°F/23°C (July), 31°F/−1°C (Jan.); Ostend (51° N, 3° E; 13 ft/4 m.) 69°F/21°C (Aug.), 33°F/1°C (Feb.). *Relative humidity:* Brussels 94 per cent; Ostend 86 per cent. *Mean annual rainfall:* Brussels 33 in./840 mm.; Ostend 31 in./790 mm.

Population

Total population: (1964) 9,428,000. *Chief towns and populations:* (1964) Brussels (1,496,000), Antwerp (880,000), Liège (610,000), Charleroi (465,000), Ghent (462,000). *Distribution:* In 1961 about 30 per cent of the population lived in Communes with more than 25,000 inhabitants. *Languages:* Both French (Walloon) and Dutch (Flemish) are official languages. There are German-speaking minorities of about 100,000 around Eupen and Malmédy in the eastern part of Liège. In 1964 the Flemish-speaking provinces (East and West Flanders, Antwerp, Limburg, and Northern Brabant) had 4,779,380 inhabitants and the Walloon provinces (Hainaut, Namur, Liège, Luxembourg and Southern Brabant) 3,152,500. Brussels is officially bilingual but has a strong French-speaking majority. In all, the Flemings form about 55 per cent of the total population and the Walloons about 45 per cent. Both population density and birth-rate are higher in the Flemish-speaking areas. *Religion:* The population is overwhelmingly Roman Catholic.

17

CONSTITUTIONAL SYSTEM

Constitution: Belgium is a constitutional monarchy with a constitution dating from 1831. The present parliament was elected in 1965 specifically as a constituent assembly charged with undertaking certain reforms of the constitution. *Head of state:* King Baudouin. *Head of government:* Prime Minister Paul Vanden Boeynants (Parti Social Chrétien).

Executive: Power is vested in the King and his ministers. The King may dissolve or prorogue parliament. He appoints and dismisses his ministers and implements legislation by royal decree, but such acts are only effective if countersigned by a minister, thereby ensuring ultimate governmental responsibility. The government cannot function unless supported by a majority of members in both houses.

Legislature: Legislative powers are vested equally in the House of Representatives and the Senate. Either house may introduce legislation, but this becomes effective only when passed by both houses and promulgated by the King. The House of Representatives consists of 212 members elected for four years by proportional representation. The Senate has 178 members, two-thirds of whom are elected on the same basis as the lower house; the remaining third consists of individuals elected by provincial councils and others who are chosen or coopted by the Senate itself.

Political parties: Belgium has three traditional parties, the Catholic-conservative Christian Social Party (PSC), the Belgian Socialist Party (PSB) and the liberal Party of Liberty and Progress (PLP). The smaller parties are the Communist Party, Volksunie (the Flemish Nationalist Party) and three parties representing Walloon interests—the Walloon Front, the Walloon Workers Party and the French-speaking Democratic Front. The government formed in March 1966 is a coalition of the PSC and PLP.

Election results:

| | House of Representatives | | | | Senate | |
| | 1961 | | 1965 | | 1961 | 1965 |
Party	% of poll	Seats	% of poll	Seats	Seats	Seats
PSC	41·5	96	34.48	77	81	76
PSB	36·7	84	28·28	64	76	52
PLP	12·5	20	21·61	48	17	40
Volksunie	3.4	5	6·49	12	—	5
Communists	3·1	5	4.56	6	1	4
Others	3·0	2	4·38	5	—	1

Leading political figures: PSC—Paul Vanden Boeynants (Premier), Robert Houben (Party Chairman), Pierre Harmel (Foreign Minister), Théo Lefèvre. PSB—Antoine Spinoy, Leo Collard (Party Chairman). PLP—Willy de Clerq (Deputy Premier), Charles Poswick (Defence Minister), Robert Henrion (Finance Minister). Volksunie—Franz Van Der Elst (President and Founder).

Local government: Each Province elects a Provincial Council for a period of four years headed by a Governor, who is appointed and dismissed by the King. From among its own members the Council elects a Permanent Deputation to manage its everyday affairs. Each Province is divided into several administrative Districts (*arrondissements*) each headed by a District Commissioner appointed by the Governor, who supervises all Communes within the Arrondissements having less than 5,000 inhabitants. The Communes (*communes*) are administered by Town Councils, elected for six years, which in turn elect their Aldermen. Each Mayor is appointed by the King on the basis of proposals submitted by the Town Council.

Judicial system: The supreme authorities are the Assize Courts of which there is one for each Province, the Courts of Appeal in Brussels, Ghent and Liège, and the highest court, the Court of Cassation, in Brussels. The country is divided into legal districts bearing no relation to the administrative divisions, each having its own court of first instance (civil and criminal), and further subdivided into judicial *cantons* each with its own JP. Judges are appointed for life. Trial is by jury. There is no death penalty.

Recent History

After the second German violation of its neutrality and its subsequent occupation in the second world war, Belgium signed the Brussels Treaty (later to become the WEU) in March 1948 with the Netherlands, Luxembourg, Britain and France, and in 1949 became a founder member of NATO. Belgium has also been a leading exponent of European integration through its membership of Benelux, ECSC, EEC and Euratom. In 1922 Belgium signed a 50-year customs agreement with Luxembourg (Belgo-Luxembourg Economic Union—BLEU). Belgium's colonial disengagement from the Congo and the former Trust Territory of Rwanda-Urundi has involved bloodshed in all three countries. The Communist-inspired strikes of 1947–8, growing strife between Walloons and Flemings, frequent government changes, and strikes by doctors and police have troubled the domestic scene in post-war Belgium. In 1966 there were attempts to expel the Walloon elements of the University of Louvain from Flemish territory. In June of the same year it was decided to transfer SHAPE and the HQ of NATO's Central Command to Brussels. Mr Paul-Henri Spaak, former Foreign Minister and Secretary-General of NATO, retired from active politics in 1966.

Defence: The Sovereign is titular commander-in-chief of the armed forces. Military service lasts 12–15 months. Total armed forces number 107,000 of whom fewer than half are conscripts: army 83,500, air force 19,000, navy 4,500. The air force and navy are assigned to or reserved for NATO service. The 1966 defence budget was BF26,000 million ($520 million) representing 3.5 per cent of GNP.

Economy

Background: Belgium is a highly industrialised country. In 1959 a labour shortage and the slow rate of recovery from the 1958 recession led to the setting up of a Bureau of Economic Planning. Latterly the problem of diversifying and increasing production has been tackled by a policy of redeployment of labour resources, heavy investment towards modernisation, improvement of the competitive position of exports and continued controlled expansion of private consumption. An effort has also been made to intensify investment in underdeveloped regions that depend upon unprofitable industries. The basis of recent policy has been the Economic Expansion Laws of July 1959, offering tax exemptions, low-interest-rate loans and preferential treatment to foreign investors. To further industrial development, a National Investment Corporation was set up in 1963, authorised to invest capital in business enterprises on temporary and specially favourable terms. In the face of a shortage of investment capital (although foreign investment has remained strong) which brought on a serious crisis in public finance in 1965, subsequent policy was one of careful economy designed to keep the increase in total public expenditure below the growth in value of GNP, and to protect individual purchasing power by controlling prices and public spending.

In 1964 the Belgian GNP amounted to BF768,200 million ($15,364 million). From 1950 to 1960 the annual average rate of growth was 2·7 per cent. The Bureau of Economic Planning laid down an annual 4 per cent growth rate for 1962–5. Actual growth rates for these years were 3·8, 4·3, 3·9 and 3 per cent. Main growth industries are chemicals, rubber, heavy metallurgical and metal products, food and beverages. In 1964 the origin of GDP at factor cost was:

Sector				Percentage
Agriculture	.	.	.	6·5
Industry	.	.	.	42·5
Services	.	.	.	51
GDP				100

Annual average rate of industrial growth in the period 1961–4 was 6·5 per cent, representing a slight decline compared with the years 1958–60. The principal industries are coal mining, coke and electricity production, oil processing, steel, textiles, mechanical engineering, non-ferrous metals, cement, food, beverages, tobacco, wood and paper. Owing to specialised farming, Belgium's agricultural industry can provide 80 per cent of the nation's requirements. Expansion is taking place in horticulture and the production of vegetables. The main crops are sugar beet, potatoes, wheat, barley and oats.

Foreign trade: Belgium's foreign trade figures are quoted in combination with those of Luxembourg (Belgo-Luxembourg Economic Union); Belgium's volume of trade is actually 11 times greater than that of Luxembourg. Both countries are members of the EEC and in 1964, 63 per cent of BLEU's total exports went there and only 13 per cent to EFTA. In the same year imports from the EEC were 53 per cent and from EFTA 13 per cent (of total imports). This represented an increase in exports over 1963 of 19 per cent to the EEC and 4 per cent to EFTA, and an increase in imports from the two areas of 17 and 9 per cent respectively (1963 over 1962 increase in exports to the EEC was 20 per cent, to EFTA 4 per cent; in imports from the two areas, 15 and 12 per cent respectively).

In 1964 BLEU's imports of goods and services amounted to 37 per cent of GNP and exports to 35 per cent. BLEU's main imports in 1964 were minerals (mainly petroleum, iron ore and natural gas) 15 per cent, machinery and mechanical appliances 14 per cent, base metals 12 per cent and textiles 12 per cent. The main exports in the same year were base metals 30 per cent, textiles 15 per cent, machinery and equipment 11 per cent and transport equipment 8 per cent. The trade deficit widened from BF13·6 thousand million ($273 million) in 1963 to BF16·6 thousand million ($321 million) in 1964.

Employment: In 1964 the total working population in Belgium was 3·6 million of whom 6 per cent were employed in agriculture, 45 per cent in industry and 47 per cent in services. Unemployment in the same year was under 2 per cent. There continued to exist a labour shortage which had spread to all sectors of the economy by the end of the year. Increased mechanisation, an increased

number of labour permits for foreign workers and a crash technical programme with the aim of redirecting workers to areas with a particularly
marked labour shortage were then introduced. The bulk of the 600,000
foreign workers are employed in mining and manufacturing industries.

Price and wage trends: The rise in wages in Belgium has been matched by a
high increase in productivity. In the years preceding 1960 wages rose only
moderately; from 1961 to 1963 average hourly industrial earnings increased
by about 8 per cent a year, and in 1964 by 12 per cent. From 1961 to 1964
the retail price index rose annually by 1, 2·3, 3·5 and 4·5 per cent. In 1965,
in spite of a slight easing of demand, gross hourly earnings increased by an
average of 9·6 per cent. The cost of living index, pushed on by a poor harvest
and the first moves towards the EEC's common agricultural policy, rose by
4·1 per cent in 1965 compared with an increase of 4·2 per cent in 1964.

Consumption: In 1964 private consumption amounted to 67 per cent of GNP
at market prices and public consumption to 13 per cent.

SOCIAL SECURITY

General supervision is exercised by the Ministry of Social Welfare, except
in the case of unemployment insurance which is under the Ministry of Labour.
Benefits and contributions described below—except where otherwise stated—
refer to 1964. All contributions and benefits are tied to the retail price index.

Health insurance: Contributions are collected by the National Social Security
Office (NSSO) within the Ministry of Social Welfare, the programme is
coordinated by the National Sickness and Invalidity Insurance Institute
(NSIII) and benefits are paid by approved mutual benefit societies and a
Public Auxiliary Fund for persons not belonging to a society. All employed
persons must enrol with either a society or the Auxiliary Fund. Pensioners—
and under certain conditions students, self-employed persons and public
utility employees—are covered for medical benefits. There are special
systems for miners, railwaymen, seamen and public employees. Insurance is
financed equally by employers and employees, both paying 5 per cent of
monthly earnings up to BF11,550 ($231); the government covers 32 per cent
of medical benefit costs 95 per cent for certain serious diseases), 50 per cent of
invalidity pensions in the second and third years of payment and 95 per cent
thereafter. The insured pays the costs of services and is reimbursed by his
society to the extent of 75 to 100 per cent; pensioners receive all services free.
Sickness benefits are paid at the rate of 60 per cent of monthly earnings up
to BF11,550 for up to one or two years. The waiting period for salaried
employees is 30 days, during which time the employer must pay full wages.
Maternity benefits are 60 per cent of earnings paid for six weeks before and
six weeks after confinement, but not for the 30 days of compulsory paid
maternity leave that salaried employees receive.

Accident insurance: This covers all employed persons and is administered by
the Employment Accident Commission under the Ministry of Social Welfare
and by local accident boards and inspectors. Awards are approved by the
courts. The whole cost of the insurance is borne by the employer, who either
provides benefits directly, or through an insurance premium with employer
mutual associations or private insurance companies. Temporary disability
benefits are 80 per cent of monthly earnings up to BF10,000 ($200) for the
first 28 days and thereafter 90 per cent. For permanent disability, pensions

are 100 per cent of earnings up to BF10,000 for total disability, with a constant attendance allowance of up to 50 per cent of earnings. For partial disability, pensions are a percentage of the full pension corresponding to the degree of incapacity, which may be converted into a lump sum payment. Widow's pensions—also payable to dependant widowers—are 30 per cent of the insured's earnings. Orphan's pensions of 15–20 per cent of earnings are payable to not more than three orphans. In the absence of widows and orphans, pensions of 20 per cent of earnings are paid to dependant parents and 15 per cent to a brother, a sister or a grandchild.

Pensions insurance: The NSSO collects contributions and distributes them to the agencies administering the benefits: the National Retirement and Survivors Pension Fund, managed by an administrator representing the Ministry of Social Welfare and an employer-employee council, and the NSIII. All gainfully employed persons are covered by pensions insurance, with three separate schemes for wage-earners, salaried employees and self-employed persons. There are special schemes for railwaymen, miners, public employees and seamen. The coverage for invalidity pensions is the same as for health insurance. In 1966 pensions insurance was financed by the insured person and the employer at rates of 5.5 and 7 per cent of earnings respectively. For salaried employees, both contributions and benefits are subject to an annual maximum (1964) of BF108,000 ($2,160). The government provides annual subsidies for pension insurance, while invalidity pensions are financed by contributions to health insurance. Old-age pensions are paid at 65 (women 60) or up to five years earlier with a 5 per cent reduction per year, and amount to a maximum of 60 per cent of average lifetime earnings for single persons and 75 per cent for married persons. Invalidity pensions are paid to all persons losing two-thirds of their earning capacity in their usual occupation and amount to 60 per cent of earnings. Widow's pensions— payable to widows aged 45, two-thirds incapacitated or caring for a child— are 60 per cent of the insured's pension. Widows not eligible for a pension receive one year's pension in the form of a lump sum adaptation grant. Special allowances for orphans are paid under the family allowance scheme.

Unemployment insurance: The NSSO collects the contributions and the National Employment Office supervises the local agencies paying benefits. Insurance covers all employed persons except railwaymen, domestics and public employees. There are special schemes for miners, seamen, dockers and building workers. The insurance is financed equally by the insured and the employer at the rate of 1 per cent of monthly earnings up to BF11,550. The government pays regular subsidies of 2 per cent of earnings and makes up any deficits. Basic daily benefits, paid generally without a time-limit, are 50 to 60 per cent of the average wages of an unskilled worker. Maximum benefits are two-thirds of earnings, or up to 75 per cent if the unemployed person has four or more children. Special 'safeguard of living conditions' funds pay supplementary allowances to those employed in industries prone to periods of unemployment.

Other benefits: The NSSO collects the contributions for family allowances, which are distributed by the National Family Allowance Office. All persons are covered for family allowances, there being separate systems for employees and self-employed persons and special systems for miners, seamen and public employees. The employer pays 10 per cent of the insured's monthly earnings up to BF11,550; self-employed persons pay their own premiums. The government covers any deficits in the schemes for employees and self-employed persons by subsidies. In the case of employees allowances are paid to all children under 14 (21 if an apprentice, 25 if a student and indefinitely if invalid)—and may include dependant grandchildren, brothers, sisters, nephews and nieces—at the monthly rate (1965) of BF535 ($10·70) for the first child rising to BF1,123 ($22·40) for the fourth and subsequent children. Additional supplements are paid according to the age of the child. Birth allowances are (1965) BF7,957 ($159) for the first, BF5,488 ($110) for the second and BF2,953 ($59) for the third and any subsequent births. Self-employed persons receive lower family allowances but the same birth allowances. All employed persons are entitled to a minimum of three weeks holiday with pay, with a special holiday bonus amounting to 8 per cent of annual earnings for wage-earners and a half-month's pay for salaried employees, plus a family holiday bonus from the state, usually equivalent to a month of family allowances.

EDUCATION

Freedom of education is guaranteed by the constitution. Two complete networks of educational establishments coexist: one is organised by the state and the municipalities and is generally known as the 'official schools system', and 43 per cent of the population are registered with it; the second was set up by private initiative—generally Catholic bodies—and is called the 'free schools system', with which 57 per cent of the population is registered. After a long period of rivalry between the two systems, they are now organised and state-financed along more or less identical lines. Expenditure on education increased almost seven-fold in the period 1958–66, amounting in 1966 to BF38,311 million ($766 million). Education is free and compulsory for all children between the ages of 6 and 15. The upper age-limit is to be raised to 16.

Primary education: All municipalities are obliged to establish at least one primary school. Primary education lasts from the ages of 6 to 12, divided into three levels each of two years, and is generally completed by an examination for a certificate of primary studies.

Secondary education: All forms of secondary education begin at 12. The system is being directed towards a structure in which all pupils between 12 and 15 can study together in comprehensive secondary schools, and afterwards go on to higher secondary schools or secondary technical schools. In this period there are four major sections—humanities, science and commerce and two practical/technical streams; changes from one section to another are permitted. The system that is being replaced is that of an ordinary three-year secondary school on the one hand and six-year courses in the humanities at either state secondary schools (*athénées* for boys and *lycées* for girls) or private Catholic secondary schools (*collèges*) on the other. The six-year courses end with a certificate of humanities which is the main qualification for university entrance.

Special education: A number of institutes provide special education for physically and mentally handicapped pupils and students. The 1966 educational budget allotted BF153 million ($3 million) to this form of education.

Technical education: This begins at the age of 12. The maximum six-year courses may lead to higher technical education, preparing students for very diverse professions and finalised by diplomas equivalent to university degrees in commercial sciences.

University and higher education: Belgium's growing need for executive and scientific personnel has resulted in a rapid expansion of higher education and its adaptation to modern requirements. The basis of this is both an immediate and a long-term programme (1964–8) aimed at developing existing universities and higher education establishments and the organisation of new colleges. There are state universities at Ghent and Liège and two state-subsidised private universities—the Catholic University of Louvain and the Free University of Brussels. Besides these there are state colleges at Antwerp and Mons, agricultural colleges at Gembloux and Ghent, a polytechnic college at Mons, the State School of Veterinary Medicine in Brussels and the Catholic University Schools of St Louis in Brussels and of Notre-Dame de la Paix in Namur. The universities are composed of five traditional faculties—philosophy and letters, law, science, medicine and applied science—as well as the schools and colleges of higher education attached to them. Courses last from four to seven (medicine) years and are generally divided into two parts, the *candidature* and the *licence*—the latter being comparable to a Master's degree.

In 1965 40 per cent of all Belgian students were scholarship holders. In 1966 state expenditure on higher education was BF4,382 million ($87·6 million).

Educational institutions, 1963–4:

	Institutions	Students
Primary	9,164	979,869
Secondary	1,402	272,244
Technical	2,564	276,007
Universities	4	38,366

Adult education: There is a vast network of facilities for adult and self-education involving both public authorities and a number of private bodies. In 1962 there were nearly 2,700 public libraries.

MASS MEDIA

The press:

Dailies: Le Soir, Brussels, independent, 301,000; *Het Laatste Nieuws*, Brussels, PLP, 297,000; *De Standaard-Het Nieuwsblad*, Brussels, Catholic, 276,000; *Het Volk*, Ghent, PSC, 222,000; *La Lanterne*, Brussels, ind., 200,000; *Gazet van Antwerpen*, Antwerp, PSC, 180,000; *La Dernière Heure*, Brussels, PLP, 171,000; *La Libre Belgique*, Brussels, Cath., 170,000; *La Meuse*, Liège, ind., 150,000; *De Nieuwe Gids*, Ghent, Cath., 120,000; *De Gentenaar-Landwacht*, Ghent, Cath., 120,000; *Volksgazet*, Antwerp, PSB, 102,000.

Weeklies: Femmes d'Aujourd'hui, Brussels, woman's, 1,500,000; *Chez Nous*, Brussels, Cath., 300,000; *Rosita*, Antwerp, wom., 276,000; *Zondag Nieuws*, Brussels, ind., 250,000; *Ons Land*, Antwerp, illustrated, 245,000; *La Croix de Belgique*, Brussels, Cath., 182,000; *Libelle*, Antwerp, wom., 171,000; *Panorama*, Antwerp, family, 161,000; *Ons Zondagblad*, Ghent, ind., 151,000; *Ons Volk*, Brussels, Cath., 146,000; *Zondagsvriend*, Antwerp, Cath., 137,000; *Pourquoi-Pas?*, Brussels, humorous/satirical, 110,000.

Broadcasting: Belgian broadcasting is a monopoly of Radiodiffusion-Télévision Belge-Belgische Radio en Televisie, a public utility managed autonomously to which the state transfers funds raised through taxes on radio and TV receivers.

CYPRUS

GEOGRAPHY

Features: This diamond-shaped island has a low, narrow chain of mountains in the north and a rather broader and higher range in the south, with a lowland area between. Agriculture is concentrated in the central plains; industry, of which there is little, is concentrated mainly in and around the large towns. *Area:* 3,570 sq. miles/9,300 sq. km. *Mean max. and min. temperatures:* Nicosia (35° N, 33° 30′ E; 720 ft/220 m.) 97°F/36°C (July and Aug.), 42°F/6°C (Jan. and Feb.); Famagusta (35° N, 34° E; 75 ft/23 m.) 95°F/35°C, 43°F/6°C. *Relative humidity:* Nicosia 67 per cent; Famagusta 71 per cent. *Mean annual rainfall:* Nicosia 15 in./380 mm.; Famagusta 17 in./ 430 mm.

POPULATION

Total population: (1964) 588,000, composed of 77 per cent Greek Cypriots, 18 per cent Turkish Cypriots and the remainder of minorities such as Armenians and Maronites. *Main towns and populations:* (1964) NICOSIA (103,000), Paphos (58,000), Limassol (47,000), Famagusta (38,000), Larnaca (20,000). *Language:* Both Greek and Turkish are official languages. *Religion:* About 76 per cent of the population belong to the Greek Orthodox Church, 19 per cent adhere to Islam and the remainder to Armenian, Gregorian Catholic and Maronite minorities.

CONSTITUTIONAL SYSTEM

Constitution: Cyprus is a republic within the British Commonwealth. The 1960 constitution attempts to safeguard the interests of the two communities. The basic articles of the constitution cannot be amended; other articles may be amended by a two-thirds majority of the representatives of both communities in the House of Representatives; it is obligatory for all Cypriots to join either the Greek or Turkish communities. *Head of state:* President Archbishop Makarios. *Vice-head of state:* Vice-President Fazil Küçük.

Executive: Executive authority is vested in the President who is always a Greek and the Vice-President who is always a Turk. Both are elected for five years by direct vote of their respective communities. They work through a Council of Ministers (seven Greek and three Turk) who are not members of the legislature but are appointed by the executive. In January 1964 the Turkish members left the Council and have been replaced by Greeks. The President and Vice-President may either separately or jointly veto legislation concerning foreign affairs and certain questions of security or defence, and may return part or all of other legislation for reconsideration. The deputies to the executive are the President (Greek) and Vice-President (Turkish) of the legislature.

Legislature: Legislative authority other than that reserved to the Communal Chambers is vested in the House of Representatives whose 50 members are elected for five years by the Greek and Turkish communities in the ratio 35 to 15. After the outbreak of civil strife in December 1963 the Turkish deputies ceased to attend the House and both Greek and Turkish representatives extended the statutory tenure of office both for themselves and the executive after July 1965 for a period of one year at a time. The House of Representatives—in which only the Greeks were present—has also legislated to dispense with the separate electoral rolls.

Communal Chambers: Each community has a Communal Chamber controlling such matters as religion, education and the important cooperative societies, and imposing taxes and levies. In March 1965 the Greek Chamber dissolved itself, and the Greek members of the House of Representatives legislated to take over its functions and establish a Ministry of Education.

Election results: In the July 1960 elections the Greek community returned 30 members for Makarios' Patriotic Front and five members for the exclusively Greek AKEL, the Cypriot Communist Party (not opposed in the elections by the Patriotic Front in accordance with a pre-election agreement). The main anti-Makarios Greek party, the Democratic Union, is not represented in the legislature. In the communal elections 20 representatives of the Patriotic Front, three AKEL representatives and three other members were returned for the Greeks and 30 members of the National Union for the Turks. All 15 Turkish members of the House of Representatives were from Küçük's National Union.

Leading political figures: Spyros Kyprianou (Foreign Minister), Polycarpos Yeorkadjis (Minister of the Interior and Acting Minister of Defence), Renos Solimides (Finance Minister), E. Papaioannou (Secretary-General of AKEL), Osman Örek (Vice-Chairman of the National Union and Minister of Defence).

Local government: There was provision in the 1960 constitution for separate Greek and Turkish Municipal Councils in the five largest towns. But since the withdrawal of the Turkish members from the House of Representatives, the Greek members have legislated to unify the administration of the Municipalities.

Judicial system: The lowest courts of criminal and civil jurisdiction are the six Assize and six District Courts. The High Court of Cyprus was amalgamated with the Supreme Constitutional Court in the period after December 1963. It now comprises a President and four other judges. The Supreme Court was empowered under the constitution to amend, confirm or return to the House of Representatives any law or decision of the House that either the President or the Vice-President of the Republic deemed to be discriminatory against either community. The Supreme Court is also the highest court of appeal and has final and exclusive jurisdiction in all cases. Judges are appointed by the Supreme Council of Judicature. There are also communal courts and an ecclesiastical tribunal of the Greek Orthodox Church. Cyprus maintains capital punishment.

RECENT HISTORY

Cyprus became a British Crown Colony in 1925 having been administered by Britain since 1878. The constant demand of the Greek majority for Union with Greece (Enosis) erupted in 1955 into a campaign of violence led by the Greek underground army (EOKA). The British government imposed a state of emergency on the island until the signature of the London and Zürich agreements between Greece, Turkey, Cyprus and Britain in February 1959, providing for Cyprus to become independent. In December 1959 Archbishop Makarios was elected the island's first President and Dr Küçük Vice-President. Cyprus became an independent republic in August 1960 and in March 1961 it joined the Commonwealth. In December 1963, after the Turkish rejection of Makarios' thirteen points for constitutional amendment, fighting broke out between the Greek and Turkish communities, which led to the introduction of a United Nations peace-keeping force and mediator. At the end of 1966 the Force still remained, its mandate being renewed every three months. Since the Turkish members left both the Council of Ministers and the House of Representatives in January 1964 (see under *Legislature*) they have bitterly contested each new measure passed by these now exclusively Greek bodies. These measures are not deemed constitutional amendments by the Cyprus government but rather temporary provisions for the administration of the country.

Defence: Under the February 1959 agreements Britain retains full sovereignty over two military base areas, Akrotiri and Dhekelia. British sovereignty is guaranteed by a treaty between Britain, Cyprus, Greece and Turkey, by which Cyprus undertakes not to unite with any other state, and to prohibit activity designed to promote either such a union or a partition of the island. Britain, Greece and Turkey are also signatories of a Treaty of Military Alliance, whereby each guarantees the independence, territorial integrity and security of the Republic of Cyprus, and agrees to consult if there is a breach of these provisions. If they cannot agree on joint action, any one of them is entitled to take unilateral action with the sole aim of restoring the status quo.

The constitution provides for an army and for security forces (police and gendarmerie) totalling 2,000 men each and divided 60:40 and 70:30 respectively between the Greek and Turkish communities. Under the Treaty of Alliance Greece should maintain 950 officers and men, and Turkey 650 officers and men in Cyprus to train the Cypriot army. Military service is now compulsory in the National Guard for all Greek Cypriots between 18 and 50. The (Greek) National Guard is staffed by Greek army officers and totals some 11,000 men and is commanded by the former head of EOKA, General Grivas, who also commands the 10,000 strong Greek Volunteer Force. There are also several thousand armed Turkish Cypriots on the island. The strength of the UN Force is about 5,000.

ECONOMY

Cyprus is heavily dependent upon agriculture, mining and receipts from the supply of goods and services to the British bases. The 1962–6 economic programme succeeded in rapidly increasing the island's economic development. In 1965 GNP was estimated to have increased by about 24 per cent over 1964, compared with a decrease of about 8 per cent in 1964 over 1963. The estimated per capita GNP for 1965 was £250 ($700), the highest per capita in the Eastern Mediterranean next to Israel.

In 1965 agriculture contributed about 29 per cent of GDP and employed 40 per cent of the active working population. The main products are wheat, barley, olives, citrus fruits, carrots, potatoes, carebs and grapes. In 1965 manufacturing industry contributed 16 per cent of GDP and employed 13 per cent of the active working population. Minerals account for over 40 per cent of total domestic exports; main deposits are iron pyrites, copper, salt, asbestos. There is no heavy industry but a wide variety of light manufacturing industries and increasing interest in the establishment of new industries and expansion of existing ones. Tourism is becoming an increasingly important source of revenue.

In 1965 the main exports were mining products, fruit, vegetables and wine. In the same year the main imports were motor vehicles, fabrics, fuels and building and construction materials. The main export markets in 1965 were the EEC (33 per cent of total exports), Britain (31 per cent) and the Commonwealth (2 per cent). Imports were distributed as follows: Britain 34 per cent, the EEC 33 per cent and the Commonwealth 5 per cent.

SOCIAL SECURITY

The 1956 Social Insurance Scheme is compulsory for all employees except those in small-scale agricultural enterprises. It covers old-age and survivor's pensions, sickness and maternity insurance, and unemployment insurance. The scheme is financed by equal weekly contributions from employers, employees and the state of 60 mils[1] ($0·20) for males and 30 mils ($0·10) for females. Administration is in the hands of the Ministry of Labour and Social Insurance, with the Ministry of Health providing medical services through public clinics and hospitals. Accident insurance is financed by the employer alone either through the direct payment of benefits or through insurance premiums. Contributions to accident insurance are voluntary unless compulsorily prescribed for the employer. The Ministry of Labour and Social Insurance exercises general supervision. Benefits stated below refer to early 1964.

Health insurance: Medical benefits are free medical treatment, hospitalisation, maternity care and medicines. Weekly sickness benefits are paid after a three-day waiting period for a maximum of 26 weeks, and amount to £1·2 ($3·40), plus allowances of 600 mils ($1·70) for the first dependant and 300 mils ($0·80) for the second. Maternity grants amount to a maximum of £5 ($14).

Accident insurance: Government provides part of the necessary treatment. Temporary disability benefit paid for up to 26 weeks amounts to two-thirds of earnings up to a monthly maximum of £15 ($42) which may be converted into a lump sum. For permanent disability a lump sum grant of 48 months' earnings—72 months if the disabled is under 18—is paid for full disability with a minimum of £100 ($280) and a maximum of £800 ($2,240). For partial disability a proportion of the lump sum is paid. Survivor grants, allocated by court decision, are equal to 42 months' earnings—less any accident benefits paid to the insured before death—of a minimum of £100 and a maximum of £600 ($1,680).

Pensions insurance: The old-age pension is paid at 65. The full weekly pension provides the same amount for the insured and dependants as the weekly sickness benefit. Widow's pensions are the same and are paid at 50, or over 40 when the last child exceeds the age-limit, or if the widow is incapable of

[1] 1,000 mils = £1.

self-support or is caring for a child. Weekly orphan's benefits are 600 mils for the first and 300 mils for the second child under 14, or 18 if studying. Full weekly orphan's benefits are 600 mils for each full orphan.

Unemployment insurance: This is paid at the same rate and under the same qualifications as sickness benefits, except that married women and persons under 18 or over 65 are ineligible.

EDUCATION

In 1965 82 per cent of the population over the age of seven were literate. *Primary education:* This is free but not compulsory from six to 12. *Secondary education:* This lasts from 13 to 18. Secondary schools charge fees, but most of them are state-aided and fees are kept low.

Other education: There are 13 technical-vocational schools and a teacher-training school for each community.

Educational institutions, 1964–5:

	Institutions	Staff	Students
Primary—Greek	536	2,500	69,742
—Turkish	227		16,700
Secondary—Greek	43		24,885
Technical-vocational—Greek	9		2,372
Teacher-training—Greek	1	n.a.	88
Secondary—Turkish	15		
Technical-vocational—Turkish	4		7,600
Teacher-training—Turkish	1		

MASS MEDIA

The press[1]:

Dailies: Nicosia: Greek—*Haravghi*, AKEL, 18,000: *Makhi*, independent, 16,000; *Eleftheria*, ind., 14,000; *Phileleftheros*, liberal, 8,000; *Agon*, ind. Turkish—*Bozkurt*, ind., *Balkin Sesi*, nationalist. English—*Cyprus Mail*, ind.

Weeklies: Nicosia: Greek—*Kypros* (w), non-party, 16,000; *Alithia*, ind. *Tharros*, ind.; *Ethniki*, Democratic Union organ, 5,000; *Nei Keri*, left. Turkish—*Zafer*, ind.

Broadcasting: The Cyprus Broadcasting Corporation controls all radio and TV broadcasting. Radio transmissions are in Greek, Turkish and English. There is also a programme for the UN Peace Force.

[1] Circulation figures given only where available.

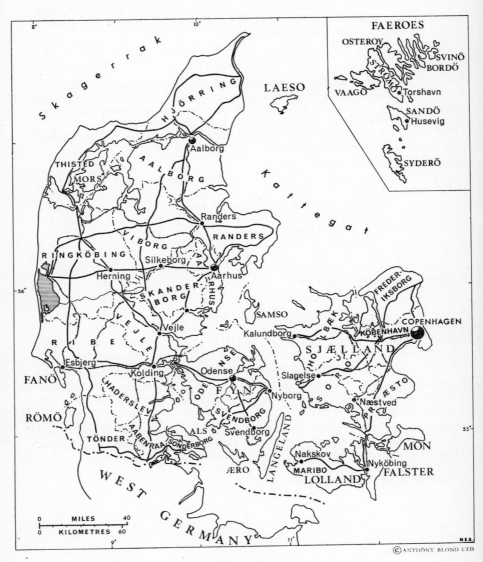

DENMARK

DENMARK

GEOGRAPHY

Features: Almost all the country lies below 500 ft/150 m. The area of greatest elevation is the north-south moraine which divides the Jutland peninsula into a rather shady and less fertile western part and a much more fertile eastern part. Eastern Jutland and the islands that constitute the rest of the country (of which some hundred are inhabited) are boulder-clay-covered with the exception of the granite island of Bornholm off the coast of Sweden. Apart from western Jutland Denmark is covered mainly by soils which support an intensive agriculture. Fuels and minerals are lacking. Industry is concentrated around Copenhagen and to a lesser extent Esbjerg, Odense and the other major towns. *Area:* 16,600 sq. miles/43,000 sq. km. Overseas Territories: Greenland and Faroe Islands. *Mean max. and min. temperatures:* Copenhagen (55° 30′ N, 12° 30′ E; 40 ft/12 m.) 72°F/22°C (July), 28°F/−2°C (Jan.). *Relative humidity:* Copenhagen 84 per cent. *Mean annual rainfall:* 23 in./580 mm.

POPULATION

Population: (1965 est.) 4,756,000. Overseas Territories: Greenland (1960) 33,000; Faroes (1960) 35,000. *Chief towns and populations:* (1960) COPEN-HAGEN (1,349,000), Århus (177,000), Odense (130,000), Ålborg-Nørresundby (119,000), Esbjerg (58,000), Randers (55,000). *Distribution:* In 1965 about 46 per cent of the population were living in towns and the remainder in rural Communes. *Language:* Danish is the official language. In North Schleswig there is a German-speaking minority of 30,000. The main language of the Faroes is Faroese which is akin to Norwegian and Icelandic.

Religion: The overwhelming majority of the population adhere to the state Evangelical-Lutheran Church.

CONSTITUTIONAL SYSTEM

Constitution: Denmark is a constitutional monarchy. The present constitution dates from 1953. *Head of State:* King Frederik IX. *Head of government:* Prime Minister Jens Otto Krag (Social Democrat).

Executive: Executive authority is vested in the King and his ministers. The King appoints as Prime Minister the leader of the party likely to obtain a majority in parliament. The King then appoints the other ministers on the advice of the Prime Minister. No act of the King is valid without ministerial responsibility. No minister may remain in office after a vote of no-confidence. If a vote of censure on the Prime Minister is approved, the whole government must resign, unless a new election is ordered.

Legislature: Denmark has a unicameral parliament (Folketing) consisting of 179 members elected by proportional representation for four years. Both Greenland and the Faroe Islands send two representatives each to the Folketing.

Referendum: Since 1953 certain bills may be submitted to referendum at the initiative of one-third of the Folketing. *Ombudsman:* The Public Affairs Commissioner (*ombudsman*) appointed by parliament observes the activities of the ministers, the civil service and parts of local government administration with a view to bringing defects in the system to the attention of the responsible authority, and investigating complaints of abuses against personal liberty.

Political parties: The main Danish parties are the Social Democrats, the Liberal Democrats, the Conservatives, the (Marxist) Socialist People's Party, the Radical Liberals and the Liberal Centre founded by left-wing Liberal Democrats in 1964. The Slesvig Party, which boycotted the 1966 elections, represents the German-speaking population of northern Schleswig. The present government is a Social Democrat minority government.

Election results:

Party	1964 Percentage of poll	Seats	1964 Percentage of poll	Seats
Social Democrats .	41·9	76	38·3	69
Liberal Democrats .	20·8	38	19·3	35
Conservatives . .	20·1	36	18·6	34
Socialist People's Party	5·8	10	10·8	20
Radical Liberals . .	5·3	10	7·2	13
Liberal Centre . .	—	—	2·4	4
Independents . .	2·5	5	1·6	—
Single-tax Party . .	1·2	—	0·7	—
Communists . .	1·3	—	0·7	—
Slesvig Party . .	0·3	—	—	1
Greenland/Faroes (each)	—	2	—	2

Leading political figures: Social Democrats—Jens Otto Krag (Prime Minister and Foreign Minister), Per Haekkerrup (Parliamentary Leader). Liberal Democrats—Paul Hartling (Party Leader). Conservatives—Paul Sörenson (Party Leader). Socialist People's Party—Axel Larsen (Party Chairman). Radical Liberals—Karl Skttye (Leader in Folketing).

Local government: Copenhagen is governed by an elected council (Borger-representation) and an executive council (Magistrat) headed by a Chief Burgomaster. The Municipalities adjacent to the capital, as well as the Provincial Boroughs (*købstaeder*) are each governed by an elected council (*byråd*) headed by a Mayor. The County Authorities (*amtskommuner*) are each governed by an elected council (*amtsråd*), the chairman of which is a government appointee, the County Sheriff (*amtmand*). The Counties are further subdivided into Districts (*sognekommuner*) each governed by an elected District Council (*sogneråd*). The Copenhagen City Council and the other Municipalities have full responsibility for municipal affairs. In the country Districts local affairs are divided between County and District Councils.

Greenland is administered jointly by an elected Provincial Council (Landsråd) and by a Danish Governor (Landshøvding). The Faroe Islands are self-governing through an elected assembly (Lagting) and an island government (Landsstyre). Foreign affairs amongst other matters are handled by the Danish government, which is represented by a Commissioner (*ombudsman*).

Judicial system: The lower courts (*underretter*) are usually constituted by 1–22 judges. Only one judge tries a case. All cases not falling within the lower courts' jurisdiction are initiated in the two high courts (*landsretter*). The Eastern High Court has jurisdiction over the islands, and the Western High Court over Jutland. At least three judges try a high court case. In criminal cases that are not minor police cases (*politisager*) the judges are assisted by lay assessors (*domsmaend*)—three in high court cases, two in lower court cases, and in those which may involve sentences of eight years or more by a jury of 12. The Supreme Court (Højesteret) functions only as a court of appeal; it is constituted by at least five judges. There are two special courts—the Commercial and Maritime Court, and for labour disputes the Permanent Arbitration Court. Judges are appointed by the Crown and may be dismissed only by judicial sentence. There is no death penalty.

RECENT HISTORY

In 1948 Denmark granted home rule to the Faroes. In 1949 it became a founder-member of NATO. In 1953 a new constitution was introduced abolishing the upper house and permitting female succession to the throne. In the same year Greenland became an integral part of the Danish Kingdom and Denmark joined the Nordic Council. In 1960 Denmark joined EFTA and the next year negotiated for full membership of the EEC. Denmark has provided troops for UN forces in Sinai and Cyprus.

Defence: The King is head of the armed forces. Military service lasts from 12 to 14 months. All front-line Danish forces are assigned to or earmarked for NATO service. Strength of the services: army 30,000, Navy 7,200, air force 12,600. There are no foreign bases or nuclear weapons on Danish soil. The 1966–7 defence budget was DKr11,915 million ($268 million), representing 3·3 per cent of GNP in 1965–6. In 1962 all Danish and German forces in the Baltic area came under a unified NATO command (COMBALTAP).

ECONOMY

Background: Denmark is basically an agricultural country with a comprehensive cooperative marketing system. Economic growth since 1957 has been characterised by a change of emphasis from agriculture to industry, with improved utilisation of manpower and rapid growth of industrial investment. However, the economy has suffered inflationary tendencies for most of this period, leading to competitive losses in industry and strong pressures on foreign exchange reserves since 1964. From 1958 to 1964 the real value of GNP rose by nearly 6 per cent, a great improvement on 1950–7. This growth involved a substantial redistribution of labour and other resources from agriculture to manufacturing industry. In 1964 the value of GNP at 1958 prices was DKr47,530 million ($6,791 million).

The origin of GDP at factor cost in 1964 was:

Sector				Percentage
Agriculture	.	.	.	13
Industry	.	.	.	40
Services	.	.	.	47
GDP				100

33

From 1961 to 1964 industrial production increased by an annual average of 9 per cent; in 1965 it rose by 6–7 per cent. The chief industrial products are machinery, manufactured foodstuffs (including beverages and tobacco), chemicals and ships. The main agricultural products are livestock, barley, sugar beet, potatoes and dairy products.

Foreign trade: The current account of the balance of payments has fluctuated considerably in recent years. The large deficits of 1961–2 were replaced by a surplus in 1963, but reverted to another large deficit in 1964. The position improved slightly in 1965 and a surplus was expected in 1966, owing largely to an expansion of exports and invisible earnings. In 1964 industrial exports rose to over 50 per cent of total exports, while agricultural exports declined to under 35 per cent; this represented an almost complete reversal of the relative contributions of the two sectors within a period of ten years. The major imports in 1964 were machinery (16 per cent of total imports), fuels (11 per cent) and textiles (10 per cent). Distribution of trade has developed in favour of EFTA of which Denmark is a member. In 1964 exports to EFTA and EEC countries were 45 and 29 per cent respectively. Imports in that year amounted to 35 per cent from the EEC and 33 per cent from EFTA. Imports accounted for 29 per cent of GNP in 1964 and exports for 23 per cent.

Employment: From 1958 to 1964 unemployment fell from over 9 per cent of insured workers to 2 per cent while the total labour force increased rapidly. In 1964 the latter was 2·2 million, of whom 18 per cent were employed in agriculture, 40 per cent in industry and 42 per cent in services. During part of 1965 unemployment fell to a record 0·4 per cent.

Price and wage trends: From mid-1960 to mid-1965 consumer prices rose by an annual average of 6 per cent and hourly industrial earnings by 10 per cent. The main contributory factors to these rises were a shortage of labour, a rise in export prices and increased home demand. To counteract persistent inflation a stabilisation policy was introduced in 1963, including collective long-term wage agreements. There were budget surpluses in 1964 and 1965, and credit restrictions and a turnover tax were introduced in 1965. Despite these and other fiscal and monetary measures, the pressure upon resources remained strong throughout 1965.

Consumption: In 1964 private consumption amounted to 64 per cent of GNP at current prices and public consumption to 14 per cent. This represented an increase over 1963 of 6·2 per cent in private consumption and 3·2 per cent in public consumption, compared with a decrease of 0·2 per cent and an increase of 3·6 per cent respectively for 1962/3. Estimated increases in private and public consumption in 1965 were 4 and 5 per cent respectively.

SOCIAL SECURITY

The Ministry of Social Affairs exercises general supervision over health, accident and unemployment insurance and direct national administration over the pension scheme. Contributions and benefits stated below refer to 1964 except where otherwise stated.

Health insurance: This is administered by approved self-governing sickness funds directly supervised by the Health Insurance Directorate within the Ministry of Social Affairs. Membership of the funds for medical benefits is voluntary. Members are of two categories, depending upon whether income does not (category A) or does (category B) exceed a specified maximum equal to the annual earnings of a fully employed skilled worker. Those who do not choose to become members must pay DKr24 ($3·50) annually to their local fund, but they receive no benefits. The insurance is financed 70 to 75 per cent by the insured person at the average annual rate of DKr100 ($14·50), and the rest by the state in the form of subsidies which mainly cover benefits for category A members. There is a special system for railwaymen. Medical benefits are generally provided by services contracted to and directly paid by the funds, and include general and specialist care, hospitalisation, maternity and some dental care, home nursing, transport (these services are free for category A members, while category B members receive partial reimbursement) and 75 per cent of the costs of vital medicines. Adult dependants must insure in their own right for medical benefits. The daily sickness benefit scheme is compulsory for virtually all persons engaged in manual employment. Persons under 45 who are not covered, or who are excepted because their wages are guaranteed in case of sickness, are entitled to insure voluntarily for a daily benefit (1965) of up to DKr23 ($3·30). Otherwise daily sickness benefits are (1965) DKr26 ($3·80) for persons over 18 with dependants, payable for six days per week for a maximum of 78 weeks in any three years. Maternity benefits are the same for both employees and voluntarily insured, but payable for 14 weeks including eight weeks before confinement for employees, and for two weeks after confinement for voluntarily insured.

Accident insurance: This is directly supervised by the Directorate of Accident Insurance under the Ministry of Social Affairs and financed by employers— who insure with an approved private insurance company or employers' mutual association—and by the state which pays a subsidy of 40 per cent of the costs for low-income employers. The insurance covers all employed persons and all self-employed persons in fishing and shipping. Other low-income self-employed persons may voluntarily insure by paying their own premiums. There are special systems for seamen, railwaymen and public employees. All cash benefits are adjusted with annual changes in the retail price index and are related to annual earnings of up to DKr10,000 ($1,450). Most medical benefits are provided under ordinary sickness insurance with accident insurance providing only appliances, and sometimes necessary specialist care. Temporary disability benefits are paid for up to three years at 75 per cent of earnings. For permanent disability, full pensions are two-thirds of average earnings for 100 per cent disability, a percentage of the full pension proportionate to the loss of earning power for 50 to 99 per cent disability and lump sum benefits for 5 to 49 per cent disability. Widow's pensions—also payable to widowers—are 50 per cent of the insured's earnings for the first two years and 30 per cent thereafter. Orphan's pensions are paid to the first two orphans under 18 at the rate of 10 per cent of the insured's earnings (20 per cent for full orphans).

Pensions insurance: This is administered at the local level by local authorities. The insurance covers all residents; there is a special system for public employees. The scheme is financed by all income-tax payers at 1·5 per cent of taxable income, which is not paid if the contribution would work out at less than DKr50 ($7·25) annually. All pensions are adjusted if there is a change of 1 per cent in the retail price index. Old-age pensions are of two forms. At the age of 67 (women 62) or 60 under exceptional circumstances, all residents receive a minimum 'national pension' of 6 per cent of the current national-average wage (9 per cent for an aged couple). These rates were equal to monthly pensions of DKr87 ($12·60) and DKr130 ($18·80) respectively in 1963. Those who need full maintenance receive the 'income-regulated national pension'. This depends on amount of income; the maximum level giving entitlement to full pension varies according to locality and marital status. This pension was worth up to DKr400 per month in 1963 with supplements of 50 per cent of pension for a wife aged 60 (15 per cent if she is younger), 25 per cent of pension for each child under 15 (18 if a student), 5 per cent if the pensioner is aged 80 and 10 or 15 per cent respectively if the pension is deferred for two or five years. Invalidity pensions are paid to those who have lost two-thirds of their normal earning capacity. This pension is the same as the old-age supplementary pension with the same dependant's supplements, plus special invalidity supplements of 15 per cent of pension and constant attendance allowances of from 25 to 40 per cent of pension. Widow's pensions, paid to women widowed after 55 or after 45 if they have two children, are the same as the supplementary old-age pension, with the same child's supplement.

Unemployment insurance: This covers most employed persons between 18 and 60, who belong to state approved trade union unemployment funds. The Directorate of Labour in the Ministry of Social Affairs directly supervises the programme through public employment offices. The insurance is financed by employees (0·2 to 4 per cent of earnings according to the fund), employers (DKr45 ($6·50) per employee annually) and the state (subsidies covering about 60 per cent of the total costs). Benefits are payable up to 90 days in one year, and for a further 160 days in a year from separate 'continuation funds'. Benefits—varying according to the fund, marital status and length of membership, plus supplements for children under 14 (18 for students), rent and fuel allowances—are a maximum of 80 per cent of the average daily earnings of the trade or trade group for unemployed persons with dependants.

Other benefits: Family allowances are usually credited against income tax, and the scheme is directly administered by the Ministry of Finance. Allowances are paid at the annual rate of DKr400, 450 and 500 ($58, 65·25 and 72·50) respectively for the first, second to fourth, and fifth and subsequent children under 16. In case of divorce there are also provisions for obtaining advance alimonies from public funds pending collection from the responsible partner, if the income of a single parent and dependant child falls below a certain level.

EDUCATION

Primary and secondary education: Education is mainly public and is compulsory from the ages of seven to 14, during which period it is comprehensive, differentiated only in emphasis on subjects in the sixth and seventh years. However, in schools with more than 14 classes children are separated according to their academic abilities. At the end of this period, given sufficient pupils, there are voluntary eighth, ninth and tenth years in vocationally slanted classes. Otherwise there is a three-year practical course of education (*realskole*) imposed upon the seventh year. At the end of the second year of this, pupils take a public examination to determine whether they proceed either to the *realeksamen* (a school-leaving examination) after one additional year of practical education, or to the three-year secondary schools terminating in matriculation (*studentereksamen*).

Special education: Special education is provided at government boarding schools, which also accept day-pupils, for all children with severe physical handicaps. The State Welfare Service for Mental Defectives provides education for mentally defective children.

Vocational education: Apprentices must be at least 14 before beginning their training, which is combined with general and vocational education. Additional technical education takes place in evening classes. At the conclusion of the apprenticeship there is for some the opportunity for training at Technical Colleges (*technika*) for three-year courses. Technical Schools (*tekniskeskoler*) offer six- to twelve-month courses to skilled industrial workers as do the Colleges of Technology in Copenhagen and Århus. Commercial Schools (*handelsskoler*) run by trade organisations lead to examinations that when passed offer advancement for businessmen through business colleges. Having gained a diploma here or having passed the Realeksamen or Studentereksamen the student may proceed to an Advanced Business College. Success in a one- or two-year course may lead to one of the two Higher Commercial Colleges (*handelshøjskoler*) in Copenhagen and Århus.

University and higher education: The University of Copenhagen provides five faculties—theology, law and economics, medicine, arts and science. It is administered by the Ministry of Education but retains extensive autonomy. Århus University has the same five faculties. It is a private foundation whose activities are subjected to regulations laid down by statute, decree or ministerial order after discussions with the University authorities. Entry to the universities is open to all who have passed the Studentereksamen and education is generally free. Attendance at lectures is to a large extent voluntary and there is no prescribed period before the examinations. Both universities draw on private grants and the government's Youth Education Fund for allocation of grants or loans to students of limited means.

Higher technical education takes place at the Technical University of Denmark and the Danish Academy of Engineering, both in Copenhagen. Other higher education institutes are the Royal Veterinary and Agricultural College in Copenhagen, the two independent dental colleges in Copenhagen and Århus, the Royal Danish School of Pharmacy in Copenhagen, the Danish College of Education for teacher-training and the Royal Academy of Fine Arts, also in Copenhagen.

Educational Institutions 1963–4:

	Institutions	Staff	Students
Primary and secondary schools	2,594	32,205	688,570
Universities and colleges of higher education . .	14	1,993	27,895

Adult education: The Folk High Schools (*folkehøjskole*), of which there were some 70 in 1963, are private institutions receiving large state grants. They offer five- to six-month winter courses. Students, who are generally between 18 and 25, may obtain state grants. The schools are free to arrange their own syllabuses within the terms of reference of general education and hold no examinations and give no certificates. Continuation schools (*efterskoler*) are similarly organised and offer similar education, but with greater emphasis on elementary school and practical subjects to the 14–18 age-group. Grants can be obtained from the state or the local authority. There were 110 of these schools with 10,000 pupils in 1963. Youth Schools (*ungdomsskoler*), maintained by local authorities, cater for the same age-group but are slanted more towards the problems of youth and have a vocational bias. In 1963 there were 550 Youth Schools with 38,000 students. Evening schools and Evening High Schools provide very varied education which is free save for a small registration fee; in 1962–3 10 per cent of the adult population was in attendance at such schools. In 1964 there were nearly 450 public libraries.

MASS MEDIA

The press:

Dailies: Berlingske Tidende, Copenhagen, independent-Conservative, 173,000; *BT,* Copenhagen, ind.-Cons., 163,000; *Politiken,* Copenhagen, Ind.-Radical Liberal, 139,000; *Aktuelt,* Copenhagen, organ of Socialist Party, 101,000; *Ekstrabladet,* Copenhagen, ind.-Rad. Lib., 82,000; *Jyllands-Posten,* Århus, ind.-Cons., 62,000; *Århuus Stiftstidende,* Århus, ind.-Cons., 59,000; *Ålborg Stiftstidende,* Ålborg, ind.-Cons., 51,000.

Periodicals: Familie Journalen, Copenhagen, family, 363,000; *Hjemmet* (w), Copenhagen, fam., 344,000; *Sondags BT* (w), Copenhagen, ind.-Cons. fam., 192,000; *Se og Her* (w), Copenhagen, fam., 180,000; *Flittige Haender* (w), Copenhagen, woman's, 145,000; *Finanstidende* (w), Copenhagen, financial, 6,000.

Broadcasting: Sound and TV services are the monopoly of Radio Denmark (Danmarks Radio). Radio Denmark is directed by a Radio Council responsible to the Minister for Cultural Affairs. The Minister appoints a majority to the Council as representatives of viewers, listeners and government, and the political parties represented on the Parliamentary Finance Committee appoint one member each. Radio Denmark is financed out of a Broadcasting Fund derived from radio and TV licences. Old-age and disablement pensioners may be exempted from payment of radio licence fees and have TV licences at half-rate.

FINLAND

GEOGRAPHY

Features: The whole country, consisting geologically of metamorphic rock of the Baltic Shield, is of low relief, only a few areas in the extreme north-west reaching over 1,500 ft/450 m. and most of the centre and south lying below 600 ft/180 m. The country is much affected by glaciation. There are two main regions: the south, with innumerable lakes and islands, short streams and low relief; and the region north of about latitude 64°N, which has few lakes, longer streams and is of greater altitude.

Almost the entire country is forest-covered, providing the main source of wealth. Agriculture is largely confined to the coastal plain areas. Iron ore is mined at Kolari in the north and copper from Lake Juo; other minerals are sparse and no fuels of importance are present, most power being derived from HEP. Industry is concentrated in the coastal towns, e.g. Helsinki and Turku, the only large inland centre being Tampere. *Area:* 117,800 sq. miles/305,400 sq. km. (excluding inland water areas amounting to an additional 12,200 sq. miles/31,600 sq. km.). *Mean max. and min. temperatures:* Helsinki (60° N, 24° E; 30 ft/9 m.) 71°F/22°C (July), 15°F/−9°C (Feb.); Sodankylä (67° 30′ N, 26° 30′ E; 590 ft/180 m.) 68°F/20°C, −5°F/−21°C. *Relative humidity:* Helsinki 85 per cent; Sodankylä 85 per cent. *Mean annual rainfall:* Helsinki 28 in./710 mm.; Sodankylä 22 in./560 mm.

POPULATION

Total population: (1966 census) 4,638,000. *Chief towns and populations:* (1966) HELSINKI (501,000), Tampere (143,000), Turku (138,000), Lahti (81,000), Oulu (78,000), Pori (57,000). *Distribution:* In 1962 41 per cent of the population lived in urban areas and 59 per cent in rural districts. *Language:* Both Finnish and Swedish are official languages. The Swedish-speaking minority numbers about 7 per cent of the population. *Religion:* 92 per cent adhere to the state Lutheran Church; 1·4 per cent belong to the Eastern Orthodox Church.

CONSTITUTIONAL SYSTEM

Constitution: Finland is a republic; the constitution dates from 1919. *Head of state:* President Urho Kekkonnen. *Head of government:* Prime Minister Rafael Paasio (Social Democrat).

Executive: The President is chosen for six years by an electoral college elected by direct suffrage. He appoints the ministers and usually acts on their advice. He has however considerable independence on such issues as the dissolution of parliament and the appointment of certain senior officials. The President determines foreign policy, making his decision in the Council

39

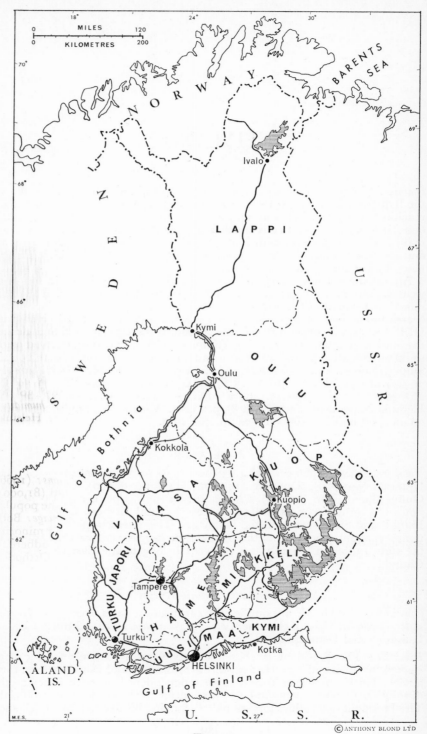

FINLAND

FINLAND

of State (Valtioneuvosto) upon the report of the Foreign Minister. The
President also has power to initiate legislation and every law passed by
parliament must be confirmed by him. The Prime Minister and ministers
who together form the Council of State are responsible to parliament.
Presidential acts must be countersigned by the competent minister, except
in cases involving the prosecution of the President or ministers.

Legislature: Parliament (Eduskunta), consisting of one chamber of 200
representatives elected by proportional representation for four years, is
the ultimate source of legislative power. Parliament appoints an Ombudsman
to supervise the observance of the law.

Political parties: No political party in Finland has had an absolute majority
since the Social Democrats in 1916–7. Consequently cabinets are either
coalitions or minority governments. The seven major parties are: the Centre
Party (formerly the Agrarian Party); the Social Democrats; the Finnish
People's Democratic Union (FPDU—an amalgam of the Communist and
Socialist Union parties); the National Coalition (conservative); the Liberal
People's Party (a merger of the Finnish People's Party and the Liberal
Union); the Swedish Party; the Workers' and Small Farmers' Democratic
League (WSFDL—left-Socialists). The present government is a coalition of
the Social Democrat and Centre parties, the FPDU and the WSFDL.

Election results:

Party	1962 Percentage of poll	Seats	1966 Percentage of poll	Seats
Social Democrats	19·5	38	27·7	55
Centre Party	23·0	53	21·1	49
FPDU	22·0	47	21·1	41
National Coalition	15·1	32	13·8	26
Swedish Party	6·4	14	6·0	12
Finnish People's Party	5·9	13	} Liberal People's Party 6·5	9
Liberal Union	1·0	1		
WSFDL	4·3	2	2·7	7[1]
Finnish Small Farmers' Party	2·2	—	1·0	1

[1]The WSFDL had an electoral alliance with the FPDU.

Leading political figures: Social Democrats—Rafael Paasio (Prime Minister
and Party Chairman), Mauno Koivisto (Finance Minister). Centre Party—
Johannes Virolainen (Party Chairman and former Prime Minister), Ahti
Karjalainen (Foreign Minister), Sulo Suorttanen (Defence Minister).
FPDU—K. L. Kulo (Party Chairman), Ele Alenius (Deputy Finance
Minister).

Local government: Finland is divided into Provinces (*läänit*) each under a
Governor (*maaherra*) appointed by the President. The Provinces exert general
supervision, particularly in financial matters, over the Communes (*kunnat*),
the basic units of local government whose councils (*kunnanvaltfustot*) are
elected for four years. The provincial administration also has a judicial
personality, particularly as court of appeal in taxation matters. Regarding
internal matters the Province of Åland is self-governing.

Judicial system: The lowest courts are the District and Municipal Courts (*kihlakunnan-oikeudet* and *raastuvanoikeudet*). In towns these are administered by the Mayor (*pormestari*) and his Assessors (*asessorit*). In the country the decision depends upon a judge and a jury of from seven to 12 peasant proprietors, with the judge alone deciding unless the jury unanimously differ, in which case their decision prevails. Appeal from these courts is to the Superior Courts (*hovioikeudet*) composed of a President and an appropriate number of members, and finally to the Supreme Court (Korkein oikeus) composed of a President and 21 judges. The Supreme Administrative Court (Korkein hallinto-oikeus) consists of a President and 20 judges appointed by the President of the Republic, and is the highest appeal court for administrative cases. The judiciary is independent of the executive; the Supreme Court appoints the judges and they may only be removed by judicial sentence. There is no capital punishment.

RECENT HISTORY

Finland was at war with the Soviet Union in 1939–40 (the Winter War) and again from 1941 to 1944. By the terms of the armistice she ceded 12 per cent of her land area to the Soviet Union and 10 per cent of her population was displaced. Since then she has maintained a policy of neutrality qualified by a special emphasis on preserving good relations with the Soviet Union. This is epitomised by the 1948 Finnish-Soviet Agreement of Friendship and Mutual Assistance which was renewed in 1955 for a further 20 years. In 1955 Finland joined both the United Nations and the Nordic Council and in 1961 became an associate member of EFTA.

Defence: The President is commander-in-chief of the armed forces. The 1948 Finnish-Soviet Agreement forbids Finland to permit the use of its territory as a base for aggression against the Soviet Union and commits Finland to defend its territory, if necessary with Soviet aid, in such an event. However, aid is not given automatically, since a separate agreement regulates the form and extent of assistance. Should the Soviet Union be involved in a war that does not affect Finnish territory, Finland is committed not to enter any alliances directed against the Soviet Union. Finnish defence forces are limited by the 1947 Peace Treaty with the Allies to 34,400 men for the army, 4,500 men and 10,000 tons for the navy and 3,000 men and 60 combat planes for the air force. By the end of 1963 the maximum forces for army and navy had not been fulfilled. The Treaty also forbids the possession of nuclear weapons, guided missiles, bombers and submarines. The ban on missiles was revoked in 1963. Compulsory military service is for 240 days, and for officers, NCOs and specialised personnel 330 days. The defence estimates for 1966 were Fmk348 million ($108 million).

ECONOMY

Background: Finland has vast supplies of timber and water-power but very few other national resources. It is heavily dependent upon foreign trade. The economy is based on a narrow range of products and has suffered serious inflation since the second world war. The Finnish mark was devalued in 1949 and 1957 chiefly as a result of economic stagnation. By the end of 1958 the economy had started to expand again but in 1961 the rate of growth had once more slowed down. Recovery during 1963 was followed by a boom in 1964. From 1959 to 1963 GNP at current prices increased by an annual average of nearly 10 per cent. The period 1964–6 was characterised by a slower annual average growth rate, severe inflation and acute balance of payments deficits. The main growth industries in recent years have been building and construction, metals and engineering.

The origin of GDP at factor cost in 1965 was:

Sector	Percentage
Agriculture . . .	19
Industry	44
Services	37
GDP	100

Between 1960 and 1964 the annual rate of increase of net domestic production was over 5 per cent. The chief industries are wood, paper and pulp, mining and power. In the same period agricultural output grew by about 2 per cent a year. The chief agricultural activities are cattle, hay, fodder, roots, barley and vegetables.

Foreign trade: Finland's consistent balance of payments deficits have been alleviated only by progressive increases in foreign indebtedness. The current-account deficit in the five-year period 1960–4 was Fmk1,260 million ($390 million) and about Fmk500 million ($155 million) in 1964. Attempts to broaden the narrow range of export products have been hampered by persistent balance of payments deficits. In 1964 over 70 per cent of total exports was derived from wood and timber. In recent years machinery and transport equipment (mainly ships) have amounted to between 12 and 15 per cent of total exports. The structure of imports is considerably more varied. In 1964 food and raw materials accounted for over 20 per cent of total imports, chemicals and semi-finished products for nearly 30 per cent and manufactured goods for nearly 40 per cent. Imports in 1964 amounted to 23 per cent of GNP and exports to nearly 20 per cent. Finland has concessional tariff agreements (Nordic Council) pending with the EEC for pulp and paper and is involved in progressive tariff reductions with EFTA. The origin of Finnish imports in 1965 was about 36 per cent of total imports from EFTA, about 30 per cent from the EEC and about 17 per cent from the Soviet Union. The destination of exports in the same year involved 17 per cent to Comecon countries, 30 per cent to the EEC and 34 per cent to EFTA (of which 23 per cent to Britain).

Employment: The total labour force in 1965 was estimated to be nearly 2·2 million. In 1964 manpower in the service sector increased by nearly 8 per cent, in industry by 1 per cent and in agriculture there was a decline of 5 per cent; this has been the pattern since 1960. In 1964 agriculture, forestry and fishing employed an estimated 31 per cent of the total labour force, industry 32 per cent and services 37 per cent. Unemployment in the same year rose to about 1·4 per cent, being highest in forestry.

Price and wage trends: From 1960 to 1964 the most notable contributory factor to the rise in the domestic price level was the increase in labour costs, which in 1964 rose by 10 per cent, accounting for nearly 60 per cent of the year's total increase in costs. The increase in the average price level in 1964 was over 7 per cent; in 1965 it was expected to fall to about 4 per cent. The cost of living index rose by an annual average of nearly 5 per cent from 1958 to 1964, the greatest rise being in 1963–4.

Consumption: In 1964 private consumption amounted to 56 per cent of GDP at market prices and public consumption to 13 per cent.

c

SOCIAL SECURITY

All benefits and contributions described below relate to 1964 except where it is otherwise stated.

Health insurance: This is compulsory for the whole population. Contributions are paid equally by the insured person, the employer and the state, and amount to 1 per cent of taxable earnings. The scheme is administered by the National Pension Institute and local insurance committees. There are sickness benefits and daily allowances, the former including up to 60 per cent reimbursement of doctor's fees, part-repayment of X-ray and travelling costs and half the price in excess of Fmk4 on medicines. Hospital fees are not included since about 80 per cent of state and communal hospital fees are financed by public funds and these hospitals provide 95 per cent of all hospital beds. Sickness benefits are paid throughout illness. Daily allowances amount to 45 per cent of normal wage or salary up to Fmk15,000 ($4,650) with a statutory minimum daily allowance of Fmk4. Extra allowances of not more than 50 per cent of the daily allowance are paid for dependants—15 per cent for spouse and 10 per cent for every child under 16. These allowances begin eight week-days after the onset of illness and may be paid for a maximum of 300 week-days. Maternity allowances are the same and are paid for 54 week-days before and after birth. A maternity benefit of Fmk50 ($15·50) is paid either in cash or in kind.

Accident insurance: All employees and their families are covered against occupational accidents and diseases, as are in some cases apprentices and vocational trainees. Contributions are paid by employers in the form of insurances taken out with appropriate insurance companies. Premiums amount to 0·15 to 1 per cent of the employee's earnings according to the degree of risk. The state pays compensation to its employees directly out of state funds. Any person may voluntarily insure if he is not statutorily insured. Benefits are full medical care and requisite disability appliances. Daily allowances are paid for one year, amounting to 60 per cent of wages with a maximum daily benefit of Fmk16·7 ($5·20), and to 80 per cent of earnings if there are dependants, with a maximum daily benefit of Fmk22·2 ($6·90). Proportional partial benefits for the degree of incapacity over 20 per cent are also paid. When the daily allowance ceases, persons with disability estimated at 10–30 per cent receive a lump sum compensation amounting to a maximum of 60 per cent of annual earnings with dependants and 45 per cent without. Those with a degree of disability over 30 per cent receive two-part pensions, a basic annuity and a supplementary annuity, both related to the degree of disability with a maximum pension of 60 per cent of earnings for full disability. Dependants' supplements are 30 per cent of pension for one dependant and 20 per cent for any others up to 100 per cent of pension. Full annuities are paid to hospitalised victims regardless of the degree of disability. An additional minimum daily allowance of Fmk6·25 ($1·90) is paid to those needing the assistance of another person. Widow's and full orphan's pensions are 30 per cent of the deceased's annual earnings, and pensions for a child under 17 or any other dependant 15 per cent, the sum of such pensions not to exceed 80 per cent of a full annuity. There are provisions for increasing pensions in accordance with the cost of living.

Pensions insurance: This is administered by the National Pension Institute. The employer contributes 1·5 per cent of pay and the insured person 1·5 per cent of taxable earnings. Anyone not paying tax need pay no premiums, but everyone is entitled to full disability or old-age pensions. Basic monthly old-age pensions amounting in 1964 to Fmk37 ($11·50) are paid to all at 65, with an increase of 12·5 per cent for each extra year worked up to 70. Additional means-tested assistance pensions of Fmk139, 126 and 113 ($43, 39 and 35) are paid monthly to those receiving little or no other income. Further monthly allowances of Fmk48–71 ($14·80–22) are paid to those in need of daily assistance. For married couples, assistance pensions are again means-tested with an upper limit 60 per cent higher than for a single person. If only the husband receives a pension and the wife is over 60 or unable to work because of child care, then his full assistance pension is increased by 30 per cent. These rates are both increased by 10 per cent for each dependant child under 16. Identical pensions and supplements are paid in the case of permanent disability, long sickness and as old-age supports for unmarried women between 60 and 65. All pensions increase with each 5 per cent rise in the cost of living index. Graduated pensions covering old age and disability offer additional pensions to most fully employed and temporarily employed persons, and are financed by employers either through insurances or pension funds and foundations, and tied to the general wage and salary level.

Unemployment insurance: This is administered by state-recognised National Unemployment Funds organised on a vocational basis and is financed in the ratio of 10:4:1 by the state, a Central Unemployment Fund financed by employers, and by the insured themselves. Any persons between 15 and 59 may take part in the scheme, and also on certain conditions aged 60 and over. In 1963 nearly 30 per cent of all employed persons belonged to 58 funds. The maximum daily allowance is Fmk10 ($3) for members with dependants and Fmk7·5 ($2·30) for other members, payable for a maximum of 150 days in every 12 consecutive months. After two consecutive years of assistance, no more assistance is paid for six months, during which period contributions must again be fully paid. Clothing and travel allowances are also paid and compensation is provided for short-time employment.

Other benefits: War invalids receive compensation for all necessary treatment, including disability appliances, daily sickness and injury benefits, disablement annuities dependent upon the degree of disability above 10 per cent, and additional allowances for dependants and additional care necessary. Children's allowances are paid by the state, with a 4 per cent charge on the employee's wage or salary made to employers. The monthly allowance is Fmk186 ($58) for the first, Fmk214 ($66) for the second and Fmk252 ($78) for all subsequent children under 16. Special children's allowances of Fmk84 ($26) are paid quarterly for orphans and children suffering from mental and physical disabilities, and of Fmk42 ($13) for illegitimate children and children under 20 who are studying and not receiving other state funds. Other benefits include a minimum of one week's free holiday for mothers of poor families, military service allowances, lodging subsidies and home-founding loans.

EDUCATION

Primary education: Education is free and compulsory from the ages of seven to 15. For the first four years all children undergo virtually the same basic education. Then on the basis of the primary school certificate and an entrance examination about 50 per cent pass on to secondary education. The remainder

45

continue in primary school and are given an education which has an increased bias towards civics and prevocational training. Primary schools are maintained by the municipalities with the state paying the bulk of the costs; the size of the contribution depends upon the location of the school, a larger contribution being paid in rural areas. School meals are free.

Secondary education: Secondary schools are divided into five-year junior secondary and three-year senior secondary grades. Junior secondary education prepares children for higher vocational education such as technical and business colleges and for apprenticeships in certain branches of government service. Those who continue to senior secondary school have a choice between a language and a mathematics division, ending with the Student examination (see under *University and higher education*). Secondary schools are maintained by the state and the municipalities, and although the bulk are private schools, the state covers about 70 per cent of their expenses by subsidy. Secondary education is not free; fees are relatively low at state schools, but higher at private schools. Annual state boarding grants are awarded on merit.

Vocational education: This takes place through training in vocational schools and through apprenticeship. Vocational schools give training in commercial, technical, agricultural and other occupations. Most are owned—with substantial state aid—by municipalities, but the state, employers and other associations also maintain them. Courses last on average from 18 months to two years. Generally students must pay their own tuition and lodging fees. However, grants may be obtained from many Communes and numerous private associations and foundations, and there are state training grants and interest-free loans for persons of small means pursuing studies in state-owned or state-supported vocational schools, or other approved courses, or apprenticeship training.

Special education: Debile and dull children are taught in special classes of elementary schools. Imbeciles and idiots are free from compulsory education, but where possible are taught in special institutions maintained on a day-school basis by the state, the Communes and voluntary associations. There are six residential schools for deaf and three for blind children organised under the public education system. Teacher-training for special education is provided at the Pedagogical University in Jyväskylä.

University and higher education: Entrance to the universities is through the Student examination and special entrance examinations. The University of Helsinki is an autonomous institution. The Finnish-language University of Turku is privately founded; its Swedish-language counterpart, the Åbo Academy (Turku), is also privately founded. The state-founded University of Oulu has an attached teacher-training college. The (Finnish) Helsinki School of Economics and its Swedish counterpart are independent colleges, as are Turku's two corresponding institutes. Further institutions in Helsinki are an institute of veterinary medicine, a school of education offering two-year courses for elementary school-teachers, and an institute of technology under the jurisdiction of the Ministry of Commerce and Industry. The Institute of Pedagogics at Jyväskylä trains teachers and provides doctorates and confers the same degrees in humanities as the Universities of Helsinki and Turku. The School of Social Science at Tampere is under the jurisdiction of the Ministry of Education.

Undergraduate courses last from four to seven years. Annual state grants are provided for students of small means. They are paid (1963) at the rate of Fmk890 ($276) for full grants, Fmk570 ($177) for partial grants and Fmk170 ($53) for grants to purchase study equipment; the first two are supplemented by grants of Fmk220 ($68) for those living away from home.

Educational institutions, 1963–4:

	Institutions	Staff	Students
Primary	6,752	26,824	583,386
Secondary . . .	550	12,703	249,327
Secondary vocational . .	627	7,219	73,558
Universities, etc. . . .	14	3,142	32,624

Adult education: Adult education is provided by People's High Schools and Workers' Institutes. People's High Schools are boarding schools providing courses in the winter months. Workers' Institutes provide evening courses. The main emphasis is upon a general education in civics for young people. These institutes are privately managed, but a large proportion of expenses is covered by state subsidies. In 1961 there were over 4,000 public libraries in Finland.

MASS MEDIA

The press (1964):

Dailies: Helsingin Sanomat, Helsinki, independent, 256,000; *Uusi Suomi,* Helsinki, National Coalition, 94,000; *Aamulehti,* Tampere, Nat. Coal., 88,000; *Turun Sanomat,* Turku, Finnish People's Party, 74,000; *Satakunnan Kansa,* Pori, Nat. Coal., 13,000; *Sanomalehti Kaleva,* Oulu, ind., 10,000; *Hufvudstadsbladet,* Helsinki, Swedish People's Party, 70,000; *Ilta-Sanomat,* Helsinki, ind., 65,000; *Kansan Uutiset,* Helsinki, Social Democrat, 55,000; *Savon Sanomat,* Kuopio, Centre Party, 54,000; *Vaasa,* Nat. Coal., 50,000; *Karjalainen,* Joensuu, Nat. Coal., 36,000; *Suomen Sosiaalidemokraatti,* Helsinki, Soc. Dem., 37,000; *Keskisuomalainen,* Jyväskylä, Centre Party, 78,000.

Periodicals (Helsinki): Yhteishyvä (w), Cooperative, 339,000; *Apu* (w), illustrated, 275,000; *Seura* (w), illus., 176,000; *Maaseudun Tulevaisuus* (3w), non-party agricultural and political, 167,000; *Viikko-Sanomat* (w), illus., 165,000; *Me Naiset* (w), wom., 165,000; *Eeva* (m), wom., 127,000; *Suomen Kuvalehti* (w), illus., 108,000; *Hopeapeili* (m), wom., 83,000; *Metsälehti* (w), forestry, 50,000; *Viuhka* (w), wom.; *Talouselämä* (w), economics, 9,000; *Mercator* (w), commerce and industry, 3,000.

Broadcasting: The Finnish Broadcasting Company (Oy Yleisradio Ab) is a state monopoly and controls all radio and TV, including commercial broadcasting. Broadcasting is financed by radio and TV licence-fees and profits from TV advertising.

47

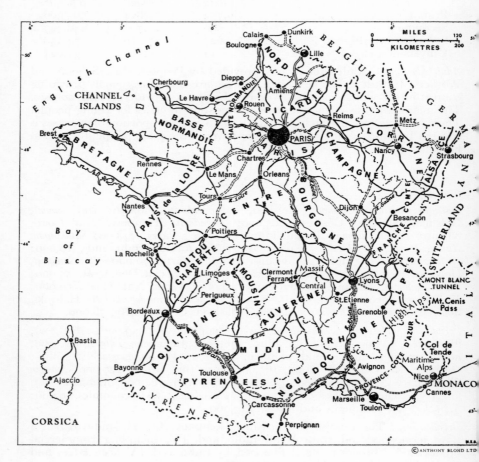

FRANCE

FRANCE

GEOGRAPHY

Features: France is the largest country in Western Europe. The most extensive of its regions, and the most important economically, is the Paris basin, bounded in the west by Brittany, in the south by the Massif Central and in the east by the Vosges. The greater part of the area lies below 600 ft/180 m. and, particularly in the east, is composed of a series of alternating ridges and valleys. The Brittany peninsula is a low dissected plateau mainly below 600 ft. The Aquitaine basin to the south is triangular in shape; its general altitude increases away from the Garonne both towards the Massif Central and the Pyrenees.

The Massif Central is upland with an average height of 3,000 ft/900 m. with parts rising to over 6,000 ft. The eastern region is composed of alternating fault-guided uplands and depressions; the central area includes the volcanic zone of Auvergne and Cantal; in the south are the limestone plateau of the Causses and deep gorges, e.g. Lot and Tarn; in the north-west is the extensive plateau of Limousin.

To the east of the Massif Central lies the lowland corridor of the Rhone-Saone Valley which provides a vital communication link between the Mediterranean and northern France. This corridor opens out onto the Mediterranean and there is a wider coastal plain to the west than to the east. South-west lies the east-west band of the Pyrenees. East of the Rhone are the French Jura and Alps. In the north-east lie the Vosges (the French counterpart of the Black Forest).

As France covers a considerable latitudinal range a wide variety of crops can be grown. The chief agricultural areas are the loess-covered chalk and limestone lands of the Paris basin (e.g. Artois, Picardy and Beauce), the terraces of the Garonne, the coastal lands of Brittany and scattered parts of the eastern Mediterranean lands and the Rhone Valley. The principal coalfields are in Lorraine, and the Franco-Belgian coalfield of the north; a number of small coalfields also produce good-quality coal in the Massif Central. Oil and natural gas are worked in the Rhone Valley and Aquitaine. The country has considerable resources of HEP; its chief minerals are the low-grade Jurassic iron ores of Lorraine. The principal industrial regions are on the Lorraine ore field, the northern coalfield, and around the towns of Paris, Marseilles, Lyons, Clermont-Ferrand, St Etienne and Bordeaux.

Area: Metropolitan France 212,740 sq. miles/551,200 sq. km. The Overseas Departments are French Guiana, Guadeloupe, Martinique and Réunion. Overseas Territories: Comoro Islands, French Polynesia, French Somaliland, New Caledonia, Saint-Pierre and Miquelon, Southern and Antarctic Territories, Wallis and Futuna Islands.

Mean max. and min. temperatures: Paris (48° N, 2° 30′ E; 160 ft/50 m.) 76°F/24°C (July), 32°F/0°C (Jan.); Bordeaux (45° N, 0° 30′ W; 160 ft/ 50 m.) 80°F/27°C (July and Aug.), 35°F/2°C (Jan.); Nice (43° 30′ N, 7° 30′ E; 40 ft/12 m.) 81°F/27°C (July and Aug.), 40°F/4°C (Jan.); Grenoble (45° N, 5° 30′ E; 735 ft/22 m.) 81°F/27°C (July), 27°F/−3°C (Jan.). *Relative humidity:* Paris 87 per cent; Bordeaux 90 per cent; Nice 68 per cent; Grenoble 82 per cent. *Mean annual rainfall:* Paris 22 in./560 mm.; Bordeaux 33 in./840 mm. Nice 32 in./810 mm.; Grenoble 38 in./965 mm.

POPULATION

Population: (1965 est.—Metropolitan France only) 49,000,000. *Chief towns and populations:* (1962) Greater PARIS (8,389,000), Marseilles (784,000), Lyons (536,000), Toulouse (331,000), Nice (295,000), Bordeaux (254,000), Nantes (246,000), Strasbourg (234,000). *Distribution:* In 1962, 36 per cent of the population lived in urban centres of more than 100,000 (of whom about 17 per cent in Greater Paris); 14 per cent in urban centres of 20–100,000; 14 per cent in urban centres of 2–20,000 and 36 per cent in rural Communes of less than 2,000.

Language: French is the official language. Breton, Corsican (akin to Italian), Spanish, Basque, Catalan, Flemish and German are also spoken in parts of the country, mainly border areas. *Religion:* About 60 per cent of the population belong to the Catholic Church. There are numerous other Christian, Jewish and Muslim communities.

CONSTITUTIONAL SYSTEM

Constitution: France is a republic. The constitution was adopted by referendum in 1958. *Head of state:* President Charles de Gaulle. *Head of government:* Prime Minister Georges Pompidou.

Executive: The President is elected (since 1962) by direct universal suffrage for seven years. He appoints and dismisses the Prime Minister, and on the Prime Minister's advice the other members of the Council of Ministers. He presides over the Council of Ministers and signs its ordinances and decrees. He may return legislation to parliament for reconsideration. Like parliament and on the advice of the Prime Minister he may initiate a revision of the constitution. The President dissolves the National Assembly, but may not dissolve it again within one year of its reelection. During parliamentary sessions he may submit draft laws to referendum and he has emergency powers in time of crisis, but he may not dissolve parliament during this period. He communicates with parliament by means of messages that are read but not debated.

The government, supervised by the Prime Minister, decides and directs general policy. The members of the government may not hold parliamentary or any other national office. The government is responsible to the Assembly, and that responsibility may be challenged only on a motion of censure, signed by one-tenth of the Assembly's members and voted for by an absolute majority, or if the government asks for a vote of confidence. If defeated by either method, the Prime Minister must hand in the resignation of the government to the President.

Legislature: Parliament consists of the National Assembly and the Senate. The Assembly comprising 481 Deputies (including 16 for the Overseas

Departments and Territories) is elected for five years by *scrutin d'arrondissement* (two-ballot single-member constitutency system). The Senate has 273 members representing Metropolitan France, Overseas Territories and Departments and Frenchmen living abroad. It is elected for nine years by indirect suffrage by an electoral college formed of Deputies, General Councillors (see *Local government*) and the representatives of Municipal Councils. One-third of the Senate is reelected every three years. De Gaulle has stated his intention of reforming the Senate by amalgamating representatives of major economic and social organisations with its membership.

Legislation may be initiated by members of either the government (*projets de loi*) or of both houses of parliament (*propositions de loi*). Finance bills must originate in the National Assembly. Legislation must be passed by both houses before being submitted to the President for promulgation. There are three types of legislation. Parliament has the right of full and detailed legislation in such matters as civil rights, nationality, criminal law and procedure and the parliamentary electoral system. Parliament determines the fundamental principles only regarding legislation in such matters as education, social security, national defence and civil law. All remaining legislation may be dealt with by the government by executive order. If parliament should invade these residual powers of the government by legislating beyond its specified powers, the government—after consultation with the Council of State and a favourable ruling by the Constitutional Council (see below under *Specialised bodies*)—may modify or annul such legislation. The government may also rule by decree for a limited period by permission of parliament; decree laws may be applicable to parliament's field of legislation and are enacted in the Council of Ministers after consultation with the Council of State. At the end of the limited period parliament may revoke or amend decree laws which fall under its normal legislative power. Parliament authorises any declaration of war.

Specialised bodies: A Constitutional Council (Conseil Constitutionnel) composed of three appointees each of the President of the Republic, the President of the Assembly and the President of the Senate, and including as honorary members all previous Presidents of France, has the duty of deciding whether laws conform to the constitution, the examination of the regulations of the two chambers, judging disputed elections and the supervision of referenda. The Economic and Social Council (Conseil Economique et Social) is a consultative body whose 200 members are nominated for five years by business and trade union organisations. The High Court of Justice (Haute Cour de Justice), composed of an equal number of members elected from among the two chambers, has the power to try the President if indicted for high treason, and members of the government for crimes or misdemeanours committed in their term of office. The High Council of the Judiciary (Conseil Supérieur de la Magistrature) of nine members appointed by the government on the President's nomination is an advisory and disciplinary body on judicial appointments. The Council of State (Conseil d'Etat) advises the government on the drafting of bills, ordinances and decrees; it is the highest administrative court in France. The Audit Office (Cour des Comptes) is formed of independent economic experts nominated for life, and supervises the execution of finance laws.

Political parties: The leading French political parties are concentrated into four main divisions. There are also some important political figures (including the Prime Minister) who have no formal party affiliation other than loyalty to the General; these are here described as 'Gaullist'. The ruling party, Union pour la Nouvelle République/Union Démocratique du Travail (UNR/UDT), which follows de Gaulle, has a majority in the Assembly with the support of the Républicains Indépendants (RI) which broke away from the Centre National des Indépendants (CNI) after the 1962 elections. The centre parties are grouped in the Centre Démocrate, based on the Mouvement Républicain Populaire (MRP), the CNI and some members of the Radical Party (Parti Républicain Radical et Radical-Socialiste). The democratic left comes under the Fédération de la Gauche Démocrate et Socialiste (FGDS) and includes besides the minute Union Démocratique et Socialiste de la Résistance (UDSR) and some political clubs, the Socialists (Section Française de l'Internationale Ouvrière—SFIO) and the bulk of the Radicals. The small left-wing Parti Socialiste Unifié (PSU) and the French Communist Party (PCF) have an electoral alliance with the FGDS for the 1967 elections.

Election results (Metropolitan France only):

Parties and groupings	National Assembly				Senate as at 1965
	1958		1962		
	% of poll (first round)	Seats	% of poll (first round)	Seats	Seats
UNR/UDT	17·5	188	31·9	231	30
CNI/other Independents .	20·1	132	9·1	29	
RI	—	—	4·4	19	81
Extreme right . .	3·2	1	0·9	—	
MRP	11·8	57	8·9	35	38
Radicals and Centrists .	11·4	35	8·0	42	50
SFIO	15·5	40	12·7	66	52
PSU and extreme left .	1·6	2	2·3	3	—
Communists . .	18·9	10	21·8	40	14
Others	—	—	—	—	9

Leading political figures: Gaullist—Georges Pompidou (Prime Minister), Couve de Murville (Foreign Minister), Pierre Messmer (Minister of the Armed Forces), Louis Joxe (Minister for Administrative Reform), Edgar Faure (Minister of Agriculture). UNR/UDT—Michel Debré (Minister of Economic Affairs and Finance), Jacques Baumel (Party Secretary-General), Jacques Chaban-Delmas (President of the National Assembly). RI—Giscard d'Estaing (Party President). SFIO—Gaston Deferre (Party President), Guy Mollet (Party Secretary-General). Communists—Waldeck Rochet (Secretary-General). MRP—Jean Lecanuet (President of the Centre Démocrate), René Pleven. Radicals—René Billères (President), Maurice Faure. UDSR—François Mitterand (Party Leader and President of the FGDS). PSU—Pierre Mendès-France.

Local government: On completion of the present administrative reform, France will be divided into 91 Departments (*départements*), which are both state administrative districts and local communities, plus the Ville de Paris having a quasi-Departmental personality. A government-appointed Prefect (*préfet*) heads all state administrative services in the Department. In the new Departments of the Paris Region (see below), there will be Deputy Prefects (*préfets délégués*) until 1968, and in the Ville de Paris the former Prefect of the Seine will be Prefect of Paris.

The Prefect is assisted by civil servants and executes, or may initiate the cancellation of, the decisions of the General Council (*conseil général*) of the Department. The General Council is elected by the population of the Department for six years. It meets twice a year, approves the Department's budget, and with the Communes of the Department (see below) has certain rights of oversight, particularly in financial matters.

The Departments are grouped together in 21 Regions. In all Regions except Paris a Regional Prefect (*préfet de region*), chosen from the Prefects of the Departments in that Region but maintaining his Departmental powers, acts as a coordinating agent. He is advised by two Regional bodies: the Inter-Departmental Administrative Conference composed of the various Prefects of the Region, the Inspector-General of the National Economy and the Coordinating Chief Treasurer and Paymaster; and the Regional Economic Development Commission composed of representatives of the *conseils généraux* within the Region (at least 25 per cent of the Commission's membership), appointees of the Prime Minister (at most 25 per cent of membership) and representatives of social, professional, economic and trade union organisations, nominated by the organisations themselves (50 per cent of membership). The Commissions vary in size from 20 to 50 members according to the size of the Region.

In the Paris Region the chief official will be as of 1968 the Administrator-General of the Paris Region. He will not have a prefecture of his own, but will have authority over all the Prefects of the Region, and be empowered with considerable administrative and economic competence. He will be President of the Regional Administrative Conference and be advised by a Regional Assembly similar to those existing in the other Regions.

The 38,000 Communes of France are not artificial structures like the Departments and enjoy a wide degree of local autonomy. Each is administered by a Municipal Council (*conseil municipal*) elected by the list system of proportional representation for six years, which in turn elects a mayor (*maire*) for the same period. Communes may group themselves into Urban Districts and Zones.

The judicial system: Under the 1958 constitution the President and the High Council of the Judiciary guarantee the independence of legal authorities. There is a clear distinction between civil and penal justice. There are four types of court corresponding to the major branches of French law: civil courts, penal courts, professional courts and administrative courts. Minor civil cases are heard by *tribunaux d'instance* and more serious cases by *tribunaux de grande instance*, which also act as appeal courts for the courts of first instance. Police tribunals judge petty offences (*contraventions*). Minor offences (*délits*) are judged by *tribunaux correctionnels*. The *cours d'assises* try *crimes* and are empowered to pronounce the death penalty; a mixed jury of nine jurors (chosen by lot) and three magistrates must give its verdict by at least eight votes. Appeal from this court is to the Cour de Cassation only, which decides whether the judgement is in conformity with the law; if the decision is negative, the case is sent back to another court of the same instance. Appeal from the other courts, including the specialised courts, is with the *cours d'appel* and then to the Cour de Cassation.

RECENT HISTORY

A provisional government was constituted in 1944 after the liberation of France, of which General Charles de Gaulle was head until his resignation in 1946. In 1946 the constitution of the Fourth Republic was adopted by referendum. Under the Fourth Republic France became a founder-member of the ECSC, the EEC and Euratom. A search for guarantees of collective security against first the resurgence of Germany and later the threat of Soviet aggression led France to sign the Dunkirk Treaty with Britain in 1947, the Brussels Treaty with Britain and the Benelux countries[1] in 1948, and in 1949 to join NATO. After the French parliament failed to ratify proposals for the European Defence Community, it agreed to the expansion of the Brussels Treaty into the Western European Union Treaty to permit German accession to NATO.

France's withdrawal from its colonial past was bloody. A prolonged war in Indo-China (1946–54) was followed by the Algerian war of independence (1954–62). Tunisia and Morocco were granted independence in 1956, Guinea in 1958 and all remaining African possessions bar French Somaliland in 1960; riots in Djibouti during the President's world tour in August 1966 led to French proposals on the future of French Somaliland. France's former African dependencies plus the Malagasy Republic are linked with France by bilateral agreements providing for a customs union, mutual cooperation in cultural and technical fields and in defence, and the provision of French development aid.

Domestically, while the French and the Community bureaucracy provided for continuity and economic growth, the body politic witnessed a succession of 26 cabinets, which provided frequent periods of executive weakness and political frustration. During a period of near civil-war brought on by an army rebellion in Algeria, this dissatisfaction with the Fourth Republic led to the return of General de Gaulle as Prime Minister in May 1958. In September of the same year the constitution of the Fifth Republic was approved by referendum.

Since that date France has increasingly followed a policy designed to maximise its freedom of action and enhance its status as a world power. In 1962 the Algerian war was brought to an end by the Evian agreement. In January 1963 France vetoed Britain's application for membership of the Common Market and signed a Treaty of Friendship with West Germany. In 1965 de Gaulle was reelected President on the second ballot. French policy towards NATO reached its climax in early 1966 when France gave notice that it was withdrawing from the organisation, though not the alliance, of the North Atlantic Treaty. Withdrawal of French air force units from Germany began in June 1966. French military policy under de Gaulle has seen the development of an 'independent' atomic strike force—the *force de frappe*. France has not signed the Nuclear Test-Ban Treaty and new French nuclear tests took place from July 1966.

Defence: The President is commander-in-chief of the armed forces. France has selective military service for 18 months. The strengths of the armed forces are: army 338,000, navy 84,000, air force 113,000. Defence expenditure for the year 1965-6 represented approximately 4.8 per cent of GNP. The defence estimates for 1967 were F23,513 million (approximately $4,797 million). Military bases of other NATO powers on French territory are reverting to French control as France's withdrawal from the military organisation of NATO becomes effective.

---

[1] See 'Western Europe and the Atlantic World' p. 253.

54

Economy

France is well endowed with natural resources and over 80 per cent of its land is productive. It is the largest agricultural producer in Western Europe and is virtually self-sufficient in food. The process of economic recovery and development in the period after the second world war has been achieved through four national plans; 1946–52/3, 1954–7, 1958–61 and 1962–5. A new plan covers the 1966–70 period. In 1963 when inflationary pressures were causing concern, the government imposed a series of stabilisation measures aimed at keeping down consumption and prices and incomes while maintaining growth in certain key industries. These measures, including a credit squeeze, an industrial price freeze and the balancing of public finance, succeeded in slowing down the upward movement in prices and wages and reduced pressure upon resources. The policy was continued during 1965 together with indirect tax concessions to encourage industrial investment and private savings, reduction of the discount rate from 4 to 3.5 per cent, and relaxation of consumer credit. The government also founded a State Loan Fund in an effort to encourage industrial investment in order to maintain the Fourth Plan growth target of 4 per cent for the year. The Fifth Plan (1966–70) envisages a minimum annual average growth rate of 5 per cent for GDP. The plan is conceived in terms of modernisation of the structure of agriculture, industry and commerce; it also aims at the implementation of an incomes policy, the shortening of the working week by $1\frac{1}{2}$ hours, a heavy increase in foreign trade and an increase in all forms of investment.

From 1958 to 1964 annual average growth rate was 5.3 per cent. In 1964 the value of GNP was F440,500 million ($88,100 million), which represented an increase of 5.4 per cent over the preceding year. The Fourth Plan (1962–5) had a growth target of 5.5 per cent per annum. From 1962 to 1964 percentage volume increases in GNP were above the target; the growth rate in 1965, however, was expected to be only 2.5 per cent. Percentage volume increase in industrial production over the preceding year since 1959 has been 3 per cent in 1959, 7.3 per cent in 1960, 5.4 per cent in 1961, 6.4 per cent in 1962, 6 per cent in 1963, 6.5 per cent in 1964, 2 per cent in 1965 and an expected 6 per cent in 1966. The main growth industries in recent years have been consumer goods—especially cars and textiles—and chemicals, fuels a͠ building materials. The state controls about 40 per cent of all indṛ The relative importance of the major sectors of the economy in terms ⁄ contributions to GDP at market prices in 1964 were:

Sector	Percentage of GDP
Agriculture	8
Industry	40
Construction	8
Services	4⟋
Total	

France's principal industries are textiles, ⟋ower, iron and steel, mechanical engineering products (especial⟋ and wood and paper- pulping. Agriculture varies according to⟋ecause of wide differences of climate; the major products are cer⟋ock and poultry, wine and vegetables. In terms of land usage Fr⟋ins very much an agricultural nation with 62 per cent of total la⟋evoted to agriculture.

Foreign trade: Between 1945 and 1958 the balance of payments showed a constant deficit. Devaluation in 1958 contributed towards surplus balances of payments from 1959 to 1963. A large net surplus in 1965 (F4,760 million or $970 million) was partly due to an increase in exports resulting from the delayed effects of the price and wage stabilisation measures introduced by the government in 1963–4. In 1964 France's exports to EEC countries rose by 13 per cent, exports to non-EEC countries by 10 per cent; imports from EEC countries rose by 20 per cent, imports from non-EEC countries by 12·5 per cent. The effect on France's foreign trade since becoming a member of the EEC in 1957 has been for exports to EEC countries to increase from 25 per cent of total exports in 1957 to nearly 40 per cent in 1964. Similarly, imports from EEC countries have risen from 21 per cent of total imports in 1957 to 37 per cent in 1964. The contribution of exports to GNP in 1964 was 10 per cent. In 1964 the main exports were food, beverages and tobacco (16 per cent of total exports), machinery and electrical equipment (14 per cent), steel (11 per cent), chemical products (10 per cent) and textiles (7 per cent). The contribution of imports to GNP in 1964 was 11·5 per cent, of which the main items were energy and lubricants (17 per cent of total imports), machinery and electrical equipment (13 per cent), food, beverages and tobacco (12 per cent), steel (11 per cent) and chemical products (6 per cent). The relative importance of tourism is steadily declining.

Employment: Of France's total working population of nearly 20 million in 1964, 19 per cent were employed in agriculture, 40 per cent in industry and construction, and 41 per cent in services. From 1954 to 1962 the agricultural working population decreased by 25 per cent and the number of persons employed in administration, transport, commerce and other services increased by 12 per cent. Up to 1964 there was a mild labour shortage, but in 1965–6 the trend was reversed owing to the levelling-off of demand, the arrival on the labour market of school leavers from the post-war 'bulge' and the repatriation—begun in 1963—of settlers from Algeria. The average annual influx of foreign workers in 1963–4 was 134,000.

Price and wage trends: In 1964 the upward movement of prices and incomes slowed owing to the stabilisation policy (retail prices rose by a monthly average of 0·2 per cent between October 1963 and December 1964 as compared with 0·4 per cent between January 1961 and September 1963). ...comes showed a similar trend during the same period. Consumer prices ...66 are being used as the key indicator for the minimum guaranteed ...olicy which is part of the government's efforts to introduce a form of GNP policy.

Private consumption expenditure amounted to 64 per cent of ...nd public consumption to 13 per cent.

SOCIAL SECURITY

The Directora... supervision over s... mental and Regional Security in the Ministry of Labour has direct which is concerned writy except for unemployment. All funds, Depart- earnings below F12,960ontrolled by a National Social Security Fund benefit purposes. The ancial equalisation. Only that part of annual —to January 1965. ...4 (1966) is considered for contribution and ...ted below refer—unless otherwise stated

Health insurance: The general system covers all non-agricultural employees and (for medical benefits only) pensioners. There are special schemes for agricultural employees, agricultural self-employed, miners, seamen, railwaymen, public and public utility employees. Health insurance, together with pensions insurance, is financed by the insured person and the employer at the respective rates of 6 and 14·25 per cent of earnings. Medical benefits are general and specialist care, hospitalisation, laboratory services, maternity and dental care, appliances, transportation and medicines. The insured pays for medical expenses and is reimbursed 70 to 100 per cent. Daily sickness benefits are paid for up to 12 months (three years for chronic illnesses) at 50 per cent of earnings up to a maximum of F17 ($3.50) per day, rising to two-thirds of earnings after 30 days if the insured has three or more children, up to a maximum of F22·66 ($4·60). Maternity benefits are the same and are paid for up to six weeks before and eight weeks after confinement. Monthly nursing benefits or milk coupon benefits of F5·20 ($1·4) are paid for four months.

Accident insurance: The general system covers all non-agricultural employees. There are special systems for public utility and agricultural employees and railwaymen. The insurance is financed by the employer at the average rate of 3 per cent of the employee's earnings. Medical benefits are paid for directly and solely by the primary fund (*caisse*). Temporary daily disability benefits are 50 per cent of earnings for the first 28 days up to a maximum of F61·20 ($12.50) and two-thirds of earnings thereafter up to a maximum of F81·60 ($16·50). For permanent disability, pensions are 100 per cent of average earnings over the last 12 months for 100 per cent disability, plus 40 per cent of pension for constant attendance. For partial disability pensions are a variable percentage of average earnings. Widow's pensions—also payable to widowers—are 30 per cent of the insured's earnings, increasing to 50 per cent if the widow is aged 60 or is invalid. Orphans under 16 receive pensions worth 15 per cent of earnings (first two), 10 per cent (third and subsequent) or 20 per cent (full orphans). Other dependant relatives may receive pensions of 10 per cent each up to a total of 30 per cent. Total survivor's pensions may not exceed 85 per cent of the insured's earnings.

Pensions insurance: This covers all non-agricultural employees in the gen⟨eral⟩ system, with special systems for the self-employed, miners, railwa⟨y⟩ public and public utility employees, seamen and agricultural work⟨ers⟩ pensions are related to current wage values. Old-age pensions are ⟨se⟩t at the rate of 20–40 per cent of average earnings over the last 1⟨0⟩ 700 increments of 4 per cent of earnings per year for each year⟨. pensⁱ⟩oners. Supplements of 50 per cent of pension are paid for a spouse earnings if three children are being reared. Special annual sup⟨port,⟩248), plus ($143) are paid from a National Solidarity Fund to lo⟨w⟩th an annual Invalidity pensions are paid at the rate of 50 per c⟨ent⟩ds, and constant over the last 10 years, up to an annual maximum⟨ for⟩ invalids up to an constant attendance allowances of 40 per cent⟨ maxi⟩mum annual old-age minimum pension in this case of F5,643 ($1,150⟨)⟩ pensions—also payable attendance allowances of 30 per cent of earn⟨ings o⟩r 60 if invalid, at the rate annual maximum of F3,672 ($748). In Jul⟨y⟩ cent of the pension if three and invalidity pensions were F1,250 ($25⟨0⟩
to dependant widowers—are paid at th⟨e rate⟩
of 50 per cent of the insured's pension⟨
children are being reared.

Unemployment insurance: This covers all regularly employed persons. There are special systems for building and dock workers. The insurance is financed entirely by the state, with local government contributing 10 per cent of costs. Daily allowances in the larger cities—after an income test—are F4·20 ($0·86) plus supplements of F1·80 ($0·37) for a non-employed spouse or parent. In 1958 employers and certain trade unions made a collective agreement whereby employers pay 0·20 per cent of salary and employees 0·05 per cent in contribution to a fund for benefits amounting to 35 per cent of wages (more in the case of old-age or long service) for nine months.

Other benefits: Family allowances are paid to all gainfully occupied persons, social insurance beneficiaries and persons who are unable to work, having two or more children. There are special systems—paying the same allowances—for railwaymen and employees in agriculture and the public utilities. The insurance is financed by employers alone at the rate of 13.5 per cent of earnings. Allowances are paid for each child under 15 (18 for apprentices, 20 for students, invalids and girls working at home): under 10 the rate is 22 per cent for the second, and 33 per cent for the third and each further child, of the currently monthly 'base wage' (F288 or $59 in January 1965). Over 10 the allowance is 9 per cent higher; over 15, 15 per cent higher. Allowances are further increased by single salary allowances paid where the wife does not work, at 10 per cent of a fixed monthly basis (F194.50 or $39.70 in January 1965) where there are no children, 20 per cent for each of the first and second children and subsequently 10 per cent or, for the wives of employers and self-employed, 10 per cent of the monthly basis for each of the first two children, increasing by 10 per cent for each subsequent child. Prenatal allowances of 22 per cent of the base wage paid for nine months, and birth grants of 200 per cent of the base wage for each birth, are paid to all mothers. For infirm children requiring specialised education, allowances are paid at the rate of 50 per cent of the base wage. All above-quoted rates refer to the Department of the Seine which pays the highest national rates.

EDUCATION

Apart from a few advanced technical institutes and professional establishments, all public teaching is the responsibility of the state. Twenty-three educational districts (*académies*)—each embracing two to eight Departments—administer primary, secondary and technical education. Each is headed a state-appointed rector who controls the education inspectorate and is ed by various consultative bodies formed of local government repre- es, academics, administrators and teachers. Public education is free religious. Private education is state-aided. Education is compulsory age es of 6 to 14 (16 in 1967).

Seconda n: All children receive the same primary education until the developh
d'observation
is divided in*nal education:* Children are graded according to their levels. On the their first two years of secondary education (*cycle compulsory for p* cle of secondary education lasts from 11 to 15, and to either a General ity, ordinary secondary and practical secondary is divided into an A st primary school record, or by examination— vate primary school—children are admitted Transitional Section. The General Section ed in Classical and Modern Lycées, and

a B stream which is taught, in addition to those who failed the examination for secondary education—the Transitional Section—in General Education Colleges. The Secondary Education College, introduced in 1963, brings together all three streams under one roof. Those in the Transitional Section of first cycle education who show sufficient ability may later rejoin the General Section; the alternative is two years of terminal practical education of a more general and practical nature, ending at 15 with an end of studies diploma (*diplôme de fin d'études*), which mentions the child's professional speciality. Some may then proceed to the B General Stream for two years of specialised professional training, ending with the Certificate of Professional Proficiency (*certificat d'aptitude professionnelle*).

At the end of the fourth year the General Section goes on to the second cycle of education—both short and long—which takes place between the ages of 15 and 18. Short education is for two years leading to either the Certificate of Professional Proficiency, or—through wider education given in Technical and Agricultural Colleges and special sections of Technical Lycées—to the *brevet d'études* in industry, commerce, agriculture or administration, and possibly further to the *brevet d'agent technique*. Long education lasting for three years takes place in Classical, Modern, Technical and Agricultural Lycées and leads on the one hand to a *brevet de technicien* in industry, commerce or agriculture and on the other to the *baccalauréat*. The reforms of second cycle education envisage that a student, having obtained the *baccalauréat*, may either take an examination to an Advanced Technical Institute, or a course in higher education, or enter an Institute for Advanced Professional Education. A pupil with the *brevet de technicien* may either embark on higher education or enter an Institute for Advanced Professional Education for a two-year course leading to the Advanced Technician's Diploma (*brevet de technicien supérieur*).

Special education: The educational programme of the Fifth Plan envisages the expenditure of F920 million ($188 million) on providing 130,000 new school places for handicapped children in addition to the 125,000 already existing in 1965. This combined figure represents only about one-third of the total of mentally and physically handicapped and maladjusted children. Teaching will take place in special classes in primary schools, in small groups in Secondary Education Colleges and in 80 new *écoles nationales de perfectionnement*.

University and higher education: Higher education is also undergoing There are both private and public institutes for higher education admission to university education is unrestricted, the *bacca* normal qualification necessary to read for a degree. Only are empowered to confer state diplomas. There is a univ town of most *académies* (see above). Generally they j science, letters and human sciences, medicine and ph law institutes and scientific and literary colleges ha ny (St towns not possessing universities. Strasbourg U e state. Catholic and Protestant theology. There are C institutes in Paris, Lille, Toulouse, Angers an advanced technical institutes which prepa careers in the civil service (Ecole Nati (Ecole Normale Supérieur), business Etudes Commerciales), engineering Cyr) and several others. This educ

Universities: Aix-Marseille, Besançon, Bordeaux, Caen, Clermond-Ferrand, Dijon, Grenoble, Lille, Lyons, Montpellier, Nancy, Nantes, Nice, Orléans, Paris (Sorbonne), Poitiers, Reims, Rennes, Strasbourg, Toulouse.

Educational institutions, 1964–5:

Institutions			Number of students
Primary —public	.	.	6,153,000
—private	.	.	1,099,000
Secondary—public	.	.	2,208,000
—private	.	.	579,000
Technical —public	.	.	344,000
—private	.	.	193,000
Universities, etc.	.	.	403,000

Adult education: This is organised by the Ministry of Education with increasing state grants. In 1965 evening classes reached about 235,000 students and correspondence classes about 42,000. The universities and other specialised institutes run advanced classes for technicians, engineers and executives.

MASS MEDIA

The press (1965):

Dailies: France-Soir, Paris, independent, 1,257,000; *Le Parisien Libéré*, Paris, ind. 915,000; *Ouest France*, Rennes, ind. 663,000; *Le Dauphiné Libéré*, Grenoble, ind., 522,000; *Le Figaro*, Paris, ind., liberal-conservative, 501,000; *L'Aurore*, Paris, ind., 426,000; *La Voix du Nord*, Lille, pro-government, 417,000; *Le Progrès*, Lyons, pro-gov., 392,000; *Sud-Ouest*, Bordeaux, ind., 388,000; *Paris-Jour*, Paris, left-ind., 356,000; *Dépêche du Midi*, Toulouse, radical-socialist, 324,000; *Le Monde*, Paris, ind., 302,000; *La Nouvelle République du Centre Ouest*, Tours, pro-gov., 297,000; *L'Est Républicain*, Nancy, ind., 267,000; *Le Provençal*, Marseilles, soc., 259,000; *Le Républicain Lorrain*, Metz, ind., 231,000; *L'Humanité*, Paris, Communist party organ, 202,000; *La Croix*, Paris, ind. Catholic, 133,000; *Les Echos*, Paris, economic-financial, 53,000; *Combat*, Paris, centre-left, 44,000; *La Nation*, Paris, Gaullist, 20,000.

Periodicals (Paris): L'Echo de Notre Temps (m), Catholic woman's, 1,688,000; *Paris-Match* (w), illustrated, 1,451,000; *France-Dimanche* (S), popular, 1,352,000; *Nous Deux*, pop. romance, 1,121,000; *L'Echo de la Mode* (w), wom., 1,100,000; *Marie-Claire* (2m), wom. 1,000,000; *Marie-France*, wom., 772,000; *Elle* (w), wom., 739,000; *Journal du Dimanche*, Sunday edition of *France-Soir*, 700,000; *La Vie Catholique Illustrée*, Catholic illus., 508,000; *L'Express* (w), left-centre, 350,000; *Le Canard Enchâiné* (w), satirical, 326,000.

Broadcasting: Sound and TV broadcasts are controlled by a state monopoly service, the Office de Radiodiffusion et Télévision Française (ORTF) independent budget. The ORTF is administered by a director-nominated by the government upon whom devolves sole manage-ibility, and a board of governors—half representing the state being highly qualified persons and representatives of viewers press and the ORTF staff—responsible for general super-of Information and Minister of Finance have the right general control over the ORTF. Ninety per cent derived from radio and TV licences.

FEDERAL REPUBLIC OF GERMANY

GEOGRAPHY

Features: Running across the north of West Germany is the North German Plain stretching from Poland to the Netherlands, mainly below 300 ft/90 m. and with numerous morainic ridges, intervening valleys and marshlands. South of this area lies the Rhine massif, consisting of four plateaux divided by the Rhine, Moselle and Lahn: the Hunsrück, Taunus, Westerwald and Eifel, all rising to 1,500-3,000 ft/450-900 m. and composed largely of volcanic material. Between Mainz and Coblenz the Rhine has cut a spectacular gorge. South and east of this upland area are the sedimentary scarplands of Swabia and Franconia consisting of an alternation of scarps and vales and seldom rising to more than 1,000 ft/300 m. In the far south, bounded by the Danube, is the Alpine foreland, a plateau of outwash material from the main Alpine ridges and dissected by the streams flowing northwards to the Danube. It rises steadily in elevation as far as the Alps.

Germany has a wide variety of geology, soils and climate and so a varied agriculture. The best of the agricultural lands are in the embayments that flank the Hercynian uplands lying south of the North German Plain, e.g. the Cologne area and other parts of Westphalia and Saxony; then come the Rhinelands and the more fertile parts of the scarpland zone. The country has considerable resources, the most important of which is the rich Ruhr coalfield (bituminous); Cologne lies on a coalfield (lignite) and there are other smaller fields. There is oil in the Rhine Valley. Iron ore is mined, especially in the Salzgitter area, though quality is poor. There are extensive salt and potash deposits in various parts of the country. The main industrial regions are associated with the Ruhr coalfield and the Salzgitter-Brunswick, Frankfurt, Mannheim, Stuttgart, Cologne, Hamburg areas and West

Area: Federal Republic 96,000 sq. miles/248,530 sq. km. West Be miles/480 sq. km. Together these areas constitute about 53 p area covered by the German Reich in 1937. The Soviet S (East Berlin) and Soviet Zone of Occupation in German or 'German Democratic Republic') cover 155 sq. mil 41,630 sq. miles/107,900 sq. km. respectively (23 per N, territory). The territories placed by the Potsdam C Polish and Soviet administration—the territorie Line—pending a final peace conference toget 114,300 sq. km. (24 per cent of Reich territo

Mean max. and min. temperatures: Frankf 340 ft/104 m.), 75°F/24°C (July), 29°F/ 50 ft/15 m.) 71°F/22°C (July), 30°F/

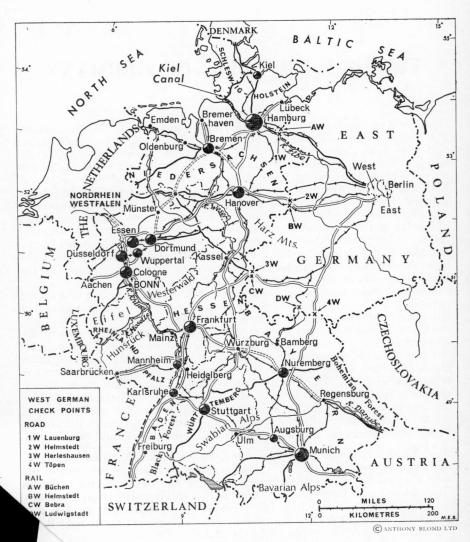

WEST GERMAN
CHECK POINTS
ROAD

1 W Lauenburg
2 W Helmstedt
3 W Herleshausen
4 W Töpen

RAIL

A W Büchen
B W Helmstedt
C W Bebra
D W Ludwigstadt

© ANTHONY BLOND LTD

GERMANY

62

11° 30' E; 1,740 ft/530 m.) 72°F/22°C (July), 23°F/−5°C (Jan.). *Relative humidity:* Frankfurt-am-Main 86 per cent; Bremen 87 per cent; Munich 87 per cent. *Mean average rainfall:* Frankfurt-am-Main 24 in./610 mm.; Bremen 26 in./660 mm.; Munich 34 in./860 mm.

POPULATION

Total population: (1965) Federal Republic 59,000,000 (including West Berlin 2,197,000). (East Germany 17,012,000, including East Berlin 1,072,000. The number of Germans remaining in the Eastern Territories is perhaps 700,000.) At the end of 1960 expellees and refugees from the Eastern Territories, the Sudetenland, East Germany and East Berlin and other areas of German settlement in Eastern Europe totalled 24 per cent of the total population of the Federal Republic (including West Berlin and the Saarland).

Capital: Berlin is the capital of all Germany. Bonn (59,000) is the seat of the Federal Government. *Main towns and populations:* (1965) Hamburg (1,857,000), Munich (1,211,000), Cologne (855,000), Essen (727,000), Düsseldorf (700,000), Frankfurt (691,000), Dortmund (656,000), Stuttgart (633,000), Bremen (592,000), Hanover (559,000), Duisburg (490,000), Nuremberg (472,000). *Distribution:* In 1965, 34 per cent of the population lived in cities of more than 100,000 inhabitants, 16 per cent in towns of 20–100,000 inhabitants, 29 per cent in towns of 2–20,000 inhabitants and 21 per cent in centres of less than 2,000 inhabitants.

Language: The official language is German. There is a small Danish-speaking minority in Schleswig-Holstein. *Religion:* About 51 per cent of the population adhere to the Evangelical Church and about 44 per cent are Roman Catholics.

CONSTITUTIONAL SYSTEM

Constitution: West Germany is a federal republic composed of 10 *Länder* and Berlin. The 1949 Basic Law (*Grundgesetz*) is the constitution of the Federal Republic, but ceases to be in force on the free adoption of a constitution for the whole of Germany. The constitution may be amended only by two-thirds majority of both houses of parliament. *Head of state:* Federal President Heinrich Lübke. *Head of government:* Federal Chancellor Kurt-Georg Kiesinger (Christian Democratic Union).

Executive: The Federal President (Bundespräsident) is elected for five years by a Federal Convention (Bundesversammlung) consisting of the members of the lower house of parliament (Bundestag) and an equivalent number of representatives of the Länder parliaments elected on a proportional representation basis.

The President nominates the Federal Chancellor (Bundeskanzler), who determines general government policy, for election by the Bundestag and appoints and dismisses the Federal ministers on the Chancellor's advice. The Chancellor-nominee is elected by the Bundestag—without debate—by a simple majority, and must then be appointed by the President. If the nominee is not elected the Bundestag has 14 days in which to elect another Chancellor by simple majority. If there is no election in this period a new vote must take place immediately in which the person receiving the largest number of votes is elected; if this number constitutes a majority the President must appoint him, but if not then the President may either appoint him or dissolve the Bundestag. This procedure ensures that the Chancellor has the confidence of the Bundestag.

The Bundestag may only express no confidence in the Chancellor by a majority election of a successor, in which case the President is obliged to dismiss the incumbent and appoint the person elected as Chancellor. If the Bundestag refuses the Chancellor's request for a vote of confidence, or if the vote goes against him, the President, on the Chancellor's request, may dissolve the Bundestag within 21 days, which right of dissolution lapses if the Bundestag elects a new Chancellor. If the Bundestag does not elect a new Chancellor and refuses to pass a bill that the government deems urgent, then the Chancellor may request that instead of dissolution the President proclaim a six-month 'state of legislative emergency' (*Gesetzgebungnotstand;* it may be declared once only in the same Chancellor's term of office) to which President and Bundesrat must agree. During this period the government, with the support of the Bundesrat, may pass any bill (except a constitutional amendment) rejected by the Bundestag.

The Federal government (Bundesregierung) is composed of the Federal ministers and the Chancellor, who may not hold any other salaried office, engage in a trade or profession, or be managers of or—without the consent of the Bundestag—directors of a profit-making concern. The Basic Law makes no provision for a vote of confidence in individual ministers.

Legislature: The present Bundestag has 496 Deputies elected for four years by a mixed system of proportional representation and the single-member simple majority method. A party must obtain at least 5 per cent of the national vote or gain three seats by direct election in order to qualify for representation in the Bundestag. In addition there are 22 members representing West Berlin who have consultative non-voting status only. The upper house (Bundesrat) has 41 members representing the Länder apportioned on a population basis and four with consultative status only for West Berlin. The members of the Bundesrat serve for no fixed period of time, being subject to appointment and recall by the Länder governments. The votes for each Land must be cast uniformly according to a prior resolution of the respective Land government. The Bundesrat discusses every bill that is introduced by the Federal government before it is presented to the Bundestag and may itself in certain circumstances introduce legislation. The approval of the Bundesrat is necessary for such Federal legislation as that affecting Länder administrative arrangements, important financial legislation and certain other matters. The Bundesrat gives its approval by a majority, otherwise differences between the two chambers may be settled by a joint committee. If the committee proposes any amendment the bill must be again voted by the Bundestag.

The Federation (Bund) legislates exclusively in foreign affairs, defence, currency, post and telecommunications, customs, etc. Upon certain other matters both Länder and Bund are permitted to legislate (concurrent legislation); the Länder may legislate to the extent that the Bund makes no use of its rights. In such matters as the press, cinema and the public services, the Bund lays down the general framework within which the Länder may legislate. Legislative matters reserved exclusively to the Länder are education, radio and TV broadcasting and control of the police, although in grave emergency situations the Federal government may place the police of any one Land or number of Länder under its own jurisdiction.

Political parties: The present government is a coalition of the Christian Democratic Union (CDU), its Bavarian wing the Christian Social Union (CSU) and the Social Democrats (SPD). The liberal-nationalist Free Democratic Party (FDP) constitutes the official opposition, although a large minority of the SPD voted against or abstained from voting in the election of Chancellor Kiesinger in 1966. Coalitions formed in the Länder do not always follow the Federal prototype even where the election results would permit.

The Federal Constitutional Court (see below under *Judicial system*) placed a constitutional ban on the neo-Nazi Socialist Reich Party (SRP) in 1951, and on the Communist Party (KPD) in 1956. The successors to the SRP were first the German Reich Party (DRP) and now the National Democratic Party (NPD). The latter gained increased electoral support in local and Land elections in 1966 in Hesse and Bavaria. The Communist-influenced German Peace Union (DFU) has declined in recent elections to the point of extinction. The right-wing All-German Party (GDP), a fusion of the German Party (DP) and the Refugee Party (GB/BHE)—focal points of right-wing and nationalistic discontent in previous years—amalgamated with the CDU on the national level prior to the 1965 elections and lost its last Land representation—to the benefit of the NPD—in the 1966 Hesse elections. Among local parties are the South Schleswig Voters' Association (SSW), the Saarland People's Party (SVP) and the Bavarian Party (BP).

From its inception in 1949 until December 1966 the Federal Republic was governed by coalitions dominated by the CDU/CSU under first Konrad Adenauer and from 1963 Ludwig Erhard. After the resignation of the FDP ministers over proposed tax increases in October 1966 the Erhard government resigned and was replaced by a 'grand coalition' (CDU/CSU-SPD), with Kurt-Georg Kiesinger as Chancellor, in December 1966.

Election results:

	Bundestag			
	1961		*1965*	
Party	*Percentage of poll*	*Seats*	*Percentage of poll*	*Seats*
CDU	35·8	192 (201)[1]	37·9	196 (202)
CSU	9·6	50	9·7	49
SPD	36·2	190 (203)	39·3	202 (217)
FDP	12·8	67	9·5	49 (50)
GDP	2·8	—	—	—
DFU	1·9	—	1·3	—
NPD	—	—	2·0	—
DRP	0·8	—	—	—
Others	0·2	—	0·3	—

[1] Figures in parentheses denote party strengths with the inclusion of the 22 non-voting Deputies of West Berlin.

Leading political figures: CDU—Kurt-Georg Kiesinger (Chancellor), Gerhard Schröder (Minister of Defence), Ludwig Erhard (Party Chairman and former Chancellor), Rainer Barzel (Parliamentary Leader), Eugen Gerstenmaier (President of the Bundestag), Konrad Adenauer (former Chancellor and Party Chairman). CSU—Franz-Josef Strauss (Finance Minister and Party Chairman). SPD—Willy Brandt (Vice-Chancellor and Foreign Minister and Party Chairman), Herbert Wehner (Party Vice-Chairman and Minister for All-German Affairs), Carlo Schmid (Minister for the Bundesrat and the

Länder), Karl Schiller (Minister for Economic Affairs), Helmut Schmidt (Parliamentary Leader and also Party Vice-Chairman). FPD—Erich Mende (Party Chairman and former Vice-Chancellor and Minister for All-German Affairs), Rolf Dahlgrün (former Finance Minister). NPD—Friedrich Thielen and Adolf von Thadden (Party Leaders).

Local government: The *Länder* are autonomous but not sovereign states. Each Land has its own constitution. Each Land elects a parliament for four years, which is generally called the Land Diet (*Landtag*), but in Bremen and Hamburg where the function of Land and Municipality is combined (a left-over from the days of the Hanseatic League), it is the City Council (*Bürgerschaft*). In Bavaria there is a second chamber (*Senat*) of 60 members representing professional and religious interests. Each Land has a government (*Landesregierung*) presided over by a *Ministerpräsident* (the corresponding organs for Bremen and Hamburg are an executive *Senat* headed by a Mayor (*Bürgermeister*) and Deputy Mayor). Generally the ministers of the Länder are appointed by the Mayor or Ministerpräsident and are responsible to the Land parliament. There is a Constitutional Court (*Verfassungs-* or *Staatsgerichtshof*) in Bavaria, Hesse, Bremen, Rhineland-Palatinate, Baden-Württemberg and the Saar, whose members are professional and lay judges and persons elected by the Länder parliaments. North Rhine-Westphalia, Lower Saxony, Bavaria, Hesse, Rhineland-Palatinate and Baden-Württemberg are divided into from three to eight Governmental Districts (*Regierungsbezirke*), each headed by a *Regierungspräsident* appointed by and responsible to the Land government. These bodies supervise all the smaller units of local government. There are no separate legislative and judicial bodies at this level.

Functions—such as road-construction, secondary education, police administration and hospitals—that are too large for the basic unit of local government in Germany, the Commune (see below), are the concern of the Regierungsbezirke and the Counties (*Landkreise*). A metropolitan community with a minimum population of 25–100,000 may detach itself from the Landkreis in which it is situated and constitute itself a City-County (*Stadtkreis*) or County-free City (*Kreisfreie Stadt*) and combine under a single authority those functions otherwise divided (within the County) between the County and the Communes. Each Landkreis elects a County Council (*Kreistag*) which in turn elects a chief executive officer called the *Landrat*. The corresponding authorities in the Stadtkreis are the City Council (*Stadtverordnetenversammlung*) and the Lord Mayor (*Oberbürgermeister*), who is assisted by a number of Deputies (*Beigeordneten*).

The Communes (*Gemeinden*) have considerable autonomy. Although they execute the legislation of both Bund and Länder, they are supervised by the latter only, through the Regierungsbezirke. Villages, towns and cities are all Communes—unless populous enough to become a Stadtkreis—and each elects a Communal Council (*Gemeinderat, Gemeindevertretung*, or in the City-Communes *Stadtrat*) and in some cases an executive body (*Magistrat*) headed by a Mayor (*Bürgermeister*), or in the City-Communes by an Oberbürgermeister. Most City-Counties and City-Communes as well as the City-States of Berlin, Bremen and Hamburg are further divided into Boroughs or Administrative Districts (*Bezirke* and *Ortsämter*).

Judicial system: The court of first instance is the District Court (*Amtsgericht*) in minor civil and criminal cases, with a single professional judge sitting either alone or with two lay judges (*Schöffen*) in criminal cases according to the degree of seriousness. The next highest court, the Regional Court (*Landgericht*), has in civil cases both original jurisdiction as a court of first instance in more important matters and also acts as an appeal court in cases decided by the Amtsgerichte. In criminal matters the Landgericht also has original and appellate jurisdiction. For original jurisdiction in serious criminal cases the Landgericht is composed of three professional and two lay judges, or of three professional and seven lay judges when constituting a *Schwurgericht* in the most serious cases. The lay judges (known as *Geschworene* in a Schwurgericht) deal with both law and fact in conjunction with the professional judges, and decide by majority vote.

The Appeal Courts (*Oberlandesgerichte*) are the highest Land courts and are composed of criminal and civil sections made up of three judges each. The Oberlandesgericht is the final instance for District Courts and the second instance for Regional Courts. It does not retry cases but either confirms the verdict of a lower court or sends it back for retrial. The final court of civil and criminal jurisdiction is the Federal Court of Justice (*Bundesgerichtshof*). It is the final court of appeal for all cases originating in the Landgerichte, except those tried by the Schwurgericht, for which it is the first court of appeal, there being no intermediate review by the Oberlandesgericht. The Federal Court of Justice also has original jurisdiction regarding treason which comprises both internal treason (*Hochverrat*)—offences against the internal constitutional order—and external treason (*Landesverrat*)—aid to a foreign power.

Other Federal courts deal with administration, labour, social and financial matters. The Federal Constitutional Court (Bundesverfassungsgericht) checks constitutionality of executive, legislative and judicial action, advises in Bund/Länder disputes and safeguards individual liberties. Its members are elected by Bundestag and Bundesrat and may not hold Federal/Land executive/legislative appointments.

Other Federal judges are appointed by the President on selection of committees of Federal and Land ministers. Länder judges are appointed by the Land Justice Minister and a similar selection committee. Federal judges may be dismissed only by the President after judicial sentence by a two-thirds majority of the Constitutional Court. There is no capital punishment.

Berlin: Berlin has a special legal status, governed by agreements (revised) of May/July 1945, as an area of Four-Power Occupation. Since 1948 when the Soviet representative walked out the authority of the Four-Power Kommandatura has in practice been applied only by Britain, the United States and France in the Western Occupation Sectors. Similarly West Berlin's own municipal organs acting in subordination to the Kommandatura exist *de jure* as the government for the entire city, but operate *de facto* only in the three Western Sectors. Although Berlin is defined by the Basic Law as a Land of the Federal Republic, Federal legislation is not binding on Berlin; it may, however, be adopted and applied by the West Berlin government. There are also the restrictions upon the Berlin representatives in the Bundestag and Bundesrat (see above, *Legislature*).

Berlin's constitution dates from 1950. The executive authority of Berlin is the Senate (Senat) headed by the Governing Mayor (Regierender Bürgermeister) with a Bürgermeister as his deputy and a maximum of 16 Senators (Senatoren) as administrative departmental heads. The Senat is responsible to the House of Representatives (Abgeordnetenhaus). The House is elected for four years by the list system of proportional representation with the same 5 per cent minimum as in national elections and numbers

200 members; in fact only 140 members are elected by the West Berlin electorate, the remainder being reserved for the East Berlin electorate. In the 1963 elections the SPD received 61·9 per cent of the vote and 89 seats (compared to 52·6 per cent and 78 seats out of 133 in 1958), the CDU received 28·9 per cent of the vote and 41 seats (37.7 per cent and 55 seats in 1958) and the FDP 7.9 per cent and 10 seats (they received no seats in 1958). The German Socialist Unity Party (SED), formed from a forced merger of the Communist and Socialist parties in the Soviet Sector of Berlin and the Soviet Zone of Germany in 1946, is permitted to operate but has no seats in the House. Willy Brandt was the dominant political figure in West Berlin from 1957 until his resignation on becoming Federal Vice-Chancellor and Foreign Minister in the Kiesinger government in December 1966. He was succeeded as Governing Mayor and SPD Chairman by his deputy, Heinrich Albertz.

The judicial system in Western Berlin is identical to that of the Federation. There are nine Amtsgerichte and one Landgericht. The Supreme Court of Berlin is the Kammergericht. Final appeal in civil and criminal cases is to the Bundesgerichtshof. The court structure is the same for Administrative Courts, the final court being the Bundesverwaltungsgericht. Like certain Länder West Berlin has a Constitutional Court. West Berlin comprises 12 of the 20 traditional Boroughs (*Bezirke*) of Greater Berlin. Each Bezirk has a Borough Council (*Bezirksverordnetenversammlung*) with some financial and local administrative powers, composed of 45 members elected by proportional representation for the same period as the House of Representatives. Each Council elects a Borough Office (*Bezirksamt*) composed of a Mayor (*Bezirksbürgermeister*) and a number of salaried officers (*Bezirkstadträte*).

RECENT HISTORY

After the second world war the German Reich was divided into four Occupation Zones administered by the United States, the Soviet Union, Britain and France; Berlin was constituted a separate area of occupation under the same four powers. Parts of the Soviet Zone were placed under Soviet and Polish administration pending a final peace conference. With the advent of the Cold War, four-power cooperation virtually ceased and instead two states, the Federal Republic comprising the occupation areas of the three Western powers, and the 'German Democratic Republic' formed from the Soviet Zone (which is recognised *de jure* only by the Soviet bloc countries), were set up in September and October 1949 respectively. In the period 1948–9 the Soviet Union blockaded the allied access routes to the Western Sectors of Berlin and brought about a split in the City administration.

West Germany joined the Council of Europe in 1951 and became a founder-member of the ECSC in 1952 and in 1957 of Euratom and the EEC. After the failure in 1954 to set up a European Army under the European Defence Community the Brussels Treaty was revised in October 1954 (Paris Agreement) to permit the membership of the Federal Republic and Italy, and to facilitate the former's rearmament and membership of NATO. At the same time the Federal Republic was recognised by the United States, Britain and France as the only state entitled to speak for Germany in international affairs, and the Occupation Statute was rescinded. With the ratification of these agreements in May 1955 West Germany regained its state sovereignty and became a member of NATO. In January 1957 the Saarland returned to full German control.

After the breakdown of the Foreign Ministers Conferences on the joint administration of Germany in 1949, four-power contact on German reunification continued, but Stalin's proposals of March 1952 were not seriously considered by the West. The next Foreign Ministers Conference (in Berlin) did not take place until early 1954, and followed upon the East German uprising of June 1953, Soviet suppression of which entailed increased Soviet commitment to a separate East German regime.

There have been subsequent major conferences on German reunification and related subjects at Geneva—twice in 1955 and again (when both the Federal Republic and East Germany were represented as advisors) in 1959. The last Geneva Conference took place during a sustained Soviet and East German offensive against Berlin in 1958–63, which had as one result the building of the Berlin Wall in August 1961, aimed at stopping the flow of refugees from East Germany. In January 1963 France and the Federal Republic signed a Treaty of Friendship. In the same year the Federal Republic ratified the Test Ban Treaty.

Because of the division of Germany, the Federal Republic is not a member of the United Nations, but has an observer in New York. Until 1967 it was the policy of the Federal Republic either not to recognise, or to withdraw recognition of, any state that recognised the German Democratic Republic (the Hallstein Doctrine); the only full exception to this was the Soviet Union, with which diplomatic relations were established in September 1955. Now a modification of the Doctrine permits West Germany to recognise Soviet bloc states which were forced to recognise the GDR at birth. The Federal Republic has provided large-scale compensation—in both cash and kind—to the victims of Hitler Germany, and in particular to Israel.

Defence: The commander-in-chief of the armed forces is the Defence Minister in peace-time and the Federal Chancellor in war-time. Under the Paris Agreements (October 1954) the Federal Republic bound itself not to construct on its own territory atomic, biological or chemical weapons. Service in the Federal armed forces (Bundeswehr) is for 18 months. Total strength in 1965 was 460,000 of whom about one-half were conscripts: army 299,000, navy 32,000, air force 93,000, territorial and local defence forces about 36,000. All operational forces except those of the last category are NATO-assigned. Other NATO forces in West Germany are mainly British, U.S. and French. The 1966 defence budget was DM17,363 million ($41,341 million) representing nearly 6 per cent of GNP.

West Berlin: There are about 11,000 Allied troops here. Articles 5 and 6 of the North Atlantic Treaty define an attack upon the occupation forces in Europe of any member of NATO as an attack upon the Alliance as a whole. Berliners are not liable for military service with the Bundeswehr, and the Federal Republic has scrupulously observed the occupation status since there are no West German soldiers there, nor is advertising for the Bundeswehr permitted. Within Berlin itself there is a special police force (Bereitschaftspolizei), as well as regular police, to provide additional internal security.

ECONOMY

Background: After the second world war the German economy recovered quickly following financial reforms. Since then the rate of economic growth has surpassed that of any other European country. This 'economic miracle' has taken place under the government's policy of a 'social market economy', i.e. a system of free competition subject to social obligations, with considerably more state participation than is generally admitted. In the period 1960–5 the main threat to the economy was an acute shortage of labour, which contributed to extremely high wage rates and considerable investment in labour-saving machinery. The labour shortage, coupled with an over-rapid growth of overall demand in relation to production, caused a sharp increase in prices. The pressure of demand also had its effect on the balance of payments, which swung into deficit in 1965. In order to check the expansion of demand, and to ease the pressure on the balance of payments, the Federal government applied a strict budgetary policy in 1966 in contrast to the expansionary policy followed in 1965. Between 1958 and 1964 GNP at constant prices grew at an annual average rate of 5·8 per cent. In 1964 GNP was DM413,400 million ($103,350 million). The average annual rate of industrial growth in 1958–64 was nearly 7 per cent. In 1964 industrial output increased by over 8 per cent compared with a 3·8 per cent increase in 1963. The contributions of the different sectors of the economy to GDP in 1964 were:

Sector	Percentage of GDP
Agriculture, forestry and fishing . .	6
Industry including construction . .	51
Services	43
GDP	100

The Federal Republic is predominantly industrial. Its principal industries are coal-mining, iron and steel production, machine construction, electrical, steel and metal, chemicals, textiles and food. Its main growth industries are manufacturing, coal-mining and building; next in importance come trade, transport and services. Agriculture, forestry and fishing have expanded less rapidly, and Germany remains, both in absolute terms and in proportion to population, by far the largest food importer in the Common Market. The main emphasis of agricultural production is on animal products. The main crops are oats, wheat and potatoes, and there has been a considerable rise in Germany's production of eggs and poultry in the past few years. Forestry constitutes an important part of the country's economy.

Foreign trade: In 1964 total exports amounted to 16 per cent of GNP and imports to 14 per cent. Main exports in 1964 were finished manufactured products (84 per cent of total exports) and semi-manufactured goods (9 per cent), and main imports agricultural products (24 per cent of total imports), finished manufactured goods (40 per cent), semi-manufactured goods (17 per cent) and raw materials (19 per cent). The bulk of the Federal Republic's trade is with the EEC. In 1964 37 per cent of total exports were to, and 35 per cent of imports were from the Common Market. In the same year exports to EFTA and the United States amounted respectively to 27 per cent and 7 per cent of total exports; 18 per cent of total imports came from EFTA and 14 per cent from the United States. Trade with the rest of the world has not increased at the same high rate. Since 1952 the Federal Republic has maintained a favourable balance of trade. In 1965, however, its balance of trade surplus of DM1,200 million ($300 million) was the lowest figure for ten years. The overall balance of payments deficit which first appeared in 1964 became more marked in 1965, the last quarter of that year, however, seeing the beginnings of an improvement, mainly due to a vigorous increase in exports to Italy and France and a slower expansion of imports.

Employment: Full employment has been maintained since 1949, but there exists an acute shortage of labour which is expected to continue. In 1964 the total labour force was nearly 27 million, of which 11 per cent was employed in agriculture, 49 per cent in industry, and 39 per cent in the services sector. From 1962 to 1964 the annual average net immigration of labour was over 300,000, main countries of origin of foreign workers being Italy, Spain and Greece. The heavy flow of labour from East Germany in the post-war years has been reduced considerably since 1961. The present level of unemployment (0·5 per cent in 1965) represents the minimum of frictional unemployment.

Price and wage trends: Between 1950 and 1960 the average annual rise in net earnings far exceeded the rise in the cost of living index: net earnings rose by 119 per cent, and the cost of living by 28 per cent. In the period 1960–5 average hourly earnings rose by 60 per cent, prices by 18 per cent and real income by 38 per cent. In 1965 the level of agreed wage rates rose by about 7 per cent, although actual earnings rose by about 11 per cent. The most rapid rise in agreed wage rates was that of over 10 per cent in the manufacturing industry. The main pressure for wage increases, exacerbated by the acute labour shortage, has been in the 4 million strong metal-working industries. In 1965 prices also rose owing partly to the general excess of demand and higher unit costs, and in spite of some stabilisation in the price of manufactured goods the cost of living rose by 4 per cent.

Consumption: In 1964 private consumption accounted for 56 per cent of GNP and public consumption for 15 per cent. In 1963–4 the percentage increases for both fluctuated; private consumption rose by 2·6 per cent in 1963 and 5.3 per cent in 1964, and by an estimated 6·3 per cent in 1965; public consumption rose by 8·3 per cent in 1963, but decreased by 0·6 per cent in 1964 and was expected to increase by 6 per cent in 1965.

West Berlin: The rate of economic growth in West Berlin has matched and often exceeded that of the Federal Republic, particularly in industrial production. Like the Federal Republic, West Berlin suffers from an acute shortage of labour. In 1965 its cost of living index rose by 3·3 per cent and the balance of trade deteriorated. The trend in prices, incomes and consumer expenditure corresponded to that of 1965 in the Federal Republic. Unemployment was marginally higher.

Social Security

Social insurance in the Federal Republic and West Berlin is run on a national basis. About 30 per cent of wages and salaries—including employers' insurance contributions—are retained for social purposes. Figures for contributions and benefits stated below relate to 1964. All insurance is under the general supervision of the Federal Ministry of Labour and Social Welfare.

Health insurance: Legislation on health matters and its enforcement are the prerogative of Länder authorities. Insurance is administered by sickness funds (*Krankenkassen*) to which all employed persons compulsorily belong other than salaried employees earning above DM7,920 ($1,980), who may adhere voluntarily. Old-age pensioners are covered for medical benefits and miners have a special system. These autonomous funds, federated at Land and Bund level, are organised on a local, Land, occupational, etc.

basis and elect on a national basis an executive committee and a representative assembly. Health insurance is financed by employer and employee who each pay 4 to 5.5 per cent of wages up to DM7,920 per year.

The state pension agencies pay two-thirds of the employer-employee contributions for pension insurance to the funds to cover the medical benefits for pensioners. Medical benefits are provided by doctors, hospitals and pharmacists contracted to and paid by the funds, and include general and specialist care, hospitalisation, prescribed medicines (a small fee is charged during the first 10 days of illness), dental and midwife care, travelling expenses and specified appliances. These benefits are provided for as long as is necessary except that hospitalisation is limited to 78 weeks in a three-year period. Sickness allowances are paid for a maximum of 78 weeks in a three-year period at 65 per cent of earnings to an annual maximum of DM7,920 plus 4 per cent of earnings for the first and 3 per cent for each of the second and third dependants. During the first six weeks of sickness, the employer must pay the difference between the benefit and 100 per cent of wages to the wage-earner and full salary to salaried employees. Maternity benefits are paid at the rate of 75 to 100 per cent of wages up to the specified maximum for four to six weeks before and six weeks after confinement. Nursing allowances amount to 50 per cent of the maternity benefit and are payable for 12 to 26 weeks. Maternity grants are DM10–25 ($2·50–6·25) according to the fund.

Accident insurance: This is compulsory for all employed persons and apprentices and most self-employed persons. Direct supervision is in the hands of the Federal Insurance Office. Insurance is administered by industrial and agricultural funds, managed and federated similarly to the sickness funds. The funds are financed solely by employers at an average rate of 1·5 per cent of employee's earnings (up to 12·5 per cent in mining). Comprehensive medical benefits are usually provided by the sickness funds for the first 18 days. Temporary disability benefits are paid at the same rate as sickness benefits, as are employer's supplements, and are also usually paid by the sickness funds for the first 18 days and thereafter by the accident funds. After 13 weeks and as long as disability is at least 20 per cent pensions are paid. Pensions for total disability are equal to two-thirds of earnings with a minimum pension of DM90 ($22·50) and a maximum pension of DM2,000 ($500) per month. In case of constant attendance the additional allowance is DM100–350 ($25–87.50) per month. Additional supplements worth 10 per cent of earnings are paid for each child under 18. Partial disability pensions correspond to the degree of disability over 20 per cent. Widow's pensions also payable to dependant widowers are worth 40 per cent of earnings if the widow is 45, invalid or caring for a child, and otherwise 30 per cent of earnings. Orphan's pensions equal to 20 per cent of earnings are paid to each orphan under 18, under 25 if a student, and indefinitely if invalid; full orphan's pensions are 30 per cent of earnings. Pensions for dependant parents and grandparents are worth 20 to 60 per cent of the insured's earnings. Total survivors' pensions may not exceed 80 per cent of earnings.

Pensions insurance: Pensions are related to working income and are adjusted to developments in productivity and incomes. Pension insurance covers compulsorily all wage-earners and apprentices, and—through a separate scheme—all salaried employees earning below DM15,000 ($3,750). There are special systems for miners, public employees and self-employed artisans and farmers. The Federal Salaried Employees' Insurance Office administers the salaried employees' scheme and the Land State Insurance Offices administer the systems for wage-earners in each Land. Both employer and employee pay a contribution of 7 per cent of earnings; this is based on a maximum amount assessed as twice the national-average earnings over the previous three years (for 1964 the annual maximum was DM13,440 or $3,360). If annual earnings amount to below 10 per cent of the annual maximum the whole contribution of 14 per cent of earnings is borne by the employer. The state pays an annual subsidy covering about one-third of the costs of the wage-earner's system and one-fifth of the salaried employees' system. Old-age pensions are paid at 65, or at 60 if the insured has been unemployed for one year, or if a woman with 10 years employment in the last 20 years.

An old-age pension amounts to 1·5 per cent of a wage-earner's 'assessed earnings' multiplied by the number of years of insurance. Assessed earnings are computed by applying the average percentage that the wage-earner's earnings were of the national average wage throughout the period that he was insured to the national-average wage in the three-year period preceding his pension claim. The national-average wage, which is adjusted annually, was DM6,720 ($1,680) in 1964. Children's supplements are 10 per cent of this figure for each child.

Invalidity pensions are paid when the insured person is no longer capable of gainful activity (general invalidity) or of earning 50 per cent of his normal wages in his usual occupation (occupational invalidity). For general invalidity the pension is assessed in identical fashion to the old age pension, and for occupational invalidity the percentage of the assessed earnings is reduced from 1·5 to 1 per cent. Children's allowances are the same as for old age pensions.

For three months all widows receive a pension equal to 100 per cent of the insured's general invalidity pension. This is thereafter reduced to 60 per cent of the general invalidity pension if the widow is 45, invalid or caring for a child, and to 60 per cent of the lower occupational invalidity pension otherwise. Orphan's pensions are 10 per cent of the general invalidity pension for each child, rising to 20 per cent for each full orphan; paid to each child under 18, under 25 if an unmarried student, and indefinitely if invalid. Total survivor's pensions may not exceed 100 per cent of the general invalidity pension.

Unemployment insurance: Benefits are administered by the Federal Placement and Unemployment Insurance Institute. Contributions are collected by sickness funds. All persons in private employment are covered save persons earning above DM15,000 ($3,750) annually, agricultural employees with yearly contracts and part-time employees. There are special systems for dock and building workers. Employers and employees each pay 0·65 per cent of annual earnings up to DM9,000 ($2,250). Benefits are paid for 13 to 52 weeks, depending upon the number of weeks of insured employment, and amount to 40 to 90 per cent of earnings, varying inversely to the amount earned. Weekly supplements for dependants are DM9 ($2·25) for a wife and first child and DM3 ($0·75) for a second child. Additional unemployment assistance, financed entirely by the state, is paid to those in extra need after a means-test.

Other benefits: All employed and self-employed persons and other social insurance beneficiaries having two or more children are entitled to family

73

allowances. Employers and self-employed persons pay 1 per cent of earnings to finance the allowances, which amount to DM40 ($10) per month for the third and each additional child. To families earning less than DM7,200 ($1,800) per year the state pays a family allowance of DM25 ($6·25) for the second child. There are a number of social services to help victims of the war, e.g. the Fund for the Equalisation of Burdens (Lastenausgleich), which is financed by a 50 per cent levy at June 1948 values (the date of the currency reform) on all property not destroyed by the war. From this fund compensation instalments have been paid and will be paid until 1976 to war victims, for the loss of immovable property and also household effects. Social assistance is provided mainly by Land and communal funds or, where hardship is due to the war, by the Bund.

EDUCATION

Education is a responsibility of the Länder governments; there is no Federal Ministry of Education, and the Bund has no authority to legislate on educational affairs. Although the Länder systems vary in detail, the basic features are uniform, and the meetings of the Permanent Conference of Länder Ministers of Culture—which has a general secretariat in Bonn—facilitates coordination. Education is compulsory from six to 18, at least eight years of which must be spent in full-time education. Most schools are state-supported, and private schools are state-supervised. Primary and vocational education is free; at the other levels where fees are payable—and free schooling is becoming increasingly common here also—grants are provided, and fees are waived for the needy. Primary education is coeducational but at intermediate and secondary schools the sexes are taught separately. Religious education given under church supervision is compulsory where parents wish it.

Primary education: The majority of children receive their entire compulsory education from six to 15 at the primary schools (*Volksschulen*). All children have a common education from six to ten (to 12 in Bremen, Berlin and Hamburg) at the Basic School (*Grundschule*). Those who pass the entrance examinations (about 22 per cent) go on to intermediate schools (about 15 per cent) and secondary schools (about 7 per cent). The remainder (about 78 per cent) go on to the upper classes of primary school (*Volksschuloberstufe*).

Secondary education: At the intermediate school (*Realschule* or *Mittelschule*) courses last for six years and provide a high level of general education. At the end of the course students take the intermediate examination (*Mittlere Reife*). Courses at the secondary schools (*Gymnasien*) last for nine years ending with the final examination (*Abitur* or *Reifeprüfung*), which is both a leaving certificate and a qualification for university entrance. About 88 per cent of successful students go on to university. The Gymnasien are of three types, emphasising the classics, modern languages or mathematics and natural science. There are also secondary schools specialising in domestic science (*Frauenoberschulen*) and economics (*Wirtschaftsoberschulen*), and those successful in the final examination of these schools are entitled to attend a particular university faculty. About 3 per cent of students enter university through courses at evening institutes. In the city-states of West Berlin, Hamburg and Bremen, the 'unified school' (*Einheitsschule*) system has been started, combining primary and secondary schools and providing a uniform basic grade with an upper grade consisting of practical, technical and economics branches. Private boarding schools such as the Waldorf Schools also provide different school programmes for the compulsory period of education.

Vocational education: Basically this is organised into the practical side, the apprenticeship (*Lehrzeit*) and the theoretical side, which is a part of the general educational syllabus. It is given mainly in four types of school— the Part-time Vocational School (*Berufsschule*), the Full-time Vocational School (*Berufsfachschule*), the Full-time Specialist School (*Fachschule*) and the Full-time Senior Specialist School (*Höhere Fachschule*). Apprenticeships generally last for three years and conclude with the Journeyman's examination in the trades and agriculture (*Gehilfenprüfung*) and industry (*Facharbeiter-prüfung*). After further practical experience the Master's examination (*Meisterprüfung*) may be taken. Attendance at the Berufsschule is compulsory for six to 12 hours per week for students from 15 to 18 years, and courses are intended to supplement their full-time professions. At the same time, within the Berufsschule, they may attend for further general education at the Continuation School (*Berufsaufbauschule*). At the end of the course students may sit a vocational training examination (*Fachschulreife*), success in which permits them to go on to the Höhere Fachschule.

The Berufsfachschulen provide full-time courses of one to three years orientated towards a particular profession, particularly in commerce, office and domestic occupations. About one-third of the Berufsfachschulen are privately run. The Fachschulen cover some 50 different professions and in general provide supplementary theoretical training to students of a minimum of 18 years, who have already had full-time vocational training. Courses last from one to eight six-monthly periods, the average course lasting for four. The Höhere Fachschulen and the Engineering Schools (*Ingenieurschulen*) provide courses of from two to three years for students over 18 who possess either the Mittlere Reife or the Fachschulreife. They prepare students for intermediate and senior positions in professions insofar as a university or equivalent education is not required.

Special education: The mentally backward are taught either in special classes attached to the Volksschulen (*Hilfschule-Klassen*)—there were 395 such classes in 1964—or in special schools (*Hilfschulen*). There are schools for physically handicapped children and those with adjustment difficulties.

University and higher education: There are in West Germany and West Berlin 20 universities, nine technical colleges (*technische Hochschulen*), five university institutes of one faculty only, 25 colleges of art and music and 17 theological and pedagogical institutes. The universities, faculties and technical colleges are ensured the right of self-administration under a Chancellor and Senate. They confer their own doctorates, acknowledge the right to teach and recruit their own staff by proposing candidates to the appropriate Land Minister of Culture. According to the Basic Law the equipment and maintenance of the higher educational institutes is a responsibility of the Länder in which they are situated, with the right of general supervision belonging to the Land Minister of Culture. University fees are about DM600 ($150) per year. About 45 per cent of all students receive some form of grant either from private or public institutions. The minimum length of courses is four years for law, economics, engineering and architecture, six for natural science and eight for medicine.

Universities, technical colleges and faculties:

Universities: Free University of Berlin, Bochum, Bonn, Cologne, Erlangen-Nuremberg, Frankfurt, Freiburg, Giessen, Göttingen, Hamburg, Heidelberg, Kiel, Mainz, Marburg, Munich, Münster, Saarbrücken, Tübingen, Würzburg. Universities are planned for Bremen, Constance and Regensburg. *Technical Colleges:* Aachen, Berlin Technical University, Brunswick, Clausthal Mining Academy, Darmstadt, Hanover, Karlsruhe, Munich, Stuttgart. *Faculties of university status:* Düsseldorf Academy of Medicine, Hanover Academy of Medicine, Hanover College of Veterinary Science, Hohenheim Agricultural College, Mannheim College of Economics.

Educational institutions 1964:

	Institutions	Staff	Students
Primary	29,992	146,336	5,204,694
Secondary . . .	3,007	63,863	1,280,743
Special	1,374	8,854	170,583
Unified and Waldorf			
schools	943	17,960	427,414
Vocational . . .	6,352	38,797	2,012,753
Universities, etc. (1965) .	76	n.a.	270,674

Adult education: The Peoples' Universities (*Volkshochschulen*) require no entrance qualifications and confer no leaving certificates, but provide evening courses emphasising general knowledge and practical subjects. Most are maintained by the Municipalities, but some in South Germany are run by voluntary associations. In 1965 there were 1,157 Volkshochschulen catering for more than 6 million people. In addition there were about 30 Residental Universities (*Heim-Volkshochschulen*), educational centres offering a home and community life, combining normal adult education with a greater emphasis on political education and civics and also providing intensive courses of advanced instruction. In 1965 there were about 10,500 public libraries maintained by the Communes and a further 11,000 run by the churches.

MASS MEDIA

The press (1964):

Dailies: Bild-Zeitung, Hamburg, independent, 4,193,000; *Westdeutsche Allgemeine*, Essen, ind., 444,000; *Hamburger Morgenpost*, Hamburg, ind., 344,000; *Ruhr-Nachrichten*, Dortmund, ind., 330,000; *Hamburger Abendblatt*, Hamburg, ind., 323,000; *BZ*, West Berlin, ind., 320,000; *Rheinische Post*, Düsseldorf, ind.-CDU, 280,000; *Die Welt*, Hamburg, ind., 274,000; *Frankfurter Allgemeine Zeitung*, Frankfurt, ind., 269,000; *Westfälische Rundschau*, Dortmund, ind., 229,000; *Süddeutsche Zeitung*, Munich, ind., 225,000; *Neue Ruhr Zeitung (NRZ)*, Essen, ind., 223,000; *Berliner Morgenpost*, W. Berlin, ind., 218,000; *Nürnberger Nachrichten*, Nuremberg, ind., 204,000; *Kölner Stadtanzeiger*, Cologne, ind., 195,000; *Rhein-Zeitung*, Koblenz, ind., 177,000; *Die Rheinpfalz*, Ludwigshafen, ind., 173,000; *Augsburger Allgemeine*, Augsburg, ind., 172,000; *Münchner Merkur*, Munich, ind., 168,000; *Kölnische Rundschau*, Cologne, ind.-CDU, 161,000; *Stuttgarter Zeitung*, Stuttgart, ind., 155,000; *Hannoversche Presse*, Hanover, ind., 151,000.

Weeklies: Hör Zu, Hamburg, illustrated and broadcasting, 3,858,000; *Bild am Sonntag*, Hamburg, ind., Sunday, 2,081,000; *Quick*, Munich, illus., 1,627,000; *Stern*, Hamburg, illus., 1,626,000; *Bunte Illustrierte*, Offenburg, illus., 1,247,000; *Neue Revue*, Cologne, illus., 1,321,000; *Für Sie*, Hamburg, woman's, 938,000; *Der Spiegel*, Hamburg, ind. political/cultural, 540,000; *Welt am Sonntag*, ind., Sunday, 484,000; *Die Zeit*, Hamburg, ind. pol./cult., 193,000; *Christ und Welt*, Stuttgart, pol./econ./cult., 175,000.

Broadcasting: The Working Association of German Radio Stations under Statutory Regulations (Arbeitsgemeinschaft der öffentlich-rechtlichen Rundfunkanstalten Deutschlands—ARD) is the coordinating body for West German radio and TV. To it belong nine regional radio stations (non-profit-making public corporations) and the two independent national radio stations, Radio Germany (Deutschlandfunk) and German Wave (Deutsche Welle) and the First German Television Channel (Deutsches Fernsehen—DF). RIAS (Rundfunk im Amerikanischen Sektor) which provides radio programmes from West Berlin for East Berlin and East Germany is represented at observer status in ARD. All regional stations provide local radio programmes and together they contribute TV programmes towards DF. The Second Television Channel (Zweites Deutsches Fernsehen—ZDF) is not a member of ARD; it provides no regional programmes and its advertising time must not exceed 10 per cent of total programme time.

The organisation of regional broadcasting is a responsibility of the Länder, and radio and TV installations are the property of the radio stations and are managed by them. Deutschlandfunk has the task of organising radio broadcasts for and to the whole of Germany and other European countries, while Deutsche Welle broadcasts in many languages to all parts of the world. Broadcasting is financed by licence fees and advertising revenue.

GIBRALTAR

Geography and Population

Features: The territory consists mostly of a mass of rock. *Area:* 6 sq. km. *Population:* (1964) 24,500.

Language: English is the official language but Spanish is spoken also. *Religion:* 87 per cent Roman Catholic, 7 per cent Anglican, 3 per cent Jewish.

Constitutional System

Constitution: Gibraltar is a British crown colony deriving a great deal of internal self-government from the 1964 Gibraltar (Constitution) Order in Council. *Head of state:* General Sir Gerald Lathbury (Governor, representing Queen Elizabeth II). *Head of government:* Chief Minister Sir Joshua A. Hassan.

Executive: Executive authority is vested in the Governor who is advised by the Gibraltar Council of five elected and four ex-officio members. The elected members are appointed from the Legislative Council by the Governor in consultation with the Chief Minister. The Chief Minister is President of the Council of Ministers which discusses policy matters in detail. Its recommendations are forwarded to the Gibraltar Council by the Chief Minister for formal approval. The Chief Minister may appoint such additional members to the Council of Ministers as he deems necessary.

Legislature: The Legislative Council consists of a Speaker, two ex-officio members—the Attorney-General and Financial Secretary—and eleven members elected by proportional representation for five years. From its number five are appointed to the Gibraltar Council. *Political party:* The Association for the Advancement of Civil Rights is led by Sir Joshua Hassan. *Local government:* Municipal affairs are conducted by the elected City Council presided over by a Mayor. *Judicial system:* There is a Supreme Court presided over by the Chief Justice and a magistrate's court.

Recent History

Britain acquired Gibraltar under the Treaty of Utrecht, 1713. By 1966 long-standing Anglo-Spanish contention over the exact status of the colony had resulted in direct negotiations between the two governments. *Defence:* There is compulsory service of four months with the Gibraltar Regiment at 18 years, and reserve training until 28. Gibraltar is a NATO sub-command and British units are stationed there.

ECONOMY

Owing to a lack of natural resources the economy depends upon the transit trade, the tourist industry and revenue from British service spending. There are small light industries such as clothing manufacture, fish and fruit canning, tobacco and beverages.

SOCIAL SECURITY

There are two contributory schemes covering accident insurance and social insurance. There are also three non-contributory schemes financed from the general revenue covering unemployment, retirement and family allowance benefits and public assistance.

EDUCATION

Education is compulsory and free from five to 15 in government schools, of which there are 14 at primary level, six at secondary and two at technical. There are also three private schools. The government and private sources provide scholarships for university study.

MASS MEDIA

The press: Gibraltar Chronicle, English daily, 3,000; *El Calpense,* Spanish daily, 2,000; *Vox,* Spanish and English weekly, 4,000; *Gibraltar Post,* independent weekly, 3,000. *Broadcasting:* The Gibraltar Broadcasting Corporation is responsible for radio and TV broadcasting.

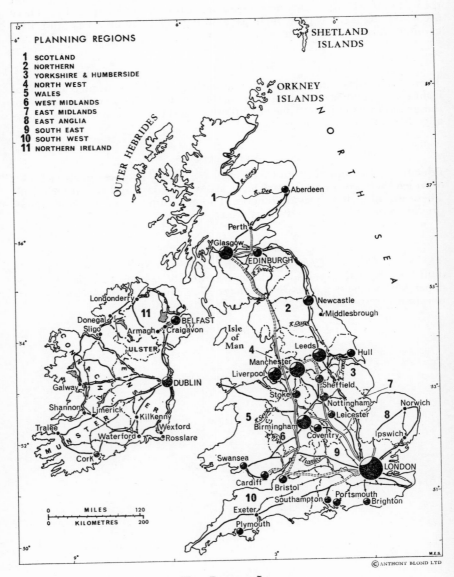

PLANNING REGIONS

1 SCOTLAND
2 NORTHERN
3 YORKSHIRE & HUMBERSIDE
4 NORTH WEST
5 WALES
6 WEST MIDLANDS
7 EAST MIDLANDS
8 EAST ANGLIA
9 SOUTH EAST
10 SOUTH WEST
11 NORTHERN IRELAND

THE BRITISH ISLES

UNITED KINGDOM OF GREAT BRITAIN AND NORTHERN IRELAND

GEOGRAPHY

Features: The principal lowland areas of England are the Lower Thames Basin in which London stands, the Severn Valley, the Somerset Levels, the Hampshire Basin, the Vale of York, the Fens and the area stretching from the Cheshire Plain to south-west Lancashire.

The main upland mass is the Pennine Ridge which extends from the Cheviot Hills and Tyne Valley in the north to the Derbyshire Dome north of Derby, in the south. This region consists chiefly of millstone grit and carboniferous limestone with an overlay of glacial clay in the north; it often reaches 2,300 ft/700 m. In the north-west is the Lake District, maximum height being 3,210 ft/980 m. at Scafell. East of the Pennines lie the North Yorkshire Moors, a Jurassic upland rising to over 1,400 ft/430 m. South of the Moors are the chalk Yorkshire Wolds reaching to Lincolnshire.

South of the Pennines lie the Midlands, an area of undulating plateau with minor hill ridges. South of the Avon Valley are the Cotswold Hills (Jurassic), south and east of which lie the main chalk hill areas of England —Salisbury Plain, Chiltern Hills and North Downs and South Downs bordering respectively the London Basin and the Weald. Devon and Cornwall contain a number of upland areas, such as sandstone Exmoor and granitic Dartmoor and Bodmin Moor.

Scotland may be divided into three regions. In the north are the Highlands, with fjord indentations and narrow raised beaches in the west and wider lowland areas in the east; there are a number of peaks over 4,000 ft/1,200 m. The Great Glen fault, followed by the Caledonian Canal, bisects the Highlands. To the south lie the Central Lowlands, mainly below 1,000 ft/ 300 m. but containing volcanic-cored uplands, e.g. Ochil and Sidlaw Hills. This area is drained by the two principal Scottish rivers, the Forth and the Clyde. Further south still are the Southern Uplands, sometimes reaching 2,500 ft/760 m. Streams such as the Nith and Annan provide routeways from the Lowlands to England.

Wales is composed largely of land over 1,000 ft/300 m., the chief lowland areas being Anglesey, the Vale of Glamorgan and southern Pembrokeshire. The southern coalfield with its narrow, deeply incised valleys and intervening plateau contrasts with Snowdonia in the north, with its peaks rising to over 3,000 ft/900 m.

Northern Ireland consists of a central core of lowland around Lough Neagh and extending to the coast south of Belfast, and surrounding hill areas—the Antrim Mountains rising to over 1,500 ft/450 m., the Mournes, 2,500 ft/760 m. and the Sperrins, 2,200 ft/670 m.

The chief arable areas of England are the Vale of York, East Anglia and Lincolnshire and parts of the south-west, Cotswolds, the south and south-east and East Midlands. Devon and Cornwall specialise in market-gardening and dairying. In Scotland the East Central Lowlands and parts of the east coast are the chief arable areas. In Wales livestock upland farming is characteristic except in the extreme south.

Minerals are found throughout Britain, except in Northern Ireland. Chief local deposits are in Nottinghamshire, Yorkshire and Derbyshire, while there are important coalfields in the Scottish Lowlands and Lancashire and smaller ones in the Midlands, Somerset and Kent. Chief iron ore deposits are in the Jurassic belt stretching from Oxfordshire to Lincolnshire. There are important kaolin deposits in Cornwall, but the country has little non-ferrous metal ore. Natural gas has been found in north-east Yorkshire and off the east coast. Scotland possesses a number of hydroelectric potential sites.

The main industrial centres of Britain are the Newcastle-Middlesbrough region, west Yorkshire and the Don Valley, south-east Lancashire, Birmingham, the Nottingham-Derby-Leicester area, London and lower Thames-side, the Central Scottish Lowlands around Glasgow, the Belfast area and the South Wales coalfields.

Area: The total area of the United Kingdom is 94,214 sq. miles/244,956 sq. km.: England 50,327 sq. miles/130,850 sq. km., Wales and Monmouthshire 8,017 sq. miles/20,844 sq. km., Scotland 30,411 sq. miles/79,069 sq. km., Northern Ireland 5,459 sq. miles/14,193 sq. km., Isle of Man 227 sq. miles/ 690 sq. km. and Channel Islands 75 sq. miles/195 sq. km. Colonies and Protectorates: Ascension, Bahamas, Bermuda, British Antarctic Territory, British Honduras, British Indian Ocean Territory, Brunei, Cayman Islands, Falkland Islands and Dependencies, Federation of South Arabia, Fiji, Gibraltar, Gilbert and Ellice Islands, Hong Kong, Leeward Islands (Anguilla, Antigua, Montserrat, Nevis, St Christopher), Mauritius, New Hebrides, Pitcairn Island, Rhodesia, St Helena, Seychelles, Solomon Islands, Swaziland, Tonga, Tristan da Cunha, Turks and Caicos Islands, Virgin Islands, Windward Islands (Dominica, Grenada, St Lucia, St Vincent). (See under *Recent History* for the independent states constituting the British Commonwealth.)

Mean max. and min. temperatures: London (51° 30′ N, 0° W; 150 ft/46 m.) 73°F/23°C (July), 35°F/2°C (Jan. and Feb.); Edinburgh (56° N, 3° W; 440 ft/134 m.) 65°F/18°C, 35°F/2°C; Cardiff (51° 30′ N, 3° W; 200 ft/60 m.) 69°F/21°C, 36°F/2°C. *Relative humidity:* London 78 per cent; Edinburgh 89 per cent; Cardiff 81 per cent. *Mean annual rainfall:* London 23 in./585 mm.; Edinburgh 28 in./710 mm.; Cardiff 42 in./1,065 mm.

POPULATION

Population: (1964 est.) United Kingdom 54,065,000: England 44,725,000, Wales and Monmouthshire 2,676,000, Scotland 5,206,000, Northern Ireland 1,458,000. Isle of Man 48,000, Channel Islands 109,000. Other Commonwealth countries about 768 million. Colonies and Protectorates about 14 million. *Chief towns and populations:* (1964 est.) Greater LONDON (8,187,000), Birmingham (1,106,000), Glasgow (1,019,000), Liverpool (729,000), Manchester (645,000), Leeds (509,000), Sheffield (491,000), Edinburgh—capital of Scotland (473,000), Bristol (432,000), Belfast—capital of Northern Ireland (410,000), Coventry (316,000), Nottingham (312,000), Hull

(300,000), Bradford (298,000), Leicester (267,000), Stoke-on-Trent (264,000), Newcastle upon Tyne (261,000), Cardiff—capital of Wales (260,000). *Distribution:* In 1961 36 per cent of the population of Great Britain lived in urban centres with more than 100,000 inhabitants, 38 per cent in urban centres of 10–100,000 inhabitants, and 26 per cent in rural areas and urban centres with less than 10,000 inhabitants. In the same year the respective percentages were 36, 40 and 24 for England and Wales; 37, 23 and 40 for Scotland; 29, 17 and 54 for Northern Ireland.

Language: English is the predominant language. In northern, central and south-west Wales, Welsh is the first language of the majority of the population. The Scottish form of Gaelic is spoken in parts of north-west Scotland and the Irish form by a minority in Northern Ireland. Manx and Cornish are virtually dead languages. In the Channel Islands a Norman-French patois is spoken in addition to English, French still being the official language of Jersey. *Religion:* About 27 million persons are baptised members of the Established Church, the (Anglican) Church of England. There are also unestablished Anglican Churches in Wales, Scotland and Ireland. The established Presbyterian Church of Scotland has about 1,250,000 members. The 'Free Churches' are the Methodists (700,000), Congregationalists (200,000), Baptists (300,000) and Unestablished Presbyterians (340,000). In addition there are over 5 million Roman Catholics (about 500,000 in Northern Ireland), about 500,000 Jews, 250,000 Muslims and numerous minority religions.

CONSTITUTIONAL SYSTEM

Constitution: Great Britain is a constitutional monarchy. The constitution is a mixture of statutes, common law and conventions. *Head of state:* Queen Elizabeth II. *Head of government:* Prime Minister Harold Wilson (Labour).

Executive: The Sovereign is head of the executive in law; in fact she acts on the advice of her ministers. She appoints the Prime Minister and other ministers on his recommendation. She summons and prorogues parliament, and dissolves it on the Prime Minister's advice. She must give the Royal Assent to all legislation that has passed both Houses of Parliament, before it can become law. These and other acts involve the use of the Royal Prerogative with its consequent ministerial responsibility. The Sovereign is titular head of the Commonwealth, the armed forces and the judiciary.

Ministers are individually and collectively responsible to parliament, even though some ministers sit in the Lords, in which case they are represented in the House of Commons by Parliamentary Secretaries. The Prime Minister is the head of the government and personally selects the ministers of the cabinet, which has supreme control over the national executive and which finally determines the policy to be submitted to parliament and coordinates and delimits the powers of the various governmental departments. The Privy Council is composed of about 300 members appointed for life, cabinet ministers being automatically members, and the remainder being senior judges and persons of eminence in public affairs in both Britain and the Commonwealth appointed by the Sovereign on the Prime Minister's recommendation. The Privy Council is responsible for submitting Orders in Council for the Sovereign's approval. Such Orders are of two types—those made by Royal Prerogative and those authorised by Parliamentary Act as a form of delegated legislation; ultimate responsibility for them rests with the minister in whose department they originated.

Legislature: Parliament is bicameral. The House of Commons of 630 members (511 for England, 36 for Wales, 71 for Scotland, 12 for Northern Ireland) is elected for five years by the single-member constituency simple majority system. The House of Lords has over 1,000 members. The Lords Temporal are: hereditary peers and peeresses who have not disclaimed their title under the 1963 Peerage Act (these number almost 900); the nine Lords of Appeal in Ordinary appointed to assist the House in its judicial function; and over 100 life peers and peeresses appointed by the Crown under the 1958 Life Peerages Act. The Lords Spiritual are the Archbishops of Canterbury and York, the Bishops of London, Durham and Winchester and 21 other Anglican bishops in rotation. Legislation may originate in either House except in the case of legislation relating to financial matters, which must originate in the House of Commons. The House of Lords has no powers of revision or delay with respect to money bills, nor can it delay any other bill longer than one year. The first British Ombudsman (Parliamentary Commissioner) was appointed in 1966, his function being to deal with complaints against central government.

Northern Ireland: The Sovereign is represented in Northern Ireland by a Governor. He acts on the advice of the cabinet of Northern Ireland. The cabinet consists of the Prime Minister and seven ministers responsible to Parliament. Parliament is bicameral. The House of Commons has 52 members elected for five years. The Senate has 26 members—two ex-officio, and the remainder elected by the lower house on a proportional representation basis. Financial legislation must originate in the lower house and may not be amended by the Senate. Any deadlock may be resolved by joint session after the Senate has twice rejected a bill passed by the Commons. The 1920 Government of Ireland Act clearly distinguishes between the respective area of legislative power of the Northern Ireland and United Kingdom parliaments (to which latter Northern Ireland sends 12 members). The legislative powers of the Northern Ireland parliament include law and order, local government, education, transport, agriculture, health and social welfare and industrial development. Foreign policy, defence, customs and excise amongst other matters are reserved to Westminster.

Administratively autonomous Crown Dependencies (Isle of Man and Channel Islands)

Isle of Man: The Isle of Man is governed by its own laws; it is not bound by Acts of Parliament unless specifically mentioned in them. The administrative body (Tynwald) is composed of the House of Keys (24 members elected for five years) and the Legislative Council composed of the Lieutenant-Governor of the island—appointed by the Crown—the Lord Bishop of Soder and Man, two Deemsters, the Attorney-General, two members appointed by the Governor and four by the House of Keys. An Executive Council of five members of the House and two of the Legislative Council, to act with the Governor, was set up in 1961.

Jersey: The Lieutenant-Governor and Commander-in-Chief of Jersey is appointed by the Crown as its personal representative and channel of communication. He may sit and speak in the Assembly of the States but not vote and has certain powers of veto over legislation. The States consist of 12 Senators elected for six years, 12 Constables and 28 Deputies elected for three years. The Bailiff, appointed by the Crown, is President of the States and the Royal Court of Jersey. The Dean of Jersey and the Attorney- and Solicitor-Generals may also sit and speak in the States, but not vote.

Permanent laws (*Projets de loi*) require the sanction of the Sovereign in Council. The government is composed of committees appointed by the States.

Guernsey: The main point of difference from Jersey is in the composition of the legislature, the States of Deliberation. It is composed of the Bailiff, 12 Conseillers elected by the States of Election for six years, the Attorney-General and Socilitor-General, 33 People's Deputies elected by direct vote, 10 elected representatives of the Parochial Douzaines and two representatives of the Isle of Aldeney elected by the States of Aldeney.

Political parties: The British electoral system tends to promote the two-party system. The present beneficiaries are the Labour Party and the Conservative and Unionist Party. The Liberal Party maintains a precarious existence between them. The Cooperative Party is not affiliated to the Labour Party nationally, but there is a joint-executive sub-committee, and most parties are affiliated at local level. The British Communist Party lost its last parliamentary seat in 1950. The Welsh Nationalist Party won its first-ever seat in July 1966 at a by-election. The Scottish Nationalist Party has no representation. In Northern Ireland the predominant party is the Ulster Unionist Party which takes the Conservative whip in the House of Commons; its opponents are the Irish Nationalist and the Republican Labour Parties. The House of Lords has a Conservative majority through the hereditary peers, but in practice there is a balance between the two parties, because only a minority of the hereditary peers usually attends.

Election results:

Parties	1964 Percentage of poll	Seats	1966 Percentage of poll	Seats
Labour . .	44·1	317	47·9	363
Conservative .	43·4	303	41·9	253
Liberals . .	11·2	9	8·6	12
Others . .	1·3	1 [1]	1·6	2 [1]

[1] Includes in both cases the Speaker of the House of Commons standing as an Independent and in 1966 one member of the Irish Republican Labour Party.

Leading political figures: Labour Party—Harold Wilson (Prime Minister and Party Leader), George Brown (Deputy Prime Minister and Foreign Minister), Michael Stewart (Minister for Economic Affairs), Denis Healey (Minister of Defence), James Callaghan (Chancellor of the Exchequer), Lord Gardiner (Lord Chancellor), Roy Jenkins (Home Secretary). Conservative Party— Edward Heath (Leader of the Opposition and Party Leader), Reginald Maudling, Enoch Powell, Sir Alec Douglas-Home, Ian Macleod, Selwyn Lloyd. Liberal Party—Jeremy Thorpe (Party Leader), Jo Grimond.

Local government: The main units of local government are the Counties and the County Boroughs (mostly with populations of over 75,000 and separate from the Counties). The Counties are further divided into Boroughs, Urban and Rural Districts—and the latter again into Parishes. Each unit elects a Council for three years by the same method as in national elections, some retiring completely at the end of the period and others electing one-third each year. The Council in turn elects a Chairman, and in some cases also Aldermen. In England and Wales and Northern Ireland the Chairman of most Boroughs is the Mayor—in the City of London and certain other important boroughs the Lord Mayor, in Scottish Counties the Convenor and in Scottish Burghs the Provost or Lord Provost. The Greater London Council and the Councils of 32 London Boroughs and the City of London administer the Greater London area. There are in England and Wales in addition 58 County Councils and 82 County Borough Councils. In Scotland there are 33 County Councils and in Northern Ireland two County Borough Councils and six County Councils.

The powers of local authorities are defined by Parliamentary Act; while they maintain much independence—in the determination of their budget, freedom from ministerial inquiry, etc.—ministers have defined rights of oversight regarding certain services. Local government finance is provided about 40 per cent by state grants, about 40 per cent by local rates and the remainder from municipal rents, and invested funds. The reorganisation of local government is at present under consideration.

Judicial system: The system in England and Wales differs from that in Scotland, while that in Northern Ireland is almost identical with the former. There is a clear distinction between civil and criminal law.

England and Wales. Criminal courts. The lowest criminal courts are those of the Magistrates' Courts or Petty Sessions. They are presided over by from two to seven unpaid laymen who obtain advice on points of law from the clerk of the court. In London and some other large cities these courts are presided over by professional salaried lawyers (Stipendiary or Metropolitan Magistrates) sitting alone. Magistrates courts try all non-indictable and some less serious indictable[1] offences. They give preliminary hearings in criminal cases and decide whether to commit the accused to Quarter Sessions or Assizes. Appeal against conviction or sentence is generally to Quarter Sessions. Specially qualified Magistrates sit in juvenile courts in cases involving persons under 17.

All Counties and 98 Boroughs have Courts of Quarter Sessions sitting at least four times a year. In Counties they are presided over by a bench of lay magistrates with a professional chairman sitting with jury of twelve, with unanimity necessary for conviction. In the Boroughs a Recorder sits alone with jury. Quarter Sessions have jurisdiction over the less serious indictable offences, excluding amongst others those carrying the sentence of life imprisonment. Courts of Assize are branches of the High Court presided over by a High Court judge sitting with jury and with jurisdiction over the most serious indictable offences. Assizes are generally held in County towns and certain other large towns and cities three to five times a year. Other Assize Courts are the Old Bailey in London and the Crown Courts of Manchester and Liverpool. The judges also deal with civil cases after the criminal cases have been heard and hear appeals on points of law from the Magistrates' Courts.

Appeal from Quarter Sessions and Assizes is to the Criminal Division of the Court of Appeal constituted by three to five judges of the Queen's Bench Division with the Lord Chief Justice generally presiding. Final appeal is to the House of Lords; the qualified peers being the Lord Chancellor, any former Lord Chancellors, retired judges who are peers and the nine Lords of Appeal in Ordinary (see *Legislature*).

There is no capital punishment in England, Wales or Scotland. Northern Ireland retains capital punishment for certain forms of murder.

[1] An 'indictable offence' is a crime or misdemeanour.

Civil courts. The lowest courts are the County Courts—of which there are about 400—presided over by a professional judge. They have jurisdiction in cases up to £400 ($1,120); this jurisdiction may be increased with the consent of the parties. More important cases go to the High Court of Justice which is composed of three divisions and staffed by puisne judges (i.e. judges without any other special office), known as Justices of the High Court. The Lord Chancellor is President of the whole High Court although in practice he does not sit in any of its three Divisions: Chancery—bankruptcy, patents, trust enforcement, wardship and adoption, etc.—nominally headed by the Lord Chancellor; Queen's Bench—breach of contract, actions for damages and tort—presided over by the Lord Chief Justice; Probate, Divorce and Admiralty—probate of wills, matrimonial and shipping cases—headed by its President. In original jurisdiction judges sit alone; in appeal cases—from Magistrates' courts, ministerial decisions and decisions of a judge sitting in chambers (i.e. decisions reached during proceedings that do not have to be heard in court)—a court is constituted by one to three judges of the Division. Appeals from County and High Courts and civil cases heard in Assizes come before the Civil Division of the Court of Appeal. This is headed by the Master of the Rolls and its members are the Lord Chancellor, Lord Chief Justice, the President of the Probate, Divorce and Admiralty Division, the Lords of Appeal in Ordinary and 11 Lord Justices of Appeal. It sits in four Divisions each of three judges. Final appeal is to the House of Lords sitting as a court of three, five or seven. The Court of Appeal and the High Court of Justice together make up the Supreme Court of Judicature.

Other courts. Coroners' Courts investigate violent, sudden or suspicious death. The Criminal Injuries Compensation Board compensates victims of crimes of violence. Courts Martial have jurisdiction over serving members of the armed forces; appeal is to the Court Martial Appeals Court and in some cases to the House of Lords. The Judicial Committee of the Privy Council is the final court of appeal from the courts of British dependencies and certain Commonwealth members.

Judicial appointments. There is no Minister of Justice. The Queen is the titular head of the judiciary, but the latter is entirely free from government control. The Sovereign—on the Prime Minister's recommendation—appoints the Lord Chief Justice, the Lord Justices of Appeal, the President of the Probate, Divorce and Admiralty Division, the Master of the Rolls and the Lords of Appeal in Ordinary. Puisne judges, County Court judges, chairmen of Quarter Sessions, Recorders and Metropolitan and Stipendiary Magistrates are mostly appointed by the Sovereign on the Lord Chancellor's recommendation. Justices of the Peace (JPs) are appointed by the Lord Chancellor—advised by the Lord Lieutenants of the Counties—on the Sovereign's behalf. Judges hold office until the statutory retirement age of 75; inferior court judges may be removed by the Lord Chancellor for misconduct or incapacity; judges of the Court of Session and High Court of Justice may be removed by the Crown for misbehaviour, or—again for misbehaviour—by the Sovereign on address of both houses of parliament.

Scotland. The lowest criminal courts are the Burgh or Police Courts and the Courts of Justices of the Peace. More serious cases are heard by the Sheriff Courts, presided over by the Sheriff-Principal or a Sheriff-Substitute, sitting in the most serious cases with jury. The highest criminal court is the High Court of Justiciary composed of the Lord Justice General, the Lord Justice Clerk and 14 Lords Commissioner of Justiciary. Cases are heard by one of these sitting with jury. Appeals in all cases are to the High Court of Justiciary and are heard by three or more judges. There is no further appeal to the House of Lords. The lowest civil courts are the Sheriff Courts, which have virtually unlimited jurisdiction. The Court of Session (with the same membership as the High Court) has universal jurisdiction and has two parts —the Outer House acting as a court of first instance and the Inner House (of two divisions of four judges each) functioning as an appeal court. Further appeal may lie with the House of Lords. The Scottish Land Court whose chairman has equivalent rank to a judge of the Court of Session deals with certain agricultural matters. The Lord Justice General and Lord Justice Clerk are appointed by the Crown on the recommendation of the Prime Minister and all other judges are appointed on the recommendation of the Secretary of State for Scotland, who is also responsible for the appointment and removal of Magistrates and may (subject to annulment by either House of Parliament) remove a Sheriff-Principal upon report of the Lord Justice General and Lord Justice Clerk.

RECENT HISTORY

Britain's post-war history has been characterised by a withdrawal from its imperial past, an emphasis on collective security, a 'special relationship' with the United States, and an avoidance—until recently—of integrated arrangements for Western European cooperation. In 1947 Britain signed the Treaty of Dunkirk with France, providing for mutual defence against any future attack by Germany; this arrangement was expanded in 1948 to become the Brussels Treaty by including the Benelux countries. In 1949 Britain became a founder-member of NATO. British forces fought in Korea under United Nations auspices from 1950 to 1953. After the breakdown of the proposed European Defence Community, Foreign Minister Eden played a leading role in converting the Brussels Treaty into the Western European Union (WEU) Treaty to permit German entry into NATO, and committed British forces to the Continent (BAOR). In 1954 Britain formed the South-East Asia Treaty Organisation (SEATO) together with the United States, France, the Phillippines, Thailand, Pakistan, Australia and New Zealand, and in 1955 the Baghdad Pact (later Central Treaty Organisation or CENTO) together with Turkey, Iraq, Iran and Pakistan and with the backing of the United States. The aim of both these organisations is containment of the Communist world. Britain exploded its first H-bomb in 1955, and negotiated a nuclear test-ban treaty with the United States and the Soviet Union in 1963; it is a member of the UN's 18-Nation Disarmament Committee.

British forces were engaged in Malaya against Communist guerillas from the end of the second world war until 1954, against indigenous terrorism in Kenya and Cyprus in the 1950s, and against Egypt in the invasion of the Suez Canal zone following Egyptian nationalisation of the Canal in 1956. British forces were committed in Malaysia against Indonesian 'confrontation' in 1963–6 and in Cyprus in the UN force in 1964.

Britain refused to join the ECSC on its formation, but was an original member of GATT, the OECD and the Council of Europe. In 1958–9, under Harold Macmillan, Britain was a prime mover in the formation of EFTA, and in 1961 began negotiations for membership of the EEC which ended unsuccessfully in January 1963 with the imposition of a French veto. A new interest developed in 1966 and new soundings of the Common Market countries began in early 1967.

In 1947 Britain granted independence to India, separating the state into India and Pakistan. In 1948 Britain terminated its mandatory responsibilities in Palestine (out of which Israel emerged), and Ceylon and Burma became independent. In 1957 Britain granted independence to the first of its African colonies, Ghana (former Gold Coast) and since then most of the other larger colonies have also become independent. In 1961 South Africa left the Commonwealth because of disagreement over its racial policies. A unilateral declaration of independence by the government of Rhodesia in November 1965 was met by the imposition of economic sanctions by the British government and by most other countries at the latter's behest. At the end of 1966 the British Commonwealth consisted of the following countries besides Britain: Australia (including New Guinea, Papua, Christmas Island, Norfolk Islands, Nauru and Cocos Islands), Barbados, Botswana, Canada, Ceylon, Cyprus, Ghana, Guyana, India (including Sikkim), Jamaica, Kenya, Lesotho, Malawi, Malaysia (Malayan Federation, Sabah, Sarawak), Malta, New Zealand (including island territories), Nigeria, Pakistan, Sierra Leone, Singapore, Tanzania (Tanganyika and Zanzibar), Trinidad and Tobago, Uganda, Zambia.

Defence: Since 1960 Britain has no longer had compulsory military service. It possesses a nuclear deterrent based at present upon a bomber force, but for the future upon Polaris submarines. This force is to be assigned to a NATO commander, as are BAOR and some naval and air-force units. There are American military bases in Britain, and Britain has a network of bases throughout the world—the main one being in Singapore—the future of some being under review. The sizes of Britain's armed forces are: army 218,000 (including 29,000 from outside Britain), navy (including marines) 97,000, air force 22,000; reserves about 11,000. Defence expenditure in 1965–6 represented 6·8 per cent of GNP; the 1966–7 defence budget was £2,172 million ($6,081 million).

ECONOMY

Background: Britain has few mineral or natural resources apart from large-scale coal deposits and a little iron-ore. Since 1965, however, potentially extensive deposits of natural gas have been discovered in the North Sea and in eastern England. Since the pound sterling was devalued in 1949 Britain has been unable to increase production significantly without causing inflation. The economic pattern in post-war Britain has consequently been one of expansion followed by deflation; growth rate of GNP has been slow—an annual average rate of 3·1 per cent from 1953 to 1964—and has been associated with constantly rising prices and incomes and a precarious balance of payments position.

In 1961 the government established a National Economic Development Council (NEDC) to promote a faster and more even rate of growth and an anti-inflationary 'pause' in wages, salaries and dividend payments was introduced as a temporary measure. In 1962 a further effort was made to introduce some form of incomes policy: a National Incomes Commission (NIC) was set up to report on inflationary incomes settlements and comment in advance on wage claims and profit levels. However, the NIC did not have the power to cancel or modify an agreement. An expansionary policy was then followed until 1964 when the economy showed signs of severe strain, with balance of payments heavily in deficit. After the general election in October the new Labour government imposed a temporary surcharge of

15 per cent—later reduced to 10 per cent in response to pressure from other EFTA countries[1]—on all imports of manufactures and semi-manufactures.

In the expectation that devaluation and severe deflationary measures would be used to curb the deterioration in the balance of payments, in November 1964 a sterling crisis was precipitated by the outflow of short-term capital. In order to maintain the official exchange rate of £1 = $2·78 (minimum) the government was forced to arrange credit facilities of £330 million ($924 million) with the IMF, and the Bank of England drew heavily on the country's gold and dollar reserves to buy pounds. The crisis subsided when the leading Western European central banks made loans totalling over £1,000 million ($2,240 million).

In 1965 the balance of payments position improved and economic activity intensified, but international monetary loans continued to be necessary. Progress toward an incomes policy was made by the new government Department of Economic Affairs, which took over from the Treasury responsibility for long-term economic measures and for achieving an incomes policy. Voluntary cooperation was enlisted from unions and employers and a National Prices and Incomes Board was set up. However, prices and incomes continued to rise faster than productivity and the April Budget of 1966 was generally deflationary. Although it was announced that the import surcharge would be removed in October 1966, Bank Rate was raised by 1 per cent in July to 7 per cent and the original goal of reducing the balance of payments deficit by the end of 1966 was not expected to be achieved until some time in 1967. Following the poor trade figures for the first half of the year, the pressure upon sterling was renewed. The severe deflationary measures taken included considerable cuts in government expenditure, certain emergency taxes and a six-month price and wage freeze.

GNP grew by 7 per cent in volume from the fourth quarter of 1962 to the fourth quarter of 1963, by 3.5–4 per cent during the following twelve months, and by only 2.75 per cent in 1965. In 1964 the value of GDP at factor cost was £24,803 million ($69,448·4 million). The origin of GDP at factor cost in 1964 was:

Sector	Percentage
Agriculture	3
Industry	47
Services	50
GDP	100

Between 1958 and 1964 industrial output increased by an annual average of 5 per cent, the expansion occurring mainly in two boom periods, 1959–60 and 1963–4. Britain's main industries are iron and steel, engineering, electronics, chemicals, textiles, transport equipment and consumer goods. The main growth industries since 1959 have been chemicals, cars and fuel, especially atomic energy. The pattern of industry has gradually changed from an emphasis on textiles, machinery and coal to a more diversified range of industries, notably chemicals, transport and other engineering products. Other important contributions to Britain's economic wealth are made by British financial services and the expanding tourist industry. The country produces about half its total food supplies, the main products including cereals, vegetables and fruit.

[1] See 'The European Free Trade Association (EFTA)', p. 619.

Foreign trade: Since the war Commonwealth markets have declined in importance whilst trade with Western Europe has expanded rapidly. Machinery and transport equipment have increased their share of total exports and other manufactured articles—ships and textiles—have decreased. Between 1953 and 1963 the volume of imported manufactured goods doubled, whereas imports of goods, beverages and tobacco expanded more slowly. During the whole of this period Britain's balance of payments position was characterised by a large deficit (except in 1958). Despite a significant rise in the value of exports, imports have grown faster. Current-account balance of payments deficit increased from £78 million ($218 million) in 1963 to £464 million ($1,200 million) in 1964, improving to a deficit of £136 million ($381 million) in 1965. The NEDC estimated in 1963 that in order to achieve a 4 per cent annual growth rate of GNP Britain would have to increase exports by over 5 per cent a year while allowing imports to increase by only 4.5 per cent a year. However, since 1961 imports have risen by about 6 per cent a year and exports by about 4 per cent. In 1965 export figures were a record, but Britain's share of world trade fell by 1 per cent to 13 per cent.

In 1964 imports accounted for 17 per cent of GNP and exports for 13 per cent. The main export items in 1964 were machinery (27 per cent of total exports), transport equipment (15 per cent) and chemicals (9 per cent). The main imports in 1964 were petroleum and allied products (10 per cent of total imports), machinery (8 per cent), meat (6 per cent), non-ferrous metals (6 per cent) and fruit and vegetables (5 per cent). Invisible items continue to make a considerable contribution to Britain's balance of payments position. Trade with the EEC has expanded at a faster rate than trade with EFTA. In 1964 12 per cent of total imports came from the United States, 32 per cent from the Commonwealth, 17 per cent from the EEC and 11 per cent from EFTA. In the same year the main export markets were: the United States 9 per cent of total exports, the Commonwealth 27 per cent, the EEC 21 per cent and EFTA 13 per cent.

Employment: In 1964 the total labour force was 24.5 million, of whom 47 per cent were employed in industry, 4 per cent in agriculture and 48 per cent in services. Full employment has been maintained since the second world war except for regional and seasonal variations. From 1961 to 1965 the annual average for unemployment was consistently less than 2 per cent (in 1965 the monthly average was about 1·5 per cent or under 400,000 persons). In recent years there has been a shortage of skilled labour in industry and building and construction which the 1966 budget sought to alleviate by means of a selective employment tax. Since the war there has been a drift of labour to the Midlands and the South, which the government has attempted to curb through Regional Planning Boards and legislation stimulating growth in stagnant and declining areas and preventing further growth of industries in over-crowded areas. In 1964 the total immigrant population, excluding Irish, was 820,000 of whom over half were of West Indian origin; geographically they are concentrated in urban areas.

Price and wage trends: From 1958 to 1964 retail prices rose by 17 per cent, weekly rates by 25 per cent and productivity by 25 per cent. In 1965 the situation considerably deteriorated; retail prices rose by nearly 5 per cent, average earnings by nearly 9 per cent while productivity increased by only about 2 per cent and average weekly hours worked decreased by over 1 per cent; substantial wage drift occurred despite the efforts of the government to implement an incomes policy. In 1965 and 1966, despite tighter hire purchase controls, price and wage increases continued to exceed the rise in productivity. In August 1966 a price and wage freeze was introduced, partly as a result of the inflationary tendencies and partly to help remedy the sterling crisis.

Consumption: From 1960 to 1964 the average annual increase in private consumption was 3.5 per cent. Public consumption increased by an annual average of 3·1 per cent in the same period. In 1964 private consumption accounted for about 64 per cent of GNP and public consumption for 17 per cent. In 1965 consumption continued to expand but in 1966 it was expected to fall sharply following deflationary policy.

SOCIAL SECURITY

The contributions for the National Health Service (NHS) and for National Insurance are collected together, but the two services are administered separately by the Ministries of Health and Social Security. Most NHS costs are met from general taxation, and the rest from contributions and rates. There are three classes of contributor, each paying a flat-rate for National Insurance, which is scaled according to age, sex and earnings.

Class I covers all employees, and contributions are paid by both employer and employee for both insurances. The flat-rate for weekly contributions paid by males over 18 to National Insurance is 10s 11½d ($1·53)[1] paid by the employer and 13s 3½d ($1·80) by the employee (this amount includes 9d ($0·10) paid by the employee and 10d ($0·11) paid by the employer as an industrial injuries insurance contribution). The contribution for health insurance is 2s 8½d ($0·40) and 7½d ($0·10) respectively. There are graduated contributions for supplements to retirement pensions and earnings-related supplements to unemployment and sickness benefits. All employees over 18 pay 4·25 per cent (pensions) plus 0·5 per cent (unemployment and sickness) on average weekly earnings[2] between £9 ($25·20) and £18 ($50·40) and a further 0·5 per cent (sickness and unemployment) on weekly earnings between £18 and £30 ($84). Supplementary sickness and unemployment contributions count towards graduated pensions. Employers pay the same contribution. It is possible to contract out of the graduated pensions scheme if a private plan offers equivalent benefits, in which case the employee pays a flat-rate weekly National Insurance contribution of 13s 4½d ($1·90) and the employer 14s 8½d ($2), with health contributions remaining the same. However, both contracted-out employees and their employers must pay sickness and unemployment contributions at the rate of 0·5 per cent of weekly earnings lying between £18 and £30.

Class II contributors are self-employed persons and those of Class III non-employed persons. Both pay own weekly premiums—for National Insurance 15s 10d ($2·20) for Class II and 12s 1d ($1·70) for Class III, health insurance premiums being 2s 10d ($0·35) in both cases.

National Insurance covers all persons for basic retirement and survivor's pensions and death grants. Classes I and II also receive sickness and maternity (grants and allowances) benefits, Class III receiving the maternity grant

---

[1] All figures refer to 1966.
[2] Average weekly earnings are assessed as one-fiftieth of gross earnings over the last complete income-tax year for all contributions and benefits under the supplementary benefit schemes.

only. In addition Class I persons are insured against unemployment and work accidents. For most National Insurance benefits it is necessary to have a minimum number of contributions before any benefit can be paid, and a specific number before full benefits are paid. Health insurance provides identical benefits to all residing in Britain irrespective of age, income, insurance qualifications or nationality.

Health insurance: The NHS is administered in three separate groups: the hospital and specialist services, the general practitioner services (local doctor, dentist, pharmacist and optician), and the local authority services (clinics, pre-natal care, school health, midwifery, ambulance, home-nursing, preventive treatment and mental sickness). These services are all provided free except for small dental and ophthalmic charges. Sickness benefits are paid at a weekly rate of £4 ($11) for men, single women and widows, £2 15s ($7.70) for married women and £2 5s 6d ($6·40) for persons under 18. Supplements are £2 10s ($7) for one adult dependant, £1 2s 6d ($3·15) for the first dependant child and 14s 6d ($2·10) for each subsequent child, plus an additional supplement under the earnings related scheme of one-third of the employee's average weekly earnings lying between £9 and £30. In no case may total benefit—including dependant's allowances—exceed 85 per cent of average weekly earnings. Sickness benefits are paid for one year, or for an unlimited period if more than 156 contributions have been paid. Wage-related supplements are paid for up to six months. Periods of sickness not separated by more than 13 weeks are treated as a single period. Persons in hospital for more than eight weeks receive a reduced rate of benefit. Maternity allowances of £4 per week are paid for 18 weeks before and after confinement. A maternity grant in the form of a lump sum of £22 ($62) is paid for each birth.

Accident insurance: This is administered by the Ministry of Social Security and financed from a common fund to which employers, employees and the state contribute. Full medical benefits are provided by the NHS. The temporary disability benefit is paid for 26 weeks at the weekly rate of £6 15s ($19) with the same dependant allowances and wage-related supplement as for sickness benefit. Married women and juveniles receive the same lower flat-rate benefits as under sickness insurance. On expiry of temporary disability benefit the insured gets a weekly disablement pension ranging from £1 7s ($3.70) for 20 per cent disability to £6 15s for 100 per cent disability. For less than 20 per cent disability the pension usually takes the form of a lump payment of a maximum of £450 ($1,620). Supplements are paid for special hardship, constant attendance and unemployability. There is a special supplementary scheme for miners.

Widow's pensions are worth £5 12s 6d ($15.75) per week for the first 26 weeks, and thereafter a maximum of £4 10s ($12·60) if the widow is disabled, caring for a child, is aged 50 at the time of her husband's death, or 40 when the last child becomes ineligible for benefits, reducing to £1 ($2·80) per week for women who do not fulfil these conditions. A widow receiving the higher rate of pension may also receive a supplementary allowance (see under *Pensions insurance*). Weekly pensions for orphans are £2 ($5·60) for the eldest child, £1 12s ($4.50) for the second eldest and £1 10s ($4·20) for all other children. This is reduced to £1 12s 6d for the eldest and 14s 6d for other children if they are not in the widow's care. Dependant or invalid widowers receive a pension of £4 ($11) per week. Parents and other relatives dependant upon the insured may also receive small pensions.

93

Pensions insurance: Retirement pensions are paid to all at the age of 65 for men and 60 for women. The weekly rates are £4 for an insured person and £2 10s for his non-insured wife if she is over 60. Supplements are paid at the rate of £1 2s 6d for the first dependant child and 14s 6d for each subsequent child. For each 12 weeks of contribution after pensionable age an increment of 1s ($0·15) is paid, which rises to 1s 6d ($0·20) if the insured has a non-insured wife of over 60. The graduated retirement pension, paid in addition to the basic retirement pension, is worth an additional 1s for each £7 10s ($21) of contributions for men, and for each £9 ($25) of contributions for women. There is no invalidity pension as such; ordinary sickness benefits and supplements for dependants are paid. Widow's pensions are paid at the weekly rate of £5 12s 6d for the first 26 weeks and thereafter at the rate of £4 per week. The supplements for orphans are the same as for accident insurance. Graduated widow's pensions are worth 50 per cent of the graduated pension earned by the husband before death, and are payable at 60. Widow's supplementary allowances are worth one-third of the husband's average weekly earnings between £9 and £30 in the last complete income-tax year before death. Widow's pensions are unaffected by other unearned income or the previous level of earnings, and family allowances (see *Other benefits*) are payable in the normal way. For full orphans there is a weekly guardian's allowance of £2.

Unemployment insurance: The flat-rate benefit, dependant's allowances and earnings-related supplement are identical with those paid for sickness and are paid for a maximum of one year; as for sickness and temporary disability benefits, lower rates are paid to married women and persons under 18.

Other benefits: War pensions are paid at the same rate as retirement pensions with similar allowances. Family allowances are paid by the state at the weekly rate of 8s ($1·10) for the second child and 10s ($1·40) for each subsequent child under 15, or under 16 in the case of handicapped children and 19 for children receiving full-time education.

EDUCATION

All aspects of education in Britain are the responsibility of the Secretary of State for Education and Science. Administration of state schools and higher education is divided between the central government departments, local education authorities and various voluntary bodies. The universities are administratively independent, their relations with the departments concerned are conducted through the University Grants Committee, and their governing bodies are appointed according to the terms of their individual charters. In England and Wales schools supported out of public funds are of three kinds: County Schools, which are wholly state-controlled; Voluntary Schools, which have been provided by a voluntary body and receive state aid; and Direct-Grant Schools which are completely independent but also receive a grant from the Department of Education and Science. In Scotland most of the schools supported from public funds are known as Public Schools; there are a few grant-aided schools conducted by voluntary bodies. In Northern Ireland County Schools and Voluntary Schools are managed respectively by the local authorities and voluntary managers, and the latter are grant-aided by the government. Physical education and religious instruction is compulsory in all schools.

94

Primary schools: State education is free and compulsory from the ages of five to 15 (in 1970–1 the minimum school leaving age is to be raised to 16). Primary education is divided into Infant Schools (five to seven years) and Junior Schools (seven to 11 years). The planning of the curriculum is largely in the hands of the head teacher and the staff. Owing to the high birth rate since 1946 primary school numbers are very high and there exists a continuing need for more teachers and school buildings. The age of transfer from primary to secondary schooling is at present under review. In Scotland primary schools take children between the ages of five and 12. Curricula are similar in scope all over Britain except in Wales where the Welsh language is taught. (See also under *Independent schools.*)

Secondary schools: Since 1944 the state educational system in England and Wales has aimed at giving all children an educational experience to suit their particular needs. Grammar Schools have come to be academic in orientation; Secondary Technical Schools are general and vocation-orientated; and Secondary Modern Schools again general but with a practical bias. The three-tier system that evolved gave rise to differential statuses being attached to each type of secondary school and was characterised by selection. In 1964 the reorganisation of secondary education was initiated in England and Wales in favour of the non-selective Comprehensive School in which a wider range of courses may be organised in a variety of ways according to local conditions and educational preferences. Basically the three alternatives are: one tier with an 11 to 19 age range, two tiers with a break at 13, 14, 15 or 16 years, or a three-tier system involving two breaks.

Scottish secondary education consists of two main categories, Junior and Senior Secondary Schools providing three-year courses (12–15) and four-, five- or six-year courses (12–18) respectively. Both types offer a general education with a wide choice of curriculum. In Northern Ireland the system is similar to that in England and Wales prior to the latter's reorganisation, the three corresponding types of schools being called Grammar, Intermediate Secondary and Technical Intermediate. Some changes in organisation are expected in both Northern Ireland and Scotland following government reports.

There is no national leaving examination in England and Wales; instead there are a variety of General Certificate of Education (GCE) Examining Boards and the recently introduced Certificate of Secondary Education (CSE) for those not taking GCE. The GCE may be taken at Ordinary (O) level generally after five years and at Advanced (A) level after seven years, but the CSE at present at the Ordinary level only. In both Scotland and Northern Ireland there are National Certificate examinations which may be taken at Junior or Senior level. A combination of O and A level certificates is the basis for university entrance in Britain.

Independent schools: Registration with the Department of Education and Science is compulsory to ensure maintenance of minimum standards. Independent schools, which are mainly boarding schools, may be primary (8–13; 'preparatory'), secondary (13–18; 'public') or primary and secondary combined. Annual fees range between £300 ($840) and £550 ($1,540). As at January 1965 there were over 470,000 pupils at independent schools in Britain (173,000 at Preparatory Schools, 101,000 at Public Schools and 196,000 at Public-cum-Preparatory Schools). The present Labour government is considering how independent schools may best be integrated into the state system.

Special schools: In England, Wales and Northern Ireland local education authorities must provide special educational treatment for the physically handicapped and the educationally sub-normal. For those categories of children attendance at special schools is compulsory between the ages of five and 15.

Vocational education: Apart from the training of teachers vocational education has developed independently of the state. However, in Technical, Art and Secondary Modern Schools there are vocational courses of all kinds, generally organised by professional associations who also act as examiners. Facilities are available for both part-time day and evening studies in addition to full-time courses. The other main category of vocational education is the apprenticeship system which aims at providing a combination of theoretical and practical instruction in a variety of trades. Day release with pay from employers is one method of training, and the government provides training centres for full-time courses to encourage industry to increase its intake of young people into skilled occupations (see Technical Colleges under *University and higher education*). Technical courses last a minimum of four years and craft courses last five years. The 1964 Industrial Training Act empowered the Minister of Labour to set up industrial training boards; by mid-1965 nine such boards had been set up in certain major industries to provide training courses.

University and higher education: Higher education is provided by the universities (both private and state-owned), technical colleges and teacher-training colleges. At the end of 1966 there were 44 universities in the United Kingdom. The universities of Oxford, Cambridge, Wales and London consist of loosely federated colleges, each of which retains much independence; Oxford and Cambridge have their own entry system. The other universities are unitary institutions each under the academic control of a Senate. Courses last three or four years for bachelor degrees. Full medical courses last five to six years.

Technical Colleges (including Art, Commercial and Agricultural Colleges) provide a wide range of courses. They are maintained by local education authorities and some of them have been given polytechnic status with an emphasis on degree-level studies. There are six National Technical Colleges linked to particular industries and administered jointly by the Department of Education and Science and the industry concerned. Teacher-training colleges are called 'Colleges of Education' in England and Wales; they are maintained by local education authorities and some have links with university education departments.

Universities (end 1966): England: Aston, Bath, Birmingham, Bradford, Bristol, Brunel (London), Cambridge, City (London), Durham, East Anglia (Norwich), Essex (Colchester), Exeter, Hull, Keele, Kent (Canterbury), Lancaster, Leeds, Leicester, Liverpool, London, Loughborough, Manchester, Newcastle-upon-Tyne, Nottingham, Oxford, Reading, Salford, Sheffield, Southampton, Sussex (Brighton), Surrey, Warwick, York. *Wales:* Wales (Aberystwyth, Bangor, Cardiff and Swansea), St Davids (Lampeter). *Scotland:* Aberdeen, Edinburgh, Glasgow, Heriot-Watt, St Andrews, Strathclyde, Stirling. *Northern Ireland:* Belfast, Londonderry.

Educational institutions, 1963:

	Institutions	Staff	Students
Primary . . .	25,369	157,699	4,728,103
Secondary . . .	6,635	154,150	3,667,223
Special . . .	856	5,588	186,169
Technical and Art . .	750	28,570	175,914
Teacher-training . .	193	4,941	18,914
Universities . . .	29	15,200	142,500

Adult education: This is available in Britain through evening institutes and adult-education centres many of which, such as extra-mural university courses, are assisted out of state funds. Others such as the Workers' Educational Association are voluntary, and some such as Correspondence and Secretarial Colleges are commercial. The range of subjects varies from handicraft and vocational studies to university degree courses. In 1966 there were 40,000 public libraries, including mobile libraries.

MASS MEDIA

The press (1965):

Dailies: Daily Mirror, London, independent Labour, 5,085,000; *Daily Express,* London, ind.-Conservative, 4,190,000; *Daily Mail,* London, ind., 2,400,000; *Sun,* London, ind.-Lab., 1,414,000; *Daily Telegraph,* London, ind.-Cons., 1,325,000; *Evening News,* London, ind.-Cons., 1,324,000; *Daily Sketch,* London, Cons., 848,000; *Evening Standard,* London, ind.-Cons., 704,000; *Manchester Evening News and Chronicle,* Manchester, ind., 475,000; *Birmingham Evening Mail,* Birmingham, ind., 409,000; *The Guardian,* London and Manchester, ind.-Liberal, 278,000; *The Times,* London, ind., 255,000; *Evening Citizen,* Glasgow, ind., 234,000; *Evening Times,* Glasgow, ind., 226,000; *Belfast Telegraph,* Belfast, Unionist, 210,000; *Financial Times,* London, ind. financial and commercial, 152,000; *Yorkshire Post,* Leeds, Cons., 118,000; *The Journal,* Newcastle, ind., 115,000; *Northern Echo,* Darlington, ind., 107,000; *Western Mail,* Cardiff, Cons., 103,000; *Morning Star,* London, organ of Communist Party, 63,000.

Sundays: News of the World, London, ind., 6,251,000; *The People,* London, ind., 5,889,000; *Sunday Mirror,* London, ind.-Lab., 5,102,000; *Sunday Express,* London, ind.-Cons., 4,226,000; *Sunday Times,* London, ind.-Cons., 1,250,000; *Sunday Post,* Glasgow, ind., 1,000,000; *The Observer,* London, ind., 797,000; *Sunday Telegraph,* London, ind.-Cons., 656,000; *Sunday Citizen,* London, Lab. and Co-op., 248,000; *Sunday Mercury,* Birmingham, ind., 220,000.

Periodicals (London): Woman (w), woman's, 3,000,000; *Woman's Own* (w), wom., 2,300,000; *Woman's Realm* (w), wom., 1,320,000; *The Universe and Catholic Times* (w), Roman Catholic, 305,000; *She* (m), wom., 300,000; *Nova* (m), wom., 159,000; *Farmers Weekly* (w), farming, 140,000; *Vogue* (m), fashion, 130,000; *Punch* (w), humorous, 128,000; *Catholic Herald* (w), Roman Cath., 104,000; *New Statesman* (w), left political and cultural, 90,000; *The Economist* (w), ind. political, business and economic, 77,000; *The Listener* (w), radio and literary, 75,000; *Illustrated London News* (w), general illustrated, 66,000; *Queen* (f), social, 58,000; *New Scientist* (w), scientific, 52,000; *Country Life* (w), cultural/social/miscellaneous, 49,000; *Spectator* (w), ind.-Cons. pol. and cul., 36,000; *Private Eye* (f), hum., 41,000; *New Society* (w), sociology and current affairs, 35,000; *Harper's Bazaar* (m), fashion, 32,000; *The Statist* (w), pol. and econ., 23,000; *Encounter* (m), cultural and current affairs, 38,000 (1966).

Broadcasting: Sound broadcasting is officially provided solely by the British Broadcasting Corporation (BBC), as are two TV services (BBC 1 and BBC 2). The Independent Television Authority (ITA) is a public body. Both BBC and ITA have independent control over such matters as programmes and administration. The government has powers of final review and may issue directives to both bodies on technical and other subjects but has no control over content of programmes. The BBC's corporation under the present Charter consists of nine governors responsible for the entire conduct of the organisation; they are advised by a number of councils. The BBC is financed by an annual sum voted by parliament based on the sale of radio and TV licences, an annual grant-in-aid also voted by parliament, and profits from the sale of BBC publications. The ITA, whose board is government-appointed, owns and operates its transmitters but studios and equipment are owned by, and programmes provided by, the programme companies under contract to the ITA. The Authority has wide controlling and regulatory powers regarding programmes. It is financed by annual rental payments made by the programme companies, which in turn derive their revenue from the sale of advertising time.

GREECE

GEOGRAPHY

Features: Greece is largely a mountainous area composed of ancient rocks (especially in the north), limestones and young volcanics. Much of the country lies over 5,000 ft/1,500 m., the only true lowland being the narrow coastal plains, Thessaly and the area north-west of Thebes. The country is divided into two main parts by the Gulf of Corinth and there is a large number of islands. Southern Greece is Mediterranean in climate and vegetation; the north is more continental, with greater temperature extremes. The chief island groups are the Ionian Isles off the west coast and the Cyclades and the Dodecanese in the east, between Greece and Turkey. In the south lies the largest island, Crete.

While the greater part of overseas earnings come from agriculture and nearly half the population is employed on the land, less than 25 per cent of the land surface is cultivable. The main cultivated areas are the lowlands and the river valleys. As in many parts of the Mediterranean region, sparse water supply frequently limits agriculture. A wide variety of minerals is produced including iron ore, pyrites, manganese and small amounts of lignite. There are no major industrial zones and industry is largely concentrated around the main towns, especially Athens and its port Piraeus.

Area: 50,600 sq. miles/132,000 sq. km. *Mean max. and min. temperatures:* Athens (38° N, 23° 30′ E; 350 ft/107 m.) 90°F/32°C (July and Aug.) 42°F/6°C (Jan.); Salonika (40° 30′ N, 23° E; 80 ft/24 m.) 90°F/32°C (July), 37°F/3°C (Jan. and Feb.); Rhodes (36° 30′ N, 28° 30′ E; 290 ft/88 m.) 83°F/28°C (July and Aug.), 51°F/11°C (Jan.). *Relative humidity:* Athens 68 per cent; Salonika 71 per cent; Rhodes 68 per cent. *Mean annual rainfall:* Athens 16 in./405 mm.; Salonika 19 in./485 mm.; Rhodes 21 in./73.5 mm.

POPULATION

Total population: (1965) 8,500,000. *Main towns and populations:* (1961) Metropolitan ATHENS including Piraeus (1,853,000), Salonika (378,000), Patras (102,000), Iraklion (70,000), Volos (67,000), Larisa (55,000). *Distribution:* In 1961 57 per cent of the population lived in rural areas and semi-urban Communes of fewer than 10,000 inhabitants, 12 per cent in Communes with 10–50,000 inhabitants and 31 per cent in Communes with a population greater than 50,000 inhabitants.

Language: 98 per cent of the population speak one of the two forms of modern Greek—*katharevousa* (purist), an artificial attempt to return to classical Greek used for official and press purposes, or *demotiki* (demotic), the spoken language and generally used in literature. There is an increasing compromise between

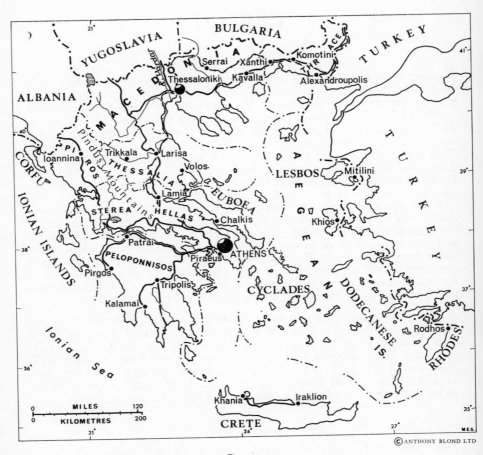

GREECE

the two. The main minority language is Turkish. *Religion:* 98 per cent of the population profess the established Eastern Orthodox faith. Freedom of faith and worship is guaranteed by the constitution, but proselytising is forbidden.

CONSTITUTIONAL SYSTEM

Constitution: Greece is a 'crown democracy'. The present constitution was promulgated in 1952. *Head of state:* King Constantine. *Head of government:* See under *Political parties.*

Executive: Executive power rests with the King and the ministers appointed and dismissed by him. The King may dissolve the Chamber of Deputies but is obliged to hold elections within 45 days of dissolution. All laws promulgated by the King must be countersigned by a minister. The ministers are responsible to the Chamber of Deputies and the government must enjoy its confidence.

Legislature: Legislative power rests with the Chamber of Deputies (Vouli) of 300 members (the number may be changed by electoral law to any number between 150 and 300) elected for four years by a proportional representation system weighted against smaller parties. Elections in Greece are usually conducted under caretaker governments composed of persons who are not members of parliament but hold important public posts.

Political parties: The leading political parties are the liberal-progressive Centre-Union (from which 45 deputies supporting Stephanopoulos against Papandreou broke away in December 1965 to form the Liberal Democratic Centre Party), the conservative National Radical Union and the moderate conservative Progressive Party; the last two contested the 1964 general election as a coalition. The Communist-backed Union of the Democratic Left (EDA) is the only other party in the Vouli (the official Communist Party (KKE) was banned in 1947). The 1965 government coalition of the Liberal Democratic Centre Party, the National Radical Union and the Progressive Party with Stephanopoulos as Prime Minister resigned in December 1966 when the Radical Union withdrew its support, and the King appointed a non-political government, with Ioannis Paraskevopoulos as Prime Minister, to superintend elections to be held in May 1967.

Election results:

Parties	1963 Percentage of poll	Seats	1964 Percentage of poll	Seats
Centre-Union	42·04	138	52·72	171
National Radical Union .	39·37	132 }	35·26	108
Progressive Party . .	3·73	2 }		
EDA	14·34	28	11·6	21
Others	0·52	—	0·22	—

Leading political figures: Liberal Democratic Centre Party—Stephanos Stephanopoulos (Party Leader and former Prime Minister). Centre-Union—George Papandreou (Party Leader and former Prime Minister). National Radical Union—Panayotis Kanellopoulos (Party Leader). Progressive Party—Spyro Markezenis (Party Leader). EDA—Ioannis Passalides (Party Leader).

Local government: This is modelled on the French system. The country is divided into 52 Prefectures (*nomoi*) headed by government-appointed Prefects (*nomarchai*). There is a Minister of Northern Greece—based in Salonika—who is a full cabinet member. Each Municipality (*demos*) and rural Commune (*kenotis*) elects an Urban Council (*demarchiakon symvoulion*) and a Rural Council (*kenotikon symvoulion*) headed by a Mayor for four years. Mount Athos is a self-governing community subject to the spiritual jurisdiction of the Ecumenical Patriarch in Istanbul.

Judicial system: The lowest court is that of the Justices of the Peace (*erenodikeon*). Each court of first instance (*protodikeon*) has a criminal court at its seat. The Court of Appeal (*efetion*) has jurisdiction in both civil and criminal cases. Final appeal is to the Supreme Court (Areios Pagos) which has four sections —three civil and one criminal—and adjudicates in quorum. There are no commercial courts; all commercial cases are tried by ordinary courts. Judges are appointed by the King—High Court judges are appointed for life and other justices are irremovable except for criminal offences. Greece maintains capital punishment.

RECENT HISTORY

In 1944 and again in 1946–9 the Greek government fought a civil war against the Greek Communists who were actively supported by members of the Soviet bloc. Greece became a member of NATO in 1952, and an associate member of the EEC in 1962. The problem of Cyprus complicated relations with Britain and Turkey in the late 1950s and relations with Turkey have again been strained since the renewed strife in Cyprus that led to the introduction of a UN Peacekeeping Force there in 1964. Under the premiership of Constantine Karamanlis (October 1955–June 1963) Greece made considerable economic and social progress. In 1965 a political crisis between the King and Prime Minister Papandreou over the investigation of a secret organisation within the army (ASPIDA) led to the latter's resignation, mob demonstrations and the defection of 45 members under Stephanopoulos from the Centre-Union Party (see above under *Political parties*). In April 1966 the Greek Foreign Minister Tsirimokos and another minister resigned from the Stephanopoulos government over the issue of the powers of General Grivas in Cyprus.

Defence: The Sovereign is commander-in-chief of the armed forces. Military service is compulsory for 24 months. Most of the army and air force is assigned to NATO. The strengths of the defence forces are: army 118,000, navy 18,000, air force 23,000. The 1966 defence budget was Dr6,175 million ($206 million) representing 3·6 per cent of GNP.

ECONOMY

Background: The economy is in the process of industrialisation; however, agriculture remains at present the basic economic activity. After the second world war political instability retarded economic growth, but in recent years production has expanded rapidly. In 1965 the value of industrial production exceeded that of agriculture for the first time. The cost of rapid expansion has been the loss of internal and external equilibrium; prices have accelerated upwards, there have been consistent balance of payments deficits and foreign exchange reserves have fallen. From 1953 to 1963 GNP increased at an average annual rate of 6·3 per cent. The growth rate of 6 per cent which was the aim of the First Plan (1960–4) was achieved. The aim of the Second Plan (1966–70) is industrialisation. The planned annual industrial growth rate for 1961–71 is 7·8 per cent; the rate achieved in the period 1961–3 was 7 per cent, increasing to 11·2 per cent in 1964. The main growth industries include iron and steel, textiles, chemicals and cement; agricultural output has declined relatively to industry, but diversification has occurred, including the introduction of cotton and rice.

The origin of GDP at factor cost in 1964 was:

Sector	Percentage
Agriculture . . .	25
Industry	28
Services	47
GDP	100

The main industries are iron and steel, bauxite and textiles. Agricultural production (by volume) increased by 3.9 per cent in 1964 compared with 9 per cent in 1963. The main agricultural products are olives, raisins, wine, tobacco, fruit, wheat and livestock (especially sheep).

Foreign trade: The balance of payments deficits up to 1963 were moderate, but in 1964–5 deteriorated considerably. The deficit on current account amounted to Dr8,100 million ($270 million) in 1965, representing an increase of about 33 per cent over the 1964 deficit; rapid growth of imports accounted for this. In 1964 exports amounted to an estimated 6·5 per cent of GNP and imports to 18 per cent. The lack of diversity of Greek exports is reflected by the contributions of tobacco (38 per cent of total exports in 1964), cotton (12 per cent), and currants (11 per cent). The main imports in 1964 were consumer goods (32 per cent), raw materials (12 per cent) and machinery (21 per cent). Over one-third of Greece's total trade is with the EEC and since 1964 this trade has expanded faster than that with other countries. Greece is currently preparing to integrate her economy with the EEC. In 1964 20 per cent of Greek imports came from EFTA and a further 11 per cent from the United States; of exports 13 per cent went to EFTA and 14.5 per cent to the United States.

Employment: The total working population in 1961 was 3·6 million, of whom 54 per cent were employed in agriculture, 19 per cent in industry and 27 per cent in services. The level of unemployment in that year was 6·5 per cent but has declined gradually since. The average annual emigration in 1963–4 was over 100,000.

Price and wage trends: The relatively favourable trend in consumer prices in 1964 was offset by the fast increase in money incomes. The rise in the consumer price index was about 1·5 per cent compared with 1·3 per cent in 1963. The liberal social policy of the government, the drift from the land and the scarcity of skilled industrial and agricultural labour all contributed to wage increases of 20 per cent in agriculture and 12 per cent in industry and services in 1964, a trend which showed little sign of slackening in 1965.

Consumption: In 1964 private consumption accounted for 71 per cent of GNP and public consumption for 12·5 per cent. Private consumption rose by 8·2 per cent in volume in 1964 compared with an increase of 10·5 per cent in 1963. Public consumption increased by 7·1 per cent in 1964 and 5·8 per cent in 1963.

SOCIAL SECURITY

The Ministry of Labour exercises general supervision over insurance. Administration of the general system of pensions, health and accident insurance is in the hands of the Social Insurance Institute (IKA). Secondary organisations functioning alongside IKA under the supervision of various ministries provide separate and supplementary insurance in these fields. Employees affiliated to such organisations need not insure with IKA. The most important of the secondary organisations are the Labour and Unemployment Insurance Organisation (OAAA), which administers unemployment insurance and family allowance benefits (IKA collects the contributions), and the Agricultural Insurance Organisation (OGA). Contributions and benefits stated below refer to 1964, and are in all cases subject to maximum monthly earnings of Dr5,250 ($175). All contributions and benefits are also related to 14 wage-classes.

Health insurance: The general system covers all employees in industry and commerce, certain urban self-employed workers and—for medical benefits only—pensioners. There are special systems for agricultural and public employees. The scheme is financed by the insured person and the employer at the rates of 3·25 per cent and 6·25 per cent of earnings (by pensioners at the rate of 4 per cent of pension) plus an annual state subsidy. Medical benefits, provided directly by IKA facilities, include care in sanatoria and nursing homes, maternity and dental care, appliances and transport—for all of which patients pay 25 per cent of costs, free hospitalisation and charges of Dr2 ($0·06) for each prescription. Sickness benefits are paid for up to 180 days (360 days for tuberculosis) and amount to 50 per cent of earnings plus 10 per cent of benefit for up to two dependants, with a maximum daily benefit of Dr60 ($2). Maternity benefits are paid at the same rate for six weeks before and after confinement with a minimum daily benefit of Dr20 ($0·66).

Accident insurance: This covers all employees in industry and commerce and is financed by the employer alone at the rate of 0·5 to 2 per cent of earnings. Medical benefits are the same as for health insurance but entirely free. Temporary disability benefits paid for the duration of the disability are the same as daily sickness benefits. Permanent disability pensions are a minimum of 60 per cent of average earnings over the last two years. Widow's pensions— also payable to needy widowers—are 80 per cent of the insured's pension. Orphan's pensions for children under 18 or invalid are 20 per cent of pension, rising to 60 per cent for the first full orphan. Pensions of 20 per cent of the insured's pension are paid to each parent or grandchild and of 40 per cent to a widowed mother if there is no spouse or orphan. Total pensions may not exceed 100 per cent of the insured's pension, or 80 per cent if the spouse is not a survivor.

Pensions insurance: Coverage is the same as for health insurance. The insurance is financed by the insured and the employer at the respective rates of 2·25 per cent and 5.75 per cent of earnings plus annual state subsidies. Old age pensions are paid at 62 years (57 for women)—a reduced pension may be obtained two years earlier—at the rate of 28 to 98 per cent of average earnings over the last two years, varying inversely according to wage class. For every 300 days of contribution above 3,000 an increment of from 1 to 2·5 per cent of the pension is paid. Dependant's supplements are 50 per cent of pension for wife—with a monthly maximum of Dr287 ($9.50)—and 20,

15 and 10 per cent of pension for the first, second and third children respectively. The maximum pension is 100 per cent of earnings. Invalidity pensions paid on loss of two-thirds of normal earning capacity are identical, except that constant attendance supplements of 50 per cent of the pension plus supplements may be paid, and there is provision for rehabilitation allowances, whereby persons suffering 33 to 66 per cent incapacity are paid the ordinary invalidity pension for up to two years. Survivor's pension is the same as under accident insurance.

Unemployment insurance: This covers all employees in commerce and industry. There are special systems for seamen and printing employees. The insurance is financed by the insured and the employer at the rate of 1 and 2 per cent of earnings respectively. Benefits are paid for a maximum of 12 months in any four-year period, at the rate of 40 per cent of wages and 50 per cent of salary, with a daily maximum of Dr40 ($1·33) and a minimum of two-thirds of an unskilled worker's wages. Dependant's supplements are 10 per cent of earnings for each, with a maximum total benefit of 70 per cent of earnings.

Other benefits: Family allowances are financed equally by the insured and the employer at the rate of 1 per cent of earnings. They are paid for each of two children under 14 (21 if invalid) at a maximum daily rate of Dr3 ($0·10) for each day worked by the parent. The maximum allowance is paid where the parent had 250 days of full employment in the previous year. The OGA insures all agricultural produce against hail and frost.

EDUCATION

Education is free at all levels, including university, higher and special education, and is compulsory for all children from 6 to 15. About 17 per cent of the population are illiterate; this represents a sharp decrease in the proportion over the last 30 years. The state allocates about 14 per cent of the annual budget to education.

Primary education: This lasts from the ages of 6 to 12 in primary schools and children then pass on to secondary education without taking an examination. *Secondary education:* A three-year course at the *gymnasium* may be followed, on passing an entrance examination, by a further three years at the *lyceum*, ending with a leaving examination which is the entry qualification for university. Secondary-school teachers are university graduates. *Vocational and technical education:* There are both private and state schools. Courses begin at the age of 12 and generally last for about three years. Technical and agricultural Gymnasia are planned to absorb about 25 per cent of the total intake of Gymnasia by 1970. *Special education:* There are centres in the main towns of Greece.

University and higher education: There are three universities—the National and Capodistrian and the National Technical (Polytechnic) Universities, both in Athens, and the Aristotelian University in Salonika. Two new universities are to be opened in Ioannina and Patras. Other institutes at university level are graduate schools for economics and commercial sciences, political science, agriculture and fine arts in Athens, and for industrial studies in Piraeus and Salonika. All are autonomous organisations governed by senates of professors, supported by and under the general supervision of the state. Courses last from four to six years. In addition there are 18 higher schools, 14 of which (with a total of 2,949 students in 1965–6) are Pedagogic

Academies offering three-year courses for elementary school teachers. There are government scholarships for undergraduates, post-graduates studying abroad and also for secondary education.

Educational institutions, 1965–6:

	Institutions	Staff	Students
Primary—			
public } private }	9,660	28,028	{ 934,125 { 42,074
Secondary—			
public } private }	648	} 9,948 } 3,485	325,620 43,264
Vocational and Technical—			
public	38	} n.a.	{ 12,120
private	223	} n.a.	{ 47,327
University level	9	1,896	56,037

Adult education: This is not greatly developed and is chiefly in the hands of private organisations such as the Greek YMCA and boy scouts.

Mass Media

The press (Athens-Piraeus area):

Dailies[1]: *Nea*, centre, 143,000; *Messimvrini*, right, 54,000; *Vima*, cen., 44,000; *Acropolis*, rt, 33,000; *Kathinerini*, rt, 30,000; *Apoyevmatini*, rt, 27,000; *Vradini*, rt, 24,000; *Ethnos*, cen., 21,000; *Athninaiki*, cen., 18,000; *Avghi*, EDA, 13,000; *Eleftheria*, Liberal Democratic Centre, 12,000; *Allaghi*, EDA, 10,000; *Estia*, progressive rt, 5,000.

Periodicals: Gynaika (f), woman's, 110,000; *Ikones* (w), illustrated, 60,000; *Aktines* (m), political/cultural/scientific, 10,000; *Nea Estia* (f), literary; *Viomichaniki Epitheorissis* (m), industrial/financial; *Elliniki Oikonomia* (m), economic.

Censorship of publications: The government exercises its control of the supply of newsprint to limit the circulations of selected newspapers.

Broadcasting: The National Institute of Broadcasting (Ethnikon Idryma Radiofonias) has been a state-supervised organisation since 1939. The Director of Broadcasting is appointed by the government. The Greek army operates a small radio station. TV is in the planning and experimental state, but a network will be set up over the next 10 years to cover 80 per cent of the population. The EIR is financed by receipts from licence fees supplemented by government grants-in-aid.

[1] February 1966.

ICELAND

GEOGRAPHY

Features: This island consists of a mountainous, part glacier and snowfield covered core, with much current volcanic activity, and a series of lowlands around the coast, especially on the north and south-west. Much of the central part of the island rises to over 5,000 ft/1,500 m. Fishing is the basis of most industry; the little agriculture that exists is mainly concerned with livestock farming. Minerals are few and power is obtained either from geothermal or hydroelectric sources.

Area: 39,770 sq. miles/103,000 sq. km. *Mean max. and min. temperatures:* Reykjavik (64° N, 22° W; 90 ft/27 m.) 58°F/14°C (July), 28°F/−2°C (Jan. and Feb.). *Relative humidity:* Reykjavik 78 per cent. *Mean annual rainfall:* Reykjavik 34 in./860 mm.

POPULATION

Total population: (1965) 192,000. *Chief towns and populations:* (1965) REYKJAVIK (94,000), (1962) Akureyri (9,500), Kópavogur (8,500), Hafnarfjördur (8,000). *Distribution:* In 1962 about 65 per cent of the population lived in towns with a population of more than 5,000.

Language: The official language, Icelandic, has maintained its separate identity since the 10th century. *Religion:* 96 per cent of the population adhere to the established Evangelical Lutheran Church.

CONSTITUTIONAL SYSTEM

Constitution: Iceland is a republic. The constitution was approved by referendum in June 1944. *Head of state:* President Ásgeir Ásgeirsson. *Head of government:* Prime Minister Dr Bjarni Benediktsson (Independence Party).

Executive: The President is elected for four years by direct vote of the people. He appoints and dismisses ministers, directs the Council of State, and has the power to introduce provisional legislation when the parliament (Althing) is not in session (this power lapses if not certified by the next session of the Althing). Presidential announcements are valid only when countersigned by a minister. The ministers together with the President constitute the Council of State. The ministers have a right to speak in either house of the Althing to which they are responsible, but can vote only if they are elected members.

Legislature: The Althing is composed of 60 members elected for four years. Forty-nine members are elected by proportional representation and the remaining 11 seats are allotted to the parties on a proportional basis. The Althing elects one-third of its members to form the upper house (Efri Deild),

107

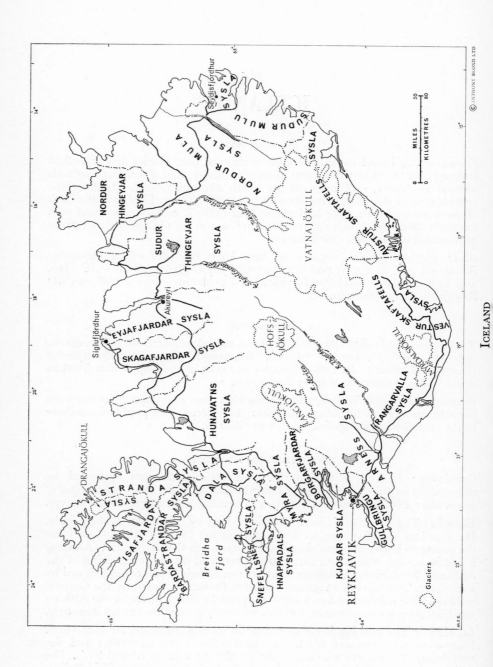

ICELAND

the remainder forming the lower house (Nedri Deild). Ordinary legislation may be introduced by either house, but the budget is composed each year by a united Althing. Legislation passed by the Althing but vetoed by the President becomes law if passed again by a two-thirds majority of the Althing. The Althing can declare no confidence in individual ministers as well as the government as a whole, and impeach ministers by resolution of a joint session of the Althing.

Political parties: There are four parties in Iceland: the Independence Party formed in 1927 from an amalgamation of the Conservative and Liberal parties, the Progressive Party (agrarian), the People's Union (Marxist) and the Social Democrat Party. The present government is a coalition of the Independence and Social Democrat parties.

Election results:

| | 1959[1] | | | | 1963 | |
| | *June* | | *October* | | | |
	Percentage of poll	*Seats*	*Percentage of poll*	*Seats*	*Percentage of poll*	*Seats*
Independence Party .	42·6	20	39·7	24	41·4	24
Progressive Party .	27·3	19	25·7	17	28·2	19
People's Union . .	15·3	7	15·2	10	16·0	9
Social Democrats .	12·4	6	16·0	9	16·0	9
Others	2·4	—	3·4	—	0·2	—

[1] Two elections were held in 1959, the latter one taking place after a constitutional amendment had altered the electoral system so as to abolish the single-member rural constituencies.

Leading political figures: Independence Party—Bjarni Benediktsson (Prime Minister), Magnús Jónsson (Minister of Finance). Social Democrats—Emil Jónsson (Foreign Minister and Party President). Progressives—Eysteinn Jónsson (Party Leader). People's Union—Hannibal Valdimarsson (Party Chairman).

Local government: Iceland is divided into 16 Provinces (*sýslur*) formed from more than 200 rural Municipalities (*sveit*). Each Province elects a Council (*sýslunefnd*) headed by a government-appointed Sheriff (*sýslumadur*) who is Chief of Police and Provincial Judge. The 14 Urban Municipalities (*baejir*) form separate administrative districts, independent of but coordinating with the Provinces. Each elects an Urban Council (*baejarstjórn*) which in turn appoints a chairman.

Judicial system: The common courts have two instances. The lower is the Provincial Court presided over by either a Sheriff or a Town Judge. The higher stage is the Supreme Court (Hæstiréttur) composed of the Chief Justice and four ordinary justices. In addition there are special courts such as the Maritime and Commercial Courts of which the higher stage is again the Supreme Court. There is no death penalty.

RECENT HISTORY

Iceland became a republic in 1944 when the population voted in favour of severing the final links with the Danish Crown. In 1949 Iceland joined NATO and the Council of Europe and in 1953 became a founder-member of the Nordic Council. A dispute over fishing limits with Britain (1958–64) was finally settled with Iceland maintaining twelve-mile territorial waters. *Defence:* Iceland although a member of NATO has no armed forces or defence budget of its own. American forces fulfil this function as part of NATO strategy.

ECONOMY

Background: Over 75 per cent of Iceland's land area is unproductive; the economy depends heavily upon fish and fish products. Since 1961 a high rate of economic growth has been maintained at the cost of inflation. In 1964 the value of GNP at current prices was estimated to be IKr17,254 million ($401 million); the annual average increase in GNP between 1962 and 1965 was over 6 per cent, mainly owing to expansion in fishing, building and construction, and (to a lesser extent) agriculture. Expansion has been influenced by a rapid increase in the labour force which from mid-1960 to mid-1964 rose by an annual average of 2 per cent. Industrial production rose sharply in 1962-3, declined in 1964 and regained its previous high level in 1965. In 1964 the value of fish and fish processing production amounted to about 25 per cent of GNP at current prices, and agricultural production to about 9 per cent. Livestock farming, particularly milk and sheep products, is the most important form of agricultural activity. The major reasons for expansion in fishing and agricultural production have been mechanisation and a high rate of investment.

Foreign trade: The surplus on the current account of the balance of payments in 1961 and 1962 followed the introduction of the 1960 stabilisation programme which included devaluation. Owing to a sharp increase in imports, deficits occurred in 1963 and 1964. Exports and imports in 1964 amounted to 41 and 43 per cent of GNP at current prices, main exports being fish and fish products (92 per cent of total exports) and main imports manufactures and equipment (72 per cent) and fuels (9 per cent). In 1963 main export markets in terms of value were: Britain 19 per cent, the United States 15 per cent, the Soviet Union 11 per cent, West Germany 10·5 per cent and Sweden 7 per cent. Imports were mainly distributed: Britain 14 per cent, the United States and West Germany 12 per cent each, the Soviet Union and Norway 10 per cent each, and Sweden 6 per cent.

Employment: The working population rose rapidly from mid-1960 to mid-1964 to a total of 73,000. In 1964 the distribution of labour was: agriculture and fishing 36 per cent, industry and construction 28 per cent and services 36 per cent. Increased employment has contributed to the strong pressure of demand.

Price and wage trends: The cost of living index rose by an annual average of 17 per cent between 1961 and 1964. From 1963 to 1964 the price of consumer goods rose by 19 per cent, wage earnings by 30 per cent and the cost of living index by 19 per cent. The government in 1965 proposed to set up an Economic Council including representatives of government, trade unions, business and farmers.

Consumption: In 1964 private consumption amounted to 64 per cent of GNP at current prices and public consumption to 8·7 per cent; this represented estimated increases of 3 and 4·1 per cent respectively over 1963, compared with increases of 7 and 7·5 per cent in 1963 over 1962.

ICELAND

SOCIAL SECURITY

The Ministry of Social Affairs exercises general supervision over the scheme, with the State Social Security Institute administering the programme through its local offices, except in the case of health insurance, where the Institute supervises the various sickness funds. Contributions and benefits stated below refer to 1964.

Health insurance: All persons aged between 16 and 66 are compulsory members of sickness funds. Insurance is financed by insured persons paying flat-rate contributions to the funds—which vary according to the locality (IKr65 ($1·50) per month in Reykjavik)—and by state subsidies (worth 110 per cent of members' contributions) and municipal subsidies (worth 50 per cent of contributions). Maternity grants and pensioners' benefits are financed from pension contributions. Benefits are provided by doctors and hospitals contracted to and directly paid by the funds. The funds must provide minimum benefits of: general practitioner services (with patients paying IKr10 ($0·23) per office visit and IKr25 ($0·57) per home visit), 75 per cent of costs of specialist treatment, free hospital care and vital medicines, with part-cost of other medicines, and 75 per cent of X-ray costs. Daily sickness benefits are a statutory minimum of IKr70 ($1·60), with supplements of IKr9 ($0·20) for the insured's wife and each of three children. Sickness benefits are paid for a maximum of 52 weeks in any two-year period. Lump sum maternity grants are IKr4,600 ($106) for each birth.

Accident insurance: This covers all employees except casual employees in non-hazardous occupations and is financed by the employer at a varying weekly rate up to IKr36 ($0·83). Benefits are all necessary care including hospital and specialist treatment. Daily temporary disability benefit is paid at the rate of IKr87.5 ($2) with the same dependant supplements as for sickness insurance, with a maximum benefit of 75 per cent of earnings. For permanent (i.e. more than 75 per cent) disability, monthly pensions are IKr1,750 ($40·25) with supplements of 50 per cent of pension for each child under 16. For partial disability of 50 to 74 per cent pensions are 50 per cent of full pension plus 2 per cent of full pension for each 1 per cent of disability greater than 50 per cent. A lump sum proportionate to the loss of wages is paid for disability estimated at 15 to 49 per cent. Death grants to survivors are IKr2,300 ($53) paid for eight years, plus a pension of up to IKr1,750 ($40·25) according to age or degree of disability, if a widow is aged 50 or invalid. Each orphan under 16 receives a monthly pension of IKr805 ($18·5).

Pension insurance: This covers all residents, with special systems for public employees and certain other occupations. Flat-rate contributions, paid by all persons aged 16 to 66 except married women, of IKr1,570–2,300 ($36–53) annually—according to sex and marital status—provide about 33 per cent of costs, weekly employers' contributions of IKr20 ($0·46) per employee provide about 15 per cent of costs, and national and local government subsidies cover 33 and 19 per cent of costs respectively. Old-age pensions paid at 67 are worth IKr1,750 per month. Supplements are 80 per cent of pension for a wife aged 67, 50 per cent for each child under 16, and increments for each year of pension-deferment up to a maximum of 67 per cent for a five-year deferment. Invalidity pensions are paid up on loss of 75 per cent of earning capacity at the same rate as for the old-age pension, with up to double the ordinary pension for those requiring special care, and the same child supplements. Widow's temporary pensions of IKr2,300 per month are paid for three months and for a further nine months—with a 25 per cent reduction—if the widow is caring for a child under 16. This is followed by a permanent monthly pension of IKr1,750 for women aged over 50 at time of widowhood (reduced by 6 per cent for each year she is less than 67). All widows receive monthly pensions of IKr155, 875 or 1,750 ($2·76, 19.3 or 40·25) if they have one, two or three children. Monthly orphan's pensions are IKr805.

Unemployment insurance: This covers all trade union members in communities of at least 300 persons, with the exception of commercial, office and public employees. It is financed by employers at the rate of 1 per cent of an unskilled worker's wage per employee with an equivalent contribution from local government and double the contribution from the state. Daily benefits, payable for up to four months per year, are IKr24 ($0·60) plus IKr6 ($0·15) for a wife and each of up to three children.

Other benefits: Family allowances are paid by the state to all residents at the monthly rate of IKr250 ($5.75) for each child under 16.

EDUCATION

Primary education: Education is compulsory between 7 and 15. At the age of 13, elementary education is completed by examination. *Secondary education:* The two remaining years of compulsory education are spent according to the examination result, in two-year Youth Schools, three-year Intermediate Schools or four-year Grammar Schools, all divided into theoretical and practical divisions. Successful pupils from the third year of the theory section of Intermediate and Grammar Schools enter either Teacher-Training Schools or Senior Grammar Schools for four-year courses, terminated by a Student examination that permits access to the university.

Vocational education: For seamen there are one- to three-year courses at both a Navigation and an Engineering School. *Trade and technical schools:* These offer mainly evening classes for three- to four-year courses. *Special education:* There are schools for the blind and the deaf and dumb in Reykjavik.

University education: The University of Reykjavik has faculties of theology, medicine, law and economics, philosophy and engineering and a research institute for fishing, industry and agriculture. University education is free of charge.

Educational institutions, 1963:

	Institutions	Staff	Students
Primary	217	1,067	24,997
Secondary	96	1,018	11,715
Technical and vocational .	42	392	3,314
Teacher-training . .	3	67	305
University	1	111	900

MASS MEDIA

The press (Reykjavik):

Dailies: Morgunbladid, independent, 32,000; *Tíminn,* Progressive, 18,500; *Visir,* Independence Party, 16,000; *Thjódviljinn,* People's Union, 11,000; *Altbýdubladid,* socialist.

Periodicals: Samtídin (m), literary, 35,000; *Vikan* (w), illustrated, 12,000; *Fálkinn* (w), illus., 10,000.

Broadcasting: Radio and TV broadcasting are a monopoly of the Icelandic State Broadcasting Service (Rikisútvarpid), an independent authority. The American Armed Forces Radio and TV Service operates a 24-hour radio station. Both the US Air Force and the US Navy operate TV services from Keflavík.

REPUBLIC OF IRELAND

GEOGRAPHY

Features: The country consists of an extensive boulder clay and peat infilled depression, including the major bog areas, surrounded by uplands—Donegal in the north-west, Wicklow Mountains in the east, Connemara in the west and the Hercynian uplands of Kerry and Cork in the south-west. In many places these uplands rise to over 1,500 ft/450 m. and reach 3,000 ft in the Wicklow Mountains and Kerry. The central plain, drained mainly by the Shannon and Boyne, has a number of low hill ridges, especially in the north-east and south-west.

There are few mineral resources. The Shannon provides HEP and the peat bogs provide fuel for a number of thermal power stations; otherwise fuel has to be imported. Industry is concentrated mainly around Dublin Bay, Cork and Wexford. The Republic is predominantly an agricultural country with its best farmlands concentrated in the south and east where climate, soils and relief are most favourable.

Area: 27,140 sq. miles/70,280 sq. km. *Mean max. and min. temperatures:* Dublin (53° 30′ N, 6° 30′ W; 155 ft/47 m.) 67°F/19°C (July and Aug.), 35°F/2°C (Jan. and Feb.). *Relative humidity:* Dublin 83 per cent. *Mean annual rainfall:* 30 in./760 mm.

POPULATION

Total population: (1966) 2,881,000. *Chief towns and populations:* DUBLIN (568,000), Cork (122,000), Limerick (56,000), Dún Laoghaire (52,000), Waterford (30,000), Galway (24,000). *Distribution:* In 1966 62 per cent of the population lived in rural areas and towns of less than 10,000 inhabitants, 6 per cent in towns with 10–50,000 inhabitants and 32 per cent in towns with populations of more than 50,000.

Language: Gaelic (Irish) is the official language and English the second official language. In 1961 27 per cent of the population was Gaelic-speaking. *Religion:* About 94 per cent of the population are Roman Catholic, 4 per cent Church of Ireland (Anglican) and less than 1 per cent Presbyterian. Although there is no state religion (the state however recognising the special position of the Catholic Church as the religion of the great majority of the population) and freedom of worship is guaranteed, the religious issue remains the fundamental basis for the continued division of Ireland from the predominantly Protestant Six Counties of Northern Ireland.

CONSTITUTIONAL SYSTEM

Constitution: The constitution, adopted by referendum in 1937, describes Ireland as a sovereign independent and democratic state (nowhere as a 'republic') and declares the national territory to be the whole island, but that pending reunification, the jurisdiction of the Irish parliament and government shall be restricted to the 26 Southern Counties. *Head of state:* President Éamonn de Valéra (Fianna Fáil). *Head of government:* Prime Minister (Taoiseach) Jack Lynch (Fianna Fáil).

Executive: The President (Uachtarán) is elected by direct vote of the population for seven years and is eligible for a second term. He appoints the Taoiseach and other ministers upon the nomination of the House of Representatives (Dáil). He normally acts upon the advice of the government, and on the advice of the Taoiseach he dissolves parliament, although at his absolute discretion he may refuse to do so. He signs and promulgates legislation and receives and accredits ambassadors. In certain functions he is aided by a Council of State (Comhairle Stáit). Under certain circumstances he has the power to refer legislation to referendum or to the Supreme Court (Cúirt Uachtarach). The government consists of seven to 15 members, collectively responsible to the Dáil. The Taoiseach, Deputy Prime Minister (Tánaiste) and Minister of Finance must be members of the Dáil, and only two members of the government at most may be members of the Senate (Seanad).

Legislature: Sole legislative power is vested in the National Parliament (Oireachtas) consisting of the Dáil and the Seanad. The Dáil has 144 members elected for five years by the single transferable vote system of proportional representation. The Seanad, which sits for the same period, has 60 members: 43 are elected as representatives of cultural and vocational interests, the two universities elect three each and the remaining 11 are nominated by the Taoiseach. Legislation may originate in either house, save money bills which must originate in the Dáil. The Seanad may delay a bill passed by the lower house for a maximum of 90 days, and may suggest amendments—except to money bills where it has only powers of recommendation—but it has no power of permanent veto.

Referendum: On petition to the President by a majority of the Seanad and at least one-third of the Dáil, certain bills passed by both houses may be referred to the electorate.

Political parties: Ireland's three main parties are Fianna Fáil (Republican Party), Fine Gael (United Ireland Party) and the Labour Party. Sinn Féin is not represented in the Dáil.

Election results:

Party	1961 Percentage of poll	Seats	1965 Percentage of poll	Seats
Fianna Fáil . .	43·8	70	47·6	72
Fine Gael . . .	32·1	47	34·2	47
Labour . . .	11·8	16	15·3	22
Others . . .	12·3	11	2·9	3

Leading political figures: Fianna Fáil—Jack Lynch (Taoiseach), Frank Aiken (Tanaiste and Minister of External Affairs), Charles Haughey (Finance Minister), Erskine H. Childers (Minister for Transport and Power). Fine Gael—Tom O'Higgins (Party Presidential Candidate in 1966), Liam Cosgrave (Party Leader). Labour Party—James Tully (Party Leader).

115

Local government: Ireland is divided into 26 Counties. In addition there are four County Boroughs and seven Boroughs divided into Urban Districts governed by elected local councils; the larger towns are governed by Town Commissioners. Finance is met from rates and state grants. General supervision is exercised by the Department of Local Government, while the Departments of Health and Social Welfare are responsible for health and public assistance administration.

Judicial system: The lowest courts are the District Courts, which have civil jurisdiction up to £50 ($140) and conduct preliminary hearings in criminal cases. Each is presided over by a District judge who must be a lawyer of 10 years' standing. Appeal is to the Circuit Court, which has civil jurisdiction to £600 ($1,680) and extended criminal jurisdiction. There are nine Circuit Court judges of whom two are assigned to Dublin. In appropriate cases the judge sits with jury. The High Court (Árd-Cúirt) has full jurisdiction. It consists of a President, six judges, the Chief Justice (Príomh-Bhreitheamh) and the President of the Circuit Court. It is normally constituted by one judge, but in exceptional circumstances a panel of three sits. It hears appeals from the Circuit Courts. The Central Criminal Court is constituted by one judge sitting with jury, and appeal from its decision is to the Court of Criminal Appeal consisting of one judge of the Supreme Court and two High Court judges appointed by the Chief Justice. The final court of appeal is the Supreme Court which comprises four ordinary judges, the Chief Justice and the President of the High Court. It sits either as a court of three or five.

Judges are appointed by the President on the advice of the government and may be dismissed only for misbehaviour or incapacity upon a resolution passed by both houses of parliament. Ireland maintains capital punishment for treason, murder of police or prison officers, for political murders and certain military offences. There is no provision for divorce.

RECENT HISTORY

After an uprising against the British in 1916 proclaiming Ireland a sovereign republic, Ireland, hitherto part of the United Kingdom of Great Britain and Ireland, was reaffirmed a republic in 1919 by the independence party Sinn Féin. Britain provided for separate subordinate parliaments for the Roman Catholic south and the six Protestant north-eastern Counties (Government of Ireland Act, 1920) which led to the establishment of the Government of Northern Ireland in 1921 (see under *United Kingdom of Great Britain and Northern Ireland—Constitutional System: Northern Ireland*). Ireland excluding the Six Counties was accorded Dominion status by Britain in 1922 as the Irish Free State. The present name of the state, Ireland (Éire) was established by the 1937 constitution (see above under *Constitution*). Ireland was neutral in the second world war. After Ireland in 1948 described itself as a republic, Britain passed the Ireland Act, 1949 declaring that Ireland had by this action placed itself outside the Commonwealth. This act also provides that no part of Northern Ireland may cease to belong to the United Kingdom without the consent of the Northern Ireland parliament. However, Ireland is not treated as a foreign state and its citizens need no passports to enter Britain.

Ireland has continually sought to end the division of the island by peaceful methods. It declined to join NATO in 1949 because of the division, but was admitted to the UN in 1955 and has provided forces for UN operations in the Lebanon, the Congo and Cyprus. In July 1961 Ireland applied for EEC membership and in 1965 signed a Free Trade Treaty with Britain. In November 1966 Séan Lemass, who earlier in the year had unsuccessfully proposed to the Northern Ireland Prime Minister a meeting of an all-Ireland parliament, resigned as Taoiseach.

Defence: The President is commander-in-chief of Ireland's defence forces, into which all the services are integrated, and which are composed solely of volunteers. The permanent defence force numbers over 13,000 with reserve forces of about 25,000. The 1966–7 defence estimates were over £10·8 million ($30·3 million) representing about 1·4 per cent of GNP.

ECONOMY

Background: A shortage of natural resources, especially coal and iron, has necessitated a heavy emphasis on agriculture. However, light industry and tourism have grown over the past decade. From 1958, the year of the first national plan, the economy expanded rapidly. By 1964–5 prices and the current external deficit were rising rapidly. Government measures taken included a reduction in the public capital programme for 1965–6, restriction of government current expenditure, discouragement of imports through credit and hire-purchase restrictions, price-control legislation, export promotion and encouragement of savings. In 1965 GNP at current prices was estimated to be £1,002 million ($2,806 million), which represented an increase of 2·5 per cent in volume over 1964 compared with an increase of 4 per cent 1964/63. From 1958 to 1963 GNP grew at an annual average rate of 4 per cent, achieving the 2 per cent target of the first economic programme. The target for the second was increased to 4 per cent to cover the years 1964–70. Both programmes followed the same basic principles—a reliance on private enterprise plus state assistance and concentration on productive investment.

The main industries are food and tobacco manufacturing and brewing; in recent years the output of lead, zinc and copper concentrates has grown considerably. The main agricultural products are livestock, vegetables and cereals. In 1964 the origin of GDP at factor cost was:

Sector	Percentage
Agriculture	22
Industry	32
Service	46
GDP	100

Foreign trade: The current deficit rose from £31 million ($87 million) in 1964 to £44 million ($123 million) in 1965. The major exports in 1964 were live cattle (25 per cent of total exports), other agricultural products (12 per cent), textile manufactures (4 per cent) and machinery and electrical goods (4 per cent). The main customers were Britain (72 per cent) and the EEC (12 per cent). The major imports in 1964 were machinery and electrical goods (17 per cent), chemicals (8 per cent), vehicles (8 per cent) and textile manufactures (7 per cent). Over half of Ireland's imports came from Britain and 16 per cent from the EEC. In 1964 Irish exports amounted to 37 per cent of GNP at current prices and imports to 42 per cent.

Employment: The total working population declined from a peak of over 1·2 million in 1936 to just over 1·05 million in 1964. This trend is primarily due to net emigration, which totalled over 178,000 in the period 1959–65 alone. Agriculture continues to provide employment for about 33 per cent of the working population, and is declining steadily as industrialisation and mechanisation in agriculture increase. In 1964 the industrial sector provided employment for 27 per cent of the working population and services 40 per cent.

Price and wage trends: Between 1960 and 1964 unit wage costs rose by 16 per cent and consumer prices by 20 per cent. The cost of living in Ireland was previously somewhat lower than in other countries of Western Europe, but as elsewhere it has risen steadily since 1945 and sharply since 1960.

Consumption: Private consumption was estimated to amount to 70 per cent of GNP in 1965 (at current prices) and public consumption to about 12·5 per cent. This represents a lower annual increase in consumption than in 1964, amounting to 6·9 per cent and 5 per cent respectively.

SOCIAL SECURITY

Social insurance is compulsory for almost all workers between the ages of 16 and 70 earning below £1,200 ($3,360) annually. Those earning more may contribute voluntarily at a lower rate and for limited benefits. The weekly contribution of 14s 8d ($1·90) in 1966 is divided equally between employer and employee and gives title to disability, unemployment, marriage and maternity benefits, medical treatment benefits and also to widow's, orphan's and old-age pensions.

Health insurance: There is no national health service. The health service is operated mainly by local councils under the general direction of the Ministry of Health. Free school examinations and services against tuberculosis and infectious diseases are available to all, and a free comprehensive medical service is provided for the lower income groups. Those in the middle-income bracket (earning below £1,200 or $3,360) are entitled to free maternity and infant welfare service and to low-charge hospital and specialist services. In general, anyone in the highest income range must pay all his medical costs. A Voluntary Health Insurance Board, established by the state but financially autonomous, is open to all, whether or not entitled to health benefits.

Accident insurance: Disability benefits are paid continuously where 156 contributions have been made and for 52 weeks where between 26 and 156 contributions have been made. Weekly benefits are 52s 6d ($7.35) for a single adult, increased by 40s ($5·60) for each dependant adult and 13s ($1·80) for each of the first two dependant children and 8s ($1·10) for each other child.

Pensions insurance: Pensions are paid to men and women after the age of 70 at a maximum weekly rate of £3 ($8·40) per person and an additional 47s 6d ($7.70) for a wife or invalid husband. Contributory widow's pensions are worth 52s 6d ($7.35) per week with additional allowances for children. Weekly benefits for orphans under 16 are 35s ($4.90).

Unemployment benefits: The claimant must be under 70 years of age and available for work. After 156 days requalification is necessary for claimants under 65. The benefits are the same as for disability.

Other benefits: Monthly family allowances for children under 16 are paid regardless of means at the rate of 10s ($1·40) for the first, 15s 6d ($2·20) for the second and 26s 6d ($3.70) for each subsequent child. Marriage benefits are lump sums of from £3 to £10 ($8·40 to $28). Maternity benefits are £4 ($11·20) for the confinement plus twelve weekly allowances of 55s ($7.70).

EDUCATION

Primary education: Education is compulsory between six and 14. The upper age-limit is to be raised to 15 by 1970. Primary education is provided free in national schools. As far as is possible the state delegates local management of primary education to the various religious denominations, while meeting most of its costs and retaining a large degree of control over its operation. No child may be refused admission to school on religious grounds or be required to attend religious instruction against parental wishes. The Department of Education is responsible for the educational programme, the approval of teacher's qualifications and payment of teaching salaries, as well as the inspection and supervision of the Primary School Certificate examination. There are a few private schools that receive no state assistance.

Secondary and vocational education: Secondary education begins at the age of 12 or 13 and lasts from five to six years. Admission is based on the result of the Primary Certificate examination or an equivalent entrance examination. Secondary schools are private institutions, which the state assists by paying grants to the school for each eligible pupil and 75 per cent of the salaries of registered teachers. The Department of Education lays down the programme for its two examinations—the Intermediate Certificate usually taken after three years' secondary education, and the Leaving Certificate taken at the end of the course at about 17 or 18 years of age. Gaelic is a compulsory subject in the Leaving Certificate except for those children who have received their primary education, before 11 years of age, outside Ireland: these may substitute another language for Gaelic. Average annual fees range from £50 to £200 ($140 to $560) for boarding schools and from £12 to £30 ($34 to $84) for day schools. Secondary education is dependent upon the ability to afford it; a few scholarships are available.

Vocational education takes the form of continuation education, supplementing primary education and providing practical training for future employment for pupils of 13–14 years of age by two- to three-year-long day-courses. Since 1963 the government has introduced a system of free comprehensive schooling that combines secondary and continuation education, and has extended vocational courses so that all students take a new form of Intermediate Certificate at all post-primary schools. After this students may change from one system to another and a new two-year technical course leading to a Technical Leaving Certificate is to be added to the list of options. Vocational education is the function of the Vocational Education Committees, elected by local authorities. Each Committee is financed by the state (about two-thirds), the local authority and to a small extent by tuition fees and miscellaneous sources.

Special education: There are special national schools for mentally and physically handicapped children, some residential and some day-schools, run by both religious orders and lay organisations. In addition there are special classes attached to ordinary national schools, mainly in Dublin.

University education: The National University of Ireland was founded in 1908 and is organised on a federal basis into constituent colleges at Dublin, Cork, Galway and a recognised college (St Patrick's Maynooth) and has about 10,000 students. Trinity College, Dublin (mainly Protestant), has over 3,000 students of whom about 28 per cent come from Britain. Both the National University and Trinity College are self-governing, but are financed through the Department of Education by annual grants-in-aid. Grants are awarded to students by the state, local authorities (with state aid) and the universities themselves.

Possession of the Secondary School Leaving Certificate usually exempts candidates from taking the entrance examinations of the universities. Gaelic is a compulsory subject in the Matriculation Certificate of the National University, but not for Trinity College. The Royal College of Surgeons in Dublin has some 800 students. As in Scotland considerable numbers of students choose three-subject general degrees in preference to specialised honours degrees. Degree courses last three or four years (six for medicine). Trinity College degrees are recognised in Britain. Medical degrees awarded in Britain and Ireland are recognised on a reciprocal basis.

Educational institutions, 1962–3:

	Institutions	Teachers	Students
Primary	4,864	14,622	502,059
Secondary . . .	557	5,908	84,916
Vocational and technical .	754	3,722	101,424
Special (1945-5) . . .	52	244	3,175

Adult education: Technical education for adults, apprentices and other persons in employment, leading in some cases to professional qualifications, is held at both day and evening courses. In 1963 there were 3,379 public libraries.

MASS MEDIA

The press :

Dailies: Irish Independent, Dublin, independent, 175,000; *Evening Press,* Dublin, ind., 145,000; *Evening Herald,* Dublin, ind., 139,000; *Irish Press,* Dublin, ind., 116,000; *Cork Examiner,* Cork, ind., 51,000; *Irish Times,* Dublin, liberal, 38,000; *Cork Evening Echo,* Cork, ind., 34,000.

Periodicals: The Sunday Press (s), Dublin, ind., 422,500; *The Sunday Independent* (s), Dublin, ind., 320,000; *Irish Catholic* (w), Dublin, Catholic, 65,000; *Irish Farmer's Journal* (w), Dublin, agricultural, 58,000; *Ireland of the Welcomes* (2m), Dublin, tourist, 55,000; *The Pioneer* (m), Dublin, Total Abstinence Society, 54,000; *Ireland's Own* (w), Dublin, family, 49,000; *The Standard* (w), Dublin, Cath., 45,000; *The Kerryman* (w), Tralee, ind., 41,000; *Hibernia* (m), Dublin, Cath. political-cultural.

Censorship of publications: A five-member Censorship of Publications Board under the supervision of the Ministry of Justice reviews books submitted by individuals or authorities (e.g. customs officials) and frequently stops publication. The Church also exercises considerable influence both directly and indirectly on book publishers and on the press.

Broadcasting: Radio and TV broadcasting is controlled and operated by Radio Éireann, an autonomous public corporation which derives its revenue from licence fees, advertising and state grants. The director-general of Radio Éireann is appointed by the government.

ITALY

GEOGRAPHY

Features: Italy is a peninsula protruding into the northern Mediterranean. In the north the Italian Alps, sometimes exceeding 12,000 ft/3,650 m. and including a number of lakes, e.g. Lake Como, provide an almost complete physical as well as political frontier; they form a broad arc from the San Remo area in the west to Trieste in the east. East and south of the Alps is the lowland drained by the east-flowing Po river (Po Valley or Lombardy Plain). This is the most extensive area of lowland in the whole of Italy. The Apennine range rising to over 5,000 ft/1,500 m. runs the whole length of the peninsula, in places close to the Adriatic, in others closer to the western coast. In this area lowlands are scattered and limited in extent and nearly all confined to the coastal belt. Sicily is triangular in shape with the highest region around Mount Etna, 10,741 ft/3,274 m. in the north-east. Almost the whole island is above 1,000 ft/300 m. Sardinia is also almost entirely mountainous.

Because of the hilly terrain, lack of water in summer and relatively poor soils, good agricultural land is very limited in extent. The two chief agricultural areas are the Campagna close to Rome, and the Po Valley. Coal resources are scarce but natural gas has been exploited on a large scale in the Po Valley and some oil has been found in Sicily. Considerable hydro-electric potential also exists in the Alps. Principal mineral ores are bauxite, mined in the central Apennines, and sulphur. Apart from the industrial development that has taken place around Rome and more particularly Naples, the main industrial region lies in the northern plain, and is concentrated in particular around Milan, Turin and Genoa.

Area: 116,300 sq. miles/301,200 sq. km. *Mean max. and min. temperatures:* Rome (42° N, 12° 30′ E; 380 ft/115 m.) 88°F/31°C (July and Aug.), 39°F/4°C (Jan. and Feb.); Milan (45° 30′ N, 9° 30′ E; 340 ft/105 m.) 84°F/29°C (July), 29°F/−2°C (Jan.); Palermo (38° N, 13° 30′ E; 350 ft/105 m.) 87°F/31°C (Aug.), 47°F/8°C (Jan. and Feb.). *Relative humidity:* Rome 81 per cent; Milan 89 per cent; Palermo 70 per cent. *Mean annual rainfall:* Rome 26 in./660 mm.; Milan 32 in./815 mm.; Palermo 28 in./710 mm.

POPULATION

Total population: (1966) 53,129,000. *Main towns and populations:* (1966) ROME (2,542,000), Milan (1,675,000), Naples (1,242,000), Turin (1,107,000), Genoa (848,000), Palermo (639,000), Bologna (481,000), Florence (454,000). *Distribution:* In 1961 25 per cent of the population lived in cities of more than 100,000 inhabitants, 35 per cent in centres of 10–100,000 and 40 per cent in centres of less than 10,000.

ITALY

Language: Italian is the official language but the German-speaking citizens of Trentino-Alto Adige and the French-speaking population of Val d'Aosta are guaranteed the right to use their native tongue as well as Italian. There are also Slav, Greek and Albanian minorities. *Religion:* Over 90 per cent of the population professes the state Roman Catholic religion. Relations between Church and state are governed by the Lateran Pact.

CONSTITUTIONAL SYSTEM

Constitution: Republic. A referendum in June 1946 abolished the monarchy, and a new constitution approved by a Constituent Assembly came into force in January 1948 (see under *Recent History*). *Head of state:* President Giuseppe Saragat (PSU). *Head of government:* Prime Minister Aldo Moro (Christian Democrat).

Executive: The President is elected for seven years by joint session of the two houses of parliament and representatives of the Regions elected by the Regional Councils (see under *Local government*). A two-thirds majority is required, but after a third ballot a simple majority is sufficient. The President appoints the Prime Minister and—on the recommendation of the Prime Minister—the Council of Ministers (Consiglio dei Ministri); he can dissolve parliament, but not in the last six months of his office; he may request either house to reexamine legislation in more detail, but if it is passed again it must be promulgated; he promulgates laws and issues decrees with the force of law. The government wields executive power. It must present itself within 10 days of its formation to a confidence vote of both houses. It is responsible to parliament, although ministers may be nominated from outside. It can be forced to resign only by a successful censure motion. Ministers counter-sign presidential acts and are individually responsible for their departments as well as collectively responsible for the cabinet as a whole.

Legislature: Parliament consists of two houses. The Chamber of Deputies (Camera dei Deputati) has 630 members elected for five years by proportional representation. The Senate (Senato), which is elected for six years (though in 1958 and 1963 it was dissolved together with the Chamber), has 321 members of whom six are life Senators. The remainder are elected by all Italians over 25 (the voting age for the Chamber of Deputies is 21) on a population basis with at least seven Senators per Region (but only one for the Val d'Aosta). Legislation may be introduced in either house, but must be passed by both houses to become law. In exceptional circumstances parliament may delegate legislative functions to the government.

Political parties: The two largest political parties in Italy are the (Catholic) Christian Democrat Party (DC) which has provided every Prime Minister since December 1945, and the Italian Communist Party (PCI). Although the latter is the largest Communist party in Western Europe and has the greatest electoral support, it has not found government representation since 1947. In October 1966 pro-Chinese elements founded a new party, the Marxist-Leninist Party of Italy (PCd'IML). The Italian Socialist Party (PSI or Nenni Socialists) and the Italian Social Democrat Party (PSDI or Saragat Socialists), which broke away from the PSI in 1947 after the latter's pact of unity with the PCI, reunited in October 1966 under Pietro Nenni into what is provisionally called the United Socialist Party (PSU), the two separate party organisations continuing to function temporarily.

123

Italy's first centre-left coalition—the *apertura a sinistra* consisting of the DC, PSDI and PRI with the benevolent neutrality of the PSI—took office under Amintore Fanfani in February 1962 and was consolidated in December 1963 under Aldo Moro including the PSI. This coalition marks an important change in Italian politics, since it constitutes the only democratic coalition that can bring about key reforms. The coalition has also resulted in the isolation and disunity of the PCI and Socialist reunification which may ultimately lead to the replacement of the PCI as the main party of the left and of the DC as the main government party.

The other parties are the right-wing Italian Liberal Party (PLI), the Italian Republican Party (PRI) based upon Mazzinian principles, the extreme-left Italian Proletarian Unity Party (PSIUP) formed in January 1964 by members who broke away from the PSI after the latter had entered the centre-left coalition government, the neo-Fascist Italian Social Movement (MSI)—the constitution forbids the reconstitution of the Fascist Party, and the Monarchists (PDIUM).

Election results: The number of seats of both Senate and Chamber was increased between the 1958 and 1963 elections by presidential decree.

Chamber of Deputies

Party	1958 Percentage of poll	Seats	1963 Percentage of poll	Seats
DC	42·3	273	38·3	260
PCI	22·7	140	25·3	166
PSI	14·2	84	13·8	87
PLI	3·5	17	7·0	39
PSDI	4·6	22	6·1	33
MSI	4·7	24	5·1	27
PDIUM	4·8	25	1·7	8
PRI	1·4	6	1·4	6
Others	1·8	5	1·3	4

Senate

Party	1958 Percentage of poll	Seats	1963 Percentage of poll	Seats
DC	41·2	123	37·2	133
PCI	21·8	59	25·5	85
PSI	14·1	35	14·0	44
PLI	3·9	4	7·5	19
MSI	5·6	8	6·2	15
PSDI	4·4	5	6·3	14
PDIUM	5·2	7	1·6	2
PRI	1·4	—	0·8	—
Others	2·4	5	0·9	3

Leading political figures: DC—Aldo Moro (Prime Minister and Party Leader), Amintore Fanfani (Foreign Minister), Emilio Colombo (Minister of the Treasury), Giulio Andreotti (Minister of Industry and Commerce). PSU—

Pietro Nenni (Deputy Prime Minister and Party Leader), Francesco de Martino (PSI Secretary-General), Mario Tanassi (PSDI Secretary-General), Roberto Tremelloni (Minister of Defence). PCI—Luigi Longo (Secretary-General), Giorgio Amendola, Pietro Ingrao, Giancarla Pajetta. PLI—Gaetano Martino (Party President). PRI—Ugo La Malfa (Party Secretary). MSI—Augusto de Marsanich (Party President). PDIUM—Achille Lauro (Party President). PSIUP—Tullio Vechietti (Party Secretary).

Local government: Italy is divided into 19 Regions (*regione*), of which five—Sicily, Sardinia, Val D'Aosta, Trentino-Alto Adige and Friuli-Venezia-Giulia—have special statutes with provisions relating to local powers and defining the extent of regional autonomy. These five Regions elect Regional Councils (*consigli regionali*), each of which elects in turn an executive arm, the Regional Junta (*giunta regionale*). The other 14 Regions are administrative areas only, as no regional statute has been passed by parliament. A government-appointed Commissioner (*commissario*) supervises state administrative functions and coordinates them with those of the Region. Italy is divided further into 92 Provinces (*province*) and about 8,000 Communes (*comuni*). The Provincial Councils (*consigli provinciali*) are elected for four years; each elects a Provincial Junta (*giunta provinciale*) headed by a President as its executive arm. The central government is represented in the Provinces by a Prefect (*prefetto*) who may veto provincial legislation, dissolve Provincial or Communal Councils and transfer their functions to a Prefectoral Commissioner pending new elections. Communal Councils (*consigli comunali*) are also elected for four years, the *giunta comunale* being headed by a Mayor (*sindaco*) who is also a central government official, although in the exercise of his central government powers he is subject to the Prefect of the Province.

Judicial system: Civil cases are dealt with in the first instance and according to their degree of seriousness by Magistrates' Courts (*giudici conciliatori*), District Courts (*preture*) and Tribunals (*tribunali*). Appeal is also consecutive and proceeds from the Tribunals to the Courts of Appeal (*corti di appello*) and —on juridical grounds only—to the Supreme Court of Cassation (Corte Suprema di Cassazione). Criminal cases begin at the District Courts and proceed from the Tribunals to the Assize Courts attached to the Tribunals (*corti di assise presso i tribunali*). Appeal is to the Courts of Appeal and the parallel Assize Courts of Appeal (*corti di assise di appello*) and from there to the Supreme Court of Cassation.

Administrative justice is separate from the ordinary system, and is composed of two judicial hierarchies both of which have judicial as well as administrative functions. One is headed by the Council of State (Consiglio di Stato), composed of 87 members and divided into six sections, and the other by the Court of Accounts (Corte dei Conti) divided into 11 sections. Appeal from both courts may be made to the Court of Cassation and, on questions of constitutionality, to the Constitutional Court. The Constitutional Court (Corte Costituzionale) set up in 1955 has 15 members of whom one-third are appointed by the President of the Republic, one-third are elected by joint session of parliament and the remainder are chosen by judges of the Court of Cassation, the Council of State and the Court of Accounts. Its main function is to pronounce upon the constitutionality of legislation passed both before and since 1948.

Judges are appointed and promoted by, and can only be removed by decision of, the Supreme Council of Magistracy (Consiglio Superiore della Magistratura). This body consists of 24 members, 14 of whom are elected by career judges, seven of whom are elected by joint session of parliament (elected members serve for four years and are not immediately reeligible) and three are ex-officio members (the President of the Republic who presides, the Chief Justice and the Chief Prosecutor).

Trial is by jury. Divorce is not legal. There is no death penalty.

RECENT HISTORY

A plebiscite held in June 1946 resulted in the abolition of the monarchy and the election of a Constituent Assembly, which drew up a new republican constitution which came into force in January 1948.

Under Prime Minister Alcide de Gasperi, Italy became a founder-member of NATO and the ECSC. This policy of Atlantic and European cooperation, from which Italy has never wavered, was continued under de Gasperi's successors, and in 1955 Italy became a member of WEU and in 1957 a founder-member of the EEC and Euratom.

Italy has had two long-standing disputes in the post-war period. That with Yugoslavia over Trieste was finally settled in 1954 when the town of Trieste was ceded to Italy and its hinterland to Yugoslavia. That with Austria over the South Tyrol (Alto Adige) has led to terrorist activities by elements of the German-speaking population—whose main contention is that the Italian government has insufficiently implemented the autonomy clauses of the regional statute (see under *Local government*)—with some aid from German and Austrian organisations, and has been considered by the United Nations. In 1960 Italian Somaliland (which became a UN trust territory after the second world war) became independent.

Defence: The President of the Republic is commander-in-chief of the armed forces in his capacity as President of the Supreme Defence Council. Selective military service lasts 24 months in the navy and 15 months in the other two services. Strengths of the services: army 270,000, navy 40,000, air force 66,000. The Carabinieri, an internal security force, number 85,000. The 1966 defence estimates were L1,239,000 million ($1,982 million) representing 3·3 per cent of GNP.

ECONOMY

Background: The influence of the State, in terms of both initiative and control, has been of paramount importance in Italy's post-war 'economic miracle' through agencies such as Ente Nazionale Idrocarburi (ENI) and Istituto per la Ricostruzione Industriale (IRI). The 1965–9 national plan aims at diversifying the economy further and eliminating structural imbalances, notably in the south. Between 1951 and 1961 the annual average increase in the growth of GNP was 6 per cent. This economically prosperous decade enabled the government to initiate development projects for the south. The Land Reform Agencies and the Southern Italy Development Fund (Cassa del Mezzogiorno) in particular helped to create a basic structure from which modern economic growth can proceed. The recession of 1963–4 involved a relative decline in volume increases of GNP at market prices; annual growth rates 1963–5 were 5·2, 2·9 and 3.5 per cent. The major growth industries since the second world war have been chemicals, textiles, cars, iron and steel, metal industries and petroleum products.

The origin of GDP at factor cost in 1964 was:

Sector		Percentage
Agriculture	. .	14
Industry	. .	44
Services	. .	42
GDP		100

Between 1958 and 1963 industrial production increased by an annual average of 14 per cent; in 1964 it rose by only 1 per cent. The recovery of industrial production in 1965 was led by the metal, coal, iron and steel and petroleum industries. Since the war agriculture has progressively declined in importance. Agricultural output increased by about 3 per cent in 1964 and 4 per cent (estimated) in 1965, the main products being olives, fruit, wheat, maize, sugar beet, livestock and wine.

Foreign trade: In 1963 Italy had a current-account balance of payments deficit of about L616,000 million ($986 million). The situation improved considerably in 1964–5, the surpluses of these two years being largely due to increased exports. In 1965 visible exports exceeded visible imports for the first time. The contribution of imports and exports to GNP in 1964 was 15 and 12 per cent respectively. In 1964–5 manufactured goods and chemical products averaged 87 per cent of total exports and foodstuffs the remaining 13 per cent. The main imports for the same period were foodstuffs 21 per cent of total imports, manufactured goods and chemical products 28 per cent, metal ores and scrap 13 per cent and crude oil 10 per cent. Trade is strongly oriented toward the EEC. In 1963–5 trade with the EEC averaged about 32 per cent of imports and 37 per cent of exports; the remainder of Italy's foreign trade was widely distributed amongst other industrialised countries, with the United States as the largest single trading partner—14 per cent of total imports and 8·5 per cent of total exports in 1964.

Employment: The total labour force in 1964 was nearly 20 million of whom 25 per cent were employed in agriculture, 40 per cent in industry and 32 per cent in services. Unemployment in that year amounted to an above-average 3 per cent. Average annual net emigration for 1961–5 was about 200,000 (312,000 in 1965).

Price and wage trends: Between 1953 and 1961 prices and wages increased moderately, but there were significant increases in 1962–4 and measures were introduced to control the impending inflation. Consumer prices rose by 4.7 per cent in 1962 compared to the annual average of 2·2 per cent for 1953–61, and in 1963 increased by 7.5 per cent, in 1964 by 5.9 per cent, and in 1965 by 4·6 per cent. Wages followed a similar trend; the increase in hourly wage earnings in manufacturing averaged 4·6 per cent a year from 1953 to 1961, but increased by 14.9 per cent in 1962, 17·1 per cent in 1963 and 11·8 per cent in 1964. The increase in 1965 was expected to slow down still further following the deflationary measures taken in 1964–5. Food and agriculture were largely responsible for the steep rise in consumer prices during this period and affected the rise in wages; automatic adjustments are now made to the cost of living. The exceptionally high wage increases in 1962–4 were in fact symptomatic of the economy reaching full employment of industrial labour, involving a large adjustment of industrial wage levels.

Consumption: In 1964 private consumption accounted for 61 per cent of GNP and public consumption for 16·5 per cent. This represented increases of 2·6 and 3·8 per cent over 1963 for private and public consumption respectively compared with increases of 9.9 and 6·7 per cent in 1963 over 1962. These two years were both higher than the average for 1959–61 (6·4 per cent a year for private and 5 per cent for public consumption) and reflected a high level of domestic demand which was not expected to be maintained in 1965–6.

SOCIAL SECURITY

The Ministry of Labour and Social Welfare exercises general supervision over Italian social security. Benefits and contributions stated below refer to 1964.

Health insurance: The general system covering employed persons and pensioners is administered by the National Sickness Insurance Institute (INAM). There are special systems for seamen, self-employed artisans, self-employed farmers, public employees, etc. administered by separate special funds. The general system is financed by the employee (0·15 per cent of earnings), the employer (9 to 11 per cent, including 2 per cent for tuberculosis insurance and an additional contribution for the medical care of pensioners) and the state, in the form of special grants. Medical benefits are for 180 days in a year and include full general and specialist care, hospitalisation, prescribed medicines, a minimum rebate of 50 per cent of the costs of dental care, midwifery and specified appliances. Sickness benefits are paid only to wage-earners (not salary-earners) at the rate of 50 per cent of earnings for 20 days, increasing to 66⅔ per cent thereafter for a further 160 days. Maternity benefits (again paid to wage-earners only) are 80 per cent of earnings for a maximum of 13 weeks before and eight weeks after confinement. Services are provided by doctors contracted to or paid directly by the INAM. Tuberculosis daily sickness benefits (separately administered through the National Social Insurance Institute—INPS) are L300 ($0·48) while the patient is in sanatorium and L700 ($1·13) thereafter.

Accident insurance: The National Employment Accident Insurance Institute (INAIL) administers the general system that covers all employees. Like the INPS, the INAIL operates its own rehabilitation centres and hospitals. Special systems for seamen and self-employed farmers are operated by separate funds. The general scheme is financed by employers at the rate of 2 to 7·5 per cent of the employee's salary according to the industry and degree of risk. Medical benefits are surgical and hospital care, rehabilitation and the provision of necessary appliances. Temporary disability benefits amount to 60 per cent of earnings for the first 90 days of disability and 75 per cent thereafter. Disability pensions are 100 per cent of earnings for total disability with a maximum annual pension of L450,000 ($720). Dependant's supplements are 5 per cent of pension for the wife and for each child under 18 or invalid. An annual allowance of L180,000 ($288) is paid for constant attendance. Partial disability pensions are paid as part of a full pension proportionate to the degree of disability over 10 per cent. Lump sum survivor grants are paid at a maximum of L550,000 ($880) according to the category of surviving dependants. Widow's pensions—also payable to a widower who is over 65 or disabled—amount to one-third of the insured's earnings. Orphan's pensions are 13 per cent of earnings for each orphan under 18 or who is disabled (27 per cent for full orphans). Any parent or other relative dependant on the insured may receive a pension of 13 per cent of earnings where there are no survivors. The sum of such pensions may not exceed two-thirds of the earnings of the insured.

Pensions insurance: The general system covering all employees is administered by the INPS. There are special systems administered by separate funds for self-employed and certain professional persons, public employees and seamen. The general system is financed by insured persons (6·6 per cent of earnings), employers (13·3 per cent) and the state (contributions equivalent to 6·6 per cent of earnings plus special grants). Old-age pensions are paid to men at 60 and women at 55. Annual pensions are equal in the case of men to 72 times 45 per cent of the first L1,500 ($2·4) of contributions, plus 35 per cent of the next L1,500 plus 30 per cent of remaining contributions. For women the equivalent sums are 33 per cent, 26 and 20. For deferred retirement, pensions are increased for men by 6 to 40 per cent for one to five years' deferment, and for women by 3 to 40 per cent for one to 10 years' deferment. Minimum monthly pensions are L12,000 ($19), or L15,000 ($24) if retirement is deferred to 65. Maximum pensions are equal to 80 per cent of previous earnings. For each child who is under 18 years or invalid a supplement of 10 per cent of pension is paid. Every December a thirteenth monthly pension is paid. Invalidity pensions are paid upon loss of two-thirds of earning capacity by wage-earners and 50 per cent capacity by salaried employees. Benefits are the same as for old-age pensions except that the minimum monthly pension is L15,000 ($24). Widow's pensions—also payable to invalid widowers—amount to 50 per cent of the insured's pension. Pensions for orphans who are invalid or under 18 are 20 per cent (full orphans 30 per cent), and for each parent and other dependants 15 per cent. The sum of such pensions may not exceed 100 per cent of the insured's pension.

Unemployment insurance: This covers all persons in private employment with the exception of domestic staff and occupational and seasonal workers. It is administered by the INPS, which also administers a wage supplement fund. Unemployment insurance is financed by employers at the rate of 2·3 per cent of earnings, with an additional 0·2 per cent being paid to the wage supplement fund. Daily benefits of L300 ($0·48) are paid for a maximum period of 180 days in one year to those credited with 52 contributions in the previous two years, with daily supplements of L120 ($0·20) for dependant spouse and each dependant child and parent. Industrial wage-earners receive two-thirds of their overall lost salary from the wage supplement fund for an indefinite period, if their hours of work are reduced to from 24 to 40 hours. If the employee is working less than 24 hours per week this supplement is paid only for three months.

Other benefits: The general system of family allowances covers all employed persons, and is administered by the Central Fund for Family Allowances under the INPS. It is financed by employers at the rate of 17.5 per cent of earnings. There are special systems for certain professional classes and agricultural employees. For the latter, employers pay L110 ($0·18) per day, and are subsidised by the state. Monthly benefits under the general system are L4,940 ($8) for the first and each subsequent child, L3,588 ($5·60) for the spouse of the insured, and L1,430 ($2·30) for each dependant parent or grandparent.

EDUCATION

In 1961 8 per cent of the population over six—predominantly in the south—were illiterate (21 per cent in 1931). Education is free and compulsory from six to 14 years. Religious and physical education are compulsory. The sexes are taught separately where possible.

Primary education: This is the same for all children and begins at the age of six. The Primary School Certificate (*elementari*) is usually taken at 11.

Secondary and vocational education: Successful attainment of the *elementari* permits a child to continue, from 11 to 14 years, at the Lower Secondary School (*scuola media unica*) which has general and practical streams; this course terminates with the *licenza media*. Those who pass an entrance examination go on to Upper Secondary Schools—*licei* and vocational schools. The *licei* have courses lasting for five years, divided into a lower two-year and an upper three-year section. Success in the final examination, the *licenza liceale*, is a prerequisite for university education. Other Upper Secondary Schools are training institutes for primary-school teachers (*istituti magistrali*), agricultural schools (*istituti tecnici agrari*), commercial schools (*istituti tecnici commerciali*), industrial training schools (*istituti tecnici industriali*), nautical training schools (*istituti tecnici nautici*) and art training schools (*istituti d'arte*). Courses last from four to five years, and after obtaining the leaving certificate the student may enter a university, university institute or fine arts academy.

Special schools: Backward children are taught in special classes attached to the elementary and intermediate schools. For the mentally and physically handicapped there are special schools, mainly private, and generally situated near hospitals or clinics.

University and higher education: Universities and university institutes are classified as state (the majority) and non-state. The former are state-financed and state-supervised, while the latter have been set up by private organisations and are recognised by the state but depend upon the private organisations for their finance. All degrees are recognised as equal. All universities have administrative autonomy within their terms of statute. The University Rector elected by the Council of Professors has virtually absolute power within the university.

There are more than 50 institutes of higher education of which over half are universities. Courses for the degree of Doctor (which is a first degree) last for four years in most faculties, five years for architecture, industrial chemistry and engineering, and six years for medicine and surgery. As at the end of 1966 some 40 new higher educational institutes were planned. Higher education is not free, but grants are provided.

Universities: Bari, Bologna, Cagliari, Camerino, Catania,[1] Ferrara, Florence, Genoa, Lecce,[1] Macerata, Messina, Milan, Milan Catholic University,[1] Milan Commercial,[1] Modena, Naples, Padua, Palermo, Parma, Pavia, Perugia, Perugia Foreigners University, Pisa, Rome, Sassari, Siena, Trieste, Turin, Urbino.[1] *University institutes:* Catania (Magistero),[2] Genoa (Magistero), L'Aquila (Magistero), Milan (polytechnic), Naples (naval, oriental studies, Magistero), Pisa (Scuola Normale Superiore), Rome (physical education, Magistero), Salerno (Magistero), Turin (polytechnic, European

[1] Non-state universities.
[2] A Magistero is a teacher-training college with university status.

studies), Venice (architecture, economics, commerce, foreign languages, literature). *Fine arts academies:* Bologna, Carrara, Florence, Lecce, Milan, Naples, Palermo, Perugia, Ravenna, Rome, Turin, Venice.

Educational institutions 1964–5:

	Institutions	Staff	Students
Primary	41,683	204,363	4,472,230
Secondary	5,794	148,489	1,995,271
Vocational	1,548	47,790	689,851
Special (1963–4)	505	44,187	4,452
Primary teacher-training	536	12,885	168,854
University and university institute faculties and fine arts academies	218	7,003	323,729

Adult education: The state-run People's Schools (*scuole popolari*) provide three types of course: lower elementary education for illiterates, higher elementary courses for semi-illiterates and refresher courses of a general culture and vocational training nature. Other adult courses have been begun by private organisations, some state-assisted and others completely financed by the organisations themselves. Supplementing these schools are other facilities for adult education such as revision courses, reading centres, music courses, family courses, itinerant courses and adult education courses proper. Since 1947 about 100,000 adults per year have passed the Elementari. The number of public libraries is small in proportion to the population.

MASS MEDIA

The press:

Dailies: Corriere della Sera, Milan, right independent, 571,000; *La Stampa*, Turin, ind., 360,000; *Il Giorno*, Milan, ind., 250,000; *Il Messagero*, Rome, ind., 209,000; *Il Resto del Carlino*, Bologna, r. ind., 182,000; *Avanti!*, Rome and Milan, PSU party organ, 180,000; *La Nazione*, Florence, ind., 178,000; *Corriere d'Informazione*, Milan, ind., 160,000; *Il Tempo*, Rome, ind., 153,000; *Paesa Sera*, Rome, Communist, 137,000; *Il Popolo*, Rome, Christian Democrat Party organ; *Il Giornale d'Italia*, Rome, ind., 100,000; *Il Mattino*, Naples, ind., 92,000; *L'Avvenire d'Italia*, Bologna, Catholic, 90,000; *Il Globo*, Rome, financial-economic; *La Voce Repubblicana*, Rome, Republican Party organ; *L'Unità*, Rome, Milan and Turin, PCI party organ.

Periodicals: Domenica del Corriere (w), Milan, general, 1,100,000; *L'Espresso*, Rome, illustrated topical; *Oggi* (w), Milan, ill., 750,000; *Tempo* (w), Milan, ill. top., 390,000; *Epoca* (w), Milan, ill. top., 350,000.

Broadcasting: The Italian Radio and Television Corporation (Radiotelevisione Italiana—RAI) is a joint-stock company responsible to the Ministry of Posts and Telegraphs, to which all radio and TV rights belong. The autonomous governmental agency IRI holds 99·8 per cent of the stock. A director-general appointed by the government exercises the greatest power within RAI. A committee appointed by the Ministry of Posts is responsible for programme standards, and a parliamentary commission for political objectivity. There are two TV channels. Broadcasting is financed by government grants, advertising profits and the sale of licences.

LIECHTENSTEIN

GEOGRAPHY AND POPULATION

Area: 61 sq. miles/158 sq. km. This little state is situated in the Alps south of Lake Constance. *Total population:* (1964) 19,000 of whom about 28 per cent are foreigners. *Capital:* VADUZ (3,800). *Language:* The official language is German. The everyday language is of Alamannic origin. *Religion:* 92 per cent Roman Catholic.

CONSTITUTIONAL SYSTEM

Constitution: The Principality of Liechtenstein is a constitutional monarchy, and under the 1921 constitution hereditary in the male line. *Head of state:* Prince Francis Josef II. *Head of government:* G. Batliner.

Executive: The government consists of the Government Leader, his Deputy and two Government Councillors. The two former are appointed for six years by the Prince on the recommendation of parliament (Diet), and the latter are elected for four years by the Diet. The government is responsible to the Sovereign and the Diet. No resolution of the Diet can be enforced as law without the Sovereign's consent. In time of emergency the Sovereign can enact parliamentary law with the Government Leader's counter-signature without consulting the Diet. *Legislature:* The Diet has 15 members elected by proportional representation for four years. *Political parties:* There are three political parties: the Progressive Citizen's Party, the Fatherland Union and the Christian Social Party.

Judicial system: Civil and criminal cases are heard in the first instance by the County Court (Landgericht) of one presiding judge. More serious criminal cases go to the Assize Court (Schöffengericht–Vergehen) and Criminal Court (Kriminalgericht), both composed of a bench of five judges. Appeal in both civil and criminal cases is first to the Superior Court (Obergericht) and then to the Supreme Court (Oberster Gerichtshof), both composed of five judges.

RECENT HISTORY

Liechtenstein has closely followed the fortunes of Switzerland. A customs union was signed between the two states in 1923. *Defence:* There is no army. Police are armed.

ECONOMY

Liechtenstein has the second-highest (to Sweden) average income in Europe. Although less than 9 per cent of the population is engaged in agriculture (compared to about 70 per cent in 1923), cattle-breeding is highly developed with a main emphasis upon milk production. Other main products are potatoes, maize, fruit and wine grapes. Tourism is a major industry, benefiting from the investment of over SF40 million in recent years. Earnings from philately amounted to about one-sixth of total revenue in 1966. The main industrial sector is the metal industry, which specialises in precision goods; ceramics is also important. Industrial trades employed about 22 per cent of the population in 1964, of whom over 40 per cent were resident foreigners, mainly Austrian, Swiss and German.

Liechtenstein is a tax-haven for holding and headquarters companies owing to its minimal capital tax of 0·1 per cent and the absence of profit, revenue or property taxes. Income from this source amounted to almost one-fifth of total revenue in 1966. Total bank balances within the country have increased twelvefold in the period 1945–63 compared to only a fourfold increase in Switzerland over the same period. The value of exports in 1965 was SF168 million compared to SF15 million in 1950. About 63 per cent of exports go to EFTA and about 22 per cent to EEC.

SOCIAL SECURITY

The system is organised on similar lines to that of Switzerland.

EDUCATION

Public education is through the eight-year Volksschule to the three-year Realschule with an educational syllabus similar to that of a Swiss secondary school. The same kind of education and further education is provided by three private schools.

THE PRESS

Dailies: None. *Periodicals: Liechtensteiner Vaterland* (3w), Vaduz, Fatherland Union, 2,800; *Liechtensteiner Volksblatt* (4w), Vaduz, Progressive Citizen's Party, 3,800; *Der Liechtensteiner* (w), Vaduz, Christian Social Party, 1,600.

LUXEMBOURG

GEOGRAPHY

Features: This small land-locked state is part of the Ardenne Massif and also of the scarplands of northern France. Mainly over 800 ft/240 m., it is dissected by a number of tributaries of the Moselle which forms its eastern border. Farmland and woodland alternate over the area and considerable quantities of Jurassic iron ore have been worked.

Area: 1,000 sq. miles/2,590 sq. km. *Mean max. and min. temperatures:* Luxembourg (49° 30' N, 6° E; 1,100 ft/335 m.) 74°F/23°C (July), 29°F/−2°C (Jan.). *Relative humidity:* Luxembourg 91 per cent. *Mean annual rainfall:* 29 in./735 mm.

POPULATION

Total population: (1964 est.) 330,000. *Main towns and populations:* (1964) LUXEMBOURG (90,000), Esch-sur-Alzette (30,000), Differdange (18,500). *Distribution:* In 1960, 23 per cent of the population lived in Communes of more than 50,000 inhabitants, 23 per cent in Communes of 10–50,000 and 54 per cent in Communes of fewer than 10,000.

Language: The official languages are French and German, but the everyday language is a West Frankish dialect, Letzeburgesch. *Religion:* Mainly Roman Catholic but with Jewish and Protestant communities in some centres.

CONSTITUTIONAL SYSTEM

Constitution: Luxembourg is a constitutional monarchy. The constitution dates from 1868; it was revised in 1919 and 1948. *Head of state:* Grand Duke Jean of Luxembourg. *Head of government:* Prime Minister Pierre Werner (Christian Social Party).

Executive: Executive power rests with the Grand Duke and a ten-strong Council of Ministers chosen by him. *Legislature:* The Chamber of Deputies numbers 56 and is elected for five years by proportional representation in four electoral districts. Legislation is first submitted to a Council of State—appointed by the Sovereign—for an advisory opinion. The Council of State elects a seven-man committee (Comité du Contentieux) every six years, which is the highest administrative court in the land. Laws affecting agriculture, labour, handicrafts, private employees and commerce must first be submitted for opinion to one or more of five Professional Chambers composed of representatives of these sectors of society.

Political parties: There are five main parties in Luxembourg of which the strongest are the Christian Social and the Socialist Workers parties. The others are the liberal Democratic Party, the Communist Party and the recently founded middle-class Popular Independent Movement. The present government is a coalition of the Socialist and Christian Social parties.

Election results:

Party	1959 Percentage of poll	Seats	1964 Percentage of poll	Seats
Christian Socials	41·9	21	33·4	22
Socialist Workers	30·35	17	37·8	21
Democrats	22·6	11	11·0	6
Communists	4·8	3	11·7	5
Popular Independent Movement	—	—	6·1	2
Others	0·35	—	—	—

Leading political figures: Christian Socials—Pierre Werner (Prime Minister and Minister of Finance), Pierre Grégoire (Foreign Minister and Defence Minister), Jean Dupong (Party President, Minister of Education, Minister of Justice). Socialists—Henri Cravatte (Deputy Prime Minister and Minister of the Interior).

Local government: The basic unit is the Commune administered by a council elected for six years. The executive heads of the Commune are a Mayor and two Aldermen (*échevins*) appointed by the Sovereign. The Communes are grouped into 12 Cantons and these in turn into *arrondissements administratifs*, each of which is administered by a government representative, the *commissaire du district*, appointed by the Sovereign.

Judicial system: The lowest courts are those of the *justices de paix*—one per Canton—with summary jurisdiction in minor police, civil and commercial cases. Appeal is to the two Regional Tribunals (*tribunaux d'arrondissements*) composed of a president and a panel of judges. These have correctional jurisdiction in all but serious crimes and act as civil and commercial courts of the first instance. Every three months the Supreme Court (Cour Supérieure de Justice) appoints the Cour d'Assises as the highest criminal court, which has six judges who also act as jurors; verdict is given by majority. The Supreme Court acts as the final court of appeal and as a court of cassation. Judges and *juges de la paix* are appointed for life by the Crown, and can be removed only by judicial sentence. Luxembourg maintains capital punishment.

RECENT HISTORY

Luxembourg signed a 50-year Customs Union with Belgium in 1922. After the German occupation from 1940 to 1944, the constitution was amended to rescind the former status of permanent neutrality. The same year (1948) Luxembourg joined with Belgium and the Netherlands in 'Benelux' and signed the Brussels Treaty. In 1949 it became a founder-member of NATO and is also an original member of the ECSC, EEC and Euratom. *Defence:* Conscription ends in July 1967. The present army of 500 regulars and 1,800 conscripts is to be replaced by a 500-man volunteer force. The 1966 defence estimates were BF483 million ($9,660,000) representing about 1·5 per cent of GNP.

Economy

Background: Luxembourg's economy has been linked to that of Belgium since the Customs Union of 1922. The steel industry dominates the economy (representing nearly 30 per cent of GNP in 1964) and Luxembourg is the headquarters of the ECSC. Owing to the preponderance of one industry and the dependence upon foreign trade the economy is susceptible to extreme fluctuation. In an effort to remedy this weakness and achieve a consistently high rate of growth the state has in recent years played a major economic role, diversifying industrial activities and modernising agriculture. However, the 6 per cent growth of GNP in 1964 compared with 1 per cent in 1963 indicated that the economy continued to be vulnerable to international fluctuations in the demand for steel. The main growth industry apart from steel since 1960 has been chemicals. Fluctuations in the growth rates of industrial production have corresponded to trends in the steel industry. The origin of GDP at factor cost in 1963 was:

Sector				Percentage
Agriculture	.	.	.	7
Industry	.	.	.	53
Services	.	.	.	40
GDP				100

The main industries, apart from iron and steel, are chemicals, tobacco, mining, beverages and manufacturing products. In 1947 agriculture's share of GNP was 12 per cent; in 1965 it was under 7 per cent. The main agricultural products are vegetables, wheat, barley, livestock, dairy products and wine.

Foreign trade: See under *Belgium.*

Employment: The total labour force in 1964 was about 138,000, of whom 42 per cent were employed in industry, 16 per cent in agriculture and 42 per cent in services. The population of Luxembourg is an aging one and there is a shortage of skilled labour not sufficiently compensated for by the relatively large numbers of foreign workers. Between 1958 and 1963 net immigration averaged over 2,600 per year.

Price and wage trends: Between 1953 and 1963 the annual rise in the cost of living was under 1 per cent, owing largely to the government's price control policy. During the same period wages rose by 5 per cent a year. In 1964 the cost of living index rose by 3.1 per cent and wages by 10 per cent. The dependence upon foreign trade, and in particular the prices of imports, is a major determining factor of all prices in the economy.

Consumption: Private consumption in 1963 accounted for 60 per cent of GNP and public consumption for 13 per cent.

Social Security

General supervision of the system is exercised by the Inspectorate of Social Institutions under the Ministry of Labour and Social Security. All pensions and family allowances are linked to a 5 per cent change in the cost of living index. Contributions and benefits stated below refer to 1964.

Health insurance: This covers all wage-earners and salaried employees (with separate systems for each) and (for medical benefits only) pensioners, and is administered by employer-employee bodies. All persons covered must become members of sickness funds; those not covered compulsorily may become voluntary members. Wage-earners pay contributions of 4 per cent of daily earnings up to BF380 ($7·60) and salaried employees 2·6 per cent of monthly earnings up to BF9,450 ($189); in both cases employers pay half this amount. Pensioners pay 2·6 per cent of pension, and the pension institutions half of this. Medical benefits are normally provided by services contracted to the funds: for wage-earners they are full general and specialist care, hospitalisation (26 weeks only), maternity and dental care and transport and 75 to 85 per cent refunds on the cost of medicines; for salaried employees they are limited to refunds on doctor's and chemist's expenses. Sickness benefits for wage-earners are 50 to 75 per cent of earnings for up to 26 weeks (in some cases 39 weeks). Maternity benefits are 70 per cent of earnings paid for six weeks before and six weeks after confinement. Salaried employees receive full wages during sickness.

Accident insurance: This covers all employees, self-employed farmers and family agricultural workers. Other self-employed may insure voluntarily. Employers pay from 0·5 to 11 per cent of earnings (up to a monthly maximum of BF15,720 ($314) for salaried employees—which limit also applies for benefits), and the government covers 50 per cent of administration costs and part of the cost-of-living pension increases. Medical benefits are treatment, surgery, hospitalisation, medicines and appliances. Temporary disability benefits are paid for 13 weeks at the rate of 75 per cent of earnings. Permanent disability pensions are 80 per cent of the previous year's average earnings for total disability with various supplements. Partial disability pensions are a percentage of the full pension proportionate to the degree of disability, which is converted into a lump sum for less than 10 per cent disability. Pensions for widows and invalid dependant widowers are 40 per cent of the insured's earnings, rising in the case of widows who are 50 or invalid to 50 per cent. Each orphan under 18 receives a pension of 20 per cent of earnings. Total survivor's pensions may not exceed 80 per cent of earnings.

Pensions insurance: This covers all wage-earners and salaried employees; administration is respectively by the Old Age and Invalidity Insurance Institution (OAIII) and the Private Salaried Employees' Pension Fund (PSEPF). There are special systems for miners, railwaymen and public employees, and self-employed artisans, farmers and merchants. Both the insured person and the employer pay 5 per cent of earnings (subject for salaried employees to the same limits as for accident insurance), and the state pays 50 per cent of the cost of basic pensions and administrative costs and part of the cost-of-living increases, and is pledged to cover any deficits. Old age pensions are paid at 60 with an option at 55 for salaried employees, and at 65 or 62 for wage-earners (miners 60 or 58); it is intended to reduce the pensionable age for miners to 55 and for steelworkers to 60. Invalidity pensions are paid on loss of two-thirds of earning capacity. Both old age and invalidity pensions consist of a basic monthly pension of BF1,690 ($34) plus increments of 1·6 per cent of total insured earnings for wage-earners or 16 per cent of total contributions for salaried employees. Supplements for each child under 18 are paid at the monthly rate of BF135 ($2·70) for wage-earners and BF370 ($7·40) for salaried employees. Monthly pensions are of a statutory minimum of BF3,038 ($60·80) and of a maximum of five-sixths of average earnings. Basic monthly widow's pensions, also payable to invalid dependant widowers, are BF1,130 ($22·60) plus 50 and 60 per cent of the increment earned by insured wage-earners and salaried employees respectively. Basic monthly pensions for orphans under 18 (23 if a student and no limit if invalid) are BF565 ($11·30) plus 20 per cent of the insured's earned increment. Total survivor's pensions may not exceed 100 per cent of the deceased's total pension.

Unemployment insurance: Unemployment is virtually unknown in Luxembourg even in times of depression. Unemployment benefits are paid to the partly unemployed.

Other benefits: There are two family allowance systems, one covering all employed persons and social insurance beneficiaries and administered by the OAIII and PSEPF, and the other—the general system—covering all other residents and administered by the Children Allowances Fund. The general system is financed by a special income tax imposed on non-employees with the government settling any deficit, and the employee system by employers at the rate of 1·7 to 5·3 per cent of wage-earnings and 2·2 to 3·3 per cent of monthly salaries up to BF15,720, the state paying BF169 ($3·40) monthly for the third child and full costs for the fourth and subsequent children. Allowances are paid for each child under 19 (23 if a student and without limit for invalid without means) at the monthly rate of BF500 ($10) for each of the first four children, increasing by BF54 ($1) for the fifth and subsequent children, under the employee system, and BF135 ($2·70) for the first two and BF500 for the third, fourth and any invalid child, also increasing by BF54 for the fifth and subsequent children, under the general system. Birth grants for all are BF5,670 ($113) for the first and BF3,375 ($67) for each subsequent child.

EDUCATION

Education is free and compulsory from the ages of 6 to 15. All schools are run by the state except for some girls' schools—mostly convents—which are state-controlled. The Ministry of Education has complete control of the curriculum, the only duty of the local government being to nominate the staff. Teaching is in German or French since Letzeburgesch has no written grammar or fixed spelling.

Primary education: This lasts from 6 to 15 years. Those who do not take or do not pass an entrance examination to the secondary or intermediate schools at the age of 12 continue at primary school. Those who successfully complete their sixth year of primary education go on to *classes complémentaires* for three-year courses. Here boys and girls are taught separately, and given a general education orientated towards later practical studies, ending with a Certificate of Primary Studies awarded by a school commission. Those who do not successfully complete their sixth year of primary studies are prepared in special classes for practical work. Certain Communes have introduced a four-year Upper Primary School.

Secondary education: Intermediate education consists of a three-year lower grade continuing, for some, in a two-year upper school. Secondary education proper is at three levels, two for boys and one for girls, all ending with an *examen de fin d'études secondaires.* For boys there are, first, Classical Lycées providing seven-year courses, divided into two-year lower and middle divisions and three-year upper divisions, with the *examen de passage* at the end of the middle grade. The Classical Lycées prepare their students for higher and university studies. The Modern Lycées offer six-year courses divided into three-year lower and upper divisions; in the upper division education is divided into industrial and commercial sections. For girls there are separate Lycées with the upper division giving university entry.

Special education: Backward children are taught in special classes. There are also institutes for handicapped children, and two institutes of education and apprenticeship for juvenile delinquents.

Technical and vocational education: Apprentices in commerce, the crafts and industry attend for part-time weekly education two- to four-year courses at the State Centres of Professional Education, ending in an examination for the *certificat d'aptitude professionelle.* Further vocational schools are the Institute of Technical Education, the Conservatory of Music and the School of Music in Luxembourg, and the State Agricultural School in Ettelbruck.

Educational institutions, 1964:

	Institutions	Staff	Students
Primary	439	1,258	33,338
Secondary	7	386	5,127
Technical and vocational (1963)	20	n.a.	4,658
Special (1963)	3	15	205

Higher education: Attached to the Athénée and the Boys' Lycée in Luxembourg City respectively are one-year courses in arts and sciences, considered the equivalent of a year at university. Success in these courses is generally a prerequisite for admission to certain professions. In addition there are two teacher-training schools and a University of Comparative Sciences in Luxembourg; the latter had 120 (temporary) teachers and 200 students in 1964. University education is normally obtained in France or Germany.

Adult education: The École Supérieure du Travail is an autonomous institution under the Ministry of Labour offering courses in law, finance and economics. There are also a number of private cultural organisations which have educational aims, in addition to adult education courses proper.

MASS MEDIA

The press:

Dailies (1965): Luxemburger Wort, Luxembourg, Christian Social Party organ, 65,000; *Tageblatt,* Esch-sur-Alzette, Socialist Party organ, 34,000; *Letzeburger Journal,* Luxembourg, Democratic Party organ, 25,000; *Zeitung vum Letzeburger Vollek,* Luxembourg, Communist Party organ.

Periodicals (Luxembourg): Letzeburger Fraen an Mammen, woman's Cath., 22,000; *Arbecht* (w), trade union, 18,000; *Letzeburger Illustreert Revue* (w), illustrated, 16,000; *De Letzeburger Bauer* (w), agricultural, 10,000; *D'Letzeburger Land* (w), independent/economic/political/cultural, 6,000; *Handelsblatt* (w), commercial, 4,000.

Broadcasting: The Compagnie Luxembourgeoise de Télédiffusion is a private body operating under state charter and financed solely by its own commercial activities; the state has no shares in the Compagnie, but the French state has a major holding through its company SOFIRAD. The Compagnie operates both home and overseas radio services through Radio Luxembourg and TV services within Luxembourg through Télé Luxembourg.

F

MALTA

GEOGRAPHY

Features: This island-group consists of limestone plateaux rising to over 1,500 ft/450 m. Agriculture is not very prosperous and there are no important minerals. *Area:* 122 sq. miles/315 sq. km. *Mean min. and max. temperatures:* Valetta (36° N, 14° 30′ E; 230 ft/70 m.) 85°F/29°C (Aug.), 51°F/11°C (Jan. and Feb.). *Relative humidity:* Valetta 76 per cent. *Mean annual rainfall:* Valetta 20 in./510 mm.

POPULATION

Total population: (1964) 324,000. *Chief towns and populations:* (1964) Sliema (24,000), Paola and Tarxien (20,000), VALETTA (19,000), Birkirkara (18,000), Hamrun (17,000).

Language: Both Maltese and English are official languages. *Religion:* 90 to 95 per cent of the population are Roman Catholic. The Archbishop of Malta is recognised as spiritual head of Malta, and the constitution guarantees the church the right to control its own affairs.

CONSTITUTIONAL SYSTEM

Constitution: Malta is an independent monarchy within the Commonwealth. The constitution was accepted as a constitution for independence by referendum in May 1964. *Head of State:* Queen Elizabeth II (represented by Gov.-General Sir Geofroy Tory). *Head of government:* G. Borg Olivier.

Executive: The Governor-General must act on the cabinet's advice except in certain specified cases. He appoints as Prime Minister that member of the House of Representatives best able to command a majority in the House and the other ministers on the Prime Minister's advice. He also appoints the Leader of the Opposition. *Legislature:* Legislative authority is vested in a unicameral parliament, the House of Representatives, whose 50 members are elected for five years by the single transferable vote system of proportional representation. *Political parties:* The two main parties are the Nationalist Party and the neutralist Malta Labour Party. All the smaller parties lost their representation in 1966.

Leading political figures: Nationalist Party—G. Borg Olivier (Prime Minister and Minister for External and Commonwealth Affairs), G. Felice (Minister of Finance). Malta Labour Party—Dom Mintoff (Party Leader and Leader of the Opposition).

Election results:

Party:	1962 Percentage of poll	Seats	1966 Percentage of poll	Seats
Nationalist Party .	42·1	25	47·8	28
Malta Labour Party .	33·4	16	42·9	22
Christian Worker's Party . . .	9·6	4	6	—
Democratic Nationalist Party . . .	9·4	3	1·4	—
Progressive Constitutional Party . .	4·9	1	1·7	—
Others	0·6	—	0·2	—

Local government: There is no local government on Malta except for a Civic Council on the Island of Gozo. *Judicial system:* Maltese civil law derives mainly from Roman law although public law is greatly influenced by the British system. The language of the courts is Maltese. The Chief Justice and other judges are appointed by the Governor-General on the Prime Minister's advice. The lower courts are the Criminal Court and the Court of Magistrates, the latter acting as a juvenile court in the case of young offenders. Appeal is to the Court of Appeal and—in certain civil matters—further to the Judicial Committee of the Privy Council. The Constitutional Court hears and determines disputes over membership of the House of Representatives—in which it has final jurisdiction—and appeals from other courts on constitutional and certain other matters. Malta maintains capital punishment but no executions have taken place since the war.

RECENT HISTORY

The Crown Colony of Malta was awarded the George Cross for its resistance during the second world war. In 1962 Malta became a member of the Inter-Governmental Committee for European Migration; it is also a member of the Council of Europe and GATT. In 1964 Malta became an independent monarchy within the Commonwealth.

Defence: Malta has small local defence forces. Immediately after independence it signed a Mutual Defence Agreement with Britain whereby British forces are to remain stationed on the island for 10 years. Malta is the HQ of NATO's Allied Forces Mediterranean, with responsibility in war of convoy-protection. Although not a formal member of NATO it has the right of consultation with the NATO Council if a threat to its political security or territorial integrity is deemed to exist, with no obligation to provide armed forces or expenses towards NATO.

ECONOMY

Background: Since independence Malta has remained heavily dependent for development upon loans from Britain. According to the 1964 Agreement on Financial Assistance between the two countries Britain was to provide £18·8 million ($52·6 million) for the three years from April 1964 and £31·2 million ($87·4 million) for the next seven years. In the 1964–9 period 75 per cent of this will take the form of gifts and 25 per cent will be loans. With the decline of the Royal Naval dockyard in Malta service spending has fallen sharply from £22 million ($61·6 million) in 1961 to £12 million ($33·6 million) in 1965, representing a decrease of 25 per cent in Malta's GNP. Partly to offset this a (second) Five Year Development Plan (1964–9) costing over £38 million ($106·4 million) aims to accelerate the diversification of Malta's economy to meet increasing employment needs, and to promote tourism and exports. Government investment aid to industry amounted to £10·57 million ($29·6 million) in December 1965 as against £3 million ($8·4 million) in February 1962.

In 1963 GNP stood at £46·2 million ($129 million) with an annual per capita income of £142 ($397). The major production increases in recent years have been in construction, rubber, chemicals, food manufacturing, textiles and tobacco. Industry continues to centre on ship repairing and building. The principal crops are onions, grapes, wheat, fodder and barley. Potatoes and fresh vegetables are the main cash crops.

Foreign trade: The pattern of trade is greatly influenced by Commonwealth preferences and the proximity of Italy and Libya. In 1964 38 per cent of imports came from Britain and 11 per cent from Italy. In the same year exports (including reexports) went 31 per cent to Britain, 12 per cent to Italy and 9 per cent to Libya. Main imports are food, manufactured goods, machinery and transport equipment, mineral fuels and chemicals. Main exports are textiles and yarns, scrap metal, rubber manufactures, oils and fats, wines and potatoes. Total domestic exports trebled between 1962 and 1965.

Employment: In 1964 the total labour force was about 87,000. Employment in the manufacturing and other industries and government service is increasing against a slow decline in agriculture, fishing, construction and quarrying. Malta is a country of high unemployment—about 8 per cent in 1963. Since the war more than 100,000 Maltese have emigrated, over 50 per cent to Australia.

SOCIAL SECURITY

Employees are covered against sickness, unemployment, old-age, widowhood, orphanhood and industrial injuries. There is a reciprocal agreement with Britain. Benefits are supplemented by free medical and other services for those whose incomes are below a certain level. Weekly contributions ranging from 3d ($0·03) for girls under 19 to 1s 10d ($0·2) for males over 19 are paid equally by employers and employees, and further contributions are made by the government. The medical service is run by the government, with the exception of four private hospitals run by religious orders. All treatment is free to people of lower-income groups and the maximum daily payment for hospital treatment is about 10s ($1·4) exclusive of modest fees for operations.

EDUCATION

Primary, secondary and special education: About 20 per cent of the population is illiterate. Primary education is free and compulsory for all children from the ages of six to 14. Instruction is in Maltese and English. All government schools are Roman Catholic. Private schools are run mainly by convents; some in receipt of government subsidies cater for both primary and (especially for girls) secondary schooling. There are special schools for handicapped children. Some children proceed to Grammar and Technical Schools, where they are prepared for the British GCE O and A levels.

Technical education: The programme for technical education is being expanded. Entrance to the five-year course is by examination taken at 11–13. The sixth form prepares pupils for A level examinations in scientific and technical subjects. Higher technological training takes place at the Malta Polytechnic. *Vocational and adult education:* Courses in craft training and industrial apprenticeship are expanding. Evening classes offer tuition in 36 subjects. Basic education in English, Maltese and other subjects is available for adults in a large number of centres in Malta and Gozo. *Higher education:* There are two teacher-training colleges with an increasing intake of students. The Royal University of Malta has seven faculties and had 78 staff and 550 students in 1964.

Educational institutions, 1963:

	Institutions	Staff	Students
Primary	195	2,274	52,010
Secondary	49	726	21,204
Technical	9	67	1,116
Special	6	24	280

MASS MEDIA

The press:

Dailies: Il Helsien, Valetta, socialist; *L-Orrizont,* Valetta, soc., 18,000; *Malta News,* Valetta, soc.; *Il-Berqua,* Valetta, independent; *The Bulletin,* Hamrun, ind.; *Times of Malta,* Valetta, pro-government.

Periodicals and bi-weeklies: Il-Poplu (bw), Hamrun, Nationalist Party; *Lehen is-Sewwa* (bw), Floriana, Catholic, 11,000; *Malta Tagnna* (w), Valetta, Democratic Nationalist; *Sunday Times of Malta* (w), Valetta, pro-gov.; *It-Tórca* (w), Valetta, trade-union, 18,000; *The Voice of Malta* (w), Valetta, soc.; *Maltese Observer* (w), Floriana, Cath.; *Forward-Il Quddiem* (f), Valetta, Progressive Party.

Broadcasting: The Malta Broadcasting Authority is an independent public body controlling the commercial radio station Rediffusion (Malta) Ltd. (on a 25-year contract with the government from 1961) and the commercial Malta Television Service Ltd. Broadcasting is in Maltese and English.

MONACO

Features: This tiny urban state is situated on the Mediterranean coast near the French-Italian border. *Area:* 1 sq. mile/2·5 sq. km. *Total population:* (1961) 22,000. *Capital:* Monte Carlo (9,600). *Language:* French and Monégasque (a mixture of French and Italian). *Religion:* Roman Catholic.

Constitutional System

Constitution: The Principality of Monaco is a constitutional monarchy. A new constitution was promulgated by the Sovereign in 1962, and any future amendments may be made only with the approval of the National Council. *Head of state:* Prince Rainier III. *Head of government:* Minister of State Jean Reymond.

Executive: Executive power is vested in the hereditary Sovereign and the Minister of State—seconded from the French government—who are assisted by three Government Councillors. *Legislature:* The Sovereign and the 18 members of the National Council, elected for five years by universal suffrage, are the source of legislative power.

Local government: The four parts of the Principality—Monaco-Ville, La Condamine, Fontvielle and Monte Carlo—are administered by an elected Municipal Council headed by the Mayor of Monaco. *Judicial system:* The Code Louis of 1919 is similar to the French Code. There is a court of the *juge de paix,* a *tribunal de première instance,* a *cour d'appel* and a *cour de révision* (court of cassation). The highest court is the Tribunal Suprême which is the administrative court and also safeguards fundamental individual liberties.

Recent History

The constitution was suspended provisionally by Prince Rainier in 1959. The new constitution of 1962 granted more power to the elected National Council. The Principality is combined in a customs union with France and in 1962 the French government set up a customs barrier to enforce stricter control on the flow of goods between the two states. This was lifted in May 1963, and many French companies established in the Principality were brought under French fiscal control.

Economy

The main sources of revenue are from the sale of tobacco and postage stamps and receipts from tourism (including the Monte Carlo Casino) and from the state's services as a financial centre. There are a number of light industries which have a market in France and increasingly so elsewhere.

SOCIAL SECURITY

The Office of Social Assistance is directed by an administrative commission under the presidency of the Mayor of Monaco.

EDUCATION

There are six primary schools, three each for boys and girls run by religious orders. There is one secondary school providing courses leading to the Baccalauréat. The Monaco Boys School and the Condamine Girls School offer short general and vocational secondary education.

MASS MEDIA

The press: The official weekly is the *Journal de Monaco.* French newspapers are widely read. *Broadcasting:* Radio Monte Carlo is a commercial body in which the French government has large holdings. Trans World Radio broadcasts—in conjunction with Radio Monte Carlo—exclusively religious programmes in 24 languages. It is maintained by voluntary subscriptions. TV is controlled by Télé Monte Carlo.

THE NETHERLANDS

GEOGRAPHY

Features: The Netherlands is unique in Europe in that some 40 per cent of its land area lies below sea level and is maintained as dry land by a complicated series of sea dykes and continual pumping. It has added considerably to its extent by the draining of the Zuider Zee. More land is being reclaimed by means of the Delta Plan now being implemented for the construction of dams to protect the islands between the Western Scheldt and mainland. Only in the extreme south-east, in South Limburg, does the altitude reach over 1,000 ft/300 m. This area is a dissected plateau covered with loess soil. The rest of the country can be divided into three main regions. First there are the Polder Lands, which stretch from Groningen in the north to the south and the Zeeland Islands. The part of this area fronting the North Sea is protected by sand dune ridges, in places reinforced; the rest is protected by dykes. Reclamation of this area began in the early Middle Ages and is still going on. The second area consists of the river valleys of the Maas, Lek and Waal; these valleys too are protected by dykes. Finally there are the sandy areas of the east, largely consisting of outwash sands and gravels of glacial and fluvial origin. In places ridges of morainic material rise above the general level of the surface to about 300 ft/90 m., e.g. in Veluwe.

The reclamation of the peat and clay areas of the west and the improvement of much of the sandy areas of the east has meant that a great proportion of the country is suitable for agriculture. The most intensive cultivation is in the Polder Lands and river valleys. The chief mineral resources are deposits of coal in south Limburg and very large deposits of natural gas in the north-east. Very few other minerals exist. The chief industrial centres are Amsterdam, the area around Rotterdam and stretching along the New Waterway to Europoort, and the urban concentration of north Brabant and north Limburg, e.g. Tilburg, Breda and Eindhoven.

Area: Land area 12,930 sq. miles/33,500 sq. km. Total area (including low-water areas, i.e. sea-level at low tide) 15,790 sq. miles/40,900 sq. km. *Mean max. and min. temperatures:* Amsterdam (52° 30′ N, 5° E; 5 ft/1·5 m.) 69°F/21°C (July), 34°F/1°C (Jan. and Feb.). *Relative humidity:* Amsterdam 83 per cent. *Mean annual rainfall:* 26 in./660 mm.

POPULATION

Population: (1965) 12,377,000. The population of the overseas territories is about 500,000. *Chief towns and populations:* (1965) AMSTERDAM (862,000), Rotterdam (728,000), The Hague (seat of government) (593,000), Utrecht (271,000), Eindhoven (182,000), Haarlem (172,000). *Distribution:* In 1965 22 per cent of the population lived in centres of less than 10,000 inhabitants,

46 per cent in centres of 10–100,000 and 32 per cent in centres of more than 100,000. *Language:* The official language is Dutch. *Religion:* (1960) Protestant 38 per cent, Catholic 40 per cent, other creeds 4 per cent.

CONSTITUTIONAL SYSTEM

Constitution: The Netherlands is a constitutional monarchy. The constitution of 1814 has been repeatedly amended. *Head of state:* Queen Juliana. *Head of government:* Prime Minister Piet de Jong (Catholic Party).

Executive: Since the constitution does not acknowledge the existence of a Prime Minister, the Sovereign appoints the ministers through the agency of a cabinet-former or *formateur* who can usually command a majority in parliament. However the Formateur does not necessarily become Chairman of the Council of Ministers (Ministerraad), i.e. Prime Minister, and sometimes does not even enter the government.

The Sovereign gives assent to all legislation. All acts of the Sovereign require the counter-signature of a minister. Ministers are responsible to parliament (Staten-Generaal) and have the right to speak in either chamber but not to vote. They are generally members of the lower chamber, in which case they are obliged to resign their parliamentary seats within three months of their ministerial appointment. Both the Council of Ministers and the Sovereign consult the Council of State (Raad van State) on legislative and administrative policy and the issue of decrees.

Legislature: Parliament has two houses. The Second Chamber (Tweede Kamer) has 150 members elected for four years by the list system of proportional representation, the whole country serving as one constituency. The 75 members of the First Chamber (Eerste Kamer) are elected by the Provincial Councils for six years with one half retiring every three. Legislation originates in the Second Chamber. The First Chamber has the power to accept or reject legislation, but only the Second Chamber can make amendments. Ceraint bills are considered by joint sessions of the two houses with the right to make amendments.

Parties	Second Chamber 1963 Percentage of poll	Seats	1967 Percentage of poll	Seats	First Chamber 1966 Seats
Catholic People's Party	31·92	50	26·51	42	25
Labour Party	27·90	43	23·55	37	22
Liberals	10·28	16	10·74	17	9
Anti-Revolutionary Party	8·72	13	9·90	15	7
Christian Historical Union	8·58	13	8·15	12	7
Pacifist Socialist Party	3·02	4	2·86	4	3
Communist Party	2·77	4	3·61	5	1
Political Reformed Party	2·29	3	2·01	3	—
Farmer's Party	2·13	3	4·77	7	2
Reformed Political Association	0·79	1	0·86	1	—
Democrats '66	—	—	4·46	7	—
Others	1·60	—	2·58	—	—

Political parties: Eleven parties are represented in the Second Chamber of which eight also have representation in the First. The two largest parties are the

Roman Catholic People's Party and the Labour Party. Three other parties—the People's Party for Freedom and Democracy (Liberals), the Anti-Revolutionary Party and the Christian Historical Union (the last two Calvinist) hold 44 seats between them. The remainder are the Democrats '66, the Pacifist Socialist Party, the Dutch Communist Party, the right-wing Farmer's Party, the Political Reformed Party and the Reformed Political Association (the last two Calvinist). The present government is a coalition of Catholic, Liberal, Anti-Revolutionary and Christian Historical Union parties.

Leading political figures: Catholic Party—Piet de Jong (Prime Minister), Joseph Luns (Foreign Minister), Jo Cals (former Prime Minister). Liberal Party: H. Wittevenn (Deputy Prime Minister and Finance Minister), Lt.-Gen. W. den Goom (Defence Minister).

Local government: The Netherlands is divided into eleven Provinces (*provincie*), each of which elects a Provincial Council (*provinciale staten*) for four years. The Provincial Council elects a six-member *college* to manage the everyday affairs of the Province. Both College and Council are under the chairmanship of a Crown Commissioner (*commissaris der Koningin*) appointed by the government. All cities, towns and villages in the Netherlands constitute Municipalities (*gemeenten*) which elect councils for four years. Each council elects an executive college whose chairman is a Burgomaster appointed by the Crown for six years. The Municipalities consult and cooperate through the Netherlands Union of Local Authorities to which all belong and which the government generally consults with regard to legislation affecting Municipal interests.

Judicial system: The lowest courts are the single-member Magistrates' Courts (*kantonrechter*) which try civil cases up to Fl500 ($137) and petty offences. The District Courts (*arrondissements-rechtbanken*) are competent in all remaining civil cases, all divorce cases and both felonies and misdemeanours; they also act as appeal courts for the Magistrates' Courts. The five Courts of Appeal (*gerechtshoven*) deal with tax matters and appeals from the District Courts; they have a number of chambers, each consisting of three judges. While the courts of first instance and the appeal courts can judge facts, only the Supreme Court (Hoge Raad) can interpret law. Judges are appointed by the Crown: they must retire at 70 There is no jury, but in some cases professional judges are assisted by skilled laymen appointed for four years. There is no death penalty.

RECENT HISTORY

The Netherlands signed a Customs Union with Belgium and Luxembourg in 1944, which has since come to be known as Benelux. In 1954 the overseas territories of Surinam (Dutch Guiana) and the Netherlands Antilles (islands of Aruba, Bonaire, Curaçao, Saba, St Eustatius and Dutch St Martin) obtained political autonomy within the Kingdom of the Netherlands, defence and foreign affairs remaining the responsibility of the Netherlands government. Independence was granted to Indonesia in 1949 and New Guinea was ceded to Indonesia in 1963. The Netherlands is a signatory of the Brussels Treaty (1948) and a founder-member of NATO, the ECSC, the EEC and Euratom.

Defence: The Sovereign is commander-in-chief of the armed forces. Military service lasts 18–20 months in the army and 21–24 months in the other services. The army of 85,000 men is assigned to or earmarked for NATO service. Navy strength is 21,000 including marines and the air force of 23,000 is also assigned to NATO. The 1966 defence estimates were Fl2,751 million ($750 million), representing 4.3 per cent of GNP.

ECONOMY

Background: The Netherlands is the most densely populated country in the world. Intensive use is made of its limited resources, coal and natural gas. The economy relies heavily upon imports, exports and entrepot trade. Apart from the recession of 1958, economic growth has been rapid since 1953; however, the economy is currently beset by inflation, an acute labour shortage and balance of payments problems. Between 1958 and 1966 the annual average rate of growth at constant prices was high at 5.4 per cent, causing a gradual exhaustion of the labour reserve, and consequent demand for labour has contributed to large increases in costs and prices since 1960.

The origin of GDP at factor cost in 1964 was:

Sector	Percentage
Agriculture . . .	8
Industry	41
Services	51
GDP	100

In recent years industrial growth has been mainly due to expansion of the metal, chemical and allied industries; the car, paper and building industries have also expanded. The major agricultural products include dairy produce and horticulture, much of which is exported. The agricultural sector continues to decline in importance.

Foreign trade: For many years there were large surpluses on the current account of the balance of payments, notably in 1958, 1959 and 1960. However, in 1964 a substantial deficit occurred (more than Fl700 million or $192 million) but in 1965 a moderate surplus of about Fl500 million ($137 million) was estimated, exports increasing by an estimated 10 per cent and imports by an estimated 5 per cent. In 1964 imports amounted to 42 per cent of GNP at current prices and exports to about 35 per cent. Over 50 per cent of trade in 1964 was with the EEC, and more in 1965. Other large sources of imports in 1964 were EFTA (14 per cent of total imports) and the United States (11 per cent). Exports, other than to the EEC, were similarly distributed— 19 per cent to EFTA and 4 per cent to the United States. Leading imports in 1964 were raw materials and semi-finished products (33 per cent of total imports), other industrial products (34 per cent), agricultural products (19 per cent) and fuels (14 per cent). Exports consisted mainly of industrial products (over 70 per cent of total exports), of which metal products, textiles and chemicals were predominant; food, beverages and tobacco accounted for a further 24 per cent.

Employment: The total labour force in 1961 was 4·3 million—10 per cent in agriculture, 42 per cent in industry and 48 per cent in services. Unemployment was under 1 per cent. Since this date the labour shortage has become more acute despite a large natural increase in the working population and an increase in net immigration of labour.

Price and wage trends: Since 1963 wages and consumer prices have risen steadily with comparable increases in labour productivity. In 1965 wages rose by 11 per cent, and in 1966 by an estimated 9 or 10 per cent; the cost of living in 1965 rose by 5 per cent, the highest increase in recent years. Throughout this period the government has attempted to control wages and prices by restricting the level of wage increases and by freezing the prices of goods.[1]

Consumption: Private consumption in 1964 amounted to 58 per cent of GNP at market prices and public consumption to 15 per cent. This represented increases of 5·7 per cent and 1·6 per cent over 1963, compared to estimated increases of 7 per cent and 1·5 per cent respectively in 1965.

SOCIAL SECURITY

General supervision is exercised by the Ministry of Social Affairs and Public Health. Contributions and benefits stated below refer to 1964.

Health insurance: Cash benefits are administered by business associations which are joint employer-employee organisations covering the various sectors of industry in which nationwide membership is compulsory (though it is possible to opt out on conscientious grounds). Medical benefits are administered by some approved sickness funds supervised by the Sickness Fund Council which is directly responsible to the Ministry. Employees earning below Fl10,900 ($2,887) annually must insure with a sickness fund. Pensioners and persons earning above this amount may insure voluntarily. There are special schemes for railwaymen, public employees, miners, seamen and certain other groups. Insurance is financed by the insured and the employer at the rate of 13 and 9–11 per cent of earnings respectively. Pensioners pay Fl5·5 or 11 per month according to marital status. The government pays subsidies for low-income voluntary subscribers. Medical benefits are provided by services contracted to and paid directly by the funds; they cover general and specialist care, laboratory services, medicines, some dental care, obstetric care, transportation, hospitalisation and appliances. Daily sickness benefits paid for up to 52 weeks are 80 per cent of earnings. Maternity benefits are 100 per cent of earnings paid for six weeks before and six weeks after confinement. Maternity grants are lump sum payments of Fl55 ($18).

Accident insurance: This is administered by the Social Insurance Bank with whom employers must insure, unless authorised by it to insure with special accident insurance associations or private companies. Insurance covers all employed persons, with special systems for seamen and agricultural employees, and is financed solely by the employer at the average rate of 2 per cent of annual earnings up to Fl10,900. Temporary disability benefits are paid for one year at the rate of 80 per cent of earnings up to Fl10,900 for the first six weeks and 70 per cent thereafter. For permanent disability, pensions are 70 per cent of earnings up to Fl10,900 for total disability, with constant attendance supplements of 30 per cent of earnings, and for partial disability pensions are equal to 70 per cent of the loss of wages. Widow's and invalid widower's pensions are 30 per cent of the insured's earnings. Orphan's pensions are 15 per cent of earnings—20 per cent for full orphans—for each child under 16. If survivor's pensions are below a maximum of 60 per cent,

[1] See 'Incomes and Prices Policies in Western Europe' (p. 394)

up to 30 per cent of earnings may be paid to parents, grandparents, parents-in-law and grandchildren.

Pensions insurance: This is administered by the Social Insurance Bank, assisted by employer-employee regional Labour Councils. Insurance covers all residents, there being a special scheme for public employees. It is financed by all insured persons of 15–64 years and employers at the respective rates of 8·1 per cent of net income and 1·5 per cent of earnings up to Fl10,900 per year. Old-age pensions are paid at 65, the full annual pension being Fl1,770 ($485)—reduced by 2 per cent for each non-contributory year. Wife's supplements of 55 per cent of pension are paid irrespective of age. Invalidity pensions range from Fl3,924 ($1,075) annually (for 80 per cent loss of earning capacity) to Fl2,454 ($672) (for loss of 55–66 per cent). Annual widow's pensions, payable at 50, with 50 per cent incapacity or with a child under 18, are Fl2,034 ($557) increasing to Fl2,910 ($705) if the widow is caring for more than one child. Orphan's pensions are paid at the rate of one-third of the widow's pension for each full orphan under 10, one-half at 10–16 and two-thirds at over 16. All pensions adjust automatically every six months for each 3 per cent change in the wage index.

Unemployment insurance: This covers both reduced pay and general unemployment benefits. The General Unemployment Fund administers the general benefits and supervises the reduced pay benefits, which are administered by business associations. All employees—except domestics and public and temporary employees—earning up to Fl10,900 annually are covered by the general system and most by the reduced pay system as well. Insurance is financed equally by the insured person and the employer at the rate of 1 to 5 per cent of earnings according to the industry, covering both general programme and reduced pay system. The government provides 0·6 per cent of total covered earnings for the general system only. Benefits are 70 per cent of average earnings in the insured's occupation with a supplement of 10 per cent for a dependant. Those covered by both benefits receive a maximum of 48 days of reduced pay benefits and then 78 days of general benefits. Those covered only by the general scheme receive 126 days of general unemployment benefits. The government pays social assistance to the needy whose benefit rights are exhausted.

Other benefits: Family allowances cover all employees, self-employed persons with limited income and social insurance beneficiaries with one or more children. For employees this is financed by the employer at the rate of 5·3 per cent of annual earnings up to Fl10,900. The self-employed and non-employed pay 2 per cent of net income, the government covering the whole cost of allowances for the first two children of self-employed persons and pensioners. Allowances are paid to each child under 16 (27 if a student or invalid) at the monthly rates of Fl19·50 ($5·4) for the first child rising to Fl32·5 ($9) for the sixth and subsequent children.

EDUCATION

Education is free and compulsory at private and state schools from 7 to 15. Privately run schools form a large part of the educational system and are financed almost entirely out of public funds. State schools are non-sectarian but provide non-compulsory religious instruction.

Primary education: Ordinary primary education lasts six years. Public primary schools are administered by municipal authorities and private primary schools by associations and institutions.

Secondary education: There are four forms of secondary education—'general continuation', divided into lower, intermediate and higher grades, and 'pre-university'.

Lower general continuation education (*lager algemeen voortgezet onderwijs*) has a first transitional year and is given in either the first two years of Elementary Vocational Schools or in two-year courses at separate Elementary General Continuation Schools. Intermediate general continuation education (*middelbaar algemeen voortgezet onderwijs*) is replacing the previous system of extended primary education and is provided as a preparation for secondary vocational education by three- or four-year courses at separate schools. Higher general continuation education (*hoger algemeen voortgezet onderwijs*) is intended to prepare students for higher vocational education and replaces the non-university preparation previously given at the Secondary Modern School (*hogere burgerschool*) and at the Secondary School for Girls. It is provided at separate five-year schools, in special departments of Atheneums, Lyceums and Intermediate Continuation Schools in the form of a two-year course subsequent to three years of pre-university education or four years of intermediate continued education, and in two-year preparatory courses at primary teacher-training colleges. There is a common first transitional year at intermediate and higher general continuation and pre-university levels.

Pre-university education (*voorbereidend wetenschapelijk onderwijs*) is given for at least six years at Gymnasiums teaching the classical humanities, Atheneums (replacing the *hogere burgerschool*) composed of literary-economic and exact science streams, and Lyceums which combine the two former.

Technical and vocational education: Schools for this form of education are mainly private; state vocational schools are maintained by Municipalities. Both are subsidised by public authorities, the state providing 70–75 per cent and the Municipalities 25–30 per cent of the public subsidy. Elementary vocational education is given at elementary technical, agricultural, domestic science and business and administration schools providing three- to four-year courses leading to apprenticeship. From intermediate general continuation education pupils may go on for a maximum of four years to courses at secondary technical, agricultural, domestic science and business and administration schools. There are also courses at this level for prospective social workers. For those completing higher continuation education or—generally after a one-year preparatory course—intermediate continuation education, technical, agricultural, teacher-training, art, business and administration and socio-pedagogic colleges offer higher vocational education through courses of a maximum of four years.

Special education: Special primary education is provided for handicapped children and also for children whose parents have no settled abode. Since 1950 both types and numbers of these schools have been greatly increased.

University and higher education: Higher education is both private and public. Public institutes are fully financed by the state and private institutes are awarded state grants covering up to 95 per cent of net costs. Leyden, Groningen and Utrecht are state universities, the University of Amsterdam is a municipal institution, and the Free University of Amsterdam (Calvinist) and the University of Nijmegen (Catholic) are private. The state administers the Technological Universities at Delft, Eindhoven and Enschede, and the

Agricultural University at Wageningen. The Institutes of Economics at Rotterdam (non-denominational) and Tilburg (Catholic) are both private. Courses generally last six years (five for law and seven or eight for medicine). Students take two examinations, the Candidate's and the Doctor's.

Students may be financed by scholarships, interest-free loans or a combination of both (mixed grants); the decision rests with the Ministry of Education and Science. These grants depend upon financial need and academic progress and are reviewed annually by the state. The maximum annual loan (1965) is Fl1,200 ($339) and if this is not enough further help is given in the form of a scholarship. The maximum annual grant is Fl4,000 ($1,096) plus exemption from the tuition fee of Fl200 ($55). Loans are repaid over ten years beginning two years after the completion of studies. However, to offset the shortage of teachers, graduates entering secondary schools have their debt reduced by 10 per cent for each year they teach.

Educational institutions, 1964:

	Institutions	Staff	Students
Primary	7,851	43,925	1,397,795
Secondary . . .	2,248	26,896	543,330
Technical, agricultural and vocational . .	1,938	n.a.	540,796
Higher	11	n.a.	58,361

Adult education: Most organisations are the result of private initiative and receive subsidies from the government. Generally adult education takes the form of social and cultural work through group discussion and short courses at residential Folk High Schools. About 50,000 people attend such courses annually. In 1964 there were 300 public libraries.

MASS MEDIA

The press (1966):

Dailies: De Telegraaf, Amsterdam, independent, 330,000; *Het Vrije Volk,* Amsterdam, Labour Party organ, 300,000; *De Volkskrant,* Amsterdam, centre Catholic, 167,000; *Het Parool,* Amsterdam, ind. soc., 164,000; *Algemeen Dagblad,* Rotterdam, liberal, 156,000; *Trouw,* Amsterdam, Protestant, 108,000; *Algemeen Handelsblad,* Amsterdam, liberal, 63,000; *De Tijd,* Amsterdam, Catholic, 59,000; *Nieuwe Rotterdamse Courant,* Rotterdam, liberal, 57,000; *De Waarheid,* Amsterdam, Communist Party organ.

Weeklies: Margriet, Leyden, woman's, 813,000; *Rosita,* Haarlem, wom., 260,000; *Elseviers Weekblad,* Amsterdam, independent, 125,000; *Wereldkroniek,* The Hague, family, 62,000; *Vrij Nederland,* Amsterdam, ind. soc., 55,000; *Haagse Post,* Amsterdam, ind., 34,000; *De Groene Amsterdammer,* Amsterdam, ind., 22,000.

Broadcasting: The Netherlands Radio Union (Stichting Nederlandsche Radio-Unie) is formed from five previously independent companies of varying political complexions. The board of the Radio Union consists of representatives of all the companies; the state exercises some supervision. Finance is by licences and advertising. The Netherlands Television Corporation (Nederlandse Televisie Stichting) comprises the same companies as the Radio Union, and its board includes their members together with others—including the chairman—appointed by the Crown. The Corporation's finance is by licence fees and is state-supervised.

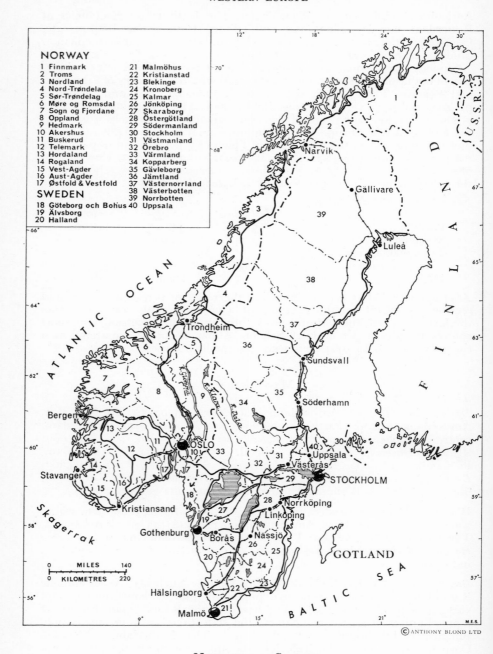

NORWAY
1 Finnmark
2 Troms
3 Nordland
4 Nord-Trøndelag
5 Sør-Trøndelag
6 Møre og Romsdal
7 Sogn og Fjordane
8 Oppland
9 Hedmark
10 Akershus
11 Buskerud
12 Telemark
13 Hordaland
14 Rogaland
15 Vest-Agder
16 Aust-Agder
17 Østfold & Vestfold

21 Malmöhus
22 Kristianstad
23 Blekinge
24 Kronoberg
25 Kalmar
26 Jönköping
27 Skaraborg
28 Östergötland
29 Södermanland
30 Stockholm
31 Västmanland
32 Örebro
33 Värmland
34 Kopparberg
35 Gävleborg
36 Jämtland
37 Västernorrland
38 Västerbotten
39 Norrbotten
40 Uppsala

SWEDEN
18 Göteborg och Bohus
19 Älvsborg
20 Halland

MILES 140

KILOMETRES 220

© ANTHONY BLOND LTD

NORWAY AND SWEDEN

154

NORWAY

GEOGRAPHY

Features: Apart from the area immediately around Oslo on the Oslo Fjord and a narrow strip along the coast from Oslo to Stavanger, almost the entire country is upland. The highest part is the Jotunheimen region, rising to over 8,000 ft/2,400 m. Much of central-southern Norway is an elevated plateau tilting to the south-east; further north the land area narrows and forms a complicated ridge of mountains sloping to the sea. All along the west coast the land is indented by a series of deep, steep-sided fjords. Most of the rivers, with the exception of those draining into the Oslo area, e.g. Glomma, are short and swift. Along the coast are numerous small islands.

Less than 5 per cent of the land is cultivated and farming is heavily localised, the chief regions being around Oslo and along the coastal plain in the south. Elsewhere farming is confined to favourable parts of the river valleys and the terraces bordering many of the fjords near their mouths. The only coalfield is in the Norwegian part of Spitzbergen. The chief mineral is iron ore, and there are a number of fields scattered throughout the country, of which the most important is around Sydvaranger (Kirkenes) and near Mo i Rana in Nordland. Industry is highly localised, being associated either with the chief ports or the large hydroelectric plants, e.g. that at Rjukan.

Area: 125,000 sq. miles/324,000 sq. km. Overseas Territories: Spitzbergen, Jan Mayen, Bouvet Island, Peter I's Island. *Mean max. and min. temperatures:* Oslo (60° N, 10° 30′ E; 310 ft/94 m.) 73°F/23°C (July), 20°F/−7°C (Jan. and Feb.); Bergen (60° 30′ N, 5° 30′ E; 140 ft/43 m.) 72°F/22°C (July), 27°F/−3°C (Jan.); Narvik (68° 30′ N, 17° 30′ E; 105 ft/32 m.) 76°F/24°C (July), 20°F/−7°C (Jan. and Feb.). *Relative humidity:* Oslo 80 per cent; Bergen 82 per cent; Narvik 79 per cent. *Mean annual rainfall:* Oslo 27 in./685 mm.; Bergen 79 in./2,000 mm.; Narvik 29 in./735 mm.

POPULATION

Total population: (1965) 3,738,000. *Chief towns and populations:* (1965) OSLO (483,000), Bergen (117,000), Trondheim (114,000), Stavanger (78,000), Kristiansand (50,000), Drammen (47,000), Skien (45,000). *Distribution:* In 1965 42 per cent of the population lived in Municipalities of less than 10,000 inhabitants, 33 per cent in Municipalities of 10–50,000 and 25 per cent in Municipalities of over 50,000.

Language: Two Norwegian languages, 'Book Language' (*bokmål*, formerly *riksmål*) which is strongly influenced by Danish, and 'New Norwegian' (*nynorsk*, formerly *landsmål*) based on Norwegian dialects, have equal official status. All official documents are published in both languages. Both are used equally on radio and TV and in the press and have the same educational standard. All children learn to read both languages and to write one. University entrance requires the ability to write in both languages. Nynorsk, which predominates in rural areas around the central range, is little used in business and only about 15 per cent of all books—including virtually no translations—are published in the language. Whether the two languages should be forcibly amalgamated or permitted to fuse naturally into a common language (*samnorsk*) is a subject of dispute. The 20,000 Lapps of northern Norway have their own language. *Religion:* The state religion of Norway is Evangelical-Lutheran to which 96 per cent of the population adheres.

CONSTITUTIONAL SYSTEM

Constitution: Norway is a constitutional monarchy. The present constitution dates from 1814 with amendments. *Head of state:* King Olav V. *Head of government:* Prime Minister Per Borten (Centre Party).
Executive: Executive power is vested in the King and a Council of State (Statsråd) consisting of the Prime Minister and at least seven other ministers (of whom at least half must profess the national faith). The King's selection must be approved by parliament. He must act in accordance with the majority of the Council. Important matters of administration must bear the counter-signature of the responsible minister.

Legislature: Norway has a modified form of unicameral legislature. The parliament (Storting) consists of 150 members elected for four years by proportional representation. It cannot be dissolved before the end of this period. The Storting elects a quarter of its members to form the upper house (Lagting) and the remainder make up the lower house (Odelsting). This division is important only for law-making; all other decisions are made by a united Storting. If legislation originating in the Odelsting is twice rejected by the Lagting, it must be voted by two-thirds majority of the united Storting. The Lagting and the Supreme Court (see under *Judicial system*) together form the Constitutional Court (Riksrett) which tries actions against ministers, representatives and Supreme Court judges.

Political parties: Norway's major parties are the Labour Party, the Conservative Party, the Liberal Party (Venstre), the Centre Party (until 1958 the Agrarian Party) and the Christian People's Party. The small anti-militarist and neutralist Socialist People's Party held the political balance in the 1961–5 Storting. The Communist Party lost its last parliamentary seat in 1957. In September 1965, 30 years of almost unbroken rule by the Labour Party came to an end when it was superseded by the present governing coalition of Conservatives, Liberals, Centre and Christian People's Party.

Leading political figures: Centre Party—Per Borten (Party Chairman and Prime Minister). Conservative Party—John Lyng (Foreign Minister and Parliamentary Party Leader), Otto Tidemand (Defence Minister). Liberal Party—Ole Myrvoll (Finance Minister). Christian People's Party—Einar

Hareide (Party Chairman). Labour Party—Trygve Bratelli (Party Chairman and Leader in Storting), Einar Gerhardsen (former Prime Minister), Halvard Lange (former Foreign Minister).

Election results:

	1961		1965	
Party	Percentage of poll	Seats	Percentage of poll	Seats
Labour Party . . .	46·76	74	43·14	68
Conservative Party . .	19·26	29	20·3	31
Liberal Party . . .	7·2	14	10·15	18
Centre Party . . .	6·83	16	9·37	18
Christian People's Party .	9·32	15	7·83	13
Socialist People's Party .	2·39	2	5·99	2
Communist Party . .	2·91	—	1·37	—
Non-Socialist lists . .	5·17	—	1·83	—
Other lists . . .	0·16	—	0·02	—

Local government: Norway is divided into 20 Counties (*fylker*) of which two—Oslo and Bergen—are urban and the remainder rural. The Counties are further divided into Rural Municipalities (*herredskommuner*) and Urban Municipalities (*by-kommuner*). The Municipalities elect Councils (*kommunestyre*) of from 13 to 85 members serving for four years. Each Council elects a quarter of its membership to serve as a steering committee (*formannskap*) with certain powers delegated to it. The committee elects a chairman who serves as Mayor (*ordfører*) for two years. The Municipalities have considerable autonomy and certain responsibilities are statutorily imposed upon them. The state supervises the Municipalities through its appointed County Governor (*fylkesmann*).

Each of the 18 Rural Counties forms a County Municipality (*fylkeskommune*)—Oslo and Bergen are Urban Municipalities coming under the authority of the surrounding Rural County—under a County Council (*fylkesting*) composed of representatives of the Municipal Councils within the County. The Council elects a fourth of its members as a County Committee (*fylkesutvalg*). A state-appointed County Governor acts as the administrative head of the County.

Judicial system: With certain exceptions, no civil case can be brought before a court prior to an attempt at mediation by a Conciliation Council (*forliksråd*). Most Municipalities elect such a council of three members for four years. It may pronounce judgement where so requested by both parties. In the five Town Courts (*byrettene*) and 94 County Courts (*herredsrettene*) civil and criminal cases are administered by a single professional judge, assisted in appropriate cases by two lay judges (*domsmenn*). In the five Courts of Appeal (*lagmansrettene*) three professional judges are assisted by two to four lay judges in civil cases and by a jury of ten in criminal cases. Appeals from the lower courts are heard by the Board of Appeal of the Supreme Court (Høyesterette Kjaeremålsutvalg) composed of three Supreme Court judges and the Supreme Court (Høyesterett) proper, which has 18 judges including the President and sits as a court of five members.

Judges are appointed by the King upon the recommendation of the Minister of Justice and must retire at 70. Otherwise they may be dismissed only by judicial sentence. There is no capital punishment for peacetime crimes.

RECENT HISTORY

After the German occupation (1940–5) Norway dropped its previous policy of neutrality and joined NATO after plans for a Scandinavian military alliance had proved abortive. In 1952 it became a member of the Nordic Council. Norway was a prime mover in the establishment of EFTA, but like Britain has negotiated for full membership of the EEC. In the UN Norway has played a leading peace-keeping role.

Defence: The King is commander-in-chief of the armed forces. To emphasise the defensive nature of its adherence to NATO, Norway does not permit the establishment of foreign bases upon its territory in peacetime. There are no nuclear weapons stationed on Norwegian territory. All men between 20 and 44 are liable to conscription for 12–15 months and additional reservist training. The defence budget for 1966 was Nkr2,134 million ($298 million) representing about 4 per cent of GNP. Strengths of the services: army 17,000, navy 7,500, air force 9,000, local defence and home guard 70,000.

ECONOMY

Background: Industrial expansion has been based primarily on the country's abundant water-power, and to a lesser extent on natural resources such as fish, timber, ores and metals. Although economic growth in recent years has been rapid, demand has tended to rise faster than capacity and has led to pressure upon both prices and the balance of trade. Anti-inflationary budgetary and monetary measures taken in 1965 did not prevent prices from rising rapidly in 1966. The government attaches great importance to long-term planning. Annual average rate of growth of GNP between 1959 and 1964 was 5·2 per cent; the target for the 1966–9 plan is 4.7 per cent a year.

In 1964 the value of GNP at current prices was NKr49,643 million ($6,930 million), an increase of 6·2 per cent over 1963. In recent years expansion has been strong in all sectors except forestry, fishing, agriculture and whaling. The origin of GDP in 1964 at factor cost was:

Sector				Percentage
Agriculture	.	.	.	9
Industry	.	.	.	38
Services	.	.	.	53
GDP				100

The main industries are iron and steel, chemicals, wood and wood processing, hydroelectric power and mining. The main agricultural products are livestock, barley and potatoes.

Foreign trade: In recent years commodity imports have exceeded exports and the resultant trade deficit has been balanced by earnings from Norway's merchant fleet (valued at about half the total value of commodity exports), tourism and the sale of whale oil. The balance of payments deficit fell sharply in 1964, mainly because of higher export earnings and lower imports of ships, but increased again in 1965. The main exports in 1964 were metal and allied products (22 per cent of total exports), forest products (16 per cent), and fish and fish products (9 per cent). The main imports in the same year were machinery and transport equipment (22 per cent), ships (about 16 per cent), raw materials, fuels and chemicals (26 per cent) and base metals

(11 per cent). In 1964 imports accounted for 32 per cent of GNP and exports for 21 per cent. In 1963 main destinations of exports were Britain (18 per cent of total exports), West Germany (15 per cent), and Sweden (14 per cent) with imports coming from the same countries—Britain 16 per cent, West Germany 17 per cent and Sweden 19 per cent. Trade with EFTA in 1963 amounted to 43 per cent of total trade and with the EEC 28 per cent.

Employment: Total employed population is expected to be 1,568,000 by 1969, with a decline in the relative share of primary industries and a growth in manufacturing, construction and service industries. In 1964 over 35 per cent of the labour force was employed in industry, 20 per cent in agriculture and 44 per cent in services; unemployment amounted to 1 per cent and was basically seasonal.

Price and wage trends: In 1964 wages rose by about 8 per cent and the consumer price index by 5.7 per cent, compared with increases of about 6 per cent for wages and under 2 per cent for the cost of living in 1963. The government has used price subsidies and set up machinery for coordination between employers and unions to determine wage increases.

Consumption: In 1964 private consumption amounted to about 53 per cent of GNP at current prices and public consumption to about 9.4 per cent.

SOCIAL SECURITY

The Ministry of Social Affairs exercises general supervision over health, pensions, accident and family allowance insurance, while the National Insurance Institution administers the programme on a national scale and supervises the local insurance funds. Unemployment insurance is supervised by the Ministry of Local Government and Labour assisted by local funds and regional labour boards. Contributions and benefits given below refer to 1964 except where otherwise stated.

Health insurance: This covers all insured residents, dependant children under 18, and a dependant spouse earning less than NKr11,000 ($140) annually, for medical benefits. Employees are covered compulsorily for sickness benefits, while non-employees may insure voluntarily. There are special systems for seamen, fishermen and public employees. Insurance is financed by the insured person at the weekly rate of NKr2·20–10 ($0·30–1·40) according to income class (non-employees pay additional premiums if voluntarily insured for sickness benefits and pensioners pay contributions only if their annual extra-pension income is above NKr1,000 or $140), by the employer at the rate of 75 per cent of the employee's contribution, and by national and local governments covering respectively 20 and 25 per cent of the contributions of insured persons. Hospital, sanatorium, laboratory and maternity services, as well as certain vital medicines, are provided free, and certain other costs are refunded. Daily sickness benefits range from NKr3 to 19 ($0·40 to 2·66) with supplements of NKr2 ($0·28) for spouse and each dependant child under 18, and are paid for 104 weeks, or indefinitely for patients with certain illnesses, e.g. polio, cancer and tuberculosis. Maternity benefits are the same as for sickness and are paid for six weeks before and six weeks after confinement. Wives of insured persons receive maternity grants of NKr200 ($28) if they are not treated in a maternity clinic.

Accident insurance: This covers all employees, students, military and fishermen. The self-employed may insure on an optional basis. The employer pays the whole contribution varying from NKr0·6 to 9 ($0·1 to 1·3) per week. Full medical benefits including appliances are provided free. Temporary disability benefit is the same as ordinary sickness benefit, and is paid for 52 weeks. The full disability pension is 60 per cent of average monthly earnings up to NKr1,667 ($233), with monthly supplements of up to NKr200 ($28) for constant attendance and of NKr75 ($10·5) for each child under 18 (21 if a student and no limit if an invalid). Partial disability pensions are paid as a percentage of the full pension proportionate to the degree of disability, and are converted into a lump sum for 15 to 29 per cent disability. Widow's pensions—also payable to invalid widowers—are 40 per cent of the insured's earnings if the widow is aged over 40 or caring for a child; otherwise she is paid two year's pension only. Monthly orphan's pensions are NKr75 for each orphan under 18 (21 if a student, indefinitely if an invalid). In the case of full orphans the first receives 40 per cent of the insured's earnings and the rest NKr75 monthly. Other eligible survivors are dependant parents, grandparents, brothers and sisters.

Pensions insurance: A common compulsory scheme for the whole population came into force in January 1967. All benefits and contributions are related to a Basic Annual Amount (NKr5,400 or $756 in 1967) adjusted in accordance with changes in the level of prices and incomes. Old-age pension begins at 70 and consists of a basic and a supplementary pension. The basic old-age pension is equal to the Basic Amount and increases by 50 per cent for married couples. Maintenance allowances of 50 per cent of the Basic Amount are paid to a spouse not entitled to his or her own pension, and of 25 per cent for each dependant child under 18. The supplementary old-age pension is calculated on the basis of all earned annual income lying between the Basic Amount and eight times the Basic Amount (i.e. pensionable earnings ranged from NKr5,400 to NKr43,200 in 1967) related to the insured's 20 best years of earnings, to a maximum equal to 45 per cent of that proportion of pensionable income exceeding the Basic Amount. Invalidity pensions, paid to those who have lost at least 25 per cent of their earning capacity, are related to degree of disability to a maximum equivalent to the old-age pension that the insured would have earned had he or she worked on until pensionable age. Full widow's pensions—also payable to dependant widowers—are paid to those unable to earn 50 per cent of the Basic Amount and are equal to the Basic Amount plus a supplementary pension. Orphan's pensions, payable to each child under 18, are 40 per cent of the Basic Amount for the first and 25 per cent for each other child; the first full orphan receives unreduced the widow's or widower's pension which would have been payable to the surviving parent, the second receives 40 per cent of the Basic Amount and the others 25 per cent each.

The scheme is financed by the insured person (paying 4 per cent of pensionable income), the employer (7 per cent), self-employed persons (6 per cent) and the state and the Municipalities (each paying 0·75 per cent). These rates refer to 1967; there will be an annual increase in the contributions of employers and self-employed persons of 0·6 per cent.

Unemployment insurance: This covers all employees earning more than NKr1,000 annually, with the exception of fishermen, family labour in agriculture and domestic service, temporary and public employees. It is financed equally by employees and employers at the weekly rate of NKr0·25– 1·20 ($0·04–0·17) according to income class, with a local government supplement of 25 per cent of the contributions of employers and employees.

The national government provides up to 60 per cent of the deficit of local funds. Daily benefits and supplements are the same as for sickness and are payable for up to 20 weeks (30 if the age of the insured is over 50) in a year. Insurance also provides financial assistance for vocational training and retraining and for moving to a new area.

Other benefits: Family allowances are paid entirely by the state for children under 16, at the annual rate of NKr400 ($56) for the second child, rising by NKr100 ($14) for each successive child. The allowance is also payable for a first child if it is an orphan or an invalid, or if its parents are divorced. All employees are entitled to a minimum of four weeks paid holiday with three days pay as a vacation allowance.

EDUCATION

Primary education: There are few private primary schools and they receive no state aid. State education is free and compulsory from the ages of seven to 14. Municipalities are empowered to extend this upper limit to 15 or 16 at their discretion, and as the nine-year school (*enhetsskole*) becomes more widespread the higher compulsory age will be 16. At present the nine-year school, expected to be general by the 1970s, coexists with the seven-year school (*folkeskole*) providing a uniform education for all children up to the age of 14. The nine-year school is divided into a six-year Junior School (*barneskole*) and a three-year Youth School (*ungdomskole*) with specialisation taking place only after the seventh year, entailing compulsory courses for those applying to the Gymnasium and technical schools. There is a voluntary tenth year. On the basis of the seven-year system pupils may attend a Continuation School (*framhaldskole*) for full or part-time studies for two or three years respectively. Primary education is continued here with a bias towards practical subjects. A number of Municipalities have made one-year attendance at Continuation Schools compulsory. The 'practical' stream of the nine-year school will replace the Continuation School.

Secondary education: Private secondary education offering short educational courses leading to state examinations has met with considerable success. Enrolment in state secondary schools (*høgre allmenskoler*) has also greatly increased in recent years. Most schools charge no tuition fees. Secondary education currently takes the form of the *realskole*, usually a three-year school, and the *gymnasium*, a five-year school, both having the same two-year foundation course. Final exams are the *realskoleeksamen* and the Gymnasium's *examen artium*, the latter being the basis for university or college education. The Realskole is to be eliminated, the first two years of secondary education being replaced by the 'theory line' of the nine-year school, leaving the Gymnasium as a three-year school.

Special schools: All children with physical or mental disabilities are educated in special schools (*spesialskoler*) administered by the Ministry of Church and Education.

Vocational schools: A number of trades have built up their own system to suit their requirements, and each system is under the appropriate ministry. State, municipal and private technical schools take people with various entrance qualifications. They provide training at all stages of apprenticeship and opportunities for higher technical education, which is administered by the Ministry of Education. The Ministry also controls the Vocational Schools for Commercial and Clerical Work (*yrkesskoler for handel og kontorarbeid*) which provide six-month or one-year day courses and two-year evening courses. Secondary Commercial Schools (*handelsgymnasier*), run by the Municipalities with state aid, provide one- to three-year courses for students having secondary school qualifications.

University and higher education: The number of students at the two universities (Oslo and Bergen) and the colleges of technology at Trondheim, agriculture at Ås, veterinary science at Oslo, economics and business administration at Bergen and teaching at Oslo, has nearly doubled between 1960–1 and 1964–5. Courses last from four to eight years. For most university courses students decide for themselves the time that they need before taking an examination.

Adult education: People's High Schools (*folkehøgskoler*) are boarding schools concentrating on general education for persons over the age of 17, the majority of whom come from country districts. All provide one-year and some two-year courses. Other adult education is largely state-aided and takes the form of lectures, direct instruction and study groups. In 1963 there were 1,109 public libraries, situated almost entirely in rural districts.

Educational institutions, 1965–6: [1]

	Schools, etc.	Staff	Pupils
Lower Primary . . .	3,508	16,996	412,157
Upper Primary . . .	192	3,129	46,329
Continuation . . .	703	1,940	30,838
Special	63	493	2,727
People's High Schools .	74	525	5,946
Secondary	322	5,276	106,918
Vocational	662	4,983	72,816
Universities, etc. . .	8	1,976	19,518

[1] Excluding private education.

MASS MEDIA

The press (1965):

Dailies: Aftenposten, Oslo, Conservative, 185,000; *Dagbladet,* Oslo, Liberal, 93,000; *Bergens Tidende,* Bergen, Lib., 75,000; *Arbeiderbladet,* Oslo, Socialist, 68,000; *Morgenposten,* Oslo, independent, 37,000; *Verdens Gang,* Oslo, ind., 35,000; *Stavanger Aftenblad,* Stavanger, Lib., 42,000; *Drammens Tidende og Buskeruds Blad,* Drammen, Cons., 31,000; *Faedrelandsvennen,* Kristiansand, Lib., 27,000; *Sunnmørposten,* Ålesund, Lib., 26,000.

Periodicals: (Oslo): Norsk Ukeblad (w), illustrated, 236,000; *Vårt Blad* (w), Co-operative, 227,000; *Allers* (w), illus., 203,000; *Illustrert Familieblad* (w), illus., 137,000; *Det Beste* (w), family, 132,000; *Fri Fagbevegelse,* organ of Norwegian TUC, 32,000; *Farmand* (w), economic/financial, 26,000; *Norsk Landbruk* (w), agricultural, 19,000; *Samtiden* (m), political/literary, 6,000.

Broadcasting: The Norwegian Broadcasting Corporation (*Norsk Rikskring-kasting*) controls and operates all radio and TV as state monopolies on a non-commercial basis. Revenue is derived from annual licences and a sales tax on receivers.

PORTUGAL

GEOGRAPHY

Features: This roughly rectangular country consists of a mountainous east and north with much lower land to west and south. The chief upland areas are the Douro uplands, which are divided in two by the west-flowing Douro; the highest parts are the Serra da Estrela, rising to over 6,000 ft/1,850 m., and the Tràs os Montes, rising to over 3,000 ft. The rest of the country is divided into a series of plains and low ridges. The chief lowland areas are along the west coast and the Tagus river.

Much of the surface of Portugal is forest-covered, and scant irrigation limits agriculture, though in recent years irrigation schemes have been developed along the Tagus and Sado rivers. Mineral deposits are scattered and of poor quality, only small amounts of coal, iron ore and pyrites being produced. Industry is limited both in variety and extent and is confined mainly to the immediate vicinities of Oporto and Lisbon.

Area: 35,500 sq. miles/92,000 sq. km. (including the Azores and the Islands of Madeira and Porto Santo). Overseas Territories: Angola, Mozambique, Portuguese Guinea, Timor, Macao, Cape Verde Islands and São Tomé and Príncipe. *Mean max. and min. temperatures:* Lisbon (38° 30′ N, 9° W; 310 ft/ 95 m.) 80°F/27°C (Aug.), 46°F/8°C (Jan.); Oporto (41° N, 8° 30′ W; 330 ft/100 m.) 77°F/25°C, 40°F/4°C. *Relative humidity:* Lisbon 72 per cent; Oporto 80 per cent. *Mean annual rainfall:* Lisbon 27 in./685 mm.; Oporto 46 in./1,170 mm.

POPULATION

Population: (1964) Continental Portugal and islands 9,180,000; Overseas Territories 12,878,000. *Main towns and populations:* (1960) Greater LISBON (1,335,000), Greater Oporto (747,000), Coimbra (46,000), Setúbal (45,000), Braga (41,000). *Distribution:* In 1960 12 per cent of the population lived in centres of over 100,000 inhabitants, 10 per cent in centres of 10–100,000 and 78 per cent in centres of fewer than 10,000 (70 per cent in centres of fewer than 2,000).

Language: The official language is Portuguese. *Religion:* Predominantly Roman Catholic.

CONSTITUTIONAL SYSTEM

Constitution: Portugal is a 'unitary and corporative' republic. The constitution of 1933 was adopted by referendum. *Head of state:* President Admiral Américo de Deus Rodrigues Tomás. *Head of government:* Prime Minister António de Oliveira Salazar.

Executive: The President is chosen for seven years by an electoral college composed of the members of the National Assembly and the Corporative

Chamber and municipal representatives of each metropolitan District and Overseas Territory, and is not eligible for reelection. He appoints the Prime Minister and the ministers proposed by the Prime Minister. He promulgates legislation passed by the National Assembly, and has the power to dissolve this body or to convoke it in extraordinary sessions. He is advised by a Council of State composed of the Prime Minister, the Presidents of the National Assembly, the Corporative Chamber and the Supreme Court of Justice, the Procurator-General and ten public figures appointed for life by the President of the Republic. The Prime Minister presides over the Council of Ministers composed of his appointees. He is responsible for general policy only to the President. The Council of Ministers may nominate, transfer and dismiss by decree the Procurator-General, the President of the Supreme Court, diplomatic and consular staff and Governors of Overseas Provinces. The life of the cabinet depends solely upon the President. Individual ministers are responsible to the Prime Minister. The Council of Ministers may legislate through the National Assembly or by decree.

Legislature: The National Assembly (Assembleia Nacional) is composed of 130 members including 23 representatives of the Overseas Territories elected for four years by direct vote for party lists. Electors include all literate males, or illiterates if they pay taxes in excess of E100 ($3·50), widows as heads of the family and unmarried women who have received secondary education. The Assembly may initiate legislation as well as pass measures proposed by the Council of Ministers or the President. Every ten years, or by special presidential authorisation, it is empowered to revise the constitution. The Corporative Chamber is composed of an unspecified number of members representing the local authorities and commercial, cultural, industrial and religious interests. The Chamber reports and advises within a specified period on all legislative proposals prior to their submission to the Assembly. Its sessions are simultaneous with those of the Assembly and no person may be a member of both bodies.

Election results: The only legally constituted political organisation is the National Union which occupies all 130 seats in the National Assembly. Groups forming a tolerated opposition are the liberal middle-class Directorio Democrata Social and the socialist Seara Nova. The Communist Party was proscribed in 1926, but is believed to have about 20,000 members.

Leading political figures: António de Oliveira Salazar (Prime Minister and President of the National Union), Alberto Franco Nogueira (Foreign Minister), General Manuel Gomes de Araujo (Defence Minister), Ulisses Cortes (Finance Minister).

Local government: The basic unit of local government is the Parish (*freguesia*). Parishes are divided into three classes. In second- and some third-class Parishes the head of the family is the direct authority. In larger first-class Parishes seven-member Parochial Councils are nominated by the president of the local Municipal Chamber (in Lisbon and Oporto by the Civil Governor). To every Parish the Municipal authority attaches a delegate (*regedor*) who acts as an observer. The Urban and Rural Districts (*concelhos*) have Municipal Councils composed of representatives of the Parishes and corporate organisations. The Councils elect two to six Aldermen for three years who together with a government-appointed President make up the Municipal Chamber. The Chamber has general administrative authority, but the President has certain independent duties of his own. In Lisbon and

Oporto the Municipalities are known as Quarters (*bairros*). The Municipalities are grouped together into Provinces. Each Province has a Council composed of representatives of the Municipal Chambers and corporative bodies. It elects a Provincial Board which is headed by a state-appointed Governor.

Judicial system: The lowest courts are those of the *juiz de paz* existing in each of the judicial districts (*comarcas*) into which Portugal is divided for the purposes of the separate dispensation of civil and criminal law. Appeal lies with the Courts of Appeal (*tribunais de relação*) in Lisbon, Oporto and Coimbra, each consisting of a president and a varying number of magistrates. Final decisions are given by the Supreme Court of Justice (Supremo Tribunal de Justiça) in Lisbon, which is composed of a president and 15 judges. Judges are appointed for life and are irremovable except in cases specified by law. There is no capital punishment except by sentence of court-martial.

RECENT HISTORY

The country has been ruled virtually since 1926 by Salazar, who in that year took charge of the exchequer, with control over the expenditure of all other ministries, after a military coup. In 1932 he became President of the Council of Ministers, a position which he has since held virtually unopposed. Portugal remained neutral in the second world war but permitted Britain and the United States to use the Azores for surveillance of the Atlantic. The country was a founder-member of NATO in 1949, joined the United Nations in 1955, and became a founder-member of EFTA in 1960. The Portuguese Territory of Goa was annexed by India in 1961. Since then Portuguese forces have been committed against insurrections in the colonies of Angola, Mozambique and Guinea. In 1958 General Delgado stood as opposition candidate in the Presidential elections and was officially credited with 23 per cent of the vote. In 1961 one of his supporters, Captain Galvão, pirated the Portuguese liner the *Santa Maria* with the aim of drawing world attention to the suppression of opposition groups in Portugal. In 1962 there was an abortive uprising against Salazar in Beja. Delgado was murdered (in Spain, possibly by Portuguese agents) in 1965. In early 1966 Anglo-Portuguese relations became strained over the supply of oil from Beira in Mozambique to the rebel colony of Rhodesia.

Defence: Compulsory military service lasts for 18–24 months in the army, 48 months in the navy and 18 months in the air force, with conscripts being liable for the active reserve until 35 years and home defence tasks until 45 years. Compulsory military service is generally to be extended to 3½ or 4 years. The strengths of the armed forces are: army 120,000 plus 14,000 African troops, navy including marines 14,500, air force including paratroopers 13,500. The para-military National Republican Guard totals a further 10,000 and there are about 500,000 trained reservists. One army division stationed in Portugal is earmarked for NATO as is part of the air force. The remainder of the army is mainly committed in the Overseas Territories in Africa. The 1966 defence estimates were E6,523 million ($224 million), representing 6·5 per cent of GNP.

ECONOMY

Background: Portugal has few natural resources and in many respects is still a developing country.[1] Three development plans—1953–8, 1959–64 and

[1] See 'The Dictatorships of Spain and Portugal', p. 320.

1965–7—have been implemented. They have been relatively successful; the annual average rate of growth of GNP in the period 1953–64 was 5·1 per cent and the structural change towards an industrialised economy has been considerable. Growth has been concentrated mainly in the non-traditional branches of the economy such as metals and metal products, chemicals, petroleum products, pulp, paper and hydroelectric power. There has also been substantial growth in the traditional industries of textiles and processed foods. Agriculture and the extractive sectors of the economy—mining and quarrying—have changed little in the last decade. In 1965 the economy continued to expand, GNP at current prices increasing to E111,047 million ($3,841 million), exceeding the growth target of 6·1 per cent laid down in the current development plan.

Sector contributions to GNP at factor cost in 1964 were:

Sector	Percentage of GNP
Agriculture, forestry and fishing	23
Industry	43
Services	34
Total	100

From 1958 to 1964 industrial production increased by an annual average of 7·7 per cent, the highest of all EFTA countries. In the same period agricultural output increased by an annual average of only 1·5 per cent. The main Portuguese industrial and agricultural products are chemicals, pulp, paper, cork, fertilisers, hydroelectric power, cotton and other textiles, wine, sardines and other canned fish, fruit, cereals and vegetables. The economy is heavily dependent upon foreign investment, both financial and technical, and Portugal's overseas territories make a considerable contribution to the balance of payments and the supply of raw materials.

Foreign trade: In 1964 exports of goods and services were estimated to amount to 16 per cent of GNP and imports to 24 per cent. The main exports in 1963 were food, beverages and raw materials (50 per cent of total exports), textiles (22 per cent) and wood and cork manufactures (11 per cent); the main imports were food and raw materials (43·5 per cent) and iron and steel (27 per cent). Chief exports in 1963 were distributed 24 per cent to EFTA, 22 per cent to the EEC, and 12 per cent to the United States; and chief imports 22 per cent from EFTA, 34·5 per cent from the EEC, 9 per cent from the United States and 14 per cent from the Overseas Territories. Between 1953 and 1963 the share of manufactured goods in total exports rose from 43 to 59 per cent, imports of raw materials more than doubled and imports of machinery and transport equipment also increased considerably. At 1962 the trade deficit for the Escudo Area—about E2,500 million ($86·7 million)—was increasing despite improvement in the overall balance of payments, and was largely due to an increase in imports, the favourable trend in the overall balance being attributable to a reduction of government expenditure abroad and an increase in receipts from tourism.

Employment: In 1960 the total working population was 3·35 million, of whom 43 per cent were employed in agriculture, 29 per cent in industry, and 26 per cent in services; unemployment was 2 per cent. Between 1960 and 1963 the labour market was characterised by a shortage of skilled manpower, seasonal unemployment, a marked reduction in the agricultural population as a result of reorganisation of industry and decline in certain industries such as mining. In 1962 the government, recognising the urgent need for more and better-trained labour, set up a Manpower Development Fund and an Institute for Industrial Research began a national training programme for foremen. Technical education is being steadily expanded.

Price and wage trends: Inflation since 1960 has been due mainly to shortage of labour and rising demand. Largely on account of recent increases in minimum wages, the general trend for wages has been to move upward at a faster rate than prices. Productivity slowed down from an increase of 14·5 per cent in manufacturing industries in 1960 to 7·9 per cent in 1961 and 3·1 per cent in 1962. Wholesale and consumer prices in 1962 increased in Lisbon by under 1 per cent and 2·7 per cent respectively, and wages by 7 per cent. Since 1962 this pattern of price and wage increases has continued to contribute towards inflation.

Consumption: In 1963 private consumption accounted for 75 per cent of GNP and public consumption for 14 per cent. In recent years the trend has been for private consumption to expand more rapidly than public consumption. A major item of public consumption since 1960 has been defence.

SOCIAL SECURITY

Social security covers old-age, invalidity, death, sickness, maternity, family allowances and occupational injury. In the case of the last, insurance covers all employed persons; otherwise it covers all employees in industry and commerce. There are special systems for fishermen, some liberal professions and railwaymen and public employees. All insurance except for accident insurance is financed by a single contribution amounting to 5.5 per cent of earnings by the employee and 15 per cent by the employer. The maximum monthly earnings for contributions and benefit purposes are E4,000 ($140). The Ministry of Corporations and Social Welfare exercises general supervision through its Directorate of Social Welfare, while local administration is through joint employer-employee regional funds coordinated by a central national fund. The employer bears the whole burden of accident insurance either through the direct provision of benefit or by paying insurance premiums to authorised insurance companies. All contributions and benefits stated below refer to 1964.

Health insurance: Free medical services are provided for one year to the insured person and his dependants, either directly by funds or through public institutions and physicians contracted with funds. These benefits include general and specialist care, maternity care, hospital care, surgery and listed medicines; they may be extended for three further years with the patient paying 50 per cent of costs. Daily sickness benefits payable for one year are 60 per cent of earnings (80 per cent for tuberculosis). Maternity benefits are 100 per cent of earnings payable for up to 60 days before and after confinement.

Accident insurance: Benefits include those medical benefits paid under health insurance plus transport. Daily allowances are one-third of earnings up to E100 ($3·50) per day for the first three days, increasing to two-thirds thereafter. The full disability benefit for total disablement is two-thirds of earnings, subject to the above maximum which may be supplemented by

13 per cent of earnings for constant attendance. Partial disability pensions are a percentage of the full sum proportionate to the degree of disability. This is converted into a lump sum if the pension is below a certain amount. Widow's pensions—also payable to dependant widowers—are 25 per cent of the insured's earnings. Orphan's pensions are 15 per cent of earnings for each of the first two children under 16, up to a total of 40 per cent for three or more children. Full orphan's pensions are 25, 45 and 60 per cent of earnings for one, two or three and more children respectively. In the absence of children, pensions are paid to other dependant survivors.

Pensions insurance: Old-age pensions are paid at 65 and are equal to 2 per cent of total lifetime insured earnings plus 10 per cent of average insured earnings over the best 10 years. Minimum pensions are 20 per cent and maximum pensions 80 per cent of basic earnings. Refunds are paid to those not qualifying for pensions, plus special assistance if they are needy. Invalidity pensions are paid to those having lost 50 per cent of their earning capacity. They are the same as for old-age pensions, except that the minimum pension is 30 per cent of earnings since first insured. A survivor's pension is a lump sum of six months' earnings of the insured and is divided equally between the spouse and children, or otherwise between the insured's heirs. Special assistance is again provided for those not entitled to a lump sum.

Unemployment insurance: None.

Other benefits: Family allowances are paid at a full rate if the employee has 20 days of employment per month. They are paid for children under 14 (24 if a student and indefinitely if the child is an invalid) at the monthly rate of E40 ($1·40) per child if the insured's monthly earnings are E600 ($21) or less, up to E100 ($3·50) if monthly earnings exceed E2,000 ($70). For each other needy dependant monthly allowances are E30 to 60 ($1·05 to 2·10) according to earnings. Allowances of E200 ($7) are paid for each birth.

EDUCATION

According to official figures 70 per cent of the population over the age of seven is literate. There are both state and private schools, but all education is geared to state examinations. Religious education is compulsory. The sexes are taught separately wherever feasible.

Primary education: This is compulsory and in state schools free from the ages of six to 11 (13 from 1970). Primary education ends with an examination and leaving certificate. *Secondary education:* This is voluntary and fees are charged, although fees in state schools are low and scholarships are provided for the needy. Private education is expensive and private schools are generally boarding schools. Those who pass an entrance examination study at *liceus* and other grammar schools for seven years. The course is divided into two parts. The first part is five years of general education with a terminal examination, which determines entry to the second part consisting of two years of specialised pre-university education ending with a secondary leaving examination which is a prerequisite for university entrance, although the universities hold their own matriculation examinations.

Vocational education: There are technical, commercial and industrial schools with nine-year courses, and higher commercial schools with four-year courses. *Special education:* Most special education is in the hands of private organisations.

University education: There are universities in Lisbon, Coimbra and Oporto, and also a technical university in Lisbon. Arts and science courses last five years, law and engineering six years and medicine seven years. University fees are low and are either paid entirely by the state or reduced in the case of needy students.

Educational institutions, 1963:[1]

	Institutions	Staff	Students
Primary	18,048	27,325	883,039
Secondary	511	7,443	146,070
Vocational	401	7,191	142,449
Special	66[2]	65	935
Teacher-training	29	312	3,641
Universities	4	n.a.	22,207

[1] State and private.
[2] Classes.

Adult education: In certain trades special evening courses are free and compulsory. Other adult education is provided free by the state. A policy of making the attainment of the primary school certificate compulsory for employment was hampered by the shortage of teachers.

Mass Media

The press (1963):

Dailies: Lisbon—*Diário de Noticias*, independent-conservative, 130,000; *Diário Popular*, ind., 80,000; *Diário de Lisboa*, ind.-cons., 40,000; *Novidades*, Catholic, 35,000; *Jornal do Comércio*, cons., 13,000; *O Século*, ind.-cons., 9,000; *Diário do Governo*, official government gazette; *Diário da Manhã*, organ of the National Union; *República*, ind.-republican; *A Voz*, pro-monarchist Cath.-cons. Oporto—*O Comércio do Porto*, commercial industrial, 60,000; *Jornal de Noticias*, ind., 50,000; *O Primeiro de Janeiro*, rep. Coimbra—*Diário de Coimbra*, rep.

Periodicals: Lisbon—*Arado* (m), agricultural; *Brotena*; *Revista Contemporanea de Cultura* (m), cultural; *O Educador* (w), educational; *O Gráfico* (m), illustrated; *Noticias do Comércio* (f), commercial; *Ocidente* (m), literary illus.

Censorship of publications: Newspapers and periodicals in Portugal and its colonies must submit all material before publication to the Inspecção Geral dos Espectáculos, a department of the Ministry of the Interior, and each issue must state that it has been passed by the censor. The Ministry has power of suppression of any newspaper or periodical. Books are not censored before publication, but the authorities are thought to be considering extending pre-publication censorship to books. In 1965 the Ministry of Education banned the Portuguese Writers' Association after it had awarded its 1965 novelists' grand prix, for *Luuanda*, to José Vieira Mateus da Graça (pen-name Luandino Vieira), an Angolan-born white Portuguese imprisoned for opposition to government policy in Angola.

Broadcasting: The state operates one national radio station (Emissora Nacional de Radiodifusão), two educational radio stations and one regional radio station. There is in addition one station (Rádio Renascença) operated by a Catholic organisation and about 20 operated by commercial organisations. TV is operated by the state-controlled Radiotelevisão Portuguesa.

SAN MARINO

GEOGRAPHY AND POPULATION

Features: A hilly country situated on Monte Titano in the northern Apennines south of Rimini. *Area:* 24 sq. miles/62 sq. km. *Population:* (1963) 17,000. *Capital:* San Marino (3,000). *Language:* Italian. *Religion:* Roman Catholic.

CONSTITUTIONAL SYSTEM

Constitution: San Marino is an independent republic whose existence as such traditionally dates back to the 4th century. *Head of state and head of government:* See under *Executive. Executive:* Executive power is vested in two Captains-Regent (Capitani Reggenti) who are elected every six months from and by the legislature to serve as joint heads of state; reelection may not take place until three years after a period of office. The Captains-Regent exercise power in conjunction with the Council of State (Congresso di Stato) made up of 10 departments. *Legislature:* Legislative power is vested in the Great and General Council (Consiglio Grande e Generale) of 60 members elected by universal suffrage for five years. *Election results:* The results of the 1964 elections were: Christian Democrats 29 seats, Communists 14, Social Democrats 10, Socialists 6, others 1. The leader of the Christian Democrats and State Secretary for Foreign Affairs is Federico Bigi. *Judicial system:* The judicial authority is the Council of Twelve (Consiglio dei XII).

RECENT HISTORY

San Marino remained neutral in the second world war. The Treaty of Friendship with Italy, first concluded in 1897, was renewed in 1953 and again with amendments in 1961. The country was ruled from the end of the second world war until 1957 by a coalition of the Communist and Socialist parties. With the formation of a new independent Social Democrat party, it has been governed since that date by a coalition of the Christian and Social Democrat parties. In August 1966 the government was voted out of office over the issue of postal votes for San Marinesi living abroad but was later reconstituted. *Defence:* All able-bodied citizens between 16 and 55, except students and teachers, are obliged to serve in the militia.

ECONOMY

San Marino has been united with Italy in a customs union since 1862. Its chief products are wheat, wine, textiles, cement, paper, leather and furs. Tourism and postage stamps are also an important source of revenue. Its main exports are wine, wool products, furniture, animal hides, ceramics and building stone.

SOCIAL SECURITY

There is no social insurance system. For health treatment the San Marinesi rely upon services provided in Italy, mainly in Rimini.

EDUCATION

There are 35 elementary schools, one technical school and one high school. Diplomas from these institutions are recognised by Italian universities.

MASS MEDIA

The press: Italian newspapers are distributed. *Broadcasting:* There is no San Marino broadcasting service, but Italian programmes can be received.

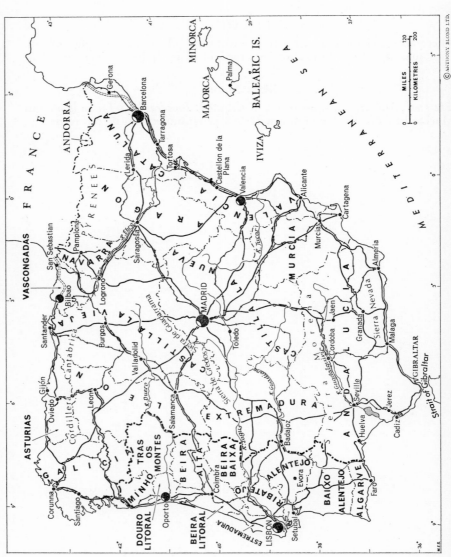

SPAIN AND PORTUGAL

SPAIN

GEOGRAPHY

Features: Spain is geographically compact, in spite of its size. In the north lies the east-west ridge of the Pyrenees which rise to over 11,000 ft/3,350 m. Chief north-south routes lie along the Mediterranean coast and through the relatively low-level route from San Sebastian to the Ebro Valley. This mountain region is continued westwards by the lower but broader Cantabrian Mountains which rise to 5–8,000 ft/1,500–2,450 m. In the south-east the Sierra Nevada and other ridges skirt the coast and, rising to over 10,000 ft/ 3,000 m., cut off most of the interior from sea influences. The isolation of the interior is further enhanced by the series of mountainous ridges bordering the very narrow coastal plain both in Catalonia and Valencia. Behind these coastal ranges is the main Spanish plateau or Meseta which averages an altitude of some 2,200 ft/670 m. in Castille and somewhat higher in New Castille. This central plateau is divided into a large number of smaller regions but in general terms can be said to consist of a series of basins and intervening areas of mountainous ridges of which the most important and highest are the central sierras, Sierra de Guadarrama and Sierra de Gredos, both rising to over 7,000 ft/2,100 m. The main areas of land below 1,000 ft/ 300 m., apart from narrow stretches of coastal plain, are the Guadalquivir and Ebro Valleys and the areas in the vicinity of Valencia and Cartagena.

Except in the more rugged and higher parts of the mountains and plateaux, farming is widely practised, with the emphasis on cereals in the plateau. The more intensive irrigation farming is concentrated in the lower parts of the major river valleys and along the coast, e.g. Valencia. Coal and iron ore are produced mainly in the north, Ovideo being the centre of the principal coalfield. Quantities of pyrites, potash and other chemicals and minerals are also produced and the country has some HEP resources. Industry is mainly concentrated in Catalonia, especially around Barcelona, and also along the north coast.

Area: 195,000 sq. miles/504,900 sq. km. (including Balearic and Canary Islands). African territories: Ifni, Spanish Guinea, Spanish Sahara. *Mean max./min. temperatures:* Madrid (40° 30' N, 3° 30' W; 2,190 ft/665 m.) 87°F/31°C (July), 33°F/1°C (Jan.); Santander 43° 30' N, 4° W; 200 ft/60 m.) 73°F/23°C (Aug.), 43°F/6°C (Feb.); Barcelona (41° 30' N, 2° E; 310 ft/95 m.) 82°F/28°C (Aug.), 42°F/6°C (Jan.); Seville (37° 30' N, 6° W; 100 ft/30 m.) 97°F/36°C (Aug.), 41°F/5°C (Jan.) *Relative humidity:* Madrid 79 per cent; Santander 84 per cent; Barcelona 73 per cent; Seville 78 per cent. *Mean annual rainfall:* Madrid 17 in./430 mm.; Santander 44 in./1,120 mm.; Barcelona 24 in./ 610 mm.; Seville 23 in./585 mm.

POPULATION

Population: (mid-1966 est.) 31,871,000. African territories (1960) 471,800. *Chief towns and populations:* (1964) MADRID (2,559,000), Barcelona (1,696,000), Valencia (583,000), Seville (532,000), Saragossa (377,000), Bilbao (351,000). *Distribution:* In 1960, 28 per cent of the population lived in Communes with more than 100,000 inhabitants, 29 per cent in Communes with 10–100,000 and 43 per cent in rural areas and Communes with fewer than 10,000.

Language: The official language is Spanish. The large Catalan- and Basque-speaking minorities are not permitted to use their own language for official purposes. *Religion:* Roman Catholicism is the official religion. The 1966 Organic Law (see under *Constitutional System*) provides that religious liberty for non-Catholics will be a state-protected legal right, thereby replacing the previous limited toleration of non-Catholic activities. A special law defining the specific freedoms of non-Catholics is to be introduced.

CONSTITUTIONAL SYSTEM

Constitution: Spain is a monarchy. The 1947 Ley de Sucesión states that the present Head of State will be succeeded by a King, subject to certain conditions (see under *Head of state*). The constitution consists of seven Fundamental Laws (Leyes Fundamentales del Reino) which may be modified or repealed by referendum only; the last was adopted by referendum in December 1966.

Head of state: Generalissimo Francisco Franco Bahamonde. The Head of State may nominate his successor, who will have the title of King or Regent. If the Head of State dies or is declared incapacitated by two-thirds vote of parliament (Cortes), his functions are taken over by a Regency Council (Consejo de Regencia) comprising the President of the Cortes (chairman), the senior prelate of the Council of the Realm (Consejo del Reino) and the senior Captain-General of the armed forces. The Regency Council convenes after three days the Council of the Realm and the Council of Ministers (Consejo de Ministros) who must together decide by two-thirds majority which person of royal blood is to be presented to the Cortes for election as King. If a King is chosen, subsequent succession is by primogeniture. If the candidate is rejected the same body may propose a new one. If he too is rejected, or if the accepted King is under 30, a Regent may be appointed, and a time-limit specified for the duration of the Regency. All functions of the Head of State devolve upon King or Regent. The Head of State must be Spanish, Roman Catholic, not less than 30 years of age, and must swear obedience to the Fundamental Laws (see under *Constitution*) and loyalty to the principles of the National Movement (see under *Political parties*).

Head of government: See under *Executive*.

Executive: The Head of State exercises supreme political and administrative power. Until the implementation of the Fundamental Law adopted in December 1966, Franco will continue to combine the functions of Head of State and Prime Minister. This law provides for a division of executive power with a Prime Minister (Presidente del Gobierno) to be selected by the Head of State from a list of three presented by the Council of the Realm (see below). The Prime Minister will direct general government policy. The other ministers will be appointed and may be dismissed by the Head of State, on the proposal of the Prime Minister. On the expiry of the Prime Minister's term of office (five years) the other ministers must retire. The Prime Minister may be removed by decision of the Head of State in agreement with the Council of the Realm or by proposal of two-thirds of the Council.

The Head of State has hitherto participated directly in government as the President of the Council of Ministers (according to the 1966 Fundamental Law the Council of Ministers will be both collectively and individually responsible for government decisions). The Council of Ministers is advised on important administrative questions by the supreme advisory body, the Council of State (Consejo de Estado) consisting of ex-officio members and an undefined number of permanent members appointed by the Head of State. Specialised advisory bodies include the National Economic Council.

In all important matters the Head of State is advised by the Council of the Realm, consisting (under the 1966 law) of seven ex-officio members (including its chairman, the President of the Cortes) and ten persons, representing the various types of Deputies in the Cortes (see below). Under the 1966 Law he will sanction government decrees authorised by the Cortes as having the force of law. Upon a resolution of the Council of the Realm based on a two-thirds vote of the National Council or the Standing Committee of the Cortes, he will adjudicate whether an act of the government is a *contrafuéro*, i.e. contradictory to the principles of the National Movement or the Fundamental Laws. He may adopt special powers during national emergency.

Under the 1966 Fundamental Law the Head of State will appoint for a six-year term the Presidents of the Supreme Court of Justice, the Council of State, the Court of the Exchequer and the National Economic Council by the same procedure as that for the appointment of the Prime Minister; they will be removable in the same way as the Prime Minister. The President of the Cortes will be appointed by the Head of State from a list of Deputies of the Cortes presented by the Council of the Realm, and will be removable by two-thirds majority of the Cortes.

Legislature: The Cortes is constitutionally defined as the organ through which the Spanish people play their part in government. By the 1966 Fundamental Law it has 600 members (*procuradores*) of whom 100 (two for each Province) are elected (for the first time since the Civil War) for four years by heads of families and married women throughout the country. Its members include ex-officio persons, elected representatives of official trade unions (not exceeding 150), representatives of Provincial Municipalities appointed by Provincial Assemblies, representatives of cultural and professional bodies and not more than 25 persons appointed by the Head of State. Nominees of the Head of State may be dismissed. The other appointed and indirectly elected members hold office for three years and may be reelected.

Legislation may be initiated by either the government (*proyectos de ley*) or by members of the Cortes (*proposiciones de ley*). In either case bills presented are debated by the relevant Commission of the Cortes and are then voted by plenary session of the Cortes. Partial or total amendment may be proposed by any member, while the government may withdraw a bill at any time. The Head of State, subject to the approval of the Council of the Realm, must either promulgate or return legislation within one month of its approval by the Cortes. The 1966 Fundamental Law provides that the two Vice-Presidents and four Secretaries of the Cortes shall be elected by members for the term of the legislature.

Political parties: In 1937 the various political groups constituting the Movimiento Nacional (National Movement) in opposition to the Spanish Republic merged into the single party Falange Española Tradicionalista y de las Juntas de Ofensiva Nacional-Sindicalista (JONS), which remains the only legally constituted party. The President of the Movement is the Head of State, and its highest assembly the National Council (Consejo Nacional), traditionally dominated by the Falange. By the 1966 Fundamental Law the National Council is to comprise 50 members elected by heads of families and their wives, 40 appointed by the Head of State, 12 appointed by the Cortes and six by the Prime Minister, and its national leadership is to be exercised by the Prime Minister on behalf of the Head of State. The main function of the National Council is to give corporate expression to the National Movement and to synthesise conflicting opinion within the nation. The trade unions (*sindicatos*), the Youth Movement (Frente de Juventudes) and the Women's Organisation (Sección Femenina) are incorporated in the Movement.

Election results: There has been no general election since before the war.

Leading political figures: Generalissimo Francisco Franco Bahamonde (Head of State), Fernando María Castiella y Maíz (Foreign Minister), Juan José Espinosa San Martin (Finance Minister), Lt-Gen. Camilo Menéndez Tolola (Army Minister), Admiral Pedro Nieto Antúnez (Navy Minister), Lt-Gen. José Lacalle Larraga (Aviation Minister), Manuel Fraga Iribarne (Minister for Information and Tourism).

Local government: The Municipalities (*municipios*) are governed by a Mayor (*alcalde*) and Municipal Council (*ayuntamiento*). One-third of the Council members are chosen by heads of families and their wives, one-third are elected by the official trade unions and the remainder are coopted by those two groups. Spain's 50 Provinces (*provincias*) are composed of groups of Municipalities; each is headed by a Provincial Assembly (*diputación provincial*) composed of a President and a number of elected members representing the Municipalities. The Provinces are governed by a state-appointed Civil Governor (*gobernador civil*).

Judicial system: The lowest courts are those of the Justices of the Peace (*juzgados de paz*) whose jurisdiction is coterminous with Municipal boundaries. Their civil jurisdiction ranges over out-of-court settlements and claims for sums under P1,000 pesetas ($16·60). They also try minor criminal offences. Municipal and Regional Courts (*juzgados municipales y comarcales*) with jurisdiction over towns or Regions sit as lower courts of first instance in civil cases up to P10,000 ($166), and have criminal jurisdiction for trial of petty offences and fraud. The courts of first instance in civil matters (*juzgados de primera instancia e instrucción*) have jurisdiction within defined judicial districts (*partidos judiciales*) over remaining civil cases and hear appeals from the Courts of the Justices of the Peace; in criminal cases they institute proceedings and report to higher Provincial courts for judgment. They may also pronounce finally on appeals from the two lower courts in minor criminal cases.

The Provincial Courts (*audiencias provinciales*) act as criminal courts and also pass final judgement on cases sent up from the lower courts. The jurisdiction of the District Courts of Appeal (*audiencias territoriales*) extends over one or more Provinces. This court functions as a plenary court for certain criminal cases, acts as a disciplinary body, and through three chambers deals with civil and criminal cases. The Supreme Court (Tribunal Supremo) in

Madrid acts as a plenary court in criminal matters and cases covering civil responsibility of high officials; it is the highest legal body and as the Judicial Council is concerned with legal appointments. As a court of justice it has six chambers which hear different types of appeals.

The judiciary is independent of the executive. Judges may be dismissed only by criminal proceedings and in cases specified in law conducted before the Supreme Court. Supreme Court judges are appointed by the Minister of Justice on recommendation of the Judicial Council. There is no divorce. Capital punishment is maintained but rarely implemented.

RECENT HISTORY

After Franco's victory in the Civil War Spain remained neutral in the second world war, although 'volunteer' forces (the Blue Division) fought against the Soviet Union. In 1946 the majority of states retracted recognition from the Franco regime under the terms of a UN resolution. This was revoked in 1950. Now only Yugoslavia and Mexico continue to recognise the government of the Spanish Republic in exile, although Spain has diplomatic relations—as yet—only with Cuba amongst Communist states. In 1953 the United States made an agreement with Spain whereby in return for economic and financial aid the United States was allowed to establish air and naval bases in Spain. In 1955 Spain became a member of the UN, in 1959 of the OECD and in 1960 of GATT. A defence treaty was signed with Portugal in 1958. Spain has never sought membership of NATO, but in 1962 and again in 1964 applied for EEC association. In 1963 the African Provinces of Spanish Rio Muni and Fernando Po were granted local autonomy within the colony of Spanish Guinea. In 1966 talks began with Britain on the future status of Gibraltar; in December Spain refused a British proposal to refer the legal issues in dispute to the International Court of Justice in the Hague.

Defence: The Head of State is the commander-in-chief of the armed forces and head of the Supreme Defence Council. There is no Defence Minister, the service ministers being also senior service commanders. Military service is compulsory for 16 months in the army, 18 months in the air force and two years in the navy. Strengths of the services: army 212,000, navy 42,000, air force 37,000. Defence expenditure represented 2·4 per cent of GNP in 1965–6 and the 1966–7 defence estimates were approximately P28,346 million ($472 million).

ECONOMY

Background: The main impetus to expansion since 1945 has come from industrial development although nearly half the country's commodity exports are agricultural products. The high growth rate achieved during the 1950s upset stability; prices rose considerably and there were repeated balance of payments deficits. The stabilisation programme that followed initiated a period of balanced growth between 1959 and 1963, but price inflation occurred again in 1964–5. The 1964–7 development plan was introduced with the basic aim of raising the standard of living and maintaining stability. Between 1954 and 1962 GNP grew by an annual average of 4·5 per cent. The 1964 plan's target of an annual growth of 6 per cent was achieved in 1964 and expected to be maintained in 1965. The main growth industries in recent years have been manufacturing (iron and steel, chemicals and construction materials) and tourism (in 1966 there were over 14 million tourists).

The origin of GDP at factor cost in 1964 was:

Sector				Percentage
Agriculture	.	.	.	21
Industry	.	.	.	36
Services	.	.	.	43
GDP				100

In 1964 industrial output increased by an estimated 11·6 per cent compared with an increase of 11·4 per cent in 1963. The continued rise in industrial production in recent years has been partly due to a high level of productive investment, both private and public. Agricultural output has tended to fluctuate with the weather, but generally has not expanded at the same high rate as industrial output. The main agricultural products are grapes, cereals, fruit, vegetables and livestock products. The annual targets for the 1964–7 plan include 5·5 per cent for industry and 4·5 per cent for agriculture.

Foreign trade: In 1964 the overall balance of payments surplus was P19,560 million ($326 million); this represented a threefold increase over 1963. A major contribution was made by tourism, receipts from which increased by 40 per cent in 1963–4. Exports accounted for 5 per cent of GNP in 1964; foodstuffs averaged 46 per cent of the total, raw materials 20 per cent and manufactured products 34 per cent. Imports in 1964 were 13 per cent of GNP; manufactured products averaged 55 per cent of the total, raw materials 18 per cent and foodstuffs 17 per cent. In 1964 36 per cent of total imports came from the EEC, 18 per cent from EFTA and 16 per cent from the United States; 39 per cent of exports went to the EEC, 25 per cent to EFTA and 10 per cent to the United States.

Employment: The total labour force in 1963 was 12 million, of whom 37 per cent were employed in agriculture, 34 per cent in industry and 28 per cent in services; about 1 per cent were unemployed. There is a general scarcity of skilled labour. In 1963 over 200,000 persons emigrated from Spain (186,000 in 1962), mostly to other European countries.

Price and wage trends: From 1962 to 1964 the average annual increase in the cost of living index was 7·4 per cent; in 1965 the February-April increase over August-October 1964 was 18 per cent. The major cause of this steep rise was the substantial price increases of agricultural and food products, deriving from the agricultural price support policy. Wages, after increasing by 20 per cent in manufacturing industries in 1963, increased by a further 12 per cent in 1964. Anti-inflationary measures were taken by the government at the end of 1964 and spring 1965; they included liberalisation of imports. However, the upward movement in prices was not arrested and spread significantly to industrial products in 1965.

Consumption: In 1964 private consumption accounted for 70 per cent of GNP and public consumption for 8 per cent. The 1964–7 plan envisages an annual growth of 5·5 per cent in private consumption.

SOCIAL SECURITY

The Ministry of Labour directs and supervises the social security system. Industrial mutual benefit societies have been integrated with the National

Welfare Institute (NWI) to provide uniform benefits. The NWI administers the pensions, health, accident and unemployment insurances, and the family allowances scheme through a national equalisation fund. In the case of accident insurance, employers must take out insurance with the National Industrial Accident Insurance Fund. Special bodies administer the special schemes outside the general scheme. Benefits and contributions stated below refer to 1964. Contributions of up to 3·9 per cent of annual earnings up to P66,000 ($1,122) are paid by the insured and of up to 12·1 per cent by the employer. These contributions finance the health, unemployment, pensions and family allowance systems. The Government pays a subsidy from the national budget.

Health insurance: This covers industrial and commercial employees earning less than P66,000 annually. There are special systems for agricultural workers, foresters, students, fishermen, domestic workers and others. Medical benefits are provided by the facilities of the NWI or doctors contracted to it, and include general and specialist care, medicines, dental and maternal care and transport—all provided for 39 weeks in one year (26 weeks for dependants). Sickness benefits are 50 per cent of earnings (60 per cent if the insured has dependants) and are paid for up to 39 weeks in one year; however, mutual benefit societies may provide benefits after this period for up to five years. Maternity benefits are paid for six weeks both before and after confinement and amount to 60 per cent of earnings (increased 60 per cent per child in case of multiple births). Weekly nursing allowances of P7 ($0·10) are paid per child for 10 weeks (15 weeks in case of multiple births).

Accident insurance: This covers all employed persons and is financed solely by the employer, the premium varying with the degree of risk. Medical benefits are all necessary care and the provision of appliances and rehabilitation, provided for an indefinite period. Temporary disability benefit is 75 per cent of earnings paid for up to 18 months. In the case of permanent disability pensions are: 75 to 100 per cent of earnings if the insured is totally disabled for all work, with a minimum monthly benefit of P1,000 ($17); 55 per cent of earnings if the disability totally prevents him from pursuing his usual profession; and 35 per cent of earnings for partial disability. Widow's pensions —also payable to widowers—are 50 per cent of earnings. Orphan's pensions amount to 10 per cent of earnings for each orphan under 18 (no age limit if the orphan is disabled), and 60 per cent of earnings for the first full orphan and 10 per cent for each other one. Pensions are paid to the parents or grandparents of the insured where there are no closer relatives. The total sum of pensions may not exceed 100 per cent of the insured's earnings.

Pensions insurance: This covers all employees in industry and commerce. There are special systems for those also covered by the special health insurance systems. Old-age pensions are paid at 65; one month's bonus is paid twice annually. Pensions are paid by government and mutual benefit societies, and amount to a minimum of P1,000 ($17) per month. Invalidity pensions are paid at 50 to those who have lost two-thirds of their normal earning capacity (30 if the insured is blind or has lost two limbs). Benefits are the same as for old age. Widow's pensions are paid at 65 or lower in the case of an invalid and amount to 50 per cent of the insured's pension.

Unemployment insurance: This covers all employees in industry and commerce, save short-term and casual employees. Benefits are paid, on condition that the insured has six months of contributions in the previous 18 months, for six months (sometimes 12) and amount to 75 per cent of earnings.

Other benefits: Family allowances cover all employees in industry and commerce with one or more children. Allowances are paid for each child under 21 (no limit if invalid) at the monthly rate of P40 ($0·68) for the first, rising by P20 ($0·34) for each succeeding child. Monthly allowances are also paid for the spouse and other dependant relatives. There are special grants for marriage, education and large families.

EDUCATION

The official figure for illiteracy in 1964 was 7 per cent over the age of 14. Religious education is compulsory at all levels of education and the Church has the right to inspect its teaching. All instruction is in Castilian Spanish. The sexes are taught separately except in sparsely populated areas. In 1964 approximately 11 per cent of the national budget was spent on education.

Primary education: Primary education is free and compulsory from six to 14. 75 per cent of children attending school go to state schools, about one-third of which are single class-room schools. Primary education ends with the Elementary Bachillerato.

Secondary and vocational education: This is optional. Secondary education lasts from 10 until 17 years. Secondary schools (*institutos*) are divided into an upper and lower division and further divided into branches for sciences and letters. Courses end in the state leaving exam, the General Bachillerato. In 1963–4 20 per cent of secondary-school pupils attended free state schools and 40 per cent each private lay-schools and schools run by religious orders, both of which are fee-paying. Equivalent to the General Bachillerato is the Labour Bachillerato which can be obtained after seven-year courses—divided into elementary and senior grades—at agricultural, industry and mining, maritime and fishing and (for women) 'administration' schools. The majority of these schools are run by the state, but certain private centres are officially recognised.

There are over 500 state-run industrial trade schools, most of which offer courses up to the grade of Master Tradesman. There are also six Labour Universities—one private and the others supported by mutual benefit societies (see above under *Social Security*)—which provide training in industrial trades and prepare pupils for the Labour Bachillerato. Technical courses last five years in the higher grades, entry being dependent upon attainment of the General Bachillerato, and three years at the intermediate grade, the conditions of entry here generally being the possession of the Elementary Bachillerato or attainment of the Master Tradesman's grade.

Special education: Special education for physically and mentally handicapped children is given in schools run by both state and private organisations.

University and higher education: Universities are not autonomous. Rectors and teaching staff are appointed by the state. There are 12 state universities; the University of Madrid alone confers the doctorate. In addition a number of non-state universities are recognised by the state under the Concordat with the Holy See. Amongst other higher-education institutes there are 13 advanced education colleges and 18 academies of art and music. University courses last from three to six years. University education is not free, but the state provides grants for the needy of an average of P5–6,000 (about $100).

Universities: Barcelona, Bilbao (commercial), Comillas (Pontifical),[1] Granada, Laguna, Madrid, Maria Cristina Madrid,[1] Murcia, Navarre,[1] Oviedo, Salamanca (Pontifical),[1] Salamanca (literary), San Sebastian,[1] Santiago, Seville, Valencia, Valladolid, Saragossa. *Advanced educational colleges:* Madrid (engineering, mining engineering, telecommunications, contemporary Hispanic studies, social studies, military staff school, Catholic Institute for Arts and Industries), Valencia (agriculture), Oviedo (mining), Barcelona (industrial engineering), Tarrasa (textiles), Sarriá (chemistry).

Educational institutions, 1962–3:

	Institutions	Staff	Students
Primary	100,970	106,028	3,201,716
Secondary	2,161	41,133	737,284
Special	n.a.	641	10,066
Vocational and technical .	82	n.a.	67,435
Universities (1963–4) . .	18	n.a.	78,917

Adult education: In 1963 legislation was introduced making it compulsory for all Spaniards born after 1946 to pass a literacy test in order to be able to vote, to occupy government posts or obtain government contracts. The army provides special general education for conscripts. In addition there are evening classes run by private organisations.

Mass Media

The press:

Dailies: La Vanguardia Española, Barcelona, independent, 220,000; *ABC*, Madrid, independent Catholic monarchist, 186,000; *Pueblo*, Madrid, syndicalist, 150,000; *Ya*, Madrid, ind. right-wing Cath., 130,000; *Levante*, Valencia, Falangist, 69,000; *Madrid*, Madrid, popular, 68,000; *Solidaridad Nacional*, Barcelona, syn., 63,000; *El Correo Español-El Pueblo Vasco*, Bilbao, Fal., 60,000; *ABC*, Seville edition, ind. Cath. mon., 49,000; *Las Provincias*, Valencia, ind. rt, 45,000; *Jornada*, Valencia, Fal.-syn., 31,000; *Hierro*, Bilbao, Fal., 25,000; *Sevilla*, Seville, Fal., 24,000.

Periodicals: Madrid—*La Actualidad Española* (w), general; *La Codorniz* (w), satirical-political; *Comercio* (m), publication of Madrid Chamber of Commerce; *Cuadernos para el Diálogo* (w), politics/culture; *Digame* (w), humorous/general entertainment; *Ecclesia* (w), ecclesiastical; *El Economista* (w), financial/economic. Barcelona—*La Familia* (m), family; *El Hogar y La Moda* (f), woman's; *Lecturas* (w), light reading.

Censorship of publications: Although the 1966 Press Law abolished the principle of previous censorship all newspapers, periodicals and books must be submitted before publication to the Ministry of Information which may suspend publication pending legal procecution. Importing of any publication is by government licence.

Broadcasting: The Dirección General de Radiodifusión y Televisión is an agency of the Ministry of Tourism and Information and controls all sound and vision broadcasting both official and commercial. Advertising is limited to five minutes per hour. All stations broadcast the national news service of the main official station, Radio Nacional de España (which covers all continental Spain, the Island Provinces and the African territories). The remainder of the programmes on commercial stations are independent.

[1] Non-state university.

SWEDEN

GEOGRAPHY

Features: Sweden can be divided into four major regions. Of these the largest is Norrland and stretches from the Dal river in the south to the Finnish and Norwegian frontiers north of the Arctic Circle. The main north-south frontier with Norway consists of a NE–SW range of mountains of Caledonian age, rather more of the belt being in Sweden than Norway. In places these mountains rise to over 5,000 ft/1,500 m. To the south-east the western edge of the Baltic Shield drops gradually to the coastal plain flanking the Gulf of Bothnia. The whole area is drained by a number of streams flowing from the mountains south-eastwards to the sea and providing considerable HEP potential. To the south of this region lies the Lakes Depression, a lowland area with alternating lakes, glacial ridges and lowlands. South again is the infertile Småland plateau. Finally, in the far south is the small region of Skåne, an undulating area of fairly low relief.

The most productive agricultural areas are the Lakes Depression and Skåne and the extreme southern part of the coastal lowlands of Norrland. Sweden is poorly endowed with fuels though there are large resources of HEP, especially in the north. There are large iron-ore deposits in the Kiruna-Gällivare areas in the far north and the Bergslagen area of the east. Small amounts of other minerals are also produced. The main industrial area lies in and north and west of Stockholm, around Gothenburg and on the shores of the major lakes. In the north the chief centre is Luleå.

Area: 173,400 sq. miles/449,800 sq. km. *Mean max. and min. temperatures:* Stockholm (59° 30' N, 18° E; 150 ft/45 m.) 70°F/21°C (July), 22°F/−6°C (Feb.); Gällivare (67° N, 20° 30' E; 1,200 ft/365 m.) 70°F/21°C, 1°F/−17°C. *Relative humidity:* Stockholm 80 per cent; Gällivare 78 per cent. *Mean annual rainfall:* Stockholm 22 in./560 mm.; Gällivare 22 in./560 mm.

POPULATION

Total population: (1965) 7,695,000. *Chief towns and populations:* (1965) Greater STOCKHOLM (1,179,500), Greater Gothenburg (520,500), Greater Malmö (260,000). (1964) Norrköping (93,000), Västerås (85,000), Uppsala (84,000). *Distribution:* In 1960, 52 per cent of the population lived in centres of fewer than 10,000 inhabitants, 17 per cent in centres of 10–50,000 and 31 per cent in centres of more than 50,000.

Language: The official language is Swedish. *Religion:* The 1951 religious freedom law considers all citizens to belong to the established Evangelical-Lutheran Church unless they freely withdraw (only 1 per cent of citizens have exercised this right).

CONSTITUTIONAL SYSTEM

Constitution: Sweden is a constitutional monarchy based on a number of fundamental constitutional laws dating from 1809. *Head of state:* King Gustav VI Adolf. *Head of government:* Prime Minister Tage Erlander (Social Democrat).

Executive: Executive power is vested in the Council of State of the King and his ministers (Statsråd). The King selects as Prime Minister the party leader having strongest support in parliament (Riksdag). No act of the King is valid unless countersigned by a minister. The Prime Minister selects his ministers whose nomination like his own is not subject to formal parliamentary approval. The cabinet (Regeringen) consists of 15 to 16 members of whom a maximum of five are ministers without portfolio. The government may dissolve parliament and order extraordinary elections (this happened in 1958).

Legislature: The Riksdag has two chambers. The Upper Chamber (Första Kammaren) has 151 members elected for eight years by the County Councils (*landstingen*) and the councils of six large towns (*stadsfullmäktige*). One-eighth of the Upper Chamber is renewed annually. The Lower Chamber (Andra Kammaren) has 233 members elected by proportional representation for four years. Legislation may originate in either chamber and must be approved by both to become law. Financial items may be reintroduced into both houses simultaneously and passed by aggregate vote of the two houses. The Justitieombudsman is appointed by parliament as a 'public watchdog' over the constitution, legislation and administration. He has a military counterpart, the Militieombudsman.

Referendum: The constitution provides for a consultative referendum if government and parliament agree to it.

Political parties: Five parties are represented in both houses—the Social Democrats, the Liberal Party (Folkpartiet), the Centre Party (formerly the Farmer's Party), the Conservative Party and the Swedish Communist Party. Two smaller parties are the (anti-socialist) Citizens Front (Medborgerlig Samling) and the Christian Democratic Union. The present government is Social Democrat.

Election results:

| Party | Lower Chamber | | | | Upper Chamber |
| | 1960 | | 1964 | | 1966 |
	Percentage of poll	Seats	Percentage of poll	Seats	Seats
Social Democrats . .	47·8	114	47·3	113	78
Liberals . . .	17·5	40	17·1	43	26
Centre Party . .	13·6	34	13·4	35	19
Conservatives . .	16·5	39	13·7	33	26
Communists . .	4·5	5	5·2	8	2
Citizens Front . .	—	—	1·5	1	—
Christian Democrats .	—	—	1·8	—	—

Leading political figures: Social Democrats—Tage Erlander (Premier and Party Chairman), Torsten Nilsson (Foreign Minister), Gunnar Sträng (Finance Minister), Gunnar Lange (Minister of Commerce), Sven Andersson (Defence Minister). Liberals—B. Ohlin (Party Leader). Centre Party—

Gunnar Hedlund (Party Leader). Conservatives—Yngve Holmberg (Party Leader). Communists—Carl-Henrik Hermansson (Party Leader).

Local government: There are about 1,000 Rural and Urban (Primary) Communes which elect councils (*kommunalfullmäktige* and *stadsfullmäktige*) of 15 to 60 members each by proportional representation for four years. Each council elects an executive committee (*kommunalnämnd* or *drätselkammare*) of at least five members for a four-year period not running concurrently with that of the council. All Primary Communes have both autonomous and state-delegated functions, the latter being regulated by special legislation.

The Province (*län*), of which there are 24, has two functions. First, all the Communes in the Province are grouped together into a County Commune (*landsting*)—which covers the same area as the Län—for local government purposes, primarily for health and educational matters. The Landsting elects a County Council (*landstinget*) for four years by proportional representation, which in turn appoints an executive committee (*förvaltningsutskott*). The larger towns are outside the authority of the Landsting and conduct their own local government. The Landsting has no supervisory powers over the Primary Communes within its area.

Secondly, the Province is an area of central government administration in those issues, e.g. the police, reserved to the state. Each Province has a provincial administration (*länstyrelse*) headed by a Governor (*landshövding*) appointed by the state for life. Stockholm has a separate but similar status, both as an urban Commune and as the twenty-fifth Province under a City Governor. The provincial administration has no concern with local government except that it acts in a supervisory capacity in the case of delegated functions and it is the first instance of appeal against decisions of a Communal Council; the second instance is the Supreme Administrative Court.

Judicial system: The courts of first instance (*underrätter*) for criminal and civil cases are the County and City Courts (*häradsrätter* and *rådhusrätter*). In the more serious criminal cases the court is constituted by one professional judge sitting with seven to nine lay judges (*nämndemän*). The decision of the professional judge is decisive except where there is a contrary decision by at least seven of the lay judges, in which case their decision prevails. In minor criminal cases there are only three lay judges and petty cases are tried by the professional judge alone. This procedure is also followed in civil cases heard in the County Courts; in the City Courts civil cases are decided by a panel of three professional judges. The next instance is the Court of Appeal (*hovrätt*); these courts are divided into two to eleven chambers each composed of a president (*lagman*) and three to four other judges. Special courts are the Supreme Administrative Court, the Law Court, the Labour Court and the Water Rights Court. The highest court is the Supreme Court of Justice (Högsta Domstolen) composed of 24 members (*justitieråd*) and divided into three chambers each constituted by five judges. Full sessions are held for certain cases. Judges are appointed by the government and cannot be dismissed except by judicial sentence. There is no death penalty except for certain war crimes.

RECENT HISTORY

Sweden remained neutral in the second world war, and has since remained free from military alliances, while seeking to further peace and reduce international tension both within and outside the United Nations. Sweden

is a founder member of EFTA, the OECD, the Council for Europe and the
Nordic Council, and in 1961 applied for associate membership of the EEC.
The country has provided both observer and combat units for United Nations
forces in Korea, Gaza, the Lebanon, the Congo and Cyprus, and is a member
of the UN's Eighteen Nation Disarmament Committee.

Defence: Sweden aims at neutrality in the event of war, to this end maintaining
very strong defence forces in relation to the size of the country. Military
service ranges from 10 months for privates to 18 months for officers up to the
age of 47. Total mobilisable strength is about 750,000 (regular forces total
about 157,000, over half of whom serve only 15 to 40 days per year): army
122,000, navy 11,500, air force 24,000. In 1964 a permanent force of 1,600
was placed at UN disposal. Sweden has no nuclear weapons. Defence
expenditure represented 4·6 per cent of GNP in 1965–6, and defence
estimates for 1966–7 were SKr4,410 million ($856 million).

ECONOMY

Background: Sweden is richly endowed with resources: vast forests in the
north, agricultural lands in the south, large deposits of iron ore, lead and
zinc and abundant supplies of hydroelectric power. There is considerable
state control of major industries and a good record of post-war employer-
union relations. The period since the second world war has been characterised
by rapid economic development; but in 1965 the economy, fully exploited,
showed signs of strain, especially in the labour market. Restrictive monetary
and budgetary policies were followed between 1964 and 1966. In 1964 GNP
was worth SKr75,085 million ($14,495 million) at market prices. In the per-
iod 1953–8 the annual average rate of growth was 3·4 per cent. This increased to 5·1 per cent in 1958–64 but was expected to decline to under 4 per cent
in 1965–6 owing to the optimum level of economic activity reached in 1964.
The origin of GDP in 1964 was:

Sector	Percentage
Agriculture, forestry and fishing	7
Industry	40
Construction	10
Services	43
GDP	100

The main industries include metals and metal products, transport equipment
and wood products. Industrial production has increased at an annual
average rate of about 4 per cent since 1946. The major growth industries
have been power, mining and manufacturing, especially chemical and
electrical engineering, and building and construction. In 1965 industrial
production rose by 6 per cent compared with an increase of 9·5 per cent in
1964. Many factors contributed to the slow-down of industrial production in
1965: a shortage of labour, the full utilisation of resources, a decline in
overseas demand and the government's restrictive economic policy, including
restraint of credit and raising of indirect taxes. The industries most affected
were woodpulp, iron and steel, and engineering products. Agriculture was
expected to account for under 5 per cent of GNP in 1966. The main agricultural products are wheat, barley, cattle, pigs, root and green crops.

Foreign trade: Sweden is heavily dependent upon foreign trade. In 1964 exports contributed 21 per cent to GNP and imports 22 per cent. The main exports during this period were forestry products (28 per cent of total exports), and machinery, apparatus and transport (in all 38 per cent). The main imports included raw materials and fuels (30 per cent), machinery, apparatus and transport (30 per cent), metals and metal products (14 per cent), and food, beverages and tobacco (11 per cent). The balance of payments during this period was relatively stable with a deficit on the trade balance generally covered by income from shipping and other services. In 1965 both imports and exports reached record levels but there was a sizeable deficit on the current account of the balance of payments, in sharp contrast to earlier years; this resulted from an increase in the visible trade deficit and a decline in net invisible earnings. The main export markets in 1964 were EFTA (37 per cent), the EEC (32 per cent) and the United States (5 per cent). The chief suppliers of imports in the same year were the EEC (37 per cent), EFTA (30 per cent) and the United States (10 per cent).

Employment: Of a total working population of 3·8 million in 1964, 12 per cent were employed in agriculture, 41 per cent in industry and 45 per cent in services. Unemployment in the same year amounted to 1 per cent; however, an acute labour shortage has since developed, and labour continues to move from the north to the south. In 1965 the numbers employed in agriculture, forestry and fishing declined 6·3 per cent over 1964. Service industries took over two-thirds of this redistribution of labour and industry the remainder.

Price and wage trends: Consumer prices increased by an annual average of only 3 per cent in the period 1958–64, the lowest increase in Scandinavia, but since 1964 the consumer price index has risen more steeply. In 1965 the increase was about 6 per cent, due largely to heavier indirect taxes introduced in July (excluding this variable the index rose by 3·8 per cent in 1965 compared with 4·5 per cent in 1964). Wages and salaries increased rapidly in 1965 despite the two-year wage agreements concluded in 1964, which had covered most wage and salary earners. Following the relatively stable period of 1958–61 there were increases of about 10 per cent in both 1964 and 1965 (the agreements had provided for increases of about 4 per cent in 1964 and 4·5 per cent in 1965).

Consumption: Private consumption in 1964 amounted to 57 per cent of GNP and public consumption to 19 per cent. Notwithstanding the increase in indirect taxation in 1965, private consumption rose faster than GNP (nearly 4 per cent); increases in 1963 and 1964 were 5 and 5·3 per cent respectively. Public consumption continued to expand at a similar, relatively high rate in 1965 (6·5 per cent) compared with 5·9 per cent in 1964 and 7·7 per cent in 1963.

SOCIAL SECURITY

Expenditure on social services in Sweden is over one-sixth of net national income. Social services absorb about one-third of the net expenditure of the state budget and about the same proportion of local and municipal budgets. Benefits stated below refer to the period 1965–6.

Health insurance: At the age of 16 every Swede becomes a member of a Regional Social Insurance Office. The National Health Service, which covers everyone, is financed by the insured person, the employer and the state at the rates of 50, 30 and 20 per cent respectively. For sickness insurance

SWEDEN

the insured person pays an average of SKr70 ($13) per year. For this he receives free hospital treatment for an unlimited period (but for only 180 days if over 67), a 75 per cent refund of medical care (doctor's fees and travelling expenses), free provision of vital medicines and a 50 per cent discount on any outlay of over SKr3 for others, refund of most travelling expenses and reduced fees for hospital care and treatment in nursing homes. Contributions for sickness benefit insurance are additional and related to earnings. Those earning SKr1,800–2,600 ($347–502) pay SKr65 ($12) annually and receive only the basic daily benefit of SKr5 ($1). This is also paid to housewives. Those earning above SKr2,600 receive an additional supplementary sickness benefit; the total daily benefit for a person earning above SKr21,000 ($4,050) is SKr28 ($5.50). These rates are to be increased in 1967. Housewives with children and students may also receive sickness benefits if voluntarily insured. Small additional allowances are paid for children. Confinement is free, a maternity allowance of SKr900 ($174) is paid for each child—even if stillborn—and increased by SKr450 ($87) for each additional child in the case of twins etc; and the mother if gainfully employed receives a daily allowance of SKr1–23 for a maximum of 180 days.

Accident insurance: All employers carry occupational injury and sickness insurance for their employees and families. Accidental injuries healing within 90 days—90 per cent of all cases—are covered by sickness insurance. Industrial injury insurance covers the costs of artificial limbs, medical, dental and hospital treatment and provides a daily care allowance— maximum SKr5—for persons unable to look after themselves. Life annuities for industrial injuries depend upon previous income up to SKr15,000 ($2,900), and the degree of disability, and the highest payable is SKr11,000 ($2,123). Widows and dependant widowers receive life annuities of one-third of the deceased's earnings while remaining unmarried (reduced by one-quarter after the age of 67), children receive annuities of one-sixth until 16 and parents also receive one-sixth if they were dependant upon the deceased. The total sum of annuities may not exceed five-sixths of total income up to SKr15,000.

Pensions insurance: Increases in basic national pensions (in addition to which supplementary pensions are paid) are planned for 1968. Basic old-age, disability, widow's and orphan's pensions are paid out of the national pensions scheme, financed by the state, local authorities and special fees. Old-age pensions are payable to all at 67, but are decreased by 0·6 per cent for every month they are paid before 63, and likewise increased for every month they are belatedly drawn up to 70. The national basic old-age pension for a single person is SKr4,330 ($835) and the maximum annual payment for a married couple is SKr5,810 ($1,121). There are additional allowances of a maximum of SKr1,325 ($256) for each child, for housing, and of SKr1,590 ($309) for disablement.

The supplementary pension scheme, financed by employers in the case of employees while the self-employed pay their own premium, is based upon a pension-carrying income, i.e. that part of income lying between a varying minimum Basic Amount (SKr5,300 or $1,013 in January–April 1966) and 7½ times that amount. Each year pension points are awarded by dividing the pension-carrying income by the Basic Amount. To obtain the maximum supplementary pension, points must have been acquired over 30 years. This pension's purchasing power is maintained.

Under the national scheme disabled persons over 16 whose capacity to work has been reduced by at least 50 per cent receive early retirement pensions having the same benefits as those for old-age, and free and subsidised aids. Supplementary disability pensions are calculated on assumed and actual earnings as for the supplementary old-age pension. Disabled persons also receive means-tested allowances for retraining and reemployment, and financial aid towards starting private business and purchasing invalid carriages.

The full national annual pension for a widow with children under 16 living at home is SKr4,339 ($838) and for a full orphan SKr11,855 ($358). Under the supplementary pensions scheme, widows and children without parents receive 40 per cent of the deceased person's old-age or early retirement pension. Widow's pensions are reduced to 35 per cent if a child's pension must be paid simultaneously, the child receiving 15 per cent. Pension is increased by 10 per cent for each additional child.

Unemployment insurance: This is administered by the trade unions through state-subsidised unemployment benefit societies to which the claimant contributes. Benefits are paid only in the case of enforced unemployment, and generally not for more than 150 days. The maximum daily benefit is SKr40 ($7·70) plus SKr2 for each child under 16. Allowances are also paid for retraining and removal to another area.

Other benefits: A tax-free annual cash-grant of SKr900 ($174) is given for every child under 16. Home-furnishing loans—maximum SKr5,000 ($965)—are available to prospective married couples; about 15 per cent benefit in this way. Minimum paid holidays are four weeks. In addition there are low-cost holidays with travel allowances and spending money for some housewives, rent allowances varying with size of income and number of children, and annual maintenance advances for children of divorced parents and some illegitimate children of up to SKr11,850 ($357) until 16 years.

EDUCATION

Primary education: Education is free and compulsory from seven to 16. The new school provided for by the 1962 reform is a comprehensive school (*grundskolan*) divided into lower (grades 1–3), middle (grades 4–6) and upper (grades 7–9) departments. There are no examinations and no streaming below the upper department, and generally one teacher is responsible for all subjects. In the first two grades of the upper department pupils are offered a limited selection of subjects but no regrouping of classes. In grade 9 pupils are offered nine courses of study divided into four sections—theoretical, social, technical-mechanical and economics, all except the first having both practical and theoretical streams for further study. The teaching of individual subjects in the upper grades is by university-trained teachers. The *grundskolan* is the responsibility of the local authorities but receives state funds for the costs of operation and construction. It is expected to be universal in 1972–3 when the upper grades will finally replace the seven-year Elementary School, the Junior High School and girls' schools, features of the former system with which the present coexists. Free school meals are common in primary schools and in some secondary schools. For children over 16 still undergoing primary education extended children's allowances of SKr75 ($14) per month are paid plus additional travelling or lodging allowances where there is no primary school in the district.

Secondary schools: Entry into the Senior High School (*gymnasium*) depends upon the final marks gained in the ninth year in the primary theoretical section. Courses last for three years with greater specialisation in the last two years and terminate in a written and oral final examination (*student-examen*) qualifying for university entrance. There are also Technical and Business High Schools providing vocational education and a diploma qualifying for university entry. Parallel with the *grundskolan* are three types of continuation school providing two-year courses for those successfully completing the social, technical and economics section of the ninth primary grade. These courses have no examinations and pupils need not attend them directly on completion of primary education.

Secondary, technical and vocational students aged between 16 and 21 receive monthly study grants of SKr75 and travelling or lodging allowances and sometimes study grants for the academic year of a maximum of SKr5,000 repayable at 5·25 per cent interest. Students aged over 21 receive larger supplementable monthly study grants of SKr175 ($34), paid without means test and without application where the annual taxable income of student and parents or husband and wife is below SKr8,000 ($1,544).

Special education: Slow learners are instructed in special forms at normal primary schools, and the educationally sub-normal may be taught at free special day and boarding schools subsidised by County Councils and government grants. Compulsory special education begins at seven and may last until 23, vocational training following eight or nine years of general schooling. Children with severe mental deficiencies get training and therapy in child-care homes. Totally and near-totally deaf children are taught at compulsory, state-financed schools for ten years, the last two being spent in vocational education. Preparatory schools for the deaf, mostly maintained by local authorities and special welfare societies with some state support, are voluntary. Children with some hearing capacity are sent to special schools, and special classes attached to primary schools, where they reach almost the same levels as children in normal Elementary Schools. There are also special schools for the blind. State supervision is exercised over all special schools.

Vocational education: Vocational education is traditionally given in the job. Several private companies have established their own workshop schools and industry plays an important part in vocational training in the ninth primary grade. In recent years vocational training has been much increased by the state and local authorities.

University and higher education: Sweden has five universities: Uppsala, Lund, Stockholm, Gothenburg and Umeå, all with a wide range of faculties. There are professional schools, with university college status, of medicine (Caroline Institute, Stockholm), dentistry (Stockholm, Malmö), economics (Stockholm, Gothenburg), technology (Stockholm, Gothenburg, Lund), pharmacy (Stockholm), agriculture (Uppsala), veterinary medicine, forestry, music and art (Stockholm). Courses last from three to seven years. Almost all tuition is free. Financial aid to students is given by the state on a large scale: the maximum grant is SKr3,710 ($716) per term plus additional allowances of SKr663 ($127) per child. Of this a maximum of SKr875 ($169) is a study grant, and only this need not be repaid.

Educational institutions, 1963–4:

	Schools and Institutions	Staff	Students
Primary	n.a.	58,671	856,023
Secondary	437	17,818	197,943
Special	111	n.a.	5,000
Vocational and technical .	64	n.a.	92,869
Higher	28	4,325	54,244

Adult education: There are about 100 Folk High Schools with 12,000 pupils offering courses of from seven to eight months. Run as boarding schools by County Councils, cultural, social and religious organisations with substantial state aid, they provide certificates for entrance into general educational establishments. Adults wanting a Senior High School diploma can study at Senior High Schools for adults or take correspondence courses. Aid for examinations is also provided by evening school. State grants are available during the final stage of studies, and also study loans of a maximum of SKr5,000 ($965). In 1964 there were 2,217 public libraries.

MASS MEDIA

The press (1965):

Dailies: Expressen, Stockholm, Liberal, 456,000; *Dagens Nyheter,* Stockholm, Lib., 384,000; *Aftonbladet,* Stockholm, Social Democrat, 272,000; *Göteborgs-Posten,* Gothenburg, Lib., 272,000; *Svenska Dagbladet,* Stockholm, Conservative, 152,000; *Sydsvenska Dagbladet Snällposten,* Malmö, Cons., 95,000; *Nya Wermlands-Tidningen,* Karlstad, Cons., 76,000; *Kvällsposten,* Malmö, Cons., 73,000; *Göteborgs-Tidningen,* Gothenburg, Lib., 68,000; *Arbetet,* Malmö, Soc. Dem., 65,000.

Periodicals: Året Runt (w), Stockholm, family, 464,000; *Vecko-Revyn* (w), Stockholm, Society, 390,000; *Allers Familiejournal* (w), Helsingborg, family, 370,000; *Nya Damernas Värld* (w), Stockholm, woman's, 300,000; *Husmodern* (w), Stockholm, wom., 284,000; *Bild-Journalen* (w), Stockholm, film, 250,000; *Min Värld* (w), Stockholm, wom., 250,000; *Se,* Stockholm (w), man's, 248,000; *Teknikens Värld* (f), Stockholm, technical, 117,000; *Industria* (w), Stockholm, industrial/financial, 42,000.

Broadcasting: The Swedish Broadcasting Corporation (Sveriges Radio) is a non-commercial limited company in which the government has no financial holdings. The only obligation to afford time to the government is in the case of important government announcements. The Corporation has the sole right of decision upon programmes, while the government has ultimate control of the range of activities as a whole, hours of broadcasting, etc. The government influences the general administration of the Corporation through its appointment of the chairman and half the board members. The director-general of the Corporation—chosen by the board—has ultimate responsibility for both radio and TV programmes. The government appoints a Radio Council which reviews programmes after their transmission and submits an annual report to the government upon complaints from organisations and private individuals. Transmission is financed by licence fees, radio and TV having separate budgets.

SWITZERLAND

GEOGRAPHY

Features: In the north-west of the country lie the Swiss Jura Mountains, an area of NE–SW trending ridges and valleys; elevations are seldom over 3,000 ft/900 m. and the whole area is heavily wooded. To the south and east of this region lies the Swiss Plateau, some 30 miles in width and consisting in the main of numerous flat-bottomed, wide river valleys with intervening areas of higher land, rising steadily towards the Alps in the south. The region also contains a number of lakes, e.g. Geneva and Constance. Nearly two-thirds of the country is covered by the Alps. Switzerland contains part of the central Alpine mountain zone, where peaks are highest and narrowest with deep intervening valleys and lakes; altitudes in excess of 10,000 ft/3,000 m. are common.

In spite of the large proportion of mountainous land just over half the country is farmed, though much of this area consists of Alpine summer pasture only. The areas of greatest agricultural concentration are in the valleys and in parts of the Swiss Plateau. The country possesses few minerals, the main economic resources being hydroelectric potential and tourism. Industry is largely concentrated in the Plateau area, especially around Zurich, St Gallen and Geneva.

Area: 15,940 sq. miles/41,290 sq. km. *Mean max. and min. temperatures:* Bern (47° N, 7° 30′ E; 1,880 ft/575 m.) 74°F/23°C (July), 26°F/−3°C (Jan.); Andermatt (46° 30′ N, 8° 30′ E; 4,730 ft/1,440 m.) 60°F/16°C, 18°F/−8°C; Lugano (46° N, 9° E; 900 ft/275 m.) 83°F/28°C, 29°F/−2°C. *Relative humidity:* Bern 87 per cent; Andermatt 70 per cent; Lugano 78 per cent. *Mean annual rainfall:* Bern 39 in./990 mm.; Andermatt 53 in./1,345 mm.; Lugano 68 in./1,725 mm.

POPULATION

Total population: (1964) 5,800,000. *Chief towns and populations:* (1964) Zurich (439,000), Basle (213,000), Geneva (176,000), BERN (167,000), Lausanne (132,000). *Distribution:* In 1960, 26 per cent of the population lived in Communes of more than 50,000 inhabitants, 16 per cent in Communes of 10–50,000 and 58 per cent in Communes of fewer than 10,000.

Language: There are four national languages—German, French, Italian and Romansh—spoken by 72, 20, 6 and 1 per cent of the population respectively. All the German-speaking population speak one of the many dialects known collectively as Schweizerdeutsch. *Religion:* In 1960, 57 per cent of Swiss citizens were Protestant and 41 per cent Roman Catholic.

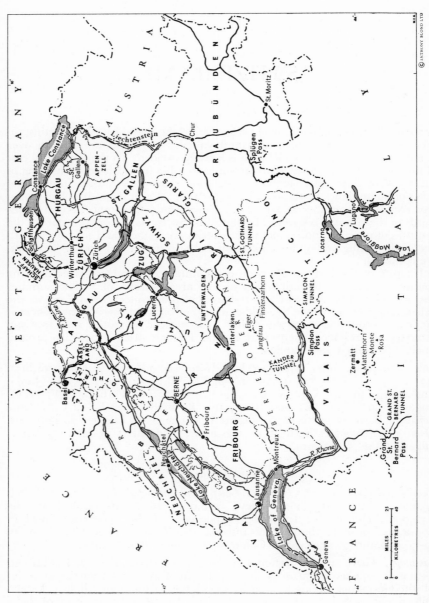

SWITZERLAND

CONSTITUTIONAL SYSTEM

Constitution: The Swiss Confederation is a federal republic of 22 Cantons, sometimes known as the Twenty-five States since three Cantons are divided into Half-Cantons. The present constitution with modifications dates from 1874.

Head of state and government: The seven-man Federal Council collectively. President of the Confederation and of the Federal Council is Roger Bonvin.

The executive: The President and Vice-President of the Swiss Confederation are elected annually by the Federal Assembly, the Vice-President generally becoming the next President. The President of the Confederation is also President of the Federal Council (Bundesrat) on a *primus inter pares* basis. He conducts the meetings of the Council and like the six other members heads one of the seven executive departments of the government. The Council is elected by the Federal Assembly for four years following a general election, and the members are jointly responsible for government as a collegial body. Any Swiss citizen except the clergy is eligible for election to the Council with restrictions on the number of representatives from one Canton. On appointment, members sever all political affiliations. The various regions, languages, religions and political parties are considered in the election. The Council is responsible to the Federal Assembly but neither a vote of censure nor a referendum can cause the resignation of the Council; Councillors are generally reelected until they resign.

The legislature: The Federal Assembly (Vereinigte Bundesversammlung) is bicameral. The National Council (Nationalrat) of 200 members (previously 196) is elected for four years by proportional representation by all males over 20. The Council of States (Ständerat) numbers 44. There are 2 representatives for each Canton (Half-Cantons have one each) and they are elected for varying periods by Cantonal legislation. The two Councils have equal authority. Legislation is prepared for their consideration by a committee system and must be approved by both houses before submission to the people (see under *Referendum*). Federal legislation is principally concerned with social insurance, international affairs, defence, export and import duties and internal communications. Federal revenue comes mainly from indirect taxation. There is also a temporary system of direct Federal taxation.

The Cantons: The Cantons and Half-Cantons are sovereign states to the extent that their powers are not limited by the Federal constitution. Each Canton has a government (*Regierungsrat* or *Conseil d'État*) varying from five to 11 members, elected for one to five years by the male population (except in Geneva, Neuchâtel and Vaud and in Basle City where women over 20 are also entitled to vote in Cantonal and Communal elections). In all but three Cantons, legislation must be submitted to referendum if a sufficient number of the population so demand. In Basle every Cantonal law is so submitted. In the Cantons and half-Cantons of Unterwalden, Glarus and Appenzell the people exercise their power directly at an annual convocation of the citizens (*Landsgemeinde*). The Cantons derive their revenue from direct taxation.

The Communes: The 3,095 free Communes of the Swiss Confederation are the basic organs of direct democracy. In the Communes the citizen has the right—and in some the obligation—to be present at assemblies to decide on local questions.

Referendum: In addition to the Cantonal referendum there exists the national referendum to which all Federal legislation must be submitted if there is a petition of 30,000 citizens against it within 90 days. The people may demand an amendment to the Federal constitution with a petition of 50,000 signatures, which becomes effective if it is passed both by a majority of the electorate and a majority of the Cantons; this so-called 'Initiative' is often exercised. The citizens within a Canton may similarly propose amendments to the Cantonal constitution as well as the adoption of new Cantonal legislation.

Political parties: The chief political parties are the Swiss Socialist Party, the liberal Radical-Democrat Party, the Catholic Conservative Party and the conservative-agrarian Peasants, Artisans and Citizens Party. The smaller parties are the liberal National Association of Independents, the anti-centralist Liberal-Democrat Party, the Democratic Party, the Protestant People's Party and the (Communist) Worker's Party.

Election results:

| | National Council | | | | Council of States |
| | 1959 | | 1963 | | 1965 |
Party	Percentage of poll	Seats	Percentage of poll	Seats	Seats
Socialists . . .	26·3	51	26·6	53	3
Radical-Democrats .	23·7	51	24·0	51	13
Catholic Conservatives	23·3	47	23·4	48	18
Peasants, Artisans and Citizens Party . .	11·6	23	11·4	22	4
Independents . .	5·5	10	5·0	10	—
Liberal-Democrats .	2·3	5	2·2	6	3
Democrat Party . .	2·2	4	1·8	4	3
Protestant People's Party	1·4	2	1·6	2	—
Worker's Party . .	2·7	3	2·2	4	—
Others	1·0	—	1·8	—	—

Leading political figures: Roger Bonvin (President of the Confederation and of the Federal Council and Head of Finance Department), Hans Schaffner (Head of Public Economy Department), Willy Spühler (Deputy President of the Confederation and Head of Foreign Affairs Department), Nello Celio (Head of Defence Department), Hans-Peter Tschudi (Head of Home Department), Ludwig von Mools (Head of Justice and Police Department), Rudolf Gnaegi (Head of Department of Transport, Communications and Power).

Local government: The Cantonal and Communal Councils are the main sources of local government. Some larger Communes elect an assembly and an executive council. In smaller Communes there is a council only. In most Cantons a number of Communes are grouped together in Districts (*Amtsbezirke*) each having a Prefect (*Regierungsstatthalter*) as representative of the Cantonal government.

Judicial system: The system varies with the Cantons, but Zurich may be taken as a model. The Canton elects its own magistracy and retains its individual procedures. Civil cases are heard in the first instance in District Courts (*Bezirksgerichte*) presided over by one judge. Each Canton has an Appeal Court (*Obergericht*) and a cassation court reviews procedural questions.

The Federal Court gives the final decisions in major Federal civil cases. Minor criminal cases are dealt with by the District and Appeal Courts. More serious cases are a matter for the Jury Court (*Schwurgericht*) of three judges and 12 jurors and the Appeal Court. The Federal Tribunal has 26 full and 11 to 13 supplementary members elected by the Federal Assembly for six years. It has seven sections and exercises jurisdiction in suits between the Confederation and Cantons, corporations and individuals, and between Cantons. It tries offences against the Confederation and is the Court of Appeal against decisions of certain Federal authorities or Cantonal authorities applying Federal law. There is no capital punishment.

Recent History

Switzerland remained neutral in both world wars. The country is the headquarters for many international organisations and has been the site of many major international conferences of the post-war period. It is a founder-member of EFTA, and joined the Council of Europe in 1963 and GATT in 1966. It is also a member of the OECD but has not applied for membership of the UN although it maintains an observer there. In 1961 Switzerland applied for associate membership of the EEC.

Defence: The Head of the Defence Department is head of the armed forces. Switzerland is alliance-free but its neutrality is based upon a high degree of military preparedness. Military service is compulsory between the ages of 20 and 60. Initial military service lasts four months, and the remaining period is spent in the reserves. In 1966 the army had 1,000 regulars and 20,000 trainees with 629,000 reservists who can be mobilised in 48 hours. The air force had 5,000 regulars, 5,000 serving trainees and 40,000 reservists. Defence expenditure represented 2·5 per cent of GNP in 1965, and the 1966 defence budget was SF1,669 million ($387 million).

Economy

Background: Switzerland has few natural resources and the cost of transporting goods to and from the country is high. Its economic structure has been developed on a basis of high-value specialised industrial products. This is reflected in both the deployment of resources and the pattern of exports. Tourism and financial services make a significant contribution to Switzerland's balance of payments position. By 1965 various measures taken to combat rising inflation had largely succeeded in stabilising the economy at the cost of a slower rate of economic growth. The annual average rate of growth at constant prices from 1958 to 1964 was 5·8 per cent. In 1965 the rate was expected to be about 4.5 per cent following the government's efforts to establish a better balance between domestic demand and supply and more stable prices. The moderate success of this policy by 1965 was due to restriction of entry and investment of foreign capital, limitation of bank lending activity, control of new security issues on the capital market, restriction of building, and licensing of employment of foreign workers. The industries most affected by the fall in demand were consumer goods, chemicals and building and construction.

Industry is predominantly export-oriented and based on a few specialised products, including watches, jewellery, machinery and metal products. Industrial production fell from a 5 per cent growth rate in 1964 to 2·3 per cent in the first nine months of 1965. In the period 1958–64 industrial output expanded considerably, but was followed by a decline. Agriculture throughout this period showed some fluctuation, declining in 1963–4. The main agricultural products are wheat, potatoes, livestock and dairy products.

The origin of GDP at factor cost in 1964 was:

Sector	Percentage
Agriculture	10
Industry	52
Services	38
GDP	100

Foreign trade: Switzerland generally has a deficit on current balance of payments. The specialised nature of the economy requires the country to import nearly all the raw materials needed for its industries. In 1964 imports of goods and services amounted to 31 per cent of GNP. Machinery, basic manufactures and raw materials accounted for over 60 per cent of total imports, and food and chemicals contributed a further 16 per cent and 8 per cent respectively. In the same year exports amounted to 29 per cent of GNP, and manufactured goods accounted for 90 per cent of all exports. Over 62 per cent of all imports came from the EEC in 1964, of which nearly half came from West Germany; 15 per cent came from EFTA. However, only about 40 per cent of total exports went to the EEC and nearly 20 per cent to EFTA.

Employment: The total working population in 1960 was 2·5 million and unemployment—except for seasonal unemployment—was virtually nil. The large number of foreign workers has been restricted in recent years (in 1965 an estimated 35,000 foreign workers were admitted compared with 117,000 in 1961).[1] Out of the total labour force in 1964 industry employed 51 per cent, agriculture 11 per cent and services 38 per cent.

Price and wage trends: The percentage increase in the cost of living rose gradually in 1962–3 and sharply (4·8 per cent) in the first 10 months of 1965 with particularly large increases in the prices of dairy products and meat. Hourly wages increased by 8·2 per cent in 1963 and 9.9 per cent in 1964. During the period 1958–64 labour productivity kept pace with wage increases, but tended to decline from 1964 onwards. However, the strong competitive position of exports has been more or less maintained.

Consumption: Private consumption in 1964 amounted to 59 per cent of GNP and public consumption to 12 per cent. This represented increases of 4.5 per cent and 5.9 per cent respectively over the previous year, compared with increases of 5·1 per cent and 8·2 per cent in 1963. This trend was expected to continue and is a measure of the government's success in restoring a balance between supply and demand.

SOCIAL SECURITY

Benefits and contributions stated below refer to 1963 unless otherwise stated.

Health insurance: The decision whether to impose compulsory insurance under public law on some or all sectors of society rests with the Cantons, which can in turn empower the Communes. As a general rule only foreign workers and those whose income is below a certain level are compulsorily insured.

[1] See 'Immigrant Labour in Western Europe', p. 439.

Compulsory insurance is usually for medical treatment and medicines only. Where daily sickness benefits are paid they never cover loss of wages. Five Cantons have no compulsory insurance. Insurance is administered by over 1,000 state-recognised sickness insurance funds to which 85 per cent of the population belong. These are either public funds founded by Cantons and Communes, or private funds organised as cooperative societies, associations or foundations. Transfer between funds is possible. Minimum benefits, fixed by the Federal government, include refund of most treatment and medicine expenses, certain minimum benefits for tuberculosis, maternity benefits, a minimum daily payment of SF2 for total incapacity to work (generally upgraded to 50 per cent of wages for a maximum of 720 out of 920 consecutive days). Sickness-allowance and medical-care insurances are separate and funds may provide either or both. Sickness insurance benefits are financed by insured persons (81 per cent), Cantonal, Communal and Federal subsidies (12 per cent) and voluntary employer's contributions (about 3 per cent), interest and other sources.

Accident insurance: This is compulsory for employed persons. There are three schemes—a state scheme for handicraft and industrial workers, a predominantly Cantonal scheme for agricultural workers, and a scheme for the crews of sea-going ships. Insurance covers non-occupational as well as occupational accidents and diseases. Benefits include medical care, a daily allowance of 80 per cent of wages and extras of up to SF50 ($12) per day, payable until recovery or certification of permanent disability; and in the case of total invalidity an annual pension of 70 per cent of annual earnings up to a maximum of SF15,000 ($3,450) rising to 100 per cent where special care is necessary. In case of death survivor's pension, based upon maximum annual earnings of SF15,000, is 30 per cent for widows, 15 per cent for orphans up to 18 (20 if still studying or training) and 25 per cent for full orphans, the sum of such benefits not to exceed 60 per cent. Contributions for occupational accidents are paid entirely by the employer and for non-occupational accidents by the insured person, with the state paying one-eighth. Supplementary benefits related to the cost of living are paid by the state.

Agricultural workers are insured with recognised private insurance companies, and contributions, paid entirely by the employer, are offset by Cantonal and state supplements. Benefits regulated by the Cantons include lump sums of SF10,000 ($2,300) in case of death and SF20,000 ($4,600) for total disablement, daily allowances of SF5 ($1·10) for one year for incapacity to work, and refund treatment costs up to SF2,000 ($460) per accident. Seamen's insurance is aligned with the compulsory state accident insurance, with benefits generally higher. Workers not covered by any of these schemes are sometimes insured under compulsory Cantonal schemes or insured voluntarily by employers with private insurance companies.

Pensions insurance: The old-age and survivor's insurance scheme is compulsory for the whole population. Contributions amount to 4 per cent of total income which is paid half by the employer for employees, while self-employed people pay the whole contribution themselves reduced on a regressive scale to a minimum of 2 per cent for persons with annual earnings of SF600–12,000 ($140–2,800) and to SF12 (about $3) per annum for those earning less than SF600. Graduated annual pensions are paid at 65 to men and 62 to women and amount to SF1,500–3,200 ($350–740) for single persons, SF2,400–5,120 ($550–1,180) for married couples, SF1,200–2,560 ($275–590) for widows, SF600–1,920 ($140–440) for orphans, and supplementary pensions of

SF600–1,280 ($140–295) for wives and SF600–1,920 for children. The scheme is administered by equalisation funds which are public institutions established by the Confederation, the Cantons and associations of employers and self-employed persons. The funds are financed by contributions of the insured, the Confederation and the Cantons, and interest earned by the funds. Invalidity insurance is financed half by the employers and the insured and half by public authorities (of which 75 per cent is paid by the Confederation and the rest by the Cantons). The insured pays 0·4 per cent of annual income and administration is through the old-age and survivor's scheme. Invalidity benefits include rehabilitation, special schooling, vocational guidance, medical care and pensions.

Unemployment insurance: This is administered by public, trade union and joint employer-worker funds. Membership of such funds is compulsory in 23 Cantons. Insurance is financed by member's contributions, subsidies from the Cantons and the Confederation and by a Central Equalisation Fund; employers do not pay a contribution. Members' contributions—SF13–79 ($3–18) per year—vary according to the fund. On fulfilment of certain conditions benefits of 60–85 per cent of insured daily earnings up to SF32 ($7) are paid.

Other benefits: Monthly household allowances of SF60 ($14) and family allowances of SF25–30 ($6–7) are paid by the Confederation to agricultural workers. These are financed by employers (1·3 per cent of wages), the Confederation and the Cantons. The Confederation and the Cantons also finance the same family allowances for farmers with annual income of less than SF5,500 ($1,265). Payment of family allowances to employees is compulsory by law in all Cantons; monthly allowances range from SF10 to 35 ($2·30–8). Similar allowances are paid in some Cantons to self-employed persons within a certain income range. Public servants also benefit in a variety of ways. All Swiss subjects in military service benefit from an income-replacement scheme financed solely by its members (contributions are 0·04 per cent of annual income) which provides total benefits of up to 90 per cent of average daily earnings prior to military service. Military insurance proper is very highly developed, covers most risks and offers a wide range of benefits.

EDUCATION

Although education is a responsibility of the Cantons, each of which has its own educational authority and system, the system as a whole is fairly uniform. Children begin at the ages of six to seven and continue until 14 to 16. The Federal constitution guarantees free primary and secondary education, that this education remains under the supervision of the civil authorities, and that no child is compelled to attend religious instruction against its parent's wishes. Instruction is in the language or languages of the Cantons.

Primary education: For four years (i.e. until 10 or 11) this is the same for all children in all Cantons. At this age children may take an examination.

Secondary education: Those who do not take the primary finishing examination or who fail it continue primary education until 15 or 16. The successful enter secondary schools in which the curricula are based in varying degrees on the requirements of the Maturity examination. At the age of 15 or 16 secondary-school children take a Cantonal examination, then either leave or go on to the age of 18 or 19 when they take the Federal Maturity examination, the main qualification for university entrance. Streaming permits students from both upper primary and secondary schools to embark upon technical and commercial secondary education. Children enter commercial schools at 14 and technical schools at 15 and after courses lasting three to five years may obtain diplomas or the Commercial Maturity Certificate. Secondary technical education is supplemented by a higher stage preparing the student for technical diplomas and licentiates and doctorates in economics and social sciences.

Vocational and technical education: Vocational training in industry, handicrafts, commerce, agriculture and domestic science is regulated by Federal law; all professional certificates and diplomas must be valid for all of Switzerland. The Federal authorities encourage vocational education by direct subsidies and other measures. The minimum age to begin apprenticeship is 15 and during the whole period of training the apprentice must attend a professional school, leading to a final examination conducted by the Cantons and then to a Federal certificate of proficiency. After this there are opportunities to pursue examinations for the certificate of Master Craftsman. The Cantonal Colleges of Technology (*Techniken*) train engineers of non-university level for engineering, chemistry and watchmaking; courses last three or three-and-a-half years.

Special education: This is provided for all severely mentally or physically handicapped children. Costs are financed partly by invalidity schemes. The mentally handicapped are taught separately from the maladjusted.

Higher education: There are seven universities, all maintained by the Cantons —Basle, Bern, Lausanne, Geneva, Zurich, Neuchâtel and Fribourg. In addition there is a School of Technology affiliated to the University of Lausanne, the Federal Institute of Technology in Zurich (the only school founded by the Confederation), and the School of Economics and Public Administration in St Gallen. Geneva has several institutes affiliated to the University—a school of engineering, a school of interpreters and a graduate institute of international studies. Courses last from four to six-and-a-half years. About 30 per cent of students at higher educational institutes are foreign. Attendance at courses is compulsory. Grants and loans are obtainable from local authorities.

Educational institutions, 1964:

	Institutions	Staff	Students
Primary	n.a.	17,714	577,055
Secondary	n.a.	6,583	142,987
Technical	46	393	9,516
Universities	10	2,569	30,441

Private schools: Besides private day schools there are over 400 boarding schools in Switzerland, many of which have an international reputation. All private schools lay a greater stress on overall training than is possible at state schools. About 10 per cent of pupils are foreign.

Adult education: Adult education is provided mainly by private organisations, in particular by the Migros Cooperative Society. These concentrate mainly on the cultural and social side of education. Courses run by Cantons and Communes are few and in their initial stages of development.

Mass Media

The press:

Dailies: Tages Anzeiger Zürich, Zurich, independent, 160,000; *Feuille d'Avis de Lausanne*, Lausanne, ind., 81,000; *Neue Zürcher Zeitung*, Zurich, Radical-Democrat, 80,000; *La Tribune de Genève*, Geneva, ind., 67,000; *National-Zeitung*, Basle, Rad.-Dem., 66,000; *La Suisse*, Geneva, ind., 51,000; *Luzerner Neueste Nachrichten*, Lucerne, ind., 47,000; *Berner Tageblatt*, Bern, ind., 47,000; *La Tribune de Lausanne*, Lausanne, ind., 45,000; *Der Bund*, Bern, ind. Rad.-Dem., 41,000; *Emmenthaler-Blatt*, Langnau, ind., 38,000; *Vaterland*, Lucerne, Catholic-Conservative, 34,000; *Die Tat*, Zurich, ind., 33,000; *Schweizerische Handelszeitung*, Zurich, financial/commercial/industrial, 10,000.

Periodicals: Pro (m), Zurich, consumer, 1,305,000; *Touring* (w), Bern, Touring Club Suisse, 440,000; *Der Schweizerische Beobachter* (w), Basle, ind., 406,000; *Eva im Haus* (q), Zurich, woman's, 369,000; *Ringiers Unterhaltungsblätter*, Zofingen, family, 314,000; *Schweizer Illustrierte Zeitung* (w), Zofingen, illustrated, 221,000; *Werkzeitung der Schweizer Industrie* (m), Lucerne, 207,000; *Zeitbilder* (w), Zurich, 154,000.

Broadcasting: The Swiss Broadcasting Corporation comprises three broadcasting societies, the Société de Radiodiffusion et de Télévision de Suisse Romande, The Radio- und Fernsehgesellschaft der Deutschen und der Räto-Romanischen Schweiz, and the Società cooperitiva per la radiotelevisione nella Svizzera Italiana. Each of these relays a service in its own language. The Swiss Broadcasting Corporation is financed by 70 per cent of licence fees and the proceeds from commercial TV and provides programme services.

TURKEY

GEOGRAPHY

Features: Only a small part of Turkey, north of the Dardanelles, lies in Europe. The greater part belongs to Asia Minor and consists of a plateau area (Anatolian Plateau), generally with elevations in excess of 2,500 ft/760 m., divided from the Black Sea in the north by the Pontine Mountains which rise to over 12,000 ft/3,650 m., and from the Mediterranean Sea in the south by the Toros Mountains which rise to a similar height. The major areas of lowland border the Dardanelles and the lower parts of the major river valleys.

The main agricultural areas are along the coastal plains, in the lower river valleys, and in scattered basins in the interior. A number of minerals are worked, of which the most important are coal (Zonguldak area), copper, iron ore and oil. There are no large industrial regions by general European standards but there are a number of small ones around the main towns and in the Karabuk area where the main iron and steel industry is situated.

Area: 301,400 sq. miles/780,600 sq. km. (of which 9,150 sq. miles/23,700 sq. km. lies in Europe). *Mean max. and min. temperatures:* Ankara (40° N, 33° E; 2,820 ft/860 m.) 87°F/31°C (Aug.), 24°F/−4°C (Jan.); Istanbul (41° N, 29° E; 60 ft/18 m.) 81°F/27°C (July and Aug.), 36°F/2°C (Jan.). *Relative humidity:* Ankara 72 per cent; Istanbul 81 per cent. *Mean annual rainfall:* Ankara 14 in./355 mm.; Istanbul 32 in./815 mm.

POPULATION

Total population: (1965) 31,391,000. *Main towns and populations:* (1965) Istanbul (1,751,000), ANKARA (902,000), Izmir (417,000), Adana (291,000), Bursa (213,000), Eskişehir (174,000). *Distribution:* In 1960 78 per cent of the population lived in centres of fewer than 10,000 inhabitants, 10 per cent in centres of 10–100,000 and 12 per cent in centres of more than 100,000.

Language: The official language is Turkish. Arabic and Kurdish are spoken along the frontiers with Syria and Iraq. *Religion:* Over 98 per cent of the population adhere to Islam.

CONSTITUTIONAL SYSTEM

Constitution: Republic. The 1961 constitution was adopted by referendum after the overthrow of the Menderes government in 1960. *Head of state:* President Cevdet Sunay. *Head of government:* Prime Minister Süleyman Demirel (Justice Party).

Executive: The President is elected for seven years by a two-thirds majority of the Grand National Assembly (Büyük Millet Meclisi) from among the

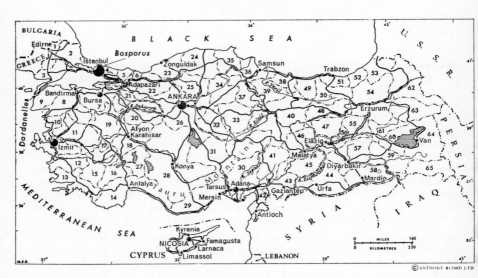

TURKEY

1. Edirne	14. Antalya	27. Isparta	40. Sivas	53. Çorum
2. Kirklareli	15. Denizli	28. Konya	41. Maraş	54. Erzurum
3. Tekirdağ	16. Burdur	29. Icel	42. Hatay	55. Bingöl
4. Istanbul	17. Uşak	30. Seyhan	43. Gaziantep	56. Elâziğ
5. Kocaeli	18. Afyon	31. Niğde	44. Urfa	57. Diyarbakir
6. Sakarya	19. Kütahya	32. Kirşehir	45. Adiyaman	58. Mardin
7. Bursa	20. Eskişehir	33. Yozgat	46. Malatya	59. Siirt
8. Ralikesir	21. Bilecik	34. Çorum	47. Tunceli	60. Bitlis
9. Çanakkale	22. Bolu	35. Sinop	48. Erzincan	61. Mus
10. Izmir	23. Zonguldak	36. Samsun	49. Giresun	62. Kars
11. Manisa	24. Kastamonu	37. Amasya	50. Gümüşane	63. Ağri
12. Aydin	25. Çankiri	38. Ordu	51. Trabzon	64. Van
13. Muğla	26. Ankara	39. Tokat	52. Rize	65. Hakâri

members of the Assembly and is not eligible for reelection. On election the President disassociates himself from his party and his membership of parliament is terminated. He selects the Prime Minister and the other ministers on the recommendation of the Prime Minister. No act of the President is valid unless countersigned by a minister. He may return legislation—except budget and constitutional laws—to the Assembly for reconsideration but if it is passed again he must promulgate it. The Council of Ministers is responsible to parliament. Ministers are jointly and individually responsible for policy. If the Council of Ministers is defeated on a vote of confidence three times within 18 months, the Prime Minister may request the President to order new elections.

Legislature: The Grand National Assembly is composed of two houses. The National Assembly (Millet Meclisi) of 450 members is elected by proportional representation for four years. The Senate (Senato) has 185 members: 150 are elected for six years by proportional representation, 15 are appointed by the President of whom 10 must have no party affiliation, and 20 are life senators. Legislation originates in the National Assembly and although the Senate has the right of amendment and proposal the final vote is always with the National Assembly. To become law a bill must pass both houses.

Political parties: The main parties are the conservative Justice Party—the direct successor of Menderes' Democratic Party—and the Republican People's Party, founded by Kemal Atatürk, which favours a considerable degree of state enterprise. In addition there are two traditionalist and religious parties, the Republican Peasants' Nation Party and its offshoot the Nation Party, the liberal New Turkey Party and the extreme left-wing Turkish Workers' Party. The Communist Party was outlawed by the government in 1945. The Justice Party forms the present government.

Election results:

| | National Assembly | | | | Senate |
| | *1961* | | *1965* | | *1966* |
	Percentage of poll	*Seats*	*Percentage of poll*	*Seats*	*Seats*
Justice Party . .	34.7	158	52·87	240	92
Republican People's Party	36·7	173	28·75	134	50
Peasants' Nation Party .	13.9	65	2·24	11	1
Nation Party . . .	—	—	6·26	31	2
New Turkey Party .	13.7	54	3.72	19	1
Turkish Workers' Party	—	—	2·97	15	1
Others	1·0	—	3·19	—	3

Leading political figures: Justice Party—Süleyman Demirel (Prime Minister), Ahmet Topalŏglu (Minister of Defence), İhsan Sabri Çağlayangil (Minister of Foreign Affairs), Cihad Bilgehan (Minister of Finance). Republican People's Party—İsmet İnönü (Party leader).

Local government: Turkey is divided into 65 Provinces (*iller*) which are subdivided into Counties (*ilçe*) and Communes (*bucaklar*). Each Provincial Governor (*vali*) is appointed by the President upon the recommendation of the Minister of the Interior. He appoints the officials of the Province and as chief administrative officer of the Province he is assisted by a staff of advisers and a Provincial Standing Committee chosen from the Provincial Council

H

which is elected for four years and over which the Governor presides. The chief officer of the County is the *kaymakam* and of the Commune the *bucak müdürü*. Each Commune comprises a number of villages each of which has a headman (*muhtar*) and a council of elders. Every Provincial and County capital and town of over 2,000 inhabitants is a Municipality (*belediye*) and is headed by a Mayor (*belediye reisi*) assisted by an elected Municipal Council.

Judicial system: The lowest civil courts, the Magistrates Courts (*sulh hukuk*) have one judge and deal with cases concerning two parties but not the public. The civil courts of first instance (*asliye hukuk mahkemeleri*) are also single-judge courts dealing with cases that involve the public besides the two parties. The Commercial Courts (*ticaret mahkemeleri*) are sited in the major cities. They have a president and two assistant judges and deal with commercial cases involving sums above £T1,000 ($111); cases involving sums below this amount are dealt with by the courts of first instance. The lowest criminal courts are the single-judge Criminal Peace Courts (*sulh ceza mahkemeleri*). Misdemeanours are dealt with by the Criminal Courts of First Instance (*asliye ceza mahkemeleri*), also single-judge courts. The Assize Courts (*ağır ceza mahkemeleri*) composed of a president and four assistant judges have jurisdiction in all cases involving penalties of five years or more. The Labour Courts (*iş mahkemeleri*) deal with management-labour disputes and are composed of one judge and one representative of each of the two disputing parties. The Courts of Appeal (*temyiz mahkemeleri*) examine all court decisions when requested by the parties; they have several chambers each composed of a presiding judge and several members. Members of the Courts of Appeal are elected by the High Council of Judges. Jurisdiction in military cases is exercised by the *askeri mahkemeleri* which consist of a president and two military officers; there is a special military appeal court.

The highest administrative court is the Council of State (Devlet Şurasi) empowered to give its opinion upon projected legislation to the Council of Ministers. The Court of Jurisdictional Disputes (Uyuşmazlik Mahkemesi) gives final judgement upon jurisdictional matters between the civil, administrative and military courts. The High Council of Judges (Yüksek Hakimler Kurulu) of 18 regular and five alternate members is concerned with all cases relating to the character and functions of judges. The Constitutional Court (Anayasa Mahkemesi) has 15 members and five alternate members. It rules on the constitutionality of legislation passed by the Grand National Assembly and its judgement is final. It is also empowered to try the senior officers of the state.

The judiciary is independent of the other organs of the state. Judges serve until they are 65 unless they are incapacitated by ill-health, convicted of a crime or pronounced unsuitable to remain in office. Capital punishment is maintained.

RECENT HISTORY

Turkey was a non-belligerent ally of Britain and France during the second world war. Turkish troops fought as United Nations forces in Korea. Turkey was admitted to NATO in 1952, signed a Treaty of Alliance, Political Cooperation and Mutual Assistance with Greece and Yugoslavia in 1954, and joined Iraq, Iran, Pakistan and Britain in the Baghdad Pact (now known as Central Treaty Organisation or CENTO) in 1955. In 1960 a military coup overthrew the government and the former Prime Minister (Menderes) and the Foreign and Finance Ministers were executed for violations of the constitution. A new constitution was adopted in 1961 and Turkey reverted to civil government. In 1964 Turkey became an associate member of the EEC.

Renewal of strife in Cyprus in December 1963 led to Turkish aerial bombardments of Cyprus based upon the country's rights under the Treaty of Guarantee (see CYPRUS, *Defence*). Turkey's relations with Greece have remained strained. In 1964, in accordance with its rights under the terms of the treaty, Turkey denounced the 1930 Agreement of Establishment, Commerce and Navigation which regulated the status of Greek nationals in Turkey on the grounds that given the Greek government's attitude over Cyprus the Agreement no longer corresponded to present circumstances. As a result Greek nationals were expelled, but not those Greeks who were Turkish citizens.

Defence: The President is head of the armed forces. Military service lasts for two years. The army totals 360,000, the bulk of which is NATO-assigned as is most of the air force of 53,000. The navy has a total strength of 37,000. Defence expenditure in 1965–6 represented 4·3 per cent of GNP and 1966–7 defence estimates were £T3,378 million ($375 million). American military bases are established in Turkey under NATO agreements.

ECONOMY

Background: The Turkish economy is basically agricultural in character. Progress towards industrialisation was slow and uneven until the 1963–7 development plan, whose main objectives were to increase the rate of industrialisation, raise the proportion of investment financed by domestic savings, stabilise and improve the balance of payments situation, maintain price stability and allow the market mechanism to play a greater role in determining prices. The plan foresees a rapid growth of the tourist industry and a far greater utilisation of the country's resources, which include immense hydroelectric potential and considerable—largely unexploited—mineral wealth (coal, copper, manganese, chromite and antimony). From 1953 to 1964 the annual average rate of growth at constant prices was 3·2 per cent. The annual average increase for 1962–4 was over 5 per cent, and in 1965 the growth rate was estimated to be 5.3 per cent. The 1963–7 plan envisages an overall annual growth rate of 7 per cent during these years, accompanied by a more systematic long-term approach to economic development. The main growth industries in recent years have been chemicals, plastics, cement, paper, rubber, metals, machinery and equipment. Other important activities include food and textiles, but these have expanded at a much slower rate. The origin of NDP at factor cost in 1964 was:

Sector				Percentage
Agriculture	.	.	.	39
Industry	.	.	.	23·5
Services	.	.	.	37·5
NDP				100

In 1964 industrial production increased by 8·6 per cent compared with increases of 8 per cent in 1963 and 7 per cent in 1962, a rate of increase expected to continue for the duration of the 1963–7 plan. Agricultural production showed an increase of 7.4 per cent in 1963, a decline of 0·2 per cent in 1964 and an increase of 1 per cent in 1965. The main agricultural products are cereals, tobacco, hazelnuts, cotton and wool; despite the declining importance of agriculture, the government is seeking to improve it through mechanisation and irrigation.

Foreign trade: Between 1963 and 1965 Turkey's balance of payments position improved considerably, but still showed a deficit of about £T1,027 million ($114 million) in 1965. Exports amounted to 5.5 per cent of GNP in 1964 and imports to 7 per cent. The main exports in 1963–4 were tobacco (20 per cent of total exports), fruit and nuts (22 per cent) and cotton (22 per cent). The main imports during this period were machinery (30 per cent of total imports), metals (11 per cent), oil and petroleum products (11 per cent) and transport equipment (10 per cent). Distribution of trade in 1964 strongly favoured Europe, especially West Germany (about 15 per cent of total trade), Britain (about 11 per cent) and the Soviet Union and other Eastern European countries (about 9 per cent). Trade with North America in 1964 was unbalanced; 17.5 per cent of total exports went there and 29 per cent of total imports originated there.

Employment: In 1960 the total labour force was 12·5 million, of whom 78 per cent were employed in agriculture, 10 per cent in industry and 12 per cent in services. In 1965 there were an estimated 160,000 Turkish workers in foreign countries, 80 per cent of them in West Germany.

Price and wage trends: The seasonal variation in the price of agricultural products is considerable. From 1962 to 1964 the cost of living index for Istanbul rose by about 28 per cent; from November 1964 to December 1965 the increase was about 11 per cent. Rapid rise in demand, tax increases and higher import tariffs contributed to these high increases. Wages rose by about 10 per cent in 1964 but the increase was expected to be smaller in 1965.

Consumption: Private consumption in 1964 accounted for 75 per cent of GNP and public consumption for 15.5 per cent.

SOCIAL SECURITY

Social security is administered by the Workers' Insurance Institute under the general supervision of the Ministry of Labour. Amounts stated below refer to 1964. Insurance covers all employees in industry and commerce in undertakings of over 10 persons, and is being gradually extended to cover small undertakings. Domestic and agricultural employees are excluded. There are special schemes for railwaymen and public employees. Maximum earnings for contributions and benefits are £T100 ($11) per day in all cases.

Health insurance: Employers and employees each pay 4 per cent of wages. Medical benefits are usually provided directly by the Institute for a maximum period of six months (18 months if such treatment will reduce disability) and include free general medical care, hospital treatment, medicines, transportation, appliances and maternity care. Sickness benefits are paid for up to 18 months, and amount to 50 per cent of daily earnings, rising to 66⅔ per cent if the insured has dependants. Maternity benefits are equal to two-thirds of daily earnings and are paid for six weeks before and after confinement. Nursing grants are £T150 ($16·66) decreasing to £T100 ($11) where the mother is hospitalised.

Accident insurance: This is paid entirely by the employer at the rate of 0·3 to 5·2 per cent of the employee's earnings according to the degree of risk. Medical benefits of the same order as for sickness are provided for a maximum of 20 months. Daily benefits for temporary disability (the same as for daily sickness allowances) are paid for 18 months. For total disability, pensions are paid at the rate of 60 per cent of earnings, with a minimum monthly pension of £T200 ($22). This is supplemented by a further 30 per cent for constant attendance. For less than total and more than 10 per cent disability, a percentage of the full pension related to the degree of disability is paid. If this sum amounts to less than £T20 ($2·20) per month, it is converted into a lump sum. Widow's pensions, also payable to disabled widowers, are 30 per cent of the insured's earnings. Orphan's pensions are 15 per cent of total earnings, and 25 per cent for full orphans, payable to each child under 18, under 25 if a student, and indefinitely if the child is an invalid.

Pensions insurance: Pensions are financed by employee and employer at the rates of 5 and 6 per cent of the employee's earnings respectively (rising to 6·75 and 8·1 per cent respectively in heavy industries). Pensions are paid at 60 for men (55 in heavy industries) and 55 for women. Old-age and invalidity pensions are 35 per cent of average earnings during the whole period of insurance rising to 50 per cent for one or more dependants. Minimum monthly pensions are £T200 ($22) or £T250 ($27.70) with dependants. Old-age pensions are reduced by 0·75 per cent for each year that insurance has been paid for less than 35 years and increased by 1 per cent for each year of insurance beyond the age of 60. Invalidity pensions are reduced by 1 per cent for each year that the insurance is less than 20 years. Pensions amounting to two-thirds of the insured's pension are paid to widows and invalid widowers at any age. Part and full orphan's pensions are respectively 25 and 40 per cent of the insured's pension. Parents receive 25 per cent if the sum of all pensions does not exceed 100 per cent of the insured's pension, with a minimum of £T200 a month. Any person who does not qualify for a pension is entitled to a lump sum refund of his own and his employer's contributions.

Unemployment insurance: The Turkish Labour Code requires an employer to pay a dismissal indemnity equal to 15 day's wages for each year worked over three.

EDUCATION

Even though the number of schools and teachers has increased ten-fold and the number of pupils by thirty-fold in the period 1923–61, Turkey's problem remains a quantitative and qualitative shortage of both schools and teachers. The national budget cannot provide the necessary additional resources; education already has second priority to defence in budget expenditure. The result is that a considerable proportion of children go without primary— and even more without post-primary—education. Although the literate population has quadrupled since 1927, Turkey still has the highest illiteracy rate in Europe—about 60 per cent in 1963. All schools, including private schools, are under the Ministry of Education. State schools are free.

Primary education: This is compulsory for all children between six and 12. The course is divided into lower and upper cycles and ends with a certificate of primary studies. In 1963, 30 per cent of children of primary-school age were not attending school at all.

Secondary and vocational education: Secondary education is divided into two stages: the three-year Middle School and the Lycée, to which there is an entrance examination. Lycée courses last for three or four years and success in the final diploma is the means of entry into the universities. Parallel to these schools are technical and commercial schools and girl's institutes offering three- to six-year courses in agriculture, engineering, building, commerce, domestic science, etc. In recent years there has been an increased emphasis on vocational education.

Universities and higher education: There are seven universities in Turkey: the Universities of Istanbul, Ankara and Trabzon, the Technical University of Istanbul, the Aegean University of Izmir, the Atatürk University in Erzurum, Eastern Anatolia (built with American assistance in Turkey's most under-developed region) and the Middle East Technical University in Ankara (established in cooperation with the United Nations). All are financed by the state, but are constitutionally guaranteed academic and administrative autonomy. University education is free. There are in addition 13 institutes of advanced professional education, including the State Conservatory in Ankara, the Academy of Fine Arts in Istanbul, schools of commerce and economics in Izmir, Istanbul and Ankara and a mining school in Zonguldak. University courses last at least four years (six years for medicine and engineering). Grants covering lodging expenses are paid mainly to students from outlying areas. Students receiving training overseas must contract to spend a number of years on their return with the government department that financed their course.

Educational institutions, 1963–4:

	Institutions	Teachers	Students
Primary (state and private)	27,172	77,553	3,644,089
Middle (state and private)	828	14,164	361,998
Lycées (state and private)	221	6,137	108,482
Vocational and higher professional	735	10,253	155,701
Universities	7	3,267	48,515

Adult education: Besides evening trade schools for adults with little primary education, there are two important forms of adult education. The People's Houses (*halkevleri*), established throughout the country, provide libraries and are concerned mainly with language and literature, fine arts, drama and history. The Village Institutes (*köy enstitüleri*) teach with regard to the needs of the area. Children with primary education are given general and vocational education in order to make them village school-teachers.

MASS MEDIA

The press (1965):

Dailies: Hürriyet, Istanbul, independent, 600,000; *Tercüman*, Istanbul, ind., 200,000; *Milliyet*, Istanbul, ind., 130,000; *Akşam*, Istanbul, ind., 110,000; *Cumhuriyet*, Istanbul, ind., 90,000; *Son Havadis*, Istanbul, Justice Party, 50,000; *Ulus*, Ankara, RPP, 40,000; *Dünya*, Istanbul, ind., 40,000; *Ege Ekspres*, Izmir, JP, 20,000; *Demokrat Izmir*, Izmir, RPP, 15,000; *Adalet*, Ankara, JP.

Periodicals: Hayat (w), Istanbul, family, 170,000; *Ses* (w), Istanbul, 80,000; *Akis* (w), Ankara, ind. political, 40,000; *Forum* (f), Ankara, political/ economic; *Doğan Kardeş* (m), Istanbul, quality children's.

Broadcasting: The Turkish Radio and Television Institute (Türkiye Radyove TV Kurumu) is an autonomous public corporation that controls all radio and TV services. Its seven-man Board of Governors is composed of representatives of the Institute itself, prominent cultural institutions, the universities, the Minister of Finance and the Minister of Tourism and Information. The director-general of the Institute is nominated by the board of governors and must be approved by the President of the Republic, the Prime Minister and Minister of Tourism and Information. The Institute has an independent budget financed by licence fees and is free to obtain foreign investment. TV is in a formative stage.

VATICAN CITY STATE

GEOGRAPHY AND POPULATION

Situation: Within the City of Rome on the right bank of the Tiber. *Population:* (1966) 890 of whom 566 are of Vatican nationality. *Language:* Italian. *Religion:* The Vatican is the centre of the Roman Catholic Church.

CONSTITUTIONAL SYSTEM

Constitution: The Vatican City State is the last remaining Papal state. The 1929 Lateran Pact between the Italian state and the Vatican (official residence of the Pope and centre of the Vatican City State) gave the Holy See the full use of property rights in and exclusive power and sovereign jurisdiction over the Vatican City State. *Head of state and the Catholic Church:* Pope Paul VI.

Executive, legislature and judicial system: The Pope is elected for life by a two-thirds majority of the Sacred College of Cardinals. He has absolute legislative, executive and judicial power. Executive power is exercised by a Governor who is directly and exclusively responsible to the Pope. Judicial power is delegated in the first instance to a tribunal, to the Sacra Romana Rota in appeal and ultimately to the Supreme Tribunal of the Segnatura. One of the Offices of the Church, the Secretariat of State, represents the Holy See (and hence the Vatican City State) in international relations.

RECENT HISTORY

Vatican neutrality was respected by all combatants in the second world war. The 1947 constitution of Italy reaffirmed its adherence to the Lateran Pact of 1929. In 1962 Pope John XXIII convened the Second Vatican Council to promote reconciliation and unity among Christian Churches. His successor, the present Pope Paul VI, visited the Holy Lands and India in 1964 and addressed the United Nations General Assembly in 1965.

MASS MEDIA

The press: Osservatore Romano is a semi-official Italian language daily under Vatican direction and covering both general news and the affairs of the Holy See. The official bulletin, *Acta Apostolicae Sedis,* is published monthly in Latin.

Broadcasting: Radio Vatican was founded in 1931 and is situated in Vatican City. A special treaty between Italy and the Vatican grants full extra-territorial privileges to another transmitter at Santa Maria di Galeria twelve miles north-west of the Vatican.

COMPARATIVE STATISTICS

COMPARATIVE STATISTICS

Except where otherwise stated, these tables are quoted (with permission) from *Basic Statistics of the Community. Comparison with some European countries, Canada, the United States of America and the Union of Soviet Socialist Republics* published by the Statistical Office of the European Communities, Brussels and Luxembourg, 6th ed. 1965. Some figures will be found to differ slightly from those given in the section entitled 'Basic Information' where other sources were used.

Symbols used:
— nil
· not available
( ) estimated
'Germany' indicates the Federal Republic including West Berlin, except where otherwise stated.

POPULATION AND LABOUR FORCE

POPULATION, 1964

Country	Area ('000 sq. km.)	Population ('000)	Density (per sq. km.)	Estimated population ('000) 1970	1975	1980
Austria	83·8	7,195	86	7,365	7,518	7,671
Belgium	30·5	9,378	307	9,610	9,815	10,000
Denmark	43·0	4,718	110	4,919	5,117	5,299
Finland	337·0	4,580	14	4,778	4,914	5,035
France	551·2	48,430	88	49,837	51,723	53,815
Germany	248·5	58,290	235	60,270	61,300	62,100
Gt Britain	245·0	54,066	222	56,790	58,638	61,425
Greece	131·9	8,480[1]	65	8,730	8,862	9,056
Iceland[2]	102·8	190	2	.[3]	.	.
Ireland[2]	70·3	2,818	41	.	.	.
Italy	301·2	52,125	173	54,318	56,402	58,439
Luxembourg	2·6	328	126	330	335	340
Netherlands	33·5	12,124	362	13,067	14,104	15,258
Norway	323·9	3,695	11	3,895	4,075	4,270
Portugal	91·5	9,107	100	9,669	10,110	10,567
Spain	504·7	31,339	62	32,386	33,551	34,491
Sweden	449·8	7,661	17	7,997	8,276	8,531
Switzerland	41·3	6,000	145	5,348	5,609	5,860
Turkey	780·6	31,118	40	32,917	37,913	43,790
Soviet Union	22,402·2	227,781	10	250,000	263,000	280,000
United States	9,363·4	192,072	21	209,000	226,000	245,000

[1] 1963.
[2] 1961. Source: National statistical abstracts, 1964.
[3] Signifies 'not available'.

EMPLOYED CIVILIAN LABOUR FORCE BY MAIN SECTORS

Country	Year	Agriculture '000	%	Industry '000	%	Services '000	%	Total '000
Austria	1963	700	21	1,356	40	1,275	38	3,367
Belgium	1964	216	6	1,641	45	1,709	47	3,622
Denmark	1964	397	18	920	40	935	41	2,282
Finland	1960	721	35	621	31	692	34	2,033
France	1964	3,653	19	7,652	39	7,946	41	19,465
Germany	1964	3,084	11	13,022	49	10,417	39	26,692
Gt Britain	1964	948	4	11,887	47	12,171	48	25,356
Greece[1]	1961	1,960	54	698	19	958	27	3,616
Iceland[2]	1964	.	36	.	28	.	36	73
Ireland[2]	1964	.	33	.	27	.	40	1,059
Italy	1964	4,967	25	7,996	40	6,426	32	19,938
Luxembourg	1964	19	14	63	46	56	40	138
Netherlands	1961	425	10	1,805	42	2,059	47	4,324
Norway	1964	302	20	516	35	649	44	1,483
Portugal	1960	1,446	43	959	29	867	26	3,354
Spain	1963	4,501	37	4,044	34	3,337	28	12,004
Sweden	1964	470	12	1,543	41	1,706	45	3,779
Switzerland	1960	280	11	1,267	51	961	38	2,512
Turkey[1]	1960	9,737	78	1,267	10	1,530	12	12,534
Soviet Union	1964	(39,710)	(38)	(31,250)	(30)	(33,040)	(32)	(104,000)
United States	1963	5,559	8	22,356	31	40,194	55	72,275

[1] Including unemployed.
[2] Source: OECD Reports, July 1965.

UNEMPLOYMENT, 1959–64
(*Percentage of total labour force*)

Country	1959	1960	1961	1962	1963	1964
Austria	4·6	3·5	2·7	2·7	2·9	2·7
Belgium	6·3	5·4	4·2	3·3	2·7	2·2
Denmark	6·1	4·3	3·9	3·3	4·3	2·9
Finland	2·3	1·5	1·2	1·2	1·5	1·5
France	·	·	·	1·1	1·0	1·0
Germany	2·4	1·2	0·8	0·7	0·8	0·7
Gt Britain	2·3	1·7	1·6	2·1	2·6	1·8
Greece	·	·	·	·	·	·
Iceland	·	·	·	·	·	·
Ireland	8·0	6·7	5·7	5·7	6·1	5·7
Italy	5·6	4·2	3·5	3·0	2·5	2·7
Luxembourg	·	·	·	·	·	·
Netherlands	1·8	1·2	0·9	0·8	0·9	0·8
Norway	2·2	1·7	1·2	1·4	1·7	1·5
Portugal	·	·	·	·	·	1·0
Spain	·	·	·	·	·	1·1
Sweden	2·0	1·4	1·2	1·3	1·4	1·1
Switzerland	·	·	0·1	0·1	0·1	0·1
Turkey	·	·	·	·	·	·
Soviet Union	·	·	·	·	·	·
United States[1]	5·5	5·6	6·7	5·6	5·7	5·2

[1] Except for 1959 excluding Alaska and Hawaii.

Source: *UN Statistical Yearbook, 1965*, ILO (cited hereafter as *UN Yearbook, 1965*)

NATIONAL PRODUCT

PER CAPITA GDP AT CONSTANT FACTOR COST, 1959–64
(1958 = 100)[1]

Country	1959	1960	1961	1962	1963	1964
Austria	102	110	114	115	120	126
Belgium	102	108	113	118	123	129
Denmark	105	111	117	122	122	130
Finland	106	115	122	125	128	134
France[2]	102	108	112	117	121	126
Germany[2]	106	114	118	122	124	131
Gt Britain	104	109	110	110	113	119
Greece	.	.	.	.	.	.
Iceland[3]	99	100	100	106	111	.
Ireland[2]	105	111	117	120	124	130
Italy	106	113	121	127	134	136
Luxembourg	102	.	.	.	.	.
Netherlands	103	112	112	117	119	127
Norway	103	108	114	116	121	129
Portugal	105	112	119	125	132	140
Spain	.	.	.	.	.	.
Sweden[2]	105	108	114	117	123	130
Switzerland[2]	106	110	115	117	120	124
Turkey	101	101	99	102	106	108
Soviet Union[4]	106	112	117	122	125	124
United States[5]	105	106	106	111	113	117

[1] Owing to varying weight-bases from country to country these figures should be interpreted with caution and taken to indicate general trends rather than precise annual changes.
[2] GDP at market prices.
[3] GNP at market prices.
[4] Net material product at market prices.
[5] GDP at market prices.

Source: *UN Yearbook, 1965*

VOLUME INDICES OF GNP AT MARKET PRICES, 1953–64
(1958 = 100)

Country	1953	1956	1959	1960	1961	1962	1963	1964
Austria	72	91	103	111	117	118	124	131
Belgium	88	98	103	108	113	119	125	131
Denmark	88	93	107	114	122	129	131	141
Finland[1]	82	97	107	117	126	129	135	(141)
France	80	93	103	111	115	124	129	137
Germany	72	92	107	116	123	128	132	141
Gt Britain	90	97	104	109	113	114	119	126
Greece	74	89	103	108	122	128	139	(151)
Iceland	.	.	.	.	.	.	.	.
Ireland	.	.	.	.	.	.	.	.
Italy	78	90	107	115	124	132	139	143
Luxembourg	.	.	.	.	.	.	.	.
Netherlands	82	97	105	115	119	123	127	137
Norway	87	98	104	109	116	120	126	135
Portugal	83	94	105	114	121	130	136	(143)
Spain	.	.	.	.	.	.	.	.
Sweden	85	96	105	109	115	120	126	135
Switzerland	84	99	107	113	122	128	134	141
Turkey	86	89	104	108	106	112	121	126
Soviet Union	.	.	.	.	.	.	.	.
United States	92	99	106	109	111	118	123	129

[1] Volume indices of GDP at factor cost.

ORIGIN OF GDP AT FACTOR COST, 1964 (%)

Country	Agriculture, forestry and fishing	Industry (incl. construction)	Services	GDP at factor cost
Austria	10·4	51·6	38·0	100
Belgium	6·6	42·6	50·8	100
Denmark	12·6	40·4	47·0	100
Finland[1]	19·4	41·9	38·7	100
France	8·9	40·8	50·3	100
Germany	5·8	51·3	42·9	100
Gt Britain	3·5	47·4	49·1	100
Greece[1]	28·9	26·8	44·3	100
Iceland	·	·	·	·
Ireland[2]	22·0	32·0	46·0	100
Italy	14·4	44·0	41·6	100
Luxembourg[1]	7·1	52·9	40·0	100
Netherlands	9·3	40·9	49·8	100
Norway	8·9	38·1	53·0	100
Portugal[1]	22·8	42·8	34·4	100
Spain	20·8	36·2	43·0	100
Sweden[2]	7·0	50·0	43·0	100
Switzerland[2]	10·0	52·0	38·0	100
Turkey[3]	39·0	23·5	37·5	100
Soviet Union	·	·	·	·
United States	3·3	38·5	58·2	100

[1] 1963.
[2] Source: OECD Reports, July 1965.
[3] NDP at factor cost.

EXPENDITURE ON GNP, 1964
(*$'000 million*)[1]

Country	Private consumption	Public consumption	Gross fixed asset formation	Change in stocks	Net exports of goods and services	GNP at market prices
Austria	5·2	1·2	2·1	+0·1	−0·0	8·5
Belgium	10·3	2·0	3·1	+0·1	−0·0	15·5
Denmark	5·7	1·3	1·9	+0·2	−0·2	8·9
Finland	.	.	.	.	.	(6·5)
France	56·5	11·7	18·5	+1·5	−0·1	88·1
Germany	58·5	15·6	27·4	+1·2	+1·3	104·0
Gt Britain	59·4	15·2	16·2	+1·5	−0·4	91·9
Greece	.	.	.	.	.	(4·8)
Iceland	.	.	.	.	.	.
Ireland[2]	1·8	0·3	0·5	+0·5	−0·1	2·6
Italy	30·3	8·2	10·5	+0·2	+0·4	49·6
Luxembourg	.	.	.	.	.	(0·6)
Netherlands	9·7	2·6	4·2	+0·5	−0·2	16·8
Norway	3·5	1·0	1·8	+0·0	−0·1	6·3
Portugal	.	.	.	.	.	(3·2)
Spain	12·4	1·4	4·0	+0·2	−0·3	17·7
Sweden	10·0	3·2	4·1	+0·2	+0·0	17·5
Switzerland	7·5	1·6	3·8	+0·2	−0·2	12·9
Turkey	.	.	.	.	.	(7·4)
Soviet Union	.	.	.	.	.	.
United States	400·6	118·5	107·3	+3·9	+8·5	638·8

[1] Approximate figures obtained by using average official exchange rates for 1964. These rates do not necessarily reflect the relative purchasing power of individual currencies.
[2] Source: *United Nations Statistical Yearbook, 1965.*

EXPENDITURE ON GNP, 1964 (%)

Country	Private consumption	Public consumption	Gross domestic fixed asset formation	Change in stocks	Net exports of goods and services	GNP at market prices
Austria	60·8	14·0	24·4	+1·1	−0·3	100
Belgium	66·7	12·7	20·0	+0·6	−0·0	100
Denmark	63·9	14·5	21·6	+2·1	−2·1	100
Finland[1]	56·1	15·6	27·2	+1·5	−0·4	100
France	64·2	13·3	20·9	+1·7	−0·1	100
Germany	56·2	15·0	26·4	+1·1	+1·3	100
Gt Britain	64·7	16·6	17·6	+1·6	−0·5	100
Greece[1]	71·0	12·5	19·1	+2·4	−5·0	100
Iceland[2]	64·0	8·7	28·8	−0·4	−1·9	100
Ireland[2]	71·0	13·0	19·0	+2·0	.	100
Italy	61·1	16·5	21·1	+0·5	+0·8	100
Luxembourg[1]	60·5	12·7	32·1	+0·4	−5·7	100
Netherlands	57·6	15·2	25·2	+3·1	−1·1	100
Norway	56·7	15·6	28·7	+0·4	−1·4	100
Portugal[1]	75·1	14·3	17·6	−1·2	−5·8	100
Spain	69·8	7·8	22·8	+1·3	−1·7	100
Sweden	57·1	18·5	23·4	+1·0	+0·0	100
Switzerland	58·5	12·1	29·5	+1·5	−1·6	100
Turkey[1]	75·2[3]	15·5	14·1	[3]	−4·8	100
Soviet Union	.	.	.	.	.	.
United States	62·7	18·6	16·8	+0·6	+1·3	100

[1] 1963.
[2] Source: OECD Reports, July 1965.
[3] Change in stocks is included in private consumption.

FOREIGN TRADE

EXCHANGE RATES AND CURRENCIES, 1966[1]

Country	Currency	£1	$1
Austria	Schilling (Sch)[2]	72·80	26·00
Belgium	Belgian Franc (BF)	140·00	50·00
Denmark	Krone (DKr)	19·30	6·60
Finland	Finnish Mark (Fmk)	9·02	3·22
France	Franc (F)	13·69	4·90
Germany	Deutsche Mark (DM)	11·20	4·00
Gt Britain	Pound Sterling (£)		0·36
Greece	Drachma (Dr)	83·00	30·00
Iceland	Krónur (IKr)	120·60	43·00
Ireland	Pound Sterling (£)		0·36
Italy	Lira (L)	1,750·00	624·75
Luxembourg	Luxembourg Franc (LF)	140·00	50·00
Netherlands	Gulden (or Florin) (Fl)	10·14	3·60
Norway	Krone (NKr)	20·00	7·16
Portugal	Escudo (E)	80·17	28·95
Spain	Peseta (P)	167·50	60·00
Sweden	Krona (SKr)	14·40	5·18
Switzerland	Swiss Franc (SF)	12·13	4·33
Turkey	Turkish Pound (T£)	25·26	9·00
United States	Dollar ($)	2·78	

[1]Average market rates for the year.
[2]Abbreviations of names of currencies in some cases different from normal practice are used in this book for greater comparative clarity.

EXTERNAL TRADE, 1964

Country	$ million	Imports % of GNP	$ per head	$ million	Exports % of GNP	$ per head	Balance[1] ($ million)
Austria	1,863	22·0	259	1,444	17·1	201	−419
Belgium Luxembourg	5,901	37·1	608	5,580	35·0	575	−321
Denmark	2,605	29·2	552	2,082	23·4	441	−522
Finland	1,505	(23·0)	329	1,291	(19·7)	282	−214
France	10,067	11·5	208	8,990	10·3	186	−1,076
Germany	14,613	14·1	251	16,213	15·7	278	+1,600
Gt Britain	15,438	16·7	285	12,341	13·4	228	−3,096
Greece	885	(18·3)	104	309	(6·4)	36	−577
Iceland[2]	(120)	43·0	.	111	41·0	.	−10
Ireland[2]	941	42·0	.	591	37·0	.	−350
Italy	7,231	14·6	139	5,956	12·0	114	−1,275
Netherlands	7,055	42·0	582	5,808	34·6	479	−1,247
Norway	1,982	31·7	536	1,290	20·6	349	−692
Portugal	761	(23·9)	83	515	(16·2)	57	−246
Spain	2,259	12·8	72	955	5·4	30	−1,305
Sweden	3,853	22·1	503	3,672	21·0	479	−181
Switzerland	3,616	28·0	603	2,667	20·6	445	−949
Turkey	542	7·3	17	411	5·5	13	−131
Soviet Union	7,734	.	34	7,681	.	34	−56
United States	18,622	2·9	97	25,987	4·1	135	+7,366

[1] + denotes export surplus.
 − denotes import surplus.
[2] Source: OECD, 1966. Provisional figures.

TOTAL IMPORTS BY AREA OF ORIGIN, 1964 (%)

Importing Country	Area of origin			
	EEC	EFTA	USA	Rest of world
Austria[1]	58·8	14·4	5·2	21·7
Belgium[2] Luxembourg	53·3	13·1	8·9	24·7
Denmark[1]	35·4	33·3	8·7	22·6
Finland	29·7	32·1	5·2	33·0
France[2]	37·4	11·6	11·3	39·8
Germany[2]	34·9	18·1	13·8	33·2
Gt Britain[1]	16·6	11·3	11·6	60·5[3]
Greece	42·3	19·5	11·4	26·7
Iceland	(17·6)	(37·8)	(12·0)	(32·6)
Ireland	(16·0)	(51·0)[4]	(8·0)	(25·0)
Italy[2]	32·7	14·3	13·6	39·5
Netherlands[2]	52·0	13·7	11·0	23·3
Norway[1]	28·8	40·5	7·5	23·2
Portugal[1]	33·1	21·4	10·5	35·1
Spain	35·9	18·4	15·6	30·1
Sweden[1]	37·4	30·0	10·0	22·6
Switzerland[1]	62·0	14·7	8·7	14·6
Turkey	28·7	16·7	28·8	25·8
Soviet Union	5·4	4·1	2·1	88·4
United States	15·2	10·5		74·2

[1] EFTA.
[2] EEC.
[3] Of which 32% to Commonwealth.
[4] To Gt Britain.

TOTAL EXPORTS BY AREA OF DESTINATION, 1964 (%)

Exporting Country	Area of destination			
	EEC	EFTA	USA	Rest of world
Austria[1]	47·5	18·4	4·0	30·0
Belgium[2] } Luxembourg }	62·6	12·6	8·1	16·7
Denmark[1]	28·1	45·0	6·3	20·7
Finland	30·6	34·2	5·8	29·4
France[2]	38·8	16·6	5·2	39·3
Germany[2]	36·5	27·2	7·4	28·9
Gt Britain[1]	20·6	12·9	8·7	57·8[3]
Greece	37·5	13·2	14·5	34·8
Iceland	(21·0)	(38·3)	(15·0)	(25·7)
Ireland	(12·0)	(72·0)[4]	(9·0)	(11·0)
Italy[2]	38·0	18·3	8·5	35·2
Netherlands[2]	55·7	19·4	3·9	21·1
Norway[1]	26·2	43·1	9·3	21·4
Portugal[1]	20·7	25·1	10·5	43·9
Spain	38·9	25·2	10·1	25·6
Sweden[1]	31·6	36·7	5·4	26·2
Switzerland[1]	40·5	18·2	9·2	32·2
Turkey	33·5	23·6	17·8	25·1
Soviet Union	6·2	5·0	0·3	88·5
United States	17·2	9·5		73·4

[1] EFTA.
[2] EEC.
[3] Of which 27·2 % to Commonwealth.
[4] To Gt Britain.

TOTAL IMPORTS, 1957–64

($ million)

Country	1957	1958	1959	1960	1961	1962	1963	1964 $ million	1964 % of world trade
Austria	1,128	1,074	1,144	1,416	1,485	1,552	1,675	1,863	1·2
Belgium Luxembourg	3,416	3,136	3,442	3,957	4,219	4,555	5,112	5,901	3·7
Denmark	1,359	1,359	1,595	1,799	1,864	2,123	2,120	2,605	1·6
Finland	900	729	835	1,063	1,151	1,228	1,208	1,505	0·9
France	6,122	5,609	5,087	6,279	6,678	7,520	8,726	10,067	6·3
Germany	7,499	7,361	8,477	10,103	10,941	12,279	13,019	14,613	9·2
Gt Britain	11,398	10,488	11,154	12,714	12,314	12,578	13,497	15,438	9·7
Greece	525	565	567	702	714	701	804	885	0·6
Iceland					72	83	102	121	·
Ireland[1]					720	754	872	974	
Italy	3,674	3,216	3,369	4,725	5,223	6,067	7,590	7,231	4·6
Netherlands	4,105	3,625	3,939	4,531	5,112	5,347	5,967	7,055	4·4
Norway	1,274	1,309	1,321	1,459	1,614	1,654	1,821	1,982	1·2
Portugal	502	480	474	544	654	587	651	761	0·5
Spain	862	827	795	723	1,092	1,570	1,955	2,259	1·4
Sweden	2,428	2,366	2,413	2,899	2,921	3,114	3,389	3,853	2·4
Switzerland	1,966	1,707	1,924	2,245	2,714	3,022	3,255	3,616	2·3
Turkey	396	315	442	468	509	622	691	542	0·3
Soviet Union	3,938	4,350	5,073	5,630	5,828	6,450	7,059	7,737	4·7
United States	13,223	13,208	15,414	15,014	14,628	16,240	17,014	18,622	11·7

[1] Based on monthly averages. Source: *UN Yearbook, 1965.*

TOTAL EXPORTS, 1957-64

($ million)

Country	1957	1958	1959	1960	1961	1962	1963	1964 $ million	1964 % of world trade
Austria	979	918	964	1,120	1,202	1,263	1,325	1,444	0·8
Belgium Luxembourg	3,171	3,053	3,295	3,775	3,924	4,324	4,839	5,580	3·2
Denmark	1,174	1,267	1,375	1,470	1,514	1,630	1,870	2,082	1·2
Finland	835	775	835	989	1,054	1,104	1,149	1,291	0·7
France	5,047	5,121	5,607	6,863	7,220	7,362	8,083	8,990	5·2
Germany	8,575	8,807	9,804	11,415	12,687	13,264	14,616	16,213	9·4
Gt Britain	9,683	9,276	9,691	10,349	10,754	11,059	11,855	12,341	7·1
Greece	220	232	204	203	223	249	290	309	0·2
Iceland[1]	··	··	··	··	72	84	94	(111)	·
Ireland[2]	··	··	··	··	504	487	548	622	··
Italy	2,550	2,577	2,913	3,648	4,183	4,665	5,055	5,956	3·4
Netherlands	3,997	3,217	3,607	4,028	4,307	4,584	4,962	5,808	3·4
Norway	822	743	809	879	930	973	1,073	1,290	0·7
Portugal	288	289	290	325	331	367	417	515	0·3
Spain	476	486	503	727	709	734	736	955	0·6
Sweden	2,137	2,088	2,207	2,564	2,738	2,923	3,202	3,672	2·1
Switzerland	1,562	1,547	1,693	1,892	2,053	2,229	2,430	2,667	1·5
Turkey	345	264	355	320	347	381	368	411	0·2
Soviet Union	4,382	4,298	5,441	5,563	5,998	7,035	7,272	7,681	4·4
United States	20,682	17,751	17,449	20,358	20,629	21,286	22,922	25,987	15·0

[1] Source: UN Yearbook, 1965. [2] Based on monthly averages. Source: UN Yearbook, 1965.

INDUSTRY

INDICES OF INDUSTRIAL PRODUCTION, 1954-64[1]
(1958 = 100)

Country	1954	1955	1956	1957	1958	1959	1960	1961	1962	1963	1964
Austria	75	88	93	98	100	106	117	121	125	131	140
Belgium	92	99	105	105	100	104	112	119	125	135	145
Denmark	87	89	90	96	100	112	121	128	139	.	.
Finland	88	98	101	104	100	109	123	136	145	151	161
France	.	82	89	96	100	101	110	116	122	128	138
Germany[2]	75	86	93	97	100	107	120	127	133	137	150
Gt Britain	.	.	.	.	100	105	113	113	114	119	127
Greece	.	.	.	.	100	.	.	.	128	137	152
Iceland	.	.	.	.	.	.	.	.	.	.	.
Ireland[3]	.	.	.	.	.	110	118	129	137	144	158
Italy	77	84	90	96	100	111	128	142	156	169	170
Luxembourg	85	96	103	104	100	104	114	117	112	113	124
Netherlands	.	.	.	.	100	109	122	126	133	139	151
Norway	81	93	99	100	100	104	114	120	125	132	141
Portugal	76	81	88	94	100	106	116	127	134	146	.
Spain[3]	.	.	.	.	.	103	106	122	133	149	171
Sweden	85	91	94	98	100	106	116	124	126	129	136
Switzerland	.	.	.	.	.	.	.	.	.	.	.
Turkey	.	.	.	.	.	.	.	.	.	.	.
Soviet Union	66	75	82	91	100	111	122	134	147	158	169
United States	92	103	107	107	100	113	116	117	126	133	141

[1] Excluding construction.
[2] Excluding West Berlin.
[3] Source: *UN Yearbook, 1965*.

WAGES IN MANUFACTURING, 1960–4 ($)[1]

(h—*hour*, d—*day*, mo—*month*, m—*males*, f—*females*, mf—*both*)

Country	Rate	1960	1961	1962	1963	1964
Austria[2]	mo, mf	85·70	93·00	99·00	105·00	114·70
Belgium	d, m	5·00	5·20	5·50	6·00	6·60
	d, f	2·80	3·00	3·20	3·60	4·00
Denmark[3]	h, mf	0·86	0·96	1·06	1·14	1·24
Finland[2]	h, mf	0·66	0·71	0·75	0·80	0·91
France[3]	h, mf	0·42	0·44	0·48	0·52	0·56
Germany[4]	h, mf	0·65	0·72	0·80	0·87	0·92
Gt Britain[5]	h, m	0·88	0·93	0·98	1·03	1·10
	h, f	0·51	0·54	0·57	0·59	0·63
Greece	h, mf	.	0·25	0·26	0·27	0·31
Iceland	.					
Ireland	h, mf	0·48	0·50	0·54	0·58	0·64
Italy[6]	h, mf	0·37	0·39	0·46	0·53	0·59
Luxembourg	h, mf	0·89	0·93	0·94	0·99	
Netherlands	h, mf	0·50	0·55	0·61	0·69	0·74
Norway[6]	h, m[5]	0·89	0·96	1·06	1·10	1·17
	h, f	0·60	0·65	0·74	0·76	0·82
Portugal	d, mf	1·01	1·10	1·15	1·21	.
Spain	.					
Sweden[2,6]	h, mf	1·12	1·19	1·31	1·40	1·35
Switzerland[3,4]	h, m[2]	0·92	0·99	1·06	1·15	1·24
	h, f	0·53	0·55	0·66	0·64	0·69
Turkey[6]	d, mf	.	.	1·56	1·65	1·74
Soviet Union	.	.	.	.	.	
United States	h, mf	2·26	2·32	2·39	2·46	2·53

[1] The time of year to which these figures refer varies from country to country. All figures are converted from national currencies at the rates quoted on page 222.
[2] Including mining and quarrying.
[3] Including family allowances.
[4] Adults only.
[5] Adult manual workers only.
[6] Including payments in kind.

Source: *UN Yearbook, 1965* (ILO)

HOURS WORKED IN MANUFACTURING, 1959-64

(d—*per day*, w—*per week*, m—*per month*)

Country	Period	1959	1960	1961	1962	1963	1964
Austria[1,2]	w	43·7	43·5	43·3	42·6	42·5	42·7
Belgium	w	·	·	41·4	41·0	41·2	40·9
Denmark	·	·	·	·	·	·	·
Finland[2]	w	43·3	44·4	44·6	42·9	44·1	44·0
France	w	45·0	45·7	46·0	46·2	46·3	46·1
Germany[1]	w	45·6	45·6	45·3	44·7	44·3	43·6
Gt Britain[3]	w	48·2	47·4[4]	46·8	46·2	46·8	46·9
Greece[1]	w	·	·	44·7	44·1	43·4	43·9
Iceland	·	·	·	·	·	·	·
Ireland	w	45·2	45·4	45·2	44·6	44·6	44·1
Italy	d	8·0	8·1[4]	8·1	8·0	8·0	7·9
Luxembourg	·	·	·	·	·	·	·
Netherlands	w	48·8	48·8	46·5	46·5	46·6	46·1
Norway[2]	w	43·4	42·9	42·1	42·2	42·2	42·6
Portugal	w	41·9	43·2	43·8	44·0	44·0	·
Spain	w	44·2	43·5	43·5	44·6	44·8[4]	44·1
Sweden	m	169·0	167·0	165·0	165·0	·	·
Switzerland[1]	w	46·6	46·1	45·8	45·6	45·5	45·4
Turkey	·	·	·	·	·	·	·
Soviet Union	·	·	·	·	·	·	·
United States	w	40·3	39·7	39·8	40·4	40·5	40·7

[1] Hours paid for.
[2] Including mining and quarrying.
[3] Adult males only.
[4] Revised method of estimation from this year onwards.

Source: *UN Yearbook, 1965* (ILO)

TOTAL PRODUCTION OF PRIMARY ENERGY, 1964

('ooo tons coal equivalent)

Country	Coal[1]	Lignite	Crude petroleum	Natural gas	Primary electricity	Total primary energy
Austria	100	2,879	3,808	2,100	5,270	14,157
Belgium	19,374	—	6	78	63	19,515
Denmark	—	(660)	—	—	10	(670)
Finland	—	—	—	—	3,469	3,469
France	48,257	1,324	4,068	6,393	12,438	72,480
Germany	143,353	31,400	10,972	2,738	4,143	192,606
Gt Britain	196,733	—	186	10	5,018	201,947
Greece	—	1,172	—	—	296	1,468
Iceland	.	.	.	.	.	.
Ireland	.	.	.			
Italy	357	412	3,818	9,161	14,722	28,470
Luxembourg	—	—	—	—	15	15
Netherlands	11,480	—	3,246	991	—	15,717
Norway	443	—	—	—	17,729	18,172
Portugal	445	53	—	—	1,757	2,255
Spain	12,064	1,291	—	—	8,767	22,122
Sweden	63	—	116	—	17,210	17,389
Switzerland	—	—	—	—	9,018	9,018
Turkey	4,449	828	1,317	—	674	7,268
Soviet Union	415,000	68,000	318,890	134,140	34,600	970,630
United States	449,472	879	541,970	446,600	73,435	1,512,376

[1] These figures are given ton for ton except in the case of the EEC countries.

AGRICULTURE

INDICES OF AGRICULTURAL OUTPUT, 1956–64[1]

(Average 1952/3–1956/7 = 100)

Country	1956/7	1957/8	1958/9	1959/60	1960/1	1961/2	1962/3	1963/4
Austria	107	112	116	108	122	126	129	134
Belgium Luxembourg	100	107	110	103	113	111	121	122
Denmark	101	111	110	110	116	121	125	118
Finland	100	107	110	112	127	125	119	130
France	102	102	105	112	124	117	129	125
Germany	102	105	110	107	121	109	123	127
Gt Britain	106	105	101	110	118	123	130	132
Greece	112	128	122	125	117	138	134	146
Iceland	.	.	.	.	.	.	.	.
Ireland[2]	.	.	104	.	108	122	119	122
Italy	103	101	116	116	107	116	115	118
Netherlands	98	105	115	117	118	118	121	118
Norway	108	101	101	98	102	104	100	105
Portugal	102	105	99	101	102	102	111	108
Spain	104	109	110	117	119	121	128	134
Sweden	101	99	95	98	100	104	100	99
Switzerland	98	99	108	106	110	110	110	107
Turkey	105	105	124	126	132	124	131	147
Soviet Union	.	.	.	.	.	.	.	.
United States	103	100	108	110	111	111	111	118

[1] Net of imported feeding stuffs and cattle.
[2] Source: *UN Yearbook, 1965*.

LAND UTILISATION, 1963

Country	Agricultural area		Arable land[1]	Permanent meadows and pastures
	'000 hectares	% of total area	% of agricultural area	
Austria	3,990	47·6	43·1	56·9
Belgium	1,685	55·2	56·1	43·9
Denmark	3,088	71·7	89·2	10·8
Finland	2,809	8·3	96·7	3·3
France	34,159	62·0	61·6	38·4
Germany	14,121	56·8	59·5	40·5
Gt Britain	12,401	50·8	59·4	40·6
Greece	9,021	68·4	43·2	56·8
Iceland[2]	2,500	(24·0)	0·9	23·0
Ireland[2]	.	68·0	.	.
Italy	19,584	65·0	74·4	25·6
Luxembourg	135	52·5	52·9	47·1
Netherlands	2,303	63·7	44·0	56·0
Norway	1,030	3·2	83·0	17·0
Portugal	4,130	46·5	.	.
Spain	22,157	43·9	94·0	6·0
Sweden	3,867	8·6	86·4	13·6
Switzerland	2,165	52·4	19·5	80·5
Turkey	54,377	69·7	48·0	52·0
Soviet Union	609,200	27·3	37·1	62·9
United States[3]	441,366	47·1	41·9	58·1

[1] Including land under permanent cultivation (orchards, vineyards, etc.).
[2] 1964.
[3] 1959.

TRANSPORT

RAILWAYS, 1964

Country	Length of line operated (km.)	Passenger/km. (million)	Ton/km. (million)
Austria	5,593	6,615	7,987[1]
Belgium	4,485	8,065	6,978
Denmark	2,486	3,399	1,550
Finland	5,389	2,357[2]	4,863
France	37,790	37,808	65,260
Germany	30,504	42,081	61,154
Gt Britain	27,349	31,820[2]	26,152
Greece	1,745	729[1]	360[1]
Iceland	—	—	—
Ireland[3]	3,300	.	.
Italy	16,213	27,926	14,662
Luxembourg	365	191	671
Netherlands	3,238	7,812	3,885
Norway	4,308	1,712	1,874
Portugal	3,571	2,258	762
Spain	13,407	11,820	7,440
Sweden	13,001	5,174	11,756
Switzerland	2,914	8,507	4,906
Turkey	8,009	3,816	4,405
Soviet Union	128,600[1]	195,100	1,854,100
United States[1]	350,517	297,758	907,622

[1] 1963.
[2] 1962.
[3] 1964. Source: *Irish Statistical Abstract*, Dublin, 1965.

CIVIL AVIATION, 1964

Country	Number of airlines	Number of aircraft	Passenger/km. (million)	Available seat/km. (million)	Load factor (%)
Austria	1	10	181	380	48
Belgium	1	52	1,627	3,015	54
Denmark ⎫ Norway ⎬	1	46	2,964	5,463	54
Sweden ⎭					
Finland	1	24	309	593	51
France	2	127	6,513	11,981	54
Germany	1	50	3,150	5,573	57
Gt Britain	4	184	9,762	16,794	58
Greece	1	15	438	842	52
Iceland[1]	1	.	652	.	.
Ireland[1]	1	.	794	.	.
Italy	1	54	3,405	6,270	54
Luxembourg	—	—	—		
Netherlands	1	40	3,000	5,916	51
Portugal	1	8	492	775	64
Spain	2	66	1,952	3,321	59
Switzerland	1	32	2,143	3,970	54
Turkey	1	160	160	288	56
Soviet Union	1	.	30,900	.	.
United States	14	1,148	85,172	140,257	61

[1] Source: *UN Yearbook, 1965.*

J

MERCHANT SHIPPING, 1964
(*'000 tons gross*)

Country	Total merchant ships	Of which tankers
Austria	—	—
Belgium	796	214
Denmark	2,431	884
Finland	964	295
France	5,116	2,209
Germany	5,159	839
Gt Britain	21,490	8,002
Greece	6,888	1,603
Iceland[1]	174	—
Ireland[1]	130	—
Italy	5,708	1,982
Luxembourg	—	—
Netherlands	5,110	1,638
Norway	14,477	7,664
Portugal	702	160
Spain	2,048	591
Sweden	4,308	1,463
Switzerland	164	—
Turkey	680	110
Soviet Union	6,958	1,716
United States	22,430	4,505

[1] Source: *UN Yearbook, 1965*.

INLAND WATERWAYS TRANSPORT, 1964

Country	Length of inland waterways in use (km.)	Number	Capacity ('ooo metric tons)	Ton/km. (million)
Austria	358	356	268	995
Belgium	1,530	5,911	2,766	6,107
Denmark	—	—	—	—
Finland	6,645[1]	.	.	.
France	7,658	9,671	3,623	12,469
Germany	4,468	7,612	4,995	40,609
Gt Britain	1,460[2]	.	.	242[2]
Greece	—	—	—	—
Iceland	—	—	—	—
Ireland	—	—	—	—
Italy	2,467	2,712	165	.
Luxembourg	37	—	—	—
Netherlands	6,374	20,547	6,141	22,715
Norway	—	—	—	—
Portugal	—	—	—	—
Spain	—	—	—	—
Sweden	642[2]	.	.	.
Switzerland	21	462	433	37
Turkey	—	—	—	—
Soviet Union	140,700	.	.	124,400
United States	.	.	.	.

[1] 1960.
[2] 1963.

CONSUMPTION

COMPOSITION OF PRIVATE

	Food	Beverages	Tobacco	Clothing and other personal effects	Rent and water charges	Fuel and light	Furniture, furnishing and household equipment
Austria	31·5	8·0	2·9	13·8	5·2	4·0	7·7
Belgium	26·6	4·9	2·0	10·6	10·8	5·9	8·8
Denmark	22·8	10·4		9·6	8·2	2·6	10·3
Finland	37·0	5·6	4·1	13·4	7·6	3·2	6·6
France	30·5	6·7	1·8	12·4	7·2	3·4	6·7
Germany	36·0		.		9·1	4·7	.
Gt Britain	27·1[4]	6·0[4]	6·6	10·8	9·9	5·0	6·6
Greece[5]	43·0	3·4	3·8	14·8	9·2	3·3	5·6
Iceland	.	.	.	.	.	.	.
Ireland	.	.	.	.	.	.	.
Italy	40·6[4]	5·7[4]	3·8	9·0	7·5	2·7	2·9
Luxembourg	34·9		2·1	.	11·2	4·9	.
Netherlands	30·0	3·3	3·7	15·8	8·0	5·6	9·6
Norway	28·2	4·9	3·1	14·7	7·8	3·8	7·8
Portugal	.	.	.	.	.	.	.
Spain[5]	44·3	3·4	0·9	11·8	4·2	2·5	6·1
Sweden	27·0	6·2	3·3	12·3	9·3	4·9	7·3
Switzerland	.	.	.	.	.	.	.
Turkey	.	.	.	.	.	.	.
Soviet Union	.	.	.	.	.	.	.
United States	20·5[4]	3·0[4]	2·2	8·9	13·3	3·6	6·8

[1] Included under Recreation and Entertainment.
[2] Netted out from other items in this table.
[3] Broken down under other headings.
[4] Non-alcoholic beverages included under Food.
[5] 1962.

CONSUMPTION, 1963 (%)

Household operation	Personal care and health expenses	Transportation and communication	Recreation and entertainment	Miscellaneous services	Domestic private consumption	Expenditure of residents abroad	Less: expenditure of non-residents in the country	Private consumption
3·0	4·4	9·6	7·7	2·2	·	1	2	100
4·6	6·2	8·3	7·8	3·2	99·7	2·0	1·7	100
·	·	11·7	·	·	·	3·2	·	100
2·1	3·9	7·1	6·2	1·0	97·8	3·0	0·8	100
3·8	8·7	8·3	6·8	3·2	99·5	2·1	1·6	100
·	3·7	8·3	·	·	·	3	3	100
2·9	2·4	10·7	7·1	4·2	99·3	1·8	1·1	100
2·2	2·3	6·6	6·0	1·6	101·8	0·8	2·6	100
·	·	·	·	·	·	·	·	·
3·7	5·1	10·1	7·3	1·6	·	3	3	100
·	5·8	8·7	·	·	103·1	3·2	6·3	100
4·5	6·0	4·2	5·1	4·2	100·0	2·4	2·4	100
3·8	4·3	9·9	7·3	2·8	98·4	4·0	2·4	100
1·3	1·3	10·7	10·8	8·9	106·2	0·6	6·8	100
2·3	3·8	14·2	7·4	1·6	99·6	1·7	1·3	100
·	·	·	·	·	·	·	·	·
4·2	8·2	14·5	5·7	8·2	99·1	1·2	0·3	100

CONSUMER PRICE INDEX, 1959–64
(*1958 = 100*)

Country	1959	1960	1961	1962	1963	1964
Austria[1]	101	103	107	111	114	119
Belgium[1]	101	102	103	104	106	111
Denmark[1]	102	103	107	115	122	126
Finland	102	105	107	112	117	129
France	106	110	114	119	105[2]	108
Germany	101	102	105	108	111	114
Gt Britain	101	102	105	110	112	115
Greece	102	102[3]	103	103	106	107
Iceland	101	103	108	120	135	162
Ireland	100	100	103	108	110	117
Italy	100	102	104	109	117	124
Luxembourg[1]	100	101	101	102	105	108
Netherlands[4]	102	103	105	108	113	119
Norway	102	102	105	111	114	120
Portugal (Lisbon)	101	104	106	109	111	115
Spain	107	109	111[5]	118	128	137
Sweden	101	105	107	112	115	119
Switzerland	99	101	103	107	111	114
Turkey (Istanbul)	126	133	138	143	153	157
Soviet Union[6]	99	99	98	99	100	100
United States[7]	101	102	103	105	106	107

[1] Excluding rent.
[2] Beginning 1963, 1962=100.
[3] Beginning 1960, 1959=100.
[4] Excluding compulsory social insurance and wage tax.
[5] Beginning 1961, new index.
[6] Excluding Alaska and Hawaii.
[7] Index of state retail prices.

Source: *UN Yearbook, 1965* (ILO)

INTERNAL CONSUMPTION OF PRIMARY ENERGY PRODUCTS AND EQUIVALENTS, 1964
(million tons coal equivalent)

Country	Coal and lignite	Crude petroleum	Natural gas	Primary electricity	Total energy
Austria	8·5	7·3	2·3	4·2	(22·3)
Belgium	23·6	18·1	0·0	0·0	41·7
Denmark	6·1	12·0	—	0·3	(18·4)
Finland	2·3	6·0	—	3·2	(11·7)
France	68·7	68·3	6·4	13·2	156·6
Germany	156·3	91·1	2·6	4·5	254·5
Gt Britain	196·7	89·2	0·1	4·9	(290·9)
Greece	1·4	4·1	—	0·3	(5·8)
Iceland	·	·	·	·	·
Ireland	·	·	·	·	·
Italy	10·9	61·3	9·2	15·1	96·4
Luxembourg	4·2	1·0	0·0	0·4	5·6
Netherlands	14·6	29·6	1·0	0·0	45·2
Norway	1·1	5·6	—	17·2	(23·9)
Portugal	1·1	2·7	—	1·7	(5·5)
Spain	16·2	16·3	—	8·1	(40·6)
Sweden	3·3	23·6	—	17·1	(44·0)
Switzerland	2·8	9·8	—	8·8	(21·4)
Turkey	5·0	5·1	—	0·7	(16·6)
Soviet Union	391·0	225·5	133·0	34·6	(784·1)
United States	383·0	677·8	566·0	73·0	(1,699·8)

SOCIAL STATISTICS

HEALTH SERVICES, 1963

Country	Doctors		Pharmacists		Hospital beds	
	'000	per 100,000 population	'000	per 100,000 population	'000	per 100,000 population
Austria	12·6	175	2·2[1]	31	77·7	1,083
Belgium	13·2	142	5·8	63	77·0	825
Denmark	6·4[1]	137	1·5[2]	31	44·6[1]	955
Finland	3·1[1]	69	10·0[1]	32	43·2[3]	960
France	52·8	110	19·8	41	455·5[3]	981
Germany	83·0	144	18·6	32	615·7	1,064
Gt Britain	56·4[2]	107	21·1[2]	40	550·7	1,022
Greece	11·3	133	2·2[2]	26	49·8	587
Iceland	.	.	.	.	.	.
Ireland	.	.	.	.	.	.
Italy	86·1	170	32·6	64	485·3	937
Luxembourg	0·3	97	0·2	52	3·9	1,200
Netherlands	13·6	113	0·8	7	87·6	728
Norway	4·6	126	0·7	20	40·4	1,090
Portugal	7·5	83	2·3	25	52·5	578
Spain	37·7	121	12·5	40	135·3	434
Sweden	7·6[1]	101	0·8[1]	10	120·6[1]	1,591
Switzerland	7·4	129	1·1	20	67·7[2]	1,247
Turkey	9·0[1]	31	1·5[1]	5	50·1[1]	170
Soviet Union	463·5	205	.	.	2,044·0	903
United States	289·2	149	.	.	1,702·0	900

[1] End 1962.
[2] End 1960.
[3] End 1961.

HOUSING

Country	Year	Number of occupied dwellings ('000)	Average number of rooms per dwelling	persons per room
Austria	1961	2,153	3·5	0·9
Belgium	1961	3,016	4·8	0·6
Denmark	1960	1,483	4·4	0·7
Finland	1960	1,211	2·7	1·3
France	1962	14,538	3·1	1·0
Germany	1961	15,564	4·1	0·9
Gt Britain	1961	15,834	(4·7)	(0·7)
Greece	1961	1,918	2·8	(1·5)
Iceland[1]	1950	31[2]	4·4	1·0
Ireland[1]	1961	676	4·4	0·9
Italy	1961	13,007	3·3	(1·1)
Luxembourg	1960	95	5·1	0·6
Netherlands	1960	2,801	5·2	0·8
Norway	1960	1,075	4·2	0·8
Portugal	1960	2,201	3·6	1·1
Spain	1960	7,332	4·3	0·9
Sweden	1960	2,582	3·4	0·8
Switzerland	1960	1,580	4·8	0·7
Turkey	1960	719	.	.
Soviet Union	1960	(50,900)	(2·8)	(1·5)
United States	1960	53,024	5·0	0·7

[1] Source: *UN Yearbook, 1965.*
[2] Total occupied and unoccupied dwellings.

J*

FACILITIES IN DWELLINGS

		% of total dwelling units with:		
Country	Year	Electricity	Inside running water	Bathroom
Austria	1961	98·3	63·6	29·6
Belgium	1961	98·5	76·9	23·6
Denmark	1960	98·4	88·2	39·4
Finland	1960	88·6	47·1	15·7
France	1962	93·0	77·5	28·0
Germany	1961	99·4	96·7	51·9
Gt Britain	1961	·	·	78·3
Greece	1961	53·1	28·6	10·4
Iceland[1]	1950	89·2	92·7	49·8
Ireland[1]	1961	83·0	51·0	33·2
Italy	1951	82·7	35·9	10·7
Luxembourg	1960	99·9	98·1	45·7
Netherlands	1956	97·9	89·5	30·3
Norway	1960	·	·	45·2
Portugal	1960	40·5	28·9	18·6
Spain	1950	80·5	34·2	9·2
Sweden	1960	·	90·2	61·0
Switzerland	1960	100·0	98·8	69·1
Turkey	1960	87·3	·	43·2
Soviet Union		·	·	·
United States	1960	99·8	92·9	88·1

[1] Source: *UN Yearbook, 1965.*

MOTOR VEHICLES IN USE, 1 JANUARY 1965

Country	Passenger cars		Commercial vehicles ('000)	Motor-cycles ('000)
	'000	per '000 of population		
Austria	703	98	123	249
Belgium	1,200	127	234	168[1]
Denmark	681	144	230	104[1]
Finland	403	88	88	101[1]
France	8,320	171	1,695	400[1]
Germany	8,676	146	891	804
Gt Britain	8,582	158	1,862	1,240
Greece	89	10	68	.
Iceland[1][2]	26	133	6[3]	.
Ireland[1][2]	254	99	51[3]	52
Italy	4,632	88	620	2,906
Luxembourg	56	169	10	9[1]
Netherlands	1,030	84	220	150[1]
Norway	415	112	136	72[1]
Portugal	211	23	78	29
Spain	652	21	315	.
Sweden	1,682	219	144	107[1]
Switzerland	830	140	96	204
Turkey	67	2	100	.
Soviet Union	926	4	3,465	.
United States	71,864	360	14,329	775

[1] 1964.
[2] Source: *UN Yearbook, 1965*.
[3] Including public service vehicles.

RADIO AND TV SETS AND TELEPHONES IN USE, 1 JANUARY 1965

Country	Radio receivers '000	Radio receivers per '000 population	TV receivers '000	TV receivers per '000 population	Telephones (end 1963) '000	Telephones (end 1963) per '000 population
Austria	2,128	295	572	79	866	120
Belgium	2,815	299	1,375	146	1,364	146
Denmark	1,619	342	1,020	215	1,248	264
Finland	1,470	320	623	135	729	159
France	14,981	308	5,414	111	5,336	111
Germany	17,494	297	10,024	170	7,560	131
Gt Britain	16,015	294	13,155	242	9,272	171
Greece	850	99	.	.	356	42
Iceland[1]	.	460	.	.	.	275
Ireland[2][3]	313	184[4]	221	184[4]	195	72
Italy	10,209	195	5,230	100	4,851	94
Luxembourg	115	347	25	76	68	208
Netherlands	2,659	218	1,836	150	2,023	168
Norway	1,071	289	407	110	838	228
Portugal	1,127	123	151	17	485	53
Spain	.	.	1,250	40	2,268	73
Sweden	2,548	331	1,964	255	3,054	420
Switzerland	1,183	200	493	83	1,998	340
Turkey	2,165	69	.	.	286	9
Soviet Union	71,800	313	12,900	52	6,600[3]	29[3]
United States	228,000	1,143	67,000	334	84,453	443

[1] Source: *UN Yearbook, 1965.*
[2] Source: *Irish Statistical Abstract, 1965.*
[3] 1964.
[4] Including both radio and TV.

PART TWO
GENERAL

POLITICAL AFFAIRS

WESTERN EUROPE AND THE ATLANTIC WORLD

JACQUES MALLET

FACING each other as they do on opposite sides of the Atlantic, Western Europe and the United States are linked closely and profoundly in a common civilisation founded on individual freedom and respect for the principles of democracy. Two world wars have strengthened and broadened their relations in the fields of defence, foreign policy and economy. These relations now constitute one of the principal facts of world politics. They are central to European politics, whose future is inseparable from that of the Atlantic world. European integration and the Atlantic Alliance have been weaving the same strand of history for the past twenty years.

Having been the catalyst and mainstay of the process of European integration that began after the second world war, the United States has in recent years become an involuntary source of discord between European countries. These countries no longer have the same conception of their relationship with the United States, and it is on this point that they are nowadays most divided. The future of European unity and that of the Atlantic Alliance, which is still the basis of their common security, thus depend on whether a solution is found for this problem. While it may be true that the unity of Western Europe has an essential contribution to make to the cohesion of the West, it is impossible to imagine a united Europe if the Atlantic Alliance were irreparably divided, just as it is inconceivable that there could be a strong Alliance with a disunited Europe.

A look at the history of the relations between Europe and the United States since 1945 will provide a better understanding of today's difficulties and throw some light on the attitudes of each. It will also show why a new balance within the Atlantic world is needed, which will reflect the spectacular economic recovery of Western Europe—a recovery that the area owes to American aid, to its own efforts, and to the success of the Common Market. The post-war period is over. The age of American 'protection', benevolent as it was, is finished for Europe. The time has now come for the 'Dialogue des Continents',[1] a dialogue which will inevitably involve competition and occasional disagreements.

This will mean the establishment of a partnership between the United States and the European Community on the lines proposed by President Kennedy in 1962; that is to say, the gradual creation in all fields of a relationship between 'two distinct but equally powerful entities, each bearing its

---

[1] Title of a work by Pierre Uri published in 1963 under the aegis of the Atlantic Institute.

share of common responsibilities in the world'.[1] Before examining the details of such a partnership it may be useful to review the development of Western Europe and the Atlantic world which has made it not only possible but necessary.

UNITED STATES AID

On 8 May 1945 the capitulation of the Third Reich put an end to fighting in the Old World. Western Europe came out of it victorious, thanks to five million American soldiers and American equipment. But in fact Europe was the great loser of the war. Hungry, ruined, uncertain of the future, the Old World watched its power and prestige melting away. Europe was confronted also by a new world balance: two giant states of continental proportions were dividing up the leadership of the world between themselves. The technical, industrial, financial and military power of the United States, strengthened already by the first world war, had been prodigiously increased by the second, whilst at the gates of the European West a new empire was being established, almost as menacing as Hitler's. Entrenched in the heart of Europe, the Soviet Union, in the famous words of Winston Churchill, was ringing down 'an iron curtain between us and everything that is in the East'. In short, Europe had become nothing more than a pawn in someone else's game.

The United States understood that it was in its interest, as well as that of the 'free world', to help and to protect Europe. The Marshall Plan and the Atlantic Alliance are the two dominant factors of this period of European history, which may be called the 'American period'. The Americans remained in Western Europe, where their presence was desired, and committed themselves to helping it. This was something new. In doing so they broke with the short-sighted policy of isolationism which they had pursued after the first world war. In 1945 the United States had the courage and the wisdom not to fall into this error again. It had appeared quite soon after the premature suspension of the Lend-lease legislation that, in spite of various kinds of aid, the countries of Europe were unable to get themselves out of the economic and financial depression into which they had been dragged by the war. Europe underwent a serious balance of payments crisis; it had largely exhausted its gold and currency reserves. The United States, on the other hand, whose gold reserves were continually growing—they were soon to reach two-thirds of the world's stock—whose balance of payments on current account ran to an average surplus of $6,800 million a year, and whose developing industries needed new markets to match their growth, was led, logically, to give Europe the wherewithal to feed itself and to revive its economy. One cannot be rich on one's own. In the Marshall Plan, American interest, it goes without saying, went hand in hand with an undeniable spirit of generosity.[2]

But political motivations were still more important. Franklin Roosevelt had cherished the hope of organising peace in agreement with the Soviet Union and Great Britain, within the framework of the world institutions set up in 1945. These hopes soon faded. General Marshall, who had become

[1] Joint declaration of the Action Committee for the United States of Europe (under the chairmanship of Jean Monnet) adopted by the representatives of the principal democratic parties and free trade unions of the Common Market countries, 26 June 1962.

[2] 'The hungry nations are turning to us. We do not have the right to disappoint them.' (President Truman).

Secretary of State in January 1947, had come from China convinced that
the Communists would sooner or later take power there. The failure of the
Moscow Conference on the peace treaty with Germany and Austria, and
subsequently of the Paris Conference, confirmed the split between the
Soviet Union and the Western powers. Given the possibility of a conflict
with the Soviet Union, it was necessary at all costs to ensure that Europe,
and its human and industrial potential, should not fall into the opposite camp,
which would have destroyed the balance of world power. Going back on its
earlier policy—of world free trade or isolationism—the United States made
its European policy the focal point of its entire foreign policy.

It was on 5 June 1947 that General Marshall, in his famous speech at
Harvard University, announced the vast programme of aid to Europe
which was to bear his name. In it he made a double appeal: to American
opinion, asking it to consent to the necessary financial effort, and to the
countries of Europe, exhorting them to unite. The originality of the Marshall
Plan lay not so much in the substitution of gifts for loans, nor in the great
scale of these gifts—Marshall Aid to Europe between 1948 and 1952 amounted
to $13,812 million[1]—as in the replacement of bilateral aid by collective aid.
In other words the Marshall Plan gave a considerable boost to European
integration, for national efforts had to be coordinated if the aid were to be
properly used. Some Americans at that time brought up the possibility of a
customs union and of a Europe unified 'on federal lines'.[2] But General
Marshall himself insisted that the way the Europeans were to organise the
distribution of aid should be left to them.

Thus instead of keeping to the old policy of 'divide and rule' the United
States, which between the wars had been largely indifferent to, or suspicious
of, the first attempts at European unity, this time took the initiative in
support of such unity, and at a time when European statesmen themselves
were feeling an urgent need of it. Belgium, the Netherlands and Luxembourg
had already formed a customs union and founded Benelux (5 September
1944). On 16 April 1948 the agreement setting up the Organisation for
European Economic Cooperation (OEEC) was signed in its turn at Paris
by seventeen Western European countries.[3]

The activity which had started in the economic field, and whose purpose
was the rational distribution of Marshall Aid, the freeing of trade and
payments, and the coordination of development plans, was soon to find its
natural extension on the political level—the Council of Europe, constituted
on 5 May 1949 by ten countries.[4] The European Movement which met in
congress at the Hague in May 1948 had since then been calling for the election of an Assembly on the basis of universal suffrage. The Consultative
Assembly of the Council which met in Strasbourg in August 1949 with
Paul-Henri Spaak as its first president may have seemed a long way from
this ideal, but it was a European initiative. The Americans refused to become

[1] Of which $2,753 million went to France, $3,421 million to Britain, $1,511 million to
Italy and $1,389 million to Germany.

[2] Notably John Foster Dulles in a speech made on 17 January 1947.

[3] I.e. almost all the countries of Western Europe except Spain. Germany was to join in
1949. Marshall Aid had been offered to the whole of Europe, including Eastern Europe.
But the Soviet Union had refused to take part in the new organisation and constrained
Czechoslovakia to follow her example. (See also 'The Organisation for Economic Cooperation
and Development (OECD) p. 624.)

[4] Belgium, Denmark, France, Britain, Ireland, Italy, Luxembourg, the Netherlands,
Norway and Sweden. Greece and Turkey joined in August 1949, Iceland in 1950, West
Germany in 1951, Austria in 1956, Cyprus in 1961, Switzerland in 1963 and Malta in 1965.

involved, while indicating that they were disappointed by the timidity of the European negotiators.

There were also other more burning problems. The United States, having demobilised prematurely, became daily more aware of dangers presented by the Soviet Union to which Winston Churchill had already drawn President Truman's attention in 1945.

Within three years the Soviet Union, in defiance of the engagements it had undertaken towards its allies, had annexed large areas of Finnish, Polish, Ruthenian, Bessarabian and Prussian territory, and the whole of Estonia, Lithuania and Latvia. Similarly, in three years several nations had been taken over by the Communists as a result of the presence of the Soviet army and against the peoples' wishes: Poland, East Germany, Hungary, Rumania, Albania; that is to say, a million square kilometres and 95 million people had been absorbed by a new 'Eurasian' empire.

The collapse of democratic government in Czechoslovakia in February–March 1948 finally succeeded in mobilising European public opinion. The countries of Western Europe understood then that they had to work together if they were to survive. Realisation of the common peril no doubt contributed decisively to accelerating the process of European integration. Indispensable as it was in any case for the recovery of the European economy, unification now seemed an urgent necessity in face of the Soviet threat. This does not mean that Europe merely united against the Communists; the joint aims were positive, not merely defensive. But the threat of Stalin, paradoxically, helped the Western Europeans to unite, to recognise their mutual needs and to organise their recovery. Thus fear, along with destitution, was the great midwife of the European Community.

In the military field, a first attempt at European organisation was made in March 1948, when Britain, France, Belgium, the Netherlands and Luxembourg signed a defensive alliance, the 'Brussels Treaty'. But in face of the enormous strength of the Soviet Union, these countries soon realised that, alone, they were practically speaking defenceless. They had neither the men, nor the money, nor the arms to carry out their policy. So on 4 May 1948 they had to make an urgent appeal to General Marshall that the United States should provide without delay for the signatories of the Treaty 'what they lacked in strength'. The appeal was answered immediately. This fact deserves to be underlined, for the Europeans' request came up sharply against a deep-rooted political and diplomatic tradition in the United States. It needed all the persuasion of General Marshall and President Truman to get the Senate to adopt on 11 June 1948 the Vandenberg resolution author-ising the United States to undertake a military commitment in peace-time outside the American continent. This made it possible for the North Atlantic Treaty to be signed on 4 April 1949. A few days later the Soviet Union lifted the first Berlin blockade, which had lasted for 323 days.

The Atlantic Alliance thus constituted brought together, in addition to the five countries of the Brussels Treaty, Scandinavia (except Sweden and Finland), Italy and Portugal[1] and on the other side of the ocean the United States and Canada. Its object was to get a collective defence effort going round the North Atlantic in peace-time under one command. According to Article Five of the Treaty the parties agreed that 'an armed attack against one of them would be considered as an attack directed against all the parties'.

---

[1] At the request of the United States, Greece and Turkey were admitted to the Treaty by the protocol of 22 October 1951; Germany joined on 9 May 1955.

To this legal guarantee of intervention—which is not, however, automatic[1]—a material guarantee was added: the permanent maintenance of powerfully armed American divisions on the European continent.[2] The physical presence of the United States in Western Europe in peace-time assured the European allies of active American support in the event of an attack from the East.

The historic importance of the North Atlantic Treaty cannot be exaggerated, especially as an expression, on the military and political levels, of a common civilisation. It constitutes a decisive turning-point in the history of the Western world, and also in that of the United States, which until then had been reluctant to 'become involved' in any permanent way in the Old World. The guarantee of the Atlantic Alliance and the presence of American soldiers—as well as the world monopoly in atomic weapons that the United States enjoyed up to 1953—were probably instrumental in protecting Western Europe from Soviet attack, and in saving the area from the fate of Czechoslovakia. Since the signing of the Treaty, the security of Western Europe has been constantly assured, and in this sense, thanks to the Treaty's military organisation, the North Atlantic Treaty Organisation (NATO), the Atlantic Alliance has been a great success within the area it covers. It has allowed the countries of Western Europe to work in peace towards their economic recovery and towards the building of a united Europe, sheltered by the American shield. Thus European integration since the war is, in a sense, the offspring of the Atlantic Alliance.

The Marshall Plan also achieved its aim: the rapid reconstruction of the European economy. It is generally recognised that without help from the United States, Europe would never have been able to rebuild its ruins nor its industrial potential. In addition to direct American aid the 'exchange value' in European currency of the dollars offered by the United States[3] made it possible to carry out a large proportion of each country's new investment plans (especially in France), thus stimulating a new economic expansion. By 1953, in most of the recipient countries, production was 25 per cent higher than in 1938.

However, United States aid did not succeed in checking the *relative* decline of Western Europe's importance.[4] Europe's dependence was manifest in the continual deficit in its balance of payments (which in spite of the gift of $22,300 million in six years went through three crises, in 1947, 1949 and 1951). The European deficit with regard to the dollar area remained around $3,000 million. Economists even came to view this deficit, which they called the 'dollar gap', as a permanent structural feature of the economy of the area. With economic dependence went total military dependence; political dependence could not fail to ensue. In a word, the countries of Western Europe were protected and assisted countries. Economically,

[1] Article Five of the Treaty limits itself to saying that each signatory, in the event of an attack against another member country, will engage in 'such action as it judges necessary'. It is the 'subsidiary bodies' provided for in Article Nine of the Treaty, set up between 1949 and 1960 and together constituting NATO, which, by binding the United States to the defence of Europe, have given to the non-automatic engagement of Article Five a material certainty of intervention.

[2] Six American divisions are still stationed on Federal German territory.

[3] And from 1950 onwards, when military aid took over from economic aid, 'offshore' orders (American army purchases, orders for equipment from European industries payable in dollars) also contributed greatly to narrowing the 'dollar gap'.

[4] One example among many: in 1913 Western Europe manufactured 46 per cent of the world's steel; in 1952 it manufactured 19 per cent (M. G. de Carmoy, *Fortune de l'Europe*, Paris, 1953).

militarily and politically the Atlantic world was dominated by the United States. This 'hegemony' was not the result of a deliberate policy; it was the consequence of weakness on the one hand and considerable power on the other. In the long run, such a situation was to the advantage neither of the United States nor of the European countries; on both sides it created complexes—in the former a sense of continually being the 'givers' and in the latter of continually being the 'takers'—which were to have unfortunate and lasting consequences for relations between them.

BIRTH OF THE EUROPEAN COMMUNITY

To remedy this unhealthy and potentially dangerous situation the Western Europeans needed first of all to stimulate the economic expansion of their countries, and secondly to regain their self-confidence and with it a feeling of independence. Britain had played a major role in setting up the first European organisations—a useful stage, but one of limited effect. It was followed by a new stage of European history that may be called the 'French period', for this time it was France that took the initiative. Many continental statesmen felt in any case the necessity for going 'faster and further'. After the Federal Republic of Germany had been established in September 1949, the United States and Britain were anxious to put an end to the International Ruhr Authority and to the limitations imposed on Germany's industrial production, which was needed for the recovery of Western Europe as a whole. A solution had to be found to this urgent problem, and Dean Acheson, the then American Secretary of State, was convinced that this solution had to be put forward by France, the country principally concerned by the revival of Germany.

The great merit of the late Robert Schuman, the French foreign minister, and of Jean Monnet, who was in charge of the French economic planning commission, was that they immediately took the opportunity offered, and looked for new solutions instead of reusing the old formulae. The Schuman Declaration of 9 May 1950, the real birth of the European Community, immediately transformed the relations between Germany and France. Five years almost to the day after the unconditional surrender of Germany, France proposed that the two countries' entire production of coal and steel should be placed under a common High Authority, an organisation which other European countries would be able to join if they wished. The decisions of this common authority, proposed Robert Schuman, were to bind together France, Germany and the other countries of the new Community. In this way the economic means of war—steel and energy—would be made to serve peaceful ends. Common institutions, with limited but real powers, would supervise the running of a Common Market in a limited but basic sector of the economy. This was also to be the first stage of a European Federation.

Both Chancellor Adenauer and Dean Acheson gave this revolutionary proposal the warmest encouragement. As Britain, however, rejected the principle of supranationality, negotiations on the Schuman Plan involved only six countries, and the Treaty setting up the European Coal and Steel Community (ECSC) was signed by them in Paris on 18 April 1951. With its coming into effect at the beginning of January 1952, economic integration had begun. The ECSC was a vast experiment; the institution of the Common Market later extended the experiment, on a more flexible basis, to the whole of the economy. The Treaty of Rome, signed on the Capitoline Hill on 25 March 1957, was a direct consequence of the Schuman Plan, and the

European Economic Community and Euratom which it set up fulfilled Schuman's aims of 1950. The European Community has now in fact pursued these aims for sixteen years in spite of many obstacles and difficulties. Indeed, the success of the Common Market was itself to have the logical consequence of Britain's requesting membership in August 1961, and President Kennedy's 'Partnership' plan of July 1962.

One can thus see developing on the continent from 1950 onwards a new policy whose inspiration was originally French. It allowed the simultaneous development of Atlantic cooperation and European integration. Little by little its far-reaching activities began to affect not only world trade (for the Community is the world's largest importer) but the other countries of Western Europe, leading for example in 1959 to the creation of the European Free Trade Association (EFTA), composed of Britain, Sweden, Norway, Denmark, Austria, Switzerland and Portugal.

The United States approved and supported this policy because it increased Europe's capacity for resistance to communism, and at the same time contributed to the strength of the Atlantic Alliance by giving it a more satisfactory balance. The United States had always felt the excessive disparity between itself and its partners to be a weakness in the Alliance. Furthermore, a rather over-simplified concept of the 'United States of Europe' has always attracted American opinion, which has even been prepared to draw parallels between the efforts of the Six to work together and the creation of the United States out of thirteen British colonies in 1776. From 1950 up to the beginning of 1963, the support given by the United States to the policy of European integration never failed, whether it was a question of the OEEC or the Schuman Plan or the Common Market. This support was essentially political in nature, and strong enough to make the Americans accept, from Europe, a certain degree of 'trade discrimination'. This is a good example of what it means to accept the logic of an idea.

The European Defence Community project of 1952–4[1] clearly showed how far the unity of the Alliance and that of Europe were interdependent: any European crisis was of necessity an Atlantic crisis, and any Atlantic crisis became a crisis for Europe. France's European partners, and in particular Germany, could conceive of European unity only in the framework of integration within the Atlantic Alliance, as did the United States itself. In Germany's case this was for obvious security reasons—its exposed situation on the frontier of the Soviet world, and the even more exposed position of Berlin. France, until 1958, did not conceive of it otherwise. The whole European Economic Community rested, in fact, on this fundamental unity of foreign policy. Fidelity to the Atlantic Alliance and to its military organisation NATO constituted the unwritten law of the Six; it allowed economic union to be founded on a solid political basis. This is one of the major lessons of recent history.

---

[1] As the Korean war made German rearmament essential, France proposed that a European army should be formed. The Treaty setting up the European Defence Community, signed on 27 May 1952, was rejected on 30 August 1954 by the French parliament, a victim of the conjunction of Gaullist and Communist votes. In the end the Paris agreements (23 October 1954) gave West Germany her sovereignty within certain limits (notably prohibition of the manufacture of nuclear armaments) and reconstituted a German national army integrated in the Atlantic Alliance.

From Common Market to Atlantic Partnership

The European and Atlantic crisis of 1954 highlights the vitality of the European Community and the irresistible attraction of the process of integration. Less than a year after the EDC had collapsed, the Six began to move forward again. On 2 June 1955 the revival of the movement took place at the Messina Conference; negotiations for setting up a Common Market and Euratom were begun. The Treaty of Rome came into effect on 1 January 1958, and the first lowering of duties took place at the beginning of January 1959. Trade among the Six grew at a rapid rate; production increased within the Community faster than anywhere else in the Western world; the countries of the Common Market Europe enjoyed unprecedented prosperity. Business and industry drew up investment programmes, production agreements and trade agreements on the basis of a vast single market of 180 million consumers. In short, the Treaty of Rome brought on to the international scene a new economic power: the principal commercial power and the second industrial power in the world, after the United States and before the Soviet Union.

The consequence of all this was a fundamental change in the respective situations of Europe and the United States. Ten years after the Marshall Plan, Common Market expansion was much more rapid than American expansion. The Common Market countries not only caught up with their balance of payments deficits, but built their reserves up to very high levels.

'The "dollar shortage" is no more; instead, Europe is accumulating dollar holdings, while America itself, despite an ample surplus of exports over imports, nevertheless has a deficit in its balance of payments as a whole—caused mainly by its private investments abroad, its continued foreign aid and its payments for overseas soldiers and arms to protect the free world. Where Europe was then [at the time of the Marshall Plan] dependent on assistance, Europe is now *furnishing* assistance to other developing countries . . .'[1]

The success of the Common Market has had a second consequence of no lesser importance. It is what President Hallstein of the Common Market Commission has called the 'Copernican Revolution' in British policy towards the Europe of the Six. At first Britain thought to create a vast free trade area made up of the Six and the eleven other countries of the OECD, in which the political cohesion of the new Community would probably have dissolved 'like a lump of sugar in a cup of tea'. The Six were not prepared to resign themselves to this form of drowning. The United States was not in favour of it, and thus France was able to put an end to the negotiations, in December 1958, without causing much more than a ripple of disapproval. In some sense the Common Market had taken off from the ruins of this still-born project. Having begun therefore by being suspicious, hostile and sceptical about its prospects, Britain, with its usual realism, turned to thoughts of joining it as soon as it achieved success and became a reality.

'Why don't you join the Common Market?' General de Gaulle had asked Macmillan at Buckingham Palace on 5 April 1960. 'It would be unthinkable,' the latter is said to have replied. 'What was unthinkable in April 1960 became the centre of Macmillan's thoughts and actions only a few months later,' adds Robert Kleimann, who records the anecdote in his book on the Atlantic crisis.[2] The British made this difficult choice of their own free will.

[1] Pierre Uri, *Partnership for Progress*, New York and Evanston, 1963. The American deficit in the balance of payments reached about $2·5 milliard in 1961.

[2] Robert Kleimann, *La crise atlantique*, Paris, 1964.

Contrary to what is sometimes said, there is no reason to suppose that their decision was suggested by the United States; but when the Americans heard of Britain's intentions they were delighted, and greatly encouraged the British to carry out the idea. Macmillan put his request for admission in August 1961; negotiations began in Paris on 10 October; they were finally 'suspended' on 29 January 1963 after General de Gaulle in his famous press conference of 14 January had noted that Britain was undoubtedly 'an island' and declared that it could not join the Community. This crisis was a highly dangerous turning-point for the European Community, in so far as from that moment the two roads—Atlantic and European—began visibly to diverge.

It was some time earlier, at the end of 1961, that the policy subsequently called 'the Grand Design' was worked out by President Kennedy's entourage.[1] Basically it was a reply to a double challenge: the success of the Common Market and the rebuilding of the European economy on the one hand (coinciding with the American balance of payments crisis); and on the other the prospect—somewhat alarming for Washington—of an enlarged Community, a vast preferential trade area possibly taking in the whole of the Commonwealth, and covering by virtue of this a third of the world's commerce.

President Kennedy and his advisers understood the need for the United States to react promptly to 'these challenges and opportunities'. Instead of seeking to solve these new problems that Europe was posing for the United States in isolation, withdrawal and protectionism by reducing all American spending abroad; instead of replying to the European challenge with an anti-European policy—President Kennedy sought a general expansion of trade in which American exports could grow. This had indeed become a national necessity. In his famous speech of 4 July 1962 at Philadelphia he proclaimed: 'I will say here and now, on this Day of Independence, that the United States will be ready for a *Declaration of Interdependence*—that we will be prepared to discuss with a united Europe the ways and means of forming a concrete Atlantic Partnership, a mutually beneficial partnership between the new union now emerging in Europe and the old American union founded here a century and three quarters ago.'

The first stage of this partnership was to be commercial. The American part took the form of a new piece of legislation—the Trade Expansion Act signed on 11 October 1962—giving the President unprecedentedly wide powers of negotiation for tariff reductions. The objective was ambitious: the proposed general reduction on tariffs of 50 per cent could go as far as 100 per cent on products of which the United States and the enlarged European Community together handled 80 per cent of world exports.

But the aims of the Partnership, as President Kennedy outlined them, were even vaster. He saw in a united Europe a partner with whom the United States could deal on a basis of full equality with reference to all the huge tasks that went with the setting up and the defence of an Atlantic community, tasks that neither side could accomplish alone. The new alliance being planned between the enlarged European Community and the United States would make an impressive force: four hundred to five hundred million people, representing twice the total production of the Sino-Soviet bloc, 90 per cent of the industrial production of the free world, 90 per cent of world trade in manufactured goods. Together the United

[1] On the genesis of the Partnership project see Joseph Kraft, *The Grand Design*, New York, 1962.

States and the Community would constitute, the President pointed out at the signing of the Trade Expansion Act, the largest confluence of economic powers in history.

One of the keystones of this great scheme was Britain's membership of the Common Market: first, because its effect would be to allow the widest range of products on which duties would be suppressed altogether under the terms of the Trade Expansion Act; secondly because Britain's entry and thus also of the Commonwealth, along with the membership or association of the other countries of Western Europe, was a guarantee that Europe would practise an 'outward-looking policy' and that the Community would remain linked with the United States within an even closer Atlantic association. In these circumstances it is easy to understand the disappointment and anger of the United States Government at the French veto on Britain's entry of 14 January 1963, and the fairly general feeling on the other side of the Atlantic, in the days that followed this decisive move, that the failure of the negotiations between the Common Market and Britain meant shipwreck for the 'Grand Design'.[1]

It would be useful to seek the reasons for this failure, in order to discover what lessons it contains. Observers generally agree that they are political rather than economic reasons, in spite of the undoubted importance and difficulty of the agricultural questions that were not resolved in the negotiations with Britain. The French veto is certainly explained in part by the Nassau Conference of 18 December 1962 in the course of which Macmillan, two days after his meeting and misunderstandings with General de Gaulle, had betrayed, in the latter's eyes, the interests of Europe for a 'dish of Polaris'.

THE TROUBLED PARTNERSHIP

It has been said that France refused Britain entry into the Common Market because she saw in her the 'Trojan horse of the United States'. This comes back to saying that the problems of the Atlantic Alliance were at the root of the crisis that was set off on 14 January 1963 (in the same way that they explain to a great extent the rejection by France's partners of her 'Fouchet Plan' ('Europe des Patries') for political union in April 1962). Responsibility for the failure of the negotiations and the misfortunes of the Partnership, considered in this light, is perhaps not entirely French. Did not Britain herself have a share? And is even the United States completely exempt? In spite of certain encouraging declarations by MacGeorge Bundy and George Ball suggesting that the American government might one day be willing to renounce its right of veto over the use of atomic force in favour of an integrated European atomic force, the United States did not understand, or did not wish to understand, that when requesting that the financial burdens of responsibility of the free world be shared, it should also have proposed a gradual sharing of the burden of political decision-making.

Furthermore, the American government never exactly defined its concept of the Partnership. Did it mean the substitution of the European Community

[1] To save the Partnership scheme from complete disaster the President's advisers reaffirmed, at the beginning of 1963, the United States' desire to continue the Kennedy round of tariff negotiations in GATT which followed on the Trade Expansion Act. They also advocated with renewed vigour the plan for a multilateral force (MLF). This plan consisted in forming a fleet of cargo vessels with international crews provided with Polaris missiles. Professor H. Kissinger of Harvard University has said of this project: 'Wrong problem, wrong answer . . .'

by an Atlantic Community? Or the collaboration of these two distinct entities for the accomplishment of common tasks? The notion of an 'Atlantic Community' gave room for all kinds of confusion. Similarly, did the Trade Expansion Act recognise the realities of the Common Market—much more than a simple free trade area, since it aims to realise a common economic policy?[1] Would the United States, conscious for the first time of the commercial disadvantages which the Common Market might involve for American industry, continue to maintain its ten-year-old policy of support for European integration on any other level than that of theory? The fact that this question had become a genuine one revealed how serious the crisis of confidence in the Atlantic world had become. President Kennedy, and subsequently President Johnson, certainly took pains to reply to these doubts, and it would be wrong to question their good faith. Nevertheless, the American conception of the Partnership, as well as the British attitude to Europe, was not unequivocal nor without contradictions.[2] In reality, the Partnership was probably 'more an orientation than a policy, more a long-term aim than a concrete programme.'[3] It failed precisely because it was not a policy with clear aims and specific methods, and also because it did not come sufficiently high among President Kennedy's priorities.

Above all this there hangs the great atomic shadow. This is the central theme of the 'great debate', in Raymond Aron's words, of the Atlantic Alliance, a debate which in all probability is only just beginning. The solution to this problem has been sought in various plans for a European deterrent force, which would benefit from help from the United States and would be closely associated with NATO. It would presuppose West Germany's association with the common effort to the greatest possible extent compatible with the Bonn agreements forbidding production of nuclear weapons in Germany. It would require in addition the creation, stage by stage, of a common political authority. Ultimately it would depend on the decision of Britain, which alone could give real military effectiveness to such a force. In any case, whether such a plan is the answer or not, the Partnership will be nothing if it is not founded on political and military bases as well as on trade and finance.

It is hard to disagree with General de Gaulle, in this connection, when he declared at Schloss Brühl in Germany on 4 September 1962: 'The alliance of the free world, in other words the reciprocal commitment of Europe and the United States, cannot in the long run preserve its sureness and its solidity if there does not exist, in the Old World, a bastion of power and prosperity of the same order as that which the United States constitutes in the New World.' Present French policy has, however, its contradictions too, for it seems as if France is systematically refusing the means of fulfilling these aims. What they involve are the gradual development of a politically federated Europe and an integrated system of European defence.

[1] See 'From Economic Union to Political Union' (pp. 594ff).

[2] In 1962 Walter Lippman gave this singularly bold ultimatum to the European countries: 'The United States needs this free trade area in which to develop her foreign commerce, earning in this way the money that is essential for financing the civil and military tasks which she has had to take on pretty well all over the world. It is quite clear that if Bonn and Paris were to scuttle the great idea, drastic reductions in American commitments abroad would ensue . . .' (L'Unité Occidentale et le Marché Commun, Paris, 1962.)

[3] Robert Kleimann, op. cit.

THREE NEW FACTORS

France has, however, done well to point out that changes in the world are bound to have an effect on the shape of the Atlantic Alliance. In the first place, since 1959 and the Soviet development of ICBMs, the world has been living in a balance of terror. The United States is now in the front line. In these circumstances, the question has arisen whether the Americans would be willing to commit their whole strength to defend Europe against attack, which might involve the immediate destruction of their own cities. At the present time Europeans have no reason to doubt the American pledge, solemnly reaffirmed by President Kennedy in his speech at Frankfurt on 25 June 1963: 'The United States will risk her cities to defend yours because we need your freedom to protect ours.'

But what of the future? Will the Americans always give the same value to European interests as the Europeans themselves? There may be European interests that do not always coincide with theirs or American interests which do not necessarily coincide with the Europeans'. Furthermore, since the escalation of the Vietnam war Europe seems no longer to be at the centre of American strategy, in so far as the centre of gravity of the cold (or warm) war has moved from Europe to Asia. Under these circumstances the urge, or indeed the need, to seek a *rapprochement* with the Soviet Union may grow more and more pressing for the United States. Thus the countries of Western Europe cannot allow themselves to rely entirely and forever on American protection.

Another new factor of major importance has also affected the European scene since the formation of NATO in 1949: the internal changes in the Communist bloc. First of all there was the 'de-Stalinisation' begun by Khrushchev and continued by his successors; secondly the split between Moscow and Peking; and thirdly, the attempts of the 'peoples' democracies' to liberate themselves from Soviet supremacy (under cover of the Sino-Soviet disagreement). From all this a softening-up of Soviet foreign policy has resulted. It may be true that Soviet military potential is still formidable[1]— but there are many reasons for believing that the present Soviet leaders have given up for the time being any thought of aggression against Western Europe. In any case, the feeling of a Soviet threat has lessened in a large sector of European opinion. Some even go as far as to conclude that the threat has disappeared, that NATO is no longer indispensable and that from now on it is possible to envisage some form of close cooperation with the countries of Eastern Europe. The direction of European policies cannot but be profoundly changed by this development, although it is still too early to make any final judgements on where it will lead.

General de Gaulle had, however, drawn some definite conclusions when he notified his allies (10 March 1966) of his decision to withdraw France from NATO—that is, from the military organisation of the Atlantic Treaty. This is the third factor that has upset the Alliance. The attenuation of the Soviet threat, the development of the French force-de-frappe, combined with the General's rigid conception of national sovereignty, have brought

---

[1] The military strength of the Warsaw Pact, the Eastern answer to the Atlantic Treaty under Soviet command, represents 185 divisions of which 65 are armoured divisions; its air strength comprises 11,300 bombers and 6,000 fighters. 750 missiles with nuclear warheads are permanently trained on Western Europe. Brezhnev declared on 29 March 1966 at the Twenty-third Soviet Communist Party Conference that the defence system of the Warsaw Pact was to be extended still further.

France to refuse any integration in defence as being tantamount to sub-ordination to the United States. Although the French government has stated that it will be faithful to the Alliance itself—and there seems no question about this fidelity—its decision about leaving NATO has led to a serious crisis among the allies.Many countries fear that the French withdrawal will simply weaken allied defence and compromise the security of the West, and, indeed, of France itself. They are above all afraid that France's action may incite the United States to withdraw its forces from Europe and go back to its traditional isolationism.

France appears to stand alone in this crisis. Not one of its fourteen Atlantic partners, including its five European partners in the Community, has approved or imitated its attitude. Some of them may, however, disapprove more of the form than of the content of France's action. Responsibility for the crisis can perhaps be shared between the United States, which has tried to maintain the status quo for too long without taking any new initiative, and France which, while it has been demanding reform of the organisation of the Alliance since 1958, has never made any concrete proposals to its partners and has finally rejected negotiation in favour of a split. In short, perhaps France revealed the extent of the Atlantic crisis rather than creating it, exacerbating a problem that had been latent for years. The question is whether France's action will make reform easier[1] or more difficult.

Serious differences between Europe and the United States are also likely in the economic field. The particular difficulty for Europe is that the area has, as a whole, a heavy deficit in its balance of trade (although not in its balance of payments) and that it is faced by powerful competition from firms over which the American administration has little control. In addition, the divergences between the interests and policies of European countries in their commercial or financial relations with the United States do not help to strengthen their position in the trade negotiations now under way in Geneva (the 'Kennedy Round'). Against a centralised administration and giant firms, Europe can only muster budding European institutions, and very much smaller enterprises whose 'technological gap' is increasing year by year.[2]

MAKING PARTNERSHIP A REALITY

All this does not make the Atlantic Partnership in any way less essential; it merely underlines the need to make it develop on economic, military, political and cultural lines simultaneously. At the same time the basic conditions of the Partnership for both sides must be clearly understood.

The United States must, in the first place, understand and accept what the Common Market is for and continue to encourage its development, even if this were to mean, for a while, some commercial disadvantages—for example, in the agricultural sector. Secondly, the United States must accept, in practice, the principle of equality; this means that from now on it should start looking for a new form of Atlantic organisation that would gradually lead to the sharing of decisions.[3] From the countries of Western Europe, the

---

[1] Any reforms must, of course, respect the principles which give the Alliance its originality and its strength: permanent consultation, collective defence, unity of command in peace-time.

[2] See 'Science and Technology in Western Europe' (pp. 357ff).

[3] In the framework of the Atlantic Organisation, the United States has been reluctant to engage in political consultations with its allies, generally being content with informing them of its decisions. It is also true that it holds—outside NATO—95 per cent of the nuclear potential of the free world.

Partnership requires that they clearly define their attitude to the United States. While they may legitimately intend to establish a new form of independence, with a capacity to make their own joint decisions, this must not be done merely to oppose the United States. The European Community may lead to a 'second force' being created within the West; it could not become a 'third force', more or less neutralist, practising a see-saw policy between West and East. This also means, however, that European integration should develop more quickly, especially on the political and military side, where it has not yet begun. For without a minimum of equality there can be no Partnership, and there can be no equality between the United States and a number of small or medium nations aggravating their weakness by their disunity, as President Kennedy clearly saw.

The difficulty in carrying out these aims lies in the fact that one of the principal obstacles to Western European political unity is the disagreement between France and its European partners on Atlantic questions. At the same time the United States will not begin to consider the sharing of decisions (which, as we have seen, is France's main complaint against the United States) while it sees that Europe, as such, is incapable of making them. To get out of this contradiction it may first of all be necessary to reestablish a climate of confidence and cooperation between Europe and the United States—and in particular between France and the United States—which would then contribute to reestablishing confidence between the European countries themselves.[1] The important thing is that the United States and Europe should both admit frankly that neither can resolve the problems of the world economy and world peace alone. It has to be a joint effort.

A great deal will also depend, for the Alliance and for Europe, on the methods and direction of Britain's policy towards Europe in the next few years. The Partnership will become much easier to maintain the day that Britain, relinquishing its 'special relationship' with the United States, but without forgetting either its Atlantic allies or the Commonwealth, makes its first choice Europe—the day when, with the agreement of France, it joins the Common Market and accepts the rules of European economic and political union. It is up to the Europeans themselves, therefore, and France and Britain in particular, to see that American leadership in the Atlantic world gradually gives way to a real partnership. At present it is largely the divisions in Europe that make partnership impossible. Only Europeans are in a position to end them.

[1] The Action Committee for the United States of Europe proposed, at its meeting in Bonn on 1 June 1964, setting up a 'Committee of Understanding' between Europe and the United States for all the questions handled by the European Economic Community. Success in the 'Kennedy Round' negotiations—in which the Common Market Commission speaks for all the Six—would also be an important stage on the road to an effective Partnership.

BIBLIOGRAPHY

Ball, George W. *Les Etats-Unis et l'Europe*, Centre de Recherches Européennes, Lausanne, 1962.

Beloff, Max. *The United States and the Unity of Europe*, Brookings Institution, Washington, DC; Faber, London, 1963.

Benoit, Emile. *Europe at Sixes and Sevens: The Common Market, The Free Trade Association and the United States*, Columbia Univ. Press, New York and London, 1961.

Birrenbach, Kurt. *The Future of the Atlantic Community: Toward European Partnership*, Pall Mall Press, London; Frederick A. Praeger, New York, 1963.

Cottrell, Alvin J. and Dougherty, James E. *The Politics of the Atlantic Alliance*, Pall Mall Press, London; Frederick A. Praeger, New York, 1964.

Hinshaw, Randall. *The European Community and American Trade*, Pall Mall Press, London; Frederick A. Praeger, New York, 1964.

Humphrey, Don D. *The United States and the Common Market: A Background Study*, Frederick A. Praeger, New York, 1962; Pall Mall Press, London, 1965.

Kissinger, Henry A. *The Troubled Partnership*, McGraw-Hill, London; Doubleday, New York, 1966.

Kleimann, Robert. *Crise atlantique*, Trévise, Paris; issued in the United States as *Atlantic Crisis*, W. W. Norton, New York, 1964.

Kraft, Joseph. *The Grand Design: From Common Market to Atlantic Partnership*, Harper and Row, London and New York, 1962.

Lichtheim, George. *Europe and America: The Future of the Atlantic Community*, Thames and Hudson, London, 1963.

Monnet, Jean. *Europe-Amérique: Relations de partenaires nécessaires à la paix*, Centre de Recherches Européennes, Lausanne, 1963.

Munk, Frank. *Atlantic Dilemma: Partnership or Community?*, Oceana, New York, 1964.

Steel, Ronald. *The End of Alliance: America and the Future of Europe*, Deutsch, London; Viking Press, New York, 1964.

Uri, Pierre. *Dialogue des continents*, Plon, Paris, 1963; issued in Britain and the United States as *Partnership for Progress*, Harper and Row, London and New York, 1963.

Wasserman, Max J. and Hultman, Charles W. *The Common Market and American Business*, Technical Press, London; Simmons-Boardman, New York, 1964.

WESTERN EUROPEAN DEFENCE: NATO IN DISARRAY

ANTHONY VERRIER

THE North Atlantic Treaty Organisation (NATO) is the military organisation of the Atlantic Alliance, which was founded by a treaty signed in Washington on 4 April 1949. The signatories were Belgium, Canada, Denmark, France, Britain, Iceland, Italy, Luxembourg, the Netherlands, Norway, Portugal and the United States. Protocols to the North Atlantic Treaty added Greece and Turkey in October 1951 and the Federal Republic of Germany in May 1955. The object of NATO is the deterrence of war in Western Europe through an integrated defence system. By Article 5 of the Treaty an attack on one member of the Alliance is construed as an attack on all.

Today NATO is the subject of intensive analysis among its members, and one of them, France, has disengaged militarily from it, believing that an integrated defence system is no longer needed in Western Europe. The disagreement between France and its allies lies in their differing interpretations of the role that should be played in Europe by the United States. President Johnson's administration is increasingly preoccupied with the Far East rather than with European security, while de Gaulle is anxious to exploit the current détente in Europe in order to establish a new defence system to make France (and its neighbours) increasingly independent of either the United States or the Soviet Union.

France still adheres to the North Atlantic Treaty, however, and its military withdrawal from NATO, which took formal effect on 1 July 1966, has left the French government with some links with NATO itself. French units assigned to NATO were withdrawn, as were French staffs in NATO commands. France withdrew from the Military Committee of senior officers and officials and ordered the removal from French soil of NATO's military headquarters, logistic facilities, Defence College and American and Canadian contingents in France. France remains, however, in the NATO Council of ministers; is continuing to participate in the NATO Air Defence Ground Environment radar scheme; will continue by arrangement with the Federal German government to station troops in the latter's territory; and has not abrogated Article 5 of the Alliance.

The collective NATO reaction to these French acts has been to deplore them; to find new sites for headquarters, facilities, College and forces (in Belgium, the Netherlands, Britain and Italy respectively); and to remove French forces from NATO contingency planning. The United States has also removed nuclear weapons hitherto provided for French forces (under American control), but, like its allies, has expressed the hope that France will one day resume its full place in NATO.

THE FOUNDATIONS: 1949–52

The reason for NATO's foundation in 1949 was not an outright attack by the Soviet Union on the United States or any West European state. Even the two most flagrant cases of Soviet subversion and coercion, both of which occurred in 1948—the extinction of democratic government in Czechoslovakia and the attempt to bring all Berlin into the Communist orbit by a ground blockade of American, British and French forces there—were not direct attacks in the geographical sense on Western Europe. Nevertheless, it was natural to believe in 1949 and it is reasonable to suppose now that Western Europe was the first priority for further penetration by the Soviet government. The disturbed political situation in France and Italy, where disciplined Communist parties were exploiting legitimate public grievances, suggested that the next step in Soviet policy would be a deliberate and subversive attempt to overthrow the governments of those countries, rather than to support a direct military attack on one, as in Greece.

But although an outright attack on Western Europe may have been unlikely in 1949 (it is certainly unlikely today), the 'Atlantic' nations were never in greater peril of losing their democratic institutions than in the months preceding NATO's foundation. It should, however, be emphasised that the danger came largely from within, and was based on factors and events by no means solely the work of Soviet agents. It is this background to present events in NATO which largely explains and partly justifies President de Gaulle's argument that a merely military alliance to deter or contain the Soviet Union in Europe can never succeed in resolving the continent's historic quarrels and tensions, nor pave the way for a political and economic community which will resolve them for good. This view of Europe's problems, legitimate enough, has been negatively exploited by de Gaulle, making it appear that his real objective is to oppose the United States. Not unnaturally, this has not until lately made Washington more sympathetic to European ideas of independence, whether feasible or not.

NATO was founded as a reflex action before the apparent probability of a further extension of Soviet power in Europe. The true nature of the threat was only faintly reflected in the debate about European unity; the means of responding to the Soviet challenge at once assumed an entirely strategic form and, in many ways, a traditional one too. At one of the earliest NATO ministerial meetings—in Lisbon in 1952—the decision was taken to raise no less than ninety-six first line and reserve divisions. It was said then that such a force would be able to engage a Soviet 'invasion' army on approximately equal terms for long enough to deter Moscow from despatching overwhelming numbers—but risking in the process an American nuclear strike. Thus was born the strategic doctrine of 'the pause', which has confused NATO planning ever since, has blurred the distinction between deterrence and defence, and has obscured the essentially complementary roles of the United States and its European allies.

The Lisbon decisions, although never implemented, remain significant to-day for two other principal reasons. Firstly it was tacitly assumed that West Germany (then garrisoned by and subject to the United States, Britain and France) would eventually join NATO: wider considerations apart, ninety-six divisions predicated a substantial contribution from Western Europe's most populous area, particularly since that from the smaller members was seen largely in maritime terms, while Italy's role was defined as guarding those East European and Balkan defiles whose accessibility to Soviet forces had so troubled Churchill in the latter stages of the second world war. The assumption of a West German contribution nonetheless remained tacit, because in 1952 it was still impolitic openly to consider transforming a beaten foe into an indispensable ally. But from 1952 onwards may be traced the course of West Germany's acceptance into the Atlantic Community, a transition from defeat and degradation to economic recovery and political influence brought about partly at least by the old-fashioned asset of military manpower.

It was doubtless this fact which enabled the Federal German Republic to accede to NATO in 1954 with so little dissent, an event which overshadowed the collapse of the attempt to form a European Defence Community. Today the Federal Republic's contribution of approximately half the divisions on NATO's central and northern fronts does much to explain the West German influence in NATO and why successive governments in Bonn from Adenauer's onwards have pressed for a share in the Alliance's nuclear armoury, at least in terms of defining its strategic role and laying down how it should be controlled.

The second significance of the Lisbon decisions of 1952 lies in the fact that the United States representatives at the Lisbon meeting were in at least two minds, and seem to have been governed by what the Australian historian Coral Bell has aptly called 'a policy of aspiration'. On the one hand, the ninety-six-division goal was intended to show that, despite American nuclear monopoly, conventional forces should attempt to deter or contain Soviet aggression. On the other hand, the nuclear monopoly distorted rational thought about the kind of conventional force which could meet Soviet forces on approximately equal terms: and rational thought in this sense meant considering not only a NATO force which could deploy and fight in Europe, but one which was within the political and economic competence of the Alliance's members to raise, equip and maintain. But even with a West German contribution, there was little chance of ninety-six divisions being raised unless NATO governments were prepared to put their forces on a war footing for an indefinite period. There was never the slightest chance of this being done unless the major members gave a lead. But the United States was heavily engaged in Korea; Britain was deeply involved in the Middle and Far East; France was saddled with Indo-China.

Moreover, each of these three powers was discovering that the deployment of military manpower did not automatically strengthen its strategic position: the United States could only achieve stalemate in Korea; Britain, despite success in Malaya, was often frustrated elsewhere—witness the inability to control political unrest in the Suez Canal Zone and at Abadan; France was being worn down in an effort to beat skilled guerillas in Indo-China by methods suited only to 18th-century siege warfare. Thus even in 1952 NATO's major members not only looked to their Eastern rather than their European moat, but they were already wondering whether the possession of nuclear weapons might not solve strategic problems which conventional forces seemed unable to do. It is this division of interests and of confusion about strategic methods by the United States, Britain and France that has contributed largely to disarray within NATO throughout its history, and that has led de Gaulle to maintain that only those members of it which have genuine European interests should arbitrate its future or decide upon its successor. But it is important to state again that these seeds of discord were sown in early days, not under de Gaulle.

AMERICAN NUCLEAR SUPREMACY: 1952-7

Since NATO quickly took the form of a predominantly military alliance, and because United States administrations in the mid-fifties were unwilling to consider the many *limitations* of nuclear weapons, it is not surprising that the Alliance began to suffer from internal stress far more quickly than its Communist counterpart, the Warsaw Pact, although the latter was not formed until 1955. In the Warsaw Pact there has never been any doubt as to who is in control, who provides the most advanced weapons and best equipped troops, establishes the strategy and commands the higher echelons. Because of the complete Soviet domination of the Warsaw Pact, the debate about the balance between nuclear and conventional forces could proceed unhampered by political considerations: as a result, the respective roles of conventional forces for defence and nuclear weapons for deterrence (or, when the Soviet nuclear armoury began to rival that of the United States, for retaliation) could be clearly defined.

The traditional Soviet military regard for artillery also played a useful rôle when tactical or battlefield nuclear weapons appeared in the Warsaw Pact order of battle in the mid-fifties. Not only was Soviet command of these weapons, as of all others of the nuclear variety, complete and unquestioned, but the strong influence of the artillery arm on Soviet military thought led in practice to a separation of 'battlefield' nuclear weapons from conventional formations. Thus the Warsaw Pact commanders have been spared the indecision from which their NATO counterparts suffer.

This indecision derives from the fact that all of NATO's major formations are equipped with nuclear weapons, which appear in the order of battle as so many artillery units. Thus it is natural for NATO commanders to believe that these nuclear weapons would be readily available for use in war, a belief which is all the more understandable when it is realised that the Alliance's force levels goals have never been met. Yet, as of now, all these 'battlefield' nuclear weapons in NATO's armoury are still controlled by United States officers and subject to the decisions of the president of the United States.

These differences between NATO and the Warsaw Pact are cited mainly to emphasise that the former, designed as a military alliance, has been governed increasingly by political factors, by contenders for influence with the United States from among its members, while the latter, although designed ostensibly as a political arrangement, as a sign of the 'free association' of Communist governments, has operated almost exclusively as a straightforward military pact. These factors are highly relevant to any consideration of the possible future development of the two alliances, which may increasingly assume a complementary rather than a competitive form.

To say this, however, is not to deny that NATO's achievement in surviving at all is remarkable. During the fifties, the most negative period of the cold war, recurring changes in American policy and strategy put the Alliance to considerable strain. As the Soviet achievement of a large yet flexible nuclear armoury became apparent to the West, American administrations clung earnestly to the concept of absolute nuclear deterrence—and they did so because the price of meeting the Soviet strategic 'double' of nuclear *and* conventional strength would have been a military contribution from the United States which President Eisenhower's post-Korea administration was unwilling to make. The advent of tactical nuclear weapons, first provided for the US 7th Army in the mid-fifties, strengthened the views of those who argued that manpower savings could in consequence be made. And while the United States was unwilling to do so, it was not surprising that its allies were constantly defaulting on their conventional requirements, with the always significant exception of West Germany. French forces in NATO were purely nominal, and the British Army of the Rhine began to decrease steadily in size, a process which was accentuated when national service came to an end in Britain in 1960.

In historical terms, American strategy as a determinant of international relations and not merely of war was most openly expressed by Secretary of State John Foster Dulles in January 1954, when he declared that in future the American response to threats of all kinds and from all quarters of the world would be massive nuclear retaliation. Since such retaliation had been eschewed in Asia—despite the opportunities there offered for its testing in the strategic crucible—it was generally supposed that Dulles meant that any Soviet threat in *Europe* which could be defined as militarily aggressive would be met at once with nuclear weapons. In the fifties, therefore, NATO was beset with a problem from which few alliances have been free; it was dominated by one member, which was nevertheless loath to be committed utterly to the support of its allies, because the logic of the Dulles doctrine meant that only the United States would decide what constituted a threat meriting nuclear punishment. Since such an act might in turn lead to a Soviet nuclear riposte—or, after 1959, provoke a Soviet 'pre-emptive' strike on American territory with ICBMs—it became increasingly clear to all concerned that only a direct threat to *American* security would bring the Dulles doctrine into play.

There were two alternatives to this doctrine: to change it and achieve the right balance between nuclear and conventional forces, or to develop a separate *West European* nuclear system to deter threats below the Dulles level. The first choice meant that NATO's principal members, other than West Germany, would have had to abandon or reduce their non-European commitments and to start thinking seriously about the role of conventional forces in maintaining European security. This was a choice that the United States would not make, Britain has so far not made, and France has very belatedly made. The second choice is that which faces NATO now, and accounts mainly for its disarray, since it means not only the formation of a new nuclear force, but, as a consequence, seeing Western Europe's relations with the Soviet Union in entirely new terms.

Thus, although American strategy and leadership in NATO during the fifties was undoubtedly effective in preventing war with the Soviet Union, it stultified strategic thought within the Alliance as a whole. And because lip service was still paid to the idea of 'adequate conventional forces', the Federal German influence grew apace, even though the future of Germany as such remained as obscure as in the days of the Berlin blockade. Indeed, Germany's future became more obscure or, at any rate, less susceptible to any notion of 'reunification', because each increase of West German influence in NATO led to a corresponding hardening of the Soviet attitude towards a peace treaty. The 'stronger' NATO became, as American tactical nuclear weapons and West German divisions were added to the order of battle, the further receded any hopes of a settlement of the German issue. Russian fears of West German irredentism were doubtless exaggerated in the fifties, and certainly served as a smokescreen for Moscow's continued grip on Eastern Europe. But there can be no doubt that a NATO strategy based almost exclusively on nuclear deterrence had by 1957 frozen any useful discussion of Germany's political future, and had placed the Alliance in a real dilemma, though not yet in its present disarray.

THE NUCLEAR BALANCE: 1957–62

In 1957 the Sputnik orbited the globe, a symbolic event as much as a scientific achievement, and one calculated to make the always technologically obsessed Americans especially sensitive to what now appeared to be their own vulnerability to Soviet nuclear blackmail; if a satellite could orbit, might not a nuclear bomb? The realisation that the American strategic deterrent was no longer the most powerful in the world produced two major reactions, neither of which need have led to further divisions in NATO if American foreign policy had not been in pawn to the Defence Department. But the decision to close the 'missile gap' and the academic debate about the limitations of nuclear weapons produced almost exactly the opposite effect to that intended. An intensive American programme began, designed to create two forms of 'invulnerable' deterrent to a Soviet nuclear attack on the United States: a missile force targeted on Soviet cities and buried in hardened sites in the deserts of Omaha, Nebraska and Nevada; and a fleet of missile-carrying submarines, whose targeting would vary with the boats' location, and would in theory give an American president the choice of striking either at Soviet cities or at 'forces', that is at large military concentrations, logistic facilities and the like.

The net effect of these measures was to convince the Soviet Union and European NATO in roughly equal proportions that the United States had lost interest in Europe; this appreciation may be said to have led to Khrushchev's decision to renew pressure over Berlin and, in 1961 and early 1962, bring the cold war to its most dangerous pitch since 1948. After the Berlin wall was built, the Kennedy administration realised that European security—and the preservation of legitimate Western interests— was more than the sum of nuclear weapons. Thereafter, the strategy of the flexible response began to be preached and practised. The European NATO reaction, coinciding with de Gaulle's return to power and the British government's restatement of its 'east of Suez' role, was to begin an agonised analysis of strategies for a situation where France and West Germany were threatened by Soviet aggression and might find themselves unsupported by their supposed allies.

It was at this moment that the American debate on the limitations of nuclear weapons and the need to devise a strategy of 'flexible response' was reaching its peak. It is interesting to note that it was the work of historians which probed most deeply. Both Henry Kissinger's *Nuclear weapons and Foreign Policy* (1957) and Robert Osgood's *NATO the Entangling Alliance* (1962) made the point that although nuclear weapons were uniquely destructive and might therefore be uniquely effective as deterrents to major war, they had no more relevance to limited war, or wars conducted at a disadvantage to states possessing a strategic nuclear system, than any other 'dominant' weapon, be it dreadnought, submarine or heavy bomber.

Unfortunately, few writers approached Kissinger and Osgood in imagination and in perception of NATO's essential dilemma of being controlled by a power which seemed increasingly bent on increasing its own security. Although the brief period of Kennedy's presidency saw American foreign policy given a clarity of outline and depth of interpretation unmatched before or since, it proved insufficient to check European members' convictions that the strategy of the flexible response, with balanced nuclear and conventional forces, was merely a device to leave them in the lurch. The 1961 Berlin crisis, when Khrushchev coolly called the American nuclear bluff in the weeks preceding the building of the Berlin wall, only deepened these fears, and led in the Federal German government to a growing demand that exclusive control of the Alliance's nuclear armoury should pass out of American hands, and that a nuclear missile force should be deployed in Western Europe and targeted on Soviet cities.

The Loss of American Leadership: 1962–6

Despite these additional stresses within NATO, there was a brief period in its history when strategic imperatives and academic analysis marched together and, under Kennedy's leadership, even began to convince Western European governments that there could be flexibility in American diplomacy as well as in American deployment of military strength. The period between Kennedy's success in the Cuba crisis of October 1962 and his death thirteen months later was one of hope and confidence in NATO and, indeed, throughout much of Europe. Khrushchev and Kennedy were moving towards a genuine understanding of nuclear deterrence; the strategy of the flexible response and a forward defence of territory by strong and mobile conventional forces seeped into NATO planning, giving in the process a further impetus to West German influence, but one sensibly modified by Kennedy's firm grasp of the reins of leadership and a growing awareness in Bonn of the true value of the nuclear/conventional balance. British and French ground forces in NATO remained unaffected by the new strategy, it is true, the former because of the determination of the British government to regard the Rhine Army as a strategic reserve which simply happened to be stationed in Germany, the latter through the French government's initial flirtation with nuclear strategy and the vicious aftermath of the Algerian war.

But despite these continued defections, a new spirit could be discerned across the whole strategic spectrum, and for a time it was not sanguine to suppose that a détente might presage arms control for the European theatre, leading in turn to a settlement of the German issue. The limited test ban treaty signed in Moscow in July 1963 pointed the way to a Europe which might still be an armed camp to the economist or idealist, but could also be one where a geographical and not merely strategic distinction had been drawn between nuclear weapons which were to be removed from the central area and conventional forces which were to be monitored by both sides. For NATO a more significant initiative was Kennedy's revived but careful pressure for an 'Atlantic' strategic deterrent, to replace the wholly American version deployed on the Alliance's behalf.

The 'Atlantic' force was intended to have an American element—some Polaris submarines—and to complement the nuclear weapons stationed or buried in the United States. Hence all NATO's members were invited to participate in this 'Atlantic' or 'multilateral' force (MLF), which although still subject to American veto would express Alliance strategy through a full sharing of all problems and options relevant to the deterrence or containment of Soviet *military* strength; to the 'assured destruction' of Soviet *cities* should Armageddon come purely American strength was reserved. The proponents of the MLF thus hoped to convince NATO that the Soviet missiles targeted on Western Europe were matched by an equivalent force and that the MLF's weapons could be deployed against military and not simply civilian targets, thus giving further flexibility to NATO's Supreme Commander in maintaining the right balance between his nuclear and conventional force. In the diplomatic sphere, Kennedy also hoped that a multilateral force could pave the way for common trusteeship of nuclear weapons in NATO and thus solve the problem that was said to haunt him—that of the proliferation of nuclear weapons among nation states. Kennedy never intended that nuclear decision-making should pass out of his or his successors' hands.

Thus there were disingenuous elements in all these proposals (which were not new, but had never before been made in such propitious circumstances). But it should be emphasised that the essential point about Kennedy's approach was that NATO's education in nuclear realities would have the twin effects of convincing its representatives that nuclear decisions were not to be taken except *in extremis* (thus demonstrating to them the risks run by the United States on their behalf), and of extolling the merits of conventional forces in a post-Cuba world. Possibly these concepts were too sophisticated for NATO to swallow; more probably their implications were politically unacceptable, even if strategically impeccable; certainly it is the case that only the West German government and several of the Alliance's smaller members were prepared to consider them. It is this situation which obtains to-day, aggravated by the British government's determination that in any NATO scheme for physical control of nuclear weapons West Germany shall not rank equal with Britain.

THE PRESENT AND THE FUTURE

Thus the situation to-day is that NATO's disarray springs from internal dispute about the role of the United States. Under Kennedy true leadership was shown, but it was too brief and too crippled by the past to succeed. Under President Johnson it has been made clear that Kennedy's 'Grand Design' for Europe is of less importance than the containment of Chinese Communism. What then of the future? Except in France and among left-wing academic strategic analysts, most examinations of NATO assume that the Alliance must survive and that the United States must continue to lead it. This attitude is natural among those who have laboured to see Kennedy's objectives achieved and have borne with fortitude the patent determination of President Johnson to follow a policy more in accord with his country's immediate interests. The desire to keep NATO alive in Kennedy's terms is also rational, since it is clear that NATO without the United States could only achieve strategic self-sufficiency by destroying the present European power balance.

Nevertheless the orthodox defenders of NATO will have to come to terms with several political possibilities. That de Gaulle's line of reasoning— modification of American monopoly of power in NATO logically follows if that monopoly is indecisively exercised—is relevant not only to NATO's future, or to that of its successor, is borne out by reference to the first of these possibilities, namely American policy over nuclear weapons.

It is now the stated policy of the Johnson administration, as expressed at the Geneva disarmament conference, to seek a non-proliferation agreement with the Soviet Union on the basis that several national nuclear powers exist and that their number can remain limited provided other states with nuclear weapons become 'entities' or groups of states with common interests in deterrence and regional security. In Kennedy's days, United States representatives tried to encourage Britain and France, the states possessing nuclear weapons too puny to rank them among nuclear powers, to abandon this form of status symbol entirely; today and for the foreseeable future, American policy appears designed to bring the British and French nuclear systems together, possibly as the basis of a European Defence Community more 'Gaullist' in concept than the proponents of an 'Atlantic' community could ever have supposed.

The second and complementary political reality is the negative power of both Britain and France to prevent the continuation of the Alliance in its present form. Although British governments have outwardly been among NATO's staunchest supporters, and de Gaulle is obviously determined to find a successor to it, the policies emanating from London and Paris in the last decade have not differed much in practice. As well as the mutual determination to preserve or seek nuclear 'independence'—and thus deny the United States her leader's role in NATO on such occasions as it has been asserted—there has been the consistent British refusal to accept the Alliance's conventional strategic requirements and de Gaulle's persistent search for an accommodation with the Soviet Union, based on the premise that the latter is a *European* power, which will reach a reasonable settlement of the German problem provided the United States military presence is removed from the continent. In this connection, it should be noted that the American proposals for a non-proliferation treaty accept that some 'erosion' of the 'Western Alliance' is a fair price to pay for Soviet acceptance of them; to be meaningful at all, such erosion can only mean the withdrawal of the United States from NATO, or its absence from a successor. Indeed the American proposals tabled in 1965 at Geneva specifically provided for such a successor.

At one time British and Gaullist opposition to American policy aroused something akin to despair in the White House. Not now: after it became obvious that Britain could not or would not spare resources for both Europe and her theatres 'east of Suez', she was urged by the United States to concentrate her defence effort on the latter. The theory of the nuclear 'entities' is virtually an invitation to de Gaulle to seek that European Defence Community which is enshrined in his vision of an area ranging from 'the Atlantic to the Urals', united by a common interest in security and trade, though not artificially bound by any doctrine of supranationality. It may be argued, however, that an idea of this kind is far removed from practical politics, and that the departure of American troops from Western Europe would as adversely affect its security as would the creation of a Western European Defence Community armed with nuclear weapons.

But two factors should be remembered in considering the proposition advanced here that NATO's ultimate successor may well be a European Defence Community which extends at least as far east as the Soviet frontiers. The United States and the Soviet Union may not share common international objectives, as President Johnson apparently believes, but they have accepted a strategic stalemate in relation to each other. The effect of this, produced by the mutual establishment of virtually invulnerable retaliatory nuclear systems, has been to reveal what propaganda and fear have disguised since 1945, namely that both powers' interests in Europe are based on security, not ideology. If that were not so, the United States would have 'rolled back' Soviet forces at the time of the Hungarian rebellion in 1956— as Dulles promised—and the Soviet Union would view with alarm and would seek to prevent the growing identity of interest and even political sympathy between Europe's separated brethren in West and East. Neither of these things has happened. The United States is secure from the Soviet Union by virtue of its assured retaliatory system, and vice versa; more to the point, the Soviet Union is secure from the misguided intentions of the leaders of any *Western* European nuclear force or defence community by virtue of its seven or eight hundred intermediate-range ballistic missiles targeted on their cities and the strongest and most homogeneous army in the world outside China.

Given these strategic and political factors, it is perfectly reasonable to contemplate the day when NATO and the Warsaw Pact will evolve into a European Defence Community on Gaullist lines. In the interim—possibly in the seventies—it may well be that a *Western* European Defence Community will emerge: its virtual possession of a nuclear armoury, subject to a negative American veto but lacking anything in the way of an American 'presence', should not be ruled out. There would, however, be genuine Soviet opposition and a sharp return to cold war conditions if the West German government were given responsibilities in such a nuclear force greater than its allies'. It is in this connection that future British defence policy is of great significance.

It has been implied in the preceding that what *may* evolve out of NATO as it stands today—a Gaullist Europe—need not evolve if American leadership is reasserted and European security is once again regarded as of overriding importance in the White House. Although the inconsistency of American policies towards European security is matched only by British indifference to it, there is no reason why the world's most powerful democracy should not take a more active interest in European problems. But if American leadership is to revive and NATO be reborn in a new, healthier and possibly more enduring form, several imperatives must be obeyed. These are as follows.

1. American leadership of NATO must be reestablished by emphatic presidential elucidation of the dangers of national nuclear proliferation. The possibilities inherent in the 'entity' concept ought to be recognised— namely that the natural preoccupation of the United States and the Soviet Union with their nuclear deterrents will lead lesser states to combine in the establishment of their own. In short, American 'disarmament' policy must change; this change should be accompanied by an unequivocal statement that there will be no American troop withdrawals from Europe.

2. A reversion to the Kennedy–McNamara policies of 1963 requires that the role of West Germany in a genuine NATO nuclear force is no greater and no less than that of any other member, the United States always excepted. French intransigence on the score of an American veto is probably insuperable; British intransigence on the score of West Germany's status is not.

3. If the United States is to revive its European leadership, it must reconsider its Vietnamese policy. This is necessary for three main reasons, namely: even the American strategic cornucopia is not boundless; a resumption of the dialogue with the Soviet Union over Europe's future is not possible while the two super powers differ about whether the war in Vietnam is revolutionary or aggressive; it will not be possible for the European members of NATO to believe that the United States has once again considered them as its major allies unless they are free of the pressure to sympathise with the containment of unrest 10,000 miles away. It may be natural for a president of Johnson's disposition to make a revival of American leadership of NATO contingent on stretching its boundaries to the Mekong delta,

but it is not a tactic which is likely to make for genuine partnership—nor to convince the Soviet Union that a resumption of the European dialogue is possible.

4. Even if the political problem of nuclear sharing in NATO is solved, that of a balance between deterrence and defence remains—as it has throughout the Alliance's history. Hence one basic concomitant to a revival of American leadership is a clear British declaration that European commitments come first and that Britain must accept Germany as an ally. But it is equally clear that Britain is not able to execute a global strategic role *and* give priority to the European theatre. Therefore it is as imperative that Britain realises that non-European commitments must eventually be terminated as it is for the United States to accept that the solution to NATO's disarray lies in a revival of its leadership.

BIBLIOGRAPHY

Bell, Coral. *Negotiation from Strength*, Chatto and Windus, London, 1962; Alfred A. Knopf, New York, 1963.

Buchan, Alistair. *Nato in the 1960s*, Weidenfeld and Nicolson, London; Frederick A. Praeger, New York, revised ed. 1965.

Buchan, Alistair and Windsor, Philip. *Arms and Stability in Europe*, Chatto and Windus, London; Frederick A. Praeger, New York, 1963.

Hunt, Brig. K. *NATO without France*, Institute for Strategic Studies, London, 1966.

Kissinger, Henry. *The Troubled Partnership*, McGraw-Hill, New York, 1965.

Knorr, Klaus (ed.) *Nato and American Security*, Princeton Univ. Press, Princeton, NJ, 1959.

Mackintosh, J. Malcolm. *Strategy and Tactics of Soviet Foreign Policy*, Oxford Univ. Press, London and New York, 1962.

Mulley, F. W. *The Politics of Western Defence*, Thames and Hudson, London; Frederick A. Praeger, New York, 1962.

Osgood, R. E. *Nato: the Entangling Alliance*, Univ. of Chicago Press, Chicago, 1962.

Steel, Ronald. *The End of Alliance*, André Deutsch, London; Viking Press, New York, 1964.

ARTICLES

The following articles are listed as they appeared in the monthly journal *Survival* (Institute of Strategic Studies, London), in which form they may most conveniently be found.

Ailleret, General. 'The Character of Strategy', May–June 1965.

Foster, William C. 'National Security and Arms Control', November–December 1964. 'New Directions in Arms Control', August 1965.

Fulbright, J. William. 'Foreign Policy; Myth and Reality', May–June 1964.

Gilpatric, Roswell L. 'American Defence, The Long View', May–June 1964.

Owen, Henry. 'What's Past is Prologue', September 1965.

K*

GERMAN DISUNITY

PHILIP WINDSOR

GERMANY has always been the centre of the Cold War. The 'German question' and its progeny the 'Berlin problem' have been the two issues in international politics which have been permanently capable of touching off a third world war or defining the conditions for an enduring peace. Germany is the one area where the armed forces of the world's two dominant powers have stood facing each other for twenty years, ready to fight at a moment's notice or the slightest infraction of their territorial position.

The conflict between the Soviet Union and the Western powers, which has spread over many parts of the world and covered a wide range of ideological and political issues, originated in a conflict about what to do with Germany. It may be argued, indeed, that the Cold War began before the second world war, when, from Munich to the Nazi-Soviet Pact, the major European powers were manoeuvering to avoid a war with Germany or ensure that if it came it would be directed away from themselves. Since then the major powers have been united only against Germany; they have never agreed on a policy towards Germany. Germany's industrial power and military potentialities have ensured this: each side in the Cold War required the country as an ally against the other, and both have hoped at different times to gain control over the whole country, the Soviet Union offering reunification on terms which would have made Soviet domination virtually certain, the Western powers insisting that the only acceptable basis for reunification was one which would have allowed the whole country to join NATO. But equally, both sides have recognised that the division of Germany was an adequate basis for the security of Europe—so long as it kept East and West apart. A clear frontier was safer than an ill-defined area of competition. So the Cold War has oscillated between these two positions. It has either been a competition for the alliance of a reunified Germany, or else an agreement not to go to war, but to stay put on the basis of a divided Germany.

The 'division of Germany', therefore, is not and has not been a simple or straightforward historical phenomenon: on the contrary, it has meant different things to different people at different times. This goes for West Germany too. There has never been a general national attitude towards relations with East Germany, or with the Soviet Union, or with Germany's Western allies; nor has there been any general agreement, except for very short periods, about the best strategy for reunification. But West German *policy* has, generally speaking, been more coherent than the conflicts within the country might have suggested, and if it was largely shaped in the early years by the nature of relations between the victorious powers of 1945, it has also done much to influence their relations in subsequent years. West German policy falls into three principal phases. The first was a period of major decision that lasted for some ten years after the second world war; the second was a period of immobilism and gradually growing frustration that led to demands for a change. The third began in 1966 and is likely to lead to a fundamental reappraisal of West Germany's foreign policy in general, and of relations with East Germany in particular. These periods, from 1945 to 1955 and from 1955 to the present, will be described in more detail later. The changes in German foreign policy themselves reflect the inconsistent, even contradictory nature of the policies of the external powers, and in discussing German foreign policy it is necessary to remember that it was to a high degree and for a long time more dependent on the interests and relations of the other countries involved in the situation than that of any other important power.

The Western allies—to use a term which glosses over differences of opinion and interest which have at times been fundamental—have usually insisted that they did not accept the division of Germany, and that the objective of their policies was reunification 'in security and freedom'; but since 1955 at least the basis of their relations with the Soviet Union has been a tacit acceptance of the fact that Germany would not be reunified in the foreseeable future. Other agreements would have to come first, so long as these were not based upon an explicit acceptance of the two Germanies. The Soviet Union, on the other hand, has, also since 1955, been reconciled to the division of the country and to a stabilisation of the Cold War along those lines. But it has attempted to force an explicit recognition of this division on the Western powers—to make them recognise East Germany. It was in attempting to do this that the Soviet Union precipitated the crises over Berlin and brought the world very near the edge of that war which neither side, once it accepted the division of the country, had any cause to fight. And while both sides risked war to establish a position that already existed, they found it impossible to reach any agreement which could have alleviated the situation because of a clash of priorities; the Western powers refusing to admit that agreement with the Soviet Union implied the recognition of East Germany; the Soviet Union insisting that recognition in one form or another was an essential condition of any agreement in Europe.

In all this West Germany was bound to become at once the most conservative and the most radical of the Western allies. The most conservative because it held out more obdurately than any other country against agreements with the Soviet Union which implied even the most attenuated recognition of East Germany, and refused (and still refuses) to recognise that the lands beyond the Oder-Neisse Line which have formed a part of Poland since 1945 are Polish. They are merely 'under Polish administration', and in deference to German feelings and because the cession to Poland of these lands in 1945 was officially an interim measure, the other Western powers also take this view—though President de Gaulle has taken care to make it clear that he accepts the Oder-Neisse Line as the Eastern frontier of Germany. But West Germany is also the most radical of the Western allies because it has continually identified any progress towards a settlement of the Cold War in Europe with progress on the reunification of the country. In fact it has taken an all-or-nothing position, which, though based on the reasonable premise that German reunification was the prime objective of German foreign policy, has also done much to perpetuate the Cold War and ensure that reunification could not come about.

Thus the pattern of relations that developed around the division of Germany was as follows. The Soviet Union insisted that any European settlement must be based on the recognition of East Germany, and was prepared to start a war-bearing crisis to secure this end. The Western powers, though they tacitly recognised the division of the country, were not prepared to recognise East Germany—if for no other reason than that this would have been fatal to their alliance with West Germany, and every Soviet demand only strengthened their formal commitment to the eventual reunification of the country. The relations between the two power-blocs alternated between a grudging rapprochement based on the *status quo* and sharp periods of crisis which heightened their outward determination to change the *status quo*. In all this West Germany played an essential part, insisting that the actual position was intolerable but ensuring that it could not be changed; at the same time East Germany exploited its position in the Soviet power-bloc to pursue a policy of unremitting hostility to the Federal Republic—even while pleading ad nauseam for the 'normalisation' of relations between the two German states—so making it impossible for any West German politician to contemplate concessions or demand anything less than full reunification. This pattern was that of a total impasse, and at times it looked as if it could go on for ever. But in 1966 it began to break up, and at the end of the year the situation seemed more fluid than at any time since the early 1950s. Ten years of deadlock appeared to have come to a sudden end, and the history of Germany to be entering a new phase, the third major period of development since the war.

The War-Time Agreements

The origins of these 'periods' lie in the war-time agreements between the partners of the Grand Alliance. At the end of the war, all three of the major allied leaders were playing for time. None of them was anxious to reach a quick settlement of the German problem. As the end of the war approached Stalin was preparing a number of Communists in the Soviet Union to take over the Soviet Zone during the period of occupation and turn it into a springboard for a reunified Germany under Communist domination. In part, his calculations were certainly influenced by the apparent intention of the United States government to limit the occupation of Germany to a very short period—a couple of years in Roosevelt's view. For the same reason Churchill was anxious to keep the United States committed to Europe for as long as possible, and avoid commitment to any plans which could mean a quick withdrawal—and a renewed struggle for the control of Europe. Roosevelt, torn between a desire to ensure the permanent subjugation of Germany, an anxiety to cooperate with the Soviet Union to secure the future peace of the world, and the immediate necessity of mediating between those two suspicious and unequal powers the Soviet Union and Great Britain, had no clear policy at all. There is no evidence that the United States had drawn up any plans other than cooperation with the Soviet Union.

In these circumstances the history of the war-time conferences and agreements is easier to understand. Their enormous oscillations between plans for the total pastoralisation of Germany and plans for industrial reparations over the foreseeable future, their almost arbitrary and certainly outrageously careless drawing of different zonal boundaries and/or different successor states, their total lack of appreciation of the importance of Berlin and the access rights of the occupying powers are now of no more than academic interest. The fundamental truth seems to be that as the end of the war drew nearer, the major allies became increasingly conscious of their own divergencies and correspondingly anxious to avoid a definitive settlement which would drag their conflicts into the open. Hence the astonishing transition from the Yalta agreement of February 1945 which envisaged 'the complete . . . dismemberment' of Germany to the attempts at Potsdam a few months later to create a unified administration in which all the allies would participate in running a single country. Hence too the fact that when agreement on these lines was found impossible to reach, the zonal boundaries degenerated into partition lines between East and West Germany. But the agreement which the allies drew up at Potsdam in the summer of 1945 is still the only guiding principle that they have in common for their future policy towards Germany. They are still officially bound to work for the creation of a unified German government, and in official theory no peace treaty can be signed between Germany and the victors of the second world war until the country has been reunified; the relations between the allies and the two German states are officially only provisional relations with provisional states until such time as a reunited country replaces both of them. Officially, of course, the United States, the Soviet Union and Great Britain are still allies.

The blatant unreality of the Potsdam Agreement does not mean that it is unimportant. It is the only official document which recognises that the three countries (France was not invited to Potsdam, which meant a further element of confusion and unreality) have a common interest in the future of Germany or a common obligation not to come to arbitrary decisions on their future policies towards the whole country without consulting each other. It means that any threat of a separate peace treaty between one of the powers and one part of Germany is, and will be seen to be, a hostile act to the others —as when Khrushchev threatened to conclude a separate peace treaty with East Germany during the Berlin crisis of 1958–9; and this in turn means that no one side in the Cold War can do very much to change the *status quo* without running immediate risks of a third world war. In effect the Potsdam Agreement is a guarantee of conflict which prevents any gradual series of changes from taking place to the detriment of either side or its own part of Germany. It is one of the supports on which the whole structure of international relations during the Cold War has depended. And it has ensured that what Dean Rusk has called the 'truce lines' of 1945 have become the boundaries of two separate German states. This paradox is understandable in the light of subsequent developments.

THE STRUGGLE FOR GERMANY

Development of the East–West split

Churchill and Truman met Stalin at Potsdam just outside Berlin in July 1945 at about the time that the Western occupying forces were entering Berlin for the first time. The war in Europe had been over for two months, and during this period the Russians had had ample time to organise Berlin, as the future capital of Germany, in their own interests. In Berlin, and in the Soviet zone of Germany, they had created an 'Anti-Fascist Coalition' of all political bodies which were prepared to cooperate with the new authority, and had already promulgated certain social reforms as well as setting up a new and, in the circumstances of the time, extremely efficient administrative organisation. There is plenty of evidence that this was intended as a trial run for eventual takeover of the whole of Germany, and that the Soviet Zone was to be a model of social reform and of German participation in the administration which would attract the inhabitants of the other zones. This was the shape that Stalin's dual policy towards Germany finally took. But at the beginning it depended on the simple stratagem of keeping the Communist Party in the background: the Anti-Fascist Coalition was to be an amorphous grouping of all political parties in which none had a distinct identity. A month before Potsdam, however, there was a change of line that is still hard to understand. Out of the blue Marshal Zhukov, the Soviet military governor, ordered the formation of 'free political parties and trade unions', and the German Communist Party, the KPD, which had hitherto been managing the Anti-Fascist Coalition in the background, emerged along with other political parties as a separate force. The discreet extension of Communist power which was originally expected had turned into an open struggle for the control of Germany between Communist and anti-Communist forces.

This struggle was to take two forms: on an official level, between the allies, it centred on the economic administration of the country and turned into a sharp dispute, primarily between Britain and the Soviet Union, about reparations deliveries (since the British Zone contained the Ruhr); on a half-acknowledged level it was an attempt by the Communist Party to win control of the German population by forcing a merger with the Social Democrats, traditionally the largest and most powerful party in the country, and this struggle centred on Berlin. For the Soviet Zone rapidly came under almost complete Communist control, and the merger was pushed through there without any trouble.

But Berlin was the one part of Germany which was administered by all the allies (though even here the city was divided into national sectors) and if the KPD, with Soviet backing, could gain control of the capital city while it was under the control of all four allies they could both demonstrate to the rest of the country that Western occupation did not mean protection and at the same time take the biggest single step towards extending their control. Between 1945 and 1946, therefore, two simultaneous conflicts were going on: the inter-allied conflict which was fought out in the Allied Control Council and at the foreign ministers' conferences, and the political struggle in Berlin. This is a vital period because much of the subsequent course of German history was then determined. On the political level, the final result was a decisive defeat for the Communists. The Social Democrats, from an almost hopeless political position and without any real support from the Western allies until the last moment, and faced with the threat of kidnapping and intimidation organised from East Berlin, resisted a Communist attempt to force a merger of 'the two proletarian parties', and finally managed to have elections held in the capital in which—in the three Western Sectors—they won an overwhelming victory. The Communists found themselves in a minority in the new city government of Berlin.

This defeat followed a decisive *démarche* of Molotov's at the Paris Foreign Ministers' Conference in July 1946. At that moment, confident of electoral victory, he had rejected a series of French proposals for what amounted to the economic dismemberment of Germany and had insisted on an all-German government and a peace treaty. In so doing, Molotov put an end to the half-alliance between France and the Soviet Union which had hitherto immobilised the development of Western policy towards Germany; France was now to find itself increasingly drawn to the Anglo-American development of a separate West German economy, while the Soviet Union had been deprived by the election results in Berlin of the one alternative to separate development on which it had placed its hopes, all-German elections resulting in an all-German government.

The result of these events was the enduring division of the country, and the beginnings of a split in Berlin itself into its Eastern and Western halves. The creation of a separate West German economy, based first on the Anglo-American Bi-zone, and later on the three Western Zones, was not intended as an attempt to divide the country, any more than the Anti-Fascist Coalition was intended to divide the Soviet Zone from the rest. But the effect in both cases was the same: what began as an attempt to set up a working model for the whole of the country ended by making it impossible for the occupying powers to agree on an overall policy. And what looked like a secondary effect at the time turned out to be just as important: the French determination that if dismemberment was not a feasible policy then Germany must be integrated into a Western European economic structure that would make it impossible for the country to enjoy unfettered control of its enormous economic resources. Such integration was the alternative to dismemberment, and there is no doubt that it was originally intended to be restrictive, though it was also coupled with a conscious determination on the part of some Frenchmen to create the kind of Western European union which is associated with the names of Monnet and Schuman. But the division of Germany went hand in hand with European integration, and this did much to ensure that the division was permanent.

Equally the split in Berlin ensured that conflicts of policy between the allied powers would be intensified by a struggle for the control of the capital, and that local conflicts in the political life of Berlin itself would be magnified into inter-allied disputes. For the next few years—until *after* the Berlin blockade of 1948–9 at least—the Western allies continued to regard Berlin as the last hope of allied cooperation, and to do everything in their power to avoid a division of the city; but this very concern, coupled with the military weakness of their isolated position in Berlin ensured that the Soviet government would be able to apply pressure to Berlin as a means of furthering its own policies, and generally treat it as a hostage to allied agreement.

Marshall Aid, currency reform and the Berlin blockade

Neither of these developments was very clear in 1946: a unified government continued in the city until 1948; the Anglo-American Bi-zone did not begin to function effectively until 1947; the French Zone did not join it until 1948; the real battle for the future of Germany was not joined until the Berlin blockade. But in fact the next two or three years saw the playing out of the fundamental decisions that had been taken by the end of 1946. Two closely connected events were of decisive importance in this development: currency reform and Marshall Aid.

A major factor in British, and subsequently French, support for the unification of the Western Zones was the growing belief that the Soviet Union was determined to ruin Western Europe economically. General Marshall's speech in June 1947 offered them a guarantee against this; it offered indeed the prospect of economic salvation along with a solution, for the time at least, to the problem of what to do with Germany. And equally it removed a major cause of French obstruction—the fact that hitherto German resources had offered practically the only source from which France could hope to rebuild its own economic strength. American help was a surer form of help, and one that would be to the political advantage of France as well, in marked contrast to its own German policy. But the success of Marshall Aid, and of the whole European Recovery Programme, depended on restoring the strength of the West German economy. Germany was perhaps the biggest single cause of Britain's economic weakness after the war, and the compromises in the reparations agreements that had been reached at Potsdam had meant for a time that both Britain and the United States were subsidising German reparations to the Soviet Union. Reparations payments from the American and British Zones had been suspended in 1946, but the drain on American as well as British resources which West Germany represented in 1947 could have led to the total economic breakdown of Western Europe, while the Bi-zone itself could not hope to recover while it suffered from an outdated currency system that had survived the war. There is in fact evidence that the decision to substitute a new and realistic currency in the Bi-zone had already been taken in 1947, but it was not until the United States and Britain had had a final confrontation with the Soviet Union at the end of the year, and won the support of France at the London Conference in February 1948, that they went on to consolidate the economic division of the country and introduce the new currency.

The results were spectacular: an overnight boom in West Germany, as the currency reform suddenly restored internal confidence, produced a stable price structure and enabled the country to take part in the export and investment programme of Western Europe. But the currency reform also led directly to the Berlin blockade. By now the Western powers had set up a de facto German government in their zones, and Berlin was the one place where the original nature of the occupation still persisted. But the blockade was not really a trial of strength between the two sides in the Cold War, fought out on the one remaining battleground. Soviet purposes seem in retrospect to have been far vaguer than that, and there are some indications that the Soviet leaders were surprised to find a full-scale crisis developing out of a bit of vengeful obstruction. As the crisis developed there is no doubt that they set out to exploit it—but rather by trying to reverse the electoral decision of 1946 and win the population of West Berlin over to their support, by alternating threats and promises, than by making any deliberate effort to force the Western allies out of Berlin. The blockade is of the greatest interest psychologically. It enabled the inhabitants of West Berlin to stand up to Communist intimidation, it forged their political cohesion under the leadership of an ex-Communist mayor, Ernst Reuter, and it forced the Western allies into a demonstrative commitment that they had not made before. After the years of Nazi rule and the comparative helplessness of the occupation, it gave West Berlin, and through it West Germany, a chance to reassert itself, to throw a psychological bridge back to the Germany that had existed before 1933. In these respects it did for Germany something of what the Battle of Britain did for Britain after the years of appeasement in the 1930s.

The blockade had however very little effect on the division of Germany. It completed the isolation of Berlin and helped indirectly to establish an East German constitution at about the same time in 1948 that the West German Basic Law was being drawn up. Apart from that, the struggle for Germany had virtually finished before the blockade began, and the negotiations that put an end to the siege did little more than consolidate the status quo. Both sides acknowledged stalemate. Berlin was not incorporated into East Germany, but West Berlin was specifically prevented from becoming a part of West Germany too. The two German states had come into existence, and neither the Soviet Union nor the United States was willing to risk a new conflict by trying to force further changes.

The policy of 'peaceful co-existence'

But though the struggle was over, the conflicts of policy were not. After his defeat in 1949, Stalin reconsidered his foreign policy. He gave up all attempts to drive the Western powers out of Germany, but he still hoped to secure the reunification of the country—on terms, of course, which would bring it within the Soviet sphere of influence. In 1952 he proposed a new attempt at reunification, even making Germany an offer of military sovereignty which was left carefully undefined. The offer was rejected out of hand by the Western powers; whereas Stalinist foreign policy never abandoned the hope of reunifying Germany, the Western powers had by now reconciled themselves to its indefinite partition. The real change came after Stalin's death. After two years of confused manoeuvres and delays, his successors also made up their minds to accept the division of Germany—and this was what was really meant by 'peaceful coexistence'. In effect, Khrushchev was telling the Western leaders that he was satisfied with the *status quo* in Europe.

But the Western powers had also progressed during this time. In 1952 they were determined to harness the military potential of Germany to their own alliance system through the restrictive mechanism of the European Defence Community, just as they had already begun to harness its economic potential through the process of European integration. By 1955, when the plans for the European Defence Community had finally been rejected in France, they were ready to incorporate West Germany into NATO. The Soviet Union, though it did everything it could to oppose this, still showed subsequently that it was willing to settle for an acknowledged partition. This was the essence of Soviet policy after 1955—and along with the integration of the Federal Republic into NATO it makes 1955 a crucial year. But it was asking too much of the Western powers to expect them to acknowledge the division of Germany—to recognise, that is, the East German regime. In any case, their commitments to the Federal Republic, the terms of the treaties under which Germany entered NATO, prevented this. The result was that after 1955 there was a neat reversal of positions. The Soviet government, which had hitherto made German reunification an important aim of its foreign policy, now insisted that the final division of Germany should be a basic condition of 'peaceful coexistence'; while the Western powers, who had been content to accept the division of Germany in the early years after the war as part of the price of Western European recovery, were now adamant in their insistence that Germany must some day be reunified. Meanwhile they refused to countenance any form of recognition of the East German government. It was in this context that Khrushchev tried to force his views on the West by putting renewed pressure on Berlin.

The crises that developed over Berlin between 1958 and 1961, when the Wall was built, should not, however, be confused with a revival of the Cold War. The struggle over Berlin arose from the Soviet attempt to dictate the conditions of peaceful coexistence to the Western allies. In Soviet eyes at least, it was an attempt to divide Europe into clear spheres of influence and have done with the Cold War; and the Western powers' insistence that this division was not final, and that some day Germany would be reunified, looked to the Eastern European leaders remarkably like an affirmation of their will to carry on with the Cold War. The fact that West Germany fully shared and supported the Western view, was indeed its chief protagonist, only exposed the Federal government to the constant suspicion (voiced openly in the Soviet Union and Eastern Europe but shared by a great proportion of the Social Democratic parties in Western Europe) that it had an active interest in the Cold War, and that its only hope for the reunification of Germany lay in prosecuting the struggle with undiminished zest.

GERMANY'S CHOICE

The process of integration into the Western system had not gone without question in West Germany. Even before the Federal Republic was established in 1949, the two leading parties had taken up opposing positions. From the beginning Adenauer, who had established a dominating position in the Christian Democratic Union (CDU), was determined to identify the new Republic with the Western world as closely as possible. Recognising that it could achieve its own independence and ultimate sovereignty as a grant from the allies, he sought to make it in effect a part of the Western alliance—even though there was no prospect that Germany would be allowed to join NATO, and though in 1949 very few politicians were prepared to consider the possibility of German rearmament seriously. But after the outbreak of the Korean war in 1950, Adenauer offered the United States a German contingent in the defence of Europe, and it was thereafter only a matter of time. The sense of inevitability of German rearmament was no doubt one reason why France, the original proponent of the EDC, dragged its feet on the issue and finally rejected it, only to see Germany join NATO in a far more independent form in 1955. It was also no doubt a primary consideration in Stalin's offer of reunification in 1952; but the choice of integration into Western Europe, combined with the long-term prospect of rearmament, had long been made by then. Adenauer was building up to a position of negotiation from strength, relying on the alliance of the United States and on partnership with the countries of Western Europe to create a base from which reunification might eventually be achieved. All the events of the next few years seemed to confirm that only 'strength' paid off.

But to the Social Democrat opposition these years seemed crowded with missed opportunities. Their early leaders, Kurt Schumacher, and Ernst Reuter in Berlin, both deplored the rigidity of Adenauer's foreign policy. Reuter was much more insistent than Schumacher on the need for Western protection—it is scarcely an exaggeration to say that Schumacher regarded all the allies with equal suspicion—but he also insisted that West Germany must be prepared to renounce the advantages of 'living in the West' for the sake of the East Germans, particularly after the East German rising of 1953. He repeatedly denounced the pursuit of prosperity for its own sake which rapidly became a characteristic of West Germany's restricted international position, and called on the inhabitants of the West to 'sacrifice their last shirt' for the chance of reunification of the country. All Social Democrats were in the beginning distrustful not only of German rearmament (to which they stayed uncompromisingly hostile until Khrushchev's Berlin crises helped them change their minds) but also of Germany's integration into Western Europe. This, they argued, prevented any chance of reunification and condemned the inhabitants of East Germany to the harsh and miserable existence that the Ulbricht regime had imposed on them.

After the East German rising, Reuter was particularly bitter in his criticism not only of the Bonn government but also of the passivity of the Western allies. 1953, if not 1952, provided, in his analysis, the chance of a fresh approach to the Soviet Union, which at that time might have been glad to wash its hands of its East German colony. It is hard to judge how excessive a hope this was, since no approach was made, and since much has been made known since 1953 of the confusion and uncertainties of the new Soviet leadership at the time. But in fact the rising of 1953 did no more than confirm that both sides had accepted the division of the country; and though the Soviet Union was to engage in some frantic diplomatic activity to prevent Germany from joining NATO in the next two years, the Geneva conferences of that year only confirmed in the end that all the major powers were content with the existing situation—and that the West Germans were too.

In fact, West Germany was choosing between security under a Western guarantee and the doubtful hope of reunification through Soviet goodwill during these years, and made a very definite choice. But the implications of this choice were not always seen clearly, except by the very few men who helped to frame Adenauer's foreign policy. 1955 was a turning-point in the history of post-war Germany, not only because it marked the Federal Republic's final integration in the Western world and the abandonment by the war-time allies of all discussion of reunification, but also because Adenauer drew from these circumstances the conclusion that the time had come to open diplomatic relations with the Soviet Union. One of the guiding principles of German foreign policy ever since the inception of the Federal Republic in 1949 has been the 'Hallstein Doctrine'—that West Germany refuses to maintain diplomatic relations with any country that recognises East Germany. The opening of diplomatic relations with the Soviet Union, the country that had not only created East Germany but made a ponderous declaration of its full sovereignty in 1955, might seem to be a flagrant breach of this doctrine. In fact, it was at the basis of it. West Germany, which claims to be the custodian of the sovereignty of the whole of Germany—a claim which is recognised by the Western allies—is bound for this very reason to safeguard the future interests of the reunified country, to assume the onus of negotiating Germany's position, and to mediate as far as possible on behalf of Berlin and the East Germans, even if only indirectly, by maintaining close relations with the Soviet Union.

In other words, the implications of Adenauer's foreign policy were not only that reunification was ruled out, that West Germany should be able to obstruct any Western move that seemed to imply recognition of East Germany—such as President Kennedy's proposal for an international access authority to safeguard Western rights in Berlin in 1962—but also that the Federal Republic should renounce all direct influence over East Germany, but yet assume a sort of responsibility for its future in its relations with the Soviet Union and the Western world. The result was that German foreign policy was for long periods condemned to a purely passive and negative role, and that 'negotiation from strength' became practically a self-defeating slogan. Its final failure was demonstrated in the Berlin Wall in August 1961, which was built to keep East Germans inside East Germany, but also divided the whole country more completely than ever.

REAPPRAISAL OF GERMAN FOREIGN POLICY

Adenauer's foreign policy was brilliantly successful in the short term and in the limited field of ensuring the prosperity and security of West Germany.

As a step to the longer-term objective of reunification it was a complete failure: indeed every short-term success ensured the longer-term failure more completely. By 1955 Adenauer had achieved everything that could have been hoped for ten years previously; ten years later nothing had changed, except for a deterioration in Berlin. Meanwhile the pressure for an active policy towards East Germany had been growing in the country. It is commonly thought that the pressure for reunification has been dying, and is bound to die away, in West Germany, as the regional pressure groups disappear and the hopelessness of the cause becomes more obvious. But the reverse has rather been true. In the early 1950s most Germans were too busy, or too anxious, to care deeply for reunification. Since then, the course of the Berlin crises and the growth of a new and articulate generation unburdened by the psychological legacies of Nazism have combined to produce a growing demand that something be done. It is no longer considered an adequate foreign policy simply to dislike East Germany and hope for its demise: this is beginning to be seen as a form of self-indulgence for which the inhabitants of the East German state pay the price. If there is little active pressure for reunification, there is a growing pressure for a new attempt to improve the conditions of life in the other half of the country, if necessary at the expense of the Hallstein Doctrine.

This pressure has been growing particularly since the building of the Berlin Wall, and it is the main result of the Berlin crises of 1958–61, which seemed for so long to threaten fundamental changes in the face of Europe, but in the end changed practically nothing. What they did do was help to change Germany's foreign policy. The Soviet government tried to force the Western powers to recognise East Germany; they refused; West Germany was made for a time to feel insecure, and seemed to question the American commitment; East Germany was brought to the verge of collapse by the loss of many thousands of refugees, whose determination to leave while there was still time was stimulated by the Berlin crisis itself. Then the Wall was built to prevent them getting out and things looked very much the same as before. But this was not how it was seen in Germany, where the building of the Wall had an enormous psychological effect. The East Germans were now in a worse condition than ever before, or so it was believed; in fact there is little doubt that conditions in the East improved very considerably after the building of the Wall, and even that a relative and intermittent freedom of expression began to develop. But West Germany had condemned itself to impotence by a doctrinaire refusal to develop a realistic policy in Eastern Europe. The pressure for change came from different quarters—from Arnold Beitz, the managing director of Krupps, who had established his own forms of semi-diplomatic contact with the Polish government; from Willy Brandt the Mayor of West Berlin, leader of the Social Democrats and since 1966 foreign minister, who argued for a form of 'Berlin initiative' in contacts with East Germany; from Erich Mende, the leader of the hitherto rightist Free Democrats and sometimes a powerful influence on the government, who demanded a much more wide-ranging series of contacts with East Germany; from some influential figures in the Protestant church and in some universities; and eventually from some members of the Christian Democrat cabinet itself. When Adenauer was eventually persuaded to resign, the Erhard government responded to these pressures by announcing a 'policy of movement' in Eastern Europe. It seemed that a new departure was beginning in German foreign policy.

But West Germany had not escaped the choice between integration in the Western system and an independent foreign policy that had dogged it for so long. This was the period of American attempts to create an Atlantic Community on the basis of an integrated NATO, attempts which Germany supported and which inevitably circumscribed its freedom of manoeuvre in other spheres. The policy of movement did not in fact amount to very much. It was in essence an attempt to isolate East Germany from the other Eastern European countries by cultivating economic and cultural relations with them, and by attempting to persuade them to recognise the links between Bonn and West Berlin, since draft trade agreements with these countries specifically include Berlin as part of West German 'territory'. In other words, it was an attempt to concentrate the Cold War against East Germany, not an attempt to unfreeze the general German situation. It was a continuation of Adenauer's foreign policy carried out by a partial reversal of the Hallstein Doctrine. Given the Soviet Union's overall control of Eastern Europe, and the concerted hostility of the Warsaw Pact countries to West Germany at a time when it looked as if Bonn might be given some sort of share in nuclear planning as part of the process of Atlantic integration, this kind of policy could not get very far. It has laid the basis for improved relations with some Eastern European countries, notably Czechoslovakia and Hungary, but it has not affected the position of East Germany within the Eastern system, and it has increased, as it was designed to, the gulf between East and West Germany.

The reaction inside West Germany has, however, not been one of disappointment or a return to the past, but a growing demand for greater efforts. During 1966 astonishing changes took place in the West German approach to the question of dealings with East Germany. Disillusion with the policy of movement swept away the taboos. At the end of 1966 the governments of both East and West Germany were clearly undecided in the face of these pressures, but both, and the West German government in particular, encouraged by the prospects of a more general East-West détente in Europe than there had ever been hope of before, had the opportunity of a more adventurous policy.

For the context of decision has changed radically. This is not so much because of the prospects of détente themselves: it is the West German government which has in the past been the chief objector to forms of détente that might perpetuate the East German regime. The real change is in the break-up of the post-war pattern of increasing integration inside the two divided blocs. In part this is a long-term process, going back to Khrushchev's decision to 'de-Stalinise'; but in part it has only a very recent history, going back only to the failure of Kennedy's 'Grand Design',[1] the disarray of the Atlantic Alliance, and collapse of Khrushchev's plans for the Comecon. Neither side can see its own way clear, and this leaves room, particularly to the major European nations, for independent initiatives. Changes in the structure of relations in Europe do not depend on a prior agreement between the two power-blocs, which would in turn result from months of negotiation among allies, but are more likely to come about in a piecemeal and messy way. In this context West Germany has a new interest in developing its relations with Eastern Europe, and in particular with East Germany. This interest is reinforced by the realisation that security has become a residual concern, and that it would not be construed as disloyalty to the Atlantic Alliance or to the United States if Bonn developed its own foreign policy in Eastern Europe. Indeed, the United States government might welcome it.

[1] See 'Western Europe and the Atlantic World', pp. 259f.

It is too early to guess what the future course of such a policy might be, or when the two German states might begin even tentative steps towards a rapprochement. But what is clear is that the third phase in the history of Germany's division is beginning. The long period of immobilism has led to demands for a change, and the West German government is still feeling its way, but it looks as if radical changes will soon be taking shape.

BIBLIOGRAPHY

Bell, Coral. *Negotiation from Strength*, Chatto and Windus, London, 1962; Alfred A. Knopf, New York, 1963.

Brentano, Heinrich von. *Germany and Europe*, André Deutsch, London; Frederick A. Praeger, New York, 1964.

Freund, Gerald. *Germany between Two Worlds*, Harcourt, Brace, New York, 1961.

Grosser, Alfred. *The Federal Republic of Germany*, Pall Mall, London; Frederick A. Praeger, New York, 1964.

Jakobsen, H. A. and Stenzl, Otto (eds.) *Deutschland und die Welt*, Deutscher Taschenbuch Verlag, Munich, 1964.

Moch, Jules. *Histoire du réarmement allemand depuis 1950*, Robert Laffont, Paris, 1965.

Nettl, J. P. *The Eastern Zone and Soviet Policy in Germany 1945–50*, Oxford Univ. Press, London and New York, 1951.

Speier, Hans. *Divided Berlin*, Thames and Hudson, London; Frederick A. Praeger, New York, 1961.

Strauss, Franz Joseph. *The Grand Design*, Frederick A. Praeger, New York, 1965; Weidenfeld and Nicolson, London, 1966.

Windsor, Philip. *City on Leave: A History of Berlin 1945–62*, Chatto and Windus, London; Frederick A. Praeger, New York, 1963.

PARLIAMENTARIANISM IN WESTERN EUROPE

RICHARD MOORE

THE natural—and to some extent proper—pride of the Briton in his parliamentary institutions has made him reluctant to admit the merits of Continental constitutional systems. He believes that under the Fourth and Third Republics French politics were little more than a series of scene-changes punctuated by brawls between the stage hands. He is hardly aware of the parliamentary politics of any other Continental state and indeed British newspapers make little enough effort to keep him informed. If he is rather more aware than most of the facts of political life he may concede that parliamentary democracy works well enough in Northern Europe, where however it is dull, but cannot be successfully imported into the states of Central and Southern Europe. He fortifies his conviction that the British system is best with the belief that it has no rivals, only inferior imitators in distant places where the Speaker's wig has been more faithfully copied than the Speaker's authority.

As the only European power of the first rank which has remained faithful to parliamentary government throughout the present century, Britain has something to boast of. But she should recognise that if her parliamentary liberties have been an inspiration to her neighbours in times of crisis this is largely because the spirit of her political institutions is basically similar to the ideals which they also have sought to establish over several hundreds of years.

The parliamentary tradition has its classical origins in Athens and Rome. Here and there in the Middle Ages it had a local form which flourished, as in the Venetian Republic, the Icelandic Althing and the Swiss Confederation. The States General in the Netherlands proved the stamina of parliamentary institutions in the struggle with Spain, and the English Revolution of the 17th century made the House of Commons a centre of power. It was left to France to turn the particular into the general and to proclaim a doctrine of government by assembly as an idea of universal application.

It is to 1789 more than to any other date that the democrats of Europe look. The convenient, if misleading, shorthand of Left and Right originated then, and the assertion of popular representation, not as a practical convenience but as a moral imperative, was made by the revolutionaries. The corruption of democracy—popular dictatorship based on a totalitarian theory—made its terrifying appearance soon after, in the Committee of Public Safety.

British politics are to this day influenced by that tremendous convulsion in which the most powerful and glittering despotism in the world fell before the assault of democracy. From the fall of the Bastille onwards no European revolution, however hostile to liberty, has not had to use some of the language of democracy and no clique or junta clinging to power has long been able to deny all the aspirations of the great revolution. It can be claimed with some confidence that in Western Europe today those aspirations are nearer to being fulfilled than ever before. The spread of the suffrage to all classes and both sexes (save in Switzerland where women do not vote in Federal elections), new prosperity, the growing sense of European community which has found such tangible and impressive form among the Six, have been accompanied by the establishment or continuation of parliamentary government in all save two of the Western European states. Only in Spain and Portugal does the national assembly remain an unimpressive and unrepresentative rubber stamp for an arbitrary authority.

VARIETY OF EUROPEAN DEMOCRACIES

The American dream of making the world safe for democracy has not yet been fulfilled, however, even in some of the European states where it is the official foundation of government and the established principle of the great majority of politicians. There is a fascinating variety in the parliamentary methods of Europe, but as regards the power and security of parliamentary democracy, each country (excluding the Iberian dictatorships) may be placed in one of three main categories.

The first can be described as those fortunate countries where the principles of parliamentary democracy and the constitutional order are not seriously challenged by any significant section of opinion. In this category come Britain and the Irish Republic, all the Scandinavian countries except Finland, the Netherlands, Belgium, Luxembourg and Switzerland.

The second category consists of those countries where there is no immediate threat to the constitutional order and little overt hostility to parliamentary democracy but where the system has yet to gain the full sympathy of the people and where the recent past is not liberal. Democracy in these countries has an imported air and its language is not always appreciated; West Germany and Austria are in this case.

The third group consists of those countries where a large part of public opinion organised in political parties or in other institutions is hostile to the principles of liberal democracy and exploits its parliamentary forms only to encompass their destruction. France, Finland, Italy, Malta, Cyprus, Greece and Turkey are so placed.

Within each category there are differences of degree. In the Irish Republic, among the countries of the first category, the shadow of the IRA is still not entirely banished from politics. The practices of the Ulster Unionists do not bear a close scrutiny. The linguistic fanaticism and racial prejudice of the Volksunie in Flanders are incompatible with parliamentarianism. There is a large Communist Party in Iceland and women don't have the Federal vote in Switzerland. Republicanism is stirring in Sweden where the constitutional order has been monarchical. In all these countries there is widespread scepticism about the pretensions of political parties and the efficiency of parliaments. But nobody expects a coup to be attempted, much less to be successful, in any of these countries and that is a rare enough phenomenon in the modern world to allow them to claim the title of unchallenged democracies.

Germany and Austria both wear borrowed clothes. The temptations and opportunities to discard them are apparently greater in Germany, a divided country of immense industrial strength, than they are in Austria, which is free of the foreign presence but obliged to recognise both by treaty and by her puny circumstances that she cannot be adventurous. In fact German democracy is a much more healthy growth: the 'proporz' system in Austria which has divided offices between the two big party organisations has stifled the growth of parliament by silencing opposition. At the same time the nationalist spleen of Austria has no chance of working itself off through diplomacy or economic competition. The result is the survival of extremist terrorist conspiracies aimed at the Italians in the Alto Adige but also possessing internal ambitions. However, Germany unlike Austria is coming to understand that parliamentary government is not incompatible with efficacy.

The countries where the enemies of democracy are still vocal and numerous are a very mixed bag. The two minor examples, Cyprus and Malta, are both essentially ecclesiastical states. Archbishop Makarios openly rules in Cyprus while the Roman Catholic Church in Malta has a decisive if less apparent influence. Cyprus is unusual in combining extreme Greek nationalism with the desire to merge with a larger country, and the inevitable hostility which this provokes among the Turkish minority makes constitutional government almost impossible. In Malta Mr. Mintoff and his large following do not accept the constitutional order and in turn are held to be beyond the pale of the devout.

In Greece the Communists, although disguised, are powerful. In the summer of 1965, using the widespread unpopularity of the crown, they came near to power. Military conspiracies and political strikes compete against the Athenian passion for political discussion, which is one of the most effective antidotes to tyranny if not a basic requirement of democracy. In Turkey a religious-minded majority use the democratic forms to defeat the social and economic measures which the intellectually liberal-educated class believe to be essential. Islam was the decisive ally of Mr. Demirel in the 1965 elections. The progressives here, as in some Arab and Latin American countries, find their friends in the army. The paradoxical result is reached that the most Western-minded Turks tend to be hostile to Western political institutions.

Finland is often regarded as a model Nordic country but in fact her democracy is precarious both internally and externally. The parliament sometimes fails to produce a government at all, and one then has to be composed of civil servants. The Communists hold a quarter of the seats. The Russians every now and again intervene to stop a movement they regard as unfavourable to them or to forbid the appointment of a prime minister whom they regard as hostile. It is interesting that Finland, menaced from outside and with 'une chambre introuvable', shares some characteristics with the Fifth Republic. In Helsinki, as in Paris, there is a prime minister who matters very much less than the president. The left without the Communists is nothing and as in France the Finnish Communists owe far more to the memory of a civil war than to widespread devotion to Marxist dogma.

FRANCE

The perennial fascination of French politics was for a time reduced by the consensus government of de Gaulle. Aghast at Algeria and irritated by the exaggerated evils charged to the Fourth Republic, the French public asked for a father figure and got him. The General's impeccable style made the surrender to his authority seem less abject. His careful use of words—unlike the far right with which he was unfairly compared, he always spoke in the name of the Republic—and his undeniable electoral victories made it difficult to make moral objections to his claims.

But the mood soon passed. By the end of 1965 France was moving back to government not by consensus but by conflict and horse-trading. There is a fierce fondness for political life in France which is occasionally silenced but easily reawakened. The Palais Bourbon was often dismissed as a comedy and sometimes passionately loathed but it seldom failed to draw an interested audience and its virtues were as real as its vices. Walter Bagehot thought the French parliament of his day was full of Disraelis. Certainly the standard of debate, if not always of behaviour, remained high to the end of the Fourth Republic. The instability of which de Gaulle and the Anglo-Saxons make mock was more apparent than real. In the first ten years of the Fourth Republic there was a much higher turnover of ministers in London than in Paris, with the admittedly important exception of the office of prime minister. Under the French system able ministers could spend years in the same post while in England they were reshuffled with alacrity.

There is no reason to suppose that France, free of the Algerian albatross, could not manage her own inimitable kind of democracy without benefit of the General's guidance. The danger to the present system, similar to an elective monarchy in which parliament has minimal influence, lies—as it did during the Algerian war—in the possibility that France may be subjected to external pressures as a result of de Gaulle's threats to break with his neighbours and allies. It is the exigencies of war, now happily remote, which have proved fatal to the parliamentary system in the past. Hope for French parliamentary democracy may now be all the higher since the deep ideological divisions in France have recently taken on an almost benign appearance. French commentators have begun to speak of 'political families' rather than parties and there is something reassuring in the phrase.

ITALY

While ideological conflict is less virulent in France, in Italy it still continues to hold a central place in political life. With the largest, and until Togliatti died, the most intelligently led Communist Party in Western Europe, and as the home of the Roman Catholic Church which has learned to refine its ideas and its political methods to the point of the exquisite, Italy could hardly be otherwise. There as in Britain before 1914 politics are meant to be passionate and expected to be intricate. Ideas matter and eloquence tells. The time of the technocrat—in politics it should not be dignified as an age— is not yet.

In the 1963 election Togliatti spoke to a crowd of twenty thousand for four hours, beginning his appeal for votes with a survey of the ills the Renaissance brought to Italy. He and some at least of his principal opponents understood the subtle interaction of new thoughts and old ideas, of present problems with past facts, which are the background wisdom of parliaments. It is hard to think of a single great parliamentarian who was not a considerable historian. But in Italy the irony is that the principal opposition party is hostile to the parliamentary order. Although Togliatti was approaching democracy when he died, arguing that successful Marxism demanded liberal methods of discussion, the conversion is far from finished. The totalitarian core remains in the Communist Party and is encouraged by the weakness of the democrats. That weakness is more one of intellectual, if not always honest, doubt, than of practical failure. Against this, it is a very important fact that the ravaged economies and shattered societies of Western Europe in 1945 were rebuilt by parliamentary governments. The *Wunderwirtschaft*, the Italian boom, the French escape from stagnation, owed much to Marshall Aid and purely technical factors but one of the underlying strengths of liberal democracy in Europe is that it has presided over the success stories of recovery.

Recently clerical reaction has found a new form in Italy. This is to make a sentimental appeal to those who combine generosity with simple-mindedness and to suggest that the gulf between the democratic and totalitarian order is not fixed. Elements in the Church are showing themselves as flexible towards Marxist as they once did towards Fascist authoritarianism. De Gasperi, the organiser of the victory of Italian democracy, understood that the success of liberal institutions in his country depended on reconciling the intellectual liberal and Social Democratic minority to the Roman Catholic majority and getting the Church to recognise that religion was not only compatible with, but safer under, a parliamentary than an authoritarian regime. When he died in 1954 he had advanced far but recent events have reopened the party to power for illiberal forces. For instance, the apparently innocent demand for greater power for the provinces in an over-centralised state conceals a demand to transfer into Communist and Nenni Socialist hands an armed police in four provinces which would cut Italy in half.

COMMON PROBLEMS

If French democracy is threatened by the consequences of her foreign policy—would her constitution and confidence stand the break-up of the European Community or the Atlantic alliance?—Italian democracy is threatened by internal dangers. On the whole, however, internal and external threats have diminished throughout Western Europe. Extremism is generally at a discount. The revival of fascism, like the slump, has often been prophesied and has never occurred. Since 1948 no European country has seen its parliamentary liberties destroyed by Communism. Perplexing problems rather than imminent perils are now the dominant features of European politics. The dangers of passionate conviction are being replaced by the difficulties of debilitating doubt. How far and in what ways can parliamentary institutions be said to be undermined by these problems and doubts?

Purely technical difficulties are more noticeable but probably less important than a failure of nerve and loss of confidence. It is true that the scale of modern government, the ramifications of a modern economy and the fluidity of a modern society make the day-to-day work of running a nation much more difficult than before 1914. What relevance has an annual budget in the era of five-year plans? How can a minister supervise a bureaucracy running into hundreds of thousands? What sure foundations for educational policy or penal law are there when moral values and social status are as mobile as they are today? Such problems are common to all the Western European states; it may further be asked whether the technical aspects of these problems or those of morale present the greater difficulty.

SCANDINAVIA

If mere scale or a top-heavy administration were the central weakness the Scandinavian countries might be expected to have come near to solving their problems. Their populations are small and in the economic sphere especially have a well-established practice of cooperation. There are no great political tensions—only a general dissatisfaction. Democracy is an unchallenged sovereign but not a very inspiring one. The design is brought up to date: ombudsmen are introduced; the Storting (Norway) and the Folketing (Sweden) televise their most important debates; the Danish second chamber has been abolished and the Swedish one is on the way out; Swedish parties are granted substantial subsidies to propagate their ideas; in Denmark a sophisticated version of the referendum designed to give a parliamentary minority the right of appeal to the country has been tried out. Political youth movements are enormous. The press in both the capitals and the provinces probably reaches a higher average standard than anywhere else in the world. All this is impressive, but unsatisfying.

The basic dissatisfaction in the Scandinavian countries springs from their isolationism and ineffectiveness on the European stage. Successful in many ways 'as nowhere else in the world' as Mr. Gaitskell once said, they still make little impact and are aware of it. There is a touching but slightly absurd interest in the debates of the General Assembly of the United Nations, since there in the lobbies with Dahomey and Panama, Denmark may seem to matter and Sweden to sway decisions, but most politically-minded Scandinavians sense if they do not recognise that for model democracies to play so small a part in extending democracy through the European mechanism to the supranational stage is an unfortunate reflection on their values.

There are 'excuses': professional neutrality in the case of Sweden; fear of losing their cultural identity; traditional distrust of Catholic Europe and recent dread of Germany. But excuses are not reasons and to the most self-consciously rational people on earth the situation is deeply disturbing. If Scandinavian democracy is to become much more than a well-oiled mechanism it must be willing to help to power future European democracy.

BENELUX

If the Nordic countries suffer from too quiet a life, some of the other small states have been too recently and for too long unquiet not to relish some repose. Such is Ireland's case, where pragmatic policies are replacing heroic stands. But Dublin has understood that the future destiny of Ireland is in the European Community and if her attitude to the Council of Europe is any guide will be in the forefront in developing its political and constitutional aspects. The Netherlands show the same spirit. The resistance of the Dutch government and Dutch opinion to Gaullism is well known. In Belgium the determination of M. Spaak to force the European idea forward and not just to concentrate on the commercial side of the Common Market is also famous. What the Low Countries are trying to do is to develop, on a European level, the parliamentary institutions which, for all their defects, have so much helped their own countries.

The Dutch parliamentary tradition is an old and proud one. It proved its value first in bringing the cities and towns together to defend their liberties and secondly in reconciling the religious communities one to another. Voting follows the confessional line to a very large extent in the Netherlands, but the necessities of parliamentary life have compelled the Protestant lion to lie down with the rapidly growing Catholic lamb. The Netherlands is historically biased towards the Protestant north. Her parliament, by allowing her Catholic citizens a full share in public life while permitting only slow change by consent, has preserved her unity as no other system could.

The parliamentary system is inevitably superior to one of personal or presidential rule in any seriously divided country. A man must be Protestant or Catholic, atheist or Marxist, a Fleming or a Walloon. Parliament must be a mixture and therefore less menacing to minority and majority alike. The collapse of the Belgian state would seem to be inevitable if her parliamentary system were to go. Under this system it pays the parties to straddle the linguistic gap, although the bulk of Belgian Socialists are Walloons and the mass of Catholic voters are Flemings. The incipient violence of a factious state which feels itself to be two nations is thus restrained.

The Benelux leaders, made aware by the second world war of the helplessness of small powers in modern circumstances, see in the European constructions now being built a chance to bring the spirit of compromise into international relations, not in temporary phases of good feeling but as a permanent characteristic of European civilisation. They have learned their political lessons in a harsh school, but of all the European governments they have been the aptest pupils. From the foundation of the Council of Europe there has been hardly any wavering. A simple thesis has been argued: Europe must be built and to be true to herself and her interests the building must have democratic foundations. So the Dutch by a virtually unanimous vote of their first chamber called for the direct election, at an early date, of the members of the European Parliament, at a time when many among the 'Five' were inclined to temporise with de Gaulle and his hostility to supra-nationalism.

GERMANY

If the politicians of some of the smaller states of Europe are seeking to enlarge the rôle of democracy, in some of the larger ones they are only just beginning to make it work. Germany gives some grounds for optimism. The Federal Republic provides by far the most civilised government Germany has had since she became a unified state. The competition may not be great but the achievement is considerable. The physical devastation and moral ruin of 1933–45 make as unpromising a background as could be imagined to the attempt to develop a German democracy, but in fact four general elections have witnessed the elimination of extremism. The reaction of the electorate has been healthier than that of their leaders. There was a public outcry when Herr Strauss raided *Der Spiegel*, and in the end, in spite of the protecting arm of Dr. Adenauer, he had to go. When Adenauer tried to gain control over the second German television service he was defeated by the Bundesrat (the second chamber).

All these gains could conceivably be reversed, but it does not seem likely. There is not merely material success but the beginnings of liberal sensitivity in Germany, the cultivation not only of the forms, but of the spirit of democracy. Few countries have shown themselves more aware of some of the new dangers to constitutional government. Reversing the general trend towards centralisation, Germany has given great powers to her Länder. She is helped by the memory of the princely states of old Germany, but it was a bold decision all the same. It is significant that the anti-democrats have made the federal system one of the main targets of their abuse. An attempt has also been made to protect the interests of the opposition and to put checks on the government's handling of spy cases. There is a Bundestag committee of six members, three from the CDU/CSU, two from the SPD and one from the FDP, which has the power to investigate spy cases and to see all the files.

The greatest weakness of the young German democracy is that it has not captured the imagination. It is pedestrian. The debates in the Bundestag are duller than those in most British county councils. Ministers sit on a platform and lecture the deputies. There is little humour and less wit. It is no answer to say that the best work is done in committee. No doubt it is, but as the committee meetings, although they publish a record, are not open to the press and public, they have small chance of enlivening public discussion. The Bonn system has many virtues, but it cannot provide that sense of participation, or of public drama, which is the strength of the British and French systems at their best. The challenges to power in Germany are still so concealed from the public in internal party conflicts that they do not necessarily reflect public opinion. Only when the Bundestag is seen to provide the 'grand inquest of the nation' will it have met the essential requirements of a parliamentary system.

Still, in many respects Bonn can demonstrate its superiority to Westminster. The political education provided may be less stimulating but the administrative powers of parliamentarians over ministers are much greater. In Germany, as nearly everywhere else in Western Europe, the age of specialisation is recognised by giving opportunity to specialists. Deputies work through a permanent committee system, not merely examining legislative proposals, but scrutinising general policy and the actual facts—not always related—in their own spheres.

BRITAIN

In Westminster there is an obstinate resistance to providing the structure and the means by which MPs could really exercise some control over governmental administration. It is not enough to boast of question time and motions on the adjournment when the opportunities for MPs to discover the really important questions to ask are so painfully restricted. The mother of parliaments is still regarded with respect on the Continent but also with a growing awareness of her arthritic condition.

Popular superstition still accords to the Commons a much more powerful rôle than it in fact enjoys. While MPs deny themselves the means which would allow them to examine effectively the administration and general policy of the government, as well as its legislative proposals, they will have little independent power. The interests will lobby in Whitehall rather than Westminster, and no argument however powerful will shake the Prime Minister from office while party discipline is as solid as it is today. The decline in the authority of the House, a matter of informed comment for over half a century, is masked by the dramatic confrontations across the floor. The pride of elected persons against which Lincoln warned more than a hundred years ago provides a cushion of conceit against reality.

Just how ineffective the House has now become in many of its most fundamental functions is revealed by the fact that not since 1921 has a single government estimate been rejected. The control of taxation, in classical parliamentary theory the keystone of the power of the representatives, has almost completely evaporated. This gradual degradation of parliament in Britain is the more painful in that the Commons remains capable of checking its own decline. There has been no shock to the constitutional system which has left British politics nervelessly twitching. Throughout the last war Churchill never failed to remind the House that he was its servant and indeed there was a notable revival of parliamentary influence during the war. The defeat of the proposed tax on books, the agitation on the rights of aliens in 1940, deservedly raised the good opinion of the House in itself.

Conclusions

Because the parliamentary tradition is so strong in Britain the weaknesses of the House of Commons suggest that they are the result of the age rather than the place. The inadequacy of parliaments is in fact as common a characteristic of modern Europe as their theoretical power, and cannot be corrected, as the Scandinavian examples show, by mere changes in the mechanism, valuable though these can be.

Parliamentary government depends for its vitality on belief in the power of words to alter facts. Darwin and Freud as much as Marx have made us doubt this possibility. The scientific age has little faith in the reality of reasoning as a means of arriving at value-judgments. Now politics are a matter of values. They are concerned with preferences much more than with probabilities and the more democratic a society the more this is true. But if at the same time the people believes that its motives and understanding are crude and limited, the values propounded by politicians will be mediocre. A parliament concerned always with gallup polls which collate the superficial judgments of the mass will seldom rise to heights. It is the growing belief that parliamentary government is necessarily, as opposed to usually, unheroic which undermines its authority. This may seem to be unlikely in the consumer age but the general response to Kennedy—more to the legend than to the fact—proves the deep-seated longing for courage and style in democratic leaders.

If modern parliamentarians seem petty it is often because they are concerned with petty problems. Matters which should be settled at a local level are drawn by the processes of administration to the centre and there, if not decided, at least debated. The preference for technicalities over ideals frightens parliamentarians away from the discussion of questions of principle. It is striking that of all the assemblies that have shown most deliberative vigour in the sixties the Vatican Council must claim a high place. St. Peter's may seem an odd place for the practice of the parliamentary arts but practised they most certainly have been.

This has been possible because, although divided on many issues, prelates live within a common frame. Strong feelings can be expressed and tough wrangles on profound matters sustained because of this. It is no accident that at the time when party feeling was far stronger than it is today, when personal rancour and division on deep questions were on almost daily display, the Commons was called 'the best club in London'. The characteristic of a club is not that the members like one another but that they agree to abide by certain rules. It is the absence of common rules which makes the parliamentary arena so often seem a sham and empty show.

The remedy would seem to lie in the development of parliaments at the European level. This is the common ground of the parliamentary democrats of Europe left, right and centre. This is the sole post-war cause which has captured the imagination of most of the young people of Europe. This is the only scale large enough to enable parliamentary institutions to grapple with modern economic problems.

Of course there will remain, especially in the larger countries, much to be done on a national scale. But it is becoming increasingly apparent that if parliamentary government is to be the pattern of the future it must move where power is moving, towards supranationalism. The failure of de Gaulle in 1965 and 1966 to disrupt the Community is of profound significance not only for the economic and diplomatic but for the constitutional future of Western Europe. His opponents took their stand on the Treaty of Rome and they consciously defended its constitutional principles. On any pragmatic view the struggle at Luxembourg was over a mere matter of detail. But as the House of Commons understood so well when it defeated the monarchy in the 17th century, the words, and the forms they clothe, are vital.

BIBLIOGRAPHY

Hill, Andrew and Whichelow, Anthony. *What's Wrong With Parliament?*, Penguin, London 1964.

Neumann, Sigmund (ed.) *Modern Political Parties*, Univ. of Chicago Press, Chicago and London, 1955.

Wheare, K. C. *Legislatures*, Oxford Univ. Press, London and New York, 1963.

Williams, Philip. *Crisis and Compromise—Politics in the Fourth Republic* (France), Longmans, 3rd ed. 1964; Shoe String Press, Hamden, Conn., 1964.

Institute of Electoral Research. *Parliaments and Electoral Systems*, London, 1962.

COMMUNISM IN WESTERN EUROPE*

JOSEPH R. STAROBIN

ANY appraisal of the Communist parties in Western Europe must begin with a distinction that may appear semantic but really touches on one of the most exposed nerves of this movement which claims a unique understanding of history, indeed the capacity to 'make' history, and yet which contemporary history has so badly lacerated. Communism is a factor, sometimes serious, sometimes vestigial, in Western Europe today; but 'Western European Communism' does not exist. There is no historically evolved fraternity of parties accustomed to mutual exchange and fitting their national particularities into a common strategy, based on a joint analysis of the economic and social terrain that since 1945 has become increasingly integrated.

The Communists are a collection of forces whose estrangement from one another has been concealed by a common ideology. Some parties are mere sects under ambitious (and often picturesque) chieftains, as has been the case in the Netherlands, Switzerland and Luxembourg. Others are the left wings of expiring or reviving nationalisms, as in Iceland or Cyprus and perhaps in Belgium. Some are the vestiges of movements whose followers have turned to left-wing Socialist parties en masse, as in Denmark and Norway. Certain parties may yet have a future, as in Spain and Portugal, whereas in Western Germany Communism is a ghost that broods over calamitous error and tragedy from which a once proud movement could not recover. Some parties, as in Sweden, strive desperately to achieve rejuvenation, rejecting even a formal solidarity with their ideological kinsmen. In France and Italy, where the Communists lead formidable electoral blocs, they cannot integrate themselves into their political communities with any real hope of influencing policy unless they undergo an inner transformation. This applies also to Finland and Greece where the Communists manage important electoral fronts, in the former case legally, in the latter illegally. Such a transformation, however, must call into question basic ideas and modes of behaviour, not the least of which is their attitude toward Western Europe as an entity.

The gathering in mid-June 1965 of nineteen Communist movements at Brussels was the first of its kind. Two years before, the Communist parties of the Six together with the British had met in the same city, whereas in Rome in 1959 only the Six had held their first meeting. The Dutch party in June 1965 refused to sign any part of the common declaration, even that aspect which projects a European security system, including both East and West, to replace NATO. The Swedish party did not attend at all, because it 'had

*Adapted, by permission, from the October 1965 issue of *Foreign Affairs*, New York. Copyright by the Council on Foreign Relations, Inc., New York.

L

just decided that no position can hereafter be adopted in its name, nor any declaration published, unless decided by its own elected organs.'[1] This 'isolationist' stand may in fact undo the regional, purely Nordic gatherings of Communists such as last took place at the end of 1962.

If, as Richard Lowenthal has observed, 'international Communism no longer has a single world-wide organisation, a single centre of authority, or a single orthodox doctrine,'[2] it is also true that the 'polycentrism' advocated by the late Italian leader, Palmiro Togliatti, has not taken hold. Part of the explanation lies in the curious relations between the two strongest movements, the French and the Italian. When at the end of May 1965 the new Italian general secretary, Luigi Longo, met his French counterpart, Waldeck Rochet, for the first time since the passing the previous year of both Maurice Thorez and Togliatti, it was noticed that they chose Geneva for their meeting place. Geographical convenience? Perhaps. The neutral ground was, however, appropriate. The two parties had been in sharp disagreement, both as regards what each of them was doing on its own terrain and the impact which divergent policies plus differences in style and stance had on each. The Longo-Rochet meeting appears to have been a turning-point, however, with the increasing abandonment by the French Communists of previous attitudes and the signing of a *protocol d'accord* in the winter of 1965—66. French Communism is now undergoing important changes in policy, such as the Italians have long shown within Italy, a new independence of Moscow, and a readiness to meet the French Socialists not only for electoral advantage but also to explore ideological reappraisal.

BETWEEN EAST AND WEST

The disarray of the Communist parties of Western Europe dates from their failure to make the integration and unification of their part of the world their own basic policy initiative at a time when, at the end of the second world war, they stood at the peak of their strength. The 'internationalism' of the Communists (so important an attraction to the survivors of war-torn Europe in the twenties) never really developed as a solidarity toward one another, except possibly during the struggle in Republican Spain and to some extent in the resistance to Hitler. Their 'internationalism' ran almost exclusively from each party toward the Soviet Union.

Western Europe was viewed essentially as a peninsula of the Eurasian continent which the Soviet armies had been unable to reach in time. The Communist parties saw themselves not as architects of a new relationship with the Socialists and Roman Catholics in the refashioning of this old centre of Western civilisation on some authentically autonomous basis, but as outposts to be held intact in terms of several calculations: the United States was assumed to face a post-war crisis on the scale of 1929–33 which would open the Western European economy to drastic socialisation; to avert this crisis (or find a way out of it) the United States would launch an anti-Soviet war. In 1949, the Communists asserted that in case of war Western Europe would be turned into a guerrilla area and the Soviet armies welcomed to the English Channel. The Communists conceived of their task as holding fast to post-war positions (they were almost everywhere members of the government) until the Soviet Union's economic recovery could stalemate Anglo-

[1] *Le Monde*, 11 June 1965.
[2] 'The Prospects for Pluralistic Communism', an essay in *Marxism in the Modern World*, Stanford University Press, 1965.

American military power. The Soviet acquisition of the atomic bomb appeared as a milestone in this strategy. The coming to power of the Chinese Communists gave it an intercontinental dimension. The Sino-Soviet alliance seemed to give Communism an Archimedean lever by which the earth itself could be moved.

The task of the Communist parties was thus to 'tread water' politically in anticipation of a transformed relationship of forces, in which the struggle for world supremacy was the cold war itself. This required avoiding the seizure of power in any country where, as in Greece, it threatened to involve the weakened Soviet Union. It also required a rigorous Stalinisation of each party, both to endure the historical interval and to communise Europe. As coordinates in this strategy the Communist parties were thus not simply Soviet agents, but supporters of the Soviet Union until such time as they could become its allies. The nuance is important because it helps explain the inner rationalisations of men who could claim that in facing the Axis they had been patriots.

But Stalinisation had to be unconditional. New leaders who had come to Communism in the Resistance and who proved hard to bureaucratise were everywhere shunted aside. In Norway, this took the form of a shabby conspiracy against the foremost Communist leader, Peder Furubotn. In France it forced the retirement of Charles Tillon and the disgrace of the veteran André Marty. Everywhere the Communists were prey to their own version of McCarthyism, which grew endemically in the atmosphere of a beleaguered force making a difficult passage toward either Armageddon or Canaan.

The trauma of the past decade (it was ten years in February 1966 since Khrushchev opened Pandora's box at the Soviet Party's Twentieth Congress) does not lie only in the successive detonations that have exploded the edifice of Stalinism. It lies in the realisation that all the circumstances which underlay the Communist options have been proven wrong, a fact which is not assuaged by the many miscalculations of Communism's opponents.

Western Europe has undergone a remarkable economic and social transformation, at rates of growth which exceed those of the Communist world. The decline of petty agriculture as well as of the small-merchant economy; swift urbanisation and the new mobility of labour; the rise of truly large-scale industry on new technological foundations fostering differentiations within the working class and a new technocratic middle class—all of it with a measure of planning and supranational institutions—these had the double effect on the Communists of turning their ideology into an anachronistic dogma while reducing their own appeal to marginal exploitation of transitory dissatisfactions.

This rise of Western Europe has been contemporaneous with the decolonisation of Africa and Asia. But far from collapsing when its colonial bulwarks were removed, as Lenin's essay on imperialism posits, Western Europe has flourished. In this entire process, the United States has come to have a relevance for European development far greater than is true of the Soviet Union and its disintegrating bloc. Quite apart from whether the United States has built a 'great society,' it serves, by the nature of the problems with which it has been grappling, as a mirror to Western Europe. The Old World faces on its own terms those changes through which the New World has been going, but to whose threshold the Soviet world has yet to come.

The Communists are able to derive some mileage by an over-simplified hostility to American imperialism; they capitalise on both the contempt and the jealousies characteristic of outmoded aristocratic and disintegrating lower-middle classes, the traditional ingredients of Europe's view of America. But the process of American life, its significance as the most advanced society in which socialising factors are at work within a democratic framework, has escaped the analysis of European radicals. Neither Europe's Socialists nor its Communists have ever seriously probed America's significance. They have always borrowed from a small fringe of American imitators who were permanent 'expatriates in their own country' and viewed the United States through European lenses. The leading Communist theoretician in France, Roger Garaudy, admits, as though it did not much matter, that he really pays no attention to American life and knows little about it.

Confronted by an era of coexistence in which the Soviet Union can neither assist them nor serve as an example—and indeed must answer for the monstrous legacy of Stalinism—the Communists have also had to face the bewildering sequences of the Sino-Soviet schism. At the outset many felt an instinctive sympathy for the Chinese. They seemed to be calling for an honest analysis, and their stress on the autonomy and self-respect of each party promised to give the Russians their long overdue comeuppance. China's pristine Leninism evoked a certain nostalgia among those who harked back to the memory of the early twenties, before Stalin had conquered and, to paraphrase Swinburne, the Communist world had 'grown grey with his breath.'

But the tone of the quarrel has been repulsive, 'reminiscent of village fights in bygone days and of soldiery on leave,' as one Swedish Communist put it in 1963. China and the Soviet Union have seemed to be as much concerned about border regions in untracked deserts as about differences in world revolutionary strategy. If national antagonisms are products of capitalism in decline, as Leninists have insisted, how explain their survival and indeed their intensification as Communist power has multiplied? More important, what the Chinese have seemed to be demanding is that the Communists in Western Europe 'tread water' and become outposts of China's ambitious project of encircling the West as though it were some sort of Kuomintang village to be undermined, surrounded and taken by a combined offensive from within and without. This was exactly the effort on which the Communists in Europe expended a quarter-century's accumulated political and human resources. 'Treading water' is an impossible task, especially for those Communists in Western Europe who want to achieve something with what they have, in this generation.

As for the Soviet party's counsel that national roads to socialism now lie open, the difficulty lies in the fact that it has been heard before, and twice abandoned, once in the late thirties and again in the mid-forties. If the Socialists and Roman Catholics whom the Communists want to persuade are interested at all in the agonising reappraisal now under way, they also place the burden of proof on the Communists. They are not at all sure (except in a few countries) that the Communists are needed. The situation is quite unlike the period of 1945–6 when their own wartime trauma drove Norwegian and French Socialists, for example, to consider fusion with the Communists.

Thus the question today is not whether the Communist parties side with the Soviet Union. Most of them do, while trying to keep their distance from the gyrations and imperatives of its policy toward China. As for the pro-Chinese trends, these exist as moods and tendencies, flourishing mainly where Communism has already been reduced to sects. Only in Belgium is there a significant pro-Chinese party (gaining perhaps a tenth of the vote of the official Belgian party) and exploiting mainly Walloon separatism and Flemish nationalism. The real distinction to be made among the Communist parties, as they confront an era for which their 'previous condition of servitude' did not prepare them, is whether they can undergo that inner transformation which the new European reality demands. Yet the paradox is that where they seem prepared for this inner change—in Italy, Belgium and, more reluctantly, in France—the question arises whether they must not abandon what is distinctively Communist about them. They are compelled to re-examine what, in fact, is meant by socialism in the first place, indeed, whether Western Europe needs it at all. Each stage of reappraisal opens up ideologically forbidden dilemmas.

THE COMMUNIST PARTIES OF SCANDINAVIA

In the Scandinavian countries, the chief trend is toward left-Socialist formations seeking a fraternal bond with the prevailing Social Democratic parties. As long ago as 1958, the Danish Communists expelled their long-time and foremost leader, Aksel Larsen, on the grounds of 'Titoism.' There-upon he organised a Socialist People's Party, took most of the Communist intellectuals and trade unionists with him, and in the November 1960 elections gained five times as many votes as the official party and all its seats in the Folketing, the Danish parliament.[1] This reversal was confirmed in the September 1964 balloting. The official party is left with some trade union influence and a daily newspaper, Land og Folk, once the leading paper of the left and now a heavy burden. When Ib Norlund, the official party's chief theoretician, is asked about his party's prospects, he foresees a long period of 'perseverance and endurance'. As for relations with Larsen, they are so hostile as to impede the mobility of the orthodox Communists, such as there is of it.

In Norway, the left-Socialist trend originated in 1961 within the traditional Labour Party. The consequence has been that even as the Norwegian Communists have retired some older leaders and have striven to dovetail their electoral tactics with the reigning Labourites they find the field pre-empted by the Socialist People's Party. The weakness of the Communists was indicated in the autumn 1965 elections for the Storting, when the Labour government was turned out partly because the left-Socialists interposed their own candidates, unpersuaded by the Communist effort to bring about some sort of unity. Moreover, the Norwegian party has been unable to rehabilitate its former leader, Furubotn, and his influential group; he was expelled as a 'British spy' or worse in 1949, but in fact he was a Norwegian cross between Peer Gynt and Joseph Stalin—at least this is how the Swedish Communists put it.

Iceland and Finland are special cases. In the former the Communists have been protagonists of Icelandic cultural revival. They have found common ground with two successive divisions among the Social Democrats, and had enjoyed until 1958 posts in the Icelandic government. Finland,

[1] The Socialistisk Folksparti gained 149,000 votes and 10 seats, compared with the official Danish party's 30,000 votes; in 1946 the latter had a quarter of a million votes and 18 deputies.

with its tormented history in relation to both Tsarist and Soviet Russia, is more readily understood as an Eastern European country, except that a Communist attempt to seize power in 1947 à la Prague was thwarted, without reducing its important mass following. The Finnish Communist Party does exert its electoral influence in its own name. It has for years dominated the SKDL, the Democratic Union of the Finnish People, a front organisation which embraces a variety of socialist-minded organisations and individuals. The intellectual weekly *Tilanne* has lately brought the ferment of the European left to a country where the Communists have been unusually rigid and cautious towards the changes within the Soviet Union. This has prepared the ground for a rather astonishing development—the breakdown of Communist control inside their own front. In February 1965, a non-Communist, Dr. Ele Alenius, was elected secretary-general of the SKDL, defeating the country's best known Communist, Hertta Kuusinen. Alenius has been calling for an end to the monopolistic influence of the Communists, and a fusion of all Finnish Socialists, independence toward the Soviet Union (within the limits of Finland's special position) and concentration on the new features of Finland's changing industrial-agrarian patterns to which the traditional verities have given little answer. No doubt this stance had much to do with the growth of the SKDL vote, within the framework of a Social-Democratic victory, in the early 1966 general elections.

The evolution of the Swedish Communist Party (CPS) has, unusually, taken place without splits such as envenomed Danish life, although the new leadership, under C. H. Hermansson, the former editor of *Ny Dag*, came to the helm at his party's twentieth congress in January 1964 after the most severe ideological reappraisal. Typical of the debate was the demand by Sven Landin, the former chairman of the parliamentary group and a leading 'rebel', that the Communists 'should endorse the democratic pattern of government that has evolved in our country and the consequences thereof should be reflected in its actions and standpoints.'[1]

The Communist change happened to coincide with parliamentary elections in which the CPS gained slightly.[2] More important, it achieved a balance of power in the Riksdag: after the 1964 elections the reigning Social Democrats lacked an absolute majority. This put the Communists in the limelight, and Hermansson and his aides acquitted themselves well in the national TV debates, showing a certain frankness and modesty. It has already been noted that the CPS simply did not attend the conference of the other parties in Brussels in June 1965, an independence attuned to Swedish traditions. On the other hand, Hermansson has been sharing platforms in Copenhagen with the dissident, Aksel Larsen, and with the left-Socialists in Oslo, much to the distress of the official Communists, especially in Denmark.

The constitution of the CPS is now being revised. A new category of membership has been created, making it possible for sympathisers to support the CPS without the usual party discipline, which further dismantles the old Leninist conceptions. Some serious thought is being given to a change of

---

[1] Sven Landin, 'Regeneration', *Ny Dag*, 9 November 1963. Also 21 December 1963. Ake Sparring, in 'Communism in the North', *ibid.*, believes 'there is every sign that the CPS is in the course of transforming itself from a Communist party of the traditional type into something that for want of a better description may be called a left-wing Socialist party.'

[2] The vote increased from 4·5 per cent to 5·2 per cent, compared with the low of 3·8 per cent in the 1962 local elections. The Communists had 8 seats in the Riksdag after the 1964 elections but managed only to restore the same percentage as they had in 1921. In 1946 they had 11·2 per cent of the vote and 15 members in the parliament.

name. This would not be unprecedented, since many Communist parties in Eastern Europe and Latin America have changed names without changing substance. But in the current Swedish atmosphere, the change would be more than nominal. The phrase 'structural reforms' (taken from the Italian Communist lexicon) crops up in conversation with Hermansson. He maintains that the Communists 'must never follow other than the democratic traditions of Sweden' and that 'further measures of a socialist character' must be taken 'in a normal way, via a majority.' He does not blink at the crucial if hypothetical question that embarrasses the French—namely, whether in any government in which the Communists were a leading factor they would agree that socialist changes might be reversible. Hermansson grants that 'we must follow the results of any vote against us.' He speaks of a new relationship with the Social Democrats, from whom his party should not be separated by a 'Chinese wall' or, he adds, 'a Russian wall or a Berlin wall'. Yet the new Communist leader is far less persuasive when explaining why Sweden needs a Communist movement at all, and what exactly a socialist Sweden would do that cannot be done by its welfare state. In speaking of the need for 'clear socialist ideas' and concepts of 'industrial democracy' or the insufficiencies of housing for all who need it, one wonders why any of this requires a Communist movement to bring it about.

THE MINOR COMMUNIST PARTIES

No particular pattern emerges from a study of the minor parties except that, while some have fallen into a fossilisation that preserves them intact, in other cases there are curious signs of stirring.

The Netherlands offers an example of petrification. Its Communist movement had vigorous socialist antecedents, many of whose leaders were forerunners of Lenin. During the war it reached its peak of 12 per cent of the vote, and its newspaper, De Waarheid, shot up from a circulation of 7,000 to a quarter of a million in 1946. Its chief figure, Paul de Groot, has shown an uncanny capacity for personal as well as political survival and has strewn the landscape with groups and factions, expelled over the years on every conceivable charge; their chief failure, it seems, lay in their inability to oust him. De Groot has abstracted one guiding element from the Sino-Soviet cataclysm, namely, to remain independent of everyone else on the basis of a pure and simple Stalinism, nurtured in his own political hothouse.

In Austria, on the other hand, a party that came out of the war with 5 per cent of the vote (despite the Soviet occupation, or perhaps because of it) has vegetated until recently. Last spring, however, this party took a swing toward full-scale 'revisionism'. After a deplorable incident in which an old rank-and-filer died after a beating by neo-Nazi thugs, a revulsion swept Austria and it brought the unprecedented sharing of a common platform between the Communists and the Social Democratic leaders of the country. Accident and circumstance often combine in Western Europe with such issues as the fear of neo-Nazism to place the Communists in a spotlight which nothing in their routine activity would warrant.

This consideration may also explain a certain electoral revival of the Belgian Communists, who seem to have begun a liberalisation within their own ranks as early as 1954, prior to the general trend. Faced with the disintegrating effects of separatism between the Walloon and Flemish sectors of the population, Belgium's unity as a nation is again at issue. The Belgian

Socialists have lost heavily by their unwillingness or inability to mirror either the demands for linguistic autonomy of the Walloons or the grievances of the Flemish, long the underdogs in Belgian life. The Communists have championed a restructuring of the country on the basis of a federation of the two peoples and the three distinct regions (for Brussels has by now a cosmopolitan character of its own). In Belgium, the Communists derive a certain satisfaction in being 'more Italian' than the French Communists to whom, of course, they are culturally very close. Perhaps this characteristic explains a slight increase of their vote in the May 1965 elections,[1] despite the defection of the pro-Chinese who have had the gall to take the identical name as the official Belgian Party and present themselves as the true believers.

The Spanish, Greek and West German parties have the common characteristic of suffering prolonged illegality, following grave defeat on the heels of very great influence in an earlier time. In Greece, however, the Communists play an active role through a 'front organisation', the EDA (which they do not entirely control), an organisation that has gained enough of an electoral position in the past half-decade to play a critical part in the tumultuous division of right and left. Part of the continuing trauma of the civil war is that the right tends to authoritarianism and the left to a 'popular front'. Were not the Communists racked by endemic factionalism (thousands of them live in far-flung exile from Soviet Central Asia to the Balkans, fiercely quarrelling about the past and the future) they could play an even greater part in this fluid political scene; their strength in Cyprus indicates that. The Spanish Communists, managing to maintain a greater continuity of leadership and policy than the Greeks, despite an equally painful exile of many cadres, is striving to make headway in the new generation of turbulent opposition to the Franco regime among students and workers, and in the Roman Catholic Church. The Communists project a policy of 'reconciliation' and 'alliance', with an appropriate emphasis on new roads to socialism, as is now prevalent in the West. They hope to influence the political landscape in Spain, fearful that it is changing without much reference to them.

As for West Germany, where the party retains its old name, the KPD, and so many old leaders and old habits, it strives to offset the rigorous ban of the mid-fifties with a bewildering variety of ineffectual 'fronts', especially on the peace issue. But it remains so much under the thumb of the East German Socialist Unity Party (SED) leadership that much of its activity comes to nought. Significantly, when the East German intellectual, Professor Robert Havemann, recently proposed that the KPD seek legality on the basis of at least the revisionism of the Swedish Communists, he was severely chastised, and this was, no doubt, one of the factors in his disgrace. The German, Spanish and Greek parties all have the nuisance of one or several pro-Chinese sects to contend with, proliferating in the sectarian atmosphere even as attempts are made, in the Spanish and Greek cases, to gain a more ambitious role.

The British Communist Party, with its characteristic attempt to maintain an aloofness and mediatory role in the Sino-Soviet dispute, has a position in the international Communist arena that its own activities in Britain do not merit. As its national congress of 1965 showed, its membership vegetates, as it has done for years, in the lower thirty-thousands. Its influence in key British unions continually declines while among university circles it is seriously in competition with a variety of ultra-left and pro-Chinese trends.

[1] With 4.6 per cent of the vote, the Belgian Communists now have a third of their 1946 vote, and have been outstripped by the Volksunie, the Flemish nationalist movement.

Its leaders would like to break away from the 'politics of protest' and become a movement dealing with the 'politics of power', as the veteran R. Palme Dutt put it. Therefore a policy of alliance with the Labour left wing is projected, and the British 'road to socialism' (which dates from 1951) is affirmed. But all this achieves little result. The rejection of the seventy-odd Communist candidates for Parliament in the March 1966 elections showed that the Communist gestures are gratuitous. Despite efforts to refresh its leadership and strike a new name and format for its daily paper, British Communism continues at best its quality of a non-malignant anachronism.

THE COMMUNIST PARTIES OF ITALY AND FRANCE

The Italian and French Communist Parties are unusual in that they can either take part influentially in politics or present serious obstacles to other political forces.[1] Despite fluctuations from more than 2,000,000 to something over 1,600,000 members, the Italian Communist Party (PCI) now has a quarter of the vote. It gained a full million in the November 1963 balloting. Its hold on local governments has declined since the Socialists joined a national coalition with a wing of the Christian Democrats. But the Communists still share in governing 1,100 communes with 8·5 million people. They are also decisive—in uneasy alliance with the Socialists—in the largest labour federation, the Confederazione Generale Italiana del Lavoro. The centre-left government may at any time find its survival depending on Communist votes. Italy's president, Giuseppe Saragat—the Social Democratic Party leader and old foe of the Communists—owes his election to them.

The influence of the French Communist Party (PCF) is far less pervasive. The party's membership has declined from the post-war peak of 800,000 to perhaps 250,000, of whom a third are reliable cadres. But its vote, except in some Gaullist plebiscites on Algeria, has remained at some 25 per cent of the total, giving it great political leverage. After Gaston Defferre failed in his effort to create a Socialist-Democratic federation of the non-Communist parties, the field was taken over by François Mitterand, whom the Socialists and Communists supported, and who gave a serious challenge to General de Gaulle in the presidential elections of December 1965. The paradox of the Communists' position lies in the fact that they are trying to find some common ground with de Gaulle, and not without success and with a suave reciprocity on the General's part. They share with him a strong animosity to supranational tendencies in Western Europe and a virulent anti-Americanism, even if the intellectual sources of both attitudes are quite different from those of de Gaulle. Maintained for twenty years as a party that could make its weight felt in the balance wheel of Soviet politics, the PCF—even if its left-Socialist admirers and rivals are constantly bewailing its *immobilisme*—can use its strength to impede long overdue realignments within French life, justifying its evasion of inner change on grounds of foreign policy. Gunnar Myrdal has called the Italian Communist movement 'a vast Tammany Hall', a metaphor which credits its common touch in Italian life, its capacity to wheel and deal, if not its principles. Annie Kriegel, in her study of the PCF's origins,[2] stresses that the French Communists achieved a 'pseudo-

[1] In both Italy and France small 'Marxist-Leninist' splinter groups under Chinese guidance have recently come into being. Though some of these formations have attracted prominent figures, they are divided amongst themselves and carry little weight as yet.

[2] Annie Kriegel, 'Aux Origines du Communisme Français, 1914–20', Mouton & Co., Paris and The Hague, 1964. *Cf.* the commentary of Eric Hobsbawm in *New Left Review*, London, May–June 1965.

L*

solution' to the basic dilemma of inheriting both reformist and anarcho-syndicalist tendencies, by sublimating them in a revolutionary party which did not enjoy a revolutionary situation. What the PCF became and what has enabled it to survive was the strategy of 'turning itself into a sort of imaginary global society, on the model of the Soviet Russian universe.'

The Italians, as their admirers in Western Europe like to point out, have formed a 'modern movement'. Most of its members are new and the largest body of its leaders came out of the resistance to Fascism in 1943–5. These young men, in their late thirties and forties, who have taken over from the veterans that survived Mussolini, are anxious to achieve something more than to wait for a favourable turn of events in the Communist world, with which they are deeply disillusioned. By contrast with France, where the old guard held on longer and the younger leaders were either bureaucratised or shunted aside, the Italian Communists give the impression of having created an 'open society'. They argue among themselves, form groups and publish the vote count in their central committee meetings; they mingle easily with political opponents. One Italian Socialist leader who otherwise opposes them declares in private conversation that the PCI's top cadres 'are cynical and strong, but men of a humanistic culture, not at all "killers", and far from Stalinism.' Some have a relatively recent immersion in Communist thought. Some have a technocratic bent, and others (as their Socialist opponents like to remember) were schooled in the last days of Mussolini's 'Social Republic'. There is an agnostic quality in the Italians, perhaps understandable in so Catholic a country, but also a profound admiration for the ability of the Roman Catholic Church to adjust to new realities, as it had been doing with Pope John's ecumenical movement. Proud of Togliatti's heritage, the Italians have made a legendary figure out of their founder, Antonio Gramsci, who died in Mussolini's prisons in 1937. In France, Khrushchev's famous denunciation of Stalin in February 1956 has never received an official imprimatur, and it was left to an opposition journal, *Unir* (which circulates 20,000 copies), to publish it. But the Italians now know from Togliatti's own writings that the venerated Gramsci had the deepest reservations about Stalin's treatment of the Old Bolsheviks, and they have food for reflection in the thought that, had Gramsci escaped to Soviet exile, he might well have perished in Stalin's purges.

Yet the vital dissimilarities of the two movements lie in something deeper: their divergent attitudes toward the problem of their own transformation. In France, the Communists have conducted desultory discussions with the Socialists and have begrudgingly granted that transitions to socialism would require a multiplicity of parties. The example of 'the Prague experience', the Czechoslovak coup of February 1948, has been renounced. Yet the PCF has much less difficulty making local alliances with Guy Mollet, the Socialist leader, throwing votes as bargains may require, than it has in re-examining its own past. The Communists emphasise unity of action with the Socialists but they do not really respect them as allies. Self-hypnotised by its own image as France's leading party, the PCF has great difficulty working with those on the left who have different origins or nuances of view. One example is Emmanuel d'Astier, an original Gaullist, who sought common ground with Marxism, but whose fellow-travelling newspaper, *Libération*, was run to the ground when d'Astier, who had long served the Communists as head of the 'peace movement', finally kicked over the traces.

Much of this is now changing, partly as a result of the new understanding with the Italians, partly as a function of the success of the 1965 elections, partly perhaps because of the 'new look' that Waldeck Rochet has offered. The French Communists are now seriously debating ideological revisions with the Socialists. They are demonstrating their independence of Moscow, as did Louis Aragon with his critique of the treatment of the Soviet writers, Daniel and Sinyavsky, all of which gives the PCF a new stature for the National Assembly elections of 1967. But their effort to ride the Gaullist horse as the general undoes the NATO alliance makes it difficult to come to terms with the basically 'European' attitude of their own allies. This is true even though the French Communists now pay lip service to the view which the Italians have held for years, that 'Europe' is a fact within whose framework the Communists must seek representation and democratisation.

The French Communists now devote a great deal of attention to Roman Catholic opinion, for a good deal of trade union life and much that is new among French farmers stem from Catholic concerns. Roger Garaudy, who recently took part in a round table on 'Christians and Marxists Speak of God', went further than his party has ever gone in recognising the importance of 'transcendence' in the human experience. He also went rather beyond the traditional PCF policy of the 'outstretched hand' toward the Catholics by urging Marxists 'to understand, to integrate and to realise the human basis of Christianity', while calling on Catholics to admit the 'purifying virtue' of Marxism. And he envisaged not so much a dialogue as a 'perspective of mutual instruction and emulation.'[1]

Italy, too, has seen a significant repercussion of both the changes in the Catholic world with *Pacem in Terris* and the acknowledgement by the Communists that separation of church and state does not exhaust the problem. In preparation for the PCI's Tenth Congress at the end of 1962, the party declared that 'today it is no longer a matter of overcoming the prejudices and sectarianism which constitute an obstacle to the collaboration of socialist and Catholic forces in obtaining immediate political and economic gains'. The issue was much more profound, that is, 'a matter of understanding how the aspirations toward a socialist society may find a stimulus in the religious conscience itself as it confronts the dramatic problems of the contemporary world. Herein the problem of religious rights in a new society presents itself in a new way.'

Left-Catholic circles, especially those around the influential Florentine weekly, *Politica*, quickly recognised that something new was being said. Moreover, when the former Soviet ideological boss, Leonid Ilyichev, came out with a famous pronunciamento denying any common ground between Marxism and Christianity and renewing the Soviet anti-religious campaign, the Italian Communists gave this the cold shoulder. The upshot has been an unusual volume, *Dialogo alla Prova*[2], in which Catholics and Communists have confronted each other's views and sought a meeting of minds. This volume has been circulating widely in both spheres of Italian life.

In 1964 the Italian leader Giorgio Amendola came forward with the concept of a new, unified party of the left, which he believes should embrace Socialists and left-Catholics. His proposal has become the major subject of the internal Communist debate, officially endorsed by Longo and the entire PCI leadership. Amendola made what he called 'a critical determination'— namely, that 'neither of the two solutions proposed to the working classes

---

[1] Publication of Garaudy's piece in the Catholic weekly *Témoignage Chrétien* brought a rebuke to the journal from the archbishop of Paris, 30 March 1965.

[2] Florence, 1964.

of the capitalist countries of Western Europe over the past fifty years (the Social Democratic and the Communist solutions) has revealed itself able, as of today, to realise a socialist transformation of society. . . .' Continuing in this vein, Amendola declared, 'I do not see how one will succeed in achieving today or tomorrow . . . what one has been unable to do in fifty years. A political organisation which has not reached its objectives in half a century, with the cooperation of three generations of militants, must seek the reasons for this failure and must know how to transform itself.'[1]

Thus the issue of the self-transformation of Italian Communism is posed. Yet what it means, and whether the badly divided Italian Socialists will respond, and whether the left-Catholics will find common ground with them, remains very much to be seen. Amendola clearly wants to shake off the old baggage. Whether a large body of the rank-and-file, reared in another tradition, will allow the change that most of the PCI leaders clearly see as necessary is another matter. In a sense, the Italian party is the victim of its own strength relative to those with which it hopes to unite. Many Socialists resent the PCI's hostility to the centre-left experiment, just as many Communists feel that the road toward the PCI's participation in government lay through tacit support of the centre-left and an effective pact of action with the Socialists, rather than a vague, if sensational, prospect of a unified party. The PCI's eleventh congress in January 1966 did not resolve its dilemmas. The diverse currents were contained, with secretary Luigi Longo's hold on his charging horses strengthened. But the Communists were powerless to prevent the Socialists under Pietro Nenni's lead from merging with the Social-Democratic Party. The prospect of the PCI's comparative isolation, despite its autonomous strength, continues. In a land where socialism has been a byword and a banner for a very long time, it still requires precise definition. The Italians are probably the only Communists who have the courage and the incentive to make this effort. Yet the very popularity, indeed promiscuity, of the old language may inhibit it.

[1] *Rinascita*, Rome, 24 November 1964.

BIBLIOGRAPHY

Adams, T. W. and Cotrell, Alvin J. 'Communism in Cyprus', *Problems of Communism*, XV, 3, Washington, May–June, 1966.

Caute, David. *Communism and the French Intellectuals*, André Deutsch, London; Macmillan, New York, 1964.

Devlin, Kevin. 'The Catholic-Communist Dialogue', *Problems of Communism*, XV, 3, Washington, May–June, 1966.

Griffith, William (ed.) *Communism in Europe*, MIT Press, Cambridge, Mass., 1964.

Horowitz, Daniel L. *The Italian Labor Movement*, Harvard Univ. Press, Cambridge, Mass., 1963.

Kousoulas, D. G. *Revolution and Defeat: the Story of the Greek Communist Party*, Oxford Univ. Press, New York, 1965.

Labedz, Leopold (ed.) *International Communism since Khrushchev*, John Wiley-MIT Press, Cambridge, Mass., 1965.

Lowenthal, Richard. *World Communism: Disintegration of a Secular Faith*, Oxford Univ. Press, London and New York, 1964.

Olmsted, Mary S. 'Communism in Iceland', *Foreign Affairs*, New York, January, 1958.

Weber, Herman (ed.) *Der Deutsche Kommunismus: Dokumente*, Kiepenheuer and Witsch, Berlin, 1963.

Wood, Neal. *Communism and the British Intellectuals*, Gollancz, London; Columbia Univ. Press, New York, 1959.

Communism in the North and *Red Opposition*, Swedish Foreign Policy Institute, Stockholm, 1965.

THE DICTATORSHIPS OF SPAIN
AND PORTUGAL

JOSÉ ANTONIO NOVAIS

SPAIN

DISINTEGRATION OF A REGIME

SPANISH ministers, and General Franco himself, constantly repeat that Spain has entered a period of evolution. In reality, this 'evolution' is the disintegration of Francoism.

Since 1947 Spain has officially been a kingdom, but without a king. General Franco, 'Caudillo of Spain by the Grace of God', holds all effective power: he is head of state, head of government, national leader of the Movement and generalissimo of the armed forces. He appoints and dismisses his ministers. He is answerable 'to God and History' alone for his actions.

Francoism is the expression of General Franco's will, but also that of the various forces which seconded the military uprising of 18 July 1936 against the legal government of the Republic. The range of supporters of the new regime was sufficiently wide—including Constitutional Monarchists and Christian Democrats as well as Fascists—to enable Franco to form a series of coalition governments, wherein predominated, depending on circumstances, the 'Fascist' or the 'Democratic' elements. This coalition broke up in 1957. The Falange (the Movimiento Nacional or Movement)[1] was almost eliminated, and for the first time the Christian Democrats did not participate in the government. A new force appeared on the scene—'the technocrats', whose members are for the most part members of or closely related to the Secular Institute of Opus Dei, a religious organisation which since 1957 has played an important part in Spanish politics.

On the other hand, General Franco has been very good at adapting himself to the changing circumstances of international politics. From 1939 to 1942 he played the Hitler card for all it was worth, but in 1942 started to veer towards the Allied camp. After the second world war he managed to unite the country behind him in the face of world-wide boycott. The Cold War atmosphere was, however, of advantage to him, enabling him in 1953 to sign both a Concordat with the Vatican and military agreements with the United States. The latter made it possible for him to set Spain's stricken economy on the way to recovery. The consequence of Franco's policies was that Francoism came to be accepted by the Western world.

The Economic Stabilisation Plan of 1959 brought Spain out of its economic misery, though at the expense of the Spanish worker. A development plan

[1] See p. 176.

was started in 1964, but results have been far from satisfactory. In spite of this, however, the standard of living has risen constantly, thanks to tourism and the remittances of Spanish workers employed abroad. Today Spain is on the threshold of a 'neo-capitalist' society, which combines the totalitarian system of the Fascist period with the liberal economy imposed by the technocrats to attract foreign capital and establish contact with the rest of Europe.

General Franco (b. 1893) is aging. Public opinion is awakening. The groups that are in power, the victors of the Civil War, are preparing to succeed him (neither the vanquished nor the new forces of the opposition having at present any part in political life). Thus we see the first stage of the regime's disintegration. Three factors contribute to this: first, tensions that have arisen between the various groups of victors with opposed political and economic interests and engaged in a race for the succession, and indeed tensions within each such group; secondly, the geographic and economic situation of Spain, which incline the country towards a political system similar to those of other West European countries; thirdly, the slackening of the reins of power not only with the passage of time but also under the pressure of public opinion, which is increasingly dissatisfied with present political and economic methods and structures. Though time has shown that large-scale change within the regime is unlikely since Francoism is essentially not open to improvements, some changes have taken place, especially in the last few years, though they have been minimal. To see why this is it is necessary to look at these changes in some detail.

POSITIVE ASPECTS OF CHANGE

The Press Law, April 1966

The Press Law came into force on 9 April 1966. Censorship prior to publication is abolished, and freedom to appoint newspaper editors without government approval is granted. The law is still, however, very restrictive. Limitations on editorial freedom are considerable and the official news agency EFE has a monopoly of foreign news. Article 2 reads:

> 'Freedom of expression and the right to disseminate information, which is recognised by Article 1, will not be limited in any way other than that established by law. The lawful limitations are the following: respect for truth and morality; compliance with the Law of the Principles of the Movement and all other Fundamental Laws;[1] the requirements of national defence, state security and the maintenance of law and order at home as well as peace abroad; due respect with regard to institutions and individuals when political or administrative actions are criticised; the independence of the courts and the safeguarding of privacy and personal and family honour.'

According to Article 69 of the Press Law, newspaper editors may be suspended for six months and fined a maximum of P250,000 ($4,170) and publishing houses may suffer suspension for three months and a maximum fine of P500,000 ($8,340).

Nevertheless, the new Press Law has had noticeable effect in increasing the amount of information available to the public. Strikes, cases tried by the Public Order Tribunal, criticism of the government-controlled Labour Organisation, an unfriendly reception given to Prince Juan Carlos on a foreign tour, illegal gatherings of students, outspoken praise of or attacks on the monarchy—more often the former—are incidents which, since the

[1] The Leyes Fundamentales (see p. 174).

Civil War, could generally only be heard of by rumour or through the foreign press. Now one can read about such matters in any Spanish paper, although reports are slanted in accordance with the varying ideologies of each. But this is where the freedom of the press begins and ends. It is quite logical that this should be so as the newspaper proprietors are identified with the regime. More than a third of all newspapers belong to the Movement, and of the others most are Monarchist and Christian Democrat. Of the news agencies, Prensa belongs to the Movement, Logos belongs to the Christian Democrats, and EFE is government-controlled.

Other liberal measures

The present official recognition of the right to strike is not due to the slight modification of Article 222 of the Criminal Code, which in its former version considered strikes the equivalent of sedition,[1] but is a direct consequence of the general strikes in the Asturias in the autumn of 1963, which the authorities were unable to prevent. Other liberal measures include the creation in December 1963 of the Public Order Tribunal to deal with political offences (previously the responsibility of military tribunals), a project for a Statute for non-Catholics, and admission of the press to the debates of the Cortes Committees. All the same, only one representative of each news agency is allowed to be present, while newspapers are not permitted to send their own correspondents and the foreign press is still barred. The suppression of the official Spanish Students' Union and its replacement by bureaucratic, ineffectual Student Associations has led to proliferation of illegal student associations; university professors have been dismissed for attending the latter.

NEGATIVE ASPECTS OF THE REGIME

While the official ban on political parties remains, there has recently been a proliferation of political parties. The traditional opposition parties, the Socialists, Communists and left Christian Democrats, have been joined by splinter groups from the Movement: left-wing Falangists, Carlists, Christian Democrat youth organisations, Social and Democratic Action and others. Power is still in the hands of Franco, and effective police vigilance makes it virtually impossible to meet, distribute pamphlets or organise strikes or demonstrations without attracting the immediate attention of the police. The social structure remains identical with that of the 19th century. All political and economic power still resides in the army, the Church and the 125 families of the conservative right which monopolise banks and industry.[2]

The Labour Organisation and trade-unionism

The only legal trade unions are those included in the state-controlled Organización Sindical ('Labour Organisation'), of which both workers and employers are obliged to be members. These so-called 'vertical' unions function at three levels: that of the worker (the 'social section'), that of the employer (the 'economic section') and that of the government-appointed officials who control the organisation. In a text-book still used in Spanish

[1] In its present version Article 222 establishes a distinction between political and economic strikes, considering only the former to be equivalent to sedition. But the question remains confused since the Labour Organisation is state-controlled.

[2] According to a recent survey banks control 56·4 per cent of the capital of Spanish limited companies.

schools, the theory of Spanish syndicalism is explained as follows: 'In accordance with National-Syndicalist doctrine, the Spanish Labour Organisation is a corporative institution corrected by the political line, which eliminates the insufficiencies of corporativism but takes advantage of its positive features.'[1] After 28 years in force, 'vertical syndicalism' has however proved to be totally impractical, which even its own officials have admitted.

The Franco regime has relentlessly persecuted all working-class movements that have not had official patronage. Members of trade union organisations that date back to before the Civil War (the socialist UGT and the liberal CNT) and of the clandestine trade unions that have arisen since (the Communist Workers Syndical Opposition, and the Workers Syndical Alliance composed of socialists, anarchists and Christians), as well as militant Catholics of the Workers Catholic Action movement, have been imprisoned at various times.

One of the most original Spanish trade union movements appeared in 1965: the Workers Movement. Originating around 1962 within the Workers Commissions under the Labour Organisation, this movement has grown on the factory floor. It is fighting for trade unionism within working class unity, disregarding all questions of political ideology. On 31 January 1966 the movement brought out a manifesto which was sent to all national authorities. This document constitutes the most remarkable political phenomenon that has occurred under Francoism, since it is the first serious attempt to organise wage-earners outside the Labour Organisation, while at the same time rejecting on principle the expedient of working clandestinely. This truly democratic movement has taken the government completely by surprise. It has so far been left alone and not been mentioned in the press. None of the hundred persons who signed the manifesto has been imprisoned.

The Church, ally and enemy of the regime

An article written by the abbot of Monserrat, Dom Aureli Escarré, published a few years ago in *Le Monde* under the title *Spain has lived through 25 years of victory, not of peace*, constituted the first open sign that the Spanish Church was beginning to reassess its relationship with the regime. The Second Vatican Council has since strengthened the position of those who are decried as 'progressive Catholics'. The Council stands for religious freedom, the separation of church and state, ecumenical collaboration, a dialogue between Catholics and Marxists. The application of its guide-lines would go against Spanish law. The Concordat signed in 1953 paradoxically impedes the application of the Council's principles. Six months after the Council was concluded, the Spanish Statute of Religious Freedom had not yet been approved and the Spanish head of state had not given up his right to nominate bishops, in spite of requests to do so from Pope Paul VI.

While the Spanish hierarchy[2] continues to live in a 'triumphal' era and still calls the Civil War 'the Crusade', the Catholic militants, the lower clergy and the young priests have taken to heart the lessons of the Council. New Catholicism in Spain is closer to the real problems of the people. Groups of priests and laymen, strongly influenced by the new Protestant and Catholic theology, identify themselves openly with the protests of

---

[1] E. Fuentes Quintana and J. Velarde Fuentes, *Política económica*, Doncel, Madrid, 1965.

[2] Described by a distinguished Spanish theologian as follows: 'Spanish bishops live politically in the shelter of and are defended by the regime; ideologically they remain in the last throes of the Counter-Reformation; in their pastoral activities they are hide-bound clericalists; their social ideas are paternalistic.'

workers and students. On 9 January 1966 twenty-two Jesuits sent a letter to the Spanish Commission of Bishops stating that 'in good conscience it is not only right but necessary' to fight against the political and economic structures of Spanish society 'though it be clandestinely'. The publications of these Catholic movements, though as yet representing a minority, are markedly independent, informative and critical. Among the most important are *Juventud Obrera*,[1] *Ecclesia* (organ of Catholic Action), *Signo*, *Boletin de la HOAC*, *Aun* and *Mas*.

ECONOMIC STABILISATION

The tourist boom and remittances of Spanish workers employed abroad produced a surplus in the balance of payments in 1964 of $296 million enabling the government to launch a development plan the same year. Under these circumstances, and ignoring the advice of the country's best economists—Tamames, Velarde and Figueroa—the so-called 'liberal' ministers of finance, commerce and industry encouraged a rapid increase in imports and the removal of tariff barriers, ignoring certain important structural problems of the economy, notably the agricultural situation and the lack of exports. A balance of payments deficit of $147 million in 1965 (imports 33 per cent higher and exports 1 per cent lower than in 1964) necessitated a sharp brake on expansion in the first months of 1966. Inflation and the balance of payments situation had been caused by a falling off of the increase in tourism (though the absolute figure remained high—14,251,000 in 1965 as compared with 14,102,000 in 1964), a decline in the number of workers outside the country and so in workers' remittances, and a large increase in public expenditure. There was a high exodus from the country-side (500,000 in 1965) and agriculture remained backward. In this situation consumers showed a desire in 1965 to catch up with the European standard of living. The cost of living increased by a monthly average of 13·2 per cent in 1965; a 9 per cent increase in salaries was provoked mainly by collective contracts; there was no improvement in taxation methods, which still rely some 61 per cent on indirect taxation.

Nevertheless, two facts show an undeniable improvement: per capita income has risen above $500[2] (Tamames gives the figure of $535) and the standard of living has quite clearly risen. In this connection it is worth comparing the standard of living in Spain with that in other countries, according to figures supplied by the OECD and the Statistical Office of the European Communities.

	Persons per room[1]	Passenger cars per '000 population[2]	Telephones per '000 population[3]	TV sets per '000 population[2]	Annual income per capita ($)[4]
Spain	0·9	21	73	40	570
Portugal	1·1	23	53	17	450
Italy	(1·1)	88	94	100	970
Great Britain	(0·7)	158	171	242	1,700

[1] 1964. [2] 1 January 1965. [3] End 1963. [4] 1964.

[1] The number for May 1966 was suppressed by order of the Archbishop of Madrid following the advice of the Government Information Office.

[2] Though according to a recent survey by the Spanish National Institute of Statistics 80 per cent of the population receive less than the national per capita figure, and 40 per cent of the population considerably less.

SPAIN VIS-À-VIS THE COMMON MARKET AND NATO

Spain's foreign policy has been based on two pacts: the Iberian Pact signed with Portugal in 1940, and the bilateral agreements of 1953 with the United States, which have brought General Franco's government into the Western defence system. Spain's 'African policy' and that of 'brotherhood with the people of Latin America' remain largely rhetorical.

Since more than 60 per cent of Spanish exports go to the Common Market countries, the European Community is of vital importance to the Spanish economy. For the Franco government admission is, of course, not only of economic importance, but also involves its political prestige. On 9 Feburary 1962 the Spanish government requested association with the Common Market with a view to full membership in the future. The Common Market let four years go by without replying. In fact, the political structure of a regime like that of Franco is not permissible within the rules laid down by the Treaty of Rome. At the beginning of 1966, however, Paul-Henri Spaak, then President of the Council of Ministers, offered Spain, on behalf of the Community, a wide-ranging economic treaty, pointing out that membership was out of the question. The Spanish government replied that for reasons of prestige it was unable to accept this proposal. Since then Spanish diplomacy has aimed at getting bilateral agreements with the Six individually. At the same time Spain is developing closer relations with the countries of Eastern Europe, including the Soviet Union.

'Spain has never requested admission to NATO', Foreign Minister Castiella has said many a time. Nevertheless the main reason why Spain is not a member of this organisation is the opposition of the Scandinavian countries to Francoism. After the crisis of the French withdrawal in 1966, however, Franco appeared to be seeking to join with the support of the United States. For this purpose Spanish diplomacy can rely on Spain's important strategic position: it can exert pressure on Gibraltar and the airspace crossed above Spanish territory by the planes going to the base which Germany has constructed in Beija, Portugal.

In any case, the future of Spain's foreign policy is linked to what will happen in the post-Franco era. Only then will it really be decided whether Spain will or will not be able to participate fully in the Western European system.

THE PROBLEM OF SUCCESSION

According to the law of succession to the position of Head of State, General Franco's successor must be 'Spanish, more than thirty years old, Catholic and of royal blood'. Moreover, he must swear allegiance to the Leyes Fundamentales and 'loyalty to the principles underlying the National Movement'. If there is no person of royal blood available who fulfills all these conditions, a regent of the kingdom may be appointed.

This law presents an endless tangle of dynastic problems, since a number of pretenders have staked out their claim to the throne: Don Juan, son of Alfonso XIII, the last king of Spain; his son Don Juan Carlos; Don Javier, leader of the Carlists, and his son Don Carlos-Hugo, husband of Princess Irene of the Netherlands; Don Francisco José, and others. Moreover, whether the country will today accept a law passed in 1947 is open to question.

General Franco himself does not comment on the situation. The most he has ever said is that 'the Movement will succeed itself', and that the laws

which will solve the problem of the succession are being worked out.[1]
Given the present-day power structure in Spain and current pressures, it
would seem logical to expect that Franco's successor would be a member of
the dynasty of Bourbon Battenberg, either Don Juan or his son, who would
thus establish the continuity of the liberal monarchy of the last Spanish
kingdom. But the question remains whether a monarchy will prove acceptable to all those Spaniards under 45 who have never known one.

PORTUGAL

A REPUBLIC 'SUI GENERIS'

'Portugal is not a country, Portugal is a tragedy,' says the poet. Responsibility
for the limitations of personal freedom, widespread illiteracy, low economic
development, medieval living conditions for the overwhelming majority
and no possibilities of emigration rests largely with one man, Don Antonio
de Oliveira Salazar. Manuel Rino, Director of Information of the Portuguese
National Secretariat of Information, explained to *Le Monde* in January 1966
that on 29 May 1926 the army, led by General Gomes da Costa, ended
political anarchy without shedding a drop of blood. He added that the
military did not know what to do with the power it held and therefore, a
few months later, asked Dr. Salazar to take charge of the exchequer. Salazar
accepted this ministerial post on the condition that he would control the
spending of all other ministries. Six years later (1932) Salazar became
President of the Council of Ministers, though in fact he had been the arbiter
of Portuguese politics from the time of the military coup. In this position
Salazar remains to this day.

1933 is the crucial date in the history of the regime. It gave birth to the
constitution—approved by plebiscite—by which the regime abides in theory,
and to the National Statute of Labour which, according to official texts,
laid down the guide-lines to the nation's corporative organisation. The
result was a republic 'sui generis, unitarian and corporative'—as defined by
Salazar—which tolerates freedom of religion, prohibits that of association
and that of the press, has abolished the death penalty (though unofficially
the security police, Policia Internacional de Defensa do Estado (PIDE)
interprets this precept with some elasticity) and outlaws strikes. At the helm
of this republic stand, on paper at least, four institutions: the Head of State,
the National Assembly, the Government and the Courts. In practice, all
power is in the hands of Salazar. He appoints the President of the Republic,[2]
makes all the decisions and exercises all controls. He also directs the only
legal political party, the Union Nacional, whose slogan is 'all for the Nation,
nothing against the Nation.' Salazar, the 'modest dictator', is a living myth
in Portugal, exercising personal austerity in his way of life and careful
pragmatism in administration, eschewing publicity and rarely making
speeches.

[1] Statements made to the *Chicago Tribune*, April 1966.

[2] The Presidents have been General Carmona (1928–51), Marshal Craveiro Lopes
(1951–8) and Admiral Américo Thomaz (since 1958). According to the constitution the
President must be elected for a term of seven years by a complex electoral body consisting of
members of the National Assembly and the Corporative Chamber and representatives of
municipalities and overseas provinces.

The PIDE

The power of Salazar rests on the powerful PIDE, through which democratic elements are successfully kept in check. The PIDE has considerable means and is responsible to no-one; its methods are secret but are known to include torture. Portuguese law allows for a prisoner to be held in solitary confinement for six months before he is brought before a magistrate. No-one will know anything about a man arrested by the PIDE; no newspaper will publish the news, and relatives and friends may hear only months later that he has been condemned or that he has died 'of natural causes' in prison.

The PIDE acts, discreetly, but at times the system fails. In 1961 Captain Galvao, a former governor of Angola who had spent several years in prison because he had denounced corruption within the regime, drew attention to conditions in Portugal when he hijacked the *Santa Maria*, one of the most important ships of the Portuguese merchant fleet. On 13 February 1965 General Delgado, a former presidential candidate, was murdered in Badajoz, Spain. One year later Spanish magistrates formally accused agents of the PIDE of having perpetrated this crime.

The press under censorship

Although the constitution (Article 8, paragraph 4) points out that self-expression is one of the rights of the citizen, all newspapers carry a notice saying: 'This issue has been passed by the Censorship Commission'. Censorship is extremely strict with regard to all matters concerning government policies, the overseas territories and the war being waged in them, though it is tolerant, as is usual in dictatorships, with regard to administrative problems and above all public services. In spite of the censorship some newspapers— not those with the largest circulation—subtly express their own ideology; these include *As Novidades* (Christian Democrat), *Republica* (Republican and the chief opposition mouth-piece) and *A Voz* (monarchist).

POLITICAL SITUATION

Official political groups

Apart from the Union Nacional there exists a 'Fascist' minority group led by Carlos Eduardo de Soveral, which publishes the magazine *Tempo Presente*, subsidised by the Government Press Office, and a neo-Fascist group of the Jeune Europe type led by Fernando Quedes and Goulart Nogueira.

In recent years the Secular Institute of the Opus Dei has seen its influence increase considerably, mainly in the economic sphere, although it suffered a serious setback through the 'Ortega Pardo scandal'. This involved a well-known member of the Order who represented Spanish banks in Lisbon and was on the boards of several important companies and banks; he fled to Venezuela in October 1965 with $225,000 and a suitcase full of jewels. Among those who are also said to be members of the Opus Dei are Cavaleiro Ferrera, former cabinet minister under Salazar; Arthur Cupertino de Miranda, a rich banker; Daniel Barbosa, a former finance minister; and Teixeira Pinto.

Opposition political groups

In spite of being outlawed, and in spite of constant persecution by the PIDE, political parties are continually extending their activities, and their ranks are swelled by a new generation of students, young professional men and the wave of militant Catholics who have understood their political future more clearly in the light of the pronouncements of the Vatican Council.

Nevertheless, the importance of these political parties should not be exaggerated; as in every dictatorship, their members are a minority.

The most important group is Acción Democrática y Social, which put up 40 candidates in the last elections, though these were eventually withdrawn. Its most distinguished figures are a former minister, Azevedo Gómez y Cunha Leal, a lawyer, Arlindo Vicente, and the Bishop of Oporto (who lives in Lourdes). There is also a dissident monarchist party led by Francisco Sousa Tavares, not to be confused with the 'semi-official' monarchism of the Pretender Duarte Nuno, who subscribes to the policies of Salazar. Finally there is the Communist Party, which is ruthlessly persecuted and whose secretary-general, Alvaro Cunha, has fled the country.

Most of the men known to be more or less of the left are in exile, mainly in Brazil, where they have formed the Frente Porgugués de Liberación Nacional, the Movimiento de Acción Revolucionaria and the Frente de Acción Popular. In the colonies the main exiled opposition parties are the Frente de Libertacão de Mocambique (FRELIMO) in Dar-es-Salaam, the COREMO in Lusaka, the Movimento Popular de Libertacão de Angola (MPLA) led by Agostinho Neto and the Frente de Libertacão Nacional de Angola (FLNA) led by Holden Roberto.

National Assembly elections, November 1965

In the weeks preceding elections to the National Assembly opposition political parties are allowed to organise meetings and publish manifestoes. This freedom is aimed at public opinion abroad, but opposition parties are hopelessly handicapped by lack of effective organisation and of press coverage. For the elections of 7 November 1965 Salazar amended the constitution, limiting the suffrage to persons able to read and write and paying a minimum amount in taxes—i.e. about 16 per cent of the population of Portugal and 7 per cent of that of Portugal and its overseas territories combined. The reason for this amendment was that in previous elections General Delgado had obtained 23 per cent of the poll.

The Acción Social Democrática put up 40 candidates and published a manifesto pronouncing itself in favour of self-determination in the colonies and certain freedoms, demanding that those responsible for the death of General Delgado should be punished, and calling for the liberation of political prisoners. At the same time another manifesto of Catholic inspiration circulated, denouncing 'a regime which calls itself Catholic but which violates the rights considered basic by Christians'.

The opposition candidates requested that the elections be postponed by one month because, not having had access to the electoral lists, they did not have sufficient time to organise even the most minimal campaign. Since their demand was rejected, they decided to withdraw their candidature. According to official sources, 70 per cent of the electorate went to the polls. Of the 130 members of the Union Nacional who were elected, 23 represented the overseas territories.

The question of Salazar's succession remains unanswered. No effort so far has been made to pave the way. The prospects at present are that when Salazar dies he will leave behind him a political void.

THE WORLD'S LAST COLONIAL EMPIRE

Angola, Mozambique, Portuguese Guinea, São Tomé and Principé, Macao, Timor and Cape Verde—in Africa, Asia and the Atlantic, Portugal possesses vast territories, twenty times larger than the mother country, with huge unexploited resources, which Salazar is not prepared to relinquish 'while there remains', in his own words, 'a single Portuguese to defend them with his blood'. For apart from being the pride of Portuguese history these territories are a source of salvation for Portugal's deficient economy; they also have strategic importance, which is of considerable use when it comes to bargaining with other countries.

The question of independence for the Portuguese colonies is brought up at the United Nations from time to time. On 21 November 1965 the General Assembly approved a resolution (66 votes in favour, 26 against and 16 abstentions) in support of a world-wide boycott on trade and arms-deals with Portugal, which furthermore required all countries to break off diplomatic relations with Lisbon.[1] But this resolution was never put into practice. Meanwhile Portugal's war against the leading Angolan liberation movement, the Uniao das Populacões de Angola (UPA), continues to cost 40 per cent of the national budget and hundreds of lives every year and obliges Portugal to borrow from other countries.

As for the situation of the native peoples of the colonies, Salazar claims that government attitudes are humane, that all the native peoples are Portuguese and that an enormous effort is being made to 'assimilate' them. In fact, in order to achieve the same rights as the whites, the Negroes—*pretos* in Portuguese—have to fulfil three requirements: they must know how to read and to write and they must be regularly employed. It is sufficient to say that more than 75 per cent of the population in the colonies is illiterate.

ECONOMY

The first development plan was launched in 1952, but was dishearteningly ineffective. The situation of agriculture remains unchanged. Arable land is owned 66 per cent by 8 per cent of land-holders, and the remainder is shared between some 427,000 small farmers. Farms are of unproductive size: there are large estates in the south and innumerable small-holdings in the north. According to the latest statistics, there are only some 60,000 farms of a reasonable size. Fifty per cent of the agricultural labour force produces 7 per cent of the national product. Agricultural products of one kind or another constitute 60 per cent of all exports (mainly cork and wine). Agricultural wages are extremely low—E29 ($1) per day—and unemployment is widespread. The average annual income of a peasant is E3,700 ($127).

Investment in agriculture is practically non-existent. Since the yield of each unit is very small and property very much divided, the produce obtained is sufficient for home consumption only, and nothing is left over to be sold. Movement of labour is discouraged inside the country and forbidden abroad. Thus at the expense of miserable living-standards for half the population, the stability of the escudo is maintained. If peasants were free to leave the land, a shortage of manpower would cause a rise in agricultural wages which would inevitably affect prices and labour costs. The bar on emigration is however frequently ignored. There are innumerable clandestine organisations which transport workers to France after providing them with false passports. The trip costs P10,000–20,000 (£60–120) and

[1] Portugal is a member of EFTA, NATO and the United Nations, and is allied to Britain (Windsor and Mentheu Pacts) and Spain (Iberian Pact); a Concordat with the Vatican was signed in 1940.

sometimes more. This means that emigrants must work for roughly one year in order to find the money to emigrate. The Spanish press frequently mentions the discovery by the police of some vehicle laden with Portuguese workers.[1]

The demographic structure, typical of underdeveloped countries, constitutes a grave obstacle in the way of the country's economic growth. Four-fifths of the population lives in villages and small country towns. With almost 10 million inhabitants, Portugal has only two large cities— Lisbon (800,000) and Oporto (400,000), and four medium-sized towns which together have 200,000 inhabitants.

The economic life of the country is concentrated in the 50-kilometre-wide coastal strip which stretches from Setubal to Braga. In fact, not even this privileged strip has enjoyed a harmonious economic development. The agriculture of Beira, Litoral or Miño is as backward as that of Tras-os-Montes or Alentejo. Nevertheless, all the cities and almost all industrial centres, as well as all large banks, large companies and most capital are contained in this coastal strip. It also holds all the universities (Lisbon, Oporto and Coimbra), most colleges, all the important newspapers and publishing houses, as well as a population that is almost entirely literate.

The industrial sector is scarcely developed. Mineral resources are few (discounting the mineral resources of Angola and Mozambique, which are for the most part still unexploited). The most important industry is that of textiles, based mainly (83 per cent) on raw cotton acquired at low cost from the colonies. The most important export industry is canning, and tinned sardines are the second largest export after cork.

The backwardness of the Portuguese economy and the absence of a minimum of political freedom required by the Treaty of Rome means that the possibility of Common Market membership, to which Portugal, like some other EFTA members, aspires, is non-existent. Moreover, the association of Portugal to the Common Market would require special arrangements for its own weak industry which would be quite unable to compete successfully with the highly developed industries of the Common Market countries. Furthermore, Portugal would provide so small and so poor a market (of 9–10 million Portuguese, not even half may be considered potential consumers) that the country is of little interest to the Common Market countries.

[1] One of these smugglers of men who, though they speculate with the poverty of the peasants, are well thought-of in Portugal, told the present writer that his most successful transaction involved taking 200 peasant men and women, dressed up as priests and nuns, across Spain in four coaches clearly marked: 'Third Pilgrimage to Lourdes from Alentejo'.

BIBLIOGRAPHY

Atkinson, W. C. *A History of Spain and Portugal*, Penguin, London and Baltimore, Md, 1960.

SPAIN

Payne, Stanley G. *Falange: A History of Spanish Fascism*, Stanford Univ. Press, Stanford, Calif., 1961; Oxford Univ. Press, London, 1962.
Thomas, Hugh. *The Spanish Civil War*, Harper, New York, 1961; Penguin, London, 1965.
Welles, Benjamin. *Spain: The Gentle Anarchy*, Frederick A. Praeger, New York; Pall Mall Press, London, 1965.

PORTUGAL

Anderson, Perry. *Le Portugal et la fin de l'ultra-colonialisme*, François Maspero, Paris, 1963.
Delgado, General Humberto. *The Memoirs of General Delgado*, Cassell, London, 1964.

de Figuereido, Antonio. *Portugal and its Empire: The Truth*, Gollancz, London, 1961.
Fryer, Peter and Pinheiro, Patricia McGowan. *Oldest Ally: A Portrait of Salazar's Portugal*, Dobson, London; Hillary House, New York, 1961.
de Oliveira, A. 'Salazar's Portugal', *Angola: Views of a Revolt*, Oxford Univ. Press, London and New York for Institute of Race Relations, 1962.
Pintado, V. Xavier. *Structure and Growth of the Portuguese Economy*, EFTA, Geneva, 1964.
Zeiger, Henry A. *The Seizing of the Santa Maria*, Popular Library, New York, 1961.

ECONOMIC AFFAIRS

THE ECONOMIC CHARACTER OF
WESTERN EUROPE

MARIANNE GELLNER

THE countries of Western Europe share certain common features which are rooted in geographical proximity and historical experience, and which have been strengthened in the last two decades by political as well as economic pressures, exerted both from without and from within. These common features of the Western European countries have been reflected in a remarkable similarity in their domestic economic policy objectives, widespread recognition of a community of interest, both in relations with each other and with the rest of the world, and the new common problems and opportunities presented by a rapid and accelerating rate of technological change.

EUROPEAN NEO-CAPITALISM

The common point of departure underlying domestic policy objectives in Western Europe lies in the existence of capitalist systems based predominantly on private ownership and private enterprise except in certain basic sectors. Within this framework, and with the lessons of the 1930s vividly in mind, Western European governments have concentrated in the last two decades on evolving and perfecting policy instruments that supplement and guide the market mechanism in pursuit of certain broad objectives. These may be defined as the fullest utilisation of national growth potential, full employment, stability of prices, balance of payments equilibrium, and the raising of living standards on a broad base. The achievement of sustained growth without inflation such as will be consistent with external balance and the demands of social justice has thus been the general aim of economic policy.

The emphasis and expression given to each of these policy objectives has differed, of course, from country to country, depending on national circumstances. Moreover, national attitudes towards these objectives have also changed over time. In the earlier post-war years, for example, the collective memory of pre-war experience weighed heavy and lent special significance to the objective of full employment in Britain, but to the maintenance of price stability in West Germany, and to the build-up of an improved economic infrastructure and industrial efficiency in France. More recently, accelerated economic growth has come to the forefront of British policy objectives whereas more equal income distribution has gained emphasis in West Germany and France. Rather different considerations have necessarily applied to the less developed countries—Greece, Turkey, Spain, Portugal and Ireland—where the need for fundamental structural change represents the primary economic problem.

As a broad generalisation, however, it can be stated that the primary concern of government intervention in the free market mechanism has progressed both in content and in method since the post-war 'Keynesian revolution'. The latter brought the recognition that governments should be both able and expected to pursue policies that would ensure economic stability. The emphasis was on avoiding mass unemployment; the main concern was for controlling the trade cycle, chiefly by adjusting aggregate demand to the available supply. More recently, attention has been extended, over and above the shorter-term concern over trade cycles, to factors that govern long-term economic growth and the problem of 'creeping' inflation under full employment conditions, raising policy issues related to the supply and allocation of labour and capital.

Moreover, the traditional juxtaposition of centralised government direction of the economy on the one hand, and the free sway of private initiative disciplined only by market forces with the minimum safeguards on the other, is being overtaken. Instead, the view is gaining ground that there is room for government intervention on quite a broad front as a normal and essential supplement to the working of the price mechanism, and the search is generally for the widening of public participation in economic policy determination through reinforced parliamentary control and three-cornered consultation and cooperation between government, management and labour, with the proviso that the principle of free wage bargaining is maintained. This reappraisal of the functions of government, development of new organisational machinery and refinement of economic policy instruments have marked out Western Europe as the testing ground for advanced industrial mixed economies, i.e. economies which rely primarily on market forces but where the state plays a significant role and the emphasis is on government initiative for a better command of the economic and social environment.

A notable expression of this evolution in attitudes has been experimentation in national planning—pioneered by France, the Netherlands and Norway during the period of post-war reconstruction and adopted since then by one Western European country after another with the important exception of West Germany. But although the latter has been fighting shy of acknowledging the virtues of a 'guided' market economy, stressing only the social security aspect of government intervention, its economic working has in practice not been far removed from the general trend. To sum up, the general trend has been away from reliance on the autonomous and automatic functioning of the market towards a more purposefully organised private enterprise system geared to the attainment of general policy goals. It has been reinforced by the desire to minimise economic uncertainty in an age of rapid change and has entailed a move away from doctrinaire orthodoxy towards greater flexibility in the management of national economies.

External Pressures and International Cooperation

The basic internal driving forces behind the post-war developments just described were, of course, social pressures for the progressive attainment of general prosperity. No less important in shaping the character of the present-day Western European economies have been external pressures and the general world environment.

On the political side, a rapid readjustment was necessary to the polarisation of world power in the United States and the Soviet Union. Further, the need was felt for an effective answer to the economic challenge of the communist system, which hardly touched the economic might and social fabric of the United States but pushed uncomfortably against the door of Western Europe. An acceptable framework had to be found for the re-entry of Western Germany into the family of nations. Traditional relations with the primary producing countries were being thrown out of gear by the loss of empires and the emergence of the north–south confrontation between the world's rich nations and the poor.

On the economic side, the philosophy on which the post-war international trade and monetary system has been based—that of multilateralism and anti-restrictionism—exerted an important influence on the formulation of national and regional policies in Western Europe. So did the historic Marshall aid offer of the United States. There ensued, on the one hand, the flow of capital from the United States to Western Europe (Marshall aid proper amounted to $13,000 million over four years but the total transfer of official capital in the first post-war decade, including military expenditure, was nearly twice as large); this—and the accompanying flow of technical know-how—helped to give Western Europe some leeway and the confidence to gain the initial impetus for economic expansion. At the same time, the Marshall offer provided the incentive for Western Europe to get together in the Organisation for European Economic Cooperation (OEEC).

The OEEC was important primarily during the first post-war decade of acute world dollar shortage. Its main significance undoubtedly lay in opening the way—through the European Payments Union and trade liberalisation measures—for a dramatic revival in intra-European trade, but it probably helped to establish new habits of thought in a much wider sense. In the Convention for European Cooperation,[1] signed in Paris on 16 April 1948, are, in fact, enshrined Western Europe's present-day economic goals with the one significant difference that 'development of production' and 'efficient use of resources' were then thought of in relation to post-war recovery and the dollar shortage rather than as a part of the conscious pursuit of long-term economic growth.

The international monetary system—the gold exchange standard—set up at the Bretton Woods conference in 1944 was brought fully to the test only after the *de facto* attainment of convertibility of the major European currencies at the end of 1958. Its weaknesses and possible reform have been under discussion for several years, mainly in the context of the protracted difficulties experienced by the two reserve currencies, the dollar and sterling. Here it is necessary to point out only that while allowing more freedom than the old-style gold standard, the system has narrowed the scope for national policies when domestic and balance-of-payments requirements come into conflict. Apart from putting constraint on changing the parity of national currencies (European exchange-rate adjustments after the devaluations of 1949 were confined to three rounds—two successive devaluations of the French franc in 1957 and 1958, and the 5 per cent revaluation of the German and Dutch currencies in 1961) there have been subsidiary limitations, notably in monetary policy, whose effect on international capital movements has had to be taken increasingly into account.

Lastly, there has been the constraint on national policies imposed by the generally accepted code of international trade as formalised in the General

[1] See 'The OECD', p. 624.

Agreement on Tariffs and Trade. This upholds the principle of non-discrimination (no new preferences except for the formation of customs unions or free trade areas), forbids beggar-your-neighbour policies, has virtually eliminated the use of quota restrictions except in agriculture and a few specific commodities, and also excludes increased tariff protection as a policy weapon in all but exceptional circumstances.

EUROPEAN INTEGRATION

Such is the broad national and international setting against which the six Common Market countries—France, West Germany, Italy, Belgium, Luxembourg and the Netherlands—set out on their experiment in European economic integration, first initiated in the creation of the European Coal and Steel Community in 1953, and fully institutionalised with the coming into operation of the Treaties of Rome on 1 January 1958 for the establishment of the European Economic Community (EEC) and Euratom.[1]

The failure of Britain to negotiate association with the European Economic Community (in 1957-8) led to the present economic division of Western Europe with the formation in 1959 of a second trading group, the European Free Trade Association (EFTA), with the more limited aim of establishing free trade in industrial goods between Britain, Scandinavia, Austria, Switzerland and Portugal.

Another institutional change was the transformation in 1961 of the OEEC into the OECD with full United States and Canadian membership and the subsequent accession, in 1964, also of Japan. This was the result partly of the shift in European policy coordination towards the EEC and EFTA, and partly also of a changed trans-Atlantic relationship from European dependence on the United States to interdependence, heralded by the gradual move to convertibility and thus removal of European discrimination against the dollar (1956-61). Moreover, a platform was needed for the examination of problems common to the world's industrial nations.

By January 1966 the EEC and EFTA had reduced their internal industrial tariffs by 80 per cent of the level applying in the respective base years, and the EEC had moved some two-thirds of the way towards a common external tariff. EFTA was due to remove the remaining internal tariffs (with minor exceptions) in January 1967, and the Six emerged from the 1966 deadlock between France and the other Five with the resolve to complete their customs union for trade in industrial goods in July 1968, concurrently with the institution of their jointly managed market in agriculture.

Part Three of this book is entirely devoted to the history, significance and consequences of the European integration moves which constitute a momentous and extremely difficult new departure in European affairs. Suffice it here to note that as yet the new Europe has not found a secure basis and that, despite any appearances to the contrary, a permanent division between six and seven of the Western European countries can hardly be visualised. As stated in 1966 by the then British minister of economic affairs, George Brown, the question is not 'whether' but 'when' Britain will enter into partnership with the Six, and what kind of enlarged European Community will result.

It is also too early to make any definitive judgements about the impact of the EEC on the Western European economy. As yet, policy harmonisation

[1] See 'The Structure of the European Community', p. 570.

in the EEC has hardly got off the ground, and the full incidence of tariff discrimination created by the two new trading groups is yet to come. However, certain general provisional conclusions may be made. First, that the movement for European integration has reinforced existing expansionary forces, not least by capturing the imagination of the business communities within the six Common Market countries themselves, and also in Britain and the United States, thus bringing, incidentally, an unprecedented influx of foreign investment capital. Besides providing an avenue for further progress in intra-European trade liberalisation (which had previously encountered difficulties), it has helped to focus attention on the questions of international policy coordination arising from increased economic interdependence and has provided the opportunity of gathering experience in dealing with national policy issues within an open trading system.

STRUCTURAL ASPECTS

Western Europe occupies some three per cent of the world's land surface, contains some ten per cent of the world's population and accounts for about one-quarter of the world's income. Per capita income in Western Europe ranks high but amounts today still to only about half the United States level. Western Europe produces nearly one-quarter of the world's manufacturing output and over one-fifth of the world's food supplies. It accounts for a major share of world trade, no less than two-fifths of the total and about two-thirds of the trade of the free world's industrial countries. Table 1 summarises the part played by industrial Western Europe in the world economy.

TABLE 1

STRUCTURE OF WORLD ECONOMY, 1960
(per cent of world total)

	Industrial Western Europe[1]	North America	Sino-Soviet bloc	Rest of world
Population	8·6	6·8	34·6	50
Real GNP	25	31	22	22
Av. per capita income as % of world average	292	458	64	43
Exports	38	21	12	29
Imports	39	16	12	33
Industrial production	24	35	28	13
Agricultural production	15	21	32	32

[1]The EEC and EFTA (excluding Austria and Portugal).

Source: A. Maddison, *Economic Growth in the West*, London, 1964, p. 159

Although by world standards the differences in economic structure and income levels between the individual Western European countries are relatively narrow, they are nevertheless substantial. The level of per capita income ranged in 1964 from over $2,000 a year in Sweden and Switzerland to below $300 in Turkey (conversion at official exchange rate). In the three major industrial countries of Western Europe, i.e. Britain, West Germany and France, per capita income levels were below those of Sweden and Switzerland. Recently France and Germany have overtaken Britain.

In the less developed Mediterranean countries and Ireland large reserves of underemployed labour still exist on the land and agriculture accounts for between a quarter and two-fifths of GDP. Italy, with its rapidly expanding industrial north, may be counted with the group of industrial countries north of the Alps. Within the latter group, a striking contrast exists between Britain and the rest. In Britain agriculture accounts for less than 4 per cent both of the labour force and of the GDP. Many continental countries have not only a broader agricultural base, but also lower average labour productivity in agriculture. In the six Common Market countries the proportion of the labour force in agriculture ranges from 10 to 25 per cent and the contribution of agriculture to GDP from 5 to 15 per cent. This partial structural backwardness, not only in Italy but also in France, West Germany and other countries, is often linked with regional problems and its persistence is closely tied to the politically explosive issues surrounding agricultural protection which it has proved hard to dent.

Nevertheless, labour productivity in agriculture has been rising rapidly in continental Europe, and at an accelerating pace (more rapidly, in fact, than in the other economic sectors); the transfer of manpower from agriculture to other occupations has begun to move apace and has been helping to alleviate the labour shortage which has become an outstanding common feature of Western Europe in the 1960s.

Another important characteristic of industrial Western Europe is its relatively high dependence on foreign trade. Among the major Western European countries France is less orientated to foreign trade than Britain and West Germany, although there has been a notable upswing in French foreign trade since the break with traditional protectionism which accompanied the second devaluation at the end of 1958 (as part of the reform programme instituted by President de Gaulle in readiness for French participation in the EEC). But even when the substantial trade between Western European countries is discounted—and this intra-trade is relatively more important, of course, on the continent than for Britain—the region's trade with countries outside it exceeds in value the total trade of the United States. More particularly, Western Europe predominates as a market for world exports, taking some 40 per cent of the developing countries' exports against some 20 per cent taken by North America. The external influences which Western Europe and North America exert on each other are transmitted not primarily through trans-Atlantic trade, but via the developing countries and, above all, through capital movements which have acquired a new dimension in recent years.

POST-WAR GROWTH

The rate of economic progress in Western Europe since the second world war has been remarkable by world standards and in very striking contrast to the relative stagnation in the inter-war years. It has brought structural changes and an almost uninterrupted rise in output and productivity. Britain, Ireland, Belgium and Luxembourg have lagged behind; the fastest growing countries have been West Germany, Austria, Switzerland, Italy, Greece and Spain. Outside the Communist world, only Japan has exceeded the growth record of the fastest growing Western European countries. The average growth rate of the United States during the period 1954–64 was comparable to those near the lower end of the European range, as is shown in Table 2.

TABLE 2

GROWTH OF GNP, 1954–64

(average annual compound rate)

EEC	%	EFTA	%	Other W. Europe	%	Other selected countries	%
W. Germany	6·3	Switzerland	5·7	Greece	6·6	Japan	10·0
Italy	5·8	Austria	5·4	Spain	6·4	Soviet Union	6·1 [1]
France	5·0	Denmark	4·4	Turkey	4·9	Canada	4·5
Netherlands	4·4	Portugal	4·7	Iceland	4·8	United States	3·6
Belgium	3·4	Sweden	4·0	Ireland	2·5		
Luxembourg	3·0	Norway	3·8				
		Britain	2·8				
Av. EEC	5·5	Av. EFTA	3·5	Av. total Western Europe [2]	4·8	Av. developing countries	4·4 [3]

[1] 1955–63.   [2] Excl. Finland.   [3] 1950–60.

Sources: United Nations and United States Agency for International Development

The less developed countries have started, of course, from a much lower level. As far as the average performance in industrial Western Europe is concerned, anything like a parallel can be found only in the United States in the period before the 1914–18 war. A comparison with long-term trends shows remarkable disparities. It has been shown that the GDP of France, West Germany, Italy and Sweden, for instance, grew in the 85 years 1870–1955 at an average annual rate of between 1·4 and 2·6 per cent; Britain's growth rate in the same period was 1·8 per cent; and the United States, growing faster than any European country and faster than in the 1950s, recorded an annual growth rate of 3·7 per cent.[1]

It may seem surprising that the apparently very good progress in most countries during the last decade should have been achieved at a time when concern over economic growth in Western Europe had hardly begun to come to the fore, and that the recent shift towards greater attention to economic growth should have been considered necessary even in countries that might have expected to be well satisfied with their post-war growth record. The reason appears to be essentially twofold. In the first place, the sustained rapid expansion which has been characteristic of many Western European countries, but which has eluded Britain, appears partly to have been the almost inadvertent result of policies pursued for other ends, and partly due also to exceptionally favourable circumstances; signs have also begun to make themselves felt, in West Germany and elsewhere, that progress in future may be more difficult. Therefore, an important economic issue in Western Europe today is whether accelerated growth can be maintained over the long run. Second but no less important, is the fact that a general appreciation has emerged of the advantages of faster economic growth in helping towards desired objectives and towards overcoming resistance to change, whether on the national or the international plane. In Britain and Belgium there has been the added incentive to 'planning for growth' provided by poor post-war performances as compared with their neighbours.

[1] Angus Maddison, *Economic Growth in the West*, London, 1964.

SPECIAL FACTORS DETERMINING GROWTH

Economists are by no means agreed as to the weight that should be attached to once-for-all influences which limit the usefulness of recent experience as a guide to the future and could also go some way towards explaining the differences in growth performance between Britain and the continent. One set of these special factors concerns elements of recovery, readjustment and catching up after pre-war stagnation and war-time disruption. Parallel with this runs the thesis that much of the unprecedented expansion in European and world trade, which acted as a stimulus to growth, was due to trade liberalisation policies whose effect must, by definition, sooner or later come to a halt.

The aftermath of war had a significant impact on every aspect of European economic life in the late 1940s and well into the 1950s. The effect of war was not so much physical destruction (in West Germany industrial investment during the war is estimated to have exceeded war damage plus the value of obsolescent plant), as the existence of pent-up demand, not least for housing, and other profound dislocations, some of them the result of the political aftermath of war. Post-war recovery and readjustment contributed for a time to relatively rapid economic advance once resources were successfully reharnessed to the requirements of the respective peace-time economies. Recovery in European trade lagged somewhat behind that of production and in some industrial sectors, for instance energy and steel, and above all in housing, supply tended to be slow in catching up with demand. The post-war recovery element is usually discounted after about the mid-1950s, but West Germany did not attain a 'normal' peace-time footing until some years later (this is reflected in Table 2 above).

A readily identifiable once-for-all expansionary influence in the world economy (which still has some way to go before it will have worked itself out) has been the progressive abandonment of trade barriers. Over the last decade or so trade liberalisation is estimated to have contributed about one-half of the increase in intra-trade between the world's industrial countries, the other half deriving from growing incomes. Liberalisation policies have gone further in Western Europe and have played an important part in shaping the two outstanding characteristics of world trade in the 1950s and 1960s: the fact that trade in manufactures has expanded more rapidly than world industrial production, and the related trend for intra-trading between industrial countries to expand more rapidly than trade between these countries and the developing world.

Moreover, machinery and transport equipment have been the most expansive among the manufactured goods entering world trade and—contrary to pre-war experience—the advanced countries (Western Europe, North America and Japan) after the war provided a faster growing import market for capital goods than the developing primary producing countries. That this expansionary world environment has stimulated economic activity cannot be doubted. West Germany constitutes an outstanding example of a country which has benefited from export-led growth.

ASPECTS OF DEMAND AND SUPPLY

The stimulus exercised on Western European economies by buoyant export markets was transmitted through boosting total demand. Post-war structural changes in the national economies also influenced demand but their primary impact was on the supply side. The most important and direct way in which this made itself felt was through an unusually rapid increase in industrial employment. The influx from the East of some 10 million expellees and refugees into West Germany—which continued until the erection of the Berlin Wall in 1961—added to the labour force and augmented the initially large reserves of unemployed labour there; the still sizeable unemployment at the beginning of the 1950s in several other countries, notably Italy, Belgium and Denmark, was absorbed at varying rates in the succeeding decade and a half.

In West Germany the average rate of unemployment was over 7 per cent in 1950, and still over 5 per cent in 1954, but had fallen below 1 per cent in 1960 and has remained well below this margin since, against a cyclical range of $1\frac{1}{2}$–$2\frac{1}{2}$ per cent in Britain, one of the European countries where full employment conditions have been maintained throughout the post-war years.

The release of labour from agriculture into other occupations, especially significant in Italy, became of added importance in industrial Western Europe as full employment conditions asserted themselves in one country after another. Yet this trend—for which there is still ample scope—could not prevent the emergence of pressure on prices as labour costs overtook productivity gains. One symptom of the tight labour situation has been the appearance of immigrant workers, mainly from Italy, Spain and Greece, but also from Turkey, Yugoslavia and elsewhere, in France, West Germany, Switzerland, Sweden and Belgium, to name the most important host countries. In the summer of 1964 a total of over three million such foreign workers was recorded (there was an additional unknown number of 'black market' workers).[1] It may be added that, while there are limits to this trend, it does mean the spread southward of Western Europe's wealth—through the remittances sent home by foreign workers—just as the rapidly growing tourist trade within Western Europe benefits substantially such countries as Italy, Spain and Greece.

The accelerated expansion of the non-agricultural labour force in many of the major industrial countries of Western Europe was accompanied by high rates of investment and high returns on investment in terms of output. In the eight years to 1963, investment as a proportion of GDP ranged between about 20 per cent and 25 per cent in the majority of industrial countries on the continent; in Britain the proportion was about $16\frac{1}{2}$ per cent (and in the United States about $18\frac{1}{2}$ per cent). At the same time, investment in housing, which is non-productive and was boosted on the continent by exceptional boom conditions, has been, by and large, considerably higher there in relation to the national income than in Britain. It is not intended here to enter into the question of the relationship between investment and growth. It may, however, be stated that, under the stimulus of favourable demand conditions or expectations, capital, entrepreneurial, technical and institutional resources and organisation needed for labour absorption and/or modernisation have often proved remarkably resilient.

The Role of Government

The role of government in national economies throughout industrial Western Europe has had a decisive influence. Total current government expenditure in these countries has ranged between 20 and 30 per cent of

[1] See 'Immigrant Labour in Western Europe', p. 436.

GDP; of total annual investment, governments have controlled directly some 40–60 per cent (against some 30 per cent in the United States). Monetary and fiscal policies have been exhaustively employed to control private demand in the interest of price stability and competitiveness. Fiscal policies have also been much refined and extended to serve other major and subsidiary policy aims, some directed towards supplementing or stimulating private investment and generally fostering productive efficiency, others towards equalisation of income and social security. The welfare aspect of government policy has, indeed, been outstandingly prominent in several Western European countries (France, West Germany and Austria) and has exceeded the United States effort by a good margin in all of them.

Another striking contrast between the United States and industrial Western Europe has been in the sphere of publicly owned or nationalised enterprises. The extent of these varies widely in Western Europe but is almost everywhere far greater than in the United States. In almost all the Western European countries public utilities, rail, air and urban transport and telecommunications are government or municipally owned. France and Britain have nationalised coal industries and government ownership extends at the present time beyond the basic infrastructure into manufacturing (e.g. iron and steel, motor vehicles, chemicals, oil refining, shipbuilding) and banking and commerce, notably in France, Italy and Austria as well as in West Germany and the Scandinavian countries. In others, for instance Belgium, public ownership is strictly limited.

The historical origins of nationalised sectors in Western European countries vary profoundly. In Germany and Italy, for instance, they were a legacy from the financial collapse in the Great Depression and the subsequent Hitler and Mussolini regimes; in France and Britain large-scale nationalisation came after the second world war, in France as an aftermath of German occupation, and in both countries out of a desire to improve on pre-war economic performance.

Arising thus partly through historical accident, and often extending over a wide range of activities in individual countries, the management and policies of publicly owned enterprises—and the methods for their control—have taken very different forms, including near-autonomous nationalised enterprises run on commercial lines, as Renault in France or the IRI and the ENI in Italy. But much of the publicly owned sector is highly capital-intensive everywhere, and is therefore important as a means, or potential means, of control over investment in the context of the national economy. In several countries public enterprises account for over one-quarter of fixed investment.

GROWTH AND INFLATION

The least successful result of post-war economic policy in Western Europe has been the difficulty experienced in warding off upward pressures on prices. The United States has proved, on the whole, more successful in this respect but through most of the post-war period had a relatively slow growth rate, relatively wide fluctuations in economic activity and a persistently large margin of unused capacity. The more recent United States bid for faster growth, which was accompanied by a notable decline in unemployment, dates back only to the early 1960s.

The fact is that the test still lies ahead, in Western Europe as in the United States, as to how fast a growth can be sustained without inflation and under conditions of full employment. One important determining factor, singled out by economic analysis based on post-war European experience, is the rate of growth of productive potential (which may be measured by labour and capital inputs and productivity). When rise in output exceeds growth potential, rising costs and excess demand tend to combine to create inflation.

As indicated earlier, in this respect the problems facing the industrial countries of Western Europe have tended to become similar over recent years. Hence the recent emphasis, in economic policy discussion throughout Western Europe, on more efficient use of resources, with special attention to investment patterns, rationalisation, labour mobility, research and development, and education. Hence also the current attempts in Britain and France to evolve incomes policies, already attempted in the Netherlands and Sweden. The hope has been that acceptable and effective means of controlling prices and incomes might obviate the need for excessive reliance on restrictive fiscal, monetary and credit measures which are seen to militate against long-term expansion, not least by undermining business confidence. In Britain, with its vulnerable and over-extended balance-of-payments position, issues such as these appear at present particularly important. Ultimate success in Britain, as elsewhere, will largely depend on future relations within Europe and in the wider international environment, for in a liberal world trade and payments system account must be taken of growing international interdependence in framing national and international policies.

BIBLIOGRAPHY

Dewhurst, J. Frederic and others. *Europe's Needs and Resources: Trends and Prospects in Eighteen Countries*, Macmillan, London; Twentieth Century Fund, New York, 1961.

Granick, D. *The European Executive*, Weidenfeld and Nicolson, London; Doubleday, New York, 1962.

Maddison, A. *Economic Growth in the West: Comparative Experience in Europe and North America*, Allen and Unwin, London; Twentieth Century Fund, New York, 1964.

Shanks, M. (ed.) *Lessons of Public Enterprise: A Fabian Society Study* (esp. Chapter XVII, 'Lessons from Abroad' by Peter Lowell), Jonathan Cape, London, 1963.

Shonfield, A. *Modern Capitalism: The Changing Balance of Public and Private Power*, Oxford Univ. Press for Royal Institute of International Affairs, London and New York, 1965.

Tew, B. *International Monetary Cooperation 1945–65*, Hutchinson Univ. Library, London, 10th revised ed. 1965; Hillary House, New York, 1965.

Williams, Lady Gertrude. *Apprenticeship in Europe*, Chapman and Hall, London, 1963.

Yates, P. L. *Food, Land and Manpower in Western Europe*, Macmillan, London; St Martins Press, New York, 1960.

ECE. *Economic Planning in Europe*, Geneva, 1965. *Economic Survey of Europe* (including a study, 'The economic significance of the public sector in some Western European economies'), Geneva, 1960.

OECD. *Growth and Economic Policy: An Unpublished Report of Working Party No. 2 to the Economic Policy Committee*, Paris, 1964.

OEEC. *Europe and the World Economy*, Paris, 1960.

WESTERN EUROPE'S ROLE
IN WORLD TRADE

JOHN PINDER

SINCE the Renaissance the peoples of Europe have sustained an extra-ordinary output of restless energy. Three of its consequences—the age of discovery, the industrial revolution, and the age of imperialism which these two begot—made Europe the centre of the world economy. Despite the self-destruction of the two world wars and the withdrawal of its East European neighbours into isolation, Western Europe still has a greater share of world trade than any other region and is second only to North America in its industrial production.

Europe's role in world trade is determined largely by the strength of Europe's industry, and it is therefore helpful first to take the measure of this. Well over nine-tenths of the world's industrial production is accounted for by the five main regions that may be classed as 'industrialised': North America, Western Europe, Eastern Europe (excluding Russia), Russia and Japan.[1] Of these North America, Western Europe and Russia, in that order, are by far the most important. Table 1 below shows the relative

TABLE 1

WORLD PRODUCTION AND POPULATION BY MAIN REGION:
SELECTED PRODUCTS, 1963

	Steel (million tons)	Cars (million)	Lorries (million)	Energy consumption (billion tons coal equivalent)	Population (million)
North America	107	8·2	1·6	1·7	208
Western Europe	107	6·7	1·1	1·0	347
Russia	80	0·2	0·4	0·7	225
Eastern Europe	26	0·2	0·1	0·4	120
Japan	32	0·4	1·0	0·1	96
Other	34	0·4	0·2	0·8	2,164
World	387	16·2	4·3	4·7	3,160

Source: *UN Statistical Yearbook*, 1964

shares in world production of representative commodities. Western Europe, North America and Russia are fairly equally prominent in steel; this reflects

[1] See the Production Summary Table in the *UN Statistical Yearbook*, 1964. This shows that the five industrialised regions accounted for over 92 per cent of world industrial production in 1958. The relative strength of industrialised and less-developed countries has not changed substantially since then.

TABLE 2
REGIONAL NETWORK OF WORLD TRADE, 1964 ($ billion)

Exporting Area \ Destination	Western Europe	North America	Japan	Eastern Trading Area[1]	Australia, New Zealand, South Africa	Latin America	South and South-East Asia	Middle East	Africa	Other less developed[2]	World total[3]
Western Europe		6	1	3	3	3	3	3	2	2	25
North America	10		2	1	1	4	3	1	[4]	1	23
Japan	1	2		—	—	2	1	1	1	1	7
Eastern Trading Area	3	—	—		—	1	1	1	—	—	7
Australia, New Zealand, South Africa	3	1	1	—		1	—	—	—	—	5
Latin America	4	4	1	1	—		—	—	—	1	9
South and South-East Asia	2	2	1	1	—	—		—	—	—	7
Middle East	4	1	1	—	—	—	—		—	—	7
Africa	3	1	—	—	—	—	—	—		—	4
Other less-developed	2	1	—	—	—	—	—	—	—		3
World total	31	16	6	6	5	8	9	5	4	4	96[5]

[1] Eastern Europe, the Soviet Union, China, Mongolia, North Korea and North Vietnam.
[2] Mainly the West Indies, Oceania and Maghreb.
[3] Includes a relatively small amount of exports to unspecified destinations.
[4] Signifies less than $500 million.
[5] It will be noted that this is the total of inter-regional trade, not the world total of international trade; the intra-regional trade is excluded.

Source: GATT, *International Trade*, 1964

Russia's concentration on heavy industry and shows a more favourable relative position than her overall industrial strength would allow. The consumer societies of North America and Western Europe, on the other hand, produce between them over nine-tenths of the world's cars. With lorries, North America comes first, then Western Europe and Japan, then Russia. In consumption of energy, which is a useful general indicator, North America is far ahead of Western Europe and Russia, which in turn are far ahead of any other region.

Although the five industrialised regions contain a minority of the world's population, they are by no means, as many people imagine, a tiny minority. They number about one billion[1] people, against some two billion in the less-developed regions: a disparity of only two to one. Western Europe alone accounts for well over a tenth of world population. The populations of the less-developed regions are, however, increasing faster than those of the industrialised regions, and the numerical disparity will therefore increase unless this trend is reversed or until large enough sectors of the less-developed world become industrialised.

Western Europe, the cradle of the industrial revolution, accounts then for probably over a quarter of the world's industrial production. When the industrial revolution came, the European trading network already covered practically the whole world; and the imperial system consequently developed rapidly on the economic basis of Western Europe's need for raw materials and foodstuffs and the lack of manufacturing capacity in the rest of the world. Against this background, it is not surprising that Western Europe is still the most important region in world trade and that it trades on a large scale with all the other regions.

The main essentials of the world pattern of trade are shown in Table 2 above. In using this table, the reader should remember that the figures for international trade within each region have been omitted. These figures are large with respect to Western Europe ($46 billion), the Eastern Trading Area ($13 billion) and North America ($9 billion), and significant for South and South-East Asia ($2 billion), Latin America and the Middle East ($1 billion each). But it is misleading to include them when examining the trading relationships between the different regions. An example will show why. Western Europe, as defined in Table 2, is divided into nineteen countries while North America is divided into two. If the inter-state trade of the United States were shown, giving fifty-one states in North America, the trade within North America would become enormously greater; conversely if the EEC were to be shown as one unit, Western Europe's internal trade would be sharply reduced. It does not seem sensible to increase a region's apparent weight in world trade merely because it is divided into a great many separate states.

This explains why Table 2 shows that Western Europe accounts for about a quarter of world exports and a third of world imports, whereas a share of 40 per cent is more often quoted, based on figures that include trade within each region as well as between regions. But it is not necessary to exaggerate in order to demonstrate the importance of Western Europe in world trade; for this region's imports and exports taken together account for almost three-fifths of the world's inter-regional trade.

A glance at Table 2 shows that the only other region of great importance in world trade is North America. Indeed, the imports and exports of Western

[1] Here and throughout this book the word 'billion' denotes one thousand million.

Europe and North America between them account for over four-fifths of the world's inter-regional trade. While the structure of the two regions' trade has important similarities, there are also three main differences: North America has a trade surplus of some $7 billion, while Western Europe has a deficit of $6 billion; while both are mainly exporters of manufactures, North America also exports large amounts of foodstuffs and raw materials; and while the trade of both is widely spread, that of Western Europe is more evenly distributed among the other regions than is that of North America.

Since the characteristics of Western Europe's trade vary greatly according to the region with which the trade is carried on, it is necessary to examine it region by region in order to understand the rôle of Western Europe in world trade and the policies that it is in the interest of West European countries, jointly or severally, to adopt.

WESTERN EUROPE'S TRADE WITH THE UNITED STATES

North America is by far the most important trading partner for Western Europe, taking a quarter of the latter's exports and supplying a third of its imports. Table 2 shows, indeed, that this trade across the Atlantic in both directions is much the heaviest of all the flows of inter-regional trade.

But if North America is important to Western Europe, Western Europe is still more important to North America, taking 42 per cent of the latter's exports in 1964. It was natural, therefore, that the establishment of the EEC as a single market with a common tariff should have evoked a powerful reaction in the commercial policy of the United States; for the EEC already accounts for over one-half of North America's exports to Western Europe and if, as in 1961-2 seemed imminent, Britain and some other European countries were to join, it would account for the overwhelming bulk.

It was a healthy sign that this reaction was a positive and trade-creating rather than a negative one. The Trade Expansion Act of 1962, which was the basis for the Kennedy Round of tariff negotiations in the GATT, both enabled the United States' president to negotiate big tariff cuts and was a declaration of his intention to do so. The cuts were to be of up to 50 per cent across the board and the president could eliminate tariffs altogether on products for which the United States and the EEC together supplied the dominant share (80 per cent or more) of world exports. If Britain were a member of the Community such products would include most of those whose manufacture requires a fairly high level of technology. As it happened, Britain's application to join was rejected and the 'dominant supplier' authority became a dead letter. At the time of writing, negotiations are continuing and the alternatives seem to lie between more modest cuts than President Kennedy envisaged (say 20-30 per cent) and complete failure. The French government seems to be opposed to the full cuts, as to any other measure of collaboration with the Americans; and France's partners in the Community are not likely to press their more cooperative attitude to the point of a majority vote for the cuts in the EEC's common tariff, partly because the present French government would probably walk out of the Community in such circumstances, and partly because the other Five are far from being as enthusiastic about the idea of substantial tariff cuts as the American policy-makers hoped.

The reason for this lack of enthusiasm is worth exploring, because it illustrates a point that is fundamental to an understanding of what is desirable and what is practical politics in the organisation of world trade.

Industries which feel weak or backward will obviously not wish to be exposed to free trade or even to freer trade. The solution proposed by the free traders is that each country should set its exchange rate at the point where half its industries will be relatively weak and the other half relatively competitive; the competitive half will thrive in each country and everyone will be better off.

But in freeing trade with a country at a more advanced level of technology, as is the United States in relation to Europe, it is in the advanced capital-intensive or science-based (i.e. research-intensive) industries that the more backward economy will suffer; if trade is completely free there is a danger that these industries will be driven out of existence. This has two consequences, one for political attitudes and the other for economic and political realities. The attitudes in favour of a freer trade are usually found in the more advanced and progressive industries. The others tend to be on the defensive; even if they might in fact gain from freer trade, they do not believe they would. It is therefore hard to generate political momentum for freeing trade with a country at a more advanced technological level, because the normal lobby for liberalisation will be absent. Nor can it justly be said that this attitude is misguided. For if the capital-intensive or science-based industries are prevented from developing, then the economy will not be able to progress to a higher level of technology. The consequences will be economically, and eventually politically, grave.

This is, of course, an example of the orthodox 'infant industries' exception to the classical theory of free trade. But the case is far from being exceptional. In a world of constant economic growth and technological progress, the more modern industries of any country other than the most advanced, that is to say the United States, can be classed as 'infant'. The exception has become the norm for all those industries outside the United States, on which progress towards a higher technological level depends.

It may be argued that this reasoning is valid for the less-developed countries, but that the technological level of Western Europe is already so high—second only to that of the United States—that Western Europe has no need of such protection: that to invoke it is as uselessly greedy as for a millionaire to claim all the benefits of a welfare state. But such a contention rests on an underestimate of the industrial strength of the United States in relation to Europe and on a lack of foresight about the future of this relationship if Europe fails to develop its advanced industries rapidly.

The industrial strength of the United States in the more advanced industries rests substantially on two factors: the average size of firm and the size of expenditure on research and development (R and D). A very big firm can draw full advantage from economies of scale, not only in production but also in other fields of operation such as marketing and R and D. The latter is of crucial importance in science-based industries such as electronics, chemicals, nuclear energy and aerospace. Among the 500 largest firms in the world, outside the Communist countries, 306 are American; the turnover of the biggest, General Motors, is about the size of the GNPs of Austria and Switzerland combined. American spending on R and D, two-thirds of it financed by the Federal government, is about four times that of Western Europe in money terms (an OECD report suggests that higher costs in the United States might reduce the real difference to two instead of four times). It follows that unless Western Europe makes rapid progress in its expenditure on R and D (which in order to be effective will probably have in large measure to be jointly financed) and in its scale of operations, which will be reflected in a rapid growth in the size of firms, the United States will remain dominant in the industries of the future. Western Europe will have made the mistake that Britain made when it remained rooted for too long in the industries that were its glory in the 19th century: textiles, coal and ship-building. Europe must, on the contrary, develop the new industries both for its future economic health and for its ability to carry its weight politically. It is also in the general interest of other regions of the world that the sources of supply of the products of these industries should be diversified; and it is indeed in the interest of the United States, with its devotion to the competitive system, that monopoly and as far as possible oligopoly should be avoided, by the development of strong competitors in the advanced industries elsewhere.

In these circumstances, then, it was probably a good thing that the idea of abolishing tariffs on the products of the more advanced industries as part of the Kennedy Round came to nothing. For free trade during the years of their development would certainly inhibit the growth of such industries in Europe. It is, however, likely that cuts of up to fifty per cent in the tariffs of the EEC, Britain and the United States would be generally beneficial. These tariff levels, despite post-war reductions, still derive in large part from a period of world slump and defensive protection, and reductions on this scale would give impetus to the expansion of world trade without disrupting the growth of Europe's more capital-intensive or science-based industries. Such reductions, as is argued later, would also play an important part in strengthening the economies of the industrialising countries.

TRADE WITH JAPAN

One country which would certainly derive immense benefit from such tariff reductions is Japan. Fifteen years ago Japan would have been classed with the low-wage, less-developed countries. Since then an increase of 10 per cent a year in GNP has been by no means unusual, and Japan's economic growth has been such that the country is approaching the economic level of the more advanced parts of Western Europe. This extremely rapid industrialisation has been accompanied by a reduction in the barriers facing Japanese exports, linked with Japan's becoming a Contracting Party to the GATT, and Japanese exports more than tripled in the decade 1955–64 (from $2 billion to $6·7 billion). The case of Japan is a very significant one, because it illustrates the problems relating to the foreign trade of a developing country and the way in which they can be solved.

The main problem that the Japanese case illustrates is the converse of that which arises for Western Europe in its trade with the United States. The industrialising country has low incomes per head and therefore a narrow home market, so that it needs export markets if its industries are to develop fast. But because it has low incomes and correspondingly low wages, its labour-intensive manufactures (typically textiles and clothing) are highly competitive with the same industries in much more advanced countries. The latter are first driven out of their export markets and then, unless they are restrictively protected, suffer heavy losses at home. It does not need to be emphasised that Japan has in the past demonstrated this process with shattering effect.

Now it is to the advantage in the long run of the more advanced countries that they should move out of traditional labour-intensive manufacture and into capital-intensive and research-intensive manufacture; and under conditions of full employment this adjustment is far from entailing the agony for those who have to adjust that it undoubtedly entailed during the years of depression. But if it occurs too quickly, it does cause hardship for those concerned, as well as a waste of industrial and social capital. Naturally, and indeed rightly, the infliction of such pain on their citizens has been resisted by the more advanced countries, and the impact of growing imports from Japan has been softened by various means: the gradual rather than sudden erosion of protection; the introduction of devices for easing industrial redeployment in the more advanced countries (redundancy payments and retraining facilities for workers, compensation for employers who reduce capacity); and the control of both the quantity and the quality of exports by the Japanese themselves (politically much easier to remove when no longer required than are the protective devices of the importing countries).

The more advanced countries can, then, play a notable part in helping the less-developed countries to industrialise if they open their markets to imports of labour-intensive manufactures; and they can do this, with the help of some gradualism and some assistance from the state, without hurting their own citizens. It is to the advantage of the more advanced countries to open their markets in this way, and indeed speed the process by finding ways to accelerate the painless change required, not only because faster industrialisation of the less-developed is in the interests of the more-advanced, but also because such change is healthy for the economies of the latter countries themselves.

As a result of its extraordinary post-war economic growth, in which the growth of foreign trade played a decisive part, the foreign trade per head of Japan's population is now not far short of the levels of North America and Western Europe, and Japan therefore contributes substantially to the widening of the world market. This increases correspondingly the scope for the growth of large-scale industry in the advanced regions of the free world (Western Europe and North America as well as Japan) and for the expansion of the export earnings of the developing countries and of Australia and New Zealand. The fact that Japan has more or less reached the economic level of Western Europe, and is no longer a low-wage country by European standards, makes the further freeing of trade with Japan much less of a problem for Europe. As far as trade with Japan is concerned, therefore, tariff cuts of the order of size envisaged in the Kennedy Round would be of benefit to both sides.

TRADE WITH EASTERN EUROPE AND RUSSIA

The future development of Western Europe's trade relations with Eastern Europe and Russia does not seem likely to be so problem-free. Trade between centralised command economies and decentralised market economies involves well-known difficulties. The planners of the Communist countries cannot forecast accurately their exports to market economies, which therefore fit uneasily into their economic plans; and both their exports and imports are subject to central administrative decisions which lay them open to the constant suspicion of unfair competition in export markets and of arbitrary protection against imports. The pricing systems of the Soviet-type economies are, moreover, irrational by the standards of market economies, which reduces the probability that trade will result in net advantage to both sides; and, although the commercial behaviour of Communist countries seems on the whole to have been remarkably good,

341

there is always the nasty feeling that this trade is controlled by governments whose intention is to undermine the economic and political systems of Western countries. This feeling is, needless to say, reciprocated by the governments of Communist countries in their dealings with the West. On top of all this there is the practical difficulty for the Eastern countries, given their relative economic backwardness and the unresponsiveness of their economic system to consumer tastes, of producing manufactures of a standard that will sell in the West, which tends to limit the scope for rapid expansion of their exports to Western Europe to those primary products—mainly oil and foodstuffs—on which some West European countries maintain tight restrictions.

In spite of these problems, however, the exports of Eastern Europe and Russia to Western Europe more than doubled between 1955 and 1964; they comprise one half of the exports of this group of countries (excluding their intra-Comecon trade); and they are likely to continue to increase. The difference between the two systems will probably remain radical for many years ahead, and thus make it necessary for both sides to keep import controls in reserve to obviate any disruption. But given this limitation, Western Europe is likely to look favourably on a steady expansion of the trade.

The motive is more political than economic. This trade is relatively much less important to the West of Europe than to the East—exports to Eastern Europe are only about an eighth of Western Europe's total exports to other regions. But it is of deep interest to the Western half of Europe to develop a satisfactory relationship with the Eastern half, and this depends on a liberalisation of the regimes in the Eastern countries. An evolution of their economies towards the more decentralised Yugoslav system would contribute greatly to more normal relations, and greater trade with Western Europe should help towards this end, by bringing their planners to grips with the problems of market economies. The process of liberalisation, if it continues, will as in the past be mainly generated by the forces within the Communist countries rather than from outside, but Western countries would be unwise to forego the opportunity of helping the process by an expansion of East–West trade.

TRADE WITH AUSTRALIA, NEW ZEALAND, SOUTH AFRICA AND CANADA

We have now examined Western Europe's trade with the other major industrial regions of the world. Before turning to the less-developed regions, however, it is necessary to consider certain countries that fall into neither category. These include Australia, New Zealand and South Africa, which are grouped separately in GATT statistics from which Table 2 is derived. Table 2 shows that Western Europe's exports to these three countries are about the same size as its exports to Eastern Europe and Russia combined and that, like Eastern Europe and Russia, they send about half their exports to Western Europe. Canada, while grouped in the statistics with the United States, towards which its economy is predominantly orientated, nevertheless shows some common characteristics with Australia and New Zealand, and in particular its participation, as a Commonwealth member, in the preference system.

During the negotiations for British entry into the Common Market, the EEC negotiators, in particular the French government, appeared to wish to minimise relations between an enlarged EEC on the one hand and Australia, New Zealand and Canada on the other. Relations with countries that are large producers of temperate foodstuffs certainly present thorny problems to those who have high-cost peasants or farm surpluses on their hands. But these problems can be solved if there is seen to be a basic identity of interests; and there is in fact a remarkable complementarity between the needs and the assets of Western Europe on the one hand and of Australia, New Zealand and Canada on the other. For the latter have vast space and natural resources but need people and capital, while Western Europe has an abundance of people and capital but lacks space and natural resources. It is to be hoped that, irrespective of the nature of Britain's future relations with the EEC, Western Europe will take care to develop closer relations, including closer trading relations, with these countries.

TRADE WITH THE LESS-DEVELOPED REGIONS

Western Europe sends about half its exports to and buys nearly half its imports from the less-developed regions (see Table 2). The extent of Western Europe's interests throughout the world is shown by the even distribution of its trade between these five regions: in 1964 both exports to and imports from each of them lay between $1·8 billion and $3·8 billion. The whole less-developed part of the world is, therefore, very important to Western Europe both as a market for its manufactures and as a source of raw materials and foodstuffs.

Western Europe is equally important to the less-developed regions. It is outstandingly the largest customer for each of them, apart from Latin America, where Western Europe is on a par with North America, each taking a third of Latin American exports. Western Europe takes over a third of the exports of South and South-East Asia, for which both North America and Japan are also major markets. Elsewhere Western Europe is predominant, providing a market for three-quarters of Africa's exports and nearly two-thirds of those of the Middle East and of 'other less-developed countries'—mainly the West Indies, Oceania and Maghreb (see Table 2).

Much of Western Europe's trade with these regions takes place within the framework of preferential systems that originated in the former French and British empires. Some two-thirds of the people both of Africa south of the Sahara and of South and South-East Asia (about 700 million in all) belong to Commonwealth countries whose exports enter Britain almost all free of duty, thus enjoying a preference against those exports of their competitors on which a duty must be paid. For the great bulk of raw materials and tropical foodstuffs, this is not as great an advantage as it may sound, because Britain's tariffs on these products are mostly low or zero, and the British market is anyway but a small part of the world market; but Britain's tariff on imports of manufactures is high, and the free entry for textiles, clothing and other labour-intensive manufactures is of considerable benefit to those Commonwealth countries, mainly India, Pakistan and Hong Kong, that manufacture these goods in large quantity.

The preferences granted by the EEC to its Associated Overseas States have a very different impact. The EEC tariffs on tropical products are in general much higher than in Britain; the EEC market is much bigger; and the Associated Overseas States contain many fewer people (some 57 million, mainly in Africa) than the overseas Commonwealth. The preferences therefore offer a great advantage to a small minority.

During the Brussels negotiations for British entry into the EEC it was agreed that Commonwealth countries in Africa should be offered associate status, and that certain tariff cuts should be made by the enlarged EEC for the benefit of Commonwealth countries in South and South-East Asia. This was a neat way of solving a tricky negotiating problem, but it is doubtful whether either this solution or the existing systems of Commonwealth and EEC preferences are in the long-run interests of Western Europe. The existing systems discriminate deeply in favour of a minority of the population of Africa (EEC preferences), to a lesser extent in favour of a majority of the population of tropical Africa and South and South-East Asia (Commonwealth preferences), and against other African or Asian states and almost the whole of Latin America. The proposed solution of the Brussels negotiations would have sharpened discrimination in favour of most of tropical Africa and against virtually the whole of Asia and Latin America.

This would be a step in the wrong direction. It will be recalled that Western Europe's exports are distributed evenly among the less-developed regions, with Africa ranking only fourth among the five for Western Europe as a whole and third for the EEC. Discrimination against Asia and Latin America does not make sense from this point of view. It would be wiser to place the whole less-developed part of the world (apart from China, which has a different economic system and presents a different problem) as far as possible on a similar footing: to phase out the tariff preferences rather than to intensify them.

WESTERN EUROPE'S FUTURE ROLE IN WORLD TRADE

It is clear from this survey of Western Europe's trading relations with all the other regions of the world that West European countries are great and world-wide traders with a consequent interest in the expansion of trade with each region. How, then, should Western Europe's role in world trade develop over the coming years? Is the old ideal of free trade still the goal, or should the expansion of the world economy be built on some other foundation?

To answer these questions it is necessary first to consider the relationship between economic progress and the scale of economic operations. As technology advances and production becomes more capital-intensive and research-intensive (or science-based), the scale of production and the size of enterprise required to maximise efficiency become constantly larger. It is widely believed that the separate states of Western Europe are already too small to give scope for the full development of modern industries such as is to be seen in America; and if this were not so today, it certainly would be tomorrow, because there is no prospect that the escalation of optimum scale will come to an end. The EEC offers a solution for the time being, but it will not be many years before either this market is also becoming too cramped, or there is a situation of oligopoly in the EEC's key industries (cars, steel, chemicals, electrical appliances) which is approaching uncomfortably near to monopoly, or both. By then the expansion of trade with other regions will have become not just helpful, but essential to continued economic progress.

Now the examination of problems in Western Europe's trade with other regions showed that free trade was not desirable with regions at different economic levels (levels of productivity and income). It is better to protect the new industries against competition from regions at a higher level of technology, and it is legitimate to protect one's more labour-intensive

344

industries against competition from low-wage countries, although the latter protection should be removed as soon as the old industries can be phased out to make way for the new. Thus it is necessary that a group of countries should have similar economic levels, if they are to embark on the abolition of tariff and other barriers that hinder their mutual trade. It was likewise explained that protection is required in the case of trade with countries having radically different economic systems (e.g. Eastern Europe and Russia). It may be said, then, that countries should be fairly homogeneous economically (i.e. have similar economic levels and systems) before they can establish a free trade system.

It is, moreover, argued by those who established the EEC that since almost all governments now intervene constantly in the economy in order to promote growth, price stability, full employment, welfare, fair competition and other objects, free trade must be accompanied by the establishment of institutions of supranational government which will coordinate the natural policies and, where necessary, themselves form and execute common policies on behalf of the whole area. This argument seems to the present writer convincing. It is not likely that free trade could be achieved, as it was in the days of laissez-faire liberalism, simply by removing the barriers; the activism of modern governments makes a more positive form of integration necessary. A further condition of free trade, then, may be that the countries proposing to adopt it should be ready to establish supranational institutions so as to deal jointly with problems of economic policy. If this is so, it will probably also be necessary for the three or four largest states of the area to be of fairly equal size, for if the supranational institutions were to be dominated by one or even two member states with much greater political weight than all the others, the latter would naturally fear that important political decisions would be taken without enough regard for their interests. The member states will also need to have similar political systems, or they will be unable to work together properly in the supranational institutions.

There are, then, five conditions that should be satisfied by countries proposing to adopt mutual free trade: similar economic levels and systems, similar political systems, comparable political weight among the three or four largest members, and readiness to accept supranational institutions. This amounts to what might be called a reformed theory of free trade, with conditions of economic and political compatibility among the countries concerned, which would then be said to form an economic union as well as a single market.

If Western Europe must eventually establish a free trade relationship with other parts of the world, in order to give scope for the continued growth of modern industries, and if the five conditions stated above must be satisfied, what regions are likely to become suitable partners in the long run?

The United States will be both economically and politically compatible if Western Europe can catch up technologically and develop enough political weight, which will probably depend on the enlargement of the EEC to include Britain and other EFTA countries. Japan will likewise be compatible if it catches up with Western Europe's economic level and continues its present course politically. Russia and Eastern Europe would also have to catch up with Western Europe, and their tendency towards liberalisation would in addition have to go a great deal further before their economic and political systems could be regarded as compatible with those of the West; this would take a long time, but the possibility should not be ruled out.

Out of the five industrialised regions of the world, then, it seems quite likely that two others will become economically and politically compatible with Western Europe during, say, the rest of this century, and just possible that all four others will. Thus there is a possibility that the industrialised part of the world will comprise a balanced group of regions from which an economic union could suitably be formed; but it seems more likely that only two or three of the regions will then be compatible, and that their political weights would not be well enough balanced to enable them to operate the necessary supranational institutions. Both Western Europe and the other industrialised regions therefore have a strong interest in helping regions now less-developed to advance their economic levels, as Japan has been doing, until they become compatible partners for free trade and economic union. If no more than one or two of the less-developed regions could do this, the prospect of a multi-regional area of free trade and economic union would be greatly improved.

Before a rapid acceleration of industrialisation and growth, such as has been seen in Japan, can be envisaged, it is necessary for a country to have an educated middle class, a basic economic infrastructure and a certain amount of industry. If its industries are to be modernised, moreover, it will probably need a large home market, which implies a fairly large population. The latter will be necessary also, if any of the less-developed regions is to contribute to the political balance in the institutions of a multi-regional economic union.

The only less-developed regions in which these conditions at present apply are Latin America, the Indian sub-continent and China. China may for the time being be ruled out because there is no sign that its political and economic systems will become compatible with those of Western Europe during this century. In Latin America, India and Pakistan, however, there would seem to be real hope of development towards the economic partnership that it is Western Europe's interest to see. Both these regions have enough education, infrastructure and industry for 'take-off'. India (470 million) and Pakistan (100 million) both have large enough populations; and if the Latin American countries are smaller (Brazil 80 million, Mexico 40 million), the Latin American Free Trade Area, while not an economic union, is helping to give their industries scope for expansion. Finally, there is a reasonable hope that the political and economic systems in India, Pakistan and Latin America will not be incompatible with those of Western Europe.

The reader may accept these propositions but find it difficult to believe that such countries could grow so fast as to catch up on Western Europe. Similar difficulty would doubtless have been found, forty years ago, in believing that Japan would catch up. It may of course be found that Japan is unique and that scepticism is justified by the event. But it is equally possible that what may be called a 'foxtrot' (slow-slow-quick-quick-slow) rhythm of growth applies. Experience has shown that between 'take-off' and 'maturity' growth rates can be exceptionally fast; and it is not hard to believe that, once economic progress has gained momentum, it is easier to catch up on somebody else's technology than to forge ahead beyond new technological frontiers. Since prosperity and expanding markets in the less-developed regions are in any case in Europe's interest, it seems only reasonable for Europe to do what it can to promote their development.

It therefore follows that West European trade policies (and aid policies too) should be such as to facilitate the rapid economic growth of less-developed regions, particularly Latin America and the Indian sub-continent.

This does not mean that Africa and the rest of Asia should be neglected, but that the regions with the best prospects of growth should receive better treatment than the other regions, rather than, as at present, being grossly discriminated against. Both tariff preferences and aid distribution are tilted by the EEC drastically in favour of Africa and against Latin America and Asia; Britain's aid likewise gives too little weight to Asia and virtually none to Latin America, while Commonwealth preference discriminates against the Latin Americans. All this makes little sense if the needs of the bulk of the population of less-developed regions are considered; it makes even less if the long-term interests of Western Europe are taken into account.

If, however, Western European trade and aid policies, while furthering economic growth and the expansion of trade in all regions, concentrate in particular upon these goals in respect of Latin America and the Indian sub-continent, there is a fair prospect that, not much later than the end of this century, four or five of the world's regions will be sufficiently compatible to consider major steps towards mutual free trade and economic union. For this is likely to be the case with North America, Western Europe and Japan; it could be true of Russia and Eastern Europe, if the political trends of the last ten years continue; and there is some hope that in one or more of Latin America, India and Pakistan, industrialisation will have gone fast enough to justify free trade with regions now classed as more-advanced. An advance towards free trade and economic union on this scale, involving regions with up to or even more than one half of the world's population, could not only give the scope required for the development of technology and the continuation of economic progress; it could also generate a great power of attraction for any regions remaining outside, and provide a framework in which to settle world political problems that now seem insoluble.

Western Europe has indeed, since 1945, done much to turn its back on national rivalries. The construction of economic union has contributed more than anything else to this end. The economic basis for this union was the evolution of technology to the point where Western European nation-states had become too small to remain economically separate. But the technological revolution continues and will continue, and before long even the world's greatest states and the EEC itself will be too small. As this happens, the nations of Western Europe will, if they have the vision, be able to play a decisive part in forming a multi-regional area of free trade and economic union.

BIBLIOGRAPHY

Dell, Sidney. *Trade Blocs and Common Markets*, Constable, London; Alfred A. Knopf, New York, 1963.
Johnson, H. *The World Economy at the Crossroads*, Oxford Univ. Press, London and New York, 1965.
Kaser, Michael. *Comecon*, Oxford Univ. Press for Royal Institute of International Affairs, London and New York, 1965.
Layton, C. *Trans-Atlantic Investments*, The Atlantic Institute, Paris, 1966.
Myrdal, Gunnar. *An International Economy: Problems and Prospects*, Routledge and Kegan Paul, London; Harper and Row, New York, 1956.
Pinder, John. 'The Economic Meaning of the Commonwealth', *Moorgate and Wall Street Review*, London, spring 1966. 'EEC and Comecon', *Survey*, London, January 1966.
Tinbergen, Jan. *International Economic Integration*, Elsevier, Amsterdam, 1954. *Shaping the World Economy*, Twentieth Century Fund, New York, 1962.
GATT. *International Trade*, Geneva, issued annually.
Political and Economic Planning. *East-West Trade*, London, 1965. *Trade Policy towards Low-income Countries*, London, 1967.
United Nations Statistical Yearbook, New York.

THE EUROPEAN CAPITAL MARKET

WILLIAM CLARKE

'THE lamps are going out all over Europe; we shall not see them lit again in our lifetime.' Sir Edward Grey's deep forebodings of 3 August 1914 might, with a little adjustment, have been applied with just as much truth to the European capital markets in 1930. One by one they were closing their doors to foreign issues. Not for another thirty years were they to be re-opened. And even now the capital markets of London, Paris, Zurich, Brussels, Frankfurt and Milan are still only a shadow of what their predecessors stood for not only before 1914, but even in the late 1920s. Western Europe has regained her economic strength. Several European currencies are more than looking the once mighty American dollar in the face (some are positively staring it out). Yet the savings and the wealth of Europe are still not being mobilised for investment elsewhere on anything like the old scale.

GROWTH OF THE EUROPEAN CAPITAL MARKET
It is not necessary to go back to the origins of the Amsterdam stock exchange in 1613 or of the London Stock Exchange in the 1670s to get the full flavour of what the European capital market once was. In fact it was not until the middle of the 19th century that both London and Amsterdam really came to fruition and that others, particularly Paris and Berlin, followed suit. Holland led the field in the 18th century, Britain in the 19th. But only after the Napoleonic wars were both countries beginning to benefit from the major shift in economic wealth resulting from the industrial revolution. For the first time money had started to accumulate in commercial hands. The wealthy princes of Florence, Lucca, Venice and Genoa were being joined by manufacturers from the north of England. Joint stock companies had been established. Soon the savings accumulating in the hands of this new industrial class were being invested in shares in a variety of enterprises finding their way to the Amsterdam and London stock markets. By the middle of the 19th century, the volume of foreign shares available in both centres had begun to expand significantly. Soon foreign government issues were a normal part of the London scene. Foreign bonds were available in Amsterdam, Paris and Berlin.

In the second half of the 19th century the process blossomed to a remarkable degree. Between 1850 and 1914 it is estimated that British investment abroad rose from £500 million to close on £3,700 million, and that of this the bulk was made up of bonds issued on the London capital market. It had gone to help build railways, harbours, plantations and other developments all round the world. Paris had done the same, financing (to its later cost) the major share of the Russian state railways. In contrast to the post-war practice since 1945, the underdeveloped countries of that time raised funds

348

directly in London, Paris or Berlin, received cash and immediately spent it on the developments they needed. European manufacturers were paid cash and everyone was happy, or reasonably so. Now these capital markets are no longer operating on the old scale, the poorer countries' needs seem to be far greater and the burden is increasingly falling on European governments direct or on exporters or both.

There was a recovery of sorts throughout the 1920s, after the interruption of the first world war, though the lending by some of the European markets became somewhat feverish towards 1929. Money was eventually being lent on ridiculous terms and occasionally to borrowers who, at other times, would not have merited attention. But this did not last. By the early 1930s, foreign lending was virtually a thing of the past. Confidence had been shattered in the 1929 crash. Britain imposed a rigid exchange control over foreign lending in 1932 and extended the regulations four years later. Other centres did the same. Tariff barriers were raised and exchange controls introduced. So things continued until war broke out in 1939.

AFTER 1945

During the early post-war period, Europe had much to contend with in reconstruction at home and did not take much heed of the needs of others abroad. From 1948 onwards vast amounts of American dollars flowed to Western Europe, and Europe's own savings were put to the same purpose. Cities were rebuilt and industries reformed. Trade recovered within Europe. But it was not until 1956 and later that it could be said that prosperity had finally returned.

The first financial centre to behave in the old way was Zurich. Switzerland had escaped not only the war-time destruction but also the post-war erosion of money values. The cost of living remained remarkably stable; Swiss banks were as discreet as ever; and it was not long before the natural inflow of capital from outside, coupled with Switzerland's own savings, allowed the Swiss authorities to introduce foreign issues on the Swiss capital market again. The market was strictly controlled, but it was a beginning. Yet not until the major Western European currencies regained convertibility at the end of 1958 did other capital markets follow Switzerland's lead. Amsterdam eventually allowed a significant volume of foreign borrowing in 1961, though none in 1959 and 1960 and hardly any in 1962 and 1963. The London market was active throughout this period, and particularly during the 1950s, but most overseas issues were for Commonwealth borrowers. For virtually the first fifteen years after the war only four basically foreign loans were arranged: for Iceland, Norway and the World Bank (twice).

It is now clear that 1958 was a turning point for Western Europe and for the European capital market too. It was the year of General de Gaulle's return to power in France. The subsequent prosperity and stability in France inevitably led to the convertibility of the Western European currencies on 29 December and, a few days later, to the launching of the Common Market. Soon economic 'miracles' were blossoming all over Western Europe. Western Germany's was the first, soon to be followed by those of Italy and France. Output rose steadily, gold flowed in and payments moved into surplus. What caused this economic upsurge is less significant to our purpose than the consequences, which were almost immediate. Given the confidence provided by convertibility, traders, manufacturers and investors all began to move money across frontiers with an ease and assurance not seen in Europe for over twenty-five years. Both short-term and long-term money was involved. Big firms began to leave surplus funds in different centres depending on the rate of interest offered. Some borrowed money in Amsterdam. Several British companies raised funds in Zurich; the World Bank borrowed in Milan; Japan raised money all round Europe; several European groups raised dollar funds in London; Copenhagen made a Swiss franc issue in London. The world was getting smaller again and money was on the move.

THE EURO-DOLLAR MARKET

The form that this money took needs some explanation. A major distinction is normally made between short-term funds that go to make up a so-called money market and longer-term funds that oil the wheels of so-called capital markets. In practice money spills over from one to the other; money borrowed in one place for a short period is put to work elsewhere for a long period. To describe Europe's capital market as one separate water-tight compartment would therefore be quite misleading; this market includes funds arising in what is known as the 'Euro-dollar market', whose growth has been one of the significant features of the economy of Western Europe over the last decade.

Euro-dollars are neither confined to Europe, nor are they entirely made up of dollars. But the shorthand term has a point. Most of the deposits happen to be dollars and most of them happen to be in Western European hands. The whole process is a return to the type of operation that was common throughout the 1920s. It can take place only when currencies can be freely held and transferred from one foreign holder to another. Although the American dollar was in this position earlier, it was not until the major Western European currencies were made fully convertible at the end of 1958 that this deposit business could develop fully. Holders of surplus currencies who knew that they would need the use of them in a certain specified time found that London banks, for example, were willing to accept them and pay an attractive rate of interest.

This business mainly began with dollars held in Western Europe. German traders, for example, who had earned dollars, instead of switching their earnings into Deutschmarks at once and getting dollars again when they needed them at a later stage, decided to place them with a London bank and earn interest into the bargain. Why, it may be asked, did they not place their dollars with American banks? The answer is simple and significant. Under Regulation Q of American banking legislation the rate of interest American banks could offer on deposits was limited. This gave ample scope for enterprising foreign banks to offer rates that American banks could not match. Since this situation arose just when the United States was running an extremely large deficit with the rest of the world, there was a growing supply of dollars being earned abroad, particularly in Western Europe. Although London banks were the most prominent, Italian, Swiss and Japanese banks have also been active in this new market. The latest estimate of the market's total published by the Bank for International Settlements in Basle put it at about 9,000 million dollars. Of this about 7,000 million was in dollars and the balance in other currencies such as sterling, Swiss francs, Deutschmarks and Dutch florins.

Most of the dollars deposited with the London banks were invested for the appropriate period in ways that brought the banks concerned a useful profit margin after taking account of the interest rate they themselves were paying. Short-term funds went into short-term projects. But there is evidence to suggest that some banks were tempted to finance longer-term projects with some of these shorter-term dollars and other currencies. In other words some of these currency deposits were financing capital developments. This occasionally led to the difficulty that deposits returned to their original owners left projects financed by banks in jeopardy unless the same amount of short-term funds could be borrowed elsewhere. But not all the dollars earned in Western Europe and other parts of the world were invested by the earners for as short a period as this. Some holders of these deposits were willing to invest them for much longer periods—for five years and upwards.

These funds soon began to spill over from the so-called money market into the capital market; and it was at this point that dollar holdings began to be relevant to the revival of Europe's capital market. While currencies had been inconvertible and thus difficult to transfer, the proportion of foreign applications for share and bond issues was bound to remain low. But as soon as confidence had been restored in the major currencies it was not only possible to expect foreign applications for loans but issues could also be contemplated in foreign currencies. The London market, for example, had an issue in Swiss francs and a whole stream of issues in American dollars. In virtually every case foreign applications predominated.

FACTORS LIMITING DEVELOPMENT OF THE EUROPEAN CAPITAL MARKETS

Thus the European capital market began to revive in different ways in the early 1960s. Western European prosperity had returned; savings were beginning to accumulate again; confidence in currencies had recovered. Above all, most financial centres—Zurich, Paris, London, Brussels, Milan, Amsterdam, etc.—still possessed well-developed institutional structures. All had sophisticated banking systems; most had a variety of other types of savings institutions; a few of them (particularly London, Paris and Amsterdam) had a large number of foreign banks and a closely knit nucleus of financial and trading companies of all kinds.

And yet, in spite of all this, the restoration was far from complete. Although the American dollar had come increasingly under pressure in the exchange markets of the world between 1958 and 1963, during that same period the foreign issues in the New York market far surpassed the volume of money being raised in Europe. Nor was this all. The number of issues in New York on behalf of European borrowers was remarkably high. This hardly made sense, at a time when America was in deficit and Europe in surplus on their balance of payments—and the Americans were not slow to complain. The phenomenon was in fact a reflection of the efficiency, cheapness and capacity of the New York market and the relative narrowness of most European capital markets. As Mr Douglas Dillon, the United States Secretary of the Treasury, summed it up at the end of 1963: 'These markets, taken as a whole, are not as efficient and effective as they might be, and as they will need to be, to play the role in the financing of European economic growth of which they are potentially capable'.

This was a serious indictment, and on balance true. In considering the factors holding back Europe's financial markets from fulfilling themselves, it will now be necessary to make a distinction within these markets, which have so far been taken as a whole. This distinction is, briefly, that London has the capital market mechanism and little savings, while the Continent has the savings but not a fully efficient market mechanism.

The common thread running through the Continental capital markets, apart from Switzerland's, is that they have suffered both inflation and war to a degree that has left scars not only on the markets and their organisation but, more important, on local investors. Confidence both in money and in bonds and shares was undermined throughout the 1930s and '40s and had a profound impact on savings and investment habits. Hence the Frenchman's predilection for small gold bars under the mattress. Neither have government policies in individual countries helped. Taxation decisions in particular have often restricted the operations of the financial markets. In some cases there have been high taxes on new securities. In others the tax burden has fallen on interest and dividends. The result has been the same in each case: to restrain financing through the capital market.

The influence of some of the savings institutions has also been important. For example, private insurance companies are a major influence in countries with a history of reasonable price stability. But they do not play a significant role in France, Germany, Italy or Belgium. As an important American report (prepared by the United States Treasury for the US Congress)[1] on Europe's capital market concluded in 1964, the assets of British insurance companies are almost four times as high as those of German companies and almost six times as high as those of French companies. The report stated that this is particularly significant: 'This reflects a rather basic institutional difference in that private insurance in continental Europe has been supplanted to a very considerable extent by social insurance. Social insurance plans are often financed out of current receipts; thus they do not always result in large capital accumulations which might be invested in securities'. This is yet a further example of the way in which public policies have affected private savings.

The above goes some way to explaining why surplus savings within these Continental economies are not always channelled towards the capital markets as efficiently as they are either in London or New York. But the difficulties do not end there. The structure of the individual capital markets is often capable of further improvement too. In France, for example, official control is dominant, largely a reflection of the unhappy monetary history of the country over the past thirty or forty years. But beyond the influence of the French Treasury lies the organisation of the market itself. A distinction is made between the so-called *banques d'affaires* and the big commercial banks. The former can acquire direct stakes in business enterprises, but it is the latter that make all the running with regard to new issues. They form consortia to underwrite the issue and use their banking network to mount a widespread sales campaign. This becomes both expensive and time-consuming and is probably one of the main reasons for the high issue costs of the French market. In Belgium the difficulties are slightly different. For one thing share-ownership, in spite of a recent expansion of interest, is still relatively narrow and activity in the stock market is concentrated on a small number of issues. For another the commercial banks are somehow restricted in their underwriting of new issues.

In Italy there is the problem of a narrow market, a continuing lack of confidence of investors and the consequent volatile nature of the stock market.

[1] See bibliography, p. 356.

Although prosperity has returned to Italy, the country still has an under-developed south in need of money and her ability to provide capital for foreign borrowers must remain limited. The control of the Bank of Italy over stock market issues is both strict and detailed. In Germany, although there is more freedom in making issues, the habits of industry (in providing most of its own capital from ploughed back profits) and of government (in influencing insurance and banking and in providing incentives for certain types of savings institutions) have combined to restrict the real functions of the capital market. Issues are firmly in the hands of the big three German banks (Deutsche Bank, Dresdner Bank and Commerzbank), the costs of an issue are high and competition is not great.

Only the London and Zurich capital markets emerged from the examination of the United States Treasury, quoted above, with reasonable results. Both had regularly accommodated a fair volume of foreign issues, whereas Frankfurt, Paris, Brussels and Milan had produced marginal results. The US Treasury report stated: 'London capital market facilities are among the most highly developed in the world'. But as we have already seen, Britain no longer has the vast volume of private savings she once had, and what little she can spare has had to go to swell investment in Commonwealth countries rather than in foreign territories generally.

Towards Development

The present situation seems to satisfy no-one and has already led to a major effort on the part of the Bank of England to try to put the London machinery to good use again without undermining Britain's balance of payments. The first steps were taken in 1962 when the Governor of the Bank of England, Lord Cromer, began to develop a new approach to the problem, concerned with the encouragement in London of an entrepot business in capital. This would have some useful advantages, he argued. It would take some of the burden off exporters who had been troubled with having to arrange export finance simply because the old system of getting foreign customers to raise money directly in Europe's capital markets had broken down. It would help to channel Europe's savings through the London capital market, thus making use of a neglected machinery. And it would provide London's merchant banks and others with a small profit margin (and valuable foreign exchange earnings). Since this was also the period when surplus dollars were piling up in Western European hands and the Euro-dollar market was developing fast, it was hardly surprising that the first efforts to put London's machinery into operation in this new way concentrated on dollar issues.

This meant that foreign borrowers came to the London market for money and were given dollars instead of pounds. Since, in addition, the bulk of these dollars were subscribed by holders of dollars outside Britain, the operation did not affect Britain's balance of payments. The first of these new-style issues was launched in May 1963 when the Belgian government raised 20 million dollars in London. This was followed in rapid succession by a Copenhagen issue in Swiss francs and by Japanese, Norwegian, Austrian, Italian and Danish issues in dollars. In 1963 as a whole foreign issues in London totalled about 100 million dollars and in 1964 they jumped to nearly 350 million. In hardly any case did British subscriptions provide more than 5 per cent of the total money raised.

This was a major step forward, but much remained—and still remains—

to be done. What has still to take place on a large scale is a succession of foreign issues in Western European centres (including London as an integral part of Europe) in European currencies. Some efforts have been made, particularly in Germany. London has taken a minor step by giving her partners in EFTA the same right to borrow money in London as members of the Commonwealth. Since there are hardly any spare funds available, this means little in practical terms for the time being. Another move was made at the end of 1964 when the city of Turin made an issue in London which introduced a new element. It was designated in sterling but gave investors an option to take principal or interest in pounds or Deutschmarks.

Another solution to the problem raised by the various currencies in Europe and a means of tapping the European market as a whole was attempted by the Kredietbank in Brussels. The basic measuring rod for the issues organised by this bank was a so-called 'unit of account', units being made up of several European currencies. A large number of such issues have been successfully launched. But not everyone is happy about the implications of such loans. Several central banks are opposed to them on the grounds that with such diverse legal backgrounds and with such varying strengths in the different currencies, the banks supporting them may be piling up difficulties for investors in several years' time. Another way of getting round these diversities was suggested some time ago by Dr Abs, the managing director of the Deutsche Bank in Frankfurt. His idea was that of parallel loans—the simultaneous floating of several loans by one issuer in different centres with each participating country raising loans in its own currency.

From what has so far been said, and considering the efforts being made to float loans simultaneously in different centres, it becomes clear that Western Europe's major monetary difficulties derive from the fact that it is still split into too many countries, with too many currencies, too many different financial systems, too many restrictions on the movement of capital and too great a difference between the efficiency of individual capital markets. Costs of market issues are low in Italy, the Netherlands and Britain and high elsewhere. There have in the past few years been currency fears for both the Italian lira and the pound. These differences are hindering the natural development of an integrated European capital market that will not only rival New York but help to shoulder some of the same burdens. An assessment of the prospects of such a market may here be made.

Effect of the Common Market

The major attempts to reduce differences as well as natural barriers to the movement of money in Western Europe have emerged from the development of the Common Market. Since the aim of this is to establish a customs union based on a complete elimination of internal tariffs, it is clear that financial and taxation policies in the different countries will equally be brought into line. It is for this reason that the Six have already launched themselves on a plan to reduce restrictions on the movement of capital among themselves. The financial implications go even further than this. Agreements on agricultural prices would be extremely difficult if members of the Six were allowed to contemplate the possibility of changing their exchange rates. Thus exchange rates have come to be regarded as frozen among the Six for some considerable time and this explains why the pressure on the Italian lira in 1963–64 caused such concern within the European Commission in Brussels. Thus the Common Market is already bringing about a closer cooperation among its members and a growing alignment in the financial field.

The individual bourses of the Six are also meeting regularly to achieve the same thing. Here the problems are more detailed: the type of information investors must have when issues are made; legal backing in each country; control over share documents; and alignment of taxation. Fortunately the meetings of representatives of the Common Market bourses have already been broadened to include, on occasions, the representatives from London and other European bourses outside the Six. Here again the same problems get an airing and progress is being made slowly but persistently. A secretariat has even been appointed in Paris, with a small nucleus of executives.

There remains the problem of how London's highly efficient financial machinery can be grafted on to the Continental markets. For a time, during the negotiations held in 1961-3 for the accession of Britain to the Common Market, it was possible to contemplate an answer to the problem. Had Britain become a full member of the Six, her economy would have been integrated with her partners in Europe and so would her financial markets. The City of London, which still claims to be the major *international* market in the world (in gold, security arbitrage, shipping, commodities, insurance, etc.), could have been expected to widen its domestic base overnight, to have been able to tap a wider area for savings, and to have gradually become the centre of Western Europe's financial operations. This may still happen. But while Britain remains outside the Six, the difficulties faced by the City's operations will be formidable. The main difficulty is that Britain lacks the surplus funds essential for any active capital market. Whether London can succeed in tapping Europe's savings by the continuous issue of foreign bonds for non-British subscription remains to be seen; however, this is not the same thing as being the centre of a wide, integrated economic area.

It was during Britain's 1961-3 negotiations with the Common Market that the future of Western Europe's currencies began to be contemplated. M. Jean Monnet had already been looking forward to the creation of a common Western European currency for some years before Britain joined the discussions. In those earlier years it was a hope rather than an immediate possibility, but the talks with Britain opened up quite a different prospect. The Americans in particular became enthusiastic, contemplating the American dollar on one side of the Atlantic and a common Western European currency (including the pound) on the other, both becoming the two key currencies in world trade and payments. This was a plan that was well ahead of its time. It tended to overlook the difficulties in grafting sterling on to the European currencies (the main problem would have been whether Europe would have been willing to shoulder Britain's sterling liabilities); it also overlooked the wide measure of integration of the British and European economies needed before central banks and individual treasuries would be willing to share their responsibilities with others. But all these ideas, which eventually collapsed with de Gaulle's veto on Britain's entry into the Common Market, served to demonstrate what large tasks lay ahead if Europe's capital markets were to achieve their full potential.

GOVERNMENT POLICY AND PRIVATE INVESTMENT

It is possible, however, that the biggest obstacle to the development of these markets lies not in the currency field or even in the political, but in the widespread influence of government policy on the channelling of private funds for investment. During the period of European reconstruction it was desirable for official policy to direct funds into certain areas of the economy, but public and semi-public institutions, once so necessary, may in future have to lose some of their dominance, particularly in Germany, France and Italy, if private investors are to be allowed more initiative. As the United States Treasury report already quoted succinctly put it: 'It would be incongruous if the Europe which supplied private risk capital for the development of North America out of the low income levels of the 18th and 19th centuries should fail to make its proportionate contribution to wider reaches of the developing world in the latter third of the 20th century'. This is the true measure of the challenge in front of the capital markets of Europe.

BIBLIOGRAPHY

Aschinger, F. E. *Zurich as a Centre of Finance*, Neue Zürcher Zeitung, Zurich, 1959.

Cairncross, A. K. *Home and Foreign Investment 1870–1913*, Cambridge Univ. Press, London and New York, 1953.

Clarke, W. M. *The City in the World Economy*, Institute of Economic Affairs, London, 1965.

Dunning, J. D. 'Capital Movements in the 20th Century', *Lloyds Bank Review*, London, April 1964.

Einzig, Paul. *The Euro-Dollar System*, Macmillan, London; St Martins Press, New York, 1964.

Foreign Dollar Loans in Europe, Macmillan, London; St Martins Press, New York, 1965.

McMahon, Christopher. *Sterling in the Sixties*, Chatham House Essays, Oxford Univ. Press, London and New York, 1964.

Macrae, Norman. *The London Capital Market*, Staples Press, London, 1957; Simmons-Boardman, New York.

A Description and Analysis of Certain European Capital Markets, US Treasury for Joint Economic Committee, US Congress, Washington, 1964.

Bank of England Quarterly Bulletin, London, June 1963.

Report of the Committee on Finance and Industry, HMSO, Cmd 3897, London, 1931.

Report of the Committee on the Working of the Monetary System, HMSO, Cmd 827, London, 1959.

SCIENCE AND TECHNOLOGY
IN WESTERN EUROPE

LAURANCE REED

FOR five centuries the countries of Western Europe have set the pace in science and technology, and judging by the results of pure research only (research carried out solely to advance scientific knowledge) it appears that they still do. Since the creation of the Nobel Prize in 1901 the area which we now call Western Europe has gained 156 prizes for science—49 for physics, 53 for chemistry and 54 for physiology and medicine, which compares with an American total of 67 and a Soviet total of nine. Taking the awards for 1960–5 alone, Great Britain, France and Germany between them have taken 16 prizes to the United States' 13 and the Soviet Union's three. However, the advance of knowledge (science) is one thing, and its exploitation (technology) another. Western Europe has today not only lost its supremacy in technology but is becoming increasingly dependent on foreign techniques to maintain industrial competence.

RELATIVE DECLINE IN WESTERN EUROPEAN TECHNOLOGY

This dependence is most marked in the advanced technologies, aerospace, cybernetics and atomic energy, where much of the original groundwork was done in Europe. Germany pioneered missile technology in the 1940s but in the 1960s the United States and the Soviet Union are the only space powers. Several European countries have succeeded in putting satellites into orbit on the back of American technology but only France has done so unaided, and Europeans must rest content with a 29 per cent share in a world satellite communications system, *Intelsat*, realised and controlled by the United States although originally conceived by an Englishman.

In recent years the European aircraft industry, concentrated in Britain and France, pioneered rear-engine design, automatic landing systems and VTOL (vertical take-off and landing) flight. Yet of the 15,000 aircraft built in the world every year (9,000 for commercial use) and of some 18,000 engines needed to fly them, 60 per cent are manufactured in the United States, 25 per cent in the Soviet Union and less than 15 per cent in Western Europe. According to *Jane's All The World's Aircraft* in the year 1965–6 Britain sold 11 BAC One-Elevens, 16 Tridents, four VC 10s and Super VC 10s and France 14 Caravelles while the American Boeing and Douglas companies sold a total of 455 jet airliners.

The position is the same in the computer industry where the American giant International Business Machines (IBM) bestrides the scene with 70 per cent of the European market. The only independent industry remaining this side of the Atlantic is in Britain. Even here home manufacturers control barely 50 per cent of their own market and according to orders placed at the beginning of 1966 the value of imported machines will exceed the value of home-built machines by 1970. The number of computers installed in a country is the best available indication of the penetration of automation and modernisation. In 1966 Western Europe had 5,520 installations, 900 for scientific applications and 4,620 for business. A total of 18,000 is projected for 1970, a figure already surpassed in the United States where installations are expected to exceed 45,000 by then.

Nuclear energy is the only major science-based industry where Western Europe has succeeded in holding its own after a sustained effort involving 88,000 scientists and engineers, a capital investment of around £1,300 million ($3,640 million), and government expenditure in 1965 of over £300 million ($840 million). Britain and the six Common Market countries had an installed nuclear generating capacity of 2,378 MWE[1] in 1965, with an estimated capacity of 11,273 MWE by 1970. Britain alone accounted for 1,395 MWE—an amount greater than the Western world's combined total including the United States—and has recently had a technical breakthrough with an advanced gas-cooled reactor system (AGR) capable of generating electricity at a price 10 per cent below the most effective coal-fired station. Yet here too the nuclear export business, currently estimated as worth more than $2 billion[2] a year, is wholly dominated by two American companies, Westinghouse and General Electric, and Britain with all its expertise has succeeded in selling only two nuclear power stations abroad, Latina in Italy and Tokai Mura in Japan.

Apart from this unfavourable flow of research-intensive exports further evidence of Western Europe's declining influence in technology is revealed in patent statistics which provide a very crude indication of the productivity of research. In France the total number of patents taken out by French applicants has remained static around 15,000 a year since 1950, while those taken out by foreign applicants climbed from 8,000 to 25,000 in 1962. France managed to increase the number of French-held patents abroad by over 5,000 in the same period but this did not keep pace with the penetration of foreign techniques in France. In 1961 French holdings in the United States amounted to 2 per cent of domestic patents, whereas those of the United States in France were equivalent to 45 per cent of France's domestic patents. No less than two-thirds of all patents operative today are in fact held by foreign applicants and France's deficit in her technological balance of payments (the difference between what is bought and sold in know-how, patents, licences, etc.) has risen from F93 million ($465 million) in 1953 to F335 million ($1,675 million) in 1962. Similarly, Germany had an unfavourable balance of $85 million in 1963. Britain on the other hand, according to statistics recently released by the Board of Trade, had a small overall surplus of £2·9 million ($8·1 million) in 1964, which makes it the only European country with a favourable account in technological royalty transactions. However, in common with the others, Britain had a deficit with the United States of £18 million ($50·5 million). Taking Western Europe as a whole, payments to the United States exceeded receipts by $111 million in 1957 and by $206 million in 1961—a ratio in the latter year of more than 5 to 1.

[1]Megawatts of electricity.
[2]The word 'billion' here and elsewhere in this book means 'one thousand million.'

The 'brain-drain' is another indication of decline. The international migration of scientists is an old phenomenon and for years a large number were attracted to European laboratories. Since the war however Western Europe has suffered from a continuing net loss of scientific manpower, a loss it can ill afford when it adds only 42,000 graduates each year to its existing stock of scientists and technologists compared to the 88,000 in America and the 140,000 in the Soviet Union. In the period 1956–61 it was estimated that scientists and engineers were leaving Europe to go to the United States at the rate of 2,230 a year—some 6 per cent of the output of graduates. Since then the number has probably been very much larger. In terms of both quality and quantity of manpower lost Britain and Germany suffered worst and both have made strenuous efforts to win their scientists back. It is not known precisely how many eventually return but some provisional data indicate that of those who go 40 per cent go for good.

The economic and social conditions most favourable to technological progress have received detailed study only in the past few years. Reliable statistics are still scanty and can be used to support almost any theory. At this stage it would be injudicious to single out any one factor as responsible for the European decline in technology. There has not in fact been an absolute decline, only a decline relative to the United States and to a lesser extent the Soviet Union, so it seems reasonable to infer that the size of a country provides at least part of the explanation. This conclusion is supported by certain facts.

THE ABSOLUTE SCALE OF R AND D EFFORT

In 1962 the United States engaged 435,600 scientists and engineers on research and development (R and D) and spent some $17 billion. In contrast, the most industrialised area of Western Europe containing a comparable population, Belgium, France, West Germany, the Netherlands and Britain, had only 147,500, spending $4·5 billion. Even if these figures are adjusted to take account of higher research costs in the United States, the resources devoted to R and D are still two to three times as great in the United States as in Western Europe. But in making this comparison it must be remembered that to treat Western Europe as an integral unit is not a fair basis for reference since science is geared to national objectives and there is a considerable amount of duplication in the area. The true extent of the R and D gap is only appreciated when measuring the total American expenditure against individual national expenditures in Europe. In the case of France the ratio is of the order of 16 to 1 and in the case of Belgium no less than 130 to 1.

In research there are always a number of lines of inquiry, and the greater number it is possible to pursue, the more probable the chance of reaching a satisfactory result. Ingenuity is only part of the story. Indeed a multiple strategy sometimes proves indispensable to success since it is the combined results of a number of lines of inquiry that yield the answer. Another advantage of numbers is the chance to reduce the 'lead time' (the time to take a new idea from the initial decision through research, development and design to first regular production). A short lead time is a major advantage in any technically progressive industry. It forces international competitiors to make a comparable effort simply to keep abreast of the leaders—a minimum 'threshold' level of R and D effort. To move from the defensive to the offensive an even greater effort is required.

Some people claim that the absolute level of activity is therefore decisive. One commentator, who sees science as the decisive factor in international power, has gone so far as to maintain that a nation's capacity to maximise its political potential through technology depends on the relative number of its first-class minds and the relative number of technicians it has to apply their work. Since the number of both ultimately depends on the total size of population, the big battalions will always win in an age when all governments strive to maximise their scientific resources.[1]

This theory rather underplays the importance of factors other than size in conditioning the rate of inventive activity. It also ignores the possibility of small countries acquiring the results of research done by others. Japan, in the past, has built extremely successful technologies on imported know-how and the United States itself leaned heavily on European research before the second world war.

Even so there are political and strategic considerations involved here and quite apart from these there are valid scientific and economic objections to over-reliance on foreign know-how. Science is not easily divisible and progress often proceeds from interaction between several branches. Development in one area may affect progress in an apparently unrelated field. The problem for a country which tries to specialise is that it loses the bearing of one branch on another which in the long run may affect its chance of staying ahead in the selected field.

There are several economic difficulties. First, licensing agreements often restrict exports by confining the licence to the home market of the licensee. Secondly, in international transfers of technology there is a considerable time-lag which in a field where technical progress is rapid may represent a great disadvantage. Thirdly, in the past technical information (other than military secrets) has been the most mobile factor in international transactions. For pure research this is still true, but for applied research the iron curtains have been rung down. R and D is big business and a substantial proportion of information is now kept wholly secret.

National autarky in science is not a viable policy even for the biggest nation, but even where imported know-how is preferred it is still necessary to maintain a minimum level of research in order to assimilate, utilise and improve upon the information obtained. Imported know-how is rarely a substitute for indigenous research.

All these considerations contribute to the tendency of Western European countries to stretch their resources thinly over a broad scientific front with the result that their R and D effort often remains below the 'threshold' set by international competition.

Spin-off from Advanced Technology

On both sides of the Atlantic a substantial proportion of total resources is committed to the military/space sector. In the United States the proportion is considerably higher, 60 per cent as against 30 per cent for Western Europe as a whole—a ratio of 7 to 1. One school of thought sees this disparity as an advantage for Europe, regarding this effort as a diversion from growth-orientated research which would raise the value of real per capita output.[2] To consider this effort as a diversion is to assume that if there were no defence-related expenditure the same scale of funds would in fact be

---

[1] B. K. Blount, 'Science as a Factor in International Relations', *International Affairs*, Vol. XXXIII, London, January, 1957.
[2] R. A. Solo, 'Gearing Military R and D to Economic Growth', *Harvard Business Review*, XL, 6, Boston, November/December 1962.

made available for growth-orientated research. In practice it proves very difficult to obtain anything like the same amount of funds for research where there are no strategic or prestige considerations at stake and where technical possibilities and sales prospects are uncertain. Furthermore, many believe that defence-related expenditures support 'lead' technologies that force the pace of development of others and stimulate a rate of technological progress superior to what could be achieved by more direct means. Now any project of great technical difficulty sets new scientific and technological parameters. It sets new problems whose solutions throw fresh light on old ones, it channels skill and imagination into the creation of new materials and processes and stimulates supporting research out of which new inventions may come. The problem of harnessing nuclear energy, for instance, has been an important stimulus in materials technology, and advanced air projects have also been important especially in electronics; but the forcing function of space research is unequalled, partly because of the great technical difficulties posed by space conditions and partly because of the wide span of industries embraced under a space programme.

There are several examples of the transfer to commercial use of products, processes and materials originally developed for space applications, but it is true that none has been very significant so far. On the other hand, 'spin-off' (indirect results of research in the form of new scientific and technological information useful in other fields) has provided a considerable stimulus to progress in electronics, metals, fuels, the life sciences, ceramics, machinery, plastics, instrumentation, thermals and cryogenics. Whether this material and intellectual 'feedback' is important enough to be advanced as a major justification for a space programme is debatable, but in so far as European nations individually have found it difficult or impossible to undertake space research they have been at an overall technological disadvantage compared with those large enough to do so.

The Size of the Market

The narrowness of European domestic markets is one of the most formidable obstacles to technological progress. The intensity of research and the speed at which innovations are taken up by industry is governed by the question of profitability. Private venture research requires mass production and markets if costs are to be redeemed. If the risk inherent in any research project is to be acceptable a large, sophisticated and *assured* market is essential. These conditions have not yet been satisfied in Western Europe's present patchwork economy.

The position is made worse by the 'threshold' set in international competition. The threshold level of R and D is an *absolute* level of resources, not a *ratio* of sales. If a European company copies the research sales ratio of a competitor with a larger home market then research expenditure may fall below the threshold. If, on the other hand, to keep lead times short enough to survive, expenditure is brought up to the threshold, research costs may become out of proportion to sales outlets, profitability be diminished, and companies be forced out of business unless research becomes government-backed.

Since the war pressure has been kept up for the elimination of tariffs and quotas, and with some success. It is doubtful, though, whether the tariff wall constitutes the most serious obstruction to goods with a high technological content. Really superior technical equipment is often purchased almost regardless of price and rides comfortably over these barriers. Indeed for aircraft it is customary in Western Europe to waive the duty on most imported machines. Behind the tariff wall there are more insidious restrictions which dissever the market as thoroughly.

One of these is created by conflicting legal and technical standards, which makes it impossible to undertake mass production of complex equipment on the scale research requires. Another is caused by differing procurement procedures of public buyers—governments and the agencies they fund, universities, local authorities, nationalised industries. The influence of the public buyer is particularly pervasive in European technology because of the size of the public sector. Almost all the transport and fuel and power industries are nationalised and in Italy and France the government has a sizeable stake in the manufacturing industries.

There is no Western European equivalent of the 'Buy American' Act which requires the Federal government to give preference to American firms over foreign even where the price is higher (as much as 50 per cent higher in the case of defence goods). In practice, however, the procurement procedures of European governments have an equivalent effect, fracturing the market and nullifying tariff concessions. Indeed they are all the more treacherous for not being incorporated in formal legislation. Each grants a preferred treatment to domestic suppliers for one reason or another, strategic, social, technological or simply because they have a direct interest in the industry. In Britain, although it is not officially admitted, state-funded buyers must give a 25 per cent preference to home computer manufacturers. In other cases open bids for government contracts are never allowed.

It has been proposed in the Kennedy Round of tariff negotiations in GATT that this favouritism should be discarded and strictly commercial criteria applied. If this were done at this stage it would almost certainly lead to further encroachment in the European market by American technology by virtue of the advantages American firms enjoy in a huge home market. This has already occurred in civil aircraft, a field where governments despite themselves have had to apply commercial criteria in the attempt to maintain the competitiveness of their international airlines. Yet the costs of R and D, even where government-financed, are reaching the point where production is only economic when the equipment is taken up by the public buyer in more than one country. So long as European governments buy 'national' they will find themselves shoring up industries which never make any money and Europe's scientific resources will be needlessly squandered in an endless round of duplication. The Plowden Committee report on the aircraft industry estimated that British governments contributed £88 million ($245 million) to civil aircraft and engine development between 1945 and 1959 and by July 1965 had recovered only £25 million ($70 million). In the end the position becomes untenable. The logical practical solution is for European governments to coordinate their procurement policies on a European basis.

THE SIZE OF FIRMS

In the United States and Western Europe over 85 per cent of industrial research is concentrated in large firms. European companies tend to spend a higher proportion of their research budgets externally in Research Associations but this is not enough to alter the fact that the intensity of research in European industry is very much less than that in American industry. This is partly explained by the fact that much public research in the United States is done in the business enterprise sector under government contract whereas in Europe it is more usually done either by the government itself in state-owned laboratories or in the higher education and non-profit sectors, and partly by the greater size of large American concerns.

Industrial concentration is not an unqualified blessing but it is an advantage in industries requiring heavy investment and in those in which technical development calls for large-scale production to reach the technical optimum. Large-scale enterprise is also an advantage in research, particularly at the development end of the innovative process. Much the same arguments in favour of the absolute scale of activity at the national level apply to the business enterprise sector. It is no accident that Europe's technological balance of payments is most adverse in mechanical and electrical engineering, where American preponderance is at its greatest. The expansion in size of European concerns is restricted chiefly by market conditions. Many have reached dimensions corresponding to the size of their national markets but further expansion is difficult to base on the vagaries of an external market.

NATIONAL EFFORTS

In recent years a closer appreciation of the importance of science and technology in economic growth has precipitated a wholesale reorganisation of science at the national level in Western Europe. Every country has set about improving scientific infrastructure, increasing expenditure and evolving a science policy. France, Britain, Germany and Belgium provide the most notable instances.

France under the Fifth Republic has made the most systematic attempt of all European countries to build up scientific and technical resources. Substantial changes were made in 1958. At the ministerial level there is now the Minister Delegate for Scientific Research and Questions of Nuclear and Space Research, and an Interministerial Committee for Scientific and Technological Research which coordinates the expenditures of the various branches of government. This Committee is assisted by the Advisory Committee for Scientific and Technological Research (CCRST), a group of twelve scientists chosen for their competence in scientific and technical fields. All these bodies share a common secretariat, the General Delegation for Scientific and Technological Research (DGRST), an organ of conception and design responsible for investigating the scientific resources of the country. Science policy is carefully coordinated with the overall economic Plan. In the Fifth Plan research expenditure is to be stepped up from 1·5 to 2·5 per cent of GNP, and under a method known as 'actions concertées' oceanography, micromolecular chemistry and automation have been singled out for special emphasis. This arrangement enables DGRST to impart special stimulus to these sectors and to coordinate public and private research on them as closely as possible.

In Britain responsibility for science and technology is divided between the Ministry of Education and Science and a new Ministry of Technology. The new Ministry was set up in 1964 to encourage and stimulate research and innovation in industry. It has concentrated its early efforts on strengthening the computer and machine-tool industries, enlarging the scope of the UK Atomic Energy Authority into research other than nuclear physics, and extending the work of the National Research Development Corporation which exists to assist the development of projects in which the cost/risk is

N

too great for private venture research. Britain has consistently spent more on scientific research than its European neighbours at 2·2 per cent of GNP. Recently there has been talk of holding expenditure below 3 per cent.

In Germany science suffered badly under Nazi rule. Many of Germany's ablest scientists were driven out of the country and after the war the Allies forbade certain research activities, nuclear physics, aviation and ship-building research. The Basic Law guarantees freedom of research and divides responsibility for science between the Federal and Länder governments. Coordination between them is accomplished by two administrative agreements, that on the establishment of a Scientific Council (Wissenschaftsrat) of 1957, and that on the promotion of science and research of 1964. The Federal government has five major promotion programmes—general promotion of science, nuclear research and development, space research, defence research, and assistance for studies. Several of these are carried out jointly with the Länder. The Federal Ministry for Scientific Research, established in 1962, centralises the nation's science policy and spent £237 million ($659 million) in 1966. Total expenditure on scientific research amounted to 1·9 per cent of GNP in 1965 and it is proposed to increase this to 3 per cent by 1970.

Belgium carried out her reorganisation in 1959. A Ministerial Committee for Science was set up under the chairmanship of the prime minister. This is a decision-making and coordinating body which formulates and carries out the country's science policy. Preparation and execution of decisions of the Ministerial Committee which affect several departments are carried out by the Interministerial Commission for Science Policy, also created in 1959. This consists of high-level civil servants representing departments concerned with science and is presided over by the president of the National Council for Science Policy (CNPS). The Council has 27 members representing scientific research, higher education and social and economic sectors and counsels the government in its elaboration of a science policy. The state's contribution to national research in Belgium is only about 40 per cent of the total, considerably lower than the European average of 60 per cent. Overall expenditure is to be increased to 2 per cent of GNP by 1970, which will bring it to the level of Western Europe as a whole.

INTERNATIONAL COLLABORATION
Bilateral agreements

Whatever steps are taken at the national level in Europe, for reasons of scale they are unlikely to match American and Soviet achievement unless complemented by vigorous action on the international plane, both to effect a satisfactory division of labour and to provide industrial and market conditions more favourable to progress. France, despite the nationalistic tone of its science, has understood this well and pursues a forceful international science policy. France has set up a network of bilateral agreements with a number of countries, with the United States on space research, with Britain and Germany in aircraft production and with the Soviet Union on colour TV, and under an agreement signed in Moscow in June 1966 on space research, meteorology and telecommunications.

Bilateral accords are very widespread in Europe, especially in the aerospace industry. British aerospace companies alone have over 30 such agreements with other European companies. France and Britain collaborate on a number of military projects but the most important, the *Concord* supersonic airliner, is in the civil field. The *Concord* agreement was signed in November 1962 and links BAC-Sud Aviation/Bristol Siddeley-SNECMA. The plane will carry 136 passengers and fly at mach. 2·2 (1,450 mph). The first prototype is due to fly in February 1968 and deliveries to commence in 1971. The costs of development have soared to £500 million ($1,390 million) from an original estimate of £150 million. It is claimed that potentially there is a market for 200 aircraft, but as at September 1966 no firm orders had been placed and deposits had been paid to reserve delivery positions on only 64. Success will depend ultimately on *Concord*'s lead-time over its American and Soviet counterparts. The problems of controlling costs in international projects and Britain's straitened economic circumstances have together dampened enthusiasm for further Anglo-French projects which have been canvassed. However, two are still under consideration—the development of a giant computer and the development of a European airbus. It is probable that Germany and other European countries will be associated with the airbus project.

NATO and OECD

Multilateral collaboration has long been promoted by the scientific community in Europe. Effective governmental participation in international science dates only from 1945, however. Sometimes governments have been persuaded to back international science ventures for purely prestige reasons, but more usually they have done so because the research in question was by nature transnational (oceanography, meteorology, radio astronomy), because it called for resources in men, materials and money on a scale beyond the means of a single country (space research, nuclear research), or because it contributed to political and economic objectives common to several countries.

Two major organisations have been concerned with the overall organisation of European collaboration in science—the North Atlantic Treaty Organisation (NATO) and the Organisation for Economic Cooperation and Development (OECD). NATO, apart from work on defence research, promotes a modest civilian programme through a Science Committee headed by an Assistant Secretary-General for Scientific Affairs. OECD through its Directorate of Scientific Affairs promotes applied research at the international level and has carried out some important studies on scientific and technological education and manpower, and general science policy.

OECD, through its specialised agency the European Nuclear Energy Agency (ENEA), has also organised collaboration on three nuclear projects: the Norwegian heavy-water boiling reactor project at Halden, the *Dragon* high-temperature reactor at Winfrith Heath in Britain, and the Eurochemic nuclear fuel processing plant at Mol in Belgium. These three projects, with a total investment of $120 million, employ more than 500 scientists and technicians. Halden has completed eight-and-a-half years as an international joint undertaking involving 11 nations and an overall expenditure of $11·8 million. The reactor was originally used for experimentation but is now employed as an irradiation testing facility for prototype power reactor fuel elements. The *Dragon* project links 12 nations in an eight-year experiment costing $70 million. It reached its full design output of 20 megawatts in April 1966. The system has proved so successful that it is claimed it will generate electricity as cheaply as fast breeders. Eurochemic, the European Company for the Chemical Processing of Irradiated Fuels, is an international shareholding company which remains under the control of governments through a Special Group of the Steering Committee of ENEA. It associates 13 countries and signed its first contracts for reprocessing in 1965.

CERN, EURATOM and ESRO

The most celebrated and successful organisation in the nuclear field is the European Organisation for Nuclear Research (CERN). This was set up in 1953 to carry out research into high-energy nuclear physics through the construction of two high-power accelerators—one a 28-GeV (billion electron volts) proton synchroton. There is also a proposal to build a 300-GeV machine costing £140 million ($389 million). CERN employs 1,500 scientists and technologists and has a budget of around £11 million ($31 million) which is increasing by 12 per cent per annum. The 12 participating countries share the cost in proportion to their national incomes. The success of this organisation is largely due to its purely scientific orientation.

Another important organisation in nuclear energy is the European Atomic Energy Community (Euratom). Signed by the Six, the Treaty came into force in 1958 for an unlimited duration. The aim of the Community was to create conditions necessary for the speedy establishment and growth of nuclear industries, and in particular to develop research, establish uniform safety standards, facilitate investment, ensure the construction of basic facilities and the supply of ores and nuclear fuels, and to bring about a common market for Western Europe's nuclear industry.

Euratom's role has primarily been as a research and development organisation complementing and coordinating national programmes. It has a research budget for the five years 1963–7 of $455 million. Research is carried out either by direct contracts with industry or research institutions, or by 'association contracts' or through Euratom's own Joint Research Centre. The association contract formula enables work done under national programmes to be put on a Community basis by the direct participation of Euratom. Association contracts account for 35 per cent of research expenditure and include several studies on thermonuclear fusion and backing for a German nuclear-powered ship, the *Otto Hahn*, due at sea in 1967.

The Joint Research Centre possesses four research establishments. Ispra in Italy has been mainly concerned with the Orgel project which involves research on natural uranium-fuelled atomic reactors using heavy water as a moderator and an organic liquid as a coolant. Petten in the Netherlands is a general competence centre while Geel in Belgium specialises in nuclear measurements, standards and the development of instruments and methods. The fourth establishment, the Transuranium Institute at Karlsruhe, is devoted to research on plutonium.

In the industrial field free trade already exists in nuclear raw materials, reactors and equipment and a regulation providing for the free movement of qualified atomic workers has been brought into force. A target programme has been published and although it is not specifically provided for in the Treaty ways have been found for Euratom to support the construction of six power plants in the Community. Important work has also been done in standardising health and insurance regulations.

Space is a new area for European collaboration. The European Space Research Organisation (ESRO) came into full being only in 1964 and owes its origin to the initiative of the same group of scientists who created CERN. It associates 10 European nations in a purely scientific endeavour. A number of establishments are being set up—the European Space Technology Centre (ESTEC) at Delft (the Netherlands) which is to carry out the design, development and construction of rocket nose cones and satellites, the European Space Data Centre (ESDAC) at Darmstadt (Germany), the European Space Research Institute (ESRIN) in Italy and a European Space Launching Range (ESRANGE) at Kiruna (Sweden) amongst others. A budget of £110 million ($306 million) is provided for the first eight years, contributions being on the basis of national incomes. Apart from launching sounding rockets at the rate of 60 a year the programme includes plans for sending satellites aloft. The first to go up will be *ESRO 2* (Hawker Siddeley Dynamics/Engins Matra), due to be launched on an American Scout rocket in April 1967. There are also plans for several lunar satellites and an ambitious 'Large Astronomical Satellite' (LAS) is to be launched in 1971. The organisation is primarily a supplier of facilities, placing its laboratories and equipment at the disposal of scientists from the universities and laboratories of member states.

ELDO

The European Space Vehicle Launcher Development Organisation (ELDO) also came into operation in 1964 on the initiative of the British government who were seeking a peaceful use for their *Blue Streak* rocket originally developed for military purposes. The objectives are the development and construction of space vehicle launchers and their equipment for supply to eventual users, of whom ESRO is intended to be one. ELDO links six European nations and Australia. The initial programme was for the joint construction of a three-stage rocket, *Europa 1*, Britain to supply the first stage, France the second and Germany the third, Italy the test satellites, Belgium the ground control stations, the Netherlands the telemetry systems and Australia the launching site. At the beginning of 1966 ELDO ran into serious difficulties. The original programme for *Europa 1* had slipped back two years, its cost had escalated from £70 million to £160 million ($445 million) and its capability was rapidly becoming technologically obsolete. The programme was revamped and the rocket given additional power so as to place satellites in synchronous orbit from an equatorial launching range in French Guiana. Costs were also more fairly proportioned according to national income and a financial ceiling of £118 million ($328 million) was placed on expenditure between 1967–71. The reason for these setbacks is the half-hearted approach of European countries to space research and its exploitation and the failure to formulate any coherent, long-term space policy.

POTENTIALITY FOR TECHNOLOGICAL GROWTH IN WESTERN EUROPE

The Common Market holds the promise of the creation of standards of size more favourable to technological progress in Europe. On the market side the dismantling of tariffs proceeds ahead of the Rome Treaty's time-table but progress in eliminating non-tariff barriers has been less satisfactory. Conflicting technical standards, especially in the electrical industry, still present serious distortions and the harmonisation of procurement procedures in the public sector is not provided for at all.

On the industrial side company amalgamations have increased rapidly since 1958 and research has been an important motive behind these mergers. It was one of the main arguments in the Agfa-Gevaert link-up; the American competitor to these two companies, Kodak, spent almost as much on research as Gevaert's total sales. The majority of such mergers, however, have been confined within national boundaries by legal and fiscal obstacles which have hindered the growth of European-sized companies. The attitude of the EEC Commission to industrial concentration is to favour amalgamations that promote technical progress provided they do not lead to monopoly positions, and among proposals for removing artificial obstacles to trans-national mergers is a proposal for the creation of a European company law code.[1]

Unlike the Treaty of Paris establishing the Coal and Steel Community (ECSC), the Rome Treaty, rather surprisingly, makes no mention of scientific and industrial research. It is on France's insistence that the Treaty's chapters on economic growth have been interpreted as implying a joint effort on scientific and technical research, and action in this sphere is outlined in the first draft programme on medium-term economic policy. The growing R and D gap between Western Europe and the United States has recently prompted calls for a European Community in Advanced Technology with a common purchasing agency. This idea has attracted strong support in Britain where supporters have seen it as a way of associating Britain, still the foremost technological power in Europe, with the process of integration prior to entry into the Community.

At first glance the extent of European scientific and technological collaboration seems impressive, but it must be pointed out that the ventures described above do not amount to more than 4 per cent of total Western European efforts—a scale too small to redress the balance with the United States and the Soviet Union. Nor have these projects been all that they might. Their shortcomings all derive from one central weakness—the absence of any European science policy. The principle difficulty in formulating such a policy is that a 'policy for science is meaningful only in the context of the broad political and social objectives that science serves, and can be effectively implemented only by bodies responsible for achieving such objectives.'[2] The promise of the European Community is that it contains the germ of political union in which a policy of scientific advance can be formulated. Such a policy is a precondition for Europe's remaining a technological third force capable of competing against or partnering others on a basis of equality.

[1] Agence Europe, 'European Company—EEC Commission Thinking.' *Europe Documents* No. 375. Luxembourg, 5 May 1966.
[2] OECD, *Science, Economic Growth and Government Policy*, Paris, 1963.

BIBLIOGRAPHY

Cleaver, A. V. 'The Future of ELDO—an Industrial Point of View', *Spaceflight*, VIII, 9, London, September 1966.
Dedijer, S. 'Why did Daedalus Leave?', *Science*, CXXXIII, 3470, London, 30 June 1961.
Freeman, C. 'Research and Development in Electronics Capital Goods', *Economic Review*, No. 34, London, November 1965.
Freeman, C. and Young, A. *The Research and Development Effort in Western Europe, North America and the Soviet Union*, OECD, Paris, 1965.
Gatland, K. W. 'Europe in Space', *Spaceflight*, VIII, 6, London, June 1966.
Jewkes, J. et al. *The Sources of Invention*, St Martins Press, New York, 1958; Macmillan, London, 1961.
Morris, A. 'Reflections on Atomic Integration', *Nuclear Engineering*, XI, 119, London, April 1966.
Polach, J. G. *Euratom*, Oceana Publications, New York, 1964.
Robbins, J. A. 'Is Standardization Common Market Trade Barrier?', *Electrical Times*, CXLIX, London, 31 March 1966.

Welles, J. G. and Waterman, R. H. 'Space Technology: Pay-off from Spin-off', *Harvard Business Review*, XLII, 4, Boston, Mass., July–August 1964.

Agence Europe. 'Community Scientific and Industrial Policy—French Suggestions', *Europe Documents*, No. 309, Luxembourg, 16 March 1965. 'Size of Businesses and Amalgamations in EEC', *Europe Documents*, No. 359, Luxembourg, 10 January 1966.

HMSO. *Report of the Committee of Inquiry into the Aircraft Industry*, London, 1965.

OECD. *International Scientific Organizations*, Paris, 1965. *Government and Technical Innovation*, Paris, 1966. *Country Reports on the Organisation of Scientific Research. Reviews of National Science Policy*. 'Overseas Royalty Transactions in 1964', *Board of Trade Journal*, CXCI, London, 29 July 1966.

UK Council of the European Movement. *European Cooperation in Advanced Technology*, London, 1965.

ENERGY IN WESTERN EUROPE

RICHARD BAILEY

ABUNDANT supplies of energy at low cost are a major factor in creating a climate for economic expansion. In the past industrial development depended very largely on the availability of coal, and it was no accident that the major industrial countries of the world were also its principal coal producers. In the last decade new sources of energy, notably oil and natural gas, have captured a number of the traditional markets for coal. At the same time the development of nuclear energy represents a completely new source of supply for the future. Energy supplies have been affected by the development of Western European integration. Three different six-nation Communities have been set up, each in charge of a different sector of the fuel and power economy. These are for coal under the European Coal and Steel Community, atomic energy under Euratom, and oil and natural gas under the European Economic Community. This division between three different organisations is particularly unfortunate at a time when the need is to coordinate energy policies. The remaining West European countries, which are not members of the EEC, face the same broad problems in the field of energy. Ample supplies of cheap energy are necessary for economic expansion, but an excess of supplies over potential demand may very well depress prices to a point where the return on capital investment, whether coal, oil or nuclear energy, may prove to be uneconomic. If this happens, the prospects of a future shortage of energy will be increased. For this reason accurate forecasting of energy supplies and demand are of the utmost importance in formulating energy policy.

Energy forecasting is a notoriously difficult operation, depending as it does on successfully calculating what will happen to a number of variables. The use of energy depends on the general level of economic activity, which must be forecast before deciding on the level of energy demand. Again, variations in the weather can upset energy calculations. A hard winter can make all the difference to the stock position of the coal industry. The future balance of demand between the different fuels will depend to a great extent on questions of availability, price and the way in which governments intervene in the energy market. But perhaps the biggest problem is how to balance the needs of the long-term situation which may be one of scarcity, with those of meeting current demand from abundantly available fuels, all of which, except coal, may have to be imported. Here the situation of each of the major fuels will be described at Community and national levels. The reasons for the failure of the Six to arrive at a common energy policy and the present and future relationship of Britain to the Community as a user and producer of energy will be analysed.

THE ECSC

The European Coal and Steel Community was established by the Treaty of Paris signed on 18 April 1951. It is important not only for its work in connection with its two industries but as the forerunner and prototype of Community-type integration. The objectives set out in the Schuman Declaration of 1950[1] were the unification of markets and control over basic resources. This was to be secured by the elimination of six obstacles: customs duties and quantitative restrictions on coal and steel movements between the member countries; discriminatory transport rates; price discrimination for domestic and export sales within the Community area; cartels and agreements in restraint of trade; government subsidies; and government control of prices. From the economic point of view the ECSC is a common market run by a nine-member High Authority with considerable executive powers. The movement of coal and the other products covered by the Treaty was achieved almost at once, although the member countries maintained control over their import policies. The major task of the High Authority has been less to create a free trade area with no tariff barriers between members and harmonised national tariffs against imports from third countries, than to ensure the application of free and undistorted competition between member countries.

The Treaty of Paris made no specific reference to the various fuels which compete with coal. When it was signed in 1951 Europe was still in an era of fuel scarcity and ministerial thinking in the six ECSC countries and in Britain was dominated by the fear that shortages might become worse. The direction of trade in coal between the Six was mainly from Germany to the other members. France, Italy and the Netherlands relied entirely on Germany for outside supplies of coking coal. Germany provided three-quarters of the supplies of coke for the Community, most of which went to France, the Saar and Luxembourg. France, the second largest producer of coal in the ECSC, was in most years a net importer. Belgium, on the other hand, was a net exporter of coal, selling to France and Italy while importing from Germany. Throughout the early years of the ECSC's existence, substantial amounts of coal were imported from non-members, particularly the United States.

A major consequence of opening the Common Market for coal was a rationalisation of the flow of trade. Before the fifties the famous triangle taking in the Ruhr, Lorraine and north-east France, in which most of the coalfields of the Community were situated, had been divided up historically between no less than five sovereign countries. Once this artificial political division had been broken down, trade flowed naturally between areas complementary to each other. For example, Ruhr coal moves freely to Lorraine, and coal from Lorraine to southern Germany. The most difficult task of the High Authority was to ensure free competition. This entailed the ending of double-pricing arrangements, discriminatory freight rates and other non-tariff barriers and the introduction of new pricing regulations. The rules that prices must not be fixed so as to apply 'unequal conditions to comparable transactions', and that sellers must publish the prices chargeable to all buyers in the Community, are basic to the principle of equality on which ECSC practice is founded. The other side of the High Authority's role in securing fair competition is its anti-cartel activity. A major conflict lasting several years took place before the biggest cartel in the coal industry

[1] See 'The Structure of the European Community'.

—GEORG—which handled sales of all Ruhr coal—was brought into line with Community practice.

OIL SUBSTITUTION

Altogether, however, the High Authority has met with only partial success in dealing with coal. Under the conditions in which it was set up the main concern was to encourage output of coal and facilitate imports from third countries. In the second half of the fifties the sellers' market in all fuels came to an end. The competitiveness of prices of different fuels became a matter of much greater significance and coal was faced with competition from imported fuels. New discoveries of oil in Venezuela, West Africa and Libya, finds of oil and natural gas in the Sahara, together with an easing of supplies from the Middle East, represented a formidable increase in the competition facing the coal industries of the ECSC. In 1960 the Robinson Committee reporting to the OEEC pointed out that 'a large part of the aggregate demand for energy in general is transferable from one energy source to another over a period', but in the short run 'the pattern of consumption is to some degree stabilised not only by the existing preferences of consumers but also by the existing types of installations and equipment for the use of particular fuels'.[1]

The rate of increase in consumption of oil in Western Europe generally since 1959 has been faster than that of industrial production. This means both that most of the increased use of energy has been met by oil, and that other fuels have continued to be replaced by it. Among oil products nearly half the demand is for fuel oils, about a quarter for gasolene and diesel oil, and the remainder for petroleum, aviation spirit, kerosene and other products. This pattern of demand reflects the tendency to use a heavy fuel wherever possible for large-scale heating, steam raising and other industrial install-ations. This has been made possible by the development of more efficient plant for the burning of the heavier fuel oils and the increasingly large scale of oil-using plant. The inducement to change over to oil-fired plant lies partly in the relatively low cost and partly in the saving of labour and general convenience compared with coal. This pattern of consumption has neces-sitated considerable adaptation of the refining industry in Western Europe. It has been necessary to vary the make-up of total crude supplies in order to yield greater proportions of the heavier oil products, to make use of advanced refining techniques, to improve the quality of gasolene, and to find alternative uses for surplus light fractions—for instance, in the petro-chemical industry, and as feed stocks in new gas-making processes.

For the countries of Western Europe the increased use of oil poses a number of problems. For some the security provided by indigenous supplies of coal has to be weighed against relative cost and other advantages of oil. Second, the pace at which one kind of fuel can gain ground on and replace another without the change causing undue social or economic difficulties involves a number of policy considerations. Thirdly, reliance on imports raises the question of how far these can be controlled and of the reliance that can be placed upon the different sources of supply. In this last connection there is the problem posed by the increasing offers of supplies of cheap Soviet oil to the European countries.

The importance attached to these various questions depends very much on whether a long or short term view of the energy position is being taken.

[1] *Towards a new Energy Pattern in Europe*, OEEC, Paris, January 1960.

Discussion of the world's oil reserves takes place by reference to what are known as 'proved reserves', that is, those quantities of crude oil which have been shown by drilling activity to be physically present and to be commercially recoverable by existing methods. Throughout the history of the industry, reserves have been continuously added to at a faster rate than the increase in consumption. But growth in proved reserves has fallen off in recent years, although the expenditure on exploration by the oil industry has greatly increased. This expenditure covers the exploration being carried on in offshore areas and the North Sea, and revisions taking place in existing oil-fields. The problem which the oil industry has to keep constantly in mind is that at some point, perhaps in the 1980s, perhaps later, a stage might be reached when annual discoveries of new reserves begin to fall short of annual consumption. If that happens, then the use to which oil products are put will have to be very carefully considered. The point here is not that supplies of oil will be short at some foreseeable date but that its percentage contribution to total energy requirements would have to fall.

The ways in which the Six have attempted to work out rules regarding external trade and internal competition for oil and coal will be dealt with in an account of the search for a common energy policy.

Nuclear Energy

Euratom was set up simultaneously with the European Economic Community by a separate treaty signed in Rome in March 1957. It has its own five-member Commission but shares all the other Community institutions with the EEC. When Euratom was created Europe was still in the midst of its post-war fuel and power shortage and it was thought that nuclear power on a large scale would be essential to meet the growing energy requirements of the Common Market. However, no sooner had the new organisation been set up than the European energy situation changed so that the emphasis switched from the development of commercial nuclear energy to longer-term research. Another major reason for setting up Euratom was the desire to pool the efforts of the Six in the nuclear field and so reduce the lead held by the United States, the Soviet Union and Britain. In the Community France alone had developed a nuclear industry. West Germany had only been allowed to start activities in this field in 1955 and neither Italy nor the Benelux countries had any significant nuclear programmes. There is full free trade inside the Community in all nuclear materials. Uranium and other fissionable material is the property of the Community, except for that which member states devote to military purposes, and a Supply Agency exists to share out materials should there be a shortage.

It has been the policy of the Euratom Commission to promote research on new and as yet unproved types of reactor rather than to duplicate work done in Britain or the United States. Three types of reactor have been selected for development. The first use natural uranium with a heavy water moderator and are being developed under the ORGEL[1] programme. The second type of reactor now being developed is the fast breeder type of the kind already in operation at Dounreay in Scotland. The programme provides for development either of a single reactor jointly by France and Germany or of two separate reactors following work done on the Rapsodie project by the French,

[1] Organic Cooled Heavy Water Moderated System.

Energy in Western Europe—1. Coal and Hydro-Electricity

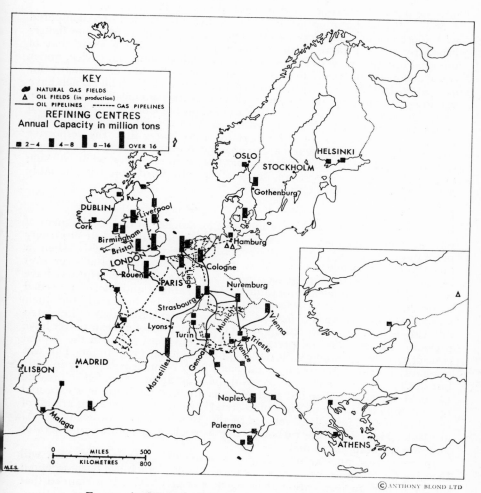

Energy in Western Europe—2. Oil and Natural Gas

and at Karlsruhe by the Germans. The third project is for a high-temperature gas reactor, and here the Community is cooperating with Britain on the Dragon project. Between them these three major programmes will cost something of the order of $200 million. In addition, Euratom has set up a Common Research Centre which in fact comprises a series of four research stations in Italy, Belgium, Germany and the Netherlands, each specialising in some particular aspect of the Nuclear Research Programme.

Some idea of the importance of the French nuclear industry compared with those of the other Community countries can be gathered from figures issued by the Euratom Commission in June 1965. These show that of the total installed power of the Community nuclear plants in service, under construction or planned, France accounts for 2,483 MWe, Germany for 917 MWe, Italy for 607 MWe, and Benelux for 231 MWe. The French have continued to develop their own nuclear industry, giving full support to some European projects but tending to look on the Community as a useful annex to their own programme rather than as a joint undertaking. The Euratom Commission's annual report for 1964 states that 'the respective efforts of the member states remain as unequal as ever with France pursuing a systematic and continuous effort to exploit her own resources, while working to acquire her own long-term needs of ores in third countries, notably Africa, Madagascar and Canada'.

Britain's nuclear energy programme

Britain has had longer and more intensive experience in the development of nuclear generation than any country in the world. The nuclear electricity programme was stepped up in the fifties after the Suez crisis when a fuel shortage appeared likely. Very large amounts of capital over and above what the electricity-generating industry would have required have been spent on the nuclear programme. The uranium and thorium needed to produce the fuel for nuclear stations have to be imported, but their foreign exchange cost is less, per ton of coal equivalent, than that of imported oil. Although earlier expectations about the economics of nuclear power have proved overoptimistic and premature, there has been a fall in the capital costs of successive stations built under the first nuclear programme. This was originally intended to provide 1,500–2,000 MW of nuclear capacity in 1965 but this target was trebled in 1957 and the programme extended to provide 5,000 MW by 1968. The last station under the first programme is expected to be completed in 1969. The commercial stations now operating are all of the Magnox type initially developed by the Atomic Energy Authority (AEA) at Calder Hall. They use carbondioxide as coolant, graphite as moderator and natural uranium as fuel.

In the second nuclear programme covering the seventies, the AEA will be using the 'advanced gas-cooled reactor' (AGR) which has been accepted for the second nuclear station at Dungeness (1,200 MW). It is claimed that the station will give cheaper base-load electricity than coal-fired stations. This reduction in running costs is associated with very high capital costs compared with those of conventional power stations. The possibilities for improving the efficiency of conventional stations have by no means been exhausted, and are in fact being vigorously examined as a result of this threatened competition. It is unlikely therefore that nuclear energy will supply more than 3 per cent of world fuel requirements in the seventies. In Britain the forecast in the government's White Paper *Fuel Policy*[1] is that

[1] Cmnd 2798.

a total of 8,000 MW might be in commission under the second nuclear programme by 1975. This forecast assumes that it will be possible to finance the heavy investment involved, and that no problems arise in relation to the supply of uranium or the disposal of waste products.

ENERGY AT NATIONAL LEVEL

By 1970 it is anticipated that all the countries of Western Europe will to a greater or lesser degree be dependent on imported energy, particularly in the form of oil. The fact that some countries are much less dependent on outside sources than others is one of the main reasons for the very different national energy policies which they pursue. Another reason is the fact that some countries, especially Britain and some of the Common Market countries, have a large financial stake in the international oil industry while others have none.

France

France has an annual coal production of some 52 million tons, considerable indigenous production of natural gas and of oil and fully developed hydro-electric capacity. She has considerable shareholdings in Middle East oil and is the largest single holder in the developed oil resources of Algeria. The French government is able to exert a very complete control over the national energy market. The mines, gasworks and electric power stations are all nationalised and the growth in national investment is the responsibility of the Commissariat au Plan. Coal imports from outside the ECSC are regulated by the ATIC, the national coal buying agency, which is able to control quantities and influence prices. Investment in the oil industry requires price authorisation by the Commission des Hydrocarbures. Further afield, the development of refining and distribution of oil from the 'Franc Zone' is now controlled by the Union Générale des Pétroles. The development of the hydro-electric programme is regulated through the nationalised Electricité de France while the exploitation and development of national oil and natural gas resources is carried on through the Bureau des Recherches de Pétrole. The French system is firmly dirigiste and while allowing competition between different fuels, it ensures that this is carried out in an orderly manner.

West Germany

West Germany is both the largest producer and consumer of energy among the Six. It possesses no significant stake in the international oil industry. Production of coal in West Germany was stabilised at 140 million tons a year but has now fallen to about 126 million tons. Coal and lignite represented 64·3 per cent of Germany's energy needs in 1964 compared with 87 per cent in 1955. Hydro-electricity supplied 3.2 per cent of the national needs in 1964 and the remainder of the country's consumption was in the form of petroleum of which about 4 per cent was locally produced and the rest imported. The use of oil in Germany is likely to increase rapidly with the development of refining capacity, especially inland refineries served by crude oil pipelines both from the east and the south. By 1975 it is expected that 40 per cent of Germany's energy will be in the form of oil.

The German coal industry suffered severely from the fall in demand that began in 1956. The effects were made worse by the fact that German importers had hurriedly concluded long-term contracts for American coal when it looked as though there might be a continuing shortage. The German government has protected its fuel market by putting a duty on imported coal, imposing a temporary duty on fuel oil, offering incentives for the use of coal in electric power stations and by the payment of 'shift premiums' direct to miners for each shift worked. In addition, the Federal government has made grants to cover increases in miners' wages, finance rebates on coal transport charges by rail and water, and has assisted in the rationalisation of the industry in various ways.

Italy

Italy has virtually no domestic coal production and depends to a much greater extent than the rest of the Six on oil, natural gas and hydro-electricity to meet its fuel needs. The big increase in industrial activity in Italy in the last decade has depended on local production of natural gas and imports of oil. For the most part industry has continued to develop in the north but some relocation has taken place in Sicily and the Mezzogiorno. Although discoveries of natural gas in the south of Italy are now being developed the gas field in the Po Valley is stated to have a life of about twenty years at present levels of production. This means that further expansions in industrial activity in Italy will be on the basis of imported fuel.

The Italians possess no shareholding in the major international oil companies and have accordingly taken steps to acquire a stake of their own in foreign oil. The instrument for acquiring this interest is AGIP, which was originally a state refining, marketing and prospecting agency set up in the twenties to search for oil and gas in Italy. It was AGIP which played a major part in finding the natural gas field in the Po Valley. The development of the field and responsibility for Italy's oil interests generally was taken over by a new state corporation, ENI, which took over AGIP and other official agencies. Under its chairman the late Signor Mattei, ENI continued to search for natural gas in Italy and at the same time embarked on a policy of bargaining for the cheapest oil imports whatever their source, and of obtaining concessions for oil production and exploration overseas. Italy's imports of Soviet oil are the largest in Europe. With imports from offshore concessions in the Persian Gulf and Egypt and oil explorations being carried out in several other countries, Italian oil products are being marketed throughout Western Europe.

The Netherlands

The Netherlands has a majority shareholding in Royal Dutch Shell, the second largest oil group in the world, a small coal industry covering some 35 per cent of its energy requirements, and a newly discovered natural gas field. This last, at Groningen in the north of Holland, contains the largest reserves of natural gas yet located in Europe. It is being developed as a premium fuel and not as a cheap general fuel that might undercut the prices of oil and coal in the electricity and industrial fuel markets. The development of the Groningen field by the Nederlandse Aardolie Maatschappi, the joint Esso–Royal Dutch Shell Group, is being carefully controlled both in regard to home sales and exports by a body which includes representatives of the Dutch state coalmines.

Belgium

Belgium has traditionally been a considerable coal producer but of recent years its industry has run increasingly into difficulties. With mining costs among the highest in Europe, the industry suffered considerably from the fall in ocean freight rates after the end of the Suez crisis which brought down the prices of imported coal and oil. The steady switch to oil by traditional consumers of coal also affected the Belgian coal industry, particularly the high-cost collieries of the Centre and the Borinage. In 1959 the High Authority gave permission for the Belgian government to introduce measures which had the effect of insulating its internal market for coal from competition from the rest of the ECSC as well as from other countries, especially the United States. Measures to rationalise the coal industry were put into effect which reduced coal output from nearly 30 million tons a year in 1954 to 21 million tons in 1964. Oil imports into Belgium have increased to bring the share of oil in the national energy consumption to nearly 40 per cent. The government has attempted by increasing the taxation of fuel oil to slow down the switch from coal to oil but with only moderate success. Belgium has no major stake in oil production abroad and is a highly competitive market for oil products, the development of which has been hindered by the need to protect the coal industry.

Luxembourg

Although a major steel producer, Luxembourg has virtually no fuel of its own and relies on Belgian and German coal, and on oil from the international companies. Its import policy for fuels is a liberal one.

Britain

Britain has the largest coal industry in Europe and the largest European interest in international oil. She also has by far the biggest research programme in nuclear energy and is the only West European country to have produced a commercially viable nuclear powered electric generating station. The National Coal Board produces around 180 million tons of coal a year against the 230 million tons of the ECSC. Britain has little hydro-electric power and before the North Sea search for natural gas began, no significant natural gas deposits. Britain's ownership of British Petroleum and the 40-per-cent shareholding in the Royal Dutch–Shell group together make a very considerable contribution to the country's invisible income which goes a long way to balance the net imports of oil on visible trade account. Imports of American coal and Soviet oil are both strictly controlled. Since the budget of 1961 there has been an excise duty of nearly £2 a ton (2d. a gallon) on fuel oil and any oil products sold in the general energy market. This is regarded as a 'revenue duty' and not as a protective measure for the British coal industry.

Various measures have been taken to help the British coal industry carry out its long-term programme of rationalisation. The difficulty is that although the National Coal Board has a much larger core of competitive coal than any of the Six, too high a proportion of its production comes from unremunerative pits. As these are concentrated in Scotland, the north-east and Wales, all of which are areas where unemployment is higher than the national average, the pace of rationalisation has had to be moderated. In the National Plan published in September 1965, it was stated that 'the importance of freedom of choice for the ultimate consumer in helping to keep down fuel cost must be recognised, but regard must also be paid to other vital national interests such as the balance of payments, security of supply, and the health of the national fuel industries'. The Plan then went on to deal with the role of different sources of energy. For coal the objective was to eliminate inefficient capacity so as to produce 'a compact and competitive industry still supplying more than half the nation's energy and offering attractive jobs'. This process of rationalisation was to be helped by various government measures taken in conjunction with the regional economic planning councils. The Board has an investment programme of about £360 million for the years 1966 to 1970, which will enable the continuation of the programme of research and development which has resulted in the production of remotely controlled and automated techniques, many of which have been brought into use in coalmining for the first time.

The Plan foresaw an increase in the demand for oil at an annual average rate of 7·5 per cent in the years to 1970. It is expected that the refinery programme during this period will lead to an increase of output sufficient to meet inland demand and bunker sales for shipping as well. The main investment by the oil companies will be in oil refineries, particularly at Milford Haven, Humberside, Tees and Thames.

The rest of Western Europe

Virtually the whole of Western Europe's reserves of coal outside those of the European Economic Community and Great Britain are in Spain. The coalfields in the Asturias, in Cordoba and Ciudad Real produce some 12 million tons of hard coal a year. Elsewhere the only indigenous deposits are of lignite and brown coal, found in Denmark, Greece and Portugal. The main source of energy produced in Switzerland is hydro-electric power. Some 50 to 60 per cent of potential hydro-electric power has now been developed and it is estimated that the cost of exploiting the rest would be so high as to be uneconomic. Austria, previously dependent on hydro-electricity as its main indigenous source of power, has now discovered considerable reserves of natural gas. The Scandinavian countries have about one half of Western Europe's remaining undeveloped hydro-electricity potential. The problems involved in its exploitation can be illustrated by the case of Sweden, where about 80 per cent of the unused potential is in the northern part of the country, while the major consuming areas are in the south. Distances of up to 500 miles have to be covered by transmission lines from the generating stations to the industrial areas. In Norway cheap hydro-electric power has been used to attract several large-scale industries, notably aluminium, specialising in electro-metallurgy. Apart from West Germany, France, Italy, the Netherlands and Britain, the only other Western European countries with any considerable oil-refining capacity are Sweden and Spain.

The place of these countries in the general pattern of Western European energy is largely as importers of fuel, especially oil, and to a decreasing extent coal. The development of long-distance electric power transmission has given a major importance to hydro-electricity resources as a means of meeting peak load demand. An elaborate system of exchanges has been worked out between Switzerland, West Germany and France, which brings hydro-electric power of the Alpine region into the distribution system of areas as far away as Luxembourg and the Rhine Valley. Exchanges by the cross-channel power-link between the Central Electricity Generating Board and Electricité de France have been in operation for several years. These transfers are of especial value in assuring supplies over the winter months. These examples of cooperation show what may very well be the pattern for the future. Western Europe may have an electricity distribution grid to which all countries are connected. Whether their power stations are coal- or oil-fired, hydro-electric or operated by nuclear energy will make no difference.

The development of a great international gas grid fed by plant working on the carbonisation of coal, on light oil distillates and from natural gas stations is perhaps rather farther ahead in the future. Long-distance pipelines from production centres have become a practical proposition with the development of the natural gas fields of Italy, France and the Netherlands. So far these have not crossed frontiers to any great extent, but the exploitation of the Groningen Field is likely to be the first step towards a new international pattern of gas distribution which will benefit the whole of Western Europe.

THE COMMON ENERGY POLICY

Although the coordination of energy policies has been envisaged ever since the creation of the EEC and Euratom, great difficulties have been experienced in reaching agreement on the form this should take. An inter-executive committee of the three European executives was set up in 1959 under the control of the Council of Ministers of the ECSC with responsibility for working out the Common Energy Policy. Since then three reports have been put forward and failed to win acceptance and the position in mid-1966 was that the Six had agreed on the outlines of the Common Energy Policy while leaving members free to pursue national policies. The first two reports put forward (the Lapie Report of March 1960 and the Short Term Proposals of 1961) were both influenced by the change from conditions of shortage to those of surplus for coal which took place between 1957 and 1960. Both reports to a greater or lesser degree had the object of protecting the coal industries of member countries.

The final 'Document de Synthèse' (1962) came at a time when the total demand for energy was increasing. The coal industry in the member countries was enjoying various degrees of protection, high-cost pits being closed down to rationalise production. The emphasis in this report was on the development of a common market in energy rather than on arriving at a coordinated energy policy. By this time the Commission of the EEC was playing a much larger role in discussions on energy policies. The fact that common policies for other sectors of the economy had been worked out or were in process of formulation gave rise to the view that given the will to reach agreement the common policy could be achieved. The third report, therefore, took less account of the problems of the coal industry and was much more concerned with long-term energy policy. This document drew in detail upon the ideas put forward by the two earlier reports, or argued in favour of a common market for energy which would be 'an open free market' offering the lowest price for energy, a market in which there would be free circulation of products. It laid stress on the importance of the security of sources of supply of imported energy, particularly of oil. The coal industry of the ECSC would be cut down to a level which was competitive with imported fuels, and any production above this would have to be subsidised by the national governments. In effect, the reduction in coal production would have been of the order of 125 million tons a year, that is, about half the Community production in 1962. The report argued that consumption taxes on fuel within the EEC should be harmonised at a low level, that taxes on all products used in transport should be brought broadly into line, and that oil prices should be published.

The report was not accepted by the Council of Ministers of the ECSC when it came up for consideration in October 1962. The coal-producing countries were sharply critical of the proposed reduction in coal output and the Inter-Executive Committee was instructed to study further the problems raised with representatives of the member governments. In particular the attention of the Committee was directed to trends in the oil market, the compatibility of cheapness of energy with security of supply, and coal subsidies.

The deadlock on the Common Energy Policy was solved to some extent by the agreement reached at a meeting of the Council of Ministers of the ECSC at Luxembourg on 21 April 1965 on energy policy and coal subsidies. The six governments agreed that the major objectives of the Common Policy are cheap power, security of supply, free choice for the consumer, fair competition in a single market between the different forms of energy, and price stability. Where one form of energy is, for technical or economic reasons, in the process of replacing another, it is accepted that this change must take place gradually. In drawing up the new policy the governments and the Community institutions are to pay particular attention to the development of uniform Community rules for trade in fuel products with non-member countries, to harmonising state aids for the coal industry, to establishing common rules and conditions for competition between different energy sources.

All this is of course no more than a general statement of intentions. When it comes down to detail the difficulties begin to emerge. The new agreement accepts the principle that government support and protection will be necessary for the coal industry but argues that this support should be aimed at making coal competitive with other forms of energy and should, in general, be gradually phased out. Although the Treaty of Paris specifically banned subsidies to the coal industry, governments are now permitted to submit schemes to the High Authority for approval and supervision. In fact a wide variety of measures is now in force for the assistance and protection of the coal industry of the six member countries. These include, apart from direct subsidies, grants towards the cost of miners' pensions, measures to promote the use of coal in electric power stations and group heating systems, the financing of coal stocks and discriminatory taxation against the use of oil.

Under the agreement governments have stated that oil and natural gas supplies should be as widely diversified as possible to ensure greater security of supply and to maintain price competition. They have also declared that they will seek a common stocking policy for crude oil and gas, and a harmonised taxation system for petroleum products. The agreement recognises the fact that a rising demand for energy within the Community will have to be increasingly met from outside sources. Against this the objection has been raised, particularly by the French, against the concept of an open market as the surest way of producing the lowest energy costs, that it gives a disproportionate bargaining power to sellers outside Europe. This is certainly the case with Middle East oil for which Europe will become a larger customer as energy demands mount. How far this can be offset by the diversification of sources of oil supply still remains to be seen. Sizeable production has been developed in the Sahara and in Libya but the fact remains that the main spare capacity for oil in the world outside the United States is in the Middle East. The fact that the principal suppliers of oil to the European market, including Libya, are all members of the Organisation of the Petroleum Exporting Countries, which includes all major oil producers except the United States and Canada, is an indication that competition in the 'open common market' which the Six hope to establish will be far from perfect.

PROSPECTS FOR THE FUTURE

The fact that Britain, as well as the ECSC member countries, is becoming increasingly dependent on imported fuels, raises the wider question of long-term energy requirements and supplies. Clearly, in the long term there is going to be considerable increase in the consumption of fuels of all kinds. Total fuel needs rose by about 70 per cent for the world as a whole during the ten years to 1966, and it is expected that they will double in the next fifteen years. If this happens the total demand for energy of all kinds will be of the order of 10,000 million tons in the early eighties, the major part of which will have to come from the fossil fuels—coal, oil and natural gas. It is unlikely that nuclear energy will make a considerable contribution to energy requirements for some time because of the very heavy capital cost involved and the possibility of a shortage of natural uranium. The failure of the Six to settle the Common Energy Policy highlights the fact that the individual governments have been content to consider their own requirements in isolation from each other. This is largely due to the fact that Western Europe is split up into many countries each of which has relatively modest requirements which under present conditions there is no great difficulty in meeting. The discovery of natural gas in the Netherlands has of course altered the situation very considerably as far as that country is concerned and for the industrial areas in Germany, Belgium and France which are likely to be importers of Dutch natural gas. However, for Western Europe as a whole, the contribution expected from the Dutch gas field covers only about one-fifth of the growth in total fuel requirements for the Six in the period 1966–70.

It would be quite wrong in the light of the longer-term estimates that are now available to assume that Western Europe is entering an era when coal will no longer be required to make a considerable contribution to energy requirements. For the Six and for Britain the main problem is to conserve indigenous sources of fuel so that the markets for coal in particular are kept large enough to enable existing capacities to survive the present period of fuel surpluses. The one thing that is not possible for any of the countries of Western Europe is to leave long- and short-term problems alike to the market in the hope that they will somehow sort themselves out.

BIBLIOGRAPHY

Bailey, Richard. 'The Energy Perspective', *Westminster Bank Review*, London, February 1964.
'Coal Support Policies in the ECSC and Britain', *International Affairs*, London, June 1966.
Schumacher, E. F. 'The Struggle for a European Energy Policy', *Journal of Common Market Studies*, Oxford, March 1964.
Annual Reports of EEC, ECSC, Euratom and EFTA.
An Energy Policy for EEC, Political and Economic Planning, London, March 1963.
Fuel Policy, Cmnd 2798, HMSO, London, 1965.
National Coal Board Annual Reports.
OECD. *Oil Today*, Paris, 1964.
OEEC. *Towards a New Energy Pattern* (The Robinson Report), Paris, January 1960.

AGRICULTURE IN WESTERN EUROPE

T. K. WARLEY

THE major problem in seeking a synoptic view of agriculture in Western Europe is that there is not *an* agricultural industry but a great number of diverse industries. Because of differences in such factors as climatic and soil conditions, stage of economic development, pressure of population on the land and national trading attitudes, the agricultural industries of the countries of Western Europe exhibit an infinite variety in terms of their importance in the national economy, the composition of their output, the relative intensities of labour, capital and land usage, the proportion of national food requirements supplied, and the standard of living that they are able to provide for those who work on the land. Moreover, the differences between the many agricultural sub-industries within national frontiers are no less striking than those between the regions and states of Western Europe. Contrast, for example, the agricultural industries of Great Britain, Denmark, Switzerland and Turkey, or the agricultural circumstances of the arable areas of East Anglia with those of the hill areas of Wales, or modern biological egg factories with farms having traditional farm-yard flocks.

However, certain factors are common to Western European agriculture as a whole, or to large segments of it.

CHARACTERISTICS OF WESTERN EUROPEAN AGRICULTURE

First, agriculture is still Europe's biggest single industry in terms both of the contribution made to aggregate and national GDP and share of total employed working population. Only in Britain and Sweden is agriculture's share of GDP at factor cost less than 5 per cent. It lies between 5 and 10 per cent in Belgium, France, West Germany, the Netherlands and Switzerland; between 10 and 20 per cent in Denmark and Italy; and contributes more than 20 per cent in Ireland and the relatively low-income countries of Southern Europe, Greece, Spain, Portugal (25–30 per cent) and Turkey (40 per cent). For Western Europe as a whole agriculture contributes approximately 9 per cent of aggregate income. In terms of employment the agricultural sector is even more important. With the exception of Britain, which is exceptional in having only 3.5 per cent of its active population engaged in agriculture, there is scarcely a country in Europe which does not have at least one in ten of its total work force employed in agriculture. In Austria, Finland, Ireland and Italy the ratio is greater than one in five, and in other Southern European countries agriculture is still the occupation of 40 per cent or more of the working population. In aggregate, the total labour input in Western European agriculture is not less than 25 million man-years, representing about a quarter of the total active labour force.

384

One immediate consequence of the economic importance of the farm sector is that no government in Europe can be indifferent to its productivity and prosperity and the numerical importance of farmers and farm workers ensures that they can exert considerable political influence.

The second characteristic of agriculture which is common to all European countries is the existence of millions of small farm businesses which have not a sufficient volume of resources and sales to yield their occupiers a level of income acceptable by contemporary social standards, still less to allow them to participate fully in the continually rising standards of living of the rest of society. This is due to two main causes. First, the very process of economic growth condemns agriculture to decline in relative terms. Although expenditure on food still represents between a quarter and a half of total consumers' expenditure in all European countries, everywhere this proportion is falling, and agriculture constitutes a falling share of total economic activity. Secondly, the propensity for total farm output and the supply of individual products to expand at a faster rate than the growth of demand has resulted in lower prices for farm products as a whole and caused hardship amongst producers of particular commodities.

The required directions of adaptation of Western European agriculture present no mysteries. Surplus agricultural labour must leave the land for occupations where its productivity is higher. There must be widespread amalgamation of holdings, substitution of capital in the form of machinery, equipment and buildings for labour, and the adoption of modern farming techniques in order that through changed land/man and capital/man ratios labour productivity and incomes can be raised. There also needs to be a change in the composition of output in favour of those products with high income and price elasticities of demand and a comparative advantage in relation to overseas suppliers.

Some of these changes are occurring. There is no country in Western Europe where agricultural employment is not declining as a proportion of total employment, and only in Greece and Turkey (where there are high rates of population increase, a preponderant agricultural sector, and a slow rate of growth of non-agricultural employment) is total agricultural employment growing. All over Europe the number of individual holdings is declining as the smaller-sized businesses are amalgamated to form more viable units. Investment in fixed and working capital and the associated adoption of modern technologies are taking place at an impressive rate. There has been a marked increase in product specialisation and concentration, and significant shifts in the composition of output, with the importance of intermediate and final livestock products (coarse grains, protein feeds, meat, milk and eggs) and fruits and vegetables tending to grow relatively to that of such products as cereals for direct human consumption, potatoes and agricultural raw materials. Indeed, labour productivity in agriculture is rising in all countries except Italy, Greece, Turkey and Portugal, at a rate substantially greater than the rate of increase in product per head in the economy as a whole.

These developments have contributed in a marked degree to the rising standards of living enjoyed by the peoples of Western Europe in recent years. Not only has there been made available to the urban population a rising quantity of food, but the release of labour from land has been a key factor in the overall expansion in output of manufactured goods and services in most countries, and the adaptation and structural changes which have occurred in agriculture have been an important cause of rising real income.

However, none of these changes is occurring sufficiently fast to raise labour incomes and resource productivity to an absolute level comparable to those in other occupations. Consequently the lower relative incomes of farmers—and in some countries their intolerably low absolute standards of living—remains one of the most intractable problems of the Western European economy.

Faced with a large sector in economic difficulties the response of governments everywhere has been to evolve policies of assistance for their agricultural industries, and the universal and direct involvement of governments in agricultural affairs is a third common characteristic of Western European agriculture.

In broad terms, governments have the choice of two types of policies. They can either attempt to speed the process of adaptation by taking measures to encourage structural change, or they can bolster farm incomes by support and protectionist policies. They have followed both courses with differing degrees of emphasis according to circumstances. Virtually all national agricultural policies have elements designed to accelerate the pace of farm amalgamations, land consolidation, capital investment, the adoption of improved practices, upgrading of the managerial skills of farmers, and an increase in the output of products with relatively favourable market prospects. The less developed countries, those in which the agricultural sector is still large, and those European countries with a substantial export trade in farm products, have lent emphasis mainly to policies of this type. The countries of Southern Europe, Denmark and, to a lesser extent, France and the Netherlands are in this group. On the other hand, most governments have also chosen to follow protectionist policies for their agricultures. Indeed, for reasons primarily of social equity and political expediency, reinforced in some instances by strategic and balance of payments considerations, the dominant purpose of agricultural policies in the remaining countries of North-West Europe since the second world war has been income maintenance.

This objective has been pursued in the main by raising prices received by farmers for their products above free market levels. The means chosen have varied, and have included import tariffs, quotas and embargoes, minimum import prices and levies, export subsidies, supply restriction, mixing regulations, deficiency payments and marketing monopolies.

PROTECTION

Estimates of the degree of protection given to agriculture are not easily made or interpreted, and in any event they vary with country, with commodity and over time. But estimates made of the percentage excess of output valued at national prices over output valued at import prices have placed the overall degree of protection in 1961–2 at around 40 per cent for West Germany, Sweden and Norway, between 25 and 30 per cent for Italy and Britain, and between 10 and 20 per cent for France, the Netherlands and Belgium. The evidence suggests that the degree of protection decreased significantly only in France during the latter half of the 1950s and early 1960s, though there was also a marginal decrease in Britain. In all other Western European countries there were increases. These were major in West Germany, Sweden and Norway, and even Denmark, which justifiably prides itself on the competitiveness of its agriculture, has reluctantly been forced to start subsidising its farmers, though as yet on only a minor scale.

The various protective policies and measures employed have had a number of common effects. First there is no doubt that the farm population of Europe has enjoyed a higher standard of living than would have been the case in the absence of protection. However, the disparities of incomes *within* agriculture have been widened, since the attempt to improve incomes by raising product price levels must necessarily confer benefits on farmers in direct proportion to their volume of sales, thereby inflating the incomes of the larger farmers whilst leaving the poorer farmers (who tend to have low incomes primarily because of their small output) relatively little better off. Secondly, income support for agriculture has involved substantial costs. Protectionist policies have tended to slow the rate of transfer of factors of production, and especially labour, out of agriculture. Hence policies of income maintenance in agriculture have conflicted with the national goals of efficient resource use and economic growth. Had redundant resources been shifted more quickly out of agriculture where their productivity was low and used in the production of non-agricultural goods and services in which their productivity was higher, an even higher rate of economic growth could have been sustained, and inflationary increases in wage rates and prices would most probably have been less severe. The growth thus sacrificed is the true cost of protectionist policies, and far exceeds the budgetary charges on national exchequers of agricultural income support programmes. Additionally, most of the specific agricultural price support measures employed in Western Europe transfer income to farmers by raising consumer food prices. Apart from the welfare consequences for low-income consumers, such policies must also have contributed to the general price inflation which has been a persistent problem of most Western European economies in the post-war period. Finally, insofar as European price and income support policies have encouraged an increase in the output of farm products which could have been produced more efficiently in other regions, the pursuit of protectionist policies in European agriculture has been at the expense of efficiency in the use of international resources.

This leads to a fourth important characteristic of Western European agriculture, namely that Western Europe as a whole is the world's most important import market for agricultural products and at the same time an important source of agricultural exports. Consequently, protectionist policies which so encourage an expansion of output as to restrict net import requirements or generate increased export surpluses are of vital economic concern to agricultural exporting nations in many parts of the world. And since trade in agricultural products represents about 30 per cent by value of total world commodity trade, policies which affect Europe's net agricultural trade position can have a marked influence on world trading activity as a whole.

In fact, whilst agricultural protectionism has played a large part in bringing about the great increase in production and gross exports of agricultural products which has occurred in post-war Western Europe (production increased by 24 per cent in the period 1955 to 1963 and gross exports by 50 per cent) demand has also increased and both gross and net imports have risen (the former by about 40 per cent, and net imports by just over a third in the period 1955 to 1963). Nonetheless, though total imports have risen in absolute terms, a major part of the rising European demand for some commodities has been filled by domestic output so that the degree of self-sufficiency has tended to increase; for some products net import requirements have actually declined (bread grains and some dairy products); and surpluses of some commodities have appeared which have had to be disposed of outside national frontiers at depressed prices. In general, the increase in Western European output induced by high price supports has been a contributory factor in the adverse trend of world agricultural prices, the relatively slow rate of expansion of agricultural trade, the accumulation of surplus stocks in exporting regions, and the unsatisfactory balance of payments position of many countries for which agricultural exports are an important part of total external trade. There is, in short, a direct conflict between the interests of the efficient agricultural exporting nations anxious to secure a rising volume of sales of farm products at remunerative prices to the Western European market, and those of the governments of European nations bent on providing their agricultural producers with an improved standard of living.

This conflict is one which has not so far proved capable of solution within the framework of GATT. GATT strives to liberalise trade by having nations adhere to the principles that tariffs should be the sole form of protection for assisted industries, that tariff levels should be bound and reduced in multilateral negotiations, and that trade should be conducted on the basis of non-discrimination with preferential trading arrangements being gradually eliminated. In practice, however, the typical situation confronting exporters of agricultural products is that protection for European agricultural industries is normally afforded by means other than simple tariffs, that the degree of protection is highly variable, is tending to rise and is not significantly subject to international influence and negotiated diminution, and that preferential trading arrangements abound and proliferate.

The EEC's Common Agricultural Policy

This state of affairs has been brought into focus by the formation of the EEC and the early effects of its Common Agricultural Policy. (The formation of the European Free Trade Association presents the rest of the world with few specifically agricultural problems since it is basically concerned with industrial products only.) The essential core of the Community's Common Agricultural Policy is that whilst free circulation of agricultural products is scheduled by July 1968 within the combined market of the six member countries, income support to farmers in the EEC will be given by maintaining a high level of product prices. The devices mainly used are a system of fixed and variable specific tariffs (levies) and minimum import prices, and internal support buying of products surplus to demand at the prices guaranteed to the Community's producers, which are then sold outside the Community. It is true that the Common Agricultural Policy also has an element of structural reform intended to increase farm incomes by raising labour productivity, but this part of the policy is subordinate to price policy, can be effective only in the long term, and has as yet hardly begun to be formulated.

Criticisms of the Community's agricultural policy have been levelled both at the principal price-raising technique which is employed and, more especially, at the price levels which have been established for producers in the EEC. The variable levy imposed on imported products to raise the landed price of the cheapest supplies on offer in world markets to the level of internal support prices is seen as a particularly pernicious protective device, penalising even the most efficient exporter outside the Community. There seems to be a real danger that in an attempt to raise the earnings of the many small-scale producers within the member states farm product prices have been set at such high levels that production will be encouraged (and consumption discouraged) to a degree where exporting countries outside the Community will be unable to participate in the increased demand which can be anticipated from population growth and economic development within Europe; that net import requirements will dwindle in absolute terms; and that export surpluses will be increased or appear which will disrupt commercial markets in other parts of the world when they are disposed of with the aid of subsidies. These fears are not without foundation, for the EEC is already about 90 per cent self-sufficient in temperate agricultural food products and in the short space of time that the EEC market regulations have been in effect some marked changes in trade volumes and directions have become apparent. Net import requirements of some commodities have declined (bread grains, poultry meat and eggs) or stagnated (feed grains), and there has been a general tendency for trade between member countries to grow much faster than trade with countries outside the Community.

POSSIBLE EFFECTS OF BRITAIN'S ENTRY INTO THE EEC

Should Britain become a member of the EEC and apply the Common Agricultural Policy, the problem would be greatly aggravated. For then the world's largest single importer of agricultural products (19 per cent of total world agricultural imports in 1963), which has traditionally allowed almost free entry for food imports, would be replacing a liberal trade policy by high protectionism, and granting preferential entry to those of her partners in the Community with export surpluses. These would include not only France, the Netherlands and Italy, but most probably also Denmark and Ireland since both countries are highly dependent on sales of livestock products to Britain and would want to follow Britain into the Community. The unfavourable consequences which Britain's application of the Common Agricultural Policy would have on the export earnings, payments balances and prospects for economic development of a number of Commonwealth countries (notably New Zealand which is overwhelmingly dependent on access to the British market) have been discussed elsewhere and need not be stressed here. But it is important to note that these ill effects would also extend to many non-Commonwealth countries around the world, notably the United States for which sales of agricultural products to Western Europe represent 45–50 per cent of its total agricultural exports.

There are, of course, many political and economic advantages to be gained by Britain in joining the Community, but adoption of the EEC's Common Agricultural Policy cannot be counted amongst them. As the policy stands at present its adoption would have adverse effects on Britain's balance of payments, the cost of living and the incomes of producers of some types of agricultural products. The adverse payments balance would arise from the higher cost of imports from other Community members, the payment to the European Agricultural Guidance and Guarantee Fund of levies collected on imports from non-member countries and the direct budgetary contributions needed to meet the balance of the Fund's expenditure.

Not knowing in advance such factors as the total cost of financing the Common Agricultural Policy in an enlarged Community, the price of supplies on the world market, the extent of trade deflection, and the response of British consumption and production patterns induced by the adoption of

European price levels and interrelationships, it is not possible to predict the magnitude of the effect of joining the Community on Britain's balance of payments with any precision. But tentative estimates point to a drain of some £200–£250 million ($560–$700 million) annually. The inflationary effect of abandoning the deficiency payment system of farm price support and moving to a high market price regime seems likely to entail a rise in the cost of living of some 2–2.5 per cent, but this burden could be spread over a number of years if the change in the support system were made gradually. So far as domestic farmers are concerned it would seem that producers of cereals and beef would benefit from considerably higher prices, milk producers would be little affected, whilst pigmeat, egg and poultry producers and some horticulturalists would be worse off under the common farm policy than under present support arrangements. At the same time it is worth stressing that as a member of the Community Britain would have the opportunity and the will to bring a liberal influence to bear on the Common Agricultural Policy in the critical matters of internal price support levels and the arrangements made to minimise its impact on the agricultural trade of Commonwealth and other countries.

GATT NEGOTIATIONS AND TRADE LIBERALISATION IN AGRICULTURE

The long-standing conflict between agricultural protectionism and the legitimate aspirations of low-cost exporters for the opportunity to increase their sales of farm products has been brought to a head in the current Kennedy Round of tariff negotiations under GATT by the United States authorities insisting that progress towards a further substantial linear cut in tariffs on industrial goods is dependent upon an effective reduction in the obstacles to expansion of trade in agricultural products.

The United States (whose broad views are shared by such other exporters as Canada, Australia, New Zealand, Denmark and Argentina) has no illusions that the long history of agricultural protectionism in Europe can be reversed. But it is bent on preventing unrestrained protectionism further eroding its share of its major export market. To this end, it wants two things. First, moderation in existing and future agricultural price support policies, and secondly, that importers should give an assurance to efficient food exporters that they will continue to have the opportunity to compete with domestic producers for a 'fair' share of total national food requirements. Specifically, the United States takes the position that margins of protection afforded domestic producers in importing countries should be bound at 'reasonable' levels, and that exporters should be given an import guarantee related to recent export volumes and an assurance that they can share *pro rata* in future growth in demand. It would like to see these arrangements embodied in a series of effective international commodity agreements between importing and exporting nations for the major commodities facing or threatened with difficult trading conditions. These are cereals, dairy products and meat, and possibly also sugar, fats and oils.

With some reluctance the Community has accepted the central proposition that continued progress in freeing trade in manufactures has reached the point where some concrete concessions must be made to temperate agricultural product exporters. Indeed, it is committed by Article 110 of the Rome Treaty to pursue commercial policies which contribute to the harmonious development of world trade. However, the Community is also required by Article 39 to ensure a 'fair' standard of living for its agricultural population and to observe the principle of 'gradualism' in bringing about structural adjustments in agriculture. The problem lies in defining in practical terms what is fair, reasonable and sufficiently gradual, in order that an acceptable compromise may be reached reconciling the trading interests of countries outside the Community with the social and political imperatives of raising the incomes of the Community's own farmers.

The counter-proposal put forward by the Community in the GATT negotiations consists of an offer to enter into international commodity agreements (first for grains and later for other sensitive products) and contains two main elements. The first is that all major exporters and importers should agree to stabilise the margin of protection they give their domestic producers. The agreed margins of protection should be fixed for periods of three years and should be subject to renegotiation at regular intervals. The second proposition is that self-sufficiency 'norms' for major products should be set for all producing countries, both exporters and importers, and that should surpluses of these products appear on world markets (defined by prices falling below specified reference levels) then those countries or groups of countries which have expanded their production beyond their agreed level of self-sufficiency should accept financial responsibility for disposing of the surplus margin as food aid to the developing countries.

Two things can be said in favour of these proposals. First, it is an important step forward in international agricultural policy that a major group of countries is prepared to expose the extent of its protection of its own farmers to international influence and bargaining. Secondly, the EEC appears to have gone some way to accepting the proposition that the real surpluses of agricultural commodities are not so much the unsaleable stocks held by low-cost exporters, but the output produced under protection in high-cost producing regions, and that in future importing regions should contribute financially to the orderly disposal of such surpluses under food aid programmes to low-income countries lacking effective purchasing power.

It is to be hoped that these proposals contain sufficient concessions to the interests of the United States and other exporters to allow future rounds of negotiations on multilateral trade liberalisation to proceed and achieve a continuing reduction in tariffs on manufactured goods. However, doubts may be entertained as to whether the EEC's formulae will in practice bring about any substantial improvement in the trade prospects facing agricultural exporting countries. This is because of particular features of the Community's two-fold proposals. On the question of the margin of support, the first point of note is that there will be a tendency to fix the margin of protection at high levels. Furthermore, under the EEC's proposals the protective margin is to be measured from *fixed* reference prices. Consequently, any fall in world market prices (reflecting underlying changes in competitive conditions or the balance between supply and demand) would in practice be offset by automatic increases in the levies imposed by the Community, with corresponding increases in the real degree of protection enjoyed by farmers in the EEC. Thirdly, exporters fear they would be in a worse position than at present if the use of compensatory variable levies were eventually extended to products which are now protected by fixed tariffs. Finally, exporters are well aware that freezing the degree of support for a product would not itself prevent domestic production rising, and gives no assurance that national self-sufficiency would not be reached or even exceeded.

Similarly, there is nothing in the Community's proposals regarding agreed food self-sufficiency ratios and joint financing of the cost of surplus disposal which guarantees that complete self-sufficiency will not be achieved and that exporters will in fact be able to meet the balance between those ratios and total requirements. That is, the commodity agreements proposed fall far short of providing exporters with an access guarantee to the EEC's market.

This last feature of the Community's proposals has proved disappointing to exporters for in recent years high hopes have been aroused that importing countries might be willing to enter into market-sharing arrangements with foreign exporters along the lines of the series of formal agreements entered into for cereals and some dairy and meat products by Britain with her principal suppliers. Under these arrangements, total current demand has been divided up between domestic producers and exporters on the basis of present shares. Overseas producers have been given an assurance they will be allowed to participate in any future growth in consumption and a further assurance that 'effective corrective action' will be taken to ensure that exporters' agreed shares of the British market are preserved. At the same time financial support to British producers has been limited to a volume of output corresponding to their assigned share of the market, and these commitments to overseas suppliers have been taken into account at successive reviews of support policy.

There is no doubt that if it were to prove possible to extend market-sharing agreements of this type then some of the conflicts between importing and exporting, high cost and low cost, protectionist and liberal countries would be resolved, and a marginally more efficient use of the world's agricultural resources secured. However, the EEC has rejected the concept of market-sharing and access guarantees out of hand. Nor is this perhaps surprising, for the Community is not as free to strike as liberal a posture on agricultural matters as is Britain with her small and relatively affluent farm population. Like most other European nations the six member countries are impelled primarily by the need to improve the incomes of their farmers. They contend that their ability to effect income improvement by admittedly necessary but socially disruptive structural reform programmes is subject to political and social restraints and to the intrinsic difficulties in implementing such programmes with sufficient speed to reduce the need for price protection. The members of the Community have had to fight hard and protracted battles amongst themselves in working out their price support systems and common price levels, and they are reluctant to retrace this ground in order to ease the problem for other countries. Moreover, since their agricultural industries are progressing through a period of rapid technological advance (which in agriculture tends to result in increased output as well as higher productivity) at the same time as the demand for farm products is growing slowly and at a decelerating rate, they are uncertain about how far they *are* in a position to give assurances at this time about their future food import requirements.

AGREEMENT ON POLICIES

Hence it would appear that in the future as in the past the impact of the agricultural policies followed in Western European countries on world trade in agricultural products will continue to be a central theme in determining economic and political relations between nations and regions. No grounds exist for optimism that complete solutions will be found. Nonetheless there are signs of a slight improvement in the way in which the problems involved are discussed, and agreement about the directions of policy changes which are required at least to prevent the situation from getting any worse.

There is, for instance, agreement that the objective of an economical use of the world's and Europe's resources will best be served if the degree of protection given to agricultural producers is not further increased. Whereas in the past national agricultural policies have typically been selfish in their purpose and implementation, there is now an awareness that the prosperity of national farming populations cannot be pursued in economic isolation. This is reflected in the willingness of Western European governments to expose their national agricultural policies to international scrutiny and influence. There is also general agreement that governments should enter into international commodity agreements. A growing number of countries are anxious to see these agreements extend beyond the mere regulation of trade prices, and into the more critical and sensitive fields of national price support and production policies, the sharing of commercial markets, and joint action by all rich nations in using food surpluses as aid to developing countries. Finally, matching the agreement on the need to bring about a better international balance in agriculture, there is a consensus (amongst all except farmers themselves who in all countries seem to favour continued protection to its alternatives) that insofar as is politically and socially possible and economically feasible, the emphasis in national agricultural policies should swing away from income support by protectionist measures and towards policies which tackle the low-income problem at its roots.

BIBLIOGRAPHY

Blau, G. *International Commodity Arrangements and Policies*, FAO Commodity Policy Studies No. 16, Special Studies Programme, No. 1, Rome, 1964.

Richter, J. H. *Agricultural Protection and Trade: Proposals for an International Policy*, Pall Mall Press, London; Frederick A. Praeger, New York, 1964.

Tracey, Michael. *Agriculture in Western Europe: Crisis and Adaptation since 1880*, Jonathan Cape, London; Frederick A. Praeger, New York, 1964.

Yates, P. L. *Food, Land and Manpower in Western Europe*, Macmillan, London and New York, 1960.

European Communities Information Service. *Agriculture in the Common Market*, Community Topics 21, London, Washington and New York, 1965.

OECD. *Low Incomes in Agriculture: Problems and Policies*, Paris, 1964. *Agriculture and Economic Growth*, Paris, 1965.

INCOMES AND PRICES POLICIES IN WESTERN EUROPE

CHARLES FORD

A NUMBER of Western European countries, including Britain, are seeking to introduce incomes policies. But nowhere can it be said that the massive difficulties involved have been successfully surmounted. In most countries a detailed and comprehensive incomes policy is out of the question. A realistic assessment of what it is reasonable to seek to do is expressed in the words of a report of a Working Party of the OECD Economic Policy Committee (which consists of senior government officials responsible at national level for economic and financial policy): '. . . To create between the various groups sharing in the national income at least approximate agreement on the broad lines of its distribution.'[1]

Whereas in 1961 an OEEC Group of Experts gave considerable prominence to the system of incomes policy applied in the Netherlands[2] and urged the introduction of wages policies in member countries of the Organisation, the OECD Report cited above commented three years later: ' . . . Some go so far as to say that some kind of incomes policy is necessary if sustained growth is to be achieved under conditions of stability. In practice, it is much more difficult to put forward a definite conclusion since, although many European countries are now trying to introduce an incomes policy, it cannot be said that any very conclusive results have been obtained up to now.'[3]

Among the events that took place between the publication of the two reports were the major changes brought about in the system of incomes policy obtaining in the Netherlands.

THE NETHERLANDS INCOMES POLICY

The system of wage control in the Netherlands involves no fewer than five different bodies at national level: the Board of Government Mediators, the Ministry of Social Affairs, the Labour Foundation, the Social and Economic Council, and the Central Planning Bureau.

Until recently, the key body was the Board of Government Mediators, appointed by the Ministry of Social Affairs. Its tasks were: (i) to establish wage rates and make other regulations on its own initiative or at the suggestion of organised labour or management; (ii) to accept, reject or modify

---

[1] *Growth and Economic Policy*, OECD, Paris, 1964, Part I, p. 14.
[2] *The Problem of Rising Prices*, OEEC, Paris, May 1961.
[3] *Growth and Economic Policy*, Part I, p. 14.

collective agreements submitted to it for approval; (iii) to extend the provisions of collective agreements to parties outside the bargaining unit; (iv) to permit derogation from the terms of collective agreements in specific cases; (v) to obtain compliance with its regulations through the courts.[1] The Board worked under general guide lines from the Minister of Social Affairs, and the Foundation of Labour had to be consulted on each decision. It was the most powerful body of its kind in the democratic world.

The three principal trade union federations and the employers' federations for industry, trade and agriculture are represented in the Foundation of Labour. The purpose of the Foundation was until 1963 to advise the Board of Government Mediators on wages questions, but it has now taken over the main policy-making functions of the Board. The Foundation also advises the Social and Economic Council. The Social and Economic Council also consists of representatives of trade union and employers' organisations, but with the addition of independent experts (fifteen trade unionists, fifteen employers and fifteen independent experts). Its task is to advise the government on social and economic questions. The Government Central Planning Bureau has the task of making annual or longer-term growth projections, etc. The Netherlands unions have argued that its annual forecasts of economic growth have consistently underestimated the actual growth rates achieved, thus minimising estimates of possible wage increases.

In 1959 a major change was introduced. Wage increases, it was decided, would in the future be determined by productivity increases in the various sectors of the economy (calculated under a strict formula based on the trend of value added per worker, at constant prices) as well as by the national average. However, the Board was still empowered to order or request a reduction in the amounts agreed in collective bargaining between trade unions and management. There was also a continuing ban upon the passing of wage increases onto prices.

The experience of this new wage policy met with considerable criticism from the Social and Economic Council. Where substantial productivity increases took place, it had been agreed that employers should participate in discussions with the Ministry of Economic Affairs to decide by how much prices should be lowered. But in fact such price reductions seldom took place. The Netherlands experience was not very different from that of other countries. Moreover, those who hoped for a reduced government responsibility for wages were deceived since '. . . never before has the government interfered so much in the shaping of wages as under the new policy.'[2] Thus the parties concerned began to agree upon a further revision of the wages policy so as to secure increased responsibility for the representatives of trade unions and employers in the determination of wages.

In January 1963 the powers of the Board of Government Mediators were substantially reduced. Since then, collective agreements have been submitted for approval to the Foundation of Labour. Collective agreements reached at industry level must continue to be harmonised with the agreements at national level through a process of so-called 'internal coordination'. Collective bargaining at industry level between representatives of management and the trade unions is pursued in the light of the central agreement reached in the Foundation of Labour. The results of this industry-level bargaining are subject to the agreement of the Foundation, and if it

[1] *The Problem of Rising Prices*, OEEC, Paris, May 1961, p. 363.
[2] W. F. van Tilburg, *Free Labour World*, ICFTU, Brussels, March 1962.

o

fails to sanction them, collective agreements are referred back for renegotiation.

Failing agreement within the Foundation, it still lies with the government to impose a wage-stop or lay down conditions for new collective agreements. In the latter case, proposals for revised contracts must then be referred to the Board of Government Mediators. In other words, although the Foundation has taken over the powers of the Board of Mediators, its responsibility is tempered by the knowledge that the government may intervene, and that if there is disagreement within the Foundation, the Board takes over its powers.

The Board retains the power to oppose a decision of the Foundation and notifies its opposition to the Minister of Social Affairs. But in the absence of opposition from the Board, the collective agreement comes into operation. The main difference from the pre-1963 system is that the Foundation now possesses a formal authority, whereas before this date, it was merely a private institution consulted by the government. Moreover, although the government retains its power to intervene, it is pledged to do so only as a last resort. It has hesitated to use its powers to curb wage increases proposed by branches of industry and has only rarely done so for fear of the development of 'black wages' (i.e. those above the maximum—referred to in other countries as 'wages drift').

Substantial wage increases took place in 1964 and 1965. Wages rose by 16 per cent and 11 per cent in these two years respectively—27 per cent in all compared with half this rate in previous years. It seems that wage increases have swollen into a flood which has completely extinguished the official 'guiding light', and which new and stronger wage dikes will be needed to hold back.

One of the key problems in applying the wages policy in the Netherlands was that with the increasing pressure during recent years on labour supplies the demand for labour was so great that the 'market prices' for labour were higher than the controlled wage levels. The result was that workers were able to ask, and get, higher wages than their trade union representatives were seeking to negotiate in collective bargaining with employers. The so-called 'black wages', i.e. those paid at wages above the legal maximum, became of increasing importance in 1963 when over half the workers were getting them.

The Netherlands experience seems to indicate that under conditions of very high demand for labour in which unemployment falls to a tiny percentage of the total labour force, the maintenance of a system of wage control creates a real danger of estrangement between the leadership and the membership of the unions. A policy of participation in the formulation of national economic policies (including incomes policies) is particularly difficult to combine with the traditional collective bargaining role of trade unions. It is all the more difficult in a country in which only a small part of the labour force is organised in trade unions.

With an increasing gap between negotiated increases and the equilibrium price for labour (i.e. what could be obtained by all-out negotiating pressures) in a situation of very tight labour supplies, the solidarity of non-organised workers and those outside the federations participating in the national machinery for wage determination could no longer be depended upon. Their pressures for higher wages could no longer be denied. Moreover, the members of unions taking part in the national wage machinery became increasingly dissatisfied.

Thus an obligation upon all employees to join an appropriate union would seem to be an indispensable corollary of incomes policies. An alternative to establishing closed-shop agreements would be to restrict certain monetary advantages arising from collective bargaining to union members only. Such a system has recently been introduced in some industries in Belgium, e.g. food, transport, engineering, steel and textiles. Collective agreements were signed in 1963–5 under which funds are established under the direction of bipartite committees (employers and unions); employers have agreed to pay into these funds an annual sum representing a percentage of total wages and salaries, and a special payment is made from the funds to trade union members only. A typical amount for such a payment is about £3 10s. p.a., but in some industries it is over £10 p.a. These are, of course, insignificant sums, but they may be increased in the future and it is of first importance that employers have recognised the principle urged upon them by the trade unions that certain advantages arising from collective agreements should be reserved exclusively for trade union members. (Legislation on American lines obliging employers to recognise unions after 50 per cent of the staff have become organised would also be an appropriate accompaniment of incomes policies.)

The OEEC Report *The Problem of Rising Prices* quoted above states that under the Netherlands wage control system bargaining parties were obliged to 'face up fully to the implications of their actions for the economy as a whole', and to 'think in terms of real incomes instead of money incomes and to concentrate attention on longer-run trends rather than the immediate past.' The main conclusions of the OEEC experts were: (i) '. . . Given the necessary political climate—and so long as conditions of extreme excess demand are not allowed to emerge—it is possible to enlist the cooperation of labour and management in a conscious effort to ensure that the average increase in wages is kept in line with overall economic considerations'; (ii) 'However, it is clear that it is much less easy to reach agreement on the economic and social criteria which should govern the size of deviations from this average.'

Although the main responsibility has since 1963 been transferred from the Board of Mediators to the Foundation of Labour, the principle of centralised assessment of industry-level bargaining has been retained and continues to be based upon similar criteria of national interest.

Employers and union organisations, as well as their members, appear to prefer some kind of incomes policy to a return to a free-for-all. This is evidenced by, among other things, the fact that the percentage of workers organised in trade unions has risen during the period of application of wages policy in the Netherlands (the post-war period). At present, about 40 per cent of workers in the Netherlands are organised in trade unions (compared with only 30 per cent in the years following the second world war). This percentage is still low compared with the Scandinavian countries but about the same percentage as in Britain. Nevertheless, it is a disturbing sign that during the last decade the membership of professional and similar unions (which are not covered by the wages policy) has risen much more rapidly than that of the three main national trade union centres whose members' wages only have come under government control. Such a tendency would be expected to result from the movement from manufacturing to the tertiary sector which is marked in advanced industrial countries. But the increase in the membership of the trade union organisations remaining outside the system of wages policy seems to be greater than could be explained by the shift of manpower into services, etc.

Why then do the unions continue to support a wages policy? The main reasons are: (i) although there have been considerable fluctuations in the share of wages in the Netherlands National Income during the last decade, during the early sixties there was a tendency for the share to increase—indeed, it rose from 68 per cent in 1959 and 1960 to 76 per cent in 1964;[1] (ii) real wages in manufacturing have risen by an average of about 3 per cent p.a. since the end of the war and over 5 per cent p.a. in 1959–64; (iii) wages policy is regarded as a device for ensuring that workers in low-productivity industries do not fall too far behind the others.

A further revision of wages policy in the Netherlands has recently been advocated by some Netherlands leaders, largely because it is increasingly recognised that the present detailed form of wages policy hardly functions and, in any case, leads to tensions between central employers' and workers' organisations and their respective affiliates. Discussion continues on the further reform of the system, but it is as yet impossible to foresee what the outcome will be. Three different views are put forward by the government, the employers and the trade unions. The general consensus is that detailed control of wages will be abolished and that a system with more or less freely established wages will come into force, but the trade unions want more and the employers and the government less freedom.

There seems to be a consensus that the detailed examination of each collective agreement should be replaced by the possibility of a general wages stop in an emergency (the trade union standpoint) or by the possibility of interfering in extreme cases and giving more detailed regulations for a few matters such as working hours, wages indexation, etc.

One of the main conclusions that trade unions in the Netherlands have drawn from the operation of the wages policy is that, despite their growing share in the GNP, wage earners have been largely unable to accumulate capital. The greater part of privately owned capital is in the hands of a small minority of the population. This has resulted from high profits which have been reinvested in the enterprise.

This has been accepted by the trade unions because it has led to growing employment opportunities. However, in July 1964, the three unions submitted a claim that employees should have a substantial share in this capital accumulation. The unions proposed that Social Investment Funds should be set up into which a part of net profits would be paid in the form of shares or cash, etc. Claims upon the Funds thus built up would be issued to employees in the form of certificates, which would give the right to distribution of dividends and interest received from the capital in the Funds.

The amounts received would vary according to the level of earnings and years of service, etc. It was proposed that the Funds should be administered by a Board upon which employees or union members would be in a majority. In order to discourage these certificates from being sold and thus increasing consumption, it was proposed to attach certain disadvantages to their sale. From the beginning of 1965, the trade unions sought to include in collective agreements paragraphs on the lines of the proposals for profit-sharing. But there was strong opposition from employers. The question was in the spring of 1966 still under the consideration of the Social and Economic Council.

[1] *Economic Survey of the Netherlands*, OECD, Paris, April 1964.

THE DISTRIBUTION OF WEALTH

Thus one of the main lessons to be learnt from the Netherlands experience is that an equitable incomes policy should embrace wealth as such and not merely the income that flows from it. Incomes policies should be consciously aimed at securing a fairer redistribution of both incomes and property. There is an increasing awareness of this problem in Britain. J. A. Meade cites the following figures concerning the distribution of personal wealth in Britain.[1]

Percentage of population	Percentage of total personal wealth		Percentage of personal incomes from property (before tax) in 1959
	1936–8	1960	
1	56	42	60
5	79	75	92
10	88	83	99

Thus 5 per cent of the population owns no less than 75 per cent of personal property in Britain and 83 per cent of personal property is owned by only 10 per cent of the population. The above table also shows that the concentration of income from property is even more striking than the concentration of ownership, since in 1959 almost the whole of income from property (99 per cent) went to only 10 per cent of the population.

It is doubtful whether every bus-driver and every engineering fitter in Britain is aware of these figures. But they are certainly aware that, despite the fact that ordinary families have more washing machines and television sets than ever before, the ownership of property such as real estate and the means of production are still concentrated in a few hands. The ensuing sense of injustice places a major obstacle in the way of persuading wage and salary earners to make sacrifices on behalf of an overriding national interest under an incomes policy which requires agreement to accept lower nominal wages than trade union representatives would normally be able to negotiate in times of full employment such as at present obtain.

In considering the distribution of wealth, it is important to recall an aspect that is usually not touched upon by academic economists—that the development of automation will lead inevitably to an increasing concentration of wealth in the hands of increasingly rich share-holders. Suppose that automation should drastically reduce the proportion of the national income that accrues to wages, asks J. A. Meade:[2]

> There would be a limited number of exceedingly wealthy property owners; the proportion of the working population required to man the extremely profitable automated industries would be small; wage rates would thus be depressed; there would have to be a large expansion of the production of the labour-intensive goods and services which were in high demand by the few multi-multi-multi-millionaires; we would be back in a super-world of an immiserized proletariat and of butlers, footmen, kitchen-maids, and other hangers-on. Let us call this the Brave New Capitalists' Paradise.

Of course, in practice, we would imagine that the employees in the automated industries would be sufficiently intelligent to continue to organise

[1] J. A. Meade, *Efficiency, Equality and the Ownership of Property*, Allen and Unwin, London, 1964, p. 27.
[2] *Op. cit.*, p. 33.

themselves into trade unions in order to ensure that they obtained an adequate benefit from the increased productivity resulting from automation, and to prevent the depression of wage standards envisaged by Meade. Moreover, it is to be foreseen that with the growth of incomes the consumption of labour-intensive goods and services referred to will be enjoyed by a growing proportion of the population, despite their increased relative costs. It has so far been the experience in the United States that the prices of services have risen more rapidly than those of manufactures probably because of the slower relative productivity growth of the former (although there is not much evidence on this). Moreover, the growth in real wages and salaries will increasingly have the effect of raising demand for hand-made and other labour-intensive products from the population as a whole and not merely from the millionaires. However, the major question posed by Meade remains relevant. Automation means increasing concentration of the ownership of property, whereas wages and salaries in such industries will represent a declining proportion of total costs (even though individual wages and salaries will not necessarily become depressed as Meade suggests). This in turn will create major political as well as economic problems, which we have not the space adequately to discuss here.

In Germany, too, as well as in the Netherlands and Britain, there is increasing discussion of the importance of the distribution of wealth as a factor vital from the point of view of equity and hence of real relevance in the determination of incomes policies. The German government has recently introduced a new law (June 1965) for encouraging private savings which enables trade unions to negotiate agreements obliging employers to pay their workers money (or give them shares) for investment purposes.

The main provisions of the new law are as follows: employers will grant their employees a share of the profits amounting to DM 312 p.a., which will be free of taxes and social charges (for employees with three or four children this can amount to DM 468 p.a.); these shares will have to be invested and shall not be disposed of for at least five years; the employee can choose freely the kind of investment he prefers; the distribution of the shares can be arranged either through individual enterprise or collective agreements; these measures also apply to office employees, judges and professional military people, as well as soldiers on military service. A law passed in 1961 contained similar proposals but in four years only about a quarter of a million workers benefited from it.

Wage Increases as a Dynamic Factor in Economic Progress

It is frequently alleged that trade union wage claims are at the root of inflationary tendencies, which leads to the conclusion that the cardinal aim of policies for price stabilisation should be to limit wage increases. Yet when we compare the economic progress made, for instance, in Germany with that in Britain, it is striking that despite the fact that wage and salary costs in Germany have risen during the last decade more rapidly than in Britain, German industrial production and exports have also risen more during the same period. Among the reasons for this are that Germany has higher investment rates, higher calibre management, more effectively organised unions (there are only sixteen unions in Germany, all organised on an industrial basis), and greater effective participation of union representatives in management (in Germany one-third of the supervisory boards of joint stock companies is elected by employees).

One of the main reasons for high investment rates in Germany is that the unions have a positive attitude towards investment, and that their claims for higher wages and shorter hours have caused employers to use labour more and more efficiently. This fact was noticed by OECD economists as long ago as 1958.[1]

It is not our purpose to argue that trade unions should oppose cooperation in an incomes policy under favourable circumstances. Balance of payments reasons may at the very least necessitate a more careful coordination of wage claims according to the needs of the external trade situation. Even temporary restraint on wage claims, *together with other incomes*, may be necessary for a time. But long-term prosperity and relative price stability cannot be achieved through permanent income limitation, as rapidly expanding industries should be enabled to permit their employees to share in the fruits of increased productivity; they will also need to attract high-calibre personnel to enable them to continue to expand, and in this way secure the release of labour from low-productivity industries and occupations.

Unions may eventually come to sign price and wage agreements with employers by which, provided employers in high-productivity industries reduce their prices, the unions agree to forego a part of their share of the fruits of increased productivity that comes to them through increased wages while increasing the part resulting from lower prices. An incomes pause should be used to secure necessary structural changes and adequate efforts to increase productivity and exports by the 'industrial partners' (as they are called on the Continent, although this does not exclude that on wages and conditions, at least, they should be sparring partners).

A POSITIVE POLICY FOR PRICES

The basic weakness of the concept of an incomes policy is that it is a *negative* device calculated (although this is rarely admitted) to hold back incomes, by which its advocates frequently mean *wages*. Such a policy is defensible as a short-term device for a country whose costs are advancing more rapidly than its competitors'. In the long run, a dynamic policy to increase productivity and reduce prices in high-productivity industries is preferable to placing impediments upon the rewards earned by labour and capital.

The private sector, however large or small it may be, is best enabled to function efficiently through the operation of the profit motive, and the labour market should be enabled to operate efficiently through proper pay differentials for skill (craft and professional), responsibility and risk, etc.

Wage demands, so far from pricing employers out of the market (as has been argued by them since time immemorial), can have the effect, after a time, of pricing them into the market again through stimulating expenditure on labour-saving investment.[2] An active labour market policy can facilitate the movement of manpower (by adequate social and other measures) from declining to expanding sectors.

A positive policy for prices is an indispensable corollary of an incomes policy. It must be founded upon a ruthless assault on the abuse of monopoly power, market-sharing arrangements and administered prices. The selective lowering of tariff barriers (or the threat of it) can be an effective means of

[1] *Annual Review of the German Economy*, OEEC, Paris, 1958.
[2] See *Economic Survey of Europe in 1962*, UN Economic Commission for Europe, New York, 1963, p. 33.

bringing down prices. Tariff cuts should be accompanied by adequate measures to ensure that the consumer benefits from the lower costs. This should be the responsibility of central bodies such as Britain's National Board for Prices and Incomes.

Food constitutes the most important element in total expenditure in working-class budgets. Stabilisation of food prices would pave the way for stabilisation of the overall price level. In discussing the reasons for the increase in prices in Western Europe in 1964 compared with the previous year, the UN Economic Survey of Europe for 1964 states: 'When and where increases in the total cost of living were substantial (i.e. over 3 per cent) increases in food prices accounted for a proportion varying between 40 and 80 per cent of the total rise.'

The Survey goes on to suggest that the causes of rising food prices deserve careful investigation and the 'price policy might well be directed more deliberately towards influencing the development of food prices.' It identifies a further vital element in price increases—high distribution costs. At the root of this is the failure to introduce sufficiently rapidly the necessary structural changes in the distribution sector. A striking example for Italy is quoted by the Survey:

1 Kg. of Peas

Price paid to Naples farmer	40 Lire
Wholesale price paid by Milan retailer	72·5 Lire
Price paid by the consumer	140 Lire

Thus the price has risen no less than three-and-a-half times between the farmer and the consumer.

Selective price controls (backed by adequate sanctions) and selective lowering of protective tariffs would seem to be the best way of protecting the consumer until such time as the long-term increase in the size of retail distribution outlets takes place.

HAVE LOWER TARIFFS LED TO LOWER PRICES?

Both EFTA and EEC are engaged on studies seeking to estimate to what extent tariff cuts have benefited the consumer through lower prices, and higher quality (or different) consumer goods. The statistical problems in making such estimations are, of course, considerable. Obviously, prices are established under the influence of multifarious factors. How can the influence of tariff reductions on prices be isolated and measured?

The reluctance of producers and distributors (especially the latter) to pass on to the consumers the benefits of lower costs is well known. An OECD report of 1964 states:

> But, though important, considerations of equity are not the only reasons; equally important has been the belief that the behaviour of administered prices contributes to cost inflation. While it is difficult to disentangle the rôle of different elements in total costs, it seems probable that the failure of cost reductions to be reflected fully or immediately in prices is an important feature of the process by which costs and prices are levered up under conditions of cost inflation.[1]

Why should reductions resulting from tariff cuts prove to be different? Of course, in any case consumers cannot expect to receive the *full* benefit

[1] *Policies for Prices, Profits and Other Non-Wage Incomes*, OECD, Paris, 1964, para. 107.

of tariff reductions, since some of the resulting increase in profits will un-doubtedly be used to improve products through increased product differenti-ation, research, etc. The question is does the consumer receive much benefit apart from this?

As increasing free trade results in a greater flow of foreign goods on to the markets of the countries concerned, the prices not only of these foreign imports, but also of similar domestic products and third-country imports with which they are in competition, should fall. Thus we cannot simply measure price changes of the goods imported from other countries within EEC and EFTA but must seek to assess the influence of the increased imports upon the prices of similar domestic products, too.

But it may be that the prices of foreign goods imported from other countries within EFTA or EEC will not be reduced to reflect lower tariffs. If so, then it will not be necessary to reduce the prices of domestic and third-country imports with which these goods compete. Indeed, frequently the same wholesaler handles both foreign imports and domestic products which are in competition with them, and he knows that the more he sells of the foreign product, the less he will sell of the domestic product with which it is in competition.

Nor must it be forgotten that tariff reductions take place under the Rome and Stockholm Treaties in gradual stages of 10 per cent at a time and that, for instance, a 10 per cent reduction in a 30 per cent tariff makes possible a mere 3 per cent reduction in price. Thus it is unlikely that traders will go to the trouble of revising price lists, etc., in order to announce such small price cuts, and obviously as tariffs come nearer to zero the room for price reductions becomes less and less.

The EEC Commission claims in its 1965 General Report that some products are cheaper as a result of increased trade and competition resulting from the Common Market. The Commission cites chocolates, cakes, biscuits and confectionery (this is, in all conscience, a very meagre list!) and adds that the prices of washing-machines have remained relatively stable since 1958 despite their embodying important technical improvements.

For a second group of consumer goods, the EEC Commission claims that increased competition within the Community has had the effect of limiting price increases. The example of knitted clothing (resulting from increased imports of Italian knitwear) is cited. But the Commission admits that for many other consumer goods the impact of the Common Market has been small, because, firstly, imports represent only a small part of the total market, and secondly, the increased imports serve merely to complete the range of goods on sale.

Finally, according to the Commission, in a few cases the tariff reductions have been absorbed by retail and wholesale distributors. The 1965 Report comments: 'It therefore seems that competition is not yet fully effective in the distributive sectors.'

Indeed, numerous official reports have drawn attention to the defects in retail distribution in some countries, e.g. the 1963 OECD Report on France:

> 1. Although concentration is not intensive in France and monopolies are rare, there seems little doubt that employers' associations at industry level play an important rôle. 2. The organisation of channels of distribution leaves much to be desired. 3. The mental outlook of the various economic agents is an important factor, conditioned as it is by an almost uninterrupted rise in prices. Price stability no longer seems normal and there is no real resistance to price changes.[1]

[1] Para. 63, p. 36.

Searching inquiry is necessary in order to establish more adequately to what extent retail distribution is responsible not only for preventing the consumer from benefiting from the Common Market but also for contributing in no small measure to general inflationary tendencies. Despite all the expectations arising from the progressive implementation of tariff reductions under EEC and EFTA, it cannot be said that such reductions have been generally passed on to the consumer. A major reason for this is that the reductions took place during an inflationary period in which most prices were rising. Moreover, inadequate distribution networks (as in France and Italy), administered prices, and very imperfect competition generally have all contributed to preventing the consumer obtaining the full benefits of tariff cuts. The most favourable verdict that may be reached is that prices of consumer goods in trade between EEC and EFTA countries have probably increased less than they would have done if tariffs had not been reduced, but that they have by no means enabled the consumer to benefit to the extent that he had a right to expect.

CONCLUSIONS

Market mechanisms for establishing rewards may be marginally modified in the light of national criteria. But we have not yet reached that degree of sophistication in assessing relative incomes to enable us to establish detailed criteria concerning who should get how much. The most we can aim at after two decades of discussion about incomes policy (a wages policy was proposed in Beveridge's *Full Employment in a Free Society*, 1944) is that prices and incomes should be subject to greater public scrutiny and those responsible for establishing them should have to account more fully for their decisions. Many more comparative international studies are needed on unit labour costs and unit costs as a whole before we can be certain that the chain of argument usually adduced in support of incomes policies—increased wages equal increased costs, equal dearer exports, equal balance of payments disequilibria—is tenable.

BIBLIOGRAPHY

Alexander, K. and Hughes, J. *Trade Unions in Opposition* (Fabian Tract 335), Fabian Society, London, 1961.
Mazzocchi, G. 'Changes in Productivity and Wages,' *Productivity Measurement Review*, No. 39, OECD, Paris, November 1964.
Meade, J. E. *Efficiency, Equality and the Ownership of Property*, Allen and Unwin, London, 1964; Harvard Univ. Press, Cambridge, Mass., 1965.
Stewart, M. and Winsbury, R. *An Incomes Policy for Labour* (Fabian Tract 350), Fabian Society, London, 1963.
A Plan for Incomes (Fabian Research Series 247), Fabian Society, London, 1961.
British Journal of Industrial Relations, II, 3, London School of Economics and Political Science, November 1964. Several articles on incomes policy.
OEEC. *The Problem of Rising Prices*, Paris, May 1961.
OECD. *Policies for Prices, Profits and other non-wage Incomes*, Paris, July 1964.

Netherlands Wages Policy
Bussy, E. M. 'Recent Wage Control Policy in Netherlands,' *Monthly Labour Review*, US Dept of Labour, Washington, May 1964.
Klant, J. J. 'Holland after the Wage Explosion,' *The Banker*, London, No. 467, January 1965.
Pen, J. 'The Strange Adventures of Dutch Wage Policy,' *British Journal of Industrial Relations*, I, 3, London, October 1963.
OEEC. *The Problem of Rising Prices*, Paris, May 1961.

PROBLEMS OF UNDERDEVELOPMENT: SOUTHERN ITALY, SPAIN, GREECE AND TURKEY

DAVID TONGE

THE European countries surrounding the Mediterranean share broadly similar climates, resources and history. Greece, Turkey, Spain and southern Italy were once among the richest countries in Europe: now they are the poorest. Although this has happened only in the last two centuries as the rest of Europe has gone through the agrarian and industrial revolutions which shifted the economic centre of gravity north-westwards, the gap is now enormous. In Greece, Spain and southern Italy average incomes are only a third of those in the European Economic Community (excluding southern Italy). In Turkey they are half as low again. In 1963 it was reported of Turkey that: 60 per cent of the population of school age and above was illiterate; 53 per cent of the villages had either no drinking water or not enough; 69 per cent of the population was without electricity; one baby in six died in its first year; there was only one nurse for every 111 hospital beds and one teacher for every 60 students; in the cities an average of nearly three persons shared each residential room; and over one million people lived in shacks.

The general situation is undoubtedly worse in Turkey than elsewhere, particularly since almost all progress is swallowed up by the rapid growth in population, averaging about three times that in Greece, southern Italy and Spain. This has led to an increased demand for food, which in turn has only been produced by cultivating yet more land. This has been done in such a way as to increase yet further the erosion of centuries of mismanagement. If the other countries do not share this terrifying battle between population and resources, they, like Turkey, all suffer from certain basic problems: too few jobs—agriculture absorbs many of those who would otherwise be unemployed but in winter may need as little as a quarter of its summer workload; inefficient industry from which a few new plants stand out in glaring contrast; enormous regional differences in income; and an abyss between the few rich and the mass living at subsistence level (a survey in southern Italy in the mid-1950s revealed that nearly half the population was obtaining insufficient food to meet minimum basic needs).

Serious attempts to tackle these countries' problems are of recent date and results are still limited, but already all of them are showing growth rates well above those elsewhere in Europe. This has been achieved by what are essentially the same methods and it might be thought that given the countries' similar geography, climate and standards of living, opportunities for co-operation between them would be enormous. But the development efforts so far made show that this is not the case and that each must proceed with its own development; in many ways these countries are too similar, they all need the same things to further their development and these can only be supplied from outside the area, in particular from the rest of Western Europe. Yet the lessons learnt from these efforts are crucial since the region is in many ways a test project in development for the rest of the under-developed two-thirds of the world. Unfortunately, however, the main reason why the backward areas around the Mediterranean are now being developed is because they all have close connections with the rest of Western Europe; their recent growth is thus no indication of what could happen in under-developed areas elsewhere. Before considering what difficulties have been encountered and what experience gained, this chapter will describe how Greece, Spain, southern Italy and Turkey arrived at their present economic plight and, by means of a detailed study of each, show that at least for them the situation is not as bad as it was.

Effects of Climate and History

In all four countries the industrial revolution was greatly delayed. Lack of natural resources such as coal and iron ore is not a sufficient explanation for this, since though Greece and southern Italy are extremely poorly endowed the same is not true of Spain and Turkey. A much more important reason is perhaps the late appearance of the agrarian revolution. For financing industrialisation it would seem that the agricultural sector must provide, as it did in England, funds in excess of its own requirements. Even more vital, farmers themselves must produce in excess of their own requirements so that the towns will have sufficient food and, at a first remove, there will be markets for the towns' products.

One reason for the late development of agriculture is of course the climate. The present pattern of long, hot summers, cold winters and often extreme temperature variations can cause severe troubles, as for instance in 1955, when spring frosts ruined the citrus crop and the following hard winter killed off thousands of olive trees. Rainfall is scarce, which may prevent plant growth, weaken animals, and, combined with hard ground and a short time for seeding, restrict the arable area; drought is a common hazard. Sea and mountains greatly modify the pattern throughout the area. Most of Sicily and the plateaux of Spain and Turkish Central Anatolia are semi-arid; conditions depend on the degree of previous exploitation but generally livestock husbandry is rare and one crop of barley or hard wheat in the winter is all that is possible. The lower mountain areas show sub-humid conditions and less destruction of the land has occurred. A small amount of mixed farming occurs, pigs graze in the evergreen oak forests, and soft wheat may be sown; with good rain it may even be possible to have a summer crop. Olives, carobs, almonds and, in the foothills, vines are common; these areas are still very sensitive to hazard. The coastal regions and north and west slopes of the higher mountains show humid conditions and fare better. Summers are long and usually dry but total rainfall is high and these last areas are well vegetated. They supply most of the Mediterranean fruit crops, while chestnut and beech trees are found in the forests.

Much of the land is thus not very promising but certainly it was once better than now. Long-term climatic variations explain this only in part as, according to the FAO, since the recovery around the time of Christ from the quite severe desiccation of 2,000 years earlier, climatic variations have been small. A much more important factor is the course of history itself. Man seems to have been his own worst enemy. Centuries of economic and political instability led to the abandoning of terraces and the aggravation of the effects of such forms of mismanagement as deforestation and root-cropping by goats. The Roman Empire fell into the hands of peoples who proved far from effective in preserving local resources in conditions very different from their own. The trade on which the wealth of the Mediterranean had been founded became disrupted and only picked up in the Middle Ages with the active use of the land route to the East.

The discovery of the sea route to the East in the 15th century soon meant that trade was diverted from the Mediterranean; at the same time land suitable for cultivation was rapidly being used up. Greece was acting as one no-man's-land between the Moslems and the West, a position which lasted long after the Moslems were displaced from the other virtual no-man's-land, Spain. And long after the fall of Granada, Spain proved far from unified. An extremely feudal structure prevailed. Vast estates and minute fragmented holdings existed side by side. Although in the 17th century Spanish industry was comparatively advanced, the lack of interest by landowners, the lack of an entrepreneurial class and the channelling of much of Spain's more active talent to the New World delayed its development. Further, as with the oil-producing countries nowadays, a copious supply of gold meant that Spain could afford not to develop its industries, and when at the beginning of the 19th century it lost these colonies it was as if a limb had been amputated. The disruption of the Peninsular wars and the wars of the Carlist Succession followed.

In Turkey, southern Italy and Greece problems were of a similar scale. Both Turkey and southern Italy were long subject to foreigners who were on the whole ignorant of the peoples they had conquered. In both countries this led to an extreme form of feudalism, complicated in Turkey by the decay of the ruling class and in southern Italy by the rigidity caused by the church; both complications applied in Spain too. Further, Turkey was in a state of almost permanent war with Russia and with the lands under its rule from which in 1829, with Russian, British and French help, Greece was formed. The new Greece continued to be at daggers drawn with Turkey and the other Balkan countries. It suffered from internal political difficulties too, and its unification was in many ways more nominal than actual. This was true of Italy as well.

Southern Italy

Centuries of neglect

Throughout its history the two parts of Italy were separated by far more than just the Papal States, with the north connected with Europe by both politics and trade, and the south (here and elsewhere in this book meaning the mainland south of Rome and the offshore islands, together often referred to as the Mezzogiorno) connected with Africa and Spain.

Successive foreign invaders, Saracens, Normans and Spaniards failed to give southern Italy the efficient administration that countries such as Austria had foisted on the north. Its agriculture was primitive and was based on the latifundia system of vast estates owned by a normally absentee landlord and often crassly managed by stewards. The displacement of the Bourbons in 1861 from the Kingdom of the Two Sicilies may have removed a tradition-bound and obscurantist regime but it failed to effect much improvement. Some land was redistributed, but mostly in large packets to town-dwellers grown rich on trade and without experience in agriculture. No improvement in the hierarchical social structure occurred; malaria prevailed. Moreover, what funds there were in the south were channelled to the north by the banks and the newly unified tax system.

Yet even at the turn of the century there was considerable concern over the problems of the south and some expenditure was especially directed to public works there. The sums involved were, however, small and produced little effect before the course of outside events increased the problem. The great depression arrived at a time when Fascist economic policies had already threatened the industrial expansion of the north. This had in any case failed to spread to the south and Fascist policies made the latter even less likely. The wide-scale industrial failures of the early 1930s led to the separation of banks from industry and, in effect, to a complete dampening down of industrial credit—just at the time when the south most needed it. The benefits obtained by the south from such infrastructural schemes as the draining of the Pontine Marshes were more than outweighed by the effects of preventing labour mobility and of over-encouraging wheat production. By 1936 industrial employment in the south was lower than at the time of unification in 1861 despite a 60-per-cent increase in its population. Nor in the succeeding years did it share in the expansion of the war industries. By 1950 the position was worse than ever. The war had destroyed one-third of southern industry and over one-half of its power stations; average annual income was less than $200, unemployment averaged 12 per cent and under-employment was incalculable.

Fifteen years of intensive effort

Since 1950, however, when the Cassa per il Mezzogiorno (the government agency for the south) was established and positive agricultural policies introduced, a really effective stimulus has been given to development. The agricultural reforms have perhaps been the least effective steps taken. They aimed at owner-cultivation and broke up many of the old estates. The land was, however, divided into excessively small units and much of the money available in fact went to providing housing and not to improving agricultural efficiency. Nor has conversion to higher-yielding crops than wheat been marked, though here the land reform agencies have achieved a limited success. But some improvement has occurred; for example, southern Italy's share in total Italian agricultural production has risen from its long-term level of one-third to two-fifths. This improvement has resulted in part from the expenditure on irrigation and afforestation but to a much greater extent from the massive public expenditure on other aspects of infrastructure —on roads, electricity, education, etc.—which has benefited agriculture only indirectly.

This expenditure on infrastructure, which has been crucial for the development of the south as a whole, was part of the government's early policy of creating conditions favourable for industrialisation. Through the years this aim has changed and the emphasis is now on giving direct encouragement to industry. The regional industrial credit institutes had been in operation for some time before 1957, but it was in this year that change really occurred. The Cassa was authorised to give grants and subsidise loans to new firms. The various fiscal reliefs dating back to 1947 were greatly strengthened. The state corporations Ente Nazionale Idrocarburi (ENI) and Istituto per la Ricostruzione Industriale (IRI) were required to locate 40 per cent of their total investment and 60 per cent of their new investment in the south. But the most important innovation was the principle of concentration of effort embodied in the 1957 and later laws. Various industrial estates in which industrialisation would be particularly favoured were provided for; thirty-nine have since been recognised, twelve major and twenty-seven minor. Expenditure on their infrastructure has been marked, land and basic facilities have been made available in them for industrialists, and particularly favourable fiscal and other incentives are offered.

In the 1965 law all these policies were intensified. The principle of concentration was reaffirmed and extended to agriculture. More state spending was committed to the south and the system of grants, interest rebates and fiscal reliefs extended; among present incentives are a 20-per-cent grant on all plant construction costs up to 6 billion (thousand million) lire—30-per-cent if equipment for new plant has been produced in southern Italy—reduced transport costs and a ten-year exemption (in Sicily fifteen-year) from profit and company taxes.

Slow immediate returns

Initially these policies seemed to make no changes to southern Italy's 19-million population and the gap between incomes in the north and south remained as large as ever. This, however, is not surprising, as the very nature of the early projects meant that returns were bound to be slow. But the continued flow of workers from the area has had two important effects. It has meant that the population of the area has remained fairly steady, and hence income increases have not merely been swallowed up in raising people's standards of living but part of them has gone to saving. It has also meant that workers elsewhere have often sent back funds to their families. Thus not only (since 1961) has southern Italy begun to generate its own funds for investment, but the inflow of resources on which the south depends has been supplemented by workers' remittances. In 1963 the inflow was equivalent to 28 per cent of local product and reassuringly the recent Italian economic downturn has shown that it is not affected by external ups and downs. Moreover, in recent years the rate of growth of southern Italy has overtaken that in the north. But it is the recent course of investment—a 25-per-cent annual compound increase between 1959 and 1963 before a slight fall in 1964 reflecting the completion of several major projects and uncertainties before new legislation—that hints at the same time at southern Italy's strength and weakness. Its strength lies in its forming part of an expanding (rapidly so until 1964) economy to which it can turn for all the funds it needs and which has protected it from balance-of-payments problems (when general deflationary measures do have to be taken they are usually designed so as to have less effect on the south). Thus the south has been able to embark on a series of massive schemes such as those at Gela (petro-chemicals) and Taranto (steel). Its weakness is that private initiative is still limited, that as a result of their self-sufficiency the projects so far completed have failed to act as a magnet for other industry.

However, as southern Italy also forms part of the EEC it again has advantages over the other Mediterranean countries. The European Investment Bank (EIB) was specially formed to direct funds to the backward areas of the Community and has devoted no less than two-thirds of its interventions to southern Italy. It is sometimes criticised for taking too limited a share in any single project and at first it seemed that it caused other organisations such as the World Bank to withdraw, but these are now showing renewed interest. Far more important, at least for southern Italy, is the scheme drawn up by a firm of economic consultants, Italconsult, commissioned by the EEC to study the problems of southern Italy. Italconsult examined the industrial areas of Bari, Brindisi and Taranto nestling together on Italy's heel. There a certain number of large plants have set up, but despite the presence of these and the availability of fiscal and financial incentives, private initiative has been weak. This, it is held, is because the plants so far established are mainly self-sufficient, vertically-integrated plants interacting little with the production processes of other industry. This last point is felt to be far more important to firms than closeness to markets or raw materials. Accordingly, Italconsult proposed the establishment of nine firms, operating in sectors not already dominated by one firm, to produce finished goods and provide work for some thirty auxiliary firms also to be established—the whole to form an extremely competitive industrial complex benefiting from its relations with nearby industry, which the firms established so far have been unable to do. The idea is a good one, particularly in view of its lack of protectionism, but the cost is enormous, about £100 million.

Despite the limitations of policy so far it seems that, barring agricultural fluctuations, growth in the south must continue to exceed that in the north. The country's first five-year plan contains this as a central assumption and outlines specific measures to ensure its occurrence by means of a continued diversion of investment funds to the south. Within five years unemployment is sanguinely hoped to fall to a level below 2 per cent. The general lines of policy are to remain the same as before, though at a later date it is intended to treat southern Italy in accordance with a still unprepared system of regional planning; this would give local authorities more powers to take the initiative in economic planning but will take a long time to introduce; given the importance of the Cassa for coordinating policy and success so far, this is all for the good.

SPAIN

Political checks to early progress

In Spain progress became marked somewhat earlier than in Italy. This was less because of agricultural development—the 19th-century redistribution of church lands merely enlarged the existing lay latifundias—than because a fragment of the gold from the new world had in fact gone, in areas such as Catalonia, to building on the embryonic industrial structure. By the early 1920s progress was rapid, but was then completely choked off by the civil war and later the ostracisation of the country; thus the 1940s was a period of stagnation. Yet during this period and the following years there did occur some large improvements in communications and, as the country's isolation required, a widening of the industrial base.

But it is only since 1956, when Spain was admitted to the United Nations, that the real changes have occurred. The market mechanism was accepted for the allocation of resources and the country was partially opened to goods, capital and skills from abroad. The initial effects of this were disastrous and reserves slumped but the 1959 stabilisation programme, effective largely because of the earlier reform of public finances, rectified the situation. Since then the government has done much to reduce the rigidities inherent in Spain's economic structure though some of its reforms have not had the results hoped for (the banking reform law, for instance, attempted to force banks to separate their industrial financing from other activities but may merely have led to the establishment of wholly-owned subsidiaries). Nor does much seem to have been done to consolidate the fragmented industrial and agricultural sectors, nor on the other hand to tackle the problem of latifundias. But the state does now exert more flexible control over the economy than it was previously able to through its own public spending, the tax system (still heavily dependent on indirect taxes) and the Instituto Nacional de Industria (INI) (a vast mass of state-run firms representing much of industry and enjoying special privileges).

Results have been considerable and since 1961 growth has been at nearly twice the rate of the 1950s; but growing pains have appeared, in particular considerable inflation. Between 1962 and 1964 prices, led by construction costs and agricultural prices, rose by one-fifth. Despite this inflation and the increase in newly-freed imports, reserves have risen throughout most of this period and cover about five months' import bill. This has not resulted from the trade balance—exports are mainly agricultural and only amount to two-fifths of the value of imports, most of which are essential—but from a massive increase in tourist receipts; these rose by 80 per cent between 1962 and 1964 when they covered 40 per cent of the import bill. Workers' remittances, the other main Mediterranean money-spinner and reason why the area is at present particularly favoured, also rose.

The 1964 Development Plan

Earlier measures are all being consolidated in the country's first development plan, which is a natural extension of recent improvements in management. It was introduced late in 1963 for the years 1964–7 inclusive. It sets a 6-per-cent annual average increase in GNP, 'to be achieved by the rational use of existing resources.' It is binding on the public sector which is to reform its accounting procedures (though the position of the INI is left vague) and indicative for the private sector. Considerable attention is to be paid to the agricultural sector via afforestation, irrigation and the consolidation of land holdings; no mention, however, is made of the latifundias nor of the price support system for agriculture which, as the OECD points out, deprives the industrial sector of much-needed funds, prevents innovations, and ossifies the present structure of agricultural production.

Industry is being helped by a regional development policy which aims on the whole at attracting industry to certain favourable areas where special incentives are made available, including provision of sites, easier recourse to official credit, investment subsidies up to 20 per cent and a reduction of taxes by up to 95 per cent. Seven industrial areas have so far been specified of which two offer particularly favourable terms. The INI itself is to act as one of the main instruments of government policy but it is intended that it will set up plant only when private firms prove incapable. It is hoped that one million new jobs will be provided during the plan period.

The importance of the plan lies most in its clear statement of the various lines of policy and the implications of the targets set. The most crucial of these is the need for a 9-per-cent annual rise in investment which, given trends in domestic saving, will necessitate a capital inflow of over £120 million annually. So far tourist receipts and the effect of the less restrictive attitude to foreign investors seem to be ensuring this while a certain amount of help is coming from the international organisations. But there are dangers: the pattern of foreign trade means that the trade balance is if anything likely to worsen, and the political troubles likely to emerge when General Franco ceases to rule the country (which in theory is a monarchy) could severely interrupt the capital flow.

TURKEY

Effects of the world wars

Turkey started to exploit some of its mineral resources in the 19th century but made little progress before it found itself in the midst of twelve years of war ending in 1922. War left the country with a devastated structure and limited funds, a position aggravated by a totally inadequate transport system, by the displacement in the 1923 population exchange with Greece, and by the abolition of the 'Capitulations' granting mercantile privileges to the foreign minorities which dominated trading. The government itself tried to encourage the private sector in 1927 by founding a business bank and giving industry tax relief and customs facilities and, later, introducing protective tariffs. The effect of these was weakened by the antagonistic attitude to foreign capital. This capital began to become crucial after the great depression when export prices fell and the country found difficulty in paying, as it had before, for the industrial goods it needed. It was forced back on itself and found itself with scarcely any capital and an extremely narrow industrial base.

So the state itself, already busy adapting itself to the Western world, took on the task of industrialisation. It founded some industries, nationalised a few foreign firms and devoted considerable funds to developing the railroads. Two narrow development plans achieved limited success. Population growth swallowed up many of the gains of this period, the second world war more. Turkey, despite its treaty commitments, did not have to fight but was forced to mobilise. This severely affected the labour-intensive agricultural sector, and together with the interruption of foreign trade was the main factor slowing down industrial growth. After the war there was a critical need for new equipment but the financing problems were large, particularly since continued outside threats caused much-needed funds to be diverted from development to defence. Further disruption resulted from the internal change to a multi-party system from the virtual dictatorship of Ataturk. Yet these problems were gradually resolved and in 1950 the economy was in full expansion.

Post-war problems

The impetus of this expansion came from the agricultural sector. In the 1950s Turkey's comparatively large foreign reserves and increased foreign aid were liberally used for the purchase of farm machinery. There was a succession of good crop years and favourable trade conditions led to the disposal of these crops abroad but in following years some severe difficulties emerged. The expansion of agricultural output had been achieved by the bringing of new land into cultivation rather than the improvement of yields. The limit of this land was reached at the same time as bad harvests— agricultural output fell in value by one-fifth between 1953 and 1954—and at the same time as reserves, worn into by the expansive spending policy of earlier years, became minimal. In the following years the economy went from crisis to crisis and it took five years for income per head to regain its

1953 level. But the 1958 devaluation and stabilisation programme set the scene for a considerable revival. Large amounts of foreign aid were received and the inflation which had characterised the preceding period came to an end. Two years later the first coordinated development programme was introduced.

This programme began with a detailed five-year plan covering the first part of a fifteen-year period over which a general perspective was taken. The first plan was for the years 1963 to 1967. In many ways it is a remarkably sophisticated document. This is less evident in the numerical part—an annual growth rate of 7 per cent is set and the precise implications of this are worked out for the various sectors of the economy—than in the underlying analysis. The plan authorities have seen with considerable objectivity the problems facing the economy and chosen sensible methods of tackling them. Land reform; a large agricultural programme; the reorganisation of the State Economic Enterprises (an amorphous collection of state-controlled industries, utilities, railways and banks, run with considerable inefficiency and altogether similar to the Spanish INI); the improvement of industrial credit facilities; the establishment of industrial zones in the backward areas; the development of tourism; education and higher quality administration; all these are considered at length and the means of introducing them laid down.

Superficially at least results have been encouraging. Price rises have been contained and the economy has expanded at an average rate of about 6 per cent. But two major drawbacks have appeared—the limitations of the authorities' effectiveness and the small quantities of foreign exchange available; besides these the incomplete realisation of some of the plan targets is of minor significance. The limited effectiveness of the authorities has been evident over a long period—an instance is the failure to raise tax yields despite a succession of tax reforms. Initially much of the ineffectiveness derived from a more fundamental fact, that Menderes' Democratic Party which long ruled the country represented the right wing and had little desire to be a reformist party. However, even after it was replaced in 1960 by a more centrally-based government, the progress of reform was slow. The bills for land reform (somewhat weak ones) and family planning are still to be passed. Now that the last election has returned the Justice Party (the successor to the Democratic Party) to power it is to be feared that progress may again be checked and an over-cautious pragmatic approach prevail.

Foreign exchange problems

The problems of foreign exchange are even more crucial. The reserve drain of the 1950s and subsequent economic ups and downs have left the country with a massive foreign debt and crippling aid-repayment liabilities. In 1965 reserves were equivalent to less than two months' import bill. The structure of foreign trade goes far towards explaining this. Imports consist entirely of vital raw materials and investment goods, and far outweigh exports (of which two-thirds consist of traditional Mediterranean products, raisins, cotton, tobacco and nuts, and one-third of a few processed foodstuffs, petroleum and copper, but no true manufactures as yet, though the system of drawback on taxes on exported manufactures introduced in 1963, despite administration problems, may be beginning to yield results). Moreover, Turkey has become a net importer of cereals (1965 would seem to be an exception to the long-term trend) and is becoming so also of oil seeds.

Yet there is hope from invisibles and Turkey seems now to be following, five years later, the course that Spain took. Tourism is still in its infancy; official figures even show that in 1964, despite three times as many people entering the country as leaving, Turkey's receipts from tourism were less than one half the amount it expended under this head. Recent heavy expenditure on facilities (and the tourist radio stations' daily exhortation to say good morning to foreigners) seems to be paying off, however; in 1965 the number of tourists rose by 40 per cent.

Workers' remittances are also on the increase. The number of emigrant workers has recently risen staggeringly; in the thirty months to mid-1965 it rose fiftyfold to 75,000 (forecasts for 1972 are for 500,000). Regrettably, however, most of those workers have come from developed areas, causing a large drain of the type of labour most needed, and until recently few remittances came through official channels. But the incentive of a premium of nearly one-third on workers' conversions of hard currency to Turkish dinars is correcting the latter and, if the increase in migration to labour-starved northern Europe can continue, then a real contribution to the balance of payments could be made. Already this is happening. In 1965 remittances from workers abroad totalled $70 million, compared with $9 million a year earlier. The planners' figures of yearly transfers of $150 million in 1967 and double that in 1972 no longer seem as hopelessly optimistic as they once did. This improvement alone could balance the foreign account.

But for the time being the country is reliant on other expedients. Attempts to curb imports by such means as compulsory deposits for the value of imports with the central banks have a generally deflationary effect since imports and domestic output are far from direct substitutes. Moreover, if deflationary measures are taken, the economy slows down without imports showing much change. And imports are necessary for the carrying through of such projects as the Eregli steel mills or the Keban dam and hence are of vital importance in the attempt to raise the standard of living of the country. There is increasing reliance on outside aid. The United States through its commodity surplus disposal schemes (Public Law 480) has provided a good deal of aid ($28 million in 1964 and $35 million in 1965), but compared with Turkey's debt-servicing bills of $145 million in 1964 and $220 million in 1965 this help is a mere fraction of what is needed. The OECD Aid Consortium has done more but until recently acted falteringly. For 1966, however, it guaranteed a figure of around $220 million (including about $70 million in debt-servicing roll-overs) while a further $180 million is expected to come from other sources as project aid and $135 million for the external financing of the Keban dam. Also the AID is providing up to $140 million for the construction of hotels and $14 million for other projects. With the Soviet Union participating in several schemes and Japan likely to do so as well, and with exports up in 1966 it seems that Turkey may now have broken free from its foreign exchange shortage; but economic independence remains a distant prospect.

GREECE

While Greece has recently been more fortunate than Turkey over its foreign exchange its needs are in some ways even greater. The settlement of one million refugees after the 1923 Lausanne Treaty with Turkey disturbed the traditional relationship between mountain and plain dwellers, by which those living in the mountains covering two-thirds of the country had been able to seek seasonal work in the plains. Pressure on the resources of the latter became intense. As a result of increased yields and the clearing of one million hectares of forest, large increases in agricultural production were obtained. These served to provide enough food but industry itself proved sluggish. The manpower available was mostly unsuitable for industrial work and natural resources were extremely limited. There was little spur for the application of capital which in any case was scarce. On top of this came four years of occupation by the Axis powers and civil war lasting, effectively, from 1944 to 1949. Later, with investment highly dependent on imports, the country's development was impeded by a lack of foreign exchange. Initially American aid partially offset this, but when the aid was stopped in 1951 investment suffered severely. Greece's foreign trade structure was (and is) similar to that of Turkey and little help was provided by exports. Since devaluation in 1953 recovery has been remarkable. Emigrants' remittances, tourism and shipowning, showing steadily more dazzling figures (1963 returns were respectively three, four and five times higher than those for 1953) have covered the trade deficit throughout this period, and only in the last year have problems re-emerged as imports began to outrun invisibles. Growth has been comparatively steady, averaging nearly 6 per cent annually between 1953 and 1958, and slightly more since.

Yet the structural weaknesses remain enormous. Industry is basically fragmented and provides little more than a quarter of GNP. The number of artisan enterprises is enormous and 75 per cent of firms with less than ten workers and employing just over half of industrial labour is only responsible, as the EIB has recently pointed out, for about one-third of production. Industrial employment has hardly risen in the last fifteen years and until recently firms had shown little tendency to grow. Until recently, too, they seemed unable to benefit from economies of scale; external economies were lacking, capital was not finding its way to industry but rather to housing and there was a generally unsatisfactory institutional framework. Gradually the authorities have acted to rectify these weaknesses.

Government measures in the 1960s

The 1960 five-year plan and the memorandum updating it in 1962 were the first steps in this direction. Emphasis was placed on improving communications and developing basic industries. The investment budgets of the state-controlled enterprises were greatly increased. A company, the Organisation for Industrial Development, was formed with public capital and through this and also directly the state intervened in industry, establishing, in line with the policy declared in the memorandum, 'basic units' in which private initiative was not originally interested. Examples of these are a petrol and two sugar refineries and a fertiliser plant: many of these basic units are now in the process of being handed over to the private sector. Investment banks were established and most of the taxes on industry reduced if not abolished, particularly for firms located outside the Athens-Piraeus cluster and those exporting part of their production. The favourable terms on which foreign investment has been treated since 1953 were consolidated.

In 1964-5 these policies were intensified. As in southern Italy, large sums have been directed to infrastructure, to improving roads, railways, ports and the electricity network; the country's association since November 1962 with the EEC has led to the provision via the EIB of considerable sums amounting in 1963 and 1964 to $37 million, $17 million of this for roads and $10 million for irrigating the Salonika plain. Further steps have been taken to channel funds to industry. The two major public bodies responsible for promoting and financing industry have been merged (the new body will also cover the tourist sector) and it is proposed that loans considered economically desirable be freed from the general charge on bank advances. Also a new law has been passed governing the creation of industrial estates and an overall development plan for the years 1966 to 1970 has been presented. The latter looks for a 7.5 per cent average annual increase in GNP. Regrettably this plan could not have been presented at a worse time. Mr Papandreou's government has been generally blamed for the present economic difficulties of the country, which have necessitated such austerity measures as an increase in turnover tax and threats to raise income tax for two years; as it was Mr Papandreou's government which commissioned the plan, a number of members of Mr Stephanopoulos's government (which fell in December 1966) were opposed to the plan on principle.

Price support for agriculture

The agricultural sector, too, has come under further scrutiny. In line with Mr Papandreou's general policy of helping the poorer classes, the farmers' agricultural mortgage debt burden and interest rates on agricultural loans have been reduced. A five-year agricultural programme has also been announced. This continues previous policies, encouraging the switch from wheat to other crops (in particular the exportable ones) by extending price support to other goods so as to regularise the market in them. It is hoped that this will stop market uncertainties from being a deterrent to switching from wheat; however other obstacles to the change remain. Many farmers are only capable of the simple techniques which wheat growing requires, while those living far away from the backward marketing system cultivate wheat in order to be self-sufficient. In any case wheat support prices have recently been very high. In both 1964 and 1965 production was about half-a-million tons higher than domestic consumption, estimated at about 1·7 million tons. Thus, further inflated by cheap imports from the United States under US Public Law 480, stocks soared to about one million tons. Storage space for this was grossly inadequate but exports were forbidden under the terms of Public Law 480. More recently, however, Greece has received special dispensation to export 0·35 million tons while it is reported that the area sown for wheat was down 12·4 per cent between the 1964–5 and 1965–6 seasons (that for barley has risen markedly). But the problem of over-production of wheat remains and the switch to new crops such as cotton, maize, sugar beet and alfalfa is slow.

Outstanding problems

Thus Greece still faces considerable problems. Industry is far from efficient, and though output may be rising, investment is lagging behind expectations; moves to improve the capital market have still only a limited effect and further efforts are of crucial importance. Employment opportunities are not being created sufficiently fast to slow down an emigration which, as in Turkey, is cutting down the amount of higher quality labour available. The calibre of the bureaucracy is still open to question and the government is unable to work through a public-dominated industrial network of the type existing, however inefficiently, in the other countries examined in this chapter. Political upheavals such as those over the defence ministry and in Cyprus are a serious problem for the effect they have not only on the administration of the country but also on foreign capital.

Private investment has so far resulted in some large and successful schemes in Greece, e.g. the complexes of Esso-Pappas (petrochemicals) and Pechiney (aluminium). It obtains protection beyond that normal in Greek law but in order to receive this must go through a cumbersome process of official authorisation (attempts have recently been made to simplify this procedure but difficulties still remain). After the crisis over the defence ministry, however, the flow of capital much slowed down. It again proved necessary to solicit aid from outside. It seems, however, that this is no problem since the settlement of the issue of pre-war debts, the consequent activation of the OECD Aid Consortium and association with the EEC indicate that sufficient external finance to supplement domestic saving will be forthcoming. Before the recent defence crisis it seemed that the Consortium might have finished its work, but it figured prominently among the bodies from which Greece expected to receive around $180 million in 1966.

The problems of obtaining adequate administration and foreign capital may be overcome on the lines of a scheme proposed in early 1966. This scheme concerned a programme for the rapid development of Crete and the western Peloponnese. Its aim was to build up agriculture and industry and above all to capitalise on the tourist potential of the area. Total cost of the programme was estimated at about $1 billion. It was to be managed by Litton Benelux, a subsidiary of an American management firm, on a twelve-year contract providing for the training of Greek staff. A ceiling was fixed for operating costs and Litton was to obtain a management fee of 11 per cent of these. It was also to be paid a commission of between $3\frac{1}{2}$ and $5\frac{1}{2}$ per cent on all foreign capital it secured. Several firms have shown interest in projects run in such a way.

THE GENERAL PATTERN

New policy trends

The success with which each of the four countries considered above has tackled its own problem of poverty has been the result of many common factors, of which the most important has been the renewed contact of each country with the outside world. For southern Italy this dates back some time; for Greece, effectively to post-war American aid; for Spain to the mid-1950s. Turkey has gradually come closer to the rest of Europe and, though like Spain its contacts may still be more limited than it would wish, like the other countries it has made good use of the advantages offered by Europe's boom. These advantages have been crucial. Before considering them it will be as well to examine the points in common in the management of the domestic economies of the four countries.

All have now embarked on comparatively sophisticated development policies. For Spain and Turkey this represents a considerable change from earlier efforts, for Greece less so, while Italy has applied well-reasoned plans for some time. All these policies, except in southern Italy, have proved less effective than hoped owing to the fact that coordinated planning is in its infancy and there are few weapons of government policy. This is particularly true now that in their overall development plans and elsewhere all countries have accepted the use of the market mechanism to allocate resources. The state is expected to remove the interferences to market forces and to improve on the mechanism itself by offering fiscal and financial inducements to stimulate private interest in desired aims. The main problem here is that at least for Spain and Turkey the state's traditional organs of power are not applicable in a market economy, and that the state has often only had limited success in removing interference to market forces. This means that the inducements offered are often insufficient and hence the state itself intervenes in industry indirectly through state enterprises (in Greece this is done through a newly formed public authority). These state enterprises are potentially an efficient instrument of government power; in Spain and Turkey they are handicapped by muddled management. Most intervention is in fields with a high capital-output ratio—in particular education, agriculture and other parts of infrastructure.

A policy of direct industrialisation is now generally favoured rather than a policy aimed at creating the conditions favourable to industrialisation (as was the aim in southern Italy in the mid-1950s). This is important since—in order of increasing seriousness—in Spain, Greece and Turkey funds are limited and the decision to concentrate on industry implies the forced neglect of other sectors. For Turkey the effects of this have been particularly grave; the country has had to spend amounts above its immediate resources and then hope that others will pay off its overdraft; even such vital sectors as agriculture and roads have still received only limited funds. This has been less the case in Spain, while in southern Italy there have recently been sufficient funds to benefit all sectors. (Southern Italy's position is different from that of the other countries since its problem is technically one of regional development within a rapidly growing economy. This makes it easier for the country to obtain funds, with the government ensuring re-allocation between north and south, but the large size of the southern region makes the problem involved and the policies necessary almost identical to those in the other countries considered, where the problem of underdevelopment is a national one.)

Slow returns in agriculture

Even the large sums spent in Italy have had scant effect on agricultural efficiency and some of the other countries have had, for instance, more success at diversifying production. This is especially true of Greece where sugar beet and pulses are now found and there has been a small shift of land from wheat to cotton. In Spain and Turkey output of cotton has also risen owing to improved production techniques, which has provided a valuable raw material for domestic industry, opened opportunities for a second crop and, in the case of Turkey, earned foreign exchange (Spanish cotton is unsuitable for sale abroad). But there have been considerable difficulties in the way of this diversification and price policies alone have proved insufficient to ensure it, probably owing to inefficiently organised markets (this problem is now being tackled). Again, much remains to be done to accelerate the introduction of, among other things, fertilisers and crop-rotation methods, both of which are essential if further erosion is to be prevented; in this case education standards are apparently a drastic impediment. It is hoped that the introduction of the EEC's agricultural policy (when it is finally agreed) will help southern Italy. It seems that the main benefit that southern Italy will receive will be funds to help it modernise its farming structure during the initial years; without such funds the policy will be of limited effect in this area, since the high fixed cereal prices planned will discourage the switch to other products.

Barriers to investment

The quality of labour has proved a major problem for industry as well as for agriculture but it is only one of the factors holding down industrial efficiency. In an effort to compensate for this and to attract industry, in all the countries under consideration the state has offered a series of financial and fiscal incentives, yet though these may be well designed their implementation has often been weak. Moreover it appears that, despite recent expenditure on infrastructure, the effect of the plant's surroundings may reduce efficiency more than can be compensated by the incentives offered by the state. In an effort to provide efficient surroundings each country save Turkey has now set up industrial estates, but the experience of Italy shows that even these may not be enough, hence the scheme proposed by Italconsult (see above). But other countries cannot hope to make use of so large a scheme and thus instead of aiming to achieve industrial growth by a concerted effort on all fronts they must rely on developing one plant or industry, hoping it will give a stimulus to others. This may fail to happen. Nor has any country yet found a reliable method of selecting the type of plant. Should the shortage of capital and surplus of labour lead one to invest in labour-intensive equipment or should the interests of efficiency be allowed to prevail and capital-intensive equipment result? Again, how is a decision to be made in the face of the facts that new industry in an established industrial conglomeration such as the Athens-Piraeus region, Barcelona or Istanbul would be more competitive but that social needs may dictate that it go to the backwoods?

Another barrier to investment is the lack of entrepreneurial spirit (though there is a mercantile class which is not interested in medium-term investment and which through speculation and depressing the farmers' terms of trade may hamper development). A further barrier is lack of capital. Even in southern Italy, despite long-standing efforts to channel funds to industry, housing often takes precedence, small borrowers are penalised and banks, as elsewhere, overprotect depositors' interests. The capital structure in each country is primitive, and though slowly improving, still acts as a drag on the economy. Thus for the moment it may be necessary for the state to play a larger role.

In general terms the state might aim to provide funds by limiting consumption, concentrating investments, or looking abroad. Given the low standards of living, limiting general consumption is little use, though by introducing highly progressive taxation (questions of tax yields apart), some results might be achieved. Progressive taxation would of course reduce the incomes of those most able to invest but there are, as the FAO has pointed out, three reasons why this might not matter: first, the rich in these countries are often not interested in industrial investment; secondly, they tend to spend large sums on luxury housing (this has a high import content so one result of progressive taxation would be to reduce non-essential imports); thirdly, it would enable the state to raise its revenue. But in total this way of limiting consumption will probably be a slow way of providing funds for investment. Better results might come from improving present uses of investment funds, from reducing the volume directed to housing and the property market—particularly in Greece and Spain— from checking leakages abroad and from reducing defence expenditure, particularly in Greece and Turkey. Again, this would probably take time and so the important role played by the outside world as a source of the funds and industrial products essential for most investment projects is likely to continue.

Europe's legacy

For Spain and to a lesser extent Turkey, further contact with the outside world has implied a considerable reversal of policy. But these countries, like Greece and southern Italy, have now made good use of their closeness to an expanding Europe. This closeness gives the area an immediate advantage over the rest of the underdeveloped two-thirds of the world—an advantage from which only Mexico, in its dealings with the United States, has been able to profit. This advantage is fourfold: first, export sales are facilitated; secondly, migrant workers can move easily; thirdly, tourism is benefited; lastly, capital transfers are facilitated. None of these factors is of course entirely dependent upon geographical closeness, but all are helped by it, the second and third especially.

The vast majority of the area's exports are primary goods, but luckily ones in general unlikely to be affected by a change in world taste, as is happening for instance to Malaya's rubber. There are, nevertheless, dangers of overproduction, most likely to affect tobacco (though Greece and Turkey have preferential access to the EEC) and oranges, of which it is feared by the EEC Commission that there may be a glut by 1970 unless a means of limiting Mediterranean production is found (the 1965 EEC crisis has not helped here). New types of export are not to be expected for the time being. Present measures particularly favouring exporters such as those in Greece are having only a limited effect, and in most countries, especially Turkey, there is little room for paring imports. Thus since these countries are adopting policies aimed at expanding exports rather than substituting for imports, the problem of paying for the latter remains crucial.

It is this that adds importance to migrants' remittances and tourist receipts. It is most unlikely that the demand for southern European labour will fall. While emigration has the debilitating effect of removing the most able-bodied from the labour force, this may be offset at a later date when labour returns better trained; in the meantime emigration helps towards paying for essential machinery. Tourism too is a help. All these countries under consideration have devoted particular attention to it; in southern Italy there are even incentives for hotels, etc. in zones of touristic interest similar to those offered to industry in the industrial estates. Though tourism offers seasonal employment only and may constitute one more cause of overexpansion in the construction industry the benefits resulting from its earnings of foreign exchange are far more important. In Spain and Greece (to a lesser extent recently), tourism and workers' remittances have more than offset the trade deficit. This has not until recently been the case in Turkey which has still the problem of balancing its external account and remains dependent on the aid that the outside world can provide.

For all four countries the difficulty of attracting outside private capital remains. The few industrial schemes to which private capital has been directed, e.g. the Esso-Pappas project in Greece, have been highly successful, but the difficulty is that private capital has been limited, and like domestic capital, often devoted to housing. Political impediments to private capital inflow such as those caused in Greece by the 1965 government crisis and in Turkey by the threat in 1965 (not, it seems, to be carried out) to nationalise the oil industry, can ill be afforded. This comparative recalcitrance where private capital is concerned has led to dependence on the aid consortia benefiting Greece and Turkey, on the interventions of the World Bank and more recently (though this does not help Spain) of the EIB. The latter, with the reservations mentioned in regard to southern Italy, has been highly effective, and were the EEC's regional policy, with its scheme for (in order of priority) occupational training, improving economic and social infrastructure, and offering fiscal and financial incentives ever to be implemented, the EIB would become the EEC's major instrument of intervention. It is still uncertain whether, besides helping the EEC's members which include Italy, this policy would be used to help the EEC's associates, Greece and Turkey.

CONCLUSIONS

While Greece, Turkey, southern Italy and Spain follow the same development paths, it appears that there are few fields in which they can cooperate. Each has set out a list of reforms it intends to undertake in order to reduce the structural rigidities inherent in its economy. These reforms have been well drawn up but, in varying degrees, less well implemented, and it is for each country alone to implement them. Again, experience has shown that each country needs from outside the same resources, funds and capital equipment, and a large amount of them. Here again these countries cannot help each other. Some positive results might emerge from joint schemes for the sale of traditional Mediterranean exports, but it does not appear that much will be gained by the related idea of a joint pressure group to avoid protection against their exports by importing countries—UNCTAD partially does this already.

Where industry is concerned there is the theoretical possibility of each country arranging to specialise on particular lines of production, thus enabling the industries of the area to benefit from the economies of scale necessary to compete in the European market. But the example of Africa has already shown the political problems of arranging such a division of productive facilities to be almost insuperable. In the case of the four countries under consideration these problems are even greater owing to the different political ties of each. In any case, the four countries are not a geographical unit suitable for such schemes.

For other countries the recent improvement in economic conditions in Greece, southern Italy, Spain and Turkey has several implications. For developed countries this improvement indicates what can be achieved by the channelling of help, whether directly through aid schemes, or indirectly through tourism, opportunities for workers, etc.; it also tends, by pointing to the importance of concentration of effort, to support those favouring the diversion of aid to the few countries nearest self-sustaining growth rather than to the more backward ones. For the underdeveloped countries as a whole, on the other hand, the lesson is a somewhat gloomy one and shows the massive amount of funds necessary before many of them will be able to break out of the vicious circle of poverty. But if the Mediterranean has mainly benefited because its favourable position in relation to Europe has enabled it to lay claim to far more aid than appears on the face of things, its development has proved an invaluable guide as to how, whatever the political and economic structure of a country, problems can be tackled.

BIBLIOGRAPHY

Barzanti, Sergio. *The Underdeveloped Areas within the Common Market*, Oxford Univ. Press, London; Princeton Univ. Press, Princeton, NJ, 1965.

Carlyle, Margaret. *The Awakening of Southern Italy*, Oxford Univ. Press, London and New York, 1962.

Grindrod, Muriel. 'Developing Southern Italy: a Fifteen Years' Survey', *The World Today*, XXI, 10, London, October 1965.

McNeill, William Hardy. *Greece: American Aid in Action 1947–1956*, Twentieth Century Fund, New York, 1957.

Stirling, Peter. *Turkish Village*, Weidenfeld and Nicolson, London, 1965.

ECE. 'Development Problems of Southern Europe and Ireland' (Part IV of *Economic Survey of Europe in 1959*, Geneva, 1960). *Economic Survey of Europe in 1962*, Geneva, 1963. *Economic Survey of Europe in 1963*, Geneva, 1964. *Economic Bulletin for Europe*, XIV, 2, Geneva, November 1962.

FAO. *Mediterranean Development Project: The Integrated Development of Mediterranean Agriculture and Forestry in Relation to Economic Growth*, Rome, 1959. Also *Country Reports*.

IBRD. *The Economic Development of Spain*, Johns Hopkins Press, Baltimore, Md., 1963; Oxford Univ. Press, London, 1966.

OECD. *Government Organisation and Economic Development: Fourth Study Conference on Problems of Economic Development, Paris, September 1964*, Paris, 1966. 'An Experiment in Planning by Six Countries', *The Mediterranean Regional Project: Education and Development*, Paris, 1965. Also *Country Reports*.

WESTERN EUROPEAN ECONOMIC AID TO DEVELOPING COUNTRIES

JOHN WHITE

THE EVOLUTION OF AID

ECONOMIC aid to developing countries is a recent phenomenon in international relations. If one takes the strictest definition of 'aid', as being the provision of resources with the primary objective of promoting the recipient's economic development, then aid was not a major element in international relations until the end of the 1950s. The strict definition is the one that is increasingly accepted. It is implicit, for instance, in the German word for 'aid', which is *Entwicklungshilfe*, or 'development assistance'.

Before the second world war the colonial powers contributed to the development of some of their dependencies, and much of what was done then would now be called 'economic aid'. In the British case, aid to the colonies goes back at least to the Colonial Development Act of 1929. This assistance, however, was provided within the framework of day-to-day colonial administration, and was not subject to the modern criteria of long-term development through planned investment. In more recent years, the colonial powers and other industrialised countries have initiated aid *programmes*, which are supposedly guided by economic priorities and which are in theory separate from fulfilment of the ordinary budgetary needs of colonial dependencies. It is in this sense that aid is a new activity, even for the former colonial powers, and it was the breaking-up of empires that made the need for it apparent.

Aid to Europe began after the second world war with US Marshall Aid, which was primarily a rescue operation akin to disaster relief—aid for reconstruction rather than aid for new development. As Europe recovered, American aid was transferred to the developing countries, and the United States soon began to put pressure on a now prosperous Europe to take over some of the burden.

In 1960 the Organisation for European Economic Cooperation (OEEC), at American instigation, set up the Development Assistance Group, consisting of the main non-Communist aid-giving countries. In the following year, when the OEEC was transformed into the Organisation for Economic Cooperation and Development (OECD), this group was formalised as the Development Assistance Committee (DAC). The creation of a formal organisation brought an important new member to the company of aid-givers—Western Germany, prosperous and justifiably proud of its own economic achievements, shorn of all traditional foreign ties, searching for a new international role commensurate with its economic power. Just as the

former colonial powers had been preoccupied with maintaining the economies of their ex-colonies, so the United States had been driven largely by its
commitment in the Cold War. Germany was not conditioned by precon-
ceptions of this sort. It was at this point that aid began to be seen as a long-
term economic activity rather than as a subsidiary element of immediate
foreign policy. The foundations were laid for the massive and concerted
effort of the mid-1960s.

CATEGORIES OF AID

One of the consequences of the evolution of coherent aid policies is increasing
sophistication in the use of various instruments to assist economic development. Aid is as subject to fads as most activities, and each of the forms of aid
listed below has at one time or another been regarded as the key to the
problem. It is coming to be recognised, however, that the problems of
development are numerous and complex, requiring a whole range of instruments for their solution.

Financial assistance

Project aid. Aid provided for the whole or part of the costs of a specific project,
usually for the foreign exchange costs, is the most familiar form of aid. The
much maligned dams, steel mills and other 'prestige' projects come under
this heading. Project aid is usually in the form of loans. It can be very useful,
provided that projects are selected in accordance with economic priorities.
Donors favour project aid because it facilitates control, thus helping to minimise such vices as corruption, but in bilateral aid it also enables donor
governments to favour their own contractors.

Programme aid and balance of payments support. Most developing countries have
a serious shortage of foreign exchange. This may be merely a symptom of a
shortage of resources of all kinds, but it may also arise specifically from the
very high import content of development expenditure, or from the debt
burden of past loans. In this case, a donor may provide 'programme' loans
for current imports. Debt postponement is sometimes counted as programme
aid, but there is a growing feeling on both sides that repeated postponement
of existing obligations is an unsatisfactory way of financing a development
programme. This is the basis of the argument for 'softer loans' (i.e. loans with
long maturities and low rates of interest).

Budgetary support. If a country is so short of resources that it cannot cover
its current budget, a donor may provide aid for general expenditure, usually
in grant form. In doing so, the donor will probably claim the right to review
the recipient's budget. This is therefore a form of aid that most independent
countries are reluctant to accept. Apart from the political awkwardness of
budgetary support, it carries the risk that it may cushion the recipient against
the need to set his own house in order.

Technical assistance

Experts and advisers. A number of developing countries, particularly in Africa,
are desperately short of the trained personnel without whom even the limited
resources available cannot be properly used. The lack has to be made good
by expatriates whose salaries may be wholly or partly paid by the country
that supplies them. Britain and France, with their traditional relationships,
are particularly large suppliers of experts and advisers.

WESTERN EUROPEAN ECONOMIC AID TO DEVELOPING COUNTRIES

Technical equipment. In a number of cases, such as the establishment of technical training institutes, the supply of experts has to be accompanied by the appropriate equipment, usually provided as a gift.

Training and education. In addition to providing technical assistance in the developing countries themselves, all the European aid-giving countries provide funds for the support of students and technical trainees from developing countries at institutions in the country providing the assistance. Again, Britain and France do most in this field, but Germany, with its highly developed system of in-service training, has provided facilities for a large number of technicians from developing countries.

Volunteers. A number of European countries, notably Britain, Germany and Norway, now have volunteer movements, in which young people work for a year or two in developing countries for minimal wages. The value of volunteers to the recipient country is the subject of controversy, but in theory they may provide middle and lower level skills where these are not locally available.

Trade and investment

Private investment. The flow of private investment resources to developing countries is a necessary complement to official aid, with special merits of its own, such as the probable accompaniment of managerial skill. But investors are often unwilling to put resources into these uncertain markets. Some aid-giving countries, therefore, have taken a number of measures to promote the flow of investment, including tax concessions and investment guarantees. The most advanced European country in this respect is Germany.

Export credits. A number of developing countries have had to finance a large part of their imports from Europe by ordinary commercial credits, which are relevant to a survey of aid since they are one of the principal causes of the heavy debt burden from which some developing countries suffer.

Imports from developing countries. The developing countries' need to export received concentrated attention at the UN Conference on Trade and Development (UNCTAD) in 1964. There are two separate problems. First, the commodities which form the staple exports of many developing countries are subject to violent price fluctuations, which makes planning difficult. The developing countries also claim that the present world trade pattern is so designed that commodity prices are bound to decline in relation to the prices of the sophisticated manufactured goods produced by the industrialised countries. Secondly, the low-cost manufactured goods which are being produced by newly developed industries compete to some extent with goods already produced in the industrialised countries. Most European countries agree in principle that their markets should be opened to low-cost manufactures from developing countries, but the domestic political implications make this difficult to put into practice.

There are two main European viewpoints on commodities, the one presented principally by Britain, the other by France. The British argue that the existing rules of the General Agreement on Tariffs and Trade (GATT) provide a starting point, with special exceptions, in favour of developing countries, in the form of steadily expanding preferences. The French argue in favour of a complex of commodity agreements, with artificially maintained prices. The initiative at present rests with a number of international institutions, such as the World Bank and the UN Trade and Development Board, which are trying to devise long-term solutions.

CATEGORIES OF DONORS

The European aid-giving countries fall into five main categories. The dividing lines are not clear-cut, and individual countries may come into more than one category.

Major ex-colonial powers

Britain and France both maintain large aid programmes, which are concentrated on their present and former dependencies. More than 85 per cent of British bilateral aid goes to the Commonwealth. About 95 per cent of French bilateral aid goes to countries of the Franc Zone. The responsibilities in these two historical commitments are so great (the Commonwealth contains more than half of the population of non-Communist developing countries) that it is very difficult for either country to spread its aid to other countries.

Lesser ex-colonial powers

Belgium, the Netherlands, Italy and Portugal all pay special attention to past or present dependencies (Portugal is a special case). In 1963, 98 per cent of Belgian bilateral official aid went to the Congo, Rwanda and Burundi. Surinam and the Netherlands Antilles figure prominently in aid from the Netherlands. About half of Italian bilateral grants go to Somalia.

These countries differ from the major ex-colonial powers in that their special responsibilities are more limited, so that the need to diversify is more obvious. The Netherlands, in particular, has made relatively large contributions to multilateral organisations and given bilateral aid to a number of countries within the framework of multinational consortia and consultative groups. The Italians and Belgians, by contrast, have not devised new forms of aid, but have fallen back on guaranteed private export credits as a makeshift channel for providing resources to countries outside their own special concerns.

Major new donors

Germany is the only European country that maintains a large aid programme which did not develop from historical commitments. This is hardly surprising, since it is the only major European economic power, with the possible exception of Italy, that did not already have widespread commitments overseas at the time when economic aid was becoming significant.

Commercial creditors

In their relations with developing countries, virtually all European countries engage to some extent in straightforward export promotion. This affects their aid programme in varying degrees, sometimes distorting it, or even operating in flat contradiction to the stated criteria of aid policy. The French and the Italians, in providing aid to countries outside their own areas of interest, frequently link government loans to the utilisation of short-term private export credits. Virtually all financial resources provided for development from Switzerland are in the form of private investment or private export credits. The Germans give their own exporters something of a free hand by deliberately keeping *official* aid representation in their embassies extremely weak. The main form of British financial aid to independent countries is entirely tied to British goods and services.

Limited aid programmes

There is a special problem for those small European aid-giving countries for which the pattern of aid is not predetermined by a commitment to former colonies. Essentially, this covers Austria, Denmark, Norway and Sweden. The problem is felt with particular acuteness by Norway and Sweden. The problem is how to make an impact with limited resources, when there is no obvious guideline leading to the selection of one or two recipient countries on which to concentrate. The first solution adopted by the three Scandinavian countries was to place most of their aid funds through the United Nations and related institutions, but recently there has been some indication of a desire for aid programmes with a clearer national identity.

THE VOLUME OF AID

Aid increased rapidly in 1961. Since then, it has remained more or less on a level, though there have been variations in individual countries. European aid has continued at the rate of approximately 2,000 million dollars a year, which is about 30 per cent of total aid provided by all the OECD countries, and about 26 per cent of world aid.

Comparative aid statistics have to be treated with caution. Figures published by individual countries, which reflect most accurately the structure of the donor's aid programme, are not necessarily comparable, because of differences in classification and budgetary presentation. The standard comparative figures, therefore, are those published by the DAC. These figures are the best available standard of comparison, though even they have to be used with caution. Their basic disadvantage is that they necessarily reduce all aid to a simple monetary value, taking little account of differences in terms, in cost of goods or personnel supplied, or in the extent to which aid given meets the real needs of the recipient.

TABLE I

OFFICIAL AID (DISBURSEMENTS) FROM EUROPEAN MEMBERS OF THE DAC, 1964

(*$ US million equivalent*)[1]

Country	Bilateral Grants and grant-like contributions	Loans[2] (net)	Total bilateral	Multi-lateral[3] (net)	Total
France	667.7	154.1	821.8	19.6	841.4
UK	235.4	210.8	446.2	44.3	490.5
Germany	149.5[4]	301.1	450.6	8.9	459.5
Belgium	76.8	1.3	78.1	1.9	80.0
Portugal	7.5	55.3	62.8	0.1	62.8
Italy	20.7[4]	40.5	61.2	− 5.2	56.0
Netherlands	13.1	19.9	33.0	16.1	49.1
Norway	2.5	0.3	2.8	14.2	17.0
Austria	1.7	5.6	7.3	5.8	13.1
Denmark	3.0	− 0.3	2.7	8.3	11.0

Source: Report by the Chairman of the DAC, 1965

[1] This table excludes Switzerland, which is not a member of the DAC, and Sweden, which became a member in 1965. According to equivalent OECD figures for 1963, total official aid from Switzerland was $6.2 million, and from Sweden $22.9 million.

[2] Loans with maturities of more than five years, net of repayment of principal.

[3] Includes purchases of bonds, capital subscriptions and voluntary grants. Multilateral contributions tend to fluctuate widely from year to year. Contributions from EEC countries, for instance, would be much higher in years in which subscriptions were due to the European Development Fund (EDF).

[4] Includes reparations.

P

TABLE 2

GEOGRAPHICAL DISTRIBUTION OF EUROPEAN BILATERAL AID, 1960-3

(as percentages of the total)

	1960	1961	1962	1963
Europe[1]	6	7	4	6
Africa	65	62	59	58
Asia	17	18	16	18
Of which South Asia[2]	(11)	(12)	(9)	(10)
Latin America	8	8	13	13
Other and unallocated	4	5	8	5
	100	100	100	100
Total aid[3] ($ million)	1,568	1,834	1,829	1,871

Source: *The Flow of Financial Resources to Less-Developed Countries, 1956–1963, OECD*

[1] Cyprus, Greece, Spain, Turkey, Yugoslavia.
[2] Mainly India and Pakistan.
[3] OECD statistics include figures for Sweden and Switzerland; also all loans with maturities of more than one year. OECD totals are therefore larger than DAC totals.

TABLE 3

COMPARATIVE PERFORMANCE OF EUROPEAN DONORS, 1964

	Grants as percentage of total aid	Multilateral as percentage of total aid	Official aid as percentage of national income	Official aid per head of population ($ US)
Austria	26	45	0.20	1.8
Belgium	98	2	0.67	8.7
Denmark	98	75	0.15	2.4
France	81	2	1.26	18.1
Germany	38	2	0.58	8.2
Italy	46	—	0.14	1.1
Netherlands	59	33	0.37	4.3
Norway	54	84	0.35	4.7
Portugal	12	—	2.24	7.1
United Kingdom	57	9	0.67	9.3

Sources: Figures derived from *UN Statistical Yearbook* and the Report by the Chairman of the DAC, 1964

FRENCH AID

The French aid programme provides a particularly clear demonstration of the way in which former colonial commitments may inhibit a donor's freedom of action, tying up resources in a manner that is at variance with current policy and interest. Under President de Gaulle, new foreign policy initiatives have been taken in relation to Latin America, South-East Asia and the Middle East. Yet in 1964, 42 per cent of French aid to independent countries went to former French dependencies in Africa south of the Sahara, 39 per cent went to Algeria and 10 per cent went to the other former French dependencies in North Africa.

The commitment to former French dependencies in Africa is complex and massive. One reason why it is so costly (see Table 3 above) is the inheritance of the doctrine of assimilation, which means that even today in these countries there is a fierce resistance to anything that might imply—in salaries, for instance, or in educational qualifications—a fall from French metropolitan standards.

The relationship between France and its former dependencies is extremely close. The aid programme is administered by missions which are separate from the French embassies, and implemented by a large corps of French experts, advisers and teachers. In 1964 there were 44,000 Frenchmen in the field under the technical assistance programme, of whom all but 2,000 were in Africa. This was more than half of technical assistance personnel supplied by all members of the DAC combined, including the United States. African recipients of French aid also benefit from large expenditure under the defence budget, and from the complex monetary and commercial mechanisms of the Franc Zone, in which the balance of advantage has shifted in recent years from France to the less developed members.

To ask what are France's motives for maintaining an aid programme of such size and complexity is not really meaningful. There is an inevitability about the French commitment which defies question. The best simple explanation was that given in the Jeanneney Report, the officially instigated critique of French aid published in 1963, which said: 'The first reason, sufficient in itself, for a French policy of cooperation with the Third World is the feeling which France has of her duties towards humanity'. In other words, French aid is part and parcel of France's traditional 'civilising mission'.

The administration of French aid was only partially reorganised when the majority of French African dependencies became independent in 1960. A further reorganisation took place in January, 1966, but the division of responsibilities remained largely historical and geographical. It was assumed that a more thoroughgoing reorganisation would take place later. A separate Ministry of State is responsible for most aid to the French overseas departments and territories.

BRITISH AID

The commitment to former dependencies has shaped the British aid programme as strongly as it has shaped the French, but in a different way. In view of the size of the Commonwealth, it is hardly surprising that the bulk of British aid should have continued to go to Commonwealth countries. What is odd is the distribution of British aid within the Commonwealth.

Until recently, the main channels of British aid were ones that had been devised for colonies, and which fitted the colonial system. Britain did not introduce a policy of aiding independent countries until 1958, when India's foreign exchange crisis, coupled with the approaching independence of a number of African countries, made a revision of policy urgently necessary. Even then, the British government made little effort to devise a coherent policy of planned and comprehensive support for its former dependencies, as the French did two years later. Britain remains exceptionally shy of anything that might be regarded as interference in the recipient countries' domestic affairs.

What the British government did was to refurbish and expand an existing category of financial assistance—loans under Section 3 of the Export Guarantees Act of 1949. Section 3 loans were originally intended as an instrument of export promotion, and they are entirely tied to British goods and services. When they were first widely used, they carried interest determined by the rates at which the Treasury could borrow, usually around 6 per cent.

The terms were progressively softened, however, until in 1965 it was announced that loans to a number of countries would be made free of interest.

In 1965 the administration of these loans was transferred to the Ministry of Overseas Development. They can be used for a very wide range of goods, but the flexibility which makes this possible presupposes a high degree of skill in the allocation of resources on the part of the recipient country. Countries without this skill, particularly in Africa, have serious difficulty in making the best use of British aid.

The main channels of aid for the colonies, or for countries so recently independent that they can still draw on their 'independence settlement', are grants and loans on the Colonial Office vote, grants and loans from Colonial Development and Welfare funds, and Exchequer loans. Loans under the first two headings are usually on soft terms. Another source of aid to colonies and Commonwealth countries that became independent after 1948 (i.e. not India, Pakistan or Ceylon) are the investments of the Commonwealth Development Corporation (CDC).

British aid was administered by a number of government departments until 1964, when the Department of Technical Cooperation, created in 1961 to administer technical assistance, was enlarged and transformed into the Ministry of Overseas Development. The Ministry's view of the British aid programme was set out in the White Paper published in August 1965, which gave Britain its first clear statement of aid policy, starting with the proclamation that the objective of aid was 'to help developing countries in their efforts to raise living standards', and that the basis of aid was a moral one.

The British aid programme is gradually being rationalised, but its distribution is still somewhat arbitrary. India and Pakistan receive far less aid, in relation to the size of their populations, than a large number of other countries. In 1964/65, the six principal recipients of British financial aid, in absolute terms, were India (£30 million), Kenya (£15 million), Pakistan (£9 million), Malawi (£9 million), Malta (£7 million) and Aden (£7 million).

GERMAN AID

Until the end of the 1950s, the Federal Republic of Germany provided comparatively little aid to developing countries. In technical assistance, German efforts were concentrated on courses in Germany for trainees from developing countries; in bilateral financial assistance, the Federal government did little beyond providing guarantees for private export credits. For some years it was thought that German official financial aid ought to be given mainly through multilateral institutions; between 1957 and 1961 the Federal Republic made large loans to the World Bank, and from 1958 onwards it was one of the two main subscribers to the European Development Fund.

The first important step in the direction of bilateral financial assistance to independent developing countries was taken by Germany, as well as Britain, in response to the Indian foreign exchange crisis of 1958. The Federal government took over responsibility for financing the giant iron and steel works which German contractors were building at Rourkela. The commitment to Rourkela remains the largest single element in the German aid programme.

In 1960 the Federal government marked the formal introduction of a policy of giving aid to developing countries by setting up an inter-ministerial committee for development assistance. In the following year, the newly created Ministry for Economic Cooperation was given the task of bringing the activities of various government departments together in a concerted aid programme. The volume of German aid increased very rapidly. Official disbursements increased by 80 per cent in 1961 alone. Commitments piled up at an even greater rate. In 1960 and 1961, Germany entered into new commitments amounting to $1,400 million, involving 65 developing countries. The rate of new commitments subsequently declined as the Federal government struggled to work off this tremendous backlog.

There were a number of reasons for the rapid growth of German aid in 1960 and 1961. Essentially, the Germans were seeking a new international role, to prove that Germany was now capable of taking its place again as an important member of the comity of nations; but American pressure, and the struggle to prevent recognition of East Germany, also played their part. Export promotion, although it is an important element in the *practice* of German aid, appears to have played very little part in the formulation of aid policy.

It took some time to get the aid programme functioning smoothly, and for the first few years German aid was characterised by long procedural delays, as was perhaps inevitable in a programme so rapidly expanded. Paradoxically, one serious cause of delay has been the determination of the Germans to ensure by every means possible that their aid programme makes a genuine contribution to development. German aid is governed by a profusion of rigid criteria and by complex control procedures, which add to the difficulty of implementing commitments. The Germans take a somewhat censorious view, for instance, of such flexible forms of aid as balance of payments support. Nearly all German financial assistance is tied to specific projects.

The difficulties that have been experienced in project finance have led the Federal government to pay increasing attention to technical assistance. In 1963, expenditure on all forms of technical assistance rose by 90 per cent, although even then it still accounted for less than 20 per cent of total aid.

The administration of German aid has suffered particularly severely from inter-ministerial rivalries. Repeated attempts to define the functions of the Ministry of Economic Cooperation have failed to give it clear operational control of the aid programme. Capital aid is still administered in part by the Ministry for Economics, with the Reconstruction Loan Corporation (Kreditanstalt für Wiederaufbau—situated in Frankfurt) as the operating agency. The Foreign Ministry is still responsible for aid representation in the developing countries themselves.

About half of German aid goes to Asian countries, though Africa is receiving a growing share. Latin America, though a traditional area of interest for German investors, receives relatively little official aid. The three most important recipients of German aid are those countries which are the targets of big multinational efforts in the form of consortia—India, Pakistan and Turkey.

MULTILATERAL AID

The institutions of EEC

EEC provides aid through two institutions—the European Development Fund and the European Investment Bank (EIB). The Fund operates exclusively in countries associated with the Community. The EIB is intended primarily to assist development in the more backward areas of member countries, such as southern Italy, but it is increasingly active in associated countries. Both institutions came into being under the Treaty of Rome.

Aid from the Community had its origin in France's need to reconcile the obligations of membership with its commitment to its dependencies. Under Part IV of the Treaty of Rome, the dependencies of all members were associated with the Community. They were given free access to the Community's markets, while retaining the right to protect their own industries, and they were to benefit from the Fonds Européen de Développement d'Outre-Mer (FEDOM). The Fund was empowered to provide grants to a total of $581 million for infrastructure and social projects over a five-year period. Germany and France each subscribed approximately one-third of the Fund's capital, with the remainder coming from the other four members.

During the life of the Fund, independence came to the French, Belgian and Italian territories in Africa south of the Sahara. In July 1963, after prolonged negotiation, a new convention of association (the Yaoundé Convention) was signed between the Community and eighteen independent African and Malagasy states. A new and enlarged European Development Fund (EDF) was established, with power to provide $620 million in grants and $46 million in soft loans over a further five-year period. The EIB was to provide $64 million in hard loans.

The EIB, in addition to providing loans under the second Convention of Association, is evolving a more significant role for itself in other associated countries. It has committed some funds to Greece, and it is to be one of the main sources of finance ($30 million committed in autumn 1965) for the Keban Dam in Turkey. Under the terms of association between Turkey and the Community, Turkey is to receive $35 million a year for five years in project loans from the EIB.[1]

The World Bank Group and UN Technical Assistance Programmes

Western Europe is the main source of finance, after the United States, for the World Bank and its affiliates, the International Development Association (IDA) and the International Finance Corporation (IFC). The Western European donors as a whole provide approximately one-third of the subscribed capital of the World Bank and the IFC, and 41 per cent of hard currency subscriptions to the IDA. A number of European countries, particularly Germany, have purchased World Bank bonds, and bond issues have also been taken up by European capital markets.

The voluntarily financed technical assistance programmes of the United Nations are also largely dependent on European contributions. In 1963 the Western European countries contributed a total of $51 million to the UN Expanded Programme of Technical Assistance and the Special Fund[2], compared with $29 million from the United States and $3 million from the Communist bloc.

COORDINATIVE MECHANISMS

Most of the European aid-giving countries are anxious to improve the coordination of bilateral aid programmes. For many of them, this takes precedence over an increase in multilateral aid. With the exception of France, all the major European donors are most heavily committed to countries in which other donors, particularly the United States, are also deeply involved.

[1] For a further account of European aid to Turkey and Greece see the chapter entitled 'Problems of Underdevelopment: Southern Italy, Spain, Greece and Turkey, pp. 414 and 417.

[2] These were amalgamated at the end of 1965 to become the UN Development Programme.

Attempts to coordinate bilateral aid programmes take two main forms—coordination of aid policy, including an attempt to reach some degree of standardisation on the terms, conditions and criteria of aid, and coordination at the operational level, usually in relation to the development of individual countries. The Development Assistance Committee of the OECD is the forum within which the notion of a common aid effort has evolved. It is likely to acquire added significance now that a number of European countries have ministers exclusively responsible for aid, for whom the DAC is the obvious meeting place.

During the first few years of its life, it was assumed that the DAC would gradually acquire an operational role in the coordination of aid, and a number of attempts were made to establish OECD working groups for individual recipient countries. By 1965, however, it had come to be generally recognised that the DAC was not well equipped for this task, largely because the OECD is not constituted in such a way that the Secretariat can take strong initiatives of its own, but it remains as a useful framework for discussions between governments.

The institution that has done most to develop the operational coordination of aid is the World Bank. The major European donors have been prominent among the countries urging the World Bank to take on this role. The Bank manages the two largest of the four existing consortia (for India and Pakistan), and a number of consultative groups for smaller countries. (The consortia for Greece and Turkey, of which only that for Turkey is active, are managed by the OECD, both countries being members of the Organisation.) The World Bank has also experimented with coordinating the bilateral financing of individual projects, such as the Kainji Dam in Nigeria and the Keban Dam in Turkey.

A number of European donors also participate in regional development schemes, which have shown themselves effective chiefly in the coordination of technical assistance. Among these are the Colombo Plan, covering South and South-East Asia, and the Committee for Technical Cooperation in Africa.

CONCLUSION

The 1960s have been designated by the United Nations as the 'development decade'. The results of the first five years of that decade, in terms of visible achievement, were disappointing. The problems of development, and of aid for development, turned out to be greater than either donors or recipients had foreseen, and there was widespread disillusionment, particularly on the side of the donors. However, some lessons have been learnt. In 1961, when the DAC was established, the European countries were providing aid for a wide variety of reasons, in varied forms, and with varied notions of the development process. One of the important achievements of the first half of the 'development decade' is that these disparate elements have to some extent been pulled together into a massive, common effort to promote the economic development of the poorer countries of the world.

There are four problems for the European donors. First, there is the question of the level of aid. This is still determined by what individual countries feel they can afford at any given moment, and little thought is given to any more rational or more distant target than that. Secondly, the administration of aid is often cumbersome and disjointed. A number of donors have made strenuous efforts to remedy this, usually by consolidating the administration of aid within a single department. The third problem is the coordination of aid, and the fourth is how to ensure that it is effectively used, in such a way that it makes the greatest possible contribution to the recipient's development. These last two problems are interrelated. They affect the European donors as a whole, with the possible exception of France. (The special relationship between France and the recipients of French aid gives rise to a somewhat different set of problems.)

It is in the field of the coordination of aid that there is most room for new policy initiatives. The solutions depend on a number of measures in areas that are now being more and more widely considered—in closer and more penetrating relations between donors and recipients, in regional organisations, in stronger official aid representation in the field, in improved evaluation of plans and selection of projects, and in a number of other areas in which an improvement in the technique of aid-giving is being sought.

The common aid effort has been built up piecemeal, and it is likely to continue that way. In India, Pakistan and Turkey, a serious effort is being made to provide aid from all sources in a concerted pattern. In Africa, however, the predominance of aid from the former colonial powers has hardly begun to give way to a coordinated and balanced programme. In Latin America, the Western European countries are not yet heavily involved, but they are likely to become so. In each of these areas, the problem of a variety of donors arises in a different form. The variety is provided mainly by Europe, and it is on the formulation of a proper relationship between Europe and the developing countries that the rationalisation of aid depends.

BIBLIOGRAPHY

Benham, Frederic. *Economic Aid to Underdeveloped Countries*, Oxford Univ. Press, London and New York, 1961.
Hayter, Teresa. *French Aid*, Overseas Development Institute, London, 1965. 'French Aid to Africa: Its Scope and Achievements', *International Affairs*, XL, 2, London, April 1965.
Little, I. M. D. *Aid to Africa*, Overseas Development Institute/Pergamon Press, London, 1964.
Little, I. M. D. and Clifford, J. M. *International Aid*, George Allen and Unwin, London, 1965.
Moyes, A. *Volunteers in Development*, Overseas Development Institute, London, 1966.
Ohlin, G. *Foreign Aid Policies Reconsidered*, OECD Development Centre, Paris, 1966.
Soper, T. 'The EEC and Aid to Africa', *International Affairs*, XL, 3, London, July 1965.
White, John. *German Aid*, Overseas Development Institute, London, 1965. 'West German Aid to Developing Countries', *International Affairs*, XL, 1, London, January 1965.
British Aid—A Factual Survey (5 parts), Overseas Development Institute, London, 1963-4.
New Directions for World Trade, Oxford Univ. Press, London and New York for Royal Institute of International Affairs, London, 1964.
The Jeanneney Report (abridged trans.), Overseas Development Institute, London, 1964.

OFFICIAL PUBLICATIONS
International
Development Assistance Efforts and Policies (Annual Reports of the Chairman of the Development Assistance Committee of OECD, Paris).
The Flow of Financial Resources to Less-developed Countries, 1956-1963, OECD, Paris, 1964.

France
La politique de coopération avec les pays en voie de développement (The Jeanneney Report), Ministry of State for Administrative Reform, Paris, 1963.

Germany
Annual Reports of the Kreditanstalt für Wiederaufbau, Frankfurt-am-Main.
Deutsche Entwicklungspolitik im Jahre 1964, Federal Ministry for Economic Cooperation, Bonn, 1965.

Britain
Aid to Developing Countries, H.M.S.O. (Cmnd. 2147), London, 1963.
Overseas Development: the Work of the New Ministry, H.M.S.O. (Cmnd. 2736), London, 1965.

SOCIAL AFFAIRS

IMMIGRANT LABOUR IN
WESTERN EUROPE

SARAH CHILD

SINCE the mid-fifties international labour mobility has become an increasingly important aspect of the European scene. The traditional pattern of small and largely seasonal movements across the frontiers of neighbouring countries has undergone a very rapid expansion and transformation. Where previously the migrant labour force consisted mainly of Italians moving to Switzerland and France and was measured annually in tens of thousands, migrants now move in hundreds of thousands from all parts of Southern and even Eastern Europe to all parts of the North, where they are joined by migrants from the ex-French and British colonies. The labour force of Western Europe now includes over four million expatriate workers, of whom some three million are themselves of European origin.

This major change in European society has occurred in direct response to basic economic pressures. Faced with the new problems of virtually full employment, and with severe labour shortages in certain sectors, the governments of recipient countries have been obliged to relax existing restrictions on immigration and in some cases to adopt positive measures to encourage it. It is only very recently that the social aspects of this solution to an economic problem have led two governments to return to a more restrictive policy. It is worth remembering, however, that although immigration is essentially an economic phenomenon, the acceleration of immigration within Europe has taken place against a political background of increasing international cooperation, and that immigration from outside Europe has been made possible by the political concepts of the relationship between Britain and France and their ex-colonies.

Within Europe, various international agreements have shown the changing atmosphere. The members of OEEC signed the first international agreement on the issue of labour permits in 1953; member governments agreed that a permit would not be refused to any foreign worker who had been offered employment, provided no suitable national could be found after a delay of a month, and that pay and other conditions of work were not inferior to those usually prevailing (unless the government concerned could show that industrial peace was threatened or that there were sound economic reasons for preventing an increase in the labour force in question). A Scandinavian common labour market was established by the agreements between Sweden and Denmark in 1946 and those countries and Norway and Finland in 1954. The Benelux union was formed in 1949; it allowed the free movement of labour in practice from its beginning, although permits were not officially abolished until 1958. The European Coal and Steel Community Treaty established a restricted form of common labour market in each of its sectors (for qualified workers when offered specific employment), and finally Article 48 of the Treaty of Rome provided for the free movement of labour within the European Economic Community at the latest by the end of the period of transition in 1970.

Immigration from outside Europe has been largely from the ex-French colonial territories to France and from the other members of the British Commonwealth to Britain. Commonwealth and colonial immigrants were entirely free from control in entering Britain until 1962, while immigrants from the French colonies and ex-colonies still have greater freedom to enter France than do European workers. Freedom of movement was always assumed to exist from British colonies to Britain, and was continued by the various acts of independence by which in the post-war years the different colonies became independent members of the Commonwealth. France gave the nationals of the North African territories complete freedom to enter France in 1945; this situation was maintained on independence for citizens of both the North and West African ex-colonies, as it is for France's remaining colonies in the Caribbean. Recent agreements between the French government and the Algerian and various West African governments to exercise controls over entry have not been enforced.

Besides these international agreements governing the movement of labour, many bilateral agreements have been signed in recent years controlling the issue of work permits, the entry of dependants, and various aspects of working conditions. The West German government, which has been particularly active in encouraging immigration, has signed agreements for group migration schemes with Italy, Spain, Greece and Turkey; the Federal Bureau for Employment and National Insurance operates local recruiting offices in all these countries. The French government has operated a similar system since 1945, with local branches of the Office National d'Immigration established in Italy and Spain.

The Distribution of Foreign Workers

The largest totals of foreign workers have been attracted to France, West Germany and Britain, although proportionately immigrant labour is far more important in Switzerland.

FOREIGN WORKERS EMPLOYED JULY-DECEMBER 1964

	As percentage of labour force	Total (thousands)	Of which non-Europeans (thousands)
France	(7·5)	(1,480)	(500)
W. Germany	3·8	1,014	42
Britain	(4)	(1,000)	(700)
Switzerland	24	721	—
Sweden	3·6	140	—
Netherlands	1	45	n.a.

Source: national statistics.
( ): estimate.

France

The number of immigrant workers in France is estimated at about one-and-a-half million. Exact information is not available; records of departures from France are not kept, and the special status of citizens of ex-colonies and the wide evasion of existing controls further complicate the picture. There are however believed to be some 450,000 Algerians in France, of whom four in five are workers, besides some further thousands of Tunisians and Moroccans. The coloured population from West Africa and the Caribbean is estimated at 160,000. Among the European immigrants the Italians probably still constitute the largest group, although the annual inflow of Italians has fallen off very sharply since 1961; immigration from Spain and Portugal is now on a much larger scale. Other substantial groups are the Poles, who arrived in large numbers between the two world wars, and the Belgian frontier workers. At least half a million dependants, with the encouragement of the French government, have accompanied the European immigrant workers, so that the total immigrant population amounts to 4 to 5 per cent of the total population of France, while the total of foreign workers constitutes well over 7 per cent of the French labour force.

Against a background of high employment, and a working population which is showing almost no natural increase but a considerable degree of geographical and occupational immobility, the French government is continuing to pursue an active policy in recruiting foreign labour. The number of permanent immigrant workers recruited annually has risen steadily from 44,000 in 1959 to 145,000 in 1964, when a further 122,000 seasonal workers also entered France.

West Germany

Although the West German economy had already absorbed some 10 million refugees from East Germany, an apparently inexhaustible demand for labour developed after the early fifties, and as the supply from the east diminished employers turned first to Southern Europe and then still further afield. The number of foreign workers rose from 100,000 in 1957 to over a million in 1964, or to nearly 4 per cent of the labour force. With 400,000 dependants immigrants then amounted to some 2·4 per cent of the population. Their numbers are increasing at a rate of about 200,000 a year, with the annual gross immigration approaching half a million.

The Italians constitute by far the largest group of foreign workers in West Germany, numbering nearly 290,000 in 1964; they were followed by the Spanish and the Greeks (144,000 each). As in France, however, the pattern is changing: net immigration in 1963 showed the addition of only 3,000 Italians as compared to over 40,000 Greeks, 28,000 Spaniards and 25,000 Turks. Immigration from other traditional sources, Austria and the Netherlands, has also been falling, while net immigration from Yugoslavia increased to over 10,000 in 1963. Recruitment has also been extended to North Africa.

Britain

As little accurate information on the numbers of foreign workers employed in Britain is available as is the case with France. Immigrants from the Commonwealth and colonies entered the country without restrictions until 1962, immigration having been substantial from 1952 onwards. Estimates based on the 1961 census of population, on research and on records kept after the Commonwealth Immigration Act required Commonwealth citizens to obtain Ministry of Labour vouchers before being admitted to the country to work, suggest that there are 3–400,000 immigrants from Cyprus, Malta and the 'white' Commonwealth countries, and some 700,000 immigrants from the West Indies, India and Pakistan. It is estimated that some

150,000 children have been born to these immigrants in Britain, making a total coloured population of about 850,000. The coloured labour force is believed to be in the region of 500,000 and the total Commonwealth immigrant labour force seems likely to amount to at least 700,000.

The British labour force also includes a substantial number of other foreign workers, estimated very approximately at 2–300,000. The largest national groups are Polish and Italian, although in recent annual inflows Spanish workers have been the most important. The total immigrant labour force in Britain is therefore likely to be in the region of one million, or some 4 per cent of the labour force as a whole, if immigration from the Irish Republic (which is totally unrestricted) is ignored. The British demand for labour continues to be very high, and the rate of natural growth in the working population is slowing down. The British government however has never pursued an active policy of recruitment of foreign labour, and in 1965 it announced that the number of labour vouchers issued to Commonwealth immigrants would be limited to 8,500 annually. No official limit has been placed on work permits for aliens, which amounted to over 47,000 in 1964. A high proportion of these are however seasonal workers; in the same year the number accepted for permanent settlement was just over 19,000.

Switzerland

The remaining Western European country with very substantial numbers of immigrants is Switzerland, where a foreign labour force of 720,000 in August 1964 amounted to nearly one quarter of the total labour force. This included, however, 206,000 seasonal workers, and the restrictive policy which has been practised over the entry of dependants can be seen in that the total foreign population was estimated at 750,000 at the same time. Nevertheless the very rapid growth of the foreign labour force, which increased by 26 per cent in 1961 and 32 per cent in 1962, led to attempts by the Federal government to limit the numbers of immigrant workers to 700,000. The failure of this policy was followed in 1965 by a decree requiring the employment of foreigners to be cut by 5 per cent. This largely affected the Italians, who constitute over 60 per cent of foreign workers in Switzerland, although once again immigration from Spain has been increasing rapidly in recent years.

THE EMPLOYMENT OF FOREIGN WORKERS

The above four countries are the main countries of destination for foreign labour, but immigrant labour is no longer uncommon in any of the prosperous countries of Northern Europe. The majority of immigrants have left countries of high unemployment and low wages in search of work and higher earnings, and the majority are unskilled. In consequence foreign workers are mainly found in the occupations least attractive to the domestic labour force, normally those unskilled occupations which are least well paid or which involve undesirable working conditions of one kind or another. There are certain exceptions to this trend in a few skilled occupations with an acute labour shortage and a wage differential large enough to attract skilled labour from abroad. But in West Germany, for example, little more than 10 per cent of the foreign workers recruited annually by the Federal Bureau are skilled.

The sector which has possibly benefited to the greatest extent from immigrant labour is that of construction. Nearly a third of the annual intake of foreign workers in France find employment in the building industry; over 20 per cent of the immigrants in West Germany are employed in building, where they made up over 7 per cent of the labour force in 1962. In Switzerland nearly a third of foreign workers are employed in construction during the summer, although the majority of these are seasonal workers and the proportion falls to 10 per cent in the winter months. In summer the West German, French and Swiss construction sectors between them employ well over half a million expatriates. The second major sector of immigrant employment is the ill-defined 'metals and machinery' or 'metal-working' sector which covers a variety of industries; a third of the foreign workers in West Germany, nearly a third of new permanent immigrants in France and some 20 per cent of foreign workers in Switzerland are employed under this heading. The textile industries in Switzerland, West Germany, the Netherlands and Britain are also among the main employment categories.

Seasonal or short-service immigrants in all countries are employed in hotels and catering (particularly the Italians and Spanish in Switzerland and Britain) and as farm labourers in Switzerland and France. A large proportion of the European immigrants who enter Britain for a year or less work in catering or domestic service; the number of Spaniards employed in domestic service in France has risen sharply in recent years and now accounts for some 10 per cent of all new permanent immigrants.

A survey of the occupations of coloured Commonwealth immigrants in Britain in 1961 showed that the largest single group was employed in hospitals as nurses and domestic workers (where the proportion was 7 in 8). Another very large group is in the transport sector as bus conductors and drivers and railway workers; it is estimated that 40 per cent of London's transport staff are coloured immigrants. There is a concentration of Pakistanis in the Yorkshire wool industry, where domestic labour has been found reluctant to work night shifts, and there are large numbers of West Indians in catering and construction, but these immigrants are on the whole well distributed over a wide range of occupations.

Mining is one example of a skilled or semi-skilled occupation in which foreign labour has been important; labour shortages in the mines in Belgium, Luxembourg, West Germany and the Netherlands have been filled by Italian miners and more recently by North Africans. The only outstanding example of a skilled occupation or profession in which immigrant workers are of vital importance is however in the British health service. Among junior doctors employed in British hospitals 40 per cent come from the Commonwealth, as do 20 per cent of student nurses.

The Social Reactions to Immigration

It would appear to be inevitable that the arrival of any large and clearly distinguishable group of immigrants will provoke hostile reactions in the host society. None of the recipient European societies has shown total freedom from resentment against immigrants, but the record has varied considerably from country to country. The degree of hostility shown has depended largely, as might be expected, on the numbers and concentration of the immigrant communities, on the extent to which their way of life has differed from that of the host society, on the scarcity of resources such as housing which must be shared with them, and also on the extent to which governments have assumed an active role in controlling and organising immigration. The most extreme social reactions to immigration in Europe have been shown in

Switzerland, where proportionally speaking immigration has occurred on a huge scale, and in Britain, where a high proportion of the immigrants are coloured and where their arrival and concentration has coincided with an acute housing shortage.

Switzerland

The very rapid development of the immigrant labour force in Switzerland, which has risen to over 24 per cent of the total labour force and which almost doubled in size between 1960 and 1964, provoked an equally rapid change in social and political attitudes to immigration. In previous years immigration had been accepted as a necessary economic evil. Work permits were issued without any fixed limits by the cantonal authorities, although with the assistance of advisory committees made up of representatives of the employers' associations and the trade unions. These committees were required to consider the need for foreign labour in the light of wage and employment levels and the general economic situation in the industries concerned, and one result of their existence was that the trade unions were relatively indifferent to the immigration question. They could theoretically exercise some control over the admission of foreign labour, which tended to balance the fact that foreign workers seldom join Swiss unions, although benefiting from collective wage agreements. The official attitude towards immigration was clearly one of non-integration, holders of seasonal work permits not being allowed to bring their dependants into the country, and holders of non-seasonal permits having first to work in Switzerland for three years.

In 1963, after a year in which the number of foreign workers had grown by nearly a third, a Federal decree was passed which limited employers to the average number of foreign workers they had employed in 1962. A year later it was decided to limit the total number to 700,000, and with this object employers were refused permission to engage further foreign labour unless their total foreign labour force had been reduced to 97 per cent of its level a year earlier. At the same time, however, the Federal government signed an agreement with the Italian government, improving the legal position of seasonal workers and in particular giving them the right to bring in their dependants after working in Switzerland for five years, while reducing the qualifying period for other foreign workers to 18 months. This provoked a public outcry, indifference to the immigrant population suddenly changing to active hostility, directed in particular against the Italians. This reaction has appeared to be based largely on a fear of loss of national identity. It has been expressed in the Swiss press through several social and economic arguments against immigration, which has been blamed for overcrowding in schools, increased crime rates, rising inflation and balance-of-payments difficulties. More extreme reactions have been centred on a political pressure group founded by a Zurich businessman with the object of banning Italian labour; among its provocative activities has been the circulation of a questionnaire, including such items as: 'Would you like to share a hospital room with a Sicilian?' and it has been the subject of official protest by the Italian Foreign Ministry.

The Swiss trade unions have now demanded the reduction of the foreign labour force to 500,000 by 1972, and all firms employing more than 15 people have been required to reduce the number of foreigners in their employ by 5 per cent.

West Germany

The difference between the German and the Italian or Spanish way of life seems unlikely to be much less marked than the difference between the Swiss and the Italian, and the relative ease with which West German society has accepted immigration must be attributed mainly to its very much smaller proportions. It is also often suggested that foreign labour in Germany is not resented because the majority of immigrants stay for a year or less. In fact this is far from being the case, as an enquiry carried out in October 1963 showed that some two-thirds of all foreign workers had been employed in the country for a year or more, and about one quarter for three years or more. The German public may of course nevertheless believe the immigrant population to be much more impermanent than it really is.

There are however other factors which may have affected the situation. The West German government has played a very active role in recruitment, and this has resulted in a certain degree of selection of immigrants, including medical checks, made in their countries of origin. The immigrants themselves, when recruited (as two-thirds are) through the Federal Bureau, are usually offered a choice of jobs and are given free transport to West Germany. The entry of dependants is freely permitted provided accommodation is available, and although the proportion of immigrants who have brought their families to West Germany is small, it is very much larger than is the case in Switzerland.

Hostel accommodation is frequently provided by German employers for single foreign workers. The provision of hostels is a vexed question in theories of integration, and it has certainly had in Germany as elsewhere the effect of isolating immigrants from the host society. On the other hand it also serves to reduce local resentment if housing is in short supply and to prevent clashes over different standards of domestic behaviour. The standards prevailing in German hostels have been raised significantly in recent years, with the help of government loans to employers, partly from the funds raised by the fees paid to the Federal Bureau to obtain foreign labour.

Another factor in West Germany is the existence of a large number of voluntary societies interested in the welfare of the various immigrant groups and operating social centres for this purpose. Largely operating under the auspices of the churches, they receive subsidies from the Federal government.

France

As in West Germany, the social reactions to immigration in France have been relatively insignificant, although France has far larger numbers of foreign workers than any other European country, larger numbers of non-Europeans than any country except Britain, and a larger foreign percentage in its labour force than any country except Switzerland. Immigrants from Southern Europe have been received with less hostility in France than anywhere else. France has of course a long tradition of Italian immigration, and there are similarities of language and custom which are probably greater than elsewhere. Immigrants from colonies and ex-colonies have not met with hostility in any way comparable with that shown in Britain in recent years, although the aftermath of the Algerian war has affected Algerians to some extent. The numbers of coloured immigrants are of course appreciably smaller than in Britain, but it appears to be the case that the French are not markedly colour-conscious, although there have recently been suggestions that the increasing inflow of immigrants from the Caribbean and West Africa may eventually give rise to trouble.

The political philosophy of assimilation which was the basis of French colonial rule is no doubt partly responsible for the ease with which France can still accept ex-colonial workers. Various practical aspects of French immigration policy have also helped. As in West Germany, a high proportion of immigrants are introduced under government auspices, through the Office National d'Immigration (ONI). The entry of dependants is encouraged provided that accommodation is available, and ONI will pay their fares to France as well as the workers'. Another organisation, the Service Social d'Aide aux Emigrants, which has been in existence since 1921, assists immigrants and is particularly concerned to encourage the reunification of families. This activity is however restricted by the housing shortage, and the standards of immigrant accommodation are very low. Large enterprises importing foreign labour with *nominatif* work contracts (i.e. in which the worker concerned is named) are required to provide hostel accommodation for single workers, but the majority of workers enter the country with a *contrat anonyme*. The government is showing increasing awareness of the housing problems; recent agreements have been concluded with Mali, Senegal and Mauritania under which French social security benefits have become payable to dependants left behind in those countries but at less than the full rate; the difference is directed into a fund for hostel building.

Another factor in France's favour in absorbing a foreign population is a very low population density. Moreover, ONI has in addition been active in directing labour to specific areas with the object of preventing large concentrations of foreign workers or indeed of national groups. This is in direct contrast to the situation in Britain.

Britain

In this over-populated country immigration has been entirely a matter of private enterprise and foreign workers are as a result highly concentrated in certain areas. Britain is an insular society in which immigrants have always been unpopular; Irish labour met with considerable prejudice until very recently, and post-war attempts to introduce Italians to reduce the labour shortage in the mines had to be abandoned in the face of the hostility of the local union branches. It is however the coloured immigrants from the Commonwealth who have in the sixties become a major cause of social and political tension.

Immigration from the West Indies during the fifties appeared to fluctuate between 15,000 and 30,000 a year, in relation to the demand for labour in Britain. In 1960, a boom year, the numbers rose to nearly 50,000. In 1961 the Conservative government began to discuss the possibility of restricting entry from the Commonwealth, and as a result the numbers of immigrants rose very sharply indeed and for the first time included as many Indians and Pakistanis as West Indians. Immigration from Asia has subsequently considerably outstripped immigration from the Caribbean. The passage of the Commonwealth Immigration Act in 1962 was bitterly opposed by the Labour Party, largely on the grounds that there was no evident economic or social necessity to restrict immigration, and that since controls were not to be enforced over immigration from the Irish Republic, the Act was clearly discriminatory against coloured people. In 1965, however, the Labour government announced that the number of work vouchers issued to Commonwealth citizens in a year was to be limited to 8,500, primarily to persons with certain qualifications—doctors, nurses, teachers, science graduates—needed in Britain. The number of vouchers taken up in 1964 had been 14,705, some 12,000 by coloured workers, and 30,000 dependants had been admitted. No restrictions were placed on the entry of dependants, but drastic powers of deportation of Commonwealth citizens were proposed for the Home Secretary. In the same year, the Labour government had introduced a Race Relations Bill making discrimination on grounds of colour illegal in public places.

The rapid change in left-wing political opinion between 1961 and 1965 reflects the intensification, in certain areas, of local resentment against immigrants. As liberal opinion has never ceased to point out, the immigrant population still constitutes a very small percentage of the population as a whole, and the coloured population is less than 2 per cent. The immigrants are however highly concentrated in the poorest districts of the main con-urbations and in two or three towns with 'immigrant' industries. In these areas the housing shortage is usually already severe, and with the additional factor of colour prejudice among landlords the only accommodation avail-able to immigrants involves living conditions which reinforce the prejudices of the local population. These living conditions in turn ensure that im-migrants will place a more than proportionate burden on the already overstrained social services; the incidence of tuberculosis becomes high, babies must be born in hospital and children taken into the care of the local authority.

Immigration into Britain has made no more than a marginal contribution to problems which would exist in any case, but the fact that so many of the immigrants are coloured has emphasised their contribution and given the problem publicity. It is possible that the West Indians alone might have been accepted by now with diminishing resentment; they are English-speaking and the number of women immigrants is now nearly equal to the men. With the advent of large numbers of Indians and Pakistanis, the possibility of integrating the immigrant communities became much more remote. These immigrants speak little English, have very different ways of life and religious practices, and in many districts still consist almost entirely of men. Where women and children have arrived, as they are now doing in increasing numbers, the advantage of the immigrants being seen to lead family lives is often outweighed by the problems presented by non-English-speaking children in the local schools. The severity of this problem for certain districts is indicated by the recent Ministry of Education circular to local authorities suggesting that the proportion of immigrant children in any one school should not be allowed to exceed 30 per cent.

Strong local feeling and the considerable (and often exaggerated) publicity given to these issues in the national press provoked the Labour government into imposing limits on the issue of vouchers which bear no relation to economic needs; it would also appear that restricting immigrants from the developing countries to their scarce professional and skilled personnel will be even more damaging to international relations. Since the entry of depend-ants has not been restricted, moreover, the increase in the immigrant population will in fact continue, and apart from some very limited financial help to voluntary committees dealing with immigration problems, there has still been no government action to assist the integration of the immigrants with the rest of the community.

The Netherlands

That it is nevertheless possible for a white community to receive coloured immigrants with very little friction has been demonstrated by the Netherlands, where we see an example of the difference that can be made by active government intervention. The Netherlands has the highest population density in the world, and its population of 12 million includes 2–300,000 immigrants from the ex-Dutch colonies in Asia, of which perhaps 10 per cent are in fact pure Dutch. The rest are mainly of mixed blood, except for some 20,000 Amboynese. The entry of these immigrants was of course a political and not an economic necessity, and in these circumstances public action is possibly easier to achieve. Whatever its causes, however, the reception of the immigrants in specially rented hotels and hostels and the provision of social workers to explain Dutch life proved a successful policy. Despite a severe housing shortage, a proportion of new building was set aside for immigrants, thus allowing them to be dispersed throughout the country, and extra help was allocated to schools with children with language difficulties. No colour bar appears to have developed in the Netherlands, despite the elements of favourable treatment for immigrants in the government programme. This achievement must be largely attributed to government action; that the Dutch are not by nature exceptionally well disposed towards foreigners has been demonstrated by various local troubles over Italian and Spanish immigrants.

Future Prospects

Nearly every country in Western Europe is now short of labour, and except during temporary periods of recession this seems likely to continue to be the case for the foreseeable future. The labour force of the six countries of the European Economic Community is increasing at less than half the rate of that of the United States; in several countries, including Britain, the labour force as a percentage of the total population is actually falling. The British National Plan (1965–70) forecasts a demand for additional manpower totalling 800,000 by 1970, while the expected increase in the labour force is 400,000; the French Fifth Plan, which also runs to 1970, requires a minimum of 325,000 foreign workers.

In recent years the labour shortages of Northern Europe have been alleviated by the movement of workers from the underemployed south, but this supply is now almost exhausted. The chronic unemployment of Italy has disappeared; the northern half of the country can employ all suitable labour from the south, and Italian firms have indeed begun to recruit Italians back from West Germany and Belgium. The Spanish and Greek governments have become concerned about the loss of skilled and young workers from key sectors, and in Spain the labour shortages which have developed in the construction and metal industries have forced wages up towards average European levels. Portugal is reported to be alarmed at the loss of skilled labour, and to be considering placing restrictions on emigration.

Alternative sources of labour within Europe are limited and expensive. The movement of workers out of agriculture and into industry is now only significant in France, West Germany and Italy, and even in these countries its rate is slowing down. There is considerable geographical labour immobility in Britain and in France, which has been a major factor in encouraging immigration, but massive social investment, particularly in housing, is required to encourage domestic manpower to move, just as expenditure on retraining is involved in any major occupational transfers.

In future the only appreciable source of readily available extra labour (with the possible exception in some cases of married women) will be from outside Europe, with all the accompanying social problems that this presents. So far, European labour shortages have been largely confined to skilled occupations. If the supply of foreign workers dries up, shortages will spread to the unskilled, low-wage employment categories. The marginal effects on certain economies and in certain sectors will be considerable; in West Germany, for example, less than 30 per cent of new jobs in the producing sectors of the economy in 1963 were filled by Germans, and in 1964 the labour force would have fallen by 50,000 without the net inflow of 150,000 immigrant workers. The general economic effects of immigration are often disputed, particularly by Swiss economists, but it seems clear that, at least in the short term, if new immigrant labour ceased to be available, the pressure on wages in the 'immigrant' industries and occupations would have important inflationary effects. If on the other hand Western Europe continues to rely on immigrant labour, but from overseas, disastrous social consequences are likely to follow if considerable social investment expenditure is not made at the same time.

In the long run the labour problems of Western Europe will no doubt be solved by a reallocation of domestic manpower and also by automation; the availability of foreign workers may indeed in recent years have allowed employers in some sectors to delay already overdue rationalisation and investment in labour-saving equipment. Immigration has nevertheless made an important contribution to European output over the last decade, and in the short term the gradual disappearance of new supplies of European expatriate labour will present severe problems to several industries and economies.

BIBLIOGRAPHY

Gwynn, John. *Switzerland's Immigration Problem. Immigration—The West German Example. French Without Tears*, Institute of Race Relations *News Letter*, London, May/June, July, November 1965.

Rose, E. J. B. 'Problems of Immigration and Integration,' *Journal of the Royal Commonwealth Society*, VIII, 5, London, 1965.

Economist Intelligence Unit. *Commonwealth Immigration* (monthly summary), London.

Fabian Society. *Strangers Within*, London, 1965.

United Nations. *Economic Survey of Europe in 1964*, Geneva.

PROBLEMS FACING THE TRADE UNIONS IN WESTERN EUROPE

R. COLIN BEEVER

PRODUCTIVITY, PRICES AND INCOMES POLICIES

PRODUCTIVITY, Prices and Incomes Policy is the name given to the British attempt since April 1965 to reduce inflationary tendencies in the economy. Attempts were made before in Britain to keep down the level of wage and salary increases; referred to as 'Incomes Policy',[1] they were angled much more at wages and salaries than at other forms of income. The new policy, by its extended title, indicates the new priorities of the British government in its anti-inflationary campaign. It is a policy that is only one part of the overall budgeting and fiscal policies incorporating many far-reaching measures such as the Corporation and Capital Gains taxes, new systems of investment allowances, the inauguration of the Industrial Reorganisation Corporation, changes in social welfare benefits and contributions, etc. These policies taken as a whole are intended to check inflationary tendencies, rectify the adverse balance of payments position and strengthen the pound sterling, and lastly, but very importantly, redistribute the national wealth to some extent and achieve a greater fairness of income between different categories.

As to the rest of Europe, only the Netherlands, Sweden, Norway and Denmark have attempted such an ambitious overall policy comprising social as well as economic reforms. In these countries, stress has generally been put on wages and salaries more than on other forms of income or on prices. The degree of stability required by different countries in the purchasing power of their currencies varies according to their balance of payments and productivity. Some countries can afford a higher rate of inflation than others, although all governments appear to regard the phenomenon as the greatest of all economic evils.

One striking fact that emerges from European experience of recent years is that the degree of inflation which actually occurs does not seem to be related to whether or not particular countries operate an incomes policy. Judging from the index of consumer prices, the Netherlands and the Scandinavian countries, which have long operated incomes policies, have had more inflation than, say, Germany, Belgium or Switzerland, which do not, and

---

[1] For the purposes of this chapter the term 'incomes policy' is taken as covering both government policy and voluntary collaboration between management and unions, initially consulting with government officials, to work out a system of wage and salary increases that the economy will bear. The Netherlands and Britain have attempted the former, and Sweden, Norway and Denmark the latter.

Britain which did not until recent years. However, Italy and France, which also do not have thoroughgoing incomes policies, have had very substantial price increases.

CONSUMER PRICE INDEX
Average for 1965 (1958 = 100)

Austria	125	Ireland	123
Belgium	115	Italy	129
Britain	121	Netherlands	126
Denmark	134	Norway	125
France	132[1]	Sweden	125
Germany	118	Switzerland	118 (approx.)

Source: *UN Monthly Bulletin of Statistics*, April 1966

[1] Author's calculation.

Denmark and Norway have operated incomes policies for many years but the Netherlands and Sweden have operated the most comprehensive policies over the longest period. Although in the latter two countries it is felt that greater stability has been achieved than would otherwise have prevailed, there is little satisfaction with the result, although in each case the unions and employers have cooperated well with the government. The basic cause of dissatisfaction has been the same as the main source of danger to the British policy—that account cannot be taken of the variations in demand for labour, especially local and regional variations.

The Swedish system is for collective bargaining agreements, usually covering a two- or three-year period, to be negotiated nationally. Negotiation may be either by the trade union national centre (the LO) and the central employers' organisation (the SAF) or by the individual industrial unions and the industrial employers' organisations. In either case it is done only in the light of prior consultations with the government and much research into what the national economy will bear. Once these national agreements are arrived at they are binding and nobody may resort to strike or lockout over their terms during the period of their validity. Industrial action was only narrowly averted in 1966, however, over the bargaining of a new agreement, which provides for the reduction of the working week from 45 to 42½ hours plus substantial wage increases phased over three years.

The basic difficulty in Sweden has been that 70 per cent of workers are on piecework and the rates for this are negotiable at local level. This causes wages drift because these rates are bid up substantially in areas where labour is short. Subsequent national agreements attempt to take account of the people left behind by getting them higher percentage increases than others. Since 1960 average hourly earnings have risen twice as fast as productivity, partly as a result of this system. The 1966 agreement provides that the wages for lower paid workers and those in weaker industries will rise with the general wages drift. Inflation is not likely to be contained on this basis and it is easy to see why the Swedes can see shortcomings in their incomes policy results.

In the Netherlands the rate of wage and other increases has been more tightly regulated, perhaps, than in any other country. Unions and employers cooperated in the Foundation of Labour to work out the levels of permissible increases nationally and the government also had a direct hand in the negotiations. There has also been a kind of national system of job evaluation on which wage levels were partly dependent and there was little inflation until about 1963. Then the unions wanted a better share of the nation's economic growth and of rising profits. Wage costs were pushed up by 17 per cent that year and have been rising fast ever since—about another 30 per cent up to the end of 1965. Productivity has been rising at about 4–5 per cent annually over this period so that inflation has been rapid. Shortages of labour in particular areas and industries were partly responsible for the complete breakdown of the incomes policy, and collective bargaining is now much tougher and much freer.

The conclusion is that incomes policy is extraordinarily difficult to work in a democratic state which has voluntary bargaining and a modern social system aiming at full employment. The lesson for governments and economists may well be that they should concentrate their policies on the eradication of the causes of inflation rather than the suppression of its symptoms such as high wage demands. This would mean the ironing out of anomalies and imbalances in the industrial and geographical labour markets.

DIVISIVE TENDENCIES AND COMMUNIST UNIONS: FRANCE AND ITALY

The trade union movement in the Common Market countries has strong divisive tendencies along both political and religious lines.[1] It is usual to have two or three major national trade union centres (or TUCs) in each of the countries, with differing international affiliations and with each centre having its own structure of affiliated industrial unions, all in competition with each other. West Germany is the only EEC member country which does not have a major problem of this sort—its trade union structure was established anew in the immediate post-war period along rational lines.

This fragmentation causes problems not only for the unions themselves, but for employers, governments and international bodies which have trade union representation. The two countries in Western Europe with the most difficult problems are undoubtedly France and Italy. In each country there are three major national trade union centres with their own industrial affiliates—the largest being mainly Communist, the second largest mainly Christian (Roman Catholic) and the smallest mainly Social Democrat.

In France the differences between the Christian and Social Democrat unions arise, today, more perhaps from organisational self-interest than from differing political policies, although the Social Democrat unions have always been rather superior in their attitude to the religious aspects—confessional trade unionism, as they call it—of the Christian unions. However, in 1964 the main body of the original Christian trade union centre in France, the Confédération Française des Travailleurs Chrétiens (CFTC), decided against continuing its policy of exclusive Christian adherence and formed a new non-Christian national centre, calling itself the Confédération Française Démocratique du Travail (CFDT). The Confédération has, however, continued its affiliation with the Christian international trade union movement. The new CFDT believes that as the second largest centre in France it can be the rallying point of democratic and anti-Communist trade unionism. This would mean its swallowing up its weaker Social Democratic rival, the Force Ouvrière (FO).

The FO does not appear ready to concede any sovereignty although it has not closed its mind to the question of working more closely with the CFDT. The difficulty is that the FO is much more rigid in its attitude to the

[1] See 'Integration and the Trade Unions.'

large Communist centre, the Confédération Générale du Travail (CGT) than is the CFDT, which cooperates industrially and, indeed, has adopted a common action programme with the CGT. The FO's unswerving refusal to have anything to do with the CGT stems mainly from the fact that the FO originated as a breakaway in 1947 when it found that the Communist line was prevailing within the CGT and that it was pursuing what it regarded as a strike policy for political ends.

Since those days the CGT has reformed its ways somewhat, because it found growing disillusionment from the workers over strikes which appeared to have no immediately attainable objectives. In the Fifth Republic, and particularly latterly, it has found itself increasingly in an ambivalent position along with the French Communist Party. Whilst being hotly opposed to President de Gaulle's domestic policies, together with its rival unions, it has found itself giving qualified approval to his international policies, particularly as regards his dissent from the other Western countries on NATO and Common Market questions. Probably this is one reason why in recent years the FO and the CFDT have, untypically, taken the lead in inaugurating strike action against some of the government's policies affecting social conditions and industrial negotiations. The CGT has sometimes been left to follow on, showing a toning down of its previous militancy.

The employers in France (as in Britain for different reasons) sometimes have to put up with rival trade unionism in their factories but the problems created are not usually serious and representation is decided by the Plant Committee elections. Employers locally tend to negotiate and cooperate with those unions holding a majority, irrespective of political considerations. A similar position as regards elections and employer attitudes exists in Italy, but it is not unknown there for some employers discreetly to back one group or another, in a variety of ways, if this helps to bring about a clear-cut decision in inter-union rivalry.

The Communist unions do not play an obstructive industrial role, generally, in France and as they are the largest organisation they are regarded by the state, for some purposes, as part of the industrial establishment and given appropriate representation along with the other unions on various bodies such as the important Economic and Social Council which is consulted by the government on many matters. The CGT is also seated on the High Commission on Collective Agreements and, through a government decision taken in 1965, on the delegation to the International Labour Organisation—a privilege gained only after years of pressure. The CGT is also seated in the Joint Commissions on unemployment and pensions schemes set up by the unions and employers themselves.

The Communist trade unions have not managed to secure representation on bodies connected with the European Coal and Steel Community or Common Market. They have been particularly keen to secure seats on the EEC's Economic and Social Committee, so far without success. The views of the Community itself, as well as the governments' views, would play a part here, but these have not been favourable, especially as the Communists have attacked the establishment of Western European integration projects from the outset. These attacks have now cooled considerably, and they were never very strong, anyway, in the Italian CGIL, which includes a large minority of Socialist trade unionists. The French CGT and Italian CGIL have set up a permanent Coordination and Action Committee. Two of its main objectives are the promotion of unity of action between all trade unions in Western Europe and recognition of the right to represent French and Italian workers in the EEC—now exclusively represented by the other, smaller national unions.

The state in Italy has discriminated against the Communist national centre rather more than is the case in France, especially on the question of representation. Perhaps this is because the political parties making up the successive governments have been more directly concerned with the future of the Catholic national centre, the CISL, and the Social Democratic national centre, the UIL. However, workers are organised to a higher degree in Italy than in France and the CGIL is a large and powerful force in the country. It is less of a dogmatic organisation than its French counterpart, however, and frequently disregards the international Communist policy lines laid down, particularly as regards Common Market questions.

The conclusion is that France and Italy are the only two countries in Western Europe with major Communist unions separately organised. This creates difficulties for the two countries and for international organisations in establishing the fruitful relations with all unions which are expected in advanced industrial societies. But this problem is less serious than the general problem of trade union disunity and factionalism in France and Italy as between the three main national centres and their affiliates. There is no immediate prospect of an end to these internal hostilities and the danger arising is the same as exists in any country where voluntary organisations are weak—an omnipotent state may fill the power vacuum, with a tendency to shrivel democracy at the roots.

TRADE UNIONS AND ECONOMIC AND SOCIAL PROGRESS

There is still a widespread belief in Britain that, economically and socially, this country is rather ahead of most countries on the Continent, with the exception of Sweden and latterly, perhaps, of West Germany. This belief is probably more prevalent among trade unionists than among employers but there is little recognition generally of the fact that, the National Health Service excepted, Britain is behind in most benefits of the welfare state, has higher unemployment than her main competitors and has been having smaller wage and salary increases than most Western European countries.

PERCENTAGE RATES OF UNEMPLOYMENT, 1965

Austria	2·7	Ireland	5·5
Belgium	2·5	Italy	2·7 (1964)
Britain	1·5	Netherlands	0·9
France	0·7[1]	Norway	1·2
Germany	0·7 (1964)	Sweden	1·1 (1964)

Source: *ILO Bulletin of Labour Statistics*, 1966 (first quarter)

[1] Author's estimate.

The Common Market countries spend more of their wealth on social security than do Britain and most other EFTA countries, including Sweden.[1] Furthermore, the Common Market countries have been getting much better wage increases than Britain and their wage costs per unit of output have

[1] See 'Integration and the Trade Unions' (p. 641). These figures relate to 1960 but the signs are that the differentials have not been reversed since and they may even have widened.

been rising faster, giving Britain an advantage in export competitiveness, again contrary to general belief. Britain is in a midway position as regards the general rise in consumer prices.

Judgments will remain subjective, however, as regards relative standards of living in European countries. Quoting the wage rates of one country alongside those of another gives no indication of the relative standards of living, even when converted to a common currency, because of variation in the cost of living. The cost of living can at present be measured only as an index, i.e. relative to the cost of living in the same country at some earlier time, because there is no scientifically accurate method of measuring it in value terms as between countries. This is one of the problems which unions face in internationalising their activities. Buying the same goods in different countries, totalling the cost and relating it to hours of labour at existing pay rates is one attempted method; but it has shortcomings in that people of different countries have different priorities in life and therefore their expenditure patterns are also different. The price of wine matters most of all to Frenchmen, of potatoes to Irishmen, of spaghetti to Italians and of fish to Norwegians. Other factors which have to be taken into consideration in considering relative standards of living are social security benefits, who pays for them and in what proportions (employers, employees and the state); the incidence of direct and indirect taxation at various income levels; and several smaller factors, often difficult or impossible to measure.

The EEC Commission and the ECSC High Authority have tried to obtain a satisfactory method of measuring relative cost of living by the 'shopping basket' concept, whereby goods purchased are based on the typical spending pattern of various nationals, but so far this has not been satisfactorily achieved. The United Nations produce a special index of retail price comparisons for the purposes of determining salary differentials for their officials. As they are mostly based on capital cities, however, they are not very typical of the countries themselves. For what they are worth the European figures are given below. The index is based on New York City = 100.

RETAIL PRICE INDEX FOR CAPITAL CITIES

Bonn	82	London	82
Copenhagen	88	Paris	101
Geneva	87	Rome	93
The Hague	83	Vienna	82

Source: *UN Monthly Bulletin of Statistics*, April 1966

The development not only of social and economic systems but of industrial relations systems varies widely in Western European countries. Some, like Britain and the Scandinavian countries, have highly developed and sophisticated collective bargaining machinery for every industry, united trade union movements and a high degree of organisation of workers. Others, like France and Italy, are badly organised and disunited, their industrial relations systems are a shambles and yet the unions have a good deal of influence at national level. Others again, such as Germany and the Netherlands, are reasonably organised, fairly tightly disciplined and with a greater stake in the smooth running of industry and the national economy than is enjoyed by trade union movements elsewhere. In all these sets of circumstances the unions have made progress in their different ways and yet their immediate objectives and priorities differ a good deal.

Unions in all the industrialised European countries, for instance, put a higher priority on holidays than does Britain, particularly annual holidays, where three to four weeks is common as against Britain's two weeks. In the Common Market countries, taking annual and public holidays together, the total annual holidays are: Italy 39 days, France 35 days, Germany 28–31 days, Belgium 25 days, Netherlands 21–22 days, and Britain 18 days. Some of these totals are established in law but frequently they are first negotiated between unions and employers in key sectors. France has recently increased the general level of the annual holiday from three to four weeks in this way.

German trade unionists put the 40-hour week high in their programme for many years and the breakthrough was achieved several years ago when it was negotiated in the huge metal-working sector of industry, to come into operation in stages, achieving the ultimate goal in 1965. However, the final stage was postponed in favour of an immediate pay rise and the 40-hour week began to operate from 1966. The German national trade union centre has at the centre of its action programme the extension of the principle of codetermination (*Mitbestimmung*) which has operated in the mining and iron and steel industries since 1951. It is trying to have the principle introduced in all large enterprises in every industry (those employing 2,000 or more workers, with a working capital of DM 75 million and an annual turnover of DM 150 million, or fulfilling any two of these criteria).

The system is that the supervisory councils (*Aufsichtsräte*) of companies have to be composed of equal numbers of shareholders and workers' representatives who elect one further independent member. The supervisory council is responsible for supervising the company's operations, reporting to the general meeting and appointing the board of directors (*Vorstand*). The board has to include a director of labour and social questions whose appointment is subject to approval by a majority of the workers' representatives on the council. The German unions have found this big stake in their major industries to their liking and they find it the most effective way of ensuring industrial democracy. Their campaign for an extension of this system is, however, meeting with heavy opposition from the employers' organisations.

AUTOMATION

Fifteen to twenty years ago when the new techniques of automation, mainly pioneered in the United States, were being studied in Europe, there was a good deal of fear among trade unions that unless it was handled very carefully it might bring an unprecedented wave of unemployment in its wake. The unions were never opposed to the introduction of automation but they insisted that it must be introduced only after full consultations with the unions and in an orderly and perhaps gradual fashion so as to avoid harmful consequences.

The fears of the unions on this score have so far proved to be without foundation. Automation has been proceeding at a fairly rapid pace all over industrialised Western Europe for some years and it has caused no structural unemployment and very little temporary unemployment or major dislocations. The experiences and problems of automation in various European countries differ little and the continental position is generally similar to that in Britain.

European experience, however, is different from that of the United States, where the unions claim that automation has brought about large-scale dislocations and is responsible, at least in part, for the relatively high unemployment rate. There are a number of reasons for this difference which must be considered.

Automation is now largely thought of in terms of computers doing work previously done by clerks and brain-workers in offices. Originally, in the United States, it was mainly thought of in terms of fully automatic processes in factories whereby manual labour was replaced by transfer machines passing on workpieces from one process to another without human intervention. This was before the use of computers on a commercial basis. Because of the scale of the home market and the limited number of companies competing in some major industries in the United States, the degree of profitable automation which could be introduced was greater than in Europe. Also the higher living standards and slower growth rate of the American economy has made it more difficult for that country to find new jobs for those displaced by automation—more markets are nearer saturation point for goods than in Europe. Neither has the United States reduced the length of its working week or extended its holiday provisions at the same rate as Europe, to offset the effects of automation. Another factor is that the American economy has little overall planning of the sort that irons out the peaks and troughs of many of the free-enterprise economies of European countries. This means less job security and less social cushioning against misfortune for most Americans.

Now that computers are available to most large or medium-sized companies for records and improved administration, etc. (it has been estimated that most companies employing over 3,000 people in Western Europe have installed electronic data-processing plant) most job dislocation potentially affects white-collar rather than manual workers. This has been offset, however, not only by full employment which ensures transfers rather than redundancy of employees, but also by the fact that the installation of this equipment can in several ways lead to more employment. First there are the obvious needs for more maintenance workers and for more staff to operate punch-card machines which prepare the data. But there is also an important side-effect in that many managements now recognise that they can quickly obtain a greater, a more accurate and a higher quality of information from their computers fairly easily—the sort of information they did not seek in pre-automation days because the man-hours involved would have been prohibitive. The effect is that enterprises and their departments can now give a better service than previously; they have a greater access to knowledge and research material and these factors, in themselves, tend to lead to expansion and hence promote employment.

Because white-collar workers frequently receive superior treatment from employers in the matters of hours of work, guaranteed pay during sickness, supplementary pensions and generally a better 'status', it has been primarily the manual workers' unions which have shown concern over the possible adverse social effects of automation if its introduction were not sensibly planned and other factors regulated. The fears, as has been said, have proved unfounded, but the thought always at the back of trade union minds is that the era of full employment and economic expansion may not last forever and that precautions should be taken to protect their members in the event of a recession. Union requests may include short-time working rather than redundancies and provision for severance pay in the latter instance. The position has also sharpened the unions' awareness of the need for their members to acquire skills through training—there is little prospect for an unskilled worker in an automated industry.

The white-collar workers are less well organised than manual workers except, perhaps, in the public services, and this makes the task of their unions more difficult in negotiating about automation. They have fewer problems, possibly, than the manual workers' unions but they, too, are concerned that their members should have the extra educational qualifications necessary for promotion in this field. Many members are worried about the extra working flexibility usually expected of them. Most white-collar workers have not previously been used to working on shifts or doing overtime—both requirements are common with computers. It is not just a question of the inconvenience, but the staffs wish to have compensatory premiums for odd hours if it is to be a regular occurrence. White-collar workers have previously been expected to take such occasional inconveniences in their stride as part of their salaried contract.

Paul Blau, chief editor of the Austrian trade union journal 'Labour and Economy' summarised the European trade union outlook in an address in December 1964. He supported automation and technological advance with reservations.

The United States have to teach us the lesson (and they have already begun to do so) that the way to private wealth in the midst of increasing public poverty does not lead us to the solution of the burning problems of our industrial society: what kind of job and work-place keeps a person happy and gives satisfaction? How must we build and administer houses, schools, hospitals, sport and cultural institutions, settlements and cities, so that children may grow up healthy, humane and open-minded, adults live and work and old people enjoy their last years? . . .

It is not enough to control technological change in such a way that we save the individual from bitter hardships and just preserve our society. Technology must be applied consciously as a tool to build the society of tomorrow.

BIBLIOGRAPHY

INCOMES POLICY

Cooper, Jack. *Industrial Relations: Sweden Shows the Way*, Fabian Society, London, 1963.
Roberts, B. C. (ed.) 'Symposium on Incomes Policy', *British Journal of Industrial Relations*, II, 3, London, November 1964.
Stewart, Michael and Winsbury, Rex. *An Incomes Policy for Labour*, Fabian Society, London, 1963.
OECD. *Growth and Economic Policy*, Paris, 1964. *Policies for Prices, Profits and Other Non-wage Incomes*, Paris, 1964.

COMMUNIST UNIONS AND DIVISIVE TENDENCIES

Bergeron, André. 'The Trade Union Movement in France', *Europe Left*, Nos 8 and 9, London, summer 1965.
Galenson, Walter. *Trade Union Democracy in Western Europe*, Univ. of Calif. Press, Berkeley and Los Angeles, 1961.
La Palombara, Joseph. *The Italian Labor Movement*, Cornell Univ. Press, Ithaca, NY, 1957.

AUTOMATION

Crossman, E. R. F. W. *Automation and Skill*, HMSO for Department of Scientific and Industrial Research (DSIR), London, 1960.
European Productivity Agency. *Automation at Renault* (*Automation* No. 12), OEEC, Paris, 1957.
OECD. *The Requirements of Automated Jobs*, Paris, 1965 (Final Report and Supplement of North American Joint Conference, Washington, December 1964).
Trade Union News, Publication Services of the European Communities, Brussels, from 1963.

THE SCANDINAVIAN WELFARE STATE[1]

VIC GEORGE

AMERICAN and European social scientists have shown a great deal of interest in Scandinavian countries since the Scandinavian 'New Deal' of the 1930s. Some saw in it the ideal compromise between unbridled capitalism and restrictive communism while others considered it with suspicion as being creeping communism in disguise. Both these sentiments are biased and exaggerated. The social policies of Scandinavian countries are not substantially different from those of other Western European countries at the same stage of industrial development.

Industrialisation is one of the basic factors that shape government social policies. It accentuates some of the traditional social problems and it creates new ones. It generates a more favourable public opinion for social reform by making the contrast between the economically active and inactive more pronounced and evident. In this way it stirs the public conscience which forces democratically elected governments into action. Above all it increases the national wealth which enables governments to implement programmes for the protection of their citizens against social and economic privation and insecurity. It is no coincidence that Sweden, the most industrialised of Scandinavian countries, possesses also the most comprehensive system of social services. It is partly for the same reason that there has been a marked convergence of government social policies in Western Europe since the end of the last war.

Political factors play an equally important role. In this respect the experience of Scandinavian countries is perhaps unique. The establishment of parliamentary government and the welfare state in Scandinavia has been a peaceful affair compared with most other European countries. The multiplicity of political parties has necessitated a long series of coalition governments resulting in a gradual erosion of party political differences. Today all Scandinavian political parties believe in the welfare state. What divides them is its extent, its comprehensiveness and the means of achieving it. This consensus of opinion would have been impossible without the striking homogeneity of the population. There are no important ethnic, religious or language minorities to generate serious conflicts among the population.

HOUSING

Three main factors account for the distinctive quality of Scandinavian housing and town planning: the late arrival of the industrial revolution, the use of hydroelectric power for industry and enlightened government policies.

[1] It was found impossible to cover the complexities of the social policies of all Western European countries in a single chapter, and this case study is offered instead. The Scandinavian countries have been chosen as exemplifying the welfare state in an advanced stage of development. Details of each national social security system in Western Europe (including benefit and contribution rates) will be found in Part One—*Ed.*

The industrial revolution arrived in Scandinavia at about the turn of the last century having swept through Britain, Germany, France, Belgium and other European countries. The social problems created by the rapid advance of unplanned industrialisation were evident to all. The Scandinavians deserve the credit for learning from the mistakes of other countries and thus saving their own countries a great deal of unnecessary suffering. The principle of laissez-faire that accompanied the industrial revolution in its early stages had undergone serious changes by the end of the 19th century when the Scandinavians began to face the social problems of industrialisation. Finally, the advance of industrialisation was less rapid in Scandinavia than elsewhere in Europe, thus creating less serious problems in housing.

The use of hydroelectric power for industry saved the cities from the decaying and blighting effect of coal on housing. It also meant smaller conurbations, though the size of the population of Scandinavian countries also had something to do with this.

Scandinavian governments are well known for the encouragement they have been giving to non-profit housing associations whose aim is to provide housing for rental or for sale on a non-profit basis. They are particularly active in urban areas and they usually provide multi-family housing. Their importance varies from one Scandinavian country to another and according to the economic conditions prevailing in the country. They have lost ground in Denmark recently owing to a change in government policy which considerably reduced state loans for house-building. Their share of the total number of dwellings built in Denmark dropped from 47 per cent in 1951 to 23·5 per cent in 1961 while in Sweden it rose from 15 per cent to 27 per cent. In Finland their share rose from 34 per cent in 1957 to 52 per cent in 1961 while in Norway the figures for 1953 and 1961 were 20 per cent and 27 per cent respectively. In Iceland non-profit housing associations are of the cooperative type and cater mostly for workers with low incomes. The use of non-profit housing associations instead of local authorities as the main alternative to private builders has certain advantages. They are in a better position than local authorities to enlist the cooperation of groups of people interested in housing and to stimulate community spirit. They are more likely to tackle housing problems to suit different local conditions and circumstances and they are less susceptible to government changes and party political pressures. On the debit side, non-profit housing associations fail to attract people of the lowest income group who usually need more assistance with housing than others. Cooperative effort, whether in housing, agriculture or social security, always attracts the better established sections of the community. Non-profit housing associations exist in other Western European countries but except in the Netherlands, Belgium and West Germany their work is limited.

The proportion of dwellings constructed by private builders is inversely related to that of the non-profit associations. State aid favours non-profit associations and it is more forthcoming when housing shortages are acute and when economic conditions are too unstable for private builders. Local authorities build very few houses in Scandinavia, with the exception of Sweden, where they built about one-third of the total number of dwellings during the period 1951–61. In the other countries their work is limited to social housing for special population groups—the elderly, the disabled, problem families, etc.

All Scandinavian countries provide grants to local authorities and non-profit associations for social housing and slum clearance. Apart from this, government policies vary. In Denmark government aid for home building is limited to guarantees of supplementary mortgage loans for certain types of dwellings. In 1961 about two-thirds of house-building was by private firms involving no state subsidy. In Finland state loans are granted to non-profit housing associations for all types of house-building but particularly for rental housing. In Norway state loans are made both at low-interest rate and at the full commercial rate depending on the type of housing and the financial status of the applicant. In Sweden state subsidy to house-building is in the form of provision of third mortgages and the guarantee of a certain interest rate for first and second mortgages.

Another form of state aid in Scandinavia is the payment of rent allowances to families with at least two children (one in Sweden) living in rented housing or in their own houses provided that the income of the family does not exceed a certain amount and the size and conditions of the dwelling meet certain requirements. Iceland is the only Scandinavian country which does not grant any rent allowances. In 1962, 11 per cent of all families in Denmark with children received rent allowances, 0·6 per cent in Finland, 6 per cent in Norway and 13 per cent in Sweden.

Rent control has been used in all Scandinavian countries for a number of years. It is applied during economic crises and housing shortages and it is relaxed in times of prosperity. Today it is used selectively for certain types of housing in the large cities where housing shortages are mostly found. The trend here is similar to that in other European countries.

Scandinavian countries have done a great deal to remedy housing shortages and to improve housing standards during the last twenty years. The proportion of housing stock constructed since 1945 was in 1965 higher in Finland—43 per cent—than in any other European country. Norway occupied a close second place—41 per cent—Sweden was above average and Denmark slightly below average. Total expenditure on housing as a percentage of GNP is higher in Finland, Norway and Sweden than most other European countries. Denmark's figure is about average, similar to that of Britain. The number of dwellings per 1,000 population built annually in Europe for the period 1950–62 was highest in the Soviet Union, second in West Germany, third in Norway, fourth in Sweden and fifth in Finland, with Denmark again average among Western European countries.

In spite of the substantial progress made since the end of the last war, there is still a great deal to be done. The position is worst in Finland where overcrowding is still a major problem mainly because the great majority of dwellings constructed were of very small size. In 1960, 27 per cent of all dwellings in Finland contained more than two persons per room—counting kitchen as a room. This was one of the highest-density figures in Europe. By contrast the other Scandinavian countries, which were building larger dwellings, had some of the lowest figures. Denmark had the lowest in Europe, 0·8 per cent, and Norway shared fifth place with Sweden. The inclusion of kitchen in the number of rooms per dwelling, however, conceals much larger housing shortages than the above figures suggest.

The determination to solve the housing problem is evident in Scandinavian countries but shortages of manpower and financial difficulties limit the number of new dwellings that can be built to replace the old, to remedy shortages and to cope with the rising marriage rate and the increasingly higher expectations of an affluent society—problems experienced by all advanced European countries.

EDUCATION AND CHILD WELFARE

All Scandinavian countries provide a number of crèches and kindergartens, mostly in towns, run by private bodies and municipalities and used mainly by children from broken homes or whose mothers go out to work. These facilities are not always free and they are far from adequate, as they are in all other industrial countries.

Children are introduced gradually to school in all Scandinavian countries. Generally speaking, young children attend school in the morning only while older children stay on till two or three o'clock. This 'long morning' type of schooling, found in other European countries too, is based on the assumption that children go to school solely for lessons and not for any play or social activities as they do at schools with morning and afternoon sessions in England and elsewhere. The proportion of married women going out to work is continually rising in all Scandinavian countries and 'long morning' schools aggravate the problem of 'latch-key' children.

Size of classes is not as serious a problem in Scandinavia as it is in many other countries of Europe. Norway and Sweden have about the lowest pupil-teacher ratios for primary education in Europe while the other Scandinavian countries occupy middle positions.

Scandinavian countries differ substantially in their methods for the selection of the élite group of students for academic secondary schooling and university education. After long public discussion and research, Sweden abandoned the selective system of education which divided children at the age of 11 into academic and non-academic secondary schools and adopted the comprehensive system for all children aged 7–16. Sweden's research findings that intelligent children are not held back in comprehensive schools will help to allay the fears of middle-class parents in other Scandinavian and European countries, such as England, where comprehensive education is being introduced. Norway is already in the process of following Sweden's example while Denmark has taken a hesitant step in the same direction by leaving the decision on the comprehensive issue to parents. Nevertheless the Danish system tries to conceal the visible effects of the selective system by keeping children of both streams in the same school. The Finnish system, however, emphasises them by transferring the brightest children to secondary schools and leaving the others behind in primary schools. Finland's selection system for secondary education is similar to the system that existed in England before the 1944 Education Act.

The selection process for university education in Scandinavia is similar to that in Britain and other European countries. It is strict and allows a small minority only of the most able secondary-school children to benefit from university education. A number of European countries have initiated programmes to assist poorer children to qualify for university education. Sweden's scheme is the most generous of all Scandinavian countries but by no means equals the English system of free grants to all students in need. The requirement that students in Scandinavia must pay back the whole or a large part of the state loan when they graduate is not conducive to the democratisation of university education. The relationship between social class and university education is as pronounced as it is in other countries. Of all students who entered university in one year in Norway recently, 23 per cent came from homes where the father had had an academic education. In Sweden the proportion was 22 per cent. In Finland a recent survey showed that only 18 per cent of university students came from working-class families while 31 per cent came from higher executive and professional classes.

Educationally sub-normal and physically handicapped children receive special education in Scandinavian countries, either in ordinary schools or in special schools depending on the severity of their handicap. Deprived and delinquent children are treated with true understanding and tolerance. Every effort is first made to help them in their family environment, they are removed from home only as a last resort and they are rehabilitated to their parents as soon as possible. These underlying principles are found in the child-care services of other countries but the machinery for implementing them is different. While in other countries decisions involving delinquent and some deprived children are taken by ordinary courts or juvenile courts, Scandinavian countries employ an administrative agency—the child welfare committees consisting of elected and coopted members. All children up to the age of 15 and the majority of those aged 15–18 committing offences are referred to the child welfare committees. The legal procedure of prosecution and defence of the juvenile courts has no place in the deliberations of the child welfare committee. It is argued, though difficult to prove, that such a system spares children the stigma of criminality and that it allows the child welfare committee more freedom than the juvenile court to deal with a child according to its need and not according to the severity of its offence. It is certainly true that child welfare committees are in a better position than juvenile courts to take a positive and a more active interest in the child welfare services of the communities they serve. The shortage of trained social workers, psychiatrists and residential establishments of a specialised nature, however, makes the implementation of child care principles as difficult as it is in Britain, the United States and other industrialised countries. Nevertheless, England indicated in 1965 that it intended to move towards the Scandinavian system: a government white paper proposed the replacement of juvenile courts by family councils similar to the Scandinavian child welfare committees.

Social Security

Broadly speaking, Scandinavian social insurance schemes occupy a middle position between the English state unified system with its tripartite method of contributions from employers, employees and the state and some of the other European schemes which are administered mostly by semi-independent bodies and are financed mainly by employers and employees.

Administration

The 19th century witnessed a mushroom growth of workers' clubs and friendly societies to insure against death, sickness and unemployment. The growth of these societies followed the trail of the industrial revolution and reached Scandinavia during the last quarter of the century. Some were based on one trade or craft and others functioned on an area basis. They were at first completely independent and membership was voluntary. Gradually they came to rely on state funds, membership became compulsory and they had to submit to state supervision. They became cumbersome and complicated as the volume of their work increased. Some countries, such as Britain, abolished them altogether and placed the administration of social security schemes in government departments. Others tried to streamline and modernise them. Scandinavian countries attempted both with the result that generally speaking the oldest types of social insurance schemes are administered by semi-independent funds while the more recent schemes are in the hands of government departments. For historical reasons insurance funds still predominate in Denmark, while government departments carry out most social insurance schemes in Iceland. Government departments are generally in a better position to administer social insurance uniformly.

Finance

Some schemes are financed by flat-rate contributions which are a regressive form of taxation, and others by tax levies related to contributors' earnings—a progressive form of taxation. Employer, employee and state contribute to the funds of some schemes while for other schemes only one or two of the parties are financially responsible. Employers are, for example, financially responsible for the industrial injury scheme in all Scandinavian countries. It is generally considered that this induces employers to reduce work hazards. There may have been some truth in this argument when businesses were small and employers paid injury benefits directly out of their own funds, but it is doubtful whether there is any validity in it today when firms are large, management and ownership are divorced and injury benefits are paid by insurance societies with whom firms have taken out a policy. Prevention of accidents depends on more positive factors than the threat of financial penalty on employers.

In Sweden and Finland employers are also financially responsible for the wage-related old-age pension schemes. The main justification for this is that employers' contributions are considered one of the best means of vertical redistribution of wealth. This is not always the case, however, because employers pass on the extra cost to consumers in the form of higher prices or to workers by withholding increases in wages. Employers' contributions in the old-age pension schemes of Sweden and Finland are, as in other Scandinavian and European countries, pay-roll taxes calculated on the number of their employees and not on their ability to pay. A more equitable form of employers' taxation, and one more likely to affect vertical redistribution of wealth, would be contributions based on profits.

While employers are solely responsible for some schemes, they are exempted completely from others for no good reason. The unemployment benefit scheme in Sweden, the sickness and maternity scheme in Iceland and the basic old-age pensions in Denmark and Sweden are financed completely by employees and the state. The general trend in Scandinavia has increasingly been for the state to assume more financial responsibility for social security schemes. A similar trend is found in many other advanced European countries.

Coverage

Coverage of social security programmes is fairly comprehensive in Scandinavia. Some schemes are compulsory and they cover everybody within the specified insurance class—industrial injury schemes, the basic old-age pension, etc. Others are voluntary and their coverage varies. Unemployment insurance is voluntary in Sweden, Denmark and Finland but trade unions make it compulsory for their members. In Denmark health insurance for medical benefits is voluntary but there is indirect pressure on people to join health insurance societies; health insurance for financial benefits is, however, compulsory.

Benefits

Modern social security schemes are a form of horizontal and vertical redistribution of wealth—from the employed to the unemployed, the young to the old, the single to the married, the rich to the poor, etc. The amount of benefits and the method with which they are paid out are naturally most important to the process of redistribution of wealth. Broadly speaking, benefits can be paid according to three main principles. First, they can be related to individual need. This enables the adjustment of the amount of benefit to the exact needs of the recipient, and may save money by the withholding of benefits from those not in need. It involves, however, the use of skilled staff who may be expensive and the application of a means test which is unacceptable in some countries, Britain, for example. The means test is used in Australia, New Zealand and Canada for some benefits and in Scandinavia for part of the old-age pension. Secondly, social security benefits can be related to average need. The state assumes or estimates what the average person needs and fixes the amount of benefits accordingly. This method is widely used in Scandinavia and Britain. It is easy to administer and it may help to promote a feeling of national social cohesion. On the other hand it is impossible to adjust to individual need with the result that for some the benefits are not needed while for others they are not adequate. The basic old-age pension schemes of Denmark, Finland and Norway involve a combination of the first and second principle, i.e. a basic pension is paid to all irrespective of need and an additional pension according to need. Thirdly, benefits and contributions can be related to earnings. It is argued that poverty and need are relative concepts and therefore social security benefits must take into account the beneficiary's standard of living. It is also in line with the principles of a capitalist economic system as it is supposed to provide an incentive to individual hard work and enterprise. Sometimes earnings-related benefits are the only benefits paid, and this is the case with some sickness and unemployment funds in Scandinavian countries. In other instances—earnings-related old-age pensions in Sweden, Denmark and elsewhere in Scandinavia—earnings-related benefits are paid in addition to the basic benefit. A number of other European countries—e.g. West Germany, Belgium and Britain—use earnings-related benefit schemes. They are becoming increasingly popular in Western Europe with rising prosperity.

Social insurance and health services have traditionally been related. Britain is the only country which has divorced its health services completely from social insurance. Scandinavian countries maintain to a varying degree the connection between insurance and health. Some types of health services —school health service, ante-natal and post-natal services, etc.—are available to all free of charge. Other services are completely free to insured members and their families only—hospital treatment in Denmark, Sweden and Norway. Other services are partially free to insured persons and their families—general practitioners' services. It is difficult to see what good purpose this connection between insurance and medical services serves in countries where health insurance is compulsory and social assistance schemes are also in existence.

A number of Scandinavian social security benefits are tied to the cost of living index. This avoids the protracted party political arguments every time benefits have to be increased to catch up with the rise in prices as happens in Britain. Real rises in the value of benefits, however, have still to be enacted by parliament in every European country. No country in Europe or else-where has yet tied its social security system fully to the wages index.

COOPERATION AMONG SCANDINAVIAN COUNTRIES

Social security benefits are provided to Scandinavian citizens by their country of residence even if it is not their country of origin. This is but one example of the cooperation among Scandinavian countries that has been actively promoted since the end of the last war and particularly since the establishment of the Nordic Council in 1953. Passports are not needed for travel from one Scandinavian country to another, drivers' licences issued in one Scandinavian country are valid in the others, and apart from certain professions work permits are not necessary for citizens of one Scandinavian country who wish to work in another. The area of cooperation covers cultural, social, economic and legal matters. It is expanding constantly, bringing increased unity among Scandinavian countries without affecting their constitutional independence.

BIBLIOGRAPHY

Dixon, C. W. *Society, Schools and Progress in Scandinavia*, Pergamon Press, Oxford and New York, 1965.

Eltz, S. *Health and Pension Insurance in Sweden*, The Swedish Institute, Stockholm, 1963.

Huus, H. *The Education of Children and Youth in Norway*, Univ. of Pittsburgh Press, Pittsburgh, 1960.

Jensen, O. *Social Welfare in Denmark*, Danish Institute, Copenhagen, 1961.

Kerr, Anthony. *Schools of Europe*, Bowes and Bowes, London, 1960; Canterbury Press, Westminster, Md, 1962.

Kuusi, P. *Social Policy for the Sixties: A Plan for Finland*, Finnish Social Policy Association, Helsinki, 1964.

Langholm, M. *Family and Child Welfare in Norway*, Norwegian Joint Committee on International Social Policy, Oslo, 1961.

Lauwerys, J. (ed.) *Scandinavian Democracy*, Danish Institute, Copenhagen, 1958.

Nelleman, A. *Schools and Education in Denmark*, Danish Institute, Copenhagen, 1964.

Skardal, D. *Social Insurance in Norway*, Norwegian Joint Committee on International Social Policy, Oslo, 1960.

Wuorinen, J. *Scandinavia*, Prentice-Hall, Englewood Cliffs, NJ, 1965.

ILO. *Housing Cooperatives*, Geneva, 1964.

Danish Ministry of Housing, et al. *Housing in the Northern Countries*, Copenhagen, 1960.

Swedish Ministry of Health and Social Affairs. *The Right to Security*, Swedish Institute, Stockholm, 1965.

United States Department of Health, Education and Welfare. *Social Security Programs Throughout the World, 1964*, Washington, DC, 1964.

EDUCATION IN WESTERN EUROPE

BRIAN HOLMES

THE countries of Western Europe share common educational traditions, two of which are specially important—the Hellenic and the Judaic-Christian. Each offered suggestions about the intellectual, moral, aesthetic and physical education of children. The intellectualism of European schools stems from Platonic-Aristotelian theories, and the importance placed on moral education from Christian writers. A number of Plato's theories continue to be debated. His belief that among individuals there are innate differences of ability justifies his contention that some people are destined to be policy-makers (guardians), others executive officers (warriors) and the majority artisans. Consequently each individual should be trained for a specific task and, since society should be stable and static, remain content to perform it throughout his or her life. None of these theories has been entirely abandoned. Nor has Aristotle's distinction between an education for the leisured-ruling classes (liberal education) and vocational training for the masses. Indeed it dominates much present-day discussion about curriculum reform. It should also be remembered that although Hellenic concepts of education stressed the all-round development of pupils they maintained that the proportion of children capable of benefiting from such an education was small.

COMMON INSTITUTIONS

The most powerful educational institutions since the Middle Ages have been the universities, originally international centres offering courses in law, theology, medicine and the liberal arts, with Latin as the common language of discourse. Grammar schools, catering for a small minority of children, were established to prepare young people for the universities and the learned professions. Many of them, like the *lycées* of France, were set up and run by the state; England, depending largely on private endeavour until 1902, was an exception. Everywhere the study of the classical languages, Latin and Greek, received much attention. The teachers in these academic secondary schools and the professors in the universities formed a community of scholars. In many countries the links between these two groups remain close principally because all of them are university graduates. The most usual name for the university preparatory school is *Gymnasium* (Austria, Cyprus, Denmark, Germany, the Netherlands, Norway, Sweden, Switzerland); in France it is the *lycée*, in Belgium the *athénée* (boys) and *lycée* (girls) and in Italy the *liceo-classico*. The name in England and Ireland is grammar or independent public school. The trend everywhere is for newer forms of university preparatory school to develop.

Systems of mass education were not firmly established until the 19th century. The points of contact between these schools and the academic grammar schools were slight since the former made no attempt to prepare pupils for university entrance. Between 1870 and 1900, however, primary education was made compulsory (and often free) in industrialised countries. The period of compulsory attendance was lengthened so that by 1920, with few exceptions, children attended school between the ages of 5–7 and 13–15. The basis of the curriculum was the 'three Rs' and by 1950 illiteracy was negligible in Western Europe except in a few countries. (In Italy, among persons over 15 it was reported to be 14 per cent in 1950; in Turkey the figure for children aged 10–14 was just over 42 per cent in 1955, and over 8 per cent in Spain. By 1960 Cyprus had reduced the corresponding figure to below 1 per cent but of the 45–54 age group 37 per cent were still illiterate.)

Gradually, during the 20th century, the schools preparing very young children for the academic secondary schools and those providing education for the mass of children in the elementary system were brought together to form a unified pattern of primary schools. By the end of the second world war most national systems included primary schools to which children went irrespective of ability until the age of 10–12. At this stage pupils were transferred to one of a number of post-primary schools or remained in the senior classes of the same elementary school. A distinction was made between 'secondary schools' which prepared pupils for university entrance and other types of post-primary schools.

Among the latter were special vocational schools where children were trained for particular occupations. In many countries an extensive system of such schools was established; the age at which children entered them varied as did the range of occupations for which they were prepared. England and Wales were exceptional; neither technical nor commercial schools developed at the second stage of education after 1902.

Teacher-training institutions in Europe developed along similar lines. 'Normal' schools were established in the 19th century to train elementary school teachers. At first, and even in 1960, in many countries, students were recruited from the elementary schools. In the training colleges a continuation of general education and professional training was provided. In England and Wales by 1940 the vast majority of intending teachers had attended a secondary school. In general the two systems, elementary and secondary (including teacher-training) were separate.

A somewhat similar duality grew up in higher education. During the 19th century special technological institutions were established to train engineers and commercial personnel. In France the *grandes écoles* achieved the highest prestige; elsewhere the technological institutions were regarded with less favour than the universities. In England most of the 19th-century civic universities evolved from technical colleges.

It may be said that post-war reform movements in Europe have attempted to break down at the second and third stages of education the traditional distinction between schools for members of a small élite and those for the masses, and between liberal education and vocational or manual training.

SOURCES OF NATIONAL AIMS IN EDUCATION

In the 17th and 18th centuries more markedly national aims in education emerged from the common Hellenic-Christian pattern. Justification for

French *culture générale*, for its emphasis on clear logical thinking expressed in French and acquired through the study of mathematics and the classical languages, may be found in the writings of Descartes. Condorcet's plan presented to the French Legislative Assembly in 1792 proposed a universal system of primary schools followed by selective secondary schools and institutions of higher education. It still forms a basis against which present debates in France can be assessed. The corps of administrators which directs educational policy with relatively little political interference is in the direct tradition of the Napoleonic system.

General education in English schools places great stress on character-training based upon non-denominational Christian precepts. Great attention is paid to leadership qualities through the prefect system, team games and extra-curricular activities. An empirical approach to learning is emphasised and the tutorial relationship in all aspects of learning between teacher and taught is important. Justification for many English traditions can be found in the writings of Milton, Locke and Thomas Arnold.

The German traditions of liberal education (*Allgemeine Bildung*) were perhaps best expressed by Wilhelm von Humboldt. The promotion of all-round culture is best achieved through the search for the good, the true and the beautiful, principally through the classics. Scientific research and knowledge for its own sake is stressed rather than teaching and examining. To this view of education as a search for truth should perhaps be added Hegel's claim that knowledge and true meaning are to be found in ideas which transcend outward appearances. One consequence of Humboldt's insistence that research should be pursued without interference from the state has perhaps been that 'true' education in the German sense has taken on an other-wordly appearance, being unrelated to the political, social and economic problems of the day which are to be solved by others who have been trained by vocational schools.

The French, British and German traditions in education continue to inform the outlook of educationalists in major areas of Western Europe. French administrative practices prevail in many countries not only in Europe but throughout the world. Certainly the schools of Belgium and of some cantons in Switzerland reflect French aims and methods. Because of the Roman Catholic Church Italy and Spain have similar attitudes to education without having been influenced greatly by French philosophy and anti-clericalism. The organisation of the schools of Germany, Austria and the Netherlands is similar, and German influence can be detected in Swedish schools. Educational policies in the Scandinavian countries tend to be similar because of a shared culture and conditions of life; indeed, in some aspects of policy collaboration between the three countries has been formalised. Differences exist, of course, and just as the Swedish schools show traces of the German spirit so the Danish schools reflect the strong links that have been forged between Denmark and England. The schools of Iceland have been strongly influenced by Danish patterns.

An identifiable British heritage finds somewhat different expression in the schools of England, Wales, Scotland and Ireland. Important differences in the Scottish system compared with the English are to be found in the long tradition of universal free education which has reduced the proportion and importance of private schools, and in the training of teachers. All teachers are required to take professional training and all male teachers of general subjects must be university graduates whose training lasts four years. Transfer between primary and secondary education is based not on examinations but an assessment of ability by teachers. The senior secondary schools enrol a high percentage (30 per cent) of the primary school leavers and offer a five- or six-year course leading to the Scottish Leaving Certificate. An ordinary grade of this examination was introduced in 1962 for pupils leaving earlier. Junior secondary schools provide a three-year course of general education. University courses in Scotland are much less specialised than in England and the proportion of students per thousand of population is higher; in 1957 it was a little over three per thousand (compare with England and Wales in Table 5 below).

The Northern Ireland Education Act of 1947 is the legal basis of a system which is not very different from the English. Fees are charged in secondary grammar schools but in 1959 certain schools reserved up to 80 per cent of their places for scholarship-holders. In the Republic of Ireland the constitution lays down that the family is the primary and natural educator and respects the inalienable right and duty of parents to provide for the religious needs of children. Parents are also free to provide education in their own homes or in private schools. In 1960 the secondary grammar schools were private institutions receiving state aid. The state provides free primary schools and the secondary vocational schools are administered by local vocational educational authorities. There is no discrimination on the basis of religion.

Turkey offers an example of a system which has been deeply influenced by both Moslem and European traditions. It is under the jurisdiction of the ministry of education. Turkish private schools obey state regulations, and private foreign schools and those for minorities operate under special regulations; their curricula are approved by the ministry and they may be inspected. The modern system owes much to the efforts of Kemal Ataturk in the 1920s and the new secondary schools were modelled on the French *lycées*. In 1959 secondary education was still not compulsory but it was free. In 1926 teacher-training was organised as part of the secondary system; technical and vocational education occupy a very important place in modern Turkey and attract large funds, and a variety of specialities are catered for in four-year vocational schools. The three-year upper secondary schools are divided into arts and science streams. Coeducation is general except in the big towns. In 1959 out of a population of 25 million there were some 30,000 university students, a proportion of just over one per thousand of population. Many of the differences between Turkey and other parts of Western Europe can be explained by the late entry of the country into the process of industrialisation.

POST-WAR DETERMINANTS OF CHANGE

After the second world war three factors created problems in the highly selective systems of education in Western Europe. First, there was an explosion of aspirations and expectations. In education these found expression in demands for an extension of compulsory school attendance and for greater equality of opportunity to enter secondary schools and universities. Secondly, the explosion of population meant that thousands more children crowded into the primary schools in the early fifties, increased the problems of 'secondary' school selection in the middle and late fifties, and created unprecedented pressures to expand on the universities in the early sixties. Thirdly, all the nations which had participated in the war had suffered great material damage, and it is against this background of rising school-age population and economic shortage that the reforms in Western European education should be viewed.

The United Nations Declaration of Human Rights signed in 1948 reflected current views in Article 26: 'Everyone has the right to education. Education shall be free, at least in the elementary stages. Elementary education shall be compulsory'. In Western Europe the demand was for 'secondary education for all'. At the national level these and similar hopes found expression in post-war constitutions and major legislation.

A provision in the French constitution of 1946 (repeated in that of 1958) guaranteed equal access to education, professional training and culture. The post-war constitutions of Italy and Germany were designed to protect the individual's civil and political rights. The 1947 Italian constitution affirmed freedom of education and opened schools to all children. The Federal German constitution granted the state power to supervise education but, because of the religious issue, parents were left free to decide whether a child should receive religious education. These general statements of intent were embodied in legislation.

POST-WAR REFORMS

Between 1945 and 1965 many of the countries forming the Council of Europe passed major educational bills. In England and Wales the wartime coalition government was first, with the 1944 Education Act. Elsewhere reforms were so fiercely debated that it was not until the late fifties and early sixties that educational legislation was finally passed.

One of the main objects of many of these reforms was to reorganise the second stage of education. The Austrian education act of 1962 laid down that children leaving the fourth primary class could go to one of several kinds of post-primary school: the senior classes of the elementary school, the main school (*Hauptschule*) or one of several types of secondary school (*Gymnasium* or modern grammar school). In Belgium experimental post-primary schools were established in 1958 to help the authorities decide on the most suitable education for individual children. The objects of the Danish reforms of 1958 were to reduce the differences between the examination and non-examination middle schools and extend education beyond the eighth class when ten pupils applied for further classes. After years of effort in France a two-year period of observation for children leaving the primary schools was established early in 1959, and the age of compulsory attendance for children entering school after 1 January that year was extended to 16 (decree of 6 January). In the Dutch parliament a bill regulating the country's highly differentiated post-primary school system was passed in July 1962; this offered the possibilities of establishing multilateral schools for the first time. Reform movements in Germany have sought to extend compulsory attendance from eight to nine years and to delay, except for exceptionally able primary-school children, the age of selection for post-primary studies. Proposals to introduce a two-year period of observation and guidance (*Forderstufe*) before a selection to a main school (*Hauptschule*), middle school (*Realschule*) or grammar school (*Gymnasium*) have been hotly debated.

In Norway and Sweden, on the other hand, legislation establishing a common or comprehensive school system was passed in 1959 and 1962 respectively. In Norway a common school (7 to 16) was introduced with the same curriculum for the first six years, and increasing differentiation from the seventh. Pupils go from this school to one of several kinds of secondary school. Sweden established a nine-year comprehensive school after which pupils may transfer to one of various types of school. Post-war legislation in Italy has been designed to make education compulsory for children between the ages of 6 and 14, and to establish middle schools offering a three-year course which will be regarded as a period of guidance.

By 1960 there were two forms of post-primary education in most Western European countries—long and short—which correspond to the traditional differences between 'secondary' and 'elementary'. Three types of school organisation were to be found at this second stage. Structure 1: three types of school—university preparation, teacher-training and technical-commercial —provide parallel post-primary courses of instruction. Structure 2: two types of school provide for university preparation and general non-vocational education. Structure 3: one type of school offers, at least up to the age of 15, a common programme for all children.

Throughout the world there has been a tendency in the post-war decades for school systems to move away from Structure 1 to Structure 2. In 1960 a large number of teacher-training institutions, e.g. in Belgium, Italy and France, were still classified as belonging to the secondary stage of education but in most cases the tendency was for closer links to be forged between teacher-training and higher education. On the other hand, manpower demands resulted in a new emphasis on technical education. Social and political theories tend to support Structure 3, and economic demands Structure 1.

Here it is possible only to describe some of the main features of reform legislation in three countries—England, Sweden and France. Each case reflects, however, important general trends.

England and Wales

Perhaps the most significant aspect of the 1944 English Education Act was the manner in which it abolished the old dual system in terms of control, finance and objectives between 'secondary' and elementary schools. Education was reorganised in three stages—primary, secondary and further—and local education authorities were held responsible to the Minister of Education for providing services at each level. Fees were abolished, a proposal to raise the school leaving age was made, and part-time education in county colleges up to the age of 18 was envisaged. In 1965 the school leaving age was raised to 16 as from 1970. According to the 1944 Act secondary education was to be provided according to the 'age, aptitude and ability' of individual children; beyond this local education authorities were free to organise secondary schools as they wished.

Since about 1946 the Labour Party and Labour-controlled LEAs have favoured a comprehensive school type of structure for secondary education (Structure 3) while the Conservative Party and its supporters have tended to favour a multi-partite scheme of secondary grammar, secondary technical, and secondary modern schools (Structure 1). Between 1945 and 1965 this debate centred on the fairness of the 11-plus procedures, while social scientists showed the extent to which the class origins of parents determine the educational opportunities of their children. Over the years opposition to change weakened and in 1965 a Labour Minister of Education and Science was in a position to ask all LEAs to submit their proposals for moving towards a comprehensive secondary school system.

Sweden

In Sweden the connection between the elementary and the secondary school turned out to be the most crucial problem for the 1940 School Committee. Since 1927 transfer from the primary schools has been possible after either four years or six. The 1946 Parliamentary School Commission appointed by the socialist government proposed to resolve this dilemma by introducing a 'unitary' or 'comprehensive' school organisation for the entire period of compulsory education. The report was fiercely debated and experiments based on the recommendations were tried out in fourteen districts. From 1949 to 1959 these activities were greatly expanded so that about one-third of the school districts had started comprehensive schools. By this time experimentation and research offered evidence that the unitary school offered an appropriate solution to the problem of differentiation. In 1963 parliament resolved that compulsory attendance at school was to be extended to nine years for all children.

The new school was called the comprehensive school (*grundskolan*) which all children were to attend, and the system was to be introduced gradually and completed during the school year 1972–3. The new school is divided into three departments, a lower department (grades 1–3), a middle department (grades 4–6), and an upper department (grades 7–9). In the lower and middle departments all the pupils of an age group take the same subjects and pupils in one class are taught by the same teacher. As far as possible these practices continue in grades 7 and 8 but in addition a number of optional subjects are offered so that for the first time pupils are divided into groups according to their option. A common nucleus of subjects is studied together, however. In the ninth grade there are nine streams and five sections, two of which are practical and two theoretical. The principle accepted is that parents choose the subjects their children are to study in the upper department. After the comprehensive school children may transfer to one of two kinds of shorter education—a two-year continuation school or a three-year vocational school—or to one of two kinds of longer education, namely an academic grammar school (*gymnasium*) with various sections or a vocational *gymnasium* (technical or commercial) lasting three years. In principle the Swedish reform delays selection and differentiation until the ninth year of school and even then choice is based upon parents' wishes in consultation with the pupil after information has been provided to them by the school.

France

The object of the French educational reforms is also to delay selection and differentiation. The concept of a period of observation and guidance was introduced into legislation passed in 1959 after many attempts had been made to introduce bills in the French parliament. The reforms are in principle based on the recommendations of the Langevin-Wallon Committee (1947) for an undifferentiated post-primary school (*école unique*) from the ages of 11 to 15. Only under the presidency of General de Gaulle was it possible to issue a number of decrees and ordinances designed radically to reform the structure of French education at the second stage. The decree of 6 January 1959 (see p. 468 above) covered all the important aspects of education. Compulsory schooling has three stages: an elementary cycle from the age of six and lasting five years; an observation cycle lasting two years provided in various types of post-primary school; and a terminal cycle of varying length provided in one of a variety of institutions. The object of the observation cycle is to assess the abilities of children so as to advise parents on the most appropriate form of subsequent education. Orientation councils are responsible for this advice which, if accepted by parents, allows children to follow a chosen course. If parents prefer another course then their child takes an examination to establish his or her ability to follow it. Possibilities of transfer from one stream to another exist and opportunities are provided for children who have not been admitted earlier to a regular orientation class to take an examination at about the age of 13 to enter special classes to prepare them for the course of studies chosen by them.

By a ministerial decree of 1962 the cycle of observation and orientation was extended from two to four years. The 1959 decree provided for shorter education courses after the period of orientation in either general secondary or technical schools. Longer education is provided in general or technical lycées, courses leading to the higher school leaving examination (*baccalauréat*). Under the 1959 reforms there were three sections in the first two years of the five-year course, seven sections in the third and fourth years and five in the fifth year. Under the scheme extending observation and orientation to four years the distinction between long and short education remains and except for the classical language option the integration of study programmes is to continue. Long general education in classical and modern lycées leads to the universities. Long technical education also leads to higher technical education for those who are successful. The tendency since 1962 has been to move towards Structure 2, providing a variety of courses in general secondary schools. In these schools, too, there is from the age of 12 (largely for rural children) a two-year transitional stream followed by terminal practical education taught by general secondary school and specialised teachers. Thus the intention is virtually to postpone selection (except for very able children who select the classical language option) until the end of nine years schooling.

Common principles

The principle of a period of guidance immediately following the primary stage of education has been accepted in many countries. By 1963 at least eight countries had either introduced, were experimenting with or were contemplating the introduction of such a period. In Germany the period under debate was from 10 to 12 in the *Forderstufe*. Experiments in Belgium offered three years of guidance from 12 to 15. In Denmark this stage was legally from 12 to 14. In Italy a reform project proposed 11 to 14. Swiss and Dutch proposals (1963) were for one-year guidance programmes between 12 and 13 and in Turkey between 11 and 14. Much of the legislation proposed that changes should be introduced gradually, so that it is still not possible to say how effective reform at the second stage of education has been.

In general it may be said that with few exceptions children in countries belonging to the Council of Europe enter school at the age of 6. England and Wales are exceptional in that attendance is from the age of 5. In Iceland, Norway and Sweden it is 7. The primary stage proper lasts between the ages of 4 and 6, transfer taking place between 10 (Germany) and 12 (Austria, Belgium, Cyprus, Greece, Luxembourg, the Netherlands and Switzerland). Transfer is at 11 in Denmark, France, England and Wales, Italy, Spain and Turkey. For some children the primary or second primary stage is prolonged: in Austria and Norway to 14, and in Iceland and Sweden to 13. Selection or transfer procedures have traditionally been based upon examination and other test results. In 1963 this was still the case in Austria, Spain, Greece, Ireland, Italy, Luxembourg, the Netherlands, Switzerland, Turkey and Britain. At that time several of these countries were proposing to change the system by replacing competitive examinations by other methods of assessing the interests and abilities of pupils. Reform movements have generally made the age of transfer less precise than formerly.

The age of compulsory school attendance varies too. By 1965 legislation had been passed raising the leaving age to 16 in the following countries: France (effective 1967), Britain (effective 1970), Sweden under the 1962 reforms, and some cantons of Switzerland. Fifteen was the age in some of the Länder of Germany, in Austria, Iceland, most areas of Norway and in the Netherlands. Fourteen was still the leaving age in Belgium, Denmark, Ireland, Italy, Luxembourg and Turkey. In Cyprus, Spain and Greece it was still 12. Encouragement to stay beyond the statutory age on a voluntary basis was given in 1963 in Belgium, Spain, Ireland, Italy, the Netherlands, Denmark and Turkey.

EFFECTS OF POPULATION PRESSURES

In practice the good intentions of the reformers were thwarted, modified or abandoned as a result of political and professional opposition and hard economic facts. Perhaps of greatest importance, however, were the forces of expansion arising from the post-war population explosion. The resulting increase in primary-school enrolments and in the proportion of school-age members of the total population in the long run, irrespective of national policies, created pressures on the secondary schools and universities.

The bulge in crude birth rates during 1945–9, taking figures for the thirties as a base, was around 30 per cent. In Denmark the crude birth rate rose from about 18 per thousand of population in 1935–9 to about 22 per thousand during the period 1945–9; in France in the same period from 15 to about 20; in the Netherlands from 20 to 26; and in England and Wales from about 15 to 18. Only in a few countries, e.g. Germany, Italy and Spain, did the crude birth rates in the late forties remain steady or drop compared with the rates during the late thirties.

The resulting increases in births in the post-war period were impressive. In France in 1940 some 559,000 babies were born, in 1945 the figure was 643,000 and by 1950 it had reached 862,000. In England and Wales in 1940 births numbered approximately 540,000, in 1945 they were 680,000, and by 1950 the figure was 698,000. These increases were of the order of 3 to 6 per cent p.a. Furthermore, infant mortality rates dropped everywhere between 1945 and 1960. The rates in Scandinavia, the Netherlands and England and Wales were always less than in France, Italy and Spain. But in France the rates dropped from some 72 per thousand live births during 1945–9 to 46 in 1950–4 and 21 in 1960. In Sweden the corresponding figures were 26 in 1945–9, 20 in 1950–4 and 17 in 1960. In England and Wales the drop was from 39 in 1945–9 to 28 in 1950–4 and 22 in 1960.

These trends account for the increases in the number of school-age children. Statistics are not readily available but throughout Western Europe UNESCO population figures show that between 1955 and 1960 the size of the 5–9 age-group remained fairly constant at around 36 millions. There was an increase of some two millions in the size of the 10–14 age-group over the same period and a rise of four millions in the 15–19 age-group. These

TABLE 1

PRIMARY SCHOOL ENROLMENTS (*thousands*)

	1950	*1955*	*1960*	Percentage increase *1950–60*
Austria	856	747	722	Fall
Belgium	804	839	919	14
Denmark	434	526	559	29
France	4,063	5,171	5,822	45
Germany (Fed. Rep.)	6,377	4,865	5,081	Fall
Greece	900	948	921	2.3
Iceland	15	17	23	53
Ireland	468	501	501	29
Italy	4,640	4,741	4,494	Fall
Netherlands	1,241	1,452	1,416	14
Norway	343	447	430	Reclassification
Spain	2,793	3,117	3,777	32
Sweden	707	844	808	14
Turkey	1,617	1,982	2,866	77
UK (England and Wales)	4,066	4,714	4,302	5.7

crude statistics show how the post-war population explosion affected the different stages of education between 1945 and 1965.

UNESCO statistics (see Table 1 above) show how the increases in primary school-age populations were reflected in school enrolments in the early fifties. By the second half of this decade the rate of increase had slowed down and in some countries had declined. Approximate figures give some idea of trends, but it should be noted that comparative educational statistics need to be used with care because of changes in systems of classification and because of the difficulties of establishing categories which apply equally to all countries.

Increased secondary school enrolments reflect not only school-age population increases but changes in government policy. Raising the school leaving age obviously made a considerable difference but many campaigns

TABLE 2

GENERAL SECONDARY SCHOOL ENROLMENTS (*thousands*)

	1950	*1955*	*1960*	Percentage rise *1950–60*
Austria	54	79	81	50
Belgium	123	237	292	137
Denmark	98	128	130	32
France	818	1,027	1,701	106
Germany (Fed. Rep.)	829	1,169	1,239	50
Greece	185	200	273	47
Iceland	5	6	10	96
Ireland	54	65	83	56
Italy	533	697	1,624	Reclassification
Netherlands	216	317	483	120
Norway	33	49	129	Reclassification
Spain	222	328	476	114
Sweden	135	177	222	75
Turkey	90	165	373	314
UK (England and Wales)	1,975	2,395	3,261	66

to encourage pupils to remain at school on a voluntary basis have also had an effect. Changes in terminology and hence the classification of school types also influence figures. As stated, opportunities to enrol in general, technical or teacher-training secondary schools exist. Some indication can be gained from enrolment figures in general secondary and technical secondary schools of policies of expansion at the second stage. Turkey provides an example of a phenomenal expansion of secondary education. The growth in enrolments in Norway reflects reorganisation under the reform laws. The approximate figures in Table 2 are derived from UNESCO sources.

Enrolments in vocational education should be treated with care because in Germany and Austria vast numbers take part-time vocational instruction. The age range of such students is very considerable. It should also be noted that there are usually at least two levels at which technical education is provided at the second stage. One level prepares technicians and other highly skilled personnel who might expect to become foremen in industry or commerce. Very approximate statistics, nevertheless, give some indication of the extent to which, as a result of expansion, technical education has been relatively neglected or received a proportion of the increase in students similar to that of the general schools, or gained on them proportionally (Table 3 below).

TABLE 3

VOCATIONAL SECONDARY SCHOOL ENROLMENTS (*thousands*)

	1950	*1955*	*1960*	Percentage rise *1950–60*
Austria	111	189	210[1]	90
Belgium	228	238	339	49
Denmark	112	121	145	30
France	242	292	550	128
Germany (Fed. Rep.)	1,832	2,482	1,866[1]	1.8
Iceland	3	2.6	2.8	Fall
Ireland	518	743	460	Fall
Italy	518	743	460	Fall
Netherlands	282	347	488	75
Norway	46	48	50	Fall
Spain	154	167	209	26
Sweden	95	120	171	80

[1]Includes part-time enrolments.

With few exceptions the tendency to expand general secondary rather than vocational secondary education is apparent from these tables. It would be unwise to say more than that this suggests that Structure 2 represents an intermediate phase of development between Structure 1 and Structure 3 in the evolution of the second stage of education in Western Europe.

EXAMINATIONS AND UNIVERSITY EXPANSION

The highly selective character of the educational systems of Western Europe was, and in 1965 continued to be, maintained by examination systems which served three functions—selection, testing acquired knowledge and providing acceptable vocational qualifications. Children face major examinations at three main points in their school career: on transfer from primary school, at the end of shorter secondary education and when they are legally able to leave school, and at the end of longer secondary education when they are about to leave school before entering a university or other institution of higher learning. It may be said that in practice the examinations which are taken at the end of shorter secondary education cover general, technical and vocational subjects. The system in England and Wales is less diversified and there is a close connection between General Certificate of Education 'O' levels and 'A' levels.

In France the examination system is particularly highly organised. Each stage of education is completed by a certificate or diploma which qualifies the student either to proceed to the next stage of education or to enter a particular occupation or profession. Thus there is a certificate at the end of primary education, certificates for various levels of technical competence and a leaving certificate for those who leave at the end of the short general education. The final *baccalauréat* is prepared for by students in the lycées or technical lycées and colleges in classical, modern or technical studies. To enter one of the higher institutes (grandes écoles) special competitive examinations have to be taken. Possession of a baccalauréat gives automatic right to any French university.

Between 1962 and 1965 this examination was the subject of considerable debate concerned with the desirability of making it the final school examination instead of the first university examination. The tradition of a two-part examination (the first part was to be abolished in favour of a qualifying test or, desirably, school records) and the desirability of adding some conditions to the requirement that entrants to the university should have a baccalauréat was also discussed. During the period 1960–65 further attempts were made to use the baccalauréat as a link between the two separate systems of teacher education, that for elementary school teachers and that for academic secondary school teachers (see p. 471 above). The fact that diplomas in technical education are considered equivalent to parts of the baccalauréat helps to break down the distinction between university preparation and other forms of long secondary education.

Throughout continental Europe the tradition remains that the final examination at the end of the classical option in the university-preparatory form of long education gives access to all the faculties of the university. Other options have been added to these final examinations. In Germany the examination is called the *Abitur*, in Austria (*Matura*), Switzerland (*Maturité*) and Italy (*Maturita*) the maturity examination, and in Scandinavia the *Student* examination. Since 1945 a movement has grown to open a second way to the universities to students from less academic secondary schools or who have studied subjects other than classical languages. In 1963 in the Netherlands a proposal was under consideration to admit to examinations of all faculties of the universities persons with any one of the certificates indicating completion of study in a pre-university school. (Previously some faculties were restricted to students with classical certificates.) Again, there has been a move to make technical diplomas equivalent to university entrance examinations. In Italy, students holding diplomas from certain vocational institutes may be admitted to the appropriate university faculties. Another way of providing an alternative way to the university is to establish special tests for students who have come up through non-university preparation schools. In some German Länder such tests are given to students from engineering schools who wish to enter higher technical schools (*Technische Hochschulen*).

In England and Wales the formal requirements for entry to a university are based upon success in the General Certificate of Education (GCE) Examination which is administered by a number of university examining boards on the advice of a schools examination council. This examination is at two levels: the 'O' (ordinary) level papers are usually taken by students after five years at a secondary school and the 'A' (advance) level papers after seven or eight years of secondary education. Passes at ordinary level are required for entry to colleges of education and are also accepted for entry to some of the higher technical certificate courses. They are in general accepted by employers as evidence that a candidate has received a good general education. (The Certificate of Secondary Education is intended for pupils at the secondary modern schools, i.e. the shorter form of secondary education.) The minimum university entrance requirements are two advance level passes, presupposing that the student will have passed a number of papers (between five and ten subjects) at the ordinary level. In 1965, except in science and technological subjects, university entrance requirements were actually higher than the minimum. Each university and department within a university is free to accept students on the basis of GCE results and an interview. Colleges within the Universities of Oxford and Cambridge have a special scholarship examination which is highly competitive.

Attempts have been made to reduce the distinction between universities and higher technological institutes. Since the war the status of the latter has risen in some countries, such as Germany and the Netherlands, where their standing had previously been inferior to that of the universities. In England and Wales colleges of advanced technology were created out of some major technical colleges. They provided, in technology, courses of a standard comparable to those given in the universities. The Robbins Committee Report of 1963 recommended that several colleges of advanced technology should be transformed into technical universities.

Throughout Europe the expansion of secondary education resulted in increases in the number of students possessing the minimum qualifications to enter university. The demand for places rose particularly when children born in the period 1945–9 reached the age of 18 or 19. Facilities, especially in the behavioural and natural sciences, could not keep pace with demand. The following approximate UNESCO figures are a significant index of the post-war expansion of education generally.

TABLE 4

AVERAGE ANNUAL UNIVERSITY ENROLMENTS 1937–40

Country	Total population (millions)	University students (thousands)	Students per thousand of population
Belgium	8½	12	1·4
France	42	84	2
Italy	45	72	1·9
Netherlands	8½	9	1·1
Sweden	6¼	9	1·3
UK (England and Wales)	46	55	1·2

TABLE 5

UNIVERSITY ENROLMENTS 1960

Country	Total population (millions)	University students (thousands)	Students per thousand of population
Belgium	9	52	5·8
France	45½	215	4·7
Italy	49½	192	3·9
Netherlands	11½	106	9
Sweden	7½	37	4·9
UK (England and Wales)	46¼	138	2·9

The changing distribution of students among the faculties during the expansion of the decade 1950–60 shows marked tendencies. The faculties which gained were education, the social sciences, the natural sciences and engineering. Enrolments in social science were almost trebled in Belgium, the Netherlands and Sweden and rose almost seven times in Turkey. Between three and four times as many students were enrolled in the natural sciences in Belgium, France and Turkey. The general trend was towards the new professional subjects—a reflection of manpower demands in the sixties.

Proportions of foreign students remained fairly constant in most countries over the decade 1950–60, but the level varied, e.g. Belgium 5 per cent, Denmark one per cent, France 10 per cent, Switzerland 30 per cent and the UK (England and Wales) 10 per cent. There was a big jump in the percentage of foreign students in Austria from 9 per cent in 1950 to 27 per cent in 1960. In 1962 Austria had foreign students from 79 countries, Belgium from 88, France from 99, Switzerland from 76 and the UK from 104. Countries with former empires drew most heavily from territories previously within these empires, e.g. France from North Africa and Vietnam. More than a thousand students from the United States were studying in each of the following countries: France, Germany and Britain. Relatively few students from Britain were studying in continental Europe but over a thousand in Ireland. Switzerland was the only country which attracted French students in any numbers. Various policies designed to facilitate the exchange of students are in operation. For example, in 1964 the French authorities agreed to accept the European baccalauréat given by six European schools in Luxembourg, Brussels, Mol, Varese, Karlsruhe and Bergen as equivalent to their own award. They also laid down equivalents between certain levels of university study in France and stages of undergraduate study in accredited US institutions. Among high-income countries the interchange of students is more pronounced at the postgraduate than at the undergraduate level.

THE CONTENT OF EDUCATION

The curricula of continental university preparation schools differ from the curriculum of the English grammar school in that a much broader spectrum of subjects is studied for a longer period. In the early classes of secondary schools the pattern is similar. During the first stage of longer education the following subjects are widely studied: native tongue, Latin for some pupils, a modern language, mathematics, history, geography, science, physical education, arts and music. Concentration for all pupils on modern languages is greatest in those countries like Denmark and the Netherlands whose language is spoken by relatively few people. The teaching of religion may be

477

compulsory (Denmark, Italy), provided but dependent on the wishes of parents (England and Wales, Germany) or excluded from the school curriculum (France).

At the second level of the academic secondary schools there is less specialisation in continental Europe than in England and Wales. In the Dutch gymnasium in the last two years of study (fifth and sixth) there are two sections, A and B. All pupils study Greek, Latin, Dutch, German, English, history, geography, mathematics, science and physical education. Those on the A side have additional Greek and Latin, those on the B additional mathematics, physics, chemistry and biology. In the modern grammar schcol Greek is omitted, and for one stream commercial and economic subjects added. The nine-year course in the German classical gymnasium has nine years of Latin, six of Greek, seven of English or French, together with mathematics, science, history, geography, physical education, art, music and an optional second language. In the modern gymnasium two modern languages and Latin are studied; one of these is replaced by additional physics, chemistry and biology in the mathematical gymnasium. In the second cycle of French long education, i.e. the fifth and sixth years of study, there are seven sections; a core of French, one modern language, history, geography, mathematics, science, physical education, art and music is taken by all pupils. Differentiation is on the basis of emphasis on classics, modern languages or science. In the last two years—the terminal classes—philosophy is studied in each of the sections together with some seven to nine other academic subjects.

In England and Wales the classical tradition has not been retained as strongly as on the Continent and the balance between the arts and sciences is somewhat distorted; in the grammar schools curricula become very specialised after the conclusion of the short general education, i.e. after 'O' levels. In the last three years of a grammar school, in the sixth forms, a pupil is unlikely to study more than four related subjects and frequently fewer. In these schools the number of pupils taking science subjects increased after the war until by 1965 arts and sciences were roughly in balance.

One of the main educational problems in Western Europe today is to provide through science and technology the kind of liberal and liberalising education which was previously obtained through the study of either classical or modern languages. The vocational schools have hardly achieved this aim. For the most part their purpose has been to prepare young people for very specific occupations. Although it is true that only in the last two years of secondary technical courses is the major part of the timetable devoted to technical subjects, in practice it has proved difficult to achieve John Dewey's ideal of providing a sound general education through vocational studies.

Another issue profoundly affects Western European education. History has traditionally been taught in most countries not only for its own sake but as a way of creating and perpetuating national attitudes. In the process history has been one of the agencies of nationalism (just as the vernaculars were after the breakdown of Latin as a lingua-franca). Attempts have been made in the present century to improve the teaching of history from the viewpoint of improving European understanding. Agencies in the Scandinavian countries, Germany and various international organisations have closely studied history text-books with a view to modifying or removing interpretations likely to lead to ultra-nationalism. In a positive way the teaching of history could make a real contribution to the development of

European attitudes among school children. A number of experimental schools now exist which attempt to promote such attitudes in a more formal manner by drawing together young people from various countries of Europe. For example, Atlantic College in Wales provides sixth-form courses for students from sixteen different countries. Through extra-curricular activities it is hoped that European understanding will be developed and that the courses provided will enable any student to enter any European university.

The forces of integration in Western European education in the sixties are growing, though more slowly than economic and political collaboration. The Council of Europe is playing a part in establishing equivalence of university diplomas that give access to the professions. It has started to work on the Europeanisation of higher education, and there have resulted a convention on the equivalence of diplomas leading to admission to universities (1954), and a convention on the academic recognition of university qualifications (1961). In the Western European Union the Conference of University Rectors was set up to ensure contacts and the exchange of ideas furthering greater unity. The Conference of European Ministers of Education is independent of the Council of Europe but uses its services to examine issues of common concern.

It is evident that the forces of political and economic integration in Western Europe will result in a wider dissemination of information about educational practices. The nations of Western Europe will wish to gear education to the achievement of shared goals, yet at the same time to use it, as in the past, to perpetuate cherished national traditions. The achievement of a balance between European unity and national diversity offers an exciting challenge. There are signs that educationists have accepted it.

BIBLIOGRAPHY

Bowles, Frank H. *Access to Higher Education*, 2 vols, UNESCO, Paris, 1963 and 1965.
Cramer, J. F. and Browne, G. S. *Contemporary Education. A Comparative Study of National Systems*, Harcourt, Brace and World, New York, 2nd ed. 1965.
Dent, H. C. *The Educational System of England and Wales*, London Univ. Press, London, 1961.
Dixon, Willis. *Education in Denmark*, Harrap, London, 1958.
Fraser, W. R. *Education and Society in Modern France*, Routledge and Kegan Paul, London; Humanities Press, New York, 1963.
Hans, Nicholas A. *Comparative Education*, Routledge and Kegan Paul, London, 3rd ed. 1958.
Holmes, Brian. *Problems in Education. A Comparative Approach*, Routledge and Kegan Paul, London; Humanities Press, New York, 1965.
Huebner, Theodore. *The Schools of West Germany*, New York Univ. Press, New York, 1963.
Husen, Torsten and Henrysson, Sten (eds.) *Differentiation and Guidance in the Comprehensive School*, Almqvist and Wiksell, Stockholm, 1959.
Kerr, Anthony. *The Schools of Europe*, Bowes and Bowes, London, 1960; Canterbury Press, Westminster, Md., 1961. *The Universities of Europe*, Bowes and Bowes, London; Canterbury Press, Westminster, Md., 1962.
Majault, J. *Teacher Training* (Education in Europe, Section II No. 4), Council of Europe, Strasbourg, 1965.
Majault, J. and Thomas, J. *Primary and Secondary Education: Modern Trends and Common Problems*, Council of Europe, Strasbourg, 1963.
Sasnett, M. T. *Educational Systems of the World*, Univ. of Southern California Press, Los Angeles, 1952.
International Bureau of Education, Geneva/UNESCO, Paris. *International Yearbook of Education*, 1933–39 and 1946–.
OECD, Paris. *Resources of Scientific and Technical Personnel in the OECD Area*, 1965.
Year Book of Education, Evans Bros., London, for University of London Institute of Education (since 1953 with Teachers College, Columbia University, NY), annually from 1932 (except 1939–45); published since 1965 as *World Year Book of Education*.

THE CHURCHES OF WESTERN EUROPE

GLEN GARFIELD WILLIAMS

AN examination of the exceedingly complicated ecclesiastical structure of Western Europe is simplified if the region is divided into six well-defined areas, within which there are, generally, considerable similarities between church life in one country and another. These areas are the Latin countries (France, Belgium, Luxembourg, Italy, Spain and Portugal), the British Isles, the Protestant European mainland (West Germany, the Netherlands and Switzerland), Scandinavia (Norway, Sweden, Denmark, Finland and Iceland), Central Europe (Austria) and the Eastern Mediterranean (Greece and Turkey). Two events have been mainly responsible for the development and consolidation of these areas.

The first event was the Great Schism of 1054: the churches of the Eastern Orthodox and Roman Catholic traditions sundered their relationships to the thundering of mutual anathemas by Pope Leo IX and the Patriarch Michael Cerularius of Constantinople. After the Schism the Roman Catholics held all of Western and most of Central Europe. The Orthodox were supreme in the Eastern Mediterranean and Eastern European areas. Both churches officially regretted the Schism at the Second Vatican Council of 1965.

The second event was the conclusion of the Peace of Westphalia which terminated the Thirty Years War in 1648. In that frightful struggle the forces of the Protestant Reformation and the Roman Catholic Counter-Reformation fought each other to exhaustion. The result was the clear definition of areas of Roman Catholic, Lutheran or Reformed (Presbyterian) influence. In England, in the meantime, the position of the Anglican Church was being consolidated against Presbyterian, Independent and Baptist movements.

The last three hundred years have seen little significant change in the ecclesiastical balance of power in Western Europe. The Roman Catholic Church is strongest in the Latin countries, in Central Europe and in the Republic of Ireland. Scandinavia and northern and eastern Germany are mainly Lutheran. The Presbyterians are strongest in Switzerland, the Rhine Valley, the Netherlands and Scotland. The Church of England cares for the souls of the majority of the English and Welsh.

It should be remembered that the obtaining of exact and comparable membership statistics for churches is a virtual impossibility, partly because precise central records are often not available and partly because churches have differing methods of assessing membership. The figures quoted hereafter refer, in a general way, to the 'community' covered by the church concerned. The figures are intended to give some idea of comparative strengths and should not be taken as precise statistics. Further, they do not refer to actual church attendance, but rather to denominational allegiance. In the large churches, especially, church attendance varies from about 2 to 10 per cent, except for special occasions such as Christmas and Easter. Usually attendance in country areas is relatively higher than in urban.

THE LATIN COUNTRIES

This area, which includes France, Belgium, Luxembourg, Italy, Spain and Portugal, is characterised by the overwhelming strength of the Roman Catholic Church. In Spain, Portugal, Italy and Luxembourg, some 99 per cent of the population is claimed by this church, in Belgium the percentage is slightly lower, at about 97 per cent, and in France it is 94 per cent. Percentages of practising Roman Catholics would be considerably lower. It would be erroneous, however, to conclude that similarity of membership percentages implies identity of atmosphere and activity in the Roman Catholic Church in these countries. Even before the events of the Second Vatican Council many French and some Belgian Roman Catholics, both clergy and laymen, were much more open to the challenges of the modern world and were less traditionalist than their counterparts in the other countries in the area.

Concordats, which ensure the recognition either of express rights of the church within the state, or of rights of the state in the sphere of religion, exist between the Vatican and Italy, Spain and Portugal. Yet distinctions are to be noted as between these three countries. In Spain and Italy the Roman Catholic Church is the established church, but while in Spain there is constitutionally no religious liberty, in Italy there is a guarantee of complete religious liberty in the constitutional provisions. Although Portugal has a concordat and it is required that Portuguese law should be inspired by Christian principles, there is no established church in that country and there is a relatively advanced degree of religious freedom.

The degree and methods of exerting influence on political affairs also vary from country to country. In Spain the Roman Catholic Church takes a clear and public part in political affairs; in Italy its influence, although none the less real than in Spain, tends to be used in a more covert fashion. This is still truer of Portugal, while in the non-concordat countries of the area the influence of the Roman Catholic Church is exerted in the form of moral pressure on public opinion rather than direct religious or canonical pressure on governments.

In the sphere of education the state schools of Portugal are non-confessional, although under Roman Catholic influence; in Spain and Italy the state schools are confessional, although it is much easier to establish private non-confessional schools in Italy than in Spain. Belgium and Luxembourg permit religious instruction in their schools, whereas in France this is permitted only as a subject contributory to the study of other subjects.

The hierarchical structure in the various countries is similar, with the archbishop of a specific diocese in each country always functioning as 'primate' of the country as a whole. In Italy the primate is the Pope. Following the decisions of the Second Vatican Council national episcopal conferences, consisting of two parts—an assembly of all bishops and an assembly of all metropolitans—are being established.

In each of the Latin countries there exist several Protestant churches, which represent at best a small, and more generally an infinitely small, proportion of the population. Most of these churches are the result of mission work established by Protestant churches from Europe and America. Until recently a number of these missions and churches worked under severe disabilities and, sometimes, outright persecution.

For its size Portugal has an unusually large number of Protestant churches and missions, although most have no more than a few hundred members. More important bodies are the Assemblies of God, the Baptists, the Brethren, the Presbyterians, the Methodists, the Lusitanian Church—which has close ties with the Anglican Communion—and the Seventh-Day Adventists, with communities ranging from 2,000 to 5,000. Most of these churches have small communities in Madeira and the Azores.

In the mid-16th century Spain experienced an indigenous movement of reformation. Small but lively, it exercised a considerable influence also outside Spain, especially in southern Italy. It was obliterated by the Counter-Reformation. Protestant missions first began to work in Spain about a century ago and churches have developed as a result. Apart from several extremely small communities and missions the largest bodies are the Baptists, the Brethren and the Spanish Evangelical Church—a united church having Presbyterian, Congregationalist and Methodist elements. Each of these bodies probably has 8,000 to 10,000 members. The Federation of Independent Evangelical Churches and the Assemblies of God number about 3,000 members each, whilst the Spanish Reformed Episcopal Church—in close relationship with the Anglican Communion—has some 2,000 members.

Religious liberty has been an essential element in the Belgian constitution since 1830 and both the larger Protestant churches—the Belgian Protestant Evangelical Church and the Belgian Christian Missionary Church—are well over a century old. They each claim about 10,000 members. The Methodists and the Belgian Evangelical Mission have some 3,000 members each, and there are smaller groups of Seventh-Day Adventists and Baptists, together with several missions.

Luxembourg, where religious affairs are still regulated on the basis of the Napoleonic Code, has a Lutheran Church of some 5,000 souls. Of recent years several active congregations of a Free Church nature have also come into being.

Protestantism in Italy is remarkable for several features. The Waldensian Church, of the Presbyterian order and having some 30,000 members, is the oldest surviving Protestant church in the world, antedating the other Reformation churches by 300 years or so. Further, it is remarkable how rapidly various Pentecostal communities have taken root, mainly in the south and Sicily, to form, together with the Assemblies of God, probably the largest Protestant groups. There are Baptist, Methodist, Lutheran and Seventh-Day Adventist Churches, whose numbers range from 15,000 to 5,000 souls.

In France also there is a history of Lutheran and Presbyterian churches dating back to the 16th century, giving France a Protestant population of about 1 million—more than 2 per cent of the population. The chief elements here are the Reformed Church of France (400,000), the Reformed Church of Alsace-Lorraine (50,000), the Lutheran Church of Alsace-Lorraine (250,000) and the Lutheran Evangelical Church (50,000). Other communities, with memberships ranging from 2,000 to 7,000, are the Mennonites, Methodists, Baptists and Seventh-Day Adventists. A number of independent missions are also very active.

The Salvation Army, which has been particularly affected by the political vicissitudes of this century, is now active in Belgium, France and Italy.

The communist revolutions and the refugees following the two world wars have meant the introduction into most of the Latin countries of Orthodox communities, mainly very small and of Russian origin. They are to be found in Spain, France, Belgium and Italy. Particularly in France and Italy some of the communities have taken root and attracted converts from the indigenous population.

THE BRITISH ISLES

Although it is convenient to consider the British Isles as a self-contained area in this study, its definition as an area is based on geographical rather than ecclesiastical considerations. Indeed, the British Isles, including the Irish Republic, present in a comparatively small compass the greatest variety of churches and ecclesiastical practices to be found in Western Europe, and possibly anywhere else except the United States. Around the privileged positions of three established or national churches is a constellation of Free Churches of various derivations. The rise, continuity and strength of the various British Free Churches is one of the important characteristics of this area.

In England itself the Church of England is at once a national and established church, counting amongst its baptised members about 65 per cent of the population. Both in its origin, doctrine and practice the Church of England is not to be identified with the churches of the continental Reformation, even though their development took place contemporaneously during the 16th century. The Anglican Church sees itself as a 'bridge', in some respects, between the churches of the Reformation and the Roman Catholic traditions and maintains its claim to preserve the Apostolic Succession. The next largest church in England is the Roman Catholic, claiming a community of some five-and-a-half million and showing signs of considerable missionary activity.

Amongst the major Free Churches the largest is also the youngest, since the Methodist Church, counting about two-and-a-quarter million in its community, came into being at the end of the 18th century, when it was separated from the Anglican Church. Today reunion talks are in progress. The older Free Churches—the Congregationalists, Presbyterians and Baptists—all of which date from the 16th and early 17th centuries, are considerably smaller. The Congregationalists and Baptists have about 200,000 members each and the Presbyterians about 70,000. Added to these there is an active group of various churches and independent congregations of Pentecostalist and revivalist nature, and, particularly as a result of the refugee movements of this century, Lutheran and Orthodox communities.

In Wales the general situation is similar and a number of the central church organisations are common to England and Wales. One or two points should be noted, however. The Anglican Church was disestablished in 1920, when the 'Church in Wales' became a separate province of the Anglican Communion. There is, moreover, a considerably higher proportion of Free Church membership in Wales than in England. Generally the Welsh-speaking sections of the older Free Churches are organised independently of the common central organisations mentioned above.

Scotland has maintained a close relationship with the continental Reformation since the days of John Knox, and Presbyterian influence is strong. Here the national church is the Church of Scotland—a Presbyterian church of over 1,300,000 members. There are four smaller churches of the Presbyterian order constituting a community of 50,000 altogether. The second largest ecclesiastical body is the Roman Catholic which, mainly as a result of the influx of Irish labour to the Scottish industrial areas, numbers nearly 800,000 members. The Anglican Church, entitled the Episcopal Church in Scotland, claims some 56,000 members; the Congregationalists follow with 35,000 members, the Baptists with 20,000 and the Methodists with about 13,500 members.

In Ireland, with minor exceptions, the organisation of the churches is not divided between the Province of Northern Ireland and the Republic. The dominant church on the Irish scene is, of course, the Roman Catholic, which claims 94 per cent of the population of the Republic and 35 per cent of that of Northern Ireland. The Church of Ireland, belonging to the Anglican Communion, has a community of about 280,000, the Presbyterian Church in Ireland about 135,000 and the Methodist Church about 33,000. The Baptists, with a little over 5,000 members, and the Congregationalists, with some 2,000 members, complete the picture of the main churches. Ever since the establishment of the Irish Free State there has been a marked tendency for non-Roman Catholics to move towards Northern Ireland. A considerable number of missions of a revivalist character flourish in Northern Ireland.

THE PROTESTANT EUROPEAN MAINLAND

In each of the three countries which comprise this area—the Netherlands, West Germany and Switzerland—there are, in fact, quite large Roman Catholic minorities. Nevertheless, these are the three countries on the Western European mainland in which the Reformation of the 16th century was strongest and where the main influence is still Protestant. The main Protestant churches in these countries derive from either the Lutheran or the Calvinistic Reformation traditions—churches of the latter order are more generally known in England as 'Presbyterian' and on the continent as 'Reformed' churches.

The national church of the Netherlands is the Netherlands Reformed Church, with a total community of about 3,300,000. This church emerged from the bitter struggles of the Dutch against the supremacy of Spain and the Inquisition. Dutch Protestants met in Emden, just outside Netherlands territory, in 1569 and prepared the basis of the church structure, which was confirmed at the Synod of Dordrecht in 1572. Although this remains the largest of the Protestant churches in the Netherlands, there have been several divisions in the church over the centuries. In 1619 the Remonstrant Brotherhood withdrew over the question of predestination. They now constitute a community of about 40,000 persons. In 1892 a larger group withdrew to form the Gereformeerde (Re-reformed) Kerken, with a community now of over 750,000.

The Mennonites, now numbering some 70,000 souls, also date back to a 17th-century origin in the Netherlands. The Lutheran Church in the Netherlands is a community of something less than 60,000. The Netherlands Baptist Union claims 22,000 members and the Union of Free Evangelical Congregations about 18,000. The Salvation Army is also active and there are several much smaller groups such as the Moravians, the Seventh-Day Adventists and the Society of Friends.

A church which is found in each of the countries of this area, as well as elsewhere, is the Old Catholic. This consists of communities which have separated from Roman Catholicism at different times. The Old Catholic Church of the Netherlands withdrew in 1724 and today has some 12,000 within its influence. The Roman Catholic population of the Netherlands is over 4 million and appears rapidly to be reaching parity with the Protestant population. It is estimated that 17 per cent of the Netherlands population of 12 million have no specific church affiliation.

In Germany, both in the Federal Republic and the Democratic Republic, the church scene is complicated by the maintenance in church as well as in civil life of the federal structure of the country. Thus each constituent territory (*Land*) has its own territorial Protestant church (*Landeskirche*), which may be of the Lutheran or Reformed traditions, or a union of the two. There are nineteen such territorial churches in West Germany and eight in East Germany. In West Germany they benefit from a number of privileges within the state and, whilst each is completely autonomous, they are closely united in organisation and activity. The Lutheran churches have a common organisation in the United Evangelical Lutheran Church of Germany (VELKD), and six of the United churches form the Evangelical Church of the Union (EKU). All the territorial churches in both West and East Germany together form the Evangelical Church in Germany (EKiD), a 'federation of Lutheran, Reformed and Union churches' constituted at Eisenach in 1948. About half the population of West Germany belongs to the constituent churches of the Evangelical Church in Germany.

The Baptists, Methodists and Union of Independent Evangelical Congregations number together nearly half a million in West Germany. There are also small Free Lutheran and Free Reformed Churches which, on doctrinal grounds, have sought to maintain their independence. The Orthodox community, mainly in 'exile churches', is about 50,000 strong. There are 40,000 Old Catholics whose church, like those of Switzerland and Austria, seceded from Rome after the promulgation of the dogma of Papal Infallibility in 1870. The Salvation Army has a widespread activity, with an officer staff of about 250. Some 44 per cent of the population of West Germany is Roman Catholic. One and a half million West Germans claim no religious affiliation at all.

The structure of the church organisation in Switzerland resembles to some degree that of Germany, since the Swiss political structure is also that of a federation of territories or cantons. In Switzerland, however, the main Protestant churches are all of the Reformed order—following the tradition of the Calvinistic Reformation, based on Geneva. The cantons of central and eastern Switzerland have remained overwhelmingly Roman Catholic. A considerable proportion of the over 2 million Roman Catholics in Switzerland —about 38 per cent of the population—reside in these territories.

In the Protestant cantons of Switzerland are seventeen state or cantonal churches. These are fully autonomous but, together with some of the Free Churches, they cooperate closely in the Federation of Protestant Churches in Switzerland. The cantonal Reformed churches have together a community of well over two-and-a-half million. In the canton of Geneva there is a Free Evangelical Church, which is of Presbyterian order but refuses the privileges of the cantonal church. The Methodist Church is the largest of the other Free Churches, with 20,000 in its community, and there are small Baptist, Independent Evangelical, Mennonite, Moravian and Seventh-Day Adventist churches. The Salvation Army is also active in many parts of the country. The Old Catholic Church of Switzerland is a body of 2,500, and there are also some very small Orthodox communities.

SCANDINAVIA

This area, comprising Norway, Sweden, Denmark, Finland and Iceland, is ecclesiastically the most homogeneous of the European region. All five countries have massive Lutheran Protestant majorities, ranging from 93 per cent of the total population in Finland to 98 per cent in Iceland. The Lutheran churches in these countries are national or folk churches, having similar, but not identical, relationships with the state. They are folk churches in the sense that they are more closely related to the people as a 'national society' than to the state as a 'national institution'. The Roman Catholic Church is present in the area in minimal proportions.

There exist considerable similarities, too, between the Scandinavian Free Churches. There are Pentecostalist groups in each country with communities numbering 115,000 in Sweden, 70,000 in Norway, 50,000 in Finland, 10,000 in Denmark and 5,000 in Iceland. There also exist active churches of the Congregationalist order, known as the Mission Covenant Churches of Sweden (250,000), Norway (20,000) and Denmark (4,000) respectively, and the Free Church of Finland (9,000); this group, peculiar in Western Europe, has close relationships with Congregationalism in Britain.

Together with the Salvation Army which, with a total community of about 100,000, works in each Scandinavian country, the Baptists, Methodists and Seventh-Day Adventists are present as follows: Baptists—Sweden 150,000, Norway 22,000, Denmark 20,000, Finland 6,000, Iceland 200; Methodists—Sweden 18,000, Norway 18,000, Denmark 6,500, Finland 4,000, Iceland nil; Seventh-Day Adventists—Finland 10,000, Norway 9,000, Denmark 7,800, Sweden 6,500, Iceland 800.

Yet in spite of so much similarity, some peculiarities in the different national situations may be noted. For example, within the Church of Iceland, where an old-fashioned piety is still practised, there has also been a very considerable spiritualist movement, which now appears, however, to be weakening. In Denmark, in addition to the churches already mentioned, there are very small groups of Quakers and Moravians. Quaker meetings have been held in south-west Norway for over a century, but the community remains only a few hundred strong. The Lutheran Free Church of Norway numbers 17,500 persons. Theologically conservative and revivalistic movements have strongly influenced the church life of Norway.

In Sweden, where the Church of Sweden claims to have maintained the Apostolic Succession, the effects of revivalist movements are also noticeable, but have been generally contained within the framework of the national church. On the other hand, similar movements have caused a deep division within the Baptist community. There is also an Esthonian Lutheran Church of about 66,000 members and a few small groups of Quakers.

Finland is the only one of the Scandinavian countries with an Orthodox community of any significant size—75,000 persons. Alongside the national church there is also a Free Lutheran Church, but it numbers only a few hundred adherents. As elsewhere in Scandinavia revivalist movements have caused different emphases to be made in different parts of the country. Particularly in some of the Free Churches this, coupled with language problems attributable to the use of Finnish or Swedish in the congregations, has caused tensions and sometimes actual divisions.

CENTRAL EUROPE

Were it not that it would overreach the geographical framework of this volume, Austria, the sole country to be considered in this area, should be taken together with Czechoslovakia, Hungary and Poland—clear indication that ecclesiastical pegs will not fit neatly into modern political holes.

Austria is a country which has been much disturbed by the political events of the last forty years. Great streams of refugees from Eastern Europe have passed into or through her territory and those who have settled there have caused some changes in the comparative numbers of the different confessions, without basically altering the picture of church relationships.

Nearly 90 per cent of the Austrian population is Roman Catholic and, since 1933, a concordat has existed between the Vatican and Austria, giving the Roman Catholic Church a privileged position. Nevertheless, wide tolerance is extended to other churches and the Lutheran-Reformed Union Church also enjoys certain privileges. This church, the Evangelical Church of the Augsburg and Helvetic Confessions in Austria, is the largest non-Roman Catholic community, with some 430,000 adherents. Of these something over 400,000 are of the Lutheran tradition and the remainder of the Reformed. The two constituent churches maintain their autonomy in a number of questions, but have a common synod for many major problems.

The Old Catholic Church of Austria comprises some 35,000 in its community, the Methodists and Seventh-Day Adventists about 5,000 each, the Baptists about 2,500 and the Assemblies of God about 1,000. There are also some small Orthodox communities.

THE EASTERN MEDITERRANEAN

As in the previous section, a part of a naturally larger ecclesiastical area has here to be considered. Greece and Turkey constitute the point at which major Orthodox influence enters Western Europe.

Greece is an Orthodox country. Its state church, the Church of Greece, formed a part of the Ecumenical Patriarchate of Constantinople until 1833, when it became a national, autocephalous (i.e. autonomous) community claiming some 98 per cent of the population. Although this is a state church, whose relationships with the state were redefined in 1923 and again in 1943, the interpretation of these relationships is still disputed at some points. There is a close identification between the Church of Greece and the Greek people, of whom it proved the strong leader during the struggle with the Turks. The second largest Christian community is the Roman Catholic, of whom some 45,000 use the Latin rite and some 3,000 to 4,000 are Uniats of recent origin, i.e. having an Orthodox tradition but remaining in communion with the Roman Catholic Church.

Protestantism is represented in Greece by the Greek Evangelical Church, of a Presbyterian-Congregationalist origin and over a hundred years old. It is a community of about 15,000. There is also a very small Free Evangelical Church and a number of somewhat indefinite and small missions, mainly of a revivalist nature and often run by Greeks who have been converted to Protestantism in the United States and who have taken their new faith back to their native land. The Greek constitution provides for freedom of religion and worship, but Greek laws prohibit proselytism. From time to time, therefore, the Protestant minorities have serious difficulties in finding a middle way between the constitution and the law.

The picture of Greece is completed by the presence of some 100,000 Mohammedans of Turkish origin.

The Turkish scene varies according to whether one thinks in terms of Turkey as a whole, with over 98 per cent of the population Mohammedans, or of European Turkey only, i.e. the territory north-west of the Bosphorus, for the great majority of Christians in Turkey are found near Istanbul (Constantinople) and in the European territories. Under the spiritual leadership of the Ecumenical Patriarch of Constantinople (often, but erroneously, looked upon in the West as the equivalent in Orthodox circles of the Pope in Roman Catholic) there were, until recently, some 85,000 Orthodox Christians. Following the deterioration of Greco-Turkish relations in the last few years many have moved to Greece and the number remaining is something near 30,000. Further, it is estimated that there are about 60,000 Armenian Christians, the great majority belonging to their national Orthodox Church. The Roman Catholic Church is also present in Turkey with a community of about 23,000. Several Protestant missions exist and there are a few foreign-language congregations.

THE JEWS

The following statistics, extracted in the case of the years 1939 and 1946 from the *Report of the Anglo-American Committee of Enquiry Regarding the Problems of European Jewry and Palestine* (HMSO, London, 1946), and for 1965 from *World Jewry* (VIII, 4, July/August 1965), will help to indicate both the present Jewish population of Western Europe and the movements caused by international events in the last thirty years.

JEWISH POPULATIONS OF WESTERN EUROPE

Thousands

	1939	1946	1965
Austria (1937: 192)	60	15	11
Belgium	90	33	35
Britain	340	350	450
Denmark	7	5.5	6
Finland	2	2	1.5
France	320	180	500
Germany (1937: 500)	215	94	30[1]
Greece	75	10	6.5
Iceland	n.a.	n.a.	n.a.
Republic of Ireland	n.a.	n.a.	5.5
Italy	50	46	35
Luxembourg	3.5	0.5	1
Netherlands	150	30	27
Norway	2	1	1
Portugal	3.5	4	1
Spain	4.5	4.5	3
Sweden	7.5	19.5	14
Switzerland	25	28.5	19
Turkey	n.a.	n.a.	55[2]

[1] German Federal Republic only.

[2] Source: *Jewish Chronicle*, September 1962.

Owing to the changes in the land areas designated by the name Germany between 1933 and 1965 the figures given under Germany are not strictly comparable. The considerable rise in the Jewish population of France between 1946 and 1965 is largely due to the influx of French Jews repatriated from Algeria, and Jewish immigration from Morocco and Tunisia during the last decade.

RENEWAL AND THE ECUMENICAL MOVEMENT

There is hardly a church in Western Europe today that is not showing evident signs of movement. It remains to be seen how far these are the feeble efforts of a mortally sick patient to relieve his discomfort, or the first stirrings of new life. Probably, although both elements are present, the latter is the dominant factor. The vast majority of the churches of Western Europe are desperately concerned about new life within their structures—whether they call it renewal or revival. The vital question is whether the desired 'new life' can be contained in the existing structures.

Of great importance is the close relationship which has developed between the movement for 'renewal' and the awareness of, if not the actual participation in, the 'ecumenical' character of ecclesiastical activity—in general terms, the whole church concerned with the whole world. For the churches of Europe, with their long histories and traditions still more or less couched in the cultures of which they are a formative part, the renewal movement in an ecumenical framework is specially painful since, for each church, it raises grave questions having both internal and external aspects. Within the churches there are many who are asking basic questions about the role, the place in society and the form of church structures. This is inevitably bringing with it increasingly strong emphasis on lay movements and, paradoxically, in some churches—even some of the Reformed tradition—a new interest in the monastic principle. One notes the rise of groups of Christians, inspired by common concerns, alongside the normal institutional life of the church. Many Protestant churches are as troubled by these para-ecclesial movements as the Roman Catholic Church was by the early 'worker-priest' movement in France.

The external, more obviously ecumenical aspects of the questions being raised by the European churches are no less grave than the internal aspects, but run the risk of being more sensational and, therefore, producing exaggerations based more on wishful thinking than on actual fact. Although the churches of the whole world have appreciably moved towards each other during this century, it must not be overlooked that ecumenical contact is still rejected or viewed suspiciously by some powerful churches; that there still exists a great confusion of concepts and ideas; that many churches are still avoiding the challenge in depth which ecumenical encounter means. Though most churches are now using the same words, in many cases the meanings they give them have still to find mutually acceptable definition. However, conversations are going on at many levels between and within the various churches, not least in Western Europe.

Another significant fact in this region is the rapid gain made in some areas by independent revivalist communities and by para-Christian groups—perhaps as a reproach to the traditionalism of the churches. In general, the churches of Western Europe are decreasing in membership proportionately to total population: there are good reasons for believing that, at least in some ways, they are becoming more vital.

Forms of Cooperative Activity between the Churches

One of the most complex problems which the non-Roman Catholic churches, both in Western Europe and elsewhere, have had to face during the middle decades of this century has been that of finding forms and methods for the exchange of insights and for practical cooperative activity. To some extent the problem already existed within the individual churches, where thinking was often uncoordinated and valuable reflections were ignored or lost. There has been a considerable increase in the number of study commissions within each church, including the Roman Catholic, and to an increasing degree account is being taken in these commissions of work being done by groups in other churches.

But many activities are now undertaken on a specifically ecumenical basis. Here, by the very nature of the case, the greatest involvement is of the Anglican, Orthodox and Protestant churches, although, particularly since the Second Vatican Council, the participation of the Roman Catholic Church is becoming more official.

In Western Europe contacts between the churches usually turn around one or more of the following points:

1. Questions of relationships between the churches. These may be treated in discussions concerning actual union between churches, e.g. Methodist-Anglican conversations in Great Britain and Methodist-Waldensian conversations in Italy; they also include problems relating to intercommunion, or the mutual recognition of ministries.

2. Studies of problems which directly relate to the life of the churches and the world in which they live. There is a great range of theological, sociological, economic, political and international and other study groups in Western Europe.

3. Practical social and relief work, in all parts of the world, for which work the Western European churches are now a major source of means and personnel. Here, at times, there is close cooperation and consultation between non-Roman Catholic and Roman Catholic churches.

Over the last twenty years or so those churches of Western Europe prepared for ecumenical activity have constructed for themselves organs of cooperation and encounter at different levels. Thus most of the countries mentioned in this chapter have some form of national ecumenical body to which the majority of the non-Roman Catholic churches belong. The degree of organisation, the powers delegated to the organisation and the spheres of activity vary greatly from country to country.

In the European region as a whole, after years of careful preparatory work, a regional ecumenical body was created in October 1964, when the Conference of European Churches was constituted. Most of the major non-Roman Catholic and many of the smaller churches, both in Western and Eastern Europe, belong to this body. The development of regional organisations, independent of but closely associated with the World Council of Churches, is a feature of present ecumenical development.

Still other kinds of ecumenical organisation are found in the region, some based on geographical considerations, e.g. the Conference of the Churches on the Rhine; some on a cultural factor, e.g. the Conference of the Protestant Churches in the Latin Countries of Europe; some on an interest basis, e.g. the Committee of the Churches on West European Migration, and so on.

The forms of cooperative organisation are numerous and increasing. There is a recognisable risk of an ecclesiastical Parkinson's Law, but this must not be exaggerated. The multifarious churches of Western Europe, having lived alongside each other for so long, are at last finding each other. Such mutual discovery will inevitably lead to the provision of new organisational forms to give it expression.

PROBLEMS FACING THE CHURCHES OF WESTERN EUROPE

Firstly, there is the complicated and ill-defined process of 'secularisation'. The term means different things in different ecclesiastical contexts. In general it includes the steady decline of the 'influence' of the churches and the tendency for Europeans, in particular, to look elsewhere for their salvation. It also involves the gradual challenging of the privileges which churches have enjoyed in many countries for centuries.

Secondly, directly connected with this and equally deeply rooted in the sometimes long histories of the Western European churches is the problem of ecclesiastical structural inflexibility at a time of rapid social change. Of this there are many aspects including questions concerning the place of the congregation, the nature of the ministry, forms of worship, Christian social responsibility in a welfare state, the expression of faith in a technical age, and many more.

Thirdly, increasingly urgent problems are posed by the various movements towards integration in Western Europe. People move with increasing ease from country to country in the course of their work—migrant workers, international civil servants or professional people in international organisations. It is easier to understand the spiritual needs of these newly uprooted people than to see how to provide for them.

Fourthly, the whole process of increased movement and mutual awareness is one of the factors contributing to the challenges facing the churches in their ecumenical experience. The Western European churches are not only conscious of this in their relationships with one another, but for many of them the question also has another dimension—that of their involvement in missionary activity in other continents. From this mission work newly independent churches (often but imprecisely referred to as 'Younger Churches') have appeared and are showing impatience with the old historical divisions, forms and structures of their European forebears. The 'older' churches are being forced to take note of this impatience.

BIBLIOGRAPHY

Coxill, H. W. and Grubb, K. (eds.) *World Christian Handbook*, World Dominion Press, London; Friendship Press, New York, 1962.

Cross, F. L. (ed.) *The Oxford Dictionary of the Christian Church*, Oxford Univ. Press, London and New York, 1957.

Hunter, L. S. (ed.) *Scandinavian Churches*, Faber and Faber, London; Augsburg Publishing House, Minneapolis, 1965.

Martling, C. H. *Europeisk Kyrkogeografi*, Diakonistyrelsens Bokförlag, Stockholm, 1962.

Molland, Einar. *Christendom*, A. R. Mowbray, London, 1959.

Slack, Kenneth. *The British Churches Today*, SCM Press, London; Alec R. Allenson, Naperville, Ill., 1961.

R

CONTEMPORARY ARTS

LITERATURE

MIRON GRINDEA

NOT so long ago it was suggested by an American historian that oral media will eventually supersede the written. In France, too, there is serious talk of evolution towards an 'unlettered literature' in which image and sound will eventually combine in an androgynous sort of universal language. TV and radio, the cinema, *son et lumière* are relentlessly replacing the printed word with projections of sound and colour; some time ago an anthology of picture poetry entitled *Svisch* appeared in Sweden; both in France and in England 'concrete poetry' is finding an increasing number of adherents. But even if one ignores these movements which may ultimately swamp literary publishing, in much post-war European literature one detects a note of discontinuity if not of total disintegration. Poets confess that words no longer seem to hold security on the printed page—they dwindle away. Novelists play upon linguistic values which they can no longer 'trust'.

The reasons for this crisis are many, but chief would seem to be the insoluble spiritual and economic pressures which followed the second world war. For Faulkner the modern consciousness is dominated by universal fear 'so long sustained by now that *we can even bear it*'; 'there are no longer problems of the spirit', he said, 'there is only the question, *when will I be blown up?*' The 'strategic' use of the first atom bomb has surely changed the writer's sensibility—and this possibly with the shortest line in modern poetry: *the baby has been successfully born* (the sole contents of a cable sent by the United States government to the British cabinet on 6 August 1945 as the first bomb was dropped over Hiroshima). But before this an entire world had already perished with the downfall of the Nazi millennium. The cruelties perpetrated not only by dictatorships but also by long-established democracies have exasperated artists and masses alike. And what culture could undergo such cataclysms without serious effects on its capacity for creative renewal?

On the other hand, the amenities which condition post-war society—with distances hardly counting and language barriers disappearing with an increasing spate of translations—may well produce a new type of literature altogether, wider perhaps in scope than Goethe's derided dream of 'Welt-literatur'. Our era of interplanetary collisions and space anchorages needs and—one hopes—breeds a *cosmic* approach to all problems of the spirit, consequently a truly *planetary* literature. Our epoch lacks creative literary giants, but the reading public is aware of a process which may ultimately make the whole globe into one country. In this context the notion of 'small' literatures is meaningless; indeed, a poem or a novel written by a Finn or a Turk can enrich our quest for meaning as much as a similar work by a Frenchman or an Englishman.

494

For convenience this survey starts with the Iberian Peninsula, moves on to the British Isles and Scandinavia and then back to the Continent as far as Turkey, and finally returns along the Mediterranean shores to where we began.

PORTUGAL AND SPAIN

Despite the fact that most writers in both Portugal and Spain have to live and create under the constant fear of censorship, the new generation is well aware of what is being achieved outside its frontiers and especially of what it can accomplish in the face of ruthless censorship. Admittedly the frequent use made of themes expressing the futility of life and the yearning for death may reflect the bankruptcy of the spirit when confronted with so much intolerance; however, creative vigour asserts itself. The rhythm in the enunciation of hidden frustrations and violence of style seem to indicate a lively future.

Since the end of the second world war Portugal has been more richly suggestive to novelists than to poets. The prolific Ferreira de Castro (b. 1898) has written at least two masterpieces, *Emigrantes*, 1928 (*Emigrants*) [1] and *A selva*, 1934 (*Jungle*), which describe life in the rubber plantations of Brazil. His political novel *A missão*, 1963 (*The Mission*) got him into trouble with the authorities, but he has achieved new prominence with an important study of the world's great works of art. In the same neo-realist tradition José Rodriques Miguéis (b. 1901) has resumed writing after a long exile abroad: his *Leah e outras historias*, 1958 and the novel *Una aventura inquietante*, 1959 express *saudades*, an untranslatable word suggesting longing. Joaquin Paco d'Arcos (b. 1902) has written in *Cronica da vida lisboeta*, 1950–1 a five-volume panorama of Lisbon during a period when the capital was exploited by spies and unscrupulous businessmen. Miguel Torga (b. 1907) is the Portuguese writer best known abroad—his name has frequently been put forward for the Nobel Prize. *Bichos*, 1941 (*Farrusco*) is a collection of animal stories of unsurpassed beauty, and *Novos contos da montanha*, 1944 describes in brief, staccato style the hard but passionate day-by-day existence experienced in the author's native Trás-os-Montes. 'I burn, and give back heat to life', reads one line in his *Iberian Poems*: Torga is also an outstanding poet. Two poignant and less familiar themes, the gradual disintegration of white people in African surroundings and the tribal life of Angolan Negroes, are dramatically treated by Castro Soromenho in the novel *Viragem*, 1947 (*The Wreckage*). An innovator, Agustina Bessa Luis, made a great impact with Proustian presentation of many characters in her first novel *A Sibila*, 1954 (*The Sybil*) and in *As relacoes humanas*, 1964.

Portuguese poetry is still dominated by the heritage of Fernando Pessoa, many of whose works appeared after his death in 1935, and José Regio (b. 1901) who founded the influential literary review *Presenca* (1927–40). Regio's *Fado*, 1941 and *Mas Deus e grande*, 1945 include some of the best lyrics of the last forty years. Following the path of the surrealist Antonio Pedro post-war poetry is successfully represented by Tomas Kim (b. 1915), Sofia de Mello Breyner Andresen (b. 1919), Mario Cesariny de Vasconcelos (b. 1923), David Mourão-Ferreira (b. 1925) and many others, all followers of the creed 'poetry is its own excuse'.

[1] Titles in brackets are those of published editions in English translation. Dates given are of original publication.

'Any man who knows how to tell his life is himself a book without equal', once wrote Portugal's veteran regional novelist Aquilino Ribeiro (b. 1885), and this fits the works of the two most outstanding Spanish novelists of today, Camilo José Cela and Ana María Matute. Cela (b. 1916) rose to prominence with his first novel *La familia de Pascual Duarte*, 1942, followed by *La colmena*, 1953 (*The Hive*), which went so far in its denunciation of Francoism and the almost total corruption of Madrid society in the middle of the second world war that the book (prefaced by the author himself as a 'pale, humble reflection of the hard and painful Spanish reality') had to be published abroad. Matute (b. 1926 and now living in France) wrote: 'a novel must hurt the conscience of society in order to alleviate its predicament'. One of her novels, *Primera memoria*, appeared in English under the title *The Awakening* in 1963 and reveals an artist of great psychological power.

Most of the avant-garde writers were in their childhood during the ravages of the Civil War. Miguel Delibes (b. 1920) feels an exile in his own country (hence the title of one of his novels, *Diario de un emigrante*, 1958); so does Carmen Laforet (b. 1921) whose epic, *Nada*, 1945 describes the pathetic coexistence of three generations—the oldest one which does not understand what is now going on, the middle one convinced that it has either won or lost the Civil War, and the confused youth who believe nothing. Juan Goytisolo (b. 1928), in his poems *Anos decisivos*, 1961 and in his novels *Duelo en el paraiso*, 1945 (*Children of Chaos*), *Juegos de manos*, 1960 (*The Young Assassins*) and *La Isla*, 1962 (*Sands of Torremolinos*) he reveals the tragic sense of isolation which surrounds most contemporary Spanish artists. Rafael Sánchez Ferlosio (b. 1927), in his novel *El Jarama*, 1955, has caught the despair of this generation.

The poet Blas de Otero (b. 1916) writes in order 'to wipe the blood and injustice from our world' (*Twenty Poems*, 1964).[1] Eugenio de Nora (b. 1923), after his *Cantos al destino*, 1945, published *España, pasión de vida*, 1954 with the zeal of a reformer hoping to see his country become 'bearable for all of us'. Space does not allow more than a mere mention of the lively and heroic Catalan literature, much of which continues in exile (Ventura Gassol in France, Josep Carner in Belgium).

FRANCE

Shortly before France was occupied by the Germans an unwise French critic stated that his country was without poets—a foolish affirmation at a time when Valéry, Reverdy, Supervielle and Eluard were still alive. André Breton (1896–1966) remained for nearly half a century the undisputed head of surrealism. Henri Michaux (b. 1889) and René Char (b. 1907) have also sought inspiration in the unconscious to attain, by the free *choc* of disintegrating words, the very sources of thought. Michaux's *Connaissance par les gouffres*, 1964 (*Light through Darkness—Explorations among Drugs*) is an extraordinary poetical attempt at detachment from the real world and a vindication of Rimbaud's pursuit of 'a derangement of all the senses'. Char, without resorting to mescalin or to other similar drugs, evolves a poetry of pure 'transvaluation of all values'. In the meantime Louis Aragon (b. 1897), the last veteran of surrealism, converted to militant communism, has in recent years perfected a poetry of philosophical content, a synthesis of human experience, classical structure and *poésie pure* which assures him a major position in European poetry. After his unforgettable war-time paean *Crève-coeur*, 1941 Aragon has passed through the dialectics not only of

[1] American edition.

Marxism, but also of unadulterated sensibility (*Les poètes*, 1960, a two-hundred-page poem). Many of his novels have appeared in English: *The Bells of Basel*, 1937, *Aurélien*, 1946, *Passengers of Destiny*, 1947, *Holy Week*, 1961.

With Saint-John Perse (b. 1887) instated in the position of patriarch (he was awarded the Nobel Prize in 1960, the year when he published the last of his very few books, *Chronique*), post-war trends in French poetry are as rich as they are significant. Francis Ponge (b. 1899) continues to be an inexhaustible coiner of rare images. He sings the mineral aspects of nature with a sovereign pride in his 'telluric' instinct. Hermetic to the extreme, Ponge is nevertheless idolised by many poets old and young. His very un-Cartesian *Dix-courts sur la méthode*, 1947 abound in memorable lines such as 'l'homme est l'avenir de l'homme'. Pierre Emmanuel (b. 1916) became, during the German occupation, a revolutionary Christian; refreshingly free from theological mustiness his poetry (*La liberté guide nos pas*, 1945, *Memento des vivants*, 1946, *Babel*, 1952, *Versant de l'âge*, 1958) attains heights of eloquence while in the novel *Qui est cet homme?* 1950 (*The Universal Singular*) the poet reemphasises the laws of the spirit. Jean Cayrol (b. 1911) is also a mystic poet and novelist of total dedication (*Poèmes de la nuit et du brouillard*, 1945, *Pour tous les temps*, 1955, and the cyclic novel *Je vivrai l'amour des autres*, 1947–50). Patrice de la Tour du Pin (b. 1911) remains engaged on his Dantesque *Somme de poésie*, begun in 1946. Eugène Guillevic (b. 1907), an unrepentant 'engaged' poet (*Terre à bonheur*, 1953) also has a lyrical beauty and a recognisable music of his own.

Space forbids the mention of dozens of poets whose experiments and achievements have preserved the forcefulness of French poetry since the end of the second world war. Amongst these Yves Bonnefoy (b. 1923) is regarded by many as the most important figure to have emerged during this period. His slender, esoteric booklets *Du mouvement et de l'immobilité du Douve*, 1953 and *Hier régnant désert*, 1956 have injected the eternal probing of the concealed function of poetic language with a new passion and an original style: 'Le Sphinx qui se tait/Dans le sable de l'Idée'.

In the field of ideas as in the evolution of the novel France indisputably appears as the most exciting, if not the most influential country in European literature. The spate of 'isms' and philosophical dissertations becomes irritating: after shaping formula after formula the enunciators of doctrines end with equal intellectual brilliance by disengaging themselves from their most alluring labels. The methods which have been launched and explored in the last twenty years, chiefly the existentialism of Jean-Paul Sartre (b. 1905) and the *nouveau roman* of Alain Robbe-Grillet (b. 1922), have already virtually been filed away in literary history. The war-time terror and humiliation gave birth to a literature as militant in its antirationalism as, in lesser dramatic national upheavals, the 19th-century romantic and the 20th-century surrealist movements.

The existentialist novel of commitment illustrated by Sartre's *Chemins de la liberté*, 1945–9 (*The Age of Reason, The Reprieve* and *Iron of the Soul*), *L'Etranger* (*The Outsider*) and *La peste*, 1947 (*The Plague*) by Albert Camus (1913–60) and *Tous les hommes sont mortels*, 1946 (*All Men are Mortal*) and *Les mandarins*, 1954 (*The Mandarins*) by Simone de Beauvoir (b. 1908) tried to render an effective philosophical treatment of man's predicament as well as a militant moral conscience on the a-priori reasoning that the external world simply refuses to keep within rational bounds—consequently the saint becomes he who lives the repudiation of all positive values. In one of his most explosive and controversial treatises, *Jean Genet comédien et martyr*,

1951 (*Saint Genet Actor and Martyr*), Sartre devoted six hundred pages to the eulogy of Genet (b. 1909), the self-depicted homosexual outcast and thief (*Journal d'un voleur*, 1949—*The Thief's Journal*), as the very incarnation of the will to the void, identical with freedom and even sacrament. Among the gospels that held sway at the most important literary cafés in Paris (Deux Magots and Café Flore) during the late 1940s and throughout the 1950s were man's 'damnation to be free' (Sartre), the absurdity of existence which justifies the individual in exhausting all the joys of the earth (Camus) and woman's perverted psychology and humiliating status due to the age-old enslavement of the 'second' sex (de Beauvoir). But while Sartre and Camus have written works of lasting literary merit, Simone de Beauvoir's fiction is marred by a didactic tendency which the author puts to better use in her essays, and since 1958, in her memoirs.

Alain Robbe-Grillet (like Breton a scientist by training), Michel Butor (b. 1926), Nathalie Sarraute (b. 1902 at Ivanovo-Vosnesensk in Russia), Marguerite Duras (b. 1914 in Indochina) and Robert Pinget (b. 1920) are the main representatives of the *nouveau roman* which breaks away from the pattern of the realist and psychological novel in dissolving the main theme into dozens of seemingly trivial details which haunt the characters' minds, as in Robbe-Grillet's *Le voyeur*, 1955 (*The Voyeur*) and *Jalousie*, 1958 (*Jealousy*), in Sarraute's *Portrait d'un inconnu*, 1949 (*Portrait of a Man Unknown*) and *Les fruits d'or*, 1963 (*The Golden Fruits*), and especially in Butor's *L'emploi du temps*, 1955 and *Degrés*, 1960 (*Degrees*), both illustrating the shifting of time fragments, essential to the building of these novels. But even the 'new wave' writers show signs of wanting to return to a more organised analysis of characters. Robbe-Grillet, who in 1956 decreed that 'the whole universe of *significances* (psychological, logical, social, functional) ought to be replaced by a more solid and more immediate world', admitted some time later that 'the *nouveau roman* was not a theory but a search', that 'the writer's interest will continue to be man's position in the world', in other words that the writer's 'only commitment is that of creating literature'. Kafka and Joyce loom large over this group of gifted writers whose work reflects the implications of total nihilism. The philosophy is that of the Irishman Samuel Beckett (b. 1906) in which man, freed from all possessions, *goes on* because he *must go on*. Beckett has enriched French literature with a series of novels written in French, *Molloy*, 1951, *Malone meurt*, 1951, *L'innommable*, 1953, *Nouvelles et textes pour rien*, 1955 and *Comment c'est*, 1960.[1]

The last decade has also witnessed the revival of the 'disengaged' psychological novel which aims at portraying the basic aspects of life in a unified, intelligible and meaningful form—'la vie, mon petit! La formule résume toute littérature', wrote Hervé Bazin (b. 1918) in a preface introducing a new series of novels entitled significantly *Rien que la vie*. The French reading public has become hostile to existentialism, believing it to have encouraged the new generation to adopt a negative, asocial attitude of inertia and amateurism. The work of pre-war writers has been rediscovered—that of André Malraux (b. 1901), for example, who in *La condition humaine*, 1933 (*Man's Estate*) takes the theme of man's tragic destiny, showing that the greater the tensions of experience the more they must be held in 'a concentrated knot of order'. Fate, therefore, can be countered by the ethic of courage. The Catholic writers François Mauriac (b. 1885) and Julien Green (b. 1900) have continued to expose man's constant guilt and apprehension of dread: longing can only be realised as torment.

[1] These novels are available in English translation.

498

The British Isles

Although it is harder in London to locate dominant trends and influences than it is in Paris, Stockholm, Amsterdam or Athens where there are distinct schools, manifestos, combative literary magazines, acknowledged 'leaders' and a corresponding number of ancient restaurants and cafés where prominent and lesser known authors can often be seen surrounded by a faithful band of followers, it is true that English poetry after 1950 presented certain distinct features, in the continental manner. An anthology, *New Lines*, edited in 1956 by Robert Conquest, unexpectedly led to a rather un-English label—'the Movement'. While often criticised for their impersonality and lack of warmth, at least three of these younger poets rose to prominence. For power and sensitivity Thom Gunn (b. 1929) stands out as the most inspired. *Fighting Terms*, 1954, was followed by *The Sense of Movement*, 1957 and *My Sad Captains*, 1961. Philip Larkin (b. 1922) also achieved a technique of masterly precision in *The Less Deceived*, 1955 and *The Whitsun Weddings*, 1966. Elizabeth Jennings (b. 1926) has developed, since *A Way of Looking*, 1955, a memorable sense of language. Her more recent volumes *Every Changing Shape*, 1961 and *The Mind Has Mountains*, 1966 carried contemporary prosody to a new lucidity (characteristically she insists on the paradox of poetry which 'arises from something intensely private but results in a passionate desire for communication').

As a mild reaction against the Movement, 'the Group' originated in Cambridge and continued its activity in Chelsea. For years poets met for no other purpose than constructive criticism of each other's verse and the search for a valid form of expression for their subjects which were often coarse and abrupt, even cruel. Ted Hughes (b. 1930) has a taste for emotional violence which makes him see nature as red in tooth and claw. With *The Hawk in the Rain*, 1957 and *Lupercal*, 1960 he has won a leading place among the young experimenters. Sylvia Plath (1923–63) is much lamented for the revelation of melody which lay behind her grim metaphors—*The Colossus*, 1961 and *Ariel*, published posthumously in 1965.

Amongst a slightly older generation a notable range of emotion, from the erotic to the traditional and pastoral, can be found in the work of George Barker (b. 1913) who considers his poetry as 'an amorous attitude', John Heath-Stubbs (b. 1918—*The Triumph of the Muse*, 1958), and R. S. Thomas (b. 1913), a Welsh vicar who sings with charm and stoic intensity the life of the Welsh countryside ('To live in Wales is to be conscious/At dusk of the spilled blood/That went to the making of the wild sky').

Going further back still, one is happily confronted with the renewed virtuosity of Robert Graves (b. 1895). With his glorying in the eternal feminine and the historical and ethnological insight that has led to such masterly prose works as *I, Claudius*, 1934, *The White Goddess*, 1948 and *The Common Asphodel*, 1949, Graves has maintained a standard of stylistic power and combative intelligence which keep his *Collected Poems*, 1957 in constant demand. W. H. Auden (b. 1907) has long abandoned his predilection for imagistic riddles and in his evolution from naïve Marxism ('we must love one another or die') to an unquiet Anglo-Catholicism has shown himself an artist capable of universal communication. Nature mysticism has found a kind of neo-Platonic apotheosis in Kathleen Raine (b. 1908) who since she began to reach a wider public in the 1940s has applied a noble skill in her search for faith and archetypal symbols.

English poetry has undergone a serious change since the deaths of Dylan

Thomas in 1953 and of T. S. Eliot in 1965. In the first place free verse is less cultivated. Another striking feature of English verse of the last decade is that most poets make no claim to profundity—on the contrary, modesty and stylishness seem to be their chief virtues; at any rate they show a sincere desire to 'speak directly to the reader in terms he can understand'. The poetical scene is diversified by yet another group of 'elders': C. Day Lewis (b. 1904) who in 1957 published *Pegassus and Other Poems*, Stevie Smith (b. 1902), a delightful miniaturist in her volumes *Harold's Leap*, 1950 and *The Frog Prince*, 1966, John Betjeman (b. 1906) whose *Collected Poems*, 1959 are of the strictest excellence, Ruth Pitter (b. 1897) and E. J. Scovell (b. 1907). An important event was the publication in 1965 of the *Collected Poems* of David Gascoyne (b. 1916), the alert, emotive and deeply charged pioneer of surrealism. Scotland and Ireland have enriched English poetry in the work of Hugh MacDiarmid (b. 1892; *Collected Poems*, 1954), Austin Clarke (b. 1896; *Ancient Lights*, 1955), and Patrick Kavanagh (b. 1905; *The Great Hunger*, 1942, *A Soul for Sale*, 1947, *Collected Poems*, 1964). Since it was published in 1922 *The Waste Land* has maintained its universal influence with its successful bid to 'digest and express new feelings and new aspects' of a decaying Europe. Although he genuinely considered Ezra Pound (b. 1885) as the *miglior fabbro*, Eliot has exerted a wider influence upon his contemporaries both as a poet and a critic. Lately younger poets have been turning more towards Pound's imagery.

The novel presents a different and richer variety of achievement. Graham Greene (b. 1904) remains perhaps the most remarkable English writer of today. Like his illustrious contemporary François Mauriac, Greene (a convert to Roman Catholicism) presents his characters in his own image so that in creating them he tries to surpass his own nature. In *The Comedians*, 1965 he continues to explore the agonies of a tormented conscience with the same mordant wit and seedy suspense which he displayed in *The Power and The Glory*, 1940, possibly the finest symbolic melodrama in modern English literature. Evelyn Waugh (1903–66), another Catholic convert who began his brilliant career with a series of devastating satires on club and country-house life in the 1920s and early 1930s such as *Decline and Fall*, 1928 and *Vile Bodies*, 1930, ended on a note of strident dilemma, although his artistry remained unmatched up to the end (*Sword of Honour* a final version of the novels *Men at Arms*, 1952, *Officers and Gentlemen*, 1955 and *Unconditional Surrender*, 1961). Writing mainly in dialogue Ivy Compton-Burnett (b. 1892) has for the last four decades released at regular intervals her family sagas in which old mythic dramas of incest and violence are reduced to a decorous world of butlers and pre-war formality (e.g. *Men and Wives*, 1948, *Mother and Son*, 1955, *Pastors and Masters*, 1965). An interest in the bizarre where reality passes over into nightmare is to be found in the fascinating fairy-tale world of John Ronald Tolkien (b. 1892). A writer of phantasies immersed in anthropological sources, Tolkien wrote a trilogy, *The Lord of the Rings* (1954–5), a classic. A younger and equally powerful moulder of allegories is William Golding (b. 1911) whose *Lord of the Flies*, 1956 takes up one of the crucial themes of modern literature, the confrontation of innocence and guilt. Golding treats the subject with consummate artistry—the work shows how soon and how easily civilisation can slip into barbarism.

Some of the younger novelists are deeply concerned with social and moral problems along the articulate, sensitive and colourful lines on which a J. B. Priestley (b. 1894) gave us his racy portraits of the common Englishman (*The Good Companions*, 1929, *The Magicians*, 1954, *The Shapes of Sleep*, 1952,

Lost Empires, 1965) or an L. P. Hartley (b. 1895) his complex studies of children and adults hiding behind the smiling faces of landed gentry (*The Shrimp and the Anemone*, 1944, *The Go-Between*, 1952, *Facial Justice*, 1960). James Hanley (b. 1901) is receiving a belated and well-deserved recognition as a versatile novelist (*The Closed Harbour*, 1952, *The Welsh Sonata*, 1954, *Say Nothing*, 1962). Anthony Powell (b. 1905) is a robust and stinging chronicler of English upper-class life—he gives us a vast, Proustian gallery of portraits in the *Music of Time* sequence which began with *A Question of Upbringing*, 1951. C. P. Snow (b. 1905) is enjoying a stable popularity for the uncompromising realism with which he has explored the various facets of power bedevilling post-war society (*The Masters*, 1951, *The New Men*, 1954, *The Conscience of the Rich*, 1958, *The Affair*, 1960, *Corridors of Power*, 1964). Angus Wilson (b. 1913) emerged as a short-story writer of cool, almost ferocious power of characterisation with *The Wrong Set*, 1949; later he expanded his gifts of observation in a series of naturalistic novels—*Hemlock and After*, 1952, *Anglo-Saxon Attitudes*, 1956, *The Old Men at the Zoo*, 1961. Another naturalistic novelist, but in a much gentler key, William Cooper (b. 1910) catches an endearing, sane portion of English life in *Scenes from Provincial Life*, 1950, and especially *Scenes from Married Life*, 1961.

Both Kingsley Amis (b. 1922) and John Braine (b. 1922) made their début with novels of irresistible originality. *Lucky Jim*, 1954 was a straightforward and very funny dissection of academic warfare in a new university town ('the welfare democracy', Amis professes, 'is a satirical arena far richer than the stratified democracy which is now yielding place to it'). *Room at the Top*, 1957 portrayed with startling clarity and pungency the growing, adventurous world of the 'lower middle-class'. Alan Sillitoe (b. 1928) began as a poet of promise, but under the influence of Robert Graves resorted to prose and depicted his native working-class surroundings in Nottingham in a first novel, *Saturday Night and Sunday Morning*, 1958, which scored a world-wide success, outshining the more artistic volume of short stories *The Loneliness of the Long Distance Runner*, 1959. Among the younger novelists should be mentioned John Wain (*Hurry on Down*, 1953, *Strike the Father Dead*, 1962), Colin MacInnes (*City of Spades*, 1957, *Mr Love and Justice*, 1960), Francis King (*The Custom House*, 1961), Stanley Middleton (*Harris's Requiem*, 1960), Julian Mitchell (*Imaginary Toys*, 1961, *A Disturbing Influence*, 1962) and Melwyn Bragg (b. 1939) who shows some of Hartley's subtle touches in his first novel *For Want of a Nail*, 1965.

Prominent among women authors, and with a solid reputation established between the two world wars, are Elizabeth Bowen (b. 1899), a masterly writer of short stories, Rosamond Lehmann (b. 1903) who excels in the lyric intensity with which she strikes a balance between reality and imagination (*The Ballad and the Source*, 1944, *The Echoing Grove*, 1953), Rebecca West (b. 1892), sharp analyst of human frailties in the *Meaning of Treason*, 1949, and Storm Jameson (b. 1894) whose novels are a convincing study of the crisis of conscience in England today (*A Road from the Monument*, 1962). Pamela Hansford Johnson (b. 1912) is both a provocative story-teller and a moralist (*The Unspeakable Skipton*, 1959, *An Error of Judgement*, 1962) and a critic (*Thomas Wolfe*, 1947). Olivia Manning (b. 1915) has achieved world-wide success with her Balkan trilogy *The Great Fortune*, 1960, *The Spoilt City*, 1962, *Friends and Heroes*, 1965; Muriel Spark (b. 1916) shows deep psychological penetration in *Memento Mori*, 1959 (God rings up a few people urging them to prepare themselves for death), *The Prime of Miss Jean Brodie*, 1961, and *The Mandelbaum Gate*, 1965 (a study of modern Israel facing the hatred of the neighbouring Arab countries); Doris Lessing (b. 1919) is intensely preoccupied with the racial and social conflicts of the last three decades and with the status of the 'free woman' faced by male stupidity, conceit and erotic clumsiness (*The Grass is Singing*, 1950, *Martha Quest*, 1952, *The Golden Notebook*, 1962). Iris Murdoch (b. 1919) has acquired European fame with a series of *romans philosophiques*, consistently entertaining and illuminated by ingenious stylistic devices (*The Bell*, 1958, *A Severed Head*, 1961, *An Unofficial Rose*, 1962).

Cyril Connolly (b. 1903) is one of the most gifted stylists in the language today; he has produced two literary gems, *The Unquiet Grave*, 1953 and *The Condemned Playground*, 1954. Related to this fine taste and delicacy of feeling are Henry Green (b. 1905) who, after describing his own experiences as a manual worker in one of his early novels, *Living*, 1929, has enriched English writing with a weird panorama of characters (*Caught*, 1943, *Loving*, 1945, *Nothing*, 1950, *Doting*, 1952) and William Sansom (b. 1912) whose short stories and novels (*The Body*, 1949, *The Face of Innocence*, 1951, *The Bed of Roses*, 1954, *The Cautious Heart*, 1958, *The Last Hours of Sandra Lee*, 1961) are unique in modern English writing for their strange interiorisation of external events and especially for their superb language. Lawrence Durrell (b. 1912) first made his impact as a poet with a predilection for concrete detail, but soon asserted himself as a prose writer. In his four-volume *Alexandria Quartet*, 1957–60 Durrell made an important experiment by taking a number of events and dealing with them from four different points of view, calling into question the whole idea of the permanence of facts.

The essay, a genre in which English writers have excelled for centuries, is still cultivated with considerable industry and charm by Harold Nicolson (*Good Behaviour*, 1955), J. B. Priestley (*All About Ourselves*, 1956) and Colin MacInnes (*England, Half English*, 1963)—and the daily Fourth Leaders in *The Times*. Sir Osbert Sitwell (b. 1892) is the unsurpassed memorialist of the last two generations, and possibly the most brilliant of a gifted family of writers.

SCANDINAVIA

The Scandinavian countries have perhaps attained the highest patterns of social welfare in modern times—yet individual neuroses and unrest go hand in hand with the wealth, the comfort, the emancipation. Anguish has been the dominant feature of every Swedish writer in a constant display of conflict from Strindberg to Harry Martinson (b. 1904), author of the first notable poem on a space theme in world literature, *Aniara*, the epic of a human-laden spaceship lost among the planets. Although Sweden, of all Scandinavian countries, was spared occupation and the upheavals of the two world wars, its literature reflects the symptoms of lassitude and despair. As early as 1916 Pär Lagerkvist (b. 1891) uttered in one of his poems the significant cri de coeur *Anguish, anguish is my heritage*. A number of poets concentrating on a review called *40-tal* ('These 40s') evolved a new, brutal image of man, bare of rhetoric and compromise, in which realism and the symbol fuse. The standard-bearers of the movement (Fyrtiotalisterna) were Karl Vennberg (b. 1910) and Erik Lindergren (b. 1910) who, after being violently attacked for their hermeticism, emerged triumphant. In his *Plea for my own Cause* Lindegren stated that 'whoever wishes to understand the ideological basis of Swedish modernism must take into account psychoanalysis, Marxist dialectics and the Uppsala philosophical school which have paved the way for a totally new poetical scrutiny of our time'.

LITERATURE

Experimentation has continued in Sweden on an increasing scale with opposing and explosive literary groups. Significantly, a poet and critic of the older generation, Artur Lundkvist (b. 1906), who introduced surrealism into Sweden, recently manifested grave concern over the levelling out of mass society resulting 'in a disgust that cannot verbalise itself'; Lundkvist also deplored the way in which 'everything becomes a disconnected *now*, a presence without past and future/which produces and destroys itself'. Gunnar Ekelöf (b. 1907), although a respectable member of the Swedish Academy, conveyed in one of his volumes of verse, *Strountes*, 1955, a desperate apprehension at the gradual erosion of language ('when one has come as far as I have in meaninglessness' is how one of the poems begins). His subsequent *Opus incertum*, 1959 exaggerated this 'anti-poetry mood'. In spite of Ekelöf's enthusiastic following, many of the younger Swedish poets such as Tomas Tranströmer (b. 1931), Göran Printz-Páhlson (b. 1931), Lars Gustafsson (b. 1936) and Jarl Hammarberg (b. 1940) manifest a sincere desire to return to certain old values ('childish thoughts come in time of need,' notes Tranströmer). Sandro Key-Áberg (b. 1922) feels the urge 'to cleanse life of pain,/ to tidy up the lonely tide of man/free of torment's spots'. At the same time, however, Emile Bengt Johnson (b. 1936), a fierce exponent of 'sound' and 'concrete' picture poetry, complains that 'language is in the way'.

American realism has exerted great influence on Swedish prose-writers, who also show the effects of both Dostoyevskian and Kierkegaardian brands of existentialism. Lars Ahlin (b. 1915) is a self-educated novelist and essayist, considered by many as the most interesting Swedish writer today. Other important writers are Vilhelm Moberg (b. 1898), author of the monumental epic *Utvandrarna*, 1952–9 (*The Emigrants*), Lars Gyllensten (b. 1921), who wrote *Kains memoarer*, 1963 (*Cain's Memoirs*) and Birgitta Trotzig (b. 1929) who reaches an extreme of anxiety when examining the limits of language ('to enter into relationship with reality (i.e. language)' means to be 'crushed into slime, to disappear completely').

The accents of resistance literature still prevail in the modernistic works of two Norwegian poets, Andre Bjerke (b. 1918) and Paal Brekke (b. 1922). Other poets who enliven the literary life of Oslo are Maria Takvam (b. 1932), Per Bronken (b. 1931), Georg Johanssen (b. 1931) and Stein Mehren (b. 1936). Danish poets corresponding in age, Benny Andersen (b. 1929, *Den musikaske aal*, 1960—*The Musical Eel*), Thirkild Bjørnvig (b. 1918, *Figur og ild*, 1960—*Figure and Fire*), Jorgen Sonne (b. 1925) and Uffa Harder (b. 1930) are technically more advanced. But it is the novel that calls for special attention. In Norway, Tarjei Vesaas (b. 1897) has gained a European reputation with his novels *Huset i mørkret*, 1945 (*The House in the Tower*) dealing with enemy-occupied Norway, *Taarnet*, 1948, *Fuglane*, 1957 (*The Birds*) and *Is slottet*, 1966 (*The Ice Palace*). So have three other Norwegian authors, Johan Borgen (b. 1902) with *Lillelord*, 1955, the story of a young prodigy whose genius was sacrificed in the first world war, Aksel Sandemose (1899–1965) with *Alice Atkinson*, 1949 and Cora Sandel (b. 1880), whose psychological studies call for social, moral and sexual reform, being directed less against the individual conscience than against society's deceit. Denmark takes legitimate pride in the growing reputation of two women writers, Cecil Bødker (b. 1927), author of an outstanding collection of short stories, *Ojet*, 1961 (*The Eye*) and Ulla Ryum (b. 1937), who began as a poet but now excels as a novelist—*Natsangersken*, 1963 (*The Night Singer*) is the story of an aging prostitute.

In both Finland and Iceland there have been new departures in poetry.

Pentti Halappa (b. 1927, *Son of the Land*, 1953) and Pentti Saarikovski (b. 1937, *About the World*, 1961) are influential figures in post-war Finnish poetry. Iceland, in spite of its small population of only 190,000, is among the most cultured countries on both sides of the Atlantic. Jon ur Vor (b. 1917) with *Vatramavar*, 1960 (*Galls of Winter*) and Sigurdur Magnusson (b. 1928) with *Hafio og kletturinn*, 1961 (*The Sea and the Cliff*) have been labelled 'atomic poets' because of their preoccupation with space exploration. David Stefansson, another leading poet, has also written a long novel, *Solon Islandus*, 1940. The doyen of Finnish novelists is Eemil Frans Sillanpää (b. 1888), who won the Nobel Prize in 1939; his novels have appeared in English (*Fallen Asleep while Young*, 1933, *The Meek Heritage*, 1938). The Nobel Prize for 1955 went to Iceland's epic story-teller Halldor Kiljian Laxness (b. 1902), author of *Sjalfstoett folk*, 1945 (*Independent People*). Antti Hyri (b. 1931) has written a 'new wave' novel, *Kevatta ja syksya*, 1958 (*Spring and Fall*).

THE LOW COUNTRIES

Lubertus Jacobus Swaanswijk (b. 1924, better known outside his country as Lucebert), Hans Andreus (b. 1926) and Remco Campert (b. 1929) figure most prominently among the Dutch poets of the '50s and '60s. Their search for a new lyricism is based on the impact of immediate sensation. While Simon Vestdijk (b. 1898) continues to astonish the younger generation by his capacity for renewal (*Vor en na de explosie*, 1960), Willem Hermans (b. 1921) has won universal acclaim with his novels *Conserve* (*Preserves*) and *The Dark Room of Damocles*, the latter an apocalyptic vision of our time. Gerard Kornelis van Het Reve (b. 1923) in his controversial novel *De avonden*, 1947 (*The Evenings*) attempts to solve the desperate problem of individual life in an aimless society. A number of Flemish writers live in Belgium, such as Jos Vandeloo (b. 1925, *Spelse parade*, 1955—*Playful Parade* and *De muur*, 1958—*The Wall*). Georges Simenon (b. 1903 at Liége), although claimed in equal measure by France, considers himself a Belgian and has expressed much of the dark, damp and disillusioned atmosphere of the Belgian landscape in his earlier novels. This Balzac of the detective story has written 200 novels and can still surprise. Within the small Grand Duchy of Luxemburg there is an active group of poets writing in German (Anise Koltz, b. 1928) and in French (Joseph Leydenbach and A. Borschette).

GERMANY, AUSTRIA AND SWITZERLAND

The most obvious effects of the collapse of Nazi Germany seem to have been a tendency to introspection and the need felt by writers to render an account both to Germany itself and to the world at large of what really happened. At the end of the war it was possible to differentiate clearly between the young, the middle-aged (those who were the most disastrously affected of all) and the elderly, such as Heinrich Mann, his brother Thomas and Franz Werfel. Ten years later a new configuration emerged, enabling a graphic distinction to be drawn between pre-war and post-war writers. Whatever their differences, Thomas Mann, Godfried Benn, Bertold Brecht and Ernst Jünger had charted the decay of Hitler's Germany, the corruption of a whole nation and culture, the brutal pursuit of power without ethical restraint. It was to them that the younger generation turned for guidance. Thomas Mann's *Doktor Faustus*, 1949 went to the heart of his still hypnotised fellow-countrymen as symbolising the unmistakable tendency of the German spirit always to find an outlet in music no matter their periodic nationalistic excesses. Jünger's novel *Heliopolis*, 1949 showed the humiliation of man in the modern city.

The fall of the Third Reich was soon to lead to an entirely new approach. Hans Werner Richter (b. 1908) founded the Gruppe 47 in Munich stating that writers had to 'narrate with brutality what happened brutally'. In his novel *Die Geschlagenen*, 1948 (*The Vanquished*) Richter describes the forced coexistence, in the same camp, of Nazis and anti-Nazis; in another novel, *Sie fielen aus Gottes Hand*, 1951 he depicted the migrations of displaced people. Herman Kasack (b. 1896) gave in *Die Stadt hinter dem Strom*, 1953 (*The City beyond the River*) a huge panorama of the whole crumbling civilisation. The destruction of Hamburg was the subject of *Interview mit dem Tode*, 1948 (*Interview with Death*) by Hans Erich Nossack (b. 1901). Among the most significant novels of the aftermath of the war was *Wo warst du, Adam?*, 1951 (*Adam, Where Art Thou?*) by the Rhenish Catholic Heinrich Böll (b. 1917). Naturally, everybody's answer in life as in the book is 'I was at the front', but Böll was not satisfied with the answer, and in an extreme state of God-forsakenness—'we must pray in order to *console* God'—continued the interrogation in yet another gloomy novel, *Und sagte kein einziges Wort*, 1955 (*Acquainted with the Night*).

Gerd Gaiser (b. 1908) in *Die sterbende Jagd*, 1953 (*The Last Squadron*) reconstructs the destruction of the Luftwaffe in Norway; he achieves deeper analysis in *Schlussball*, 1958 (*Final Dance*), the story of a family brooding over their country's defeat. In these novels Gaiser unfolds the mental chaos of post-war Germany. Günther Grass (b. 1927) belongs to the younger generation of poets and novelists (he is also a talented sculptor) expressing in unmitigated terms its hatred of bourgeois smugness and complacency, its hostility to old-fashioned nationalism and the feeling that the right is bankrupt. His best-known novel, *Die Blechtrommel*, 1959 (*The Tin Drum*), tells the story of a boy who refuses to grow after the age of three—his constant drumming symbolises the revolt against the insanity of our epoch.

The same sense of the absurdity of human pretensions unites most German poets today. Hans Magnus Enzenberger (b. 1929) whose first volume of verse is symbolically called *Verteidigung der Wölfe*, 1957 (*A Defence of the Wolves*), Heinz Piontek (b. 1925—*Wassermarken*, 1957), Gunter Eich (b. 1907), Paul Celan (b. 1920 in Rumania and now living in Paris—*Sprachgitter*, 1959), Ingeborg Bachmann (b. 1926)—all these poets show a despair which would seem a reaction against pre-war values, and the precarious political implications of a divided Germany encourage cynicism.

Austrian writers, although in general less afflicted by the crumbling of the Third Reich, have nonetheless responded to the situation. Ilse Aichinger (b. 1921) created a stir when she published *Die grössere Hoffnung*, 1958 (*The Larger Hope*) which presented the persecution and extermination of the Jews seen through the eyes of a new Alice in Wonderland. Erich Fried (b. 1921, settled in London since 1938) is an uncompromising witness of the political scene and a master of his craft both in his collected *Gedichte*, 1958 and in his novel *Ein Soldat und ein Mädchen*, 1961; Herbert Eisenreich (b. 1925), in the collection of short stories *Einladung deutlich zu leben*, 1951 (*Invitation to a Meaningful Life*), displays a profound unity of conception; Heimito von Doderer (b. 1896), often compared to Proust, wrote his greatest novel, *Die Dämonen*, in 1956.

The Swiss writers Max Frisch (b. 1911) and Friedrich Dürrenmatt (b. 1921) have in the last fifteen years brought literary world fame to the

German part of the Helvetic Confederation. Both are among Europe's most influential playwrights,[1] but have written important novels: in *Stiller*, 1954 and *Homo Faber*, 1957 Frisch chooses two heroes who have lost their identity; Dürrenmatt in *Die Falle*, 1946 and *Der Richter und sein Henker*, 1950 (*The Judge and his Executioner*) handles his obsessive themes of piety and penitence with almost wrathful vitality.

GREECE AND TURKEY

Most writers of the clandestine and highly patriotic literature of Greece provoked by four years of enemy occupation and persecution (1941–4) made a remarkable volte-face after the war and began to write works of detailed and aggressive social significance. It was during this period that Nikos Kazantsakis (1883–1957) wrote *Zorba the Greek*. A multiplicity of new themes appear in the novels of Galathea Sarantsis (b. 1920) and Margareta Liberaki-Karapanu (b. 1930), two women novelists of consistent psychological depth. Pantelis Prevelakis (b. 1909) offers a new vision of Crete in *The Chronicle of a City*. George Seferis (b. 1900) brought Greece its first Nobel Prize in 1933; his noble poetic vision is continued in the work of Odysseus Elythis (b. 1911), Nikos Gatsos (b. 1914), N. D. Karouzos (b. 1926) and Nicolas Matsas (b. 1928). Their even younger followers tend to combine ancient themes with modern, experimental imagery.

In spite of the revolution achieved by Kemal Ataturk—a feudal country went through one of the greatest linguistic and social transformations of modern times almost overnight—the new Turkish literature did not emerge until the publication in 1941 of *Garip*, a collective volume containing the experimental work of three poets, Orhan Veli (1914–50), Oktay Rifat (b. 1914) and Melih Cevdet Anday (b. 1915). 'The entire structure of literature', they said, 'must be altered from top to bottom; poetry must appeal to the multitudes'. Influenced by Apollinaire and the surrealists, Veli drew his inspiration from the 'little' man's daily life and his example is still a major influence among the younger poets. The equally important work of Nazim Hikmet (1901–62) cannot circulate in the poet's own country because he was a militant Communist and in fact died in exile in the Soviet Union. Bedri Rahmi Eyuboglu (b. 1913) exerts his influence not only as a poet but also as a painter in his native Istanbul.

Deeply steeped in ancient folktales, the young Turkish novelists continue the Islamic tradition of story-telling, evident in *Our Village* by Mahmud Makal (b. 1930), an account of peasant life in Anatolia, and in a number of realist novels such as *Ince Memed*, 1956 (*Slim Memed*) by Yashar Kemal which was acclaimed as a masterpiece of observation and local colour. Orham Kemal (b. 1914) has also acquired fame with his short stories and novels which constitute a canvas of social evolution. The short stories of Sait Faik (1907–54) sparkle with uninhibited love and fun ('If men are not to love each other, why do they build such crowded cities?'). The still younger poets and novelists, e.g. Edip Cansever (b. 1928), Metin Eloglou (b. 1927), Kemal Ozer (b. 1935) and Taksin Yugel (b. 1933), are learning to lean less and less on Western ideas and themes, and to use them as objects of comparison rather than sources of inspiration. The future of Turkish literature lies in the rich indigenous character of Turkey.

[1] See 'Theatre', p. 514.

ITALY

The Fascist dictatorship left no opportunity to Italian novelists between the wars for genuine expression and experiment. The poets Giuseppe Ungaretti (b. 1888), Eugenio Montale (b. 1896), Umberto Saba (b. 1883) and to a lesser extent Salvatore Quasimodo (b. 1901, Nobel Prize 1959) dominated the scene with their hermetic meditations and subtle technical devices. Thus the advent of peace in 1945 released the pent-up feelings and ideas of the previous three decades into a ruthless critique of society, of the corrupt governing classes and of the hypocritical bourgeoisie. Vitaliano Brancati (1907–54) with *Gli anni perduti*, 2nd ed. 1944 (*The Lost Years*) and Alberto Moravia (b. 1907) with *La mascherata*, 1947 (*The Fancy Dress Party*) and *La Romana*, 1947 (*The Woman of Rome*), led this movement. Brancati, who lived in Sicily, laid bare in two other novels, *Don Giovanni in Sicilia*, 1941 and *Il bell'Antonio*, 1949 (*Antonio, the Great Lover*) a provincial life in which men cannot integrate their rampant sexual desires with a maturer, more total relationship, but boast and brag their way towards brute animality. Moravia, too, proclaims the collapse of traditional values; he owes his popularity and influence to a totally pansexualist view of the world which invades his style as well as content.

Cesare Pavese (1908–50) is still a dominant influence through the bitter solitariness reflected in each page of his posthumously published diary *Il mestiere di vivere* (*This Business of Living*). His roots were mostly in an inescapable childhood past. Each man is an enclosed world; woman cannot enter. And so although Pavese attempted to face society as a realist, he remained the contemplative witness. In *Quasi una vita*, 1951 (*Almost a Life*) Corrado Alvaro (b. 1895) has married the political chronicler in him to the man rooted in the south in its suffering. The south has produced a powerful neo-realist movement restoring ties with European currents, restricting its scope to the hard, desperate provincial and rural life, but within that examining what makes man truly a human being, through his fundamental needs. The psychological subtleties of leisured people have no relevance in this world. Carlo Levi's *Cristo si è fermato a Eboli*, 1946 (*Christ Stopped at Eboli*) was the first example of this movement. Levi's brilliant account of his own experiences when Mussolini sent him into political exile in the primitive region of Lucania sparked off a whole series of documentaries, notably Danilo Dolci's *Inquest at Palermo*. Elio Vittorini (1908–65) in his *Conversazione in Sicilia* (*Conversation in Sicily*, 1948) marked a more lyrical and constructive tendency. The 'I' was no longer introspective but identified with the destiny of others in their fall and their salvation. His influence is still profound. In contrast with Vittorini's bitterness is the gentle realism of Vasco Pratolini (b. 1913), chronicler of the ordinary Florentine worker and vindicator of comradeship and solidarity. In *Il quartiere*, 1944 (*A Tale of Santa Croce*) and *Un eroe del nostro tempo*, 1949 (*A Hero of Today*) he achieves documentaries of supreme artistry, something Zola or Gorky never did to the same degree.

But neo-realism by no means monopolises post-war Italian literature. The fantasists and dark humourists play their part, for example Tomasso Landolfi (b. 1908) with *Raconto d'autunno*, 1947 and *Ombro*, 1954 and Dino Buzzati (b. 1906) with *In quel preciso momento*, 1951, an exploration of fantasy and the absurd which has a disturbing logic. Carlo Emilio Gadda (b. 1893), an engineer by profession, is a case apart. His profession of faith *Come lavoro*, 1950 reveals a bitter conception of life presented in a violent style softened by a devastating sense of humour. His masterpiece *La cognizione del dolore*,

1963, set in an imaginary place in South America, is a tour de force reminiscent of Rabelais and Joyce; it is as if language is in a perpetual state of formation—foreign and archaic words are used as well as new coinages to convey an extraordinary sense of the ironical and grotesque.

Women novelists who deserve mention include Alba de Cespedes (b. 1911; *Dalla parte di lei*, 1949 and *Prima e dopo*, 1956), Gianna Manzini (b. 1896; *Arco di Noé*, 1960), Natalia Ginzburg (b. 1916; *La strada che va in città*, 1942— *The Road to the City*, *Tutti i nostri ieri*, 1952, *Le voci della sera*, 1961) and Elsa Morante (b. 1918; *L'isola di Arturo*, 1957).

With Gadda there stand preeminent Italo Calvino (b. 1923), Carlo Cassola (b. 1917) and Pier Paolo Pasolini (b. 1922). With their starting-point as neo-realists each moves in his own direction. Calvino allows fantasy to exceed realism; he is sharp, witty and malicious. Cassola goes beyond the pathos of Vittorini to rigorous objectivity—his characters have no emotional complexity but act in a world of unquestionable objects. Pasolini is the *enfant terrible* of the group; his *Ragazzi di vita*, 1955, caused a sensation with its bold and detailed description of youth, while in his later works, such as *Una vita violenta*, 1959, like Gadda he puts language to a Joycean sort of test. Life in its elemental aspect intoxicates these writers, and their steady progress indicates the potential and at the same time the limitations of post-war Italian writing—provincialism means contact with lived and picturesque experience but also loss of contact with foreign experimental movements.

In the work of the poets who became established after the war there are to be found, generally speaking, an engagé tone and distinctly left attitudes. Vittorio Sereni (b. 1913) is preoccupied with the problem of man in urban society; in *Gli strumenti umani*, 1965, he forsakes the personal, subjective lyric for an attempt to render civic consciousness, a direction already apparent to some extent in his earlier *Diario d'Algeria*. In Pier Paolo Pasolini a political interest is strong (*La religione del mio tempo*, 1961; *Poesia in forma di rosa*, 1964). Other representatives of this generation are Alfonso Gatto (b. 1909), Mario Luzi (b. 1914) and Bartolo Cattafi (b. 1922). The 1960s have produced a significant avant-garde group known as the Novissimi, a selection of whose work appeared in 1961 in the anthology *I Novissimi*, ed. Alfredo Giuliani (revised edition 1965). Alfredo Giuliani (b. 1924), Elio Pagliarani (b. 1927), Edoardo Sanguineti (b. 1930), Nanni Balestrini (b. 1935) and Antonio Porta (b. 1935) are concerned with linguistic experiment before ideology and social criticism, seeking a new poetic structure to reflect a post-war social structure whose destruction of values they take for granted. The function of poetry, writes Giuliani in his introduction to *I Novissimi*, is 'not so much a form of knowledge as a means of contact,' and 'poetry must explore all possible ambiguity and comprehensiveness of language.'

CONCLUSION

In spite of widespread discontent and frustration among European writers, literature is still a matter of dedication. Many of the linguistic labours which show a wealth of technique rather than of feeling have a contemporary reference and justification. The changes and disruptions which the second world war brought about in the life of Western Europe are so deep that many nations are now making a sort of pilgrimage in search of a new ideal. We may therefore assume that man's hopefulness will continue to help writers to find truths beneath the surface of frequent adversity and ugliness.

BIBLIOGRAPHY

Bleiberg, Germán and Marías, Julian. *Diccionario de literatura española*, Revista de Occidente, Madrid, 3rd ed. 1964.

Collins, A. S. *English Literature of the Twentieth Century*, University Tutorial Press, London, 4th ed. 1960.

de Doisdeffre, Pierre (ed.) *Dictionnaire de littérature contemporaine*, Éditions Universitaires, Paris, 1963.

Einarsson, S. *History of Icelandic Literature*, Oxford Univ. Press, London; Johns Hopkins Press, Baltimore, Md, 1957.

Grenzmann, Wilhelm. *Deutsche Dichtung der Gegenwart*, Frankfurt-am-Main, 2nd ed. 1955.

Grigson, Geoffrey (ed.). *The Concise Encyclopaedia of Modern World Literature*, Hutchinson, London; Hawthorn Books, New York, 1963.

Gustafson, Alrick. *A History of Swedish Literature*, Oxford Univ. Press, London; Univ. of Minnesota Press, Minneapolis, Minn., 1961.

Jennings, Elizabeth. *Poetry Today*, Longmans, Green for British Council, London; London House and Maxwell, New York, 1961.

Sherrard, Philip. *The Marble Threshing Floor—Studies in modern Greek poetry*, Vallentine, Mitchell, London, 1956.

Viscardi, Antonio. *Storia della letteratura italiana*, Milan, 1960.

von Wilbert, Gero (ed.). *Lexikon der Weltliteratur*, Kröner, Stuttgart, 1963.

Adam International Review, London. Special issues on contempory Danish, Dutch, Swedish, Swiss and Catalan literatures.

THEATRE

OSSIA TRILLING

In many countries of Western Europe the theatre has traditionally been regarded as a spiritual need or public utility and has received the support of the state together with museums, libraries and education. In certain others, namely Britain, Ireland, France, Italy, Greece, Spain and Portugal, it was until recently thought of as a commercial undertaking subject to the demands of a free market. The broader concept began to spread to these countries after the second world war. The theatre is increasingly fulfilling its ancient role as a social and communal leveller and an intellectual forum. Britain has its National Theatre at long last; Italy has a permanent civic theatre in its capital for the first time since the Colosseum was abandoned as a resort of public entertainment, and in Milan the world-famous Piccolo Teatro has been saved for the nation after its two founders, Paolo Grassi and Giorgio Strehler, threatened to abandon it for lack of adequate municipal support; in France, where for centuries the theatre meant Paris, an ever-expanding state-aided regional repertory system is now firmly established; Eire has rebuilt the Abbey Theatre, though that, for the moment, is as far as the state has ventured; the Greek government assists and imposes conditions on the private sector to ensure that theatre-going everywhere, and not only at the National Theatre or the annual festival in the ancient 15,000-seat Epidaurus Theatre, falls within the purview of everyone's purse; even in Spain and Portugal, where religious and political censorship restricts the free growth of a genuinely popular theatre movement, the theatre receives limited encouragement from public funds.

For the most part, however, the theatre remains a minority—and a middle-class—pastime. This is especially true where education is still differentiated along class frontiers. Cinema, television and pop music are the mass-audience attractions. The tendency to suspect the dramatic art is however being fought. This is done in a variety of ways. In France, Sweden and Germany, for instance, audience organisations offer reduced-price seats and preferential ticket-booking facilities. The German Volksbühne movement ensures captive audiences to most theatres (and opera houses). Skilful written or word-of-mouth propaganda aims to reach audiences through the school and the factory. The effect is cumulative. The growth of children's theatres almost everywhere implies a recognition that the spectator of the future has to be captured as young as possible, when he is most impressionable. Where theatre-going has been a national habit for a long time, as in Sweden or Germany, the scope for experiment is greater. It is no accident that there is a wider response to avant-garde drama among the general public in these countries than, say, in France, where it remains a minority interest. In such countries, too, the stage attracts far more writers with an intellectual, poetic or philosophic bent—witness Sweden.

Austria, Germany and Switzerland

Strictly speaking the German-language theatre is indivisible, with its regular interchange not only of plays but also of artists and technicians. Nonetheless each of the three German-speaking countries has an identifiable face of its own.

In Vienna the Burgtheater, with two stages, boasts the highest acting payroll (108 not counting guest-artists) of any European subsidised playhouse. It has a recognisable acting style that leans heavily on exteriorised display and its policy in recent years has obliged it to steer clear of controversial dramatists like Brecht, Frisch or Beckett. It has concentrated on the Austrian classics (Grillparzer and Raimund) and Shakespeare, often exquisitely staged. However, in 1966 its first production of a play by Brecht was announced for the ensuing season and there was talk of inaugurating a studio-stage for minority tastes. Max Reinhardt's old theatre, the Josefstadt, privately owned but partly subsidised, has been a little more enterprising, as in the case of *Die Flucht* ('The Flight') by Lida Winiewicz and Ernst Waldbrunn, an actor turned dramatist, who himself re-enacts, in his first play, the autobiographical dilemma of a half-Jew confronted by a Nazi on the run who once saved his life.

The 'recent past' (as German-speaking people outside Switzerland prefer to call the 'Nazi terror') is a theme that is widely touched on more than twenty years after the overthrow of Hitler, even in Austria. All the same, the country's foremost living dramatist, Fritz Hochwälder (b. 1911), an original playwright blessed with a philosophical turn of mind, insisted on having his latest drama *Der Himbeerpflücker* ('The Raspberry Picker'), a farcical study of neo-Nazism, premièred in Switzerland where he lives. Few of the remaining Austrian dramatists have found a public outside the German-speaking theatre. Elias Canetti (b. Bulgaria, 1905) is without doubt the giant among them, intellectually speaking, but his playwriting career was interrupted by the Nazi interregnum and he now resides in England, like his countrymen, Erich Fried (b. 1921), a distinguished poet and translator of Shakespeare, and Jakov Lind (b. 1927), a dramatist, like Fried, who is obsessed by the unimaginable depths of cruelty of which man is capable. The regional theatres in Austria, like those in Switzerland, have a determined provincial tone, despite their international repertoire. In Bregenz and Salzburg, at the annual festival, foreign dramatists, like the exiled Polish Catholic writer, Roman Brandstätter (b. 1906) or Julius Hay (b. 1900), an exile from Communist Hungary, have been given a first hearing.

The Europa Studio in Salzburg gave the German première of O'Neill's lost play *More Stately Mansions*, the last play of his great autobiographical cycle, in Karl Ragnar Gierow's reconstructed version, first seen in Swedish in Stockholm. Leopold Lindtberg and Fritz Kortner are two of the former exiles who frequently return to Austria from Switzerland and Germany, where they live and are regularly employed, to add lustre to the art of theatrical production in their sometime fatherland.

The most widespread and best attended theatre of the German-speaking countries, as well as the most heavily subsidised, is that of West Germany. The pattern is repeated in West Berlin, once the theatrical capital of Germany and now obliged to compete for personnel and the maintenance of artistic standards with a decentralised theatre that sprawls between Hamburg and Munich, Düsseldorf and Stuttgart, Lübeck and Frankfurt. Even the smaller towns, like Bremen, Heidelberg, Darmstadt or Ulm, can afford to be go-ahead in repertoire and presentation. They often invite leading guest-directors from other cities or from abroad and vie with one another for the privilege of being the first to stage a new dramatist's work. The present revival owes much to the federal and municipal post-war rebuilding policy. Playhouses often share a stage and overheads with an opera or ballet ensemble and can thus rationalise staff, expenses and programmes. This forward-looking policy has also had the effect of luring back several of the eminent artists, like Kortner, who had been banished by the Nazis. Among them are players of the first rank like Ernst Deutsch, Elisabeth Bergner, Lucie Mannheim and Grete Mosheim. The director Erwin Piscator (1893–1966), inventor of the 'epic' and 'total' theatres, spiritual foster-father of Brecht and pioneer of the labour theatre of the 1920s and of countless technical and artistic innovations now taken for granted throughout the world, was for several years, until his death, manager of the West Berlin Free People's Theatre where he staged the world premières of several new plays by German or German-speaking authors.

The most prominent of these was Peter Weiss (b. 1916), who escaped from Nazi Germany as a youth and is today a resident and citizen of Sweden. His scarifying contemporary dramas, all written in German, have been staged in every corner of the globe. Taking his inspiration from Artaud, Brecht and Strindberg, Weiss is a poet of the theatre but with a political and philosophical axe to grind. His best-known work is *The Persecution and Murder of Jean Paul Marat as Staged by the Inmates of the Asylum of Charenton under the Direction of the Marquis de Sade*. It was premièred at the Schiller Theatre in Berlin. It exploits innumerable theatrical devices borrowed from disparate theatrical traditions, involving the use of music, mime and a combination of prose and verse, to present the philosophical dilemma of revolution in all its implications. The Berlin production, staged by guest-director Konrad Swinarski, from Warsaw, was pronounced 'very daring, for Warsaw' by Peter Brook, while his own production by the Royal Shakespeare Company, cast in a rather different mould and reflecting more closely the then fashionable vogue of the 'theatre of cruelty', won high critical distinction when performed in New York. The action is laid throughout in the bath-house of a lunatic asylum and the Stockholm production (by Frank Sundström) emphasised the claustrophobic atmosphere by having the entire auditorium decked out as a bathhouse and thus fully involving the audience in the horrors that were being enacted not only before its eyes but all around it. Piscator mounted a moving rendering of Weiss's *The Investigation*, a poetic distillation in oratorio form of the Frankfurt trial of the Auschwitz war-criminals on the same night as fifteen other German theatre managers, while Peter Brook staged a rehearsed reading of the play simultaneously in London. A dramatic and highly concentrated evocation of a terrifying chapter of human history, Weiss's play is a perfect example of the German 'Zeittheater'.

This term does not quite mean documentary theatre, but rather contemporary theatre in a political and philosophical sense. It applies more obviously to *The Representative* by Rolf Hochhuth (b. 1931) and to *In the Matter of J. Robert Oppenheimer* by Heinar Kipphardt (b. 1922), both staged by Piscator. The first of these is a contentious drama (also subsequently performed the world over) which seeks to lay a portion of the blame for the war-time massacre of the Jews of Europe on the Vatican's refusal, on diplomatic grounds, to make an overt protest; the second is a documentary condensation of the loyalty hearings of the United States Atomic Commission in which the eminent nuclear physicist and 'father of the atom-bomb' appeared as a martyred protagonist. Controversial topics of contemporary or recent historical themes have provided a whole new generation of German dramatists with much of their material. Hans Günther Michelsen (b. 1920), a former serving officer, examines the backwash of Nazism in the present-day German army in *Helm*, written, like his earlier plays, in an idiosyncratically elliptical manner that recalls the style if not the subject-matter of the plays of Samuel Beckett. This play, too, was performed at Piscator's theatre, as was *Aufstand der Offiziere* ('The Officers' Conspiracy') by Hans Hellmut Kirst (b. 1914), a thriller-type documentary about the abortive 1944 plot to assassinate Hitler. Martin Walser (b. 1927) is another writer interested in the Nazi mind both past and present, as his two plays *Eiche und Angora* ('Oak and Angora'—*The Rabbit Race* as it was called when staged in English at the Edinburgh Festival) and *Der schwarze Schwan* ('The Black Swan') show, though his method is allegorical and makes few concessions to the audience. The type of play that is often described in the West as 'theatre of the absurd' is not much in evidence in Germany. The novelist Günther Grass (b. 1927) began his writing career as an absurdist playwright. In 1965 he changed his tack to the 'Zeittheater' type of play, though using a form of poetic symbolism (e.g. in *Die Plebeier proben den Aufstand*—'The Plebeians Rehearse the Uprising'), in which he posed the problem of the role of the intellectual in a revolutionary situation. All these writers (except Michelsen), and several more like them, owe their inspiration to the Brechtian theatre and to its characteristic 'epic' manner, which seeks to inform and persuade by demonstration rather than by swaying the emotions as the traditional classical theatre seeks to do.

West German managers have shown a special interest in the East European theatre, not only inviting directors, like Swinarski or Erwin Axer of Warsaw, and designers, like Josef Svoboda of Prague, to work in their theatres, but also staging many first performances of radical East European plays, sometimes as world premières. Thus Vaclav Havel and Ivan Klima of Prague have been put on in Berlin and Düsseldorf. Slawomir Mrozek of Warsaw, though currently self-exiled to Italy, has been staged throughout the German-speaking theatre (as well as in other West European countries) and even politically conforming authors have found their way to West German stages, not least from East Germany. Hartmut Lange (b. 1937) is an example of an East German writer (Kipphardt is another) who has moved to the West; his latest drama, *Marski*, a critique in verse of life in the German Democratic Republic, was first performed in Frankfurt. Among the world premières staged in Germany are several plays by Beckett and the Americans Albee and Kopit, who found producers in Berlin long before they became established in the United States. The standards of performances are usually of the highest, partly thanks to the tradition which was maintained abroad, notably in Zurich, during the Nazi interregnum, and undoubtedly also to the technical advances that enable complex scenic effects, for example, to be simulated with ease by means of up-to-date lighting techniques. In this field several of Germany's foremost directors are as much at home in the opera-house as in the playhouse, both at home and abroad. Günther Rennert, of the Bavarian State Opera and also Artistic Adviser of the Glyndebourne Opera in England, and no less familiar on the dramatic stage, exemplifies this group of versatile theatre artists.

As the bastion of intellectual freedom during the Nazi period, Zurich became a refuge and focal point of all that was best in the German theatre that did not find its way across the Atlantic. Here, where some of Brecht's plays were first staged and where a designer of international stature like Teo Otto made his home, the German-speaking theatre's most influential dramatists, the agnostic humanist Max Frisch (b. 1911) and the Christian humanist Friedrich Dürrenmatt (b. 1921) grew to maturity. Both have found an audience far beyond their native Switzerland, and each, for all their difference of approach, the former romantic, the latter avowedly Brechtian, owe their appeal as much to their purely technical mastery as to the fact that, fundamentally, their chosen themes reflect the thoughts and anxieties of men and women today. Frisch's *Andorra* is a satire on xenophobia in general that administers a rebuke to the Nazi mentality in particular, wherever it may be found. Dürrenmatt's *The Visit of the Old Lady* has also travelled far and wide and been subjected to countless interpretations from an anti-capitalist tract to a piece of Christian pleading. Though no one label fits all their plays, what the two writers and all their plays have in common (apart from a palpable if tenuous pessimistic thread) is a desire to explore every possible theatrical expedient in order both to amuse and to instruct their audience. No writer for the theatre in French-speaking Switzerland, dominated as it is by the neighbouring theatre of France, compares with these two in ability, unless one excepts the absurdist Robert Pinget (b. 1920) who lives in Paris. The Italian-speaking population rely for their theatrical fare on radio, TV, local amateurs and touring companies from Italy.

BRITAIN

Theatrical activity has for years been concentrated in the capital. Struggling provincial repertory theatres (as they are misnamed, since their programmes are presented for short runs of from a fortnight to four weeks) have benefited since the war from increasing state aid distributed through the Arts Council of Great Britain and, with certain notable exceptions, the rather less forthcoming local authorities, enabled since 1948 to assist the professional theatre out of rates. Several of these have done solid work as a result, expanding audiences and fostering new playwrights, who also receive encouragement of a practical kind from the Arts Council and by way of foundation grants and such institutions as the new university drama departments (that in Bristol being the first). Bristol (where the name of the Old Vic as a company has been retained after the original was swallowed up by the National Theatre in London), Oxford, Coventry, Liverpool and Nottingham (which has one of the most modern and adaptable stages in the country), are the leaders of the repertory movement today. Since 1956 there has been a veritable revolution in the British theatre. It is both convenient and convincing to date its beginning to 1956, because that was the year in which the Royal Court Theatre, managed for ten years by the late George Devine, launched out with a new policy and the discovery of John Osborne (b. 1929).

Creator of the 'angry young man', Osborne was the forerunner of a whole school of new playwriting that has grown apace in the succeeding years, fertilised on the one hand by the drama and television departments of the BBC and the commercial TV stations and on the other by parallel institutions of similar intent, like the Theatre Workshop directed by Joan Littlewood in Stratford-atte-Bowe in London's East End, the Arts Theatre Club in the heart of London's West End (nicknamed 'London's pocket national theatre' by a perceptive critic), the more enterprising provincial repertory theatres, and since the 1960s the Hampstead Theatre Club. What is unprecedented about the new school is the fact that its authors are largely of working class origin and that their plays owe nothing to the conventions of the escapist theatre of entertainment which mostly relies for its success on dramatic trivia. So deeply embedded has it become in the public conscience that commercial managers and, with them, a conservative theatre censorship, have reacted to developing public taste by attempting to satisfy it rather than, as in the past, ignoring or suppressing it. Matters of public concern both social and private are now freely discussed, though the Lord Chamberlain's office still has arbitrary powers over every word spoken and action performed in a public theatre.

The growth of the new school of playwrights is partly a social phenomenon and partly a reflection of the aspirations and frustrations of the younger post-war generation. This is especially true of Osborne's earliest plays, *Look Back in Anger, The Entertainer, Epitaph for George Dillon* and *The World of Paul Slickey*. A working-class boy who became an actor and found himself equipped with a gift for concisely pungent dialogue, Osborne is both a social rebel himself and the spokesman of the rebels and the misfits or outsiders in the society he abhors. Many of his protagonists are failures, from Archie Rice in *The Entertainer* to Maitland in *Inadmissible Evidence*. Even when attracted by a historical or literary theme (*Luther, A Patriot for Me*, about the homosexual Austrian spy Colonel Redl, or *A Bond Honoured*, based on a Lope de Vega play about a repentant renegade) Osborne chooses non-conformist protagonists and invests them with a universality that goes some way to explaining why he is the British dramatist whose plays are most often performed outside Britain.

What Osborne lacks is a true poetic gift. John Arden (b. 1930) has it in abundance. His earliest plays are as full of protest as Osborne's but they have a degree of poetic and allusive truth that invites the audience to consider their verdict without instructing them which way they ought to vote. Even the hero of *Serjeant Musgrave's Dance*, who should be representing Arden's convictions about war and hatred, is painted in deliberately unattractive colours. In *The Workhouse Donkey*, a satire on power politics in terms of local government ambitions and rivalries, *Left-Handed Liberty*, an ambivalent study of King John written to commission to commemorate the Magna Carta celebrations, and *Armstrong's Last Goodnight*, which has the wily opportunist Sir David Lindsay committing crimes for the greater glory of the English King Henry VIII whom he serves, Arden, like Brecht, shows us the many facets of human nature without necessarily inviting full condemnation of any one of them. Typical in Arden is the use of the ballad, a musical penchant he shares with Brecht.

Among the principal proletarian dramatists (their dramas have been unfairly called 'kitchen-sink', a term of abuse that betrays the class prejudice of the critic rather than the nature of the play itself) are Shelagh Delaney (b. 1939), whose first play, *A Taste of Honey*, about a touching personal relationship and written at the age of eighteen, seems to have been a flash in the pan, Frank Norman (b. 1930), an entertaining painter of low life, and the late Brendan Behan, an Irishman by birth but, like the other two, put squarely on the British theatrical map by Joan Littlewood. Bernard Kops (b. 1928) and Arnold Wesker (b. 1932) are preoccupied with the role of the individual in a society that is on the eve of becoming socialist and, as Jews themselves, they excel in portraying Jewish characters. Harold Pinter (b. 1930), also a Jew, is no less adept at putting realistic Jewish types on the stage, but this is not by any means his main concern. His plays (notably *The Homecoming* and *The Caretaker*) have been called comedies of menace, and the clashes of fear, greed and misunderstanding when wholly incompatible people are brought together are brilliantly worked out through the use of a repetitive or lapidary dialogue, deliberately studded with clichés and false emphases. By contrast with the others, and despite the deceptive realism of his dialogue, which is really highly artificial, Pinter, as he himself admits, has nothing whatever of real importance to say.

Wesker is a case apart. He depicts personal and social animosities in the realistic *The Kitchen*, the discrepancy between town and country and between the educated and the less fortunate in the socialist trilogy *Chicken Soup with Barley*, *Roots* and *I'm Talking about Jerusalem*, and frustrating class distinctions in *Chips with Everything* and *Their Very Own and Golden City* (which won the Marzotto Theatre Award in 1964). He has put his beliefs into practice through the trade union supported Centre 42 which he co-founded and directs; the aim of this organisation is to bring the artistic experience to audiences hitherto deprived of it.

The list of new British working-class writers is too vast to mention in its entirety. One might, however, single out Henry Livings (b. 1929), an eloquent farceur (performed at Theatre Workshop, the Arts Theatre and at the Royal Shakespeare Company, London); James Saunders (b. 1925), a social critic with a Pirandellian streak; and David Mercer (b. 1928), whose stage plays, like his TV dramas, are packed with invention. Other writers not of proletarian origin who have climbed on to the band-wagon of the theatre of revolt include John Mortimer (b. 1923), a barrister with a flair for incisive dramatic utterance; Ann Jellicoe (b. 1928) and N. F. Simpson (b. 1919), two winners of the Observer Play Competition that coincided with the birth of the new wave and gave it a strong fillip; and Peter Shaffer (b. 1926), whose output ranges from an examination of the fascist mentality (*Five Finger Exercise*) to an historical drama about the Conquest of Peru (*The Royal Hunt of the Sun*) and a hilariously ironic comedy of 1960 manners (*Black Comedy*).

Older playwrights who are successfully performed include Graham Greene (b. 1904), unorthodox apologist for Roman Catholicism, James Boynton Priestley (b. 1894), Noel Coward (b. 1899) and the most successful authoress of thrillers of all time, Agatha Christie (b. 1890), whose *The Mousetrap*—in its fourteenth year in 1966—is the longest-running play in history.

Britain's first permanent 'open-stage' or 'thrust-stage' playhouse, the Chichester Festival Theatre, inspired by Sir Tyrone Guthrie's Canadian precedent, has set the tone for a new style of production which has baffled orthodox opinion but enables the classics to be staged far more adequately than when they are constricted into the conventional 'picture-frame' stage. England even has a permanent 'Theatre in the Round' at Stoke, founded by the adventurous Stephen Joseph. The first theatre to be built in the City of London since the City Fathers banished the 'rogues and vagabonds' from the city precincts 300 years or more ago—the Mermaid, managed by Bernard Miles—has shed the picture-frame, though the shape of the auditorium is not revolutionary in any way. The major influence from abroad has been the Brechtian theatre with its 'Alienation Effect' and its music-hall influences, apparent in the dramas of Osborne and the productions of Joan Littlewood. The Polish critic, Jan Kott, is responsible for a new existentialist interpretation of Shakespeare, mirrored in Peter Brook's stylised handling of *King Lear* at the Royal Shakespeare Theatre. The National Theatre under Sir Laurence Olivier is too young to have formed a style of its own and its Literary Manager, Kenneth Tynan, has formally denied the need for one.

FRANCE

Hardly anyone in France is writing the kind of play that the new school in England has been producing, the kind that Planchon, head of France's most radical and go-ahead regional theatre, Théâtre de la Cité de Villeurbanne, would like to stage for his mainly working-class patrons. The nearest parallel with Germany's 'Zeitstück' authors or Britain's dramatists of revolt is Armand Gatti (b. 1924) from Marseilles, whose plays require monster casts and until 1966 had been seen in the provinces and in Germany alone, with the sole exception of the abstruse *Chant public devant deux chaises électriques* ('Public Song in front of Two Electric Chairs') which was put on at the Théâtre National Populaire (TNP) in Paris and depicts the passion of Sacco and Vanzetti. Gatti is not everybody's playwright, being overfond of theatrical trickery. To his school belongs Arthur Adamov (b. Caucasus, 1908), a self-declared Marxist dramatist of the 'epic' school, which he joined after making his earliest début as an absurdist playwright, but he, too, is more honoured in the regions than in the capital, which remains the stronghold of the commercial or 'boulevard' theatre.

Paris, however, is the seat of four national dramatic theatres and two national lyric theatres in which box-office appeal is not the main criterion of success. The TNP, directed for nearly fifteen years by Jean Vilar who was succeeded in 1964 by Georges Wilson, has its faithful following with its repertoire of mainly French classical and modern foreign plays. The Comédie Française, Europe's oldest national theatre, has a more extensive repertory that includes many more plays by French authors past and present. The Théâtre de France, part of the latter until 1961, is now a separate entity managed by Jean-Louis Barrault, whose repertory is to some extent complementary to the others'. The latest national theatre is the Théâtre de l'Est Parisien in Menilmontant, directed by Guy Retoré some-what on the lines of London's defunct Theatre Workshop, with a sprinkling of new plays among the classics. Private managers also benefit from state grants, such as those allocated to premières of new works, though on the other hand the conservative taxation system which affects alike the timid and the pioneering spirit is clearly due for overhaul.

Since the 1950s France has popularised the concepts of the 'theatre of the absurd' and the 'theatre of cruelty'. Much of what is written today, whether for the private or the national sector, derives from these two streams, which were prompted by Jarry and Artaud respectively. To the former category belong the early Adamov, Jean Tardieu (b. 1903), Samuel Beckett (b. 1906) and Eugène Ionesco (b. Rumania, 1912); to the latter Jean Genet (b. 1910) and the late Jacques Audiberti (1899–1965). Belonging to neither category or only partially affected by them are the philosopher-playwrights Jean-Paul Sartre (b. 1905), Gabriel Marcel (b. 1889), Henry Marie-Joseph Millon de Montherlant (b. 1896) and Marguerite Duras (b. Indochina, 1914). Sartre began as an existentialist, as a thinker who rejected the absolute concepts of idealist philosophy and his first plays reflect the illusory nature of general truths (*The Flies, Huis Clos*). Turning Marxist he wrote the anti-racialist *La p..... respectueuse* ('The Respectful Prostitute'), the anti-capitalist

Nekrassov, the anti-fascist *Altona* (which was also interpreted as being directed against the war in Algiers) and the anti-militarist *The Trojan Women*, an adaptation of Euripides into modern French. His line of thinking has influenced the Marxist Gabriel Cousin (b. 1918), the existentialist François Billetdoux (b. 1927) and the anti-militarist Jean Cau (b. 1915).

The influence of Samuel Beckett, born in Dublin and living in Paris, has been profound. Beckett writes in French and translates his own plays into English. *Waiting for Godot* (1953) has been called existentialist, absurdist and religious. Certainly Pinter's laconic manner is unthinkable without either Beckett or Ionesco, master of the drama of non-communication or misunderstanding. Beckett's later plays have grown shorter and less communicative with the years—as the search for identity has become harder, so the means of expression have become more succinct and withdrawn. His latest drama, *Come and Go*, premièred almost simultaneously in Berlin and Paris, plays exactly three minutes!

Ionesco, a countryman of the inventor of Dadaism, is a self-proclaimed enemy of the 'engaged' or 'committed', i.e. political theatre. He plays with thought and language as a circus-clown might with his props and his earlier plays use extravagant though usually compelling theatrical symbols to portray the human dilemma, which he views in a sort of vacuum, only occasionally, as in *Rhinoceros* or *The Stroller in the Air* (both premièred by Barrault after first performances in Germany), relating it to man's political environment. *Exit the King* (as the Edinburgh Festival production with Alec Guinness called *Le roi se meurt*) and *La soif et la faim* ('Hunger and Thirst') (which marked his début at the Comédie Française in 1966) present a cataclysmic Beckettian vision of the world. Montherlant, Jansenist and aristocratically contemptuous of the bourgeoisie he affects to despise, wields a pen of extreme violence and chooses as protagonists not the downtrodden and the oppressed, but the tyrants and oppressors. Audiberti's style is wayward and his thought generally scabrous, but he is mildness itself when compared with Genet. Marcel is an orthodox Christian apologist, a writer of considerable intellectual merit but a small following, and, like Claudel before him, difficult to export. Duras, on the other hand, despite the limited appeal of her enigmatic style, has broken through with her long one-act play *Days in the Trees* that became a starring vehicle for Madeleine Renaud in Paris and Peggy Ashcroft in London in one and the same season.

A master theatrical craftsman of little profundity is the prolific Jean Anouilh (b. 1910), whose undemanding if outspoken plays offer agreeably glib entertainment to undemanding patrons of the boulevard theatre. Several of Anouilh's plays exploit the streak of cruelty present in human nature. In the case of Genet, however, this becomes a predominant factor, and all men and women appear as the victims of their sadistic and masochistic impulses. A youth spent in criminal pursuits has shaped Genet's philosophy unmistakably and the ritualistic mould into which he presses his dramatic statements (whether he is dealing with homosexual fancies, as in *The Maids*, or with the representation of the world as a brothel of mystic proportions, as in *The Balcony*) gives them a strangely irresistible magic, once one is prepared to swallow the ribald metaphor into which everything is distorted. Illusion and reality, as in Pirandello, play a major role in his theatre, as in *The Blacks*, in which Negroes don white masks to re-enact, in highly symbolical fashion, the tragedy of racial antagonisms, or as in his four-hour-long, forbiddingly allegorical reappraisal of the Algerian war, *The Screens*, which provoked the same sort of rioting in the Théâtre de France in 1966 on the part of right-thinking patriots as had been engineered in 1964 by right-wing elements during Peter Brook's production of Hochhuth's *The Representative* at the Athénée (under the title of *Le vicaire*).

If the French theatre is weak in the scenic department (despite some note-worthy work by René Allio, Jacques Noel and Jacques Dupont), it offers a strong list of supremely able directors such as Jean-Louis Barrault, André Barsacq, Jean Vilar, Raymond Rouleau (all of whom have made their mark in the opera as well), and, especially in the field of farce, Jacques Charon.

SCANDINAVIA

The pattern in Sweden, Norway, Denmark, Finland and Iceland is much the same: there is widespread activity in the state and city theatres, which stage the best work of foreign authors alongside some native drama. Sweden can point to several highly accomplished directors, e.g. Alf Sjöberg and Ingmar Bergman. The director of the famous Royal Dramatic Theatre of Stockholm, Erland Josephson (b. 1923) took over from Bergman in 1966. He is also a noted actor and playwright. The son of devout, conservative, working-class parents, Pär Lagerkvist (b. 1891) is still the successor of Strindberg as Sweden's leading dramatist. A rebel and a social critic, with a preference for a non-realistic idiom, Lagerkvist differs from most of his southern colleagues in being a firm believer in man, even though his best-known play, *The Hangman*, ends on a sad note, and even when he indicts man's cruelty and folly, as in *The Philosopher's Stone*. This inner contradiction is typical of Sweden and is often present in the prolific dramatic output of the post-war period. Denmark, except for H. C. Branner (1903–66), has nobody of comparable stature, but the theatre-going tradition is as strong as in Sweden, especially in the capital, where the Royal Theatre offers drama, opera and ballet alternately, all of the highest standard.

Norway's theatrical life is burdened by geographical difficulties, which explain the existence of Scandinavia's oldest state touring theatre, and by its having two distinct though related languages. No dramatist since Ibsen and Bjørnson has succeeded in finding more than a local audience but the visits of Norwegian troupes abroad, recently with an American negro, Earle Hyman, playing such leading roles as Othello and Emperor Jones in impeccable Norwegian, suggest that theatrical standards should not be underestimated. Finland, like Belgium, is bilingual and the capital has theatres performing both in Finnish and in Swedish. The only dramatist of note to have crossed Finland's frontiers to any extent was Hella Wuolijoki (1886–1954), who was born in Estonia and collaborated with Brecht on the latter's *Squire Puntila and his Servant Matti*. Nonetheless there is a huge output of native drama in both languages to meet local needs. Iceland, with Europe's youngest theatre, is in a similar position as regards native drama-tists, among whom Halldór Kiljan Laxness (b. 1902) alone has been staged abroad.

ITALY

Described by J. B. Priestley soon after the second world war as the worst theatre in Europe, Italy's has rapidly risen to a high position, so high indeed that an Italian company was able to perform *Hamlet* in its native tongue at London's National Theatre in 1964, an Italian director has staged Shake-speare there more than once, and many of the coveted awards distributed at the close of the annual seasons given at the Théâtre des Nations in Paris have gone to Italian players, directors and companies. Luchino Visconti, Franco Zeffirelli, Giorgio de Lullo and Franco Enriquez, skilled directors (and often designers too) of both opera and drama, are in great demand by foreign theatre-managers. Though Italy still lacks a national theatre there is talk of turning the Milan Piccolo into one, in recompense for the valuable achievements of its founder-directors. In the 1960s a network of city theatres, sometimes in league with private touring companies (a type that is rapidly going out of existence), has become well established. Vittorio Gassman's efforts to create a popular travelling theatre (every Italian company, even a resident regional theatre, is expected to go touring) on the model of France's TNP failed, but the close collaboration between the city theatres, with their main showcase at the Florentine Civic Theatre Festival, founded in 1965, has already saved Eduardo de Filippo's Neapolitan company and may be expected to bring a much-needed measure of security to Italy's otherwise shaky theatrical structure.

De Filippo (b. 1900) is best-known abroad; his social comedies, rooted in the classical Italian comedy, are highly esteemed in Eastern Europe. But since the death of Pirandello no Italian dramatist, except possibly the late Ugo Betti (1892–1953), has been successfully transplanted. Ezio D'Errico (b. 1892) is a prolific writer who uses a symbolical idiom, Diego Fabbri (b. 1911) is a Roman Catholic humanist with a strong sense of humour, and Aldo Nicolaj (b. 1920) is a poetic fantasist with mildly left-wing commitments. These three alone among Italian dramatists have had a play performed in Germany, France or the Soviet Union. No doubt the censorship, abolished in 1965, has something to do with the relative timidity of contemporary Italian drama. It explains why *La governante* ('The Governess'), a satire on bourgeois conventions built around the tragedy of a Lesbian attachment, by the Sicilian Vitaliano Brancati (1907–54), had to wait until 1965 before reaching the stage.

THE LOW COUNTRIES

In Belgium there are two distinct theatres, one French-speaking, the other Flemish-speaking. Like French-speaking Switzerland, Belgium tends to be dominated by its great southern neighbour, but there is a flourishing National Theatre which, if it has not produced any post-war dramatist of any special merit, has at least offered its patrons unusual productions of the classics, often with distinguished foreign guest-directors and designers, and occasional world premières, as in the case of Wesker's *Their Very Own and Golden City*. The death of Michel Ghelderode (b. 1898) in 1962 robbed Belgium of its most significant dramatist, while the successful author of cynical comedies, Félicien Marceau (b. 1913), a one-time wartime collaborator, moved south after the war and acquired French citizenship. The Dutch-speaking theatre's history is almost as rich in dramatic production as England's, but of the handful of authors writing in the Netherlands today two at the most have taken root abroad: the communist Theun de Vries (b. 1917) and the internationally successful Jan de Hartog (b. 1914), whose real name is F. R. Eckmar. Luxembourg depends entirely on touring companies from Belgium, France and Germany.

IRELAND, GREECE, TURKEY, PORTUGAL AND SPAIN

Brendan Behan's *The Hostage*, one of Joan Littlewood's great hits and a success in numerous European theatres, was world premièred in Dublin in 1957 as *An Giall*. No other Gaelic play, performed either at the Abbey Theatre or in any other part of the Irish Republic, has so far found an international audience. English is the language used by most Irish playwrights; the most successful, like Giles Cooper (b. 1918) and Hugh Leonard (b. 1926), live in London and make their living out of TV rather than the stage.

In Greece native drama suffers from the same disabilities as any other minority culture and the best productions, either at the National Theatre or in the many private playhouses, are of the classics or foreign plays. The Greeks, like the Finns, specialise in light comedies of local appeal and they are legion. Among directors, Alexis Minotis, doyen of the National Theatre, and Michael Cacoyannis, the film director, have acquired a reputation for their work abroad.

As so often under a paternalist régime, the Turkish dramatist given to social criticism may be an exile. This was the case of Turkey's leading poet-dramatist, the communist Nazim Hikmet (1901–63). Theatre-going is a far more popular pastime in Turkey, whose theatre is barely older than the century, than in Portugal, or even Italy. The State Theatre of Ankara tours the whole country and the Municipal Theatres of Istanbul, founded by the dedicated and evergreen enthusiast Muhsin Ertugrul (b. 1892), have a regular following: but even an established figure like Ertugrul has to be prepared for surprises, since he was once expelled from Ankara and in 1966 lost control of his complex of theatres in Istanbul.

Despite limited state aid, the Portuguese theatre survives on the shaky foundation of public apathy and an arbitrary censorship. The most adventurous activity, in Oporto, is at the mercy of police interference. The mystical *Jacob and the Angel* by José Régio (b. 1901), whose real name is J. M. dos Reis Pereira, has been staged abroad and so has the lyrically realistic *Tà-Mar* by Alfredo Cortes (b. 1880). Several plays by younger writers have appeared in print but still await the imprimatur of the authorities before they can be done in public. Even the National Theatre (a misleading name, since the company is privately owned and controlled) is not exempt from official surveillance, which explains its timorous repertoire.

The Spanish theatre is in a much healthier state despite the arbitrary censorship and lack of public interest (it is difficult in any case to compete with the appeal of the bullfights). Grant-aided theatres in Madrid are relatively new. Spain's best-known post-war dramatist was Alejandro Casona (1903–65), who went home after a lifetime's exile in Argentina on the eve of his death in Madrid, a dramatic poet full of fantasy and closely allied to the theatre of Lorca. Fernando Arrabal (b. 1932), a poet and a social critic, shows a strong absurdist influence in his work, but he lives in exile in France and writes in French. Alfonso Sastre (b. 1926) is another spiritual rebel who survives at home despite constant official persecution. There are many dramatists in Spain, as in Italy, mostly authors of innocuous comedies supplying local needs. But even though most of Europe's leading dramatists get a hearing, the authorities see to it that the controversial ones, the ones most likely to provoke independent thought, are staged within the confines of a limited sphere of intellectual and middle-class theatre-goers.

BIBLIOGRAPHY

Bentley, Eric. *The Life of the Drama*, Atheneum, New York, 1964; Methuen, London, 1965.

Brustein, Robert. *The Theatre of Revolt*, Little, Brown, Boston, Mass., 1964; Methuen, London, 1965.

Clark, Barrett H. (ed.) *European Theories of the Drama*, Crown, New York, newly revised by Henry Popkin, 1965.

Cole, Toby (ed.) *Playwrights on Playwriting*, Hill and Wang, New York, 1960.

Esslin, Martin. *The Theatre of the Absurd*, Eyre and Spottiswoode, London; Doubleday, New York, 1962. *Brecht: A Choice of Evils*, Eyre and Spottiswoode, London, 1959; issued in the United States as *Brecht: The Man and His Work*, Doubleday, New York, 1960.

Funke, Lewis and Booth, John E. (eds.) *Actors Talk about Acting*, Random House, New York, 1961; Thames and Hudson, London, 1962.

Guernsey, Otis J. (ed.) *Best Plays of 1964–5*, Dodd, Mead, New York, 1965. *Best Plays of 1965–6*, Dodd, Mead, 1966.

Guicharnaud, Jacques. *Modern French Theatre from Giraudoux to Beckett*, Yale Univ. Press, London and New Haven, Conn., 1961.

Hainaux, René and Yves-Bonnat. *Stage Design Throughout the World Since 1950*, Harrap, London; Theatre Arts Books, New York; Meddens, Brussels, 1964.

Hewes, Henry (ed.) *Best Plays of 1962–3*, Dodd, Mead, New York, 1963. *Best Plays of 1961–2*, Dodd, Mead, 1964.

Kitchin, Laurence. *Mid-Century Drama*, Humanities Press, New York, 1960; Faber and Faber, London, 2nd ed. 1962. *Drama in the Sixties*, Faber and Faber, London, 1966.

Kott, Jan. *Shakespeare Our Contemporary*, Doubleday, New York, 1964; Methuen, London, 1965.

Marowitz, Charles; Milne, Tom; Hale, Owen (eds.) *The Encore Reader*, Methuen, London, 1965.

Santaniello, A. E. (ed.) *Theatre Books in Print*, Drama Bookshop, New York, 1966.

Sartre, Jean-Paul. *Saint Genet, Actor and Martyr*, Allen and Unwin, London; George Braziller, New York, 1964.

Taylor, John Russell. *Anger and After*, Pelican, London, revised ed. 1963; Hill and Wang, New York, 1964.

Thody, Philip. *Jean-Paul Sartre*, Hamish Hamilton, London, 1960; Macmillian, New York, 1961.

Tynan, Kenneth. *Tynan on Theatre*, Pelican, London, revised ed. 1964; Doubleday, New York, 1st ed. 1964.

Ten Years at the Royal Court 1956–66, English Stage Society, London, 1966.

CINEMA

JOHN RUSSELL TAYLOR

THE cinema in the Western European countries today exemplifies in an extreme form the situation of the cinema all over the world: crisis-prone and faced with a constant general decline in cinema attendances, threatened by competition from television, which seems to challenge it on its very own territory, and for ever having orations delivered by saddened well-wishers over its grave, it nevertheless not only keeps going, but every year contrives to improve its position, not only artistically but commercially as well.

The key to this seemingly paradoxical situation lies in the erratic history of the entertainment industries since 1945. The end of the war left most film industries in the West shattered, and the few that were not—Britain, Sweden, Spain, Switzerland, Turkey—were compelled by external conditions to cater only for a home audience and be as far as possible self-sufficient. While the industries of France, Italy, Germany and other countries affected one way or another by the war and its aftermath set about reconstructing, and the neutrals continued much as before, Britain began an all-out offensive to break into major international markets, especially the American. Largely as a direct consequence of this ill-timed over-extension, Britain was the first country in Europe to suffer a large-scale economic crisis in its film industry, a crisis from which it has only slowly and gradually begun to recover, largely with the help of American finance.

Elsewhere in Europe the pattern of collapse and recovery has been fairly consistent. Practically everywhere there is a reliable bedrock of undemanding popular cinema which is cheaply produced, intended entirely for home consumption, and provides day-to-day bread and butter for its producers. Some film industries—Turkish, Spanish, Greek—rarely attempt to rise above this elementary level, and they are the soundest economically, on their given small scale. Beyond this there are the countries where artistic quality is a consideration in at least an important segment of the industry, and these are for various reasons the most precarious. Partly it is that in such countries, which tend to be the richer and more highly developed, problems like the spread of television and new teenage affluence which expresses itself in dancing, record- and clothes-buying rather than in going to the cinema, have to be faced earlier than in less highly developed countries. Also, obviously, the more films cost the more they may lose, and the more speculative the whole system of film production. Hence in general it is the larger, more important film industries, such as the British, French, Italian and Swedish, which have had the most chequered career since 1945.

The post-war pattern of events was set almost at once, by the Italian cinema. In general it is the best-founded, most secure film industries which

523

are the most conservative. Far from encouraging unpredictable novelty when they can afford to gamble, most film producers will do so only when their backs are against the wall and they are forced to say they will try anything once. Thus it was that the first post-war renaissance in the cinema came about in Italy: with almost all the industry's resources destroyed in the war, the only possibility of continuing production was to give a large number of new young film-makers the chance to follow their own artistic inclinations and make films with non-professional actors, entirely on location instead of in destroyed or unavailable studios. In this way 'neo-realism' was born, and the artistic and commercial success of the best films by this school of film-makers—Roberto Rossellini's *Open City* and *Paisa*, Vittorio de Sica's *Bicycle Thieves*—helped to put the Italian industry back on its feet, particularly by opening the doors of an extensive foreign market to its greatest artistic achievements. But then success and relative prosperity brought a new conservatism and a loss of impetus among the neo-realists. This in its turn brought stagnation and a further economic crisis, from which only a new generation of creative film-makers, seizing their chance, were able to extricate the Italian cinema for a while.

Of course it would be an extreme over-simplification to suggest that these fluctuations in the economic status of the industry were entirely due to variations in the artistic quality or entertainment value of the films produced. But the pattern of revival, collapse and new revival sketched out by the Italian industry in the post-war years, partly conditioning and partly conditioned by the qualities of the films made, has repeated itself over and over again in other countries. In Britain, for example, the first post-war revival in and expansion of the film industry received a major set-back with the economic crisis in 1948; a second revival, under the aegis of Alexander Korda's British Lion organisation and with the backing of government money, petered out in the early fifties, and it took several years before the first tentative moves in the direction of an artistic revival, with the works of such 'new wave' directors as Tony Richardson, Karel Reisz and Lindsay Anderson, and a commercial revival with, above all, the phenomenally successful James Bond films, began to make itself felt in the early sixties.

In France, similarly, the first films made after the war by some of the older figures, and the earlier works of such newer figures as Henri-Georges Clouzot, Jacques Becker and Yves Allegret, seemed to hold out the prospect of a real revival in the French cinema. But soon the industry fell a prey to artistic indecision and loss of touch with commercial realities, and the *nouvelle vague* of young newcomers to the cinema, inspired by and given their head as a result of the enormous success of Roger Vadim's *Et Dieu Créa la Femme* and its new young star Brigitte Bardot, gave the French industry only a temporary respite. Before long complaints were heard of an enormous backlog of unreleased (and in some cases, it was said, unreleasable) films; money became difficult to raise for any sort of film, but especially for anything which was felt to be at all risky, and several of the leading figures to emerge in the younger generation of film-makers found themselves idle while the industry took stock.

These are the sort of troubles which have beset the cinema almost everywhere in Western Europe, and indeed in the world, where a sustained attempt has been made to produce films somewhat more ambitious than the staple ephemeral commercial product. In the circumstances, it is perhaps surprising that so much of value has been accomplished in the last ten years, and is still being accomplished now; if fewer films are being made,

CINEMA

as is the case in most countries today, at least it is likely that a higher proportion of them will be worth seeing and have some lasting value.

BRITAIN

The current situation of the British cinema is in general one of fair artistic health and remarkable commercial prosperity. This has been achieved, it must be said, largely with the aid of American money and the increasing internationalisation of film production. Most of the notable older figures still active in film-making, such as Carol Reed and David Lean, have occupied themselves almost exclusively for the last few years with large-scale international productions such as Reed's *The Agony and the Ecstasy* and Lean's *Lawrence of Arabia* and *Doctor Zhivago*, which can be considered British films only in a very vague and hazy sense of the term. Similarly, many of the younger directors who have come forward since Tony Richardson's first feature film *Look Back in Anger* in 1959, and shown that there was a place for a new talent in the conservative British studios, have been dependent for their start and their continuing ability to make films on the support of American finance. Even Woodfall Films, the company which produced most of Richardson's films (*The Entertainer*, *A Taste of Honey*, and most successfully *Tom Jones*) was originally floated on transatlantic capital and under the supervision of a North American producer, Harry Saltzman, who later launched the record-breaking James Bond series of films.

But however these new directors have been financed, at least the chances have come. At present Tony Richardson undoubtedly leads the field in the size of his output, his international reputation (especially since the worldwide commercial success of *Tom Jones*) and the intelligence with which he has chosen his material, from works by such writers as John Osborne, Shelagh Delaney, Jean Genet, Evelyn Waugh and Marguerite Duras. His artistic stature is more a matter of controversy, since up to the present he has proved more skilful at manipulating an eclectic bag of tricks derived from the innovations of other film-makers than at evolving a recognisable style of his own. However, where he has led, others have followed, and undoubtedly during the last few years the British cinema has undergone something of a revolution. A revolution, first of all, in subject matter: after years of neglect the everyday facts of British working-class life came to be accepted as a possible subject for a serious dramatic film, largely because of Jack Clayton's *Room at the Top* (1958), and this led to a freer-ranging investigation of the whole contemporary British scene in later films. But *Room at the Top* was still technically a very old-fashioned film, and it was left for Richardson and his successors to enliven the look of the British film and throw outworn narrative conventions and stolid, literal naturalism out of the window.

Among those who have done this successfully are Karel Reisz, who created in *Saturday Night and Sunday Morning* a creditable slice of working-class life, then progressed in *Night Must Fall* and *Morgan—A Suitable Case for Treatment* to a more extravagant, less reality-shackled study of mental maladjustment, and John Schlesinger, who has traced a similar course through *A Kind of Loving* to *Billy Liar* and *Darling*. More accomplished and original than either are the single feature films of two directors from the stage, Joan Littlewood, who in *Sparrows Can't Sing* made a brilliantly bawdy, artificial comedy on the Restoration model under cover of a realistic study of working-class marital relations, and Lindsay Anderson, who in *This Sporting Life* made the only

525

British film worthy, in its dark obsessive power, to stand beside the cinema of Buñuel. Of a generation younger still the most striking figure is Richard Lester, an American who has spent all his working life in Britain and has made in *The Knack* and his two films with the Beatles, *A Hard Day's Night* and *Help!* the most sustained and successful attack yet in Britain on the old-established conventions of film continuity and what one can and cannot do with it, creating in the process a dazzling, brilliantly inventive cinema of visual humour, as topical as tomorrow's headlines and maybe as short-lived.

Meanwhile, commercial British cinema goes on, only a little influenced by the fact that many of the biggest commercial successes are films like *Tom Jones* and the Lester films, which seem to come from the other camp. Still, virtually all commercial shortcomings of the British film industry (and they are many) are wiped out in the fantastic success of *Doctor No*, *From Russia with Love*, *Goldfinger* and *Thunderball*. Like most of the 'quality' British cinema, they are based on pre-sold material—novels, plays—and in their attitude to the craft of cinema if nothing else they are extremely conservative. But as much as anything they have been responsible for the revival in the purely commercial fortunes of the British industry, and without that little else would be possible.

FRANCE

Since 1956, when Roger Vadim was given the chance to make a film very much as he liked to exploit the charms of his wife and star Brigitte Bardot, and the result, *Et Dieu Créa la Femme*, conquered the world, France has been the principal growing-point in European, if not in world cinema. At this time the old guard of the industry were firmly entrenched, and there was a regular, accepted progression to full direction by way of odd jobs around the studios and some years as assistant to an established figure. Feeling this as an unnecessary and unacceptable restraint, a number of young would-be film-makers banded together in the columns of the eccentric and influential review *Cahiers du Cinéma* to launch an attack on the stifling, stodgy 'tradition of quality' which was then dominant in the French film. One of the first side-effects of Vadim's enormous success and the demonstration thus offered that there might after all be money in the talent of these young tearaways was that a number of writers from this group, particularly Jean-Luc Godard, François Truffaut and Claude Chabrol, were given the chance to make full-length feature films within the commercial cinema. Each of them early produced a major success (respectively *A Bout de Souffle*, *Les Quatre Cents Coups* and *Les Cousins*), and these helped to bolster the confidence of producers not only in their further works, but in the potential of yet more, newer directors who were waiting for a chance to show what they could do.

During the first four or five years of the New Wave it has been estimated that about a hundred-and-fifty new directors made their début with at least one feature film, and sometimes several. Naturally there was bound to be some reaction after this outburst, and early in the sixties that reaction set in: the most commercially successful films, at home if not abroad, were still old-fashioned crime thrillers starring Jean Gabin and basic comedies with stars like Bourvil and Louis de Funès. What, then, producers began to ask, did the French industry need with these expensive, unpredictable and obscure new directors? The reaction, aggravated by an economic recession in the French film, kept a number of the leading figures of the new generation inactive for a while, especially those who, unlike the prolific Godard, pouring out one film after another and virtually making them up as he went along, needed time and careful preparation and big budgets. In 1965, however, things began to improve, and if the supply of exciting new talent seems, not very surprisingly after the tremendous outburst of the previous years, rather to have dried up, at least most of the really notable figures of the 'old' New Wave are continuing to extend and deepen their talents and to become established as the new, less rigidly stereotyped 'tradition of quality' in the modern French cinema.

Outstanding among them remain Truffaut, Godard and a third, Alain Resnais, who belongs to no particular group and has always very much made his own way in his own fashion. The least predictable of them, perhaps, is Truffaut; after his first major success with the semi-autobiographical *Les Quatre Cents Coups*, a sympathetic picture of a delinquent boy, he progressed to the eccentric and iconoclastic comedy-thriller *Tirez sur le Pianiste*, the elegantly equivocal love story *Jules et Jim*, and the surprisingly 'classical' drama of adultery *La Peau Douce*. If Truffaut has refused to be tied down to any one style, Godard has continued in film after film to elaborate and explore his marvellously casual, improvisatory approach to the cinema; his films, whether comedies like *Une Femme est une Femme*, dramas like *Vivre sa Vie*, science fiction like *Alphaville* or extraordinary, unclassifiable works like *Une Femme Mariée* or *Bande à Part*, all witness a unique at-homeness with the medium, a sheer delight in the whole process of film-making which is captivating. Resnais, the most literary of the three, came to the feature film from making short documentary films on art; his three major films so far, *Hiroshima Mon Amour*, *L'Année Dernière à Marienbad* and *Muriel*, have all been collaborations on equal terms with noted novelists (Marguerite Duras, Alain Robbe-Grillet and Jean Cayrol respectively), and have shown extraordinary technical mastery in manipulating complex time structures and an artist's eye for visual detail, even if the overall effect remains for many viewers cold and academic.

The other figures in the new wave are too numerous to mention more than a small fraction of them. Among the most interesting are Jacques Rivette, whose first completed feature, the magical and mysterious *Paris Nous Appartient*, gives high hopes for his future work; Claude Chabrol, most polished and accomplished of the group's light entertainers, who has found new popularity with a series of witty spy dramas; Agnès Varda, whose *Cléo de 5 à 7* remains the most subtly, completely feminine of films; and Jacques Demy, who achieved in *Les Parapluies de Cherbourg* a new genre, the sung film, and made such concepts as prettiness and charm again respectable in the cinema. Meanwhile, many of the older figures of the French cinema continue to make films; both such precursors of the New Wave as Robert Bresson, most severe and ascetic of film-makers, and the comedian Jacques Tati, and the real old masters of the French cinema like René Clair and Jean Renoir, both of whom have remained as active during the last ten years as during the previous thirty.

ITALY

The recent history of the cinema in Italy has had more ups and downs, perhaps, than that of any other national cinema except the British. During the last ten years or so it has struggled out of the shadow of its immediately post-war fame on account of a small number of neo-realistic masterpieces, and has weathered a number of economic crises. The most significant figures of the neo-realist era, Roberto Rossellini and Vittorio de Sica, have continued to make films on and off; though Rossellini's career has been in general decline and he has turned most recently to television, de Sica has found a new lease of life as a director of commercial comedies and dramas, especially those, like *Two Women* and *Yesterday, Today and Tomorrow*, which have starred Sophia Loren and been widely distributed in English-language versions. Otherwise the commercial cinema in Italy has followed one new craze after another: one year it was all cheaply-made costume epics with heroes called Hercules or Maciste; another it was films in episodes, filmed strip-tease revues, horror films or, most surprisingly, a whole rash of Italian-made westerns. These have each had their periods of success, and the horror film vogue in particular produced some really stylish and distinguished work from directors such as Riccardo Freda and Mario Bava. Despite this, the commercial position of Italian films has always remained uncertain, and much of the better-paid work in Italy for film technicians and actors has come from American film companies who found it cheaper to make super-spectacles like *Cleopatra* in Italy than it would have been at home in America.

Somewhat apart from all this has been the work of a relatively small number of leading creative figures in the Italian cinema, whose films are shown in art cinemas around the world. The most important of these in the period following the heyday of neo-realism have been Federico Fellini, Michelangelo Antonioni and Luchino Visconti. Fellini began working as a script-writer, with Rossellini and others, and did not direct his first film until 1950. In all his films he evokes with tremendous intensity and ebullience his own private world of flesh and fantasy. His first big success was *La Strada*, a strange, elusive story of a waif in a cruel world; his later, more ornate cinematic visions *La Dolce Vita*, *8½* and *Giulietta degli Spiriti* have created a new kind of filmic baroque. While Fellini's greatest strength is his complete disregard of conventional canons of taste, Antonioni's lies in his perfect taste and sense of moderation: everything in such films as *L'Avventura*, *L'Eclisse* and *Deserto Rosso* is done by suggestion and indirection, to create a haunting world of shifting appearances and values constantly called into question. Visconti, rather older and with longer experience in the cinema than Fellini and Antonioni, is also one of Italy's leading stage directors, and his films remain less completely conceived in terms of cinema than theirs. He has made films in many different styles; the most generally effective remain his exquisite period re-creations in *Senso* and *The Leopard*.

Of the younger Italian directors the most strikingly individual is Ermanno Olmi, who has demonstrated in *Il Posto* and *I Fidanzati* a profound insight into the lives and thoughts of ordinary people and a complete command of the technique by which he reveals them.

SWEDEN

The cinema in Sweden has remained since the war virtually isolated from that in other countries, and has been dominated almost entirely by the work of one man, Ingmar Bergman. Bergman began his film career in 1944 by writing an original screenplay, *Frenzy*, for the then leading director in Sweden, Alf Sjöberg. He rapidly graduated to direction, and became at the same time a leading figure in the Swedish theatre. In 1951 his career was interrupted by a dramatic crisis in the Swedish film industry, and for more than a year no feature films were made. In 1955, with his sixteenth film, *Smiles of a Summer Night*, he found international fame, and for the next few years was the most fashionable director in the world, not only on account of the succession of new films he was making (*The Seventh Seal, Wild Strawberries, The Virgin Spring*), but through the world's simultaneous discovery of the films he had made earlier. This enormous vogue had its inevitable reaction, and in recent years his trilogy *Through a Glass Darkly, Winter Light* and *The Silence* have had a rather rough critical passage, though his latest film, a colour comedy called *Now About All These Women*, did restore his reputation in some quarters.

The fame of Bergman has tended to overshadow all his contemporaries except the sensitive documentarist Arne Sucksdorff, and to inhibit the development of those younger than him. But now a new generation seems to be emerging, with directors like Jörn Donner and Bo Widerberg, who are able to break away from Bergman's unmistakable chiaroscuro style and his grimly obsessive Strindbergian subject-matter and show us something original of their own.

OTHER COUNTRIES

The cinematic output of most other countries in Western Europe is either numerically small or qualitatively negligible, or both. At one end of the scale are countries like Iceland, Norway, Eire, Belgium and Portugal, who make virtually no feature films unaided, though they may from time to time participate in co-production arrangements or provide locations and even (in the case of Eire especially) modern studio facilities for visiting companies. Turkey has a sizeable film industry, but the films made are confined almost exclusively to home consumption and have no artistic pretensions whatever. Finland and Switzerland make occasional films with an attractive local flavour, though both depend primarily on films from abroad for their staple fare. Denmark and the Netherlands both have small-scale but relatively thriving local film industries. Denmark possesses one of the outstanding directors in the history of the cinema, Carl Dreyer, who in 1965 broke a ten-year silence with a distinguished new film, *Gertrud*. The Netherlands has long had a thriving school of documentary film-makers, a leading figure of which, Bert Haanstra, has recently begun to make feature films, both documentary and fictional, while Fons Rademakers, a disciple of Bergman, has shown a highly personal talent in several features.

Somewhat more developed are the industries of Greece, West Germany and Spain. Greece, like Turkey, turns out many films for home consumption each year, mainly emotional dramas and comedies with music. It has, however, also produced one major film-maker in recent years, Michael Cacoyannis, who produced an impressive series of films deeply rooted in Greek life and landscape (*A Girl in Black, A Matter of Dignity*) before succumbing in *Zorba the Greek* to the blandishments of the big-budget international production, with less happy results. Spain is in a somewhat similar position; a solidly founded local industry, not vitally affected by the recent descent of Americans seeking somewhere even cheaper than Italy to make American films, and a small number of more ambitious film-makers whose films are aimed at, and sometimes reach, an international audience. Foremost among these are Luis Garcia Berlanga, maker of a number of pleasant, very mildly satirical comedies, and Juan-Antonio Bardem, whose *Muerte de un Ciclista* and *Calle Mayor* vividly evoke some aspects of middle-class life in modern Spain. West Germany, immediately after the war, found itself at something of a disadvantage before East Germany in that most of the talented directors

seemed to be working in the east. Several of them later came west, but little
has happened to shake the West German cinema out of its rut of sterile
academicism, in which even the flashy and superficial films of Rolf Thiele,
such as *The Girl Rosemarie,* come as a pleasant relief.

THE UNITED STATES IN EUROPE

Over the whole European scene there still presides the colossal shape of the
film industry of the United States. Though itself riddled with uncertainty and
liable to crisis in the last few years, it still has at its command amounts of
money virtually undreamt of in the European cinema, and though it has
less claim than ever to artistic leadership, it can still from time to time turn
out films which make a clean sweep of the world's box-offices. Nowadays
many of these films are apparently British, or occasionally French or Italian.
Whereas in the 1930s and earlier Europe's best talents would if possible be
transplanted to Hollywood, now Hollywood comes to them; many of the
most financially successful European films are largely or entirely American-
financed and, to a greater or lesser extent, tailored to the specific requirements of the American market. This is true, for example, of the James Bond
films; but the same American producer, Harry Saltzman, was in the year of
Thunderball the main financier of a new Spanish-made Orson Welles film,
Chimes at Midnight, a new French-made de Sica film, *Un Nouveau Monde,* and
Olmi's film about Pope John, *E Venne un Uomo.* Joe Levine, producer of
The Carpetbaggers and *Harlow,* has also been the guiding hand behind such
recent Italian successes as the Loren–Mastroianni–de Sica films *Yesterday,
Today and Tomorrow* and *Marriage Italian Style,* among many others. Even
continental producers like Dino de Laurentiis and Raoul Lévy have slanted
their recent productions, sometimes disastrously, towards wide American
distribution, and a European super-production like Laurentiis' *The Bible* is
conceivable only in terms of an extravagant gamble on eventual widespread
distribution as an American film.

But, as the Saltzman films suggest, it is not only in the obviously commercial cinema that American money looms importantly. Nowadays a company
like United Artists will often turn out to have a stake in improbable places,
e.g. Antonioni's *La Notte* or Louis Malle's *Viva Maria,* or Twentieth Century-
Fox in Buñuel's *Le Journal d'une Femme de Chambre.* Such participation takes
place quite separately from unmistakably American films which simply use
Europe as a location and European actors and technicians because they are
the handiest. Nor can it be said that the influence of America and American
money has been all bad. If some films have undoubtedly lost a little of their
savour by compromises reached with one eye on the American Mid-West, a
large number of worthwhile films, art and entertainment, have been made
which, without American participation, would not have been made at all.
The United States thus maintains a forceful presence in the European
cinema.

BIBLIOGRAPHY

Durgnat, Raymond. *Nouvelle Vague: The First Decade,* Motion, London, 1963.
Houston, Penelope. *The Contemporary Cinema,* Penguin, London and Baltimore, Md., 1963.
Taylor, John Russell. *Cinema Eye, Cinema Ear: Some Key Film-Makers of the Sixties,* Methuen,
London; Hill and Wang, New York, 1964.

PAINTING AND SCULPTURE

IAN DUNLOP

QUANTITY and diversity are among the most notable features of present-day European art. With the decline of Paris as the main artistic centre —it is still of course a centre—other cities like London, Barcelona, Zurich, Milan and Düsseldorf have emerged as places where artists no longer feel out of touch with the latest developments and ideas, nor feel they will suffer in critical esteem or financially from being where they are. Nowadays it is not surprising to find two artists, one from Croydon and the other from Lille, both working in similar styles and both exhibiting at a big international exhibition like the one held every four years at Kassel in Germany. Artistic styles are no longer related to nationality, in the way that expressionism, for instance, once had its base in Germany. Today's styles are international.

PARIS AS AN ART CENTRE

Before the second world war Paris was the artistic centre of the Western hemisphere. Nearly all the most significant modern artists lived there— Picasso, Matisse, Brancusi, Mondrian and Braque are just a few examples; it was the birthplace of new movements as far-reaching as cubism and surrealism; in addition it was the chief centre for dealers, collectors, critics, connoisseurs and museum directors. Like Rome in the 17th century under the Barberinis, Paris was the city where international reputations could be made or broken. Artists could live and work elsewhere, but, however high their reputations were at home, they had to exhibit in Paris to gain any international success.

In recent years Paris has been losing its authority as the main artistic centre in the West. New movements have started elsewhere, chiefly in New York. The Paris dealers are not as successful as they were and a good deal of their trade seems to have moved to London. Perhaps most significant of all, young artists, who used to go to Paris at the first opportunity, now choose the United States as a place to start their careers.

New York now dominates the artistic world. This situation began with the emigration of a number of prominent European artists to the United States at the outbreak of the second world war. Their arrival coincided with, and possibly helped the birth of a new American painting of immense vitality and influence. At first the new painting was admired by a few critics and museum officials in the United States only, but by 1960 it had become a universal success. Two important changes have come as a result. Firstly the American painter, who had lived in appalling conditions during the Depression and spent most of his early life despised by his own countrymen, had been transformed into a national hero and even into a respectable businessman. Secondly many more Americans began to collect modern art. The scale of

531

the new painting, its directness, its expansive open forms, even its vulgarity, had caught the mood of a prosperous and confident nation.

The Old World, by contrast, had to recover from the ill effects of the war. Most of the countries in which art had flourished before the war had been occupied by a power hostile to every form of modern art. Its leading artists had either died, emigrated or gone into virtual retirement while the war lasted. Picasso, Matisse, Léger and Braque were getting old and the younger artists who might have taken over from them or at least benefited from contact with them were caught up in the war and denied normal artistic activity.

In Britain artistic activity was hampered by the war but not extinguished. A number of prominent artists found employment with the Ministry of Information as official war artists. Henry Moore, for example, made some moving studies of life in an air-raid shelter. Although not much came of this work, it did at least keep artists occupied.

In Paris one or two exhibitions were mounted. In 1941 a group of young painters which included Jean Bazaine (b.1904), Maurice Estève (b.1904), Charles Lapicque (b.1898), Edouard Pignon (b.1905), Gustave Singier (b. Belgium, 1909), Alfred Manessier (b.1911) and Pierre Tal Coat (b.1905), all of whom became well-known after the war, took part in an exhibition called *Young Painters in the French Tradition*. The tradition was a mixed one—a combination of cubist space, fauvist colour, expressionistic handling and Rouault-like figuration. Behind the group could be discerned a muddled philosophy in an art engagé—a term much bandied about during and after the war. Art, these artists felt, should deal with the fundamentals of life. Abstract art was declared 'escapist', and for a time content was thought to be necessarily representational. Many of the group—Manessier, for instance —were devout Roman Catholics; others became communists.

A similar situation developed in Italy, where Renato Guttoso (b.1912), Giulio Turcato (b.1912), Emilio Vedova (b.1919) and a number of now forgotten names were sympathetic to the communist cause and for a time attempted to paint in the approved party manner. Of these the Sicilian Renato Guttuso is by far the most interesting. He has a genuine feeling for the oppressed, and during the war he joined an anti-Fascist movement. He adapted his academic training to socialist-realist subjects without undue strain. His chief merit, besides his passionate sense of commitment, is his bold and incisive line, which gives a veracity to his scenes of war, murder and brutality, where others sentimentalise. Recently he has mellowed, now depicting still-life, beach scenes and massive women.

It is difficult to take seriously any of the realist and committed art that emerged after the war. Nowadays it seems scarcely credible that a painter like Bernard Buffet (b.1928) was once greatly admired. Nevertheless, when a group of young painters that included Buffet and Claude Venard (b.1913) formed a movement called 'L'homme témoin' in Paris in 1948, they had many supporters. Buffet's banal, sentimental and mannered figures won every sort of prize and achieved some remarkably high prices, which have since become a source of embarrassment to owners and dealers alike. He is one of the many instances of the fallibility of Paris dealers and critics in assessing a painter's artistic and financial worth, a fallibility which may have contributed to the decline of Paris as an art centre.

A similar situation has occurred with a group of painters that formed the abstract wing of the post-war School of Paris, who were once overrated by the Paris public but have since had their reputations shorn by the world at large. They do not really constitute a school though they have certain tendencies in common. Each has developed his own personal idiosyncrasies, but they are all for the most part concerned with distilling nature into abstract and emotive forms. If an artist of this school were to paint autumn, for example, he would produce not trees shedding their leaves as such, but the colours and lines commonly associated with such sights.

The basic structure of this abstract style has been, more often than not, a modified cubism. It is the common denominator behind the work of painters like Nicolas de Staël, Serge Poliakoff, the Portugese painter Maria Vieira da Silva (b.1908), Mario Prassinos (b. Istanbul, 1916), František Kupka (1871–1957) and the artists who first exhibited with the Young Painters in the French Tradition like Manessier and Estève. The characteristics of this painting extend beyond Paris to, for example, the Italian Basaldella Afro (b.1912) and the Austrian Fritz Hundertwasser (b.1928), who adds a sinuous surrealist element of his own. English painters like Keith Vaughan (b.1912), Ceri Richards (b.1903), Victor Pasmore (b.1908) and Ivon Hitchens (b.1893), and some of the St Ives painters, have also produced an abstract art along these lines.

This type of painting is poetic, often extremely seductive in colour—this is particularly true of the French painters—tasteful, professional, and yet when compared with the art of the pre-war years or the art produced recently in the United States it is totally without power or vitality. Few of its practitioners have attempted to extend the range of expression open to painting or challenged our ways of seeing things. Instead they have followed set patterns and made their work as acceptable and as *chic* as possible. Some, however, are technically extremely able. Pierre Soulages (b.1919), for example, is a beautiful handler of paint. His sombre bars of black shiny pigment, criss-crossing like scaffolding round a new building, make a very strong impression. Jean Fautrier's (b.1897) subtle use of texture coupled with a delicate sense of colour is arresting when first seen, though his repetition of the same qualities bores. Jean Bazaine, Alfred Manessier and Serge Poliakoff (b.1906) are also capable of creating beautiful works, though they too are guilty of repetition.

The English painter William Scott (b.1913) and Nicolas de Staël (1914–55) are exceptions. Before the war Scott lived in France and soon acquired the French gift for colour and fluid handling of thin paint. In 1953 he went to New York and came to know Pollock, Kline, Rothko and the other abstract expressionists. He was overwhelmed, he said, by the size and directness of the new American painting. In Scott the two streams of painting, the French and the American, have combined to produce an art poised, controlled and fundamentally his own.

Nicolas de Staël, unlike most of the other members of the School of Paris, seldom repeated himself. He continually searched for better and better ways of rendering his response to nature. In 1942 he turned to abstract painting. His starting-point was a form of synthetic cubism. By building up his paint in layers sometimes an inch thick, de Staël was able to give a textural and coloured richness to his forms. In 1952 the sight of a football game set off a new train of thought. Figures, objects and landscapes entered his work. His colour, always his strong point, reached an extraordinary intensity; his painting continually catches one unawares by original harmonies and contrasts. In 1955 he committed suicide by throwing himself from his studio window in Antibes. It is impossible to say where his art might have gone, for he seemed capable of anything.

POST-WAR SURREALISM

The interpretations of surrealism, one of the leading movements of the 1930s, are as many as its practitioners. Certainly when Max Ernst, Magritte, Masson, Miró, Arp, Lam and Matta returned to Paris after the second world war, most of them from exile in the United States, there was no longer any common bond between them, not even an allegiance to the high-priest of surrealism, the poet André Breton. One strand of surrealist thought which was important in these years was the belief that art is connected with, or even the product of, the unconscious. But there was no agreement on what was meant by the unconscious, only a variety of clues. Kandinsky's theory that mental states can be transmuted directly into forms and colours, Klee's intimist paintings and his seemingly spontaneous method of working, André Masson's Japanese-like brushstrokes, were all taken up and studied by younger painters in Europe and the United States. It seemed possible that the interval between the act of creation and the act of painting could be condensed. In 1940, possibly with these examples in mind, the Cuban Roberto Matta and the American Robert Motherwell suggested to Jackson Pollock that they explore the field of automatic painting together.

Jackson Pollock (1912–56), however, preferred to go his own way, and by about 1946 he had found a satisfactory form of expression. To eliminate all figuration, perspective and compositional factors inherent in traditional painting he gave up easel painting altogether. Instead he unrolled large areas of canvas on to his studio floor and, standing on the canvas, dripped and splashed his paint as the mood took him.

At the time Pollock seemed to have broken every rule in the painter's book. 'You cannot hang an event on the wall', said Mary McCarthy. His paintings now seem neither as new nor as spontaneous as when they first appeared. Behind the apparent freedom lies the control of a painter deeply immersed in traditional practices. But Pollock's rejection of easel painting in favour of an all-over mural-like art, his use of new techniques such as staining the canvas and splashing paint, his use of new materials such as lacquers and aluminium emulsions, have had a profound effect on artists living as far apart as Japan and Finland. He is almost certainly the only artist to have emerged since the war who can compare with pre-war masters like Matisse and Picasso.

Pollock began to influence European painters in the early 1950s. In England one of his most devoted admirers is Alan Davie (b.1920) who met him early in his career and found in him the idealism and technical vituosity which was latent in his own painting. Davie is, however, an individualist and his preference for strong fruity colour and symbolic imagery has prevented his admiration from becoming mere imitation. On the continent Pollock's influence can be detected in the work of the Cobra Group which includes among others the Dutchman Karel Appel (b.1921), the Belgian Corneille (Cornelis van Beverloo, b.1922) and the Dane Asgar Jorn (b.1914), and also in the work of painters like the Dane K. R. H. Sonderborg (b.1923), the Spaniard Antonio Saura (b.1930) and the Belgian Pierre Alechinsky (b.1927). Influence is perhaps too strong a word to use in connection with all these painters; Pollock did however pave the way for some of them to gain acceptance.

Pollock was, of course, not the first nor the only artist to explore the pictorial possibilities of spontaneous gesture. Both Wols and Hans Hartung had been working along these lines. Wols (Otto Schulze Battman, 1913–51), the son of a well-to-do German civil servant, had experimented, during his unhappy years in internment camps and in hiding, with a glorified doodle. Using tiny bits of paper Wols covered the whole pictorial field before him with a spidery and nervous handwriting. 'The movements of the hands and fingers', he said, 'express everything'. On a larger scale Hans Hartung (b.1904), who like Wols was born in Germany but settled in Paris, began to use reed-like lines against dull backgrounds, reminiscent of Chinese calligraphy. By making his lines with slow or frenzied arm movements he expressed his thoughts and emotions to the outside world. Georges Mathieu (b.1922), another Parisian, worked in a similar direction. In 1950 he began to explore the possibilities of painting to music. Henri Michaux (b.1899) attempted to draw while in a semi-drugged trance. Yves Klein (1928–62) used women models as paint brushes.

Action and gesture were only one off-shoot of surrealist thinking. In England surrealism took a more conventional and recognisable form. The three outstanding figures in recent English art, Francis Bacon (b.1909), Henry Moore (b.1898) and Graham Sutherland (b.1903), have all touched on surrealism at one point or another. The interesting thing about them is that they are all deeply traditional artists. Moore's sculpture revolves around themes first formed in ancient Greece. His reclining figures, his mother and child, his warriors' helmets all have their sculptured antecedents. Sutherland has been preoccupied with Catholic iconography, like the thorns round Christ's head. Bacon has taken as his starting-point Velasquez's portrait of Innocent X, Van Gogh's Reaper, or a still from Eisenstein's *Battleship Potemkin*. Working with traditional themes and often with traditional techniques, they have all produced works in tune with contemporary taste.

The same may be said of the Swiss sculptor and painter Alberto Giacometti (1901–65). Originally he was associated with the surrealists Miró and Arp, but in 1942 he began to work from nature again. 'To my terror', he recalled, 'the sculpture became smaller and smaller. Only when it was small was it like, and all the same these dimensions revolted me, and tirelessly I began again, only to end a few months later at the same point'. From this moment on, Giacometti was caught up in a self-defeating endeavour to pin down the transient and ephemeral appearances of things. It was a Sisyphean task. His works had to be taken from him before he destroyed them. Giacometti could never be satisfied. Yet as far as his admirers are concerned his thin spindly figures are among the most poignant works of art produced this century.

The Italian Giorgio Morandi (1890–1964) also worked in a traditional vein; he has been increasingly admired in recent years. Like Giacometti he restricted himself to a few chosen subjects, in his case still-life. An aloof and solitary figure, he attempted to capture the shape and the volume of his bottles, cups and books with a delicate line and a soft impressionistic sense of colour. Working with three tones, he gradually softened the gradations between them to produce works which have an atmospheric stillness of extraordinary intensity. His works have had a great influence on other Italian painters, notably Giuseppe Capogrossi (b.1900), and have even extended to other arts such as the cinema. One of his most devoted admirers is the Italian film director Antonioni.

SCULPTURE

The medium in which traditional practices have been most closely adhered to in post-war Europe is sculpture. While most modern painters have scrutinised the nature of their art and tried where possible to remove what they believed to be unnecessary, sculptors have shown reluctance to examine the basic essentials of their medium, frequently assuming the attitudes of a craftsman rather than those of an artist.

Much post-war European sculpture looks modern, but it only looks it. The basic forms have stayed the same. Thus semi-figurative sculptors like the Italians Marino Marini (b.1901) and Giacomo Manzu (b.1908), the French Jean Ipoustéguy (b.1920) and Germaine Richier (1904–59) and the English sculptors so much admired in the 1950s, Kenneth Armitage (b.1916), Lynn Chadwick (b.1914) and Reg Butler (b.1913), are firmly webbed in traditional methods and ideas. Not wishing to be called old-fashioned, they doll their work up with superficial features of modernism, mostly lifted from painting; perhaps fearing that their work might not be recognised as sculpture they have retained such unnecessary conventions as the pedestal and a totemic central mass; not surprisingly their style falls between two stools. Their main concern seems to be with texture, with the patina of bronze, the grain of wood, or the ripples in a piece of marble.

Recently there have been encouraging signs that European sculptors are starting to examine the essentials of their medium. In England one of Moore's assistants, Anthony Caro (b.1924)—possibly under the influence of the American painter Kenneth Noland and his compatriot David Smith—gave up working in the conventional plaster and began to work directly with iron girders, metal plates and tubing, using colour to rob the surfaces of his materials of their old associations. His pupils at the St Martin's School of Art in London—Philip King, William Tucker, David Annesley, Timothy Scott and Michael Bolus—have like him abandoned the pedestal, opened up new shapes by using materials like fibreglass and plastic, and removed any signs of the making process so popular amongst the preceding generation. In authority and originality these sculptors seem far in advance of their contemporaries in the rest of Europe. Other sculptors who have attempted to break away from the conventions of traditional sculpture are the German Norbert Kricke (b.1922), Eduardo Paolozzi (born of Italian parents in 1924) and the Greek Takis (Vassilakis, b.1925) who has made highly effective use of electric motors and magnets in his work.

On the whole, present-day sculpture in Western Europe lacks any common aims or methods. Sculptors seem to follow their own paths and pay much less attention than painters to the latest ideas. As a result good sculpture is diffuse and each country in Western Europe has its own native talent. The Spanish sculptor Eduardo Chillida (b.1924) has produced works which scarcely betray his early French training, but which are austere in their simplicity and yet delicate in the subtle use of forged iron. Max Bill (b. Switzerland, 1908) is like Chillida primarily an abstract sculptor but there the similarity ends. Bill, possibly because of his immersion in Bauhaus[1] ideals, brings to his often highly poetic works a fascination for forms based on mathematical formulae. 'The human body', says the Austrian Fritz Wotruba (b. 1907), 'has never ceased to be the main source of my work; it was there at the beginning and it will be there at the end.' Wotruba treats the body in an architectural way using thick rough blocks of stone. His one-time pupil the Greek sculptor, now living in Vienna, Joanis Avramidis (b.1922) has a similar respect for the human figure yet his preference for smooth clear-cut forms is nearer Bill's approach; a faint echo of his approach can be found in the work of the Italian Gio Pomodoro (b.1930) and the Frenchman César

[1]See 'Architecture', p. 543.

(César Baldaccini, b.1921). The Dane Robert Jacobsen (b.1912) shares Chillida's taste for raw iron but chooses to use abstract unpremeditated forms.

TEXTURE

A concern for surface texture is not limited to post-war sculptors alone. Since 1940 a number of painters have added sand, plaster, rags and other bits of rubbish to their canvases. This is not a new development but derives from Picasso's and Braque's early collages and from Kurt Schwitters' dadaist montages of the 1920s.

In 1952 the Italian Alberto Burri (b.1912), who had served with the Italian forces as a doctor, transplanted the image and even the material of blood-soaked bandages straight to the surface of his canvas. Recently he has been using battered tin plates welded together, and plastic foil which he has burnt with a blow lamp. In 1954 in Barcelona Antonio Tapies (b.1923) showed his paintings for the first time; they were made of plaster-glue and sand, constructed to form reliefs on to which indecipherable signs and hieroglyphs were scratched and drilled. In Italy Lucio Fontana (b.1899) began to slit his canvases with a razor blade and blister holes into plastic paint. In France Fernandez Arman (b.1928) has produced some nauseating assemblages out of such things as plastic eyes, and Bernard Requichot (1928–61) some disturbing effects from coils of plastic wire. Zoltan Kemeny (born in Rumania in 1907, died 1965) made some intriguing metal walls that lie half-way between painting and sculpture.

Another artist who has made considerable use of textural effects has been the Frenchman Jean Dubuffet (b.1901), though there is more than this to his work. As an artist and as a man Dubuffet is ill at ease with the main drift of contemporary painting and with the rational and technological age he lives in. He dislikes a formal approach to painting and finds representational painting boring. 'Do we wish only to learn?' he asks. 'Is it not possible for the artist, like a Chinese juggler on the day of great rejoicing, to draw from his head the shimmering scarves of incongruity and deck out his home admidst the joyous tinkling bells the merry fair of Equivalences and Inconsistencies?' Not surprisingly Dubuffet has had difficulty in finding an answer. Twice he gave up painting altogether. He was shown a way out, however, by the work of children, lunatics, primitive people and those who had managed to avoid the burdens of culture that seemed to weigh so heavily upon him. Dubuffet drew his inspiration from them and managed, or so his admirers claim, to beat the innocent at their own game. Dubuffet has not worked in this genre alone. His painting has gone through many changes. At present he is working on a series of visual jigsaw puzzles which he calls *Hourloupes*.

Dubuffet has been called the greatest living French painter—which, if true, is a poor reflection on present-day French painting. He is however one of the most creative artists to have emerged in France since the war, and one of the most productive, turning out on an average one work a day.

PURE ABSTRACT ART

There has been remarkably little abstract art in Western Europe recently of the type produced at the Bauhaus in the 1920s and by members of the de Stijl Group before the war. Pioneers like Mondrian, Moholy-Nagy, Gabo and Albers emigrated to the United States. Only the Dutchman Georges Vantongerloo (b.1886) of the de Stijl movement and Max Bill of the constructivists have remained. There are signs of a semi-geometric type of abstract art returning. American hard-edge painting—the use of broad bands of strong contrasting colour placed next to each other without any gradation between —has found its followers in Europe. For instance, it has been reflected in the work of the English painters John Hoyland, Jeremy Moon, Paul Huxley and Robyn Denny. Other forms of abstract painting have been developed by the Italians Piero Dorazio (b.1927) and Giuseppe Capogrossi (b.1900) and the Irishman Patrick Scott (b.1923).

The two leading European abstractionists since the war have been the Englishman Ben Nicholson and the Hungarian Victor Vasarély, who now lives in Paris. Ben Nicholson (b.1894) is not the sort of artist one would expect to take up this form of painting. He has a Botticelli-like gift for line and a chaste sense of colour. His ex-wife, the sculptress Barbara Hepworth, shares many of his tastes. Nicholson started as an admirer of Juan Gris, but by 1935 he had embarked on a series of reliefs, mostly in white, using geometrical figures of the utmost austerity. Since the war he has allowed his natural talents greater freedom. Recognisable objects and landscapes, of a highly refined nature, have appeared in his work. Some would say he sugared the pill. But Nicholson rejects the idea that abstract art involves the withdrawal of the artist into an ivory tower. 'It is related to Arsenal v. Tottenham Hotspur quite as much as to the stars in their courses', he has said, an opinion that might be shared by such painters in England as Victor Pasmore and the Formosan Richard Lim.

Victor Vasarély (b.1908) was drawn towards abstract art by his fellow Hungarian Moholy-Nagy. The Bauhaus became his spiritual home. For a time he worked as a commercial artist and it is only since 1944 that he has devoted his whole attention to abstract painting. Vasarély has a thorough knowledge of the mechanics of his art and the uses to which they can be put. He knows how colour works, how forms interrelate, how the mind reads a visual pattern, how depth and space can be suggested, and how modern materials can be of use to the artist. His paintings are as rich in personal expression as any work of art can be. The same can be said of the young English artist Bridget Riley (b.1931). Superficially her works can be read as mere optical eye-teasers. But Bridget Riley chooses her visual patterns and ambiguities with intuitive felicity.

One important by-product of Vasarély's painting, and a direct descendant of the old constructivist teaching, has been the use artists have made of movement. In Paris the Groupe de Recherche d'Art Visuel, which includes Yvral (son of Victor Vasarély), Julio Le Parc (winner of the main painting prize in the 1966 Venice Biennale), the Venezuelan Jesus Raphael Soto (b.1923), the Israeli Agam (Jacob Gipstein, b.1928) and the Hungarian Nicholas Schöffer (b.1912) have all employed movement in one form or another, either by building small motors into their work, or by making use of the movement of the spectator as he changes his position in front of a work. Three Düsseldorf artists, Heinz Mack (b.1931), Otto Piene (b.1928) and Gunther Uecker (b.1930), have collaborated on similar constructions. The difficulty experienced by most people on seeing this type of work is to know where the machine or the science leaves off and the artist begins. Many of the exhibits at an exhibition called *La Nouvelle Tendence*, held in Paris in 1964, were undoubtedly beguiling. Whether this work has more potential than that is still an open question.

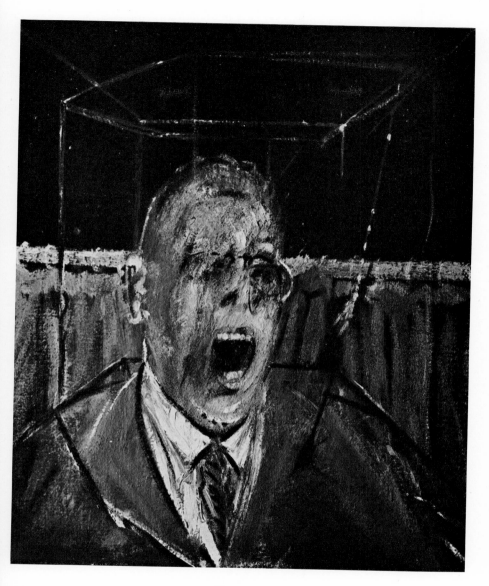

PLATE 1

Francis Bacon *Study for a Portrait,* 1952

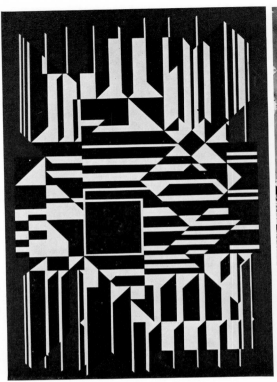

Victor Vasarély *Tilla*
(emulsion on board), 1957–62

Jean Dubuffet
Man with a Basket, 1955–6

PLATE 2

Alberto Burri
Sacco e Rosso, 1954

Alberto Giacometti
The Cat, 1954

PLATE 3

Max Bill
Rythmus im Raum, 1947–48
(execution in granite,
1962 ; collection Mr.
and Mrs. James Clark,
Dallas, Texas)

PLATE 4

Anthony Caro
Prospect, 1964
(painted steel)

Below
Henry Moore
*UNESCO
Reclining Figure*,
1957–8
(marble)

PLATE 5

Vallingby: view of shopping centre
(late 1950s, Sven Markelius)

Philharmonic Concert Hall, Berlin (1956–63,
Hans Scharoun)

PLATE 6

Festival Hall, Chianciano Terme, Tuscany:
reinforced concrete roof (1952, P. L. Nervi)

PLATE 7

Église St Joseph, Le Havre
(1949–56, Auguste Perret)

Below
Pilgrimage Chapel,
Ronchamp (1954,
Le Corbusier)

PLATE 8

Economist Building,
London (1964,
Peter Smithson)

Below
St Catherine's College,
Oxford: view of
main quad (1960–4,
Arne Jacobsen)

Pop Art or New Realism

A new form of figurative painting has its supporters among young artists in Western Europe today. Once again the initiative came from the United States, where artists began to use images taken directly from advertisements, comic strips and soup cans. The idea was that commonplace objects like the American flag, which had been seen but never looked at, could in the hands of a capable artist like Jasper Johns take on an altogether different appearance when removed to an artistic setting. The critic Harold Rosenberg described the new form as 'an advertising art which advertises itself as art that hates advertising'.

The patron saint of this movement became Marcel Duchamp (born in France in 1887 but now living mostly in New York), though Duchamp himself was less enthusiastic about his offspring. 'When I discovered ready-mades I thought to discourage aesthetics. In Neo-Dada they have taken my ready-mades and found aesthetic beauty in them. I threw the bottle-rack and the urinal into their faces as a challenge and now they admire them for their aesthetic beauty.' A fellow dadaist, Kurt Schwitters (1887–1948), who died neglected in England in 1948, has recently found many champions. Schwitters was a man of extraordinary creative gifts who thoroughly deserves greater attention.

The new figurative art, dubbed by the English critic Laurence Alloway 'pop art', began to be felt in Europe around 1960. It found its most sympathetic followers in Britain where artists like Richard Hamilton, Anthony Donaldson, Allen Jones, Joe Tilson and to some extent David Hockney and Peter Blake, began to work within the idiom, though without the frenzy of the Americans. In the rest of Europe pop art has been accepted less quickly. The German Konrad Klaphek, the Frenchmen Télémarque and Martial Raysse, the Swede Öyvind Fahlström and the Austrian Curt Stenvert were among the first to be associated with the movement.

Conclusion

On the face of it art is flourishing in Western Europe. More people seem to appreciate more art than ever before; the attendance figures at galleries and museums rise each year; more works of art are sold; artists no longer starve. While the European economies thrive there seems no danger of this happy situation ending. Yet if one tries to judge the quality of present-day art *sub specie aeternitatis* there are many causes for doubt. Art may be appreciated by more people, but it also seems to mean less. Artistic styles seem to change as fast as fashions, and revolution in the arts as in politics appears to have been institutionalised. Of course similar fears were felt when the impressionists first appeared and again with the birth of cubism, but this does not make these fears today any the less disturbing. Probably it is best not to judge today's art by any standards but its own. It is surely as pointless and as misleading to compare Matisse with Titian or Dubuffet with Rembrandt as it is to compare Oxford linguistic philosophy with the magnificent structures of Kant and Spinoza.

The modern artist has narrower objectives than his predecessors. Just as the modern philosopher has handed over many traditional philosophical questions to the scientist, so modern art has discarded the grand themes which preoccupied the old masters and returned them to literature, whence they were partly derived. Contemporary artists who have attempted to go beyond these limitations have generally failed. Picasso, for example, has made such forays, which end more often than not in pastiche. The best modern artists have generally found their subjects either within themselves, or in the nature of art itself. It looks as if these two types of art, what might be called the 'introspective' and the 'formal', will continue to be practised for some time to come. Certainly there is no artist working in Europe today who seems capable of anything more heroic.

BIBLIOGRAPHY

Amaya, Mario. *Pop as Art*, Studio Vista, London, 1965; issued in the United States as *Pop Art and After*, Viking Press, New York, 1966.

Bann, Stephen; Gadney, Reg; Popper, Frank and Steadman, Philip. *Kinetic Art*, George Wittenborn, New York, 1966.

Greenberg, Clement. *Art and Culture*, Beacon Press, Boston, Mass., 1961.

Haftmann, Werner. *Painting in the Twentieth Century*, 2 vols, Lund Humphries, London; Frederick A. Praeger, New York, 1961.

Huyghé, René (ed.) *The Larousse Encyclopedia of Modern Art*, Paul Hamlyn, London; Putnam New York, 1965.

Lake, Carlton and Maillard, Robert (eds.). *A Dictionary of Modern Painting*, Methuen, London, 1956; Tudor, New York, 1964.

Maillard, Robert (ed.) *A Dictionary of Modern Sculpture*, Methuen, London; Tudor, New York, 1962.

Seuphor, Michel (ed.) *A Dictionary of Abstract Painting*, Tudor, New York, 1957; Methuen, London, 1958.

Waldberg, Patrick. *Surrealism*, Skira, Cleveland, Ohio, 1962; Thames and Hudson, London, 1966.

American Abstract Artists. *The World of Abstract Art*, George Wittenborn, New York, 1957.

54-64, Painting and Sculpture of a Decade. Catalogue to the exhibition organised by the Calouste Gulbenkian Foundation, at the Tate Gallery, London, 1964.

ARCHITECTURE

HARRY GRAHAM

Two of the commonest views put forward about architecture today are that it is all the same—in Bristol, Tokyo and Casablanca—and that it is abysmally bad. There is unfortunately considerable justification for both these views, which are in essence one. Information is nowadays disseminated so far and so fast that the so-called 'international style' is absorbed by architects everywhere almost without their being aware of it. And unlike wine, it is usually the bad that travels. This is the architecture that is generally seen, and many people are unaware of the excellent, stimulating and sometimes beautiful buildings that abound in Europe.

Daunted by the apparently insurmountable difficulties of making the world an agreeable place in which to live, the architectural profession is in a state of mental confusion: it sees the high ideals which it has set itself constantly frustrated. As the creators of the perfect environment for the new way of life of the 20th century, a rôle which architects have rightly tried to assume, they have managed to make very little headway. In all European countries, opportunities for the sensible replanning of cities, presented by the destructions of the war, have been neglected or misused. This may have been from the economic necessity to get on and rebuild without waiting for a comprehensive or considered plan, or more often from the lack of perception of those in public control, and from the great gulf which yawns between the architects' Utopian aspirations and what society as a whole is ready to accept.

There are consequently two standards of architecture. In all countries there is some outstanding new architecture, and a great deal of depressing mediocrity, but what is completely lacking is a minimum standard of competence common to all new building. It is perhaps over-optimistic to expect that this can be achieved so soon, when modern architecture has only been generally accepted since the end of the second world war. However, the mental state of architects today, the feverish search for new solutions, both functional and aesthetic, and the consequent sense of unease, is not calculated to produce this common standard. A great deal is nowadays talked about the need for improving the 'total environment', as the realisation that the whole fabric of life is being choked by the accretions of modern industry becomes ever more forcibly evident. Nevertheless, it is precisely in the total environment that the failure of architecture is most apparent. Only when architects have evolved a common standard, by reaching a clear and confident understanding of their task, and above all by gaining the sympathy and cooperation of all the other elements in society which determine its face, can the total environment really be improved.

If one opens an architectural magazine at random, one will be unlikely to tell in what country, in what continent even, the building illustrated is to be found. Nonetheless, national characteristics can still be discerned in the various productions of Europe. These can be divided, for the purposes of a general and not too rigid classification, into the Scandinavian countries, the Teutonic countries, Italy, France and England. This is not to say that the smaller and poorer Western European nations do not have a contribution or a character of their own.

SCANDINAVIA

The Scandinavian countries have approached the common standard of excellence mentioned above more nearly than any other country in Europe. They have escaped the disadvantage of over-crowding, almost entirely avoided the massive onslaught of the industrial revolution of the 19th century from which cities in the rest of Europe are still reeling, and they have developed an enlightened welfare state long before other countries. These three factors have given them room to manoeuvre, less obsolete building to contend with, and the power and the will to plan comprehensively. Civilised values have been able to spread more widely throughout society than is possible in countries shackled with the impedimenta of the 19th century. Modern architecture is accepted, understood and admired, and that essential for a high general standard, active public taste, operates more successfully. A feeling for pre-industrial craftsmanship, which has none-the-less been united with modern technique, produces an unequalled standard of finish. This elegance and finish is well-known in Europe, through Scandinavian furniture and domestic implements, which have become for many the symbol of modern elegance.

In Sweden particularly, the feeling for architecture is inseparable from a feeling for urban design as a whole, a second essential for excellence in the total environment. In Stockholm, as early as 1904, the city began to acquire urban land, so that now it can reap the reward of being able to plan its extensions logically and comprehensively. A good example of this is the new quarter of Stockholm called Vallingby, begun in the late 1950s under the direction of Sven Markelius. It is full of lessons for the city planner, many of which have passed into the text-books, but few of which have been so successfully implemented elsewhere. Vallingby is a suburb of the city, but every aspect of its carefully thought out plan has prevented it from becoming another of the soulless adjuncts which we think of as suburbs. In addition to a great variety of house types, fitted to the existing landscape which was allowed to permeate the whole development, it has a cultural, shopping and recreational centre which the architects managed to invest with charm and vivacity. Vivacity, of course, cannot be provided by architecture alone, and in this case springs from another planning decision, to provide work not only for a quarter of the residents, but for 60,000 more people from neighbouring areas. Here, too, the segregation of pedestrians and motor-cars has been successfully achieved, and made workable by grouping the highest housing densities round the shopping centre and the railway station, which has a fast service to the city.

Although there is a high general standard of taste and competence in Scandinavia there are few masterpieces. The flavour of its architecture is very well exemplified in England by the new St Catherine's College at Oxford, built by the Danish architect Arne Jacobsen. It has clean, simple, geometric lines, an astonishingly high standard of detailing and finish, full of good ideas played down to a minor key, a place for sensible, rational people to live in: nothing in it offends, except its inoffensiveness—there is no spark of greatness.

Finland has produced, in her fastness of snow and pine-forests, a modern architecture of unique distinction and consistency. Mainly of brick and unpainted wood, robustly handled, it has a curious air of being completely modern, and yet uncontaminated by the hurly-burly of Europe. The prestige of Finnish architecture is no doubt largely due to the possession of Alvar Aalto, a man of international fame, whose work is not limited to Finland.

WEST GERMANY

Since the beginning of the century, Germany has been one of the pioneers of the modern movement. Between the end of the first world war and the advent of Hitler, a remarkably vigorous school of innovators, of whom Walter Gropius, founder of the famous Bauhaus, Eric Mendelsohn and Mies van der Rohe were the protagonists, asserted itself against the 19th-century ideas which were then still strong in all European countries. The Bauhaus' concern was with the industrialisation of buildings, good design in mass-produced articles, and a rational simplicity. Mies van der Rohe is still the acknowledged master of this idiom, and has had incalculable influence throughout the world. The other school of this period was Expressionism, the organic, romantic, curvilinear style, which still has its descendants in Europe today.

In 1933 all this ceased, and the eclectic monumentality of Fascism was imposed. In 1945 Germany had been left behind in the general progress of modern architecture, and having been a source of influence became a receiver from the rest of Europe and from America, where so many of her earlier pioneers such as Mies van der Rohe are now practising. The slogan after the war was 'a roof over one's head, nothing else matters'. Thus in spite of being one of the most prosperous of European nations to-day, the volume of building produced, and the sheer hard work which has gone into it, has left the Germans little time to do anything but accept what other countries are doing. Traditionalism, too, is still a hang-over from the Fascist period, especially to be seen in the coyness of private speculative housing and in the architecture of hotels.

Thus German architecture in the 1950s and 1960s is of no great distinction as the Germans themselves are aware. However, there is still much on the credit side, and the technical standards of building are high. As might be expected in a country where great stress is laid on education, school buildings are good, simple, practical and imaginative. In office building there are some sound achievements, notably the splendidly simple soaring triple slab of Thyssen House, in Düsseldorf, one of the finest skyscrapers in Europe; and in church architecture, particularly in southern Germany, there has been some fine work, sometimes too restlessly searching for novelty, but vigorous, diverse and inventive.

Finally, mention must be made of the German pre-eminence in theatre-building. Among several good examples, the Philharmonic Concert Hall in Berlin, by Hans Scharoun, one of the best of the 1920s generation who remained in Germany, is a building in which the principles of organic architecture are pursued with undeviating rigour. Everything is subservient to the business of performing and listening to music. The tiers of the hall rise like vineyards in a valley, in the words of the architect, and the tent-like roof forms the sky, but with a principal function of providing good acoustics. The swirling, diverging staircases are designed to deposit the audience dramatically, but conveniently, in their places where the central event is performed. The building is a triumph of consistent subservience to an idea, and of the Expressionist school of German architecture.

SWITZERLAND

The old gibe that Switzerland has produced nothing but the cuckoo-clock is manifestly unfair in regard to architecture. Le Corbusier was a Swiss by birth, though he became French by adoption, and as early as 1901 Robert Maillart began designing his bridges and other structures in reinforced concrete, of unparalleled technical daring and aesthetic panache. Altogether Switzerland has a tradition of good modern architecture, strongly influenced, as might be expected, by Germany. Again, as might be expected, building in Switzerland is of unsurpassed technical excellence; it is claimed that modern Swiss buildings are the only ones in Europe that improve with age, unlike those of France or Italy, whose maintenance is often appalling.

In the main branches of architecture, housing, schools, institutions and public buildings, there is a great deal of competence, and some quality. The Swiss are particularly adept at fitting buildings into their mountainous landscape. There are many good housing schemes stepping down a hill-side. An example is the new rural community at Hallen, near Berne, where terraced houses, with strongly modelled balconies overlooking the valley, climb the wooded hill-side, so that the upper houses use the roofs of the lower ones as gardens.

THE NETHERLANDS

The Dutch were among the pioneers of modern architecture from the beginning of the century to the 1930s and have fathered many and diverse movements—the school of Berlage and De Stijl among them. However, since the war, this early impetus seems to have fallen off almost completely; there is now a good deal of building of a solid pedestrian sort, and some unpleasant romantic anachronisms. Planning is often on a rigid grid system, reminiscent of the endless rectangular pattern of Dutch fields.

However, in the rebuilding of Rotterdam in 1953, the Netherlands produced a shopping precinct, in the centre of the town, which was considered by many to be a model for this type of planning, and has had wide influence, notably at Coventry in England. The complete segregation of pedestrians and traffic was put into practice, and great attention was paid to the details of street furniture and layout.

Another more recent work, the Children's Home near Amsterdam by Aldo van Eyck, is very remarkable. It is a geometric but irregular single-storey composition of squares, each with a pre-cast concrete saucer-dome, forming internal courts and re-entrants. It is a fascinating and stimulating building, and shows, perhaps, that the Dutch architectural spirit has only been sleeping, and is waking up again.

ITALY

Italy has always been the land of great architecture and today it still stands, as it has always done, above the other countries of Europe. The miraculous sense of visual beauty, unhampered by northern puritanism, is as strong as ever. The volume, the violence and even the flatulence of Italian architectural writings are a sign of their vitality; and although the charges of façadism and wilfulness are often levelled by purists, architecture is in the Italian blood. Italy's architecture has a great many highlights, against a background in which there are many very bad buildings—extremes are in the Italian temperament—and in which the more social aspects of architecture, such as schools, urban and suburban planning, are neglected by comparison with other European countries.

Italy's history as a conglomeration of city states makes for great variety as well as quality in the provinces. Rome, the administrative and religious capital, industrial Milan with its closer ties to northern Europe, Naples and the old Bourbon south, Turin at the other extreme, each have the individuality and the talent of a whole country.

The station at Rome, built by Montuori in 1950, is an appropriate introduction to the city's architectural treasures, which it in no way shames. It is typical of the Italians that this modern building of great power and elegance incorporates an ancient Roman wall in its design. (The English cannot even incorporate a Victorian arch.)

Pier Luigi Nervi, the great architect-engineer, stands out from a phalanx of talent to exemplify the peculiar Italian skill in the daring and dramatic use of reinforced concrete, refined and attenuated to its last limits. Nervi has been practising since the 1920s, and his works and those of his disciples cover Italy. Perhaps his most exquisite feat is the roof of the casino at Chianciano Terme in Tuscany, a vast floating saucer of intricate ribs.

In Milan, there is Gio Ponti's Pirelli building, whose knife blade silhouette is justly famous, and, not far away, the Torre Velasca, an arresting if not very beautiful tower of pink concrete with curious flying ribs supporting the overhang of the top ten floors. Nowhere in Europe is it possible to find two more dissimilar office blocks. In churches, factories, individual houses and apartment blocks (rather than whole housing schemes), museums, department stores and institutions of all kinds, ideas of such diversity are being produced that it would be impossible to reduce them to a type or a generalisation.

An important aspect of the Italian genius is to be seen in their attitude to their own architectural heritage, which has been elevated to a contemporary art. In the refurbishing of picture galleries and museums, in the incorporation of a cinema in a 14th-century palace, the Italians dare to change more radically than any other country. With that simplicity of line and subdued richness of material which is particularly Italian, they have improved and revitalised many of their old buildings. The recent rehabilitation of the Querini Stampalia Palace in Venice, by Carlo Scarpa, as a library and art gallery, is a good example. In the great Romanesque churches of Apulia, three centuries of sacred patisserie is being ruthlessly scraped off, and plate-glass is replacing opaque screens. The results are extraordinarily effective. In this way, too, the great Italian tradition is being carried on.

FRANCE

France is a country of curious contrasts in architecture. She has produced the Ecole des Beaux Arts, that anathema of modern architects, and Viollet-le-Duc, the father of modern architectural theory. She has produced marvellous works of engineering and craftsmanship, and the lowest general standard of building; some of the worst architecture in Europe, and the greatest architect of the 20th century, Le Corbusier.

That peculiar French shoddiness, which nevertheless sometimes rises to heights of unexpected elegance, is to be seen in almost all post-war buildings. All over France, grim grey slabs, with their rows of chimneys, rise from seas of ill-considered tarmac. It is as if the French had decided, after consideration, that these things do not matter, that other things are more important.

And yet the good buildings are of a very high standard. Le Corbusier, whose death in 1965 removed the presence but not the spirit of one of the giants of 20th-century architecture, had dominated the scene since the 1920s, though it was not till after the war that he had the success in his fight against tradition in France that he deserved. Since the mid-1950s, a new generation of architects, many of them trained by, or at least owing allegiance to Le Corbusier, have begun to improve the scene, and have produced some works of quality. In 1962, the reform of French architectural education was begun, and the stranglehold of the academic tradition may at last be shaken off.

Many of Le Corbusier's finest buildings are not on French soil. In France, however, there is the world-famous chapel at Ronchamp, completed in 1954, in which his peculiar and inimitable genius appears; photographs do not unfortunately convey the moving quality of this building. Almost equally famous is the Unité d' Habitation at Marseilles, a great apartment block in rough concrete which stands out with its powerful modelling immeasurably superior to all the other undistinguished slabs in Marseilles, or indeed anywhere in France. Following Le Corbusier's idea of the vertical street, the roof is a public piazza, covered with sculptured forms in concrete, making a dramatic silhouette against the Mediterranean and the dry Provençal landscape. This building, often criticised for its effect on the lives of those who live in it, has nevertheless had profound influence on the rest of Europe, constantly imitated but never equalled.

At the monastery of La Tourette, near Lyons, raw concrete is again used, and appropriately enough for a religious building it has something of the bold grandeur of the French Romanesque. It has a fairly conventional plan; cells, chapel, refectory round a court, but Le Corbusier has elevated that French shoddiness almost into a mystique; the electric light wires are not even concealed. As with his other buildings it shows that, while the influence of his architectural thinking is profound, his aesthetic approach is so personal that it can hardly be imitated without anti-climax or disaster.

In larger-scale housing projects there has been improvement and some success since the late 1950s. At Marly-les-Grandes-Terres, on the outskirts of Paris, a comprehensive housing scheme by Marcel Lods shows a greater concern for all-over planning than hitherto found in France; there is a well-thought-out separation of traffic and pedestrians, schools, medical facilities and an excellent shopping centre, but it is marred by too much rigidity, and a lack of attraction in the buildings themselves.

At Bobigny and Aubervilliers, both suburbs of Paris, the architect Aillaud has tried to get away from the rectangular approach in two slightly bizarre schemes, with round apartment towers, sinuous endless ribbons of six-storey blocks, and triangular clusters. The effect is interesting, but not really successful. A new town extension at Bagnols-sur-Cèze in Provence is another example of rational geometric planning, but this time with an improvement in architectural quality.

Finally, mention must be made of the rebuilding of Le Havre by Auguste Perret, another great name in French architecture. Perret, who died in 1954, though the work at Le Havre continued after his death, was both classicist and innovator in the field of reinforced concrete design. Le Havre is a rigidly geometrical urban layout, and a standardised frame system with precast panels of many-coloured concrete is used in all the buildings. The scheme is enormously admired by some for its lucidity, logic and precision, and hated by others as sterile classicism. It can perhaps stand as an epitome of French architecture, in which the worst and the best are represented.

BRITAIN

Britain was the last of the important countries to embrace the modern movement. In the 1920s and 1930s, when other countries were inventing and advancing, traditionalism persisted. Modern works of any merit were very few, and the humbler attempts at modernity in this period are now considered the nadir of British architecture. But since the war, modern architecture has become increasingly accepted, if not universally loved, and in the 1960s it seems that Britain is catching up after her late start. Works of considerable merit have recently been produced, and in some branches of building, particularly schools, housing and the layout of industrial estates, Britain has been setting an example to Europe.

In town-planning and renewal, little of great success has been done in the 1960s. As in most other European countries, opportunities are constantly neglected or mishandled. In London, changing so rapidly, incoherence predominates; even in the City and around St Paul's, where a conscious effort has been made, the results are not happy. This is perhaps not surprising in a country which is fundamentally inimical to urban life, and where the traditions of laissez-faire militate against comprehensive planning. In the celebrated new satellite towns of London, such as Harlow and Stevenage, a surburban atmosphere prevails and the quality of architecture is not high. However, at Cumbernauld, near Glasgow, the latest of the new towns, there is a marked improvement; this is expressed by a greater compactness in the plan, achieved with linking pedestrian streets, and a more urban scale in the town centre. These qualities are spreading in Britain, no doubt as the smallness of this overcrowded island becomes more forcibly realised.

In housing, there have been some notable successes. In London, the Churchill Gardens scheme, begun in 1947 but still being extended, is a good example of high-density urban housing, and at Roehampton a series of bold concrete towers are disposed, on the principles of Le Corbusier's 'ville radieuse', in a splendid site on the edge of Richmond Park. In Sheffield, the more recent Park Hill scheme shows the growing tendency towards compactness. Continuous blocks, following the contours of the hilly site, and bending back on themselves to form enclosures, have wide access decks on many levels, to introduce the community life of streets into high buildings. It is a vast and impressive group, but whether its social aims will work is still to be seen.

The boom in office blocks, brought to an end by government action in 1965, has produced a mass of undistinguished buildings which disfigure, in varying degrees, all the larger cities of Britain. There are, however, some exceptions to the general level, of which Thorn House, Castrol House and the Vickers tower, all in London, are examples. New Zealand House, also in London, is above average, well detailed throughout, and of a standard not normally possible with commercial developers. Yet none of these buildings, whatever their quality, seems to have been placed in the urban scene with any real thought to its effect in the town-planning sense. There is one exception to this which deserves mention—the Economist Building in St James's by Peter Smithson, completed in 1964. The composition of three towers of varying height has been used to form a small piazza raised above the pavement, with a considerable sense of urban style. The lowest block is on the street frontage, and maintains perfectly the scale of the 18th- and 19th-century façades on either side. This building, simply and robustly, if unexceptionally detailed, represents what the norm of modern architecture should be, but so rarely is.

In the 1960s, the university expansion programme has called forth the best of the architectural talents in new foundations such as Sussex, York and East Anglia, and in the older universities, especially Oxford and Cambridge. It is in this field that there have been buildings which lift England out of the common rut. At Sussex, Sir Basil Spence's new university is a good example; grouped in a broad bowl of open land, the buildings are all of massive, vigorous brickwork, capped with huge segmental arches of concrete. At York, the new university is less exciting, but makes consistent use of prefabricated components, developed in the school-building programme of the 1950s. Examples of good and sometimes outstanding university architecture could be multiplied. Mention must, however, be made of the Engineering Faculty at Leicester University by James Stirling, a now celebrated building of vigour and articulation, reminiscent of a piece of Victorian engineering.

GREECE AND SPAIN

Mention should be made of two Mediterranean countries, Greece and Spain, which have some claim to an architecture of their own. Greece has only since 1945 entered the field of modern architecture on a large scale, but is making rapid strides forward from the 'Othonian' traditional and the jazz villa. Some apartment blocks and offices in Athens have real elegance and refinement, and the government-sponsored Tourist Bureau is building excellent hotels in provincial towns, notably in Nauplion and Kalambaka.

In Spain, too, there are signs of increasing architectural vigour, making headway against a background of little distinction and the heavy preferences of Fascism. As in Greece, much of the new building is aimed at coping with the massive onrush of northern Europeans searching for sun and wine, and the devastations of the tourist industry are now bidding fair to ruin the coast-line (and later the interior) of this last backwater of Western Europe.

BIBLIOGRAPHY

Blake, Peter. *The Master Builders* (general introduction to the works and theories of Le Corbusier, Mies van der Rohe and Frank Lloyd Wright), Victor Gollancz, London; Alfred A. Knopf, New York, 1960.

Banham, Reyner. *Guide to Modern Architecture*, Architectural Press, London, 1962; D. Van Nostrand Co., Princeton, NJ, 1963.

Kidder Smith, G. E. *The New Architecture of Europe*, World Publishing Co., Cleveland, Ohio, 1961; Penguin Books, London, 1962.

Encyclopaedia of Modern Architecture, ed. Wolfgang Pehut, Thames and Hudson, London, 1963; Harry N. Abrams, New York, 1964.

World Architecture, Vols. 1–2, ed. John Donat, Studio Vista, London; Viking Press, New York, 1964 and 1965.

MUSIC

STEPHEN WALSH

IN music ends and means have always been closely interwoven. This has never been more so than in the music of today, which makes so little immediate appeal to the senses. The layman may feel that techniques as advanced as those currently in vogue are not really his concern; he may even feel that if the music cannot speak to him directly as, say, Mozart's does, then it scarcely merits his attention. But many musicians, the present writer included, have found that a comprehension of the threads of development and of the technical aims in modern composition has led them back to contemporary music with renewed fascination.

ORIGINS OF MODERN MUSIC

Modern music, at least as the present-day avant-garde understands it, begins with Arnold Schoenberg (1874–1951) and with his pupils and associates, Alban Berg (1885–1935) and (perhaps most important of all) Anton Webern (1883–1945). These composers are generally grouped under the title 'the second Viennese School', though in fact they developed independently and exerted a widely divergent influence on later trends. Schoenberg, the first composer to rationalise the use of atonality in music and the formulator of the system which he called 'composition with twelve notes', i.e. dodecaphony, was thus the fountain-head of all modern serial techniques and is still revered as a patriarchal figure by all but the most regressive of modern composers.

Schoenberg's harmonic idiom departed from the whole concept of key and evolved towards a method in which all twelve notes of the chromatic scale occupied a position of equal importance—no single note (or tonic) was allowed to predominate. During and immediately after the first world war he rationalised this in his system of 'serial' composition, the essence of which was that the twelve notes could be presented in any of the innumerable possible orders, but that once chosen the order should be maintained throughout the work (with, however, certain licences too complex to be described here).

The more rhapsodically imaginative Berg espoused dodecaphony only insofar as it suited his fundamentally romantic temperament—his violin concerto (1935), for instance, neatly sidesteps the atonal issue by using a twelve-note series with strong tonal associations (a series of superimposed triads), and by incorporating a Bach chorale in its finale. Webern, on the other hand, was an absolutist. He wrote exclusively in short forms, though few of his works could precisely be described as miniatures. Their content is explosively compressed, Webern's latent expressionism being rigorously

549

controlled in a way that is scarcely less neurotic than the more florid effusions of other post-romantic composers. This is clearly 'atomic' music, and it has been absolutely seminal for the mainstream of avant-garde work as it exists two decades after Webern's death.

OLIVIER MESSIAEN

Up to the second world war, progressive trends in music were more or less defined by the work of the Viennese School and of its disciples, some of whom were to acquire increased significance later on. But at about the time of Webern's death there emerged in Paris a composer whose work, though of a highly idiosyncratic nature, was to become even more crucial to the direction taken by the avant-garde. This was Olivier Messiaen (b. 1908). Messiaen's stylistic origins owe more to Debussy than to Schoenberg, and can be seen as a logical development from Debussy's experiments with modality and rhythm.

But whereas Debussy's innovations were largely instinctive (they consisted, in the main, of emancipating music from various tyrannies, primarily those of Western tonality and the barline) Messiaen, like Schoenberg—though on quite different lines—rationalised his methods with the utmost precision. He established certain melodic modes of his own, modes which bore no relation to those of either classical or medieval antiquity, but followed complex patterns within themselves, and were generally limited in the number of ways they could be transposed into other keys (the chord of the diminished seventh—say C, E flat, G flat, A—is a classic instance of a 'mode of limited transposition', since there are only two other ways of reproducing it). Messiaen also applied the system to rhythm by employing rhythmic shapes which were palindromic, and could therefore not be effectively inverted. The early works use these methods with more or less freedom; but in the notorious *Étude de rythme No. 2* (*Mode de valeur et d'intensités*) of 1949, the rationalisation is complete. Each element of the music (melody, rhythm, dynamics and timbre) is regulated according to a mode, so that the progress of the piece is ruled by a mathematical logic which nevertheless allows of considerable musical diversity and technical manipulation on the composer's part.

The *Étude* marked a turning point, not only for Messiaen, but for his pupils, who included at that time, and since, many of the most progressive among the younger generation of composers. Subsequently Messiaen concerned himself more and more with timbre, both in his organ pieces, which rank among the most majestic since Bach, and in works for orchestra, where the influence of birdsong (transcribed quite literally) has become a key factor. Younger composers followed this lead, and the emancipation of timbre as a functional element of composition has been one of the most important of contemporary musical developments in Europe.

PIERRE BOULEZ

The technical quicksands which beset the listener trying to understand the origins of modern compositional methods become deeper still when we turn to Messiaen's pupils, and particularly to the most prominent of them, Pierre Boulez (b. 1926). In the early post-war years the younger French composers paid little attention to Messiaen, devoting most of their studies to Schoenberg and Berg, to Debussy and intermittently to Stravinsky (the

Stravinsky of *The Rite of Spring*, the Debussy of *Pelléas et Mélisande*). Webern's technique of fragmentation and of intense serial concentration caused great excitement. But it was not until Messiaen began to exert his influence as a teacher that all these elements fused into a coherent whole. Messiaen was not himself a serialist, but his methods seemed to have strong serial connotations. The *Étude de rythme* made a particular impact, for it opened a completely new vista of the infinite possibilities of serialism.

Boulez found that by applying serialism (rather than modality) to every element of his music he could exert the most rigorous control over his material, without in any way limiting its expressive potential. In his *Structures* for two pianos (1952) 'total serialisation', i.e. serialisation of all elements including rhythm, dynamics and so on, had its first airing. *Structures* derived its technique (and one of its melodic series) from the *Étude*, but with this difference: that whereas Messiaen restricted the development of his material by decreeing that each element (for instance any given note and any given rhythmic duration) should recur with certain other elements, Boulez allowed them completely free movement. Each note of the pitch series was to appear in combination with each rhythm and each dynamic value and so on, thus making available a range of development of an entirely new and astronomically extensive type.

This kind of total serialisation has dominated French vanguard music since the early fifties, though one or two young composers still adhere to the precepts of orthodox dodecaphony as preached by René Leibowitz. Boulez's own development has been typical (though his stature, both as a composer and conductor, is not). Up to the composition of *Structures* he had been moving gradually towards the methods which that work propounds; thereafter he absorbed them as a natural means of expression, so that by the time he wrote *Le marteau sans maître* (a setting of verses by René Char for contralto and small instrumental ensemble, 1954) he had completely mastered the techniques involved. It is significant that this is the work by which Boulez is now best known, and one of very few avant-garde compositions to have achieved really international acclaim.

There is some indication that in the past decade Boulez's efforts as a composer have slackened, as though, having achieved a goal, his interest in it had diminished. His later work flows naturally into the vast homage to Mallarmé, *Pli selon pli*, which in its turn grew out of the *Mallarmé Improvisations*, one of the first works by Boulez to incorporate 'aleatory', or chance, elements. Boulez is known in principle to oppose this aspect of modern composition, feeling it to be a step towards anarchy from the position of 'democratic solidity' represented by total serialisation. His use of 'aleatory' as of electronic technique has thus been occasional rather than intensive, and has never dominated the central features of his idiom.

KARLHEINZ STOCKHAUSEN AND MUSIC OF CHANCE

Nevertheless the role of chance and improvisation in modern music has increased enormously, largely through the work of the young German composer Karlheinz Stockhausen (b. 1928). Stockhausen studied in Paris with Frank Martin, Darius Milhaud and Messiaen, and quickly became an apostle of total serialisation. But for him this proved a constricting force and led him to experiment with what he termed 'alea' (the Latin word for 'chance'). From the close though by no means symphonic organisation of *Kontrapunkte* (1953) he thus moved to the comparative looseness of *Klavierstück*

XL (1957), in which a set of nineteen note groups is scattered at random over the paper, and the performer is given a series of basic tempi, dynamic levels and so on, within which he can arrange the note-groups at his own discretion. If this sounds complicated, it pales before the complexity of *Zyklus*. Here the score is arranged on a spiral pivot, and the player is allowed to start on any page he chooses, proceeding through the work back to his starting point. Physically he is stationed within a circle of percussion instruments, moving from one to the next in order, either clockwise or anti-clockwise. Stockhausen's more recent works elaborate these spatial functions: both *Gruppen* (1958) and *Carré* (1960) are for multiple orchestral and/or choral forces placed on different sides of a square hall and playing for some of the time independently of one another (a method which recalls the work of the American composer Charles Ives, and of the eccentric though influential John Cage).

'Aleatory' techniques have spread rapidly, too rapidly perhaps for their healthy absorption into an already complex expressive medium. In many countries they have been a symptom of a hysterical movement away from an otherwise throttlingly conservative atmosphere. In Spain, for instance, the desire to supersede the traditional attachment to national culture has led to an influx of unrelated influences, from Stravinsky and Bartok to *musique concrète*, some of which have inspired worthwhile compositions, some not. The leading composers, Cristóbal Halfter and Luis de Pablo, moved speedily through the early stages of dodecaphony and total serialism, and have now both used chance and improvisation as important elements in their work.

In Scandinavia the situation is somewhat different, because here musical tradition has never been firmly established and tends to centre on one or two individual giants (Sibelius, Nielsen, Grieg, Berwald being the obvious instances from each country). For many years Scandinavian music moved sedately in the more conventional 20th-century streams, prominent influences being (apart from the native composers mentioned above) Prokofiev, Shostakovich, Bartok, and—more recently—Benjamin Britten. Gradually, however, there emerged an interest in more advanced idioms. The formation in the late forties by Hilding Rosenberg of a group of young Stockholm musicians dedicated to the propagation of modern music in Sweden stimulated a new movement which has grown spectacularly with the help of radio, in Sweden as elsewhere an important factor in the promulgation of contemporary art. At first interest centred on the tonal applications of serialism (under the influence of Berg), but composers like Ingvar Lidholm and Karl-Birger Blomdahl experimented with tone-colour and Webernian pointillism, and these developments have been harnessed by the youngest and in many ways most brilliant of present-day Swedish composers, Bo Nilsson (b. 1937), into music where sound takes on an ethereal, other-worldly quality of a most vividly imagined kind.

Electronic Music

The obsession with pure timbre, so striking a feature of European music in the fifties and sixties, led naturally to the last important current in the contemporary mainstream, that of electronic composition and *musique concrète*—the application of extra-musical sounds to musical ends. Both methods were pioneered in the United States by the French-born composer, Edgar Varèse (1885–1965), who actually gave up creative work for some years until the technical means became available by which he could realise the entirely new sounds he envisaged. The first practical use of musique concrète, however, took place in Paris in 1949, where it was developed by Pierre Schaeffer in collaboration with Radio Française. For some time Schaeffer and Stockhausen worked together, and it was during this period that Stockhausen developed the principle of electronic composition. The two techniques naturally became complementary until finally they merged, so that the most recent electronic music blends elements of both, with taped sound (as in Stockhausen's *Gesang der Jünglinge*, 1955–6, which uses boys' voices) analysed electronically, very often beyond recognition.

Stockhausen established a studio for electronic music at Cologne, one of three main centres in Germany (the others are at Darmstadt and Munich). Subsequently studios sprang up in other countries, in Spain, Sweden, the Netherlands and above all the United States, where the technique was seized on eagerly by the world's most scientifically advanced civilisation.

There is, however, still some question as to the future applicability of electronic music. Its most successful effusions have undoubtedly been in the field of background music for films and television plays, though few will deny the beauty of the best electronic works by Stockhausen (the *Gesang der Jünglinge* or *Kontakte*, 1960). A number of leading composers, among them Boulez, have coopted the technique into otherwise conventionally scored music, and works in which tape recordings play a prominent part are comparatively common. Strangely, though, electronic music has found little favour in Italy, where the avant-garde movement is otherwise strong (Franco Evangelisti's *Incontri di fascie sonore* is the best-known instance); less strangely it has encountered almost none in Britain, where there are no significant electronic composers and few facilities for electronic experiment. The tendency of British music to steer a central course between the radical and the reactionary will be discussed below.

Luigi Dallapiccola and other Italian Composers

There is an important body of Western European composers who fall between this central road and the more extreme avant-garde trends. They happen to include some of the most striking musical intellects of our day, and their stature is very largely expressed by their refusal to be diverted by fashion, and by their essentially personal use of systems which have also fed the avant-garde. One turns first to Italy, where there are a number of such composers, headed by the doyen of present-day serialism, Luigi Dallapiccola (b. 1904). Dallapiccola came to twelve-note music by his own route, and the influence of Schoenberg was complemented by certain pentatonic (five-tone) elements in his own style, and, on his own admission, by literary precedents in the work of Joyce and Proust. As in much modern Italian music, there is a strong social conscience detectable in Dallapiccola's writing, the upshot of the traumatic Fascist experience and two world wars. Dallapiccola is obsessed by the theme of imprisonment and liberty, and tends to set texts dealing with these ideas. His masterpieces are thus choral, the *Canti di prigionia* (1938–41), which uses an almost entirely percussive accompaniment, and the opera *Il prigioniero* (1944–8), which is quite strictly dodecaphonic, but with small concessions to tradition which pacify the conventionally attuned ear.

Dallapiccola's highly personal use of serialism has found a strong response among younger Italian composers, stronger, certainly, than the less committed neo-classicism of the others of his generation, Goffredo Petrassi (b. 1904), an influential teacher, and Francesco Malipiero (b. 1882), whom

Dallapiccola rather perversely regards as the greatest living Italian composer. Nevertheless the seminal influence in Italy has been that of Bruno Maderna (b. 1920), who evolved from Schoenbergian serialism a highly complex mathematical system which regulated the order of notes and rhythms with complete precision. Maderna's music, and indeed that of his pupil, Luigi Nono (b. 1924), is seldom heard in Italy, though it is well-known in northern Europe and highly respected at Darmstadt and Donaueschingen, the unofficial headquarters of the German avant-garde. Nono carries the social aspects of music to an extreme scarcely envisaged even by Dallapiccola, exorcising all purely lyrical elements and speaking throughout with a voice in which protest is easily the dominant feature. The apogee of this tendency can be seen in the cantata *Sul ponte di Hiroshima* ('On the bridge of Hiroshima'), where all purely musical forms and shapes are ruled by the need to express the emotions implicit in the work's title.

By contrast Luciano Berio (b. 1925) is a musical craftsman of the highest order, for whom timbre is a central element in musical expression. His works are characterised by their clarity of texture and by the pure beauty of their musical line (one of his best-known works in Britain is, significantly, *Sequenza I* (1958) for solo flute, while another, *Circles* (1960), for voice and percussion, is also much determined by the direction of a solo line). More recently Berio has turned to expressionism, especially in his opera *Passaggio* (1963), which exhibits intense, explosive qualities that hark back to Webern.

HANS WERNER HENZE

Since Dallapiccola's early masterpieces, Italian music has developed with tremendous virility and independence along lines that are fundamentally instrumental and choral. Ironically, the best opera composer working in Italy has been a German, Hans Werner Henze (b. 1926), who moved from his native country to Naples in 1953, and was profoundly influenced by the atmosphere of southern Italy. He studied first with Leibowitz, under whom he learned the profound respect for Schoenberg which informs his most mature works. Above all Henze is a lyrical composer (both a cause and an effect of his move to Italy) and a great deal of his music, not least the operas, shows him to be very much an heir to the German romantic tradition. He is, too, an eclectic, having taken much from Webern and Berg, and from Stravinsky (both the early works and the more recent serial works by this most flexible of composers).

Of the operas *King Stag* (Berlin, 1956) is a vast romantic fantasy in which expressionist traits are prominent, while *The Prince of Homburg* (1960) moves sharply from the extravagant lyricism of a Berg to the harder, clearer outlines of a Stravinsky, without ever losing its bearings in relation to Henze's own style. Henze is also a prolific instrumental, orchestral and choral composer, writing in a luxuriant but always profoundly expressive style. Nevertheless there are signs in the most recent works to have reached Britain—the *Fifth Symphony* (1962) and the cantata *Novae de infinito laudes* (1963)—of a hardening of outline, an effect perhaps of Stravinskian influence. The cantata, in particular, is one of the most uncompromising in harmonic language of all Henze's works, and may yet prove to be the most important.

BRITISH COMPOSERS

With Henze we enter a realm of modern music fairly familiar to audiences in Britain, where his works have been frequently performed. The younger school of British composers has tended to follow a similar course, insofar as it has adopted a free-thinking and individual attitude to Schoenbergian serialism, but has generally ignored the more extravagant manifestations of the avant-garde (this with the exception of Cornelius Cardew [b. 1936] whose work is—oddly for a British composer—better-known and more highly regarded on the continent than in England). Richard Rodney Bennett (b. 1936) has found a happy compromise between advanced serialism and the more conventional techniques. His *Symphony* (1965) perhaps sacrifices rather too much on the altar of facility and comprehensibility, but the one opera, *The Mines of Sulphur*, shows a sterner, less compromising approach to his material, as well as a feeling for theatrical situation.

If Bennett's facility has helped him to meet the many commissions which have come his way, it has also tended to bring him under suspicion in critical and professional music circles. The same could be said of Malcolm Williamson (b. 1931), whose easy flirtation with such conflicting styles as nightclub jazz and Messiaen is a serious obstacle in all but his very best works (the *Sinfonietta*, 1965, or the operas *Our Man in Havana*, 1963 and *English Eccentrics*, 1964). Two composers who have been less compromising in their stylistic concessions should also be mentioned. Peter Maxwell Davies (b. 1934) has made increasing use of medieval techniques, but in an entirely modern way that shows close affinity with the timeless colouristic world of the continental avant-garde. Maxwell Davies has written much for children (he was for a time musical director of Cirencester Grammar School) and has demonstrated a striking gift for inculcating a mastery of contemporary musical intricacies into young minds. Nicholas Maw (b. 1936), on the other hand, is an essentially lyrical user of advanced serial techniques, and his idiom has all the qualities of a natural expressive language. Maw's works are as yet little played, though his reputation has been (justifiably) critically boosted.

The generation born in the mid-thirties is a strong force in present-day British music, but is not by any means the only one. Fashion, which has brought the younger composers to early prominence, has also been fairly kind to their elders, especially to Benjamin Britten (b. 1913), more recently to William Walton (b. 1902), and also, intermittently, to Michael Tippett (b. 1905), Alan Rawsthorne (b. 1905), Lennox Berkeley (b. 1903) and— sternest of post-Schoenbergians—Elizabeth Lutyens (b. 1906). Britten, secure in his stature as the most highly regarded of Western composers, has widened his scope in recent years to include a number of intensely wrought instrumental works—a field which previously only captured his occasional attention. Yet his range remains enormous. In 1965, supposedly a sabbatical year, he produced four new works, a suite for unaccompanied cello, the *Gemini Variations*, a cycle of William Blake songs, and a choral work, *Voices for Today*. Operatically he has become, for the time being, quiescent—his only opera since *A Midsummer-Night's Dream* (1960) has been the strange, idiosyncratic adaptation of a Japanese No-play, *Curlew River* (1964), which scarcely seems to fall within the canon of his other stage works.

Walton's output since the *Second Symphony* (1960) has been comparatively slender. The symphony was underrated when it appeared, and this situation has not changed—a record published soon after the work's premier was almost as quickly deleted. In his serious compositions Walton has become a more economical writer than is generally realised, and although it is true that the massive potential of early works like the *First Symphony* and *Belshazzar's Feast* has gone largely unfulfilled, there is still real strength and a prodigious technical command in everything he writes.

T

If Walton has to some extent receded, Tippett, who celebrated his sixtieth birthday in 1965 (almost simultaneously with Rawsthorne), has palpably advanced. Tippett's career has been an unbroken stylistic search and it is still true that his music is advancing into fields quite unforeseeable from his early works, the *Concerto for Double String Orchestra* or the cantata *A Child of Our Time*. He remains the most philosophical and thoughtful of British composers, and his latest compositions, which include a tough, visionary cantata, *The Vision of St Augustine* (1966), and the more approachable though highly original *Concerto for Orchestra*, show that he is still reaching out into new fields, both musical and intellectual. Rawsthorne, arguably the best of Britain's older generation of purely instrumental composers, has not prospered so markedly as Tippett. But his works, with their taut formal organisation and sinewy invention, are played with sufficient frequency for them to be a cogent force in the concert world.

'COMPROMISE' COMPOSERS

If contemporary British music demonstrates anything at all, it is that a musical culture can and does thrive not only on the most outrageous effusions of a detached avant-garde, but on the more staid, stable elements represented by what one might term the 'compromise' composers, who take what they consider most valuable from the available sources without necessarily sacrificing individuality. In strongly progressive countries like France the rearguard tends to become swamped, but it remains essential to the health of the culture. Composers like Darius Milhaud, Georges Auric, Henri Sauguet and André Jolivet are highly prolific but no longer at the forefront of France's musical life; nevertheless, their works are nationally known and thus nationally significant.

By the time Hindemith died in 1963 his reputation as an *enfant terrible* had been dissipated by a popular streak which led him to compose too much of what he termed *Gebrauchsmusik* (bread-and-butter music). His opposition to serialism and to its more advanced offshoots brought him critical opprobrium. His later years were musically an anticlimax. Hindemith's successors at the helm of tradition in Germany, Carl Orff (b. 1895) and Boris Blacher (b. 1903), have never really established their reputations overseas. Orff is generally known in Britain by only one work, *Carmina Burana* (an early composition, 1936), Blacher almost solely by name (except that he has the distinction of having composed yet another set of variations on Paganini's famous theme). Both compose in a spare, economical idiom; both have since the war espoused the cause of opera. Orff's idiom in particular makes a virtue of the simplest musical means, so that his works have a monolithic impressiveness but little subtlety of design. His association with music for children is another aspect of this quality.

In Austria the mere local fact of the Viennese School has not produced anything approaching a virile strain of contemporary composition. Austria's most potent influence has been didactic (for example Ernst Krenek in Germany and Egon Wellesz in England) but her composers have unfortunately turned away from the progressive example set by such men. In Greece, on the other hand, there are some surprises. Modern music was brought to the country by Nikos Skalkottas, a strange hermit-like figure who studied with (and was highly regarded by) Schoenberg, but who died in 1949 at the early age of forty-five. Younger composers reaped the benefits, and there now thrives in Greece a vital and individual school of modernists, headed by Theodor Antoniou (b. 1935), who has employed total serialisation plus aleatorism in his music, and Jani Christou (b. 1926), a prolific writer of theatre and television scores, whose work seems to owe something to the time and space experiments of Messiaen and his followers.

In Belgium, whose situation might seem ideal for absorbing all kinds of influences, music has receded in recent decades. The Netherlands, on the other hand, unhampered by a firmly rooted tradition of its own, has been fertile soil for influences from both within and without. Internally the key figure is Willem Pijper (1894–1947), and it is due both to his importance as a composer and to his music's appealing character (it has certain of the qualities to be found in Sibelius, but is more firmly romantic in character) that there are now so many young composers in the Netherlands. Externally, influences have come not only from France and Germany but also from Italy (Louis Andriessen, b. 1938, was a pupil of Berio), so that there is still some difficulty in defining what precisely constitutes the Dutch musical character. Nevertheless there is evidence in the work of Kees van Baaren (b. 1906), Hans Henkemans (b. 1913) and Peter Schat (b. 1935), to name only three of many, of a technical adventurousness which is something quite new in the history of Dutch music.

BIBLIOGRAPHY

Boulez, Pierre. *Penser la musique aujourd'hui*, Editions Gonthier, Switzerland, 1963.
Hartog, Howard (ed.) *European Music in the Twentieth Century*, Routledge and Kegan Paul, London, 1957; Pelican, London, paperback ed. 1961.
Hodeir, André. *Since Debussy: a View of Contemporary Music*, Secker and Warburg, London; Peter Smith, Gloucester, Mass., 1961.
Mason, Colin (ed.) *Cobbett's Cyclopedic Survey of Chamber Music*, III, Oxford Univ. Press, London and New York, 1963.
Mellers, Wilfred. *Music in a New Found Land: Themes and Developments in the History of American Music*, Barrie and Rockliff, London; Alfred A. Knopf, New York, 1964.
Rufer, Josef. *Composition with Twelve Notes*, Barrie and Rockliff, London, 1954; Dover, New York.
Webern, Anton. *The Path to the New Music*, Theodore Presser, Pennsylvania, 1963.

PERIODICALS
Die Reihe, Vienna; English translated version Theodore Presser, Pennsylvania.
Musical Quarterly, Schirmer, New York.
Tempo, Boosey and Hawkes, London.

PART THREE

WESTERN EUROPEAN INTEGRATION

PRINCIPAL WESTERN EUROPEAN ORGANISATIONS

ANTHONY SHARP

COUNCIL OF EUROPE

Address: Place Lenôtre, Strasbourg, France. *Foundation:* May 1949. *Membership:* Austria (1956), Belgium,[1] Cyprus (1961), Denmark, France, Federal Republic of Germany (1951), Great Britain, Greece (August 1949), Iceland (1950), Ireland, Italy, Luxembourg, Malta (1965), Netherlands, Norway, Sweden, Switzerland (1963), Turkey (August 1949). *Function:* Discussion of common interests and problems and discovery of new methods and areas of cooperation between member states.

Organisation: The Committee of Ministers consists of one minister—usually the foreign minister—from each member country for the biennial meetings usually held in April and December; ministers' deputies act as permanent representatives at routine monthly meetings. The Council decides with binding effect on all matters of internal organisation and may also conclude conventions and agreements. The Consultative Assembly consists of 144 members, weighted in number between member states, either elected by national parliaments or appointed. They are generally parliamentarians and reflect party political strengths in the national parliaments. Members represent public opinion and not their governments. The Assembly meets annually in ordinary session and may submit recommendations to the Committee of Ministers, pass resolutions and discuss reports. The Standing Committee which represents the Assembly when not in session meets four times a year. Ordinary Committees deal with the various spheres of cooperation such as social problems, refugees, law, culture, etc. Under the 1950 European Convention, a European Commission is empowered to investigate claims by states (sometimes individuals) that human rights and fundamental freedoms have been violated. Its findings may be examined by the European Court of Human Rights (founded 1959) whose final and compulsory jurisdiction has been recognised by nine Council members, or by the Committee of Ministers which is empowered to take binding decisions by two-thirds majority. The Secretariat serves both the Committee of Ministers and the Consultative Assembly.

[1] No date indicates founder member.

North Atlantic Treaty Organisation (NATO)[1]

Address: Evere, Brussels. *Foundation:* April 1949 by the North Atlantic Treaty. NATO is the organisational structure set up to implement the Treaty's provisions. *Membership:* Belgium, Canada, Denmark, France,[2] Federal Republic of Germany (1955), Great Britain, Greece (1952), Iceland, Italy, Luxembourg, Netherlands, Norway, Portugal, Turkey (1952) and the United States. *Function:* To maximise the ability of members individually and collectively to resist any armed attack upon the territory of any member or a member's occupation forces in the North Atlantic area and to provide means of political cooperation and consultation and economic collaboration amongst members.

Organisation: The Council is the supreme organ of NATO, meeting twice a year at ministerial level and regularly at official level, each government being represented by a permanent representative. The Council is responsible for the implementation of the provisions of the Treaty, and may set up permanent or temporary committees to assist it in all aspects of its work. The secretary-general of the Organisation is appointed by, responsible to and chairman of the Council. He organises the work of the Council and directs the international Secretariat and its four Divisions: Political Affairs; Economics and Finance; Production, Logistics and Infrastructure; Scientific Affairs. He has direct access to all NATO agencies and to member governments and aids the settlement of disputes between members.

The senior military organ, the Military Committee, is composed of a chief-of-staff of each member country[3] and meets in Brussels at least twice a year at chief-of-staff level, and periodically at that of permanent military representative. It is responsible for recommendations and guidance on military questions to other NATO organs. Subordinate to the Military Committee are the major Commands and Planning Groups: Allied Command Europe; Allied Command Atlantic; Channel Committee and Allied Command Channel; Canada–US Regional Planning Group; and a number of other military agencies such as the NATO Defence College in Rome and the Military Agency for Standardisation in London.

Western European Union (WEU)

Address: 9 Grosvenor Place, London SW1. *Foundation:* May 1955 by a treaty based on the earlier Brussels Treaty of March 1948. *Membership:* Belgium, France, Federal Republic of Germany, Great Britain, Italy, Luxembourg and the Netherlands. *Function:* The coordination of defence policies and equipment of member countries and their cooperation in legal, political, cultural and social affairs.

Organisation: The Council consists of the foreign ministers or London ambassadors of member countries plus an undersecretary at the British Foreign Office, meeting under the secretary-general's chairmanship. It is responsible for policy-formulation, the issue of directives to the secretary-general and the Organisation's agencies, and ensuring close cooperation with the NATO Council. The Agency for the Control of Armaments is

---

[1]See also 'Western European Defence: NATO in Disarray', p. 265.
[2]France withdrew from NATO's military command in 1966.
[3]Iceland, having no armed forces, is represented by a civilian.

responsible to the Council for ensuring that undertakings not to manufacture certain weapons are observed and for controlling the level of armament stocks held by members on the European mainland. The Standing Armaments Committee[1] aims to develop the closest possible cooperation between members in the production and procurement of armaments. The Council has met quarterly since October 1963 to review the political and economic situation in Europe.

The Assembly meets twice yearly in Paris; its members are elected or appointed by member parliaments. It considers defence policy in Western Europe and other common interests of member countries and may make representations to the Council, national parliaments, governments and other international organisations. The Council presents an annual report to the Assembly with special reference to the Agency for the Control of Armaments. The Assembly has a number of permanent committees.

ECONOMIC COMMISSION FOR EUROPE (ECE)

Address: Palais des Nations, Geneva. *Foundation:* 1947. *Membership:* All Western and Eastern European countries (including the Federal Republic of Germany, the Byelorussian SSR and the Ukrainian SSR and excluding East Germany) and the United States. Switzerland participates in a consultative capacity.

Function: One of the four regional economic commissions set up by the UN Economic and Social Council, the ECE studies European economic and technological problems, collects statistics, furthers the exchange of technical information, and makes recommendations. *Organisation:* The Commission meets annually in plenary session. The various Committees are convened for brief meetings throughout the year. The Secretariat services both the Commission and the Committees and publishes reviews and surveys.

ORGANISATION FOR ECONOMIC COOPERATION AND DEVELOPMENT (OECD) [2]

Address: 2 Rue André-Pascal, Paris 16. *Foundation:* September 1961 in succession to the Organisation for European Economic Cooperation (OEEC) founded in 1948. *Membership:* Austria, Belgium, Canada, Denmark, France, Federal Republic of Germany, Great Britain, Greece, Iceland, Ireland, Italy, Japan, Luxembourg, Netherlands, Norway, Portugal, Spain, Sweden, Switzerland, Turkey, United States. Australia, Finland and Yugoslavia also participate in certain matters. *Functions:* To achieve the highest sustainable economic growth and employment among members, to coordinate and improve development aid and to help the expansion of world trade.

Organisation: The Council, composed of representatives of the member countries and meeting at both official and ministerial levels, is responsible for general policy and administration. The Executive Committee is composed of the representatives of eleven member countries elected annually by the Council; it meets at least once a week and makes a prior examination of all matters to be submitted to the Council. The Secretariat serves both bodies. In addition there are a number of standing committees covering specialised economic affairs, and the board of management of the European Monetary Agreement (EMA, the successor to the European Payments Union or EPU) and the European Nuclear Energy Agency (ENEA).

[1]Address: 43 Avenue du Président Wilson, Paris 16.
[2]See also 'The Organisation for Economic Cooperation and Development', p. 624.

T*

NORDIC COUNCIL

Address: The Council has no permanent headquarters. See below under *Organisation. Foundation:* 1953. *Membership:* Denmark, Finland (1956), Iceland, Norway and Sweden. *Function:* As a consultative body to increase cooperation between member countries.

Organisation: The Council consists of members elected by the member parliaments (Denmark, Finland, Norway and Sweden 16 each and Iceland five) and also of appointed representatives of each government. It meets annually in ordinary session in the capital of one of the member countries, and may also convene in extraordinary session. For each ordinary session, and for the management of its affairs until the next ordinary session, the Council elects from its members a Presidium consisting of the presidents of the various delegations. Resolutions of the Council take the form of recommendations to member governments, on which the governments must submit annual progress reports to the Council. During each ordinary session the delegates form themselves into five standing committees (economic, cultural, social, communications and legal), each undertaking the preparatory work in connection with matters before the Council. The standing committees may also meet in inter-sessionary periods and special committees may also then be formed. The Council has a Secretariat in the capital of each member country, all of which collaborate closely under the supervision of the Presidium.

Outside the Council there are a large number of official and unofficial Nordic and Scandinavian committees, enterprises and societies.

BENELUX

Address: 39 Rue de la Régence, Brussels. *Foundation:* The Benelux Treaty came into force in November 1960 after a number of preparatory agreements. *Membership:* Belgium, Luxembourg and the Netherlands. *Function:* Economic, non-political union of the member countries.

Organisation: The Committee of Ministers meets at least once every two months and is composed of not less than three ministers from each country. Resolutions must be unanimous (an abstention is not considered a negative vote). The Committee is responsible for decisions relating to the application of the Treaty of Economic Union, ensuring the observance of agreed conventions, and making recommendations for study by and issuing directives to the other Benelux organs. The Consultative Inter-Parliamentary Council consists of 21 members from each of the Netherlands and Belgium and seven from Luxembourg, with no executive role but able to debate general matters concerning the Union. The Council of Economic Union consists of a chairman from each member state and the presidents of the seven committees; the presidents of any of the two special committees may be coopted when their special field is under discussion. The Council of Economic Union ensures the execution of decisions of the Committee of Ministers, passes directives to the committees and special committees, coordinates their work and transmits their and its own proposals to the Committee of Ministers. The Secretariat is headed by a secretary-general who is always Dutch, assisted by a deputy from each of the other member states, all appointed by the Committee of Ministers and directly responsible to the latter's Working Group for the Administration of the Union. The Arbitration Tribunal settles disputes arising from the working of the Union; it consists of two representatives of each member state appointed by the Committee of Ministers. The Economic and Social Advisory Council advises the Committee of Ministers.

EUROPEAN ORGANISATION FOR NUCLEAR RESEARCH
(CENTRE D'ETUDES DE RECHERCHES NUCLÉAIRES OR CERN)

Address: 1211 Geneva 23. *Foundation:* 1954 on UNESCO's initiative. *Membership:* Austria, Belgium, Denmark, France, Federal Republic of Germany, Great Britain, Greece, Italy, Netherlands, Norway, Spain, Sweden, Switzerland. Poland, Turkey and Yugoslavia have observer status. *Function:* The collaboration of certain European countries on purely scientific and non-military problems of nuclear research.

Organisation: The Council consists of two representatives of each member state. The Committee of the Council has 12 members and comprises the president and vice-president of the Council, the presidents of the Finance Committee and of the Scientific Policy Committee and representatives of member states. There is a Directorate headed by a director-general who is assisted by committees.

EUROPEAN SPACE RESEARCH ORGANISATION (ESRO)[1]

Address: 36 Rue Lapérouse, Paris 16. *Foundation:* 1962; formally established 1964. *Membership:* Belgium, Denmark, France, Federal Republic of Germany, Great Britain, Italy, Netherlands, Spain, Sweden, Switzerland. Austria has observer status. *Function:* To undertake space research and provide member states with research facilities.

Organisation: The Council is the governing body and consists of two representatives for each member state. It is assisted by a Finance Committee, a Scientific Committee, a Subcommittee on Launching Programmes and six working groups. The director-general is advised by Scientific, Administrative and Technical Directorates and a Secretariat staffed from member states.

EUROPEAN SPACE VEHICLE LAUNCHER DEVELOPMENT ORGANISATION (ELDO)[1]

Address: 36 Rue Lapérouse, Paris 16. *Foundation:* 1962; formally established 1964. *Membership:* Belgium, France, Federal Republic of Germany, Great Britain, Italy, Netherlands. Australia is also a member, providing a launching range in Woomera. *Function:* To construct and develop space launcher vehicles on an international basis.

Organisation: The Council is composed of two representatives for each member state. It approves research, development and construction programmes and distributes tasks amongst members. It is assisted by a Scientific and Technical Committee and a Finance Committee. The Secretariat is responsible for formulating and executing programmes, administration and finance.

THE EUROPEAN COMMUNITIES: EUROPEAN ECONOMIC COMMUNITY (EEC), EUROPEAN COAL AND STEEL COMMUNITY (ECSC) AND EUROPEAN ATOMIC ENERGY COMMUNITY (Euratom)[2]

Membership: Belgium, France, Federal Republic of Germany, Italy, Luxembourg and Netherlands. European states associated with the EEC: Greece and Turkey. African states associated with the EEC: Burundi, Cameroun,

[1]See also 'Science and Technology in Western Europe', pp. 366–7.
[2]See also 'The Structure of the European Community', p. 569.

Central African Republic, Chad, Congo (Brazzaville), Congo (Democratic Republic), Dahomey, Gabon, Ivory Coast, Madagascar, Mali, Mauritania, Niger, Rwanda, Senegal, Somali Republic, Togo, Upper Volta. Overseas territories associated with the EEC: France—Comoro Islands, French Somaliland, French Austral Territories, French Guiana, French Polynesia, Guadeloupe, Martinique, New Caledonia, Réunion, St Pierre et Miquelon, Wallis and Futuna Islands; Netherlands—Netherlands Antilles, Surinam. Austria, Israel, Morocco, Tunisia, Algeria, Kenya, Tanzania and Uganda are seeking EEC association.

Information services: European Communities Information Service, 23 Chesham St, London SW1; Bureau d'Information des Communautés Européennes, 61 Rue des Belles Feuilles, Paris 16; Ufficio Stampa e Informazione della Comunità Europea, Via Poli 29, Rome; Bureau d'Information des Communautés Européennes, Rue de Lausanne 72, Geneva; Voorlichtingsdienst van de Europese Gemeenschappen, Mauritskade 39, The Hague; Press und Informationstelle der Europäischen Gemeinschaften, Zitelmannstrasse 11, Bonn; European Communities Information Service, 2207 Commerce Building, 155 East 44th St, New York, NY 10017 and 808 Farragat Building, Farragat Sq., Washington 6, DC.

EUROPEAN ECONOMIC COMMUNITY (EEC)

Address: Commission—23 Avenue de la Joyeuse Entrée, Brussels. *Foundation:* By the Rome Treaty, signed and ratified 1957, effective 1 January 1958. *Function:* The principal aim is to eliminate all direct and indirect barriers to exchange of goods and movement of capital and labour between members during a defined transitional period, with the purpose of harmonising and stabilising economic development and increasing the general standard of living. A common policy has been formulated for agriculture and common policies for other sectors are being discussed.

Organisation[1]: The Council of Ministers (2 Rue Ravenstein, Brussels) is composed of one representative of each member state. Decisions are usually taken by majority but where qualified majorities are required voting is weighted as follows: France, Italy, Federal Republic of Germany four votes each, Netherlands and Belgium two each, Luxembourg one. The Council of Ministers is responsible for coordination of economic policies and general policy-making. The Commission has nine members, not more than two of whom may come from the same member state, appointed by member governments. It is responsible for the execution of the provisions of the Rome Treaty. On the Treaty's non-specific provisions it makes proposals to the Council of Ministers and implements the latter's decisions. It has certain emergency powers to aid members in economic difficulties. Decisions are by majority. The Council of Association (23 Avenue de la Joyeuse Entrée, Brussels) is composed of members of the Council of Ministers and of the Commission and one representative of each of the associated African countries and is responsible for the working of the Convention of Association. The Economic and Social Committee (3 Boulevard de l'Empereur, Brussels) is composed of more than 100 representatives of employers, labour and economic groups within member states; it forms an

[1]A treaty was signed in April 1965 providing for the merging of the Councils of Ministers of the three Communities into a single Council, and the fusing of the Commissions of the EEC and Euratom and the High Authority of the ECSC into one Commission.

advisory body to the Councils of Ministers and Commissions of the EEC and Euratom with particular reference to agriculture and transport.

The European Investment Bank (85 Boulevard de Waterloo, Brussels), administered by a board of governors (generally the finance ministers of the member states), a 12-man board of directors and a three-man committee of management, grants loans to and provides guarantees for projects of economic development within the Community. The European Social Fund is administered by the Commission and provides retraining and resettlement for workers affected by the introduction of the Common Market. The European Development Fund provides development aid for the associated states and territories. The Monetary Committee has 14 members and promotes the coordination of monetary and financial policies between members. The Transport Committee, composed of experts nominated by member states, assists the Commission in its task of removing transport discrimination between member states.

EUROPEAN COAL AND STEEL COMMUNITY (ECSC)

Address: 2 Place de Metz, Luxembourg. *Foundation:* By the Paris Treaty, signed April 1951, effective July 1952. *Function:* To foster political unity by creating supranational objectives and institutions and granting access for all member states to coal and steel resources within the Community, and to create a single coal and steel market amongst member states.

Organisation: The High Authority has nine members (eight appointed by member states and the other coopted) serving for six years and acts by majority vote. It is responsible for executing the tasks entrusted to it under the Treaty through binding decisions, recommendations binding in aim but not means, and non-binding opinions. The Council of Ministers (3 Rue Auguste Lumière, Luxembourg) consists of one representative of each member state and has the general task of harmonising the action of the High Authority with the economic policies of member governments. The Consultative Committee, consisting of representatives of producers, workers and consumers, and dealers in equal number, is appointed for two years by the Council of Ministers.

EUROPEAN ATOMIC ENERGY COMMUNITY (Euratom)

Address: 51–53 Rue Belliard, Brussels. *Foundation:* As the EEC. *Function:* To speed the establishment and growth of nuclear industries within the Community by stimulating and coordinating public and private research in atomic energy, ensuring the free flow of information and encouraging the construction of reactors. It also has certain regulatory functions.

Organisation: The Commission of five members is appointed by the member governments (except Luxembourg) for four years. It is the executive arm of the Community and coordinates its work; it is responsible to the European Parliament (see below). The Council of Ministers deliberates at monthly meetings on the proposals of the Commission. The Scientific and Technical Committee has 20 members appointed by the Council of Ministers for five years. It must be consulted by the Commission on certain matters and may be consulted upon any. The Consultative Committee on Nuclear Research is an advisory body to the Council, and provides a link between the Commission and member governments.

The European Parliament

Address: Rue Beaumont, Luxembourg. *Function:* As a common organ of the Communities to supervise all executive authorities, to discuss annual general reports, and to debate all matters of common interest. It may dismiss any Community executive by two-thirds majority in a vote of censure. *Organisation:* The Parliament is composed of 142 members nominated by the national parliaments of the member states, sitting in party and not national groups. France, the Federal Republic of Germany and Italy have 36 members each, Belgium and the Netherlands 14 each, and Luxembourg six.

The European Court of Justice

Address: 12 Rue de la Côte d'Eich, Luxembourg. *Function:* As a common organ of the Communities to adjudicate in disputes arising out of the application of the Treaties. *Organisation:* The Court consists of seven members appointed for six years by member governments.

European Free Trade Association (EFTA) [1]

Address: 32 Chemin des Colombettes, Geneva. *Foundation:* 1960. *Membership:* Austria, Denmark, Great Britain, Norway, Portugal, Sweden, Switzerland. Finland is an associate member. *Function:* To bring about free trade in industrial goods and the expansion of trade in agricultural goods between members.

Organisation: The Council is composed of one representative for each member country, meeting at either official or ministerial level. It makes decisions over a wide range of issues including tariffs. Decisions must be unanimous for new obligations, otherwise a majority suffices. There are a number of specialised Council Committees. The Consultative Committee comprises a maximum of five representatives per member country. It meets a few weeks before each ministerial meeting of the Council, and may discuss anything within EFTA's sphere of activity. Its chairman reports to the Council. The Finland–EFTA Joint Council is the organ for associating Finland with Council decisions. The Secretariat services both Council and Consultative Committee.

[1] See also 'The European Free Trade Association (EFTA)', p. 614.

THE STRUCTURE OF THE EUROPEAN COMMUNITY

TONY BURGESS

THE BEGINNINGS

THE European Community may be defined as an organisation set up by a group of Western European countries with the aim of achieving eventual political union through a gradual process of practical economic integration. Although the potential of the Community may have been accepted at the best only tacitly, and as a very long-term objective, by some of the signatories of the founding Treaties, the undoubted intention of the men who drafted these documents was to establish an institutional framework which could develop, by a process of evolution, into a viable system of government for a European federation, possibly a United States of Europe.

The Treaties themselves, however, were never intended to be much more than formal statements of mutually accepted principles—skeletons needing the flesh and sinew of detailed legislation to give them life. In the sense therefore that the emerging shape of the European Community has depended, and will continue to depend, on the manner in which its member countries choose to interpret the broadly defined aims of its founders—the manner in which they choose to pad out the skeleton—it is an evolutionary growth. Even the Community's institutions themselves have to a certain extent developed empirically, and in several instances they have been able to reinterpret their terms of reference to meet new or changing situations.

Membership of the European Community is at present confined to the six original signatory states of the founding Treaties—Belgium, France, the Federal Republic of Germany, Italy, Luxembourg and the Netherlands—although its architects' intentions were that membership should be open to any European state willing to accept the obligations of the Treaties. In the event, however, the British application for entry failed when in January 1963 France exercised the veto which all existing members possess over the admission of new members, ostensibly because President de Gaulle was not satisfied that the United Kingdom was prepared to accept the spirit of the Treaties (see the chapter entitled 'Britain and the European Community'). Following the failure of the British negotiations, the applications for membership which had been lodged by Ireland, Denmark and Norway were not pursued by these countries.

So far, for simplicity, we have referred to 'the European Community', but the use of the singular is strictly inaccurate since there are in fact three separate European Communities: the European Coal and Steel Community (ECSC), the European Economic Community (EEC, more frequently known as the Common Market), and the European Atomic Energy Community (Euratom). Membership of the three Communities is identical, consisting of the six countries listed above, and although there are certain constitutional differences between the three organisations, particularly between ECSC on the one hand and EEC and Euratom on the other, similar basic principles are embodied in all three founding Treaties, and each Community has a similar institutional structure. The plans, already far advanced, for merging these three Communities into a single constitutional entity are described at the end of this chapter.

The establishment of the first of the three Communities, the European Coal and Steel Community, resulted from the Schuman Declaration of 9 May 1950. In this declaration Robert Schuman, then French foreign minister, proposed that the coal and steel resources of France and Germany should be pooled in an organisation open to all European countries. The invitation was accepted by the governments of Germany, Italy, Belgium, Luxembourg and the Netherlands, but the British government replied that it would 'reluctantly be unable to accept . . . a commitment to pool resources and set up an authority with certain sovereign powers as a prior condition to joining talks. . . .'

The aims of ECSC, which began to operate in 1953 under the terms of the Paris Treaty, were twofold. In the first place it was intended that the pooling of French and German basic production would achieve the final reconciliation of these two traditional enemies by making further conflict between them impossible on practical grounds. Secondly, ECSC was conceived as the first step towards a new political order in Europe. Out of limited economic integration its founders hoped that political unity would grow. Their choice of a gradualist approach—an attempt to create practical solidarity between European countries through concrete achievements in closely defined fields—was conditioned by disillusionment over previous attempts to unite Europe in one move under more grandiose but basically impractical designs.

The initial success of ECSC, under the leadership of Jean Monnet, who had played a major part in drafting the Schuman Declaration, led very quickly to the first attempt at political union in Europe. Shortly after the signature of the ECSC Treaty, the Community governments signed the European Defence Community (EDC) Treaty, which, by placing the six countries' military resources under joint control, would have solved the problem of German rearmament. At the same time a plan for a European Political Community was drawn up. These plans came to nothing, however, when the EDC Treaty, ratified by the other five parliaments, was rejected by the French National Assembly.

This failure notwithstanding, the logic of European economic integration, rapidly demonstrated by ECSC, was not to be denied, and the six governments, by their decision to extend the process to the whole field covered by their separate national economies, showed that they had drawn the obvious conclusion. As a result, they concluded two further treaties, the Rome Treaties, setting up the European Economic Community (which rapidly took to itself the title of the Common Market, although the earlier Paris Treaty already referred to 'the common market for coal and steel') and the European Atomic Energy Community. The aim of EEC, which with Euratom came into being on 1 January 1958, was to ensure the continued economic expansion of the member countries, and thereby the steady social progress of their peoples, by the creation of a single market for all goods and factors of production in place of the six separate national markets. The

Community governments also recognised that the establishment of the thoroughgoing customs union which they envisaged would entail the complete integration of their national economic policies over a very wide front.

Euratom's main aim, given the enormous cost of nuclear research which often places a severe strain on the resources of even major countries acting alone, was to ensure the efficient development of a nuclear industry on a Community-wide basis, to the point where it would be capable of making a major competitive contribution to Europe's rapidly expanding power needs. Euratom also concerns itself with medical and biological research in the nuclear field and the industrial uses of atomic energy, but under the terms of the Treaty its functions are strictly limited to the peaceful uses of the atom.

THE MAIN INSTITUTIONAL FRAMEWORK

The institutions of the European Community (the reversion to the singular is here deliberate in view of the functional interdependence of the three legally distinct Communities) were constituted by the founding Treaties in such a way as to form the basis of a system of government for a Europe ultimately politically united along federal lines. The system already contains an embryonic legislature (the three Councils of Ministers, the Executives in their policy-making rôle and the European Parliament), a civil service (the Executives in their administrative rôle and their ancillary bodies), and a judiciary (the European Court of Justice). Although considerable development of these bodies' powers, and clearer definition of their functions in relation to each other and to the member governments, will be required before they can fairly be described as a viable system of federal government, the potential exists in the Treaties, as the men who drafted them intended that it should. This potential has been clearly recognised and endorsed by most of the statesmen and administrators who have been responsible for implementing the Treaties.

The Councils of Ministers

Until such time as the merger of the three Communities, or at least of their institutions, is achieved, there are legally three separate Councils of Ministers, one for each of the existing Communities. The Councils are made up of ministerial representatives from each member country. In theory the actual ministers taking part in any particular meeting of the Council vary with the subjects under discussion—ministers of transport when transport policy is on the agenda, ministers of agriculture to discuss farm problems, and so on—but in practice all major Community decisions are taken by a Council consisting of the six countries' foreign ministers. Since the same persons often take part in meetings of the three different Councils of Ministers, the distinction between these legally separate bodies has tended to become blurred in the minds of observers not intimately connected with Community affairs. Nevertheless, considerable differences exist between the competence of the ECSC Council on the one hand, and the EEC and Euratom Councils on the other.

Ministers taking part in meetings of the Councils do so as the official representatives of their countries, and a major function of the Councils is to ensure that the varying national interests of the member countries are fully taken into account in the shaping of Community policy.

The decision-taking machinery set up by the Treaties founding the three Communities is based on the acceptance of weighted majority voting in the

Councils of Ministers as the norm of Community practice. A unanimous vote is required only where a specific exception to this principle is made in the Treaty concerned. In practice, these exceptions may be divided into two groups. There are a few permanent exceptions, of which decisions on the admission of new members and on amendments to the Treaties themselves are the most important, and, in the case of the EEC and Euratom, a much larger group of temporary exceptions, applicable during the initial stages of these two Communities.

The temporary exemptions from the principle of majority voting under the two Rome Treaties are all meant to terminate at or before the end of the EEC's transition period, i.e. by 1970 at the latest. Some EEC decisions initially requiring a unanimous vote were transferred to the realm of majority voting when the Common Market moved into the second stage of its transition period in January 1962, and most of the remaining temporary exceptions were removed when the Community moved into the third stage of its transition period at the beginning of 1966. The so-called 'gentlemen's agreement' on majority voting—that a majority vote would not be used in practice to override the vital national interests of any member country—which ended the Community crisis of the second half of 1965 and early 1966 does not affect the basic Treaty position on this issue.

The Rome Treaties lay down that where decisions of the EEC or Euratom Councils of Ministers require only a majority vote, the votes of the member countries shall have the following weights: France, Germany and Italy, four votes each; Belgium and the Netherlands, two votes each; Luxembourg, one vote. Of this total of seventeen votes, any twelve votes are sufficient to carry a decision based on a proposal put forward by an Executive (see below). Where a decision is being taken on a matter that does not require a prior proposal from the relevant Executive, these twelve favourable votes must be spread among at least four member states. The latter provision ensures that when the Council is not acting on a proposal of the Executive, the three smaller Community countries cannot be outvoted as a group by the three larger countries. In these circumstances the minimum consensus required would be two of the larger countries plus Belgium and the Netherlands.

In the Paris Treaty, which gave the ECSC Council of Ministers more limited powers than those later bestowed on the ministerial bodies of the EEC and Euratom (see below under *The Formulation of Community Policy*), there are no temporary exceptions to the general principle of qualified majority voting. There are, however, a number of permanent exceptions concerned with matters outside the strict coal and steel sectors. Also the system of weighting votes is rather different, being conditional on the relative importance of the member countries as coal and steel producers.

The chairmanships of the Councils of Ministers are exercised in rotation by the ministerial representatives of each member country, for periods of three months in the case of ECSC and of six months in the case of EEC and Euratom.

Although the Councils of Ministers themselves are non-continuous bodies, meeting at intervals, their sessions are prepared, in the case of the EEC and Euratom, by a Committee of Permanent Representatives of the member countries, and, in the case of ECSC, by a Coordinating Committee. Both the Permanent Representatives Committee and the Coordinating Committee are made up of the member governments' ambassadors to the Communities, and operate on a continuing basis. Each Council is also serviced by a full-time secretariat.

The Community Executives

The executive bodies of the three Communities—called the Commission in EEC and Euratom, and the High Authority in ECSC—have become, partly as a result of the responsibilities given them under the Treaties and partly as a result of their own initiatives, the mainsprings of all action at the Community level. The histories of the three Communities since their inception have been largely the history of these three bodies' attempts to translate the ideal of European unity into practice.

The individual characteristics of the three separate Executives are described below, but they each have the same overriding responsibility—to act as the guardians of the principles contained in the founding Treaties and to represent and safeguard the interests of their respective Communities as entities. In this latter task the responsibilities of the Executives are in clear distinction from those of the Councils of Ministers, where the interests of each member country are represented. To ensure that the Executives act only in the interests of the Community as a whole, their members undertake not to be swayed by the national interests of their own countries, and pledge themselves to independence of their governments, from whom they may not receive instructions. The deliberations of each Executive are secret, and decisions are taken on a straight majority vote. The Executives operate on the collegiate principle, and a decision once reached binds the Executive concerned as a body.

Each Executive has its own staff, forming the nucleus of a fully comprehensive international civil service, members of which are responsible only to their respective Executive, not to the national administrations of their own countries. The Executives are continuous bodies, the duties of whose members and staff occupy them on a full-time basis.

The High Authority of ECSC is composed of nine members, with its headquarters in Luxembourg and a total staff of about 1,000. Decisions of the High Authority are directly binding on the coal, steel, iron-ore and ferrous scrap industries of the Six, without the need for these decisions to be embodied in national legislation. The initial task of the High Authority, when ECSC was first set up, was to establish a common market for these products throughout the geographical area of the Six. This it did by abolishing all trade barriers for these products between the member countries, and by removing trade distortions such as discriminatory pricing of coal or steel based on the nationality of the buyer, unjustified government subsidies to national industries, and other impediments to rational patterns of trade.

Once a single Community-wide market for ECSC products had been established, the main emphasis of the High Authority's work changed from that of innovation to the administration of the system which it had created. It is now principally concerned with supervising the efficient operation of the common market for coal and steel products, ensuring that the Paris Treaty rules on fair competition between firms are observed, enforcing Community anti-trust legislation to prevent any firm or group of firms from attaining or abusing a dominant market position, encouraging investment and research in the Community coal and steel industries, and offsetting the social effects of the changing patterns of employment in the European coal and steel industries. The latter task has become more urgent in recent years as a result of the diminishing importance of the European coal industry, and High Authority action in this field has taken two main forms: material assistance to new industries who show interest in setting up in declining coal-mining areas, and retraining schemes and financial assistance for former workers in

ECSC industries who may be obliged to seek jobs in new industries or new areas.

Eight members of the High Authority are appointed, on the basis of unanimous agreement, by the member governments. The ninth member, who has come traditionally to be regarded as the representative of trade union interests in the High Authority, is coopted by the other eight. Each member holds office for six years, and is eligible for reappointment. One-third of the membership of the High Authority is renewed or reappointed every two years, and for this regular renewal half the members are named by cooption. Not more than two members of the body may be of the same nationality. The president and vice-president of the High Authority are appointed by the governments, on a unanimous vote, from among the members. They hold office for two years, but may be reappointed.

The Common Market Commission is also composed of nine members, with its headquarters in Brussels and a total staff of about three thousand. The main task of the Commission is to ensure the implementation of the Rome Treaty and to supervise the gradual integration of the entire economies of the six member countries, a process which involves the removal of unjustified restrictions on the free movement of goods, capital, services and labour, and the working out of common policies in sectors such as agriculture, transport and external trade. In carrying out this task, the Commission has two distinct roles—as an initiator responsible for putting forward proposals for new Community action, and as an administrative body responsible for putting into effect policy decisions already adopted by the Council of Ministers. The first of these two roles is examined more closely below under the heading *The Formulation of Community Policy*.

All nine members of the EEC Commission are appointed unanimously by the national governments. Members hold office for four years, and are eligible for reappointment; their terms of office are concurrent. Not more than two members of the Commission may be of the same nationality. The president and two vice-presidents of the Commission are appointed from among the members by the six governments acting unanimously. Their terms of office are for two years, but they may be reappointed. In the event of the six governments failing to agree on the replacement or reappointment of a member or officer of the Commission when the individual's term has expired, the person concerned remains in office until such agreement is reached. (This condition applies also to members of the other two Community Executives.)

The Euratom Commission comprises five members. Its headquarters are in Brussels, and it has a staff of about two-and-a-half thousand research workers and seven hundred administrative officials. Its task is to ensure the establishment within the Community of a viable and efficient industry for the peaceful exploitation of nuclear resources, to encourage nuclear research and the training of atomic scientists, to administer the Supply Agency through which all nuclear fuel used in the Community's civilian atomic industry is channelled, to supervise the common market for all nuclear materials and equipment which has been set up among the Six, and to lay down safety standards for the Community's nuclear industry as a whole.

In certain cases the Euratom Commission can issue regulations which are directly binding on Community firms operating in the nuclear field, and it has wide powers of inspection and control over the use of nuclear materials which pass through the Supply Agency's hands, to make sure that they are being used only for specified and peaceful purposes.

All five members of the Euratom Commission are appointed unanimously by the six governments, hold office for four years, and are eligible for reappointment. Their terms of office are concurrent; no two members of the Commission may be of the same nationality. The president and vice-president are appointed under the same conditions as the officers of the EEC Commission.

The European Parliament

The Paris Treaty, which established the European Coal and Steel Community, made provision for a Parliamentary Assembly 'consisting of representatives of the peoples of the member states of the Community', which would exercise democratic supervision over the actions of the High Authority. When the Common Market and Euratom were set up, this Assembly, which became known as the European Parliament, was given the responsibility of democratic supervision over all three Communities. At the present time it has no real legislative power, but it has made full and vigorous use of the rights of consultation covering a wide range of Community activity granted to it under the Treaties.

The Parliament consists of 142 members, delegated by the national legislatures of the six Community countries. France, Germany and Italy send thirty-six members each; Belgium and the Netherlands fourteen members each; and Luxembourg six members. The composition of the groups of delegates from the various countries reflects the broad balance of the parties in the national parliaments concerned, although Communists and members of extreme right-wing parties are not admitted to the European Parliament. Eventual election of the European Parliament by direct, Community-wide suffrage is envisaged in the Treaties, but this provision has not yet been implemented.

Perhaps the most significant aspect of the way in which the Parliament operates is the fact that its members have decided, of their own accord, to sit as political groups, not as national delegations. The three main political divisions which have emerged in the Parliament are Christian Democrat, Socialist and Liberal. There are also now a small number of French Gaullist members.

The Parliament meets in Strasbourg, and holds about ten full sessions a year, of a week each. Its specialised Standing Committees, each of which closely follows a specific aspect of the activities of the Community Executives, meet more frequently.

The Community Executives are obliged to submit annual reports to the Parliament, which can force the resignation of any of the Executives as a body on a two-thirds vote of censure. The Parliament has the right to be consulted before certain types of decisions are taken by EEC and Euratom. It also has the right to scrutinise the three Communities' budgets, and its members may put written questions to the three Executives. Representatives of the Executives and of the Councils of Ministers are entitled to address the Parliament under certain conditions at their own request.

The Parliament elects its president and officers from among its members. Except in special circumstances laid down in the Treaties, the Parliament acts by means of an absolute majority of the votes cast. The full sessions of the Parliament are held in public.

The European Court of Justice

The European Court of Justice is the final point of appeal on all matters concerning the interpretation or application of the Community Treaties.

It has the sole power to rule on the legality of acts committed by the Councils of Ministers and the Community Executives. It can decide on appeals for exemption from Community regulations, questions of Community procedure, disputes over interpretation of the Treaties or their implementing regulations, and cases where Community institutions are alleged to have exceeded their powers. It may also judge cases where one of the Executives or a member government is alleged to have failed to carry out its responsibilities under the Treaties.

Right of appeal to the Court is open to member governments and to Community institutions. Under the Common Market and Euratom Treaties, private individuals or legal persons may also appeal to the Court against Community rules which are directed at them, or which concern them directly or specifically. The ECSC Treaty allows firms or associations of firms subject to the Treaty's provisions to appeal against particular Community decisions which concern them, or against general decisions which they feel result in injustice when applied in their case.

The Court may also give judgment and award damages in cases where the plaintiff claims that he has suffered loss as a result of an act of a Community institution. Under certain circumstances the Court may also decide preliminary issues submitted by national courts in Community countries, where questions of the interpretation of the Treaties or the validity of Community decisions are raised in domestic litigation.

The judgments of the Court have direct force of law in all Community countries, without the prior need to be incorporated in the member countries' legislation. They are binding on all parties concerned, whether individuals, firms, national governments, or Community institutions. In the twelve years of the Court's history, there has been no occasion on which its decisions have been resisted by member governments, or on which a government has refused to carry out its rulings.

The Court, which meets in Luxembourg, consists of seven Judges, appointed unanimously by the member governments from among persons of high legal standing in their own countries. The Judges are assisted by two Advocates General, also appointed by the governments, and a Clerk appointed by the Court. The Judges serve for terms of six years, and may be reappointed. Partial renewal of the membership of the Court occurs every three years, affecting three and four Judges alternately. The Judges elect from among their number a President of the Court, who holds office for three years.

The Court is divided into two chambers of three Judges each. Decisions are reached through deliberations in either of the two chambers or in full court. A simple majority of the Judges is sufficient for the adoption of a ruling. No dissenting opinions are published.

The Formulation of Community Policy

The differences between the Paris Treaty founding ECSC and the later Rome Treaties founding EEC and Euratom are most clearly apparent in the provisions which each makes for the formulation of Community policy.

In ECSC the executive body, the High Authority, has considerably greater powers of direct action than were later given to the EEC and Euratom Commissions. The role of the ECSC Council of Ministers is confined over a large field of Community activity to putting forward the opinions of the governments before the High Authority takes decisions which will be binding on the coal and steel industries of the six countries. However, the Council's prior approval, based on either a simple or a qualified majority vote, depending on the issue, is required for most important decisions. With minor exceptions, unanimous approval by the Council is necessary only for matters outside the strict coal and steel sectors.

In the Common Market and Euratom, there is a far greater degree of interdependence between the Executives and the Councils of Ministers in the process of defining Community policy. In these two Communities the Councils of Ministers take the final policy decisions, although they can do so only on the basis of proposals put forward by the Commission of the Community concerned. The Councils can only modify such proposals by a unanimous vote, even in cases where a majority vote is sufficient to adopt the particular proposal as it stands. In EEC and Euratom, therefore, the Commissions have almost the sole right to propose Community policy, while the Councils of Ministers retain responsibility for the ultimate decisions on these proposals. Only in certain limited circumstances do the EEC and Euratom Commissions have the right to take independent action, usually in their administrative role in the implementation of policy already adopted in principle, or under a specific mandate from the Council.

In the process of making proposals for Community action, the EEC and Euratom Commissions possess one important faculty which has greatly facilitated agreement in the Council of Ministers in the past on a number of difficult issues. The Executive concerned has the right to modify its proposals at any time up to the moment when the Council actually reaches a decision. After observing the way in which the debate has gone in the Council on a contested issue, and taking account of the various national positions, the Executive may therefore produce a compromise solution at the psychological moment—a 'package deal' in Community jargon.

Under the Rome Treaties the Economic and Social Committee (see below under *Ancillary Community Bodies*) and the European Parliament have the right to be consulted before most Community decisions are adopted. The Consultative Committee of the ECSC (see below) has the same right in many circumstances in the formulation of ECSC policy.

ANCILLARY COMMUNITY BODIES

The three Executives and the Councils of Ministers are advised before formulating or implementing Community policy by a number of specialised or general committees. Some of these committees were envisaged in the Treaties, others have been set up on an *ad hoc* basis as the need arose.

The Economic and Social Committee, consisting of 101 members representing employers' organisations, trade unions, consumers' associations and other social and economic groups, has the right to advise the Common Market and Euratom Commissions and Councils of Ministers on many aspects of Community policy.

The Consultative Committee, consisting of fifty-one members, performs a similar task for the ECSC High Authority.

The Scientific and Technical Committee, made up of twenty-one independent nuclear experts, advises the Euratom Commission on nuclear problems. This is a purely advisory body, and its members have no official status as representatives of their countries, but it does have the right to be consulted on certain issues.

The Transport Committee, consisting of independent experts appointed by the Council of Ministers, advises the Common Market Commission on transport problems.

In addition to the above bodies, five particularly important committees have been set up within the framework of EEC to facilitate coordination of the member countries' economic policies and to speed cooperation between them in the vital monetary and financial spheres. The first of these committees, the Monetary Committee, was specifically envisaged in the Rome Treaty. The rest were established as the increasing pace and scope of economic integration in the Community made them necessary.

The Monetary Committee, made up of the EEC Commission and national experts, advises the Commission and Council of Ministers on a wide range of monetary-policy questions, including the coordination of Community policy on world monetary problems. One of the Committee's main functions is to bring together the officials of the six countries responsible for drafting national monetary policy.

The Short-Term Economic Policy Committee was set up in 1960, and modelled directly on the Monetary Committee. As its name indicates, its purpose is to facilitate the coordination of the member countries' short-term economic policies, with particular reference to the avoidance of cyclical fluctuations.

The Budgetary Policy Committee, with the Medium-Term Economic Policy Committee and the Committee of Governors of Central Banks (see below), was set up under a series of decisions taken by the Common Market Council of Ministers in April 1964. The aim of these decisions was to extend the process of economic integration between the Six to coordination of their medium-term policies, and to strengthen their existing monetary and financial cooperation. The Budgetary Committee groups senior government officials, and has the task of coordinating the member countries' budgetary policies and of advising the Common Market Commission on all problems in this field.

The Medium-Term Economic Policy Committee, composed of senior officials of the six governments, advises the Common Market Commission and Council of Ministers on the coordination of the member countries' economic policies over periods of four to five years. This committee supplements the work of the Monetary and Short-Term Economic Policy Committees.

The Committee of Governors of the Central Banks was set up to harmonise the policies of the Community countries' central banks.

In addition to the committees listed above, whose principal role is to provide expert advice for the Community Executives, Councils of Ministers and member governments on a wide range of economic, social and technical problems, four funds have been set up to promote investment in the Community and its associated countries, and to offset where necessary the social cost of economic progress. The first three of these funds listed below are administered by the Common Market Commission; only the last, the European Investment Bank, has a separate legal existence.

The European Social Fund has the task of preventing or alleviating any social hardship which might result from structural changes in the Community economy brought about by closer economic integration. In particular, the Fund promotes employment opportunities, especially in areas where traditional industries are declining, and facilitates the mobility of workers within the Community. Like the readaptation aid provided by the ECSC High Authority, the Social Fund assists workers who have had to move or change their jobs by providing vocational retraining, and resettlement and other grants. Its method of operation is to refund fifty per cent of the expenditure undertaken by the member governments for these purposes.

The Agricultural Guidance and Guarantee Fund, set up under EEC's common agricultural policy, has three tasks: to help finance modernisation schemes and structural improvements in the Community's farm sector, to undertake support buying of agricultural produce on the Community market when prices fall below those guaranteed to farmers, and to provide rebates on Community exports of farm produce when world market prices are below the Community guaranteed minimum.

The European Development Fund administers the bulk of the development aid which the Community as an entity (as distinct from member countries individually) provides for eighteen associated African countries.

The European Investment Bank, with independent status as an international financial institution, encourages investment in the economically less developed areas of the Community and helps to finance modernisation schemes or new projects of general Community interest. The largest proportion of the Bank's loans to date have been made to promote the industrialisation of Southern Italy, the Community's economically most backward area. Recently the Bank has also begun to finance development projects in countries having association agreements with the Community.

The organs of association

In addition to the Association Convention between the EEC and eighteen independent African states,[1] the Common Market also has separate Association Agreements with Greece and Turkey. Each of these arrangements has its own institutional structure consisting of a Council of Association, a Parliamentary Conference, and a Judicial Tribunal.

The three Councils of Association comprise representatives of the Common Market Council of Ministers and the Commission on the one hand and representatives of the associated partner on the other (one representative from each of the eighteen countries in the case of the African Convention). Since the Association Councils are ministerial bodies meeting only periodically, detailed day-to-day administration of each agreement is delegated to Association Committees meeting at government-official level.

The Parliamentary Conferences, which usually meet once a year to consider their respective Association Councils' annual reports, group members of the European Parliament and parliamentarians from the associated countries. Judicial Tribunals have been set up under each agreement to settle legal disputes between the parties.

The UK–ECSC Association Agreement, signed in December 1954, set up a Council of Association comprising British and High Authority representatives, which meets regularly at ministerial and expert level. The aims of the Association are to lower trade barriers in coal and steel products between Britain and the ECSC, to promote the coordination of economic policies affecting these products, and to further cooperation in the fields of technology, science and industrial hygiene.

The common services of the Executives

Three specialised service departments have been set up jointly by the three Community Executives.

[1] Burundi, Cameroun, Central African Republic, Chad, Congo (Brazzaville), Congo (Democratic Republic), Dahomey, Gabon, Ivory Coast, Madagascar, Mali, Mauritania, Niger, Rwanda, Senegal, Somali Republic, Togo, Upper Volta. Nigeria signed a trade agreement with the EEC in 1966.

The Legal Service advises the Executives on all legal matters, from the drafting of Community legislation to issues raised before the Community Court of Justice.

The European Communities Statistical Office is responsible for the collection and compilation of comparable statistics for each of the Community countries, and for the production of statistics covering the Community as a whole. The Office publishes a wide range of monthly, quarterly and annual statistical summaries, and many special reports.

The European Communities Press and Information Service deals with all aspects of public information work and press liaison in the Community countries and abroad. London, Washington and New York are among the cities outside the Community in which the Service maintains information offices.

THE COMMUNITY BUDGETS

The European Coal and Steel Community is the only one of the three Communities which currently has an independent source of revenue. This derives from a levy which the High Authority is empowered, under the Paris Treaty, to impose on the annual turnover of all firms in the Community coal, steel and associated industries. At the present time this levy is fixed at 0.25 per cent of turnover.

Up to now the budgets of EEC and Euratom have been derived from direct contributions by the member governments, although it is envisaged that these two Communities will eventually acquire independent revenues based on the proceeds of the Common External Tariff (see the chapter entitled 'Customs Union and Economic Union in the EEC'). Under the current system, the Council of Ministers fixes the size of the Community budget each year, and the total is divided among the member countries according to a scale laid down in the Treaties: 28 per cent each from France, Germany, and Italy; 7·9 per cent each from Belgium and the Netherlands; and 0·2 per cent from Luxembourg. In addition to its administrative budget, Euratom has a research budget fixed at $432 million for the five-year period 1963–7. In the first five years of its existence, Euratom had a research budget of $215 million.

THE MERGER OF THE COMMUNITIES

The logic of gradually increasing economic integration in the European Community has made the eventual fusion of the three existing Communities inevitable. To a growing extent, the process of creating a single economic unit in place of the six national economies of the member countries has been made more difficult by the functional division between the three Communities. The development of a common energy policy, for example, has not been facilitated, in spite of close cooperation between the three Executives, by the fact that coal policy is currently the responsibility of ECSC, oil and natural gas policy the responsibility of EEC, and nuclear-energy policy that of Euratom. Similarly, in the field of transport policy, the ECSC High Authority has wide powers of control over the movement of coal and steel products within the Community, but other transport matters are the concern of the Common Market Commission.

A treaty merging the three Community Executives into a single Commission of the European Communities, and creating a single Council of Ministers for all three Communities, was in fact signed by the member governments on 8 April 1965. It was due to come into force on 1 January 1966, but as a result of the political crisis which developed in the Community in mid-1965, has not yet been implemented. This treaty covers only the fusion of policy-making and administrative institutions of the Communities, and for an interim period the single Executive and the single Council of Ministers continue to implement the three separate Community Treaties.

One of the main tasks of the single Executive after the merger treaty has been implemented, however, will be to put forward proposals for a single Community treaty to replace the Paris Treaty and the two Rome Treaties. Only when a single European Community Treaty comes into effect will it be legally correct to speak of 'the European Community', rather than 'the European Communities'. The other major task which will face the merged Executive as soon as it takes office will be to supervise the integration of the currently separate staffs of the three existing Communities.

The Executive merger treaty stipulated that the single Community Executive would have fourteen members initially, but that this number would be reduced to nine when a single Community treaty came into effect, or within three years at the most. In the discussions which led up to the merger treaty, it was agreed by the member governments that the new Community Executive would have its headquarters in Brussels, and that Luxembourg would be compensated for the loss of the ECSC High Authority by becoming, in principle, the headquarters of all or most of the Community's legal and financial bodies.

BIBLIOGRAPHY

Bebr, Gerhard. *Judicial Control of the European Communities*, Stevens, London; Frederick A. Praeger, New York, 1962.

Brierley, Caroline. *The Making of European Policy*, Oxford Univ. Press, London, 1961; New York, paperback ed. 1963.

Deniau, Jean F. *The Common Market*, Barrie and Rockliff/Pall Mall Press, London; Frederick A. Praeger, New York, 3rd ed. 1963.

Forsyth, Murray. *The Parliament of the European Communities*, Political and Economic Planning, London, 1964.

Hallstein, Walter. *United Europe: Challenge and Opportunity*, Harvard Univ. Press, Cambridge, Mass.; Oxford Univ. Press, London, 1962.

Henderson, W. O. *The Genesis of the Common Market*, Frank Cass, London, 1962; Quadrangle, Chicago, Ill., 1963.

Lindberg, Leon N. *The Political Dynamics of European Economic Integration*, Oxford Univ. Press, London; Stanford Univ. Press, Stanford, Calif., 1963.

Lippmann, Walter. *Western Unity and the Common Market*, Little, Brown, Boston, Mass.; Hamish Hamilton, London, 1962.

Mayne, Richard. *The Community of Europe*, Gollancz, London, 1962; W. W. Norton, New York, paperback ed. 1963.

Noel, Émile. *How the EEC's Institutions Work*, Community Topics Series No. 11, European Community Information Service, London, 1963.

Pryce, Roy. *The Political Future of the European Community*, Federal Trust/Marshbank, London 1962.

Weil, Gordon L. (ed.) *A Handbook of the European Community*, Pall Mall Press, London; Frederick A. Praeger, New York, 1965.

European Community Information Service. *A Guide to the Study of the European Community* (bibliography), London, 1965.

Political and Economic Planning. *European Organisations: An Objective Survey*, Allen and Unwin, London, 1959. *Aspects of European Integration*, London, 1962. *Budgetary Control in the European Economic Community*, Occasional Paper No. 6, London, 1964.

CUSTOMS UNION AND ECONOMIC UNION IN THE EEC

ROY PRYCE

ALTHOUGH the Treaty of Rome is a lengthy and complex document it does little more than sketch in the programme of integration on which the six countries of the European Economic Community (EEC) embarked in January 1958. When seven and a half years later, in June 1965, the Community ground to a halt because of a crisis precipitated by the French government, much still remained to be done. Nevertheless in the intervening years, as a result of intensive effort, the member states had progressed far along the path towards a customs union. They had also made substantial progress in laying the foundations—and in some sectors a good deal of the superstructure—of economic union.

THE CUSTOMS UNION

The basis on which the Community rests is provided by a customs union: that is, the abolition of tariffs, quotas and other similar obstacles to the free movement of goods between its members and the substitution of a common external tariff for the separate national tariffs towards countries outside the Community. The mechanism by which these twin objectives are to be reached was laid down in considerable detail in the Rome Treaty. Its application in the period 1958–1965 gave rise to comparatively little difficulty. During 1958 there were fears that the French might not be willing to make the first internal tariff cuts due on 1 January 1959; however, the economic and financial reforms carried out in December 1958 under the Fifth Republic enabled France to respect its obligations. Later on the original timetable was twice speeded up by decisions of the Council of Ministers on 12 May 1960 and 15 May 1962. By 1 January 1966 the total internal tariff cuts amounted to 80 per cent of the levels in force in 1957. All quotas on industrial goods had been abolished by the end of 1961, and quotas on agricultural goods either substantially increased or replaced by levies. (See Common Market Timetable, page 583.)

The greater part of the common external tariff was agreed during the negotiations of the Treaty. Most duties were a mathematical average of existing levels applied by France, Germany, Italy and Benelux (the latter countries already having a common external tariff). The result gave a moderate level of protection, its average incidence being lower than that of either the United Kingdom or the United States. Those items on which no agreement proved possible at this stage—there were 77 headings in this category—were grouped together in 'List G' for subsequent negotiation. These were items like aluminium, zinc, cork, sulphur and vehicle parts on

COMMON MARKET TIMETABLE

(Entries in italics show measures taken under the decisions of 12 May 1960 and 15 May 1962 to speed up the Common Market timetable)

Date	Internal tariff cuts		Quota enlargements (total)	Alignment of national tariffs on common external tariff: reduction of difference (up or down)
	Total	Minimum for each product		
STAGE 1 1958	—	—	—	—
1959 1 Jan.	By 10%	By 10%	By 20%	—
1960 1 Jan.	—	—	By 20%	—
1 July	By 10%	By 10%	—	—
31 Dec.	*By 10%*[1]	*By 10%*[1]	—	—
1961 1 Jan.	—	—	By 20%	—
31 Dec.	By 10%	By 10%	*Abolition of quota restrictions on industrial goods*[2]	*By 30% (common tariff fully applied where difference amounted to 15% or less)*

By end of Stage 1: Total internal tariff cuts on each product amounted to 40%. Export duties had been abolished. This Stage ended on 31 December 1961.

STAGE 2 1962 1 July	*By 10%*	*By 10%*	—	—
1963 1 July	*By 10%*	*By 5%*	—	*By 30%*
1964 31 Dec.	*By 10%*	*By 5%*	—	—
1965 31 Dec.	*By 10%*	*By 5%*	—	—

By end of Stage 2: Total internal tariff cuts on each product were at least 65%.

STAGE 3 1966 1 Jan.	Acting on the Commission's proposal, the Council fixes the rate of remaining internal tariff cuts during Stage 3		—	—
1969 31 Dec.	To zero	To zero	—	Full adoption of common external tariff

By end of Stage 3: All internal tariffs and quotas, and restrictions on the free movement of men, services and capital, to be removed. This Stage may only be prolonged by unanimous vote of the Council on a proposal by the Commission; the total transition period may not be prolonged by more than three years.

Source: Information Service of the European Communities.

[1] By 5% only for agricultural products.
[2] Special arrangements were made for enlargement of industrial quotas.

which the interests of the member states were in conflict. But the duties on these items, with the single exception of petroleum products, were settled in a package deal concluded by the Council of Ministers on 2 March 1960.

The Treaty provided that national tariffs should be aligned on the common external tariff in three stages corresponding to the three stages of the transitional period. The first step which reduced the difference between the two levels by 30 per cent was duly taken on 31 December 1961 at the end of the first stage; the second was brought forward to 1 July 1963. The remaining step will be taken on 1 July 1968.

These successive steps have meant some raising of German and Benelux tariffs towards non-Community countries and a corresponding reduction of the higher French and Italian duties. A provisional 20-per-cent reduction in the tariff was however made in 1961, part of which was later consolidated in the 'Dillon round' of tariff negotiations in the GATT (General Agreement on Tariffs and Trade). A further reduction of up to 50 per cent on industrial items is theoretically possible in the event of a successful outcome of the 'Kennedy round' of negotiations in the same body. The difficulties encountered since these negotiations began in 1963 suggest however that the eventual outcome will at best be of much more modest dimensions.

ECONOMIC UNION

In addition to the free movement of goods, integration also implies the free circulation of workers and capital, a lifting of national restrictions on the right of firms to set up in other member countries, and of similar restrictions on services (banking, insurance, and those provided by members of the liberal professions, etc). At the same time it requires the creation of common or harmonised policies in certain sectors and a coordination of general economic, financial and budgetary policy. As the Treaty gives only an outline of the objectives to be reached and the means for their attainment, a very large part of the activity of the Community's institutions has been devoted to these matters, some of which—like agriculture—have proved to be of great complexity and considerable political difficulty.

Neither the free circulation of workers nor that of capital has yet given rise to major problems. With regard to workers the principle introduced by the Treaty is that nationals of the member states should be free to take up offers of jobs anywhere in the Community. This was regarded as of especial importance by the Italians as a way of reducing their heavy structural unemployment at the time the Treaty was negotiated. The trade unions in the other countries were less enthusiastic, fearing that employers might turn to Italians in order to depress wages or resist claims for higher pay and better working conditions. It was therefore decided to introduce free movement in stages.

A first regulation was passed in August 1961 and a second in February 1964. While the first maintained a priority for each national labour market and restricted the right of free movement to those seeking permanent employment, the second abolished this priority and extended free movement to seasonal and frontier workers, at the same time giving migrant workers the right to be joined by all their dependents in the country of their new employment. The effect of these measures has not, however, been very marked. This has been due mainly to the general tightness on the labour market produced by the high level of economic activity which characterised most of the period up to 1966.

In May 1960 the Community unconditionally freed a wide range of capital movements and conditionally freed most other types. Since then the major emphasis has been on harmonising legislative and administrative arrangements which in many cases have proved to be of more material importance than formal prohibitions in obstructing capital movements.

In contrast progress has been much slower with the right of establishment throughout the six member countries and the freeing of services. A general programme was agreed in October 1961 but it was already clear in 1965 that certain important parts of it—notably the coordination of legislative and administrative provisions and the mutual recognition of professional qualifications—would not be completed by the end of the transition period. The main reason for this was the extraordinary complexity of the problems in this sector; a contributory factor the smallness of the staff the EEC Commission had working on them. Completion of the programme will be necessary before full economic union can become a reality, and it has not yet had any major impact on the activities involved.

COMMON POLICIES

Agriculture

The formation of a common agricultural policy has been a central concern of the Community and the subject of repeated and major political difficulties. It is only due to the efforts and skill of Sicco Mansholt, the member of the EEC Commission responsible for this sector, that a steady momentum has been maintained in spite of the acute problems of drawing together what were previously six separate and divergent national agricultural policies.

The first major decision was taken in December 1960. The Council then accepted the principle proposed by the Commission of substituting a system of levies on a number of major products for the tariffs and quotas which had previously been used by the member countries to protect their farmers. The levies fulfil a dual purpose. As applied to trade in farm products within the Community they will be progressively reduced until by 31 December 1969 they will disappear to give free trade in these products between the member states. At the same time variable levies at the external frontier of the Community will give permanent protection against fluctuations in world prices, being based on the difference between internal prices (maintained in some cases by support buying and other devices) and world market prices. In January 1962 agreement was reached on detailed marketing arrangements for a series of products after a marathon session during which, as *Time* magazine reported, 'three officials collapsed with heart attacks and stubble-bearded, trigger-tempered delegates fought long into the night, stoked with double whiskies'. The products in question were grains, pigmeat, eggs, poultry, fruit and vegetables, and wine. Other regulations were later approved for beef and veal, rice and dairy products. In each case, however, a decision on the future common price level was left until later.

This was the next major hurdle and one that was successfully surmounted for the key sector of grain prices in December 1964. The German government, under heavy pressure from its own farmers, had resisted the Commission's proposals for a reduction of current German wheat prices to a level close to the average between these and the lower French prices. It gave way, however, in the face of pressure from the other members and in particular a threat from President de Gaulle to withdraw from the Community unless agreement was reached. To compensate for lower producer prices in Germany,

Italy and Luxembourg it was agreed to pay a total of some £150 million to the affected farmers up to the end of the transition period. It was also agreed that the common prices would not be applied until 1 July 1967.

This agreement was typical of a policy which has had to recognise that what is politically possible must take priority over what may be economically desirable. While Mansholt found little difficulty in resisting the more extreme demands of the farmers' organisations—which were in any case divided among themselves on all the major issues—he was well aware that the price of success was a system that would guarantee much the same level of protection as that formerly maintained by national measures. In some cases the degree of protection has increased, though it would seem more by accident than by design. It is however very difficult to assess the extent to which the new marketing arrangements have affected prices. On the whole they seem to have had less immediate effect than more general economic trends, and seasonal and cyclical factors. (While for instance egg prices rose under the impact of the new regime they soon fell again as a result of an increase in production.)

The long-term effects of the policy can only be a matter of speculation. In early 1967 no common price levels had been in force long enough for their effects to be visible. Some of the marketing arrangements for sugar, vegetable oils and fats, for instance, had only recently been agreed. Many other aspects have also to be worked out. Little has yet been done with regard to structural policy or the harmonisation of state aids; nor have any of the authorised producer groups on which the Commission sets much store yet been set up. There are also a number of external factors which may impinge on the practical effects of the common policy. The Commission for instance has proposed a binding of support amounts in the framework of the Kennedy round of GATT negotiations. It has also expressed its willingness to enter into negotiations for international agreements on certain commodities.

At the same time the general pattern of farming in the Community is rapidly changing under the impact of other factors. Since 1958, for instance, the active labour force on the farms has fallen from some 18 millions to under 12 millions, and this flight from the land is expected to continue. (In France, for example, the numbers engaged in agriculture are likely to be halved in the next twenty years.) No other sector of the Community's economy is undergoing such rapid change. But while its agricultural problems may become in the long run politically more manageable they seem certain to provide in the foreseeable future as many explosive problems as they have done since 1958. In the meantime it is a remarkable achievement that the transition to the new policies has been carried out without any disruption, and that the farmers themselves who (with the exception of the Dutch) were initially hostile to integration are now among its more fervent supporters.

Competition

While it was generally recognised by the Treaty-makers that a common policy for agriculture would have to be based on managed marketing, much emphasis was placed on the need in other sectors to ensure a maximum degree of competition. Article 85 of the Treaty prohibits agreements or concerted practices which prevent, restrain or distort competition, such as price-fixing, market-sharing, restriction of production or of technical developments and discriminatory supply conditions, if they are likely to affect trade between the member states. (It does however permit those agreements which contribute to better production or distribution or to technical progress.) Article 86 also declares an abuse of a dominant position as contrary to the Treaty.

Although these provisions were held to be immediately binding on the member states the Community institutions had to work out a common policy to put them into effect. After much discussion a system of compulsory registration of agreements was applied by decision of the Council of Ministers in March 1962. Provision was made for the 'negative clearance' of those types of agreements which the Commission deemed to fall within the permitted categories, but heavy fines were laid down for those firms which persisted in maintaining agreements judged to be incompatible with the Treaty. More than 37,000 agreements were duly registered; not surprisingly the Commission made slow progress in dealing with them. To lighten its load the Council agreed to a number of group exceptions, and the Commission for its part sought to reach decisions on certain other major categories. As a result of its pressure a number of agreements have been dissolved by their authors without a formal decision, and others adjusted to conform with the Treaty. A good deal of pressure has however been applied by industrial circles to persuade the Commission to authorise agreements promoting common action between firms faced by strong competition from outside the Community, in particular from the United States. In 1966 it was still too early to judge how readily the Commission would react to such arguments or how stringent and successful the control of restrictive trade practices would prove to be.

By 1966 the considerable reduction of internal tariffs had revealed the importance of disparities in national legislation and administrative regulations as a factor in distorting competition. The varying incidence of taxation, for instance, became a matter of increasing concern. In November 1962 the Commission put forward a first measure to deal with this problem by proposing the general adoption of an added value tax as the major instrument of indirect taxation. This had still to be agreed in 1966, though much of the initial opposition to it had by then disappeared. At the same time a start was made in the harmonisation of legislation covering other sectors, such as food and drugs and tenders for public contracts. Many trade associations were themselves actively engaged in preparing their own schemes for harmonisation on matters ranging from the hallmarking of precious metals to regulations concerning beauty parlours.

Some perceptible progress has also been made in reducing the discrimination implicit in state-controlled monopolies; a draft convention has been drawn up to harmonise the law with regard to bankruptcy; and another has been prepared on patents. Agreement on the latter, however, was held up by a divergence between the member states on whether an agreement should be limited to members of the Community or should be extended to a wider group of countries, including for instance the United Kingdom (which expressed its wish to be included).

Transport

Progress in the application of a common policy to transport has been slow and the results obtained by 1966 were small. The major reason for this was the much lower priority attached to this sector by governments and the opposition of the Netherlands to the adoption of a less liberal system than their own, and one which might consequently reduce the work for their transport concerns. ('The Dutch think they are God's own carriers'

U

commented one exasperated official after another abortive meeting.) The first major decisions were not taken until June 1965 and these provided only a framework within which detailed regulations were to be worked out in two stages, the first to stretch between 1966 and December 1969; the second up to the end of 1972. Fork rates (compulsory maximum and minimum rates between which the charges have to fall) were to be introduced for cross-frontier road and rail transport, while water transport concerns were to be required only to publish rates lying outside the limits of non-compulsory rate brackets.

Commercial policy

It is quite clear that the member states of the Community will sooner or later need to arrive at a common commercial policy and the Treaty provision (Article 111) speaks of bringing it about not later than the end of the transition period. Although the member states have had to adopt a common position with regard to a series of requests for trade agreements by other countries, including Israel, Iran and the Lebanon, and to the tariff negotiations in GATT, progress in other respects has been slow. In 1964 the Commission proposed a new series of measures pointing out the urgency in particular of common action with regard to trade with countries of the Eastern bloc, and low-wage countries. Some progress has been made in adopting uniform lists of quota-free products, in harmonising insurance and credit schemes to aid exports, and in joint consultation before the conclusion of bilateral trade agreements. But in other important respects—for instance, the harmonisation of export aids, anti-dumping measures and quotas—much remains to be done.

Social policy

One of the weakest aspects of the Treaty, social policy remains for the most part firmly in the hands of national governments. The French and Germans in particular have strongly resisted attempts by the Commission to extend the range of social harmonisation specifically sanctioned by the Treaty. Such provisions as were inserted in it owe their origin mainly to French fears that their own manufacturing costs were higher than those of other member countries because of higher social charges. It was this for instance which lay behind the obligation to introduce equal pay for men and women by the end of the first stage of the transition period. Formally this obligation has been respected though its application in practice is far from complete. The social fund, from which national governments are repaid half the cost of re-training schemes, has also been of limited significance because of the narrowness of its terms of reference. The trade unions in the Community have become increasingly restive with the lack of progress in the social field.

Economic and financial policy

As integration has advanced it has become evident that a successful economic union can only function if the member states coordinate their general economic policies to a degree that was not envisaged in the Treaty. As however these policies belong to a very sensitive area of national sovereignty the Community has proceeded with great caution in this direction. An early development was the creation in 1960 of a Trade Cycle Policy Committee consisting of senior national officials and the Commission which, on the basis of annual and quarterly reports by the latter, has sought, with moderate success, to prevent the development of imbalances within the Community's economy. In the meantime the Monetary Committee has also provided a forum for the comparison of national policies and discussion of trends and problems in this crucial sector. The finance ministers of the member states have also met regularly for a similar purpose. In 1964 at the suggestion of the Commission a new series of steps was taken to intensify these exchanges. The terms of reference of the Monetary Committee were extended to include prior consultation on important issues of international monetary policy, and a new committee composed of governors of the central banks of the Community (Deutsche Bundesbank, Banque de France, etc) was established. A Budgetary Policy Committee of senior officials was also set up with the aim of a gradual coordination in this sector.

At the same time there were other important developments. In April 1964 the Council for the first time issued, on the basis of a proposal from the Commission, a recommendation to the member states aimed at correcting what it considered to be dangerously inflationary tendencies, especially in Germany and Italy. This, in brief, suggested the pursuit of a liberal import policy; the maintenance or imposition of credit restrictions; and tight control over public expenditure, with additional taxation to cover any increased deficit. This recommendation was more important as a sign of the increasing impact of integration than in its direct effects, though it occasioned a good deal of controversy in Italy where the socialists in the centre left government resented external pressure to pursue a deflationary policy.

Italy, however, stood to gain a good deal from efforts the Commission was also making to persuade the member governments to adopt a common approach to regional policy. In December 1961 three working parties were set up to study ways of dealing with underdeveloped regions in the Community, those faced by a decline in traditional industries, and the problems of inducing firms to set up in such areas. On the basis of these reports, which were published in July 1964, the Commission worked out a first memorandum on regional policy which it presented to the Council in May 1965. It suggested that regional development programmes be worked out with a high priority given to schemes for the retraining of the local work force. In the meantime substantial aid from the European Investment Bank had been made available for the industrial development of southern Italy, the Community contributing in particular to the financing of a major new steel works at Taranto.

An even more significant development in 1964 was the creation of a Medium-Term Economic Policy Committee under the chairmanship of Dr Wolfram Langer, German secretary of state for economic affairs. The task it was given, to quote the Commission, was 'the establishment of overall medium-term economic forecasts in order to clarify decisions on economic policy'. In effect it began to work out an economic programme for the Community for the period up to 1970. Its agenda included an examination of the choices to be made in terms of basic objectives, the conditions of economic growth, ways of securing the harmonious development of the various factors of production (including professional training schemes, competition policy, investment policy, and scientific research programmes), and what would be required in terms of action by member states with regard to public expenditure and taxation. This was an exercise in indicative planning which at one stage seemed likely to have profound consequences on many areas of both national and Community policy-making. A five-year economic programme was published in April 1966. The crisis of June 1965, however, had slowed down the Committee's work.

THE CRISIS OF JUNE 1965

The occasion of the crisis was a package proposal put forward by the Commission which linked the future arrangements for financing the common agricultural policy both with measures to create an autonomous budget for the Community (out of the proceeds of the levies on imports of food and the duties derived from the common tariff) and an extension of the budgetary powers of the European Parliament. The immediate break occurred over the unwillingness of some member states (notably Italy) to commit themselves to a definite settlement of the problem of financing the common farm policy, on which France insisted. Behind this conflict lay a series of deeper issues touching on the willingness of the member states to accept the further merging of sovereignty implied by the other aspects of the Commission's package and also by the requirement in the Treaty that in the third stage of the transition period (reached at the end of 1965) weighted majority voting should be introduced for most major issues. In his press conference of September 1965 President de Gaulle made it clear that he was unwilling to accept this and that he was also determined to curb the powers of the Commission. In the meantime France had ceased to take part in meetings of the Council and had thus brought the Community to a standstill.

It was nevertheless significant that the French did not go further: the Community was consigned to the deep freeze but not to the scrap heap. Their own freedom of manoeuvre was limited by the fact that although economic union was far from completed, business circles had come not only to accept the programme of integration but also to rely on its fulfilment. Attitudes had been readjusted to the new dimensions of a common market; so too had investment and marketing policies. Moreover, more than 300 Community professional organisations throughout the Six, representing industrial trade associations, farmers' unions, trade unions, commercial, transport and other interests, had been set up to concert policy and take common action. By their own action they had extended the processes of integration even beyond the wide bounds of the formal Community system, and had also acted very often to obtain the more rapid completion of the programme laid down in the Treaties. Many of them now protested against the French action: for them a reversion to a purely national economic framework was unthinkable.

These developments combined with the firm front maintained by the other five member states during the crisis eventually led to a compromise at a meeting of the Council of Ministers in Luxembourg at the end of January 1966. The Six agreed to disagree about the use of weighted majority voting, France insisting on the continued need for unanimity; they also agreed on minor changes in the relationship between the Commission and the Council, and on a programme of work for the coming months. France then agreed to resume active membership of the Community. The basic political divergences between France and her partners had not, however, been resolved. Though impelled forward by the economic expectations engendered by its early success, the EEC seemed certain to encounter more rough weather as it neared the end of its transition period.

BIBLIOGRAPHY

OFFICIAL DOCUMENTS

Bulletin of the European Economic Community, EEC Commission, Brussels, monthly.
Eighth General Report on the Activities of the Community, EEC Commission, Brussels, 1965.
Treaty establishing the European Economic Community, Brussels, 1957.

PERIODICALS

European Community, European Community Information Service, monthly.
Journal of Common Market Studies, Basil Blackwell, Oxford, quarterly.
Opera Mundi-Europe (weekly report on the economy of the Common Market), European
Intelligence Ltd, Tunbridge Wells, Kent.

BIBLIOGRAPHIES

A Guide to the Study of the European Communities, London Office of the European Community
Information Service, revised ed. 1965.
Paklons, L. L. (ed.) *European Bibliography*, Cahiers de Bruges No. 8, de Tempel, Bruges, 1964.

BOOKS

Campbell, Alan. *Restrictive Trading Agreements in the Common Market: Texts and Commentaries*,
Stevens, London; Rothman, South Hackensuck, NJ, 1964.
Deniau, Jean F. *The Common Market*, Barrie and Rockliff/Pall Mall Press, London; Frederick
A. Praeger, New York, 3rd ed. 1963.
Despicht, Nigel. *Policies for Transport in the Common Market*, Lambarde Press, London, 1964.
Forsyth, Murray. *Cartel Policy and the Common Market*, Political and Economic Planning,
London, 1962. *Towards a Common Economic Policy for EEC*, Political and Economic Planning,
1964.
Hallstein, Walter. *United Europe: Challenge and Opportunity*, Oxford Univ. Press, London;
Harvard Univ. Press, Cambridge, Mass., 1962.
Lindberg, Leon N. *The Political Dynamics of European Economic Integration*, Oxford Univ. Press,
London; Stanford Univ. Press, Stanford, Calif., 1963.
Kitzinger, Uwe. *The Challenge of the Common Market*, Basil Blackwell, Oxford, 1962.
Mayne, Richard. *The Community of Europe*, Gollancz, London, 1962; W. W. Norton, New
York, paperback ed. 1963.
Oudemans, G. *The Draft European Patent Convention*, Stevens, London; Bender, Matthew,
New York, 1963.
Pryce, Roy. *The Political Future of the European Community*, Marshbank for the Federal Trust,
London, 1962.
Shanks, Michael and Lambert, John. *Britain and the New Europe*, Chatto and Windus, London,
1962; issued in the United States as *The Common Market Today—and Tomorrow*, Frederick
A. Praeger, New York, 1963.
Tracey, Michael. *Agriculture in Western Europe*, Cape, London; Frederick A.
Praeger, New York, 1964.
Weil, Gordon L. (ed.) *A Handbook of the European Community*, Pall Mall Press, London;
Frederick A. Praeger, New York, 1965.

591

FROM ECONOMIC UNION
TO POLITICAL UNION

PIERRE URI

THE aims of the European Communities have always been political. Does this mean that the Communities will lead to a political union between the member countries?

GROWTH OF THE EUROPEAN COMMUNITIES

Integration started with the pooling of coal and steel, which might seem a strange way to begin, for the freeing of trade in two isolated products for any length of time must cause serious economic distortion. It was a novel approach, which has, however, proved successful: by creating an unbalanced situation the member countries forced themselves to go a step further in order to restore the balance. Criticism gave a new impetus to the whole operation, by involving the critics in the business of European integration.

Coal and steel both had a symbolic value. Coal was still the main source of power for the manufacturing industries, and steel was, and still is, the mainstay of the armaments industry; together therefore they played a decisive part in peace and war. But above all they provided an opportunity to set up a new kind of institution to administer common interests. This fundamental urge is reflected in the Schuman declaration,[1] part of which is incorporated in the preamble to the Paris (or European Coal and Steel Community) Treaty, which speaks of putting an end to centuries of warfare and bloodshed and laying the foundations of institutions to guide the common destiny of the member states.

It soon became clear that the idea of a body representing the Community as a whole, which would conduct a sort of dialogue with the member states, was an important one, and could be extended to other spheres. It was next taken up in the project for a European Defence Community (EDC). This project was first conceived at the time of the negotiations on the Schuman plan. The basic aim was not only to enable France and Germany to be reconciled, but to settle the status of Germany, then still in the hands of the Allied High Commission, by direct transition from an occupation regime to a new European system under which Germany would be integrated into a much larger entity. The United States, alarmed by the threats to Western

[1] See 'The Structure of the European Community', p. 570.

Europe from outside, proposed the reconstruction of a German army of twelve divisions to strengthen the defence forces of the West. The danger of building up an independent German army and high command, and the blatant contradiction between reestablishing a national force and the attempts at creating a supranational organisation (represented by the European Coal and Steel Community), required an immediate counter-proposal. In retrospect the EDC, the resulting project, was clearly inopportune. Not only was national opinion probably not ready for it, but for years afterwards one member of the Community at least (France) was engaged in wars outside Europe, and 'exceptional' withdrawals from the proposed integrated force would have been more often the rule than integration. The draft itself, which was copied somewhat unimaginatively from the Paris Treaty, had several drawbacks. Although putting great emphasis on the supranational principle, embodied in a nine-member Commissariat, it prevented the Commissariat from working because most of the decisions needed the unanimous agreement of the member states. As the common budget was simply the sum of the defence budgets voted by the national parliaments there was also a danger of insufficient money, since the member countries would have vied with each other to keep their contributions relatively speaking as low as possible.

The difficulty of establishing common forces without a common foreign policy was, however, realised at the time, for without such a policy there could be no decision to use force. Hence the idea of a political community to complement the defence community. The European Assembly's plan to meet this need is not without historical interest, even though it was abandoned when the EDC was rejected by the French parliament. The general structural pattern of an assembly, council of ministers, court of appeal and executive, was copied straight from the Paris Treaty, but this time the executive was to be elected by the assembly. The powers of the executive were essentially the same as those of the High Authority of the Coal and Steel Community (ECSC). As far as diplomacy was concerned, it could only give advice or suggestions, and though there was a chapter devoted to European laws it gave no indication of their content.

The EDC project thus failed to grasp the basic principle to which the European Communities owe their success: the direct relationship between the structure of the institutions and their purpose.

But the structure of the ECSC itself is out of proportion to the work it has to do, as it consists of an executive, an assembly, a consultative committee, a court and a council, to serve only two industries. This is because the intention was to create not simply a model for the future but a framework into which other economic sectors and other spheres still under national control would ultimately be fitted as their time for integration into the European system arrived. Considerable powers had to be delegated to the ECSC from the start, owing to the nature of the two industries: in the coal industry inflexibility of output meeting fluctuating demand, fiercer competition from other kinds of energy, social problems, and the very narrow margin between shortage and surplus; in the steel industry, violent fluctuations in demand depending on the rate of general investment and exports, accompanied by constantly rising costs. At the same time both industries were faced with the need for new large-scale investment, involving considerable time-lag before results could appear, and for long-term investment planning in spite of rapidly changing economic conditions. Thus it was not simply a matter of delegating enough authority to pass temporary measures and to unify the different markets; a sort of economic government was required to deal with so large a variety of problems. The dramatic emergence of the Common Market, after the Rome Treaty was successfully drawn up five years later (1957), showed that this approach and this type of institution were accepted as sound; indeed, the new Community extended the range of its institutions to take in the whole of the economy.

The objectives of this treaty were again political. Whatever the real reasons had been for France's refusal to ratify the EDC Treaty, it looked at the time (1954) like failure for the idea of a united Europe. In fact, the project was rejected because of the hesitations of the French foreign minister, Georges Bidault, in spite of his then being a supporter of the European movement, and because the prime minister, Pierre Mendès-France, was anxious to settle the matter rapidly, since it was seriously dividing the country. Owing largely to a misunderstanding between him and the other NATO governments, Mendès-France decided against the project, with the result that the whole European defence project was defeated inside France by a combination of those who did not wish to give up a French national army and those who were opposed to German rearmament under any circumstances.

After this setback, the question arose how to start moving again. Most of the discussions took place in and around the High Authority of the ECSC in Luxembourg. There were, for instance, cautious suggestions that the High Authority's powers should be widened to include transport and other forms of energy (apart from coal). But it was difficult to justify this when the other industries, to which energy and transport are related, were to remain under separate economic systems; moreover, oil was an international product (coming from outside the Community) and transport, electricity and gas were service industries, so that the High Authority's experience with coal and steel would be of little use, and the difficulties would be out of all proportion to the results desired.

Jean Monnet and Louis Armand came forward with the idea of pooling atomic energy. The fundamental importance of atomic energy for the future and the vast amount of research involved commended the idea, but above all the fact that atomic energy had hitherto had largely military associations meant that the idea appealed strongly to the public. Even so, the governments still had to agree. In one way Euratom was a continuation of one of the main purposes of the Schuman plan: to establish common bases for economic development. The other main purpose was to conduct another experiment in integration in a limited sector, which would then gradually lead to general integration. It is not generally known that the idea of combining these two purposes and establishing a common market for the whole of the economy was a kind of by-product of Euratom. The broader approach was a condition imposed by Germany for accepting an atomic energy community, for Germany did not stand to gain much in this field from an association with the other ECSC members, if integration were not extended to include other economic sectors. Conversely it was the attraction of Euratom which made the French political leaders accept the idea of the Common Market. Whatever the initial attitudes, however, it was not long before the general Common Market became the more important development, on which all the other proposals, concerning energy, transport or the establishment of Euratom, depended. Once again economics and politics came together, while the close relationship between institutional structure and aims was made particularly clear in the new Treaty's plans for an economic union which would go well beyond the scope of a customs union or free trade area.

POLITICAL QUESTIONS IN ECONOMIC TERMS

Customs union and economic union

It is not easy to determine exactly where a 'customs union' ends and 'economic union' begins, for the two concepts can be defined in several ways. One definition is that a customs union concerns only the free movement of goods within a given area, and a common tariff at the border; thus according to this definition, any measure which does not strictly concern goods comes under the definition of economic union. This means not only measures such as free movement of labour and capital, but also common rules of competition applying to business concerns or governments, and, of course, common financial resources and common policies.

A narrower definition of economic union is that it requires constructive action as opposed to the mere removal of obstacles to trade; according to this definition the mere abolition of restrictions of the free movement of capital and labour from one country to the next comes into the same category as measures relating to goods, i.e. a customs union. (This is the position held by some socialists, who regard any free trade measure as being 'right-wing', and who therefore, when the dismantling of tariffs was achieved ahead of schedule in the Common Market, criticised the lack of progress in the creation of common organisations and harmonisation of economic conditions to which the left traditionally attaches importance.)

There is a third possible distinction between a customs union and economic union if the rules of competition, particularly the prohibition of cartels, are considered as an inseparable corollary of free trade. An example of this distinction may be found in EFTA, which is not an economic union but which, according to the Stockholm Convention, has a few basic rules governing competition; on the other hand, it is not concerned with agriculture and there is no common external tariff, both of which are covered by the Rome Treaty.

The problems involved in agriculture, transport and foreign affairs, however, cannot easily be classified under any of these definitions of either customs union or economic union. For example, the movement of goods can involve agriculture only if there is a general agricultural policy and marketing system; any rules for transport will involve rules governing transport prices; and a common external tariff rapidly creates the need for a common trade policy, an aspect, in its turn, of foreign policy. In other words, in order to work these largely divergent elements into a coherent whole, an overall plan is essential: there must be an automatic process by which the plan is implemented, leading to the same close interrelation of parts as obtains in an internal or national market. The more the governments are actively involved in the workings of the economy, in order to ensure expansion, stability, full employment and fair distribution of wealth, the more they will be bound to undertake in common, if they are also to establish a common market between their states.

Harmonisation and coordination

A question which then arises is how far to take joint action in any given sector. In this connection, 'harmonisation' and 'coordination' are terms which are used frequently and generally treated as synonymous, but it may be useful to define them more precisely. The difference between them (whether it be in connection with tax legislation or monetary policy or anything else) can be demonstrated by their relation to an absolute term: complete unification (of states).

In the absence of such unification, harmonisation aims at preventing distortions in competition. Where, for instance, profits taxes differ from one country to another, capital tends to be deflected from economically productive projects into investment on which taxation is less heavy. In a common market concerted action also has to be taken if competition threatens to bring about harmonisation in an undesirable way. For instance, if member countries compete with each other to have the lowest profits taxes, this would inevitably lead to increases in other kinds of taxation. This line of argument led to the insertion into the Treaties of rules to establish equal pay for men and women and standard working hours to govern the application of 'overtime' rates.

Coordination, on the other hand, does not imply the application of permanent rules. Coordination concerns policies, whether they be policies to deal with the immediate economic situation, or longer-term programmes. It does not normally mean that all member countries act in the same way. Instead they often need to act differently, but to complement each other: rates of interest, for example, may be made to vary from one country to the next according to the balance of payments position; and coordination of regional policy means granting aid to some areas and no aid to others in order to avoid a further concentration of industry in the traditional areas. A recent example of coordination in the European Community may be seen in the medium-term programmes which were drawn up jointly as a compromise between countries which have large-scale economic planning and those which do not. These programmes enable the former to base their planning on information concerning a much wider economic area instead of limiting themselves to an isolated view of their national economies. They also force those countries which, like Germany, traditionally avoid using a systematic approach to government programmes, to take all of them together—be it town-planning, transport, education or defence—enabling them to be carried out far more successfully, precisely because each item is no longer considered in isolation.

Of course, it will always be hard to agree to what extent actions should be based on joint decisions, in the interests of a smoothly operating market or a closer-knit Community. Answers to questions such as how much disparity in taxation systems can be allowed without causing damage to the Common Market; how much autonomy is permissible in trade policy to enable each country to pursue its own foreign policy; which industrial and commercial agreements have a purely local significance and which affect the Common Market as a whole; how much disparity in company law can be allowed between one country and the next—answers to all these questions will depend on individual assessments.

The best and most comprehensive solutions require a much more radical approach. For instance, differing systems of indirect taxation are not incompatible with the Common Market provided goods carry the taxes of the country of destination. But if this means that exports to another country (even within the Community) are always exempt from tax, and equalisation taxes are levied on imports, then fiscal frontiers will always remain, which in practice leads to the same kinds of control that are exercised at customs frontiers today. Leaving aside the question of the effects of these taxes on investment, the standardisation of indirect taxation throughout the Community may, therefore, be prompted more by psychological reasons than by strictly economic ones. On the other hand, as the plans for a Common Market added-value tax show, the opportunity for discussion and comparison which standardisation provides leads to schemes which are far sounder economically than many existing national systems which reflect bad habits and outdated traditions.

It always takes time to come to grips with the real, as opposed to the apparent, problems of integration. The absence of European company law or a European type of company has not prevented the existence of a common market nor the formation of joint subsidiaries by companies of different nationalities; the subsidiary companies take the form and abide by the laws of the country in which they are set up. However, the absence of European company law makes mergers between companies of different nationalities practically impossible, with the result that American companies have found it much easier than European ones to reap the benefits of the wider economic area created by the Common Market. This influx of direct foreign investment has made European businessmen realise the need, if not to standardise commercial law and the different types of company, at least to provide alongside existing systems the alternative of a new type of company with a European base.

THE POWERS OF THE COMMUNITY INSTITUTIONS

Logical necessity does not, however, automatically become political reality. In the history of the Community there have been times when progress, instead of being the result of effective and systematic action by the European Institutions, as was intended and hoped by the authors of the Treaties, was rather at the mercy of whim or the interplay of force, cunning and bargaining between the governments.

The Schuman Plan was based on the new concept of supranationalism. A myth such as this had to be created to arouse public opinion in countries which had long been kept apart and opposed to each other. In the Paris Treaty the emphasis is on the powers invested in the High Authority, though almost any decision, apart from the application of the rules of competition, financing the Community and implementing transitional measures, requires the unanimous approval of the Council. The tone is different in the Rome Treaty. It is written in more modest terms. There is a Commission which, for questions other than those connected with the implementation of the Treaty, puts proposals to the Council of Ministers, and it is the Council which takes the decisions. It looks at first sight as if the concept of supranationalism had declined in importance from the Paris Treaty to the Rome Treaty, from the European Coal and Steel Community to the European Common Market and Euratom. On closer examination, however, one finds that this power of proposal has given the later institutions even wider powers than the High Authority possesses: this is illustrated by the fact that there are hardly any matters over which majority decisions are not ultimately possible, provided they are based on a proposal from the Commission.

The Executive—the Commission in one case and the High Authority in the other—is of course not the only body to have a common responsibility towards all six countries jointly. The European Parliament which controls the Executive, and the Community's Court of Justice which settles disputes, are not simply groups of delegates from the different countries; they too have to define a Community viewpoint. The Parliament has indeed followed this pattern, for its members have grouped themselves according to political view, and not according to country or origin. Even the Council of Ministers has a kind of two-way allegiance: it must not only reconcile the interests of the different governments, but must play its part in establishing a policy for the Community as a whole.

This problem of finding the best method of reaching a collective decision affecting several countries at once is an extremely difficult one today. It presents a kind of dilemma: unanimity seems justified because each national government is responsible for certain interests—each has its own work to do and is answerable to parliament and nation—but unanimity may rule out the possibility of common decisions entirely, because the power of veto creates a potential deadlock. Some institutions, such as the Organisation for European Economic Cooperation, have worked satisfactorily under this system. However, the OEEC's important decisions were taken largely under pressure from the Americans; its main function was to administer the funds and operate the Marshall Plan. Some memorable instances on the other hand of the adverse effect of the veto and the unanimity rule can be seen in the history of the United Nations Security Council.

Should the Community then adopt a majority system immediately, for surely majority rule is the very foundation of democracy? The analogy is false, for a majority vote between governments is not the same as a majority decision within a country. All the people making up a nation have the same loyalty or responsibility to their country, even though they may hold different opinions. But governments are responsible for various interests and have pledged themselves to differing causes, and they are bound to act in what they consider to be the interests of their country. Thus a majority vote between governments is far from being an objective decision in the sense that it is within an individual country. It provides a risk of coalitions or of underhand bargaining: some member countries may join hands to obtain decisions at the expense of a minority, or there may be compromises by which votes are bought by concessions which have no bearing on the issues at stake. Neither a system of 'one-country-one-vote', as in the United Nations, nor one of weighted voting based on contributions, as in the International Monetary Fund, has proved really satisfactory.

The European Common Market, with its common authoritative body (the Council of Ministers), its rules of procedure laid down in the Rome Treaty, and its institution (the Commission) for carrying out the decisions of this body by means of discussion and control, is the most original solution yet put forward to solve the problem. The Community does not simply ignore national attitudes, psychological differences and divergent interests; it provides a strictly realistic solution in order to counter the divergences in the initial outlook and circumstances of the countries concerned; a group of men—the Commission—have been appointed to think out and propose new formulae, to create a balanced approach and to provide a concrete idea of the common interest. Supranationalism and cooperation between countries are therefore not contradictory terms in the Community system. It is based on cooperation, but cooperation better organised and made more effective because a body of men can stimulate the parties involved into joint action.

Majority rule

The Common Market has solved the dilemma that unanimity leads to deadlock, and majority voting to coalitions or bartering, by providing a method by which a genuine majority rule can be achieved. Two aspects should be emphasised. First there is the transition period. The Rome Treaty stipulates that the unanimity rule will operate for a period which varies in length according to the type of problem, and it is only after this period has expired that majority voting becomes the rule—except for certain types of decision for which it was not possible to lay down a time-table in advance. This means that member countries are encouraged to reach an agreement unanimously, and to make the necessary concessions before the time for a decisive vote comes, from which a country might lose even more. The other aspect of procedure is still more important: it is to ensure that, except in very rare and insignificant cases, majority votes by the Council are never taken *in vacuo*; they must be taken on the basis of a proposal coming from an independent body, the Commission. Therefore supranationalism in the Community, if we can still give it that name, by no means involves the loss of sovereignty, and does not mean that a country has to throw itself at the mercy of its co-members without guarantee that a common interest is being served.

The ingenious mechanism which was devised to ensure this—that majority decisions can be taken only on a proposal put forward by the Commission, and that these proposals can be altered only by unanimous agreement in the Council—has led to a dialogue between the parties concerned. There is little chance of unanimous agreement against the Commission, and it is not possible for a majority of countries to force the Commission's hand. Should the Commission consent to a majority vote which ran counter to the rightful interests of the member countries or of the Community as a whole, it would be censured by the Assembly or have its decision nullified by the Court. On the other hand, there is nothing to prevent it from continually adjusting its proposals until they are acceptable to the Council.

It is not surprising that the criticisms levelled against the system by France have not been taken up by the other Common Market countries. First, it is not true that the majority voting rule only came into force effectively with the third stage of the transition period: it was simply widened then to include a large number of decisions affecting agriculture and transport; it had already been applied without any particular difficulty in a considerable number of other spheres. Moreover, in practice, majority votes are fairly rare; they facilitate agreement instead of leading to deadlock, for the fact that it is possible to use a majority vote often makes it unnecessary to do so. (Votes have been weighted in a very simple way, using the figures 1, 2 and 4 to ensure that no country alone has the power of veto—not even the three Benelux countries together, for their combined population and output do not amount to half that of one of the three larger member countries.)

The French government has maintained, further, that the move to a majority vote (for decisions on agriculture) would enable other countries to take back the concessions they had made under the unanimous voting system. This is a surprising attitude to adopt, and quite contrary to general principles of law, since the decisions have been taken for a definite period of time and can normally be changed only by the same procedure as that by which they were taken. By criticising both the fact that the Community's institutions have been given certain powers, and the fact that majority voting has been made possible, the French government has contradicted itself and wilfully ignored the whole point of the Community system: the indissoluble link between majority voting by governments in the Council and proposals issued by an independent body (the Commission). Obviously the Commission would not want simply to abandon its responsibilities for agriculture, nor could the Council take these responsibilities away, unless the Commission itself proposed such a move.

The crisis which began in June 1965[1] was only overcome eight months later in Luxembourg by acknowledging the differences between France and her partners. France is against any extension of the majority voting rule and has stated that it will block any decision in which another country is put in the minority, by uniting with it. The other countries uphold the majority principle and will not give way on it. France, however, has reserved the right to resume its boycott if it does not agree with any particular decision. An unkind summary of the way the dispute was settled—or, if one prefers, papered over—could be made as follows: France is the only one of the member countries which is likely to find itself in the minority, but if this occurs, it reserves the right to break its Treaty obligations.

In all probability the whole system will continue to function in spite of the shock it has received. The vital problem then will be whether the Community institutions can be made to develop gradually and continuously into the institutions needed for a united Europe, and whether economic union may become political union.

The Nature of Political Union

There is much ambiguity concerning the extent to which a problem or a decision is political. In a sense everything which the Communities have achieved so far is political, not so much in the achievements of the institutions themselves, where the political content is obvious, but in the sectors of the economy which have been reorganised or given a new framework. To begin with, everything concerning agriculture—production, guidance, maintenance of farm income, the decrease in the farming population—is implicitly political, in the sense that these questions directly affect the electorate. Fiscal reforms, such as the harmonisation of the tax systems in the different member countries, are also essentially political measures because the distribution of revenue and economic power between different sections of the population will be deeply affected by them. All this is political also in that the Community's activities have not been based on logic alone but have affected and involved a whole range of national customs, feelings, pressures and arrangements. 'When we are agreed', one international civil servant has said, 'a problem is economic; when we do not agree then it is political'. There is considerable truth in this, for sometimes a problem can be settled by exact calculation, and at other times a wide range of imponderable elements have also to be taken into account.

Economic problems also of course become political problems the more closely they are related to the general aims and policies of a country. This explains the tension between international agreements and national resistance to their application. Financial policy, credit policy and incomes policy all make up monetary policy, the aim of which is to ensure overall stability, fair distribution of wealth and expansion. This is obviously an essential part of government action. Similarly, in foreign trade the Community will inevitably move from a common external tariff to a common trade policy. Simple international trade agreements have for some time now provided for less important products to make up the trade balance between the countries concerned, and generally speaking this form of arrangement no longer leads to internal political difficulties for the governments concerned.

[1] France withdrew from the Council of Ministers as a result of a disagreement with the other five member countries over the arrangements for agriculture in the Community.

A common trade policy will, however, involve a great many other highly political decisions; for instance, whether to trade with China, or with all, or some, of the East European countries; it will involve taking sides in the Arab–Israel dispute or even trying to bring the two together; it will involve a joint decision on whether to open up the European market to the developing countries instead of pursuing a self-contradictory and ineffective policy of aid without trade for these countries; it will also mean recognising the differences between Africa, South-East Asia and Latin America. So that in concrete terms, a common trade policy, if it is ever launched, would have a very strong bearing on more than two-thirds of the basic foreign policy problems of most of the member countries.

Apart from the irrationality of the 'package' nature of decisions on questions like agriculture, financial or commercial policy—questions which ought in fact to involve as highly logical and scientific an approach as possible—there are some matters in which valid political aims are completely at variance and at times even in contradiction with economic good sense: for instance, the question of associating the Community with one or other of the Mediterranean European countries, for which, practically speaking, the Community gets nothing but bills; or, of course, all so-called problems of prestige. And lastly, there are issues which by their very nature cannot be subjected to the kind of approach the Community uses because they are based on a different set of values, whether valid or not: these are diplomacy and defence, the decisions which affect the continuing existence of the member states as such and determine decisions of peace or war.

There are two basic difficulties before the Community in moving from economic to political union. First is the question of method. In the economic sphere it has been possible to introduce changes gradually so that their effects are not too severe, and by progressively increasing the number of joint decisions to soften the impact of the Community on national institutions. In diplomacy and defence, however, there seems to be a barrier which has to be broken: it involves the abandonment of all that is fundamental to the separate existence of the national governments, which fear to find themselves reduced overnight to being part of a federation, deprived of international status and with no more autonomy than provinces. The second, and more important difficulty, is that it is not easy for the peoples of the member countries to abandon their traditional national outlooks, which are often different from and even opposed to those of the other members, and accept common objectives. The difficulty is even greater when diplomacy becomes an end in itself, when a country's foreign policy consists essentially of being noticed rather than contributing to the creation of a more ordered and less unjust world.

Before answers to these difficulties can be found two points must be clearly understood. First, there are some problems such as frontiers, or relations with former colonies or overseas possessions, which are essentially national problems. No country will want to act on the advice of the others when dealing with these, still less hand over decisions on them to others. The only point in discussing them is for consultation or information. The logical line of approach would indeed be, for a country which is going its own way in these fields, to cease expecting to have the full support of the others in the name of solidarity. Most of these questions have been inherited from the past; some of them have already been settled and others may disappear as time goes on. For these purely national problems there should be a kind of transition period until they have all been solved.

The second point is that in spite of flashes in the pan, for countries as small as those of Western Europe independent foreign policies can only be illusory, unless aims are negative. These countries can independently play a destructive role, refuse to cooperate or break up common institutions, but beyond that all they can do is to strike attitudes or play games. None of them has achieved a special relationship with China, Latin America or the Soviet Union, and indeed they can have no real influence on world affairs except by joining their efforts in some common approach, since alone they have too little to offer.

Joint political action

Critics of the Community say that political action must be backed by national feelings, on behalf of which sacrifices can be demanded and made. There is, however, no real disagreement about the fundamental requirements of politics, and no one has ever maintained that anything can be achieved by setting up a disembodied technocracy. Nor has anyone imagined that nations can be merged together immediately, or a European nation born overnight which will command the same affection and loyalty as the traditional mother country. On the contrary, it is as a result of clearly recognising the difficulties that will have to be overcome that a body has been created which aims gradually to replace opposing passions with common objectives. There is an inherent contradiction in the view that political action can be defined as action for which men are prepared to die, and in the sketch of political union, put forward by its supporters, which limits such a union to periodical meetings of heads of state or government, on the grounds that new nations cannot be founded. Take the most typical example of this contradiction in action: the decision to use atomic weapons. It is just possible to conceive of a nation deciding to use them, but in doing so it risks destroying itself; it is even harder to conceive of a collective decision by several countries, but this is the only kind of decision which would offer them some chance of avoiding disaster. Thus an administrative arrangement of periodical meetings between heads of state would be hopelessly weak in the face of the urgent and dramatic decisions which they might have to take.

The question remains whether the existing system of Community institutions can be extended as it stands into the political sphere. One essential prelude to this (though by itself it would not be enough) would be the formation of an independent body to make proposals on long-term European aims, and to instigate concerted action in times of crisis. As far as the procedure for holding meetings is concerned, there is of course a great difference between meetings held at a fixed date between governments and meetings called by a commission to discuss specific proposals worked out in advance. The first, as the history of the Franco-German Treaty of 1963 has shown, is quite likely to achieve nothing except to bring into the open, and possibly aggravate, disagreements. But meetings arranged to work out a policy, or called to deal with specific emergencies, provide an impetus of their own and their importance can be adjusted according to the importance of the issues at stake—as the history of the Common Market has shown.

This could not be the final answer, however. Political union is too specific a problem to be solved by preconceived plans. The answer cannot be given in the abstract. European integration since the second world war has been a success because instead of following an abstract scheme, it proceeded by sudden bounds. It began by an agreement on coal and steel, and the logical thing would have been to extend integration to other industrial sectors.

Circumstances led instead to the projected Defence Community, but when this failed the scene of action switched suddenly to general economic integration. The use of a variety of approaches is the key to success.

If the political aims of European integration are to be achieved it must be understood that unity may develop along lines which seem impossible today. There are several possible approaches which, as often happens in history, could converge at a given time, or follow closely on each other. Perhaps institutions will arise out of the need for a European deterrent force, or perhaps direct elections to the European Parliament could have an effect out of all proportion to what would, after all, only be a change in procedure. Or perhaps one day widespread demands for a European constituent assembly will come from the peoples of Western Europe themselves. The important thing will be not to miss the opportunity when it arises.

BIBLIOGRAPHY

Albrecht-Carrie, René. *One Europe: The Historical Background of European Unity*, Doubleday, New York, 1965; issued in Britain as *Unity of Europe*, Secker and Warburg, London, 1966.
Curtis, Michael. *Western European Integration*, Harper and Row, New York, 1965.
Gladwyn, Lord. *The European Idea*, Weidenfeld and Nicolson, London; Frederick A. Praeger, New York, 1966.
Hallstein, Walter. *United Europe: Challenge and Opportunity*, Oxford Univ. Press, London; Harvard Univ. Press, Cambridge, Mass., 1962.
Kohnstamm, Max. *The European Community and its Role in the World*, Univ. of Missouri Press, Columbia, Mo., 1963.
Lindberg, Léon. *The Political Dynamics of European Economic Integration*, Oxford Univ. Press, London; Stanford Univ. Press, Stanford, Calif., 1963.
Monnet, Jean. *Les États-Unis d'Europe ont commencé*, Laffont, Paris, 1955.
Pryce, Roy. *The Political Future of the European Community*, Federal Trust/Marshbank, London, 1962.
Schuman, Robert. *Pour l'Europe*, Nagel, Paris, 1963.
Uri, Pierre. *Dialogue des continents*, Plon, Paris, 1963; issued in Britain and the United States as *Partnership for Progress*, Harper and Row, London and New York, 1963.
Zurcher, Arnold. *The Struggle to Unite Europe*, New York Univ. Press, New York, 1958.
Le dossier de l'union politique, Documents of the European Community, No. 23, Paris, July 1964.

EUROPEAN COMMUNITY LAW

WERNER VON SIMSON

THE LEGAL ASPECT OF THE EUROPEAN COMMUNITIES

The legality of the European Communities

THE three European Communities (collectively spoken of as 'the European Community'), i.e. the European Coal and Steel Community (ECSC), the European Economic Community (EEC) and the European Atomic Community (Euratom), were set up by treaties between the founding members, France, Western Germany, Italy, the Netherlands, Belgium and Luxembourg (the Six).[1] They are the result of a legal act, and their institutions exist and operate within the limits set by the treaties. The treaties in question are the so-called Paris Treaty of 18 April 1951—which came into force on 25 July 1952—and the Rome Treaties of 25 March 1957—which became effective on 1 January 1958. They have been ratified and enacted as national law in all six signatory countries.

The legal nature of the Treaties

Much argument has been devoted to the question of the precise legal effect of these treaties. Do they provide the origin and the constitution of a supranational state to whom the member states have transferred at least part of their national sovereignty, or are they no more than a common plan of action, the execution of which depends on the continuing willingness of the states to pursue it?

There can be little doubt that the purpose of the treaties was to go beyond a non-committal and freely reversible declaration of intent. They were meant to stabilise the political will of the Six in such a way as to allow for a consecutive (as opposed to a simultaneous) give and take in the introduction of the measures envisaged by the treaties. This was essential because for some of these measures the time was already ripe when the treaties were signed, while others needed further definition and agreement. Together the treaties have a fundamental aim: the creation of a unified and homogeneous market covering the territory of the six member states. The treaties are, in short, an attempt to tie the different choices of political and economic action open to each state to a common pursuit by means of a system of legal obligations.

How far does such a system hold good in the face of continuing political sovereignty of the member states?

No common sovereignty

It is now generally admitted that no common sovereignty above that of the member states has resulted from the treaties. The binding power of the

[1] See 'The Structure of the European Community' (p. 570).

treaties consists much less in their strictly legal system of rights and obligations than in a factual connection which they establish. They define a specific and highly complex political situation with its actual advantages and tempting possibilities on the one hand, and they state the conditions under which this situation is made available to the participating states on the other hand. Each individual treaty obligation is thus binding, not so much as a part of an enforceable system of law and sanction, but because it belongs to the fundamental decision of each participating state to avail itself of an agreed system of mutual political and economical advantages and possibilities—to be, in short, and to remain a member of the Community in question. Looked at this way the treaties can be described as the set of rules and conditions which define, first, the aims and powers of the European Communities and, secondly, the conditions under which a state may remain a member.

A common political will

The ultimate binding force of the treaties depends therefore on the value which the association they have created and made possible assumes in the eyes of the member states. The treaties clearly start from the assumption that this value will increase with the progress of integration of the six markets into one common market, until finally it will become economically (and hence politically) catastrophic for a state to leave the Community. The view that the incomplete Common Market has already become practically irreversible—sufficiently so to make a threat of one-sided withdrawal sound somewhat unreal to the other members—may well be justified, notwithstanding the Community's crisis of 1965–6.

Negative obligation of the Treaties

More problematic if less obvious is the power of each state to refuse to help the Communities to develop further unless their essential character is altered. For the treaties do not merely entail certain definite obligations but they also make a number of potential steps in the field of European or other international action dependent on unanimity among the member states. Not a few of the Communities' future actions which are envisaged in the treaties, and which are indeed necessary if the real purpose of the treaties is to be fulfilled, depend on new decisions which each state, legally speaking, is free to make or to withhold. In this sense the efficacy of the treaties has so far not become independent of the continuing (and even increasing) will of the member states to pursue their original plan of European integration. The speed, if not perhaps the fact, of progress is still very much subject to the attitudes of at least the larger member states.

THE METHOD OF THE TREATIES

Form of procedure

The form of procedure employed in the three treaties differs in one fundamental aspect. The Coal and Steel Community is founded on what the French call a *traité de règles* (treaty of rules); the two other Communities are based on a mere *traité de cadre* (framework treaty). R. Krawielicki, the late director-general of the Communities' legal service, has given in a recent study (see the bibliography at the end of this chapter) a detailed account of the structural differences to which this distinction leads. Since the ECSC treaty aims at the integration of only two basic industries whose conditions and problems are comparatively well understood, it was possible to write into the treaty itself the main laws which should apply in this partial common market, and to create in a number of fields direct administrative powers to be exercised by a common executive (the High Authority in Luxembourg). With the EEC, on the other hand, aiming as it does at a comprehensive amalgamation of the six national economies, such a detailed approach did not seem practicable. Conditions were much too varied and complex to allow for a specific attribution of administrative powers or even for a definiton of such powers. Nor could agreement on all the innumerable questions of detail have been reached in time to be incorporated in the treaty. The treaty therefore limits itself to defining the topics on which agreement is to be reached and legislation subsequently to be drawn up, and to devising a method of attaining this aim.

Community law and national law

Before looking at the legal provisions of the treaties a word should be said about the relationship between Community law and national law. The idea, originally advocated by some writers, that a European law above the different national laws had come into being has proved to be, in its general sense, untenable. But in two respects a supremacy of Community law over national legislation is now commonly admitted. In the first place the treaties themselves contain certain provisions aiming at a common interpretation, by the different national courts of law, of the treaties and of the rules resulting from them. If a question of interpretation arises in one of these courts, that court can, and if its judgment is not subject to the findings of a higher court must, submit the question to the Court of the European Communities before proceeding with the suit. This is to ensure that differences in national jurisdiction will not diversify the application of Community law. At the same time, in the EEC the Council of Ministers has power to issue directions to the member states suggesting the uniform development of national legislation related to the establishment or the functioning of the Common Market.

Community law and subsequent national legislation

The problem of the validity of subsequent national legislation which con- tradicts Community law has frequently been discussed. Solutions which rely on any preconceived idea about the nature of Community law tend, in the opinion of the present writer, to obscure rather than clarify the issue, because they presuppose what they ought to investigate. The effects of a law determine its nature, not the other way round. Another approach seems more promising: the distinction between the different categories of order which Community legislation and national legislation seek to establish. A regulation made under Community law resolves a legal doubt common to all six countries. No national law can cover the same ground since it is effective in one country only. It must therefore be assumed that a national law, even where its literal meaning seems to suggest the contrary, does not intend to counteract Community law but must be interpreted as being valid only in so far as it does not encroach upon it.

Who may invoke Community law?

The question has also been raised whether the provisions of the treaties (other than those expressly addressed to individuals or companies) are binding only upon the states in their relation to each other or whether a private party may in its own right seek to enforce the observation of such rules by a Community institution or by a member state. As far as the Community institutions are concerned more will be said below. Where a state acts towards an individual party in violation of a treaty obligation the question of relief is not expressly dealt with in the treaties. But a case has come before the European Court of Justice in which one of the member states had claimed payments for certain goods imported into its territory from another member state, payments which in effect, if not in name, amounted to an increase in customs duties, while the treaty provides that no such increase should occur. Could the importer rely on this provision to claim, in his national court, that the demand was illegal? The European Court, to whom this question had to be referred by the national court, affirmed that he could, although three of the member states had made strong representations to the contrary. This must be considered one of the most important decisions yet reached by the European Court.

Coercive powers

Little need be said about the means of coercion available to the Communities in the case where a member state deliberately refuses to honour its treaty obligations. They are certainly brittle, and even if they were more effective than they are, the basic need for continuing cooperation has been sufficiently emphasised to show that the efficacy of Community law largely depends on its voluntary acceptance by the member states. Another point may, however, be mentioned here. Where a member state introduces measures which, although they fall within its competence, as opposed to that of the Communities, might have an adverse effect on the Common Market, the Communities are in various ways entitled by special treaty provisions to counteract this effect or to mitigate it. This may be done by withholding benefits due under the Community treaties or by allowing discriminations against the state concerned which would otherwise be forbidden.

CONTENT OF COMMUNITY LAW

Purpose of the Treaties

The principal purpose of the treaties is the creation of a common market among the member states. This means a market in which national distinctions are partly abolished immediately and partly destined to be abolished within a specified time. Customs duties and quantitative restrictions to the movement of goods within the Common Market were either, as in the ECSC, declared illegal, or, as in the EEC, subjected to a plan of gradual removal. In the EEC also (as opposed to the ECSC) a common external customs tariff and a common trade policy were envisaged. The mobile factors of production, i.e. manpower, services and capital were to be freed from all impediments affecting their movement within the Community. For agriculture and transport similar steps were also envisaged, but in the treaty itself common policies for these sectors were all that could be agreed upon, while implementation was left to subsequent legislation.

A common economic philosophy

A very important feature of the Common Market is to be seen in the restrictions imposed by the treaties on the power which either states or individual enterprises are allowed to wield within the Market. The Market's competitive structure is specifically laid down, and the forces of government or of private economic action are bound by law to respect this structure. This conception of the Market—although not undisputed within individual member states—assumes that in it the general economic good is brought forth by individual productive efforts acting upon each other and determining their respective success or failure by such interaction. No individual effort, prompted as it must be by the prospect of individual gain, must be allowed to dominate the Market and to make itself independent of competition. In the ECSC all discriminations between producers, buyers or users of coal and steel are strictly forbidden, concentrations between producing and trading firms are subject to previous approval by the High Authority, and restrictive agreements are illegal except in a limited number of specific cases which must also be authorised by the High Authority. In practice concentrations have been allowed almost without exception, but it can be assumed that some which would not have proved acceptable have not been pursued for this reason.

As to restrictive agreements, the most important case the High Authority has had to deal with has been the sales agreements which for more than fifty years practically unified the sale of coal from the Ruhr mines. The immense difficulties which the coal industry had to encounter, contrary to all expectations at the time when the treaty was signed, and the special production problems connected with the non-renewable nature of its resources, led the High Authority to seek a gradual solution. In the end it recognised that competition in this type of market cannot be unrestricted, chiefly because some competitors have, apart from the fields which they currently exploit, further unopened fields to develop, while others simply exhaust their existing fields without the need to accumulate capital for future development. The fact that oil had emerged as a very serious competitor to coal had also to be considered. In the end the Court gave an authoritative interpretation of the relevant clauses of the treaty, admitting a limited but still effective degree of competition as best suited to serve the various and in their unlimited application contradictory aims of the ECSC treaty.

It remains true, however, that in spite of modifications called for by special circumstances a fundamentally competitive market structure is one of the main tenets of the treaties. The special importance of the adoption of this market structure and of the principle of non-discrimination lies in the fact that the whole system of economic legislation is thereby anchored in one particular economic philosophy—that of a considerable and ultimately decisive measure of free enterprise—and that the member states are precluded from pursuing political aims inconsistent with this philosophy (unless of course the member states agree to change the treaties). A homogeneous framework of production and trade in which the six previously separate economies can gradually be merged into one could doubtless not have been attained on any other basis. Once it had been attained legal powers were needed by the organs of the Community to maintain and use this basic structure.

Before looking at these powers it must be mentioned that the EEC does not go as far as does the ECSC in its measures against trade restrictions. Discrimination is not generally forbidden, but only if it takes place for reasons of nationality. Concentrations between enterprises do not require approval. Restrictive agreements are, however, declared incompatible with the common market and are consequently illegal and void, unless they fall within limited categories which it is left to the Council of Ministers to specify in accordance with proposals submitted to it by the Commission. The treaty itself contains only the general principles and it will take many years before the Commission will be able to finish its task of implementing these rules by suggesting specific legislation. A start, however, has been made.

How the Communities Work: Legislation

The rigid conceptual distinction between legislature, administration and judicial power may no longer be adequate to describe what happens in a state, but it will serve well enough to give an overall idea of the legal system operating within the Communities.

Who acts as law-giver?

The main source of law in the Communities is without question the text of the treaties. This is amplified and supplemented by what may be described as delegated legislation issuing from the institutions set up by the treaties. These orders and regulations have the force of laws and they are inferior to the text of the treaties only in so far as they have to conform to that text. A further source of law is the jurisdiction of the European Court of Justice, admitting or rejecting, as it does, such general principles of international or Community law as the parties to a lawsuit may from time to time invoke.

The text of the treaties represents the unanimous will of the member states once commonly agreed, and valid as long as it has not been changed. It has been laid down specifically in the treaties when and how the treaties can be changed, either by unanimous, or, in less important cases, by majority decision. The observance of these conditions is in some instances assured by the European Court having to confirm a change before it can become operative.

Since, as has been mentioned, a great number of details had to be left to administrative regulations or to quasi-legislative decisions it is important to know who is competent to issue these. In the ECSC the treaty itself contains a fairly detailed set of legislative provisions and it was possible to entrust the High Authority, consisting of nine members nominated according to the treaty, with the task of issuing the regulations and individual decisions for their implementation. It is worth noting that the treaty prescribes in some detail when this should be done by general administrative regulation and in what other cases it should be left to the consideration of the individual case and its circumstances. The Court has been careful to preserve this distinction which guarantees to any party concerned in the Community that the special features of its case will be considered wherever the treaty demands it. In the case of the EEC much more had to be left to future legislation, whether direct or delegated, and it was obvious that the executive, i.e. the Commission of nine members nominated by the governments of the member states, could not be the proper body to decide on these unresolved problems. In many cases new political agreements had to be made by the states and it was therefore necessary to create a legislative body, acting within the general limits set by the treaty, in which the national governments were directly represented and could express their current political opinion. This institution is the Council of Ministers, consisting of one representative of each of the six countries. Each Community has its own Council of Ministers, but there is a permanent secretariat to the three, and in practice the same members of the Council often attend the different meetings.

The process of Community legislation

Two interesting features characterise the process of legislation within the competence of the Council of Ministers. The one relates to the system of voting, the other to the mode of action by which the Commission and the Council cooperate in the task of law-making.

Voting in the Council of Ministers. The voting in the Council of Ministers is divided into such cases which involve, or are thought to involve, the states in their quality as sovereign members of the Community, and such others where the specific (and necessarily different) importance of each member state's economy is considered relevant. In the first case the Council decides with a simple majority of its members, so that four states, even if they include the three smallest, can outvote the remaining large ones. In cases where a qualified majority is required by the treaty, France, Germany and Italy have four votes each, Belgium and the Netherlands two, Luxembourg one. A further subdivision is made. Where the Council has to act upon a proposal of the Commission—a procedure, described below, which is used for most of the important cases of law-making—a majority of twelve votes will suffice, without taking into account the number of states assenting. In all other cases twelve votes, but with at least four states assenting, are required. This distinction therefore gives weight to the responsibility of each state in matters affecting its national competence, and neglects this potential interest in matters where a balance between the demands of the different economies seems a more pertinent consideration.

Legislative initiative. In a great number of instances the treaty contains regulations on the process to be followed in amplifying and supplementing its provisions. In general it is up to the Commission to take the initiative and to draft legislation which the Council then enacts, either unanimously or by majority vote according to the treaty's rule. If the Council wishes to alter the Commission's proposal it can do so only by unanimous vote. The consequence of this is that the Commission can, in such a case, decide whether to make the alteration sought by the Council part of its own proposal, thereby enabling the Council to act on a majority vote where the treaty admits it, or whether to maintain its original draft requiring a unanimous vote for its alteration.

While the initiative for law-making lies therefore with the Commission—a state of affairs which has given rise to objections by the French government—the Council can ask the Commission to take such initiative in cases where it deems this opportune to attain the aims of the treaty.

The European Parliament

The European Parliament is, with the Court of Justice, one of the two organs common to all three European Communities. Its participation in law-making and administrative procedure is very restricted and can in no way be compared to the role assigned to national parliaments in this field. Its main function is to be consulted in a number of cases which are listed in the treaties, and which are mainly, if not exclusively, instances in which the law-making competence of the Community directly affects the legal situation within the member states. The Parliament can voice its opinion on the drafts submitted by the Commission to the Council but this is in no way binding even if it may have a certain political weight with these bodies. The final draft after the Parliament's comments have been considered is not made available to it again before the Council votes on it.

The Parliament also has the right to be consulted in the case of certain proposed alterations of the treaties, and of new treaties of association. But only in the ECSC is there a genuine legislative competence in that alterations proposed by the High Authority and the Council of Ministers cannot become effective without the Parliament's approval. In the case of the two other treaties no such assent is required.

In certain circumstances the Parliament can dismiss the High Authority, or the Common Market or Euratom Commissions—this has never happened—but it has no such control over the Council of Ministers. This right of dismissal (by a vote of no-confidence) is of little importance in practice because it is too heavy a weapon to allow for any effective Parliamentary control in day-to-day matters. But it gives an opportunity, or pretext, to the Community's executive institutions to seek the approval and comment of the Parliament in order to obtain political support for disputed measures. A recent attempt, backed by the Commission of the EEC, to secure a certain degree of budgetary autonomy, and to make this move acceptable by granting a corresponding right of control to the Parliament, has foundered on the determined resistance of the French government.

ADMINISTRATION

The High Authority

In the ECSC the legal provisions are, as has been said, chiefly contained in the treaty itself. The High Authority is, therefore, less concerned with law-making than with the application of the law. Yet it also, to a certain extent, has been left to supplement the treaty by executive orders and regulations, and to specify the way in which the treaty should be implemented.

The executive functions of the High Authority, as opposed to those of the other Communities, include the right to levy a contribution on the coal and steel production within the Community, and to use this revenue to pay for its own administration, to further certain specified purposes, and to arrange for credit facilities to the coal and steel industry. The High Authority has, in relation to these industries, a direct competence to ensure and if necessary enforce the application of provisions relating to restrictive agreements, concentration of enterprises, or the control of dominating market positions. It is also competent to deal with the application of price regulations, such as non-discrimination in price policy, publication of price lists, and fixing of maximum or minimum price levels in certain circumstances. It can exert a limited influence on investment policy. In exceptional situations it can, either on its own initiative or on that of the Council of Ministers, directly control coal and steel prices by creating mutual financial equalisation funds or by introducing production or sales quota systems (either with the simple or with the unanimous approval of the Council, as the treaty may prescribe for each of these measures). The High Authority also has the right to enquire into the working of individual enterprises in connection with its tasks.

The EEC Commission

In the EEC, the Commission's competence to deal directly with enterprises or private persons exists to a much more limited extent. The treaty does not rule out such competence but the Council has the right to decide how and where this competence can be used. The chief instances of orders or regulations that have been made so far are those implementing part of the general principles relating to trade restrictions, and others specifying forbidden discriminations in the field of transport. Others will doubtless follow.

The Commission's main administrative competence, apart from that of preparing laws to be promulgated by the Council, consists in issuing regulations for the detailed application of marketing and price equalising measures. The Commission is also in charge of the gradual unification and harmonisation of trade policy among the member states and of legal matters applying to the Common Market.

Special rules apply to the various agencies instituted by the treaty, i.e. the European Investment Bank and the European Social Fund.[1]

THE RULE OF LAW

With the institution of a common executive which in the nature of things had to be fairly independent of national control—the appointment of members being the only way in which the member states could exert controlling influence—the problem arose as to how to secure the observance of the rule of law in this administration. As has already been pointed out, the Community executives do not, in contrast with national administrations, have a competence for political action, but are limited to matters concerning the rights of the individual citizen or requirements of procedure. The political rights of the executives are limited by depending on the specific attributions contained in the treaties. Some sort of judicial control is then necessary to ensure that these limits are observed together with the rule of law governing administrative action in general.

The Court of Justice of the European Communities (a common organ of all three of them) consists of seven judges appointed by mutual agreement between the member states. Judges are appointed for six years, new nominations for three or four judges alternately taking place every three years to assure continuity of jurisdiction. The Court, according to a fundamental article in each of the three treaties, safeguards the observance of law in the interpretation and application of the treaties. There is, however, no general clause allowing for judicial control of every act of the executive. An enumerative system specifies the competence of the Court and the right of member states, of Community organs other than the Court, and of individual parties to appeal against acts of the executive, or against its failure to act where the treaty requires or entitles it to do so. The Court is competent to deal with disputes between member states themselves, between member states and a Community, and between individual institutions of the Communities. It enjoys, as has been mentioned, a certain monopoly in deciding on questions of Community law. This extends to cases pending before national courts, in so far as their decision depends on the interpretation of such questions. The Court has made it a strict principle in these cases not to suggest in any way how the case before the national court should be decided, but only to give a rule of interpretation to assist the national court in its work.

It is the observance of the law and not the adequacy of administrative discretion which the Court exists to ensure. Its powers to review administrative acts are generally limited to the control of four requirements: that the act in question (which can be brought for appeal to the Court only if it has legal significance) lay within the competence of the organ by which it

[1] See 'The Structure of the European Community' (pp. 578–9).

was issued; that the essential formal requirements, including such consultations or approvals as the treaty prescribes, were observed; that the act (or failure to act) complied with the material requirements of the treaty in question and with the rules regulating its application; and finally, that the authority concerned did not abuse its statutory powers. In the case of an individual party the act which it wishes to submit to judicial review must be shown to concern it immediately and individually. If the Court finds the legal objections justified it annuls the decision of the executive. The organ concerned is then left to take measures conforming to Court findings.

The Court is further competent to deal with actions for damages claimed in respect of illegal measures taken by an executive organ or by one of its employees. It has had very little occasion to use these powers so far. It also deals with disputes between the Communities and their employees within the limits set in their employment statutes or contracts.

A private party, as has been mentioned, can attack a general measure taken by a Community organ only if and in so far as this measure affects it directly. There is, however, provision for such a party to invoke before the Court the inapplicability of a general measure to its individual case, if the case depends on the validity of this general measure. Technically, even if the Court accedes to this request, the measure in question remains valid and only its application to the specific case before the Court can be disallowed, but in effect the authority concerned has always felt prompted to adapt its general measure to the findings of the Court.

The Court has been rather generous in admitting private claims. Although its task is to apply Community law and not national law it has shown a tendency to admit as tacit rules of Community law such rules and general convictions as could be shown to belong to the law commonly observed in all the member states.

The jurisdiction of the Court serves to fill the gaps left by the treaty provisions when applied to day-to-day life. It helps to maintain the common confidence without which it would be impossible to pursue a political aim, which is defined by its realisation. The different objects, rules and decisions of the treaties form a complex whole, each provision depending for its justification on the fulfilment of another. A political development of the size and complexity of the European Communities would be unthinkable without a legal framework to assure this interdependence for all concerned.

BIBLIOGRAPHY

Bebr, Gerhard. *Judicial Control of the European Communities*, Stevens, London; Frederick A. Praeger, New York, 1962.

Catalano, Nicola. *Manuel de droit des communautés européennes*, Dalloz-Sirey, Paris, 1962.

Feld, Werner. *The Court of the European Communities: New Dimensions in International Adjudication*, Nijhoff, The Hague, 1964.

Van der Groeben, Hans and von Boeckh, Hans (eds.) *Kommentar zum EWG-Vertrag*, Vols. 1–2, Lutzeyer, Baden-Baden, 1960.

Krawielicki, Robert. 'Strukturunterschiede zwischen dem Montanvertrag und dem Vertrag über die Europäische Wirtschaftsgemeinschaft und ihr Einfluss auf die Fusion der Verträge', *Festschrift für Philipp Möhring*, Munich, 1965.

Lorenz, Werner. 'General Principles of Law: Their Elaboration in the Court of Justice of the European Communities', *The American Journal of Comparative Law*, XIII, 1, Ann Arbor, Mich., 1964.

Scheingold, Stuart A. *The Rule of Law in European Integration*, Yale Univ. Press, New Haven, Conn. and London, 1965.

Valentine, D. G. *The Court of Justice of the European Communities*, Vols 1–2, Stevens, London, 1965.

THE EUROPEAN FREE TRADE
ASSOCIATION (EFTA)

C. M. W. VASEY

THE CREATION OF EFTA AND THE
ECONOMIC DIVISION OF WESTERN EUROPE

THE European Free Trade Association, or EFTA as it is generally known, was set up in May 1960 on the basis of the Stockholm Convention, signed in July 1959.[1] It comprises Austria, Denmark, Great Britain, Norway, Portugal, Sweden and Switzerland; Finland acquired associate status in 1961. These countries, whatever their collective importance as trading nations, could hardly be described as forming a natural economic unit. The origins of EFTA are to be sought in the formation of the European Economic Community in January 1958, bringing with it the threat of tariff discrimination against those countries left outside. What brought the Seven together in Stockholm in July 1959 was the breakdown in December 1958 of the negotiations on the British plan for setting up a multilateral free trade area embracing the whole of Western Europe, which would have come into existence concurrently with the common market that the six countries of the EEC were proposing to create between themselves. The ostensible reason for the breakdown was the French refusal to accept a free trade area without a harmonised external tariff and a more extensive coordination of economic and social policies than the British, the Scandinavians and the Swiss were prepared to accept. The real reason lay somewhat deeper—in the existence of two divergent approaches to European integration, one based essentially on trade liberalisation, the other on the creation of common policies over most aspects of the economy.

The immediate purpose of EFTA was to establish an industrial free trade area by means of the progressive elimination of tariffs and quotas on goods produced in the member states. It was confidently assumed that a pragmatic system of intergovernmental cooperation would be adequate to deal with any non-tariff problems that might arise. The ultimate purpose, however, was to persuade the Six to agree to a multilateral trading arrangement which would prevent the economic division of Europe, while allowing the EEC to pursue its own development. From this point of view, the formation of EFTA was essentially a diplomatic manoeuvre, designed to facilitate an overall settlement and at the same time put pressure on the Six. It was noticeable that the British, to whom EFTA meant a relatively small accretion of strength, were always less enthusiastic than the Swiss and the Swedes. Indeed, EFTA

[1] See p. 616.

614

had hardly come into existence before the British began to have second thoughts about the wisdom of this collective approach to the problem of tariff partnership with the EEC as opposed to a direct request for membership, even if this were to involve a greater degree of integration than the British had hitherto been prepared to envisage.

In June 1961 the British announced their decision to apply for membership of the EEC. Although it was agreed that EFTA would be kept in being until satisfactory arrangements had been concluded with the EEC to meet the 'legitimate interests' of the various EFTA countries so that they could all 'participate from the same date in an integrated European market', the British decision was the signal for a general move to abandon EFTA. Britain and Denmark formally applied for membership of the EEC at the beginning of August; Sweden, Switzerland and Austria applied for association in December; and Norway applied for membership in May 1962. (Finland and Portugal never specified what kind of arrangement they would seek, but it could only have been some form of association.)

The breakdown of the negotiations between Britain and the EEC in January 1963 gave EFTA a new and unexpected lease of life. Faced with the prospect of being excluded from the EEC for an indefinite period, the Seven had no choice but to make the most of their own organisation, which had operated fairly smoothly on the economic level. (Tariffs on inter-EFTA trade had already been reduced by 50 per cent from their original levels by January 1963, though under the initial timetable for tariff reductions, tariffs need only have been cut by 30 per cent.) The result was a programme of measures adopted at Lisbon in May 1963 which included among other things a revised timetable for the remaining tariff reductions, a general review of the adequacy of the EFTA rules of competition and new activities in the field of agriculture and economic development.

The progressive internal development of EFTA following the Lisbon meeting left unsolved, however, the problem of the economic division of Western Europe, which became increasingly acute with each new tariff reduction within the EEC. Early in 1965 the Seven decided to take the initiative again. At a meeting in Vienna in May it was decided to approach the Six with an offer of permanent collaboration between EFTA and the EEC on a number of concrete non-tariff problems, such as patents and industrial standards. The immediate purpose of the proposal was to attenuate some of the harmful side-effects of the economic division of Western Europe, but it was also hoped to lay the foundations for an eventual overall settlement. In fact, the whole 'bridge-building exercise', as it was generally called, was overtaken by events. The situation was transformed by the constitutional crisis in the EEC over the financing of the common agricultural policy, which for a time effectively put an end to any hopes of opening a dialogue with the Six, and then by the British decision, announced in April 1966, to begin diplomatic soundings on the possibilities of obtaining satisfactory terms of admission to the EEC. The Austrian government had in fact been negotiating separately with the Six for association to the EEC since 1964, while the Danish government had for some time been under considerable pressure from its farmers to obtain membership of the Common Market separately. The British decision had the effect of swinging the whole Association behind a policy of direct contact with the EEC, even if Sweden and Switzerland still remained dubious.

Thus by the summer of 1966, the idea of seeking some form of arrangement between EFTA and the EEC seemed to have been abandoned once again in favour of a new attempt by the member states to join the Common Market as full or associate members. The political situation in the EEC and in Western Europe as a whole, however, would seem to make a formal British bid for membership in the near future very difficult, and only Austria is prepared to go ahead without Britain. EFTA could thus have several more years of separate development before it. To form an accurate idea of what EFTA's prospects of development are, it is first necessary to take a closer look at the Association and at the Stockholm Convention on which it is based.

The Stockholm Convention

The Stockholm Convention was drawn up in the summer of 1959. It is a highly pragmatic document, in which virtually the only specific provisions are those dealing with the removal of tariffs and quotas and the rules of origin. The other articles merely lay down a series of general rules designed to ensure that the proper functioning of the free trade area is not interfered with as a result of government action or inaction in other fields. The only institution established by the Convention is a purely intergovernmental Council with no supranational powers.

The main features of the Stockholm Convention are the provisions for the progressive removal of import duties on all goods produced in the member states.[1] The original timetable, which was based as far as possible on that of the EEC, provided for an initial tariff reduction of 20 per cent on 1 July 1960 to bring EFTA into line with the EEC, followed by three reductions of 10 per cent at intervals of eighteen months and five at intervals of one year. The target date for the final abolition of tariffs was thus 1 January 1970 as in the Treaty of Rome. This timetable was repeatedly modified to keep pace with the acceleration of the EEC tariff-cutting schedule, with the result that the first three tariff cuts of 10 per cent were brought forward to July 1961, March 1962 and October 1962 respectively, by which time EFTA was more than two years ahead of schedule. A revised timetable for the remaining tariff cuts was adopted at Lisbon in May 1963, under which the date for the final removal of customs duties on inter-EFTA trade was fixed at 31 December 1966, which is eighteen months ahead of the date for the final removal of tariffs in the EEC.

Exceptions to the general elimination of tariffs in EFTA by 1966 are of two kinds. The first reflects the differing levels of industrial development within EFTA. Thus Norway and Finland have been authorised by the Council to delay the final removal of tariffs in certain sectors until 1970, so as to give the industries concerned further time to adapt to free trade. Portugal is also allowed under the Convention to retain some tariff protection for her existing and potential infant industries until 1980. The second kind of exception derives from the fact that EFTA does not interfere with member states' fiscal policy. Accordingly, import duties applied primarily for the purposes of raising revenue are exempt from the general removal of duties. The Convention merely requires the elimination of any 'effective protective element', an obligation which applies not only to revenue duties but also to internal taxes generally.

In addition to the progressive removal of import duties, the Convention provides for the progressive elimination of quotas and other import restrictions

---

[1] Most agricultural and marine products are specifically excluded from the reduction of tariffs. The Convention lays down, however, that special arrangements must be made to expand trade in these two sectors.

except those required for non-commercial reasons, the enforcement of national laws on marketing and the protection of state monopolies. The date for the final elimination of quotas is the same as that for the removal of tariffs. In fact both Portugal and Finland have been allowed to retain a limited number of quotas, Portugal to protect her car assembly industry, Finland in connection with her system of bilateral trade agreements with the Soviet Union. The Convention also allows the temporary reimposition of import quotas during the transition period if the progressive elimination of tariffs and quotas results in an appreciable fall in production in a given industry or region—a provision that has never been used. Neither has any member state invoked Article 19, which authorises member states, under certain conditions, to reimpose quotas in the event of balance of payments difficulties. When Britain got into economic difficulties in the autumn of 1964 it imposed a flat 15 per cent import surcharge, for which there was no justification in the Stockholm Convention. The British argument that an import surcharge was less restrictive in its effects than a system of arbitrary import controls was not fully accepted by the other member states, which resented especially the fact that Britain had not consulted them before imposing it, as required by the Stockholm Convention.

The problem of providing for the removal of tariffs and quotas was a simple one compared to the problem of trade deflection as a result of the absence of a common external tariff. The Convention therefore contains an elaborate series of rules of origin (which, incidentally, take up three times as much space as the rest of the Convention) designed to ensure that the relatively high tariffs of some member states on goods imported from outside the area are not undermined by imports through the low-tariff member states. Basically, goods traded between the member states qualify for EFTA tariff treatment if the EFTA component is more than 50 per cent by value, or alternatively if certain prescribed processes have been performed in the exporting member state. In order to minimise the risk of trade deflection at the expense of traditional outside suppliers, an extensive list of industrial raw materials and semi-manufactures in which EFTA is deficient are classified as of EFTA origin even if imported from outside the area. These rules, which have been subjected to a continuous process of revision and review, have worked even more smoothly than expected, and the safety-valve provisions of Article 5 of the Convention, which allow a member state to take safeguard measures in the event of industrial production being affected by trade deflection, have never yet been invoked. This is a fact of some pride to EFTA in view of the dispute with the French during the OEEC negotiations of 1958–9 about the possibility of defining workable origin rules without a prior harmonisation of external tariffs. [1]

Although EFTA refrains on principle from any interference with member states' domestic arrangements not directly related to tariffs and quotas, the

---

[1] It is probably true, however, that by the very nature of things a free trade area does tend to encourage the downward harmonisation of tariffs on imports from outside the area. This is illustrated by the dispute over 'tariff drawback' (refund of import duty paid on imported raw materials or semi-manufactures subsequently reexported). The Convention provides that once free trade has been reached, member states may refuse the benefit of EFTA tariff treatment to imports from other member states that have benefited from drawback. This rule was finally confirmed by the Council, but only after a minority of member states had made a determined effort to get the rule rescinded on the grounds that it would penalise industry in high-tariff countries. The experts' view, which was shared by the majority of the member states, was that drawback, like any other export subsidy, was incompatible with a free trade area, and that the remedy for any country that found its export industries penalised by high duties on imported raw materials was to reduce the level of the duties in question.

Convention nevertheless recognises that government action or inaction in certain fields such as the right of establishment of foreign firms, restrictive business practices, the commercial activities of public authorities, state export aids and dumping, can nullify the benefits of free trade. Member states are accordingly free to invoke the consultation and complaints procedure,[1] which is the normal means of settling disputes, if they feel their interests are being jeopardised. In addition, the Convention gives the Council power to lay down more detailed rules for dealing with these problems in the light of experience. One of the main decisions taken at Lisbon in May 1963 was, in fact, to review all the relevant provisions of the Convention before the end of the transition period.

REVIEW AND EXECUTION OF THE STOCKHOLM CONVENTION

The 'rules of competition', as they are commonly known, may be divided into two kinds. In the first place, member states may be required to refrain from certain practices. Thus Article 13 of the Convention forbids the use of a whole range of direct and indirect export subsidies as well as any aid to industry whose main effect is to nullify the benefits of trade liberalisation for industry in other member states; Article 14 bans commercial practices by public bodies that provide the same sort of protection for domestic producers as would be banned under the Convention if obtained through the use of tariffs and quotas or state aids. The review provided for at Lisbon has not taken the form of drawing up detailed rules which are then applied to particular cases; it is a comprehensive review of member states' legislation and administrative arrangements with a view to detecting any discriminatory practices. These are then dealt with by the offending member state, frequently through bilateral negotiations with the interested parties. A similar kind of review has been made of member states' arrangements with regard to revenue duties, non-commercial quantitative restrictions and border charges in general, as well as marking regulations and other non-tariff barriers which may also distort competition.

The rules of competition of the second category assume some form of positive government action. Thus Article 15 of the Convention deals with cartels or restrictive business practices that frustrate the benefits 'expected' from free trade, Article 16 outlaws restrictions on the establishment or operation of firms that are applied in a discriminatory way for the same purpose, and Article 17, besides confirming member states' rights under GATT to deal with cases of dumping by means of countervailing duties or import restrictions, also provides that they may be asked to take action against the dumping of non-EFTA goods on their markets which threaten the interests of other member states. In the case of Article 15, the review has resulted in an agreed set of procedures which will make it possible for a firm to have a complaint considered first on an informal basis between the two countries concerned rather than be obliged to persuade its government to invoke the formal consultation and complaints procedure—which it is unlikely that any government would use. The Council has also decided to examine whether member states have the legislative and administrative means to ensure the effective implementation of Article 15, and to clarify some of the technical terms used in it. In the case of Article 16, the review has resulted in an agreed interpretation, under which member states promise to

---

[1] See p. 622.

grant automatically any request for establishment by an EFTA firm for the purposes of distribution or assembly and, within certain limits, for the purposes of manufacture as well.[1] Member states are also requested to check the existence of any legislative or administrative obstacles to the implementation of this article. In the case of Article 17, the purpose of the review is to see whether the GATT rules on dumping are likely to be adequate in the context of a free trade area. The most likely result is an agreement on how the existing rules are to be interpreted and applied, possibly coupled with a review of anti-dumping regulations in the different member states. This would be in accordance with the pattern of cooperation established so far.

The benefits of free trade are likely to be jeopardised not merely by competitive distortions, but also by conflicting economic and financial policies. Under Article 30 of the Convention, the member states recognise that their individual economic and financial policies may affect the economies of the other members, and state their willingness 'to pursue those policies in a manner which serves to promote the objectives of the Association'. The means for implementing this provision, apart from the possible recourse to the consultation and complaints procedure which is implicit in the wording of the article, are periodic exchanges of views and recommendations by the Council. In fact, the member states preferred to rely on OECD and these provisions remained in abeyance until the sterling crisis of October 1964, when Britain unilaterally imposed a 15 per cent surcharge to protect its balance of payments. The resulting crisis spurred EFTA into setting up an Economic Committee, which keeps a regular watch on short-term developments in the world economy and in the member states, and their likely effects on EFTA trade. The Committee's ability to influence British economic policy will always be limited, but it did deal successfully with the Finnish balance of payments crisis in the winter of 1965–6, when it discussed both the probable effects on EFTA of the various measures taken by the Finnish authorities and possible measures of assistance by the other member states. The Committee has also held long and detailed discussions of such problems as the techniques of long-term planning with a view to sustained economic growth and structural policies in the different member states, the aim being to encourage cooperation since it cannot be imposed.

The free trade area envisaged by the Stockholm Convention is not of course complete. Neither the abolition of tariffs and quotas nor the rules of competition apply to agriculture, which is also subject to special treatment in the Treaty of Rome. Rather than propose some form of common policy, for which EFTA lacks either the economic basis or the institutional machinery, the authors of the Convention merely laid down that one of the objectives of the Association shall be the expansion of trade in agriculture so as to provide 'reasonable reciprocity' for those member states whose economies are dependent on their exports of farm produce, which means in practice Denmark and Portugal. The size of the problem is limited in the first place by the fact that a large number of processed agricultural produce and some other goods not produced in the importing member states are classified as industrial goods and thus qualify for EFTA tariff treatment. The problem of ensuring reciprocity for Denmark and Portugal is dealt with essentially by

---

[1] Article 15 raises certain problems in connection with exchange controls, access to capital markets, the takeover of established firms and access to raw materials, which are to be further studied. The last two problems reflect the fears of a relatively underdeveloped country like Norway about the possible consequences of integration with financially more powerful neighbours.

v

means of bilateral agreements, which are considered an integral part of the Convention, any tariff concessions they contain being extended to all EFTA countries. There are nine such agreements, of which some antedate the Convention while others were concluded in 1963. The most well known is the Anglo-Danish agreement giving free access to the British market for Danish bacon and butter, which was the price of Danish membership of EFTA.

In May 1963 it was decided to set up a standing committee to carry out an annual review of EFTA trade in agriculture and to study ways and means of increasing it. In addition to seeking further tariff concessions, the scope for which is rapidly becoming exhausted, the Danes have been arguing strongly for EFTA solidarity vis-à-vis the EEC, even going so far as to threaten to leave the Association if their partners would not cooperate. This means in the first place that the latter should refrain from subsidising exports to traditional Danish markets in Germany and the Six which are being rapidly eroded under the impact of the Common Agricultural Policy of the EEC. In the second place the Danes have been arguing insistently for a common policy against dumped or subsidised agricultural exports to EFTA markets from non-members, which in practice means the EEC and Eastern Europe. The other member states have so far refused to do anything more than refer to the GATT provisions on dumping, but the Council has at least invited Austria and Switzerland to acquire the necessary legislative or administrative means to implement these provisions. This means that coordinated action between the member states on the basis of GATT is now possible if the political decision is ever taken.

The benefits of free trade are likely to be unevenly spread not only as between countries dependent on agricultural exports and those dependent on industrial exports, but also as between countries of varying levels of economic and industrial development. Tariff measures of the sort adopted in favour of Portugal, Norway and Finland, giving these countries further time to adapt their more backward industries to free trade, are partial and temporary solutions. In May 1963 the Council set up an Economic Development Committee which carries out development studies with particular reference to problems arising from the removal of tariffs and, more important, acts as a forum for promoting technical and financial cooperation between the member states, mainly at non-governmental level.

The initial range of subjects tackled by the Committee included two questions of general interest—regional planning and the techniques of industrial financing, and a number of questions of specific interest to individual member countries, such as technical advice on transport planning and export promotion for Finland, or the possibilities of developing the Portuguese machine-tool, food-processing and paper industries through sub-contracting or licensing arrangements with industries in other EFTA countries. Some of the initial projects were insufficiently prepared and of doubtful value, with the result that the Committee then limited itself to a smaller number of well-prepared projects of immediate interest to EFTA countries. These projects include an investigation of means of encouraging foreign tourism and investment in the Algarve region of Portugal, a study of certain aspects of the handling of general cargo in three EFTA ports (Oslo, Manchester and Lisbon), a comparative study of the concept of growth points in the context of regional development, and a visit to member states by representatives of the subcontracting agency set up by the Federation of Portuguese Industries with EFTA advice. Britain has asked for a comparative study of industrial training systems. All these schemes are on a very limited scale and the link with EFTA and the Stockholm Convention is sometimes tenuous. The schemes are best considered as the EFTA substitute for a common industrial and regional development policy.

INSTITUTIONS OF EFTA

The basic decision-making body of EFTA is the Council, in which each member state is equally represented at ministerial level. The Council operates in practice at two levels, the major political decisions being taken at ministerial meetings held two or three times a year in one or other of the national capitals, while the day-to-day administration of the Association is left to a committee of the heads of the permanent delegations in Geneva. The Council has also set up a number of permanent committees, composed of national officials, to deal with various aspects of EFTA activity. The Customs, Budget and Trade Experts Committees have existed almost from the beginning. To these were added the Agricultural Review and Economic Development Committees (May 1963) and the Economic Committee (November 1964). The Council has also made frequent use of ad hoc working parties to look at particular problems, ranging from the elimination of quotas to the revision of the rules of competition. The whole system of permanent committees and ad hoc working parties is organised and serviced by a secretariat under the command of a secretary-general. Although without any formal right of initiative, the secretariat plays an increasingly important role in the decision-making process, while the secretary-general has virtually acquired the role of spokesman for the Association, both on questions of European integration and on internal matters.[1] Finally, there is the Consultative Committee, composed of independent experts and representatives from both sides of industry in the different member states. This was set up by the Council in February 1961 to advise on the affairs of the Association as a whole. There is also an EFTA Parliamentarians' group, a purely informal body composed of delegates from the EFTA countries to the Consultative Assembly of the Council of Europe, which meets once during every Council session. Neither of the last two institutions has any real influence, however, in the affairs of the Association.

Unless the Convention specifically provides otherwise, decisions of the Council have to be unanimous.[2] Within the limits of the objectives of the Association, the Council's legislative powers are very wide indeed, since it has the right, and in some cases the duty, either to supplement or amend almost all the substantive provisions of the Stockholm Convention, from the rules of origin to the rules of competition. This power is not, however, likely to be used to transform the Convention. Apart from the operative provisions directly related to the free trade area, the Convention is essentially a good conduct code, and the supplementary rules adopted by the Council are never likely to go beyond agreed interpretations of the way in which the various articles are to be applied in practice.

[1] The then secretary-general, Frank Figgures, took a vigorous stand at the time of the British surcharge crisis in November 1964. A former senior official at the Treasury, Figgures resigned in November 1965, being replaced by Sir John Coulson, Deputy Under-Secretary of State at the Foreign Office.

[2] As a general rule, decisions are taken by a simple majority in cases where a member state asks to be relieved from, or refrains from complying with, its obligations under the Convention. No new obligation can be imposed on a member state by majority decision.

The Council is also the judicial organ of the Association. Disputes about the proper implementation of the Convention are settled through the consultation and complaints machinery, which may be set in motion by any member state that feels that the objectives of the Association or the benefits expected from the liberalisation of trade are being jeopardised. If the normal bilateral and multilateral consultations yield no results, the injured member state may make a formal complaint to the Council, which sets up an examining committee to establish the facts of the case. The Council then decides the case by a simple majority vote. To enforce its ruling, the Council may issue appropriate recommendations to the offending member state or authorise the other member states to suspend the application of specified treaty obligations, also by a simple majority.

In practice, the Association works in such a way that disputes rarely reach the formal complaints stage.[1] The tendency has rather been for the member states to settle difficulties between themselves on an ad hoc bilateral basis. This approach, if carried too far, has obvious dangers for the uniform application of the Convention. To meet this danger, it has been decided to encourage the member states to make greater use of the provisions for multilateral consultation in the Council, which have previously suffered from being identified too closely with the complaints procedure. Although the Council remains entirely competent to interpret the Convention, the secretary-general has been given the power to draw its attention to bilateral settlements between the member states which involve a danger of divergent interpretations.

EFTA vis-à-vis the EEC

The assumption on which EFTA was founded is that none of the member states were prepared for economic integration of the kind envisaged by the EEC. This assumption no longer holds good. Britain, Denmark and Norway have made membership of the EEC a national policy objective, while Austria, Sweden and Switzerland are apparently prepared to seek a form of association that will for all practical purposes involve complete economic integration with the EEC, subject only to political and institutional guarantees of their political and institutional neutrality. In the long run, this must mean the absorption of the EFTA countries by an enlarged EEC. In the short run, it is sometimes argued, this means that there is considerable scope for an increased degree of economic integration within EFTA, both for its own sake and to give the EEC a sharper incentive to negotiate. When the committee of the permanent delegations was instructed to study the possibilities of collaboration with the EEC as part of the bridge-building scheme, it was also asked to look at the possibilities of extending the range and scope of EFTA activities as well as of strengthening its institutional arrangements. A prolonged period of stalemate as regards the enlargement of the EEC will encourage a revival of these aims.

Yet the scope for increased integration within EFTA is limited by the nature of the Association. EFTA is primarily an exercise in trade liberalisation between a group of countries who for geographical and institutional

---

[1] The first two complaints to be carried to the stage of an examining committee were settled by the Council in May 1966. In the first case, the Council rejected a Danish complaint in connection with British exports of live cattle to West Germany; in the second, the Council ruled in favour of a Norwegian complaint about the British refusal to apply EFTA tariff treatment to fish 'grillets'.

reasons could never expect to form a full customs and economic union, with common agricultural, industrial, transport, regional development and fiscal policies and harmonised economic legislation. The basic EFTA formula of a free trade area with special arrangements for agriculture defines the limits of the Association. EFTA action with regard to non-tariff barriers and obstacles to competition is limited to this objective. The creation first of the Economic Development Committee and then of the Economic Committee has meant a broadening of EFTA activities to include mutual consultation on economic problems of common interest as well as various schemes for technical and industrial cooperation, but expansion of these activities in the future, however great, will hardly lead to a change in the nature of the present pragmatic cooperation between the members of EFTA.

It has been suggested that EFTA might venture into such fields as the establishment of a common patents law, uniformisation of industrial standards and harmonisation of national regulations concerning the manufacture and marketing of industrial goods generally. The purpose here would be to facilitate integrated European rather than purely EFTA policies, though there has been talk of separate action by EFTA if the EEC refused to cooperate. The problem facing EFTA in this connection arises from the fact that as long as the member states' basic objective is to join the EEC, the Six have very little incentive to cooperate, while the Seven have very little incentive to adopt separate arrangements except of a provisional kind. This dilemma is inherent in the provisional nature of EFTA itself.

BIBLIOGRAPHY

Camps, Miriam. *The European Free Trade Association. A Preliminary Appraisal*, Occasional Paper No. 4, Political and Economic Planning, London, 1959. *Britain and the European Community 1955–63*, Oxford Univ. Press, London and New York, 1964.

Lambrinidis, J. S. *The Structure, Function and Law of a Free Trade Area. The European Free Trade Association*, Stevens, London; Frederick A. Praeger, New York, 1965.

Business International. *The European Free Trade Association. Today and Tomorrow*, London, 1964.

EFTA. *The Stockholm Convention Examined*, Geneva, 1963. *EFTA Bulletin* (monthly) and Annual Reports, Geneva.

THE ORGANISATION FOR ECONOMIC COOPERATION AND DEVELOPMENT (OECD)

SALOMON WOLFF

ORGANISATION FOR EUROPEAN ECONOMIC COOPERATION (OEEC)

THE Organisation for Economic Cooperation and Development (OECD) has a long and eventful history, some knowledge of which is necessary if we are to appreciate the Organisation's present work and future prospects. OECD comprises Western Europe, the United States, Canada and Japan and is often taken today to represent the economic interests of the rich industrial countries. However, it must not be forgotten that it arose in the wake of another international organisation—the Organisation for European Economic Cooperation (OEEC), a union of the Western European states ruined in the second world war, which was formed to promote the best allocation of Marshall Aid dollars for the recovery of their shattered economies.

On 5 June 1947, the American Secretary of State General Marshall made his famous speech announcing massive American aid towards the economic reconstruction of Western Europe, on condition that the countries concerned pooled their efforts in attacking the problems involved. This offer was to have a far-reaching effect on the post-war development of the area. Just over a month later, on 12 July 1947, representatives of sixteen European countries met in Paris to discuss acceptance of the American offer. From this conference emerged the Committee for Economic Cooperation, which was given a double task—to make a detailed report to the American Congress on the state of the European economy and to lay the groundwork for a permanent system of European economic collaboration. The conference that launched OEEC was held early in 1948, and on 16 April of the same year the new organisation started work. A short time afterwards it moved its headquarters to the Château de la Muette on the edge of the Bois de Boulogne, which was also to be the seat of its successor, OECD.

Of the many international organisations that arose in the post-war period probably none succeeded as well as OEEC in carrying out its allotted tasks. It had eighteen member states—all the countries of Western Europe with the exception of Finland. Its contribution to the economic reconstruction of Western Europe can hardly be overestimated. When it started work, the whole of the Western European economy lay in ruins. Thirteen years later, when OEEC handed over to OECD, most of the OEEC countries had reached a degree of prosperity they had never known. In these thirteen years the total production of these countries had more than doubled. Not only were their budgets balanced but they could show substantial surpluses into the bargain, with the result that by the end of 1958 it was possible to introduce convertibility of currency. The standard of living in these countries had attained undreamt-of heights. Western Europe, which in 1948 had stretched out a begging hand to Washington, was now once again a factor to be reckoned with in the world economy.

A major factor in the 'economic miracle' that has taken place in Western Europe was certainly the generous extent of Marshall Aid. But even when this aid came to a stop in June 1953, the economic recovery of Western Europe continued to take big strides. There can be no doubt that it was the flood of dollars from America, whose distribution among individual countries was organised by OEEC, that made the first steps easier and indeed made them possible. But OEEC's most striking success was the result both of the close degree of collaboration between the member countries and of the basic principles governing this collaboration. Very soon after its foundation OEEC began to urge upon its member states the desirability of free international trade and a multilateral payments system. Dismantling of the trade and payments restrictions that had been built up during the war and the period of shortages that followed it provided the basic element in Western European economic recovery.

Liberalisation of foreign trade and the foundation of the European Payments Union (EPU) were the most important tools in this recovery. 'Liberalisation of foreign trade' meant the deliberate and progressive removal of quota restrictions, first of all between member states themselves and then from trade between them and other countries including the United States. Gradually this liberalisation policy was extended to 'invisible' trade services and to some extent capital movements. A 'Code of Liberalisation' for trade was complemented by a 'Code of Liberalisation of Current Invisible Operations'.

Free development of European trade presupposed, however, the existence of corresponding financial measures in the monetary field which had to be cleared of restrictive bilateral agreements. Thus there arose within OEEC the idea of a European clearing house, whose duty it would be to meet creditor nations' demands in a strong currency and to accord debtor nations a credit in the same currency. In the role of clearing house there appeared the European Payments Union (EPU) which started work on 1 July 1950 and was not liquidated until convertibility of the European currencies was introduced in late 1958. (Its place was then taken by the European Monetary Agreement (EMA) which had been drawn up as far back as 1955 with an eye to this contingency.) EPU practice was based on the 'unit of account', of the same value as the US dollar. Surpluses and deficits of any one country vis-à-vis its trade partners were calculated on a reciprocal basis. In this way, credits or deficits were no longer reckoned against any particular country but against EPU, which gave partial credit to debtor countries. The means for these credits were provided partly by the creditor countries and partly by the USA.

THE TRANSITION TO OECD

It might at first sight appear that the success of OEEC proved its own undoing, in that it made itself superfluous by carrying out its allotted task—the economic reconstruction of Europe—to everyone's satisfaction. In reality, however, the crisis in OEEC which led to its reorganisation was sparked off by deep-set differences of opinion among the member states about the path Western Europe should tread in the future. The OEEC member states were split into two groups. The first group, led by France, wanted to push on beyond the progressive integration of their economies to a politically united Western Europe, a United States of Europe; while the other group, led by Great Britain, felt that the most that could be aimed at was collaboration in certain restricted fields between sovereign states.

The Paris Treaty creating the European Coal and Steel Community (ECSC) was signed on 18 April 1951. This organisation formed by six countries—France, West Germany, Italy, Belgium, Holland and Luxembourg—owed its inception to the initiative of the French foreign minister, Robert Schuman. As long as economic integration remained restricted to the coal and steel industries it had little effect on the activity of OEEC. The attempt, which soon followed, to turn the 'Six' into a European Defence Community was finally defeated by the resistance of the French parliament. The move some years later to establish a European Economic Community (EEC) was crowned with a good deal more success. By the Rome Treaty of 25 March 1957, the Six laid the basis for the integration of their economies in a Common Market by means of a customs and economic union.

About the middle of 1956, even before the Common Market took definite shape, Britain started working within OEEC for the formation of a European free trade area, which would comprise all the member states and thereby largely offset the protectionist element in the Common Market of the Six. These negotiations went on until November 1958 when they were broken off at France's instigation, which led to a serious crisis within OEEC. Soon afterwards, however, at the end of 1958, the Western European currencies were able to move towards full convertibility as a result of the stabilisation of the French franc. At the same time a start was made with the implementation of the Rome Treaty by reducing tariffs between the six member states. Not long afterwards negotiations started between Britain, Sweden, Norway, Denmark, Switzerland, Austria and Portugal on the formation of the European Free Trade Association (EFTA) which finally came into being by the Treaty of Stockholm, signed on 4 January 1960. The creation of EFTA— which was intended by its promoters mainly as a means of putting pressure on the Six to get them to reconsider the question of negotiations over a multilateral association of other European countries with EEC—was not likely to improve relations between the two camps within the framework of OEEC.[1] The future of the Organisation had therefore become problematical.

It was the United States, the original prime mover behind OEEC, that now provided a solution. When the Atlantic Economic Conference opened in Paris early in 1960, Douglas Dillon, the American Undersecretary of State, proposed that OEEC should be so modified as to include the United States and Canada. The decision to do so transformed a purely European organisation into an Atlantic one. As the accession of the new members involved extensive rethinking of the whole idea of the Organisation, its nature and its tasks, almost a whole year passed while negotiations went on over the necessary changes. A preparatory committee was entrusted with drawing up the new Articles; presided over by the newly appointed secretary-general of OEEC, Professor Thorkil Kristensen of Denmark, it produced not only a new Convention but also a Report in which the various questions involved were set out in detail. This Report and the Convention itself were

[1] For details of EEC and EFTA see the chapters entitled 'The Structure of the European Community' (p. 569) and 'The European Free Trade Association (EFTA)' (p. 614).

approved at the ministerial conference held in Paris on 13 and 14 December 1960, the Report forming an integral part of the Convention. The Convention on the setting up of the Organisation for Economic Cooperation and Development (OECD) was signed on 14 December 1960 in Paris by the representatives of twenty countries—Belgium, Denmark, Germany, France, Greece, Ireland, Iceland, Italy, Luxembourg, the Netherlands, Norway, Austria, Portugal, Sweden, Switzerland, Spain, Turkey, Britain, the United States and Canada. The Convention came into force on 30 September 1961 following ratification by the signatory powers. In April 1964, Japan joined the Organisation, thus becoming its twenty-first member.

The Convention establishing OECD is couched in very general terms. American constitutional and executive practice had to be borne in mind, as questions of economic policy in America are subject to the approval of Congress to a far greater extent than they are in Europe. The aims of OECD are set out as follows in Article I of the Convention:

> The aims of the Organisation for Economic Cooperation and Development shall be to promote policies designed:
> (a) to achieve the highest sustainable economic growth and employment and a rising standard of living in Member countries while maintaining financial stability, and thus to contribute to the development of the world economy;
> (b) to contribute to sound economic expansion in Member as well as in non-Member countries in the process of economic development;
> (c) to contribute to the expansion of world trade on a multilateral, non-discriminatory basis in accordance with international obligations.

Economic policy, development aid and world trade are thus stated as the main preoccupations of the Organisation; the rest of the Convention is concerned with basic principles for running the Organisation.

INTERNAL STRUCTURE OF OECD

Internally OECD is modelled essentially on OEEC. Binding decisions can be taken only by unanimous approval of the supreme organ, the Council, in which all members are represented. Any member, however, has the right to abstain. If a country announces that it is not concerned with or interested in the question being discussed, a decision may be taken without its participation; such a decision is then not binding on the non-participating country. The only substantial difference between OEEC and OECD is that in the latter the position of the secretary-general is stronger; he not only heads the Secretariat but is also president of the Council whenever the Council is composed not of cabinet ministers but of permanent delegates from the member countries. The work of the Council is prepared for it by the Executive Committee which is formed by ten member states appointed annually by the Council.

OECD carries out its work mainly through its special committees. Of particular importance is the Economic Policy Committee which is composed of high officials of member states and which meets three or four times a year. Its discussions aim at closer coordination of the economic policies of OECD members. This committee is helped in its work by three Working Parties formed by a limited number of member states. Working Party 3 is particularly influential in that it deals with currency and balance of payments questions and exercises an unmistakable influence on the monetary policy of the leading industrial powers. The other two Working Parties are

STRUCTURE OF THE OECD[1]

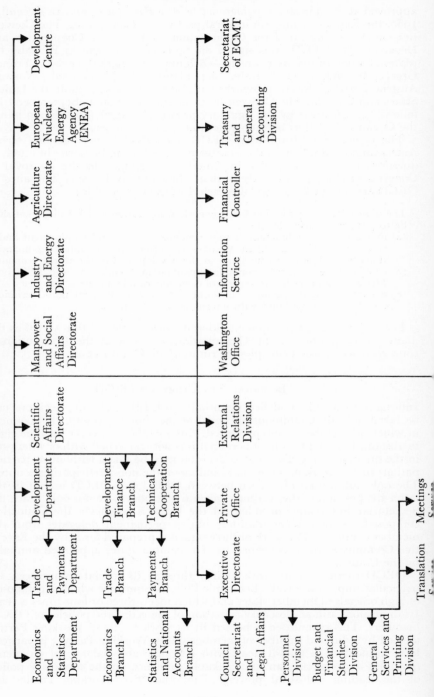

628

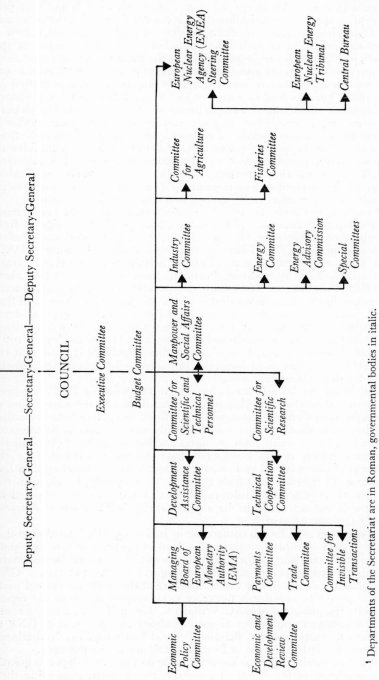

¹ Departments of the Secretariat are in Roman, governmental bodies in italic.

concerned with policies for the promotion of economic growth and with production costs and prices. In addition there is the Economic Development and Review Committee which is specially concerned with the annual review of the economic situation of individual member states. The results of this review are published by the Organisation in the form of separate reports on each country, which usually arouse a great deal of public interest. Assessment of economic development is based not only on memoranda supplied by member states but also and to a greater extent on documentation prepared by the Economics and Statistics Department of the Secretariat. This department is organised in exemplary manner and its work is of great service in promoting better understanding of economic and financial matters. Even though some of the statistics prepared by OECD are intended for confidential internal use only, the main body of information assembled is regularly released. The Organisation publishes each year some 10,000 statistical tables which are at the disposal of governments, parliaments, professional associations, trade unions, market study groups and other research institutes.

The handling of development aid problems falls within the competence of the Development Assistance Committee (DAC)—which carries on from the Development Assistance Group (DAG), a body created even before OECD was established. The following members of OECD belong to DAC: Belgium, Denmark, West Germany, France, Britain, the Netherlands, Italy, Japan, Canada, Norway, Austria, Portugal, Sweden and the USA, along with the EEC Commission. The countries represented in DAG provide some 90 per cent of funds annually available for development aid. The total flow of capital from DAC members to developing countries in 1964 was 8,710 million dollars (8,060 million in 1963) of which 5,950 million (6,090 million in 1963) came from public funds and 2,760 million (1,970 million in 1963) from private investment and credits. From these figures it is clear that the work of DAC members is of immense importance in providing financial assistance for developing countries.

It must, however, be admitted that so far the work of DAC has been largely restricted to the collection of statistical data and the supervision of contributions from member states, while its efforts to achieve better coordination of these contributions have met with only modest success. At the same time there can be no doubt that the talks carried on within DAC and the investigations which it has conducted have greatly contributed to the development of financial aid and to its more useful and rational application. The exchange of information about the steps each country is taking in this field is in itself beneficial. A substantial part of the material collected by DAC is published annually in its reports entitled *The Flow of Financial Resources of Developing Countries.*

On the occasion of its fourth conference in July 1965, DAC concluded that as a result of unfavourable harvests and a drop in the price of raw materials, an increase in the amount allotted to development funds would be necessary. The member states agreed to aim at allotting at least one per cent of GNP to development assistance. The Committee urged the states concerned to do all in their power to reach this figure or even surpass it. From the report submitted by the president of DAC, Willard L. Thorp (USA), it may be seen that the following countries are allocating about one per cent of GNP to development assistance: USA, Britain, Federal Germany, the Netherlands and Belgium, while in the case of France the figure is two per cent.

It was further established that the effectiveness of such aid depends greatly upon the readiness of the recipient countries to set about expanding their own economies. The Committee therefore recommended that, when fixing the amount of financial assistance and the conditions under which it was to be provided, the donor countries should take into consideration the efforts made by the recipient countries to make effective use of their own resources. For instance, the Committee was particularly concerned by the question of the growing indebtedness of the recipient countries. Unless this trend were reversed, the Committee felt, there was a danger that the net amount of financial assistance available would become smaller and smaller as increased allocations would be merely swallowed up in settling outstanding debts. The donor countries were therefore requested to provide their assistance preferably in the form either of outright gifts or of long-term loans at especially favourable terms. Finally, the need for better coordination of financial assistance was stressed; and to this end the creation of special consultative groups was urged.[1]

Developing countries need not only financial means but also technical know-how. Also working within the framework of OECD is the Technical Cooperation Committee, which is devoted to carrying out technical assistance programmes for the benefit of member countries such as Greece, Iceland, Portugal, Spain and Turkey. Turkey is something of a problem child of the Organisation in that she requires very extensive financial aid, and a special consortium is concerned with the administration of this aid. A similar consortium has been created to deal with Greece's problems.

A special Working Group of Technical Cooperation is concerned with technical aid to non-member countries and about one-fifth of the funds made available by the donor countries in the shape of bilateral donations are spent on technical aid. Thanks to these funds it was found possible in 1964 to send some 80,000 teachers and other experts to developing countries and maintain almost 42,000 students and trainees from these countries in Europe and North America. Recruitment of suitable instructors and technical personnel is however becoming increasingly difficult. Finally, since spring 1963 OECD has been running its own Development Centre which is doing all it can to provide the developing countries with the knowledge and experience they need for their economic development.

The other activities of the Organisation are of lesser scope than its work in the two main fields of economic policy and development assistance. A Trade Committee follows developments in international trade; however, while the old OEEC was able to do a lot of good work in this field, after it was transformed into OECD trade policy was deliberately pushed into the background, as it was generally agreed that thenceforward world trade should develop according to the principles laid down by the global General Agreement on Tariffs and Trade (GATT). Since then the Trade Committee has concerned itself mainly with the problems created by trade between the industrial states and the developing countries. World trade was further promoted by the work of the Fiscal Committee, which was in particular responsible for a 'Draft Convention for the Avoidance of Double Taxation with respect to Taxes on Income and Capital', which has served as a model for the conclusion of many bilateral agreements of the same kind.

A Committee for Invisible Transactions formed by ten experts seeks to remove obstacles in the field of international trade in services and capital. To this end it has worked out a 'Code of Liberalisation of Capital

---

[1] For more extensive discussion of the role of DAC in the giving of aid to developing countries, see the chapter entitled 'Western European Economic Aid to Developing Countries' (p. 423).

Movements' and 'Code of Liberalisation of Current Invisible Operations' and sees that they are observed.

When the European currencies went over to convertibility at the end of 1958, there came into force, as has already been mentioned, the European Monetary Agreement (EMA) to which only the European members of OECD belong. The work of EMA, which is run by a board of management, has however grown less and less important since its inception, as international monetary policy has gravitated more and more to other international organisations. Thus EMA's activity has in recent years been confined mainly to granting Turkey credits from the European Fund which forms part of it. In these circumstances it is not certain whether EMA will be preserved, or, if so, in what form.

The Manpower and Social Affairs Committee has on the other hand a very extensive field of action. It was at this Committee's instigation that OECD decided to summon its member states to review their labour market policies and to make these a part of the machinery to promote economic growth. The Committee has launched several investigations among which those dealing with mobility of manpower are specially important.

The Industry Committee deals with questions concerning the progress and expansion of industry. It comprises a whole series of sub-committees devoted to special problems of single industries such as steel, chemicals, textiles, cement, etc. Similarly, the Energy Committee supervises the work of the special committees for coal, electricity, oil and gas. These committees devoted to single branches of industry and energy are described as 'vertical' committees; they publish regular and comprehensive reports on developments in their respective fields.

Agricultural problems are in the hands of the Committee for Agriculture which meets regularly at ministerial level and so provides the ministers of agriculture of the member states with an opportunity for keeping in close personal touch with each other and with each other's problems. Although this committee is not empowered to exercise any direct influence on the agricultural policies pursued by individual countries, its researches and the discussions which are carried on within it make a valuable contribution to better mutual understanding. This is especially so since most of the member states have the same sort of agricultural problems to cope with, arising from the rethinking necessary in agriculture as a result of increased industrialisation and technical progress. There is also a separate Fisheries Committee.

OECD's field of activity extends also to scientific problems in so far as there is any connection between these and the central questions of economic and development policies. Scientific questions are dealt with by two committees—the Committee for Scientific and Technical Personnel and the Committee for Scientific Research. Some attempt is made in this connection to establish what contribution scientific research and training have to make to economic advancement.

OECD has several more committees in addition to those above-mentioned, e.g. the Insurance Committee, the Maritime Transport Committee, the Committee of Experts on Restrictive Business Practices, the Tourism Committee and also several special sub-committees. A Budget Committee prepares the decisions of the OECD Council on the internal finances of the Organisation; its expenditure is covered by the contributions made to it by member states.

OECD inherited from OEEC the European Nuclear Energy Agency (ENEA) which is an autonomous organisation aiming at promoting the use of atomic energy for peaceful purposes in Western Europe. ENEA fosters technical collaboration between its sixteen member states and has to this end created three joint projects—the Company for the Chemical Processing of Irradiated Fuels (Eurochemic) and two joint undertakings concerned with reactor technology. One of the projects concerns the twenty-megawatt boiling heavy-water reactor built at Halden in southern Norway by the Norwegian Atomic Energy Institute and the other the 'Dragon' reactor project at Windrith in the south-west of England. The sixteen member states have signed a convention establishing uniform European legal dispositions governing liability and compensation to be paid in the case of damage to persons or property resulting from nuclear accidents.

COLLABORATION WITHIN UNSPECIFIED LIMITS

As will be seen from the above account of the committees working within OECD, the Organisation's activities extend to almost all sectors of the economy, the overriding aim being to foster and promote the economic growth of member states and of developing countries alike. It is characteristic of the spirit that animates the Organisation that on the occasion of its very first meeting in November 1961 the Ministerial Council set itself a common growth target. The aim is that in the period from 1960 to 1970 the GNP of member states will rise by fifty per cent, that is to say by an average of 4.2 per cent per year, although growth rates will obviously vary from year to year and from one country to another. At the same time the Council stressed the importance of maintaining stability in balance of payments and in prices, and the desirability of higher than average rates of growth being reached and kept by the more backward member states. The Organisation was charged with assisting and supporting these countries in drawing up and carrying out their development plans.

All this was essentially a statement of aims, for OECD has little power to exercise any decisive influence on the economic policies of its member states. A considerable gap lies between, on the one hand, the size of the job OECD is expected to do and on the other, the practical means it has of doing it. While the parent organisation OEEC had certain specific functions, initially in the distribution of Marshall Aid and later in the field of European trade and monetary systems, OECD operates in no well defined or specific field of activity. On the contrary, in almost every domain of its activity it finds itself in competition with other international organisations which are much better equipped for practical action. Thus, questions of financial policy belong to the sphere of the International Monetary Fund (IMF) and the 'Group of Ten'; problems of trade policy come under GATT; while EEC and EFTA are concerned with changes in the economic structure of Europe. And these are only the most important rival organisations. OECD, it has become clear, is not well adapted to taking firm decisions requiring practical implementation.

But one must guard against underestimating the importance of OECD's activities. OECD is making a decisive contribution to economic collaboration in the Western world by providing a forum where the industrial states of the West meet to investigate and discuss their common economic problems. In this way, OECD plays the part of a joint study and research organisation where ideas, plans and information can be exchanged and where questions of principle as well as day-to-day problems can be studied, always with an eye to improving coordination between individual member states.

By the transformation of OEEC into OECD and the entry of the USA and Canada and, later, Japan, the European framework of the Organisation was transcended. But if the geographical field of activity was widened, it was at the cost of inner cohesion and practical effectiveness. The result has been that the Organisation has lost, once and for all, its chance of being instrumental in the integration of the European economy, which is now in the hands of other organisations. Thus OECD's task since then has been to attend to those economic problems which are common to all the industrial states of the West. By becoming the 'Rich Man's Club' OECD was automatically forced to concentrate its activities on aid to the under-developed countries. In this field its main task is to smooth out the difficulties that arise between the industrial states and the under-developed countries, and to try to introduce a systematic approach to the world economy.

OECD's development since its inauguration has certainly been in accordance with the intentions of its sponsors led by the USA. It was due to OECD that closer economic collaboration could be started between the USA and the economically rehabilitated countries of Western Europe. This enabled the USA to share with her European partners the numerous and heavy burdens which America's leading position led her to assume in the post-war period. This has especially been the case in the field of development assistance and also in that of monetary policy.

If powerful interests argue for the continuation and enhancement of this collaboration, it must not be overlooked that as the immediate post-war period is left further and further behind, the more do centrifugal forces make their appearance which gravely impede the process of integrated collaboration among the Western industrial states. (This phenomenon is apparent in the Communist bloc as well.) It is therefore not very likely that we can look forward to any internal strengthening of the OECD in the near future. It would seem that it will have to confine itself to serving as a meeting place for discussion. On the other hand, OECD is so organised that it could easily increase the degree of cooperation between its members should the need be felt. Indeed, the effectiveness of the Organisation's work depends exclusively on the ability and willingness of the member states to integrate their economies and to seek common solutions to their problems.

BIBLIOGRAPHY

Adam, H. T. *L'Organisation Européenne de Coopération Economique*, Librairie Générale de Droit et de Jurisprudence, Paris, 1949.

L'Huillier, J. A. *Théorie et Pratique de la Coopération Economique Internationale*, Editions Génin, Librairie de Médicis, Paris, 1957.

Kristensen, T. 'The OECD: a landmark of international co-operation', *NATO's Fifteen Nations*, Paris, December 1962–January 1963.

Marjolin, Robert. *Europe and the United States in the World Economy*, Duke Univ. Press, Durham, N.C., 1953.

Message from the President of the United States transmitting a copy of the Convention on the OECD, signed at Paris on December 14, 1960, The White House, Washington, 1961.

OECD Convention of 14th December 1960. Report of Preparatory Committee. Related Documents, OECD, Paris, 1960.

OECD. Rules of Procedure of the Organisation, OECD, Paris, 1963.

Partnership for Progress, Atlantic Institute, Paris, 1964.

Report of the Committee on Foreign Relations, United States Senate on Executive E, 87th Congress, 1st Session, US Government Printing Office, Washington, 1961.

The OECD: History, Aims, Structure, OECD, Paris, 1964.

The OECD Observer, OECD, Paris, bi-monthly.

INTEGRATION AND THE
TRADE UNIONS

R. COLIN BEEVER

THE trade union movement in Western Europe has its main strength in member countries of the Common Market (EEC) and the European Free Trade Association (EFTA). In all these countries, except Portugal, it has significant influence (usually more in EFTA than in EEC countries). In Spain, Greece and Turkey trade unions operate but are weak; in Ireland, Iceland and Finland they are fairly effective. The main reason why unions have more influence in most EFTA countries than in most EEC countries is because they are generally united in the former but divided, at national level, in the latter. This has nothing to do with the setting up or operation of the two trading blocs themselves, but is due to historical and political factors.

Broadly speaking, trade unions consider themselves political as well as industrial bodies and have usually tended to ally themselves with one political party or another. Where there has been a significant clerical element in national politics the unions tend to be divided but where there has been no active political battle involving the clerics, that is, mainly in Protestant countries, the unions tend to be united, though this is not invariable. Another element which appears to have an important bearing on the divisive tendencies of trade unions is the strength of the Communist parties in the countries concerned. This might itself be influenced, of course, by the presence of the clerical factor in politics. Thus Social Democratic, Christian and Communist political parties all have their own philosophies about the role of trade union movements and they support (sometimes financially) the setting up and maintenance of movements built in their own image. All pay lip-service to the ideal of trade union unity, but all equally firmly reject that unity on anything other than their own terms.

West Germany is the outstanding exception to these generalisations in that it is the only EEC country with a broadly united trade union movement. But this is a phenomenon of the post-war period. Clericalism in politics was a big issue before the war, as was Marxism. Now both are fairly insignificant and the new trade union movement, built up again from scratch with the help of the occupying authorities, is united in one national centre or TUC.

The country-by-country position of the unions in Western Europe is as follows (initials in parentheses are of the Internationals—to be described later in this chapter—to which the trade union national centres are affiliated). Only the major national centres are included.

EEC
West Germany. The trade unions are united in the Deutscher Gewerkschafts-bund or DGB (ICFTU) which dominates the trade union scene, although not all unions are affiliated and in recent years there has been a little competition from a revivified Christian trade union centre. The DGB is Social Democrat-oriented but with a large minority of Christian Democrat supporters and has a fairly important influence at national political level, but this has been declining somewhat in recent years.

France. In the past several attempts at unity have been made by the trade unions but these have never lasted for long and the present three-way division has existed since 1947. The largest national centre is the Confédération Générale du Travail or CGT (WFTU). It is the one union in Western Europe which has always adhered closely to international Communist policies, industrial and political. The second largest is the Confédération Française Démocratique du Travail or CFDT (CISC) which is Christian Democrat-oriented but which in 1964 adopted this new name (it was previously known as the Confédération Française des Travailleurs Chrétiens or CFTC) in order to relax its specifically Christian orientation and recruit from the whole anti-Communist field of trade unionists. The smallest of the main national centres is the CGT Force Ouvrière (ICFTU), a Social Democratic breakaway from the old united CGT. The unions do not now have a high political influence, but they have in recent years won several notable victories, some with a political flavour, through militant industrial action.

Italy. Again, the largest national centre is Communist-oriented though with a strong minority of Nenni socialists. It is the Confederazione Generale Italiana del Lavoro or CGIL (WFTU). It has, however, been notable for deviation from the international Communist line, especially over questions of Western European integration. The second largest national centre is the Confederazione Italiana Sindacati Lavoratori or CISL (ICFTU), which is Christian Democratic-oriented but affiliated nonetheless to the largely Social Democratic international, rather than to its Christian counterpart. The smallest, the Unione Italiana del Lavoro or UIL (ICFTU) is Social Democrat-oriented. Again, because of their divisions, the unions are not very influential politically but they are more strongly organised than their French counterparts industrially, and they are not timid about using their strength.

Belgium. There are two main national centres, the Social Democrat Fédération Générale du Travail de Belgique or FGTB (ICFTU) and the rather smaller Christian Democrat Confédération des Syndicats Chrétiens or CSC (CISC). Their main strengths are respectively in the Walloon areas and in Flanders and the north. They are both moderately influential politically.

Netherlands. Here the unions, although split three ways, are rather more politically influential than in Belgium, perhaps because of their cooperation in the Foundation of Labour and in the Social and Economic Council, and also because of their close cooperation with governments in working a national incomes policy, until its final collapse in 1965. The three main national centres are the Social Democrat Nederlands Verbond van Vakverenigingen or NVV (ICFTU) which is the largest, the Catholic Nederlandse Katholieke Arbeiderbeweging or KAB (CISC), the second largest, and the Christelijk Nationaal Vakverbond in Nederland or CNV (CISC) which is the smallest and Protestant-oriented. The last is one of the very few Protestant unions affiliated to the predominantly Catholic Christian International.

636

Luxembourg. Even this tiny country has its own trade union split between the largest Confédération Générale de Travail or CGT (Luxembourg), which is Social Democrat and affiliated to the ICFTU, and the LCGB (CISC) which is Christian Democrat.

EFTA

Britain has the largest trade union movement in Europe, and it is united in one national centre, the Trades Union Congress or TUC (ICFTU), which has gained increasingly in stature and influence, is represented on a wide range of public bodies, and is strongly organised industrially. It has been consulted on matters of public policy by all governments in recent years although it has close affinity with the Labour Party in that many of its members are also Party members, and the unions contribute to Party funds.

Sweden. Trade unions are united in the one national centre known as the Landsorganisationen I Sverige or LO (ICFTU), which is extremely influential politically and industrially, has the closest links with the Social Democratic government, contributes to Party funds, and has the largest percentage of organised labour anywhere. The LO closely cooperates in a national incomes policy and it reflects the modernity and scientific approach to all problems that is characteristic of Swedish society. Regarded as a model by many unions in other countries.

Norway has a similar trade union organisation to Sweden's, even down to the name of the federation, Landsorganisasjonen i Norge or LO (ICFTU), its affinity with the Social Democrats and its substantial support of them. Though of high standing, the Norwegian LO is not quite as strong industrially as the Swedish.

Denmark. The Danish trade union federation, De samvirkende Fagvorbund or DSF (ICFTU), is the only major trade union national centre and it is Social Democrat-oriented. It is organisationally fairly strong and has political influence.

Austria. The trade union federation known as Österreichischer Gewerkschaftsbund or ÖGB (ICFTU) effectively straddles the Social Democrat–Christian Democrat division in the country and is comparatively well organised and efficient, with significant political influence.

Switzerland. The federation known as Union Syndicale Suisse or USS (ICFTU) accounts for the bulk of trade union membership but has competition from much smaller Roman Catholic and Protestant national centres (both CISC). The USS, at least, has considerable (including political) influence in the country.

Portugal. There appears to be no genuine trade union movement operating in Portugal, or if there is it has no contacts with any other European movements, national or international.

OTHER WESTERN EUROPEAN COUNTRIES

Ireland. Since 1959 the unions in the North have been united with those in the Republic within the Irish Congress of Trade Unions, or ICTU. Those in the North are mostly affiliated to the British TUC in addition. Both sections of the movement are consulted by their respective governments although recognition first occurred in 1964 in Ulster. Some unions affiliate to their Labour Parties both in the North and the Republic. The unions are fairly strongly organised in many parts of Ireland and can be surprisingly militant and even stubborn when occasion demands.

Greece. The main movement is the Greek General Confederation of Labour, known as the GSEE (ICFTU). It is lacking in strength and influence largely owing to an extended history of factional infighting and leadership problems. In 1964 the Greek government put restrictions on the movement including the appointment of government nominees to administer the national centre. The ICFTU unions in the EEC protested vigorously but the movement remains virtually under government control.

Turkey. Until a few years ago the unions were all local organisations with little strength and hardly any professional staff, but having a form of arbitration operating for settlement of differences with employers. Under the new state constitution, however, they are guaranteed the right to organise, to bargain collectively and to strike. They are gaining in strength and now operate federations of unions in various fields and have some national organisation including a national centre named TURKIS (ICFTU). Political influence is very limited and political affiliation frowned upon.

Spain. The ICFTU has not recognised any trade union movement operating inside Spain under the Franco regime, stating that they are not free or independent of the state. It has campaigned consistently against the imprisonment of Spanish trade unionists. The ICFTU does recognise, and has affiliated, a Spanish union in exile, the UGT, which fights against the regime. However, it appears that the trade unions inside the country have been able to throw off some of the Falangist ties more recently and one of them, the ASO or Spanish Workers' Alliance, appears to have been active in the militant industrial movement which embarrassed the regime and caused some small measures of liberalisation in 1964–5.

Finland. The Finnish trade union movement has had a chequered history, reaching its most powerful point about 1947; at that time it had very considerable political influence and a marked effect on the country's social and economic policies and legislation. Since then the leading confederation of trade unions, the SAK (ICFTU), which has close affinities with the Social Democratic Party, has experienced a number of internal difficulties causing many unions to break away. These gave rise to a new but smaller trade union federation, the SAJ (ICFTU), which now has competing sections in most industries. There are a number of other independent unions and also a sizeable confederation of civil servants and white-collar workers, the TVK.

Iceland. Because of the nature of the country and its small population, the unions are mainly organised on a geographical rather than a trade or industry basis, but there are some which are industrially based in the larger centres of population and some other unions especially for women. Most eligible workers belong to their union and most unions are affiliated to the Icelandic Federation of Labour or IFL (ICFTU). The IFL has considerable central powers in the trade union movement and there is a well regulated code of industrial relations, both legally and voluntarily based, reaching down to even very small employers of labour.

The Three Internationals

The Trade Union International with most affiliates, membership and influence in Western Europe is the International Confederation of Free Trade Unions (ICFTU), located in Brussels, with affiliates in each of the EEC and EFTA countries (except Portugal) and in Greece, Turkey, Finland and Iceland. Apart from its largest affiliate, the American AFL-CIO, the ICFTU is almost wholly Social Democrat-oriented. It has its own European regional organisation, also in Brussels, with separate secretariat, to which all ICFTU affiliates in the region belong. Its job is to coordinate overall European activities and policies, with particular attention to the wider problems of European integration, and especially bridge-building between the EEC and EFTA. But it has no permanent machinery as such for day-to-day coordination except a very small secretariat in Paris which promotes trade union liaison with the Organisation for Economic Cooperation and Development (OECD).

However, a separate organisation of ICFTU affiliates in EEC countries has been set up, with headquarters in Brussels, known as the European Trade Union Executive, again with its own secretariat. It not only acts as a day-to-day coordinator of national trade union policies on EEC matters, but the secretariat is itself a liaison office with the EEC, making representations to the Commission and being seated on various bodies. The Executive also has a network of sub-committees for specialised duties and coordination, the three main ones being for the Common Market, Euratom and the Coal and Steel Community.

The ICFTU itself has always strongly supported moves towards European integration and all its affiliates in Europe have done so as well, those in EEC countries having been by far the most enthusiastic. ICFTU affiliates in EFTA countries have supported EFTA but have otherwise been as cautious as their governments about committing themselves to the proposition of the EEC becoming the dominant and all-embracing group.

The Confédération Internationale des Syndicats Chrétiens (CISC) or International Federation of Christian Trade Unions is a very much smaller organisation than the ICFTU but has the bulk of its affiliated membership in Western Europe. Its only really significant national centres are in France, Belgium, the Netherlands, Luxembourg and Switzerland. It also has its headquarters in Brussels but it has rather less influence there with the EEC than has the ICFTU. The CISC has its own European Organisation which is an all-embracing organisation for European questions generally.

The CISC is predominantly Roman Catholic but also has a couple of small Protestant affiliates. Its practical differences with the ICFTU are mainly organisational but its trade union policies, especially on European integration questions, are very similar. A good deal of cooperation now takes place between the two organisations. Like the ICFTU, the CISC maintains close relations with the EEC Commission and coordinates the policies of its affiliates in the Six. It has no significant affiliates in the EFTA countries, except for Switzerland.

The third international, the Communist one called World Federation of Trade Unions (WFTU) with sizeable affiliates in France and Italy only, has always been opposed to the European Community in principle for political reasons and its French affiliate has largely followed this line. The Italian affiliate, however, has taken a much more favourable view of the EEC, socially and economically at least. There are now clear indications that both national organisations are coming to accept the Community as a hard fact of life and they are attempting to achieve the same liaison and representational facilities at Brussels as their rivals—something which, hitherto, they neither strove for with any enthusiasm nor were considered eligible for by their governments or by the European Commission. The WFTU has no specific European organisation within its structure although the French and Italian affiliates meet from time to time in an ad hoc joint committee to discuss European Community problems and policies.

INTERNATIONAL INFLUENCE OF WESTERN EUROPEAN UNIONS

ICFTU and CISC affiliates have representation on various Community organs, notably the Economic and Social Committee of the EEC and Euratom and the Consultative Committee of the ECSC. WFTU affiliates have no such representation. Union representatives who are seated on the various Community committees are consulted on most major matters of economic and social policy, along with employers' representatives and other interested bodies. The unions, particularly, feel that their international cohesion and coordination is good and that they have had in the past some influence on Community policies. Latterly, whilst still strongly supporting the Communities, they have been critical of what they regard as the slowness of its progress in several directions and what they feel is an overriding of trade union views on some issues.

In EFTA there is an Advisory Committee to the Ministerial Council, which includes trade unionists among its representatives, though it is not regarded as a very influential body. But as EFTA has no specific social programme, as does the EEC, and little economic programme other than the removal of trade barriers, the scope for such influence must necessarily be very restricted. Tending to reflect their respective governments' viewpoints, all the ICFTU affiliates support 'bridge-building' between the two trading groups, but EEC unions tend strongly to believe that eventually the only solution can be for EFTA countries to join the EEC. EFTA unions do not necessarily accept this.

Of the two trading groups the EEC has undoubtedly made the more rapid economic and social progress in recent years, although not all of this, of course, is due to the operation of the EEC. Five to ten years ago the EEC countries were significantly behind Britain and the Scandinavian countries in living standards and social benefits but now the gap has been narrowed and in some particulars the EFTA countries have been overhauled. One reason for this is the high coordination of EEC trade union activities, including exploitation in negotiations of anomalies in pay and conditions as between member countries. The following table compares the EEC and UK:

SOME EUROPEAN STANDARDS OF LIVING[1]

	Germany	France	Italy	Belgium	Netherlands	UK
Index of hourly gross wages in mid-1964 (1958=100)	167	156	172	133	161	128
Average hourly earnings in manufacturing industry, 1963[2]	6s 6d	4s 9d	5s 1d	5s 2d	5s 3d	7s 5d
Index of consumer prices (all items), November 1964 (1958=100)	115	130	127	112	120	117
Index of wage costs per unit of output, 1964 (1960=100)	114	112	117	—	—	107

[1] Sources: index of hourly gross wages and consumer prices from the monthly *General Statistical Bulletin of the European Communities*, Statistical Office of the European Communities, Brussels; average hourly earnings from the *Ministry of Labour Gazette*, London, November 1964; index of wage costs per unit of output from the Statistical Appendix to the quarterly *Economic Review*, National Institute of Economic and Social Research, London.

[2] Relates to all workers in Germany, France, Italy and Belgium but to adult men only in the Netherlands and the UK. These last two figures are therefore higher than a true comparison would give.

Up-to-date figures are not available on social security expenditure as a percentage of GNP but the following figures relating mainly to 1960 give some indication of the position in the EEC and EFTA:

SOCIAL SECURITY EXPENDITURE AS PERCENTAGE OF GNP IN EEC AND EFTA COUNTRIES[1]

Germany	16.5 per cent[2]	UK	11 per cent
France	13.4 per cent	Norway	10.3 per cent
Italy	12.7 per cent	Sweden	12.4 per cent
Belgium	15.1 per cent	Denmark	11.1 per cent
Netherlands	11.7 per cent[2]	Switzerland	7.7 per cent
		Austria	14.1 per cent
		Portugal	5.5 per cent

[1] Source: *Basic Statistics of the Community*, Statistical Office of the European Communities, Brussels, 1964.
[2] Relates to 1959.

PROBLEMS OF INTERNATIONALISM

The new moves towards internationalism have posed special problems for the trade union movements. In the EEC one of these is how the union movements are going to develop a supranational trade union movement as opposed to the high degree of national coordination that they have achieved at present. Eventually they will find that they cannot keep calling for the faster relinquishment of national sovereignty by EEC governments unless they are prepared to relinquish more themselves to the international trade union movement. There are, however, personal and other questions working against a quick solution.

A second problem is that of ensuring adequate social safeguards under the provisions for free circulation of labour. The gradual introduction of the provisions in the Community has been supported by the unions but the latter have, of course, demanded close surveillance. The significant level of economic planning in EEC countries in recent years has almost brought an end to the old unemployment bogies and unemployment of any serious proportions now exists only in pockets or regions, much the same as in Britain. There is no significant overall problem. A main problem facing the unions has been to obtain sensible social safeguards in case a bad recession should hit the Community at any time. The unions have helped to work these out, together with the highly complex migratory and social security transfer regulations which the EEC has brought into being.

A third and perhaps the biggest problem of all for the unions is their exact role in the Community's economic and social planning programmes. Virtually all unions in Western Europe now support the upward social harmonisation policy of the European Community, although, until recent years, some unions in EFTA countries feared this might hold up the more advanced nations whilst the stragglers caught up. In fact, some of the stragglers have not only caught up but have overtaken others, even though the leaders were still progressing. West Germany is the prime example. Her social security benefits, generally speaking, are now among the best in Europe.

The EEC unions themselves have naturally supported upward social harmonisation and have tried to get their own interpretation of it accepted. The principle was kept deliberately vague in the Rome Treaty, although the Treaty had one or two specific commitments such as equal pay for equal work for men and women and the free movement of labour. As far as other social benefits are concerned it now seems to be generally accepted that the policy requires all EEC member countries to work towards achieving the standard of the pacemaking country in any particular social benefit. Different countries differ in their needs and priorities, however, and for this reason complete uniformity is not the goal.

Upward social harmonisation is intended to define the trends to be pursued rather than the specific objects to be achieved and is a dynamic process wherein the pacemaking countries are still free to improve their own policies and benefits, even before others have caught up.

'READAPTATION' AND THE SOCIAL FUND

Perhaps the most interesting Community experiment has been in the use of the 'readaptation' programme in the Coal and Steel Community (ECSC), later modified and adopted in the EEC and Euratom and incorporated into their policy relating to the Social Fund. Readaptation in ECSC is a combination of measures designed to protect and socially cushion workers whose employment is threatened by the operation of the common market in coal and steel or as a result of profound changes in marketing conditions. The ECSC High Authority has wide powers to arrange for the re-employment of such workers in the same or other industries, including retraining them where necessary and making all provisions, financial and otherwise, for resettlement if they are moved, by mutual agreement, to another area. At the same time high unemployment allowances are paid to workers in the interim period between one job and the next, varying between approximately 70 per cent and 90 per cent of their previous wage. The High Authority has powers which have been used widely both to finance new industry coming into an area to absorb surplus labour and to set up housing schemes for Community workers, particularly when they move to new areas.

The implications of this readaptation policy for ensuring a high rate of technical progress in the coal and steel industries in the Community countries will be apparent. Technical change has been able to go ahead apace because the danger of heavy unemployment or social dislocation arising has been kept to a minimum. Neither has it proved generally difficult to close down redundant or uneconomic coal mines, although there have been exceptions to this in Belgium.

The Community trade unions have given strong support to the ECSC's readaptation scheme and have criticised the EEC provisions as being less favourable. The EEC set up a Social Fund for 'promoting within the Community employment facilities and the geographical and occupational mobility of workers'. However, it is less easy to use this fund to relieve pressing social needs as it works more slowly and has more procedural obstacles, notably that the government of the member country concerned must initiate the special aid, cannot be reimbursed for more than half of it and in any case not before a six-month waiting period has elapsed.

Thus no payments from the Community's Social Fund are made directly to the workers and the fund cannot be drawn upon except by government request, and then only after the workers concerned have managed to persuade the government to initiate a scheme. Given these snags, however, the operation of the Fund is ingeniously designed in that it is financed from predetermined contributions from member states and it is therefore in each state's interests to try and recoup some of this considerable outlay by initiating schemes whenever they seem necessary.

The Fund finances: (a) occupational retraining, (b) resettlement allowances, and (c) grants-in-aid to workers whose employment or remuneration would otherwise suffer owing to the conversion of their firm to other forms of production. This third provision is more limited in application than the ECSC readaptation scheme but it does make specific provision for assistance where firms are converting to new forms of production and it promotes technical change. All this is acceptable to the unions as far as it goes but it is not far enough for them. They have pressed for the fund to be strengthened by reducing its dependence on the prior action of governments, by extending its operations beyond the EEC transitional period and by increasing the funds available to it. The unions are represented on a committee which assists the European Commission in administering the fund, so their views have not gone unheard even though they have been so far largely unheeded.

Social policy in the Community is much wider than the above implies.[1] Article 118 of the EEC Treaty states the aim of promoting 'close collaboration between member states in the social field, particularly in matters relating to: employment; labour legislation and working conditions; occupational and continuation training; social security; protection against occupational accidents and diseases; industrial hygiene; the law as to trade unions, and collective bargaining between employers and workers'. The unions are naturally very active in insisting that nobody accepts a lower standard of living and that most people receive better conditions in all these fields. It is an enormous and complex undertaking for the Community to try and harmonise national laws and policies in all these matters, but the process is proceeding gradually.

COLLECTIVE BARGAINING

The manner in which the unions have set up their own new machinery in the European Community and in which they have been thrown together in their work at Community headquarters and seated on official bodies has had a significant effect on their activities and on their ordinary industrial negotiations. The unions have got used to thinking in Community terms rather than national terms, both in their policies and planning and in their collective bargaining techniques. The flow of information has greatly increased between member countries' unions and major conditions which are conceded in one country are immediately used as a basis of comparison in other countries. The employers on their part are more prone to accept the validity of these Community comparisons and to make more concessions than is usual. In other fields they are often dismissed by the employers as 'irrelevant' or 'not strictly comparable'.

There is thus a marked tendency in the Community for social and fringe benefits to be improved and for the national gaps between them to be narrowed. Wages and salaries are going up rather faster than in Britain (as shown in the table on page 640) and in most EFTA countries, although there is still considerable national variation within the Community. The reasons for this lie largely in the pace of improvement of the various economies and the differing bargaining powers of their unions. In spite of Community developments, which have been fast and extensive, there is nothing approaching international collective bargaining in operation as yet. It may well come within a few years as far as some fringe benefits are concerned, but it is likely that the real power and influence of unions and of employers

[1] See the chapter entitled 'The Structure of the European Community' (pp. 578–9).

in bargaining wages and salaries will continue to be disposed of at national level for many years. After all, the Community is not an employer in the general sense and collective bargaining is still conducted with thousands of individual employers or with state corporations.

FUTURE PROSPECTS

The prospects for further developments in trade union structure and policies in Western Europe depend on a variety of factors. One of these is the political complexion of the governments of Community members. All unions strongly oppose President de Gaulle's policies towards the Community and the French and German unions generally have been feeling for some years that they are having a difficult job influencing their governments. Neither at national nor at Community level is the deference paid to their views to which they believe they are entitled and this inevitably reflects itself in the Community's various institutions.

Another factor which will be very significant for trade union interests and influence is the future structure of the EEC. If the European Parliament is eventually given greater powers of supervision and if it becomes an elected body as the unions hope, their influence will be increased because they have close ties and connections with those who may well be among the most influential Deputies. The existing Parliament has already supported several policies first propounded by the unions. If, on the other hand, as is happening at present, the balance of power in the Community tilts more towards the Council of Ministers and away from the Commission, the trade unions can expect to receive a decreasing amount of sympathy for their views.

Again, if the unions expect to attract greater deference than at present they will have to consider an even stronger and more cohesive form of supranational organisation for themselves than that existing. At present they have coordination—what they need is integration. The need is not only at the international but also at the national level. It must include an abatement of the rivalries which exist between the various national centres in each EEC member country.

As far as the unions in the EFTA countries are concerned, they play little part in the working of the Association. They have occasionally protested about this, but have not made a major issue of it. If a wider grouping comprising EFTA and EEC countries were brought into being they would certainly expect a more extensive role. Should there be further attempts to achieve EEC membership for these countries the unions would harbour at least some doubts about the wisdom of the policy but would most probably back their governments' decisions and set about gaining the maximum influence and representation for themselves alongside their EEC colleagues.

The policies which the unions have so far pursued at national and international levels in Western Europe are encouraging in that they are forward-looking and take the broad view about economic and social affairs. They fully appreciate the benefits and what they believe to be the inevitability of European integration—economic, social and political, and generally speaking they want to speed up the process.

If the unions were to lose influence it would be a setback for democratic processes. Both the EEC and to some extent EFTA have the unions to thank for the popular and articulate support which these associations enjoy. Only the unions have consistently spoken for the ordinary people in support of integration. Their opposition could certainly have made things difficult in the EEC and governments have sometimes been slow to recognise the value of this support. Union views have, of late, often been ignored or arbitrarily rejected and union requests for improved representation, even in a consultative capacity, have been negatively received. There are strong indications that now the Community's existence seems much less in danger of being jeopardised through criticism, some of the unions' demands may be backed up by more militant action than hitherto. However, there is no doubt that if French national policies were pushed so far as to represent a real danger to the Community's existence, the unions would be the first to rally to its defence.

BIBLIOGRAPHY

Beever, R. Colin. *European Unity and the Trade Union Movements*, Sythoff, Leyden; Lounz, New York, 1960. *Trade Unions and the Common Market*, Political and Economic Planning, London 1962.

Galenson, Walter (ed.). *Comparative Labor Movements*, Prentice-Hall, New York, 1952.

Kitzinger, U. W. *The Challenge of the Common Market*, Blackwell, Oxford, 1961.

La Palombara, Joseph Guido. *The Italian Labor Movement*, Cornell Univ. Press, Ithaca, N.Y., 1957.

Lorwin, Lewis L. *The International Labor Movement*, Harper and Bros., New York, 1963.

Pinder, John. *Britain and the Common Market*, Cresset Press, London, 1961.

Schur, Val. *Labour in Britain and the Six*, Economist Intelligence Unit, London, 1962.

Shanks, Michael and Lambert, John. *Britain and the New Europe*, Chatto and Windus, London, 1962. Published in the United States as *The Common Market Today—and Tomorrow*, Frederick A. Praeger, New York, 1963.

ICFTU, Brussels. *The Austrian Trade Union Movement*, 1956. *The British Trade Union Movement*, 1954. *The Danish Trade Union Movement*, 1961. *The French Trade Union Movement*, 1953. *The Norwegian Trade Union Movement*, 1956.

Swiss Federation of Trade Unions. *The Trade Unions in Switzerland*, Berne, 1947.

UK Council of the European Movement, *Our Social Services and the Common Market* (report of the Social Services Conference organised by the UK Council, London, February 1962), London, 1962.

BRITAIN AND THE EUROPEAN COMMUNITY

JOHN CALMANN

OBSTACLES TO ENTRY

PRIME MINISTER HAROLD WILSON's aim of getting Britain into the European Community, stated in a number of cautious speeches in November 1966, drew little positive response from the Continent. The five Common Market countries supposedly favourable to British entry (i.e. all members except France) merely noted the statements, and the Common Market Commission gave its guarded approval. The French reaction was particularly cool, and showed no change from the position taken by Prime Minister Georges Pompidou in London in July of the same year. It was clear that France still found difficulty in accepting Britain as a real partner in Europe. The old arguments about Britain 'not being ready for the Treaty of Rome' were gone through again, even though this time they no longer carried the conviction that they once did.

For it now seems clear that both major British political parties have committed themselves to entering the European Community. Their reasons for accepting the aims of the Community after so much hesitation are varied, but basic to both the Conservative and the Labour approaches (the Liberals have always been in favour of entry) is the understanding that the Common Market represents a new force on the continent of Europe to which Britain cannot apparently provide a more attractive alternative—a force which will change, and to some extent already has changed, relationships between the members, for the Community provides a formal and institutional recognition of the interdependence of European states. Britain's difficulty in accepting such a systematic approach to relations with its neighbours has been due to the memory of a vast empire and great influence outside Europe, a memory that maintained the illusion of self-sufficiency. As will be seen, a majority in both major British parties has gradually come to recognise that self-sufficiency is no longer possible, and that whatever the cost of entering may be, the cost of staying out of the Community will probably be higher.

It is impossible, of course, to draw up a realistic balance sheet of the advantages and disadvantages of Britain's joining the Community. What seems likely is that some industries in which Britain is fairly strong, such as chemicals and fibres, mechanical engineering and automobiles, electronics and computers, and nuclear energy, would profit from the enormously expanded market provided by the Community. On the other hand, while the standard of living of Britain's farmers might improve through the

Common Agricultural Policy, Britain's cost of living might gradually rise as a result of an increase in the cost of food—according to some estimates the rise might be between 3 and 4 per cent. The effect on Britain's balance of payments might also be considerable, in that the Common Agricultural Policy requires countries which import food from outside the Community to pay levies on such imports into a common fund to be used for various purposes within it. If Britain joined several other countries would join as well; this could lead to modifications both in the levy system itself and in the level of payments expected from each member country. It is also possible that once Britain had joined the Community the basic methods of the Common Agricultural Policy might be changed, if it were found that it was seriously detrimental to the economy of any of the member countries.

One of the advantages of the Treaty is that it leaves the political future of the Community vague. It indicates that political union in some form is desirable, but the Six have not yet progressed very far here. Far from this uncertainty being a disadvantage for Britain, as some British critics of the Community have suggested, it provides a formidable opportunity for British statesmen to contribute something of their own to the development of the Community, for it is in the field of political institutions that Britain is most respected and admired in Europe. Political possibilities may be of even greater significance in the long run, perhaps, than the advantage of a wider market and of a planned international economy.

France's reluctance to accept Britain's desire for membership of the Community as genuine derives more from its own uncertainties about Britain than from Britain's uncertainties about the nature of the Community and what it will lead to. France's views are today very different from those of its partners on this question.

At the same time, while the other five member countries believe that British membership of the Community is desirable, they are not prepared to risk anything for it, at least not as long as there is no positive sign that Britain is really committed to entry. After the break-down of the negotiations with Britain in January 1963 it emerged that the Five were not prepared to risk a split inside the Community with France while Britain itself was divided on the issue. Their attitude would become more positive if Britain took some new initiative of its own towards Europe. As will be seen later, however, one of the main difficulties in the British approach to the problem of entry is that most of those concerned with it are hypnotised by France's opposition. In so far as this opposition is real their position is understandable; it is, however, unproductive of change, and has led to an atmosphere of deadlock, in spite of Wilson's attempts to restart negotiations.

Many reasons have been given for French intransigence, and especially that of President de Gaulle, who has paradoxically enough also shown the keenest desire to collaborate with Britain in one limited field, the aircraft industry. Since this industry is one where the British are in a stronger position than the French, in that the British industry is larger and technically more varied, the President's willingness or unwillingness to work with Britain is clearly not dictated by fear of British power and resources. On the contrary, in the summer of 1966 Pompidou seemed to be saying that Britain's current economic weaknesses meant that the country would have to wait until they had passed before it could apply for membership of the Community. One of the strongest reasons Britain has for joining, however, is the feeling that some of these difficulties would be overcome through membership. The 'cold blasts', 'axes' and 'squeezes' applied by the Labour government, meant to 'shake up' the British economy, might be obtained through the strong competition offered from the Continent, if Britain were in the Community. Above all Britain needs help with its balance of payments difficulties; to cure these it needs the continued support of its European partners. But it is precisely this support which France is reluctant to offer, for what seem to be political reasons.

Britain finds itself therefore in a deadlock with France. This is a situation which the French sometimes appear ready to exploit, thereby casting doubt on the validity of their reasons for keeping Britain out and refusing to admit the possibility of renewed negotiations. Apparently France under de Gaulle still seeks a form of national independence in which few other Western European states believe today. Military strength is still, according to some French theorists, the ultimate source of power, and economic strength important mainly in that it is needed for military strength. Thus France sets aside a large proportion (about half) of its military expenditure on the *force de frappe*—its atomic weapons system—and accuses Britain of being subservient to the United States. France regards the European Community as a method of reinforcing its economy, but does not consider that membership binds it to accept all the implications of the Treaty of Rome, such as a directly elected European parliament, common funds centrally administered, or even a common trade policy towards countries outside the Community. In other words the Community is a mechanism, in the Gaullist view, to help each member-nation survive; it is not an end in itself. Britain is a European nation with which France must remain a friendly rival; Britain's weaknesses are useful to France, therefore there is no reason to help Britain overcome them. And while a serious economic crisis in Britain, reflected in mass unemployment or a large decline in imports, is something which would possibly harm France too, a series of economic difficulties which merely hamstring its government need cause the French government little or no concern.

THE NEGOTIATIONS 1961–3: THREE MAIN PROBLEMS

France's attitude to British entry was not always as adamant; during the long negotiations from the autumn of 1961 until January 1963, France appeared, at first at any rate, to be willing to consider British membership. This is not the place to discuss the failure of these negotiations, except in so far as they revealed certain basic problems which for a long time afterwards dominated British attitudes to the Community. The seemingly interminable discussions surrounding the problems of British agriculture and of Commonwealth trade held up the negotiations for about nine months (March–December 1962), and there can be no doubt that the effect of this was not merely to disillusion the British, but also to make the French, the principal protagonists on the other side, suspect that Britain did not want to accept the Community's rules. As many writers on this subject have pointed out, these rules were made very much with French agriculture in mind.

Britain's support system and tradition of importing from cheap Commonwealth producers (who, according to the French and the Common Market Commission, are subsidised also) was changed from being a technical stumbling block into becoming a major political issue on which the British government was apparently prepared to see the negotiations stand or fall. This was probably a tactical error, for it gave de Gaulle a good opportunity to consider the probable effect of membership on the balance of forces in the

Community (and in Europe generally) much more carefully. Britain's acceptance from America of the Polaris submarine and missile system at Nassau in December 1962, a meeting from which France was excluded, confirmed him in the view that Britain could not become his partner. In Britain, however, the view persisted for some time after the French veto of 14 January 1963 on Britain's entry into the Community that agriculture and Commonwealth trade were fundamental issues, and to these two was added, particularly in the mind of the Labour Party, the question of the other countries of the European Free Trade Association (EFTA) and Britain's commitment to see that an arrangement was made between them and the Community also.

Agriculture

The insistence, however, with which the British government originally spoke of safeguards for these 'essential interests', which were required before Britain could enter the Community, was probably unnecessary. The Community's objective must obviously be to protect the essential interests of the member countries; it is the Commission's business to discover what these are, and, if necessary, to try to reorientate government thinking about them in new directions. The problems of British entry, in any case, can be said to fall, like most of those with which the Commission has to deal, into 'technical' and 'political' categories. The 'technical' are those on which the governments have committed themselves to find a solution; the 'political' imply that governments have not yet been convinced of the necessity to act, and are using talks and negotiations as a method of protecting special interests, inside their own countries. Under this definition the agricultural problem, for instance, is largely a 'technical' one, and if Britain has the 'political' will to be a member of the European Community an adequate solution to it could certainly be found. In other words, if the introduction of the Community's Common Agricultural Policy into Britain were regarded as part of the business which Britain would have to accomplish after signing the Treaty of Rome, instead of making accession to the Treaty dependent on settling agriculture first, Britain would probably find that its influence on how that policy was developed would be much greater.

The fact is that the Treaty of Rome is not regarded by most member countries as a trade arrangement but as the foundation of a new system of international relations between Western European states; the aim is to encourage both the economic development of members and their political cooperation. The effects of the Common Agricultural Policy of the Community may not be entirely to Britain's liking, especially where the question of balance of payments is concerned, but until Britain joins it is almost impossible to know exactly what the effect on the country would be, or what adjustments would have to be made to solve its special problems. It has been suggested by some agriculturists that British horticulture, poultry and dairy farming might all be adversely affected by the application of the Common Agricultural Policy; given a transition period (discussed below) and a reconsideration of problems such as these by a Commission in which British interests would be heard, it can be expected with some confidence that changes in the present structure of farming in Britain would be carried out sufficiently gradually to cushion farmers against adverse effects. In the latter half of 1966, indeed, the attitude of the British government to this question seemed to change so that agriculture is now talked of more as a problem which will have to be faced than as an insuperable obstacle to entry.

The Commonwealth

The Commonwealth problem has also changed since the time of the negotiations. It was then feared that the Community would continue to give preferences to the ex-French (and ex-Belgian) colonies in Africa, while the ex-British colonies and territories, which comprised much larger areas, much greater populations and a much wider variety of economies, would be neglected. It was the British government's aim that the 'white' Commonwealth should also find at least as great an outlet for its traditional exports as these countries (Australia, New Zealand and Canada) had found in Britain; at the same time the developing Commonwealth countries like India or Nigeria would obviously have to benefit from the Community's aid programmes. At the time it also seemed that some countries, like Nigeria, would simply shun the Community, and leave the Commonwealth if Britain entered it, because they regarded it as a 'neo-colonialist' enterprise.

All this was reversed soon after the negotiations collapsed. India, Nigeria and the countries of East Africa as well as the 'white' Commonwealth established their own direct relations with the Community and many have sought to obtain some form of trade or aid agreement with it. Such an agreement between Nigeria and the Community, held up by France's six-month-long defection from the Council of Ministers in 1965, came into force in 1966; the East African countries are still negotiating theirs. Canada, Australia and New Zealand have permanent representatives in Brussels, but no formal negotiations are yet in progress. Their exports will, however, be considered in the framework of the 'Kennedy Round' of trade negotiations in GATT which are still going on. The concessions made to India, Pakistan and Ceylon by the Community during the negotiations with Britain have in part at least been put into practice since; for instance, tea enters the Community free of duty or quota restrictions. The 'white' Commonwealth countries are also being encouraged by Britain to seek new markets, as Britain cannot by itself continue to provide a tied outlet for their exports while they protect their own industries with tariffs against British products. New Zealand seems to be the only one of these countries which is still heavily dependent on the British market for its lamb and butter.

Today the problem of the Commonwealth is in many ways more political than economic. Indeed, while the question of Commonwealth trade has turned out to be less important than it seemed in 1962, the question of Western Europe's relations with the rest of the world, developing or developed, has become more urgent; as the transformation of the old imperial relationship is completed, and as Britain gradually reduces its commitments in the Far East, it will be increasingly necessary for Europeans to look at the rest of the world as a whole, and not in terms of their own former relationships with various parts of it. The Community will no longer find it so easy to restrict its aid to France's ex-colonies or those of Belgium and the Netherlands, and will be under great pressure to consider providing outlets for goods from Latin America and Asia as well as Africa. Several Mediterranean countries (Morocco, Algeria, Tunisia, Israel and Yugoslavia) are engaged on negotiations with the Community already; Greece and Turkey have become associate members. Developed countries like Canada and Australia on the other hand will have to get more accustomed to establishing their own relationship with the countries that are nearer to them, especially in the Pacific, instead of assuming that their foreign policies can be managed from London or Washington or conducted on the basis of sentimental attachments to the mother country. Developed or not, all these countries seek help, material, technical and educational, from Europe (as well as hoping to sell there), and it is obviously going to be easier to answer this need if Europeans act in concert and pool their resources for aid, than if each country competes with its neighbours in trying to conserve its former sphere of influence.

This is a long-term political problem, which can probably be most usefully discussed after Britain has joined the Community; certainly the economic problems involved in Commonwealth trade, like those of agriculture, can be regarded as 'technical' and need not be obstacles to British entry any more. On the other hand the political problems involved are not likely to decrease with time, and far from dampening British enthusiasm for the Community the need for a common approach to the rest of the world should encourage Britain to seek membership. This, of course, involves the other EFTA countries as well.

EFTA

The British commitment to the EFTA countries took the form of promising them that Britain would not leave the organisation without finding some acceptable arrangements with the Six for all the members who wished to have them. This commitment was considered particularly important by the Labour opposition in Britain during the negotiations for entry into the Community; they felt it was a legitimate reason for withholding their support for the government's position in Brussels. Since the Labour Party has taken office, however, one EFTA country, Austria, has begun negotiations on its own with the Community, which may lead to its becoming an associate member and thus to its withdrawal from EFTA. The Danes have been held back by their loyalty to the British, and this is also true of the Norwegians; in the autumn of 1966, however, the Danish government began to show interest in making a separate approach. Portugal as a developing country is a special case, and will require special treatment should it wish to join the Community; Sweden and Switzerland remain, and it is unlikely that Britain would allow its entry into the Community to be held up by the neutralist qualms of these two countries.

The difficulty that the entry of the EFTA countries represents for the European Community is that it would add enormously to the heavy load of technical and administrative problems which the Commission has to bear. It would probably be hard for all the countries to join simultaneously, or to conduct their negotiations with the Community at once. The amount of special cases and special treatments each is likely to wish to discuss is considerable, and so a carefully organised timetable would have to be prepared in order to fit their membership in with Britain's. The pressure on the Commission would increase enormously, and it is possible that it would be forced to seek new powers, and greater scope to reach decisions quickly. This is all calculated to deter the French government, which sees no need to hurry the process of patching up the division of Europe represented by the existence of EFTA and the EEC, and which would not wish for any increase in the powers of the Commission which an extension of the Community's area might bring with it. Thus the main political difficulties associated with the entry of the EFTA countries into the Community (apart from the question of Switzerland's and Sweden's neutrality, which concerns them alone) come from French fears of what will happen to the Community; it is possible, however, that French attitudes to the progress of European integration will change under the pressure of circumstances. From the point of view of the

EFTA countries themselves the problems are technical, and membership of the Community is a question of time. It can be said, therefore, with some certainty that if Britain joined the Community, arrangements for dealing with the other EFTA countries would follow automatically, and would not provide an obstacle to British membership.

A Transition Period?

Thus the three great stumbling-blocks of the 1961–3 negotiations have been transformed, both in themselves and in the way the British government, manned by a party originally hostile to the Community, looks at them. These problems will be the stuff of future talks, but it is unlikely that they could hold them up once they had begun. The adjustment to Community methods and policies would have to be made gradually; that is to say not during the negotiations themselves, but during a 'transition period', in which Britain would be a member of the Community, take part in the discussions of the Council of Ministers and contribute to the development of the common policies. In this period Britain could also adapt its agricultural system to fit in with that of the Community, seek to establish the basis of a new relationship with the Commonwealth countries and bring in its EFTA partners as well as introduce the many tariff and tax (and other) changes which the Six have already effected within the Community.

All this would require a large number of administrative changes, and could therefore not be done overnight. The length of such a transition period would be a major item of the negotiations; it would probably have to be fairly long, possibly five years or more. If there were no time-limit, or if a longer limit were set, the application of the Community's system might be spun out indefinitely by governments unwilling to sacrifice support from voters who might for a short while be adversely affected by the changes. The supporters of British entry both on the Continent and in Britain have frequently said in the last few years that the next round of negotiations should be short and successful: by allowing for a transition period this would become much easier to achieve administratively speaking.

The commitment by all major parties to seek British membership is to some extent a reflection of the fundamental recognition by the British public that the country can no longer survive on its own, that the British need their neighbours, just as in the long run their neighbours need them. The Conservative Party has repeatedly declared its commitment to getting Britain 'into Europe', but its influence in opposition is largely a propagandist one, and it cannot decide policy. There also seems to be a tendency among Tories to seek arrangements with General de Gaulle, as if British membership depended only on him; there is no interest in finding closer ties with West Germany. This attitude is also present in the Labour government's policy, which rests on French objections and apparently sees no alternative to wooing or threatening France. At the same time the Labour Party, since coming into office, has moved significantly closer to accepting the Treaty of Rome, and in November 1966 the government made it clear that membership of the Community is the principal aim of British policy in Europe.

Getting Support For Britain

The difficulty is going to be to convince all concerned of British sincerity, especially France under de Gaulle. It is widely felt among advocates of

British entry that the first aim ought to be to get active support for British membership from among the Five, who have not so far shown themselves willing to take any risks on Britain's behalf. For them to become so willing, the British government must give a clear indication that its commitment to Europe comes first. A new approach from Britain is the answer to this problem, not a passive acceptance of the status quo accompanied by complaints of French intransigence, which has been the basis of the discussion in Britain so far.

The history of British relations with the Six since the war can be said to fall roughly into three stages. First, until the end of the 1950s Britain remained suspicious and even hostile to all proposals to integrate the economies, the defence, or the political structure of Western Europe, and stuck to the 'three-circle' theory, of each of which Britain was a member: the Commonwealth, the Atlantic world and the United States, and Europe. The second stage came when Prime Minister Harold Macmillan became aware that Britain was going to be excluded from an important economic development in the shape of the Common Market, and proposed that the Six should join with Britain and other European countries in a Free Trade Area; this was rejected by the Six as being too loose a structure. The third development was the commitment to Europe which the Conservative government made in 1961 when it opened the negotiations to join the Common Market. This commitment was hidden from the public, because Macmillan feared the consequences for his party if his hand was too openly revealed; it is also possible that neither he nor his ministers, including Edward Heath, were fully aware of the political implications of starting these negotiations.

In effect the negotiations began a process of education in Britain, through which all the major political groups attached to both main parties found they had to take the development of the Community seriously. Instead of the Rome Treaty being, as Labour Leader Hugh Gaitskell seemed to think it was, a trade arrangement which aimed to hamstring governments and prevent socialist policies, it was clearly the basis of a major political institution, which in due course became important enough even for General de Gaulle to attack it. In 1965–6 it became increasingly clear that the development of such a political institution is something which has captured the imaginations not only of the British civil service, and the Foreign Office in particular, but of some members of the government. But as we have seen, Britain is apparently still faced by the stone wall of France's objections.

This is because Britain has not yet reached the fourth stage of attempting an initiative itself towards Europe, one which does not merely pose the problem of British commitment to the Community, but which offers the Six something new. One reason for this is that the 1966 Labour government is still a recent if not reluctant convert to the idea of close ties with Europe, and apparently still fears anything which would diminish what the Prime Minister refers to as 'our sovereignty'. Leaving aside the philosophical vagueness of this term, the practical implications are that the government is reluctant to commit itself as yet to a European policy which might yield some results. One advantage for the Prime Minister in taking over the Conservative position on the Common Market is that it has no immediate consequences. In fact, new ideas which could come from Britain about a possible European technological union and a new common defence organisation to replace NATO, on both of which Britain has plenty to offer its neighbours, are mentioned only in passing, or kept in files far from the light of day.

New British Initiatives

Technological union

Such ideas have, however, been mooted for some time now by active 'Europeans' in Britain and by those concerned with preparing policy in Whitehall. It is impossible here to give more than a rough sketch of what they involve but it is worthwhile to mention them even if only very shortly, because in 1967–8 it is possible that the transformation of Britain's relations with the rest of Western Europe will involve a radical new departure. By 'technological union' is meant an organisation which would attempt to pool the resources of its member countries in a number of advanced technological industries. These include air transport, computers, nuclear energy and space, all of which are fields in which European countries have already begun to work, but in which Britain still has a lead in Europe. In Britain these industries employ more people than in any other European country, and most important of all, the extent of the research and development effort in Britain in these fields is larger also. What Britain lacks at present is the ability to increase this effort, mainly because the cost of doing so is greatly beyond the resources of a country of Britain's size, and also because the country lacks the qualified manpower. Britain is trying to cooperate to some extent with France in the aircraft industry (where it has too much manpower), but the aim of a technological union would be to go well beyond the limits of bilateral cooperation in one industry. The aim would be to help those countries, which, like Germany, have access to capital but have little or no research and development effort and limited technological resources. Indeed it is in the technological field that Britain would probably find Germany most interested in becoming its partner.

The way such a technological union might work is for the member countries to set up a joint institution, which would be given funds for research and for aid to investment in the industries concerned; these funds would be fixed for a defined period, probably about five years. The institution would have powers to direct research into fields which it felt were particularly important and to make sure that the results of such work were published or made available to interested parties in the member countries; this would avoid the duplication of effort which the existence of several national programmes in Europe makes inevitable today. Britain's particular contribution could be to provide scientists and engineers for joint research schemes. The institution would also have funds to use for investment in the industries concerned, much as the High Authority of the ECSC has been able to help the modernisation of the coal and steel industries of the Community with special investment aid. The introduction of automated methods of production, frequently feared by both management and labour for its possibly disruptive effects, might be furthered by programmes financed by this common institution and aimed at training people in new methods and especially in the use of computers, and at helping workers who became redundant through the introduction of labour-saving systems. (This particular aspect of modernisation has been very successfully dealt with in the ECSC through the High Authority's 'readaptation schemes' which have helped about 200,000 redundant coal-miners in the Six. A technological union would probably not have to deal with such large numbers, but the methods used in coalmining could probably be applied in other industries also).

If Britain were anxious to discuss such a plan with Germany it might find a much more lively and positive response than for its perennial attempts to get the Germans to cover the currency loss involved in British expenditure on troops in Germany by buying British equipment. The Germans have pointed out time and time again that they are not interested in buying things they do not need, just in order to help with balance of payments problems. A much more sensible approach would be to find out what the Germans do need, and then to seek to make arrangements with them which would have attractions for both sides. For Britain there would be not only the advantage of more amiable and productive cooperation with Germany in the advanced technological industries, in which Germany's needs are great (and its dependence on the United States burdensome) but also the political asset that Britain would at last find an active partner in Europe. Other countries would of course be encouraged to join, and it is likely that Italy, Benelux and the Scandinavian countries would also be interested; and France could not long remain on its own.

An approach on defence

On the defence side, Britain is at present engaged on talks with Germany and the United States on the question of reducing the number of troops stationed in Germany—though the reasons for this are more to do with balance of payments than with strategy. (It also seems to be the belief of the United States government that this is a way of reaching new agreements with the Soviet Union.) France has withdrawn from active support of NATO though still committed under Article 5 of the NATO treaty to come to the defence of its allies in the event of their being attacked. The unreality of the present NATO system, with its heavy dependence on the American nuclear deterrent, its lack of a joint procurement system, its separate but individually ineffective national forces (as far as the European members are concerned) and its lack of a common concept of present-day strategic needs, is beginning to make itself felt in Europe; lip-service is paid to the NATO idea, but each country is beginning to seek a new understanding with Eastern Europe on its own, and the outlook for joint procurement of weapons has never been so bleak.

If Britain were to seek to create a new European defence system, based on close cooperation with Germany and allied to the United States (something which the Americans themselves seem to be advocating now) but on the basis of a new treaty, it is possible that the idea would gain considerable political support on the Continent. The object of the treaty would be to try to create a common European approach to defence problems, without France, if need be, in the initial stages. (The mistake being made currently in the Conservative Party is to suppose that a pooling of French and British nuclear forces would have the same psychological effect; the French are simply not interested in such an idea, and the rest of Europe, and especially the Germans, would regard it as an attempt by the two countries least committed to European integration to dominate the rest. The government, by comparison, remains entirely preoccupied with NATO on the one hand, and attempting to get 'off-set' payments from Germany on the other, and disregards the need for a 'European' approach to defence altogether.)

COMMITMENT WITHOUT A POLICY

In both these fields, advanced technology and defence, Britain still seems determined to 'go it alone'. In the aircraft industry, it is true, Britain is cooperating with France, but both countries are doing this with glances over their shoulders to see what chances there are of surviving on their own. This industry is too limited, and the market available probably too small for this form of cooperation to be much more than an administrative experiment. In defence the government is still not certain whether Europe is its main commitment or whether Britain needs to be involved in the Far East, and is still deeply concerned with a 'special relationship' with the United States, whose existence is, however, hard to prove. The main difficulty Britain has in getting into the Community, if such is its aim, is to get enough political support from the Five to make France feel that it will be out on a limb if a veto on British entry is attempted a second time. This support can be obtained only by positive measures, initiatives such as those described above, which would prove that Britain is now prepared to merge its future completely with that of its neighbours in the Community.

In January 1967 it was clear that French policy was aimed at holding up British entry for as long as possible. Direct refusal to consider the question had so far been ruled out, partly because General de Gaulle was afraid of the effects such a move would have on the French parliamentary elections, and partly because the French government was becoming more aware of the limitations of nationalistic policies in Europe and their isolating effects. The possibility of spinning out the preliminary talks, by introducing irrelevancies such as the price of gold, remained open to him, however, with the result that this preliminary phase appeared likely to take a long time. It was, of course, possible that Wilson and Brown, in their diplomatic assault on the Six in January and February 1967, would persuade the five countries favourable to British entry to seek to force France to accept the new member, if necessary with threats to leave France on its own. This, however, was an unlikely development. In any event Wilson's commitment to entering the Common Market, however ambiguously it has sometimes been expressed, and whatever the motives for it may originally have been, has had the effect of strengthening the position of the institutions of the European Community and their supporters in the Six, and means that the aims of some of their critics, such as General de Gaulle, who wish seriously to modify their influence on member governments and nations, are going to be more difficult to realise. Thus, in spite of his former doubts about its value Wilson's approach to the European Community has made a real contribution to its vitality and this in itself will perhaps ensure that Britain will become a member, however long it takes.

BIBLIOGRAPHY

Beloff, Nora. *The General Says No: Britain's Exclusion from Europe*, Penguin, London, 1963; Peter Smith, Gloucester, Mass., 1964.

Calleo, David. *Europe's Future: The Grand Alternatives*, Horizon Press, New York, 1965.

Camps, Miriam. *Britain and the European Community, 1955–63*, Oxford Univ. Press, London and New York, 1964. *What Kind of Europe?*, Oxford Univ. Press, London and New York, 1965.

Gladwyn, Lord. *The European Idea*, Weidenfeld and Nicolson, London; Frederick A. Praeger, New York, 1966.

Pinder, John. *Europe Against de Gaulle*, Pall Mall, London; Frederick A. Praeger, New York, 1963.

Economist, London, 14 May 1966 (issue entitled *Europe in a Shrinking World*).

EEC. *Report to the European Parliament on the Negotiations between Great Britain and the Six*, Brussels, February 1963.

Journal of Common Market Studies, III, 3, July 1965 (issue entitled *The Future of Britain's Relations with Europe*), Basil Blackwell, Oxford.

Opera Mundi-Europe: A Weekly Report on the Economy of the Common Market, European Intelligence Ltd, Tunbridge Wells, Kent.

THE FUTURE OF INTEGRATION

RICHARD MAYNE

'WE don't know where we're going—we only know we're going there together.' The words may seem reminiscent of one of the British army's less intelligent marching songs; they were in fact the answer given by a very wideawake staff member of the Common Market Commission to a journalist who asked him about the future of the Six. Like many non-committal statements, this one contained a grain of truth. Until June 1965 there seemed little doubt that the Common Market countries were engaged in an irreversible process of economic and political unification, which other nations of Europe, including Britain, were one day likely to join. The only points at issue appeared to be the speed, shape, scope and orientation of the joint endeavour. Various hypotheses were conceivable and had been conceived: there was even a discernible progression from somewhat simple models to more sophisticated concepts, from vague formulations to precise if optimistic targets. The dust kicked up by the winding column of Eurocrats and others sometimes obscured the horizon; but its scouts, at least, had occasional glimpses of the promised land.

In June 1965, however, Europe's prospects were suddenly clouded with doubt and apprehension. Two years earlier, when President de Gaulle had killed the British negotiations on the pretext that they were already dying, the European Economic Community had suffered its first crisis of confidence; now, for the first time, it looked as if it might break up. The destructive act was again that of President de Gaulle, and again he had a pretext: his five partners, he said, had failed to keep their promise to agree on farm finance regulations by midnight on 30 June; and so, instead of pursuing the search for a solution, the French government withdrew from the Common Market Council of Ministers, refusing to do more than allow the Community to mark time. The point at issue seemed to be majority voting in the Council, scheduled to begin in 1966: but the real question was the General's objection to collective decision-making. Although a compromise appeared to be reached in January 1966, large question marks still hung over the Community's future during that year.

CONFUSED UTOPIAS

The earliest days of European unification, in the late 1940s and early 1950s, were marked by a degree of semantic confusion perhaps unrivalled since the *filioque* controversy. What was 'Europe'? What was 'unity'? The failure to ask these fundamental questions, or at least to agree on the answers, led to much fruitless debate: 'federalists' and 'functionalists', in particular, charged regularly past each other in the verbal tournaments of the Council of Europe;

657

and the 'European Movement' grouped under its multicoloured banners the partisans of several mutually exclusive political creeds. Academic students of the period may tend to smile in retrospect, forgetting that their own clarity of vision owes much to the accumulated efforts of busy, preoccupied men who had to think out what they were doing while they were trying to do it.

What visions of Europe's future, then, guided those who pioneered her unity? Perhaps the simplest was a rejection of the past. 'Europe was not built' said the Schuman Declaration of 9 May 1950, 'and we had war'. The aim was more than simply to prevent war between France and Germany. In 1950, with Hitler's defeat only five years away and trouble brewing over the Ruhr and the Saar, this in itself was no mean ambition; yet beyond lurked vaster, vaguer prospects. 'For peace to have a real chance, there must first be a Europe.' 'The contribution that an organised and living Europe can bring to civilisation is indispensable to the maintenance of peaceful relations.' What, at that time, did such phrases mean?

For Jean Monnet, initiator of the Schuman Plan, the ultimate vision seemed then to be a federation of the West. It was the time of the beginnings of the 'cold war', and with them the first steps towards 'Atlantic' groupings. If the Schuman Declaration spoke of 'the European federation which is indispensable to the maintenance of peace', it was a federation conceived in a wider Western framework, perhaps even as a first model for some kind of universal order.

FEDERAL ORDER

In so far as European unity was thus regarded as the germ of law and order in the world, it clearly hearkened back to its own theoretical origins. The various unsuccessful utopians who throughout the centuries had preached the unity of Europe had most often had in mind a universal system: the reason was simply that for them Europe was the heart of the world. By the end of the second world war such cosy illusions were no longer tenable; but in the first days of the peace, from Bretton Woods and San Francisco agreements onwards, attempts were made to achieve some kind of unity on a world scale. It was natural, therefore, that some of those who later championed federalism in Europe should speak and write in terms which suggested that they saw it as a pilot plant for federalism in the world. Again, it would be easy to deride such notions, particularly in Great Britain, where the word 'federalism' seems often to be associated with crankishness, despite the federal solutions so frequently offered by British governments to post-colonial problems. Nonetheless, it can hardly be denied that the success of quasi-federal organisation in Europe would do much to vindicate the notion, and that some at least of its lessons might later stand a chance of being applied elsewhere. If, for example, a quasi-federal system succeeded in reconciling France and Germany only a few years after they had been at each others' throats, the advocates of such systems would have a partial answer to the reproach that they were starry-eyed in supposing similar progress one day possible in relations between East and West.

Already, however, exegesis of even so primitive a nature probably makes too explicit the ultimate aims of the federalist wing of early 'Europeans'. For the time being, and in the unpromising 'cold-war' context of the early 1950s, they were content to act where action was possible. This, essentially, was in the territory of the six countries that adopted the Schuman Plan—France, Germany, Italy and Benelux. 'Europe', for the moment, was what its detractors then called 'Little Europe'; and its theoretical model was at first fairly simple. The original Schuman Plan invested most of its political capital in the High Authority, based partly on the International Ruhr Authority, a short-lived organisation which was created in 1949 by Britain, the United States and France. To begin with, there was no provision even for a Council of Ministers, although this emerged very early in the Schuman Plan negotiations. 'Authority' was the key word; and the High Authority's own publicists later stressed this aspect of the organisation with almost forbidding relish. 'Supra-national' was another favourite expression at the time. In some degree it was justified as a dramatisation of what was, after all, a striking novelty; but it led to misapprehensions—among the champions of European unity as well as its opponents—about the likely shape of united Europe's political future. Even 'federalism', so often regarded in Britain as impracticably extremist, in fact prescribes decentralised as well as centralised decision-making.

THE SINGLE-STATE HYPOTHESIS

A close study of the political institutions of the United States might have helped to avoid some misunderstanding of this sort; but the slogan 'The United States of Europe' was often employed in the early 1950s by those whose vision of the future was based on the 'single-state hypothesis', as it may be called. The supposition, that is, was that as Europe advanced towards political unity, through the Schuman Plan, the European Defence Community, and so on, the member countries of the Community would gradually assume the characteristics of a single nation, perhaps with a European patriotism or even nationalism to complete the analogy with the nation-states of the past.

Monnet himself never espoused this particular doctrine. His own view of Europe, as expressed in his writings and speeches, from the first laid greater emphasis on the 'organisational' aspect of Europe and its exemplary value as embodying common rules and institutions. He did, however, liken the acceptance of law-and-order by nations in international affairs to its acceptance by the citizens of any one country in their relations with each other, and this may at times have seemed to support the single-state hypothesis with which he disagreed. Others, moreover, and especially the various promoters of Europe's cultural unity, tended to display in mild forms a European patriotism which in politics might have seemed less innocuous.

Similar tendencies emerged later in some of the theorising about the Common Market. Here the aim was clearly enough to establish among the six member countries a single market and a single economy comparable to those of a single state. From this to the single-state hypothesis of Europe's political future was not an enormous step. Even today, some such assumption seems to underlie much of what is said and written about the future of Europe, notably in the field of defence. Up to a point, it has its justification, since a European Defence Community would undoubtedly require machinery for rapid collective decision-making, especially in the nuclear field. In simplified terms, this necessity is often expressed as a question—how can Europe have a nuclear force without a European president to use the safety-catch and trigger? With the logic of this, in regard to the internal political structure of a future united Europe, it may be hard to quarrel. What seems less certain is whether in the 20th century the single-state analogy makes sense in the broader context of Europe's relations with other parts of the world, and in particular with the United States.

EUROPE AS A THIRD FORCE

This last question is one that notably fails to trouble the champions of a hypothesis cognate with the single-state analogy—that is, Europe as a third force. What precisely this phrase means is open to dispute: a Gaullist deputy, speaking in the European Parliament, once claimed that it meant no more than the emergence of Europe as an economic power following the United States and the Soviet Union. Not everyone was lulled by such a bland interpretation; for the phrase's original context made fairly clear that what its advocates had in mind was a status for Europe comparable with that which Mr Nehru sought for India—independence from both East and West. Even this description, however, remains subject to ambiguity. If 'independent' means 'no longer dependent', for example, on US aid, or 'no longer subordinate' in the Western Alliance, few 'Europeans' would reject 'independence'; nor would the United States, on its own constant showing, wish to prevent it. But when the term is used by Gaullists, the usual intention appears to be a Europe without permanent attachments; and this, if opinion polls are to be credited, finds little support from the public even in France itself.

EUROPE OF THE STATES

Gaullism contains many paradoxes. Not the least of them is the fact that many Gaullists who adhere to the third-force hypothesis of an 'independent' Europe not only reject the single-state analogy which it seems to resemble, but also spurn both 'supranationality' and 'integration'. In practice, Gaullist France has helped to promote the economic integration of Europe; but right from the beginning, the spokesmen of the regime have held, at least in theory, that Europe could only be 'united' by the collaboration of sovereign states. Their opponents, with some justice, retort that a 'Europe of the States' of this kind would find it hard to achieve 'independence', that the Gaullists, in other words, seek the end without accepting the means. President de Gaulle's own pronouncements on this subject certainly seem to expose him to this objection. Some of his subordinates appear more canny. By all means, they say, there must be some pooling of sovereignty in limited technical fields; but there can be no question of progressive political integration.

In the economic field, this sounds plausible. French Gaullist officials have conducted a long campaign of sniping at the protocol privileges of the Common Market Commission; but French sovereignty has indeed been limited in a number of matters, not least on agricultural questions where France has been one of the promoters of practical integration. It is in the field of nuclear defence, however, that Gaullist theory seems particularly caught up in contradictions. If Europe is to be 'independent' of the United States in the Gaullist sense, then it must possess its own deterrent; to deploy this with any degree of credibility, there must be a European centre of decision. This would seem to imply a fundamental sacrifice of national sovereignty to European political institutions, perhaps to a single government or president of Europe.

No explicit or coherent answer to this objection has yet been forthcoming: the most that Gaullist theory will concede is that 'one day' Europe may become 'an imposing confederation'. The difference between this and a 'federation', in the eyes of its sponsors, appears to be more than a matter of three letters. It certainly seems to exclude a European constitutional structure similar to that of the United States. Faced with this contradiction, one may either conclude that Gaullist philosophy is incoherent or try to find explanations elsewhere.

One such explanation seems possible, even if it does not show the General in a particularly good light: that is, that he intends to provide Europe's defence and leadership himself. The French *force de frappe*, in other words, would replace the United States' deterrent as the protector of 'independent' Europe; there would be no need for political integration since the ultimate decision-making centre would be Paris. Curiously enough, some such political arrangements were foreseen a century ago by Victor Hugo, when he wrote that 'in the 20th century there will be an extraordinary nation. . . . This nation will have Paris as its capital, and will not be called France: it will be called Europe'—a point of nomenclature that the General might dispute. His Common Market partners, and Germany in particular, could hardly be blamed if they found such a prospect unattractive. The *force de frappe* might well seem a poor substitute for the American nuclear umbrella; and in an 'independent' Europe of the States of this sort, some states would clearly be a great deal more 'independent' than others.

THE EMERGING SYNTHESIS

A synthesis of the divergent and conflicting hypotheses about Europe's future was beginning to emerge at the beginning of the 1960s. In part, it was the operation of what the former French premier Michel Debré, for long the lone Gaullist opposition in the Community's Parliamentary Assembly, had called the *engrenage*. This untranslatable word usually means 'the works' or 'gear-wheels': here, with reference to the Community, it has the implications of 'sausage-machine'. M. Debré was anxious that France should not be swallowed up by the process of integration.

The notion was somewhat as follows. To solve the problem of the Ruhr, the Schuman Plan had created a common market in coal and steel. To remedy the disequilibria caused in the member countries' economies by the integration of these basic products, it was necessary either to deintegrate them or to integrate the rest of the economy in a common market for all goods. Such a general common market would only produce its full fruit if the factors of production were integrated too, and freedom of movement accorded to capital and labour. Once this measure of integration was on the way, it would be logical and indeed necessary to harmonise taxes, legislation and so on, and to adopt common policies not only in such sectors as transport and agriculture where pure competition was not enough, but also, ultimately, in most fields of economic and monetary policy. To achieve all this, and to administer the resultant economic union, some political machinery would be necessary; when it was established and fully operative, the member nations would be ready to take further steps in political integration which could lead them to the 'ever closer union' prescribed by the Rome Treaty. Steadily and ineluctably, the practical fusion of interests and pooling of sovereignty would lead to full political union.

In practice, of course, so neat a pattern was too good to be true. As time went on, some of the earlier and simpler models and hypotheses were modified. The High Authority set up by the Schuman Plan seldom acted by diktat, but in fact engaged in a permanent dialogue with the national governments represented in the Council of Ministers, in order to find solutions to common and often unforeseen problems. The further steps in economic integration which seemed so logical required not only long negotia-tion but also immense administrative labours even when in principle the governments were agreed. Europe was being built piecemeal and untidily, with crises and setbacks and lacunae along the way. At the centre of the whole process, however, there remained the dialogue between a European body responsible for seeking solutions to common problems and the Council of Ministers responsible for defending national interests and taking the final decisions together. This institutional system was confirmed by the Treaties of Rome setting up Euratom and the Common Market. It differed from the original simple blueprint for the Schuman Plan, from the single-state analogy, from political federalism, from Europe of the States; it was novel and *sui generis*; it had evolved. At the same time, it promised to give the advantages of each of the earlier, simpler hypothetical systems. It was capable of reaching difficult decisions, like a true Authority. It was able to create a single economy out of six. It maintained and protected the rights of the states, but pointed the way towards possible federal developments in the political field.

By the beginning of the 1960s, indeed, it was beginning to seem reasonable to look ahead to the possible extension of this 'Community method' of dialogue to fields outside economics, and in particular to foreign policy and defence. The Bonn Declaration of 1961 by the Six expressed their willingness to seek union in these fields.

The initial Fouchet negotiations for this purpose had broken down a year later, partly owing to disagreement on the scope and nature of 'political union', but the notable success of the Common Market in recovering its momentum after the breaking-off of the 1961–3 British negotiations led many to feel that the time was growing ripe for a further attempt at unification in the political and military fields.

In a joint declaration in Bonn on 1 June, 1964, Jean Monnet's Action Committee for the United States of Europe, comprising the majority of the political parties and all the non-Communist trade unions of the Six, spelled out a number of ways in which advance might be possible: by fusing the Executive bodies of the Schuman Plan, Euratom and the Common Market; by increasing the powers of the European Parliament and providing for the direct election of some of its members; by having the Parliament ratify the nomination of the new joint Executive's president; and by extending the Common Market's institutional system to foreign policy and defence. 'This', the Action Committee added in a further declaration a year later, 'will open a new period in which European nations will gradually come to treat foreign policy and defence as joint problems, as they already deal with economic questions in the Common Market. This intermediate period is necessary for real progress to be made in the organisation of Europe. Once they have transformed relations between them in this way and come to speak with one voice on the essentials of policy, the European nations will be able to open the great debate which will ultimately enable them to decide what form a democratic government of Europe is to take.' Nothing ultimate was prejudged, therefore; but the way ahead seemed clear.

Equally clear, at least to Monnet's committee, was the future posture of Europe vis-à-vis the United States. It was neither subordination nor 'independence' in the Gaullist, third-force sense; nor was it now conceived as dissolution into an 'Atlantic Community', federal or otherwise, since this would have presupposed American willingness and ability to undertake Community-style obligations. What was envisaged, rather, was a relationship of equals between the United States and united Europe in the making—something more enduring, and more self-confident on both sides, than the traditional alliance of one vast and many smaller powers. This new relationship of equals would extend in time into the field of defence, including nuclear defence; and the proposed Multilateral Force (MLF), provided that its statute contained a 'European clause' permitting collective European action, might offer a means to this end. Thus united in equal partnership, Europe and America would be in a better position to come to terms with the Soviet Union, without any move towards a détente producing, as now, nervousness in Europe—especially in Germany—which in turn could lead to impatience in the United States. The emergence of a politically united Europe, moreover, would facilitate a détente by making unilateral national action impossible and by furnishing a political framework within which the German people could be safely and peacefully reunited without reconstituting a single and separate German state. Finally, the resultant settlement between the West and the Soviet Union would create a climate of peace which would promote and facilitate the peaceful evolution of the rest of the world. United Europe would thus have started a ripple which would carry a very long way.

Such was the hopeful synthesis which began to seem possible with the continued success of the Common Market. One key element in it—the notion of equal partnership between Europe and America—was stated most memorably by President Kennedy in his Independence Day Speech in 1961; and, as the date suggests, this notion was founded in part on the supposition that Great Britain would join the Common Market. With the breakdown of the negotiations in January 1963 this hope was drastically deferred: in the following November, President Kennedy was assassinated. Neither of these events invalidated the basic policy; but in the resultant confusion and pessimism, doubt began to grow. When in June 1965 President de Gaulle withdrew his ministers from the Common Market, many began to wonder whether the whole great endeavour which had seemed to promise order and peace in the post-war world was not being swept aside by a resurgence of short-sighted nationalism, curbed only by precarious alliances and doomed to lead to conflict, perhaps even to a third world war.

SCENARIOS

In speculating on the possible consequences of Europe's failure to achieve unity, it will be useful to borrow the nuclear strategist's device of 'scenarios' tracing alternative hypothetical sequences of events. The following grim 'scenarios' are offered in an attempt to reach some tentative conclusions about the likely course of events should European integration fail.

The Common Market breaks up

Despite the 'Gentlemen's Disagreement' which partly healed the Common Market crisis of 1965, progress in Brussels grinds to a halt. All that is achieved is on the General's terms: full satisfaction on farm policy, no majority voting, an impotent Commission, no steps towards economic union beyond farm policy, no political prospects. Each nation looks after its own interests. Strains appear in the 'common' commercial policy, especially towards the Soviet Union. France makes a long-term trade agreement with the East. Germany, increasingly uneasy, feels obliged to do likewise; and at length all the countries of the West compete to offer Moscow ever better terms, thereby losing their bargaining assets in advance of any settlement. The consequent hardening of the East-West division of Europe causes growing unrest among the rising generation in Germany.

At the same time:

Britain, although tempted by the now less 'supranational' shape of the Common Market's institutions, still tries to lay down the terms on which she will join it. She is reluctant to accept the common agricultural policy and those aspects of the customs union she feels will damage Commonwealth trade as well as increasing her own balance-of-payments problems. As a result, the veto on British entry subsists. In EFTA she finds no substitute for the economic scope the Common Market would have given her; more and more she is forced to cut the coat of her living standards to the cloth of her relatively small national industries. The Commonwealth countries are attracted more and more by the United States and the Common Market; Britain and the neutral or quasi-neutral EFTA countries find their role in the world progressively dwindling. Picturesque and slightly impoverished, Britain lives more and more on her memories, less and less in the present. The brain drain becomes a flood. . . .

Or:

France makes a new proposal to 'save' the Common Market: a Europe-wide free trade area with bilateral arrangements for French agriculture. Despite opposition from the 'Europeans', this is too popular with business circles among the 'Five' for them to resist it. Britain seizes the opportunity with both hands: on agriculture, she makes import arrangements with France similar to those with Denmark in EFTA. The United States is worried but cannot seriously object to what seems to be 'saving' European economic cooperation. When the institutions of the free trade area are established, lip-service is paid to Community principles, but that is all. For the time being, there is no direct friction as in the first scenario above; but the prospect of a politically united Europe has immeasurably receded since its immediate commercial advantages appear to be offered by free trade. No arrangements are made for Europe-wide companies, and Europe's industries fall more and more under American business domination.

Meanwhile:

NATO disintegrates

With or without a free trade area as in the last scenario, the United States begins to suffer more and more from pinpricks administered by France, and maladroit moves made by Britain. Increasingly, a Bonn-Washington axis develops. France quits NATO. The Germans, anxious to retain the French 'hinterland', and the United States, concerned about supply lines, at length renegotiate their links with France on a bilateral basis. Britain and France continue to build expensive and largely ineffective national 'deterrents'. Germany is by now enjoying a special relationship with the United States and has her own High Command. Britain continues to press for a non-proliferation treaty whose main effect is to prevent Germany acquiring any nuclear role. Germany protests in private, but is bought off by consultation arrangements. These satisfy no one. Extremists organise protests. Ultimately a new generation comes to power, with greater temptation to seek a new Rapallo or else to pursue revanchiste claims. . . .

Or:

The picture as before, with an increasing build-up of 'tactical' nuclear weapons on German soil, controlled by US Army personnel. Further poor harvests in the Soviet Union put economic pressure on the satellites and on the Soviet Zone of Germany and the Soviet Sector of Berlin. A strike occurs in an East Berlin factory and is severely repressed. The strikers reply with demonstrations; a riot turns into a revolt. Amid angry scenes in the Federal Parliament, the Bonn government protests, but nothing practical can be done. . . . Violent unrest spreads in both halves of Germany. . . .

BRIGHTER ALTERNATIVES

The above scenarios are more in the nature of scarecrows than of cautionary tales. No one supposes that events would turn out precisely in that fashion; but the fear of such things happening could have serious effects on mutual confidence and might very well make impossible the hopes of détente, particularly in a complex world situation where the temptation—in East and West alike—to go on dividing one's adversaries often obscures the need to come to terms with them. Uncertainty may not lead to war, but it cannot lead to lasting peace.

There are, however, brighter alternatives.

The Common Market develops

France's material interests ensure that she stages no more walkouts from Brussels. The logic of the Common Market in practice prevails. Britain sees and envies its success, and makes an unconditional offer to join. Even the General cannot refuse, for fear of reprisals by the 'Five'.

Or:

Continued French intransigence leads the 'Five' to make an offer to Britain: will she take France's chair? Instead of hedging and insisting on special conditions for Commonwealth trade and agriculture (which would ultimately lead, no doubt, to a free trade area as in the third scenario above), Britain accepts with alacrity. At this, France either presses unsuccessfully for trade, or is obliged to retract her anti-supranational reservations in the hope of heading Britain off. After considerable upheaval, the Common Market settles down with its original membership plus that of Britain and some other EFTA countries, France having decided that this is the lesser of two evils.

Or:

The 'Five' continue to hold the fort in the Common Market, stopping the clock where necessary, until a change occurs in the French government. France gradually becomes more flexible on the institutional aspects of the Rome Treaty system amid general euphoria; Britain applies for membership and is accepted.

NATO is suitably reformed

The fourteen non-French NATO countries counter France's proposed withdrawal with an offer to reorganise the Alliance in order to give Europe a greater voice in it. The French agree to a conference which leads to an arrangement based on European-American partnership or one temporarily including a special and separate status for France. Later, as the reality of the partnership grows, the incentive for France to exchange her special status for a place in it increases. A new French government does so.

Or:

Goaded by further French obstructionism, the United States revives the MLF project and presses ahead despite British and Russian objections. The Germans respond enthusiastically; so do several smaller European countries. France continues to make angry noises; Britain, on the other hand, decides that she had better not be left outside. An MLF treaty is concluded, and comprises a 'European' clause. France is offered a special relationship outside it similar to that formerly enjoyed by Britain. Subsequently, France opts in too.

Or:

Britain decides that the time has come to pool her defence capability with her neighbours and thus accept equality with Germany. She proposes to build a European political and defence community, to 'Europeanise' her own deterrent, and to enter the Common Market. She calls for a defence conference between herself and the Six, with an US observer. At the same time she proposes that the European participants should negotiate a treaty on nuclear defence with the United States to ensure a proper relationship between the partners. France is at first suspicious, but is surprised by British willingness to pool know-how, and decides to join the pool. Routine protests from the Soviet Union are met by the perfectly reasonable argument—already advanced by the United States in the Geneva negotiations—that one European centre of nuclear decision is safer than two. Ultimately, the progressive political integration of Western Europe, and better because more equal relations with the United States, make it possible to concert a policy of progressive détente with the East.

The Future

These scenarios are suggestions rather than conclusions. Whatever the outcome of existing uncertainties, nothing is likely to turn out so pat. The most probable future for Western Europe is no doubt a combination of some of these elements with others that cannot yet be foreseen. Part of the purpose of stating some hypotheses, in fact, is to guard against their being realised. For unless one believes that human actions are totally devoid of reason, it seems hard to imagine that certain collision courses can be knowingly chosen. The long-term interests of Europe, including Britain, are so evidently dependent on the pursuit of economic and political unity that only a confirmed pessimist can readily believe that they will be permanently ignored.

If the optimistic hypothesis prevails, what does it hold for Western Europe's future? The prospect of 250 million and more men and women working together on the most hopeful political task of this century. A Europe without barriers, almost without frontiers. The chance to profit from the goods and the leisure that modern industry makes possible. The continual stimulus of the interplay between national cultures, far more directly than at present. A lifting of the overcast of malaise that afflicts both France and Britain, former world powers now diminished. The prospect for the Germans of reunification with their families in the East. Scope for ambitious people outside the confines of their countries. The chance to make a real impact on problems, in Europe and the rest of the world, that no one country can settle alone. Europe's ability to influence its own future and no longer to depend solely, in matters of life and death, on the decisions of a distant president whom Europeans have little chance to influence and no hand in electing. The hope of securing the beginnings of a peaceful world by applying reason, not habit, to international relations.

What the first steps along such a path will be must depend on the circumstances of the moment—whether or not the Common Market continues to develop into economic and political union, whether or not Britain and the United States, in particular, can save and reform the Atlantic Alliance, whether or not these things have to be done without initial French participation, whether economics or politics or defence comes first or whether all progress together. But whatever the tactics and the timing, one thing is essential if progress is to be made at all: Britain, like the other European countries, must realise that unilateral national action is fruitless, that there is no sane way to go it alone. Once this is accepted, joint action becomes the obvious course, and problems which used to be thought of as national problems become common problems, to be solved far more effectively together. This is the essence of the Community method adopted by the Six. Only if they pursue it, and if Britain joins it, can they and she assure their economic and political future.

In the short run, this means that Britain must make up her mind to join the Common Market, if need be irrespective of the initial 'terms' of entry. Once in, she must throw her weight behind the essential method of 'Community dialogue' which has enabled the Six to make the progress they have, and she must shun the temptation to reduce the Community to a 'Europe of the States'. Only thus, perhaps, can France be coaxed back into a similar attitude. To do this requires that Britain accept equality with each of her partners, and in particular the Germans; and this in turn will ultimately require the scrapping, or the 'Europeanisation', of independent national deterrents.

With Britain's weight thrown into the balance, Western Europe can rapidly become the equal partner—equal in right if not in might—of the United States. And so a longer-term prospect opens up: a new relationship in the West, founded on growing confidence and mutual respect. Fears of 'domination by American capital', talk of 'creating a European third force', would become a thing of the past; so would Soviet attempts to continue the old policy of seeking to divide the West. Talks with the Soviet Union could then be held in a new atmosphere, untroubled by Gaullist manoeuvres, German uneasiness, or American temptations to try to settle matters alone. Gradually peaceful coexistence would become more than a phrase to cloak the balance of terror; and in the new context of the United States of Europe, the divided German people would be able to attain unity without the dangers of reconstituting a separate German nation-state. An United States of Europe would not in itself be enough to ensure world peace; but since the West and the Soviet Union already have at their disposal the bulk of the world's power, constructive and destructive alike, it would be a formidable force for stability.

BIBLIOGRAPHY

Birrenbach, Kurt. *The Future of the Atlantic Community*, Praeger, New York, 1963.
Camps, Miriam. *What Kind of Europe?* Oxford Univ. Press, London and New York, 1965.
Duchêne, François. *Beyond Alliance*, Atlantic Institute, Paris, 1965.
Hallstein, Walter. *United Europe*, Oxford Univ. Press, London; Harvard Univ. Press, Cambridge, Mass., 1962.
Kohnstamm, Max. *The European Community and its Role in the World*, Univ. of Missouri Press, Columbia, Mo., 1964.
Mayne, Richard. *The Community of Europe*, Gollancz, London, 1962; W. W. Norton, New York, 1963.
Monnet, Jean. *Les Etats-Unis d'Europe ont Commencé*, Laffont, Paris, 1955.
Pinder, John. *Europe against de Gaulle*, Pall Mall Press, London; Frederick Praeger, New York, 1963.
Pryce, Roy. *The Political Future of the European Community*, Marshbank, London, 1962.
Uri, Pierre. *Partnership for Progress*, Harper, New York, 1963.

x

NOTES ON CONTRIBUTORS

BAILEY, RICHARD. Read economics at London University. Director of Political and Economic Planning, 1954–64. Special adviser to the National Economic Development Council, 1964–6. Currently consulting economist with Industrial and Process Engineering Consultants (Great Britain). Member of Senate, London University since 1966.

BEEVER, R. COLIN. Read economics and political science at Oxford University. Research Fellow of the Council of Europe, 1957–8 and wrote thesis 'European Unity and the Trade Union Movements'. Has worked as shop steward and trade union branch and area officer, and has travelled widely in Western Europe and North America on trade union studies. Formerly Honorary Secretary of the Labour Committee for Europe in London and Editor of *Europe Left* (quarterly review of Committee). Six years as Assistant Research Officer, Amalgamated Engineering Union. Currently Research and Statistical Officer, National and Local Government Officers Association.

BURGESS, TONY. Read economics at London University. After working in advertising turned to economic journalism in 1957, writing for *Petroleum Press Service*, *Euromarket* and *Business*. Appointed to staff of European Communities Information Service in Luxembourg, 1962 as editor of the Service's English-language publications. Press Officer in the Information Service's London office, 1964–6.

CALMANN, JOHN. Born in Hamburg, emigrated with his family to England in 1937. After leaving Oxford University, where he read history, he worked for the *Wall Street Journal* in New York and then for the European Community in Luxembourg, where he was first in the publications department of the Information Service and then a spokesman for the High Authority of the ECSC. He then became editor of the English edition of *Opera Mundi-Europe*, and later carried out a study of the political aspects of European cooperation in defence technology for the Institute for Strategic Studies, London. Currently employed by a publishing house in London.

CHILD, SARAH. Read philosophy, politics and economics at Oxford University and took a diploma in politics at College of Europe, Bruges. After six years at the Economist Intelligence Unit, where as a departmental manager she was responsible for EIU research into the economic and social aspects of immigration, she resigned to do freelance work.

CLARKE, WILLIAM M. Read economics at Manchester University. On editorial staff of *Manchester Guardian*, 1948–55. On staff of *The Times*, 1955–66: Assistant City Editor, 1955–7; City Editor, 1957–62; Financial and Industrial Editor 1962–6. Editor of *The Banker*, 1966; Editorial Consultant to *The Banker* since 1966. Director of Committee on Invisible Exports. Publications: *The City's Invisible Earnings*, 1962; *The City in the World Economy*, 1965.

DUNLOP, IAN H. E. Read mental and moral science at Trinity College, Dublin. After short period as supply teacher wrote on art for *The Times*,

1964–5. Art critic for *The Evening Standard* since 1965. Publications: Catalogue notes and entries to exhibition *The New Generation*, March 1965, Whitechapel Gallery, London; *Mondrian*, 1967.

FORD, CHARLES. After reading economics at the London School of Economics became research economist for the Amalgamated Engineering Union. Since 1957 Assistant Secretary of the European Regional Organisation of the ICFTU and of the Trade Union Advisory Committee to OECD (previously OEEC).

GELLNER, MARIANNE. Read economics at the London School of Economics. On staff of the Royal Institute of International Affairs, London, 1951–62, specialising in international economics. Now engaged in demand forecasting for the British Iron and Steel Federation.

GEORGE, VIC. Honours degree in social administration from Nottingham University. M.A. (Nottingham); thesis on assimilation problems. Formerly Child Care Officer with the LCC; Senior Research Officer, London School of Economics and Political Science. Currently Lecturer in Department of Applied Social Science, Nottingham University.

GRAHAM, HARRY. Read history at Oxford and studied for five years at the Architectural Association School, London. Since 1960 has worked for various London firms of architects, and has also had his own private practice.

GRINDEA, MIRON. Born in Rumania. Studied at Bucarest University, the Sorbonne and the University of London. Settled in Britain in 1939. With Benjamin Britten, Henry Moore and Stephen Spender founded the International Arts Guild in 1943. He has edited the international literary magazine *Adam*, published in English and French, since launching it in 1941.

HOLMES, BRIAN. Read physics at London University. Ph.D. (London) for thesis on methodology in comparative education. Formerly taught physics in secondary schools; Lecturer in Education at Durham University; Assistant Editor of the *World Yearbook of Education*, University of London, Institute of Education as Lecturer and Senior Lecturer at the Institute. Currently Reader in Comparative Education at the Institute. Author of *American Criticism of American Education*, 1956; (with S. B. Robinson) *Relevant Data in Comparative Education*, 1963; *Problems in Education*, 1965. Secretary Treasurer of the Comparative Education Society in Europe and Vice-President of the American Comparative Education Society (1966–7).

MALLET, JACQUES. Studied at the Ecole Nationale d'Administration and the Institut d'Etudes Politiques, Paris. Staff member of the Information Service of the Common Market in Paris since 1958; member of the Council of the French Association for the Atlantic Community. Has written widely on international affairs, particularly on the problems of the Third World and European integration. He has made a special study of relations between the Common Market and the United States, contributing important articles to *Preuves* (February 1963) and *Revue de l'Action Populaire* (June 1963).

MAYNE, RICHARD. Ph.D. (Cantab.) Rome Correspondent of *The New Statesman*, 1953–4; Assistant Tutor at the Cambridge Institute of Education, 1954–5. On staff of the ECSC High Authority in Luxembourg, 1956–8; on staff of Common Market Commission in Brussels, 1958–62 (was closely concerned with negotiations for British membership); since 1962 Director of the Documentation Centre of the Comité d'Action pour les Etats-Unis d'Europe, Paris, directed by Jean Monnet. Regular contributor to British,

French and American periodicals and a member of the BBC Critics Panel. Author of *The Community of Europe*, 1962, and is at present working on a history of Europe since the second world war.

MOORE, RICHARD. Educated privately and at Trinity College, Cambridge; President of the Cambridge Union. Leader writer, *News Chronicle*, 1956–60; Secretary General of the Liberal International, 1961–4. Liberal Parliamentary Candidate at Tavistock, 1955 and 1959; Cambridgeshire, 1961 (by-election) and 1964; North Antrim, 1966. Currently Personal Assistant to Chairman of the Liberal Party and Political Counsellor to the Liberal International; Member of the Royal Institute of International Affairs and the Institute for Strategic Studies, London.

NOVAIS, JOSÉ ANTONIO. Read philosophy and law at Madrid University; also studied at the Official School of Journalism, Madrid. Currently Madrid correspondent of *Le Monde* and *O Estado de Sao Paulo;* Spanish correspondent for Radio Diffusion Belge, *Novedades* (Mexico) and *Avanti* (Italy). Author of many books on current affairs, has also published poetry and plays.

PINDER, JOHN. Read economics at Cambridge University. Thirteen years with the Economist Intelligence Unit, where became Director of International Operations; Director of Political and Economic Planning, London since 1964. Trustee of the Federal Trust. Publications include *Britain and the Common Market*, 1961 and *Europe against de Gaulle*, 1963.

PRYCE, ROY, Ph.D. (Cantab.) Fellow of Emmanuel College, Cambridge, 1955–7; Fellow of St Antony's College, Oxford, 1955–7. Head of the London Office, European Communities Information Service, 1957–64; Rockefeller Research Fellow, 1964–5. Currently Lecturer in Politics and Director of Contemporary European Studies, University of Sussex.

REED, LAURANCE. During service in the Royal Navy (1956–8) attended H-bomb tests on Christmas Island. Read law at Oxford. Currently a free-lance writer and working on a book on European collaboration in science and technology and its importance in international integration. Member of the Bow Group.

SHARP, ANTHONY. Read international politics at University College of Wales, Aberystwyth. In 1963 began preparation of D.Phil. thesis (Sussex University) on Geneva Foreign Ministers' Conference of 1959, research for which included six months at Free University of Berlin.

VON SIMSON, WERNER. Read law at the Universities of Freiburg (Baden) and Berlin. Advocate at the Court of Appeal in Berlin, 1936–9. Came to England at the outbreak of war and remained there till 1953, when he went to Luxembourg to become an advocate practising at the Court of the ECSC (now the Court of the European Communities). Member of the Law Faculty, University of Freiburg.

STAROBIN, JOSEPH R. Formerly a prominent member of the American Communist Party, has made special studies of communism in Latin America, Western Europe and China, where he lived for a year, 1952–3. Now Senior Fellow, Research Institute on Communist Affairs, Columbia University, New York. Author of *Eyewitness in Indochina*, 1954, and *Paris to Peking*, 1955.

TAYLOR, JOHN RUSSELL. Read English at Cambridge University. Researched on Art Nouveau book design at the Courtauld Institute of Art, London for two years. On staff of *The Times* in various editorial capacities, 1959–63;

since 1963 film critic of *The Times*. Regular contributor to *Sight and Sound*, *Plays and Players*, *The Listener* and other publications. Books include *Anger and After: A Guide to the New British Drama; Anatomy of a Television Play; Cinema Eye, Cinema Ear: Some Key Film-Makers of the Sixties; The Penguin Dictionary of Drama; The Art Nouveau Book in Britain*.

TONGE, DAVID S. Read natural sciences and economics at Cambridge University. After a training course at a New York bank specialising in international trade and a period of service in London for the same bank, he joined the Economist Intelligence Unit, London, where he now works in the European Department of the International Development Division as a researcher and consultant. His activities cover a broad range of subjects including development problems in southern Italy, long-term forecasting and preparation of publications on European countries.

TRILLING, OSSIA. Honours degree from Oxford University. Formerly actor and director. Has been writing drama criticism since 1937. Regular contributor to *The Times* and other British and foreign newspapers. Critics' Circle Councillor; Vice-President of the International Association of Theatre Critics. Co-editor and contributor to *International Theatre*, 1949; co-editor and contributor to *Dobson's Theatre Year Book*, 1948–9.

URI, PIERRE. Studied at the Ecole Normale Supérieure, the Faculté de Droit of the Sorbonne and Princeton University. Economic and Financial Councillor to the Commissariat Général du Plan, 1947–52; member of the United Nations Committee of Experts on Full Employment, 1949; Economic Director of the ECSC, 1952–9; chairman of Experts Group on the Long-term Development of the EEC, 1960–4; now Economic Consultant to the Atlantic Institute near Paris. Publications include *La crise de la zone de libre-échange*, 1959; *Dialogue des continents*, 1963; and reports on the Schuman Plan, 1951 and on the economic situation of the EEC, 1958.

VASEY, C. M. W. Read history at Oxford University; studied European institutions for one year at College of Europe, Bruges; research assistant in political science, University of California (Berkeley). Four years as journalist on staff of Agence Europe. Attached since 1966 to Secretariat of Council of Europe, Strasbourg as Secretary to the Political Committee of the Consultative Assembly.

VERRIER, ANTHONY. Special correspondent for *The Economist, The Observer* and *The New Statesman*, 1960–5, dealing predominantly with foreign affairs and defence. Currently engaged on a history of the strategic air offensive in the second world war and a study of British policy in Arabia and Asia during the last hundred years. Author of *An Army for the Sixties*, 1966 (a study of British defence requirements).

WALSH, STEPHEN. Read music at Cambridge University. Has contributed music criticism to *The Times, The Guardian, The Financial Times* and *The Daily Telegraph*. Has produced and frequently broadcasts on music for the BBC.

WARLEY, T. K. After reading horticulture at Nottingham University took a Master's degree in agricultural economics and then joined the Department of Agricultural Economics there, where he now lectures on agricultural policy and marketing. Spent the year 1958–9 at the University of California under the auspices of the OEEC, has lectured at international conferences and seminars in Germany, France and Canada, was a consultant to the EEC Commission on British Agricultural Policies in 1962, and directed an extended seminar on agricultural marketing for the Ministry of Overseas Development in 1965.

WHITE, JOHN. Read politics, philosophy and economics at Oxford University. Formerly foreign correspondent for *The Times* in Europe, Africa and the Far East. Joined the Overseas Development Institute, London in 1964 where he is currently a research officer.

WILLIAMS, GLEN GARFIELD. Graduate of Universities of Wales, London and Tübingen. Baptist minister in St Albans, Herts, 1955–9. Divisional Area Secretary for Europe, World Council of Churches, 1959–62; Executive Secretary, later General Secretary, Conference of European Churches since 1962.

WINDSOR, PHILIP. Read modern history at Oxford University and researched on German history at Oxford and the Free University of Berlin. Three years at the Institute for Strategic Studies, London; currently Lecturer in International Relations, London School of Economics. Publications: *City on Leave* and (with Alastair Buchan) *Arms and Stability in Europe*, both 1962.

WOLFF, SALOMON. Born in Minsk. Read politics at Hamburg University. Economic correspondent of the *Frankfurter Zeitung* for France, 1923–34; with the Bank Mendelssohn and Co. in Amsterdam, 1934–9; since 1940 economic correspondent of the *Neue Zürcher Zeitung* for France, European economic integration and monetary questions. Author of several books on economics and finance.

ACKNOWLEDGEMENTS

BASIC INFORMATION

Copyright sources substantially drawn upon were: Austria: *Social Security in Austria*, National Federation of Austrian Social Insurance Institutions, Vienna, 1961. Denmark: *An Official Handbook*, Press and Information Department, Royal Danish Ministry of Foreign Affairs, Copenhagen, 1964. Finland: *Introduction to Finland 1963*, ed. Göran Stenius, Press Bureau of Ministry of Foreign Affairs, Porvoo, 1963. Germany: *Germany Reports*, general editor Helmut Arntz, Press and Information Office, Bonn, 4th ed. 1965; Helmut Arntz, *Facts About Germany*, Press and Information Office, Bonn, 1966; Elmer Plischke, *Contemporary Government of Germany*, Houghton Mifflin, Boston, 1961; Elmer Plischke, *Government and Politics of Contemporary Berlin*, Martinus Nijhoff, The Hague, 1963. Ireland: *Facts About Ireland*, Department of External Affairs, Dublin, 1965. Italy: John Clarke Adams and Paolo Barile, *The Government of Republican Italy*, Allen and Unwin, London, 1961. Norway: *Norway Yearbook*, Johan Grundt Tanum, Oslo, 6th ed. 1962; *Statistisk Årbok for Norge 1966*, Central Bureau of Statistics, Oslo, 1966. Spain: *Spain at a Glance*, Spanish Information Service, Madrid, 1964. Sweden: *Social Benefits in Sweden*, Swedish Institute, Stockholm, 1966. Switzerland: Eugen Egger, *Die Organisation des Schulwesens in der Schweiz— Statistik über das Schulwesen*, Huber, Frauenfeld, 1964; Arnold Saxer, *Social*

Security in Switzerland, Paul Haupt, Berne, 1965. Turkey: Nuri Eren, *Turkey Today—and Tomorrow*, Praeger, New York, 1963; Geoffrey Lewis, *Turkey*, Ernest Benn, London, 1966. United Kingdom: *Britain—An Official Handbook 1966*, HMSO, London; O. Hood Phillips, *Constitutional Law*, Sweet and Maxwell, London, 1957. General: *Social Security Programs throughout the World 1964*, US Department of Health, Education and Welfare, Social Security Administration—Division of Research and Statistics, Washington, 1964; *Statesman's Year Book 1966–67*, ed. S. H. Steinberg, Macmillan, London, 1966; *Europa Year Book 1966*, Volume I, Europa Publications, London; *Guide to International Organisations*, Reference Division, Central Office of Information, London, 1961; Robert G. Neumann, *European and Comparative Government*, McGraw-Hill, New York, 1960; *The Military Balance 1966–67*, Institute for Strategic Studies, London, 1966; *United Nations Demographic Yearbook*, 1962 and 1965, United Nations, New York; *UNESCO Statistical Year Book 1965*, Mayenne, 1966; *Commonwealth Relations Office Year Book 1966*, HMSO, London.

ILLUSTRATIONS

Grateful acknowledgement is made to the following for their permission to reproduce copyright photographs: Marlborough Fine Art Ltd, London (Bacon, Moore); Hanover Gallery, London (Vasarély)—and with Association pour la Diffusion des Arts Graphiques et Plastiques, Paris or ADAGP (Giacometti); the Trustees of the Tate Gallery, London (Burri)—and with ADAGP (Dubuffet); Prof. Max Bill (*Rythmus im Raum*, 1947–48/62); Mr. M. Tarnay (Caro); Mr. G. E. Kidder Smith (Vallingby); Reinhard Friedrich, Berlin (Berlin Philharmonic Concert Hall); French Government Tourist Office (Église St Joseph); Architectural Press Ltd, London—with Mr. Wm. J. Toomey (*Economist* Building) and with Mr. Eric de Maré (St Catherine's College).

INDEX

Note: Part One is designed for ready reference, and only
the subsection *Recent History* in the section *Basic Information*
is indexed in addition to Parts Two and Three.

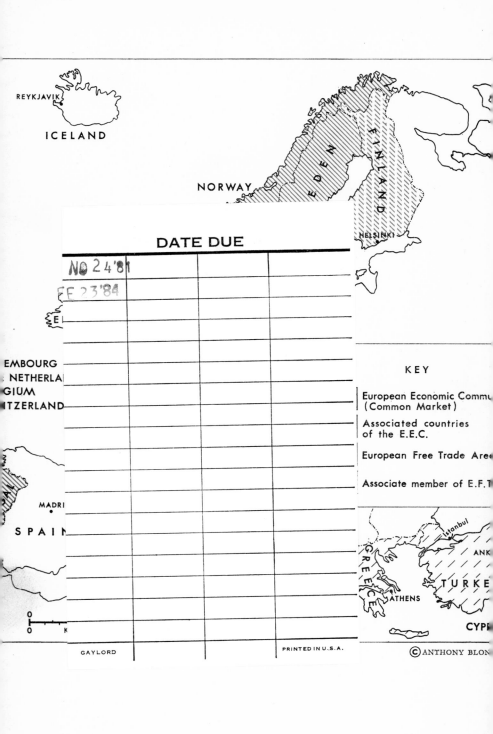

REYKJAVIK

ICELAND

NORWAY

S W E D E N

FINLAND

HELSINKI

DATE DUE

NO 24'81			
FE 23'84			
E			
EMBOURG			
NETHERLA			
GIUM			
TZERLAND			
MADRI			
SPAIN			
0			
0 K			
GAYLORD			PRINTED IN U.S.A.

KEY

European Economic Commu
(Common Market)

Associated countries
of the E.E.C.

European Free Trade Are

Associate member of E.F.T

Istanbul

ANK

G R E E C E

TURKE

ATHENS

CYPI

© ANTHONY BLON